THE SHIELD OF ACHILLES

ALSO BY PHILIP BOBBITT

Constitutional Interpretation

U.S. Nuclear Strategy: A Reader
(with Lawrence Freedman and Gregory Treverton)

Democracy and Deterrence:
The History and Future of Nuclear Strategy

Constitutional Fate: Theory of the Constitution

Tragic Choices (with Guido Calabresi)

THE SHIELD OF ACHILLES

WAR, PEACE AND THE COURSE OF HISTORY

PHILIP BOBBITT

ALLEN LANE
an imprint of
PENGUIN BOOKS

ALLEN LANE
THE PENGUIN PRESS

Published by the Penguin Group
Penguin Books Ltd, 80 Strand, London WC2R ORL, England
Penguin Putnam Inc., 375 Hudson Street, New York, New York 10014, USA
Penguin Books Australia Ltd, 250 Camberwell Road, Camberwell, Victoria 3124, Australia
Penguin Books Canada Ltd, 10 Alcorn Avenue, Toronto, Ontario, Canada M4V 3B2
Penguin Books India (P) Ltd, 11, Community Centre, Panchsheel Park, New Delhi – 110 017, India
Penguin Books (NZ) Ltd, Cnr Rosedale and Airborne Roads, Albany, Auckland, New Zealand
Penguin Books (South Africa) (Pty) Ltd, 24 Sturdee Avenue, Rosebank 2196, South Africa

Penguin Books Ltd, Registered Offices: 80 Strand, London WC2R ORL, England

www.penguin.com

First published in the USA by Alfred A. Knopf 2002
First published in Great Britain by Allen Lane The Penguin Press 2002
1

Printed and bound in England by Clays Ltd, St Ives plc

ISBN 0–71399–616–1

*To those by whose love God's grace
was first made known to me
and
to those whose loving-kindness
has ever since sustained me in His care.*

CONTENTS

BOOK II: STATES OF PEACE

The Iliad
(lines 558–720)

And first Hephaestus makes a great and massive shield,
blazoning well-wrought emblems all across its surface,
raising a rim around it, glittering, triple-ply
with a silver shield-strap run from edge to edge
and five layers of metal to build the shield itself,
and across its vast expanse with all his craft and cunning
the god creates a world of gorgeous immortal work.

There he made the earth and there the sky and the sea
and the inexhaustible blazing sun and the moon rounding full
and there the constellations, all that crown the heavens,
the Pleiades and the Hyades, Orion in all his power too
and the Great Bear that mankind also calls the Wagon:
she wheels on her axis always fixed, watching Orion,
and she alone is denied a plunge in the Ocean's baths.

And he forged on the shield two noble cities filled
with mortal men. With weddings and wedding feasts in one
and under glowing torches they brought forth the brides
from the women's chambers, marching through the streets
while choir on choir the wedding song rose high
and the young men came dancing, whirling round in rings
and among them the flutes and harps kept up their stirring call—
women rushed to the doors and each stood moved with wonder.
And the people massed, streaming into the marketplace
where a quarrel had broken out and two men struggled
over the blood-price for a kinsman just murdered.
One declaimed in public, vowing payment in full—
the other spurned him, he would not take a thing—
so both men pressed for a judge to cut the knot.

The crowd cheered on both, they took both sides,
but heralds held them back as the city elders sat

on polished stone benches, forming the sacred circle,
grasping in hand the staffs of clear-voiced heralds,
and each leapt to his feet to plead the case in turn.
Two bars of solid gold shone on the ground before them,
a prize for the judge who'd speak the straightest verdict.

*   But circling the other city camped a divided army*
gleaming in battle-gear, and two plans split their ranks:
to plunder the city or share the riches with its people,
hoards the handsome citadel stored within its depths.
But the people were not surrendering, not at all.
They armed for a raid, hoping to break the siege—
loving wives and innocent children standing guard
on the ramparts, flanked by elders bent with age
as men marched out to war. Ares and Pallas led them,
both burnished gold, gold the attire they donned, and great,
magnificent in their armor—gods for all the world,
looming up in their brilliance, towering over troops.
And once they reached the perfect spot for attack,
a watering place where all the herds collected,
there they crouched, wrapped in glowing bronze.
Detached from the ranks, two scouts took up their posts,
the eyes of the army waiting to spot a convoy,
the enemy's flocks and crook-horned cattle coming . . .
Come they did, quickly, two shepherds behind them,
playing their hearts out on their pipes—treachery
never crossed their minds. But the soldiers saw them,
rushed them, cut off at a stroke the herds of oxen
and sleek sheep-flocks glistening silver-gray
and killed the herdsmen too. Now the besiegers,
soon as they heard the uproar burst from the cattle
as they debated, huddled in council, mounted at once
behind their racing teams, rode hard to the rescue,
arrived at once, and lining up for assault
both armies battled it out along the river banks—
they raked each other with hurtling bronze-tipped spears.

*   And Strife and Havoc plunged in the fight, and violent Death—*
now seizing a man alive with fresh wounds, now one unhurt,
now hauling a dead man through the slaughter by the heels,
the cloak on her back stained red with human blood.
So they clashed and fought like living, breathing men
grappling each other's corpses, dragging off the dead.

And he forged a fallow field, broad rich plowland
tilled for the third time, and across it crews of plowmen
wheeled their teams, driving them up and back and soon
as they'd reach the end-strip, moving into the turn,
a man would run up quickly
and hand them a cup of honeyed, mellow wine
as the crews would turn back down along the furrows,
pressing again to reach the end of the deep fallow field
and the earth churned black behind them, like earth churning,
solid gold as it was—that was the wonder of Hephaestus' work.

And he forged a king's estate where harvesters labored,
reaping the ripe grain, swinging their whetted scythes.
Some stalks fell in line with the reapers, row on row,
and others the sheaf-binders girded round with ropes,
three binders standing over the sheaves, behind them
boys gathering up the cut swaths, filling their arms,
supplying grain to the binders, endless bundles.
And there in the midst the king,
scepter in hand at the head of the reaping-rows,
stood tall in silence, rejoicing in his heart.
And off to the side, beneath a spreading oak,
the heralds were setting out the harvest feast,
they were dressing a great ox they had slaughtered,
while attendant women poured out barley, generous,
glistening handfuls strewn for the reapers' midday meal.

And he forged a thriving vineyard loaded with clusters,
bunches of lustrous grapes in gold, ripening deep purple
and climbing vines shot up on silver-vine poles.
And round it he cut a ditch in dark blue enamel
and round the ditch he staked a fence in tin.
And one lone footpath led toward the vineyard
and down it the pickers ran
whenever they went to strip the grapes at vintage—
girls and boys, their hearts leaping in innocence,
bearing away the sweet ripe fruit in wicker baskets.
And there among them a young boy plucked his lyre,
so clear it could break the heart with longing,
and what he sang was a dirge for the dying year,
lovely . . . his fine voice rising and falling low
as the rest followed, all together, frisking, singing,
shouting, their dancing footsteps beating out the time.

And he forged on the shield a herd of longhorn cattle,
working the bulls in beaten gold and tin, lowing loud
and rumbling out of the farmyard dung to pasture
along a rippling stream, along the swaying reeds.
And the golden drovers kept the herd in line,
Four in all, with nine dogs at their heels,
their paws flickering quickly—a savage roar!—
a crashing attack—and a pair of ramping lions
had seized a bull from the cattle's front ranks—
he bellowed out as they dragged him off in agony.
Packs of dogs and the young herdsmen rushed to help
but the lions ripping open the hide of the huge bull
were gulping down the guts and the black pooling blood
while the herdsmen yelled the fast pack on—no use.
The hounds shrank from sinking teeth in the lions,
they balked, hunching close, barking, cringing away.

And the famous crippled Smith forged a meadow
deep in a shaded glen for shimmering flocks to graze,
with shepherds' steadings, well-roofed huts and sheepfolds.

And the crippled Smith brought all his art to bear
on a dancing circle, broad as the circle Daedalus
once laid out on Cnossos' spacious fields
for Ariadne the girl with lustrous hair.
Here young boys and girls, beauties courted
with costly gifts of oxen, danced and danced,
linking their arms, gripping each other's wrists.
And the girls wore robes of linen light and flowing,
the boys wore finespun tunics rubbed with a gloss of oil,
the girls were crowned with a bloom of fresh garlands,
the boys swung golden daggers hung on silver belts.
And now they would run in rings on their skilled feet,
nimbly, quick as a crouching potter spins his wheel,
palming it smoothly, giving it practice twirls
to see it run, and now they would run in rows,
in rows crisscrossing rows—rapturous dancing.
A breathless crowd stood round them struck with joy
and through them a pair of tumblers dashed and sprang,
whirling in leaping handsprings, leading out the dance.

And he forged the Ocean River's mighty power girdling
round the outmost rim of the welded indestructible shield.

And once the god had made that great and massive shield
he made Achilles a breastplate brighter than gleaming fire,
he made him a sturdy helmet to fit the fighter's temples,
beautiful, burnished work, and raised its golden crest
and made him greaves of flexing, pliant tin.

Now,
when the famous crippled Smith had finished off
that grand array of armor, lifting it in his arms
he laid it all at the feet of Achilles' mother Thetis—
and down she flashed like a hawk from snowy Mount Olympus
bearing the brilliant gear, the god of fire's gift.

—Homer
(translated by Robert Fagles)

Foreword

This is a remarkable and perhaps a unique book. There have been many studies of the development of warfare, even more of the history of international relations, while those on international and constitutional law are literally innumerable. But I know of none that has dealt with all three of these together, analyzed their interaction throughout European history, and used that analysis to describe the world in which we live and the manner in which it is likely to develop. Indeed, few people can match Philip Bobbitt's qualifications to write it: doctorates in both law and strategic studies, a respected record of publications in both, long experience in government, and all informed by a deep understanding of history such as most professional historians would envy.

Even as recently as a decade ago Bobbitt's approach, and yet more, his conclusions, would have seemed profoundly shocking to international lawyers and specialists in international relations alike. The conventional wisdom of the Western world, derived from Kant through Jeremy Bentham, proclaimed by Woodrow Wilson in 1918 and implemented by Franklin D. Roosevelt in 1945, was that war was a condition of international disorder that should and would be remedied by the development of international law and enforced by appropriate courts on the model of those prevalent in Western democracies. On that basis had been created the whole apparatus of the United Nations and World Courts on which we allegedly depend today for the maintenance of international order and which quite manifestly fails to provide it. Bobbitt goes back to an older and bleaker tradition: that associated with the name of Niccolò Macchiavelli, who wrote in a time in many respects very comparable to our own. Then as now the accepted paradigm of legitimate order, in his day the hierarchy of feudalism, was breaking down. A new template of legitimacy was needed, and could be provided only by a new institution, the State, termed by Thomas Hobbes "That Mortal God—our peace and defence." The State promised peace and defense to its members in return for their allegiance, their money, and, if need be, their lives. But the State could emerge and sustain itself only through success in war, and success depended on mastering the appropriate techniques—the weapons systems, the motivations, and the financial underpinning. Success in war legitimized the State, and the structures developed by the successful states—not simply the armed forces themselves but the financial arrangements required to pay for them and the constitutional relationship between rulers and ruled that made those arrangements possible—became the new paradigm for political authority and obedience throughout the European continent.

"International relations" thus became the relationship between sovereign States. But whence did those States derive their legitimacy? By the nineteenth century two very different schools of thought had developed. In Western Europe and the United States, after the English, American, and French Revolutions, it was assumed that the legitimacy of the State arose from popular consent enshrined in written or unwritten constitutions. Since these constitutions guaranteed domestic justice and order, it was further assumed that a similar mechanism would produce justice and order between states themselves. States that disturbed international order were behaving as "illegally" as were rebels against domestic order, and war against them was as legitimate as forcible proceedings against domestic rebellion. But in nineteenth century Germany a very different analysis had been developed by Hegel and his disciples. The State, they pointed out, was created not by law but by war. Since the State was not only the highest but the sole creator of legitimacy, self-preservation was the State's first duty and the primary concern of its citizens' allegiance. As the State had come into existence through war (a thesis self-evident in the case of Prussia, but no less applicable to the Untied States) so it could only survive and express itself through war. This philosophy was to shape German policy in the first half of the twentieth century. If Germany had won the two World Wars, the subsequent settlement would have borne the stamp of Hegel rather than that of Jeremy Bentham.

This is Bobbitt's starting point: "Law and strategy" he writes, "are mutually affecting." There is a constant interaction between the two. Legitimacy itself "is a constitutional idea that is sensitive to strategic events"—not least to a "strategic event" so cataclysmic as losing a war. Nevertheless, although wars may create and mold states, it is the State that creates legitimacy both domestic and external, and it is legitimacy that maintains "peace." If states can no longer maintain their legitimacy, or if their capacity to do so is called into question, then there will be another war, the outcome of which will create a new legitimacy. To ignore the legal aspect of international order is a recipe for the total and permanent war preached by Ludendorff and, more effectively, his younger colleague Adolf Hitler. To ignore the strategic aspect, as did Woodrow Wilson and his disciples, is at best to forfeit the capacity to create an international order reflecting one's own value system; at worst, to see it destroyed altogether.

In the first part of this book Bobbitt shows how the very nature of the State has been determined by the changing demands of war, and how it developed through a series of what he terms "Epochal Wars." In early modern Europe, princes had to create state mechanisms—administrative bureaucracies, legal systems, fiscal apparatus—to extract enough taxes from their subjects to enable them to conduct wars that were made increasingly expensive by the need to pay full-time mercenary forces, to build fortifications, and to buy guns. At the same time they created a common structure for reciprocal acceptance and mutual recognition, a "Society of States" that was eventually established by the Peace of Westphalia in 1648, to be updated at Utrecht in 1713 and again at Vienna a hundred years later. The legitimacy of this structure—states defined by territorial boundaries ruled by dynastic rulers "absolute" in their jurisdiction—was challenged at the end of the eighteenth century by the concept of the "nation," one that not only created a new criterion of legitimacy but could alone provide the numbers and motivation of a new age of mass warfare. But if these newly enlisted masses were to be motivated and militarily effective the State had to provide not only defense but welfare and education, and if they did not the "audit of war" would find them out. That was what happened in the First World War, which destroyed the dynastic regimes that proved unable to mobilize and motivate their peoples. But no peace was then possible until an alternative criterion of legitimacy emerged that could win universal acceptance. A three-cornered struggle had to take place between the liberal democracy of the West, the bellicose tribalism of Nazi Germany, and the authoritarian socialism of the Soviet Union. So for Bobbitt the Long War that opened in 1914 ended only with the Soviet collapse in 1990 and the apparent triumph of Western concepts of "legitimacy."

The settlements reached at Paris in 1990 that concluded both the Second World War and the Cold War that followed it might have been expected, like its predecessors at Vienna, Utrecht, and Westphalia, to introduce another long period of stable peace. Both Germany and Russia were now democratic nation-states and accepted "Western values"; not only the rule of law legitimized by democratic consent, but a further criterion of legitimacy that had developed in the West during the struggle against totalitarianism—the recognition of universal "human rights": a major derogation from the state sovereignty that had been the basis of international relations since the Peace of Westphalia. But there was another and yet more fundamental difference between this peace settlement and its predecessors. Those had established a stability between nations that rested on a balance between the powers. This recognized not so much the triumph of

Western democratic values as the overwhelming and apparently unchallengeable power of the United States: its supremacy in the weapons systems created by nuclear and information technology, its enormous wealth, and the universal attractiveness of its popular culture. America's European allies were at best subordinate and dependent associates. This, so it was hoped, would be a unipolar world of a kind not seen since the fall of the Roman Empire; but like the Roman Empire, it would be based on a rule of law.

What went wrong? It is here that Bobbitt's thesis becomes fascinating and controversial. One obvious feature of the Paris treaties was that, although they may have settled the problems that had tormented Europe for the past hundred years, Europe was now only one region in a global system whose complexities that settlement did not begin to address. Even within Europe, the settlement could not deal with the fallacy that had invalidated the Wilsonian world vision from the very beginning. Nation-states, the building blocks of the international community, are not "given": they have to be created. Nations—self-conscious ethnic communities—do not create states, though they can certainly destroy them. On the contrary, with few exceptions, states create nations. Even in Europe the problem of "state-building" in the Balkans remained, and remains, unsolved, while elsewhere in the world stable nation-states are the exception rather than the rule. More common are states that have signally failed to create nations, and can barely function as "states" at all.

Further, even the great nation-states that possessed the cohesion and discipline to fight and survive the two World Wars were already becoming obsolete. It did not require a mass effort of national dedication to produce the weapons that destroyed Hiroshima and Nagasaki, nor could a similar effort have preserved them. It was largely the realization of their reciprocal vulnerability that prevented the conflict between the West and the Soviet Union from erupting into violence, and made it possible for the Soviet Union to be defeated by American "soft power." For if weapons of mass destruction could so easily penetrate the conventional defenses of the nation-state—and to nuclear there were to be added chemical and biological threats—so could, in peacetime, economic strength and cultural dominance. Instant communications made possible by information technology were creating a global society that, though far from homogenous, was increasingly interdependent, and within which no nation-state, however powerful, could regard itself as independent and invulnerable: not even the United States, as it discovered on September 11, 2001.

So as the development of guns had destroyed the old feudal order, and the development of railways the old dynastic order, now the development of computers has destroyed the nation-state. Not the State itself, as Bobbitt is at pains to show: the State will always be necessary to provide security, fiscal organization, and law. But in the same way as princely states mutated into dynastic territorial states, and they in their turn into nation-states, now nation-states are mutating into what Bobbitt terms "market-states," and the second part of his book is devoted to describing the nature of market-states and the possible kinds of world that they may create. The plural is significant: Bobbitt provides no single scenario for the future but multiples, none of them very attractive: we are required to choose among a wide range of equally disagreeable dystopias. We are also required to choose among a wide range of possible wars, because Bobbitt is under no illusion that, any more than their predecessors, market-states will provide perpetual peace. At worst there may be cataclysms, at best a continuation of the low-key global violence to which we have become accustomed over the past ten years and from which not even the wealthiest and most power-ful communities will be able to escape. The best they can do is reduce their vulnerability, and the only victory they can look forward to is avoidance of defeat.

This book was virtually complete before the events of September 11 gave a horrible reality to Bobbitt's description of the possibilities that now lie before us. But for that, *The Shield of Achilles* might be ranked with such massive prophecies of doom as Spengler's *Decline of the West,* which scared us witless in the 1930s and is now deservedly forgotten. Such a fate is unlikely to befall this volume. Anyone who believes that the author con-templated with equanimity the future that lies before us should first read the poem from which the book takes its title. Bobbitt believes that mankind could be facing a tragedy without precedent in its history. It is not clear that he is wrong.

—Michael Howard

Prologue

We are at a moment in world affairs when the essential ideas that govern statecraft must change. For five centuries it has taken the resources of a state to destroy another state: only states could muster the huge revenues, conscript the vast armies, and equip the divisions required to threaten the survival of other states. Indeed posing such threats, and meeting them, created the modern state. In such a world, every state knew that its enemy would be drawn from a small class of potential adversaries. This is no longer true, owing to advances in international telecommunications, rapid computation, and weapons of mass destruction. The change in statecraft that will accompany these developments will be as profound as any that the State has thus far undergone.

THE END OF THE LONG WAR AND THE TRANSFORMATION OF THE MODERN STATE

This book is about the modern state—how it came into being, how it has developed, and in what directions we can expect it to change. Epochal wars, those great coalitional conflicts that often extend over decades, have been critical to the birth and development of the State, and therefore much of this book is concerned with the history of warfare. Equally determinative of the State has been its legal order, and so this is a book about law, especially constitutional and international law as these subjects relate to statecraft. This book, however, is neither a history of war nor a work of jurisprudence. Rather it is principally concerned with the *relationship* between strategy and the legal order as this relationship has shaped and transformed the modern state and the society composed of these states. A new form of the State—the market-state—is emerging from this relationship in much the same way that earlier forms since the fifteenth century have emerged, as a consequence of war. This war, the fifth great epochal war in modern history, began in 1914 and only ended in 1990. The Long

War, like previous epochal wars, brought into being a new form of the State—the market-state. The previous form—the constitutional order of the nation-state—is now everywhere under siege.

As a result of the Long War, the State is being transformed, and this transformation is constitutional in nature, by which I mean we will change our views as to the basic *raison d'être* of the State, the legitimating purpose that animates the State and sets the terms of the State's strategic endeavors.

The nation-state's model of statecraft links the sovereignty of a state to its territorial borders. Within these borders a state is supreme with respect to its law, and beyond its borders a state earns the right of recognition and intercourse to the extent that it can defend its borders. Today this model confronts several deep challenges. Because the international order of nation-states is constructed on the foundation of this model of state sovereignty, developments that cast doubt on that sovereignty call the entire system into question.

Five such developments do so: (1) the recognition of human rights as norms that require adherence within all states, regardless of their internal laws; (2) the widespread deployment of nuclear weapons and other weapons of mass destruction that render the defense of state borders ineffectual for the protection of the society within; (3) the proliferation of global and transnational threats that transcend state borders, such as those that damage the environment, or threaten states through migration, population expansion, disease, or famine; (4) the growth of a world economic regime that ignores borders in the movement of capital investment to a degree that effectively curtails states in the management of their economic affairs; and (5) the creation of a global communications network that penetrates borders electronically and threatens national languages, customs, and cultures. As a consequence, a constitutional order will arise that reflects these five developments and indeed exalts them as requirements that only this new order can meet. The emergence of a new basis for the State will also change the constitutional assumptions of the international society of states, for that framework too derives from the domestic constitutional rationale of its constituent members.

THE RELATIONSHIP BETWEEN MILITARY INNOVATION AND CHANGE IN THE CONSTITUTIONAL ORDER

Ever since Max Weber,[1] scholars have argued that a revolution in military affairs brought forth the modern state by requiring an organized system of finance and administration in order for societies to defend themselves. Accepting this premise, however, it is unclear precisely which revolution in military affairs actually brought the modern state into being. Was it the use of mobile artillery in the sixteenth century that abruptly rendered the castles and moats of the Middle Ages useless? Or was it the Gunpowder Revolution of the seventeenth century that replaced the shock tactics of pikemen with musket fire? Or the rise in professionalism within the military in the eighteenth century and the cabinet wars this made possible (or was it the change in tactics that accompanied mass conscription in the nineteenth century)? One important consequence of asking this question in this way is that it assumes that there has been only one form of the modern state: the nation-state. If, as many believe, the nation-state is dying owing to the five developments mentioned above, then this scholarly debate about the birth of the state has consequences for its death.

But if we see, on the contrary, that *each* of the important revolutions in military affairs enabled a political revolution in the fundamental constitutional order of the State, then we will be able not only to better frame the scholarly debate but also to appreciate that the death of the nation-state by no means presages the end of the State. Moreover, we will then be able to see aright the many current political conflicts that arise from the friction between the decaying nation-state and the emerging market-state, conflicts that have parallels in the past when one constitutional order was replaced by another and led to civil strife within the State and spurred novel and deadly conflict abroad. Finally, we will be better prepared to craft new strategies for the use of force that are appropriate to this new constitutional order—and vice versa.

THE RELATIONSHIP BETWEEN THE CONSTITUTIONAL ORDER AND THE INTERNATIONAL ORDER

Every society has a constitution. Of course not all of these are written constitutions—the British constitution, for example, is unwritten. Nor does every society happen to require a state. But every society—the Vineyard Haven Yacht Club no less than the Group of Eight—has a constitution because to be a society is to be constituted in some particular way. If a revolution in military affairs enables the triumph of certain constitutional order in war, then the peace conferences that ratify such triumphs set the terms for admission to the society of legitimate states, a society that is reconstituted after each great epochal war on the basis of a consensus among states. Each great peace conference that ended an epochal war wrote a constitution for the society of states.

Yet all constitutions also carry within themselves the seeds of future conflict. The 1789 U.S. constitution was pregnant with the 1861 civil war because it contained, in addition to a bill of rights, provisions for slavery and provincial autonomy. Similarly the international constitution created at Westphalia in 1648, no less than those created at Vienna in 1815 or Utrecht in 1713, set the terms for the conflict to come even while it settled the conflict just ended. The importance of this idea in our present period of transition is that we can shape the next epochal war if we appreciate its inevitability and also the different forms it may take. I believe that we face the task of developing cooperative practices that will enable us to undertake a series of low-intensity conflicts. Failing this, we will face an international environment of increasingly violent anarchy and, possibly, a cataclysmic war in the early decades of the twenty-first century.

While it is commonly assumed that the nuclear great powers would not (because they need not) use nuclear weapons in an era in which they do not threaten each other, in fact the new era that we are entering makes their use by a great power more likely than in the last half century. Deterrence and assured retaliation, as well as overwhelming conventional force, which together laid the basis for the victory of the coalition of parliamentary nation-states in the Cold War era, cannot provide a similar stability in the era of the market-state to come because the source of the threats to a state are now at once too ubiquitous and too easy to disguise. We cannot deter an attacker whose identity is unknown to us, and the very massiveness of our conventional forces makes it unlikely we will be challenged openly. As a consequence, we are just beginning to appreciate the need for a shift from target, threat-based assessments to vulnerability analyses.* What is less appreciated is the consequent loss of intrawar deterrence[†] and the implications of this loss with respect to the actual use of nuclear weapons. To illustrate this paradox consider this example: Nuclear weapons do not deter biological warfare (because its true perpetrators can be easily disguised), and yet a nuclear strike is probably the only feasible means of destroying a biological stockpile that is easy to hide and fortify in a subterranean vault. As we shall see, the possibilities of nuclear pre-emptive strikes, draconian internal repression, and fitful retaliation all accompany the scenarios of weakened deterrence and disguised attacks, and all can lead to cataclysmic wars between states that would otherwise studiedly avoid such confrontations. Even though the possibility of cataclysmic war threatens the twenty-first century, however, defensive systems can play a far more useful role than they could in the previous period, when they tended to weaken deterrence.

---

*A target or threat-based strategy depends upon retaliating against enemy assets. The threat of retaliation against known targets keeps the peace. A vulnerability-centered strategy employs various defenses to keep the peace when the targets for retaliation are unknown.

[†]Intrawar deterrence can dampen escalation, as parties already at war nevertheless refrain from aggressive acts that would lower the costs of retaliation for those acts to the retaliator.

At the same time that we have experienced these quiet yet disturbing changes in the strategic environment, there have been ongoing low-intensity conflicts of the kind we have seen in Bosnia, Rwanda, Northern Ireland, Palestine, and elsewhere, which are being transformed by the information revolution. Remote, once local tribal wars have engaged the values and interests of all the great powers because these conflicts have been exported into the domestic populations of those powers through immigration, empathy, and terrorism.

What is rarely noted is the relation between cataclysmic and low-intensity wars and the constitution of the society of market-states that will have to fight them. There can be no peace settlement without war, but there *can* be peace making. If we can successfully manage the consensus interventions of the great powers in low-intensity conflicts—as we have done, finally, in the former state of Yugoslavia—we will have constructed a new constitution for the society of market-states, thereby avoiding the systemic breakdown that provokes more generally catastrophic war. It may be that the very vulnerability of the critical infrastructures of the developed world, which invites, even necessitates, great-power cooperation, will then provide a basis for strengthening the society of states through information sharing and market cooperation.

HOW TO UNDERSTAND THE EMERGING WORLD ORDER OF MARKET-STATES

There is a widespread sense that we are at a pivotal point in history—but why is it pivotal? This book offers an answer: that we are at one of a half dozen turning points that have fundamentally changed the way societies are organized for governance. It identifies this change and shows how it is related to five previous such pivotal moments that began with the emergence of the modern state at the time of the Renaissance. It lays bare the neglected relationship between the strategic and the constitutional—the outer and inner faces of the State. Yet, this book is just as concerned with the future as it is with the past, laying out alternative possible worlds of the twenty-first century.

The modern state came into existence when it proved necessary to organize a constitutional order that could wage war more effectively than the feudal and mercantile orders it replaced. The emergence of a new form of the State and the decay of an old one is part of a process that goes back to the very beginning of the modern state, perhaps to the beginning of civil society itself. That process takes place in the fusing of the inner and outer dominions of authority: law and strategy.

Whether war or law is the initial object of innovation, constitutional and strategic change inevitably ensue, and new forms of the State are the result of the interaction. Each new form of the State is distinguished by its unique basis for legitimacy—the historical claim it makes that entitles the State to power.

A great epochal war has just ended. The various competing systems of the contemporary nation-state (fascism, communism, parliamentarianism) that fought that war all took their legitimacy from the promise to better the material welfare of their citizens. The market-state offers a different covenant: it will maximize the opportunity of its people. Not only the world in which we live but also the world that is now emerging is more comprehensible and more insistent once this historical development is appreciated and explored for the implications it holds for the fate of civilization itself.

The emergence of the market-state will produce conflict in every society as the old ways of the superseded nation-state (its use of law to bring about certain desired moral outcomes, for example) fall away. This emergence will also produce alternative systems that follow different versions of the market-state in London, Singapore, or Paris, and this development could also lead to conflict. Most important, however, the global society of market-states will face lethal security challenges in an era of weakened governments and impotent formal international institutions. And these challenges will pose difficult internal problems as well, as every developed, postindustrial state struggles to maintain democracy and civil liberties in the face of new technological threats to its well-being.

A society of market-states, however, will be good at setting up markets. This facility could bring about an international system that rewards peaceful states and stimulates opportunity in education, productivity, investment, environmental protection, and public health by sharing the technologies that are crucial to advancement in these areas. And these habits of collaboration can provide precedents for security cooperation; for example, the United States can develop ballistic missile defense technology or fissile material sensors that can be licensed to threatened countries. The technology for safer nuclear energy can be provided as a way, perhaps the only way, of halting global warming while assisting Third World economic development. A state's internal difficulties can be dealt with—perhaps can only be dealt with—through international information sharing that the market makes feasible. Markets, on the other hand, are not very good at assuring political representation or giving equal voice to every group. Unaided by the assurance that the political process will not be subordinated to the most powerful market actors, markets can become targets of the alienated and of those who are disenfranchised by any shift away from national or ethnic institutions.

The decisions that arise from the emergence of the market-state are already, or will soon be, upon us, but they are often disguised if they are not seen in the context of this new form of the State.

THE FUTURE OF THE STATE

The pattern of epochal wars and state formation, of peace congresses and international constitutions, has played out for five centuries to the end of the millennium just past. A new constitutional order—the market-state—is about to emerge. But if the pattern of earlier eras is to be repeated, then we await a new, epochal war with state-shattering consequences. Many persons see war as an illness of states, a pathology that no healthy state need suffer. This way of looking at things more or less disables us from shaping future wars, as we search, fruitlessly, for the wonder serum that will banish war once and for all (or as we plan to fight wars we know—or believe—we can win). Yet we can shape future wars, even if we cannot avoid them. We can take decisions that will determine whether the next epochal war risks a general cataclysm.

Whatever course is decided upon will be both constitutional and strategic in nature because these are the two faces of the modern state—the face the state turns toward its own citizens, and the face it turns toward the outside world of its competitors and collaborators. Each state develops its own constitutional order (its inward-facing profile) as well as its strategic paradigm (its outward-turned silhouette), and these two forms are logically and topologically inseparable. A state that privatizes most of its functions by law will inevitably defend itself by employing its own people as mercenaries—with profound strategic consequences. A state threatened with cyberattacks on its interdependent infrastructures can protect itself by virtually abolishing civil privacy or by increasing official surveillance and intelligence gathering or by expensively decentralizing. Each course has profound constitutional consequences.

THE STRUCTURE OF THIS BOOK

The Shield of Achilles treats the relationship between strategy and law. I had originally intended to publish this study in two volumes, corresponding to the different focus in each: whereas the first part of this work deals with the State, the second takes up the society of states; whereas the first is largely devoted to war and its interplay with the constitutional order of the State, the second concentrates on peace settlements and their structuring of the international order.

I have come to see, however, that there is so intimate a connection between the epochal rhythms of state formation and the abrupt shifts in international evolution that a single volume is truer to my subject. Nevertheless, for readers interested in the history and future of war, Book I, "State of War," can stand alone; for those interested in the history and future of international society, I believe Book II, "States of Peace," can be read with profit by itself.

At the beginning of each of the six Parts of this combined work, a general thesis is set forth as a kind of overture to the narrative argument that is then provided. Similarly, the poems that precede and follow each of the Parts reflect some of the motifs of the presentation.

"State of War," Book I of this work, focuses on the individual state; it is divided into three parts, which correspond to three general arguments.

Part I, "The Long War of the Nation-State," argues that the war that began in 1914 did not end until 1990. By looking at earlier epochal wars beginning with the Peloponnesian Wars, one can see how historians from Thucydides onward have determined whether a particular campaign is a completed war or only a part of a more extended conflict such as the Thirty Years' War. Epochal wars put the constitutional basis of the participants in play and do not truly end until the underlying constitutional questions are resolved. This is how it was with the Long War, which was fought to determine which of three alternatives—communism, fascism, or parliamentarianism—would replace the imperial constitutional orders of the nineteenth century. The Long War embraces conflicts we at present call the First World War, the Bolshevik Revolution, the Spanish Civil War, the Second World War, the wars in Korea and Viet Nam, and the Cold War.

Part II provides "A Brief History of the Modern State and the Constitutional Order"* beginning with the origin of the State in Italy at the end of the fifteenth century and ending with the events that began the Long War. These chapters assert the thesis that epochal wars have brought about profound changes in the constitutional order of states through a process of innovation and mimicry as some states are compelled to innovate, strategically and constitutionally, in order to survive, and as other states copy these innovations when they prove decisive in resolving the epochal conflict of an era. Sometimes the impetus comes from the constitutional side, as when the political changes wrought by the French Revolution in the late eighteenth century demanded tactical and strategic change to cope with the loss of a highly trained officer corps; sometimes the impetus was the reverse, as when the use of mobile artillery against the rich walled city-states of Italy in the early sixteenth century required the creation of

---

*By *State* I mean a political community that bears international status, like Germany or India, not a subdomain or province like Hesse or Bengal (or Texas). By *nation* I mean an ethno-cultural group.

bureaucracies and efficient systems of taxation. Most often the causality was mutual: strategic innovations (like the use of mass conscription) brought about changes in the constitutional order of the State—such as a broadened franchise and mass public education—and these constitutional changes in turn brought forth new tactical and strategic approaches that sought to exploit the possibilities created by the new domestic political environment, opportunities for innovations as different as terror bombing and the Officer Candidate School.

Part III of Book I, "The Historic Consequences of the Long War," argues that the Long War of the twentieth century was another such epochal war, and that it has brought about the emergence of a new form of the State, the market-state. These chapters address the situation of the United States, one of the first market-states, and suggest how this state will change both constitutionally and strategically as this new constitutional order comes to maturity.

Related theses can be found elsewhere. The notion that state formation in Europe occurred as a result of a revolution in military tactics (a claim made by Michael Roberts and others), the "short century" thesis (the notion that the century began in 1914 and ended with the end of the Cold War) associated with Eric Hobsbawm, and even the notion that a new form of society is coming into being (proposed by Peter Drucker, among others) are well-known. My thesis, however, implies, but also depends upon, the constitutional/strategic dynamic of five centuries, and it is this dynamic that shapes the expectations I put forward about the future structure and purpose of the market-state.

While Book I treats the individual state, Book II, "States of Peace," deals with the subject of the society of states. The society of states, as described notably by the late Hedley Bull, is to be distinguished from the state system. The state system is a formal entity that is composed of states alone and defined by their formal treaties and agreements. The society of states, on the other hand, is composed of the formal and informal customs, rules, practices, and habits of states and encompasses many entities—like the Red Cross and CNN—that are not states at all. International law is usually defined in terms of the state system. There are, of course, exceptions to this way of looking at international law, particularly in the work of Myres McDougal and his followers. In Book II, I treat international law as the practices of the society of states rather than as an artifact of the state system. I argue that international law is a symptom of the triumph of a particular constitutional order within the individual states of which that society consists (and is not therefore a consequence solely of the international acts of states). International law arises from constitutional law, not the other way around.

Part I of Book II, "The Society of Nation-States," deals with the society

of states in which we currently live. It traces the origins of this society to
the abortive peace that followed World War I and the American program
that attempted to superimpose the U.S. constitutional model on the society
of states. Part I then brings this plan forward to its collapse in Bosnia in the
1990s, and concludes with the claim that the society of nation-states is rapidly decaying. Although it is not novel to encounter a claim that the nation-
state is dying, my thesis is markedly different from others because it
derives from my general conclusion that the dying and regeneration of its
constitutional orders are a periodic part of the history of the modern state.
Those who write that the nation-state is finished are usually also of the
view that the nation-state is synonymous with the modern state itself. Thus
they are committed to maintaining that the State is withering away, a
highly implausible view in my judgment. Once one sees, however, that
there have been many forms of the modern state, one can appreciate that
though the nation-state is in fact dying, the modern state is only undergoing one of its periodic transformations.

Part II of Book II, "A Brief History of the Society of States and the
International Order," revisits the historic conflicts that have given the modern state its shape and which were the subject of Part II of Book I. In Book
II, however, the perspective has changed. Here I am less concerned with
epochal wars than I am with the peace agreements that ended those wars.
Part II makes the claim that the society of modern states has had a series of
constitutions, and that these constitutions were the outcome of the great
peace congresses that ended epochal wars. The state conflicts discussed in
Book I are taken up in Book II in terms of their peace conferences, culminating in the twentieth century with the Peace of Paris that ended the Long
War in 1990. In these chapters, the emphasis is on international law rather
than strategic conflict, though of course, consistent with my general thesis,
the two subjects are treated as inextricably intertwined.

Part III, "The Society of Market-States," depicts the future of the society of states. Its chapters hypothesize various possible worlds that depend
on different choices we are even now in the process of making. Most of
this Part is devoted to a series of scenarios about the future, adapting methods pioneered by the Royal Dutch Shell Corporation. Book II ends with
the conclusion that, by varying the degree of sovereignty retained by the
People, different societies will develop different forms of the market-state.
The task ahead will be to develop rules for cooperation when these different approaches frustrate consensus or even invite conflict—a conflict that
could threaten the very survival of some states.

Finally, I should like to provide some background regarding the title of
this work. "The Shield of Achilles" is the name of a poem by W. H. Auden.
At the end of this book I have reprinted that poem in full. It provides, in
alternating stanzas, a juxtaposition of the epic description of classical

heroic warrior society with a gritty, twentieth century depiction of warfare and civilian suffering. It is important to remember, in the discussions on which we are about to embark, that they ultimately concern violence, and that our moral and practical decisions have real consequences in the use of force, and all that the use of force entails for suffering and death. This is the first point to be suggested by the title.

The shield for which Auden named his poem and to whose description much of the poem is devoted is described by Homer in Book XVIII of the *Iliad,* lines 558–720 (see pp. ix–xiii). Many readers will be familiar with this famous passage, which has inspired paintings by Rubens, Van Dyck, West, and others as well as countless classical Greek depictions. It will be recalled that the Trojan hero Hector had claimed the armor worn by Patroclus when he slew Patroclus in battle; this armor had belonged to Achilles. Patroclus had borne Achilles' armor into battle in an effort to inspire the Greeks by making them believe that Achilles himself had taken the field. Achilles then asked his mother, the sea goddess Thetis, to procure for him another set of armor from Hephaestus, the armorer of the gods, whose forge was beneath the volcano at Mount Etna.

Hephaestus's mirror, which showed the past, present, and future, might also come to the minds of some persons. It is my aim not only to support certain theses about strategy, law, and history with arguments drawing on the past, but to illuminate our present predicament and speculate about the choices the future will present us. This is another resonance of this title to which I wish to call attention.

Hephaestus created an elaborate shield on which he depicted a wedding and feasts, a marketplace, dancing and athletics, a law court, and a battle, along with other arts of culture, the cultivation of fields, and the making of wine. This is the main point that I wish my readers to bear in mind: war is a product as well as a shaper of culture. Animals do not make war, even though they fight. No less than the market and the law courts, with which it is inextricably intertwined, war is a creative act of civilized man with important consequences for the rest of human culture, which include the festivals of peace.

CONCLUSION

Many things ought to look different after one has finished reading this book: former U.S. President Bill Clinton, British Prime Minister Tony Blair, and German Chancellor Gerhard Schroeder, who have been widely criticized in their respective parties, will be seen as architects attempting a profound change in the constitutional order of a magnitude no less than Bismarck's. As of this writing, U.S. President George W. Bush appears to be pursuing a similar course on many fronts. Foreign policy concerns, like the protection of the critical infrastructure of the developed world or the creation of intervention forces (such as those so discredited in Viet Nam and Somalia), which may now seem marginal, will be seen as centerpieces in the struggle to change, or at least manage, the shape of wars to come. The law-oriented methods of the nation-state will be seen as being replaced by the market-oriented methods of the market-state, setting controversies as different as abortion rights and affirmative action in a new context. For example, nation-states typically endorsed—or banned—prayers in public schools because such states used legal regulations on behalf of particular moral commitments. The market-state is more likely to provide an open forum for prayers from many competing sects, maximizing the opportunity for expression without endorsing any particular moral view. This is but one example of countless such contrasts.

Above all, the reader should get from this book a sense of the importance of certain choices that otherwise might be made in isolation but that will structure our future as thoroughly as similar choices in the last half millennium structured our past.

There are times when the present breaks the shackles of the past to create the future—the Long War of the twentieth century, now past, was one of those. But there are also times, such as the Renaissance—when the first modern states emerged—and our own coming twenty-first century, when it is the past that creates the future, by breaking the shackles of the present.[2]

Preparation

Still one more year of preparation.
Tomorrow at the latest I'll start working on a great book
In which my century will appear as it really was.
The sun will rise over the righteous and the wicked.
Springs and autumns will unerringly return,
In a wet thicket a thrush will build his nest lined with clay
And foxes will learn their foxy natures.

And that will be the subject, with addenda. Thus: armies
Running across frozen plains, shouting a curse
In a many-voiced chorus; the cannon of a tank
Growing immense at the corner of a street; the ride at dusk
Into a camp with watchtowers and barbed wire.

No, it won't happen tomorrow. In five or ten years.
I still think too much about the mothers
And ask what is man born of woman.
He curls himself up and protects his head
While he is kicked by heavy boots; on fire and running.
He burns with bright flame; a bulldozer sweeps him into a clay pit.
Her child. Embracing a teddy bear. Conceived in ecstasy.

I haven't learned yet to speak as I should, calmly.
With not-quite truth
and not-quite art
and not-quite law
and not-quite science

Under not-quite heaven
on the not-quite earth
the not-quite guiltless
and the not-quite degraded

—Czesław Miłosz

BOOK I

STATE OF WAR

Paradise Lost
(Book III, lines 111–125)

. . . They therefore as to right belonged,
so were created, nor can justly accuse
their maker, or their making, or their fate,
as if predestination overruled
their will, disposed by absolute decree
or high foreknowledge: they themselves decreed
Their own revolt, not I: if I foreknew,
foreknowledge had no influence on their fault,
which had no less proved certain unforeknown.
So without least impulse or shadow of fate,
or aught by me immutably foreseen,
they trespass, authors to themselves in all
both what they judge and what they choose; for so
I formed them free, and free they must remain,
till they enthrall themselves . . .

—John Milton

Introduction:
Law, Strategy, and History

LAW, STRATEGY, HISTORY—three ancient ideas whose interrelationship was perhaps far clearer to the ancients than it is to us, for we are inclined to treat these subjects as separate modern disciplines. Within each subject we expect economic or political or perhaps sociological causes to account for developments; we are unlikely to see any necessary relation among these three classical ideas. They do not appear to depend upon each other.

Of course we understand, from the point of view of any one of these three disciplines, how events in one can affect events in another. A war is won, and international law changes, as at the Nuremberg trials that followed World War II and called to account those who had obeyed orders they believed to be lawful. Or a war is lost, with the consequence that a new constitutional structure is imposed, as happened to Japan after World War II. Thus does strategy change law—and we call it history. Or the law of a state changes—as by the French Revolution, for example—and this change brings about the *levée en masse* that enables a Napoleon to conquer Europe through strategic genius; thus does law change strategy, and this too we call history. Or history itself brings new elements into play—a famine drives migration across a continent or technological innovation provides the stirrup—and an empire falls, and with its strategic collapse die also its laws. With all these examples we are familiar, but we understand this interrelationship as the by-product of cause and effect, the mere *result* of wars, famine, revolution, in which history is simply the record of events, organized according to the usual subject matters. We scarcely see that the perception of cause and effect itself—history—is the distinctive element in the ceaseless, restless dynamic by means of which strategy and law live out their necessary relationship to each other. For law and strategy are not merely made in history—a sequence of events and culminating effects—they are made of history. It is the self-portrayal of a society that

5

enables it to know its own identity.[1] Without this knowledge a society cannot establish its rule by law because every system of laws depends upon the continuity of legitimacy, which is an attribute of identity. Furthermore, without such a self-portrayal, no society can pursue a rational strategy because it is the identity of the society that strategy seeks to promote, protect, and preserve. One might say that without its own history, its self-understanding, no society can have either law or strategy, because it cannot be constituted as an independent entity.

History, strategy, and law make possible legitimate governing institutions. For five centuries, the operation of these institutions has been synonymous with the presence of the modern state, and so we may be inclined to think of the subjects of these disciplines—history, strategic studies, jurisprudence—as mere manifestations of the State. Such a reaction is natural enough with respect to law: some writers, such as Kelsen[2] and Austin,[3] have held that there is no law without the State. And other writers, such as Machiavelli[4] and Bodin,[5] present strategy as an aspect of the State, for it is the State that sets the terms of engagement pursued by generals, that fields their armies and declares their wars or announces their capitulations. It is even plausible to regard history in this way: for this reason, Hegel wrote that history ended at the Battle of Jena, with the birth of the state-nation, for history ends with the creation of an institution that makes the Absolute attainable.[6] These reactions are understandable but they are misguided.

The State exists by virtue of its purposes, and among these are a drive for survival and freedom of action, which is strategy; for authority and legitimacy, which is law; for identity, which is history. To put it differently, there is no state without strategy, law, and history, and, to complicate matters, these three are not merely interrelated elements, they are elements each composed at least partly of the others. The precise nature of this composition defines a particular state and is the result of many choices. States may be militaristic, legalistic, and traditional to varying degrees, but every state is some combination of these elements and can be contrasted with every other state—and with its own predecessors—in these ways.

The legal and strategic choices a society confronts are often only recombinations of choices confronted and resolved in the past, now remade in a present condition of necessity and uncertainty. Law cannot come into being until the state achieves a monopoly on the legitimate use of violence. Similarly, a society must have a single legitimate government for its strategic designs to be laid; otherwise, the distinction between war and civil war collapses, and strategy degenerates into banditry. Until the governing institutions of a society can claim for themselves the sole right to determine the legitimate use of force at home and abroad, there can be no state. Without law, strategy cannot claim to be a legitimate act of state.

Only if law prevails can it confer legitimacy on strategic choices and give them a purpose.* Yet the legitimacy necessary for law and for strategy derives from history, the understanding of past practices that characterizes a particular society.

Today, all major states confront the apparently bewildering task of determining a new set of rules for the use of military force. Commentators in many parts of the world have observed a curious vacillation and feck-lessness on the part of the great powers at the very time those powers ought to be most united in their goals, for the Long War that divided them has now ended. Or perhaps it is the end of the Long War that accounts for such widespread confusion. Because the ideological confrontation that once clearly identified the threats to the states of either camp has evaporated, it has left these states uncertain as to how to configure, much less deploy, their armed forces.[7] What seems to characterize the present period is a confusion about how to count the costs and benefits of intervention, pre-paredness, and alliance. What does the calculus for the use of force yield us when we have done our sums? Only an unconvincing result that cannot silence the insistent question: "What are our forces for?"[8] Because no cal-culus can tell us that. We are at a moment when our understanding of the very purposes of the State is undergoing historic change. Neither strategy nor law will be unaffected. Until this change is appreciated, we will con-tinue the dithering and the ad hockery, the affectations of cynicism and the placid deceit that so typifies the international behavior of the great powers in this period, a period that ought to be the hour of our greatest coherence and conviction. It is not that the United States did or did not decide to go into Somalia or Bosnia; it's that the United States has made numerous decisions, one after the other, in both directions. And the same thing may be said of the pronouncements of the other great powers regarding North Korea, Iraq, and Rwanda. "Ad hoc strategies" is almost a contradiction in terms, because the more states respond to the variations of the hour, the less they benefit from strategic planning.

The reason the traditional strategic calculus no longer functions is that it depends on certain assumptions about the relationship between the State and its objectives that the end of this long conflict has cast in doubt. That calculus was never intended to enable a state to choose between competing objectives: rather, that calculus depends upon the axiomatic requirement of the State to survive by putting its security objectives first. We are now entering a period, however, in which the survival of the State is paradoxi-cally imperiled by such threat-based assumptions because the most power-ful states do not face identifiable state-centered threats that in fact imperil

*This is the true import of Clausewitz's celebrated remark that "war is the continuation of politics by other means."

their security. Having vanquished its ideological competitors, the democratic, capitalist, parliamentary state no longer faces great-power threats, threats that would enable it to configure its forces by providing a template inferred from the capabilities of the adversary state. Instead, the parliamentary state manifests vulnerabilities that arise from a weakening of its own legitimacy. This constitutional doubt is only exacerbated by the strategic confusion abroad for which it is chiefly responsible. So the alliance of parliamentary great powers,* having won their historic triumph, find themselves weaker than ever, constantly undermining their own authority at home by their inability to use their influence effectively abroad. With a loosening grip on their domestic orders, these powers are ever less inclined to devote themselves to maintaining a world order. The strategic thinking of states accustomed to war does not fit them for peace, which requires harmony and trust, nor can such thinking yet be abandoned without risking a collapse of legitimacy altogether because the State's role in guaranteeing security is the one responsibility that is not being challenged domestically and thus the one to which it clings. We have entered a period in which, however, states must include in the calculus of force the need to maintain world order. This is not the first such period; indeed, the last epoch of this kind was ended by the eruption of the conflict that has just closed, leaving us so disoriented. Accordingly, there is much to learn from the study of that conflict, and also from earlier eras that were marked by changes in the constitutional form and strategic practices of the State.

Preliminarily, there are a few widespread preconceptions that must be put to one side. In contrast to the prevalent view that war is the result of a decision made by an aggressor, I will assume that, as a general matter, it takes two states to go to war. The common picture many Americans and Europeans have of states at war is that they came into hostilities as a result of the aggression of one party. It is like a class bully in a schoolyard who provokes a fistfight in order to terrorize his classmates. But the move to war is an act of the State and not of boys. States that wish to aggrandize themselves, or to depredate others, may employ aggression, but they do not seek war. Rather it is the state against whom the aggression has been mounted, typically, that makes the move to war, which is a legal and strategic act, when that state determines it cannot acquiesce in the legal and strategic demands of the aggressor. So it was with Germany, Britain, and France in 1939.[9] So it was with Athens and Sparta in 431 B.C. A corollary

---

*A great power is a state capable of initiating an epochal war, that is, a conflict that threatens the constitutional survival of the leaders of the society of states. Attacks by lesser states can be swiftly rebuffed (as Iraq learned in the Gulf War). Even a state whose forces can be decisive in a particular campaign—like North Viet Nam's—can neither initiate nor terminate an epochal war. Its attacks are insufficient to call the constitutional survival of its adversary into question or to settle such questions when they are posed by others.

to this idea is the perhaps counterintuitive notion that sometimes a state will make the move to war even when it judges it will lose the war that ensues. A state that decides it can no longer acquiesce in a deteriorating position must ask itself whether, if it chooses to resist, it will nevertheless be better off, even if it cannot ultimately prevail in the eventual conflict.

Many persons in the West believe that war occurs only because of miscalculation; sometimes this opinion is combined with the view that only aggressors make war. Persons holding these two views would have a hard time justifying the wisdom of Alliance resistance to Communism the last fifty years because it was usually the U.S. and her allies and not the Soviets who resolutely and studiedly escalated matters to crises threatening war. Besides the obvious cases involving Berlin in 1952, or Cuba in 1962, we might add the decisions to make the move to war in South Korea and in South Viet Nam, the nature and motivations of which decisions are underscored by the persistent refusals of the Americans and their allies to bomb China or invade North Viet Nam. That is, in both cases the allied forces fought to stop aggression by going to war and declined to employ decisive counteraggression.

Those persons who concede these facts and conclude that these decisions were wrong, and yet who applaud the victory of the democracies in the Cold War, are perhaps obliged to reconsider their views. For it was this peculiar combination of a willingness to make the move to war coupled with a benign nonaggression, even protectiveness, toward the other great powers that ultimately gave the Alliance victory. Sometimes this matter is confused in the debate over precisely how this victory was achieved. Was the Cold War won because U.S.-led forces militarily denied Communist forces those strategic successes that would have sustained a world revolution? Or was it won because northern-tier markets were able to build an international capitalist system that vastly outperformed the socialist system (and an international communications network that informed the world of this achievement)? Such a debate misses the point, perhaps because it is suffused with the assumptions about war and miscalculation to which I have referred. Neither military nor economic success alone could have ended the Cold War, because neither alone could deliver legitimacy to the winning state, or deny it to the loser. Moreover, neither military nor economic success was possible without the other: can one imagine a European Union having developed without Germany, or with a Germany strategically detached from the West? Even the ill-fated American mission in Viet Nam contributed to the ultimate Alliance victory: a collapse of military resistance in Indochina in 1964 would have had political effects on the very states of the region whose economies have since become so dynamic (analogous to those effects that would have been felt in Japan following a collapse of resistance in Korea in 1950). The political and economic, far from being decisive causal factors on their own, are really two faces of the same phenomenon. Only the coherent union of a constitutional order and a strategic vision could achieve the kind of results that ended, rather than merely interrupted, such an epochal war. We shall have to bear this in mind with regard to maintaining either success, political or economic, in the future.

Contemporary imagination, however, like so many aspects of contemporary life, is suffused with presentism. This is often commented on by those who lament the current lack of interest in the past, but it is equally manifest, ironically, in our projections about the future. This leads us to the third preconception that must be dismissed: namely, that future states of affairs must be evaluated in comparison with the present, rather than with the unknowable future. One encounters this often in daily life, in the adolescent's decision to quit school so "I can make more money" (because going to school pays less than working in a fast-food shop) or the columnist's claim that "if we balanced the budget, interest rates would drop and growth would increase" (because the government would not be adding to the demand for borrowed money). In those cases the speaker is making the mistake of comparing a future state of affairs with the present, and omitting to imagine what an alternative future state of affairs might be like (if he stayed in school and qualified for a better job; if the government steeply increased taxes in order to balance the budget), which would provide the proper comparison. If this seems altogether too obvious, let me give one famous example of this preconception.*

Many commentators believe that the turning point in the 1980 U.S. presidential elections came in the first debate between the candidates when Governor Reagan asked the American people to consider the question "Are you better off today than you were four years ago?" Indeed, this riposte was so successful that it was used in the 1984 debate by Reagan's opponent, Walter Mondale; and used again by George Bush against Michael Dukakis; and then used by Governor Clinton against President Bush.

Such a question, however, can scarcely be the measure of a presidential administration because the one thing we know is that things will never stay the same for the length of a presidential term, regardless of who is in power. Governor Reagan ought to have asked the public in 1980, "Are we better off now than we would have been if President Ford had held office these last four years?" This is the measure of the choice to be made, which might be phrased: "Will we be better off in four years, not 'than we are now' but 'because of the choice we are asked to make now'?"

---

*Even a thoughtful commentator can succumb to this fallacy, as when Michael Mandelbaum asserted that the NATO mission had failed because the people of the Balkans "emerged from the war considerably worse off than they had been before." James Steinberg, "A Perfect Polemic," *Foreign Affairs* (November/December 1999): 129.

The calculus employed by a state in order to determine when it is appropriate to make the move to war is, similarly, future-oriented. It asks: will the state be better or worse off, in the future, if in the present the state resorts to force to get its way? For half a millennium, the State has been an attractive institution for making political decisions precisely because it is potentially imperishable. The State, being highly future-oriented, can channel resources into the future and harness present energy for deferred gains. But this quality of futurism is also its vulnerability: the State is a clumsy instrument for persuading people to make sacrifices when objectives are in doubt, or to parry subtle long-term threats, because the interests of the people can easily be severed from those of the State when long-term objectives and goals are at issue. In the long term, as Keynes remarked, we are all dead. In periods in which the objectives to be pursued by the State are unclear, its very habits of orientation toward the future do not help to marshal the popular will, and thus the State is apt to be disabled from carrying out commitments that may be necessary for its ultimate security and the welfare of future generations to which it is, *faute de mieux,* committed. Threats such as the destruction of the ecology, the erosion of the capital base, potential threats to its critical infrastructure, and especially demographic developments all play on this vulnerability, for each such threat can call on a vocal domestic constituency that, out of reasonable motives but a present-minded orientation, can paralyze rational action. And, it should be noted, military power can quickly erode if a state does not accurately conceptualize the threats it actually faces, and thus neglects to adopt a strategy that meets those threats.

It is interesting to ask just what the United States, for example, at the end of the twentieth century took to be the objectives of its strategic calculus. According to a Pentagon White Paper at the time, there were three such objectives: deterrence, compellance, and reassurance.[10] It can be easily shown, however, that these three objectives were hangovers from the era just past, indeed that they were borrowed from theories about the objectives of nuclear strategy. What is less obvious is that, at the end of the war the Alliance had just won, objectives such as these were worse than useless because they tended to obscure the tasks that the United States had to undertake in order to redefine the goals of its national security policy. Let us look at each of the three purported objectives.

Deterrence is an extraordinarily limited theory that relies on a reasonable but extraordinarily broad assumption. That assumption is that the State will make decisions as a result of balancing the benefits to be achieved by a course of action against the costs incurred in pursuing those benefits by the particular means proposed. This assumption, in turn, depends on the commonsense observation that human beings can imagine pain greater than that they now endure, that they can imagine happiness greater than that in which they now delight, and that they will evaluate possible futures in terms of their mixtures of these two imaginary states. For instance, deterrence is a common means in criminal law, in the classroom, even in the family. "Don't even think of parking here" reads a familiar sign that reflects this approach.

As a strategy, deterrence makes most sense in the extreme case of nuclear deterrence, where the interest of the state in simple survival intersects the clarity of the danger of annihilation. Deterrence is more problematic, however, when the calculations on which it relies become more complex, or when these calculations are clouded by cultural differences and varying attitudes toward risk, or when the facts on which such calculations depend are uncertain or colored by wishful thinking. In other words, the idea of deterrence is itself so much a part of human nature that it can be applied only as it is affected by the various fallacies and shortcomings to which human nature is prey. Moreover, the strategic theory of deterrence is of a very limited application. It is scarcely deterrence, much less nuclear deterrence, that prevents the United States from invading Canada (or the other way around). Our political relations with Canada—an amalgam of our mutual history (including past wars against each other), our shared institutions, our intertwined economies, our alliances—are what render the idea of an attack by one on the other absurd enough to have been the basis for a popular satiric comedy. Rather, military deterrence is a concept that is useful *within* war or the approach to war, once political relations have become so strained that hostilities only await opportunity. It is only because we have lived for so long at war that we are inclined to miss this point, and that we have come to think of deterrence as a prominent feature of the international relations of a peacetime regime.

Drawing on work by the economist Jacob Viner, Bernard Brodie introduced into American strategic thinking the remarkable idea of nuclear deterrence. To see how revolutionary an innovation this was, we need only recall Brodie's famous conclusion. He wrote, "Thus far the chief purpose of our military establishment has been to win wars. From now on its chief purpose must be to avert them. *It can have almost no other useful purpose.*"[11] This makes a great deal of sense when dealing with nuclear weapons. The destructiveness of such weapons and their possession by our adversaries required a revolution in thinking about the purposes of our military forces. The military managers and politicians of the 1950s who were inclined to treat nuclear weapons as though they were simply bigger bombs had to learn a new, eerie form of strategic calculation. Deterrence, as a general matter, however, is a poor mission statement for a state's armed forces. No state, even one as wealthy as the United States, can afford to maintain the forces that would successfully deter all other states acting independently or in combination. One can see from the Pentagon

White Paper that this idea of Brodie's in the nuclear context—the use of armed forces to avert war—has now infiltrated the conventional, that is, the non-nuclear mission statement. Not only is it unrealistic to assert that the United States must maintain forces so vast as to be a matter of general, conventional deterrence. It also begs the one important question at the end of the Cold War: whom are we supposed to deter? Only when this question is answered can we so configure our forces as to realize such a policy. Deterrence does not come with its own specifications. If it takes two to war, then the idea of deterring wars without a specified adversary or threat is nonsense. The simple intuitive appeal of being so strong militarily that no one dares threaten you is an absurd idea for a state. Indeed, such an idea, however appealing, can actually weaken the state because the diversion of its resources into an undirected defense establishment undermines the economic and political strength the state will require should it find itself in a dangerous confrontation.

Advances in weapons technology make it possible for the leading states of the developed world to produce weapons of mass destruction that are so deadly relative to their size and cost that they can bypass even the most sophisticated attempts at defense by attrition. A corollary to this fact is that these weapons can be deployed clandestinely, so that the possibility of retaliation can be defied, and thus the strategy of deterrence rendered inoperable.

Compellance, too, is an idea that originated in the strategy of nuclear weapons and has been imported by the White Paper into the world of conventional forces. There is some considerable irony in this. Thomas Schelling introduced the neologism "compellance" as a complement to "deterrence" because this ancient concept of the use of force had become lost in the bizarre new world of nuclear strategy.[12] Schelling used "compellance" to describe the coercive use of nuclear weapons. This occurs when the threat of the use of such weapons seeks to compel an adversary state to actually do something it would otherwise not do, rather than merely refrain from doing something it would like to do (which is the purpose of deterrence). Compellance has been a purpose for armed force or, indeed, violence generally throughout the life of mankind. Yet it too is inappropriate as a mission statement for American forces. Only if we have a clear political objective can we determine what form of compellance is appropriate strategically. To say the mission of our forces is "compellance" is very like saying the mission of our minds is "thought." It is both a true and an empty sentence.

Compellance has had a good run lately. It was compellance that forced Saddam Hussein to evacuate Kuwait, once he had occupied and annexed it. It was compellance that forced Slobodan Milosevic to abandon Kosovo, a province he hitherto controlled utterly. These were worthy objectives, even if our execution of our war plans was not faultless. It would be good to have had a Bush Doctrine or a Clinton Doctrine, spelling out precisely for what reason and in what contexts the United States will compel other states by force, not only because the public in a democracy has a right to such an articulation of purpose, but also because without such limiting guidelines, compellance has a way of bringing forth countervailing force. When he was asked what the lesson of the Gulf War was, the Indian chief of staff is reported to have said, "Never fight the United States without nuclear weapons."

Interestingly, the third idea said to make up the mission of U.S. forces today is an idea also drawn from nuclear strategy. Sir Michael Howard is the father of the notion of "reassurance" in nuclear strategy.[13] In a series of essays and lectures he stressed reassurance as the key element in American nuclear strategy—an element not directed at our adversaries, but toward our allies. Much stronger forces are required, he concluded, to reassure a nervous ally who is dependent on U.S. nuclear protection than are actually required to deter a targeted enemy from attack. Like the contributions of Brodie and Schelling, this insight has been of crucial importance in the development and understanding of nuclear strategy. I doubt, however, that it can be of much use in the absence of a threat to the Atlantic Alliance, or to any of the states who have relied upon the American nuclear umbrella. Of what exactly are we to reassure our allies?

Reassurance as an idea in nuclear strategy depends on the crucial distinction between *extended* and *central* deterrence. The former term applies to the extension of American nuclear protection to Europe and Japan; the latter term refers to the threat of nuclear retaliation to deter attack on the American homeland. I have argued elsewhere that extended deterrence has driven U.S. nuclear strategy, not central deterrence. Reflecting on the evolution of nuclear strategy in *Democracy and Deterrence,* I concluded in 1983 that:

> The fate of the world does not hang on whether the U.S. or the USSR reduce their weapons or on whether they freeze their technologies. Indeed it should be easy to see that were either goal pursued too single-mindedly, there would result a much more dangerous world as other powers entered the nuclear field, approaching parity with the superpowers. Rather, our situation will be determined by whether Euro-Japanese security is enhanced, from their perspective, by our strategies, military and diplomatic; whether the public can be made to understand and support such steps as do enhance the extended environment when it has been told more or less constantly that it is the number of weapons and the advance of technology that causes (or cures) the problem. . . .[14]

I still endorse this view, but such reassurance is now far less easy to achieve because it has largely ceased to be defined. Reassurance played a crucial role during the final phase of the Long War, from 1949 to 1990, because it prevented multipolarity—the proliferation of nuclear weapons to states such as Germany and Japan—and thereby made possible the quite stable deterrence relationship between the United States and the Soviet Union. Reassurance, I will argue, has an equally vital role to play in the twenty-first century as our strategies move toward a greater emphasis on defense and deception. This will not be possible, however, if we continue to think and plan as though the stable relations that attended the possessors of weapons of mass destruction in the Cold War are somehow intrinsic to such weapons. Indeed, in my view the use of nuclear weapons is likelier in the first fifty years of the twenty-first century than at any time in the last fifty years of the twentieth century, but we are lulled into complacency about this because of the nuclear stability we experienced in that period. As one commentator has put it,

> our current strategic thought tends to project this peculiar experience into the future. It assumes that the use of mass destruction weapons will either be deterred or be confined to localized disasters caused by strategically incompetent terrorists. Competent adversaries, this thinking implicitly assumes, will have to emulate the "revolutionary" military technology that we now possess, but at the same time adhere to our old, counterrevolutionary strategy, as worked out in our superpower rivalry with the former Soviet Union. But, unfortunately, our old strategy is not an immutable law of nature. A highly competent enemy might well emerge who will seek to destroy the United States by using mass destruction weapons in a truly revolutionary kind of warfare.[15]

Thus we won't be able to reassure our peer competitors because we will fail to appreciate the true threats they face. Instead, mesmerized by "rogue states" whose hostility to the United States is essentially a by-product of our global reach that frustrates their regional ambitions, we will find ourselves increasingly at odds with the other great powers. Until we know what will serve the function of maintaining the Alliance that has become a proto–world order, we know not what to assure our allies of (or insure them against). The problem for the United States has become to identify its interests and future threats so that it can use its power to strengthen the world order that it has fought, successfully, to achieve, and that can, if properly structured and maintained, re-enforce American security to a far greater degree than the United States could possibly do alone. This is essentially an intellectual problem, just as the solution devised by the

United States and its allies to the universal vulnerability that attended the development of nuclear weapons was an intellectual solution.[16] But faced with the immense difficulties of anticipating a new strategic environment—both at the state level, where peer competitors may emerge as threats, and at the technological level, where weapons of mass destruction make nonsense out of our defense preparations—who is eager to take the bureaucratic and political risks inherent in accepting this challenge?[17] How much more likely it is that we will extrapolate from the world we know, with incompetent villains and heroic (and recent!) success stories.

Our present world, this "Indian summer"* as one writer puts it, not only presents a beguiling invitation to complacency reinforced by new technological possibilities. It also offers an opportunity to undertake some fundamental reassessments without the terrible pressure of war. Recent American successes in the Gulf War and in Yugoslavia, however, may tend to discourage any too-radical revisions.

Paul Bracken correctly concludes,

> The focus on the immediate means that a larger, more important question is not being asked: should planners redesign the U.S. military for an entirely new operational environment, taking account of revolutionary changes in military technology and the possible appearance of entirely new kinds of competitors?[18]

And Fred Iklé adds that

> . . . military planners, as well as most scholars, would shrug off these cosmic questions and instead nibble at the edges of the problem— worrying, say, about whether a tactical nuclear weapon could be stolen in Russia and sold to Iran, or whether Iraq might still be hiding some Second World War–type biological or chemical agents.[19]

A failure to take seriously the new strategic environment can have costly consequences in the domestic theatre as well. Should the use of a weapon of mass destruction occur, the state in which this happens will undergo a crisis in its constitutional order. How it prepares for this crisis will determine the fate of its society, not only its sheer survival, but the conditions of that survival. Some societies may become police states in an effort to protect themselves; some may disintegrate because they cannot agree on how to protect themselves.

The constitutional order of a state and its strategic posture toward other states together form the inner and outer membrane of a state. That mem-

---

*Written before September 11, 2001; see the epilogue.

brane is secured by violence; without that security, a state ceases to exist. What is distinctive about the State is the requirement that the violence it deploys on its behalf must be legitimate; that is, it must be accepted within as a matter of law, and accepted without as an appropriate act of state sovereignty. Legitimacy must cloak the violence of the State, or the State ceases to be. Legitimacy, however, is a matter of history and thus is subject to change as new events emerge from the future and new understandings reinterpret the past. In the following chapters, we will see how the standards against which state legitimacy is measured have undergone profound change, animated by innovations in the strategic environment and transformations of the constitutional order of states.

It is often said today that the nation-state is defunct.[20] Recently, in a single year, two books were published with almost identical titles, *The End of the Nation-State*[21] and *The End of the Nation-State: The Rise of Regional Economies*.[22] To these can now be added Martin van Creveld's distinguished *The Rise and Decline of the State*.[23] There are skeptics, however, who point out that both nationalism and the State are thriving enterprises. Moreover, for all the transfer of functions to the private sector, we don't really want the State to fade away altogether. There are many things we want the State and not the private sector to do because we want our politics rather than the market to resolve certain kinds of difficult choices. And, it must be conceded, the market itself has need of the State to set the legal framework that permits the market to function.

What is wrong in this debate over the demise of the nation-state is the identification of the nation-state with the State itself. We usually date the origin of the nation-state to the Peace of Westphalia in 1648 that ended the Thirty Years' War and recognized a constitutional system of states. In fact, however, the nation-state is relatively new—being little more than a century old—and has been preceded by other forms of the State, including forms that long antedated the Thirty Years' War. The nation-state is dying, but this only means that, as in the past, a new form is being born. This new form, the *market-state,* will ultimately be defined by its response to the strategic threats that have made the nation-state no longer viable. Different models of this form will contend. It is our task to devise means by which this competition can be maintained without its becoming fatal to the competitors.

PART I

THE LONG WAR OF THE NATION-STATE

THESIS: THE WAR THAT BEGAN IN 1914 WILL COME
TO BE SEEN AS HAVING LASTED UNTIL 1990.

*Epochal wars can embrace several conflicts that were thought to be
separate wars by the participants, may comprise periods of apparent
peace (even including elaborate peace treaties), and often do not maintain the same lineup of enemies and allies throughout. The Long War—
which includes the First and Second World Wars, the Bolshevik
Revolution and the Spanish Civil War, the Korean and Viet Nam Wars,
and the Cold War—like earlier epochal wars, was fought over a fundamental constitutional question: which sort of nation-state—communist,
fascist, or parliamentary—would lay claim to the legitimacy previously
enjoyed by the imperial state-nations of the nineteenth century.*

MCMXIV

Those long uneven lines
Standing as patiently
As if they were stretched outside
The Oval or Villa Park,
The crowns of hats, the sun
On moustached archaic faces
Grinning as if it were all
An August Bank Holiday lark;

And the shut shops, the bleached
Established names on the sunblinds,
The farthings and sovereigns,
And dark-clothed children at play
Called after kings and queens,
The tin advertisements
For cocoa and twist; and the pubs
Wide open all day—

And the countryside not caring:
The place names all hazed over
With flowering grasses, and fields
Shadowing Domesday lines
Under wheat's restless silence;
The differently-dressed servants
With tiny rooms in huge houses,
The dust behind limousines;

Never such innocence,
Never before or since,
As changed itself to past
Without a word—the men
Leaving the gardens tidy,
The thousands of marriages,
Lasting a little while longer;
Never such innocence again.

—Philip Larkin

CHAPTER ONE

Thucydides and the Epochal War

THUCYDIDES WROTE the classical masterpiece *The Peloponnesian War* during his exile from Athens. That exile began in 424 B.C. as a consequence of the loss of Amphipolis where he had been commander of the Athenian forces, ending the period in which he had served as an Athenian general in Thrace. He is believed to have begun his history of the war between Athens and Sparta in the years after 421 B.C., that is, after the signing of the Peace of Nicias that ended the Ten Years' War, as it was known to him and to his contemporaries. Yet he is not generally known to us as the author of a "History of the Ten Years' War."[1]

It is clear from the way in which he concludes his account of this war in the perfect tense before beginning his famous "second preface" that he regarded this war, and its history, as complete. It was only after 413 B.C. that Thucydides conceived the idea of the series of conflicts between Athens and Sparta as a single continuing war. At this point he decided to incorporate this first book—the history of the Ten Years' War—into the larger work.

Why was this? Thucydides did not make this decision after the final defeat of Athens; the main body of Books VI and VII was written when he was still in exile, well before the end of the war. Rather it seems to have been an Athenian raid in 414 B.C. that made clear that the issues of the Ten Years' War had not been fully resolved. So it is with all *epochal* wars—the Hundred Years' War,[2] the Thirty Years' War,[3] the Punic Wars[4]—and so it will be seen of the war of the twentieth century. Historians classify such epochal wars as constituting a single historical event because, despite often lengthy periods in which there is no armed conflict, the various engagements of the war never decisively settle the issues that manage to reassert themselves through conflict. Whereas we commonly think that the aspirations at the outset of war will determine its closure, it is in fact the dynamic interplay between strategy and the legitimating goals of the state that must be satisfied before we can say that a particular war is really over. The goals of the warring states must be compromised or otherwise the means of pursuing those goals by violence will be taken up again. When constitutional issues come into play there is little room for compromise; the loss of the issue can mean the loss of the state itself.

It may take some time, and some disagreement, before a consensus among historians is reached on the war of the twentieth century. The term "Thirty Years' War" appeared in 1649 in the English weekly newspaper *The Moderate Intelligencer,* shortly after the end of that war in 1648.[5] A journalist from that paper linked the various religious wars fought in Europe after the rebellion in 1618 of Protestant Bohemia against its Catholic ruler, Ferdinand of Habsburg, later the Holy Roman Emperor Ferdinand II. Other historians since have also tied these various wars together, though some begin somewhat earlier (1566) with the Dutch/Calvinist revolt against the Spanish,[6] which undoubtedly had a religious dimension. For these historians, the epochal war is the Ninety Years' War. Still others break up the struggle into two epochal wars: one beginning with the 1618 Bohemian revolt, and another commencing with the Swedish invasion of Bavaria in 1630, which was a more typical war among great powers. For historians of this perspective, such as Bishop Gepeckh of Freising, there were two separate wars: a Twelve Years' War and an Eighteen Years' War.[7] All of these wars have in common that they end with the Peace of Westphalia in 1648. Yet other historians, who emphasize the political and secular dimensions of the conflict, see it as continuing until the Peace of the Pyrenees in 1659 or the Peace of Copenhagen in 1660.[8] And one is not necessarily more correct than another: if the historian views the war as having arisen from sectarian differences, it is nevertheless true that by the end of the war Europe had been politicized, secularized, and rationalized to a degree inconceivable at the beginning of the struggle, when theological convictions so preoccupied Europeans that national, social, and patriotic considerations were subordinated.[9]

Similarly, although the actual phrase "Hundred Years' War" apparently was not used until the nineteenth century, historians two centuries earlier saw the conflict as a single epochal war, even if they disagreed as to its precise dates. As with the Thirty Years' War, the disagreement turns on what the ultimate issues are taken to be. Francois de Mezeray in his *Histoire de France* in 1643 considered the Anglo-French struggles to constitute a single war beginning in 1337 and lasting one hundred sixty years.[10] Most historians today start the war in 1328 (the date that Philip VI of France confiscated the French property of the English king Edward III and the year that Edward obtained a claim to the French throne) or 1340 (the year that Edward declared himself to be king of France), but some see the war between England and France as an Anglo-French civil war—because the kings of England were feudal lords of France—lasting from 1294 until 1558 (the date England lost her last holding in France and ninety-five years after the usual date for the end of the war when the English were removed from all of France except Calais).[11] The reasons given by the contending scholarly parties to this historical controversy assume the same fundamental premise: a single epochal war encompasses shorter wars, interposed with periods of little or no fighting, when a central issue links the constituent conflicts and remains unresolved until the ultimate settlement. Therefore, whether an epochal war can be said to encompass other particular wars depends on what issue the historian believes was central to all the linked conflicts, even if this issue only becomes clear in the course of the conflict itself. This is the lesson of Thucydides.[12]

Thucydides did not live to see his epochal war carried to its conclusion, when Macedon put an end to the constitutional order of Greek city-states and proved that only a larger empire could maintain itself and defend Greece. This event, like the war that preceded it, provides an overture to the narrative that follows.

CHAPTER TWO

The Struggle Begun: Fascism, Communism, Parliamentarianism, 1914-1919

WE SHOULD REGARD the conflicts now commonly called the First World War, the Second World War, and the Korean and Viet Nam Wars, as well as the Bolshevik Revolution, the Spanish Civil War, and the Cold War as a single war because all were fought over a single set of constitutional issues that were strategically unresolved until the end of the Cold War and the Peace of Paris in 1990.

The Long War (as I shall call it) was fought to determine what kind of state would supersede the imperial states of Europe that emerged in the nineteenth century after the end of the wars of the French Revolution (a war that also appeared as a series of engagements and discrete wars until the Congress of Vienna resolved the fundamental questions at issue). These states dominated Europe and eventually the world until the collapse of the European system in 1914. The Long War was fought to determine which of three new constitutional forms would replace that system: parliamentary democracy, communism, or fascism.

What propelled this cataclysm? What put these three particular alternatives in play? It was the instability of two states, Germany and Russia, within whose domestic societies these three options furiously contended. Once Germany and Russia were taken over by one of the radical alternatives to the parliamentary systems outside these states, Germany and the Soviet Union attempted to legitimate their regimes by making their systems the dominant arrangement in world affairs. As we shall see in Part I, the legitimacy of the constitutional order we call the nation-state depended upon its claim to better the well-being of the nation. Each of these three constitutional alternatives promised to do so best. Within every state, these alternatives contended, but it was the triumph of the radical alternatives in two Great Powers that led to the Long War. To understand this it is necessary to begin with the German struggle to create a nation-state.

FASCISM

After the Peace of Westphalia in 1648 full recognition was given to the sovereignty of both Catholic and Protestant German princes of the Holy Roman Empire—that, indeed, was the key solution to the conflict. Thus, despite paper provisions to the contrary, the Empire ceased to exist in practical terms. It had no common treasury, no authoritative common tribunals, and no means of coercing dissenting member states. In place of the Empire, there was only a collection of weak and disorganized states divided by religious affiliation.[1] This collection of states faced the great continental powers of France, Russia, and Austria, and the great maritime powers of Holland and England, all of whom had consolidated themselves constitutionally in the seventeenth century. These Great Powers were thus not joined by a great German state.

Not until the middle of the nineteenth century did one German state, Prussia, impose its rule on the others and create the first European nation-state.* From its beginning the German state was hostile to the prevailing international system and its creators, which had hitherto provided models for a German state. We owe to Bismarck the decisive strategy of separating German national aspirations from the liberal background that had formerly nurtured them. He accomplished this through the adroit use of war, defeating in turn both Austria-Hungary and France, the two states that had dominated German politics since Westphalia. This allowed him to place at the apex of the German state a radically conservative, militarist class whose only claim to pan-German legitimacy was that it alone was able to realize the ambitions of national unity. German nationalism[†]—a program that held that a state was legitimated by its service to a pre-eminent ethnic nation—was the prototype for fascism, as its expression in the Constitution of 1871 confirms.[2]

Bismarck did not so much unify as conquer the other German states and then proceed to transform their politics by delivering German unity under

*This development is discussed in more detail in Chapter 8.

[†]"The emergence of the German empire (in 1871) as a result of three short successful wars provided no final settlement of the problems in Central Europe. [Far from it, for] the unification of Germany gave great impetus to nationalist movements throughout the Continent. The means by which it was brought about afforded a dangerous, yet fatally easy pattern for others to follow. Since Germany had been united by force and through union had achieved a predominant position in Europe, other nationalities aspired to attain a greater preeminence than they enjoyed, and to reunite their people in the state by similar means." Nicholas Mansergh, *The Coming of the First World War, 1878–1914: A Study in the European Balance* (Longmans, Green, and Co., 1949).

a popular doctrine of militarism and ethnic nationalism. This put fascism on the table as a competitor to the parliamentary systems. But that would not necessarily have led to war had the question of constitutional legitimacy not arisen within the new German state. It is useful to remember that Bismarck's goal had been "to achieve German unity without revolution so as to fend off the social consequences of successful revolution," as Geoffrey Barraclough has put it.[3] When Bismark's successors were threatened by a Social Democratic electoral victory in 1912, they found the moment to attempt an ambitious strategic program of European conquest. Germany sought through an attack on the pre-existing empires of Europe a means of vindicating its claim to destiny that would, perforce, also vindicate its autocratic regime's claim to legitimacy. Indeed, we might think of the situation in Germany in 1914 as replicating that of Europe as a whole: within, as without, Berlin sought to defeat the movement for parliamentary self-government and the threat of revolution, the two other options contending for the future of Europe. This point is powerfully supported by the path-breaking work of the historian Fritz Fischer.[4] Whatever may have been the case when Barbara Tuchman wrote her popular and influential *Guns of August,* or A.J.P. Taylor his *War by Timetable: How the First World War Began,* it is impossible to maintain today,* in light of German archival research, that World War I was all a ghastly mistake, unintended by any of the parties, the result of complicated alliances and railroad timetables.[5]

In 1959, Fischer published an article in *Historische Zeitschrift* that would itself have considerable historical significance. Relying on archival materials from Wilhelmine Germany, including the September Program drafted by an assistant to Chancellor Bethmann Hollweg and initialed by Bethmann Hollweg, Fischer insisted that German war aims consistently pursued before and during the First World War were uncannily like those of the Nazis in the Second World War; that these war aims were the logical consequence of German political policy before the Sarajevo assassination in 1914;[6] and that these policies could only be fully understood as the effort of the Prussian elite to secure its victory over domestic elements of both liberal parliamentarianism and socialist revolution by achieving a European hegemony and a world position of epic dimensions.[7] Fischer showed further that the basic continuity in German history between 1871 and 1945 lay in its substantive goal:[8] the defense of a fascist constitutional system against liberalism and socialism.[9] This was the state that plotted the beginning of what became, after the miscarriage of its war plan in Sep-

---

*"It seemed clear that whatever else they had achieved, Fischer and his school had finally laid to rest the legend that in 1914 all the Great Powers had, in Lloyd George's now hackneyed phrase, 'slithered all over the brink into the boiling cauldron of war.'" Roger Fletcher, "Introduction," in Fritz Fischer, *From Kaiserreich to Third Reich: Elements of Continuity in German History, 1871–1945* (Allen & Unwin, 1986).

tember of 1914, the Long War. While the outbreak of war may have preceded the ideal German timetable by some months owing to the Serbian crisis in July 1914, the decision to go to war had already been taken by the only constitutional authority empowered to make that decision, as part of a program in which war was a necessary step. That this decision should come from Germany underscores the source of the question put to the world community by the Long War: for in Germany the choice among three constitutional options first flared into international violence. As we shall see, Russia somewhat later also resolved these historic constitutional options by violence. The United States, Britain, and France had already opted in favor of one of the critical paths, that of parliamentarianism, not without internal strife. Thus were the three principals of the Long War arrayed: Germany, Russia, and the three Atlantic states.

World War I did not solve the question of what sort of system would succeed to power; it only generalized that question to virtually all states. Thus one important political consequence of the war was the rise of a state embodying the ideal of socialism, bringing into the strategic and international sphere a third international ideology that arose in a domestic context. The Bolshevik Revolution may be seen, for our purposes, as bringing to the international level of conflict one of the domestic options in play in the collapsed states of post-1914 Europe.

COMMUNISM

During the course of 1917, following defeat on the Eastern Front, the authoritative capacity of the Russian state, its power to govern, ceased to exist. The Provisional Government that forced the tsar to abdicate adopted a parliamentary form, but, perhaps for this reason, it did not succeed to the authority of the tsarist state, nor was it able to establish legitimacy on its own. As Edward Acton described the situation:

> [T]raditional military discipline collapsed; the . . . police force disappeared, and the new government proved unable to establish control over the armed militia organized by workers . . . The effect of these developments was to render the liberal-dominated Provisional Government incapable of enforcing its will and to make it dependent instead upon society's voluntary acceptance of its policies. Those policies, however, proved increasingly unpopular.[10]

After introducing the full panoply of civil liberties and setting in train the democratization of local government, the Provisional Government wished to pursue the war according to the legal and moral obligations it felt it owed its allies as the legitimate heir to the sovereignty of the tsarist state. This attachment to law, so characteristic of the parliamentary democracies that served as models for the Russian Provisional Government, was fatal to its popular position because virtually all elements of the populace were united by an antipathy to the rule of law. Industrial workers who faced rapidly worsening economic conditions and the loss of their jobs frantically clamored for confiscatory government intervention on their behalf; peasants demanded to be given land and campaigned for the seizure and distribution of estates. There were also demands for separate preferential status by several of the national minorities. Antiwar feeling spread among the returning rank-and-file soldiers. On all these issues the Provisional Government had to repudiate the wishes of the people, and by so doing, it forfeited all popular support for its authority. As we shall see again in our later discussion of Weimar, Germany,* the parliamentary option had failed the nation.

> What underlay the Bolsheviks' increasing influence was the appeal of their policies . . . They committed themselves to a program of immediate peace, confiscation of noble estates, drastic reform of industrial relations and intervention to prevent economic collapse, and the principle of national self-determination . . . So widespread was popular support for its call for the transfer of "all power to the soviets" that when the party, operating through the apparatus of the Petrograd soviet, launched the armed uprising of 24–5 October, Kerensky and his colleagues [the parliamentary government] were unable to offer effective resistance . . .[11]

This widespread popularity of their program permitted the Bolsheviks to seize power, but not to hold it. Lenin and his colleagues in the Communist Party were by no means intoxicated with the niceties of popular democracy, nor with the view that the party leadership should be subordinated to the political opinions of even its own rank and file, much less those of the populace at large. Nevertheless, during the first months of office, the new government concluded the Treaty of Brest-Litovsk (despite the wish of many in the leadership to reject harsh German terms and launch a revolutionary war). The government gave legal sanction to peasant seizures of land and the local distribution of titles to these properties (despite the leadership's commitment to collective landholding). And the government felt itself forced to recognize the right of minority ethnic groups to state status, and proposed various decentralizing industrial measures "despite its view that these steps could lead to the unraveling of

*See Chapter 22.

the state." In the ensuing months there were numerous confrontations between the government and the peasants as the latter withdrew grain and raw materials from the market and the former began requisitioning supplies from the countryside. During this same period there were similar confrontations with industrial workers, whose numbers were swollen by returning soldiers. By mid-1918, 60 percent of Petrograd's workforce was unemployed.[12] It was far from clear, at this point, that the communist option would prevail. In the end, it was the conflict among the contending constitutional options for the state that actually saved the government and strengthened the Party, allowing it to centralize and finally to triumph.

This conflict—between communism, parliamentarianism, and fascism—came to a decisive juncture in Russia with the outbreak of civil war in the summer of 1918. Many of the most politically active persons were co-opted into the Soviet bureaucracy, the secret police, and the Red Army in the face of an armed challenge by the counterrevolutionary army, the Whites. The Whites represented a coalition of parliamentary and fascist groups, united by their hatred of communism. Their uprising suddenly presented the possibility that the redistribution in property relations and ownership that the workers and peasants had secured during 1917 might be reversed. This potential legal counterrevolution ignited the volunteers who joined the Red Army to defend their gains. The legal conflict—constitutional in nature—drove the strategic and, finally, the historical.[13]

When the Civil War ended, the now greatly strengthened government determined to continue the policies of "war communism"—to continue grain requisitioning and military-style discipline in the factories. This provoked a number of violent strikes, peasant riots, and, in 1921, the revolt at the Kronstadt naval base. Lenin and the party leadership reacted with the ameliorative New Economic Policy (NEP), which ended requisitioning, legalized private trade, and abandoned the semi-militarization of labor.

This was the prevailing economic program in 1927 when the first Five-Year Plan was introduced. This Plan proposed massive state investment that, with increases in agricultural and industrial productivity, was to bring about a rise in living standards. But even though investment soared, gains in productivity were slight, such that workers and peasants were now called upon to finance the state's investment in heavy industry. As it became clear that considerable coercion would be required, some of the Soviet leadership, led by Bukharin, urged a revision of industrial goals. Josef Stalin led the majority that insisted on overcoming the resistance of the society and replacing the NEP.

Requisitioning was reinstituted; when this proved insufficient, the state imposed a system of forced collectivization. Those peasants who resisted were deported to isolated regions in the north and east. Trade unions became parts of the Party apparatus, even as real wages fell; chronic shortages occurred and pressure increased for gains in production. Coercion succeeded, however, and this success was decisive in the state's attempt at transforming Russia into a communist society.

How did this state—and Stalin—succeed? We have seen that the state apparatus had been decisively strengthened during the 1920s: the army, the bureaucracy, the network of secret police had all been expanded. More importantly, however, the state prevailed because of the widespread commitment it was able to inspire in the public, drawing on its origins in the October Revolution, its victory in the civil war, and, above all, its identification of patriotism with class warfare.[14] The effect of this success was

> to radically redraw the boundary between state and society . . . Virtually every citizen became an employee of the state. Private commerce and independent artisan production were suppressed, and although collective farms notionally belonged to their members, in practice management was taken out of their hands, and they too became state employees. . . . [E]very worker was compelled to carry a labour book containing a detailed record of his labour performance; [absenteeism was a criminal offense]; and special permission was required to change from one job to another. . . . Virtually all institutions were subordinated to the state and run by party appointees. The press, the radio and publishing were run under direct party supervision.[15]

A state was thus created that vigorously and wholly embodied the other option to liberal parliamentary democracy, just as the German state had embodied the fascist alternative. The Revolution that gave it birth, and the Civil War that first threatened and then consolidated it, were both fought over precisely this choice of systems, and both the Civil War and the Revolution were provoked by military engagements occurring during the First World War and immediately thereafter. Indeed one can go further: the success of the Soviet state depended upon a ruthless state violence in order to achieve industrialization, and "Stalin's forced-march industrialization prepared the Soviet Union for an astonishing victory in World War II."[16]

There are those who think that a civil war or a revolution cannot be thought of as a strategic part of a larger, international conflict, but there are countless examples to the contrary.* Indeed, any view that epochal war is constitutional in nature virtually predicts that such wars will give rise to the eddies of civil war. A key factor in whether these conflicts should be thought of as campaigns in a more general, epochal war lies in whether great powers intervene in them. For this reason, the Spanish Civil War and

---

*Including the uprisings in the Low Countries that were part of the War of Spanish Succession. This incorporation of civil and interstate conflicts is also a theme in Thucydides.

the Korean and Viet Nam Wars, as well as the Russian Civil War, properly belong to the Long War; whereas the Ataturk Revolution, the Indian Civil War that accompanied partition, and the Nigerian Civil War do not. Intervention by the great powers is an indication that international interests are at stake—but only an indication, for there are sometimes regional or humanitarian reasons why a great power might intervene in a civil war, as Wilson did in the Mexican Revolution, or NATO chose to do in Kosovo. When Lloyd George intervened in the Russian Civil War, he meant Great Britain to intervene against the communist alternative, not against *Russia*. The interest at stake was Britain's interest in the international struggle against Bolshevism. The same is of course true of the Russian intervention on behalf of the Loyalist forces in Spain, and the German and Italian interventions on behalf of the Falange forces there.

To appreciate the Soviet challenge and its role in the Long War it is important to recall the violent antiparliamentarianism of the Bolshevik revolution and Civil War. The success of the Bolshevik government meant that by the end of the 1920s, the three competing constitutional options now contended, despite the Peace at Versailles, in an unstable international environment. Nor did this instability arise owing to upheavals in the defeated states alone. With the collapse of three of the World War I belligerents, new states appeared. Although in the West we are often inclined to think of this period as one of peace—*l'entre-deux-guerres*—the frontiers of these new states were often established through fighting, the borders between Poland, Lithuania, and Russia being an example. More importantly, in every country the three contesting options found significant popular followings. After the triumph of communism in Russia in 1917, a Bolshevik revolution followed in Bavaria in January 1919, and in Hungary between March and August. These events cast the problem for the Peace Conference then meeting at Versailles into this form: to impose conditions on Germany such that both protofascism, the Prussian militarist state, as well as communism, were made impossible.

Accordingly, the German state was dismantled. First, the army was reduced to 100,000 men (it had been, before the war and mobilization, 750,000)[17] and the general staff was dissolved. Provision was made for the trial of war criminals, including the kaiser, Chancellor Bethmann Hollweg, and Field Marshals von Hindenburg and Ludendorff. Treaty articles proscribed a German military air force and permitted only a rump fleet. Second, several new parliamentary states were created with specified boundaries, and legitimacy was conferred on them by the Peace Conference. Third, an international system of law, embodied in the League of Nations, was set up as a sort of global constitution of parliamentarianism. But none of this could finally succeed, because the fundamental idea on which the Treaty rested—that fascism and communism were illegitimate forms of nation-statehood—was not established by the end of World War I. To appreciate this we need only consult the competing national accounts of that five-year belligerency.

The Conference at Versailles offered a straightforward theory of the war: in Article 231 of the Treaty, Germany accepted responsibility for forcing the war upon the world, and underlying this was the view that the German system itself was to blame. The official German historians, however, took a different line. Between 1922 and 1926 the German government published a forty-volume collection of edited diplomatic documents (*Die grosse Politik der europäischen Kabinette*—The High Policies of the European Governments), attempting to show that Germany had not sought war in 1914. Part of the argument was that if the general staff had wanted war, there had been better opportunities in 1905 or 1909 than in 1914. Part of the argument was that Russia and France had wanted war: Russia for access to the Mediterranean, France to recover Alsace-Lorraine. In fact, every state that was involved had some self-aggrandizing war aim. Because the war aims of the European victors were in fact expressed in the Treaty, thus compromising the Wilsonian claims to disinterestedness that had, to some extent, induced the German capitulation, the Treaty itself was cited as evidence not of German culpability but of German victimization.

By contrast, Soviet commentators[18] argued that the war was the inevitable product of the last stages of capitalism. An international competition for new markets, for raw materials from colonies, and for new opportunities for investment had pitted the capitalist states against each other in the Middle East, the Far East, and Africa. Thus both communists and fascists argued that the prevailing international system required war—though they based their conclusions on different theories. Communists saw war as the natural outcome of arms races, driven by the industrialists who profited from competition in (and by) arms. Fascists saw war as a necessary struggle by means of which stronger states superseded the weak. In either case, the Treaty of Versailles could not end the war begun in 1914 because it did not, indeed could not, reconcile these perspectives.

By trying to answer the questions "What rights does a state have? When is a state legitimate?" with the utopian answers of the scientifically minded end of the nineteenth century—identifying the processes that cause a state to succeed in historical terms and thus to have its rights and its legitimacy accepted—each of these three competing ideologies offered a claim of equal plausibility. Only the complete collapse of actual states, the embodiments of these competing ideas, would answer these questions definitively. The Long War would be resumed until each of the competing systemic alternatives had been thoroughly and completely discredited in the eyes of its own people and the world. Despite all the second-guessing of the peacemakers at Versailles, it is hard to see how the resumption of war in the 1930s could have been avoided.

If Winston Churchill was right when he called the Second World War the "Unnecessary War"—because the threat of force by the West would have deterred the armed aggression by Nazi Germany, perhaps indefinitely, as proved to be the case with the Soviet Union—he was nevertheless wrong to imply that something short of a collapse of the competing systems would have given the world peace, or even an end to the outbreaks of international violence that have formed so much of the history of the Long War and thus of the twentieth century. Even in Britain, these choices were not finally made by the 1930s; perhaps this is one reason why the British were so irresolute in opposing the rise of Hitler. Indeed by the 1930s there was scarcely a country in the developed world, and few in the colonial world, that had failed to produce indigenous fascist, communist, and parliamentary parties.

CHAPTER THREE

The Struggle Continued: 1919–1945

IN 1917, Bolsheviks overhrew the Russian parliamentary state and in the ensuing decades civil conflict erupted between fascist and communist militias and parliamentary governments in Germany, Italy, and Spain, with the latter wholly unable to maintain order. The contested domestic order in each of these states would ultimately be controlled by that party that was able to leverage strategic and international maneuvering into domestic primacy. In Germany, Hitler used the universal public hatred of the Versailles Treaty as the foundation for his claims to power; in Russia, Lenin's adroit removal of Russian forces from World War I served the same role.

The relation between law and strategy, between the inner and the outer faces of the State, is maintained by history—the account given of the stewardship of the State. This account changes when the constitutional order of the State changes, as the new order sets new criteria for legitimacy. For the nation-state, these criteria were derived from its mission to improve the welfare of the nation. In a sense, all the nation-states of this era, whatever their ideology, were welfare states. For the nation-state, ideology supplies its history, and each of the contending ideologies—communist, fascist, and parliamentary—had a different account to give of the forces of history. Marx, Spengler, and Macaulay (among many others) all provided historical explanations of the political development of Europe that served to legitimate the ideological struggles of the three competing constitutional forms.

Thus it was crucial to the rise of fascism that a particular historical account be given to the strategic events of World War I, if that conflict was to be extended and renewed.[1]

Many influential groups—indeed much of German political society and of the general population—did not believe that Germany had been defeated: because Germany had been tricked into surrendering, the Allied victory in the First World War had never really been consummated. Apart from a brief period at the start of the war, there had been no military engagements in Germany. Virtually until the Armistice there had been a general expectation of ultimate victory in Germany, and, as one historian put it, "many [Germans] saw [the Armistice] not as a defeat but as a set-back which, with suitable leaders and policies, would be overcome."[2] This sense was both aggravated by and responsible for the "stab in the back" account of events, which depicted the collapse of Germany in 1919 as the act of corrupt politicians who had betrayed the nation by agreeing to an armistice. A widespread feeling of injustice took the immediate form of a campaign against the terms of the Versailles treaty, but the many sympa-thizers with this position in England and America were wrong, I think, to believe that a mere repudiation of some of the treaty's more onerous terms—rather than a renaissance of the German Reich—was the objective of the complaining parties. The reparations demanded by the Treaty were ludicrously punitive, but were eventually largely written off; more serious is the claim that Wilson's Fourteen Points had induced the German surren-der on a basis that was not genuinely fulfilled at the Peace Conference.

Speaking of the anti-Versailles groups in Germany at this time, Fischer recognized that

> over and above mere revision of Versailles, their great objective was the rehabilitation of the German Great-Power position, above all with regard to eastern Europe, to an eastern imperium guaranteeing a self-sufficient war economy . . . In such a political context the use of mili-tary force was taken for granted. . . . This objective had originated during the Kaiserreich, led to the First World War . . . and gathered momentum during the Third Reich and into the Second World War . . . which must be understood primarily as a reaction to the First World War, as a refusal on the part of [Germany] to accept the outcome of the First World War.[3]

Hitler achieved power in Germany by taking this task as his objective and by identifying repudiation of the Treaty with a rebirth of the German state. He studiedly and publicly pursued the goal of reopening hostilities. There had been of course a period during which overt hostilities ceased. Doubtless at the time of the Treaty of Locarno (1925) it must have appeared that Germany had chosen a parliamentary path and that the War had actually ended. The Dawes Plan (1924) plus inflation had eased the reparations burden on Germany, which, by the time Hitler came to power, was of little economic consequence in any case. But these appearances obscured the fact that a decision for parliamentarianism had not been made by the German nation, and that once the great economic depression cast doubt on the ability of a parliamentary state to deliver stability and pros-perity, Germany would opt for the fascist alternative to pursue precisely the same goals it had sought in 1914 by means that were dictated by the nature of fascism itself. On this view, one might say that hostilities were resumed in 1935 with German rearmament, not in 1939 with the attack on Poland.

Alan Bullock concluded his magisterial biography of Hitler with the claim that Nazism was rooted in German history, and that Hitler represented the logical outcome of nationalism, militarism, the worship of force, and the exaltation of the State.[4] I prefer to put this slightly differently: Hitler was the apotheosis of a particular malaise of Europe, which had provided the basis for the seizure of power over the German states at the end of the nineteenth century, and which inspired global ambitions. That Nazism was to some extent idiosyncratic to the German nation is a consequence of fascism itself and its derivation of the legitimacy of the state from its identification with the national ethnos and its interest. Fascism not only follows, but intensifies and exalts, unique cultural and ethnic aspects of the society that it seeks to govern. What is striking, for the purposes of the present work, is the deliberate resort to international violence on the part of all the great fascist powers, Germany, Italy, and Japan, *before* 1939.

It is an interesting historiographical issue whether the economic conditions and policies of the fascist states—their rapid rearmament, and heavy demands for the import of raw materials, fuel, and food, coupled with their chronic lack of foreign exchange and of sufficient export earnings— whether these conditions impelled the fascist states to war, as asserted by historians such as D. E. Kaiser,[5] or whether Hitler was essentially an improvising leader, seizing opportunities provided by the inept diplomacy of his adversaries, as suggested by A.J.P. Taylor's *Origins of the Second World War,* and war a mere contingency.[6] Taylor argues that the various stages of the Czech crisis were driven by Neville Chamberlain's initiatives, to which Hitler had only to react, and even that the declarations of war in 1939 were largely a result of poor timing by Hitler in his reaction to the continuing offers of appeasement by Britain and France. Others have concluded that Hitler's plan was, as William Shirer claimed, a blueprint for a series of world-dominating campaigns[7] animated by a visionary malice. And there are still other causal accounts of the origins of the Second World War by distinguished historians.[8] Perhaps all these judgments are to some degree true;* they do not entail the conclusion that, absent the causes they emphasize, war would not have occurred in any case. Putting to one side the various accounts of the origins of World War II, one may say that the

---

*Nor are these various explanations incompatible with the claim of one long war; see, for example, Taylor, *Origins of the Second World War,* who ends his book with the words "Such were the origins of the second World War, or rather of the war between the three Western Powers over the settlement of Versailles; a war which had been implicit since the moment when the first war ended" (278).

Long War could not have ended so long as fascism was alive in a great power—fascism as an outlook, as a guide to managing the affairs of state, as much an understanding of history as a political program. It is this attitude that Hitler shared with the German veterans of the First World War, that made him their hero as well as their representative. Resolute actions might have deterred Germany for a time; absent such actions, the temporary stalemate of Versailles was bound rapidly to end in violence.

To be able to appreciate the force of this attitude, this mentality, it is useful to remember three general facts about Europe before 1939, when large-scale hostilities resumed: first, that Hitler and Mussolini* were brought to power by the very parliaments they despised, and not by coups d'état, and that this occurred not because they had simply intimidated the ministries they faced down but because their programs and personalities were overwhelmingly popular, embodying the hopes and ideals of millions; second, that the programs of the fascists were defined by their opposition to parliamentary liberalism and communism, to conflicts with whom the fascists owed their ascension to power; and finally that for two years before the triumph of fascism in Germany in January of 1933, violence had been renewed on the international scene in a way that utterly discredited the Versailles parliamentary vision of world peace through law.† On these first two points, it is useful to review the record, which has been obscured by the fascist claims of a dramatic seizure of power, as well as by Western historians who are loath to admit the deep appeal of fascism to democratic publics.

In Italy the fascist ascendancy began to take shape as soon as the Versailles Conference was concluded. The Italian government that negotiated the treaty was swept away largely on that account by the election of 1919, and the new government was immediately shaken by the extraconstitutional seizure of Fiume by a group of army veterans led by the poet D'Annunzio, in protest against the Versailles agreement. The refusal of the government to arrest D'Annunzio or even to call for the withdrawal of his forces, and the Italian threats against Yugoslavia when its government wished to resume control of the city, reflected popular disenchantment with the Versailles settlement and reinforced those groups that favored direct, extralegal, anticonstitutional action.

The option of fascism was in play both domestically and internationally, and so long as it was alive in one arena, it remained a possibility in the other. In some states, notably Spain, its appeal lay principally in dealing with domestic conflict, and yet it played an international role. In Italy,

---

*As well as Tojo, by the way.

†Much as in our day the similar vision animating the U.N. has been discredited by its performance in Bosnia, Rwanda, Cambodia, and elsewhere.

what began as an international move quickly became a model for direct action on the domestic scene. Paul Hayes describes this vividly:

> [In Italy] demobilization had been followed by mass unemployment . . . Inflation, already high, rose sharply after 1918, exacerbating social tensions. Two of the worst-affected groups—landless peasants and poorly paid factory workers—soon resorted to the seizure of land or to strikes and factory occupations. The owners of property were terrified by this militancy and resentful of the government's apparent toleration of illegality. By 1920 fears of an Italian version of the events of 1917 in Russia were widespread among the upper and middle classes. It was in this situation that Fascism found its voice . . . In September 1920 . . . a wave of occupations and lockouts struck the industrial centres of the north. . . . Landowners and industrialists formed their own organizations and recruited private armies, mainly from the ranks of the unemployed war veterans. Increasing disorder lent credibility to Mussolini's vehement attacks on the lack of government authority.[9]

In this chaos, the Italian premier called the election of May 1921. When as a result the fascists were admitted to the national governing bloc, they were able to continue their campaign of violence against the socialists and communists from within the shelter of the police and the national government. Mussolini himself, however, left the coalition and relentlessly attacked the government, recognizing that the true source of his appeal lay in his posing an alternative to parliamentarianism. His campaign was equally aimed at the left and the liberals: he attacked the parliamentary system and the Versailles settlement, while managing a campaign of street terror against the parties and unions of the left. In 1922 he reoccupied Fiume and, when the government acquiesced in this move, he stepped up terrorist assaults in a number of industrial cities against leftists and trade unionists. When the left responded with a call for a general strike, Mussolini answered with an ultimatum threatening the government, challenging it to stop the strike and vowing to stop it himself if the government did not. By such maneuvering against the left, Mussolini was able to build an independent base of financial support among industrialists and landowners while at the same time making himself increasingly attractive to the very administration he was weakening. Although Mussolini always portrayed his rise to power as culminating in the March on Rome, in fact the role of the March was more complicated. Mussolini did not seize power. Rather he threatened to do so, began mobilizing the fascist paramilitaries, and thus provoked the collapse of the government. He then coolly refused to be brought into a coalition; faced down the interim government when the king refused to give permission to declare martial law; watched as a new coalition collapsed; and was finally invited by the king to be prime minister on the advice of the very parliamentarians whose ability to form a government he had frustrated.

A similar story can be told of Hitler's route to power, based also on the triangulated conflict between fascism, communism, and parliamentarianism refracted through domestic and international dimensions. Hitler's contempt for parliamentary democracy at home and the Versailles system abroad, his disgust at the political flaccidity of the parliamentary states and the pusillanimity of the Weimar politicians, his hatred of the socialist parties in Germany, and his desire to destroy the Slavic enemy where those parties held power, even his anti-Semitism, which called attention to the prominent role of Jews in parliamentary Weimar and in the communist movement—all these united the domestic and the international in a program of enormous moral and political appeal to the German people.

Hitler's skill, however, was not just in uniting these two dimensions, and thus tying his fortunes to the conflicts with (and between) parliamentarianism and communism. There were other, more established parties doing that. Indeed, the Nationalists themselves were a kind of protofascist party, who also attacked Versailles, were anti-Marxist, called for an aggressive foreign policy, and so forth. Rather it was because his was not an established party that, when the Great Depression made the Weimar Government appear helpless and confused, Hitler inherited the conservative followers of Hindenburg. His sociopathic nationalism and antisocialism only found a financial base in industrialists and landowners* after they began to doubt the ability of the established forces to maintain order against a left revolution. In Germany, as in Italy, but on a far larger and more aggressive scale, the fascists relied on street fighting and political violence against the left to provoke disorder. The civil conflict that fascism sought provided fascism's road to power much as the civil war in Russia had coalesced support for Bolshevism. When unemployment exceeded 30 percent, workers began to abandon the center parliamentary parties for the fascists and communists, the support for the latter ironically increasing the support for the former. Thus we can chart the dramatic rise in Hitler's electoral success from 1924 to 1932[10] with the parallel loss of support for the conservative forces. In July 1932, when the Nazi party won 37.3 percent of the vote, it exceeded this number in fourteen of Germany's thirty largest cities and in only one fell as low as 20 percent. In a multiparty state, with proportional representation, this is a remarkable popular showing. When Hitler ran against the conservative Paul von Hindenburg for the presidency, the latter was able to win only by relying on votes from the left-wing party, the SPD. When Hitler acceded to the chancellorship, he did so

---

*Indeed Hitler despised capitalism because the State does not control free markets.

on the same basis as the leader of any parliamentary party: he had the votes.*

Thus neither Hitler nor Mussolini seized power: both were brought to premierships by the calculations of other politicians who realized they needed them. They were needed because the parliamentary states that had "won" the First World War, or been set up by the winners, could not during their fleeting ascension settle the constitutional and moral question at issue, and were thus never secure in their claims of legitimacy in those states where this legitimacy was most closely tested. Legitimacy is a constitutional idea that is sensitive to strategic events; when the Versailles system proved itself strategically vacuous, the legitimacy of the parliamentary regimes that were its constitutional progeny suffered accordingly.

For the same reason that the Versailles peace was unstable domestically, the international scene was haunted by increasing violence. Consider the following timetable: In September 1931, on the basis of an odious and farcical pretext, the Japanese occupied Mukden and the area surrounding the Manchurian Railway. The following January they invaded the region north of Shanghai; by March 1933 they had reached the Great Wall. That same month, Japan withdrew from the League of Nations and Hitler came to power in Germany. In March 1935 Germany renounced the disarmament clauses of the Versailles Treaty and began open rearmament. In October, Italy invaded Abyssinia. In March 1936 the Germans occupied and fortified the demilitarized Rhineland, renouncing provisions of the Locarno treaty as well as those of Versailles. In July the Spanish Civil War began, accompanied by armed intervention on the part of Germany, Italy, and the Soviet Union in an explicit, violent competition. In March 1938, Germany annexed Austria. By the end of September, the German-speaking Sudeten region of Czechoslovakia had been seized. In March 1939, the rest of the Czech state was engorged. In April, Italy occupied Albania. All these states—China, Abyssinia, Spain, Austria, Czechoslovakia, Albania—were members of the League of Nations; indeed, two of them had been created by the Versailles Treaty. It is therefore not implausible to suggest that "war" did not begin with the declarations of war in 1939.

For some years before Hitler invaded Poland—a parliamentary state also created by Versailles[11]—triggering the declarations of war on September 3, 1939, by Britain and France, the world had experienced increasing armed conflict. On September 17, the Soviet Union invaded Poland.

---

*And Hitler was sustained in power by a broad base of popular support, based on fulfilling the fascist assumption of the nation-state social contract. Only Nazi Germany, of all the Western states, eliminated unemployment during the depression years of 1933–1938. Moreover, contrary to conventional assessments, this was done not by means of rearmament but in order to enable rearmament. See Dan Silverman, *Hitler's Economy: Nazi Work Creation Programs, 1933–1936* (Harvard, 1998); see also R. J. Overy, *The Nazi Economic Recovery 1932–1938* (Cambridge, 2d edn., 1996).

Though both states, fascist Germany and communist Russia, anticipated the conflict between them that ultimately came in 1941, they were united in their contempt for the international system of the parliamentary states. It seems clear that what was *not* established at Versailles was a peace, and therefore it seems reasonable to conclude that war had not really finally ended there.

There were of course other states in which these three competing paradigms struggled for supremacy—notably Japan and China—that entered the conflict at this stage, even though they had not been parties at its inception in 1914. Japanese fascism was driven by its own inner/outer struggle—the Eurocentric settlement that caused the war to pause in 1919 could not have prevented the rise of Japanese militarism, whatever the provisions agreed upon at Versailles. It is characteristic of epochal wars that parties change sides—as did Italy and Japan during the Long War, Austria during the Wars of the French Revolution, France during the Thirty Years' War—and that new parties join the conflict, while exhausted parties retire. It is interesting, however, to point out two facts about the rise of Japanese fascism that bear, even if tangentially, on the thesis of the Long War.

As we will see in Part II, the history of states reflects a complex interaction between profound constitutional change and strategic innovation. "The Long War" is a name that can be given to the strategic consequences of the constitutional development of the nation-state that began in the late nineteenth century, as this constitutional order replaced the imperial state-nations of the previous century and searched, restlessly, for the axiomatic legitimacy the old regimes had long enjoyed. Each of the three models of the nation-state—the parliamentary, the communist, and the fascist—strove for constitutional legitimacy in the domestic arena, and for a validation of that legitimacy in the international sphere. Japan also followed this course.

It was the bewildered response of the Tokugawa regime to the external pressures from Britain, France, and Holland for trading rights, and the threat posed by Russia to Japan's northern territories, that cast doubt on the vitality and internal legitimacy of that regime. The strategic crisis came in 1853 when a United States naval vessel appeared in Uraga Bay, armed beyond anything the Japanese could launch, and delivered an ultimatum demanding an opening of the Japanese trading market. China's sovereignty had already collapsed under the pressure of Western military technology after the Opium Wars of 1842, and now fears in Japan of a similar event precipitated a constitutional revolution of the kind that had occurred earlier in Europe. The Tokugawa regime could only offer continued isolation—which the West had shown it could penetrate—or appeasement, which had so notably failed to preserve sovereignty in the Chinese context.* The Meiji Restoration of 1868 thus began as a defensive response to Western threats. Although it was considered impractical to confront the Western powers in light of Japan's inferior military apparatus, a program of national defense was begun under the slogan "A strong economy: a strong army," with the goal of expelling the Western interlopers once economic self-sufficiency was achieved. Constitutional change, precipitated by strategic challenges, in turn brought forth its own strategic innovations. Conscription was introduced in 1873, which tended to encourage nationalist attitudes; with the forces thus raised, an internal rebellion in the 1870s was crushed, strengthening the allegiance of the nation to the State.[12] Gradually the objective of self-defense and renewed seclusion was replaced by the desire to become a great power on the European model. In 1890 the constitution of this transformed Japanese state was adopted. Significantly, it was modeled on the Prussian constitution.[13] It instituted a weak legislature without effective control over the budget. As a result, the political parties of the Diet were never able to claim to speak for the nation—that was reserved for the Emperor—and more and more they became perceived as corrupt, divisive forces. The Diet's efforts to control military spending by holding up the budget process were contrasted with the military's victories over China in 1894 and Russia in 1905, legitimating the role of the military as the voice of the nation, and showing the politicians up as petty and partisan.[14]

Thus, although the principal parliamentary parties "provided Japanese premiers in the 1920s, they failed to establish the mantle of legitimacy for parliamentary democracy."[15] Moreover, although the socialist parties within Japan were ruthlessly suppressed,[16] the example of Russian Bolshevism, and especially the rising specter of Chinese communism, increased the desire of the Japanese military to go on the offensive in East Asia. This group was able to discredit the parliamentary system by seizing the initiative in foreign policy: the invasion of Manchuria and the creation of the puppet regime of Manchukuo both were undertaken without political authorization.[17] When junior officers organized an abortive coup d'état in Japan itself, a wave of violence followed, including the assassination of the premier. The views of these insurrectionaries are reflected in this reminiscence:

[F]rom 1919 until the time of the Manchurian Incident in 1931, Japan fell into the abyss of spiritual darkness ... individualism, liberalism,

---

*The revolution in 1868 replaced a regime similar in many ways to the princely states of Europe that were succeeded by kingly states, as will be discussed in Part II. The Tokugawa had no standing army, no centralized bureaucracy embracing the various territorial components of the state, no permanent legations. David L. Howell, "Territoriality and Collective Identity in Tokugawa Japan," *Daedalus* 127 (Summer 1998): 105.

and democratic thought flowed freely through the muddied waters of materialism, utilitarianism, and the worship of the almighty yen. Socialism, communism and anarchistic thought spread like contagious diseases.[18]

These two facts—the role of the protofascist Prussian constitution and the alarm at socialism—are often overlooked in the debates about the relationship of Japanese to European fascism. For our purposes they provide some context to the expansion of the Long War into Asia, and Hitler's declaration of war on the United States immediately following Pearl Harbor. The defeat of the Japanese and the success of the American occupation destroyed fascism in Japan, even though the ethnic source of state legitimacy on which fascism depends had deeper roots in Japan than perhaps anywhere else. Fascism in Europe was also destroyed, not simply because it was defeated, but because the nature of the defeat, its totality and remorselessness, discredited it. Can we say then that the Long War ended in 1945?

Can we say, that is, that Yalta succeeded where Versailles had failed? It is by now a commonplace among some historians and politicians to observe that the illness of President Roosevelt, combined perhaps with his naive faith in his ability to manipulate Stalin, was responsible for the division of Europe—or at least the cession of the states of Eastern and Middle Europe to the Communist empire.[19] I am inclined to believe that this precise division was entirely a matter of the condition and location of armies in Europe, and that the date of the Normandy invasion—as to which the Americans actually had less leeway than any of the negotiating parties believed—determined the line of advance of Western forces of any magnitude. But whether or not I am correct in this conjecture, Yalta did not resolve the systemic issue: whether the order among nations, or within the conquered states, would be a rule of parliamentary law or of communism. The wartime Grand Alliance of nation-states—actually called the "United Nations"*—that prosecuted the war against Germany was a three-sided relationship dominated by fear of fascism but in no sense one coalesced around parliamentary values.[†]

---

*The term was suggested to Roosevelt by Churchill, who quoted the following stanza from Byron: "Thou fatal Waterloo/Millions of tongues record thee, and anew/ Their children's lips shall echo them, and say—/ 'Here, where the sword united nations drew, / Our countrymen were warring on that day!'/And this is much, and all which will not pass away." (*Childe Harold's Pilgrimage*, canto 3, stanza 35.)

†As Philip Bell has put it, "In the perspective produced by the Cold War, it became easy to think of that alliance as consisting of the Americans and British over against the Soviet Union; but this was a false picture of events at the time. The truth was of a meshing of interests and a criss-cross of disputes; not a clear divide, but a sort of cat's cradle of tangled threads. Roosevelt sought to work closely with Stalin, and so did Churchill. Each was prepared to do so, on occasion, against the other." P.M.H. Bell, *The Origins of the Second World War in Europe* (Addison Wesley Longman, 1986).

Bearing this in mind, is not the answer to the tedious controversy over who is responsible for the beginning of the Cold War, that "responsibility" lay in simply continuing to assert the claims of legitimacy that preceded the Second World War? These claims conflicted because they were asserted beyond the sovereignties of the democracies and the socialist states, over divided states—like Germany, Korea, and Viet Nam—and over emerging new states—chiefly in the Third World, where the legitimacy of the constitutional order was in play.

CHAPTER FOUR

The Struggle Ended: 1945–1990

THE LONG WAR now continued because it had not truly been ended. In the closing months of World War II the Red Army advanced over 1,500 miles west from Stalingrad to Berlin and beyond. Agreements reached at the Yalta Conference provided that the states thus overrun by the Soviet Army would be permitted to organize themselves according to free elections. The Soviet Union, however, relying on local communist parties in these states, set about creating regimes that would be exclusively communist in character, and that did not depend on—indeed, would not permit—the legitimacy conferred by an open electoral process. This was most dramatically demonstrated in Poland where, in January of 1945, Stalin recognized the communist-dominated Lublin Committee as the rightful government of Poland, in spite of having promised at Yalta the preceding February to include representatives of the government-in-exile in the new Polish government. Stalin continued to work for a purely communist constitutional arrangement on the basis of which, rather than through parliamentary elections, the legitimacy of the state was to be assured.

At the time of the Potsdam Conference in August, the Allies made two decisions that, though not explicitly connected, interacted so as to ensure that the Long War would not be ended at this stage. First, detailed arrangements were made for the temporary occupation of Germany according to four zones of authority, corresponding to the four great powers of the United Nations alliance (the United Kingdom, France, the United States, and the USSR). Berlin lay deep within the eastern zone that was to be governed by the Soviet Union but the city itself was also divided into four zones, each allocated to one of the Allied powers. All parties agreed that a peace settlement would follow, uniting Germany as a whole; in the interim, Germany was to be treated as a single economic unit.

Second, the British, French, and American powers agreed to a substantial extension of Polish borders westward into what had been Germany, on condition that the Soviet Union renew its pledge to provide a role for non-communist groups in the new interim Polish government, and to permit free elections, universal suffrage, and secret ballots for the selection of the permanent government. These elections were never held, and the noncommunist elements in Poland were liquidated. In February 1946, Stalin gave a widely publicized address saying that the Soviet Union had to remain prepared for war with the capitalist nations. The intentions behind this speech are still a matter of dispute, but its effect was to send shock waves through Washington. The next month, Churchill delivered his celebrated Fulton, Missouri, speech declaring that

> Communist parties, which were very small in all these Eastern states of Europe, have been raised to preeminence and power far beyond their numbers, and are seeking everywhere to obtain totalitarian control. Police governments are prevailing in nearly every case, and so far, except in Czechoslovakia, there is no true democracy . . . An attempt is being made by the Russians in Berlin to build up a quasi-Communist party in their zone of occupied Germany . . .[1]

By 1947, communist governments had indeed been set up, under strict control by the Soviet Union, in Poland, Rumania, Bulgaria, Hungary, and in the Soviet zone in Germany, and where noncommunist parties had been included in the governing coalitions of these states, they were removed. The next year a murderous coup d'état brought communists to power in Czechoslovakia. In none of these states thereafter were parliamentary-style elections ever conducted. State terror, state-controlled media of expression, and single-party politics became the pattern for each of these states. In reaction the Western allies refused to proceed toward the unification of Germany and instead set up parliamentary constitutional institutions in the western zones of Germany, virtually creating a new German state.

This familiar chronology accounts for there being no peace treaty ending World War II among all the Allies: the Western states did not wish to ratify the subjugation and deformation of the states of Central and Eastern Europe; the Soviet Union was unwilling to risk independent states in the region, a real possibility any time free elections might have been held to constitute a government. Yet these two steps were linked: unless the USSR held free elections, the West would never recognize the governments that held power in these states. Therefore there was no formula for compromise on a unified German state. The Second World War had stopped with an invitation to contend further.

That a Cold War followed therefore poses two questions: Even if there was to be no peace, was there really war? In other words, how can *war* be cold? And if there was war, why was it *cold,* that is, why wasn't it fought across the plains of Europe with the million-man armies that had contested two prior episodes? In my opinion, decisions taken by the United States are responsible for both these outcomes, ensuring that the Long War would be continued and that it would be "cold." First, on March 12, 1947, President Truman stated in a speech to Congress:

> At the present moment in world history nearly every nation must choose between alternative ways of life. The choice is too often not a free one . . . it must be the policy of the United States to support free peoples who are resisting attempted subjugation by armed minorities or by outside pressures . . . [W]e must assist free peoples to work out their own destiny in their own way.[2]

The immediately precipitating event for this statement was communist assistance to guerilla movements in Greece and Turkey and the continued Russian occupation of northern Iran. The immediate consequence of the Truman Doctrine, as it came shortly to be called, was a grant of about $400 million (or the equivalent of $2 billion in current dollars) to the governments of Greece and Turkey.

Three months later, in another act of resistance, the American secretary of state, George Marshall, announced a plan for European recovery. Altogether about $12.5 billion (or roughly $60 billion in current dollars) was spent on Western countries over the next three years.

Nor were the Russians deceived as to the import of these steps: it was war. At the refounding conference of the Comintern in September, Malenkov—who would later briefly succeed Stalin—replied:

> The ruling clique of the American imperialists . . . has chosen the path of hatching new war plans against the Soviet Union and the new democracies . . . The clearest and most specific expression of the policy . . . is provided by the Truman-Marshall plans.[3]

In Chapter 5, I will venture some guesses as to why the United States decided to contest the issue of what system—parliamentary and capitalist or communist and socialist—would prevail in Europe. In Germany, the contest had begun as a domestic one; it couldn't be avoided in 1914 or in 1933. The same was true of other states—Russia, Spain, Italy—that were drawn into the Long War. But the United States was not threatened with a change in its own system, as were the states that chose to resist in the various campaigns of the Long War—France, Britain, Czechoslovakia, and Poland. For the moment, let us take as given that the United States did decide to resist, and that this converted the mere absence of peace into war.

The second issue is why this war remained "cold." Like the decision to contest the unconsummated outcome of the Second World War, the decision to refrain from an armed conflict in Europe also required the commitment of two parties. On the American side, war meant (1) extending nuclear deterrence to Europe and Japan; (2) restoring conventional force levels in Western Europe to credible size so that this extension of nuclear deterrence could function; (3) refraining from initiating the use of force in Europe; and (4) accepting the challenge in "hot" campaigns outside Europe. If the war remained "cold," the United States believed it stood a good chance to win it because the issues, moral and political and economic, that kept the Long War going were thought to favor the West. Because the Long War was essentially constitutional in nature, only a profound change in the Russian polity was certain to resolve it. The leadership of the United States believed such a change would ultimately come about (just as their adversaries not implausibly believed the reverse).

This attitude on the part of the Americans is clearly reflected in NSC 68, the strategic planning document that was drafted to govern U.S. policy from 1950 onward:

> Resort to war is not only a last resort for a free society, but it is also an act which cannot definitively end the fundamental conflict in the realm of ideas . . . Military victory alone would only partially and perhaps only temporarily affect the fundamental conflict.[4]

In Germany and Japan total defeat had allowed such a remaking of the basis of constitutional norms. After the Soviet acquisition of nuclear weapons, however, that sort of victory was never an option because a total defeat requires a total war. The United States could not afford to risk such a conflict with a nuclear power capable of striking the U.S. homeland and destroying it. What was needed was a change of heart on the part of the persons enabling the Communist system to continue.

For the Soviet Union the commitment to contend with the West in the face of enormous hostile force (including nuclear weapons) meant: (1) developing a nuclear threat against the U.S. homeland; (2) maintaining force levels sufficient to prevent successful uprisings in the Eastern European client states and to deter any Western assistance to such uprisings; (3) refraining from any threat to the U.S. of sufficient imminence to overcome the American commitment to containment and risk the actual outbreak of hostilities in a central theatre; and (4) pressing the West wherever possible in Third World theatres.

The necessity of these particular elements of the Cold War strategies of the United States and the USSR may not be obvious, and so a little time can be spent on briefly explaining them. The important point, however, is that they can be seen to operate in each of the major crises of the Cold War, crises that took the place of battles in the various campaigns in this phase of the Long War.

To the extent that American and Soviet policy makers confronted a symmetrical set of problems in a bipolar world, their policies can be discussed in this paired, complementary way. First, with regard to the role of nuclear weapons: for the United States to maintain the conflict but avoid battle, it had to deploy a force sufficient to deter attacks by the Red Army and also sufficient to prevent the development of a West German nuclear force that would otherwise be inevitably raised to defend the Federal Republic of Germany from Soviet coercion. This deterrence was impossible to accomplish with U.S. ground forces alone, owing to the large numbers of troops required. The American public would not, in the decades-long struggle that evolved, have stationed such a vast armed force abroad. Only by developing and deploying nuclear weapons to defend American allies, rather than just the American homeland, could the United States field a force that would accomplish its strategic objectives. By the same token, the Soviet Union could not permit the United States to enjoy a continental sanctuary in case of a European conflict. Long-range nuclear weapons were the only way for the Soviet Union to take the threat of a hot war to the American continent and thus be assured of a cold war in Europe.

Second, with respect to force levels in Europe: once the U.S. homeland became vulnerable, the United States could not make its nuclear threat credible on behalf of Europe unless there were also ground forces under U.S. command in Europe that could both parry modest conventional threats (without forcing the United States to commit to a nuclear attack in political circumstances that would not justify such devastation) while at the same time serving as hostages whose destruction by a large-scale Soviet ground attack would immediately create the political will to ensure a nuclear American response.[5] On the Soviet side, the USSR had to maintain forces large enough both to deter national uprisings—a mission that did not require vast manpower—and to check any temptation by the West to assist such uprisings—which might require large forces—and to exercise some coercive political influence over Western European states, especially West Germany. To do less imposed enormous risks, because if the satellite states were to spin out of the Russian orbit, only a force of World War II proportions could bring them back in.

Third, with regard to the use of force: the United States had to find ways to refrain from actually resorting to fire in Europe, because its logistical position—six weeks across the Atlantic from delivering its full force—was so vulnerable and attenuated. The USSR also had to show restraint, because a change in U.S. policy to fight an active war in Europe would, whatever the ultimate outcome, threaten cataclysmic destruction for the

Soviet state. As a result no two states were as careful to protect the existence of the other—despite their rhetoric—as were the United States and the Soviet Union once the Soviets acquired the ability to attack the U.S. homeland.

Fourth, with respect to the constraints placed on where the Long War was allowed to break into violence: the situation of both parties tended to confine conflict to areas outside Europe. So long as the United States was unwilling to use nuclear weapons beyond the well-defined limits of its vital interests, the USSR could maintain the conflict outside Europe and, it seemed for a while, even prevail in certain theatres. The United States, however, could neither acquiesce in nor escalate these conflicts: the former amounted to a loss in a campaign of the Long War, with incalculable effects on the cohesion and vitality of the Western alliance (which came to include Japan and other Asian states); the latter strategy would have cracked completely the domestic popular basis that, with some fissures, held together so remarkably for almost half a century, offering a rebuke to the Tocquevillian thesis that parliamentary republics cannot sustain a consistent foreign policy.

An awareness of these four, mutual parameters—the nuclear competition, the level of conventional forces in Europe, the avoidance of conflict on the Central Front, and the eagerness to engage in the Third World—will assist us in briefly reviewing the short history of the Cold War, this last of the campaigns of the Long War. But before recounting this nerve-wracking if ultimately triumphant history, one observation must be made about the Alliance and Soviet strategies described above. Neither of these strategies discloses a plan for terminating the conflict; neither shows how its side will actually win. (In the parlance of contemporary Washington, neither side had "an exit strategy.") Each side seemed to hope that the other side would collapse of its own internal contradictions and to believe that, if only the conflict could be joined and endured, history would vindicate one but not the other. Astonishingly, this appears to be what actually happened (although it was hardly obvious at the time that this would be the case).

The first engagement of the campaign occurred, not surprisingly, in Germany. The Marshall Plan, which was begun as a program of reconstruction for Britain, France, and other Western European states, was soon extended to Germany. By 1948 German nationals had assumed economic responsibilities for the new "Federal Republic," sustained by American support. In late June a new currency, the deutschemark (DM), was introduced to replace the inflation-ravaged reichsmark (RM). In retaliation the Russians introduced a new currency in their sector. The Western powers were unwilling to allow this currency, over whose monetary policy they had no control, to enter the West through Berlin and so they introduced the new DM into West Berlin. This assertion of constitutional sovereignty in the divided city provided the spark for the first crisis of the Cold War. The next day, the Russians cut off all access by road, rail, and canal between Berlin and the West. The blockade lasted for eleven months. British and U.S. aircraft made almost 200,000 flights to Berlin, carrying 1.5 million tons of food, coal, and other stores.[6] In May 1949 Stalin lifted the blockade. Although American forces had been mobilized to fight their way into Berlin—and although the Russian forces could easily have interdicted the airlift—neither of these eventualities occurred. One might say that a "crisis" is the form of battle that is customary in a cold war, and that distinguishes it from a "hot" one. Engagements in a cold war therefore can include either conventional battles (like the Communist drive toward Seoul in 1950) or crises (like the Cuban Missile Crisis in 1962).

The second engagement of this new phase of the Long War occurred in Asia, following a pattern that was to repeat itself in many different parts of the Third World. Beginning as a civil war, largely apart from the Long War, but fought, as in Europe, between parliamentary, fascist, and communist constitutional alternatives, the struggle for control of China entered its final phase with the withdrawal of the Japanese. Nationalist armies were given vast amounts of Western aid, but the corrupt and rigid system for which they fought proved unable to successfully deploy its superior forces. Promising land reform, an end to the dictatorships of regional warlords, and the extermination of a pervasive system of corruption, the Communists steadily gained support from China's people. In 1949—the same year as the Berlin airlift—Mao Zedong achieved complete control of China, and the American-supported forces of Chiang Kai-shek[7] fled to the island of Taiwan, a former Chinese colony. Although the extent of Russian support for Mao has been exaggerated, this event was undoubtedly a terrible blow to the West. The United States did not wholly acquiesce in this development, however, and began to grope its way toward rules of engagement in Asia consistent with the parameters I have outlined above. Taken all in all, these rules have been a notable success—not as dramatic as in Europe—but probably as positive as could be reasonably expected.

Events in China structured everyone's expectations in the next campaign: Korea. The USSR had declared war on Japan only a few days before the Japanese surrender in 1945, but did not fail to send troops into the Korean peninsula as the war ended. The United Nations (the international organization, not the wartime alliance) assumed responsibility for the peninsula and designated the United States and the Soviet Union to administer the south and north of Korea respectively. South Korea was more populous than the North, and the United States hoped that having established a democratic constitution in the South, popular free elections to unite the country would bring parliamentary institutions to the whole peninsula. The Northern leader, Kim Il-sung, refused, however, to take up the 100 seats in the National Assembly allocated to the North. After months of discussions with the Russians, Kim returned to Moscow with a well-prepared plan for the invasion of the South. Stalin had doubts about such an invasion, according to Khrushchev, and feared the Americans might return to the peninsula in force. Mao's opinion was solicited, and it was he who, in the end, persuaded Stalin that the United States would not intervene.[8]

On June 25, 1950, the North Koreans launched a successful surprise attack on South Korea, capturing the Southern capital and trapping the South Korean forces within a narrow perimeter around a Southern port. In legal terms, this was an attack on the United Nations. The U.N. Security Council—with the Russian member absent in protest over the refusal to seat the Communist Chinese representative—voted to send assistance. After a dramatic landing in the rear of the North Korean forces, the American commander launched a counterinvasion of North Korea, driving north almost to the Chinese border. The Chinese then intervened in staggering numbers; urgent requests to Washington from the U.S. commander for nuclear weapons support were denied and the line of defense was not stabilized until the U.N. forces had been pushed back to a latitudinal parallel roughly marking the original division of the country. For two years there was a bloody stalemate, ending in an armed truce in 1953. This armistice was secured by the presence of U.S. forces and the extension of nuclear deterrence to the Korean peninsula. Perhaps as much as any other factor, this development led the Chinese to demand assistance from the Russians in producing nuclear weapons, a demand that the Soviet Union refused. This rebuff, disclosing as it did many other conflicts of interest between the two states, led to the break between the two great Communist powers and eventually to the triangulation of the Soviet/American/Chinese relationship. But before this could occur, the United States would be tested a third time in Asia.

Mao's assessment of U.S. fortitude had proved to be a fateful error. Had it not been for the Korean conflict with its massive Chinese commitment of forces, China would likely have successfully seized Taiwan,[9] owing in part to the greater difficulty of delivering effective U.S. resistance to Taiwan than to Korea. Such a step would have had incalculable consequences, but fortunately this did not happen, though there continued throughout the 1950s to be threats to Taiwan from Beijing. No longer, however, could China count on Soviet support.

Stalin died in 1953, and the first of a series of meetings "at the summit," in Churchill's phrase, took place in Geneva in 1955 among the parties to the Cold War. This led to the signing of the Austrian State Treaty, by which Four Power occupation forces were withdrawn and Austrian neutrality confirmed. Like the War of Spanish Succession, which it so much resembled, the Long War had its moments of successful diplomatic détente, and, also like the War of Spanish Succession, it was often driven by the local, national aspirations of populations in the occupied (or disputed) states. Khrushchev's secret speech to the Twentieth Party Congress in February 1956, denouncing Stalin and Stalinism, was soon circulated and led to a surge of hope in the states of Central and Eastern Europe that a new order was possible. Riots broke out in Poznan in June that brought the return to power of the Polish leader Gomulka, previously imprisoned for ideological deviations from Stalinism. A greater threat to the Russian satellite system occurred in October when the Hungarian leader Imre Nagy took power. In November he announced that Hungary would end its alliance with the Soviet Union and pursue a neutralist foreign policy. Political prisoners were freed; there was talk of holding genuinely free elections under a multiparty arrangement. In strategic terms this was by far the most important development in Europe since the Berlin blockade. The Russians agreed to a tactical withdrawal but almost immediately returned to Budapest in force and crushed the Hungarians. Although Nagy was given asylum in the Yugoslav embassy during the conflict, he was eventually imprisoned and executed on June 16, 1958.[10] Carefully adhering to the parameters that were emerging to govern the East-West conflict, the Americans expressed "profound distress" and claimed to be "inexpressibly shocked" by developments[11] but did nothing.

These events not only were significant in themselves, as they crucially threatened the alliance system of the Warsaw Pact, but were important also for their relation to events in Germany. When an uprising ultimately broke out in East Berlin, it too was swiftly crushed with memorable brutality.

The successful prosecution of war depends, as Clausewitz wrote, upon the proper coordination of political leadership, armed forces, and the passions of the people. If the East German people, ignited by the same emotions that inspired the Poles and the Hungarians, had brought about a new leadership for the German Democratic Republic (GDR)—if they had chosen parliamentarianism for Germany—this would have forecast the end of the Long War. It was, after all, over Germany's fate with respect to the three alternative systems of twentieth-century government that the Long War began and continued to be fought. As it was, the USSR took special care to see this did not happen.

After the uprisings in Poland, Hungary, and East Berlin, the Soviet Union began to threaten to conclude a unilateral peace treaty with the GDR. From a legal point of view this would have forced the Western powers to negotiate with the East German state—which they did not recognize—for access to West Berlin. Such an assertion of constitutional sovereignty would have greatly inflamed the conflict: it would have amounted to an attempt to end the Long War through partition, much as the

Thirty Years' War was ended. In 1648 the Peace of Westphalia had divided up the states and princes of Germany on religious lines; a Soviet peace treaty with the GDR would have done the same thing along ideological lines. This perspective helps explain why the West reacted with such horror to the prospect of a "peace treaty" and indeed provoked a panic among American leaders that is otherwise hard to understand today.[12] Many assumed that recognition was tantamount to the seizure of West Berlin by the East Germans. At any rate, President Kennedy made it clear that he regarded this threat as the latest feint in the strategic competition between East and West* and promptly announced an increase in the strength of U.S. forces in the area by 217,000 men, roughly triple the previous number, bringing American troops to their highest levels in Germany in the post–World War II period.[13]

Ten days later, the Russians replied to Western diplomatic notes, observing that "[f]or many years the United States has been evading a peaceful settlement with Germany, putting it off to the indefinite future. The American Note shows that the U.S. Government prefers to continue adhering to this line."[14] Of course this was perfectly true. The United States had decided to resist the partition of Europe, to continue the Long War, and thus was unwilling to agree to a peace. On August 7, Khrushchev ridiculed the American position:

> What provisions of the Soviet draft of a peace treaty with Germany could give the American President a pretext to contend that the Soviet Union "threatens" to violate peace? Could it be those which envisage the renunciation of nuclear weapons by Germany, the legalizing of the existing German frontiers, the granting of full sovereignty to both German states, and their admission to the United Nations? If anyone allowed himself to resort to threats it was the U.S. President.[15]

Many persons hearing these remarks must have asked themselves why the United States was overreacting; and unless the dimensions of the entire conflict are appreciated, the American position seems petulant, absurd. It was in fact, as the perspective of the Long War shows, nothing of the kind, but reflected instead an acute appreciation of the fundamentally constitutional issues at stake. Moreover, there was, lurking beneath the cloak of sovereignty that such a treaty would throw over the East German state, a vexing problem. To recognize the GDR would have been to permit them to control not only access to West Berlin, but access out of East Berlin, as any

---

*"Our presence in West Berlin, and our access thereto, cannot be ended by any act of the Soviet Government . . . The [Western Alliance] had been built in response to challenges: . . . European chaos in 1947; of the Berlin blockade in 1948; of Communist aggression in Korea in 1950." Broadcast by President John F. Kennedy, July 25, 1961.

state is permitted to do with its own borders. At this time, about 300,000 East Germans were disappearing into West Berlin and thence to West Germany each year. Since 1949 three million persons had gone through Berlin to the West. This continued flow of young, talented, educated, and professional people was damaging in and of itself; it could at any time, however, erupt into a complete hemorrhage. The purpose of the Russian treaty was to stanch this flow, and thus to prevent a greater one. On the night of August 12–13, 1961, a concrete barrier up to six feet high and topped with barbed wire was erected in the Potsdamerplatz by communist "shock workers." Similar barriers of greater height were raised at other points along the boundaries of the Eastern and Western sectors of the city. Building the "Berlin Wall" was a bold move by the Soviet Union and the wall's survival was, as Khrushchev later claimed, a "great victory."[16] This engagement, like the Viet Nam War, must be scored a communist success, even if, as in Viet Nam, the United States could not prudently have done more than it did. The West, though it brought up bulldozers backed by tanks and some infantry, never attempted to breach the wall and confined itself to complaints at the U.N.

Roughly one year later, American photo reconnaissance disclosed that the Russians were in the process of installing ballistic missiles in Cuba with an intermediate range (1,000–1,400 miles). The Cuban Missile Crisis has been widely misdescribed as provoking the United States into a threat to launch nuclear weapons against the Soviet Union if Russian missiles were not removed from Cuba.[17] Actually, the president's carefully worded ultimatum stated that if nuclear weapons were used against the United States from Cuba, the United States would retaliate against the USSR, a very different matter, and a position well within the parameters of the tacit U.S./Soviet rules of engagement.* This ultimatum was coupled with a blockade of the island and preparations for invasion. In that context, the statement was not an ultimatum so much as an invitation to deal, and this is exactly what happened. In exchange for the removal of the weapons, the United States pledged not to invade Cuba; and the United States undertook to remove intermediate-range ballistic missiles (IRBMs) based in Turkey that were targeted against the Soviet Union. Like the Berlin Wall, this was a tactical success for the Russians—Khrushchev uses the same words in Russian to describe both events in his memoirs[18]—but was it not also, like the Berlin Crisis, a strategic calamity for the USSR?

It may be difficult to see such crises as taking the place of "battles" within the Long War. We are accustomed to thinking of battles fought with shock and fire and leaving behind casualties. But if we bear in mind the

---

*By contrast, the Soviet deployment presaged a shift in the correlation of nuclear threats, opening up the future possibility of accurate, ground-launched weapons minutes away from the U.S. offensive sites, and potentially under the control of a satellite state.

perspective of the Long War, however, which was punctuated by conventional battles as well as crises, we can see that its crises really had more in common with the battles of the eighteenth century than with the crises of the nineteenth. In the eighteenth century the extreme expense of highly professionalized armies made them far too precious to be risked in battle once technological innovations in warfare made actual fighting so lethal; advantages accruing to the defense imperiled any army that actually sought battle.[19]* Battles became actions of maneuver, culminating in the tactical withdrawal of one party once it was forced into an untenable position. Similarly, in the second half of the twentieth century, nuclear weapons—which, once mutual and secure against pre-emption, gave to the defense an asset of infinite value—made the hot battles of the First and Second World Wars too risky for the U.S. and the USSR. Crises served as battles of maneuver, with one side—as in Cuba—retreating when it became clear that, if things played out, that side would find itself in a losing position from which there was no escape.

Some historians believe that Kennedy, but for the constraints imposed by anti-communist domestic political pressures, was willing to go further to end the crisis by simply accepting Soviet nuclear missiles in Cuba. Such a concession, coupled with the crisis/battles over the Berlin Wall and the Bay of Pigs, would have amounted to an American strategic defeat, in Long War terms. A remark allegedly made by Robert McNamara during the Crisis, that "a missile is a missile is a missile" (equating Soviet missiles in Cuba with American missiles in Turkey), is, obviously, dealing with the issue from a far different perspective than that presented here.[20] Perhaps, from the view of systems analysis, IRBMs are more or less fungible, regardless of who possesses them, if they are placed to threaten similar or comparable targets. Should those missiles have been fired, one can imagine that Moscow would have been destroyed at about the same time as Washington. From the perspective of the Long War, however—where crises stand in place of battles—to have accepted the Soviet adventure in Cuba would have been an American loss precisely because it would have amounted to an acceptance of a kind of "equivalence," publicly conceding to the Soviet Union that it had every bit as much right to threaten the United States as the United States had to threaten it.

For the United States to achieve its strategic goals—for it to win the Long War—it had to contain communism within its Second World boundaries and thus prevent this movement from taking over fresh societies that would enrich its system with the accumulated human capital and other resources of the states it took over. If *containment* could be managed,

---

*Thus, "[a]rmies in Europe by the later eighteenth century thus concerned themselves predominantly with problems of siegecraft, fortification, marches, and supply . . . Most of their time was passed in profoundest peace." Michael Howard, *War in European History,* 72.

then—so the Americans believed—the steady impoverishment of the socialist system would begin to tell. Like an engine requiring oxygen but producing carbon monoxide, the Soviet system would steadily grow more anaerobic until it collapsed. For the USSR to achieve its objectives—its leaders believed—it had only to maintain communism in a great power until the steadily declining business cycles and ever more severe economic depressions of the capitalist states provoked internal revolutions. Sergei Khrushchev recently quoted his father as saying—in classic nation-state terms—"between communism and capitalism, that system will win that presents the better life to the people."[21]

The Soviet Union had world-dominating ambitions in a sense, but Russian strategic goals were not to be realized in conquests of the kind that brought them the satellite regimes of Eastern Europe. This distinction is underscored in a memorandum from Charles Bohlen* to Paul Nitze[†] in 1950:

> It is open to question whether or not, as stated, the fundamental design of the Kremlin is the domination of the world. [Putting it this way] tends ... to oversimplify the problem.... I think that the thought would be more accurate if it were to the effect that the fundamental design of those who control the USSR is (A) the maintenance of their regime in the Soviet Union and (B) its extension throughout the world to the degree that is possible without serious risk to the internal regime.[22]

This nicely captures the inner/outer nature of a constitutional conflict. Widespread extension of communism was unlikely so long as the United States continued its commitment to containment. In this light, the internal exile of millions of East Germans and the public humiliation of a Third World client though tactical successes were hardly strategic triumphs for the Soviet Union, the former because it tended to destabilize the Communist system in the Warsaw Pact states, the latter because it alienated revolutionary parties abroad. (And indeed the Cuban Missile Crisis—and the Sino-Soviet split—were two of the factors cited by the group that ousted Khrushchev in October 1964.) This difficulty for the Soviet Union should remind us that its interests were not entirely coextensive with those of the ideological adversary against which the West struggled. To defeat communism did indeed mean that the Soviet Union would have to be defeated, but

---

*Chief Soviet expert and the Counselor of the U.S. Department of State; later U.S. Ambassador to the Soviet Union.

[†]Head of policy planning for the U.S. Department of State (1950–53), and principal author of the highly influential National Security Council document (NSC-68) that provided a blueprint for Allied resistance to the Soviet Union.

it did not follow that every triumph for communism strengthened Russia. The success of a communist insurgency that took over an otherwise independent state might or might not be in the interests of the Soviet Union, much less Russia; the new regime might, as happened in Yugoslavia, turn against its Soviet sponsors, just as the Vietnamese communists quickly turned against China. In terms of the historic struggle between communism and parliamentarianism in the Long War, however, success for a communist takeover would amount to a defeat for the United States and her allies in any case because communism, and not merely any particular state, was the enemy. Some commentators of this period were fond of pointing out that communism was not a "monolith," a fact they took to imply that the United States should not engage itself in struggles against communist movements not directly controlled by the Soviet Union. Viewed from Moscow, the increasing fragmentation of the world communist movement was indeed a source of alarm. But from a Long War perspective, this insight is, at best, beside the point.

In some ways, the U.S. role was easier than that of the Soviet Union, although it scarcely appeared so at the time. By the mid-sixties the United States had become deeply involved in Southeast Asia. To Eisenhower, Kennedy, and Johnson the principle of containment required military assistance to the newly established Republic of South Viet Nam and, at least, a stalemate to the efforts of communist North Viet Nam to unify the country by force. By 1969 the United States had stationed 500,000 troops in the region, and by 1968 had defeated the communist insurgency in the South (although this fact was little credited by the public and the media at the time). But the American strategy of graduated response did not defeat the North Vietnamese, who were highly motivated, had secure bases in the region outside South Viet Nam, and were well supplied by other communist states. When it became apparent that American public opinion would not support the lengthy and costly commitment required to defeat North Viet Nam, President Johnson halted the bombing of the North and opened peace talks in Paris; not surprisingly the North Vietnamese stalled the negotiations in the hope of a further decline in U.S. popular support for the war and perhaps the election of an American president who would cut and run. In the ensuing five years, public opinion in the United States pressed ever more passionately for a disengagement. Eventually a ceasefire and peace treaty were negotiated that provided for an American withdrawal and a guarantee of nonaggression by the North Vietnamese. When the withdrawal was completed in 1973, however, the North immediately renewed its attack, correctly judging that the U.S. Congress would not permit the United States to re-introduce forces in the region in retaliation for the treaty breach. By 1975, the Congress, doubtless reflecting American public opinion, had even cut off military assistance to its ally in the South, and communist forces were able to overrun South Viet Nam as well as Cambodia and Laos.

It was a military defeat of historic consequence and continues to distort the American debate over war powers and foreign policy. But it was not, however, a decisive defeat for the American position in the Long War, of which the Vietnamese War was but a single, peninsular campaign. Indeed if we bear in mind the strategic objectives of the United States in the Long War, her ability to prevent a North Vietnamese victory for thirteen years, virtually without assistance from any major ally, in a remote theatre dominated by a civil war, was a remarkable achievement. American strategy revealed both the tactical weaknesses of containment—that it surrendered initiative to the adversary, allowed the enemy to choose the terrain and type of battle, committed the United States to marginal theatres of little intrinsic significance to American fortunes—as well as its strategic strengths, namely, that delay coupled with conflict on the periphery tended to play into the long-term interests of the West. During those thirteen years pro-Western governments consolidated their power in Indonesia,[23] Malaysia, and Singapore while economic growth ignited in the region's key pro-Western states, South Korea, Japan, Thailand, and Taiwan. By 1975, the year of the worst U.S. military humiliation since 1943, the threats to all these states and territories, from within and from a hostile China, had far receded from their level in the late 1950s. In every one of these now prosperous and fast-growing states, the essential issues of the Long War had been decided in their domestic polity and had been resolved against communism (although the long-term fate of Taiwan may still be in jeopardy, depending on what path the mainland Chinese leadership chooses).

The Communist victory in Viet Nam did strengthen communist movements everywhere, as we know from the remarks of a wide variety of national liberation and communist state leaders. And the small "dominoes" of Laos and Cambodia did fall once the Americans withdrew. But the long struggle required to achieve that victory hardened the divisions between the Soviet Union (whose client was North Viet Nam) and China (which supported the Khmer Rouge in Cambodia and invaded Viet Nam in February 1979). As in the Korean War, the imposition of civilian restraints on military operations in Viet Nam, though much criticized, succeeded in keeping Long War objectives in mind and in not permitting the goal of victory in battle to obscure the pursuit of victory in war.

Between 1968 and 1980, the Soviet Union invaded Czechoslovakia and deposed a communist regime in Prague; embarked on a breathtaking buildup of nuclear weapons; invaded Afghanistan, deposed and murdered its communist leader; attacked Chinese positions across the Ussuri River and maintained a force in readiness there of some fifty divisions; offered the United States a condominium in international affairs; and signed the

Helsinki Accords, effectively ratifying the Soviet sphere of influence over Eastern Europe. Many persons saw this period as one of Soviet dynamism, and from a certain perspective, this was undoubtedly so. But viewed from the perspective of the Long War, it represented a collapsing position. Mao's designated successor, Lin Piao, of all people, read this well enough when he observed:

Since Brezhnev came to power, with its baton becoming less and less effective and its difficulties at home and abroad growing more and more serious, the Soviet revisionist clique has been practicing imperialism more frantically than ever. Internally it has intensified its suppression of the Soviet people. Externally it has stepped up its collusion with the U.S., intensified its control over and its exploitation of the various east European countries . . . and intensified its threat of aggression against China. Its dispatch of hundreds of thousands of troops to occupy Czechoslovakia, and its armed provocations against China are two [such] performances.[24]

What the Chinese clearly saw, and what the West appeared to miss, was that Russians were anxious to rid themselves of socialist solidarity in favor of a world role within, and legitimated by, the great power system.[25]

When Gorbachev succeeded Brezhnev in 1985, after two brief intervening premierships, the Soviet Union found a leader with the energy and will to break openly with the Communist method of total state planning. Gorbachev's initial goal was the restructuring of the Soviet economy, a restructuring that he originally advertised as a reorganization of the government bureaucracy to make it more efficient and to bring about greater quality control without fundamentally altering the basis of the command economy. This restructuring he called "perestroika." Gorbachev's campaign of reform ran into such opposition within the bureaucracy and the Party, however, that in 1986 he called for greater openness in debate in order to mobilize public pressure for reform. This policy he called "glasnost." Within the Soviet Union a civil breakdown began to occur as credibility drained away from the Communist Party; the economy worsened, and food shortages began to appear as uncertainty enveloped the underground market. In a second attempt to harness popular opinion in order to bring about reform, Gorbachev called for greater democracy and pluralism. This, however, prompted the Baltic states to agitate for their independence. In Poland, a noncommunist government was formed in the summer of 1989 and, in October, the communist government of Hungary bowed to demonstrations and accepted a new constitution. In the interim, Hungary had permitted East Germans to use the Hungarian borders to escape to Western Europe. This refugee exodus led to massive antigovernment demonstrations within East Germany and, on November 9, 1989, crowds broke through the Berlin Wall. In October 1990 Germany was unified. By June 1990, democratic elections in Czechoslovakia had produced a noncommunist government, and a parliamentary constitution followed.[26]

The Long War was over. It officially ended in November 1990 when the thirty-four members of the Conference on Security and Cooperation in Europe (CSCE)—including the United States, the Soviet Union, the United Kingdom, France, and Germany—met in Paris and signed an agreement providing for parliamentary institutions in all the participating states. This was the Charter of Paris, which was the centerpiece of the more comprehensive Peace of Paris.

Formal peace was signed with the agreements at Paris in November 1990. Then a reunited Germany, a chastened Soviet Union, a reconciled Poland and Czechoslovakia, a benevolent Britain, France and United States, all behaved with a rational civility hardly seen in European relations. Unfortunately because of the collapse of the Soviet Union shortly thereafter and the confusion that followed it, the event passed almost unnoticed.[27]

On December 25, 1991, the Soviet Union formally dissolved. Now all the great powers that had begun the turbulent search in 1914 for a legitimate and legitimating constitutional order to succeed the empires of the nineteenth century had reached consensus. Between 1914 and 1990, the population of the world tripled—but an estimated 187 million persons, about 10 percent of the population of 1900—were killed or fated to die by human agency.[28]

The end of the Long War is not the end of the need for history-making by the State if by that one means the achievement of a final state paradigm, nor the end of war. But it does represent, as Francis Fukuyama memorably showed, the final "perfecting"—in the legal sense—of the nation-state.[29]

It is possible to live within the culture of war for so long that the end of a particular war seems like the end of all violent political struggle, and the temporary quiet that follows seems to promise a perpetual, peaceful, and exhausted stasis. This feeling is all the more likely if it accompanies what appears to be a moral consensus. The Long War was in a deep sense a moral struggle. Each of the three contending state systems was the outcome of a particular nineteenth and twentieth century attitude about mankind, attitudes that I will roughly call the biological, the sociological, and the legal. The fascists believed in a sort of social Darwinism for states, by which the competition for survival among species was mirrored in the struggle among, and the domination of, genetically determined national groups among human beings. For all their differences about political action, on this fundamental social scientific point they were united. The communists took a sociological view of man, by which man could not only be wholly described according to his behavior in groups, but could be changed by manipulating the incentives of groups transcending states. Though they differed dramatically on many theoretical points, and endlessly debated whether socialism should be strengthened in a single state at the expense of world revolution, whether the Marx of the *Grundrisse* or the Marx of the later works was to be preferred, and so on—for the whole point was that the theoretical could guide the practical—they agreed on this assumption. The partisans of the liberal democracies also agreed on a basic element of the parliamentary attitude: that the impartial rule of law, and not simply the political power of the individual or group, should govern the outcome of state decisions. Each of these attitudes is not so much a reaction to the others, as it is to the nineteenth century self-consciousness that delegitimated the dynastic territorial states of the eighteenth century. Each tries to escape the problem of this loss of legitimacy by bringing an external, validating resource to bear. Each promises that it can best deploy the State to enhance the welfare of the nation. And to some degree, the residue of all these attitudes was present in every society—perhaps in every human heart—that contended in the Long War. What had ended was not just the Cold War, but a century of conflict over the basis of the State itself. And this accounts for the sense of bewilderment that followed. It wasn't like the usual end of an ordinary war but rather like the end of a way of living.

From a strategic point of view, the example of the West, and especially the United States, must rank among the most successful and skillful coordinations of force and statecraft for the achievement of political goals ever recorded. What Gordon Craig and Felix Gilbert said of the Truman administration and the strategic campaigns of the late forties can be said of the U.S. presidents generally with respect to the Cold War:[30]

> The effective mobilization of public support for its European commitments and the skillful use of economic resources to gain its objectives, and finally, . . . the imposition upon its military operations of limitations determined by political considerations—all in all [constitute] an exercise in strategy that would almost certainly have won Clausewitz' approbation.[31]

For roughly forty-five years, across nine administrations drawn from both political parties, the Americans were able to summon great resources and—unusually, it is said, for a democracy—great stamina and great restraint. What can be said of the United States–led Alliance during the Cold War can be said of the West generally with respect to the Long War.

When Clausewitz wrote his most famous and most widely misconstrued sentence, "War is the continuation of politics by other means,"[32] he intended to remind his readers that the destruction and human sacrifice that attends war could only be justified to the extent that war was absolutely necessary to accomplish political goals. One might go further and say that it is a corollary to this truth that if the political question that impels states to war is not resolved in that war, then the peace that ensues may be only a pause. Each of the campaigns of which the Long War was composed had strategic consequences for the next, just as the First World War set the stage for the Second, and so on. Now the fundamental constitutional problem of the Long War has been answered. Government by consent, freely given and periodically capable of being withdrawn, is what legitimates the nation-state. Government under law—not government that is above the law—provides the means by which states are legitimated.* So the next question intrudes itself: what are the *strategic* consequences of the peace?

What will this new world look like, and how should a state make its way in it? Will such a world be so chaotic without the overarching framework of the Long War that we will look back on the era of the Cold War as a golden age? By means of what new framework ought we to understand events and, ultimately, decide when to use force? These are the questions taken up in Part III, and they are on the minds of thoughtful persons throughout the world. Sometimes it is said that such questions are more difficult now that the armed struggle among great powers is over. If the conventional approach is to assess the threat then because the threat has changed—indeed, to a very large extent vanished—it is said we shall be at a loss until a new threat appears.

But this observation, which might be rephrased as "If No Copernicus, Then No Newton" (if no problem, then no answer), doesn't go to the issue of deciding per se. It might explain and even justify decisions that seem ad hoc, or patternless, but it neither explains nor justifies the abrupt and repeated reversals of policy in the West since the end of the Long War. While such an explanation might excuse the cynical apathy that governs so many Western foreign ministries, it scarcely excuses the loss of life and loss of confidence in our institutions that has been the result. The flip-flopping of Western decisions regarding Russia or Yugoslavia or Iraq is characteristic not so much of mystery as of changing incentives.

Then, it is sometimes said, it is a matter of "leadership." In its first term

---

*And for this reason, the communist leadership of the People's Republic has the most to fear from internal dissent.

for example, the Clinton administration did not inspire critics by a slavish devotion to consistency in foreign policy. It is also said that the world is more complex now, that no single paradigm, such as that of containment that guided the West during the Long War and to which I have tried to draw attention, could possibly be useful today.

I am skeptical about these "explanations." This is not the first time that an epochal war has ended, and certainly not the first time that profound constitutional questions have been decided by strategic developments, nor that constitutional innovations—like parliamentary democracy—have driven strategic change. In Part II, we will look at the strategic and constitutional consequences of earlier, state-shaping struggles. These make up a history, a way of understanding the development of the State, and of understanding the actual state we are currently in. Finally, in Part III, we examine the State we are becoming, the historic consequence of the Long War.

May 24, 1980

I have braved, for want of wild beasts, steel cages,
carved my term and nickname on bunks and rafters,
lived by the sea, flashed aces in an oasis,
dined with the-devil-knows-whom, in tails, on truffles.
From the height of a glacier I beheld half a world, the earthly
width. Twice have drowned, thrice let knives rake my nitty-gritty.
Quit the country that bore and nursed me.
Those who forgot me would make a city.
I have waded the steppes that saw yelling Huns in saddles,
worn the clothes nowadays back in fashion in every quarter,
planted rye, tarred the roofs of pigsties and stables,
guzzled everything save dry water.
I've admitted the sentries' third eye into my wet and foul
dreams. Munched the bread of exile; it's stale and warty.
Granted my lungs all sounds except the howl;
switched to a whisper. Now I am forty.
What should I say about my life? That it's long and abhors
*   transparence.*
Broken eggs make me grieve; the omelette, though, makes me vomit.
Yet until brown clay has been rammed down my larynx,
only gratitude will be gushing from it.

—Joseph Brodsky, 1980
(translated by the author)

PART II

A Brief History of the Modern State and Its Constitutional Orders

THESIS: THE INTERPLAY BETWEEN STRATEGIC
AND CONSTITUTIONAL INNOVATION CHANGES
THE CONSTITUTIONAL ORDER OF THE STATE.

Epochal wars produce fundamental challenges to the State. A warring state that is unable to prevail within the then-dominant strategic and constitutional practices will innovate. In such wars, successful innovations—either strategic or constitutional—by a single state are copied by other, competing states. This state mimicry sweeps through the society of states and results in the sudden shift in constitutional orders and strategic paradigms in the aftermath of an epochal war. By this means, a new dominant constitutional order emerges with new bases of legitimacy, and older forms decay and disappear.

A History Lesson

Kings
like golden gleams
made with a mirror on the wall.

A non-alcoholic pope,
knights without arms,
arms without knights.

The dead like so many strained noodles,
a pound of those fallen in battle,
two ounces of those who were executed,

several heads
like so many potatoes
shaken into a cap—

Geniuses conceived
by the mating of dates
are soaked up by the ceiling into infinity

to the sound of tinny thunder,
the rumble of bellies,
shouts of hurrah,

empires rise and fall
at the wave of a pointer,
the blood is blotted out—

And only one small boy,
who was not paying the least attention,
will ask
between two victorious wars:

And did it hurt in those days too?

—Miroslav Holub
(translated by George Theiner)

CHAPTER FIVE

Strategy and the Constitutional Order

THE IDEA OF a "military revolution" in Europe was first introduced by Michael Roberts in his now-famous inaugural lecture at the Queen's University of Belfast in January 1955.[1] Roberts identified four profound changes in warfare in the period 1560–1660. First was a revolution in tactics, as archers and then infantry armed with muskets ended the dominance of feudal knights and massed squares of pikemen. To put this in other words, *fire* replaced *shock* as the decisive element on the battlefield. Second, a dramatic increase in the size of armies occurred, with the forces of several states increasing ten times between 1500 and 1700. Third, strategies changed as the possibility of decisive action in the field replaced the static and inconclusive siege tactics of the previous century. Fourth, war became more of a depredation on the civilian society: the vastly greater costs required to field such larger armies, the damage wrought by foraging troops, and the destructiveness of battles made civil life grimly more like that of Brecht's *Mother Courage,* written of the Thirty Years' War, than of *Lepanto,* Chesterton's brightly lit account of the famous naval battle of a century before.

Roberts's thesis quickly achieved the status of orthodoxy—Sir George Clark enthusiastically adopted it unqualifiedly in his *War and Society in the Seventeenth Century* published three years later[2]—and thus became a target for various qualifying theses* in the ensuing years. But by far the most important development was the claim that the need for cash and an

---

*Roberts was criticized for slighting developments in naval warfare and charged with underestimating the continuing impact of siege warfare throughout the century, overestimating the impact of Gustavus Adolphus's reforms and ignoring altogether the similar, parallel changes made in the French, Dutch, and Habsburg armies. See Geoffrey Parker, *The Military Revolution* (Cambridge University Press, 1996), 1–2, citing among others David Parrott, "Strategy and Tactics in the Thirty Years War: The Military Revolution," *Militargeschichtliche Mittelungen XVIII* 2 (1985): 7–25 and John Lynn, "Tactical evolution in the French army, 1560–1660," *XIV French Historical Studies* 14 (1985): 176–91. See also David Parrott, "The Military Revolution in Early Modern Europe," *History Today* 42 (1992): 21–27; and John A. Lynn, "The Trace Italienne and the Growth of Armies: The French Case," *Journal of Military History* 55 (1991): 297.

administrative infrastructure to fund and manage the larger armies and new technologies caused a revolution in *government* from which, in the seventeenth century, the modern state emerged. Roberts himself had drawn attention to issues of state formation, national identity, centralization, and the development of state bureaucracies, and this aspect of his argument was picked up by others.[3] Geoffrey Parker, Roberts's greatest student, observed a strikingly similar pattern that culminated in the establishment of the Ch'in imperial dynasty.[4] And he concluded that there occurred in European armies such a massive growth in manpower, accompanied by a profound change in tactics and strategy, and on European societies such a greatly intensified impact of war, that equally profound changes in the structure and philosophy of government came about.[5]

To manage the sheer size of seventeenth century armies—Gustavus Adolphus had 175,000 men under arms—states could no longer rely on the traditional ways in which troops were raised. Roberts suggested that governments met this challenge through constitutional centralization, first taking control of the recruiting, equipping, and supplying of troops (which in turn required a more extensive and accountable administrative structure); then establishing permanent standing armies; and finally funding this vast military and administrative expansion through the sophisticated credit and financial systems that are a key characteristic of the modern State. By 1660, it was claimed, the military revolution had had its effect: the modern style of warfare had come into being and with it the modern State, exemplified by the progressive regime of Protestant Sweden.

This thesis was criticized, however, by Parker.[6] He attacked the idea that the military advantage had shifted to constitutionally progressive regimes, and wrote admiringly of the Spanish, who, he claimed, were at the forefront of new weapons technology and the introduction of smaller, more tactically flexible units. Indeed, it was the Spanish army, as early as the 1570s, that had taken on the characteristics of a permanent standing army, with its extensive structures for financing, training, logistics, and command. In subsequent work, Parker focused on a differing explanation for the increase in army size than that proposed by Roberts: rather than reflecting a response to the more ambitious and decisive strategies of the seventeenth century, Parker traced the growth of armies to developments in fortification in the sixteenth century. It was not so much the development of artillery capable of blasting down fortresses as it was the change in the fortresses themselves, enabling them to employ this technology defensively, that set the terms of the sixteenth century battlefield. This change produced the *trace italienne,* characterized by low formidable walls, broken by complex bastions to enable fire against sapping trenches, and surrounded by obstacle-strewn but visually clear fields that permitted fortress artillery to rake a besieging force with fire. Parker argued that commanders, contemplating these new fortifications, were compelled to increase greatly the numbers of troops in order to man the ever more complex and lengthy siege lines and, if on the defensive, to garrison fortresses for an aggressive defense. For Parker then, the revolution began a century earlier.

In contrast to this claim, Jeremy Black argued that the military revolution actually occurred a century *later* than that proposed by Roberts.[7] The development of the ring bayonet, which effectively replaced the use of pikemen by giving the musketeer a pike of his own; a surge in the number of troops engaged in battle; the standardization of equipment, including uniforms; and vastly more comprehensive logistical infrastructures all impressed Black as having a decisiveness that was absent in the transient reforms of earlier periods. Moreover, rather than seeing the creation of the modern state as the outcome of an earlier military revolution, Black concluded that the modern administrative and bureaucratic state that emerged in the early eighteenth century was the driving factor behind *strategic* change.

Challenging the thesis of a military-governmental revolution altogether, David Parrott attacked the claim that the expansion in the size of armies was indeed accompanied by a comparable expansion and centralization of the State. In fact, he argued, the great majority of forces that fought in Europe before the end of the seventeenth century were not raised by states at all, but rather were recruited and managed by an extensive system of private entrepreneurs. He concluded that there was no direct correlation between the growth of the forces being maintained and the development of the State. The principal reason for the large numbers of troops in Europe was to allow the military contractors who maintained them to recover their expenses by means of enforced contributions from local populations. The great seventeenth century commander Wallenstein, Parrott noted, told the Holy Roman Emperor in 1626 that he could maintain a self-financing army of 50,000 but not one of 20,000 because the larger force could man garrisons and extract contributions. Parrott proposed that we see the increase in military forces and expenditure as leading not to state-building, but to an unprecedented willingness of the State to offload its responsibilities onto private contractors. When the seventeenth century did witness an increase in the centralization of state authority, Parrott disparaged this as a reaction to the military developments of the preceding period.

In the chapters that follow, I will trace developments in strategy from roughly the end of the fifteenth century onward and relate these developments to changes in the constitutional structures of the states of Europe. For these purposes, we need not attempt to resolve many of the questions about the "military revolution." Whether in fact the numbers of troops employed in the sieges of Strasbourg, Breisach, or Turin were greater than those deployed in the preceding century, and whether the forces available for any particular battle in the Thirty Years' War really were as large as those nominally under Swedish command, are matters not directly germane to the present task. It is undeniable that developments in strategy changed the ferocity of and resources required for war from the beginning of the sixteenth century onward, even if we do not know precisely how these demands were met. What we must attempt to answer is Parrott's question: what is the relationship between strategic development and constitutional innovation? And if there is a causal relation, then we must answer Black's question: which way does it run? Does the state change, and with it the strategies it employs? Or do changes in the strategic environment force states to change their organization in order to cope with these developments? And if we can answer those questions, then we can perhaps decide at what point this profound change occurred—the question that divided Roberts and Parker and Black.

This agenda, however, is not as tractable as it may at first appear. Take Parrott's question. It seems undeniable that there is a relationship between strategic and constitutional change, and the reason for this is not hard to gather. Strategic developments in a geography of proximate societies like Europe can present a similar, acute problem to states that otherwise may greatly differ. The endowments of states such as Spain and France may have little in common—that is, their material resources, cultural traditions, and political leadership may be absurdly unalike—but the cannon that confronts one will confront both. A new development in military tactics or technology will quickly spread through the available colleges and arsenals of all states. Every state must either mimic or innovate in response to such a development. And yet isn't Parrott right in implying that there is no single relationship between state formation and strategy because history provides far too many counterexamples of retrenchments that follow growth, of successful military innovations that lead nowhere constitutionally, and profound constitutional changes that seem to have no impact on military matters? To take but two examples: Consider the Polish army's practices during the seventeenth century that considerably diverged from those of the European states discussed by Roberts, Parker, and Black, yet were highly successful against the Swedes. Nevertheless, these innovations forced neither military nor constitutional changes on the rest of Europe. One might add also the Hungarian tactics against the Turks in 1686, which were similar in style to those of the Poles. Or consider the downsizing of European forces after Waterloo. Of the great powers, only Prussia elected to follow Napoleon's example and retain a large standing army; the others were far too wary of having so many soldiers garrisoned at home with large numbers of weapons that could be turned against the state.

Nor can one easily answer Black: if, as Parrott asserts, there is no linear, causal relationship between changes in the State and changes in strategy, how can we determine in which direction the causal relation holds? And if we don't know that, how can we say at which precise point the decisive revolution occurred—for if the constitutional changes in the State are dominant, the point at which those changes occur dates the revolution, but if the strategic change is determinant, then *its* hour of change is decisive. And so we cannot answer Roberts and Parker either.

Nor can they answer each other, for on the facts as we know them—that the nation-state has been the outcome of modern history, and that modern warfare has proceeded from loosely organized bands of mercenaries to the vast, professionalized standing armies of the present—there is no decisive fact that cannot be accommodated by each of the various proposed theses. If we focus on the Battle of Nördlingen in 1634, for example, the Swedish innovations so praised by Roberts look ineffectual against an apparently traditional Habsburg force—but it was just such innovations that won battles at Breitenfeld (1631), Lützen (1632), and Wittstock (1636). A partisan of either position can parry such evidence with the ease of a sociobiologist asked for evidence of adaptive traits. Biogenetic evolution is punctuated; why can't the evolution of states also be? And therefore what counts as a significant event is one that fits a general account whose terminus is the world we know now. Other events, other battles, are pruned away as evolutionary dead ends.

Can it be a sheer coincidence that Roberts, one of the most distinguished contemporary historians of the Swedish empire, locates the military revolution in the campaigns of Gustavus Adolphus, while Black, a prominent historian of the regimes of the eighteenth century, finds his revolution there, and Parker, whose evidence goes beyond his special distinction in the history of the Spanish empire of the sixteenth century, nevertheless discovers in that century, in the Spanish campaigns in Flanders, the true beginning of the military revolution? It seems the more one learns about a period, the more pivotal and unique it appears. This appearance might simply be owed to that situating perspective that can accompany scholarly immersion. But in the case of historians as able and judicious as these, that seems an insufficient conclusion. Mightn't it also be that each of these historians is right because they are all right? More than one revolution has occurred because more than one constitutional order of the state has arisen. In the following narrative, I will discuss the transformations of the State that have accompanied military revolutions. I count six of these, not one—and thus do not answer Roberts's, Black's, and Parker's question by choosing one single date for a military revolution, but by choosing all three, as well as some others—because the states that were brought into being are constitutionally distinct with respect to six different periods.

I propose, in the brief historical narrative that follows, to treat the relationship between state formation and strategic change as that of a *field,* as contrasted with those causal relations that are usually characterized along a *line*. A field relationship is mutually effecting between two or more subjects. Significant events in the development of strategy will be shown to have important constitutional manifestations, and significant constitutional changes will enable and sometimes demand strategic shifts, including shifts in the deployment of technology and tactics. Whether the one causes the other, or vice versa, depends entirely on where you stand and when you decide to begin. If we begin at the end of the eighteenth century, for example, it seems clear that the constitutional changes of the French Revolution made possible, even required, the *levée en masse* and wouldn't tolerate a heavy reliance on foreign mercenaries; bound by these requirements, Napoleon fashioned a new strategic approach to warfare. If we begin in the middle of the nineteenth century, it seems equally clear that the technological impact on military affairs of the industrial revolution—the ability of railways to move troops, the awesome results of rifled firearms and mass-produced naval hulls—made possible, perhaps even required, the mobilizing nation-state capable of harnessing industry to wage war. If we stand in Poland, we see the evolutionary process differently than if we view events from the perspective of Spain. But this is not because they are disconnected, but rather because the connection is not linear, with one a dependent variable of the other. Individual choice and sheer contingency have a role to play that is a necessary part of, not an annoying intrusion on, such field relations. It is choice, after all, that determines where we begin our story, and where it is set.

CHAPTER SIX

From Princes to Princely States: 1494-1648

"Dinanzi a me non fuor cose create se non etterne e io etterna duro."
"Before me nothing was created but eternal things and I endure eternally."[1]

FROM THE FALL of Rome in A.D. 476 to the crowning of the Frankish leader Charlemagne by the pope on Christmas Day 800, the former territory of the Roman Empire was successively flooded by waves of barbarian invaders from eastern and central Europe. Literacy, trade, and simple security dramatically receded toward the Mediterranean. By the end of the first millennium, however, the central island of the old empire had re-emerged, lapped by Muslim conquests in Spain and North Africa, Norse settlements from the North Sea and Baltic coasts to Sicily, and the incursions of tribes from the eastern steppes that had come as far as Rome and then ebbed to the edges of Vienna. The remaining center, composed of the lands colonized by Germanic tribes in what is now France, as well as Italy and central Europe, huddled together, its populations largely Roman Catholic in religion, and its local rulers the dynastic tribal successors of the Germanic invaders. Within this center two parallel structures developed: the universal Church spanning local cultures, and the fragmented feudal system of local princes. The legal relations of these two entities were in principle separate: the Church system of religious, educational, bureaucratic, and charitable life co-existed with the military and proprietary prerogatives of the nobility, though in fact the feudal administrative structure depended on Church personnel, and the Church was itself a landowner of immense wealth and political presence.

The defining legal characteristic of medieval society was its horizontal nature, reflected across these two pervasive dimensions of ecclesiastical and feudal power. From a modern and secular perspective, these two systems are difficult to imagine as operating simultaneously. Medieval society, however, was not divided into separate states, with each prince a sovereign within his own territory, ruling hierarchically all within that territory and no persons or territories remaining outside the domain of some prince. On the contrary, political society was organized into four co-existing functional sectors: the nobility, the clergy, burghers, and peasants—although some of these sectors were themselves organized vertically, and the authoritative heads of one sector might have had a certain legal authority over the members of the other sectors, as, for example, the Church had jurisdiction over wills and marriages in all sectors. Vertical power, however, was horizontally limited; for example, while a king could demand military service from the feudal vassals who were obligated to him, and while some of these lesser lords owned land to which peasants were attached, a king had no direct authority over his vassal's peasants. Similarly, the urban stratum of medieval society, comprising artisans, merchants, and townspeople of various functions, was in many aspects of life independent of both the clergy and the nobility. A great number of these townspeople were Jews, who though often operating under severe civil restrictions, were largely autonomous. It is to these cities that we owe the concepts and practices of trade, manufacturing, banking, and the organizations of guilds. Some cities were self-governing; some were under princely patronage.

In this diverse commercial environment the need for legal norms is hardly surprising, but what was it about medieval Europe that made it the birthplace of the state system and its attendant norms of international law, when there were many other diverse, commercial environments—the Levant, the Far East—where this did not happen?

First, the medieval church provided a bureaucracy that encouraged regularization across many diverse cultural communities, and also was able to lend itself to the various political authorities in order to supply an administrative apparatus for their needs. The word "clerk," which we associate with a governmental and legal establishment, derives from "clergy" and the practice of filling administrative posts with churchmen. Second, and more important, the two-dimensional nature of medieval Europe meant that the universality of Christendom was coextensive with the radically diverse and disparate ethnic, tribal, and cultural mix. In other cultures only one of these elements prevailed, either the imperial or the fragmentary. In the case of an imperial hierarchy such as medieval China, relations with outsiders always remained just that: no "society" could develop within which they were included. This was the experience of the medieval traders in the Far East and with the Muslim courts. In the case of the diverse but fragmented societies cohabiting the same territory without an overarching superstructure, their very proximity tended to exaggerate conflict and prevent a common culture from developing. This was the case with the pre-Moghul Indian states. In both cases very advanced cultures failed to develop a state system and an international law because neither ever developed an overarching international culture.

In medieval Christendom, however, a universal, overarching institution existed that provided a society of diverse and competitive princes with both the means and the motive to develop a body of comprehensive legal practices. In the first place, legal rationales could bolster a prince's claim to territory or prerogatives. In a system of states without an overarching structure, there was no appeal to higher authority; in Europe, appeal could be made to the Church. Moreover, the omnipresence of ecclesiastical dominion often provided a motive for resistance to that dominion and the availability of legal arguments provided a resource to be deployed *against* the Church without having to reject ecclesiastical authority per se. As Adam Watson has put it:

> The . . . legal justification for territorially defined realms made it increasingly easy for kings in the west to defy a particular pope (or in some areas emperor) though without formally repudiating the universal authority of these offices.[2]

In the second place, the superstructure of Christendom was itself an international legal culture. Popes were elected by cardinals from many different localities, and the Holy Roman Emperor was chosen according to the votes of the diverse electoral princes of the empire, including three archbishops.* It has even been asserted by some historians that the origin of the constitutional idea of a separation of powers lies in the struggle between papal and temporal authority, and the argument that the Church should determine the law as a guide but rely on independent lay rulers to execute and apply these rules.

Finally, the universal scope of the Christian community imposed restraints on a prince's reasons for going to war. Wars among Christians needed a legal justification. It is instructive to compare Aquinas's rules as to what constitutes a just war, addressing as he was a society of diverse princes, with those of Augustine, who spoke to an imperial audience. Aquinas's rules are an effort to "enhance the security of legitimate possession." Indeed we can trace the current preoccupation in international law with justification for war to this period when it was the aim of the medieval Church to limit the use of force to the maintenance of world order, where the "world" was Christendom.

---

*Although the ecclesiastical electors were usually cardinals within the Church, their status as electors was derived from their authority as archbishops of the sees of Cologne, Mainz, and Trier.

War against non-Christians provided the exception to these efforts at limitation. Here also the unique combination of competing princes and a universal order militated in favor of a developing multinational culture. A crusade had to be proclaimed by the pope, and there were strict rules governing such proclamations as well as the relationships that obtained among the participating princes. The crusades are an example of this interplay between local identification and universality, one that is often misunderstood by a sort of anachronistic psychological Marxism that would expose them as a mere façade for plunder. As Christiansen has retorted:

> To present [the Crusades] as . . . matters of interest disguised as matters of conscience . . . is too easy. It avoids the unavoidable question of why men who were never reluctant to wage war for profit, fame, vengeance or merely to pass the time, without any disguise or pretext, nevertheless chose to claim that certain wars were fought for God's honour and for the redemption of mankind.[3]

It is important to observe that war in each of the theatres of European expansion was sanctioned by papal authority: the *reconquista* of the Iberian peninsula, the efforts to recover Palestine and re-establish the Roman Christian kingdoms in the Near East, and the expansion north and eastward against the pagan Slavic lands. All of these were Christianizing missions, given legal warrant and therefore legitimacy in the eyes of other princes by the sanction of the Church. As we shall see, it was the withdrawal of the universal Church from its legitimating role, leaving in its wake a society of political entities that were unable to assert an objective legitimate status, that in part produced the modern state.

The princes of this period were not territorial in the sense of having a fixed settlement and identification with that locality and its people; that would come later. At this time, the sense of their subjects was too local to be national; and the princes' sense of themselves and their property was determined by inheritance and to a much lesser extent by solidarity with a particular land or its inhabitants. They were not the monarchs of nations. The Henry V who fought at Agincourt to recover his property on the continent is unlikely to have spoken the sentiments of a nationalist, Renaissance author like Shakespeare in exhorting his men. For Harry, yes; but not necessarily for England and St. George. Nor were these princes of *states;* rather they governed realms, each with a rudimentary administrative apparatus that was impermanent and fixed only to the person of the prince. As princes without nations and without states, they were in some ways well suited to give birth to what would become international law because they had legal relations with each other that required legal rules. Princes made contracts: the law of contracts for princes became the international law of treaties; princes made war and the international laws of war arose from the laws of torts and crimes among princes; the international law of territorial conquest and session arose from the laws of property and the inheritance of estates among princes.

On this distinctively medieval pattern is the present international law based. This accounts for many traits that persist in that law, as the law of the society of princes became the law of the society of states.

PRINCELY STATES

Medieval Christendom was not yet a society of politically distinct states. But at first in Italy, and then throughout the area, the complex horizontal structure of feudal society crystallized into a vertical pattern of territorial states, each with increasing authority inside defined geographic borders.[4]

This change was begun by the conquest of Constantinople in 1453 by the Ottoman Turks, when two events of profound consequence for the Italian cities occurred: first, the steep, high walls of Constantinople, hitherto thought to be impregnable, were battered into rubble by gigantic wrought-iron tubes that fired balls made of stone; second, a large population of talent, including a group of classical scholars, largely Greek, who were the inheritors of the premedieval tradition, were driven out of ancient Byzantium and forced to immigrate to the university towns of Italy. The only comparable injection of such talent into a thriving society might be the exodus of European refugees during the 1930s and the consequent quantum change in the quality of American universities and eventually American cultural life.*

The classical ideas of these scholars found an eager audience in Italy: parallels to the Greek city-states and the Roman city-republic appealed to the pride of the Italian city-realm. Moreover, an enormous cultural energy was released once Italian society, whose periodic eruptions of piety had never quite exhausted its love of power and pleasure, was shed of the sheer weight of hypocrisy that the medieval Church had steadily accumulated on its behalf. Finally, classical ideas—or rather Renaissance notions about such ideas—provided a rationalization of events, as the city-realm began to thrive on its independence and assertiveness, that seemed more in accord with reality than did medieval universality and the dual allegiance to the ecclesiastical and the feudal. Questions that could be answered only

---

*This was also true of British intellectual life; one has only to think of von Hayek, Gombrich, Popper, Pevsner, among others.

by reference to biblical and dogmatic texts increasingly seemed to lack the urgency of questions that could only be answered by reference to the world. The trajectories of artillery are, for example, a matter of physics, not of church doctrine. The "bombards" of the Turks presaged the change in government that would bring into being the new idea of the State.

But the huge cannon of Mehmed II that destroyed the fortress walls of Constantinople was difficult to transport and slow to arm. The French king, Charles VIII, however, financed the development of a cannon so light that it could be easily transported.[5] Cast bronze replaced wrought iron when it was discovered that the method used to found church bells could also create cannon.* The catalyst for constitutional change occurred when Charles VIII invaded the Italian peninsula in 1494 with a horse-drawn siege train of at least forty artillery pieces. Contemporaries of this event immediately appreciated its implications: in 1498 the Venetian senate declared that "the wars of the present time are influenced more by the force of bombards and artillery than by men at arms" and desperately began trying to organize to meet this challenge. Others, too, recognized this moment as a turning point. Francesco Guicciardini, the Florentine diplomat and statesman, wrote in the 1520s:

> Before the year 1494, wars were protracted, battles bloodless, the methods followed in besieging towns slow and uncertain . . . Hence it came about that the ruler of state could hardly be dispossessed. But the French, in their invasion of Italy, infused so much liveliness into our wars that whenever the open country was lost, the State was lost with it.[6]

Facing such a strategic challenge, Italian cities could no longer simply rely on their high walls and fortified towns to protect them. Machiavelli, writing in 1519, said that after 1494, "[n]o wall exists, however thick, that artillery cannot destroy in a few days." Suddenly walls, towers, moats—all were rendered obsolete.[7] As a result, princes and oligarchs made a pact with an idea: the idea was that of the State, and its promise was to make the ruler secure. The State—a permanent infrastructure to gather the revenue, organize the logistical support, and determine the command arrangements required for the armies that would be required to protect the realm—was established to govern according to the will of the ruler. In time, however, it would become clear that it was not the prince's immortality that was gained by this move, but the State's. Just as Renaissance princes had found

---

*As John U. Nef put it, "[t]he early founders, whose task had been to fashion bells that tolled the message of eternal peace . . . contributed unintentionally to the discovery of one of man's most terrible weapons." Quoted in Bernard and Fawn Brodie, *From Crossbow to H-Bomb* (Indiana University Press, 1973), 48.

they needed more secure, more professional armed forces than the seasonal contributions of medieval knighthood could provide, so the new Renaissance state would gradually turn to less idiosyncratic guidance than that offered by princes in order to aggrandize its wealth and power.

Thus, the modern state originated in the transition from the rule of princes to that of princely states that necessity wrought on the Italian peninsula at the end of the fifteenth century. It is certainly true that there were states before this period; but these, like the city-states of Thucydides, did not self-consciously think of themselves as juridical entities separate from (and sometimes operating in opposition to) the civil society.[8] For Thucydides the State is never a thing—it has no "legal personality" as we might say. The State is always an irreducible community of human beings and never characterized as an abstraction with certain legal attributes apart from the society itself. The modern state, however, is an entity quite detachable from the society that it governs as well as from the leaders who exercise power. This detachment gives the State its potential for immortality.

We can date the appearance of such a way of looking at the State to the time when the legal and material attributes of a human being were ascribed to the State itself. All the significant legal characteristics of the State— legitimacy, personality, continuity, integrity, and, most importantly, sovereignty—date from the moment at which these human traits, the constituents of human identity, were transposed to the State itself. This occurred when princes, to whom these legal characteristics had formerly been attached, required the services of a permanent bureaucracy in order to manage the demands of a suddenly more threatening strategic competition. (The first permanent legations, for example, accredited to a particular court rather than merely serving as temporary emissaries, date from this period.) This strategic competition provoked what Finer has defined as the essential characteristic of the modern state: that

> the paramount organ of government is subserved by specialized personnel; one the civil service, to carry out decisions, the other—the military service to back these by force where necessary and protect the association from other similarly constituted associations.[9]

Strategic competition on the Italian peninsula provoked military innovation by Italian cities that were rich but weak. In the armies of the great powers, France, Aragon, and England, the number of soldiers raised by feudal levy was compounded with that raised by hiring mercenaries. Since the fourteenth century, however, the Italian cities had relied entirely on privately organized professional armed forces. Single groups—the *compagna di ventura*—were recruited, supplied, and paid by their commanders, the *condottieri,* who sold their services to the highest bidder. The necessity for, and later the ambition of, the *condottieri* was a crucial element in the creation of the first modern states. For it was these mercenaries whose expensive services animated the need for the princely state, and whose ambitions then exploited the legitimating resources of that state, once the transfer of legal personality from the person of the prince to the princely state had occurred.

The *condottiere* was a contract employee. The word derives from the Italian for "contract," *condotta*. The necessity to employ mercenaries became general on the peninsula once a few cities hired such forces because the shifting alliance structure of the region meant that no city could rely on the mercenaries of another.[10] Once the superiority of the professionalized forces of the *condottieri* became clear, this innovation swept through all the cities of the peninsula as one after another mimicked the innovation lest it be engulfed by it. This necessity forced princes and oligarchs and ruling councils to rely more heavily on a bureaucratic apparatus, first to fund the *condotte* and later to provide for the acquisition of artillery. The *condottieri* themselves soon saw the advantage in turning their force on the authorities by whom they had been hired and supplanting them.

To rule the city he had seized, however, the usurping *condottiere* needed legitimacy. The *condottieri* took their contracts from a prince or oligarchy and hence from them alone derived the *condottiere*'s legal status. The princely state, however, once severed from the prince who brought it into being could provide a legal status for the *condottiere* apart from that of an employee of the prince or ruling council whom he had deposed. Thus this irony gave birth to the modern state and its unique problem, its problematic relation to the elusive status of legitimacy: only a State, however rudimentary, could provide the prince with the infrastructure necessary to maintain expensive mercenaries, but once this infrastructure was erected, it could also provide others with the means of exercising the power they had seized,[11] and legitimate their doing so.

This reification of the State reshaped the international society that had come into being in the Middle Ages. The Italian peninsula was a perfect laboratory for such a new society: the principal political actors spoke a common language; they were physically proximate; none was so powerful as to make diplomacy irrelevant; repeated invasions by French, Spanish, and Imperial forces, throughout the period of this transition, were unable to establish an hegemony that could overcome a careful balance of opposing powers, which necessitated complex negotiations and intercourse; and, most importantly, the rulers of these cities faced a need for law that only an international society could satisfy, namely, the legitimation required by those who seized power by force or held it without the imprimatur of dynastic right. In these geopolitical circumstances, the Italian Renaissance produced the first princely states and, almost as a corollary, the inheritance by these entities of the legal status hitherto reserved for the persons of princes. Far too little attention is customarily paid by legal scholars to the effects of other states on a state's own constitutional system. In the Italian laboratory we can see the mimetic, competitive, reactive relationships among these states and the significance of these relationships for the constitutional order.

The Italian peninsula was dominated by five city-realms: Rome, Naples, Milan, Florence, and Venice. The center of the Renaissance in Italy was Florence, whose situation was similar to that of the other city-realms. It was her solution to that situation that provided other cities with the form on which the princely state was modeled. What were the characteristics of the Italian situation within which Florence and other cities found themselves?

First, the cities were defined geographically, as opposed to the usual springing dynastic inheritances of princes. Realms that were increased (or decreased) by the happenstance of inheritance and marriage often yielded disparate, unconnected properties scattered across Europe. This tended to fracture rather than consolidate a common culture. Second, the cities were wealthy—Florence had an annual income greater than that of the king of England and the revenue of Venice and its *Terra Ferma* at the middle of the fifteenth century was 60 percent higher than that of France, more than double that of England and Spain[12]—in a world that had recently come to a money economy. These cities could afford a bureaucracy and profit by it. Third, the wealth of the cities was coveted by others; yet the cities had populations too small to create effective militias, and therefore required mercenaries. Fourth, the Italian rulers of these city-realms faced a new and menacing technology that threatened to make obsolete the sheltering walls and turrets that protected them from their French and Habsburg predators.

This transition from prince to princely state provides us with an initial example of a strategic imperative animating a constitutional innovation—an instance, that is, where the insistent question of security in a specific context (geography, wealth, small population) yields a new legal solution and requires a story to rationalize that solution. If the constitutional innovation of the modern state was in part a response to the threat posed by mobile artillery to the walled cities of Italy, the precise shape of that response—the princely state—was not governed by strategic considerations alone, but also by the felt need to ensure legitimacy for the leadership that wedded its future to this new creation.

A vulnerability rooted in questions of dynastic legitimacy underlay all the principal city-states of Italy. Consider the situation of the cities' leaders in 1454. In Milan, the dynastic line had ended in 1447; one candidate for the succession was Francesco Sforza, a *condottiere* and the husband of the last male heir's illegitimate daughter. The Holy Roman Emperor, Frederick III, claimed the Duchy of Milan as forfeit to the Empire, there being no rightful dynastic claimant. The Kings of France and Spain also pressed claims.

Florence was effectively ruled by the Medicis, a banking house whose head, Cosimo, had returned in triumph from exile in 1434 to dominate the Signory, an oligarchical body. By his command of capital, Cosimo was able to affect events throughout Europe, including, for example, the Wars of the Roses (through loans to Edward IV), and to paralyze Naples and Venice by withholding credit that would have been used to finance mercenaries. Yet the Medici ruled by competence, not royal bloodlines, and thus always had to refresh their legitimacy through further successful acts on behalf of Florentine society.

In Venice, the ruling group of merchant oligarchs, the Signoria, had led the city to an expansion on the mainland, seizing towns and fortresses from the Milanese—in an effort to make Venice self-sufficient in food—and also from the Empire, Naples, and the Papacy. Unlike the other cities, Venice was an international maritime power, but her new acquisitions made her vulnerable to a coalition of forces that would, ultimately, destroy her power. Precisely because she was a republic—Venice provided a model often referred to in the *Federalist Papers* by the American constitutional founders—she could not claim dynastic legitimacy, which became a more pressing issue once she expanded beyond her historic city lagoon.

In Rome, the papacy was held by a Catalonian family, the Borgias. The fact that elections had been manipulated to permit more than one generation of a family to control the papacy only underscored the obvious: the pope, Alexander VI, behaved like a Renaissance prince, delegating papal authority to his children, and using the powers of the papacy, including excommunication, as diplomatic tools. Yet he did not have the legal imprimatur of a prince. Instead he became one in fact by virtue of a papal election, which cast doubt on not only his own legitimacy as a putative political monarch but also on his power to confer legitimacy on his heirs.

Naples was in the possession of the Spanish king after a century of disputed successions, recurrent revolutions, turmoil, and anarchy. It provided an example to the other cities of what might happen to them if the great kings outside Italy were to invade the peninsula, as well as providing a base to Spain from which further adventures might be launched.

Let us grant then that these cities were insecure and could profit from the legitimacy and focus of energy that a State could provide—why at this time? Surely there had been insecure oligarchies of dubious legitimacy before? Why did it take the psychological and cultural change that produced perspective in drawing and melody in music and the nude in modern painting—why did it take the Renaissance to create the princely state?

Partly it was a matter of contrast with what had gone before. Renaissance skepticism about the deference owed to medieval authority fortuitously fed the necessities that led to the princely state. If the universal Church could not confer legitimacy, much less security, on the realms of the Renaissance prince, this was as much liberating as it was dismaying. The philosopher of the Renaissance who was most interested in the interplay between the internal constitution of the State and its external, strategic security wrote:

> If the various campaigns and uprisings which have taken place in Italy have given the appearance that military ability has become extinct, the true reason is that the old methods of warfare were not good and no one has been able to find new ones. A man newly risen to power cannot acquire greater reputation than by discovering new rules and methods.[13]

This insight led its author, Niccolò Machiavelli, and others, to the constitutional outlook that framed the princely state.

It was a sharp break with the perspective it superseded. Whereas the new Renaissance state intertwined the legal and the strategic, the medieval world had mingled the religious and military. As Sir Michael Howard has expressed it:

> Knighthood was a way of life, sanctioned and civilized by the ceremonies of the Church until it was almost indistinguishable from the ecclesiastical order of the monasteries . . . equally dedicated, equally holy, the ideal to which medieval Christendom aspired. This remarkable blend of Germanic warrior and Latin *sacerdos* lay at the root of all medieval culture.[14]

In a society in which all activity had religious significance, the knight served God by serving his liege and by waging war according to rules laid down by the Church and delegated to temporal authority. The military relationship between vassal and lord, knight and liege, also reflected the economic relationship: the vassal was allotted property and accepted the obligation to provide military service to the lord in war. Thus arose a legal relationship that depended upon both economic realities and military imperatives. Both of these were transformed at the end of the medieval era; whether as a result or as a cause, the spiritual structure collapsed as well.

> When rapid expansion of a money economy shook the agricultural basis of medieval society, the effects of this development on military institutions were immediate. . . . [T]he great money powers of the period, the Italian cities, came to rely entirely on professional soldiers. . . .

New classes of men, freed from the preceding military traditions, were attracted into the services by money, and with this infiltration of new men, new weapons and new [tactics] could be introduced. [This evolution was accelerated by the development of artillery, which was expensive and favored the offense at the expense of fortifications and the feudal castle.] The moral code, traditions and customs, which feudalism had evolved, had lost control over the human material from which the armies were now recruited. . . . War was no longer undertaken as a religious duty, the purpose of military service became financial gain.[15]

Entrepreneurs are hardly likely to provide services for their customers that entail their own annihilation and the sacrifice of their capital. In Machiavelli's first diplomatic mission on behalf of the city of Florence, he negotiated the fees of a *condottiere* engaged in the efforts to regain Pisa. Observing at Pisa the mercenaries sent by the king of France, an ally of Florence in the campaign, he noted that these troops refused to advance against the city, mutinied, and finally simply disappeared. Indeed, during the last months of 1502, Machiavelli was present at Sinigaglia when Cesare Borgia persuaded a number of hostile *condottieri* to meet with him and had them murdered once they arrived. These events confirmed for Machiavelli the weaknesses of reliance on the *condottieri* and the need for a ruthless and decisive political leader.

Machiavelli devised the following proposals: (1) Florence should have a conscripted militia: the love of gain would inevitably corrupt the *condottiere* who would avoid decisive battles to preserve his forces, betray his employers to a higher bidder, and seize power when it became advantageous; (2) the prince had to create institutions that would evoke loyalty from his subjects which in other countries was provided by the feudal structure of vassalage, but which had in Italy been lost with the collapse of medieval society; (3) legal and strategic organization are interdependent: "there must be good laws where there are good arms and where there are good arms there must be good laws."[16] "Although I have elsewhere maintained that the foundation of states is a good military organization, yet it seems to me not superfluous to report here that without such a military organization there can neither be good laws nor anything else good";[17] (4) deceit and violence are wrong for an individual, but justified when the prince is acting in behalf of his state; (5) permanent embassies and sophisticated sources of intelligence must be maintained in order to enable successful diplomacy; and (6) the tactics of the prince, in law and in war, must be measured by a rational assessment of the contribution of those tactics to the strategic goals of statecraft, which are governed by the contingencies of history. All of these conclusions compel a final one: princes must develop the princely state.

The princely state enables the prince to rationalize his acts on the basis of *ragione di stato*. He is not acting merely on his own behalf, but is compelled to act in service of the State. Notice how the very word *state* undergoes a transformation in this period from its Latin root *status* meaning a "state of affairs," to the State as an institutionalized "situation." By extending the power of the prince, the State replaces the lost relationship of vassalage and its obligations to an overlord with a citizen's duty, a crucial change if Machiavelli's conscript army was ever to become a reality. He urged a system in which a civil bureaucracy would replace the strategic and legal roles of vassals. Civil servants would provide a more reliable infrastructure.[18] Perhaps the most important official reflection of Machiavelli's statecraft is the statute of December 1505, which ordered the organization of a Florentine militia. This law was drafted by Machiavelli, and the preamble announces some of Machiavelli's fundamental views, especially the idea that the foundation of a republic is "justice and arms," that is, the intertwining of constitutional and strategic capabilities. It is significant also that a *statute* embodies these ideas because a princely state requires laws, whereas a prince acting alone needs only decrees. This is an essential movement toward the formation of public rather than private authority.

The medieval system had been a rights-based system. Each member of that society had a particular place that determined rights, obligations, and a well-defined role. It is a familiar but erroneous portrait of the medieval era that depicts its society as uniform and colorless. Rights-based systems can in fact yield enormous diversity, because though conformity may be enforced by law, it is not necessarily enforced by that most pitiless of masters, the individual ambition; thus such systems often encourage creativity, as the natural exuberance of individuals attempts to circumvent the rigidity of their assigned roles and the received wisdom. Yet these systems often strike us as irrational in practice because they do not attempt to match talent and performance with role. Perhaps that is why contemporary philosophers today who urge us to adopt rights-based systems often must resort to hypothesized situations like the Rawlsian veil of ignorance, behind which each person must choose a distributive system he or she would prefer without knowing what particular person one turned out to be.

What rights-based systems reject, then, is rationality applied to the contingent situation. Thus the Franciscans imprisoned Roger Bacon for his scientific speculations; the Dominicans preached crusades against the cultivated nobles of Toulouse; the Benedictines erased masterpieces of classical literature in order to copy litanies, and sold pieces of parchment for charms.[19] And even though Aquinas, Duns Scotus, and William of Ockham were rigorous logicians, only Aquinas applied this rigor to the analysis of their political condition.

The spirit of the Renaissance, by contrast, was quickened by curiosity, piqued of course by the recovery of classical models that provided an alternative to the medieval paradigms, but driven relentlessly by a need for inquiry into the place of temporal man himself. Copernicus and Galileo; Vesalius and Harvey; Leonardo and Michelangelo; Petrarch and Boccaccio—all had this in common: a desire to see man's *contingent* situation as it is. This draws the light of rationality back onto the viewer. In the medieval period, there had been a universal system of customary law, based on the rights of inheritance, charters, and grants. Customary law is the common law of practices. We are inclined today to think of common law as generated by courts, but this is really an abbreviation: common law is simply the customary law of the judiciary; it grows and is modified by the exercise of court practices. The medieval period was almost entirely ruled by a kind of common law, but the generating institutions of that law were seldom judicial courts.

When these institutions began to malfunction—as, for instance, when the introduction of a money economy broke down the rights-relations of lord and vassal with regard to military service[20]—and new practices developed (such as the professional, mercenary army), the questioning figures of the Renaissance tried to design institutions that would improve on the merely customary (for example, Machiavelli's plan for a conscripted militia drawn from the Florentine population).

Precisely because the inherited institutions were rights-based, they could not promote new arrangements that were violative of the customary methods. A prince alone could not rewrite the constitutional rules of his society's governance to meet his own needs; that would require an institution that objectified the needs of the prince but was distinct from the prince himself. In Italy, the development of such an institution was catalyzed by the strategic threats facing the city-states.

From 1494, Italy became the prize for which Spain and France contended, with local allies, in the first modern epochal war. All eyes were focused on the security of these fragile cities. Men of letters and artists were urged to design countermeasures to the bronze cannon that invaded Italy in 1494. Leonardo's notebooks of this period contain sketches for a machine gun, a primitive tank, and a steam-powered cannon,[21] and Michelangelo repeatedly submitted drawings of fortifications that he thought would withstand bombardment by the new technology of artillery.

The medieval world had been roughly split in two halves. In the west, there were realms where dynastic power had devolved on princes who were hemmed in by customary law, the autonomy of their vassals, and the local rights of towns. These were realms where legitimacy was solid, but the power of the prince circumscribed. In the east, in central Europe, princes were subject to the dual universality of the pope and the emperor, both elected rulers representing complex sets of competing interests. As cities in Italy and princely realms in the Netherlands and parts of Germany began to assert their independence and to accumulate wealth and power, they found themselves subject to assaults on their legitimacy, because their assertions of independence were not endorsed by the papacy or the empire.

> Western kings, in particular, came to realize the significance of the [Italian innovation] and of the much greater power which Italian rulers were able to concentrate in their own hands. . . . True, the most conspicuous Italians, from the Medicis, the Sforzas and the Borgias down to dozens of smaller rulers, had power without legitimacy. The western kings had legitimacy without much effective power . . .[22]

The Italian solution, adopted, for example, by the pope himself, was the princely state. The pope became a prince, and the Roman Church his state. Western kings envied the power that this innovation was able to concentrate in the hands of the prince. Thus,

> [t]hose rulers who understood best the political lessons to be learnt from Renaissance Italy set about turning the legitimate but shadowy medieval overlordship of their realms into a [princely state] on the grand scale, with themselves as the real and absolute masters within the boundaries of their kingdom.[23]

These possibilities presented themselves: either a prince could seize power and form a state; or if one had the good fortune to inherit a kingdom, one could transform it from a realm into a princely state. (A realm, in contrast to a state, has only customary political structures; for example, it has no permanent bureaucracy, diplomatic corps, or armies.) Which option was available was largely determined by history and geography. Thus the first option was the way of the city rulers who had not come to power by virtue of dynastic inheritance (this was the pattern of the Sforzas, the Borgias, the Medicis), but it was also, to a certain degree, the situation of Henry Tudor, who, though presenting dynastic claims, ended a civil war by force. The second choice was made by Louis XI, the king of France, the largest and richest realm in the west. After he inherited the throne, he systematically reduced the power of the nobility, the Church, and the parliaments of his realm by force and deceit, and established a princely state on the Italian model that was particularly attractive to the towns and cities that he enriched even as he circumscribed their political independence.[24] Similarly, in Spain, the dynastic marriage of Ferdinand of Aragon and Isabella of Castile brought a legitimate inheritance of great wealth and territory, which was transformed by Ferdinand's internal, centralizing policies, and by what can justly be called a Florentine foreign policy. This transformation yielded a princely state of transcontinental ambition. Fueled by the wealth of the Americas, Spain reached its apogee during this period. By contrast, the Habsburg king, Maximilian, inherited realms that were not geographically contiguous, and his election as emperor simply found him opposed by princes—in Bavaria, Saxony, Prussia—who were themselves in the process of creating princely states. In this situation, Maximilian wished to subsume the princely states of his competitors in a new European imperium.

One conspicuous feature of the Italian system was the balance of power. We owe this concept to the Medici (balances are, after all, a banking concept), but, as we will see, this idea only came into being in the modern world when there was an international society—the Italian society of princely states—and, of course, the reflection upon the nature and requirements of that society by a shrewd and lucid ruler. Francesco Sforza proposed an alliance to Lorenzo de Medici in order to oppose the growing power of Venice, which had seized territory on the Italian mainland. Sforza suggested that if Venice were not rebuffed, she would by her conquests become so much richer that she would be able to hire *condottieri* capable of enlarging the Venetian state even further and by this process eventually dominate the Italian peninsula. Lorenzo agreed, but he qualified his consent by observing that Venice must not be destroyed, because this would weaken the forces that might one day be needed to coalesce in order to oppose the power of Rome or the Empire. Doubtless Lorenzo also did not want to so strengthen his own ally by giving Milan sole control over the rich valley of the Po, as to tempt Sforza into his own bid for hegemony. Therefore the reply from Florence contained the historic phrase "the affairs of Italy must be kept in balance." This is the compensating idea to Machiavelli's observation that the princely state always has an urge to expand.[25]

The development of princely states alone was not enough to create an international society beyond Italy. Rather this came about, bringing with it notions of a law among states, owing to the need to maintain a balance of power in order to protect against the strongest princely state, Spain. First, however, the overarching power of the universal Church had to be broken, so that states could develop on a territorial basis with subjects who looked to the state rather than elsewhere for allegiance. The universal Church, in medieval times, was the uniting system within which an international society of princes could begin to develop; once these members became princely states, the Church (and the Empire) were a hindrance to the development of a society of states.

The story I have just told is a straightforward one. At its center was the realization by the Italian city-realms of the late fifteenth century that the high, fortified walls that had protected their citizens and their riches would be battered to bits by the introduction of artillery into siege campaigns. Once this fact became apparent, reliance on mercenary forces became problematic: if troops had to leave their fortresses and actually fight decisive battles to protect the city, then mercenary *condottieri* were dubious men for the job. Why should they risk not only their lives but their investment on behalf of a temporary employer? They would have to be compensated for such risks. These two realizations—which were plain to contemporary commentators—form the parentheses within which the princely state existed. It was created in order to provide a secure infrastructure and revenue base for hiring mercenaries; it flourished to serve the needs of the mercenaries themselves, especially the maintenance of legitimacy; it withered and was everywhere superseded because it could not field forces to match the commitments of states that were larger, richer, and, above all, animated by transcendent motives less vulnerable to the transient allegiances of paid captains. Machiavelli's hope that reifying the State would encourage loyalty and sacrifice was not misplaced, but his view that a citizen militia relying on these qualities could substitute for mercenaries was.

The princely state allied the dynastic conventions of medieval feudalism with the constitutional innovation of a distinct and objectified state. This was a secular move, as is most dramatically evident in the secularization of the papal states. When it was followed by a sectarian reaction— motivated in part by disgust at this transformation of the papacy and the Church—princely states attempted to call forth the sacrifice and endurance required by the new forms of warfare by relying on sectarian appeals. To a large degree, they succeeded, and the result was the epochal Thirty Years' War. States the size of cities, however, could not muster the revenues necessary to wage war on the new, vast scale that they themselves had inadvertently brought into being, and the Italian plain ceased to be the incubator of constitutional orders.

The ultimate solution to the artillery threat to the fortified town lay in a new design for fortresses. The *bastioned trace*—a "trace" being a blueprint or outline—is believed to have originated in Italy and has come down to us as the *trace italienne* for that reason. With this design military architects remade the vulnerable fortress wall into a formidable defensive platform for fire. The high walls that had hitherto characterized fortified cities were made lower and thicker to present less prominent and less fragile targets to besieging artillery. Doing so, however, entailed an additional vulnerability because close assaults could exploit the dead zones along the walls or within the interstices created by square or circular towers. The solution was found in erecting projecting bastions on which could be mounted weapons that covered these blind spots. Then the walls themselves, whose surfaces were slanted to deflect bombards, were buttressed on the inside by earth, so that their defenders could rely on the walls to absorb the force of projectiles. A ditch outside the exterior wall heightened the effect of the fortress wall without making it high enough to crumble or topple when struck. Because the defenders were now firing from behind as much as twenty feet of earth, they were masked from the ditches directly below. These designs forced the besieger to pay a heavy price in time and manpower, but they also extracted costs from the besieged:

> These new fortresses, characterized by thick sunken walls and a snowflake-shaped plan that enabled the defenders to sweep every foot of the walls with enfolding cannon fire, proved capable of resisting artillery bombardment and assault alike. To ensure their control over these expensive, powerful and strategically important fortifications, the central governments of Renaissance states increasingly garrisoned them with regular standing armies. . . . To recruit, train, pay and supply these troops required unprecedented amount of money, larger military and fiscal bureaucracies and correspondingly higher taxes. The military expenditures of the Spanish monarchy, for example, increased roughly twentyfold between 1500 and 1650, a 300% increase even after adjusting for inflation.[26]

Although the first bastion design dates from the 1480s, it was the French invasion of Italy in 1494 that produced the *trace italienne* and the desperate efforts of the princely states to erect them. In 1553, faced with the prospect of an attack, the city of Siena tried to fortify itself using the new architecture. When the attack came the next year, even though few of the projected walls had been finished, so much had already been spent on fortification that Siena had no funds left to raise a relief army and the city surrendered unconditionally in 1555.

Such fortresses drove up the size and cost of armies in two ways: large numbers of troops were required for lengthy sieges because the fortress was too formidable a redoubt to be left in the rear of an advancing army; and this meant that, to be most effective, the new fortresses required large garrisons that could successfully pursue an evacuating force. As a consequence, the dominant constitutional form began to move away from the smaller, princely states to kingly states, a transition that can be seen as the Italian strategic innovations moved north in the 1530s. By then over a hundred Italian engineers were working in France on the kingdom's northern defenses. By 1544 more than a dozen such fortresses lay along the border with the Netherlands, defended by more than a thousand artillery pieces.

At the same time, other Italians were working for the Habsburg realm at a staggering cost. The fortified center of a single city, Antwerp, with nine bastions, cost one million florins ($150,000) and between 1529 and 1572, some forty-three kilometers of defenses of the new style[27] were built in the Netherlands at a cost of ten million florins ($1.5 million).*

The French introduction of mobile artillery into Italy in 1494 had set in train a series of events by which princes and oligarchs found it necessary to set up bureaucracies, first in order to raise money for mercenaries and fortress renovation, and then to give those same mercenaries and oligarchs legitimacy. Once created as a mere instrument of the prince, the State took on a life of its own, and a succession of constitutional orders arose that interacted with changes in the strategic environment.

Whereas princely states became progressively discontinuous, as dynastic inheritance and marriage added property, and progressively more sectarian, as these states sought to unite ecclesiastical and political bases of legitimacy, the new forms of kingly states were geographically centralized and coolly rational where religious matters were concerned.

One can go further. Once the princely state came into being, territorial conceptions of strategy replaced those of purely dynastic motivation. This development was masked in the Italian experience because the cities were the states: their fortification was a minimum criterion for survival. As we shall see, however, in the struggle of kingly states massive fortress lines became the centerpiece of military policy and contemporary techniques of siege warfare dictated the forces sufficient to garrison such lines.[30] To summarize the development described in this chapter, we may turn to Paul Kennedy, who writes of this period:

> The post 1450 waging of war was intimately connected with [state formation] . . . There were various causes for this evolution . . . But it was war, and the consequences of war, that provided a much more urgent and continuous pressure toward "nation-building" than these philosophical considerations and slowly evolving social tendencies. . . . Above all, it was war—and especially the new techniques which favored the growth of infantry armies and expensive fortification and fleet—which impelled belligerent states to spend more money, [to develop] new

---

*The impact on the constitutional shape of the State of these intricate, often elegant fortress designs is a matter of some scholarly dispute[28] but even the most eloquent of Parker's critics concedes that "war compelled the state to grow in power if it was not to perish. France's 17th century conflicts became wars of attrition, during which the Bourbons fielded ever larger forces. In such contests, when victory depended upon the ability to maintain huge armies in the field for years on end, resource mobilization held the key. Greater armies demanded greater quantities of funds, food, and fodder so the existing state apparatus scrambled to mobilize them. Despite its efforts, the state fell short of satisfying the army's appetite and was forced into a turbulent but necessary transformation in order to muster and maintain its troops. The process brought into being the centralized bureaucratic monarchy."[29]

organizations for revenue collecting, [to effect] the changing relationship between kings and estates in early modern Europe.[31]

By means of a state, oligarchs and princes could enhance their preparations for security, while attaching themselves to an institution that would legitimate their acts. Soon this new institution had spread to other regions, prompting Christopher Marlowe to write of England,

> *Albeit the world thinks Machiavelli is dead,*
> *Yet was his soule but flowne beyond the Alpes,*
> *And now the Guize is dead, is come from France*
> *To view this lande and frolicke with his friends.*[32]

CHAPTER SEVEN

From Kingly States to Territorial States: 1648–1776

Being once perfected how to grant suits,
How to deny them, who t'advance, and who
To trash for overtopping, new created
The creatures that were mine, I say, or chang'd 'em,
Or else new form'd 'em, having both the key
Of officer and office, set all hearts i' th' state
To what tune pleased his ear . . .[1]

FROM EARLY in the sixteenth century until the middle of the seventeenth two conflicts intertwined: the religious struggle that began with the Reformation and which provoked horrific civil wars throughout Europe; and the efforts of the Habsburg dynasty to establish a true imperial realm in Europe. These two interacting dramas culminated in the Peace of Westphalia in 1648, which ratified the role of the kingly state as the dominant, legitimate form of government in western Europe. During this period of more than a century, the kingly state—a domain of absolute authority that made the king the personification of the State—achieved pre-eminence, although the seeds of its successor, the territorial state, were sown by the same treaties that ratified the kingly states' dominance. Before the kingly state could prevail, however, the international scope of the Church and the Holy Roman Empire, whose weakening had facilitated the emergence of the princely state, had to be shattered. The Habsburg drive for hegemony put these stakes on the table by uniting two goals—to restore Catholic universality and to make the Holy Roman Empire a universal power—and it was the Habsburg defeat that brought the kingly state to triumph.

KINGLY STATES

In the year 1500, Europe comprised some 500 or so princely domains, independent cities, and contested territories. By the middle of that century, the princely states that had superseded this rich variety of constitutional forms were already being transformed themselves by the advent of kingly states. Three such states in particular—Sweden, France, and England— embodied this nascent, potential constitutional successor to the princely state. Like Spain, all three had greatly expanded the permanent bureaucracies of the princely states, introducing and maintaining standing armies, and they had centralized taxation specifically directed toward the ability to finance war.[2] As Charles Tilly concluded, European "state structure appeared chiefly as a by-product of rulers' efforts to acquire the means of war."[3] Not coincidentally these states commenced to codify their civil and criminal laws at this time, a constitutional ramification of the objectified State. The precise state structure that emerged during the period from roughly 1550 to 1660—the kingly state—was only one possibility. The imperial realm, a dynastic conglomeration of princely states, also presented an option. This was the constitutional form pursued by Habsburg Spain. France, whose development of the kingly state set the pattern for all others once it had shown itself to be strategically dynamic and overpowering, provided one constitutional model of the kingly state. Sweden also effected an historic transition from princely to kingly state when Gustavus Adolphus and his gifted minister Oxenstierna collaborated to transform a succession crisis into the consolidation of this new constitutional form. All of this unfolded when strategic developments decisively undermined the constitutional role of the princely state at the end of the century.

In 1494, the year that Charles VIII began his campaign in Italy, he did so at the head of a multinational army,* paid regularly by royal finances whose collection and disbursement had been reformed in order to provide a fully stipendiary force in the field for the life of the campaign. "With hindsight we can describe Charles VIII's force as the first 'modern' army, in that it consisted of the three arms deployed in various mutually supporting tactical combinations, and was very largely made up of men paid from a central treasury."[4]

The military lessons that the French invasion had prompted the princes and oligarchs of Italy to learn—the requirement of larger professional

---

*Which is to say a multiethnic army; throughout I will use the term *nation* as referring to a cultural, ethnic group that may or may not have a state. The Kurds, for example, constitute a nation though they as yet have no national state; the state of Aruba is composed of only a fragment of a nation, even though it is a member state of the United Nations. The Hebrew nation long antedates the founding of Israel and survived Roman occupation. The Cherokee nation never had a state. *Nationalism* is a political movement of peoples, not states. Recall Jonah's cry, "Of what nation are you?"

mercenary forces, the need for artillery, new fortress design—were applied by unified Italian administrative organizations supported by consistent finance. When France developed the princely state, however, she could draw on a great national culture, nourished by a vast and contiguous estate that could staff and pay for its bureaucratic apparatus, which in turn provided the mechanisms for raising even greater revenue. It is often said that the Valois successes in the Italian invasion can be attributed to the introduction of mobile artillery, and this is doubtless true. France had no monopoly on the manufacture of artillery, however. (Nor were there many "French" in the French army, it being mainly composed—like the forces of the Italian cities—of foreign mercenaries, chiefly Swiss.) Rather it was a combination of French reforms and the diplomatic paralysis of the Italian cities that led to the inevitable military outcome. In 1494 Charles VIII had moved against Naples, which had a secure dynasty and lay near to many of the richest cities in Europe, of which she was one, and had defeated the Neapolitan forces by February 1495. Initially, each of the neighboring cities had sought to defend its own autonomy rather than unite with Naples. Milan, in fact, gave the French army free passage. Florence revolted against its regime, and the citizens set up a republican government that was in effect a French satellite.

The princely state in Italy had been developed by families who wished to re-enforce their legitimacy to govern, and who required a more efficient means of marshaling wealth in order to defend their claims by means of expensive mercenaries. The kingly state took the Italian constitutional innovation—fundamentally, the objectification of the state—and united this with dynastic legitimacy. The result was a formidable creation that dominated Europe for the next century. Confronting the princely state and the imperial realm as competing constitutional forms, the kingly state proved able to vanquish these forms strategically and, as a consequence, historically. As before, the development of constitutional forms came about in tandem with a revolution in military tactics.

Prior to this period, the progress of operations in war had become increasingly drawn out. The combination of missile fire and rapid movement, so lethally effective at Agincourt in the fifteenth century, had been succeeded in the sixteenth century by the Swiss tactics using massive formations of pike and musket. The Swiss order of battle ranged men in twelve or more rows, practically immobilizing them once deployed. Spain used these tactics for the relentless and terrifying assaults of the *tercio,* a tightly packed rectangle, often fifty files wide and forty ranks deep, whose heart was formed of pikemen wielding fifteen-foot spears, flanked by musketmen (arquebusiers) who protected the formation from cavalry attacks. The armies of which these formations were composed were hardly more mobile: they depended upon magazines located in fortresses and thus could not stray far or for long from their very limited communications with these fixed points. The fortresses themselves, reconstructed along the lines discussed earlier, could no longer be easily reduced by artillery, which meant that siege campaigns became more drawn out and were themselves a complex logistical process of assembling artillery and stores. Campaigns now came to revolve around sieges, and great battles were seldom fought. Europe appeared to be locked into a situation of military stalemate: a heavily defended fortress sheltering perhaps 10,000 troops had to be seized by an advancing army, but barring surprise (as in the capture of the Dutch towns in 1572 by the Sea Beggars) or treachery (as at Aalst in 1576, where the town was sold by its English garrison to the Spanish), this could be a matter of many months, even years.

The introduction of small arms, which dates to the middle of the sixteenth century, eventually changed this situation and brought a revolution in tactics. Reliance on firepower on the battlefield led not only to a changed role for the cavalry—because infantry now became a potentially decisive force—but also added urgency to the move to larger armies. Such a move depended upon consistent finance, centralized government organization, and logistics planning of a high order. When Michael Roberts coined the phrase "military revolution" to describe these innovations, his characterization became perhaps the single most influential concept in the studies of early modern warfare in Europe.[5] He argued not only that these tactical changes were responsible for a dramatic shift in the strategy and scale of warfare, but also for a change in the societies that undertook such warfare.

What was this revolution in tactics and what brought it about? It is associated, at least in its initial appearance, with Maurice of Nassau, who led Europe in the development of a year-round professional force. The Dutch, owing to the great wealth amassed from their maritime trade, were able to afford a standing army. That meant that the state could specify the conditions of training, and this fact actually made possible the revolution in warfare that is associated with Maurice, the Dutch leader.

Maurice's cousin, William Louis of Nassau, wrote him a letter from Groningen dated December 8, 1594—which has been preserved—in which he first suggested the technique of an infantry countermarch. William Louis had just read Aelian's description of a drill practiced by the Roman army; inspired by this account, William Louis suggested that six rotating ranks of musketeers could replicate with gunfire the continuous hail of missiles that the Romans had achieved using javelins and slingshots. By this means, it would be possible to create tidal waves of fire through a coordinated fusillade, replacing individual aiming. Maurice modified the ancient Roman practice by alternating ten ranks in order to maintain constant musket fire, and the technique of rolling musket volleys soon became the standard battle tactic of European armies.[6]

This innovation was perhaps as crucial in the transformation of the state during this period as the development of fortresses had been in the previous era, or the use of artillery against fortified cities before then. Muskets capable of piercing armor plate at 100 yards had been introduced earlier in the century, but the rate of fire was torturously slow, owing to the complicated process of reloading. If this problem could be solved, however, muskets promised to remake armies because muskets required little experience to use compared to the long bow and were as effective against cavalry as the pike. Moreover, large tight squares of pikemen made attractive targets for the not-very-accurate muskets.

If the innovation of fortress design had been to take a target—the fortified city—and transform it into a platform for fire, then the Spanish *tercio* did much the same thing for shock: it took infantry otherwise vulnerable to charges from cavalry and made them a sort of gunless prototank, invulnerable and inexorable. These slow-moving formations would crush anything in their way, unless it was another such massive square, in which case neither side would gain a decisive advantage. Battles tended therefore, like sieges, toward stalemate. The tactics of the period provided no effective means of penetrating this type of defense in depth.

Maurice, however, saw

> that fire power was now the decisive element rather than shock: that the pike was there to protect the musket, not the other way round. It was thus necessary to devise both formations which would maximize fire power, and procedures to ensure its continuous and controlled delivery. Instead of pike squares several thousand strong . . . Maurice adopted elongated formations of musketeers . . . countermarching in their files, reloading as they did so, so that their front rank was always giving continuous fire.[7]

In the armies that adopted this innovation—the forces of the anti-Habsburg coalition—the infantry was deployed in shallower, more linear firing formations that allowed for more tactical flexibility than did the *tercio,* with its massive squares of infantry composed of central blocks of pikemen forty to sixty soldiers deep, encased on all sides by deep sleeves of musketeers who protected them from assault. To perfect these tactics, intricate drills were practiced in order to speed up the rate of fire until Gustavus Adolphus introduced a variation that concentrated fire on massive simultaneous volleys by multiple ranks, opening up the opposing pike formation to a cavalry charge. While Spanish cavalry were still practicing the traditional *caracole*—in which successive ranks of horsemen charged toward an enemy line, fired their handguns and then wheeled off to the flanks—Swedish cavalry restored the attack with the saber, directly charging into those ranks decimated by a focused musket volley.

These innovations required a great degree of control by the commander, a prerequisite of which is discipline in the ranks. "It was discipline and not gunpowder," Max Weber concluded, "which initiated the transformation. [G]unpowder and all the war techniques associated with it became significant only with the existence of discipline."[8] That in turn was only possible with forces that were constituted over a long term, were constantly drilled, and sought their identity in the professional esteem of the corps, rather than the glory of feudal knights or the personal enrichment of mercenaries. This required a state apparatus, but not just any sort of state. Rothenberg reminds us that, up to this time,

> the greatest obstacle to the conduct of consistent military operations could be found [not just in problems of logistics and siege warfare, but] in the social characteristics of most armies. Altogether, the ascendancy of the tactical defense, the strength of the new fortifications, and the mercenary character of troops explain why warfare in Europe had become so drawn out and indecisive.[9]

Therefore, when Maurice of Nassau attempted to exploit the use of infantry firepower through a technique that put a premium on fast arming, he introduced further innovations, which required standardization in weaponry and the extensive training of troops. Only thorough practice could train troops to withstand the terror of cavalry charges without losing their nerve and either breaking and running, or at the very least disrupting the complicated rhythm of the volley and permitting themselves to be assaulted at close quarters. When Gustavus Adolphus adopted these tactics, putting his troops in line (rather than in the classic squares that had dominated European battlefields), he changed their tactical mission. By teaching his forces to use a countermarch in which musketeers rotated their positions by slowly moving through the ranks of their own men, moving backward to reload, then moving forward through stationary reloaders, he enabled his line to take the offensive rather than being forced to remain static. These tactics had the effect of restoring the infantry to its status as a battle-winning force and reducing the significance of the artillery-encrusted bastioned fortresses. Such tactics, however, required the continuity of substantial forces in being. Only a standing army would have the professionalism to execute such complicated and harrowing tactics. Roberts argued that these standing armies tended to enhance monarchical power, and militarize the nobility as well as much of the general populace through conscription. Thus there was, he argued, a mutually reinforcing relationship between the professionalization of the military required by these tactical innovations and the rise of the kingly state. Roberts wrote that "the new principle of concentrating military power under the absolute control of the sovereign" was a consequence of "the transformation in the scale of war [that] led inevitably to an increase in the authority of the state . . . Only the state, now, could supply the administrative, technical, and financial resources required for large-scale hostilities."[10] Speaking of this period, William McNeill concurred that "new weaponry began to favor larger states and more powerful monarchs," and he referred to the "centralizing effects of the new technology of war."[11] As Jeremy Black has observed of Roberts's thesis,

> the chronology of military change is apparently matched by a more general political chronology . . . Thus the modern art of war, with its large professional armies and concentrated yet mobile firepower, was created at the same time as—and indeed made possible and necessary by—the creation of the modern state.[12]

The strategic innovations of ever more expensive fortress design and complex infantry fire crushed those constitutional forms that could not adapt in order to exploit those innovations: first princely states, with their modest revenue bases; then the discontinuous Habsburg empire of princely states that risked decisive battles in so many theatres that it was bled dry by the new, more dynamic and lethal warfare.

The chief advantage of the kingly state over the princely states it dominated was sheer scale. Yet this advantage was not enjoyed by the Habsburg empire, which assembled a vast collection of princely states into a single constitutional unit. It is important to see how, despite enormous wealth and experienced forces, who were, as at Nördlingen, capable of devastating victories, the Habsburg imperial constitutional form was nevertheless vulnerable to the escalating possibilities of violence posed by the revolution in tactics.

The sheer quantitative advantage that imperial and kingly forms shared should not blind us to the constitutional, qualitative difference between the kingly state and the princely state. Henry VIII may have broken with Rome in order to marry again, a princely prerogative, but the fact that he could make himself head of a new national church is indicative of a change in the nature of monarchy.

When at the end of this period, the last of the great figures of the kingly state proclaimed, *"L'état, c'est moi,"* he was saying no more than other monarchs of the kingly state could have claimed; but he was saying a great deal more than the proudest Medici or Sforza. The kingly state had a voice distinct from that of the princely state. We can hear it clearly in the work of

Jean Bodin, one of the most influential European political philosophers. In his preface to the *Six Books Concerning a Republic,* written in 1576, Bodin attacks Machiavelli—the poet of the princely state—for suggesting that the leader of a state is bound to different moral rules than an ordinary man. Machiavelli's idea is fundamental to the notion of the State as something other than a human being, and thus something in whose service the prince must obey imperatives other than those that govern ordinary human behavior. Bodin challenges this advice as tending to weaken the monarch's authority. Whereas for the princely state the great leap is from the prince as person to the prince plus an administrative structure—the prince and the State—the transformation to the kingly state (the state already having been objectified) reverses this move and makes the monarch the apotheosis of the State. To put it differently: the princely state severed the person of the prince from his bureaucratic and military structure, thereby creating a state with attributes hitherto reserved to a human being; the kingly state reunites these two elements, monarch and state, and makes of the king the State itself: *"L'état, c'est moi."*

If such a king were seen as immoral, Bodin argued, this would undermine the state's legitimacy. Moreover, he wrote:

> In addition to the counselors of tyranny [e.g., Machiavelli], there are others . . . who are no less dangerous and are maybe even more so. These are the ones who under the pretext of the people's liberties cause subjects to rebel against their natural princes, and thereby open the way to factious anarchy which is worse than tyranny ever was.[13]

These "others," perhaps even more "dangerous" than Machiavelli, were writers who claimed the right of resistance for the people. Bodin insisted that all authority had to be vested in a sovereign, a single will. The king could impose any law on his subjects with or without their consent; to hold otherwise meant that the State was something less than sovereign, that it could be thwarted as when a man with a severe physical disorder finds himself unable to command his limbs to move. A king's will is the sovereign of the State just as a man's will is the sovereign of his body. This is the credo of absolutism, and it is the constitutional doctrine of the kingly state.

Perhaps we today are inclined to exaggerate the actual absolutism of the kingly state.[14] Things may look more monolithic from a distant perspective. Doubtless a more consensual and complex arrangement prevailed at the time than may now appear. For our purposes, however, it is enough to observe that contemporaries of this period perceived both an enormous change under way in the centrality of the State as well as a crisis of legitimacy besetting that State. For it was a significant change to place the State

in man, especially when it had been scarcely a century since the State was
torn from the local princes who were so soon to be made redundant by it.
Hobbes saw this clearly, and made it his life's work to give reasons why
the monarch was not simply another man—owing to the move to an objectified State—and why the obedience owed the State could be owed to a
man. In the *Behemoth,* he complains:

> Lastly, the people in general were so ignorant of their duty [they had
> been seduced and corrupted], that no one perhaps of ten thousand knew
> what right any man had to command him, of what necessity there was
> of King or Commonwealth, for which he was to part with his money
> against his will; but thought himself to be so much master of whatso-
> ever he possessed, that it could not be taken from him upon any pre-
> tense of common safety without his own consent. [Moreover] king,
> they thought, was but a title of the highest honor, to which gentlemen,
> knight, baron, earl, duke were but steps to ascend to, with the help of
> riches . . .[15]

To overcome this attitude had been one of the chief goals of the constitutional form of the kingly state. Some form of constitutional response was
certainly necessary owing to those strategic innovations that were marginalizing the princely states as well as imposing new demands upon them.
The kingly state established itself as an absolute yet legitimate state form
in the era that witnessed the permanent schism of the ecclesiastical regime
(which had been the main barrier to the emergence of the kingly state) and
the destruction of the imperial regime (which was the kingly state's main
rival to succeed the princely state as the dominant constitutional order in
Europe).

This outcome was far from obvious in the first half of the sixteenth century when Charles V attempted to consolidate a Habsburg empire against
the opposition of the French king Francis I. In a way, the princely state can
be said to have originated in the rivalry between the Habsburg dynasty and
that of the Angevin/Valois of France, because the invasion of Italy in 1494
had been undertaken to support a French claim to the throne of Naples
against the claims of Aragon; to this claim was later added the assertion
of a French dynastic right to the Duchy of Milan against the Sforzas and
their Imperial patrons. The opposition to French claims became unified,
however, and vastly increased with the consolidation in one Habsburg heir,
Charles V, of a staggering dynastic inheritance. Thereafter the modest
princely states of the Italian peninsula were no longer principal players.
Instead, Charles's vast continental realm of dynastic properties was eventually opposed by an alliance of princely states led by the champions of
the emerging constitutional order of kingly states. Thus the competing

variants of the State all contended, and, thanks to the sheer scope of Charles's inheritance, these forms played for stakes that would be historically decisive.

Charles was born at Ghent in 1500. His father was the Habsburg archduke of Austria, son of Maximilian, the Holy Roman Emperor, and of Mary, daughter of Charles the Bold of Burgundy. Charles's mother was the daughter of Ferdinand, King of Aragon, and Isabella, Queen of Castile. Thus Charles promised to unite within one person an Austrian-Spanish realm that included the Low Countries, to which he might add the German emperorship and even lay fair claim to Burgundy. It was an astounding example of the dynastic conglomerations that were acquired through inheritance and the alliances of marriage. Such a "realm," as I have used the term, was in essence a personal union of territories. To the modern eye some of these dynastic states seem very odd indeed, and would appear to have little hope of survival; their various geographic components seem too disparate in terms of culture, language, and institutions. This observation, however, anticipates the outcome of a struggle that Charles V and his successors had first to play out: it is only because the universalism of the Empire and the Church was shattered during that struggle that it seems to us that national culture, language, and local institutions are the stuff out of which viable states must be made. Indeed it was Charles's goal to reverse this development and restore the unity of a Catholic Europe.*

One might say that the inheritance of Charles V created the conditions for a perfect experiment to determine whether in fact the State could encompass many different nations once the Reformation had so greatly sharpened the cultural differences among the peoples under his rule.

When Charles was crowned emperor in 1519, he had inherited not only vast dynastic properties from his grandfather, Ferdinand of Aragon and his other grandfather, Maximilian, but also quarrels over the thrones of Naples and Milan, respectively; plus a third dispute over the crown of Navarre from one grandmother, Isabella, as well as a fourth dynastic claim, from his other grandmother, over lands lost to France by her father, the Duke of Burgundy. In all of these disputes his antagonist was the losing candidate for the emperorship, Francis I, who had become king of France.

What is important for our study is that both Charles and Francis failed to achieve their strategic objectives, so that by the end of this period in the mid-sixteenth century, it was clear that a dynastic realm agglomerating princely states across Europe could not succeed in creating an imperial state. Such an entity simply could not manage sufficient control of its do-

*"I was not invested with the imperial crown in order to take over yet more territories, but to ensure the peace of Christendom and so to unite all forces against the Turks for the glory of the Christian faith." Charles V in 1521, quoted in Jacques Barzun, *From Dawn to Decadence* (HarperCollins, 2000), 93.

mestic resources in order to maintain standing armies capable of the prolonged campaigns required to vindicate dynastic claims that were often geographically remote and politically fraught.

It took an entire century, however, for the new constitutional form of the kingly state to triumph, ascending a helical staircase whose steps connected religious conflicts on one side and dynastic ones on the other. For at the same time that Charles V was concluding the compact of Noyon with Francis I, which provided him with safe passage to his new Spanish inheritance, Martin Luther was proclaiming his doctrines for the reform of the Church. In the ensuing two decades—that is, until the beginning of the more radical career of John Calvin, which made matters considerably more difficult—religious strife rendered the domestic bases of both Francis and Charles ever more insecure, so that when their conflict ended with Francis's death in 1547, the main objective of Charles's policy was the suppression of the Protestant cause, which he himself had done much indirectly to support when his pursuit of hegemony in Europe had united antiimperial German princes with religious reformers. Charles's motives at this moment were expressed in a letter to his sister:

> [I have decided to attack the Protestant League because] if we fail to intervene now, all the Estates of Germany would be in danger of breaking with the faith . . . After considering this and considering it again, I decided to embark on war against Hesse and Saxony as transgressors of the peace . . . [a]nd although this pretext will not long disguise the fact that it is matter of religion, yet it will serve for the present to divide the renegades.[16]

The hostility of France toward Habsburg designs did not die with Francis, however personal the quarrel with Charles. Indeed the possibility of alliance between German princes and Henry II, Francis's successor, drove Charles to agree to the Treaty of Passau, whose provisions led to the Augsburg settlement in 1555.

Augsburg is an historic agreement because it provided that rulers were to determine the religious denomination of their respective states (the constitutional principle of *cuius regio eius religio*), matching Lutheran princes with Lutheran subjects and Catholic rulers with Catholic peoples. According to this principle, the decisions of the ruler as to which sectarian preference to adopt were binding also upon his subjects with the concession that dissatisfied persons were welcome to emigrate to more congenial states. This, with the migrations that followed, sealed the dominance of the princely state over the feudal princes who had ruled within a universal Christendom, and intensified the sectarian basis of the princely state. Augsburg enshrined the constitutional form of the princely state because it attached to the State an attribute—religious affiliation—hitherto associated with a human being, the prince.

Charles, in frustration and despair at these developments, which forever fragmented Europe and ended his dream of a restored, single Christendom, abdicated in October 1555. He left his Spanish dominions (including the Netherlands) to his son, Philip II, and arranged for the imperial crown to be assumed by his brother Ferdinand, who possessed the Austrian lands of the Habsburgs. A putative constitutional successor to the princely state—a dynastic empire accumulating many princely states—had thus far failed.

> Although foreigners frequently regarded the empire of Charles V or that of Philip II as monolithic and disciplined, it was in fact a congeries of territories . . . There was no central administration . . . The absence of such institutions which might have encouraged a sense of unity and the fact that the ruler might never visit the country, made it difficult for the king to raise funds in one part of his dominions in order to fight in another.[17]

But the princely states of Italy had not succeeded either, for these states had been extinguished by the wars between Charles and Francis, with whom the comparatively small states of the Italian cities could not compete, even though they had pioneered the techniques by which the energies and resources of their conquerors were concentrated. The sack of Rome by Habsburg mercenaries in 1527 is perhaps the best date for the death certificate of the innovative Italian states whose "precocious development of an urban economy"[18] had produced the wealth that could employ, and the vulnerability that would require, mercenary forces and had thus begun the process of modern state formation. The next historic constitutional event, the development of the kingly state, could not be completed so long as civil war threatened those great states that were candidates for absolute monarchical rule. A domestic, constitutional imperative—consolidation—drove the strategic aims of the State; when this was accomplished the strategic innovations by which this prerequisite was achieved still required further constitutional change before the kingly state, a unified, autocratic, monarchical state—the "absolute" State of early modern Europe—could fully emerge. Such states, though legitimated by dynastic rules, had to be reconfigured by the demands of war for mass taxation and state efficiency.

The Peace of Augsburg had the unfortunate effect of giving free rein to savage repression by those sovereigns who stayed within its rules, and thus the Inquisition and the civil wars in France, Germany, and the Netherlands began in earnest at this time. The ensuing Thirty Years' War made evident the weakness of both the princely and the imperial options for the state.

But the kingly state did not truly triumph as a stable and powerful entity until constitutional centralization became a reality. The Peace of Westphalia, ending the Thirty Years' War, ratified this new political creation, uniting the legitimacy of the dynastic realm and the Italian administrative innovations of the Renaissance, with the permanence of a fixed and contiguous national population. Westphalia provided France—the first and most successful kingly state—with a period of domestic consolidation, and effectively ended the Habsburg drive for empire. Ironically, it also set the stage for the next constitutional form of the state, the territorial state,* as if the triumph of one constitutional order somehow germinates the form that will ultimately vanquish it.

In France, as in the rest of Europe, the experience of the Italian Renaissance had paved the way for the Reformation. The Italian Wars begun by Charles VIII in 1494 had brought the French into contact with a spirit that is reflected in the colorful chateaux that replaced the dark feudal castles of medieval France, and in the works of Rabelais, and, somewhat later, Montaigne. In time this spirit must catch fire in theology: five years before Luther's 95 theses, a lecturer in Paris had published a commentary on St. Paul in which the doctrine of justification by faith was asserted.

In response to these developments, Charles's successor, Francis I, and his successor, Henry II, favored a policy of Protestant suppression; this became in time a policy of persecution. The accession of Francis II produced no change. When, in 1560, a Protestant conspiracy to seize the government was exposed, a new round of persecution began. The death of Francis II in 1560 brought an eleven-year-old, Charles IX, to the throne. Neither he, nor his mother, Catherine de Medici, nor her other son, Charles's successor, Henry III, seem to have had any especially intense sectarian convictions. Their chief goal was simply to maintain themselves in power between two powerful contending parties. In the event, they presided over forty years of civil war, including the St. Bartholomew's Day massacre of Protestants on August 24, 1572, which is as good a date as any to mark the end of the princely state in France. The massacre was a consequence of stratagems attributed to the Florentine Queen Mother whereby the leader of the Protestant party was to be killed, and the blame laid on the leader of the Catholic party. The last Valois monarch, Henry III, finally murdered the head of the Catholic League, and was

---

*An early version of the territorial state was prematurely attempted in the sixteenth century by William the Silent with respect to the Low Countries, but absent the strategic innovations necessary to exploit the nationalism that Westphalia ultimately made possible, William was never able to make the seventeen provinces of the Netherlands into a viable federation. Instead the sectarian nature of the princely state repeatedly asserted itself. In 1579 the northern provinces formed a union to promote Protestantism, from which union the modern state of Holland ultimately emerged; in the same month the southern provinces concluded a treaty undertaking to maintain Catholicism in what has become Belgium.

himself assessinated by a Burgundian monk. After four further years of fighting, Henry of Navarre, a Calvinist Bourbon prince who was the next in the dynastic line, agreed to a nominal conversion to Catholicism—his was the famous phrase, "Paris is worth a mass"—and was crowned at Chartres in 1594. Having subdued the last remnants of civil war, Henry propounded the Edict of Nantes on April 13, 1598, granting religious toleration to all sects. His assassination in 1610 by a deranged monk cut short this experiment in multiculturalism, and made way for the full development of the kingly state in France, which depended upon a united, rather than internally tolerant but divided, populace.

The architect of the French kingly state was the remarkable minister Armand-Jean du Plessis de Richelieu. One significant contrast between the kingly and princely states can be detected in the contrasting concepts of *raison d'état* and *ragione di stato,* principles of the kingly and princely constitutional orders, respectively. Among the Italian princely states, *ragione di stato* simply stood for a rational, unprincipled justification for the self-aggrandizement of the State, whereas *raison d'état* achieved a parallel justification through the personification of the state, and leveraged the imperatives of this justification to impose obligations on the dynastic ruler. This enabled Richelieu to pursue a policy abroad that was in pragmatic harmony with his domestic policy, though distasteful to his ruler. Such an approach contrasted also with the constitutional imperatives of the Habsburgs: Olivares, Richelieu's Spanish counterpart, was not allowed the same latitude, dealing as he was with a dynastic ruler who was not committed to the personification of the state but rather to the reverse, one who instead saw his realm as an objectification of himself. "If constitutions do not allow this, then the devil take constitutions," Philip IV once exclaimed in frustration. Thus Olivares's strategic designs were largely governed by Philip's personal religious convictions, a limitation that ultimately proved fatal to the plans of both men. Richelieu, on the other hand, contended that state decisions were not to be confused with questions of personal religious preference: the State (and therefore the king who embodied the State) had special responsibilities for preserving peace and the general welfare, and the king was divinely appointed to this role. History does not record Richelieu's reply to a prominent Jansenist who asked, "Would [the king] dare to say to God: let your power and glory and the religion which teaches me to adore You be lost and destroyed, provided the state is protected and free from risks?" but we can imagine his reply: "Take this up with God—it is He who has imposed this responsibility on me."

THE THIRTY YEARS' WAR

Richelieu used the epochal war we know as the Thirty Years' War (1618–1648) as the means by which the new French state was forged and French hegemony in Europe achieved. Indeed, the Thirty Years' War can be understood as the interlocking of two great struggles, to which France supplied the decisive key. This is partly explicable for geopolitical reasons: France happened to lie along both the borders of the territories where two separate wars were fought. For our purposes, however, it is equally important to observe that France underwent the transformation of the princely Valois state into the Bourbon kingly state, a centralization, secularization, and nationalization of state authority along absolutist lines famously identified with the principle of *raison d'état*. By contrast, the two conflicts for which France provided the crucial nexus were themselves efforts of two different Habsburg states to perpetuate, on the one hand, and to greatly expand, on the other, the princely states that were the legacy of the division of the realms of Charles V.

The first of these historic struggles was the Dutch war against Spain by which the Habsburg provinces of the northern Low Country rebelled in a religious, nationalist uprising against Madrid. The second struggle occurred in Germany, where the Emperor Ferdinand II, who was also a Habsburg prince, sought to subdue and re-Catholicize the German principalities that formed the empire (including his own hereditary kingdom of Bohemia), in order to forge a single princely state.

The seam along which these two struggles met was a long corridor between the Habsburg provinces in Northern Italy and those in the Netherlands. This corridor provided the indispensable line of re-enforcement for Spain once the Dutch successfully denied Spanish access to Northern Europe by sea. Along this line ran the border between France and the Holy Roman Empire, that congeries of cities, principalities, and estates that was the remnant of the Roman Empire after Otto the Great combined the kingship of the Germans with the emperorship of Rome. Since 1438 the emperor, "Erwahlter Romischer Kaiser,"* had been a member of the Habsburg dynasty.[19] To keep this strategic passageway secure necessarily meant the continental encirclement of France, and the strict control of the German principalities of the western Empire, including the rich Palatinate and its capital of Heidelberg.

In the Peace of Augsburg (1555) that ended the first modern epochal war, the Habsburgs had appeared to relinquish their pursuit of a dynastic empire that would control Europe but in the Peace of Cateau-Cambrésis

---

*A translation of "Electus Romanus Imperator," not, as is usually the case in English histories, the "Holy Roman Emperor."

(1559), they had wrung consent from Valois France to its encirclement, though one divided between Spanish and Austrian Habsburg branches to be sure. The cordon that bound France and connected Habsburg lands was a precarious line subject always to the vagaries of dynastic inheritance and political disintegration.

The new French dynasty that came to power with the accession of the Bourbon prince Henry IV in 1589 aimed at breaking this encirclement. From the first decade of the seventeenth century until mid-century, with only the short interlude of the de Medici regency, France sought ways to sever this geopolitical cordon, to penetrate Germany and to cut the link between the Low Countries and Spain. First through the means of financial subsidies and covert aid, then later through open warfare, France entered both these great struggles and linked them together as politically as they were linked logistically.

France's own constitutional evolution had made her the first kingly state in Europe. Efforts at constitutional centralization were undertaken by Ferdinand in Germany and by the Habsburg king of Spain, but both these princes clung to a dynastic fragmentation, which dissipated national unity, and a sectarian ideology, which constricted diplomatic and military freedom of action. Both were prisoners of the archetype of the princely state at a time when a new, more aggressive constitutional form of regime was being born. Spain's failure to restrict Dutch independence and the emperor's failure to destroy the independence of the German princes sealed the decline of their respective monarchies and delivered Europe to the ambitions of France. By contrast, France's adroit maneuvering during this period allowed her to exploit to her advantage these essentially constitutional struggles facing Spain and the Empire, and to succeed to the leadership of Europe when the heirs of Gustavus Adolphus were unable to build on his successful effort to make Sweden a dynamic kingly state.

The Thirty Years' War (1618–1648) was an epochal war composed* of the Bohemian and Palatine War (1618–1623); the War of the Graubünden (1620–1639); the Swedish-Polish War (1621–1629); the Danish War (1625–1629); the War of Mantuan Succession (1628–1631); the Swedish War (1630–1635); the War of Smolensk (1632–1634); and the French and Swedish War (1635–1648). The reason why it is convenient to treat these sometimes overlapping, sometimes episodic conflicts as a single war, despite intervening peace treaties, changes in the parties, and even some switching sides, is that a single constitutional issue was at stake throughout: would the princely states of the Habsburg dynasty impose their constitutional form of the state—the militantly sectarian and multinational

---

*Just as the Long War, discussed in Part I of Book I, was composed of World War I, World War II, the Korean War, the Cold War, the wars in Southeast Asia, and other more minor conflicts and crises.

dynastic state—on the contested areas of Germany and the Netherlands, whose constitutions were in play? That is, would the United Provinces of the Netherlands emerge as a Spanish possession, re-Catholicized, an example of the archetypal princely Habsburg state? Would the German and central European Protestant states of the empire be remade into a Catholic, German princely state under the Austrian Habsburg heir? Or would the secular relationships among the national, absolutist monarchs of the new kingly states of France, Sweden, and Britain prevail instead?

The behavior of France and Spain is exemplary in its contrast between these two forms of the State. In the struggle to reunify the states of Germany under Catholicism, Richelieu (a cardinal and devout Catholic) resolutely continued the foreign policy of Henry IV and opposed Spanish re-Catholicization in Germany as a long-term threat to France. Yet when Olivares wished to aid the Protestant Huguenots in France, as a way of weakening the French state that was assisting the Netherlands in its efforts to throw out the Spanish, Philip would not consent. Nor would he permit an end to the hemorrhage in the Low Countries that, more than anything else, destroyed Spanish power in Europe, because the Habsburgs could not in good conscience abandon this territory to heresy. Nor could they strike a bargain with heretics, such as was brokered by the imperial warlord Wallenstein, that would have pacified the Empire. Thus were the interests of Spain sacrificed to the interests of the Habsburg dynasty, including its hereditary claims in Italy and the Netherlands, and to the sectarian convictions of Habsburg rulers. At the same time, Richelieu was pursuing a domestic policy of persecuting the Protestant Huguenots while hiring the Protestant Swedes as allies, and giving subsidies to the Protestant Dutch on the condition that they abandon their support for the Huguenots. One cannot imagine the Spanish forging an alliance with the infidel Ottoman Turks, as Richelieu did, enabling France to harass the Austrians by proxy and thereby divert Habsburg resources from the struggle in Germany.

The 1618 revolt of the Protestant aristocracy in Bohemia against their new Habsburg ruler, Ferdinand II, had escalated rapidly, quickly encompassing many issues. Eventually it embraced the struggle for independence of the Low Countries from Spanish rule, a revolt that had begun in the 1540s; a revolt by the electors and princes of the Holy Roman Empire against the Habsburg emperor; and a religious war between the Evangelical Union, made up mostly of German principalities, and the Catholic League. Confirming its status as an epochal war, Gustavus Adolphus said of this conflict, "All the wars of Europe are now blended into one."[20]

In the early stages of the war, the Habsburg emperor Ferdinand's forces were successful, and by the late 1620s, Wallenstein, the imperial war commander, seemed to be poised to seize all of Germany. This provoked Gustavus Adolphus, the Swedish king, to enter the conflict on the side of the

Protestants. His manifesto was that of the head of a kingly state, however, not that of a religious fanatic. Upon joining the war he explained his rationale simply: "It will be sufficient to say that the Spaniard and the house of Austria have been always intent upon a Universal monarchy. . . ."[21]

Gustavus Adolphus, with his minister Axel Oxenstierna, had in Sweden created one of the first and most formidable kingly states. Through a series of reforms, the treasury and tax system, education and the courts—indeed the entire state administration of Sweden was centralized. The nobility, which had so bedeviled Gustavus's father, was induced to take up state service as an ideal.

Yet this would hardly have seemed likely in 1611 when Gustavus, still a minor, inherited the throne usurped by his father, Charles IX. The Swedish Diet took this opportunity to extort the Charter of January 1, 1612, from him, which bound the monarchy to rule in terms of the constitution, a restraint that had not troubled Charles. The charter provided that the consent of a Council was required for all new laws, major acts of foreign policy, and the summoning of the Diet. No new taxes could be imposed, and no new troops levied, without the consent of the relevant constitutional parties. Gustavus Adolphus had no choice but to accept this document in an apparent blow to royal authority and in favor of aristocratic constitutionalism. But what appeared to be a casting away of royal power was apparent only: accepting the charter brought not only reconciliation but also the services of Oxenstierna, its main drafter, to the chancellorship. Together these two very different men—"Gustavus dynamic, impetuous, 'ever *allegro* and courage'; Oxenstierna imperturbable, tireless, unhurrying; the one supplying inspiration, the other ripe wisdom and many-sided administrative ability"[22]—creatively exploited this reconciliation to fashion a powerful, absolutist state. There was a resolute effort by the king to abandon the arbitrary rule of his father with its judicial murders and political tribunals. In time the ability and popularity of the king induced a consensus in the society that enabled him to rewrite the charter in practice. He did not feel bound to obtain the consent of the State Council in high matters of state, nor did he so much submit to the Diet requests for new taxes and conscription as insist on their confirming these orders.

> It is not a question of whether I have the right to make impositions without advice, nor of what your privileges may permit; what we have to look to is the temper of the commonalty and the necessity of the times; and it is not a question of what they are bound to pay, but of what they can pay.[23]

Roberts sums up the constitutional development well:

Thus against all probability, Gustavus emerged from the crisis of his accession with regal authority essentially unimpaired; and monarchy remained personal, after 1611 as before. But with a difference. In the first place, the attempt which Charles had made to exercise direct supervision over all branches of government was abandoned; the business of state was now too heavy for such methods . . . There had to be delegation, and Gustavus recognized this. In the second place, there was a difference of personality, tone and manner. Charles IX had ruled against the grain of the nation: Gustavus ruled with it. His popularity, his personal prestige, enabled him to enlist the institutions of government—the Council, the Diet, the provincial administration, the Church—behind the policies he considered necessary; and consultation produced an appearance of collaboration which was not wholly illusory, since it in fact reflected something like a national consensus. Without such a consensus, the sacrifices which his policies demanded would scarcely have been tolerable to his people.[24]

Thus Sweden moved from the condition of a princely state—wherein the state apparatus functions to implement the will of the prince in virtually all matters—to a kingly state, in which the state apparatus is delegated direct supervision over state matters, and in which the king plays a role of inducing patriotic collaboration by essentially becoming the state in a person. The two qualifications on regal authority described by Roberts are in fact like two halves of a scissors: the absolutist regime requires both more delegation and greater consensus. Gustavus and Oxenstierna provided this constitutional innovation at a time when it was necessary to do so in order to effect the strategic innovations that would determine the course of the Thirty Years' War.

The internal factor [that accounts for Sweden's swift rise to dominance from unpromising foundations] was the well-known series of reforms instituted by Gustavus Adolphus and his aides. . . . In developing the national standing army . . . in training his troops in new battlefield tactics, in his improvements of the cavalry and introduction of mobile, light artillery and finally in the discipline and high morale which his leadership gave to the army, Gustavus [produced] perhaps the best fighting force in the world when he moved into northern Germany . . . during the summer of 1630.[25]

When Sweden entered the war, Gustavus introduced new tactics on a scale that only such a state can field and in so doing he utterly transformed the fortunes of the Protestant side. Gustavus Adolphus, perhaps more than any other leader, used the potentiality of the kingly state to exploit the military revolution begun by gunpowder. His father had been enamored of Maurice's tactical theories, but his attempts actually to employ them in a campaign against Poland had met with disaster. The son realized that constitutional as well as strategic reform was necessary. Rejecting the idea that conscripts could never fight on equal terms with professional mercenaries, Gustavus personally drew up the Ordinance for Military Personnel in 1620, which instituted a reformed conscription. A draft was cheaper than hiring mercenaries; it could invoke patriotism in order to win sacrifice on the battlefield; it relied on a relationship between subject and monarch so that the duties it imposed were matters of obedience to orders and not interpretations of a contract. The king could prescribe what weapons and formations his men would use, regardless of their personal preferences. As Roberts has observed, "The Ordinance of Military Personnel was much more than a successful regulation . . . It was a social landmark. . . . Not the least important of [its] characteristics was the state's unremitting control of its subjects." The scope of the Thirty Years' War was too broad for Sweden's manpower, and mercenaries were mainly employed; but the kernel of the armies was always Swedish. The mercenary forces Gustavus enlisted were put through training under Swedish officers to relearn their trade along Swedish lines. Gustavus and Oxenstierna had drafted the Articles of War of 1621 as a code of military law. These differed from earlier instruments in that they were devised as direct orders from a sovereign and not a matter of negotiation between the prince and military entrepreneurs. To take two examples: there were explicit provisions commanding troops to entrench when ordered to do so, and there was a code of military justice providing for courts martial.

Gustavus Adolphus modified Maurice's linear formations, though with much the same objectives of flexibility and increased fire in mind. Like those of the Dutch school, Gustavus's battle orders provided for two or three lines, small units, and a high proportion of officers and NCOs, but where Maurice's lines were ten deep, Gustavus limited them to six to make the troops easier to command. Cavalry was drawn up at no more than three deep at the battle of Lützen, and it was intended to operate in a revolutionary way. By 1627 Gustavus had begun to attach musketeers to his cavalry to discharge volleys into the enemy ranks, enabling the cavalry to charge through the gap in the pikemen that was thus opened up; the musketeers would reload while the cavalry charged and returned. Similarly, he used pikemen in a charge once an opening in the opposing formation had been blasted through by musket volleys. Not Maurice's rolling fire, but instead a series of shattering blasts was Gustavus's goal, and so he trained his men in the salvo whereby platoons of musketeers fired simultaneously instead of successively. This rhythmical alteration of shot and charge, of fire and shock, depended upon disciplined coordination no less than Maurice's choreographed sequences, and therefore it too required careful and extensive training.[26]

Gustavus's tactics served a strategy of annihilation, and thus represented a profound change in thinking from Wallenstein's strategy of attrition or the siege tactics of Maurice.[27] Gustavus sought a decisive resolution through massed force in order to strengthen the State rather than allowing its power to be diffused through lengthy and indecisive campaigns.

When, despite Gustavus's death at Lützen in 1632, the fortunes of war did not shift, Olivares dispatched a new Spanish army to aid the Austrians in 1634. That year the Spanish defeated the main Swedish army at Nördlingen. This, however, had the effect of bringing French forces into the war in 1635. Now Spain turned directly to confront France, and Olivares looked across the Pyrenees at Richelieu. "Either all is lost, or else Castile will be head of the world," wrote Olivares in that year as he planned an invasion of France on three fronts for 1636.

At this point, however, the fundamental strategic weakness of the constitutional order of the Habsburg realm made itself felt. Unlike France, Spain was not a kingly state. Nor was the Empire, though Wallenstein appears to have hoped to make it so. Wallenstein's goal was to secure a stable, absolute monarchy for the whole of Germany. His great wealth—from confiscated Protestant estates—enabled him to propose that he would raise a large army at his own expense and lend the emperor the money to maintain it. This would render the emperor free of Maximilian I, elector of Bavaria, and of Tilly, Maximilian's general, as well as of the other German princes who cherished their independent roles. In our terms, Wallenstein—meritocratic in his promotions, indifferent to religious affiliations—sought to transform the empire into a German kingly state. Neither his emperor nor the princes and electors would permit that, however, and despite Wallenstein's remarkable military gifts, eventually these men conspired in his assassination.

Nor were Olivares's efforts to consolidate the Iberian state as successful as those of his French counterpart. Indeed, the most disastrous failure to mobilize resources lay in Spain itself, where the crown's fiscal rights were in fact very limited. Each of the three realms of the crown of Aragon had its own laws and tax systems, and as a result each had considerable autonomy.

This lack of centralization was further accentuated by the geographic dispersion of the Habsburg constitutional order. Such de facto decentralization tended to surrender initiative to Spain's adversaries owing to the Habsburg refusal to abandon any part of the realm no matter how lengthy and precarious the lines of communication. During the next decade, Dutch and French forces attacked the Spanish Netherlands at two points; the Portuguese revolted in 1640; Swedish and German troops pressed Habsburg forces in northern Germany; a Catalan rebellion began; and there appeared to be some possibility of a complete breakup of Spain itself.

Mainly, though, the conflict settled in Germany, where more than five hundred separate garrisons carried out a savage war designed to deny their enemies any material support, and to seize for themselves whatever forage they could discover. The war that had hitherto been fought principally by German states with foreign assistance now entered its characteristically "epochal" phase as a struggle between the great kingly states of Sweden and France versus Habsburg Austria and Spain. France's defeat of Spain at Rocroi in 1643 and Sweden's victory over the imperial armies at Jankau forced the Habsburgs to the peace tables. Although a Franco-Spanish conflict lingered on for ten more years, the central war in Europe was ended in 1648.

The final destruction of the princely state—of which states the vast Habsburg assemblage was a conglomerate—was the result of the settlement of the Thirty Years' War itself. The Westphalian Peace, as we shall see in Book II, replaced the vision of a dynastic continental empire with the reality of the kingly state. With some exceptions, the Peace gave Ferdinand III, the Habsburg emperor, a free hand in his hereditary territories, including of course the right to suppress Protestantism. At the same time, the treaties removed the pre-eminence of the Habsburg dynasty in Germany. It would now be possible to speak of the interests of the Empire as deriving from the electors, princes, and free cities represented in the Diet. All princes were confirmed in their "territorial superiority in matters ecclesiastical as well as political."[28] All princes gained the right to conclude treaties with foreign powers. Thus did the Reformation destroy the universal lay structure, just as the Renaissance had destroyed the universal Church. In *Paradise Lost,* Milton would re-create Machiavelli's prince in the guise of Satan.[29] At Westphalia the sectarian princely state had similarly been cast out.

The Peace of Westphalia "is null, void, invalid, damnable, reprobate, inane, empty of meaning and effect for all time," declared Pope Innocent X,[30] reflecting a shrewd and percipient assessment of the implications of the treaty for a universalist Catholic Europe. Rather than an imperial, hierarchical states system that might operate in tandem with a pan-European *reconquista,* the Peace* created a system based on absolutist sovereignty, which meant a system predicated on the legal equality of states.

---

*This is discussed in greater detail in Chapter 20.

The peace legitimated the ideas of sovereignty and dynastic autonomy from hierarchical control . . . The reverse of the coin was that it de-legitimated all forms of hegemony and the vestiges of hierarchical con-trols . . . By sanctifying Europe's centrifugal forces by providing a legal basis . . . the documents licensed an anarchical dynastic states system and the internal consolidation of its members.[31]

Princely states persisted in Italy and in Germany because of powerful competing cities in both places and owing to the presence of the papal states in the former and irreconcilable religious division in the latter. These thwarted the consolidation necessary for the creation of a kingly state in both places. The princely state by contrast was "in essence a personal union of territories. In institutional terms, the state was unified only in the person of the prince. Most rulers had enclaves of territory within their states which owed allegiance to another prince."[32] Generally, in Europe, however, this constitutional form gradually gave way, in the period of the sixteenth and early seventeenth centuries, to another idea, wherein the dynastic heir ruled an impersonal state in which the function of kingship was inseparable from that of an enduring, immortal state. After the ratifica-tion of the constitutional form of the kingly state at Westphalia, no war arising primarily from religious issues occurred in Europe among the sig-natories. The victory of the kingly state was accompanied by the broad introduction of rationalism into European thought. Thus Bossuet,[33] one of the proponents of the autocratic power of Louis XIV, is also notable for maintaining that government was a work of reason and intelligence.

Bossuet claimed that there were four characteristics of monarchical power: it was sacred; it was paternal; it was absolute; and it was subject to reason. We might re-characterize these qualities of the monarch as legiti-mate by means of divinely guided dynastic succession (sacred); owing a duty to the State that superseded the personality of the monarch (paternal); owing no hierarchical duty to any other institution, domestic or external (absolute); secular and rational rather than dogmatic (subject to reason).

Over the period of the rise, triumph, and fall of the kingly state—roughly from 1567 and the outbreak of the Dutch revolt against Spain, until 1688 and the expulsion of the Stuarts from England—the armies of France, England, Sweden, and the Dutch Republic tripled or quadrupled, sending government expenditures soaring. These immense strategic de-mands provided a constitutional impetus toward absolutism. Vastly more money and planning also were required for the sieges of the Thirty Years' War than anything preceding it. To capture Hertogenbosch in 1629, for example, the Dutch had to construct over twenty-five miles of trench works.

During the Thirty Years War, capital levies were imposed by both sides
on cities and towns . . . The discovery that taxes collected regularly by
any permanently existing governmental unit . . . could be multiplied
many times by assigning them to the service and repayment of a specific war debt laid the basis for far-reaching innovations in public
finance throughout Europe in the second half of the seventeenth
century.[34]

Six institutional structures typified the kingly state: a standing army[35]
(or navy, in the case of England); a centralized bureaucracy; a regularized
statewide system of taxation; permanent diplomatic representation abroad;
systematic state policies to promote economic wealth and commerce; the
placement of the king as the head of the church. But note these differences
between the kingly state and the territorial state that eventually replaced it:
the former had standing armies, but these were armies in which foreign
mercenaries still predominated, at least numerically. The kingly state had a
centralized bureaucracy but positions in it were sold to raise revenue.
Diplomacy was made more formal and representation more stable, but a
principal duty of the legation remained to negotiate marriage contracts for
the royal family. Finally, although the kingly state regulated and protected
its local industries, it did so not in order to enlarge private wealth, and
thereby increase tax revenues, but to boost its own power, and it often
reneged on its debts.[36]

TERRITORIAL STATES

The outcome of the Thirty Years' War finally established the pre-eminence
of the kingly state, although in such a way as to seed the next development
in statecraft, the territorial state. Partly this had to do with the way the war
was fought.

In the Thirty Years War, warfare reached the nadir of brutality and
pointlessness portrayed in the etchings of Callot and the black humour
of Grimmelshausen's prose. In order to survive at all, mercenary forces
had to batten on the civil population. In order to survive at all, civilians,
in their turn, their homes burned and their families butchered, [swelled
armies] governed not by strategic calculation but by the search for
unplundered territory.[37]

Such horrors fed the need for a state constitutionally grounded in territorial identity. When brutalized inhabitants fled the countryside and popu-

lated the besieged cities, they looked to the state for protection. There has been an active debate over the magnitude of the actual population loss owing to the Thirty Years' War.[38] Some historians say about one-third of Germany's population was lost and the war has been variously estimated as having depleted the population of the Empire by 20–40 percent. Ward notes that of 35,000 villages in Bohemia at the beginning of the war, scarcely more than 6,000 remained at the end. Some war zones lost over half their population; in a corridor running from Pomerania in the north to the Black Forest, the loss of civilian population reached 50 percent. Even these estimates are clouded by the enormous number of refugees. Some cities that were places of refuge then became targets, as happened to Magdeburg, which lost almost its entire population in the sack of 1631. All these events, including the collapse of an independent and prosperous peasantry that had local ties and did not identify with the larger states, as well as the consequent rise of large-scale estate farming, tended to enhance the viability of and desire for territorial states. Finally, the Peace of Westphalia encouraged mass migrations, as populations sought the protection of sympathetic kings of the same religious sect as themselves.

Craig and George begin their study of diplomatic history by observing that the "Thirty Years War [brought] to the fore the most modern, best organized, and, if you will, most rationally motivated states: the Netherlands, Sweden, and France."[39] The political practices of this wartime coalition were ratified "by the Westphalian settlement as the rules of the new commonwealth in Europe [which] rules then developed by *ad hoc* practice into the constituent legitimacy of the European society of states."[40] Each of the members of the coalition had had to be persuaded to cooperate, rather than being obliged to do so, which secured for each a de facto equality as a state.

Of these three allied states, one would take the kingly state to new heights (France), while another (the Netherlands) would develop the internal institutions and external attitudes of a territorial state. France remained a kingly state, struggling to assert its primacy in a society of states that would be increasingly inhospitable to such states, while its competitor kingly state, Sweden, fell successively to the flaws inherent in such states: the caprice of inheritance, the megalomania of rulers, the lack of domestic levers of mobilization, the unity such states evoke from their adversaries, and the suspicion they evoke in their allies. For a century and a half after Westphalia, the military and political struggles in Europe were divided between two theatres, east and west, in which these kingly states asserted themselves, and within which the supremely successful territorial states— the Dutch and their successors, the British in the west and Prussia in the east—rose to pre-eminence. The first half of this era culminates in the

Treaty of Utrecht, which enshrines the political system of the territorial states, and the second half ends with the French Revolution, which utterly effaces the greatest kingly state, France.

The Peace of Westphalia recognized the legal status of a great many states; representatives of over a hundred attended the congress. The most important aspect of this recognition is that, extrapolating from the Peace of Augsburg, the Peace of Westphalia augmented the sources of constitutional legitimacy of the State, which hitherto had been conferred by the customary system of dynastic inheritance and conquest. By simply removing from over three hundred autonomous territories in Germany the umbrella of authority hitherto supplied by the Holy Roman Emperor, the two Westphalian treaties legitimated a vast number of states on two novel bases: one, that the "state" was organized on a recognizable constitutive basis that did not conflict with the status quo; and two, that the congress (and thus the new European society) found it acceptable. This recognition embraced such small principalities as Parma, Baden, and Hesse, but also ecclesiastical lordships such as Cologne, Mainz, and Salzburg, as well as city-republics such as Venice, Genoa, Lucca, Geneva, and Berne. It included states whose affairs were governed by dynastic princes, elected officials, collective bodies, and mixtures of these models. At the same time, this society of states refused to recognize national groups that inhabited provinces such as Catalonia, Scotland, Brittany, Sicily, and Bohemia, where larger states had absorbed them. From the perspective of the present work, the great English historian C. V. Wedgwood could hardly be more wrong in her conclusion that the Thirty Years' War was "the outstanding example in European history of a meaningless conflict."[41] From the point of view of constitutional law and strategic conflict, the Thirty Years' War and the Peace of Westphalia ended the interstate dimension of the religious struggles of the previous era and set the strategic agenda for a century. Indeed one might even say that by generalizing the Augsburg principle of *cuius regio eius religio* to all the states of Europe,* the result of this conflict was the inevitable identification of a particular population with a particular state, a development that in time led to the nation-state and the struggle for self-determination. Thus the Westphalian settlement's calculated omission of a unified Germany led directly to the Long War of our century.

The territorial state had special concerns that contrasted with those of the kingly state. Whereas a kingly state was organized around a person, the territorial state was defined by its contiguity and therefore fretted constantly about its borders. For the territorial state, its borders were everything—its legitimacy, its defense perimeter, its tax base. The territorial state depended on vigorous trading systems because its domestic market

---

*Excluding of course the Ottoman Empire.

might often be insignificant, and also because it derived a significant amount of its revenue from taxing imports. Such states, of which the United Provinces of the Dutch was the initial example, pursued similar diplomatic and strategic objectives, including rational borders; free seas and open markets; an international consensus that no state should be allowed to dominate the affairs of the others; secular state preferences in the international arena; and a continuous diplomatic dialogue. Above all, the territorial states depended upon an active and engaged society of states. Only an international society could confer legitimacy on the constant territorial adjustments required by the balance of power, once legitimacy was founded on formally ratified treaties and agreements and not simply inheritance or conquest. As with the other historic changes in the constitutional orders of the European powers, however, it required the strategic collapse of the dominant form for the new order to be widely adopted.

With Louis XIV the kingly state reached its final apotheosis. He inherited four mutually supporting elements of such a state: a widely supported theory of divine right; a rich, well-organized, and highly centralized state apparatus; an unquestioned dynastic legitimacy; and a regal temperament. Bossuet, his court chaplain and resident political philosopher, expressed the view of many of his contemporaries that a king is a minister of God, to Whom alone he is responsible. On a somewhat different basis, the English political philosopher Filmer wrote: "That which is natural to man exists by divine right. Kingship is natural to man, therefore kingship exists by divine right."[42] This theory fitted perfectly the attitude and temperament of the new king.

His greatest asset was the structure of the French kingdom that Richelieu and Mazarin had shaped that enabled Louis, with his incomparable finance minister Colbert, to exploit its resources for war. The establishment of the French war ministry, whose *intendants* supervised and inspected the financing, supply, and organization of troops;* the creation of an entire military physical plant and infrastructure including barracks, hospitals, officer academies, ship repair yards, parade grounds, magazines, and arms depots: these formed the sinews not only of the military authority of the State, but of its political and constitutional status as well. Other states ardently copied the French model. As Kennedy puts it:

> [A]ll this forced the other powers to follow suit, if they did not wish to be eclipsed. The monopolization and bureaucratization of military power by the state is clearly a central part of the story of "nation-building"; and the process was a reciprocal one since the enhanced

---

*Our word *martinet* comes from the name of an inspector general of this period who imposed rigid and exacting standards of training and discipline.

authority and resources of the state in turn gave to their armed forces a degree of permanence which had not often existed a century earlier.[43]

Richelieu had died in 1642, having orchestrated the coalition that defeated the Habsburg drive for empire in Europe. The following year Louis XIII died, leaving as his heir a five-year-old boy. For eight years Mazarin struggled to maintain the state in the face of a civil war known to history as the Fronde. When the young king attained his majority in 1651, Marshal Turenne was able to restore order in Paris and to declare the Fronde to be rebels against the king's person. By 1653 the movement was dead, and Mazarin, the object of its hatred, had been restored to power as prime minister. But although suppressed, just as the English Restoration suppressed the Protectorate, these movements against the absolutism of the kingly state, their patriotic appeals to "the country," and their hatred of foreigners at court, can be seen in retrospect as harbingers of the ultimately triumphant form of the territorial state.

In 1654 Louis XIV was crowned at Reims. The next year when Parlement attempted to criticize the edicts of the king, he appeared suddenly before them and is said to have made his celebrated declaration, the motto of the kingly state: *"L'état, c'est moi."* Whatever his actual remarks, he scolded the members and left without waiting for their reply, a maneuver that had been previously attempted with such disastrous effects by another champion of the kingly state, Charles I of England. In this case, Mazarin and Turenne were able to suppress any insurrectionary reaction. Louis returned to the field, where he led his troops in their campaigns.

Louis did not share power. He never summoned the States-General or the Parlement. The nobility, the Church, and the towns were all made subservient to the absolute authority of the king. An administrative apparatus operating through ministers who were no more than agents of the Crown, initiated by Richelieu, was put securely into place. Once Louis was secure from internal challenges, with the administrative despotism of a sophisticated kingly state thus in place, he began to make war on the settlements of Westphalia in order that he might become the arbiter of Europe.

"Everything was calm everywhere [when I ascended the throne]," Louis XIV later recalled ruefully; "peace was established with my neighbors, probably for as long as I myself might wish . . . my age and the pleasure of being at the head of my armies perhaps made me desire rather more external activity."[44]

At some point Mazarin and his kingly protégé conceived the plan of uniting the Bourbon and Habsburg dynasties through marriage and eventually bringing Spain within French control. Toward this end Mazarin began negotiations with Philip IV for the marriage of his daughter, Maria Theresa, to Louis. These negotiations were accelerated by French strength in the field and a show of French interest in the young princess of Savoy. When Louis was reconciled to the prince of Conde, his principal rival, who had attempted to seize power in 1650, the king made a tour through the south of the country to Bayonne, where his marriage with the Spanish *infanta* took place. He then made a triumphal entry to Paris with his bride. When Richelieu's successor, Cardinal Mazarin, died in 1661, Louis did not replace him, choosing instead to be his own prime minister. Louis was twenty-three. All the elements of the kingly state—political unity, absolutism, centralized administration, dynastic legitimacy, secularism—were in place.

Louis abolished or ignored all rival authorities and councils. The local authorities, the nobility, the Church, and town government were all placed directly in relationship to the Crown, and all were made responsible to his will. The bureaucratic structure of the kingly state created by Richelieu had been perfected by Mazarin, who sought and promoted the talented managers necessary to run it—Fouquet, Colbert, le Tellier. There were more men of remarkable ability, promoted on merit, who were wholly dependent on the king for their status and authority. Speaking of the most celebrated of this cadre, Mazarin is said to have declared upon his deathbed, to Louis, "Sire, I owe everything to you, but I pay my debt in giving you Colbert."

Colbert, who succeeded the masterful Fouquet, was from 1661 to 1672 supreme in virtually every domestic department. He increased methods of indirect taxation, thus capturing some of the hitherto exempt classes; gave incentives to trade and manufactures; invited foreign talent to settle in France; produced road and canal projects by the score; created a fleet that was, in size at least, the equal of any in Europe; financed the fortifications with which Vauban, the great siege architect, overcame the very tactics he had taught the rest of Europe and secured Calais, Dunkirk, Brest, and a whole line of interior fortresses; and most significantly, produced a revenue surplus each year with which Louis could pursue his foreign policy. This permitted France to enlarge the standing army first established in 1640. Louis's domination of Europe was largely based on the fact that by 1666 he was able to maintain a force of almost 100,000 men, which he would soon triple. This, however, would have been fruitless without the centralized civilian structure put into place during this period by Louis's ministers.

Bankruptcy, indiscipline, corruption: these were the characteristics of French armies, as of most others, before . . . 1661. Yet by 1680 the French forces were nearly 300,000 strong and the wonder of Europe . . . Basically [this] was the work of two outstanding and tireless bureaucrats, le Tellier . . . and his son . . . Louvois. [Their] most important innovation . . . was the creation of a civil bureaucracy to administer the army.[45]

All French soldiers, of whatever rank, were subject to civilian control in every aspect of defense preparation: procurement, weapons manufacture, the hiring and fitting out of privateers, no less than logistics.

When Philip IV of Spain died in 1665, Louis laid claim to various lands in the southern Netherlands, relying on his wife's dynastic rights.* The War of Devolution (1667–1668) ensued when he invaded these territories. The Spanish could not mount a serious resistance, but the French invasion prompted the Dutch and the English, then in the midst of a trade war, to conclude a peace at once and to enter into an alliance in order to prevent Louis from seizing the entire southern Netherlands. At Aix-la-Chapelle in 1668 Louis agreed to a settlement, gaining a number of fortified cities in Flanders. This was merely a prelude.

For the next four years, Louis planned his campaign against the Dutch. In 1667 Colbert had imposed discriminatory tariffs against Dutch products; in 1671 these were sharply increased. French diplomacy deftly detached the British (in the secret Treaty of Dover) and the Swedes from Dutch alliances. Then, in 1672 Louis struck on land while the English fleet attacked the Dutch at sea. This invasion brought William III to power in Holland, a man who embodied the ideals of the territorial state to the same degree that Louis XIV represented the kingly state. It is an irony that is not uncommon in strategic affairs that the very success of Louis's forces so terrified the Dutch that they turned to their most intransigent and dynamic leader. He, by playing on the fears of other states that Louis would upset the balance of power in Europe—fears that were excited by Louis's successes in the field—was able to organize a general coalition against the French. In 1673 the Spanish joined the Dutch; the next year a number of German states joined the alliance. In 1674 the English parliament forced Charles II to withdraw from the war, and in 1677 William married Charles's niece, Mary, the daughter of his brother and heir.

Louis redoubled his efforts. At the Peace of Nijmegen in 1678, he took back Franche-Comté and made further gains in the southern Netherlands and Alsace. Along these lines, Louis—with the guidance of Vauban—built the "iron barrier" of fortifications that presaged the Maginot Line of a later century. Louis was determined to press on to the Rhine. Of the cities that he then seized in 1681 the most important was Strasbourg, which was followed by the siege of Luxembourg. When the English threatened a general

---

*Though he had renounced these, her dowry—agreed at the Peace of Pyrenees in 1659—had never been paid.

European war, Louis raised the siege in return for an agreement that for thirty years he would remain in possession of the territory he had claimed. This was the Truce of Ratisbon, which ratified all of Louis's gains since 1678.

Louis chose this time to revoke the Edict of Nantes and renew the persecution of Protestants. Although this might seem reckless, perhaps explained only by the deepest religious convictions, in fact neither conclusion is warranted. It was Louis, after all, who, when the emperor and pope appealed to him for help in driving the Turks from Vienna in 1683, replied laconically that "crusades [are] no longer in fashion."[46] Moreover, Pope Innocent XI condemned the revocation of the Edict and correctly saw that Louis intended to use this step as a means of ultimately asserting his supremacy over the French Church. This was precisely Louis's objective, and it is doubtless also true that he correctly read the mood of his people, who had collaborated in many ways since the death of Mazarin in petty and malicious attacks on Protestants.* Thus Louis managed to succeed in further centralizing in his person the aspirations, and the prejudices, of his subjects.

This step had the unintended effect, however, of destroying his closest ally, James II, who had been trying to maintain a kingly state in Britain. James had attempted to intercede with the pope, soliciting his support for the Revocation, a move that scarcely endeared James to his own subjects, some 300,000 of whom were non-Anglican Protestants.[47]

In 1686 the League of Augsburg was formed to maintain the agreements of Westphalia, which, it was felt, were jeopardized by Louis's ambitions. The emperor, the kings of Spain and Sweden, the Dutch, Bavaria, and the Rhine provinces all joined, as did the pope the following year. Louis replied by demanding that the League adopt the Truce of Ratisbon as the permanent peace settlement, and James was unwise enough to support this claim. Along with other factors (including James's scarcely concealed Catholicism), this provoked leading English figures to invite William III to replace James, and thus Louis's chief opponent, and the chief protagonist of the territorial state, came to power in London.

The resulting War of the League of Augsburg, begun when Louis responded to the developments against him by invading the Rhineland and burning Heidelberg, was the greatest international conflict since the Thirty Years' War. For the first time Louis faced armies that were a match for his own. By 1697 both sides were exhausted and agreed to the Peace of Ryswick. Louis was obliged to surrender some of the towns he had seized

---

*Absurd interpretations were put on the Edict: Protestants were forbidden to hold burial services during the day because no clause in the Edict expressly permitted them; new churches were forbidden because the Edict merely ratified those in existence at the time.

before the war, including Luxembourg, and to recognize William III as king of England, but he retained Strasbourg and Franche-Comté. Ryswick was a victory for the territorial states, and for the constitutional geography of a multipolar Europe in which small states held the balance of power. For that reason, every diplomat of the period must have realized that when the issue arose of the succession to the Spanish throne—for which Louis had so long prepared himself—Ryswick would be challenged.

The War of the Spanish Succession arose owing to an essential shortcoming in the system of kingly states, its dependence on dynastic legitimacy and on the will of a single person. As it happened, "[o]n no other occasion in the history of modern Europe have so many questions of vital concern to its peoples depended on the death or survival of one man."[48]

That man was the Spanish king, Carlos II, the last descendant of the male line of the great emperor Charles V. He had long been an invalid, and had not produced an heir. The prospect of his death, which appeared imminent over an unexpectedly long reign, excited and alarmed the dynasties of Europe because of the possibility that either Bourbon France or the Habsburg empire would attempt to amalgamate with what was still the richest and by far the most populous collection of human beings owing allegiance to a single European sovereign, the kingly state of Spain—encompassing the Iberian peninsula (minus Portugal), Belgium, a huge overseas colonial empire, and various parts of Italy, including Milan. The pieces that Louis had carefully assembled—his Spanish wife, a dowry controversy, a secret partition agreement with the Austrian Habsburg king Leopold I that provided for a division of the Spanish empire between them if Charles should die without an heir—now all seemed to fall into place.

There remained two formidable obstacles. Spain's partners in the Peace of Ryswick would not tolerate the blow to the balance of power that would occur from uniting Spanish overseas possessions with either France or the Empire. It is a matter of some dispute whether the occupation of the Americas had continued to be nearly as enriching to Spain as it proved at first; compared to the ever-escalating expense of garrisoning a continent and the costly maintenance of long lines of threatened communications across the Atlantic, this may not actually have been so. But in light of the greatly increased costs of maintaining competitive military forces on the continent of Europe, no territorial state could risk diverting this treasure, however costly it had become to extract, to a hegemonical kingly state so plainly on the march.

Shortly after Ryswick, England, Holland, and France had attempted to settle the question of Spanish succession. It is interesting to observe the two sets of negotiating states in these treaties: the territorial states, personified by William III, carefully trying to maintain a balance of power; the kingly states, represented by Louis, keeping intact those dynastic inheritances that might, in the fullness of time, augment the kingly state. William's vision of the European community would eventually triumph at Utrecht when the epochal war waged by Louis finally ended.

Lossky portrays the two men with great insight, and accomplishes also a vivid portrayal of a Europe constituted by Westphalia, compared with that which would emerge at Utrecht.

> Louis' aim was quite simple: to increase the grandeur of his State and of his House, so that his own preeminence as "the greatest king in Christendom" would be beyond dispute. He believed that each country had its own "true maxims of state," rooted in the natural order, whose ultimate author was God. Good statesmanship consisted in following these maxims . . . Only an absolute monarch stood a chance of following the true maxims consistently. Wherever kingly power was limited, it was virtually certain that private interest would becloud the real interest of the State. . . . There was more room for change in [William's] world than in Louis' . . . [William came to see] the struggle on [a] plane that helped him attain to that comprehensive view of the war, and eventually of all Europe, which made him natural leader of the coalition. He ceased to belong to any one country. He sacrificed Dutch interests to English, English to Dutch; when necessary, he was ready to sacrifice the interests of both to those of the coalition; and towards the end he preferred the welfare of all Europe to the smooth running of the coalition.

> The correspondence of William and his narrow circle of friends frequently contains expressions like "the general interest of Europe" and "the public good." These are no mere phrases: often the writer is aware of a conflict between "public good" and State interests, and he invariably sides with the former. Louis, probably, would have resolved such a conflict the other way around, had he been aware of its existence anywhere except in the imagination of misguided men.[49]

The Spanish and King Carlos II objected to the arrangement negotiated by William and Louis in the Partition Treaty, however, as did the Emperor Leopold. When Carlos died in November 1700, it was discovered that he had left the entire of his dominions to Louis's grandson. Carlos evidently believed that France, as Europe's strongest military force, was most able to prevent a future dismemberment of the Spanish monarchy. And there was this codicil: if Louis chose to honor the Partition Treaty instead and to reject the bequest, all the Spanish holdings were to go to Leopold's younger son, whose family, conveniently, was not a party to the Partition Treaty.

When the Spanish king died and Louis was informed of the will, he called his councillors together and solicited their views. The memoirs of the foreign minister, Torcy, who was present, recount the debate:

> It was easier to foresee than to prevent the consequences of the decision in question. [In signing the Partition Treaty with the British and Dutch, the king] had engaged himself to reject every disposition whatever made by the King of Spain in favor of a prince of the line of France. . . . [T]he consequence of such a violation was inevitable war. [But if Louis rejected the will, the whole of Spain's dominion would go to the Habsburgs, a union that, when last held by Charles V, was deemed] heretofore so fatal to France [that war here too was inevitable].[50]

It was absurd that France should make war on Spain because its late king had tried to give his dominions to a French prince. Furthermore, Louis was well aware that he would fight such a war to enforce the Partition Treaty without allies. Only weeks before Carlos's death, William III had written to the Dutch Grand Pensionary that it "would be quite against my intention to be at present involved in a war for a treaty which I concluded only with a view to prevent [a war]."[51] Finally the prospect of the union of the two kingdoms was too tempting for a man of Louis's nature to reject. On Tuesday, November 16, 1700, Louis exuberantly introduced his grandson to the court as Philip V of Spain. The Spanish ambassador exclaimed, "There are no more Pyrenees. They have vanished and we are but one nation."

The wrath of the disappointed emperor was not in itself a reason to rouse the territorial states to defy Carlos's will. They declined to insist, with Leopold, that the Partition Treaty be enforced. Then Louis went too far: he declared that his grandson could not renounce his rights to the French throne. Anticipating the reaction, Louis quickly invested the Spanish fortresses of Luxembourg, Namur, and Mons on the Dutch border; and he transferred to France commercial advantages formerly granted by Spain to England. The French ambassador to Madrid became a kind of proconsul through whom Louis effectively administered Spain. A council of four was set up to reform Spanish finances and administration along French lines.

Thus began the War of the Spanish Succession. Initially, Louis decided to carry the front to Vienna, an audacious plan that miscarried with the victory at Blenheim of the virtuoso partnership of John Churchill, Duke of Marlborough, and Prince Eugene of Savoy. In 1706, an Anglo-Portuguese army seized Madrid. This was followed by further defeats for the French at the hands of Marlborough and Eugene: Ramillies (1706), Oudenarde (1708), and finally Malplaquet (1709), all enormous battles with tens of thousands of casualties. France was invaded, and the hard winter of 1709 starved countless peasants to death. Louis sued for terms. The allies, however, now insisted that Louis send French troops to drive Philip, Louis's own grandson, from the peninsula. This the French king refused to do. Philip was able, in part owing to the success of French reforms, to garner widespread popular support in Spain and in 1710 twice won victories. When the unexpected death of Leopold's successor brought his son to the imperial throne, the entire picture changed. Now the territorial states faced the prospect of a new Habsburg ruler reassembling the dynastic properties of Charles V. When Louis agreed to promise that the Spanish and French crowns would never be united, the territorial powers were willing to accept the obvious preference of the Spanish for Philip V. Only the Austrians wished to continue the struggle, and, after long negotiations, the war was ended by the treaties of Utrecht in 1713 and Rastadt in the following year.

For our present study, the importance of the Treaty of Utrecht cannot be overstated. By its terms it is the first European treaty that explicitly establishes a balance of power as the objective of the treaty regime. The letters patent that accompanied Article VI of the treaty between England, France, and the king of Spain whose dynastic rights were being set aside acknowledged the "Maxim of securing for ever the universal Good and Quiet of Europe, by an equal weight of Power, so that many being united in one, the Ballance of the Equality desired, might not turn to the Advantage of one, and the Danger and Hazard of the Rest."

This treaty permitted adjustments at the margin, but not the wholesale annexation of a national state; inhabitants now cared whether they were French, German, or Austrian.[52] More importantly, securing the territorial state system had now become an important diplomatic objective; after Utrecht, the recognition of any state required its assurance to an international society that the system generally was not thereby jeopardized. That meant that "hereditary right and the endorsement of the constituent local authorities were no longer sufficient by themselves to secure sovereignty over a territory."[53]

It had required an international society to accomplish these achievements, including the effective ratification of the constitutional triumph of the territorial state. So much else that we now take for granted in the international system flows from this watershed event. For example, the authority of multinational congresses (of which Utrecht itself was the most far-reaching in the eighteenth century) and our view of law as the legitimation of acknowledged customary practice (because this revolution in legitimation came about not through a hierarchical appeal but through consensus) both date from this time. In one respect, however, the Peace of Utrecht stood for a system that is very different from the system of international rule making and rule following we have today: Utrecht gave a significant role to war. At Utrecht and thereafter, the balance of power not only permitted but required occasional territorial adjustments, though resort to war was tempered by the further requirement that these adjustments be ratified by the society of states.

This society was motivated by a commitment to preserve its own peace and stability. As ever, strategic means were deployed to secure constitutional ends, but these ends were subtly shaped by the necessities imposed by the development of innovative strategic forms. After Utrecht, the eighteenth century saw many wars, but all of them were

> minor wars of adjustment: the final means, after other pressures and inducements had not succeeded, of compelling . . . modifications of the balance between the states of the system . . . [T]he commitment to preserving a balance of power led to the transfer of territories from one sovereign to another regardless of tradition, the wishes of the inhabitants [or dynastic rules].[54]

This crucial and unusual role for war as an integral part of the diplomatic system would, of itself, have led to an increasing professionalization of war making, but that development was accelerated by other factors having to do with innovation in war-making itself. These factors led to the success of the two territorial states best able to professionalize their capacity to make a new kind of war and maintain their independence from the wars of others: England and Prussia.

Historians debate whether territorial states made the development of professional armies possible—armies that were trained by the State, paid year round from a state treasury, employed within a career structure that was designed and maintained by the State—or whether the changes in warfare brought about by the deployment of such armies made the development of territorial states a necessity. The kingly state was well suited to deploy forces that comprehended the revolution in tactics of the seventeenth century—Gustavus Adolphus showed that beyond doubt—but such states could not maintain these forces in the field for decade after decade, which the collapse of the French economy in 1708–1709 also showed. Only forces that were socially cohesive, drawn from a single territory, recruited to fight for "their country"—a phrase uniquely associated with the territorial state—rather than for highly paid mercenary captains, and above all used for the limited objectives of limited wars, as opposed to the ambitious dynastic enterprises of the megalomaniacal kingly states, could make up a standing army capable of being supported over the long term. The triumph of the territorial state coincided with developments in weapons technology—the replacement of the matchlock musket by the flintlock, whose simple and reliable design made possible a discharge of three rounds per minute and thus the establishment of three ranks capable of simultaneous fire, and the invention of the ring bayonet, which eliminated pikemen from the battlefield—and together led to the successes of Marlborough and Eugene and thus directly to Utrecht.

The Peace of Utrecht,* composed of the whole complex of treaties embracing Utrecht, Rastadt, and, a few years later, Passarowitz and Nystad, subordinated the traditional legal criteria of inheritance and hierarchical allegiance (religious or political). In their place was a unity of strategic approach—a judgment by the society of states as to what was an appropriate strategic goal and what constitutional forms were legitimate. This is how it looked to Voltaire, writing in about 1750:

> For some time now it has been possible to consider Christian Europe, give or take Russia, as *"une espèce de grande republique"*—a sort of great commonwealth—partitioned into several states, some monarchic, the others mixed, some aristocratic, others popular, but all dealing with one another; all having the same basic religion, though divided into various sects; all having the same principles of public and political law unknown in the other parts of the world. Because of these principles the European [states] never enslave their prisoners, they respect the ambassadors of their enemies, they jointly acknowledge the preeminence and various rights of [legitimate rulers], and above all they agree on the wise policy of maintaining an equal balance of power between themselves so far as they can, conducting continuous negotiations even in times of war, and exchanging resident ambassadors or less honourable spies, who can warn all the courts of Europe of the designs of any one, give the alarm at the same time and protect the weaker . . .[55]

Such practices are usually taken to be the necessary preconditions of modern public international law; indeed the most influential commentator on international law of the period, Vattel, virtually repeats this characterization of European political society in the summary of his *Law of Nations*.[†] What is equally interesting, however, is the passage with which Vattel ends this summary:

> England . . . has the honour to hold in her hands the political scales. She is careful to maintain them in equilibrium. It is a policy of great wisdom

---

*A more detailed account can be found in Chapter 21.

†"Europe forms a political system in which the [states] inhabiting this part of the world are bound together by their relations and various interests in a single body . . . [making] of modern Europe a sort of *'republique'* whose members—each independent, but all bound together by a common interest—united for the maintenance of order and the preservation of liberty. This is what has given rise to the well-known principle of the balance of power . . ." Vattel, *Le Droit des Gens,* Book III, Chapter 3, sections 47–48.

and justice, and one which will be always commendable, so long as she makes use only of alliance, confederations, and other equally lawful means.[56]

The Treaty of Utrecht was often called by contemporaries the *"Paix d'Anglais"* and for good reason: it represented the success of a constitutional order that had passed from the Dutch to the English with William of Orange at about the same time that the trade wars against the Dutch ceased and British merchants secured the majority of maritime trade. William's policies required an unprecedented level of state expenditure: the rate of taxation was doubled to pay for a large and growing navy and an army the size of those of continental states. Once Britain effectively defeated the Jacobite movement in Scotland in 1746, she became a territorial state free of the vulnerabilities, as well as the temptations, of continental acquisitions. Even though the electorate of Hanover had been brought to London along with a new dynasty in 1714, Britain did not seek territorial expansion on the continent. And while it was a less than constant leader in preserving the balance of power—acting forcefully in 1717 by organizing the triple alliance of the Hague to check Spanish ambitions but refusing in 1731 to act on behalf of the balance—Britain was a principal beneficiary of the new international order. Within that order Britain meant to improve her position outside the continent. Rather than seek European conquests, Queen Anne declared, "It is this nation's interest to aggrandize itself by trade."[57] For the rest of the century, when Britain and France clashed, the principal impact was felt overseas.

It is sometimes difficult to see this through the fog of engagements on the continent. Despite important battles abroad—the French besieged Madras, while the British had notable successes in America and French overseas trade was virtually halted by blockade—it was French success in the southern Netherlands that brought the British to the negotiating table and forced them to return Louisbourg, the key to Canada. It was clear to all parties, however, that the great stakes lay outside Europe, even if the key to winning them might lie within. Some French strategists argued that America could be conquered by attacking Hanover; others, that this was only a diversion from maritime engagements that depended upon a pre-eminent navy. Meanwhile, in London, opposition members denounced continental involvement to defend "the despicable electorate" of Hanover, while others argued that America could be won on the banks of the Elbe by tying down French resources. Everyone was agreed, however, that America was the stake.

The Seven Years' War sustained this argument. All-out war began in North America in 1755 (as a young lieutenant colonel, George Washington, and his men fired the first shots of the war) and quickly spread to the

European continent. Pitt's strategy of using Prussia to bleed French land forces on the continent while the British Navy destroyed the French at sea proved to be a spectacular success. One by one the French overseas posts were taken once their communications had been cut by British seapower. The Peace of Paris in 1763 brought Canada and Florida to Great Britain. Then the American colonies revolted, and France concluded a formal alliance with the United States, "not," as Louis XVI put it, "with any idea of territorial aggrandizement for us, but solely as an attempt to ruin [British] commerce."[58] By 1780, the Spanish, Dutch, and French were all arrayed against Britain. The American victory at Yorktown in 1781 was the accomplishment of an army that was half-French and of a French fleet that blocked relief for the surrounded British forces (though this is not the standard account in American schoolbooks). For the first time since 1692 the British lost control of the seas.

To American eyes, British policy appeared as a lapse by the British into the ways of the kingly state: George III and his ministers were just so described in the Declaration of Independence. If this was the case, the British had steadied by 1786 and concluded a new commercial treaty with France, restoring by this and many other efforts the British position as arbiter of the balance of power. Despite the younger Pitt's famous remark in 1792 anticipating a long period of peace, this step came just in time.*

One other state especially benefited from the new society in Europe organized around the balance of power by the territorial states. Prussia was best able to exploit the revolution in technology and tactics in warfare, as Britain was best able to benefit from the commercial advantages of relative tranquility on the continent and of maritime expansion beyond. Prussia, by happenstance as much as planning, had been shaped by its ruling family into an instrumental, highly effective territorial state seeking its aggrandizement in carefully selected limited wars, always adding territories that would increase rather than divert the power of the center, avoiding dynastic overextension, and above all, separating the person of the ruler from the state that he and the state's system of bureaucracy served. This last, of course, is the constitutional watermark of the territorial state, and contrasts sharply with its constitutional predecessor.

The kingdom of Prussia began its modern course in 1618, when the electorate of Brandenburg and the duchy of Prussia were united under a Hohenzollern prince.[59] Prussia was hitherto a small state on the Baltic in Poland, to the east of the Vistula, once inhabited by Lithuanian tribes who were conquered and converted by the Knights of the Teutonic Order. During the Thirty Years' War, the Brandenburg electorate had played an

*"Unquestionably, there was never a time in the history of this country, when, from the situation in Europe, we might more reasonably expect fifteen years of peace than at the present moment." Quoted in John H. Rose, *William Pitt and the Great War* (G. Bell and Sons, 1911), 32.

insignificant role until the succession of Frederick William, known as the Great Elector. It was he who transformed the electorate into a kingly state, observing the example of Louis XIV. At the Peace of Westphalia, the Great Elector was able to gain valuable accessions of contiguous territory, and in 1653 he secured a small grant to raise an army of a few thousand men from the estates in which the landed aristocracy was the main voice;* in return, the nobility were confirmed in their privileges and were given full jurisdiction within their lands and a guarantee of preferment as to official posts; in addition, the towns were confirmed in their judicial immunities and guild rules.[60] To finance the army the estates agreed to the assessment by royal officials of land values on which a modest tax was levied—the *Generalkriegskommissariat*. In so doing the estates compromised their traditional right to tax themselves. Frederick William promptly used this reform to leverage higher taxes; when some estates objected, he levied taxes by force. By these measures he was able to create a highly centralized absolutist monarchy and its necessary accompaniment, a standing army, which by 1672 was 45,000 strong.[61] Virtually all state resources were subordinated to the building up of the army. The royal bureaucracy responsible for levying taxes to support the army extended its control over many aspects of Prussian commercial life: in the towns where the tax was raised by an excise on goods, and in the country where levies against harvests and rents supplied revenue, these Prussian officials constituted a supervisory arm of the king and intensified the increasing centralism of Prussian economic life. The Prussian victory against the Swedes at Fehrbellin in 1675 had shaken Europe,[62] and the Great Elector's successor, Frederick III, was recognized as King Frederick I of Prussia by the emperor. Superficial as this recognition may appear to us, it fulfilled a prerequisite for the formation of a territorial state by giving to the subjects of the Prussian crown a common name. Frederick's son resumed the policy of strengthening the army.

This figure is well known to historians from Macaulay's description: Frederick William I did indeed, it seems, walk into private houses and inspect the family dinner, and cane idlers when he happened to meet them on the street, and did fly into inexplicable rages as well as fits of depression. But he also first introduced universal conscription into military service, while exempting the bourgeois taxpayers, taking care to send peasant soldiers back to their farms at harvest time, and nurturing a textile industry with state purchases. By the time of his death in 1740, Prussia had a highly efficient bureaucracy, large financial reserves, and the fourth largest army in Europe (although the state ranked only tenth in territory and thirteenth in population).

*The estates being composed of those classes having a definite share in the body politic (nobles, clergy, commons). There was no permanent assembly of the Estates in Prussia at this time.

In the same year, 1740, the Austrian emperor Charles VI died. With Charles, the male line died out and the throne passed to his daughter Maria Theresa. The last years of Charles's reign had been clouded by his fears for her succession, and so he had persuaded the other European powers to subscribe to the Pragmatic Sanction, an agreement according to which they promised to observe and defend the integrity of Austrian possessions under Maria Theresa. Among the signers was Frederick II, the new king of Prussia.

Nevertheless, without warning, Frederick invaded Silesia, an Austrian possession that lay between the Brandenburg and Prussian lands of his state. In the ensuing three wars, he managed to retain Silesia, despite overwhelmingly adverse odds, and thereby almost doubled the size of his small kingdom. The following excerpt is from Frederick's memorandum on the matter to his ministers:

> Silesia is the portion of the [Austrian] heritage to which we have the strongest claim and which is most suitable to the House of Brandenburg. The superiority of our troops, the promptitude with which we can set them in motion, in a word, the clear advantage we have over our neighbors, gives us in this unexpected emergency an infinite superiority over all other powers of Europe. . . . England could not be jealous of my getting Silesia, which would do her no harm, and she needs allies. Holland will not care, all the more since the loans of the Amsterdam business world secured on Silesia will be guaranteed. If we cannot arrange with England and Holland, we can certainly make a deal with France, who cannot frustrate our designs and will welcome the abasement of the [Austrian] house. Russia alone might give us trouble. If the empress lives, . . . we can bribe the leading counsellors. If she dies, the Russians will be so occupied that they will have no time for foreign affairs . . . All this leads to the conclusion that we must occupy Silesia before the winter and then negotiate. When we are in possession we can negotiate with success.[63]

To this remarkable document, Craig and George say only, "This memorandum really requires no comment. Here is a mind completely dominated by *Staats raison,* a mind that admits no legal or ethical bonds to state ambition." Although this term translates to "reasons of state," it has a connotation unique to the territorial state, in contrast to *raison d'état* and to *ragione di stato,* which, as we have seen, reflect their respective constitutional origins. *Staats raison* is a rationale given on behalf of the State, an imperative that compels its strategic designs (such as the seizure of a proximate province for geostrategic reasons). It identifies the state with the country, the land. The *raison d'état* is a reason invoked on behalf of a king, justifying his acts as being those imposed on him by the State (such as aid to Protestant princes by a Catholic king); it identifies the king with the State when he takes on the role of the state. *Ragione di stato* are reasons that distinguish the state code of behavior from the moral code of the prince (such as deceit or treachery) when the state takes on the role of the prince and the prince is relieved of his moral obligations as an individual. Each phrase, though it translates into the same English words, belongs to that constitutional order within which it acquired use—the territorial state, the kingly state, and the princely state, respectively.

Frederick's seizure of Silesia had profound effects on the future of Germany, for when Austria lost Silesia, with its large population and important commercial resources, the western half of the Austrian empire ceased to be predominantly German, and Prussia became the primary force in Germany. Two further wars confirmed Frederick's gains: the War of the Austrian Succession (1740–1748), in which various states abandoned the Pragmatic Sanction and joined Prussia in a bid for Austrian territories in the Netherlands, Italy, and Bohemia, and the Seven Years' War (1756–1763), in which Prussia was supported only by Hanover and Great Britain (which took the war to North America and India, where British success was finally achieved). The Prussia of the Great Elector who inherited parcels of territory along the vulnerable north German plain, repeatedly crossed and recrossed by brutal mercenaries of every contending power in the Thirty Years' War, had become one of the great powers of Europe in little more than twenty years. Moreover, the Great Elector's Prussia, which had been so carefully modeled on the French kingly state, was transformed by his great-grandson, now called Frederick the Great, into a territorial state of singular intensity. It was Frederick, who entertained no self-doubts about his role at the apex of Prussian political society, who nevertheless described himself not as the incarnation of the State but as its "first servant."[64]

What sort of power was the Prussian state? It was highly stratified; it carefully husbanded its resources; it emphasized loyalty to the State rather than to the dynasty; it encouraged economic growth in manufactures, trade, and agriculture rather than stripping these enterprises of their wealth for the Crown; and it derived all of these imperatives from a desire to create and maintain an army well beyond what most observers would have regarded as its means. In Frederick's view, the State must assure a careful balance between classes within the State, and between economic power and the diversion of economic resources to the military. To accomplish this he insisted that only members of the nobility could serve as officers, and that noble lands could not be sold to peasants or townsmen; that peasant lands must not be absorbed by bourgeois or noble acquisition, and that only those peasants who could be spared from agricultural duties should be recruited to the army; and that townspeople were most useful to the state as producers of wealth and thus "should be guarded as the apple of one's eye." Frederick's soldiers felt no great loyalty to him as a person. Indeed, in his political memoir, he confides that, during the first Silesian wars, "he had made a special effort to impress upon his officers the idea of fighting for the country of Prussia."

In all of these respects, Frederick the Great typified the ruler of a territorial state.[65] His objectives were territorial and statist, rather than dynastic and personal or religious. It is intriguing that even the training of troops reflected the attributes of the state Frederick created, but not so surprising because the state itself had been crafted to provide resources and a structure for warfare. This is evident in the iron discipline that Frederick instilled in the Prussian forces. The goal of this discipline was to make the army into an instrument that could respond to a single strategic will. Frederick once remarked that his soldiers must be more afraid of their officers than of their enemies.[66] Officers and men must understand that every act "is the work of a single man." "No one reasons, everyone executes." Men who are trained to march smartly can also turn quickly and in unison in battle. At Lentzen, Frederick's men suddenly began a flank attack with an about-face.[67] An army thus trained can achieve tactical mobility, becoming skilled in quickly shifting from marching order to battle order, remain steady under withering fire, and, most important, respond to a unified strategic vision. An army trained in this way, Frederick repeatedly said, could provide full scope to the art of generalship.[68]

What kind of generalship was that to be? The answer is consistent with the answer to the question "what kind of statesmanship does the territorial state exact from its leaders?" Strategy, which is the art of the general, is the answer to the question posed by constitutional imperatives, the objects of the statesman. But constitutional imperatives, like the constitutional order itself, change in response to the demands of innovations acquired by strategy. A state that presents a new model, constitutionally, like the territorial state—which identifies the State with the land of its people—will succeed or fail depending on how it is able to adapt new forms of strategy to serve that model. And these new strategic forms will inevitably impose themselves on the constitutional order. The strategic innovations of Frederick and the Prussian state were so dramatically successful that they changed the shape of warfare—and of the State itself—for all Europe. Palmer observes of this new form:

> Battle, with troops so spiritually mechanized, was a methodical affair. Opposing armies were arrayed according to pattern, almost as regularly as chessmen . . . on each wing cavalry, artillery fairly evenly distributed

along the rear, infantry battalions drawn up in two parallel solid
lines . . . each . . . composed of three ranks each rank firing as at a
single command while the other two reloaded . . .[69]

According to Frederick, marching order was determined by battle
order: troops should march in columns so arrayed that by a quick turn the
column presented itself as a rank, firing in lines with cavalry on its flanks.
Because a battle order of long unbroken lines was as vulnerable as it was
murderous, Frederick designed the "oblique order," which involved the
advance of one wing by successive echelons while the other wing remained steady, minimizing exposure to the weaker end. This either gained
a quick victory by a flanking attack, rolling up the enemy's line or, if failing, tended to minimize losses as the hitherto static wing maneuvered to
cover the withdrawal of the extended wing. Such a general tends to avoid
cataclysmic engagements; he looks for set battles, preferably sieges, and
tries to acquire fortresses. Forts, Frederick wrote, were "mighty nails
which hold a ruler's provinces together." Generalship of this kind is after
all *territorial,* both tactically and strategically: "To win a battle means to
compel your opponent to yield you his [territorial] position."

These military ideas were a dimension of Frederick's overall views as a
statesman, and it was Frederick who succeeded William III as the model of
the territorial state leader.[70] He carefully maneuvered to augment his state
with territory that would actually contribute to the wealth[71] or territorial
integrity of the state—rather than vindicate dynastic claims—and that
could be gained at reasonable costs in concert with the other powers of
Europe. The most striking example of this was the result of the First Partition of Poland, whereby, only nine years after the end of the Seven Years'
War, Prussia, Austria, and Russia made substantial territorial acquisitions
while avoiding conflict. Frederick gives us his view of this incident in his
History of My Own Times:

> This was one of the most important acquisitions which we could make,
> because it joined Pomerania and Eastern Prussia; as it rendered us mas-
> ters of the Vistula we gained the double advantage of a defensible fron-
> tier to the kingdom and the power to levy considerable tolls on the
> Vistula, by which river the whole trade of Poland was carried on.[72]

Once this vital property was gained—it closed Prussia's territorial gap
along the Baltic coast—Frederick immediately moved to improve it.
Craftsmen, artisans, manufacturers, educators were all sent to colonize the
area; marshes were drained; the Vistula was connected to the Oder and to
the Elbe by a great canal.

Frederick was both a beneficiary and a strong supporter of the Utrecht system, even if he had made his debut on the European stage by a successful *coup de main* within that system.

> The ambitious should consider above all that armaments and military discipline being much the same through Europe, and alliances as a rule producing an equality of force between belligerent parties, all that princes can expect from the greatest advantages at present is to acquire, by accumulation of successes, either some small city on the frontier or some territory which will not pay interest on the expense of the war [required to take it].[73]

He saw clearly enough that war should be undertaken in proximity to one's own frontiers, because of the "difficulty of providing food supplies at points distant from the frontier, and in furnishing the new recruits, new horses, clothing and munitions of war."[74] Above all, he relied on forces that, however well-drilled, had no moral enthusiasm or political conviction. For this reason he could not rely on his armies to live off occupied countries because they would desert if dispersed to forage, and their morale would collapse if their supplies were not regularly refreshed. For the same reason, his alliances were solely matters of strategic calculation, and thus he could never depend on support from ideologically sympathetic local parties in the countries he invaded. In order to preserve the authoritarian constitutional structure of the Prussian state, Frederick dared not excite the energy that lay dormant in nationalism. Indeed, this was the challenge of the territorial state: to make the State, rather than the person of the king, the object of constitutional and strategic concern without permitting the people to claim the State as their own. "My land," "my country," but not "my nation." All of this stands in stark contrast to the style of warfare epitomized by Frederick the Great's successor as the leading commander in Europe, Napoleon Bonaparte.[75]

In contrast to the absolutism of the kingly state, the territorial state was a state of definite limits. We have seen this to be the case in the composition and maintenance of its armies. The governments of territorial states were limited in the revenue base they could derive from their subjects because the territorial state depended for its legitimacy on a compact with the estates of the realm, and not on the axiomatic dynastic rights of an absolute ruler. Nor could these governments draw on the entire human resources of the state: typically the aristocracy was privileged to officer the army and the state. (The kingly state was more meritocratic in this respect.) The people, insofar as they were a material factor in the strategic calculations of the territorial state, were simply taxable assets to be encouraged, and not too much disturbed, by the occasional warfare of the state. Frederick the Great wrote that he "wanted to fight [his] wars without the peasant behind his plow and the townsman in his shop even being aware of them."[76] The role of the citizen did not require that he take part in war. Sound political economy counseled that armies should be composed of men who were the least necessary, economically, to the well-being of the state. The aristocratic officer corps scarcely demanded from the marginal persons they commanded any of the characteristics of esprit that the officers expected of themselves. Rather they relied on good physical care, medical attention, adequate housing, and regular pay to motivate their troops. The rise of large standing armies under the kingly state had resulted in the systematic use of billeting. Troops were assigned to private houses, taverns, and stables. After the Seven Years' War, however, the new territorial states of Europe increasingly housed their forces in barracks, isolated from the surrounding populations. It was expected that enlisted men would freely desert if allowed to reconnoiter in small parties and that both officers and men would change sides if presented with the promise of more attractive employment.

Professional armies were expensive and the extensive drill required by eighteenth century tactics meant that the territorial state had a great investment in each soldier. Large-scale pitched battles were seldom risked. Marshal Saxe in his *Reveries de Guerre* (1732) made the much-quoted statement: "I do not favor pitched battles, especially at the beginning of a war, and I am convinced that a skillful general could make war all his life without being forced into one." Armies in Europe at this time became, in Clausewitz's words, like "a State within a State, in which the element of violence gradually faded away."

The delimited territorial state thus produced a delimited warfare, fought with limited means for limited objectives. Wars of position prevailed over wars of attrition, and precisely because battles were so deadly they were largely avoided and were not decisive when they occurred. Thus even though there were technological breakthroughs, particularly in the ability to deliver firepower, and therefore casualty rates rose appreciably during this period, the abundant possibilities for decisive military action ironically prevented the hegemony of any one state. Small sovereignties that had been active participants in earlier eras however—Cologne, Wurtemberg, Münster, Bremen, Genoa, Hesse—virtually disappeared. War became an activity of the Great Powers because only they could control territory significant enough to finance its defense in an era in which territory itself was the medium of exchange of power.

Prior to the arrival of the territorial state, rights of succession had been the principal source of interstate dispute. These were legal rights, based on ancient titles, marriages, cessions, that didn't merely provide the monarch with a patrimony, but established his right to rule. As Holsti has put it, "The territories that reverted to a prince, king or queen were less significant than the rights that inhered in them."[77] But in the eighteenth century, concerns for succession began to relate less to the right to rule—who had the better claim to succeed—than to the power to control territory. To paraphrase Luard slightly, control over territory no longer resulted from a credible claim; the claim resulted from a credible control over territory.[78] We have only to compare the careful preparations of Louis XIV to place a Bourbon prince on the throne of Spain—the thwarted dowry, the Spanish wife, the secret agreement with the other principal contending family—with Frederick's casual pretexts regarding his Silesian claims. Once he decided to move against Austria, Frederick directed a subordinate to work up a case that Silesia really belonged to Prussia; on being presented with the results, Frederick replied with amusement that the official had proved to be a good charlatan.

Indeed even in the selection of monarchs, sorting out the dynastic priority among competing legal claims became subordinated to aligning the decision with overriding strategic purposes. Dynasts themselves in this era ceased to think of territory in terms of family patrimony but rather as a commodity—the currency of great power relations that it had become. Dynastic rights were now fig leaves for territorial claims.

This was the era of the great territorial partitions: in 1772 of Poland by Russia, Austria, and Prussia; in 1773, of Swedish possessions by Russia, Denmark, and Prussia. Territory could be traded to avoid or terminate a war, disregarding entirely its legal associations with family compacts, marriages, and titles.[79] In place of the princely pursuit of titles and their appurtenant rights, once the coin of European patrimonial conflict, states struggled to gain or hold territory per se. Territorial conflicts became the chief source of war in this period, not simply because land was essential to national power—providing a population from which to conscript, a base of revenue and trade—for this had always been the case, but rather because legitimacy too now came from the sheer control of territory. A state that could consolidate its holdings, shedding noncontiguous family properties that were vulnerable to predation, could build itself a strategic position of relative invulnerability, and this alone was enough to assure its position among the other powers of Europe. Otherwise, it faced steady losses of its territory, even the threat of partition by a coalition. The balance of military technology and tactics was such that no state could hope for the wholesale patrilineal annexation of another—the vindication of a dynastic claim—yet every state was vulnerable to having a province picked off at its borders. The stereotypical view of eighteenth century conflict as indecisive reflects, as Jeremy Black effectively showed, an oversimplification of the political context.

18th century conflicts do appear inconclusive because they were frequently coalition conflicts and . . . coalition warfare could inhibit a determination to achieve decisive results. [Moreover] governments did
not necessarily wish to make their allies too powerful by weakening
their rivals excessively.[80]

This reticence lay in the nature of the constitutional basis for the territorial
state and not in a lack of decisive military technology or ambition.

Pikemen had been hitherto used to protect musketeers from attack by
cavalry and by other pikemen; now bayonets fulfilled this role and more
because they added a firepower the pike could not provide. It had always
been difficult to maintain the necessary ratio between pikemen and musketeers once a battle began; the bayonet effectively solved this problem. The
deployment of the flintlock musket, in which powder was ignited by a
spark caused by the striking of flint on steel, produced a lighter, more reliable weapon that, with the aid of cartridges, doubled the rate of fire. Both
of these changes swept through the armies of Europe: Prussia adopted the
bayonet in 1689, one year after Louvois had instructed Vauban to produce
a prototype; Denmark followed suit in 1690. At the battle of Fleurus that
year some Imperial units attracted universal attention when they repulsed
repeated French cavalry charges though unsupported by pikemen and
armed only with muskets. The French abandoned the pike in 1703, the
British the next year. The Austrians adopted the flintlock in 1689, the
Swedes in 1696, the Danes and the British by 1700.

From the late seventeenth century onward, especially in Prussia, Holland,
and Britain, a new kind of regime was supplanting the king-centered states
of which Louis XIV's was exemplar. The primacy of infantry fire made a
well-trained and well-disciplined force more valuable than ever but, constitutionally, the state that fielded that force had to justify doing so on some
basis more substantial than the vanity of the monarch. During this period,
successful military powers were changing the compact that legitimated the
state, and this, in the field relationship I have been describing, led to strategic innovation. The crises of legitimacy that brought William of Orange to
the British throne and crushed the reign of James II epitomized this
change, but it was going on in many states.

The new order was distinguished by a view of the State as a solar system rather than the reflection of the personality of a sun king. Hume expresses this point of view in his 1753 essay "Commerce," in which he
takes up Machiavelli's subject, the State, and transforms it into a mar-
veling disquisition on the state as an invisible mechanism, enabling growth
and the creation of wealth. No less a champion of this idea, though it may

be shocking to say so, was Frederick the Great, who ceaselessly portrayed himself as the servant of the State, frugally husbanding its material assets and prudently attending to the increase of its efficiencies. This era, the Age of the *ancien regime*—before the dawning of an acute national self-consciousness but after the mannered rejection of the hubristic pyrotechnics of the kingly state—was characterized by the adroit use of strategic and tactical positioning.

Its military aspect was in perfect harmony with the constitutional modesty of its regimes. If, at other turns of the wheel, a strategic innovation or constitutional cataclysm signaled the new era, the introduction of the territorial state came with the exhaustion that followed the end of the vast European civil conflict, the Thirty Years' War. We can almost date its inception to the beheading of the monarch of the English kingly state, Charles I, in 1649.

The territorial state was characterized by a shift from the monarch-as-embodiment of sovereignty to the monarch as minister of sovereignty. A striking example of this occurred in the well-known "Diplomatic Revolution" of 1748, in which reasons that related entirely to perceptions of the national interests concerned were allowed to predominate over the dynastic traditions of the Bourbon and Habsburg houses, and as a consequence, France and Austria found themselves allies for the first time.

In the period after Utrecht a number of decisive changes occurred, in terms of army size, weapons, and most especially the administration of the armed forces, their training and control by the State. Thus it can be argued that the constitutional imperatives of the territorial state were partly the cause, and not merely the consequences of these changes.[81] The period from 1660 to 1760 saw a significant increase in the number of men permanently under arms in Europe, an increase that is more dramatic once we recall that for most of this period European population figures were static. Greater administrative capability was felt in the field: for example, the Austrian conquest of Hungary from 1683 relied on the creation of a series of magazines. Large-scale mapping took place as surveys grew in importance, an obvious consequence of the territorial state's preoccupations.

But not every state was able to reconstruct itself along such constitutional lines; in Poland, for example, the nobility was unable to reconcile itself to fidelity to the State as an entity of which the monarch was the first steward, and it simply destroyed the state structure that might otherwise have successfully resisted partition. Everywhere that control of the troops—everywhere the state monopoly on legitimate violence—fell from the hands of the State, the advantages of this military revolution eluded the country, as happened in Sweden and Hungary. Yet even the rigid stability of the successful territorial states would soon be shaken by a new, more dynamic constitutional form and its accompanying strategic whirlwind.

CHAPTER EIGHT

From State-Nations to
Nation-States: 1776–1914

A swamp still skirts the mountain chain
And poisons all the land retrieved;
This marshland I hope yet to drain,
And thus surpass what we achieved.
For many millions I shall open regions
To dwell, not safe, in free and active legions.
Green are the meadows, fertile; and in mirth
Both men and herds live on this newest earth,
Settled along the edges of a hill
That has been raised by bold men's zealous will.
A veritable paradise inside,
Then let the dams be licked by raging tide;
And as it nibbles to rush in with force,
A common will fills gaps and checks its course.
This is the highest wisdom that I own,
The best that mankind ever knew:
Freedom and life are earned by those alone
Who conquer them each day anew.
Surrounded by such danger, each one thrives,
Childhood, manhood, and age lead active lives.
At such a throng I would fain stare,
With free men on free ground their freedom share.[1]

THE INCESSANT COMPETITION of the new European society of territorial states required enormous and ever increasing expenditures on professional armies. Although the territorial gains permitted by the balance of
power to any single state could not possibly justify such expenses, without
an extensive professional army any single state risked piecemeal losses to
the other states that could be catastrophic (such as happened to Poland

when it lost 29.5 percent of its population and 35.2 percent of its territory in 1772).

The diplomatic relations among eighteenth century states were conducted according to a precise diplomatic code of behavior; so were their wars. Neither left much room for innovation. The increasing burden on states thus could not be significantly relieved externally; that meant that there would be increasing pressure for constitutional change, internally, as each state struggled to wring greater and greater effort from its own society.

Those territorial states, like Britain, that were able to survive eventually transformed themselves into state-nations in the nineteenth century. Those states that had not made the transition to the territorial constitutional order—that remained kingly states in their constitutional life (like France or Sweden)—could not call on the leadership of elites to support the increasing demands of the State. At some point, the groups on which the kingly states depended simply refused to support the State any further. Each monarch was then faced with a difficult choice for the social order: either cut back on military expenditure and give in to what every state feared as external threats but which the kingly state saw as a threat to dynastic sovereignty itself, or ally with elements in the threatened society that were traditionally outside the leadership. Every kingly state eventually made the choice to do the latter, and everywhere this occurred, the old order was destroyed.[2] Thus at the end of the eighteenth century, Europe entered a period of intense crisis from which it did not emerge until 1815.

> Adherents of the revolution, who could be found all over the European world in 1790, liked to see themselves as part of a single movement . . . [b]ut the revolutions of the 1790s were not brought about by revolutionaries, nor were they the product of a revolutionary movement. They were situations resulting from the collapse of the previous order; the situations produced the revolutionaries . . . The collapse of the old order resulted, in general, not from attacks by those excluded from its rewards, but from conflicts between its main beneficiaries—rulers and their ruling orders.[3]

For this reason the first states in the new international order to be transformed into the next state constitutional form, the state-nation, were those that had made the least accommodation to change hitherto; by mid-century, however, virtually every great power had followed suit. Although it might have horrified some of the statesmen of these countries to be told so, they were all following in the path of the military genius and dictator Napoleon Bonaparte.

THE STATE-NATION

What is a "state-nation," this curious phrase that seems no more than a typographer's inversion of a familiar term in political science? A state-nation is a state that mobilizes a nation—a national, ethnocultural group—to act on behalf of the State. It can thus call on the revenues of all society, and on the human talent of all persons. But such a state does not exist to serve or take direction from the nation, as does the nation-state. This is quite clear in the case of Napoleonic France, which incorporated many nations within its territory, but suppressed nationalism wherever it encountered it outside France.* It is equally true of the British Empire. By contrast, the nation-state, a later phenomenon, creates a state in order to benefit the nation it governs. This, of course, raises the familiar late-nineteenth century (and twentieth century) question of self-determination: when does a nation get a state? This question is nonsense to the state-nation. One might say that the process of decolonization in the twentieth century was the confrontation of nascent nation-states like Ireland or India or Indochina with state-nation forms, like Britain and France.†

To understand the development of the state-nation, the French example is particularly illustrative, for there a single leader can be shown to have appreciated the strategic demands that put the old regime under such pressure (indeed these same demands threatened to destroy the revolutionary Directory) and to have instituted the constitutional innovations that transformed the State. Here, also, an epochal war provided the occasion for the adoption of these innovations throughout Europe.

The Wars of the French Revolution and the Napoleonic Wars (1792–1815) pitted France against all the other major states of Europe, sometimes in coalition, sometimes standing alone. This epochal war—throughout the nineteenth century *it* was known as the Great War[4]—can be conveniently broken down into twelve successive interconnected conflicts:

(1) The war of the First Coalition (1792–1797) was a war begun by Austria against revolutionary France. In September 1791 the French National

---

*Napoleonic imperialism was paid for by plunder . . . A nation proclaiming liberty, fraternity and equality was now . . . conquering non-French populations, stationing armies upon them, sequestering their goods, distorting their trade, raising enormous indemnities and taxes and conscripting their youth . . . In Italy between 1805 and 1812 about half the taxes raised went to the French." Kennedy, *The Rise and Fall of Great Powers*, 133, 135.

†"In 1914 London declared war on Germany on behalf of the entire empire. But long before post–Second World War anti-colonial nationalism stripped away Britain's Asian and African colonies, the 'white' dominions of Canada, Australia, and New Zealand were resisting rule from London. By the time of the Chanak crisis with Turkey, in 1922, London had discovered that it could not count on automatic support from the empire. After 1926 British military planners no longer considered the British Commonwealth to be a reliable basis for military plans." Joseph S. Nye, Jr., "The Misleading Metaphor of Decline: Analogies between the United States and Post-Imperial Britain are Inaccurate and Mischievous," *The Atlantic* 265 (March 1990): 89.

Assembly dissolved itself and announced that the Revolution was over; a new Assembly was elected and a constitution put in place. The Revolution, however, was only getting underway. The French king and queen secretly appealed to the queen's brother, the Habsburg ruler of Austria, Leopold II, for assistance. Leopold had already allowed French émigré forces to organize and arm; on July 6, 1791, he invited the other powers to join a coalition to stop the course of the Revolution. On August 21 Austria and Prussia announced that they regarded the situation in France as a matter of interest to all European sovereigns. For its part, the French Legislative Assembly was in a truculent mood. "It may be," one member wrote to his constituents in December, "that as a matter of sound and wise policy the Revolution has need of a war to consolidate it."[5] On March 1, 1792, the Assembly voted for war. Prussia supported Austria, and their joint armies invaded France in the summer of 1792.

At Valmy, a hundred miles from Paris, the French won a decisive victory. A new Assembly was chosen, to be called a "convention" after the American constitutional convention.* The Convention proclaimed France a republic, offered French aid to all nations that wished to overthrow their oppressive regimes, and condemned the French king to the guillotine. Following the withdrawal of allied forces after Valmy, the French invaded Austrian territories, occupying Brussels and annexing Savoy and Nice. The Convention declared war against Great Britain and the Dutch Republic in February 1793 and against Spain in March. British subsidies induced a number of states to join the expanding allied forces: Portugal, Piedmont-Sardinia, the Papal States, and the Kingdom of Naples, as well as various German states allied with Prussia and Austria.

The force built up by this alliance shook the French armies. Their commander, Dumouriez, the victor at Valmy, was defeated in March and subsequently defected to the enemy, taking with him the minister of war. In October the Constitution of 1793 was suspended, and the Reign of Terror began. After putting down revolts in Lyons, Marseilles, and Toulon, French forces faced the coalition and won a resounding victory at Fleurus on June 25. As soon as it became apparent that France could not be easily crushed, the European coalition faltered. The Prussians made peace in March 1795; Spain, three months later. The Netherlands were defeated by France and occupied. Only Britain and Austria refused to concede.

In 1796 the young French general Napoleon Bonaparte opened his first Italian campaign, defeating the Austrians repeatedly until in April 1797 they agreed to a truce, followed by a peace treaty between the two states.

---

*Which created the first state-nation.

"Napoleon's Italian campaigns of 1796–7 seemed almost miraculous; twelve victories in a year, announced in bulletins which struck the world like thunderclaps."[6] The First Coalition now dissolved completely, but the British still refused to make peace.

(2) A new campaign was begun against Britain through Egypt (1798–1801) by Bonaparte, who sought a route by which to conquer India and to menace the Ottoman possessions in the Near East. While this was going on, France began a series of campaigns on the Italian peninsula. These commenced (3) the War in Central Europe (1798–1799). France attacked and conquered Switzerland (1798), the Papal States (1798), Piedmont-Sardinia (1798), and Naples (1799). The ambitions of Bonaparte toward the Levant succeeded in alarming the tsar, who responded to a proposal from London that he organize a second alliance. This proposal, drafted by Pitt, laid out the program that was the blueprint for the ultimate settlement in Vienna sixteen years later.

(4) The War of the Second Coalition (1798–1802) was prosecuted against France by Britain, Austria, and Russia. Prussia did not join, nor, as Pitt had hoped, did the three great powers pledge themselves not to make peace separately. By the summer of 1799, allied forces had driven France from German territory and inflicted severe defeats on the French in Italy and Switzerland; France itself appeared threatened with invasion and the ruling Directory was discredited. In October, however, French forces rallied and forced the Russians out of Switzerland while defeating and expelling an Anglo-Russian force that had attempted to invade the Batavian Republic (as the Netherlands had now become under French occupation). On October 22, the disillusioned tsar withdrew from the coalition.

That same week, Bonaparte suddenly reappeared in Paris from Egypt; in November a coup d'état ended the Directory and established the Consulate; by the close of 1799 Bonaparte had made himself first consul and head of the French Republic.

He could not claim legitimacy for himself on dynastic grounds, but he had no intention of relying on assemblies either (and thus was not interested in the form of the territorial state). Nor did he wish to remain the *condottiere* of the Directory. Throughout his dictatorship he showed a canny appreciation for the symbols of the French state and of how the French nation could be put at the service of that state. "Clearly, the decisive factor throughout was Napoleon's hold on the imagination of the French people at a moment when they felt themselves threatened by a renewal of Jacobin terror [at home] and invasion [from abroad]."[7]

With Bonaparte's victory at Marengo in June of 1800 and Moreau's at Hohenlinden in December, the second allied coalition fell completely apart. France succeeded in signing a peace treaty with Austria at Luneville in February 1801 and with England at Amiens* in 1802.

Bonaparte's handling of the continental states arrayed against him reflected a shrewd appreciation of their constitutional basis. So long as he faced territorial states, he could outmaneuver their coalitions by offering one of their members substantial territorial cessions; that state realized that if these were refused, another state might accept offers made to it, thus bringing down the coalition and weakening the bargaining power of the resisting state. Russia, Prussia, and Austria each revealed a willingness to settle with France if offered a sufficient territorial inducement.[8] This tactic had been well understood by Frederick the Great, but in him it was deployed for the limited territorial objectives of the territorial state. With Bonaparte, this technique was used in service of the unlimited, imperial objectives of the state-nation.

France was transformed into a new constitutional entity. After Amiens, Bonaparte declared, "Citizens, the Revolution is now settled in the principles which started it," meaning that a new state had been created that embodied those principles. That state, however, was far different from what had been envisioned in the heady days of 1789.[9] A referendum was now proposed to determine whether Bonaparte should be consul for life. This plebiscite resulted in an enthusiastic endorsement for a quasi-imperial regime. Fresh hostilities that reopened against England in May 1803 moved France further along the constitutional path of the state-nation. The French Senate in 1804 sent an address to Bonaparte after an assassination attempt, urging that the Consulate for Life be changed to an hereditary empire subject to a new public referendum. "The government of the Republic," the address stated, "is now entrusted to an emperor. Napoleon Bonaparte, first consul, is Emperor of the French."

But only when each of Napoleon's victim states had become persuaded that it must change in order to save itself, did a *society* come into being that can properly be called a society of state-nations. In the meantime, there lay twelve more years of war. The same week in May that Bonaparte assumed the title of Napoleon I, Pitt returned to power in England and at once began to organize yet another alliance against France. British subsidies succeeded in bringing first the Russians, in November 1805, and later the Austrians, in August, into a league that fought (5) the War of the Third Coalition (1803–1807).

On October 20 the Austrians were crushed at Ulm, and on November 13, the French army entered Vienna. Only ten days earlier the British and

---

*It was the resignation of the Pitt cabinet over the king's refusal to assent to a law removing the disabilities of Catholics that cleared the way for a treaty with the French. *New Cambridge Modern History*, vol. IX, 260.

Russians had induced Prussia to join the coalition. On December 2, Napoleon defeated the combined Austrian-Prussian armies at Austerlitz. On December 15 Napoleon offered the formerly British seat of Hanover to Prussia and wrecked the Third Coalition. That same month harsh terms were imposed on the recalcitrant Austrians: the Habsburgs were excluded from Italy; an indemnity of forty million gold francs was paid; and Germany was reorganized—Bavaria, Wurtemberg, and Baden became states allied with France and, with a dozen German states, formed the Confederation of the Rhine with Napoleon as Protector. The Confederation pledged 80,000 troops to France in case of war. When Napoleon announced that he would no longer recognize the Holy Roman Empire, it was dissolved. The Habsburg ruler henceforth styled himself Francis I, Emperor of Austria.

Throughout the summer of 1806, Napoleon negotiated with Britain and Russia, the only members of the Coalition still in the field. When Prussia dispatched an ultimatum to France on learning that Napoleon had offered to return Hanover to Britain in these negotiations, Napoleon immediately struck back. At Jena on October 14 the Prussian forces were destroyed, and two weeks later Napoleon occupied Berlin.* Napoleon now turned against Russia. At the battle of Friedland the Russians were defeated, and the tsar, Alexander I, agreed to a truce that matured into the Peace of Tilsit. This agreement brought Russia not only out of hostilities but into alliance with France. In November 1807, Russia declared war on Britain.

(6) The Franco-Austrian War was a desperate attempt by Austria to exploit French preoccupation with a Spanish uprising, supported by Britain in (7) the Peninsular War (1807–1813), and to seize the initiative in Central Europe. Like the Prussians, who seethed under French oversight, the Austrians prepared for a nationalist struggle against French imperialism. Indeed, it has been remarked that "[h]itherto, Napoleon had fought governments; after 1807 he found himself fighting nations,"[10] a crucial development in the evolution of the state-nation from territorial states. Napoleon's victory at Wagram, however, dashed Austrian hopes before Prussian forces could even be brought into play. Austria was forced to cede territory to the Confederation of the Rhine, to Saxony, and to the Italian kingdom. Russia, which had taken Finland from Sweden in (8) the Russo-Swedish War of 1808, was now given Austrian territory in Poland. In March, Napoleon signed a marriage treaty with the daughter of Emperor Francis, and a proxy marriage took place in Vienna two days later.

The Franco-Russian alliance had not kept Austria from making war against France, as Napoleon had planned; nor had it provided Russia with the promised partition of Turkey, where Russia had been at war since 1806

---

*At the tomb of Frederick the Great Napoleon paid tribute to his predecessor. "Gentlemen," he said to his assembled marshals, "take off your hats. If *he* were here, *we* would not be here."

in (9) the Russo-Turkish War. Thus in 1812, Napoleon concluded treaties with Prussia and Austria requiring those states to provide 20,000 and 60,000 troops, respectively, to attack Russia. By spring he had accumulated forces totaling 600,000 men. Alexander responded quickly: he made peace with the Turks; received secret assurances from the Prussians and Austrians that they would not in fact make war against Russia; formed an alliance with Britain; and negotiated an accord with the Spanish insurgents. One may say that (10) the Russian Campaign of 1812 laid the foundation for (11) the War of the Fourth Coalition (1812–1814), which ultimately defeated Napoleon and deposed him. The final campaign in this epochal war was begun with the flight of Napoleon from Elba, an island to which he had been exiled by the Coalition. The One Hundred Days (12) ended shortly after the French defeat at Waterloo.

Napoleon inherited the strategic problems created by the French Revolution. It is true that a revolution in war had been underway for some time, but it would be a mistake to conclude that the strategic innovations of this era would have occurred quite as they did without Napoleon's leadership, or that the state-nation he brought into being was simply the result of revolutionary ideology. As the Duke of Wellington put it,

> [Napoleon] was the Sovereign of the country as well as the military chief of the army. That country was constituted upon a military basis. All its institutions were framed for the purpose of forming and maintaining its armies with a view to conquest. All the offices and rewards of the State were reserved in the first instance exclusively for the army.[11]

It is important to understand precisely what strategic innovations Napoleon relied upon, and then to briefly chronicle his experience with them. That will lead us to an understanding of the state-nation form he created.*

The most important of these military innovations was the adoption by the Convention of something approaching universal conscription—the *levée en masse*—which produced an enormous increase in the number of soldiers. This changed the type of soldier available to French commanders, but it also enabled them to fight a different sort of campaign, and to fight more campaigns.

> Describing the posture of Austria and Prussia at the outset of the French Revolution, Clausewitz noted that the two countries resorted to the kind of limited war that the previous century had made familiar in Europe. People at first expected to deal only with a seriously weakened French army; but in 1793 a force appeared that beggared all imagination.

---

*And how it differed from the state-nation model created by Washington, Hamilton, and Madison.

Suddenly war again became the business of the people—a people of thirty millions, all of whom considered themselves to be citizens ... and consequently the opponents of France faced the utmost peril.[12]

This political and social change led to far larger armies and thus to important developments in strategy and tactics. After 1800 Napoleon normally fought his campaigns with more than 250,000 troops, in contrast to the 75,000-man armies of the early and middle eighteenth century.

Second, the reform of the artillery arm by Gribeauval* and du Teil—whose brother was one of Napoleon's patrons and instructors—had created the most efficient and mobile artillery in Europe. Third, the separation of armies into autonomous and self-sufficient divisions that could proceed along several different roads simultaneously gave greater speed and flexibility to strategic movement. Fourth, the use of light skirmishers, who were detached from the line and could be shifted to harass, mask, or exploit, operated to confuse an enemy accustomed to fixed formations in which an encounter implied contact with an element of the main force. Fifth, the change from the line, which had emphasized defensive fire, to the attacking column, which emphasized shock—that is, the change from *l'ordre mince* to *l'ordre profond*—increased the sheer violence of battle as well as making use of less trained soldiers whose enthusiasm could compensate for their understandable reluctance to stand mutely while absorbing fire. The column could deploy large numbers of raw recruits, whereas the firing line required a steadiness and discipline that only highly trained troops could muster. Altogether, there was a "revolution in war" composed of the great increase in the number of soldiers, far larger and more sophisticated administrative services, innovative infantry tactics and technical improvements in artillery that "for the first time made possible the close co-ordination of infantry, cavalry and artillery in all phases of combat."[13]

Such armies awaited a commander who could disperse them along many routes, bringing them together at a decisive moment to crush the enemy in one state-shattering battle. Paret has speculated about the effect of these innovations had there been no Napoleon, that is, how they might have been used to create a French territorial state:

---

*"By boring out the barrels instead of casting the bore into the piece [Gribeauval] achieved finer tolerances, with less windage (the difference between the diameter of the cannonball and the diameter of the bore) to sap the power of gunpowder. A ball of given weight thus required less powder and smaller powder charges and allowed the walls of the chamber to be thinner." In addition, Gribeauval shortened barrels and also modified gun carriages to enhance mobility. John Lynn, "Jean-Baptiste de Gribeauval," in *The Reader's Companion to Military History*, ed. Robert Cowley and Geoffrey Parker (Houghton Mifflin, 1996). The French also standardized the calibre of cannon and fabricated interchangeable parts.

All that we know . . . suggests that had Napoleon been killed before Toulon . . . France would have ceased or at least slowed its efforts to destroy the European balance of power. Without his insistence on the immense exertions demanded by Europe-wide wars, the government would probably have been content with securing France's "natural" frontiers . . . Had further wars been waged, [the] Revolution and the transformation of war would still have left France the most powerful country in Europe but a country integrated in the political community, rather than dominating and indeed almost abolishing it.[14]

This strikes me as exactly right: but for Napoleon, France would have joined the society of territorial states instead of attempting to supplant it. And this speculation is important for our wider study, because it suggests that a revolution in military affairs is not sufficient, without further human agency, to bring a new constitutional order into being.

The French entered warfare in 1792 to defend their Revolution against invading reactionary forces; they continued these wars to spread the gospel of revolution to other states; and finally France pursued war to aggrandize the French state, which was represented as the embodiment of the Revolution. It is usually said that this progression represents a complete shift— from missionary crusade to imperial engorgement—but this fails to appreciate the constitutional outcome of the Revolution, the new state-nation. For such a state, the expansion of the State—the state that represents the nation—is not at all incompatible with popular sovereignty, nor is the state-nation's subjection of other states, either as satellites or as colonies. All energies are bent to the triumph of the state as apotheosis of the nation, and thus the champion of the people.

That the armies of France, which had once been welcomed by nationalists in Germany and elsewhere, were to become the target of local patriotic hostility tends to obscure this point, but that is only because we see this from the perspective of the nation-state and of national liberation movements. The nationalism of the state-nation, which created the imperial state, focused the will of the nation in serving the state, building in a kind of paradox at the inception: the great state-nations existed to promote liberty and equality, constitutionalism, and the rule of law; and yet in order to aggrandize the State, which was the deliverer of national identity and political liberty, other nations were subjugated and alien institutions superimposed upon them.

Napoleon transformed strategy on the basis of two strategic insights that he ultimately also used to create a new constitutional vision of the State. The first of these insights had been prefigured by du Teil, who, in his work *De l'usage de l'artillerie nouvelle dans la guerre de campagne*

(1778), had argued that concepts familiar in siege warfare could be employed on the battlefield, especially the way in which artillery fire could be concentrated to exploit a breach in the enemy's line of battle. Napoleon expanded this idea to an entire battle, and then, in his greatest innovation, to the enemy state itself. "Strategic plans are like sieges," he wrote; "concentrate your fire against a single point. Once the breach is made, the balance is shattered and all the rest becomes useless." Napoleon argued for the greatest concentration of force possible at a single point because this compelled the other side to give battle with armies sufficiently strong that their destruction would mean *political* collapse, threatening the very State itself. His strategy called for deep salients into enemy territory with large numbers of French troops. These penetrating maneuvers were managed by bringing autonomous divisions along many different routes to converge at a single point. As Sir Michael Howard has vividly described it,

> [t]his decisive concentration arose from an initial dispersal of forces, a deployment so wide that it was impossible to discern in advance where Napoleon intended to strike. In 1805 these corps were quartered all over western Europe—northern France, the Netherlands, Hanover—and were brought together with perfect timing to surround the Austrian army at Ulm. Then they dispersed, to converge on the Austrians and Russians at Austerlitz. The following year they advanced northward, spread out like beaters, to destroy the Prussians at Jena.[15]

Because they were autonomous and relatively smaller, these corps could be expected to live off the land, and travel on roads that could not otherwise accommodate armies of the size that would achieve Napoleon's goal.

The result was a new mobility, which made possible the concentration of superior force at the decisive point. Against a greater enemy force, Napoleon sought the point at which their forces were divided. Typically, in the coalitions of territorial states, it was a point between different national forces—and defeated each in detail, as happened in Italy in 1796 and almost again at Waterloo. Against an inferior force, Napoleon sought the point at which the enemy's communications were most vulnerable, so that either the opposing commander was forced to fight at a disadvantage or capitulate, as happened at Ulm in 1805.[16]

Napoleon himself, like all great innovators perhaps, doesn't seem to have appreciated the strategic and political reasons why the armies of the territorial states had ever bothered to use the old tactics before he arrived to teach them new ones. In exile, Napoleon criticized the dispersal of forces by a French general in the 1799 campaign as a vicious habit that made it impossible to achieve important results. "But that was the fashion in those days," he said sarcastically, "always to fight in little packets."[17] Fighting with much smaller armies within a system that permitted only minor gains and penalized risk, the territorial state performed according to a completely different strategic agenda. Napoleon freed French strategy from these restraints by adopting a different constitutional role for the French state that shattered the system that had imposed these restraints in the first place. This set the stage for Napoleon's second insight.

The strategic aim of preserving a balance of power, which is associated with the society of territorial states, reflected a quite different underlying political culture from one that sought collective security. Although we often think of maintaining the balance of power in a negative sense— states coalescing to defeat any attempt at hegemony—it also has an aspect of adjustment, in that whenever a member state is enlarged by gain, the others are given compensation to maintain the balance. This was the case, for example, in the partitions of Poland in 1772 and 1793. Thus the system is relatively tolerant of violence, so long as it is limited both as to means and ends. A collective security system, by contrast, is wholly intolerant of interstate violence and calls on all members to check an attack from any source. It is perfectly conceivable that the latter should have developed after the continental struggles to contain Charles V, and later Louis XIV, but this did not happen, partly no doubt because the leader of the coalition against the hegemony of the Habsburgs then became the state that drove for hegemony itself, and partly because the new society of states in Europe was still too fragile to evoke so strong a collective commitment from its members. Yet only such a system could have contained a state-nation of such dynamism as France under Napoleon's leadership.

In Napoleon history found an extremely aggressive and warlike personality mixed with an extraordinary talent for improvisation. He did not "regard war as an emergency measure, a measure of the last resort with which to repair the failures of diplomacy; instead it was the central element of his foreign policy."[18] He was thus able to turn the system he found in Europe against itself by playing on the competition among states inherent in the territorial system. Paret describes this well:

Nowhere was Napoleon's integration of diplomacy and violence more effective than in the manner in which he pursued the traditional goal of politically isolating a prospective opponent. . . . In December of [1805,] having seduced Prussia into neutrality, he defeated the Austrians and Russians. In 1806, England and Russia watched as the Prussian army was destroyed. The following spring he defeated the Prussian remnants and their Russian allies while Austria was still arming; and in 1809 Austria was once more defeated while potential supporters were still debating whether to come to its aid.[19]

Of course such a strategy depended on Napoleon first establishing his credibility—that he could, and would, actually put at risk stakes of his own such that battle would be on a scale and of such a ferocity as would jeopardize the survival of the state—and second, on molding a state that would permit such vast investments as to make these threats credible (as no territorial state could do).

There is a story told of the young Napoleon Bonaparte that is instructive in this respect. While a lieutenant in the artillery, he was present at the siege of Toulon, which he visited during a furlough. This city, then the center of resistance to the Revolution, sits at the midpoint of a bay forming a natural harbor and partly enclosed by heights at the harbor entrance. Napoleon is alleged to have advised the besieging revolutionary commander to move his artillery batteries from their position overlooking the city to the distant point that commanded the entrance to the bay. When this apparently counterintuitive advice—moving the besieging artillery beyond a range where it could shell the city—was taken, it had the effect of creating anxiety in the commander of the British fleet that lay in the harbor. He feared that French guns might cut off his means of exit. Accordingly he withdrew the fleet to a point beyond the mouth of the bay. When the British ships withdrew, however, morale among the citizens of Toulon collapsed, for they too had counted on an escape by sea should that prove necessary, and the city quickly surrendered. The remark attributed to Napoleon, as he pointed on the map to the remote edge of the harbor precipice, is "*There* lies Toulon."[20]

Just as Napoleon generalized to battle and then to the campaign itself the lessons of an artillery siege, so he generalized to the prevailing European political system the mentality of the siege commander who plays upon the morale of the defenders to give him victory at a reasonable cost. This strategy nicely suited Napoleon's tactical sense: he was uninterested in the capture of fortresses or the occupation of terrain, because these could not force the collapse of will that the destruction of the enemy's army accomplished. A dramatic defeat not only led to further reversals and withdrawals, but eventually had the effect of forcing the opposing government to withdraw its support from the multistate coalition. To achieve such a defeat, Napoleon had to entice the enemy into committing his main force in battle. This could only be accomplished through deep penetrations of enemy territory with the greatest force possible, often leaving his own communications and rear completely exposed. One example of this can be found in the Austerlitz campaign of 1805. Napoleon induced the main Austro-Russian army to launch a premature offensive, not waiting for Russian and Austrian reinforcements, by playing on the Austrian desire to reoccupy Vienna. Another example can be found in the 1806 campaign against Prussia, in which Napoleon advanced toward Berlin, creating a threat to which the Prussians had to respond, in a tactical context in which they were diverted by their anxiety about their capital. In both these cases, he did not aim at mere territory, but instead struck at the state: the state was forced to fight, for essentially political reasons, and inevitably found Napoleon well-prepared militarily for the confrontation that he alone truly sought.

Indeed Napoleon's defeat in Russia came about when he was unable to force the Russians to commit their main army to a climactic battle to save Moscow. To the contrary, the Russians burned their own capital and left Napoleon's army to starve in it. Although Russia was very much a member of the European society of powers, she was not a territorial state, and her dynasty did not constitutionally depend on the support of the nobility or the army. Russia was perfectly capable of a defense in depth because she was not defined, constitutionally, by her territorial extent. Because she faced a French army that was hopelessly overextended while she herself had all of Russia to withdraw into, she did so, laying waste to her own territory as Russian forces retreated.* When on September 14, 1812, Napoleon entered an undefended Moscow, and it was set ablaze that night by the Russians, the tsar astonishingly refused to negotiate a peace. As French communications and supply links collapsed, Napoleon abandoned Moscow on October 19, but heavy snowfalls transformed the retreat into a catastrophe: the French suffered more than 300,000 casualties from exposure, starvation, and the harrying fire of Russian forces.[21]

Napoleon thus was defeated in Russia not because the territorial state had found a successful strategy to parry his innovative techniques. Nor were territorial states eager to adopt Napoleonic methods. Indeed the states who opposed France well realized that a fundamental shift in the nature of the state was a prerequisite to fielding a nation in arms by mass conscription, whose officers had been given open access to commissions, and which often was fed by requisition—although it gradually did appear that this could be done without the revolutionary upheavals that took place in France. When these changes did come, they spread to other states the state-nation model of government of which the Napoleonic state was an early example.

---

*A similar argument might be made regarding the Peninsular Campaign by Wellington, who adopted tactics that would not have been politically feasible had he been a Spanish or even Portuguese commander.

The new monarchies who came to power, after the Revolution of 1830, Louis Philippe and Leopold I, sought the sanction of "the people" as king "of the French" and "of the Belgians," rather than of France or Belgium. Even the reactionary Tsar Nicholas I, three years after crushing the Polish uprising of 1830–1831, proclaimed that his own authority was based on nationality (as well as autocracy and Orthodoxy)—and his word *narodnost,* also meaning "spirit of the people," was copied from the Polish *narodowosc.*[22]

This model was very different from that of the nation-state, and Napoleon himself, as well as the architects of the Vienna state system that institutionalized his defeat, were careful not to nurture such states. For a time Napoleon enjoyed a reputation as a liberator, arising from his 1796 campaign in Italy,[23] in which, as a general of the Revolution, he prised Lombardy from the Austrians and established the Cisalpine Republic, whose capital was in Milan. But in the beginning of 1799, having annexed Tuscany and Piedmont, and having established republics in Rome and Naples, the Directory studiedly refused to assemble an Italian nation-state. Once Napoleon seized power he annexed Piedmont directly to France in 1802, and the Ligurian Republic, whose capital was Genoa, in 1805; in 1801 he had decreed a constitution for the Cisalpine Republic and was named president of what he agreed to call the Italian Republic. Belgium—the Austrian Netherlands—had been occupied in 1795 and formally annexed to France in 1797. The left bank of the Rhine had been annexed by France in 1797 and by 1803 all but three of the ecclesiastical princes had lost their sovereignty, as had all but six of the fifty-one imperial towns and cities. Several south German states were carved out or enlarged, but there was never any question of creating a new German state.

The kingdoms of Westphalia and Bavaria and the Grand Duchy of Warsaw were all French satellites. For a time Holland was made a kingdom under Napoleon's brother Louis, but when this monarch showed too much independence, the Dutch state was annexed directly to the French Empire. Joseph Bonaparte was first King of Naples, and was then replaced by the French marshal Murat when Joseph became king of Spain. In all of these states, important reforms were accomplished: serfdom was abolished (in varying practical degrees), French-style prefectures were set up in some of the German states, a civil code was introduced, and new written constitutions were promulgated. But at no time was there any contemplation of creating actual states whose legitimacy derived either from the fact that their institutions were expressions of national will or that they sought responsibility for the welfare of the nation. Napoleon's remark regarding the Polish Sejm (parliament) is instructive: "As for their deliberating assemblies, their *liberum veto,* their diets on horseback with drawn swords, I want nothing of that. . . . I want Poland only as a disciplined force, to furnish a battlefield."[24]

Nor did the Peace Settlement of 1814–1815, following Napoleon's defeat, seek to create national states: quite the opposite. The claims of Holland were extended to include Belgium; Piedmont was enlarged to include Genoa and Nice, then handed over to the House of Savoy; Austria annexed Lombardy as well as Venice; Pius VII recovered the Papal States; and Poland was reorganized into little more than a province of Russia, three-quarters of the size of the Grand Duchy of Warsaw, while most Poles continued to live under Prussian or Austrian rule. The Federal Diet in Frankfurt was not to be a popularly elected parliament; on the contrary, it was to be a body of state representatives of thirty-nine different German governments, including Austria and Prussia, both of which lay partly outside the German Confederation. Sweden and Norway were joined in a forced marriage. And, interestingly for our study, England secured to herself the Cape of Good Hope, Ceylon, Malta, and the Ionian Islands. Insofar as the wishes of the national peoples involved were contemplated at all, they were calculatedly frustrated.

Despite Napoleon's loss, however, the state-nation had triumphed and its imperatives were to govern not only the Peace Settlement but the peace itself. The myth that united strategy and law in every period became now a national myth, epitomized by the merging of the State into the personal and quasi-religious roles once occupied by princes.

> National history was depicted by writers both of school textbooks and of popular works as the history of the Nation's military triumphs. Other Nations were defined by these authors in terms of military relations. Foreigners were people with whom one went to war and usually defeated, and if one had not done so the last time, one certainly would the next. [O]ne found personal fulfillment in making "the supreme sacrifice" so that the national cause might triumph . . .[25]

It is important to appreciate the characteristics of such a state in order to understand the nature of the international society composed of such states. Napoleon had forced every territorial state eventually to conform itself to the state-nation model if it was to compete militarily. Armies of conscripts, meritocratic and bourgeois ministries, broad-based taxation without exemptions for the nobility, all spread across Europe, just as mercenary and nonstate elements vanished from the forces of the great powers.[26] Most importantly for our purposes, the triumph of the state-nation meant that the legitimacy of this constitutional form was recognized by the congress of states that wrote the peace. The creation of this congress we owe to one remarkable figure more than to any other, and it is perhaps only from the present perspective that we can truly appreciate his achievement.

Robert Stewart, Viscount Castlereagh, the British foreign minister from 1812 to 1822, was born in 1769, the same year as Napoleon, his great adversary, and Wellington, his principal political and personal ally. This proud, uncharismatic* man understood the requirements of the new society of state-nations and labored selflessly to bring about its harmony. At the time, he was little understood and greatly vilified; both Byron[27] and Shelley† wrote remarkably cruel lines to immortalize their hatred of him, and even today he has yet to find a diplomatic biographer sufficiently attentive to his conceptions for Europe. For the most part such biographers are either apt to be defensive in tone[28] or they are mesmerized by the voluptuous characters of his cynical contemporaries, Talleyrand and Metternich.[29] From our current perspective, however, one can see in Castlereagh's work an achievement of such magnitude that it becomes clear how, despite the incomprehension of his successors and the hostility to his designs of his continental collaborators, it survived to give Europe peace for forty years. To appreciate this, let us revisit the endgame of the epochal French War, and its resolution at Vienna.

Having abandoned Russia, Napoleon was on the defensive in 1813. As he retreated from the Rhine late in that year, Wellington crossed the Pyrenees and successfully attacked Bayonne. Holland rose in revolt and expelled the French imperial civil and military officers. Early in November the Austrian foreign minister, Prince Metternich, made a peace overture that would have acknowledged French conquests through 1796, leaving Belgium, the German left bank, and Nice-Savoy under French rule. Napoleon rejected these terms. On December 21, the armies of the coalition crossed the Rhine, beginning the invasion of northern France. But in February, encouraged by recent victories in the field, the French emperor again rejected peace offers, this time confining France to the boundaries of 1792. Only at this juncture was Castlereagh able to secure an allied agreement, signed March 9 at Chaumont in Champagne, that the war should be fought out until a definitive victory had been won and, more importantly, that the alliance would continue after its victory. The language of the treaty is significant:

---

*"Last night I toss'd and turned in bed, But could not sleep—at length I said, I'll think of Viscount C—stl—r—gh, And of speeches—that's the way." Thomas Moore, "Insurrection of the Papers," from Richard Kenin and Justin Wintle, *The Dictionary of Bibliographical Quotation* (Knopf, 1978), 146.

†"I met Murder on the way—/He had a mask like Castlereagh—/Very smooth he looked, yet grim;/Seven blood-hounds followed him;/All were fat, and well they might/Be in admirable plight,/For one by one, and two by two,/He tossed them human hearts to chew/Which from his wide cloak he drew." Percy Bysshe Shelley, *The Mask of Anarchy: Written on the Occasion of the Massacre at Manchester* (Reeves and Turner, 1887), 57.

The present Treaty of Alliance having for its object the maintenance of a balance of Europe, to secure the repose and independence of the Powers, and to prevent the invasions which for so many years have devastated the world, the High Contracting Parties have agreed among themselves to extend its duration for twenty years from the date of signature.[30]

This treaty held the coalition together until the Peace of 1814–1815 was completed, providing the basis for the First and Second Treaties of Paris and for the Congress of Vienna. Chaumont is the source of "the first notable experiment in institutionalizing the principles of concert and balance in behalf of European peace,"[31] where the key word is "institutionalize." The Congress system took the wartime coalition of collective security and applied it to peacetime, in much the same way that the North Atlantic Treaty Organization has operated in our own time, persisting beyond the Cold War to provide a framework for subsequent collective action in Iraq, Bosnia, and Kosovo.

It was Castlereagh's strategic innovation to use the wartime coalition to maintain the peace. To accomplish this, he undertook the following, highly difficult objectives: (1) he had to dismantle the Napoleonic superstate, while preserving the state-nation of France to such a degree that it would legitimate its new regime (rather than stigmatizing it as the collaborationist party that had sold out France to her enemies); (2) he had to persuade the allies that their cooperation in the face of tantalizing French offers and menacing French threats had ultimately been worthwhile, which meant that while British allies would receive substantial territorial gains, the British would not; (3) he had to institutionalize the directorate of the Congress so that it met regularly to continue multistate collaboration, and yet somehow keep it from turning into an instrument of internal repression when member-states felt threatened by revolutions in various European countries; (4) he had to win credible commitments of armed force of such overwhelming magnitude that no single power or coalition of two of the five great powers could be reasonably hopeful of success through war; (5) he had to do all these things while facing stiff opposition in his own party from George Canning, whose rhetorical gifts and skill at playing on public opinion he could not hope to match, and from Whigs who portrayed him as a mere henchman of the reactionary Metternich, and (6) he had to act in concert with Prussians who wanted a Carthaginian peace, Russians who were entertaining the idea of a continental hegemony at German expense, Austrians who felt threatened by the new development of the state-nation and its ability to exploit national sentiments, and the French, who saw England as their primary persecutor and the frustrator of their continental dreams.

Nor was the environment of the Congress suited to his virtues. Castlereagh was honorable and undevious;[32] Metternich and Talleyrand were notably, even ostentatiously, neither. Castlereagh was tolerant in religious matters (though an Anglo-Irish peer, he had long supported Catholic emancipation, and resigned from the government in 1801[33] when the king refused to sign the emancipation act) and modest in his deportment; by contrast, Tsar Alexander I, the most flamboyant and politically indispensable personage at the Congress, persuaded every single party attending to sign a declaration in behalf of a "decent Christian order" (except the Ottoman sultan, the Pope—who refused to sign along with Orthodox and Protestant monarchs—and Great Britain), kept spectacular mistresses, and was acknowledged even in this society as a narcissistic megalomaniac. Yet, despite all these obstacles, Castlereagh did to a very large degree succeed.

Castlereagh played, first, on the awareness of all parties that a few states, collectively, possessed preponderant armed force and second, on the fact that while any one of these states could mobilize an entire nation to inflict horrific damage on the others, any further international conflict was sure to arouse the will of nations to seize their states because the mobilization of entire national peoples produced a larger and more critical audience for public decisions. Between these two apprehensions, fear of military defeat and fear of domestic upheaval, Castlereagh strung his diplomatic strategy. As we will see, it really had very little to do with the "balance of power" as that term had been used in Europe since Utrecht, although labeling it as such gave it the status of precedent.

As we have observed, the eighteenth century armies fielded by territorial states were (compared to their successors) relatively small and highly professional. Prior to the 1790s a military treaty might call for the provision of a force of 18,000 or 24,000—reckoned in the Roman units of 6,000 soldiers associated with the legion. In a previous chapter, the increase in size brought about by Frederick the Great was noted; yet on only two or three occasions did he ever commit more than 50,000 men to a battle. The French *levée en masse,* a nationwide mobilization, transformed this scale. In 1808, on the eve of the campaign that ended at Wagram, Napoleon commanded some 300,000 troops in Spain, another 100,000 in France, some 200,000 in the Rhineland, and another 60,000 in Italy. One expert has calculated that between 1800 and 1815, the number of Frenchmen called up reached two million, of whom an estimated 400,000 died either in service or as a result of service in war.[34] By the time of the Hundred Days, the Coalition was able to field quickly 750,000 men, of whom 225,000 converged on Waterloo. Such magnitudes transfixed the attention of every political leader in Europe. Armies of this size meant that a campaign prosecuted on a continental scale would risk destroying the state that waged it, as indeed the French state had been destroyed, but only if opposing forces of comparable size could be mustered.

This was the true *balance* in Castlereagh's calculations: a collective security force of such immense magnitude that it would deter any great power from aggression. As Ford has observed, Castlereagh's "position rested on the belief that genuine national interests, clearly recognized, could create in Europe an equilibrium of forces capable of rendering war unfeasible for any one power, or even for a coalition unless directed against a single aggressor."[35]

To maintain such a coalition credibly required a commitment from all the major states. Even if the benefits to the common good justified a common effort, what was to prevent any single state from opting out of such an effort and still enjoying the fruits of general security? If the cost of a European conflict was so horrific, why wouldn't a state simply let the others fight—or not fight, for that matter? For if one state kept out, why would its rivals bleed themselves white in a conflict for the common good? If one state did keep out, why wouldn't the others do likewise, leaving the field to the most aggressive state? This problem required Castlereagh to exploit the second overwhelming impression of the wars that had just ended: wherever the war had been taken, large and hostile popular insurrections had been touched off. These occurred in Belgium in 1798, Naples in 1799 and 1806, Spain in 1808, and the Netherlands in 1811–1812. There is some dispute whether these were national uprisings or simply revolts of a familiar kind against the requisitioning by troops of foodstuffs, horses, and equipment. It is of no matter: in either case, war on an international scale meant unleashing popular national forces that the state could not control.

This was the problem of the state-nation, which, unlike the nation-state, had no broad-based elective assemblies to mediate strategic decisions and, speaking comparatively, little free press to articulate and educate public opinion. The state-nation, however, did have positive characteristics that Castlereagh understood perfectly. Its leadership was cosmopolitan, it could take decisions quickly and make commitments over the long term, and it possessed a mercantile and industrial tax base that could benefit from defense preparations and direct military expenditures. It was, in short, ideal for the innovation of the Congress, which Castlereagh introduced at Vienna, having insisted on provisions for this mechanism in the preceding treaties among the allies.

There had of course been other conferences and congresses before Vienna; two or three, the Westphalian conferences at Münster and Osnabrück in 1648, and that at Utrecht in 1713, have been discussed, and form the subject of Part II in Book II. Those congresses, however, met for the sole purpose of arranging peace settlements—where settlement was the objective, including parceling out the territorial spoils of war. The Congress of Vienna was something new.* Of this Congress Metternich wrote,

> No great political insight is needed to see that this Congress could not
> be modeled on any which had taken place. Former assemblies which
> were called congresses met for the express purpose of settling a quarrel
> between two or more belligerent powers—the issue being a peace
> treaty. On this occasion peace had already been made and the parties
> meet as friends who, though differing in their interests, wish to work
> together toward the conclusion and affirmation of the existing treaty.[36]

Relying on the Treaty of Chaumont, a secret article inserted in the first Treaty of Paris had reserved the determination of Europe's ordering to the great powers of the Coalition. Castlereagh now concluded the Quadruple Alliance of November 1815, which reiterated the key features of Chaumont but stipulated that the great powers would hold periodic conferences,

> for the purpose of consulting upon their interests, or for the considera-
> tion of measures which . . . shall be considered the most salutary for the
> purpose and prosperity of Nations and the maintenance for the Peace of
> Europe.[37]

"Thus," as Craig and George put it, "the new order was in a sense given both a constitution and a constitutional watchdog (as defined by the final act), and a concert of powers to watch over it."[38]

At Vienna, diplomats of the great powers met repeatedly with each other and with parties as various as the Vatican emissary, the sultan of Turkey, rival Italian factions, thirty German princes, and representatives of the Jews of Frankfurt am Main. Meanwhile, ten special commissions dealt with specific questions ranging from the organization of Germany and Switzerland to topics such as population statistics, diplomatic rules, and the vexing matter of the slave trade. There was no plenary session of all the delegates until the signing of the final comprehensive treaty, called—as with the Helsinki Accords in our own day, which the Congress prefigured—the Final Act. The historian Jacques Droz has concluded,

> [t]rue, it was scarcely possible to talk of limiting State sovereignty in
> favour of an international organization. Nonetheless, the results
> achieved at Vienna were inspired by a certain concept of international
> relations which excluded the use of force and which consequently rep-

*For a more detailed discussion of the Congress, see Chapter 22.

resented a considerable advance on the highway robbery of the eighteenth century.[39]

The course of the Congress did not run entirely smooth. The tsar and the Prussians were not quite willing to abandon their goals of using the Congress to win historic territorial concessions. Tsar Alexander's ambition was to gain a Polish kingdom that would recover for Poland all of Prussia's share in the partitions of 1793 and 1795, with the tsar as king. Prussia, for its part, wished to annex the whole of Saxony.

On January 3, 1815, Castlereagh concluded a secret agreement with Austria and France to resist, by force of arms if necessary, these extreme claims. It has been questioned by historians whether this was in fact merely a bluff; Castlereagh would have been hard put to secure the approval of Parliament for such a war. However that may be, the agreement, which was quickly leaked, had the desired effects both of bringing France into the Alliance, and of persuading Prussia and Russia promptly to moderate their demands. Within six weeks the Polish and Saxon questions had been resolved by compromise, and the Final Act was signed on June 9, 1815.

Of all the powers of the coalition, Britain took away the least in territorial gains. It annexed nothing on the continent. It returned scores of overseas areas seized and occupied during the years of warfare. At Ghent, moreover, Castlereagh had concluded a treaty with the United States that ended the War of 1812 on terms so generous in light of the British capture of Washington that American students are routinely taught that the United States actually won the war. This far-sighted statesman had, more than any other person at the Congress, created a permanent system of consultation, a genuine "concert of Europe."

On November 20, 1815, the coalition partners committed themselves for twenty years each to contribute 60,000 men should there be any attempt to overturn the settlement. In the meantime, however, Alexander had drawn up the Treaty of the Holy Alliance, a union of the tsar's religious convictions (Castlereagh called it "a piece of sublime mysticism and nonsense"[40]) and Metternich's reactionary intrigue. This treaty, though innocuous enough on its face, in fact sought to organize the powers of Europe for intervention against internal revolution. Such a step was viewed by Castlereagh as a subversion of the true purpose of the Congress and in a diplomatic note of October 19, 1818, Castlereagh protested that

> nothing would be more immoral or more prejudicial to the character of governments generally than the idea that their force was collectively to be prostituted to the support of established power without any consideration of the extent to which it was abused.[41]

Confronting this nineteenth century version of the Brezhnev Doctrine, Castlereagh continued to cling to the hope that peace could be maintained among nations whose internal systems remained their own affair. Two months after the Holy Alliance was concluded, Castlereagh renewed the Treaty of Chaumont and arranged for the periodical calling of international congresses. The first of these meetings, the Congress of Aix-la-Chapelle in the autumn of 1818, seemed to reinforce his hopes. He and Wellington attended for Britain; for Austria, the emperor Francis I and Metternich; for Russia, the tsar and Nesselrode; for Prussia, Frederick William III; for France, Talleyrand's successor (Talleyrand having resigned to become Louis XVIII's royal chamberlain). Although the Quadruple Alliance was reaffirmed, a new agreement, the Quintuple Alliance, was formed to admit France into the society of great powers "to protect the arts of peace." All occupation forces agreed to leave French soil; progress was made on a more generous definition of Jewish rights, the abolition of the slave trade, and mediation between Sweden and Denmark. Yet beneath this harmony, there lay a fundamental division of purpose as to the proper scope of the emerging directorate of the five powers.

The three eastern monarchies held the view that political revolutions were the responsibility of governments, like other public order problems—crime, for example, or epidemics and panics. When, therefore, a revolution broke out within the European world, it was the responsibility first of the state government, but second, if necessary, of the international directorate—the *Concert of Powers,* as the phrase was first used at Aix-la-Chapelle (Aachen)—to stabilize the situation. All this they had learned from Napoleon, who had used the rhetoric of revolution to bridge state boundaries, and had effectively exploited civil discontent as a strategic weapon.

Castlereagh did not share this view. For one thing, he knew that the British Parliament would not support a policy of constant intervention in other states, particularly to prop up repressive regimes. This meant that the directorate would proceed without British consent—that was part of the rules—and that this would gradually isolate Great Britain. Second, he saw that enlarging the agenda of the Concert moved the powers away from the two contexts of concern on which he had relied for their cooperation, for while revolutionary activity might arise from national feeling and might by contagion threaten neighboring regimes, it did not necessarily arouse a national people to arms against their neighbors. Once the focus was off this threat to international security, the states of the coalition would not need to hang together and would soon split into rival camps, in part on the basis of their differing attitudes about political reform. It was at Aix-la-Chapelle that Castlereagh condemned all efforts "to provide the transparent soul of the Holy Alliance with a body."[42] Even a new revolt in France, he added, would openly justify intervention only if it were judged that the result would be the arming of the nation for conquest elsewhere. By adroit diplomacy he was also able to prevent discussion of the question of intervention against the Latin American colonies that were in revolt against Spain.

When the following year, however, military revolts occurred in Spain itself and in Naples—a rising of the Cadiz regiments against Ferdinand VII, a revolt of the Carbonari against Ferdinand I—there was no deflecting the debate over intervention. By means of the diplomatic note of May 5, 1820, Castlereagh was able temporarily to prevent intervention in Spain. With regard to the Neapolitan uprising, which alarmed the Austrians, who held significant and restive territories in Italy, Metternich was able to win consent of the other powers to a military expedition, and a new conference was promptly proposed by the tsar. Castlereagh did not oppose Austrian intervention, but strongly opposed intervention by the alliance, and he tried to avoid the convening of a new conference.

The tsar insisted, however, and Castlereagh was forced to be content with sending low-level representation. The Congress of Troppau, in October 1820, met in Silesia to consider the revolutions then in progress against the Bourbon monarchs of the Two Sicilies and Spain. On November 19, Metternich laid before the congress a document, already signed by Russia, Prussia, and Austria, which dealt with the question of revolutions in general and the right of the alliance to deal with them by force. This *Protocole* had been drawn up by the Russians, and announced the intention

> to prevent the progress of the evil with which the body social is menaced, and to devise remedies where its ravages have begun or are anticipated . . . When States [which have undergone a change due to revolution] cause by their proximity other countries to fear immediate danger . . . the Allied Powers . . . will employ . . . measures of coercion if the employment of such coercion is indispensable.

From London, Castlereagh acted quickly. He called in the Russian ambassador and stated:

> On viewing . . . the spectacle now presented by the Troppau reunion, it is impossible not to consider the right which the Monarchs claim to judge and to condemn the actions of other States as a precedent dangerous to the liberties of the world. . . . [N]o man can see without a certain feeling of fear the lot of every nation submitted to the decisions and to the will of such a tribunal.[43]

Then he rewrote the State Paper of May 5, 1820, which had come straight from his own pen. Phrased in sometimes lengthy and complex sentences, it nevertheless goes directly to the heart of the matter with two lucid arguments. First, are the great powers prepared to apply such principles for intervention to themselves? Second, while it was true that the revolution that brought Napoleon to power had unleashed a conflict with an entire nation in arms, this was due to the particular state involved, France, and not simply to the fact it was triggered by a revolution: of "that spirit of military energy which was the distinctive and most formidable character of the French Revolution . . . the late revolutions have as yet exhibited no symptom." Indeed the massed opposition of the great powers to a national revolt was precisely what could evoke such a force: "The apprehension of an armed interference in their internal affairs may excite them to arm, may induce them to look with greater jealousy and distrust than ever to the conduct of their rulers . . ." Finally, he concluded:

> What hope in such a case of a better order of things to result from the prudence and calm deliberations among a people agitated by the apprehensions of foreign force, and how hopeless on the other hand the attempt to settle by foreign arms or foreign influence alone any stable or national system of government![44]

It was possible, Castlereagh believed, for a nation to create "a better order of things"—a state-nation—without terrorizing one's neighbors. Britain had done so. But this was only possible if the nation was not menaced by foreign threats.

The reader will recognize from this paper the two wellsprings of Castlereagh's policy described earlier—the consequences of provoking a nation in arms, and the danger of nationalism—as well as his conclusion that, in such an historical context, peaceful change in one state need not jeopardize the interests of others. Tying these ideas together implied that intervening to arrest change was actually the surest route to a general conflagration. Moreover, Castlereagh's first point suggests that the great powers are in some sense obliged to obey the same rules they would prescribe for others, a dimension of collective security regimes that is often overlooked. If it was strategically shrewd to avoid a massive intervention in order not to unite a nation in arms, it was also a strategic consequence of the constitutional objectives of the Coalition: to preserve a society of states that were secure from territorial trespass.

The *Protocole* was withdrawn. Metternich was able to deflect Russian offers of assistance in dealing with the Neapolitan revolt, and a new venue, Laibach, was chosen for the concluding stages of the conference. The Congress of Laibach, which in January 1821 authorized Austrian intervention, is often taken as marking the ruin of Castlereagh's project. As Sir Harold Nicolson wrote, "The Great Coalition was thus finally dissolved;

the Concert of Europe had disintegrated; the Holy Alliance had succeeded in destroying the Quadruple Alliance; the Congress system had failed."[45] This was not Castlereagh's view at the time, however, and in any case, it tends to overemphasize the purely formal aspects of his program.

At Troppau, Britain had opposed any project for sending troops into either Spain or Naples, and the allies had deferred to British objections regarding a proposed intervention in Madrid. But the other powers at the congress had also voted to authorize military action by Austrian forces in Italy and to ask that a Russian army of 90,000 men stand by to march there from Poland if necessary. At Laibach, Ferdinand himself appeared before the conference and Metternich sought and obtained permission for Austria to act alone in Italy. Austrian troops—not, it must be emphasized, troops from the coalition—restored the regime in Naples. When the Circular of December 8, 1820, out of Laibach reiterated the claims of the alliance to intervene against revolutionary activity, Castlereagh responded with his own paper, the British Circular of January 19, 1821. In it the allies read that

> the British government would . . . regard the principles on which these measures rest to be such as could not be safely admitted as a system of international law. . . . [The government does] not regard the Alliance as entitled, under existing treaties, to assume, in their character as allies, any such general powers.

The distinction is crucial:* Castlereagh was prepared to accept Austrian intervention as the act of a state that had, after all, substantial security interests that were jeopardized by events in the Italian peninsula. A great power was permitted to intervene in its sphere of influence, acting on its own behalf. He was not prepared to agree to the alliance acting in concert on Austria's behalf in order to pacify an Austrian possession. Metternich professed horror that the December circular had been leaked; he presaged Nicolson in his exclamation, *"Les bienfaits de l'Alliance Européenne etaient suspendus."* He could not resist including in the final declarations from Laibach a ban by the allied sovereigns on all revolutions. Yet it was also announced that another conference would be summoned the next year at Florence (it was actually held at Verona) to reconsider the occupation of Naples and Piedmont. Castlereagh responded to this declaration on the floor of the House of Commons on June 21, 1821. He reiterated his objections but stated that he did not think a new protest was required. He

---

*And one that eluded much thinking about the United Nations in our own era: Article 51 of the U.N. Charter is either the sine qua non of a collective security regime, or the United Nations is really a vehicle to ensure the balance of power via the Security Council. Usually commentators get this point backwards, thinking Article 51 inimical to the integrity of the system.

subsequently made clear, and Metternich confirmed, that each regarded the alliance as the best means of preventing aggressive action by a great power. Both men planned to convene a new Congress of Vienna to discuss the Spanish question, following the ministerial meeting in Verona that was devoted to Italian affairs.

There Metternich hoped to collaborate with Castlereagh to *prevent* Russia from supporting French intervention in Spain. The tsar, whose close relations with Castlereagh were unique in the diplomatic world, had asked to meet with him in Vienna. It is clear that the latter dreaded the upcoming meetings in Verona, where he would be required to repeat the British position on what was no longer a live question, and at one time he entertained a proposal by Metternich that he simply skip Verona and come to Vienna in late August, before the sovereigns met, in order to have preliminary conversations with Metternich.

Castlereagh was, at this time, perhaps the most unpopular man in English public life. He had for a long time been forced to carry pistols to protect himself, and his life had often been threatened. To Liberals he was the embodiment of repression abroad; in his own party, of which he was effectively the prime minister during this period, he was isolated by his long-standing hostility to Canning, and indeed to the whole world of public relations that Canning represented, and his closest connections in public life were confined to the king and the Duke of Wellington.

On August 9, he seems to have had something like a breakdown. That day he saw both the king and the duke—the latter said, in his characteristic way, "I am bound to warn you that you cannot be in your right mind," to which Castlereagh replied, rather pathetically, "Since you say so I fear it must be so." The duke offered to stay with him, but Castlereagh would not consent to this. Wellington then tried without success to contact Castlereagh's doctor. Castlereagh paid a visit to the king, who was preparing to leave for Scotland. The king, also alarmed, alerted Liverpool, the titular prime minister, who refused to credit the report that Castlereagh, always so notably self-possessed, had become deranged. An interview with the doctor ensued; he was not greatly concerned. Castlereagh went to his country house and was kept in bed during the 10th and 11th. He was bled and given "lowering" drugs, which might be called tranquilizers nowadays; however, they had the effect of inducing a violent delirium. The next morning, the 12th, he cut his throat with a small knife and died immediately. At his burial in Westminster Abbey, large hostile crowds filled the streets, and malicious cheers were given as the coffin was carried into the Abbey.

This event utterly changed all that followed. At Verona, Metternich was isolated—Castlereagh's replacement at the conference, the Duke of Wellington, having arrived only when the issues had already been decided.

At Vienna, there was no powerful influence to divert Russian support from France, which wished to take the initiative of intervening in Spain where a fresh revolt at Cadiz had broken out. Chateaubriand, the architect of French intervention in Spain, understood this.

> I believe that Europe (and in particular France) will gain by the death of the first minister of Great Britain. Castlereagh would have done much harm at Vienna. His connections with Metternich were obscure and disquieting; Austria deprived of a dangerous support will be forced to come near to us.[46]

Moreover, Castlereagh was replaced at the Foreign Ministry by Canning, who despised the Congress system, had no relationship with the tsar, whom he loathed, and who was determined to reduce the Alliance to its component parts. In support of his policy, he had decided to enlist public opinion, which he did in a series of declarations that inspired liberal reformers throughout Europe.

Whether or not Castlereagh could have achieved the legal and strategic point at Vienna on which he insisted—that the Alliance could not intervene as an Alliance in domestic affairs—can we agree that his system basically failed? Ford's conclusion that "[a]fter Verona, now one and then another major state took the initiative, employing means and encountering responses most of which would have been familiar to 18th century statesmen"[47] suggests a reversion to the diplomacy of territorial states.

This remark, like Nicolson's, implicitly dismisses much of the point of Castlereagh's efforts, and in any case bears only glancingly on the subject of our inquiry. Whatever the form of the congresses—and these have lingered on to our own day and were a prominent feature of the nineteenth century—Castlereagh's great innovations were not procedural only. This fact is made clearer if we appreciate the difference between Castlereagh's objectives and those suggested by the phrase *balance of power,* so often associated with the Vienna settlement.

For Castlereagh, the term *equilibrium* had a different meaning from that of the phrase *balance of power* as that phrase was understood at Utrecht and by the territorial states. He sought to introduce a benign, shared hegemony based on a mutual recognition of rights underpinned by law. His goal was a constitutional transformation of the society of states, and this objective contrasted sharply with the system of territorial states and its competitive rather than collaborative design. Indeed one can see retrograde "balance of power" thinking as responsible for Napoleon's initial success: while Austria attempted to check French aggression, Prussia and Russia carved up Poland; at the same time, Britain helped herself to France's overseas possessions. The first three coalitions were flawed, as

Paul Schroeder has argued in *The Transformation of European Politics: 1763–1848*,[48] not, as is usually maintained, owing to the failure of the allies to coalesce militarily but rather in their inability to concert their basic interests. The "balance of power" of the ancien régime, "a balance among hostile forces," does not promote such harmony, and perhaps does not hold it even to be possible.[49]

It was only when European statesmen adopted the goals of political cooperation and compromise that victory over France was achieved. "The final coalition against Napoleon preserved its unity, paradoxically, by putting agreed political aims before purely military concerns." After 1815, Castlereagh's vision of equilibrium—a system of collective security—was enhanced by the readmission of France to the concert.

It is customary to think of the Vienna settlement in Metternichian terms: as a restoration of reactionary constitutional ideas. But this view arises as much from the political perspective today associated with contemporary realism as it once did from the politics of radicalism. Indeed one sees it most formidably in Henry Kissinger's descriptions of the Vienna settlement.[50] Schroeder, on the other hand, argues that the Vienna system was in fact "progressive, [and] oriented in practical, non-Utopian ways toward the future." This system proved itself able to handle the Spanish and Greek crises, and emerged intact from the revolutionary crises of 1848. It faced its most damaging threats from the shortsightedness of Canning and Palmerston, who wished for roles in the already outmoded theatre of the competitive balance of power. Castlereagh's *equilibrium* amounted to an imaginative transformation of the power politics of the territorial states. The difference can be appreciated when one notes that, during the turbulence of 1848, the members of the concert did not use the various revolutions as an opportunity to aggrandize themselves at the expense of their rivals, in contrast to the behavior of the great powers during the revolutionary wars of a half century before. As John Lynn has perceptively summarized:

> Many have responded by arguing that the Congress respected and established a balance of power to Europe. However, balance of power thinking was hardly original; it had underlain treaty settlements for the preceding century and a half and they had not brought lasting peace. Something else was involved. Rather than create a balance among hostile forces, the statesmen of Europe created an international system based on compromise and consent . . . regulated through a series of periodic international conferences. In short, the Congress of Vienna did not bring a return to the old international politics of the eighteenth century, but accepted and furthered new approaches to the international system . . .[51]

In 1793, when he was twenty-four, Castlereagh had written his uncle: "The tranquillity of Europe is at stake, and we contend with an opponent whose strength we have no means of measuring. It is the first time that all the population and all the wealth of a great kingdom has been concentrated in the field."[52]

On this insight—his appreciation of the emergence of the new state-nation on the international scene—he built a constitutional system that long outlasted the conflicts he was called upon to resolve. Until the advent of the nation-state made it unfeasible, the Concert of Europe was able to cope with every crisis between 1815 and 1854 by finding a solution that prevented the outbreak of war. This was true in the Belgian crisis of 1830, the Near Eastern crisis of 1838, and the first Schleswig-Holstein crisis of 1850, to take only the most dramatic disputes.

In his last interview with the king, Castlereagh is recorded as having said, in despair, "Sir! it is necessary to say goodbye to Europe; you and I alone know it and have saved it; no one after me understands the affairs of the continent."[53]

This remark is sometimes attributed to his mania; and there is no doubt that he may have exaggerated matters when he politely included his sovereign in the role of statesman, a claim that must have pleased, if mystified, the insular king; but is there not something to it? And doesn't it, with the youthful remark of thirty years earlier, fittingly bracket the remarkable insight of this lonely, much vilified, and rarest of personalities? When his system ultimately failed, after 1870, it was in part because the object of his insight, the society of state-nations, was to be replaced.

The period of the ancien régime had been forcibly ended by the French Revolution. This constitutional transformation demanded a commensurate revolution in strategy. The new French state could not avail itself of the hierarchical and aristocratic military structure of the territorial state. Once a new strategy was found, its triumph was made possible by the political mobilization of the mass of the French people on behalf of their national identity and on behalf of the state that did so much to define that identity. Thus in this instance constitutional innovation drove strategic innovation, which relied ultimately on the popular effects of the constitutional change that had set the new strategy in motion in the first instance.

Therefore we are unable to say precisely that causality flows in one direction only between military and constitutional innovation. As Black observes:

War is often seen as a forcer of . . . governmental . . . innovation in the shape of the demands created by the burdens of major conflicts. . . . [I]t can be argued [however] that many military changes reflected political-governmental counterparts rather than causing them.[54]

Nevertheless, it is true that, as David Parrott notes, "the direct link between military change and state development remains: developments in the art of war are still attached to the idea of progress in achieving a modern administrative/bureaucratic state."

Yet what is missing in such an account is the role of history itself with respect to law and strategy. Law and strategy are mutually affecting. All of these historians realize that, though none identify the reason this is so. The causal model these scholars have in mind, by which strategic innovation forces constitutional change, or sometimes vice versa, tends to obscure the fact that the link between the two is not merely causal but relational. Every change in the constitutional arrangements of the State will have strategic consequences, and also the other way around, so that innovation in either sphere will be reflected in the degree of legitimacy achieved by the State, because legitimation is the reason for which a constitution exists, for which the State makes war.*

One can say, with Charles Tilly, that the European "state structure appeared chiefly as a by-product of rulers' efforts to acquire the means of war."[55] And one can agree with Downing[56] that the fiscal military state is the consequence of the pressures of sustained war and military expenditure that required an immense degree of administrative professionalism and vast global resources to maintain specialized battle fleets in remote seas. But one can also say with Davdeker[57] that the democratic revolution brought about the bureaucratization of the force structure, thus changing command, control, and communications systems to a revolutionary degree.

Because history provides the way in which legitimation is conferred on the State, history is the manifestation of the interactions of law and strategy as history affords the means by which the State's objectives are rationalized. History determines the basis for legitimacy. Nowhere is this relation between history, strategy, and law clearer than in the example of the form of the state-nation that dominated the European scene from the period of the Napoleonic wars until that form was shattered by the collapse of the Vienna system and the rise of the nation-state. As will be seen in Book II, the search for legitimation was the common factor between the

---

*Two metaphors are helpful in understanding the State: (1) that the State acts as a network, conveying decisions made by the responsible parties so that it is both the medium of constitutional and strategic change, and also the expression of constitutional and strategic change; and (2) that the State depends on society the way a virus depends on the nuclear material of a cell, so that it is both made in time—has a birth and life and decay—and made of time, that is, what we know of it is the narrative of this morphology, the story of its adaptation to the conditions of society. The State, that is, both composes history (1) and is composed of history (2).

epochal wars of the French Revolution and the Congress of Vienna that arranged the peace.

If the warfare of the territorial states was characterized by concerted efforts to minimize risk, the warfare of the state-nation can be said to seek the high returns that only come from accepting great risks. Rather than depend on proximity to magazines, Napoleon moved with lightning speed across distances too great to allow such reassurance; rather than dividing his troops, so as not to chance their annihilation, he concentrated his forces and defeated his enemies piecemeal. Napoleon exploited the use of light troops and skirmishers, the introduction of self-sufficient divisions that could travel separately until the moment of concentration and then suddenly mass in a decisive convergence, and the creation of light yet powerful field artillery, all to achieve the mobile strategy required for a cataclysmic confrontation with adversaries who would have preferred wars of position. Finally, Napoleon simply fought with forces vastly larger than any the eighteenth century had seen. Frederick the Great lacked the resources either to destroy his enemies or to completely impose his will on them.[58] By September 1794, the army of the French republic had, at least on paper, 1,169,000 men, about six times the size of Frederick's armies at their largest.

The territorial state of Frederick the Great would never have risked the potential internal upheaval of assembling such forces; arming the people was the last thing Frederick wished. Nor could such forces have been trained in the exacting drill of his tactics. It was the revolutionary state that made the *levée en masse* possible—which Napoleon later exploited—because mass conscription made the State the focus of the nation. Untrained and to a large degree untrainable in the tactics of the territorial state, these lightly armed soldiers, many even without proper uniforms, were unsuitable to the strategy as well as the constitutions of such states; their service began as an unavoidable necessity when the Revolution, literally and figuratively, decapitated the officer class, yet this service continued and became the heroic pride of the state-nation.

The constitutional transition to the state-nation should not be confused with that which resulted in the nation-state. To repeat: the nation-state takes its legitimacy from putting the State in the service of its people; the state-nation asks rather that the people be put in the service of the State. The state-nation is not in the business of maintaining the welfare of the people; rather it is legitimated by forging a national consciousness, by fusing the nation with the State. Consider Napoleon's speech to the troops before entering Italy: ". . . All of you are consumed with a desire to extend the glory of the French people, all of you long to humiliate those arrogant kings who dare to contemplate placing us in fetters; all of you desire to dictate a glorious peace, one which will indemnify the Patrie for the immense sacrifices it has made; all of you wish to be able to say with pride as you return to your villages, 'I was with the victorious army of Italy!'" Such states are imperial by their very nature and mercantile, whether or not they actually have colonies. The Congress of Vienna, which met to undo the constitutional damage done by Napoleon, in the end ratified his most profound transformation, making Europe safe for three-quarters of a century for a form of the State that would scarcely have been recognized by the ancien régimes it is sometimes purported to have restored.

The state-nation provides a novel constitutional basis for colonization, an idea utterly antithetical to the nation-state, which holds that a national group is entitled to its own state. Schroeder perfectly captures the nature of the Napoleonic state-nation when he describes the decade of Napoleonic hegemony in Europe—the *Rheinbund,* the collection of satellite states, the continental system—as an exercise in European colonization.[59] Later the real action would take place elsewhere, in areas where European technology and especially European customs of command and control overwhelmed national peoples and made them imperial subjects.

> It is in [the] global context that European military history is of most consequence. The technological changes that were to bring clear military superiority for the Europeans, such as steam power on sea and land, breech-loaders, rifled guns and iron hulls, did not occur until after 1815 . . . Military strength was central to this rise in Western power, both within and outside Europe, and was to give shape to the 19th century world order.[60]

In the year 1800, Europeans controlled 35 percent of the land area of the world; by 1878 this figure had risen to 67 percent. What made this possible—what gave imperialism legitimacy and energized the colonial officials who officered native regiments and administered remote and disease-infected regions, and what above all drove the states that paid for that infrastructure—was a certain constitutional order of the State. It was not only superior technology[61] but superior strategic habits (including discipline in battle, map making, supplying credit and financing quartermaster provisioning over long lines of communication, and above all, political cohesion) that ensured the European triumph because strategic habits were "more difficult to transfer or replicate than technology, resting as [they] did on the foundation of centuries of European social and institutional change."[62] This change forged a form of the State that apotheosized its glory within a system of great powers, bending the energies of often diverse national peoples to its service. Napoleon unsentimentally realized this source of his legitimacy: "My power depends upon my glory and my glories on the victories I have won. My power will fail if I do not feed it on new glories and new victories. Conquest has made me what I am and only conquest can enable me to hold my position."[63] Deriving legitimacy from delivering benefits to the state-nation was recognized also by institutions as diverse as the East India Company—which was nationalized in 1858— and the Suez consortium.[64]

Every era asks, "What is the State supposed to be doing?" The answer to this question provides us with an indication of the grounds of the State's legitimacy, for only when we know the purpose of the State can we say whether it is succeeding. The nation-state is supposed to be doing something unique in the history of the modern state: maintaining, nurturing, and improving the conditions of its citizens. That is a different assignment from enhancing the national interest. Burke, speaking in 1774 for the state-nation in his most famous address, put it this way: Parliament was not "a congress of ambassadors from different and hostile interests . . . but . . . a deliberative assembly of one nation, with one interest, that of the whole."[65] That nation is a corporate body with a national interest that is distinct from the accumulated interests of groups or individuals within that body. By contrast, the nation-state exists to determine the desires of its different constituencies and translate them into legislative action. The flow of legitimacy is from the people's judgment—the nation's—to the state; hence the importance to the nation-state of the broadening of the suffrage and the vexing problem of the nation-state, the question of self-determination, that is, the people's judgment on statehood itself.

The transition from state-nation to the nation-state brought a change in constitutional procedures. The plebiscite, the referendum, and indeed the whole array of participatory procedures do not derive from the American or French revolutions. In Federalist Paper #63 Madison could write that the distinction of the American government "lies in the total exclusion of the people, in their collective capacity, from any share" in the government. By the end of the American Civil War, however, the requirements of legitimation had changed. Similarly, in Europe, it was, again, the relation between constitutional change and strategic innovation that made this transformation both necessary and possible. This relation was manifested in, and accounted for by, history.

It is fascinating to recall that, as early as 1809, General Gerhard von Scharnhorst, the director of the Prussian War Academy and the creator of the Prussian general staff system, advocated such Napoleonic measures as a national army, general conscription, the appointment of commoners as officers, the abandonment of linear tactics in favor of light infantry and columns, and, astonishingly, the fomenting of popular insurrection in areas controlled by the French. Frederick William III was unwilling to endorse such a radical state-national program;[66] it was left to Scharn-horst's successors in Prussia to effect the next "revolution" in strategic and constitutional affairs, which brought the nation-state into being in Europe.

THE NATION-STATE

The state-nation mobilized and exploited whatever national resources it happened to find itself in charge of (including the colonial resources of otherwise stateless nations). It was not responsible *to* the nation; rather it was responsible *for* the nation. The nation, for its part, provided the raw material with which the state-nation powered the engines of state aggrandizement. Nowhere is this contrast more apparent than in the history of empire that began as colonization in the seventeenth century, was transformed into imperialism by the middle of the nineteenth century, and then was ultimately undone by the ethos of the nation-state and its demands for the constitutional recognition of national identities.

By the middle of the nineteenth century, most of the empires of European states were in place: the great subcontinent of India was already the most important possession of the most important empire. Ironically, at about the time the nation-state emerged in Europe with the creation of Germany and Italy, imperialism abroad intensified. This is the period, as Michael Doyle has observed, that "is associated with the full transfer of rights of sovereignty (usually marked by either treaty or conquest)"[67] to the governing imperial state and it is usually dated from the 1880s and the scramble for African possessions. In only a few decades the state-nation would be destroyed in Europe proper, and with it the Concert of European states that had maintained peace.

The turning point occurred in the late 1840s, when, for similar but unrelated domestic political purposes, European politicians seized on the idea of national self-determination as the key element underpinning a program of political reform.* This idea was antithetical to the Vienna system and cast doubt on the legitimacy of that system. Challenges to the system's program of strategic restraint further discredited the Vienna system. The Crimean War, the Italian wars, the unification of Italy, but most especially the unification of Germany were ever escalating challenges to the Vienna Concert that arose from the campaigns for popular sovereignty, so that by the last of these conflicts, in 1870, the state-nation in Europe was in rapid retreat.

It may seem to us today altogether natural that states should occupy

---

*And not just European politicians: Lincoln's nation-state was the first fully realized example of this constitutional order.

fixed and contiguous places on maps, but that, as we have seen, was not always the common conception. And it may also seem obvious that the geographical division of the world into states should fit the division of mankind into nations. But this too was not always so. As H. G. Wells put it, that the political world should be divided into nation-states, and that this must be so in order to ensure stability,

> would seem to be self-evident propositions were it not that the diploma-tists at Vienna evidently neither believed nor understood anything of the sort, and thought themselves free to carve up the world as one is free to carve up such a boneless structure as a cheese.[68]

One could argue—as indeed Castlereagh did as a young man when he voted to disband the Irish parliament—that the coincidence of political boundaries with ethnic ones is actually a recipe for conflict. Nevertheless, it became a common belief among very different societies after the upheavals of 1848 that governments existed to better the lot of national peoples. Some have argued that this shift to welfare nationalism was a conscious strategy on the part of ruling elites to distract the masses from the exploitative practices of the industrial age. There is doubtless some truth in this, but nationalism was itself also a motivating factor among revolutionaries, and, in any case, that it was a card effectively played by politicians in several very different circumstances does not tell us why it proved so effective and transformative.

During 1848, Poles, Danes, Germans, Italians, Magyars, Czechs, Slovaks, Serbs, Croats, and Romanians rose in arms, claiming the right of self-government. In February, a revolution occurred in France, and one of the great powers suddenly appeared to have taken up the cause of popular nationalism against the Vienna system. In March the French foreign minister declared that the new French Republic did not recognize the peace treaties of 1815 and would defend by force the rights of oppressed nationalities against any aggressor. This pledge was not immediately fulfilled, but a new leader emerged who was able to exploit sentiment in Europe for the nation-state and the self-determination of peoples. Louis-Napoleon Bonaparte, nephew of the Emperor Napoleon, was elected president of the Republic by universal suffrage in December 1848. Barred by the constitution from a second term, he mounted a coup d'état in December 1851. A fresh plebiscite was held on a new constitution; 7.5 million persons voted yes, against 650,000 voting no, with 1.5 million abstentions. The seizure of constitutional power had been legitimated by an appeal to the people.

The use of the plebiscite to ratify changes in the constitution had been previously initiated by Napoleon I, but the differences in the two occasions are illuminating.

When Napoleon I used the plebiscite, he was attempting to legitimate his own role within a revolutionary state; when he sought to legitimate his role vis-à-vis other states, by contrast, he had himself crowned emperor by the pope. When Louis Napoleon resorted to the plebiscite, he first used it to legitimate a new constitution, and later in 1852 in order to confer the title of emperor and to make this title hereditary. In other words, Napoleon III (as Louis Napoleon then became) employed the plebiscite to legitimate not only his role, but the new role of the State itself. Moreover, the universal suffrage of Napoleon III, vastly larger than that called upon by Napoleon I, not only ratified constitutional changes, but was also the basis for legislative elections. The use of the national referendum to determine the constitutional status of a state is more than anything else the watermark of the nation-state. For on what basis other than popular sovereignty and nationalism can the mere vote of a people legitimate its relations with others? It is one thing to suppose that a vote of the people legitimates a particular policy or ruler; this implies that, within a state, the people of that state have a say in the political direction of the state. It is something else altogether to say that a vote of the people legitimates a state within the society of states. That conclusion depends on not simply a role for self-government, but a right of self-government. It is the right of which Lincoln spoke at Gettysburg.

Napoleon III desired to break out of the Vienna system, which he perceived, with some justice, as having been built to confine French ambitions, and he wished to invigorate the principle of national self-determination, which he believed, with somewhat less justification, to have been the guiding ideology of his late uncle. Accordingly, he carefully chose the place where he would confront the system: not Belgium nor the Rhineland nor the Italian states. Aggression against these states could be justified on grounds of frustrated nationalism, but such an attack would have united the Concert against him. Rather he chose to move against the Ottoman Empire. As Gildea has shrewdly concluded, the "Empire could be used safely as a laboratory for testing the principle of nationalities, and the precedent could then be applied to other parts of Europe."[69]

The ten million Orthodox Christians in the Ottoman Empire came under the protection of the tsar. But there were Roman Catholic Christians in the empire as well, mainly in Lebanon, where French missionary efforts had been steadily increasing their numbers throughout the 1840s. Napoleon III seized on this issue and demanded that the Ottoman governor remove the keys to the Holy Places from the Orthodox patriarch and give them to Catholic clergy, and further that a Latin patriarchate be established in Jerusalem. When the Ottoman authorities acceded to these ultimata, Russia responded by insisting on guarantees for Balkan Orthodox Christians, whose national movements the Russians had begun to aid. In July, the tsar moved forces into the Danubian principalities of Moldavia and Wallachia. Finally war broke out between Turkey and Russia, and in November 1853, the Turkish fleet was destroyed off the southern coast of the Black Sea. Napoleon III seized this opportunity to propose an alliance with Britain to prevent Russia from driving the Ottoman Empire from the Dardenelles and thus opening the Mediterranean to Russian fleets. Great Britain pledged to maintain the integrity of the Ottoman Empire.

In Britain, public opinion ran high against Russia. Although the Aberdeen cabinet was disposed to do nothing, its most formidable member, Lord Palmerston, resigned on the issue and took his case to the public. He was returned on a wave of popular feeling in favor of war. An alliance was concluded with France, and a combined fleet was sent to the Black Sea in January 1854.

Palmerston's strategic objectives were by no means confined to simply opposing Russia over the straits. In a secret memorandum he prepared for the cabinet in March 1854, he wrote of the Russian empire's

dismemberment. Finland would be restored to Sweden, the Baltic provinces would go to Prussia, and Poland would become a sizable kingdom. Austria would renounce her Italian possessions but gain the Danubian principalities and possibly even Bessarabia in return, and the Ottoman Empire would regain the Crimea and Georgia.[70]

Such a program appealed to Napoleon III's desire to inflame Polish, Romanian, and Italian nationalism, but it required a total military defeat of the Russians, which France could not afford: to lose Russia completely would sacrifice important protection France might need against Prussia. The hazards of destroying the Vienna system began to dawn on French policymakers.[71]

In September 1855 Sevastopol fell to the British and French. Palmerston, who had become prime minister the preceding February, was eager to press the attack, but he was also fearful of a separate peace between France and Russia. Finally he gave in to the rest of the cabinet and to the views of Queen Victoria and Prince Albert, and concluded a peace treaty. The terms were harsh: Russia lost her protectorate over the Danubian principalities, as well as about a third of Bessarabia. These areas became the state of Romania, the formation of which markedly increased the intensity of nationalist sentiment in other Balkan states. The provision that no warships could traverse the straits in peacetime was extended to the entire Black Sea.

Russia's defeat completed her constitutional transition to a state-nation. Because service in the army was rewarded by emancipation, serfs had to be recruited for long periods; otherwise, the number of those bound to the land would have plummeted. Thus recruitment provided only about 700,000 men. There was no reserve. Such measures did not fill the needs of contemporary warfare, which required universal, short-term conscription, followed by service in the reserve. An adequate system, however, would move all serfs through the army in a generation. Therefore modern conscription and reserve service meant the emancipation of the serfs. And this is precisely what happened, in yet another example of strategic imperatives flowing back into the constitutional structure that strategy is supposed to serve. In 1861 the serfs were freed; universal military service followed in 1874. Six years' active service and a nine-year reserve commitment created a total force of 1.35 million. Various other efforts were made to focus the energies of the entire nation on service to the state. Thus evolving, Russia entered a period from which most of the great powers were just emerging; it would take another military catastrophe, in 1916, to bring a nation-state into being.

With the successful conclusion of the Crimean War, Napoleon III moved from being a mere egoist to becoming the most prominent personage in Europe. Ever mindful of his public, he next turned to Italy, where the strategic objectives of France could again be married to the support of local nationalist sentiments. In 1859, France intervened in Italy after Napoleon III concluded a secret agreement with Cavour, the Piedmontese prime minister, providing that the kingdom of Piedmont would be extended into a Kingdom of Upper Italy to include Lombardy, Venetia, and the Romagna. France would receive Nice and Savoy. A Kingdom of Central Italy, composed of Tuscany, Parma, Modena, Umbria, and the Marches, would be given to Napoleon's cousin, Prince Napoleon. As with the French demands against the Ottoman Empire, French intrigue had singled out another vulnerable multinational state-nation: the Austrian empire.

Fighting broke out in April, most of the warfare taking place between French and Austrian forces. The battles of Magenta and Solferino were actually French victories, not those of the Piedmontese or Italian volunteers. The decision to cease fire was also French, and an agreement was signed between Napoleon III and the Austrian emperor Francis Joseph on July 11, 1859. This truce clearly sacrificed Italian nationalism to French ambitions. Lombardy was given to Piedmont but Venetia remained with the Austrians. Nothing was said of the French agreement with Cavour. The settlement ignited a firestorm of reaction among the Italians, who had not been consulted. Cavour resigned his premiership. Assemblies called by Tuscany, Parma, Modena, and the Papal Legations* met and requested annexation by the kingdom of Piedmont.

---

*The northern Papal states.

At first Napoleon III demurred and fell back on a call for a European congress to settle the question of central Italy. This approach might have strengthened the system of collective security in Europe, but then, in December, he changed course. Relying on Britain, where Palmerston and his foreign secretary, Lord John Russell, supported the principle of self-determination, Napoleon III renewed the agreement between France and Piedmont. Cavour returned to power in less than a month.

Piedmont annexed the Duchies and the Legations and promptly organized a plebiscite, based on universal suffrage, held in March 1860. The Piedmontese king, Victor Emmanuel, took over the new territories by decree. Elections to a single Italian parliament were held in Piedmont-Sardinia, Lombardy, the Duchies, and the Legations. The first task of this legislature was to ratify the annexations to Piedmont as well as those to France. The French annexations of Nice and Savoy had been similarly endorsed by local plebiscites.

The French annexations, however, had enraged the Italian partisan leader Garibaldi (a native of Nice) and other Italian revolutionaries, and he mounted an insurrection in Sicily in April. The success of this insurrection, which was quickly joined by discontented peasants recruited by promises of land reform, prompted Cavour to dispatch officials to prepare plebiscites for annexation in the newly liberated areas. These officials Garibaldi expelled or avoided. When Garibaldi marched on Naples, Cavour planned a pre-emptive coup, but this failed, and Garibaldi entered Naples in September.

Fearful of losing the leadership of the emerging unification movement to Garibaldi's partisans, Piedmont sent forces into the Papal States and defeated a Catholic army at Castelfidardo in mid-September. When Bourbon forces in the south began to gain ground against Garibaldi, the latter called on Piedmont for assistance. This permitted Cavour to announce to the parliament on October 2, 1860, that the revolution was at an end. Sicily and Naples were annexed after a plebiscite by universal suffrage on October 21.

Italian unification was not quite complete. French troops remained in Rome, kept there by conservative pressure on Napoleon III, and it was not until the German victory at Sedan in 1870 that they were finally withdrawn. Nevertheless, without French determination to drive Austria from Italy, unification would not have happened at this time. Whether it was wise of Napoleon III to accomplish this is open to question; by weakening Austria, he removed the strongest check on Prussian ambitions to unify Germany, a development that could only threaten France in the long run. Moreover, France—with the enthusiastic if passive collaboration of the British—had dealt a severe blow to the Vienna system. By relying on a national insurrection to destroy the forces of a great power, these states had ignored the ominous predictions of Castlereagh about a general war. In so doing, these state-nations, and the society of such states, had begun to give way to the nation-state. There is some evidence that the leadership in these states perhaps believed they had found in the ideology of popular sovereignty and national aspirations a way of preserving their own states from revolt. After 1870 the greatest of the nation-state builders, Bismarck, made clear to all what had happened. As Michael Doyle has insightfully observed:

> Leadership could win nationalism over to the state . . . and when revolution and nationalism were no longer synonymous, war could be fought on a wave of national feeling that, to everyone's surprise, did not ignite liberal revolution. The tiger of the nation-state did, however, require lavish feeding. Provinces and people could no longer be treated casually as the chips in dynastic politics, they were the children of the nation. Thus as war became more efficient, unleashing the power of the whole people, so peace became more difficult.[72]

But in 1860, at the conclusion of the Italian wars, this was not obvious to all observers. The most that could be said was that the rules of the Concert had been tested in the Crimea—an "out-of-area" problem, so to speak, as the Concert did not strictly apply beyond Europe or include the Ottoman Empire—and had been abandoned in the Italian peninsula apparently without the dire consequences of which Castlereagh had warned. The Crimean War alone, however, caused more deaths than any other European conflict between 1815 and 1914. Moreover, within eleven years of the conclusion of the Italian War, three major wars were fought in Europe: the war between Denmark and the German states in 1864; the Austro-Prussian war of 1866; and the Franco-Prussian war of 1870. As a consequence a new nation-state was forged and a new society of states eventually came into being, with a new sort of question at the center of every member state: which political system best improved the welfare of the national people?

The construction of the new nation-state of Germany occurred when Prussia was able to conquer and annex the other members of the German federation, excluding Austria. Although it is commonly said, by Kissinger[73] among others, that the peace of Vienna lasted until 1914 because no general war broke out until then, the wars by which Germany was unified virtually destroyed the Vienna System and with it the system of consensus as to the legitimacy of the state-nations that were its constituents. German unification was made possible, first, by the reform of the Prussian military that moved Prussia from a territorial state to a state-nation. This was primarily accomplished under the leadership of Scharnhorst and Gneisenau. Second, this state-nation was made the political and diplomatic leader of a national movement to unite the German people, ultimately transforming its constitutional basis and its strategic objectives into those of a nation-state. This effort was led by Otto von Bismarck and Helmuth von Moltke.

The transformation of warfare by Napoleon I and the state-nation had been fully appreciated by Prussian analysts, who were well aware that new methods of war and the preparation for war would have a profound social and political impact on Prussian society. The army of Frederick the Great had been a force of professionals isolated from the rest of society, ruled by iron discipline, and led by officers drawn solely from the nobility. To transform this army into that of a state-nation, Prussia undertook universal conscription of a more radical type than had previously been attempted anywhere.

Conscription had been adopted in most of the other countries in Europe as each transformed itself into a state-nation, and put its nation in arms. In every country outside Prussia, however, this amounted to the drafting of the poor because substitutes for service could be hired. In Prussia, however, all groups in the population were required actually to serve. This provided enormous manpower; it made the army into a true citizens' armed force; it made possible the strategic and tactical innovations urged by Scharnhorst and Gneisenau, and their successor, Moltke. Most importantly, it set up a constitutional conflict between liberal, decentralizing parliamentary elements that wished to maintain the voluntary militia and Prussian royalist military groups that intended to use the new standing army to create a pan-Germany in the image of Prussia.

Helmuth von Moltke, like Scharnhorst and Gneisenau, was not a Prussian by birth. His father had been an officer of the king of Denmark.* Moltke was educated as a Danish cadet, but his experiences at school had been unhappy and his relations with his father were distant, so in 1822 he applied for a commission in the Prussian army. In 1823 he passed the entrance examination to the War College, which was at that time directed by Clausewitz. In 1826 he returned to his regiment but was soon assigned to the Prussian general staff, where he remained for more than sixty years. In order to buy and maintain horses, without which he could not serve on the general staff, Moltke earned money by translating six volumes of Gibbon's *Decline and Fall of the Roman Empire*. Financial need had earlier compelled him to write short novels, and his letters from Turkey, where he had served as a military advisor, are still read as classics of German literature.

---

*Who, as the duke of Schleswig-Holstein was also a German prince (with such fateful consequences as we shall see).

With the exception of those few years in Turkey, Moltke never saw action, indeed never commanded a company or any larger unit, until, at the age of sixty-five, he took command of the Prussian armies in the war against Austria in 1866. If it was said of Bismarck that he was a "kind of Minister-President with a uniform hidden under his suit,"* the very opposite might have been said of the highly reserved and rather sensitive Moltke.

Prussian mobilization for the Italian wars had been a fiasco. In the ensuing years until 1866, Moltke devoted himself entirely to preparations for future military operations and remained aloof from the political scene. In 1860 the Prussian king William I, and the minister of war, von Roon, had proposed a thoroughgoing reorganization of the Prussian military. This plan envisioned increasing the standing army by raising the length of military service from two years to three, while converting the militia to a reserve force, which in turn meant the abolition of those militia-like sections of the armed forces, the territorial army, in which liberal politics had generally prevailed. In May the Prussian parliament agreed to vote additional military credits on the understanding that the government was withdrawing the reorganization plan and would use the money only to strengthen existing units. New units had already been formed, however. Further military credits were then denied; a parliamentary dissolution followed and a new election was held in December 1861. This and another election in May 1862 only reinforced the parliamentary opposition to military reform. In September 1862 Otto von Bismarck was called in by the crown to break the deadlock, a *"konfliktminister"* who, it was assumed, was willing to violate constitutional rules in order to quell the opposition. It was at this time that he made his famous statement directly attacking the prevailing constitutional order in Europe:

> Prussia's frontiers as laid down by the Vienna treaties are not conducive to a healthy national life; it is not by means of speeches and majority resolutions that the great issues of the day will be decided—that was the great mistake of 1848 and 1849—but by iron and blood.[†]

He followed this in January by saying menacingly that if the Parliament refused to agree, conflict would follow, and "conflicts become questions of

---

*Ironically the general staff, who viewed Bismarck as a meddler, sarcastically referred to "civilians in cuirassiers' tunics," a reference to Bismarck's habit of dressing in uniform, especially after 1870. Gall, 366.

[†]Quoted in Gall, 204. The very vividness of this remark aroused much criticism at the time. Von Treitscke, hardly a liberal, wrote his brother-in-law, "You know how passionately I love Prussia, but when I hear so shallow a country squire as this Bismarck bragging about the 'iron and blood' with which he intends to subdue Germany, the meanness of it seems to me to be exceeded only by the absurdity" (Gall, 206). And even Bismarck's ally von Roon complained of "witty sallies" that did their cause little good.

power. He who has the power in his hands goes forward, because the life of the State cannot stand still even for one moment."[74]

When new elections in October 1863 strengthened the Opposition in Parliament, Bismarck simply ruled without an approved budget. This period of nonparliamentary rule allowed the army to institute its reforms and, ultimately, to implement its innovative strategy. Holborn concludes:

> The constitutional conflict was still raging when the battle of Konig-gratz was fought. The parliamentary opposition, however, broke down when the Bismarckian policy and Moltke's victories fulfilled the longing for German national unity. Moltke's successful strategy, therefore, decided two issues: first, the rise of a unified Germany among the nations of Europe; second, the victory of the Prussian crown over the liberal and democratic opposition in Germany through the maintenance of the authoritarian structure of the Prussian army.[75]

Prussian innovations in strategy were well designed to serve both these purposes, and indeed could not have succeeded without the new constitutional structure because they depended upon a highly motivated, highly disciplined force of immense size under a central command with spaciously delegated constitutional authority.

The Napoleonic strategic revolution had been carefully studied by all the armies of Europe. As early as 1815 it had become the new dogma, and its imperatives were in part responsible for the development of the state-nation that it called into being. Napoleon Bonaparte had stood the strategic ideas of the eighteenth century on their head. These ideas held that, as territorial gain was the object of warfare and war was prosecuted by expensive, professional armies, battles were to be avoided. Wars became intricate ballets of position, each army maneuvering to force the other from one less favorable territorial position to another, occupying the ceded ground. This was the strategic paradigm of the territorial state. The Napoleonic campaign denied all these principles. Instead of avoiding actual clashes, such campaigns sought battle, and the larger and more destructive the better, because it was by battle that the forces of the enemy could be destroyed. Only this would cause the collapse of morale that would force the enemy government to sue for peace and put that government at the mercy of French terms. It was not territory that Napoleon I sought, but the political and economic resources of the conquered nation, so these could be exploited by the French state. This was the strategic paradigm of the state-nation.

A liturgy of Napoleonic principles soon replaced the study of the campaigns of Frederick the Great. In the widely read writings of the Swiss theoretician Jomini, Napoleon's ideas were reduced to a set of rational rules and geometric axioms. The Prussian school of strategy, however, drew a different conclusion from Napoleon's campaigns. The most important lesson for the Prussians was the link drawn between the political objectives of war and its strategic prosecution, a connection summed up in the concept of the "moral" element in warfare. Napoleon's Prussian students stressed the role of spontaneity in his decisions and the ineluctable nature of the unpredictable. To these theoretical insights, they added the tactical possibilities opened up by the technology of the Industrial Revolution. This technology included techniques for manufacturing armaments that greatly increased the lethality of fire; the telegraph, which expanded the immediacy and range of communications; and, perhaps most significantly, the railroad, which promised to transform logistics.

In the Italian wars of 1859, a French force of 120,000 reached the theater of operations in eleven days by rail; had they marched, it would have taken two months. Generally it was calculated that troops could be transported by railway six times as fast as the armies of Napoleon I had marched. In addition to the railroad, there was now in place a dense road system that had come into being in the course of the explosive development of European industrial trade. Not only the movement of men, but also their resupply with matériel was affected by the railroad and road network. Forces arrived in good shape; they could be maintained for months on end by their home economies; the injured could be evacuated; home leaves and furloughs became possible, with all the consequences for morale in the field and politics in civil society.*

The limits to the size of armies that Napoleon I had shattered had reimposed themselves in his Russian campaign. There was a limit to what foraging and pillage could accomplish to effectuate resupply. But with provisioning by rail there was in principle no limit imposed by logistics on the size of armies that could be fielded. Only the national economy and the demography of the society remained constraints. In 1870 the North German Federation deployed against France exactly twice the number of men Napoleon had led into Russia: 1,200,000. By the time Germany fielded an army in the next war, that number would double again.

Technological developments either enhanced the importance of sheer numbers—like new technologies of lethal firepower—or made those numbers more effective, like the development of the telegraph that gave commanders greater control of their forces. By the 1860s firearms had undergone considerable improvement since their introduction as slow-firing muskets. The smooth-bore, muzzle-loading musket, whose awkwardness had inspired the elaborate quadrilles of Maurice of Nassau, was

*Indeed it was the military vote in 1864 that re-elected Lincoln. James M. McPherson, *Ordeal by Fire, Volume 2: The Civil War* (McGraw-Hill, 1993), 456–58.

replaced by the breech-loading, rapid-firing, rifled firearm. Rifling, the grooving inside barrels that increased the range and accuracy of a weapon fivefold, was in use by the 1840s, by which time the percussion cap had replaced the flintlock. In 1866 the Prussians fought with the Dreyse "needle gun," the first rifled breechloader. This fired three shots to a muzzle-loaded rifle's one, and could be fired lying down. "For the first time in the history of war the infantryman could kill his adversary at a range of several hundred yards without presenting a target himself."[76] According to Strachan, between 1840 and 1900 the range and rate of small-arms fire had increased tenfold.[77] In artillery, analogous developments took place. By 1870 Krupp was producing new steel breech-loading rifled cannon with ranges in excess of three thousand yards.

These technological developments challenged the prudence of the Napoleonic confrontation. How could an attacking force close with the enemy if they were battered to pieces miles before even sighting them? Just as importantly, how could the commander deploy forces in these huge numbers as anything more than a giant, confused mass? In 1865 Moltke wrote:

> The difficulties in mobility grow with the size of military units; one cannot transport more than one army corps on one road on the same day. They also grow, however, the closer one gets to the goal since this limits the number of available roads. It follows that the normal state of any army is its separation into corps and that the massing together of these corps without a very definite aim is a mistake. . . . A massed army can no longer march, it can only be moved over the fields. In order to march, the army has first to be broken up, which is dangerous in the face of the enemy. Since, however, the concentration of all troops is absolutely necessary for battle, the essence of strategy consists in the organization of separate marches, but so as to provide for concentration at the right moment.[78]

Napoleon I had demonstrated at Ulm the power of dividing the army into columns that advanced to a critical point for juncture. Napoleon, however, had held that an army must be massed days before battle. Partly this was dictated by the time it took for columns to re-form in battle formation. But partly also it was the result of Napoleon's preference for interior lines, an undivided force, frontal assault at the crucial moment, and central tactical command. Such tactics seemed suicidal now in the face of the advances in firepower that a defensive position could deploy with such lethal effectiveness. Scharnhorst was among the first to adapt the Napoleonic principle of concentrated forces to new conditions through the use of concentric movements. In Moltke, strategy found a commander who would use concentric operations and detached corps on a scale undreamt of before. As Rothenberg has observed:

> Confronted with the deadlock imposed by new weapons and extended frontages, Moltke . . . developed the concept of outflanking the enemy in one continuous strategic-operational sequence . . . By seizing the initiative from the outset, he intended to drive his opponent into a partial or complete envelopment, destroying his army in a great and decisive battle of annihilation or encirclement.[79]

Outflanking maneuvers of this kind—because they had to encompass the enormous lines made possible by armies in unprecedented numbers—would call for enormous numbers as well. The army with the greatest resources in manpower and supply would enjoy a decisive advantage. This required not only a sense of national purpose (which the state-nation was well-suited to provide) but also a sense of participation in the politics that led to war (which only the nation-state could fulfill). "[T]he greater the sense of participation in the affairs of the State, the more was the State seen as the embodiment of these unique and higher value systems which called it into being, and the greater became the commitment to protect and serve it."[80]

Thus popular participation became the instrument that both created the nation-state and was itself reinforced by the institutions of the State it created. This phenomenon is evident in the history of the creation of the nation-state Germany by the Prussian state-nation.

Bismarck had begun by identifying Prussia as the apotheosis of the German; accordingly there was nothing "more German than the development of Prussia's particular interests."[81] But this was by no means clear to the other members of the German federal diet, including especially the Austrians. It was Bismarck's task to somehow separate the Austrians from the mission of unification and then carry out that mission so successfully as to silence opposition to Prussian leadership among the other apprehensive German states.

Bismarck became minister-president in 1862. The following November, King Frederick VII of Denmark died, and the main line of the Danish royal house became extinct. The provinces of Schleswig, Holstein, and Lauenburg had been attached to the Danish kingdom in much the same way that Hanover had been attached, for dynastic reasons, to the British kingdom: Frederick had been duke of Schleswig-Holstein, and as duke of Holstein and Lauenburg as well had been represented in the German Confederation. As with Hanover, Holstein and Lauenburg were by language and geography German. Two national movements, the German and the Danish, competed for support in the duchies, whose independence had been guaranteed by the 1852 Treaty of London, to which the great powers were signatories.

In March 1863, the Danish parliament rashly incorporated Schleswig* on the nationalistic grounds that most of the population of Schleswig was Danish, conceding that Holstein and Lauenburg held special rights. In reply, acting in the name of the Confederation on behalf of the German minority in the duchy, Prussian and Austrian forces invaded Schleswig in January and Jutland in March. Anglo-French opposition to the invasion was frustrated by English fears of encouraging a French move against the Rhine. In August the new king of Denmark, whose forces had been overwhelmed despite some initial misfires by the Prussian general, surrendered his rights in Schleswig.

Having contrived a successful military alliance with Austria over Schleswig, Bismarck proceeded to use this success as a hammer to break first the Confederation and then Austria herself. The apparent Austrian-Prussian rapprochement put Prussia in a good position to renew the Franco-Prussian free-trade treaty that Prussia had negotiated in 1862, playing on French fears of a Habsburg/Confederation-wide competing market. Bismarck now proposed expanding this treaty to include the entire Confederation, excluding Austria. Eventually even the southern, pro-Austrian states came along because they were unable to survive without the markets and outlets controlled by North Germany.

Bismarck then used the Austro-Prussian military success to drive a wedge between Austria and the rest of the German states. Austria and most of the southern German states in the Confederation had expected to bring Schleswig into the Confederation along with Holstein. Bismarck rejected this and instead negotiated an agreement with Austria partitioning the duchies, Austria to administer Holstein and Prussia, Schleswig, on an ad interim basis. In so doing, he was playing on the unreformed constitutional structure of the multinational Habsburg state that was perforce insensitive to the contradiction of accumulating isolated, ethnically distinct provinces.

This agreement, the Treaty of Bad Gastein, discredited Austria within the Confederation, as well as put her in the impossible position of attempting to administer a remote and recalcitrant state that lay between Prussia and Denmark. Bismarck took covert steps to exacerbate this difficulty, as well as stimulating Prussian public opinion to call for the annexation of both duchies into Prussia. Attempting a retreat from its position, Austria then reasserted its support for an independent duke and proposed that the

*In the following discussion of the Schleswig-Holstein dispute, perhaps one should bear in mind Palmerston's remark: With regard to Schleswig-Holstein, he said, "only three men had grasped it in all its ramification: one was dead, the second had been driven mad by it, and the third, he himself, had forgotten all about it." But the only way to understand Bismarck's adroit use of this strategic problem is to give at least some of the problem's complicated background.

decision be left to the Confederation. This Bismarck knew would result in a rejection of Prussian claims to the duchies, because the Confederation would vote for a separate state constructed from a union between the duchies. Prussia therefore denounced this move as a breach of the treaty and a cause for war. Bismarck promptly concluded a treaty with Italy to attack Austria and add Venetia to the Italian national state; he also began talks with Hungarian nationalists. Next he attempted to isolate Austria within the Confederation by bidding for the support of the German liberals, to whom he proposed a national parliament elected by universal suffrage. When Austria asked the Confederation to reject Prussia's proposals, Prussia responded by announcing that the German Confederation had ceased to exist, and called upon the German states to join a new Confederation, the North German Confederation, that excluded Austria.

The Prussian king, William I, had wished to avoid war with the Austrians and as a consequence the Prussians began their mobilization late, such that there was doubt whether an effective offensive could be mounted. But whereas the Austrians could employ only one railroad line for their mobilization in Moravia, Moltke used five to transport Prussian troops from all over Prussia to the battlefront. Thus on June 5, 1866, the Prussian armies spread over a half circle of 275 miles. Moltke began at once to draw them closer toward the center, but steadfastly refused to order a full concentration in a small area. It was not until June 22 that officers of the Prussian vanguard handed their Austrian counterparts notice of the Prussian declaration of war.

The Austrian army moved from Moravia in three parallel columns, reaching their destination on June 26. Their commander, Benedek, was a product of the old school: fearless, stolid, he relied on formation in depth and the advantage of an interior line of operations. He failed, however, to derive the chief advantage of such a concentration when he delayed attacking either of the two equally strong Prussian armies facing him. Moreover, Benedek's early concentration inhibited his mobility. Once the opportunity had passed it was too late for the Austrians even to retreat behind the Elbe at Koniggratz and Benedek was forced to accept battle with the river at his rear. Like a Wagnerian overture, Moltke continued to hold off the final climax, keeping his armies one day's distance from each other until the night of July 2. At that time, he ordered the two Prussian armies to operate not merely against the flanks, but against the rear of the enemy: a strategy of encirclement. This did not completely come off, but at Koniggratz the Austrian army did lose the war as well as a fourth of its strength. Because Benedek did not retain enough space to advance against one portion of the Prussian army and then turn against the other, but instead was so hemmed in that he could not attack one force without being immediately attacked in his rear, the advantage of the interior line was forfeited.

Had the local commanders actually carried out Moltke's orders for encirclement, it is possible the Austrian army would have been entirely destroyed, as occurred when Moltke's battle plan was executed against the French at Sedan.

Peace preliminaries were signed on July 27. Bismarck's principal war aims—the dissolution of the German Confederation and the removal of Austria from German affairs—had been accomplished by a course so circuitous, so Machiavellian, that historians continue to debate whether or not Bismarck actually intended the diplomatic campaign as it unfolded.[82]

Putting aside as unprofitable for our study an analysis of the psychological intentions of the Prussian president-minister, three questions remain: (1) How was Prussia able to convert a somewhat reckless act of Danish nationalism into a decisive weapon of destruction against the Confederation, on whose behalf Bismarck was allegedly acting? (2) How was Prussia able to use an alliance with Austria, and a successful war prosecuted by the two allies, to destroy Austria's role in German nationalism? (3) Is there anything about the nature of Moltke's strategy that helps us answer (1) and (2); that is, did the military imperative in this instance shape the sort of state that Bismarck was pursuing, such that it enabled, indeed brought to life a ruthlessly decisive diplomatic and political opponent of both the Confederation and the Austrian empire? The answers to all three questions revolve around legitimacy, popular nationalism, and self-determination, and their interplay with the new constitutional structure coming into being, the nation-state.

First, Denmark and all the states of the German Confederation were inflamed by nationalism. There were both German- and Danish-speaking residents in Schleswig-Holstein, in significant numbers. It had long been a goal of Danish nationalists to recognize constitutionally what was already a fact dynastically; namely, that the Danish king was the ruler of the duchies. Danish dynastic succession had been strengthened by the Treaty of London in 1852, which recognized Christian IX as the successor to Frederick VII. The role of the duchies, however, remained a point of contention between the two national movements. As early as 1855 a constitution had been adopted for a Greater Denmark that gave a central parliament in Copenhagen legislative rights over the duchies.

Protests had been immediately lodged against this move by the Confederation on behalf of Holstein, which was a member of the Confederation, and also by Austria and Prussia, which were signatories to the Treaty of London. When the Federal Diet threatened the Danish king with an enforcement order (a *Bundesexekution*) with respect to Holstein and Lauenburg, Frederick compliantly abolished the new constitution, but this had the unfortunate effect of separating Schleswig from the other two territories, because it was not a member of the Confederation. At the end of

March 1863 the Danes formally objected to the section of the Treaty of London that dealt with Schleswig, and announced they would henceforth recognize special status for Holstein and Lauenburg only. When the Confederation now threatened to reinstitute the *Bundesexekution* order with respect to Schleswig, it exceeded its lawful authority. The Confederation was not a signatory to the Treaty of London, and Schleswig was not a member of the German Confederation. The Confederation was thus discredited in the eyes of German nationalists and forced to rely on the two German great powers to enforce matters against the Danes.

The Danes promptly adopted a new constitution incorporating Schleswig, and it was at precisely this point that Frederick VII died. The Treaty of London, which had been guaranteed by the great powers for just this eventuality, was now called into question because the legal requirements for succession had not been fulfilled by the Holstein parliament. German opinion was virtually unanimous that the treaty did not apply. Into this breach the duke of Augustenburg, who had relinquished his rights under the treaty, now stepped forward and offered his son, who was presented to the Confederation as Duke Frederick VIII. This was rapturously hailed by the citizens of Schleswig-Holstein as vindicating *their* rights to self-determination. A constituent assembly gathered spontaneously and swore allegiance to Frederick VIII. The majority of members of the German Confederation declared for Augustenburg and for the recognition of an independent principality for Schleswig-Holstein. This was the situation in November 1863. Prussia thus was offered the opportunity of championing the national movement, a role for which Bismarck had previously clamored.

Now, to the astonishment of all observers, Bismarck objected. As his principal biographer puts it,

> instead of leading Prussia to the head of the national movement, instead of mobilizing Prussia's military might for the German cause, the might that after all was supposed to have been strengthened and was to be strengthened further to this end, the Prussian head of government appealed to the sanctity of international treaties. And instead of supporting the actions of the Confederation and upholding Prussia's claim to a leading role with that organization, he was obviously concerned only to put relations between Prussia and Austria back on their old, pre-1848 footing . . .[83]

For Austria had never been keen on the idea of self-determination. The vindication of national passions would hardly be welcome to a multinational empire, with the obvious implications for Venetia, Bohemia, and

Hungary. Moreover, Schleswig-Holstein was far from Austria, lying between Prussia and Denmark and obviously well within Prussian control. In view of this, Vienna was extraordinarily pleased, if surprised, when the Prussian minister-president suggested a close collaboration between the two states and rejected the proposal for an independent principality.

It was a virtuoso performance. By demonstrating the impotence of the Confederation to the German national movement, Bismarck wholly discredited it as the vehicle for unification. The German Confederation could not deliver a German state against the Danes. But by luring Austria into a repudiation of the Augustenburg plan, Bismarck demonstrated that Austria too could not be relied on to vindicate German nationalism. By securing an alliance with Austria, he divided it from France, the one party that might have saved the Habsburg Empire once Prussia turned on it. And by selecting a field of confrontation so remote from Austria as Schleswig-Holstein, Bismarck guaranteed that, when the time was right, he could force a conflict with a now isolated Austria and annex the duchies to Prussia.

In creating an alliance with Austria, he excluded the German Confederation. This was accomplished by persuading the Austrians that the principle on which they must stand was the sanctity of international law; the Confederation, after all, was not a signatory to the Treaty of London. Moreover, Bismarck claimed to be upholding the rights of the state-nation against the national movements that threatened it, in this case the Danish. When, Prussia having proposed to annex the duchies, Austria was forced to fall back on the pro-Augustenburg position, she fatally embarrassed herself with the German national movement and gave Prussia the casus belli that permitted Moltke's armies to take the field.

All this falls into place if we appreciate Bismarck as the architect of the nation-state, as opposed to a champion of nationalism. Perhaps the most important insight into his aims is contained in his own words: "If revolution there is to be, let us rather undertake it than undergo it."[84]

Despite his frequent and passionate claims to the contrary, Bismarck was not inclined to protect the state-nations of Europe, including its empires. Rather he aimed to destroy the Concert built out of them with a new creation, the nation-state.* In so doing he was internationalizing the constitutional struggle in which he was engaged in Prussia, and he was deploying a strategic style of confrontation that was uniquely suited to the popular resources and moral passions of the nation-state.

---

*"It is not surprising that the principal legal codes of the world were introduced by the two greatest State builders of the 19th century: Napoleon and Bismarck," *The Quality of Government*, R. La Porta, F. Lopez de Silanes, A. Shleifer, and R. Vishny (National Bureau of Economic Research, 1998).

The mortal risk to the Vienna system of state-nations lay in the kind of warfare conducted by the nation-state. As Lothar Gall has observed of the 1866 campaign:

> The danger, as Bismarck knew, was considerably increased by the type of war that the Prussian military leadership, under the influence of . . . Moltke, envisaged waging. From the start it was no limited engagement in the style of eighteenth century warfare that they planned, one answering to possibly wide-ranging but at the same time precisely defined and hence limited political objectives; what they had in mind was an unlimited, "total" war that aimed to destroy the opponent's military might as completely as possible.[85]

It is no coincidence that the appearance of the nation-state—in the United States owing to the Civil War, in Europe owing to the unification of Germany—was accompanied by the strategic style of total war.* If the nation governed the state, and the nation's welfare provided the state's reason for being, then the enemy's nation must be destroyed—indeed, that was the way to destroy the state. Whereas Napoleon and the state-nation had reversed this, as for them it was necessary to destroy the state by threatening the state apparatus with annihilation, for the nation-state it was necessary to annihilate the vast resources in men and matériel that a nation could throw into the field, quickly through encirclement (Moltke's method), or less quickly if necessary through the attrition of economic resources (Sherman's method). It was only when nuclear weapons made the divided superpowers mutually and mortally vulnerable that the nation-state and the style of total war it dictated were undermined (at least as to these powers and their allies).

Moltke's strategy led to the overwhelming defeat of the Austrians at Koniggratz and Sadowa on July 3, 1866, and the peace of July 27 of that year. This time there was no congress to sort out the results. The Prussian peace terms were moderate, nonnegotiable, and perfectly understandable in light of the objective of creating a nation-state, though puzzling from the perspective of a state-nation (as indeed they completely bewildered William I). Austria made no surrenders of territory. Even the customary war indemnity demanded of the loser was quite reasonable, much of it being composed of a cancellation of Prussian debts. The principal changes

---

*In 1870, while serving as an observer with the Prussian army during the Franco-Prussian War, the American civil war general Philip Sheridan advised Bismarck that his treatment of the French was too mild. You must cause the civilian "inhabitants so much suffering that they must long for peace, and force their government to demand it. The people must be left nothing but their eyes to weep with over the war." P. A. Hutton, "Paladin of the Republic," in *With My Face to the Enemy,* Robert Cowley, ed. (G. P. Putnam's Sons, 2001), 357.

were political: Hanover, Hesse, Nassau, and what had been the free city of Frankfurt all were to lose their independent status and become provinces of Prussia, as were the disputed duchies of Schleswig and Holstein.

Bismarck next turned to the question of the southern states of Germany. The peace treaty of Prague in 1866 confined Prussia to an area north of the river Main. His strategy for annexing the states beyond the Main appeared at the time extraordinarily indirect and improbable, but it was made successful nonetheless by virtue of a remarkable stroke of political luck. For Bismarck did not threaten these states directly—which would have united Austria and France against him—but rather brought them under his control by virtue of a conflict over Spanish succession, of all things. If we keep in mind his goal of building a new constitutional order, however, and put to one side the more usual goals of simple territorial aggrandizement and accretion, his success does not seem all that roundabout. It was only necessary for him to build, by every means at his disposal, a sense of the German nation in the southern states, and then wait for the international opportunity that would allow him to unite that sense with Moltke's army corps.

Bismarck first concluded a set of secret military alliances with the south German states. Then he announced a proposal for a common customs union, to be governed by a parliament elected on the basis of universal suffrage for the entire area of the union, which included Southern and Northern Germany. He then covertly disclosed to the press a secret deal wherein Napoleon III had agreed to purchase Luxembourg from the king of the Netherlands. When news of this broke, a wave of patriotic emotion carried the southern states into the new parliament in June 1867.

Of course, in such a parliament, as he was well aware, he immediately began to confront the same political opposition he had encountered in the Prussian parliament. Popular opinion was far more influential in the nascent nation-state than it had been in the state-nation, but Bismarck had to risk its antagonism and even opposition if he was to harness its energy. In the election to the new parliament Bismarck's allies were crushed, just as his forces had been routed repeatedly in Prussian elections. Bismarck bided his time.

In 1868 Queen Isabella of Spain was overthrown; the successful insurgents now looked for a new monarch. They offered the crown to Prince Leopold of the Catholic branch of the Hohenzollerns, Prussia's dynastic family. This in itself did not fire Bismarck's ambitions for the Prussian ruling house, contrary to the conclusions of historians analyzing this offer from the state-nation's point of view. Napoleon I may have wanted his relatives on all the thrones proximate to his; Bismarck was after something else. Rather, he feared that if the Hohenzollern candidate rejected the offer, the Spanish would turn to the Wittelsbach dynasty of Bavaria, the principal south German state that opposed his long-range plans. If this happened, Bismarck told a nonplussed William I on March 9, 1870, the Spanish ruling house would maintain "contacts with anti-national elements in Germany and afford them a secure if remote rallying point."[86]

This did not persuade William, who was often baffled by his minister-president. In the middle of March the king cast the only vote in the Prussian Crown Council against the Hohenzollern candidacy of Prince Leopold. The king's opposition was sufficient; on April 20 Leopold and his father sent the Spanish government a formal notification of their refusal. By June, however, Bismarck had been able to turn this around, all the time keeping to the pretense that this was purely a dynastic affair. The acceptance by Leopold on June 19 was followed by the consent of the Prussian king two days later. Now the trap was baited.

What Bismarck counted on was an intemperate reaction by Napoleon III. If this could be provoked, then

> German national feeling would all of a sudden come into play: the nation would feel humiliated through its protecting power, Prussia, and would demand appropriate counter-measures. [That] would result in all misgivings and reservations with regard to Prussia and Prussian control being thrust into the background, at least temporarily. One could then expect to see a kind of national united front comprising the vast majority of existing parties and political forces with corresponding repercussions on the future shape of Central Europe.[87]

On July 4, two days after the announcement by the Spanish of the Hohenzollern acceptance, the Prussian ambassador was summoned to hear a sharply worded threat from the French foreign minister as well as the prime minister. The ambassador agreed to report these directly to the Prussian king at Bad Ems, where William had gone for a holiday. Two days later the French foreign minister announced in the Chamber of Deputies that

> [w]e do not believe that respect for the rights of a neighbor people obliges us to suffer a foreign power to disturb the present balance of power in Europe to our disadvantage . . . [The French government relies on] the wisdom of the German . . . people. . . . [But] should things turn out otherwise we shall know . . . how to do our duty without hesitation and without weakness.[88]

At this point the French ambassador, Benedetti, hurried to Bad Ems. On July 9 he delivered a formal complaint to the Prussian king. As arranged by Bismarck, the king replied simply that he had given his consent as the head of the Hohenzollern family and not as king of Prussia; the decision had been one for Leopold's branch of the family to decide. The conciliatory king nevertheless then promptly wrote to Leopold's father on July 10 suggesting that his son withdraw. On July 12 Prince Leopold announced that he was no longer a candidate.

However they may have appeared, so far things were going Bismarck's way. He knew he could count on the king's genuine aversion to war and his willingness to compromise. Now Bismarck's judgment of Napoleon III and the French leader's invincible vanity, as well as recent developments on the French political scene, came to bear. Through the Prussian ambassador in Paris the French government demanded not only formal approval of the withdrawal but also a declaration on the part of the king that in consenting to the candidature he had had no desire to offend the interests and honor of the French nation, and, further, that he would enter into a binding commitment never to give his consent to such a candidacy in the future. It was now possible for Bismarck to spring the trap by disclosing these demands to the German public and demonstrating that France was attempting to use the king's obvious love of peace and willingness to compromise to humiliate him and with him Prussia and the German nation that relied on Prussia as its military arm. Thus when the king sent his reply to the French through Bismarck, the latter cut the "Ems Dispatch" to only two sentences and distributed it to all Prussian diplomatic missions late in the evening of July 13 for immediate publication. A legend has grown up around Bismarck's behavior at this point—Winston Churchill renders it unforgettably[89]—that Bismarck doctored the dispatch. The "revised" message went:

> His Majesty the King has refused to receive the French ambassador again and has informed the latter through the duty adjutant that His Majesty has nothing further to say to the ambassador . . .[90]

The original had spoken only of "an adjutant" and the part about having nothing to say had referred explicitly to the present state of information. This was the final snap of the trap. French reaction, which would have been imprudent enough in the hands of Napoleon III, was now a matter of French public opinion. Bismarck could count on France responding so vehemently that Prussia could take its newly won national solidarity into the field. The French mobilized on July 14, 1870, and declared war on July 19, 1870. With this declaration, the formal legal requirements of the alliance treaties with the south German states were triggered, probably unnecessarily for ever since the publication of the Ems Dispatch, German national opinion had been passionately behind the Prussian king.

There was some further maneuvering. Bismarck leaked to *The Times* a handwritten draft of a treaty by Benedetti that spoke of France acquiring Belgium (without disclosing the date, which was 1866), and this doubtless reinforced the decision of the British not to get involved. But the main brake on intervention by third parties was the general understanding of the situation by the great powers: as in 1866 they completely misread what was actually happening. The leaderships in these states were convinced that this was a war to adjust international tensions, that it involved a local territorial conflict that would be resolved by a limited war. They had lived so long within the rules of the Vienna system that they appear to have thought them self-executing. All states knew it was in the self-interest of the state-nation system to avoid the destruction of any other state; the con- stitutional form of the state-nation and its precarious relation to the public demanded this restraint, as Castlereagh had taught. They were unprepared for a strategic challenge shaped by a new kind of state, whose constitu- tional legitimacy required the destruction of the system that had prevented German national unification. If Prussia was to establish itself as the legiti- mate state of the German nation, the system of collective security that had kept the German people fragmented must be smashed and a new method of validation for the State put in its place.

The German mobilization order came on the night of July 15, 1870. When complete the Prussian army had over a million men under arms. Against this the French—who fielded a professional, veteran force, experi- enced in combat, with modern weapons—could at best call on 350,000. In eighteen days, six Prussian rail lines and three additional lines for South Germans transported ten corps, 426,000 troops, to the front. By August 18, one of the two main French armies had fallen back on the fortress of Metz, which capitulated after a long siege. The other French force, attempting to relieve the fortress, was intercepted, driven against the Belgian frontier at Sedan, and surrounded. It surrendered on September 1 with Napoleon III and 104,000 men, who became prisoners of war.

The Germans invested Paris on September 18 but held only a narrow corridor to the capital. The French still had significant resources. Four new armies were raised in the French provinces. Bismarck, concerned that time was inevitably on the side of the French, who commanded the sea and could thereby bring fresh supplies from abroad, demanded an immediate bombardment of Paris. Moltke demurred, on grounds that he lacked suffi- cient guns for an effective attack, and argued that an unsuccessful bom- bardment would merely strengthen resistance. The king, however, sided with Bismarck, and as more heavy artillery arrived, Moltke commenced a furious shelling of the city on January 5, 1871. Armistice negotiations began on January 23 and Paris surrendered on January 28.

William I was proclaimed emperor of Germany in January at Versailles, the southern states having signed treaties the preceding month creating a united German state. Sovereignty lay in the Bundesrat, but the leading role of Prussia was obvious: of the sixty-one votes in this assembly, Prussia had seventeen, Bavaria six, Saxony and Wurttemberg four each, Baden and Hesse-Darmstadt three each, and all the others one apiece. Bismarck became the imperial chancellor, the only responsible federal minister, replicating on the national scale his precarious but decisive role in the Prussian parliament. In September he had electrified Europe by demanding the cession of Alsace-Lorraine. It is still debated whether this was the result of an attempt to capitalize on German nationalist sentiment or was rather the natural aggrandizement of a supremely successful military campaign. In all likelihood it was neither: restoring these ancient lands, which had been taken from Germany by France, was a way of creating a certain kind of state, a state that the nation felt belonged to it.

This was not lost on all other national leaders. In England, Benjamin Disraeli—who did as much to create the nation-state in Britain as any other nineteenth century leader—remarked with much prescience to Parliament in February 1871:

> This war represents the German Revolution, a greater political event than the French Revolution of last century . . . Not a single principle on the management of our foreign affairs, accepted by all statesmen for guidance up to six months ago, any longer exists. You have a new world . . .[91]

Unification was both the outcome of, and in some cases the cure for, nationalism. German nationalism, which sought to embody the political and cultural aspirations of the German people, was employed as a means of stifling Danish and Polish nationalism. Italian nationalism crushed the incipient national revolts in Naples and the national ambitions of Venetia. In both Italy and Germany, it would be as correct to say that a single state-nation conquered the others and transformed itself and them, as to say that a new state arose from the coming together of independent, ethnically connected states.

After 1871, a new society of nation-states gradually emerged. Its mood was one of easily inflamed nationalism and ethnic truculence. This reflected the public mood, excited by the press on a scale impossible before the spread of free compulsory public education and vastly increased literacy. Three new ideas vied in the public mind for attention and allegiance: Darwinism, which had been easily adulterated into a social credo of competitiveness and national survivalism; Marxism, with its hostility to the capitalist relationships of the industrial age; and bourgeois parliamentarianism, which promoted the rule of law in a national and an international society that was becoming increasing credulous about the role that law could play. It was thus an age of faith in law even if the bases for legal consensus were at the time being quickly eroded, an age of anxiety in class relationships, an age of ethnomania within states. The contrast with the world it replaced could not have been greater.* One can scarcely imagine a leader of a state-nation speaking as Bismarck did in explaining the new spirit of the age:

> Who rules in France or Sardinia is a matter of indifference to me once the government is recognized and only a question of fact, not of right. . . . [F]or me France will remain France, whether it is governed by Napoleon or St. Louis. . . . I know that you will reply that fact and right cannot be separated, that a properly conceived Prussian policy requires chastity in foreign affairs even from the point of view of utility. I am prepared to discuss the point of utility with you; but if you posit antinomies between right and revolution; Christianity and infidelity; God and the devil; I can argue no longer and can merely say, "I am not of your opinion and you judge in me what is not yours to judge."[92]

This is the authentic voice of the nation-state. Regimes may come and go, but the nation endures. International law conformed itself to this new society: how a government came to power was of no relevance so long as the fact of its control over a nation could be established.[†] Self-determination—the right of nations to have states of their own—became the only principle recognized in international law that detracted from the axiomatic legitimacy of the government that was in control.

It was obvious at the time that the nation-state bore certain strategic risks that were inherent in the kind of political society on which such a state depends.[‡] In his last public statement, in 1890, Moltke issued an ominous and melancholy warning. With such states, the old warrior said, which depended upon and at the same time inflamed popular passions, future wars could last "seven and perhaps thirty years."[93] This Tiresian forecast takes us back to Part I and the Long War.

There are, of course, other examples of the transition from state-nation

---

*As Michael Doyle has observed, "The Europe of 1870, which was to retain its major features until 1914, was a Europe very different from that of 1815. It was almost exactly what the statesmen of 1815 feared Europe might become, though they would have been amazed to discover that many of the changes had been led by men of their own kind—the aristocratic (now nationalist leaders) [of the nation-state]." Michael W. Doyle, *Empires* (Cornell University Press, 1986), 242–43.

[†]See e.g., the Montevideo Convention.

[‡]Chief among these is that the creation of states from proximate national elements can pose a threat to their neighbors. Thus Bismarck claimed that "restoring the Kingdom of Poland in any shape or form is tantamount to creating an ally for any enemy that chooses to attack us." Therefore, he concluded that Prussia should "smash those Poles till, losing all hope, they lie down and die; I have every sympathy for their situation, but if we wish to survive we have no choice but to wipe them out." Gall, v. I, 59.

to nation-state. Lincoln brought about the first of these constitutional transformations. As James McPherson aptly puts it, "The United States went to war in 1861 to preserve the *Union;* it emerged from war in 1865 having created a *nation.*"[94] This constitutional transformation, like the others we have studied, was accompanied by a revolution in strategy. Indeed, it may be said that it was Lee's adoption of the state-nation tactics of Napoleon I—tactics at which Lee excelled—that ultimately proved fatal to the Southern cause in the American Civil War. In the Wars of the French Revolution, Napoleon had been able to blast a hole in the enemy's line with canister fired by massed batteries of artillery, using fire against a line in much the same way a breach in a fortress wall might be opened. But by the time of the Civil War, infantry were armed with the Minié ball rifle, which had a greater effective range than canister. Moreover, with a range four times that of the smooth-bore musket carried by Napoleon's troops, the rifled barrels of the Union soldiers at Gettysburg doomed the frontal assaults that had been favored by the *Grande Armée.* Neither cannon nor charges could dislodge an entrenched defensive position,[95] and indeed the campaigns of 1864–1865 were marked by extensive entrenchments and field fortifications.[96] By the end of the Civil War, major battles had more in common with operations on the Western Front in World War I—the initial campaigns of the nation-state's epochal war—than with early Civil War battles like First Manassas or Shiloh. But it was not the constitutional and strategic developments in America that gave Europe its model for the nation-state, in any case.*

One state more than any other in Europe had used the new developments in warfare to change itself. The Prussian solution to the danger of arming the public and the requirement of vast numbers of soldiers to exploit the opportunities of decisive battle was to militarize the entire society. After the 1873 depression, the German state nationalized the railroads, introduced compulsory social insurance, and increased its intervention in the economy—in order to maximize the welfare of the nation.[97] Throughout the nineteenth century Britain refused to adopt a mass conscript army; it was Prussia that militarized as it industrialized. The railways, telegraph, and standardization of machined tools that industrialization made possible allowed for dizzying increases in the speed and mobility of military dispositions. The use of the telegraph, in concert with the railroad, allowed generals to mass widely dispersed forces quickly and to coordinate their operations over a vast theatre. During the Civil War, the Union Army shifted 25,000 troops, with artillery and baggage, over 1,100 miles of rail lines from Virginia to Chattanooga, Tennessee, in less than ten days. An

---

*Lincoln's multiethnic nation, founded on the principle of a nation of citizens—including African-American former slaves—was the antithesis of a European nation.

entire society could be mobilized for war, replenishing the front when necessary as the conflict progressed. But this was only possible if that entire society could be made a party to the war. This was the contribution of the nation-state. Far from being the paradoxical fact it is sometimes presented as, Bismarck's championing of the first state welfare systems in modern Europe, including the first social security program, was crucial to the perception of the State as deliverer of the people's welfare.* If the wars of the state-nations were wars of the State that were made into wars of the peoples, then the wars of the nation-states were national wars, championing causes that had deep popular support, and that were fought on behalf of popular ideals. The legitimation of the nation-state thus depends upon its success at maintaining modern life; a severe economic depression will undermine its legitimacy in a way that far more severe financial crises scarcely shook earlier regimes.[98]

Bismarck essentially bargained with the peoples of the various states of the North German Confederation to deliver German nationalism by means of Prussian aggression. There was no a priori reason why Prussia, feared and in many German quarters hated, was the natural leader of German nationalism nor any reason why Austria could not have been Germany's champion. The difficulty for Austria lay in the fact that it was necessarily a state-nation: its empire was composed of so many nationalities that it could not, constitutionally, adapt. The difficulty for the liberal states of the Confederation was that they could not marshal the material resources to exploit the military revolution wrought by industrialization. Only Prussia was without both these handicaps. Thus Prussia was the first European state to successfully unite the strategic and constitutional innovations of its time. Koniggratz, Gravelotte, and Sedan redeemed the Prussian pledge, and, in the doing, created a modern nation-state defined by the ethnicity of its people.

This new form of the state undertook to guide and manage the entire society, because without the total effort of all sectors of society, modern warfare could not be successfully waged. Not only the power of the State but its responsibility as well were extended into virtually all areas of civil life. All aspects of life were accordingly promised to improve. We hear its voice in Wilhelm II's famous assertion, *"Herrlichen Zeiten führe ich euch noch entgegen"* ("they are marvelous times towards which I will yet lead you"),[99] a public relations remark one can scarcely imagine in the mouth of his dignified and reticent grandfather.

---

*This concern for the welfare of the citizen was reflected in military matters: the first systematic use of battle dress to hide rather than advertise a soldier's presence dates from this period. In contrast, the state-nation's exaltation of sacrifice to the State had caused uniforms to reach their ornamental peak. The British adopted khaki for colonial campaigns in 1880 and for home service in 1902. The Germans went to field gray in 1910. See John Lynn, "Camouflage," in *The Reader's Companion to Military History,* 68.

CHAPTER NINE

The Study of the Modern State

All wars are so many attempts to bring about new relations among the states and to form new bodies by the break-up of the old states to the point where they cannot again maintain themselves alongside each other and must therefore suffer revolutions until finally, partly through the best possible arrangement of the civic constitution internally, and partly through the common agreement and legislation externally, there is created a state that, like a civic commonwealth, can maintain itself automatically.

—Kant, *Idea for a Universal History
with Cosmopolitan Intent* (1784)

OPEN ANY TEXTBOOK on constitutional law and you will find discussions of the regulation of commerce and the power of taxation, religious and racial accommodation, class and wealth conflicts, labor turmoil and free speech, but little or nothing on war.* The same is true of treatises on jurisprudence and legal theory. Yet who would deny the constitution-shaping experiences of war on the modern state? Think of the constitution of Japan, which was imposed by war; or that of Napoleonic France, which was extinguished by war; or that of the United States, which was established as a reaction to a revolutionary war and then transformed by a civil war. Even the discussion of the American Civil War is traced by such treatises mainly for its doctrinal effect, though in fact a civil war is the most revealing of the constitutional structure of the State because it lays open the anatomy of the body politic.

---

*My colleague tax professor Calvin Johnson has reminded those of us who teach constitutional law of the crucial role taxation played in the framing of the U.S. Constitution. Indeed it was the failure of the Articles of Confederation to establish a revenue base that led to the Philadelphia proposal of 1789. But what were the taxes *for*? To wage war in order to defend the new American state against attack because that state faced potentially mortal threats on every front.

Open any textbook on war and you will find chapters on strategy, the causes of wars, limited war, nuclear weapons, even the ethics of war, but nothing on the constitutions of societies that make war—nothing, that is, on what people are fighting to protect, to assert, to aggrandize. A constitution is not merely the *document* that manifests the ways in which a society recognizes the rights of family, of property, of land and personal security, of commerce, of ethnicity and religious commitment, and of government itself: rather a constitution *is* these ways. Societies, all societies, are constituted in a certain way, and this way is their constitution. States, which direct the political affairs of most national societies, are also constituted in a particular way, and this is not merely reflected in their law, it *is* their law. But even the more sophisticated contemporary books on geopolitics do not deign to mention law, unless it is to denigrate lawyers and "legalistic" thinking. And so it is that the fundamental force fields of the State—the relation between law and war, and between legitimacy and violence: relations that yield the State's most basic expression of its identity, indeed that gave birth to the modern state—are rarely even mentioned, much less addressed. These relations, these force fields, are simultaneous: it is only when the State is authorized by the society to defend that society with violence that the State is also accorded the monopoly on violence domestically, and is accorded the right by the society of states to resist external coercion. History discloses no examples of states that have given up the constitutional authority to deploy domestic or international violence without ceasing to be states.

The State has two primary functions: to distribute questions appropriately among the various allocation methods internal to the society, determining what sorts of problems will be decided in what sorts of ways;[1] and to defend that unique pattern of allocation by asserting its territorial and temporal jurisdiction vis-à-vis other states. These two tasks are, respectively, the work of constitutional law and strategy. History—the self-understanding of the society—is what enables the legitimation of constitutional law and strategy because history provides the means of giving an account of the State's stewardship—whether the State has fulfilled the requirement of its particular constitutional order.

In the preceding chapters it has been argued that there is a mutually affecting relationship between strategy and constitutional law such that some strategic challenges are of so great a magnitude that, rather than merely requiring more taxes, or more bureaucrats, or longer periods of war service, they encourage and even demand constitutional adaptations; and that some constitutional changes are of such magnitude that they enable and sometimes require strategic innovation. One cannot say whether, because of the development of light infantry and novel artillery tactics, the eighteenth century state was superseded by a state that could exploit the human material of the masses, as for example occurred with the Prussian constitutional reforms of 1806, or whether, owing to the revolutionary constitutional changes of 1789 in France that destroyed the army of the ancien régime and brought forth a surge of popular enthusiasm for the new state, new military policies, like the *levée en masse* and Napoleon's tactics, came into being. Both are persuasive accounts of the birth of the state-nation and the death of the territorial state. Both of these narratives culminate in the copying of the new constitutional order of the State and of its strategic inventions by other states that cast off the old forms.[2] Strategy and the constitutional order are mutually entailed. The common element to these two subjects lies in the state's quest for legitimacy.*

This quest leads us to the legitimating role of history: history is the medium by which the legitimacy of the constitutional structure is married to the success of the strategy of the state. For example, it was the constitutional order of the Habsburg state—dynastic, Catholic, multinational—that made the continued Spanish possession of the Netherlands so insistent a strategic goal, despite the fact that this region was far from Spain, and had different religious as well as different cultural and linguistic traditions. The Habsburg defeat not only ended the era of the princely state, it began the era of the kingly state of notably different constitutional arrangements. History gives the prestige of inevitability to decisive events, and cloaks state action, inner and outer, with legitimacy when a successful strategy is in harmony with the triumphant constitutional order. A crisis in legitimacy can be provoked either by external events or internal ones—usually the two go together—when the State becomes separated from its history. This happened to the Austro-Hungarian Empire in the late nineteenth century when it was unable to link its imperial state with any single national identity. A supple, flexible state will be portrayed in a way that allows for greater continuity with various strategic and constitutional innovations and thus offers a wider range of possible adaptations to necessity; a more rigid state will find its history is a straitjacket, confining it so tightly that only a political Houdini (like Bismarck) can break loose to survival.

---

*An alternative to finding the common basis for legitimacy in contemporary constitutional orders is to compare the constitutions of various states. Comparative constitutional law courses are usually paralyzingly boring; they typically consist of arid comparisons of the provisions of different written constitutions—which ones protect trial by jury, which ones have a bicameral legislature, and so forth. In this, comparative constitutionalism resembles comparative religion where the lecturer professes to think that the anthropologically collected dogma of a particular sect more or less sums up the content of religious faith. Such comparative constitutional law courses (and I dare say the comparative religion ones too) are lifeless because they lack the animating aspect of the subject being studied. With respect to constitutionalism, they lack its link between the common method of legitimation (unique to that era) and the different values that characterize different states. People do not sacrifice their lives to protect the electoral college. Nor do people make the sacrifices asked by religious faiths because they share deep convictions on any but the most basic theological matters.

The interplay between the military revolution that won the Long War—the development of nuclear weapons, an international communications system, and the computer (which made possible strategic deception and intelligence penetration to unprecedented effect)—and the constitutional changes that are both the consequence of that development as well as its enabling structure provide the subject of Part III. Suffice it to say at this point that the sense of identity of the nation-state, a state that defines itself by its axiomatic linkage to a people and its portrayal as their benefactor, is under considerable assault. Few contemporary groups, except those, such as the Palestinians or the Kurds, who are without states, seek their fulfillment in a relationship between their ethnic group and the nation-state. Indeed it is increasingly difficult for the nation-state to fulfill the functions that it added to its portfolio when it superseded the state-nation: not simply the maintenance of an industrial war machine of immense cost that is unable to assure the physical security of its citizens, but also the maintenance of civil order by means of bargaining among constituencies, the administration of juridical norms that embodied a single national tradition, and above all the management of the economic growth of the society in order to provide a continuous improvement in the material conditions of life for all classes.

These tasks were the nation-state's raison d'être. Yet today, market regulation by the State has become unpopular, many citizens have been effectively marginalized in the political life of their societies, and private business organizations have taken the initiative regarding international development. It is they who determine whether the economic policies of a state merit confidence and credit, without which no state can develop. At the same time, there are new security demands on the State that require ever greater executive authority, secrecy, and revenue. The constitutional shape that will emerge from this latest phase of transformation could be configured in several different ways. But before an understanding of these possibilities can be gained and the moral implications of the choices they present appreciated, we have needed to study in Part II the recurrent way in which the constitutional transformations of the State interact with its strategic innovations. Now we are in a position to ask what new demands for legitimation will be made upon the State, and how the experience of the Long War has fitted us to cope with these demands, to repeat the mixture of adaptation and innovation that has shaped the State heretofore.

My aim in presenting such a narrative is not so much to provide a standard history—there are better books for this, cited in the notes—but to depict the story of particular individuals acting within the choices presented by history. This avoids, I hope, the technological determinism of much politico/military history,[3] and its attendant assumptions about progress, without pretending that statesmen could reinvent the choices that faced them, choices—but not decisions among those choices—dictated to a great degree by the relationship between constitutional forms and strategic capabilities. All the transitions that are charted in Part II trace the State's constitutional and strategic change as it adapts, metamorphoses, thrives, and decays in ever-changing strategic circumstances, always striving for legitimacy in the new context in which it must compete.*

Over the long run, it is the constitutional order of the State that tends to confer military advantage by achieving cohesion, continuity, and, above all, legitimacy for its strategic operations. And it is these strategic operations, through continuous innovation, that winnow out unsuccessful constitutional orders.

*See Plate IV, page 347.

Excerpt from "Elegy for the Departure
of Pen, Ink and Lamp"

I never believed in the spirit of history
an invented monster with a murderous look
dialectical beast on a leash led by slaughterers

nor in you—four horsemen of the apocalypse
Huns of progress galloping over earthly and heavenly steppes
destroying on the way everything worthy of respect old and defenseless
I spent years learning the simplistic cogwheels of history
a monotonous procession hopeless struggle
scoundrels at the head of confused crowds
against the handful of those who were honest courageous aware

I have very little left
not many
objects
or compassion

light heartedly we leave the gardens of childhood gardens of things
shedding in flight manuscripts oil-lamp dignity pens
such is our illusory journey at the edge of nothingness

pen with an ancient nib forgive my unfaithfulness
and you inkwell—there are still so many good thoughts in you
forgive me kerosene lamp—you are dying in my memory like a deserted
 campsite

I paid for the betrayal
but I did not know then
you were leaving forever

and that it will be dark

—Zbigniew Herbert
(translated by Bogdana and John Carpenter)

PART III

THE HISTORIC CONSEQUENCES OF THE LONG WAR

THESIS: THE MARKET STATE IS SUPERSEDING THE NATION-STATE AS A CONSEQUENCE OF THE END OF THE LONG WAR

The end of the Long War has been quickly followed by the emergence of a new constitutional order. This new form is the market-state. Whereas the nation-state, with its mass free public education, universal franchise, and social security policies, promised to guarantee the welfare of the nation, the market-state promises instead to maximize the opportunity of the people and thus tends to privatize many state activities and to make voting and representative government less influential and more responsive to the market. The United States, a principal innovator in the development of the market-state, must fashion its strategic policies with this fundamental constitutional change in mind.

Homage to a Government

Next year we are to bring the soldiers home
For lack of money, and it is all right.
Places they guarded, or kept orderly,
Must guard themselves, and keep themselves orderly.
We want the money for ourselves at home
Instead of working. And this is all right.

It's hard to say who wanted it to happen,
But now it's been decided nobody minds.
The places are a long way off, not here,
Which is all right, and from what we hear
The soldiers there only made trouble happen.
Next year we shall be easier in our minds.

Next year we shall be living in a country
That brought its soldiers home for lack of money.
The statues will be standing in the same
Tree-muffled squares, and look nearly the same.
Our children will not know it's a different country.
All we can hope to leave them now is money.

—Philip Larkin

CHAPTER TEN

The Market-State

One has already to know (or be able to do) something in order to be capable of asking a thing's name.

—Ludwig Wittgenstein*

DIFFERENT CONSTITUTIONAL orders are responsive to different demands for legitimacy. Legitimating characteristics, such as dynastic rights, that are sufficient for one constitutional order are inadequate for another. The reason that the constitutional order of the nation-state is undergoing a transformation is that it faces a crisis of legitimation. When the American state changes to reflect a new constitutional archetype,[†] it will do so in response to demands for new bases for legitimacy, demands that arise in part as a consequence of the strategic innovations that won the Long War. In light of this new constitutional form of the State, the Americans will desire an appropriate national security paradigm. The reason the United States needs a new national security paradigm is that the Wilsonian internationalism[‡] that guided us throughout the Long War was derived from the constitutional order of the nation-state. Obviously, Wilsonian

---

*¶20, *Philosophical Investigations,* 2nd ed. (Macmillan, 1958).

[†]I should emphasize that such a transformation does not mean that the present U.S. constitution will be replaced. It has already weathered one such transformation in the constitutional order, that from state-nation to nation-state, and its underlying theory of popular sovereignty, personal liberty, and individual equality is perfectly compatible with the multicultural market-state. On some issues, though, such as federalism and the regulatory powers of Congress, it may be interpreted in the new archetypal context in ways that are more restrictive of government; while in others, notably national security, the power of the executive may gain. But none of these developments require a departure from the available constitutional arguments that currently make up American constitutional law, even if the outcomes of constitutional decision making were to undergo some considerable change.

[‡]"In a sense, the same world view that ultimately drove a reluctant President Woodrow Wilson to intervene in World War I was also the logic of intervention in Viet Nam." Kai Bird, *The Color of Truth: McGeorge Bundy and William Bundy, Brothers in Arms* (Simon and Schuster, 1998); see Tony Smith, *America's Mission: The United States and the Worldwide Struggle for Democracy in the Twentieth Century* (Princeton University Press, 1994).

internationalism was not the only option available to nation-states as diverse as Fascist Italy and Communist China; perhaps less obviously, determining the rough shape of the new constitutional form the United States is in the process of adopting will not by itself determine how and when the U.S. should use force in international affairs. That determination will require an examination of the special situation of the United States, a unique state with unique advantages and burdens.

These three subjects—the source of the constitutional crisis of legitimation and the nature of the new constitutional order; the practical choices a State faces in defining a national security paradigm; and the crafting of such a paradigm that is compatible with that order and responsive to our particular position—are the subjects of the three final chapters of Book I.

THE CRISIS OF THE NATION-STATE

As we saw in the historical narratives of Part II, the nation-state is a relatively recent structure. Indeed, the modern State itself is of fairly recent vintage in the life of civilized mankind, dating as it does from roughly the end of the fifteenth century.[1] Before that period European governance divided jurisdiction among ecclesiastical authorities, independent cities, feudal rulers (whose own relationships were far from simple), and various oligarchies. Only when a strategic threat to the wealthy and sophisticated cities of Italy provoked a crisis of survival did these societies turn to the institutional bureaucratization of governing authority that became the modern state. The reification of the State that resulted conveyed to a state structure the two characteristics of sovereignty that had hitherto exclusively been possessed by the person of the prince—a monopoly on the legitimate use of violence domestically (the role of lawgiver) and the independence of will in foreign affairs (the right of sovereignty).

We then saw a series of changes in the structure of states, a morphology of constitutional orders or archetypes. These changes culminated in the form of the nation-state late in the nineteenth century. It was only then that the idea took hold that a State is properly—that is to say, legitimately—formed by the boundaries of its national people and not simply by the conquered or inherited territory of rulers. At each stage in this morphology, constitutional change was accompanied by strategic innovation, as those states that were able to consolidate power within a unitary jurisdiction of taxation, regulation, and administration developed new strategies or copied the strategic breakthroughs of their competitors. It was the strategic successes of the European state that made its archetypal constitutional structures the models for the world until finally the most recent form—that of the nation-state—was turned against a receding form, the colonial state-nation, and the European model became global and virtually universal.*

Why should it be that now, at the moment of its most widespread adoption, this model should be superseded? We have seen how the constitutional archetype of the nation-state presented states with three competing options: fascism, liberal parliamentarianism, and communism. The unresolved issue as to which of these options would best assure the legitimacy of the nation-state caused the Long War to persist for most of this century; now, at the moment of resolution, why would a new constitutional question be put to the conflict-weary states of the world?

It was only in 1989 that Francis Fukuyama wrote:

What we may be witnessing is not just the end of the Cold War, or the passing of a particular period of postwar history, but the end of history as such: that is, the end point of mankind's ideological evolution and the universalization of Western liberal democracy as the final form of human government.[†]

How can it be that, so soon after this historic success, the fundamental form of the nation-state, of which the liberal democracies are a triumphant exemplar, would metamorphose into a new archetypal model? The reason lies in the Long War itself and the strategic innovations by which that war was won by the liberal democracies.

The nation-state has accumulated various responsibilities. The legitimating promises of earlier, preceding constitutional forms are often inherited by successive archetypes as entrenched expectations and entitlements. The princely state promised external security, the freedom from domination and interference by foreign powers. The kingly state inherited this responsibility and added the promise of internal stability. The territorial state added the promise of expanding material wealth, to which the state-nation further added the civil and political rights of popular sovereignty. To all these responsibilities the nation-state added the promise of providing economic security and public goods to its people. The failure of the Soviet Union to live up to this expectation, as much as any other cause, contributed to its delegitimation in the eyes of its nation. Very simply, the strategic innovations of the Long War will make it increasingly difficult for the nation-state to fulfill its responsibilities. That will account for its delegitimation. The new constitutional order that will supersede the

---

*For this reason Part II was, until its final chapter, so "Eurocentric."

[†]Francis Fukuyama, "The End of History?" *The National Interest* (Summer 1989): 3. It is instructive to note that Hegel, from whom Fukuyama takes the electrifying phrase "the End of History" thought much the same thing when the state-nation triumphed at the battle of Jena.

nation-state will be one that copes better with these new demands of legitimation, by redefining the fundamental compact on which the assumption of legitimate power is based.

Three strategic innovations won the Long War: nuclear weapons, international communications, and the technology of rapid mathematical computation. Each has wrought a dramatic change in the military, cultural, and economic challenges that face the nation-state. In each of these spheres, the nation-state faces ever increasing difficulty in maintaining the credibility of its claim to provide public goods for the nation.

SECURITY

The State exists to master violence: it came into being in order to establish a monopoly on domestic violence, which is a necessary condition for law, and to protect its jurisdiction from foreign violence, which is the basis for strategy. If the State is unable to deliver on these promises, it will be changed; if the reason it cannot deliver is rooted in its constitutional form, then that form will change. A State that could neither protect its citizens from crime nor protect its homeland from attack by other states would have ceased to fulfill its most basic reason for being.

The Long War was characterized by many strategic innovations, two of which are especially pertinent to the problem of maintaining external and internal security. First, the Long War was a total war, that is, a struggle in which war was waged directly on the civilian societies supporting the states at war. Without the "total participation [of the belligerent populations] in field and factory as well as in the armed forces, the struggle could not be carried on at all."[2]

The strategy of total war is, as has been noted, characteristic of the nation-state. Indeed in the constitutional transition that accompanied the American Civil War, we can observe one state (the Confederacy) that represented an earlier order (the state-nation, whose strategies are indistinguishable from those of Napoleon) fighting another state (the Union) that came to stand for a new insurgent order, the nation-state, whose strategies (such as Sherman's March to the Sea) prefigure those of the Long War. The nation-state mobilizes the total resources of the society in pursuit of its political goals, and it is the *nation* of its adversary that it attacks in order to achieve victory.

In November 1917 Georges Clemenceau was summoned, at age seventy-six, to be prime minister of France in the midst of World War I. His speech to the Chamber of Deputies was composed the night before he assumed office. He wrote with a quill, at his bedside table, wearing a small silk cap. He began, *"Nous nous présentons devant vous dans l'insigne pensée d'une défense integrale . . ."* for he had long been a critic of the previous administration's divided command arrangements, in which the Allies were responsible for their own sectors. But then he scratched out *"défense"* and replaced it with *"guerre."* Not "total defense" but "total war."

This famous address to the chamber reflected the new perspective and responsibility of the nation-state (of which Clemenceau, in opposition to the French imperialists of his day, was a passionate advocate). To a packed chamber (Winston Churchill was in the gallery) Clemenceau said,

> We present ourselves before you with the unique thought of total war . . . These Frenchmen whom we are forced to throw into battle, they have rights over us. They want none of our thoughts to be diverted from them, they want none of our acts to be foreign to them. We owe them everything, with no reservation. All for France bleeding on its glory, all for the apotheosis of law triumphant.[3]

Similarly, in October 1941, President Franklin Roosevelt decided to produce an atomic bomb. Hitler[4] and Stalin[5] and the Japanese cabinet[6] made similar decisions. Of these decisions there was little public knowledge at the time. But such decisions are entirely consistent with the entire strategic pattern of the nation-state.

> Certainly since Grant and Sherman, American commanders had accepted that modern wars—which is to say wars between modern societies capable of fielding and supporting vast modern armies—would not be won by the elegant Napoleonic maneuvers of a Lee or Jackson, isolating, distracting and dividing armies in the field, but by the relentless destruction of a society's ability to carry on. The theory of strategic bombing holds that air power will accelerate this process by leapfrogging the lines of defense and directly attacking the supporting society . . . The atomic bomb was developed [by the United States and the United Kingdom] as a weapon that, like other counter-city incendiary bombs, could be used to compel the Axis political structure to collapse.*

Even though the development of nuclear weapons brought the strategy of the nation-state to its apogee of effectiveness—"the apotheosis of law triumphant"—and ended the Long War by stalemating the superpower

---

*Philip Bobbitt, *Democracy and Deterrence,* 20. The fiftieth anniversary of Hiroshima was accompanied by an intense debate over the rightness of the decisions to use atomic weapons against Japan. Utterly absent in that debate was the fact that there was no decision as such; that is, the use of these weapons was only the orderly continuation of a campaign of terror bombing that itself was only the continuation of the strategy of total war, the strategy of the nation-state. It is characteristic of the successor to that constitutional and cultural form that commentators should be asking whether or not the Japanese couldn't have been bargained into peace without the use of nuclear weapons. This sort of question is almost unintelligible in light of the struggle of the nation-state and its role in the Long War, but fits nicely within the assumptions and strategies of the market-state.

military conflict, these weapons will progressively undermine the nation-state's ability to protect the nation from foreign attack. Even if most states cannot expect to match the American arsenal, an increasing number will have access to a variety of low-cost launchers, nuclear warheads, and other weapons of mass destruction. Of course such states would not be able to win an all-out war with the United States, Britain, Russia, France, or China (the largest members of the nuclear club), but by threatening to use such weapons against U.S. forces abroad, or her regional allies, or even against American continental territory, such states can paralyze American policy.

As one commentator has observed, "Certainly had Saddam Hussein been possessed of a working nuclear arsenal, the United States would have been far less willing to station half a million troops, a sizable fraction of its air forces, and a large naval armada within easy reach of Iraq's borders,"[7] an observation that will not be lost on most world leaders. The consequence of this development for the projection of conventional forces is profound. It's not so much that nuclear weapons render the promise of security to the citizens of the nation-state unbelievable per se; rather it is that *only* the possession of weapons of mass destruction can hope to validate that promise, with the unavoidable result that no nation-state can afford to be without the protection of such weapons, because their conventional forces are utterly vulnerable to threats from the states that do possess these weapons. With the Long War ended, once the nuclear umbrella of the United States ceases to be extended to cover Japan, Germany, and other states against attack, the drive to acquire weapons of mass destruction will become irresistible. Widespread nuclear proliferation may take time, and there are enormous domestic barriers in the developed world to proliferation to major states such as Germany and Japan. But the arrival of nuclear weapons to regional powers—Israel and Iraq, North and South Korea, India and Pakistan, the Central Asian former Soviet states and the non-Russian Slavic ones, Iran and others—will inevitably engage all the major states. In such a world, over whom is the United States supposed to extend its nuclear protection? For without this guarantee, the nation-states once protected will seek their own nuclear weapons. When this happens, the citizens of every nation-state that possesses such weapons become a target for nuclear attacks against which there is no defense, precisely because there is no other way to use force successfully against such states. This is an historical experience with which Americans have long lived, and one that has so greatly contributed to the demise of the nation-state here. Then the nation-state faces an impossible dilemma: if it does not have nuclear weapons, it cannot guarantee the security of its citizens from foreign attack; if it acquires such weapons, its civilian population will be specifically targeted for annihilation. Finally, it must also be noted that the presence of nuclear weapons in the arsenals of states motivates the development of other weapons of mass destruction—such as chemical, biological, and cyber weapons—as options that are less costly to obtain and the origin of whose use is easier to disguise. Here too it is the decisive impact of nuclear weapons in the Long War that now drives this development.

I will write in a subsequent section about the failure of the nation-state to provide internal security against crime and terrorism. For now, let me suggest that this is a consequence of the *national* character of nation-states, which isolates and alienates substantial minorities of their citizens even to the point of defining some criminal behavior in essentially ethnic ways. For example, why in the West is marijuana criminalized but martinis are not? Why is polygamy criminalized but not divorce? The ethnic focus of the nation-state, its pervasive analogy to the family, creates a role for antisocial elements, "misfits," that is connected to violence because violence is the currency of the state. In every society there are such people, and such groups; in the nation-state they become the enemy of the State (and vice versa), because the State itself is fused to a national conception of the culture. Nevertheless, without the Long War and the strategic concept of total war the horrors of present urban life might not have come into being, for much of contemporary crime is a kind of protowar against the State, waged against civilians. Groups of bored and armed young men, quasi-mercenaries (as in Colombia) or quasi-soldiers (as in Somalia), are not so different in kind from the small bands that fought the wars of the Middle Ages, except that in the Middle Ages chivalry to some degree tempered the impact on noncombatants, whereas today "terrorists"—as the nation-state calls them—specifically target civilians.[8] Bandits, robbers, guerrillas, gangs have always been part of the domestic security environment. What is new is their access to mechanized weapons, another product of the technological environment of the Long War, and the unique political role of such groups, which pits them against noncombatants as a means of war against the State itself.[9] Against these threats, the nation-state is too muscle-bound and too much observed to be of much use. The mobilization of the industrial capacity of a nation is irrelevant to such threats; the fielding of vast tank armies and fleets of airplanes is as clumsy as a bear trying to fend off bees.

WELFARE

The revolution in modern communications that began with the telegraph changed warfare and virtually ensured the emergence of the nation-state.* Ultimately, developments in communications technology also were decisive in the Long War. It has been argued, by Mary Fulbrook among others,

---

*This point is well documented in Daniel Headrick's *The Invisible Weapon: Telecommunications and International Politics, 1851–1945*[10] and other recent scholarship.[11]

that it was the manifest incompetence of the East European regimes, as reflected in the implicit contrasts made available by West European television to the publics of those regimes, that ultimately delegitimated the governments of the Warsaw Pact.[12] Eric Helleiner's book, *States and the Reemergence of Global Finance: From Bretton Woods to the 1990s*,[13] convincingly argues that the government policies of nation-states have played a decisive role in the stunning globalization of commodity pricing, interest rates, and the availability and pricing of credit.[14] I should like to connect these works of scholarship by suggesting that it was the change in the nature of the states fighting the Long War, a change brought about in part by communications technology, that moved those states gradually and then rapidly to shift away from controls on the private movement of capital and ultimately to permit the virtually uninhibited flow of capital among developed states. Very simply, the victorious Western nation-states of the Long War, plus West Germany and Japan, by relying on the market to allocate resources efficiently within their domestic economies effectively extrapolated this approach to all the states of their alliance. What had been true within a single state proved true among states. The attempt to control currencies and investment in the socialist states turned out to be a crippling mistake, draining away investment that might have been indifferent to the human rights shortcomings of such regimes, and walling those states off from international trade that required convertible currency. The nation-state, which had established its reputation as a provider of welfare to the nation by guaranteeing a unified national market and providing protection against foreign competition and access to foreign markets, was supercharged when the liberal democracies applied the same principles to their interstate trade and finance. The effect of the reduction on direct controls and taxes on capital movements, the liberalization of long-standing regulatory constraints on financial services, the expansion of relationships with offshore financial harbors, and the disintermediation that accompanied these steps made states much wealthier. At a price.*

The price these states were compelled to pay is a world market that is no longer structured along national lines but rather in a way that is transnational and thus in many ways operates independently of states. At the

*Louis Pauly, "Capital Mobility, State Autonomy and Political Legitimacy: Transcending National Boundaries," *Journal of International Affairs* 48 (1995): 369. Karl Marx anticipated this when he wrote, "The bourgeoisie, by the rapid improvement of all instruments of production, by the immensely facilitated means of communication, draws all, even the most barbarian, nations into civilization. The cheap price of its commodities are the heavy artillery with which it batters down all Chinese walls, with which it forces the barbarians' intensely obstinate hatred of foreigners to capitulate. It compels all nations, on pain of extinction, to adopt the bourgeois mode of production; it compels them to introduce what it calls civilization into their midst, i.e., to become bourgeois themselves. In one word, it creates a world after its own image." Karl Marx and Friedrich Engels, "Manifesto of the Communist Party," in *The Marx-Engels Reader,* 2nd ed., ed. Robert C. Tucker (W.W. Norton, 1978), 477.

micro level, this is true of the multinational firm, which moves its location to optimize conditions for its operation, taking into account the nation-state only as a source of tax breaks and incentives to be sought, or as a nettle of regulations to be avoided. Far from being dependent on the local government, these corporations are seen as providing desperately needed jobs and economic activity, so that the state is evaluated on whether *its* workforce has the necessary skills, and whether *its* infrastructure has been suitably configured to attract the corporation. At the macro level, this development applies to capital flows, in the face of which every country appears powerless to manage its monetary policy. Walter Wriston, the former chairman of Citibank, described and defended the process of capital decontrol as follows:

> The gold standard [of the nineteenth century], replaced by the gold exchange standard, which was replaced by the Bretton Woods arrangements, has now been replaced by the information standard. Unlike the other standards, the information standard is in place, operating, will never go away and has substantially changed the world. What it means, very simply, is that bad monetary and fiscal policies anywhere in the world are reflected within minutes on the Reuters screens in the trading rooms of the world. Money only goes where it's wanted, and only stays where it's well treated, and once you tie the world together with telecommunications and information, the ball game is over. It's a new world, and the fact is, the information standard is more draconian than any gold standard . . . For the first time in history the politicians of the world can't stop it.[15]

Approximately four trillion dollars—a figure greater than the entire annual GDP of the United States—is traded every day in currency markets. The consequences of these trades for the economic well-being of any particular nation-state can be decisive. There is a grotesque disparity between the rapid movement of international capital and the ponderous and territorially circumscribed responses of the nation-state, as clumsy as a bear chained to a stake, trying to chase a shifting beam of light.

Finally, communications—in the broadest sense of that term, encompassing all human logistics—have increased the dangers posed by transnational threats (like those of new diseases once confined to remote incubators, or wounds to the global environment that once took centuries to materialize, or abrupt population shifts and migrations that were once locally confined, to take but three examples). Moreover, the global communications network itself presents a new and fraught fragility as to which merely national protection is pathetically inadequate.

The most important consequence of these developments is that the State seems less and less credible as the means by which a continuous improvement in the welfare of its people can be achieved. Many states, including most notably the United States, have experienced considerable difficulty in achieving stability even regarding their own budgets. Their difficulties with chronic deficits and ever-mounting debt are instructive. Of course there is nothing wrong with a state taking on debt. Every corporation does this. If taxes can be analogized to equity contributions, then it can properly be said that a state should maintain the balance of debt and equity it thinks appropriate at any given time. During the development of the American West, and during the Second World War, the U.S. government acquired debt as an even greater proportion of its national wealth than today. What marks the current period as different is the way in which the funds thus acquired have been used: the proceeds of this borrowing have been returned as consumption—that is, to improve the immediate welfare of the people—rather than to fund investment in infrastructure; and much of that consumption has been expatriated as earnings to foreign firms. A nation-state government simply finds itself unable to either balance its budget (because it cannot reduce welfare outlays to all sectors) or redirect the proceeds of its borrowing, because only by borrowing money can it continue plausibly to claim that it is bettering the welfare of its people, much as the manager of a Ponzi scheme, by distributing to investors the proceeds of fresh participants, can continue to claim that his stock portfolio is thriving. Such policies have an inevitable end, as everyone recognizes. There is no reason why a state cannot grow out of its deficit, but to do so, however, it will have to increasingly abandon the objective of the government's maintaining the ever-improving welfare of its citizens.* That is, it will have to change the crucial element of the basis for its legitimacy as a nation-state. As we will see in a later discussion, this is precisely what the Bush administration in the United States and the Blair government in Great Britain were in the midst of doing at the beginning of the twenty-first century.[16] From this perspective President Reagan and Prime Minister Thatcher were among the last nation-state leaders. Although they offered radically new policies, they appealed to the same basis on which to judge those policies—whether they improved the welfare of the people—as did their great welfare-state predecessors. Bush and Blair, however, are among the first market-state political leaders. They appeal to a new standard—whether their policies improve and expand the opportunities offered to the public— because this new standard reflects the basis for a new form of the State.

Although it may surprise many readers, the corporation was a nation-

---

*U.S. projected revenue surpluses, for example, cannot survive projected Social Security expenditures unless that program is scaled back.

state vehicle to improve the welfare of its citizens. Replacing the great trusts and partnerships of the state-nation, the corporation bureaucratized the management of business, making it feasible for the State, through regulation, to temper the profit motive with concern for the public welfare, replacing the enterprising if ruthless entrepreneur with the modern manager. This varied in degree from nation-state to nation-state, but throughout the First World the corporation was the legal structure by which the political objective of improving welfare was grafted onto the market.

The revolution in debt financing of the 1980s dramatically changed this. By mobilizing hitherto uninvolved shareholders and drawing on capital raised by high-yield (junk) bonds that promised—and delivered—excellent rates of return, wave after wave of mergers and takeovers transformed the management of large corporations. The "fat" that new managers were able to squeeze out of the companies they took over in order to pay the interest on the debt by means of which they had bought a controlling percentage of shares, in some measure came from the nonprofit, public welfare role of the corporation. Huge savings did not accrue through shutting down private dining rooms, whatever the corporate raiders said. Savings on this scale came from downsizing and layoffs. The productivity gains made possible by the computer chip and the immediacy of information brought about by the revolution in communications combined to replace corporate managerial control (which tended to favor stability over enhanced competitiveness) with control by the capital markets. The corporation had failed to maximize the opportunities of its shareholders because it insulated business decisions from competition. Indeed there was really no way that even the most enlightened managers could both protect the welfare of the community and create the lean, nimble enterprises capable of prevailing in the global marketplace.

CULTURE

The third promise of the nation-state was that it would protect the cultural integrity of the nation. Whether this applied to national liberation movements in Third World colonies whose cultures had been suppressed or to ethnic groups like the Czechs or Poles, who found themselves submerged within a larger national culture, or to the Germans, whose culture was fragmented among many states, or to the Italians, to whom all of these disabilities at one time applied, the nation-state promised a wholeness. One nation, one state.

Here too the strategic innovations of the Long War played a transformative role. Mass electronic communications made possible mass ideological propaganda on a scale and of an immediacy hitherto impossible. Of course propaganda has long been a military tool: Napoleon's battle dispatches no less than his calls for liberty and equality were studiedly drafted to move public opinion. Romanticizing war-making served his political goals. Napoleon did not believe that public opinion would decide the issue at Waterloo or Austerlitz or Borodino, however. By contrast, the morale of the entire nation is crucial to the prosecution of twentieth century warfare. That is why the morale of any enemy public—as opposed to the morale of the army and its ruling elites for Clausewitz and Napoleon—must be crushed by the nation-state at war. For the same reason the morale of one's own nation must be inspired and reassured.[17] The globalization of communications, however, wrests control of this morale from the instrumentalities of the nation-state. Foreign broadcasts, for example, are the primary news source for 60 percent of educated Chinese, despite the efforts of the People's Republic of China to control the content of information going to its public. Access to the Internet will inevitably increase this figure.

On behalf of the victorious nation-states of the Long War, propaganda has been chiefly directed at advertising the ideology of democracy, equality, and personal freedom. With respect to democracy, it may be that, in the words of one analyst, such advertising has persuaded "too much,"[18] for few nation-states can provide examples of the kind of democracy that is propagandized. In any case, it is well-documented that the publics of the Western democracies do not generally believe in many of the practical constitutional underpinnings of the parliamentary states. For example, the publics in the United States and the United Kingdom do not believe in an adversarial political system ("Why can't the politicians put partisan differences aside and do what's best for the country?"); they do not believe in the protection of criminal rights ("If he's not guilty, why do you think he was arrested and indicted? A criminal should not go free on 'technical' grounds"); they do not believe in the adversarial role of lawyers ("If we could just sit down without the lawyers, we could sort out our differences. A lawyer only wants you to hear his side of the story") and cannot bring themselves to believe that an ethical attorney would defend a client he believed to be guilty or take a position on a legal question solely because it was in his client's interest to do so.* Americans, by significant majorities, believe there should be prayers in the public schools, that news reporters should be forced to reveal their sources when presented with a subpoena, that a refusal to testify on one's own behalf is tantamount to a confession of guilt, and that politicians generally—though not, it should be noted, one's own congressman—are professional liars and that federal judges

---

*See Matthew Parris, a former MP, "Ministers pander to a misguided populace," *The Times* (London), August 4, 2001. This shortfall in public opinion is by no means confined to the nation-state. The market-state too will have to contend with the fact that their publics also do not believe that the market should determine prices or wages or that anyone should profit from scarcity. Publics are often reported to think that increased productivity will increase unemployment. And there seems to be a consensus among the publics of many states that an immigrant should not take a job for which there is already a willing indigenous worker. See Parris, ibid.

should not have life tenure—all attitudes that are considerably at variance with the constitutional operation of the system that, taken as a whole, Americans revere.

Nor can the nation-state assure equality, if by that is meant the equal treatment of different cultural communities. The boundaries of the states of the world do not, and could not, coincide with the various cultural communities that make up their populations, communities that are bound by common religion, language, or ethnicity, because these communities themselves are often overlapping and multiple but seldom coextensive. Moreover, the nation-state is, oddly, the enemy of "nations" as such, or ethnicity, because, at least in its most popular form, it must ally one, and only one, ethnic group with the State, which also must be unitary, with one and only one sovereign. Bismarck's nation-state, not Lincoln's, has generally been the model for the world.

Or to put it another way, we will inevitably get a multicultural state when the nation-state loses its legitimacy as the provider and guarantor of equality. And this legitimacy it must lose if equality is understood as an equality among ethnic groups. This is apparent in such appalling but doubtless well-intended experiments as the Australian adoption and relocation of Aboriginal children, as well as the useful but regrettable American practice of affirmative action. In both cases, a dominant national group is setting the terms of assimilation on the basis of which the State will assure equality to individuals and, by setting those terms, implicitly denying equal status to the group that is thought to be in need of assistance. Without affirmative action, the presence of some ethnic groups will be diminished in some meritocratic professions and institutions; with affirmative action, many will be confined to a second-class status that is re-enforced by the hostility of those who are displaced. Either way, it is the cultural standards of "merit" that set the terms of the debate, that is, that require "affirmative" action in the first place, or that seek to block that action on grounds that it is unjust.

These two opposing but interacting phenomena—the oppression of minority groups by the nation (that is, by the dominant ethnic group with whom the State is identified) and the resistance to an assimilation that might overcome oppression—are damaging to the legitimacy of those nation-states that are based on the promise of assuring equality among all national members.* As a result, it is increasingly difficult in multicultural, multiethnic states to get consensus on public-order problems and the maintenance of rule-based legal action, which are core tasks of the State.

Finally, the techniques of mass propaganda also threaten the claim of the State to ensure the conditions of freedom.[19] This is most easily seen in

---

*Fascist nation-states, of course, made no such promise.

the immense power of the modern electronic media and the press. More than any other development it is the increased influence of the news media that has delegitimated the State, largely through its ability to disrupt the history of the State, that process of self-portrayal that unites strategy and law and forms the basis for legitimacy. This perhaps is most egregiously evident in phenomena like the digitized re-creation of President Kennedy's assassination in a movie "showing" a government plot to kill the president, but it is also evident in the nightly news broadcasts, where confident and placid presenters portray the political events of the day as repetitive, formulaic entertainments. Journalists themselves soon become the important characters in the historical narrative portrayed by journalism; politicians and officials merely provide the props. The story of government becomes the story of personalities in conflict with the media itself, and the story of official evasion and incompetence unmasked by the investigative entrepreneurs of the news business.

The press and electronic media, far more than the drab press releases of any government, are the engines of mass propaganda today, and it should be borne in mind that the press, when it is not controlled by the State, is driven by the need to deliver consumers to advertisers,[20] and whether State-owned or not, is animated by the conditions of competition among all news media. Whatever the individual aspirations of its reporters and editors, the ideology of media journalism is the ideology of consumerism, presentism, competition, hyperbole (characteristics evoked in its readers and watchers)—as well as skepticism, envy, and contempt (the reactions it rains on government officials). No State that bases its legitimacy on claims of continuity with tradition, that requires citizen self-sacrifice, that depends on a consensus of respect, can prosper for very long in such an environment. It must either change so as to become less vulnerable to such assaults, or resort to repression. Some nation-states do the latter; the liberal democracies, whose claims to ensure civil liberties are as much a part of their reason for being as any other functions, cannot do this. At best they can manipulate information and resort to deception, thus poisoning the history on which they themselves must ultimately depend. This is the province of the "spin doctor" whose role in government has become correspondingly more important.

International telecommunications are also responsible for the exposure of human rights abuses and the resulting demands on the nation-state that it obey laws not solely of its own choosing. In the war in Kosovo, to take a single example, NATO entirely bypassed both the U.N. Charter and the laws of Yugoslavia in order to stop ethnic cleansing by Serb officials who could claim, doubtless correctly, that they were only obeying the orders of a lawfully elected government in Belgrade. It now appears that even reconciliation commissions cannot confer effective amnesties for acts by officials within their own countries. They may, it seems, be prosecuted after all by courts in other countries as happened to General Pinochet when he ventured abroad for medical treatment. These developments show no sign of abating.

There are other strategic innovations that arose during the course of the Long War that will have an important effect on shaping the new constitutional archetype that will succeed the nation-state. Foremost among these innovations was the introduction of the computer. It was an early computing device and a team of mathematicians, for example, that allowed the British and later the Americans to read the classified communications of the Nazis and the Japanese during World War II.[21] This permitted the strategic deceptions at Normandy and at Midway without which the war certainly could not have been won at the time and in the dramatic way that it was won by the Allies. The Long War did not merely co-opt but actually caused this technology to be developed. The Internet, for example, a system of linked computer networks, was the outgrowth of an American defense agency effort to create a communications system that would survive a nuclear attack.

Computer technology has decentralized the availability of information and at the same time opened up new channels of information to the nation-state. More information now flows to every public official than he or she can possibly assimilate. Computer accessibility to government and government information has had the ironic effect of so overloading officials that they must ignore more pleas for audiences and reply perfunctorily to more appeals than any despot making his progress through a crowd of peasants.

Moreover, insofar as computer technology has breached the security of the State and ever more widely distributed the information government once claimed to possess solely, it has contributed to the decline in prestige of the State. The Xerox copier not only threatens national currencies; it threatens the currency of the bureaucracy, which is the control of the flow of information. What national leader can be confident, as he faces a live interview, that the confidential memo he saw yesterday will not be thrust in his face if he denies its contents today? This may be an important contribution to openness and honesty in government, but it cannot be a step that strengthens the nation-state, a structure that must often maintain itself by taking decisions and then, and only then, persuading its public. Most dramatically, the Internet will frustrate government attempts to use law to enforce moral rules—the very raison d'être of the nation-state. Canada, for example, was unable to enforce its strict blackout rules on the news coverage of sensational criminal trials; Singapore, despite searches of tens of thousands of files, has not been able to stem the receipt of pornography.[22] Espionage using electronic file transfers—that is, replacing the "dead drops" of spies that were concealed in hollowed-out trees with the parking of computer files on nonsecure e-mail sites—allows a single agent to turn over more information to his control in an instant than could be analyzed in a decade. The nation-state is maddened by such developments and, like the bear with painful dental caries in Milosz's memoir, becomes dangerous to itself and others in its frustration.

These various developments, and others, have led to a disintegration of the legitimacy of the nation-state. In summary, no nation-state can assure its citizens safety from weapons of mass destruction; no nation-state can, by obeying its own national laws (including its international treaties) be assured that its leaders will not be arraigned as criminals or its behavior be used as a legal justification for international coercion; no nation-state can effectively control its own economic life or its own currency; no nation-state can protect its culture and way of life from the depiction and presentation of images and ideas, however foreign or offensive; no nation-state can protect its society from transnational perils, such as ozone depletion, global warming, and infectious epidemics. And yet guaranteeing national security, civil peace through law, economic development and stability, international tranquility and equality, were the principal tasks of the nation-state. Developments born in strategic conflict can, however, as they have done before, also lead to a regeneration of the State. What would a new constitutional order look like?

THE EMERGENCE OF THE MARKET-STATE

The State has proved itself to be a remarkably resilient institution, periodically transforming its structure. When faced with mortal threats, states have resorted to the expedient of constitutional change, remaking themselves when strategic innovations by their competitors threatened to overwhelm them or when internal stresses enlivened by these strategic developments threatened disintegration from within. In our own era we are witnessing the emergence of the *market-state* and the shift to that form from the constitutional order of the nation-state that has dominated the twentieth century. The strategic innovations by which the Long War was won have forced each of the great northern-tier powers to adapt. Some— like the states of former Nazi Germany and the former Soviet Union— have adapted so profoundly that we might say that constitutionally they were obliterated, to be replaced by different kinds of states.

The market-state is a constitutional adaptation to the end of the Long War and to the revolutions in computation, communications, and weapons of mass destruction that brought about that end. As the Long War made abundantly clear, the conception and production of the most qualitatively superior forces required not merely an industrial society but a creative society, with the capital to exploit that creativity. Now that creativity and capital has been turned against the nation-state itself.

What are the characteristics of the market-state? Such a state depends on the international capital markets and, to a lesser degree, on the modern multinational business network to create stability in the world economy, in preference to management by national or transnational political bodies. Its political institutions are less representative (though in some ways more democratic) than those of the nation-state. The Open Markets Committee of the Federal Reserve and the electronic referendum (to take two extremes) are more characteristic of the market-state than the elegant electoral representative institutions envisioned by Hamilton and Madison or the mass election campaigns of Roosevelt and Johnson. Like the nation-state, the market-state assesses its economic success or failure by its society's ability to secure more and better goods and services, but in contrast to the nation-state it does not see the State as more than a minimal provider or redistributor. Whereas the nation-state justified itself as an instrument to serve the welfare of the people (the nation), the market-state exists to maximize the opportunities enjoyed by all members of society. For the nation-state, a national currency is a medium of exchange; for the market-state it is only one more commodity. Much the same may be said of jobs: for the nation-state, full employment is an important and often paramount goal,[23] whereas for the market-state, the actual number of persons employed is but one more variable in the production of economic opportunity and has no overriding intrinsic significance. If it is more efficient to have large bodies of persons unemployed, because it would cost more to the society to train them and put them to work at tasks for which the market has little demand, then the society will simply have to accept large unemployment figures. Mark Tushnet has noted this development:

> Small-scale programs with modest aims characterize the new constitutional order: any deficiencies in the provision of health care or in income security after retirement are to be dealt with by market-based adjustments rather than ambitious redistributive initiatives. Similarly, poverty is to be alleviated by ensuring that the poor obtain education and training to allow them to participate actively in the labor market, rather than by providing generous public assistance payments.[24]

If the function of law in the nation-state is process-oriented, churning out impartial rules and regulations to promote desired behavior, the market-state pursues its objectives by incentive structures and sometimes draconian penalties, not so much to assure that the right thing is done as to prevent the social instability that threatens material well-being. The market-state is classless and indifferent to race and ethnicity and gender; its yardstick for evaluation is the quantifiable. Indeed, to a far greater extent than the nation-state, the market-state is culturally accessible to all societies: the statistics and media images that carry its messages do not require proficiency in any particular natural language.

If the nation-state was characterized by the rule of law—and as we shall see in Book II, the society of nation-states attempted to impose something like the rule of law on international behavior—the market-state is largely indifferent to the norms of justice, or for that matter to any particular set of moral values so long as law does not act as an impediment to economic competition. The cliché "level playing field" captures this concern. Does this agnosticism make the market-state an ideal form for the varying states of the world, including the diverse Third World, where values differ greatly from those of the developed world and from each other, or is it ill-suited to states, like Iran or Saudi Arabia, that wish the State to embody the cultural values of the people (that do not want a "level playing field" for all competitors)? In either case, the market-state's essential indifference to culture poses some difficulties for the operation of the State. Foremost among these is the fact that it will be much harder to get the publics of such states to risk their lives and fortunes on behalf of a state that is no longer the champion of their cultural values. The sense of a single polity, held together by adherence to fundamental values, is not a sense that is cultivated by the market-state. This cultural indifference does, however, make the market-state an ideal environment for multiculturalism.

Operating through the state-nation, the State sought to enhance the nation as a whole. In the era of the nation-state, the State took responsibility for the well-being of groups. In the market-state, the State is responsible for maximizing the choices available to individuals. This means lowering the transaction costs of choosing by individuals and that often means restraining rather than empowering governments. Thus we see measures like the proposal to limit the percentage of GDP taken by government, and other forms of capping the tax rate, and actions by courts that have struck down affirmative action plans[25] or limited the federal power to regulate commerce and disallowed certain criminal sanctions (like those against contraception or abortion).[26]

In the market-state, the marketplace becomes the economic arena, replacing the factory. In the marketplace, men and women are consumers, not producers (who are probably offshore anyway).

> What can a hospital attendant, or a schoolteacher or a marriage counselor or a social worker or a television repairman or a government official be said to make? . . . More important than the producers . . . are the entrepreneurs—heroes of autonomy, consumers of opportunity—who

compete to supply whatever all the other consumers want or might be persuaded to want . . . competing with one another to *maximize everyone else's options.*[27]

Some entrepreneurs will fail; all consumers will find their options limited, to varying degrees, by their resources. But both failure and limitation are necessary to choosing; there can be no real choices without the possibility of getting it wrong, and indeed choice itself is a consequence of scarcity.

Is governance easier in the market-state, because so much less is demanded of it, or more difficult because the habits of the good citizen are lost? Perhaps both. As is frequently pointed out, contemporary political reporting is not presented against an historical background of complex competing values, but increasingly in terms of the power relationships of the personalities involved, as if politics were like a simple sporting event—who's winning and who's losing, or, as shown by the little arrows in a popular news magazine, who's up and who's down. This is characteristic of the market-state, with its de-emphasis on the programmatic and legalistic aspects of governance.

And is this not what politics is—not simply how it is reported—in the market-state? When the publics of nation-states, to say nothing of their leading individuals, believed wholeheartedly in the mere materiality of their history—that they were in the grip of vast causal forces, economic, psychological, sociological, over which they had no control—then politics for the public, like ethics for the individual, became mainly a matter of protecting the interest of the group within which one found oneself. When the publics of market-states come to believe that their histories are chosen, a matter of interpretation, deconstruction, and sometimes cosmetic reconstruction, then politics, again like ethics, becomes a matter of insurance—quantifiable and probabilistic. On the other hand, a meritocracy where no one can remember what the moral bases for merit were, but where it can be measured and ruthlessly assessed nonetheless, promises a competitive dynamism that few nation-states could match today.

Recent movements in American jurisprudence—law and economics, feminism, critical legal studies—all agree on this first principle: power is the basis for legal decisions. Whatever the intellectual merits of such movements, a society that is strongly influenced by them is going to have a hard time finding nurses or teachers or soldiers without devoting vastly more financial resources to their recruitment and retention. And yet the diversion of more resources to the human services sector by the State is far *less* likely in a society that values entrepreneurial, material success above all. "The market is not a good setting for mutual assistance, for I cannot help someone else without reducing (for the short term at least) my own options."[28] On the other hand, teamwork and harmony are far better indicators of an organization's long-term prospects for success than many other indices, and so such a society may well excel at encouraging those institutions that are best able to motivate persons to cooperate.

Long before the time of princes, long before there were states, "everywhere was an America," John Locke wrote. By this he meant a world entirely free of any civilized institutions, as he believed America to have been when Columbus discovered it for European society, a world, that is, of opportunity, a world to be made. Perhaps we now stand at a similar moment of discovery.

The market-state is, above all, a mechanism for enhancing opportunity, for creating something—*possibilities*[29]—commensurate with our imaginations. The rocket technology developed to deliver weapons in the Long War has propelled man into a perspective from space; his communications technology, also developed for strategic reasons, has sent back an image from that perspective.[30] I am inclined to think that something of the market-state's indifference to fate and sensitivity to risk is related to this reorientation, where the illusion of limitless opportunity meets the reality of choice.

Similarly, the decoding of human genetic material will change the way we look at excellence and achievement. We are inclined to forget that the doctrine of the divine right of kings rested on an admiration amounting to awe for the fatalistic assumption of chance; it was discredited when Enlightenment thinkers shifted the basis for the evaluation of that doctrine from one of the grateful acceptance of divine providence (for who could know better than God who should rule), which is actually confirmed by the apparent randomness of inherited merit, to a more self-confident, humanistically centered basis in the rational assessment of ability. We are at present undergoing a similar shift as the basis for human assessment in the various competitions of the meritocracy shifts from a passive acceptance of inherited abilities to a quest for the enhanced, or engineered, faculties made possible by molecular biology. Here, too, the market-state's apparent indifference to the state's role in ensuring justice fits the new, wide open landscape of apparent opportunity. A State that tried to sort out who should be allowed to grow taller or be endowed with perfect pitch would soon find itself hopelessly overcommitted financially or the center of group warfare; in other words, it would find itself in the situation of the nation-state at present. The market-state, with its sublime indifference to such questions and its refusal to guarantee outcomes, is more survivable in the new world of genetic technologies. These technologies have the power to enhance autonomy as never before, freeing men and women from their own genes, and providing choices only dreamt of until now.

In each of the phase transitions that we observed in the history of the modern state, a new form of strategic vision emerged to accompany the new constitutional order. As the State moved to state-nation from territorial state, for example, arguments derived from the premises of collective security arose to accompany those arguments that derived from the balance of power that, in a previous transition, had emerged to dominate other, earlier strategic arrangements. In this way, states added to the array of available strategic programs, as earlier strategic visions were replaced and decayed into mere policies.

What strategic motto will dominate this transition from nation-state to market-state? If the slogan that animated the liberal, parliamentary nation-states was to "make the world safe for democracy" (the security paradigm that decayed into the policy of democratic enlargement, among others), what will the forthcoming motto be? Perhaps "making the world available," which is to say creating new worlds of choice and protecting the autonomy of persons to choose.

Universalizing opportunity, however, does not mean making every state rich; nor does it even mean making sure no state becomes poorer. Rather, it means the opening up of opportunities on the largest scale possible in the expectation that this will maximize the growth of wealth generally. It may require that every state refrain from steps that would make any other state poorer to a degree greater than the gain in enrichment taken as a whole, but this is not as onerous as it may at first appear. For example, the state that develops a substitute for oil may well make another state, one that produces oil, poorer. But the gain in the total enrichment of the global environment is greater than the loss, because there are now two sources of energy supplies where before there was only one. A state need not be required to subsidize the growth of other states—as perhaps the oil-producing states once did when oil prices were artificially low—even if a rise in prices may harm some states while benefiting others, and even if the total balance sheet of world wealth is static, i.e., only a transfer of wealth is accomplished, one without net growth to the world taken as a whole. For in this case, the state that became poorer is not poorer than it would have been had the subsidy never occurred. Some states are going to be poorer in a world of market-states, but they need not be poorer than they would have been absent the emergence of the market-state; indeed, within the world of nation-states, the poorest states are already getting poorer.

The transition to the market-state is bound to last over a long period and put into conflict the ideals of the old and new orders. It should be emphasized that just what particular form of the State ultimately emerges from this process cannot confidently be predicted. It is a failure of imagination, however, to assume that the only thing that will replace the nation-state is another structure with nation-state-like characteristics, only larger. It is in some ways rather pathetic that the visionaries in Brussels can imagine nothing more forward-looking than equipping the E.U. with the trappings of the nation-state. Just now, it seems to be the Euro, a currency that, like all currencies, will be reduced to an accounting mechanism in the face of the ubiquitous Visa card. The key idea of the modern state is the exclusiveness of its jurisdiction. It is natural that commentators then should infer from the exclusivity of membership in the E.U. that jurisdictional exclusiveness must follow, but this rather misses the point of the modern state's development in the first place, its ability to deliver legitimacy. Facing the pressures described in this chapter, the State is likelier to resort to the pattern of accommodation and change we have seen in earlier periods than to self-destruct by dissolution into a larger mass. If the E.U. were to persist in its current course, it would be attempting to thwart the emergence of a market-state. Instead, it may be that the Union itself will adapt, enabling rather than attempting to suppress this new constitutional order.

It should also be emphasized that I have not argued, and do not wish to argue, that the State has changed in the precise ways it has *because* of strategic challenges to itself. Many elements in the development of the State account for the fact that it has changed in exactly the ways it has; moreover, the State might have innovated in other ways; the innovations that did occur might have occurred anyway. I claim only that a coherent and helpful account can be given of the constitutional changes the State has undergone in periods of strategic threat, and of the strategic innovations that accompanied the new constitutional orders that have emerged. That said, what guesses can we make about how states will adapt to this new form?

The market-state will live within three paradoxes: (1) it will require more centralized authority for government, but all governments will be weaker, having greatly contracted the scope of their undertakings, having devolved or lost authority to so many other institutions, including deregulated corporations, which are in but not of the State, NGOs (nongovernmental organizations such as the Red Cross, the MacArthur Foundation, the Natural Resources Defense Council), which are in but not of the market, and clandestine military networks and terrorist groups, which set up proto-markets in security and function as proto-states at war; (2) there will be more public participation in government, but it will count for less, and thus the role of the citizen *qua* citizen will greatly diminish and the role of citizen as spectator will increase; (3) the welfare state will have greatly retrenched, but infrastructure security, epidemiological surveillance, and environmental protection—all of which are matters of general welfare— will be promoted by the State as never before. These three paradoxes derive from the shift in the basis of legitimacy from that of the nation-state to that of the market-state. Let me speculate about possible policies for one state, the United States, within this new constitutional order.

SECURITY

Some consequences of the strategic innovations that won the Long War require a stronger and more centralized government than before. For example, nuclear weapons strategy, clandestine intelligence collection, and covert action sometimes require a level of secrecy that is incompatible with open government or even the relation between parliamentary oversight and the citizenry that links government to the people. Unless the president has the authority to launch nuclear weapons, the system of assured annihilation is changed into a very different scheme of risk taking that might well tempt an adversary into making threats—or executing them—in the hope of paralyzing the United States. It is simply absurd to think that a system of nuclear deterrence could be maintained if the president had to go to Congress for a declaration of war before launching a retaliatory or pre-emptive strike. But how can the difficult problem of nuclear command and control be reconciled with the new constitutional demands of the market-state for transparency and citizen participation? The answer may lie in changing our expectations about what legitimate delegation consists in and accepting very broad predelegations of authority, as it were, that can be withdrawn by the normal statutory process but that otherwise remain in place. This changes the burden between the branches of government, admittedly; after such a predelegation, the Congress would have to muster a two-thirds majority to remove power from the president by overriding his veto of legislation repealing the delegation, should he choose to resist. We are already moving from a system in which the State is the principal actor on behalf of the nation to one in which the State is the facilitator of practical affairs. The market-state seeks a role as enabler and umpire, and shuns the role of provider and judge. Broad legislative delegations—such as "fast track" trade authorizations and the consolidated budget—are above all simply practical and efficient. Increasingly, the justification for state action will turn on its relation to minimizing transaction costs. Redistributive and meliorist policies will come under intense attack on these grounds.

This decoupling of state *apparat* and national community is consistent with developments in war itself. If war becomes again, as it once was, an affair of states rather than of peoples—if it becomes, in Michael Howard's words, "denationalized"—this may not be such a bad thing. It is true that this move tends to isolate the executive from the body politic, making it "a severed head conducting its intercourse with other severed heads according to its own laws."[31] There will be little sense of the mass participation that characterized the Long War and that united nationalism and militarism in the creation of the nation-state. But if this is no longer a military necessity, should our constitutional forms continue to demand it? Can participation be supplanted by mere observation, coupled with Internet opinion polling, rather than voting and serving? What seems likeliest is that expectations will change, ultimately corresponding to the change in strategic requirements that no longer require vast armies of conscripts—though again I note that the precise way in which this accommodation will play out is not predestined.

Other responsibilities of the market-state may also lead to a similar delegation of power, e.g., the monitoring of epidemics and diseases, of international migration, of terrorism, of espionage, and of threats to the environment. All of these spheres of governmental activity are ill-suited to effective oversight by the market. Some depend on maintaining the secrecy of crucial information, while others require a single governmental voice in a dialogue with other governments. In both cases, transparency and public knowledge are sacrificed.

The successful discharge of the responsibilities just discussed is only possible in a constitutional system with a powerful, centralized, and, above all, *trusted* executive. Innovations of the 1970s, like the independent counsel, or detractions from the unitary executive generally, as well as the contempt with which claims of executive privilege are customarily greeted, are hardly compatible with the kind of decisive executive demanded by the market-state. It's not that the president must be above that law: that would be utterly and obviously contradictory of the principles of the American constitution. Nor should the presidency be inferior to the judiciary, the Congress, or the press, the executive's principal competitors. It's rather that our expectations about what the law should be have been shaped by the endgame of the nation-state and its close identification of the State with the nation. When these expectations change, the glamour and prestige of the presidency will suffer. As an institution, it will find itself in competition with the media to a greater degree even than with its traditional competitors in the other two branches. It will be important to ensure that the president's ability to govern, in the limited areas of responsibility given to the market-state, be enhanced. Fragmenting the constitutionally unitary executive branch can scarcely be a positive step in the direction of enhanced presidential authority.

Some areas of responsibility are amenable neither to complete determination by market processes nor to handling by the federal government. These might devolve to the states and localities with the expectation that they will be delegated to associations, NGOs, nonprofit foundations, charities, and the like that operate with the greatest legitimacy at the local level because participation seems more available to local citizens.

The important difference between the devolving federal state and the local state is that the latter can experiment in the market. In some local states genetic research, abortion, and sexual orientation will be largely unregulated; in others, regulations governing these activities will be enforced by market actors licensed by the local state; and in some states the regulations will be enforced by police sanction. What is all too clear, however, is that a federal police presence is far too unwieldy, too nonlocal to handle the single issue most American citizens fault their government over, the issue of crime. If there was any doubt about this, it was settled in the public's mind by the U.S. government's handling of the Branch Davidian case in Waco, Texas, where eighty-one persons, thirteen of them children, died as a consequence of the government's efforts to serve a warrant.[32] Nor has the continuing futility of the government's "war" on drug use redeemed its prestige.

The devolution and the licensing of private firms to enforce regulations are troubling in a society that has steadily moved to make its criminal laws nationally uniform and to restrict the legitimate use of force to trained men and women acting under strict official discipline. In this, however, as in much else the United States can more easily adapt to such devolution than other states. Its system of federalism provides a ready structure for devolving power out of Washington; virtually all law enforcement is already a matter of state jurisdiction. Moreover, the Second Amendment to the U.S. Constitution—aptly termed by one distinguished constitutional scholar "the embarrassing second amendment"[33] for the discomfort it causes persons who are accustomed to supporting both gun control and civil liberties—reflects a fundamental, residual locus of armed force in the people themselves.[34] If, as Martin van Creveld speculates, "the day-to-day burden of defending society from low-intensity conflict will be transferred to the booming security business,"[35] this mixture of devolution and privatization will become commonplace in the market-state. This is a harrowing prospect, but one with which we may have to learn to cope.

We will also have to cope with the increasing willingness of corporations to sell sensitive military technology to potentially dangerous foreign states. American, French, German, and British companies have all done so and, despite the fact that some of them have been exposed and their officers even indicted, these practices are likely to continue. Indeed many companies vigorously lobby their governments to permit these sales, lifting restrictions against technology transfers as a mere concomitant to deregulation and the drive for market share. Nor can the international banking system's critical support for the operations of denationalized terror networks be ignored. The nation-state was poorly situated to cope with this informal, virtual treasury as receipts and disbursements leapfrogged national regulation. It remains to be seen whether the market-state, with its sensitivity to any costs imposed on transactions by regulation, will do any better.

POLITICS AND REPRESENTATION

The emotional fusion between the People and the State begun by the state-nation and reconceptualized in the nation-state was intensified by the Long War. Governments undertook responsibilities in entirely new areas of the social and economic activities of their citizens, and the nation endorsed the actions of the State through a variety of means, including a vastly expanded voting franchise, an institutionalized role for labor unions, and greatly increased taxation. In the market-state, both sides of this reciprocal equation will change: there will be fewer formal mechanisms for endorsement by the public and the State will undertake to do less.[36]

Though I shudder to think so, I believe we can expect more reliance on the plebiscite, the initiative, and the referendum, especially as these become so easy and cheap to undertake once interactive cable television becomes universal in the United States. To some extent, we are already living under such a regime. What I have in mind is not the extensive use of referenda at the state level[37] but rather the heavy reliance on frequent polling by American office holders. These are a kind of virtual-reality referenda, allowing the politician to test the results of a proposal. Like aircraft landing simulators, these polls give guidance to the politician without his actually putting himself at risk by calling for a referendum that he would have to support (or oppose),[38] and with the results of which he would then have to live.

At the same time, the market-state does not suffer from the acute shame experienced by the nation-state when the subject of campaign finance is discussed. When Chief Justice Earl Warren wrote that "Congressmen do not represent interests or trees, they represent people,"[39] he was expressing an axiom of the nation-state. Doubtless he believed it, but it would be hard to maintain this view in light of today's functional patronage of candidates by contributors. If there are any readers innocent of this process, it goes like this: campaigns are funded by contributions from persons and groups with interests in the behavior of the candidate if she (or he) is successful. These campaigns are far too expensive to be funded by any candidate personally save the wealthiest individuals, and even these, if they are successful, lose no time in paying themselves back through postcampaign fund-raisers. Politicians of unquestioned rectitude, who would not dream of accepting a bribe—a payment for their personal benefit in exchange for a vote or action on behalf of the payor—have long now accustomed themselves to promising assistance (and sometimes votes) to persons and groups who give them money in the full expectation that the word of the politician is good. Their very rectitude is, ironically, the door opener to the contributor, because it guarantees the payee will deliver as promised. Whether there is anything wrong with this I am hesitant to say. Shouldn't the right-to-life candidate's campaign be the beneficiary of the funds collected to promote a right-to-life policy? Shouldn't the congressman anxious to alleviate unemployment in his district vote for a public works project there, and isn't such a man a suitable person for local business interests to support? But there persists a disquiet among those who believe the civics lessons of the nation-state, which hold that the votes of the public ought to be the only coin of the political realm. I believe a time will come in the transition from nation-state to market-state in which we will reflect on our current fund-raising practices with revulsion and an amazement that we tolerated them for so long.

But that does not mean that we will replace these practices, which seem so violative of the ethos of the nation-state; it is likelier that we will keep the practices and change the ethos. The market-state is not so squeamish. Indeed, *its* civics lessons hold that there should be no limits on campaign spending from any source so that the true opportunity costs of a candidate's defeat are reflected in the probability of his victory. The market-state merely tries to get the "best" person for the job in the way that universities try to get the "best" students: they set up a market that selects persons on the basis of predictions about their subsequent success. Fund-raising is to governing what SATs and high school grades are to college grades, accurate (if circular) predictors of a later performance that is, in the era of the "permanent campaign," a repetition of the test itself. Governance becomes a matter of maintaining popularity, which requires further advertising, which requires further fund-raising. The candidate who is tied to important interests by virtue of his fund-raising is precisely the person whose vote will most closely reflect those interests. The more money he raises, the more attractive the candidacy, because successful fund-raising reflects the relationship between the importance of the interests he represents and his ability to represent them (as those interests judge it—and who are better placed to do so than they?). And this is just as well, because initiatives, plebiscites, and referenda are, like all elections, very expensive. The more frequently they come, the greater the match between economic interests and public policy; indeed, this is one of the attractions of the market-state. That this places enormous power in the hands of the media only underscores the change in its constitutional role with the emergence of the market-state.

We can expect an improvement in the quality of the civil service as taxpayers come to demand better performance from government and to appreciate the need for better compensation in order to secure that performance. Like the rise in tuition costs—which is mainly a matter of responding to the increased expectations of students in the context of fixed faculty productivity—a rise in government costs is almost unavoidable. Government bodies do not make decisions more efficiently, for example, because they have computers any more than professors give better comments on essays because these comments are composed on a word processor. This rise in costs will perhaps be counterbalanced by a narrowing domain of the matters we allocate to government. With respect to those responsibilities that governments of market-states retain, we shall expect better performance.

WELFARE

The nation-state undertook to be responsible for economic planning for the society, income redistribution, and democratic accountability, and it promised to underwrite (in varying degrees) employment, health care, education, and old-age security. The nation-state is rightly thought of as a new constitutional order, for not only are these responsibilities a significant departure from those of the state-nation, they also reflect the unique source of the nation-state's legitimacy, its promise to provide for the material well-being of the nation. This promise was made by parliamentary, communist, and fascist governments alike. The market-state need make no such commitments because its relationship to its society is formed on a different basis.

It is obviously true, however, that single-parent families, declining literacy, teenage pregnancy, and drug, alcohol, and tobacco abuse, represent significant *economic* costs to a society. Apart from the lost productivity of workers who put themselves in, or find themselves in, such difficult situations, there is the tremendous cost involved in providing family subsistence (or day care), unemployment compensation, medical insurance, remedial education, and so forth. Ought not the market-state to be concerned with these problems, even if the reason for its concern is different from that of the nation-state? It depends on how effective you think the state—any sort of state—is in addressing such issues.

The nation-state, it is implied by some critics, created its budget problems because in undertaking to improve the welfare of all of its citizens, it both hobbled the opportunities for its most productive workers (through regulatory and redistributive legislation) and inadvertently crippled its neediest and least productive workers by tying them to programs that locked them into a cycle of dependency. Thus, it is alleged, the state became progressively less able to pay a bill that wasn't worth paying in any case. If there appears to be a consensus today that none of the problems listed in the paragraphs above—teenage pregnancy, drug abuse, etc.—could actually be cured by massive government programs, let alone by those that are likely actually to be initiated,[40] this reflects a profound shift in the expectations we believe can be imposed on the State.

The first casualty of this shift in opinion is the legitimacy of the nation-state. The State cannot covenant to improve the welfare of all of its citizens if it is generally believed that there are a great many persons in desperate straits whom government cannot—and, for various reasons, perhaps should not—attempt to assist. In the face of such a consensus of delegiti-mation, the acceptance of a new constitutional order becomes virtually an imperative and the shape of that order must be one that is compatible with that consensus. Thus the second casualty of this shift in view of the basis of the State is any large-scale effort by government to address social dys-function (though it is assumed by market-state ideology that increased opportunity means increased wealth, and that this will ameliorate many social ills).

It may be that we can expect in the United States (and elsewhere) the sharp and permanent diminishment of the welfare state, with its safety net of public housing, free medical care, aid to dependent children, and unem-ployment allowances. Whether or not these programs are cut back, a simple refusal to maintain their ever-increasing costs with ever-increasing funding will in the not-too-distant future reduce their ameliorative impact significantly. At the same time, regulatory reform will proceed at a quick-ened pace. Regulation can be viewed, from an economic perspective, as a tax[41] no less than direct taxes. Either a business can be taxed to pay for garbage removal or it can be required to remove its own garbage: either way, it pays. In a situation of perfect information there is no difference in the effect on the ultimate allocation of resources whether the tool of regu-lation or taxation is used. The difference occurs when deregulation is accompanied by tax cutting. Thus regulatory reform is not merely an effort to unchain innovative entrepreneurs and to remove noisome and idiotic rules from the workplace; when coupled with tax-lowering politics, it is also part of a larger effort to reduce the percentage of GDP taken by gov-ernment (directly or indirectly).

For that portion of the nation-state's agenda that cannot be offloaded by the market-state, there is the alternative of privatization. In the American context, this term does not mean auctioning off state-run commercial enterprises (like British Rail) to private investors, but rather contracting out traditional government duties. In some cases, such as operating prisons and hospitals, this is simply a roundabout way of introducing more careful financial accountability and more efficient practices into public enter-prises. But in other cases—notably education—it amounts to a more pro-found change. The nation-state was inevitably hostile to private education (many nation-states banned or attempted to ban private schooling) because it tends to remove such an important cultural experience from the inclusive objectives of the national agenda. In the market-state, however, with its skepticism about government and its compact with individual choice, the prospect of turning over education to parents is welcomed enthusiastically. Voucher systems—which effectively use the state as a tuition collector, rebating the collected fees to private and public schools that are chosen by parents—are likely to become the standard, not the exceptional, means of school selection. The default rule will perhaps always provide some publicly managed schools—though federalism makes possible the option of doing away with public schools entirely—but the days of virtually universal mass public education, like the similar experience of universal military conscription, are probably unlikely to continue. The voucher scheme is precisely the sort of expansion of opportunity the market-state undertakes to provide: more options, less coercion by law.

These speculations about how the market-state will play out in the United States must not be taken to obscure the point that different cultures will adapt the market-state in different ways. The Soviet Union, Great Britain, and Fascist Japan were all nation-states, after all, no matter how greatly their policies and politics differed. Different cultures will adapt the market-state in distinct ways. The American emphasis on individual rights, a laissez-faire business and trading system, and restless personal freedom will take the market-state in one direction; other societies will find the market-state just as adaptable to preferences for group responsibility, a state-inflected market, and long-term social stability.

The United States is remarkably well situated to become a market-state. Its multiculturalism, its free market, and its diverse religious makeup—all of which resisted the centralizing efforts of the nation-state—and, above all, its habit of tolerance for diversity give it an advantage over other countries in adapting its state to this new constitutional order. Insofar as the American people are able to resist calls to take back the state in order to unify the culture and reform dissenters, the agnosticism of the market-state will be well accepted. Nostalgia aside—which I feel more than most—it is important to identify which cultural and political struggles are simply hangovers from the dying nation-state and its resistance to the form of the new market-state and which are genuine choices that the market-state brings to life.*

---

*One way to chart the changes in the State is to note the way that the language of strategy has infiltrated nonmilitary organs of society. The use of terms like "campaign" in a political context dates from the era of the state-nation in which the nation was enlisted in the politics of the State. Now, with the emergence of the market-state, one can read books with titles like *The Business Principles of Sun Tzu* or *The Leadership Secrets of Attila the Hun* and even *Elizabeth I CEO*. A distinguished American judge and former law professor has gone so far as to describe Jesus Christ as a "moral entrepreneur." Richard A. Posner, *The Problematic of Moral and Legal Theory* (Harvard, 1998), 42.

CHAPTER ELEVEN

Strategic Choices

One also expects "elegance" in its "architectural," structural make-up. Ease in stating the problem, great difficulty in getting hold of it and in all attempts at approaching it, then again some very surprising twist by which the approach, or some part of the approach becomes easy, etc. Also, if the deductions are lengthy or complicated, there should be some simple general principle involved, which "explains" the complications and detours, reduces the apparent arbitrariness to a few simple guiding motivations, etc. These criteria are clearly those of any creative art and the existence of some underlying empirical, worldly motif in the background—overgrown by aestheticizing developments and followed to a multitude of labyrinthine variants—all this is much more akin to the atmosphere of art pure and simple than to that of the empirical sciences.

—Von Neumann on the qualities of a good mathematical proof*

THE END OF the Long War has also brought an end to the usefulness of the strategic paradigm that structured so much of American policy during the more than three score and ten years of U.S. involvement in the larger world, from the reversal of his own isolationist policies by President Woodrow Wilson in 1917, to the proclamation of a Wilsonian "New World Order" by President George Bush in 1990. That paradigm was formed by the cluster of understandings about the American purpose in the world, the threats the United States faced in that world, and the strategies to be employed to achieve those purposes and respond to those threats. These understandings continue today to provide the partly conscious model by which Americans grasp world events. This model has roots in American continental expansion westward, in the idealistic imperialism of Theodore

*Quoted in William Poundstone, *Prisoner's Dilemma* (Doubleday, 1992), 28.

Roosevelt, and the haunting cadences of Abraham Lincoln. It only came to life, however, once the United States was brought face-to-face with an attack by a great power whose involvement with the dynamic of state changes in Europe juxtaposed a competing paradigm that was threatening and invigorating. On March 12, 1917, Germany sank the U.S. merchantman *Algonquin* on the high seas; on March 18, she sank three more American merchant vessels; on April 1, the *Aztec,* another merchantman, went down. These attacks—and not the more famous sinking of the liner *Lusitania* two years earlier—propelled the United States into armed conflict, and the Americans have been endeavoring to "make the world safe for democracy" ever since.

A paradigm such as this does more than provide a model for describing events: it offers an explanatory worldview within which each new phenomenon can be fitted without altering the entire scheme. There will be zones of disagreement, of course, but the overall understanding is largely accepted by all parties to the debate. In the present chapter we shall study various new proposals for the American role in international affairs that describe themselves, or are described by others, as new "paradigms." I think it can be shown that each of these is actually more of an implementing "policy"—like containment—than a new worldview, and also that each of the policies is really simply an application of the current paradigm, often even a repetition of a position within that paradigm that has appeared at an earlier period. *Policies* are distinguished by their pursuit of particular objectives, the identification of a particular threat, and their proposal of a particular strategy. For example, the purpose of containment was to defeat international communism. The perceived threat was communist aggression in Central Europe and in Asia on the one hand and threats of subversion in the formerly colonial states of the Third World on the other. The strategy employed was nuclear deterrence and conventional defense in the First World and military assistance augmented by covert aid to surrogates in the Third World. Alternative policies, like the liberation of communist clients and the rollback of the Soviet occupation of Central and Eastern Europe, or, at the other extreme, acquiescence and appeasement, were frequently proposed. These alternatives were not incompatible with the Wilsonian worldview, but after debates that look, in retrospect, less closely divided than they perhaps were, these alternative policies were decisively rejected by a series of administrations from both American political parties. Large elements of these parties actually preferred such alternatives but they were never able to fundamentally alter the policy of containment over a period of four decades and nine administrations. There were occasional departures from the rough guide I have just sketched, but even with these apparent departures U.S. policy was remarkably consistent over this long period.

But with the Long War won, why do we need a structuring paradigm at all? Why not simply make decisions on an ad hoc basis, recognizing that, in any case, these decisions will not be randomly made or irrational, but will be guided by our best judgments as to what appears to increase American power and freedom of action? The answer lies in the relationship of strategy to law. Legitimacy, not merely power, was what the Long War was fought over. Until that fundamental question could be settled, conquest and defeat alone could not end the war. Legitimacy is the ground of law; it arises from consistent practices and tacit acceptance and gives law its authority. A United States that cannot explain why it seeks the enlargement of democratic practices among all states—and yet supports the suppression of the Algerian elections that would have brought Islamic fundamentalists to power—will not be able to rally a worldwide consensus in favor of democratic enlargement. A United States that can offer no reason why Russia should be treated as a successor state for the purposes of the Soviet Union's Security Council seat but as a dissolved state for the purposes of the Strategic Arms Limitation Treaty* will perhaps have its way in such matters for a time, but only so long as our power can compel assent. It is better, even from the perspective of our power—in the long run—to write the rules, though they may sometimes be applied against our wishes, than to abandon rule following in favor of policies that have no more general appeal than that we want them followed, at least for the time being.

We can extend our influence beyond our temporary hegemony if we take this moment to craft a system of rules with our allies that is compatible with our basic understanding of state responsibility. Yet without some general understanding of our strategy in the world, we cannot begin to even draft such rules.

What are some of the candidates for this new paradigm? I will describe five general approaches and attempt to place various contributions from the recent literature on this subject within them. This is especially hard to do because these proposed paradigms are really nothing of the sort: rather, they are simply policies in service of the old paradigm that guided our behavior during the Long War. As a result, there is much overlapping among writers as they stray from a particular position that is comprehensive and internally consistent because they recognize that, as a practical matter, something more fundamental is pulling them away from a doctrinaire consistency. I put proposals in categories in order to ease the reader's understanding of what options are on the table for today's leadership, not because I am dealing with a series of clear-cut manifestos. On the other hand, it is also important to realize that the proposals that are proffered to

---

*Successor states "succeed" to the rights and obligations of their predecessors; dissolved states do not.

become a new American paradigm for our behavior in the world are so far short of this advertising that no leader, no matter how nearsighted, is likely really to rely on them to master the challenges that have arisen in the back-wash of the end of the Long War. This basic impracticality is sometimes hidden in the persuasive, reassuring prose of editorial writers and the aggressive debating of political candidates who do not have the responsi-bility of day-to-day decision making but are confident that things would run more smoothly if they did.

One might label these five approaches as (1) the New Nationalism, (2) the New Internationalism, (3) the New Realism, (4) the New Evangelism, and (5) the New Leadership. Each of these general programs has a distinct paramount goal for U.S. policy; each proposes a particular strategy to achieve that goal; each reflects a perception of a crucial threat to U.S. interests to which the proposed paradigm is responsive.

THE ANARCHIC SOCIETY
AND THE NEW NATIONALISM

In 1977 Hedley Bull's path-breaking book *The Anarchical Society* appeared.[1] Almost at once it was recognized as describing something essential about the international world of national states, something that recalled Hobbes's description of mankind in a state of nature. Hobbes and Bull described a world whose fundamental feature was that it was without law. It was a world of all against all and each one against every other one. In such a world the primary goal was to be fittest in a competition for sur-vival, and so it is also with the proposed new paradigm that has recently found favor with a new generation of political leaders on the right.

This strategy for the competitive survival of the United States focuses our resources on confronting only those threats that truly put the United States itself at risk. Alan Tonelson, in an influential article in *Foreign Affairs,* "Superpower without a Sword," recommends that American forces limit their mission to deterring nuclear attacks on the American homeland, defending the American landmass from conventional incur-sions, and maintaining the flow of oil from the Persian Gulf, "at least until a serious national energy plan is in place." This is the core of his strategic plan, augmented by "token handholding" forces in Europe and East Asia, the maintenance of units capable of launching precision-strike weapons against rogue states to destroy weapons of mass destruction, and small special forces to handle evacuations, hostage rescues, and the like. It pro-vides a well-thought-out example of an increasingly influential position in American affairs.[2]

A similar proposal became part of the "Contract with America," the legislative agenda offered by Republican candidates for the Congress in 1994. During a debate in the House in February 1995 one Republican representative was quoted as saying, "You call it isolationism. I say it's America first!," apparently unconscious of the resonance such a phrase must have for many, because the America First Committee was the 1940 vehicle for isolationism before Pearl Harbor. Nevertheless, the congressman was right, I think, in distinguishing this position from isolationism. A fuller canvass of this position will show that it does not in fact offer a new paradigm—and isolationism for the United States would certainly be that—so much as a policy variant on the interventionist role for America that we have pursued since entering World War I.

The strategy urged by this approach would be more parsimonious in defining what constitute American "vital interests" because the new nationalist believes that most international conflicts and injustices do not concern our survival and therefore they can be safely, and should be prudently, ignored. The principal threat to the United States is thought to be economic, and, perhaps because they are asserting a strategic view, proponents of this position tend to adopt an essentially mercantilist view of international economic competition. That is, whereas strategic affairs are commonly zero-sum, with the measurement of the victor's spoils never exceeding those of the defeated's losses, economic perspectives are typically thought to enable the creation of wealth for all trading partners. When a strategic perspective on economic trading is introduced, however, gains and losses are necessarily relative to the positions of the various competing states. It matters not so much that both the United States and Japan are wealthier after a decade of record U.S. trade deficits; what matters is that the relative position of the United States vis-à-vis Japan has declined. Treaty arrangements like NAFTA and GATT are anathema to the New Nationalist because they sacrifice the pre-eminence of the American market in order to generate wealth, while many foreign markets remain to a large degree closed to U.S. products.

There is a populist flavor to this position that disdains the establishment policies of intervention abroad and free markets at home. Thus Patrick Buchanan:

> Put bluntly, it is blue-collar Americans whose jobs are lost when trade barriers fall, working-class kids who bleed and die in Mogadishu and along the DMZ when the shooting starts. But the best and the brightest tend to escape the worst consequences of the policies they promote from military service to unemployment. This [and not better information or understanding] may explain why national surveys show repeatedly that the best-educated and wealthiest Americans are the staunchest internationalists on both security and economic issues.[3]

Tonelson adds:

> On the merits, the essence of the America First approach [urges that] a
> focus on rebuilding and husbanding America's material wealth is our
> best foreign policy bet in the turbulent world we've entered, and the
> establishment knows it. [It is] a full-blown alternative [that] would
> break decisively with internationalism by abandoning the quest for
> worldwide security, prosperity and democracy as the best guarantors of
> American well-being. Instead, it would conclude that in a world likely
> to remain highly unstable, America's future is best assured by restoring
> and consolidating its own military and economic strength . . .[4]

Owing to this focus on domestic rebuilding, it is not surprising that it
was the NAFTA debate, more than any traditional security crisis, that
seems to have rallied the partisans of this approach. Precisely because
NAFTA was advertised as a way of stemming illegal immigration from
Mexico, it tended to invite nationalist reaction. The proponents of the
treaty were put in the position of asserting a kind of blackmail: either we
assist the Mexican economy or our own security would suffer. But this
argument plays into the hands of the proponents of the set of policies I
have been describing as New Nationalist because it implicitly accepts that
the relative attractiveness of the United States must decline in order to
keep Mexican immigrants at home.

In any case, proponents of this view argue, the United States really has
no alternative. We may claim, as did the first Bush administration, that we
are forging a new world order, but the stark reality is that assets of the
scope required by such an undertaking no longer exist. The Pentagon continues to maintain that the American military is capable of fighting a Gulf
War–size regional conflict and at the same time coming to the aid of allies
in a similar-size undertaking elsewhere (as in Korea) while being able to
initiate small-scale intervention of the sort launched against Panama or in
relief of the Kurdish forces in northern Iraq; this is the "two and one-half"
war scenario. But, it is argued by New Nationalists, the facts are otherwise.

In the last decade of the twentieth century, the U.S. military saw a 40
percent drop in active personnel. The Army's 10 combat divisions lack a
full complement of officers, tankers, and gunners, and the Air Force as of
2001 was 700 pilots short.

Planned force levels do not provide this "two and one-half war" capability. When Iraq invaded Kuwait in 1990, U.S. active forces contained 18
Army divisions, 9 Marine expeditionary brigades, 15 Navy aircraft carrier
battle groups, and 22 Air Force tactical fighter wings. Of these, 8 Army
divisions, 6 Marine brigades, 6 carrier groups, and 10 tactical wings were

**COMPARISON OF ACTIVE FORCE LEVELS WITH
"DESERT STORM" GULF WAR DEPLOYMENTS**

MILITARY UNIT TYPES PLANNED LEVELS	ACTIVE FORCE LEVELS IN 1990	ACTIVE FORCES IN "DESERT STORM"	CLINTON 1999 ACTIVE
Army Divisions	18	8	10
Army Independent Brigades/Regiments	7	3	4
Marine Brigades	9	6	5
Carrier Battle Groups	15	6	11
Air Force Fighter/ Attack Wings	22	10	13
Total Military Personnel	2,070,000	427,000	1,453,000[5]

sent to the Persian Gulf. The outgoing Clinton administration proposed a force structure composed of 10 Army divisions, 5 Marine brigades, 11 carrier groups, and 13 tactical wings in the total active force.

To refight the Gulf War in 2001 would take 80 percent of all U.S. Army divisions, more than 75 percent of Air Force fighter attack wings and Marine air wings, and 50 percent of our aircraft carriers. If during such a conflict the North Koreans attacked across the 38th parallel, all of our reserves would have to be called up, and mobilization of the Selective Service pool would be required.

Moreover, this gap between means and ends is growing larger, owing to the end of the Long War and an expansion of U.S. military missions. First, the collapse of the Soviet Union increased the number of independent actors on the world stage, some of whom had been restrained from fomenting conflict by Soviet local control. They, unlike the Soviet Union, have every incentive to believe that American resolve to intervene in their depredations is far more modest than our rhetoric, and thus the testing of U.S. commitments is, ironically, likely to increase rather than decrease after our victory in the Long War. "Since 1990 we deployed forces about 45 times," according to former Secretary of State Alexander Haig. "During the entire 50 year span of the Cold War we had only 16 deployments."[6] Second, our national will to send troops abroad appears to be inversely correlated with the habit of our leaders to support humanitarian interventions. Polls routinely show large majorities opposed to intervention in Haiti,

Somalia, Rwanda, and elsewhere. The American public not unreasonably appears to be more intent on revitalizing the social and economic framework at home, a focus of attention that is to some degree self-fulfilling, because as fewer and fewer resources are allocated abroad—resources that have to be voted by the representatives of the public—attention to other states' problems becomes more and more difficult.

But perhaps the most salient argument for this proposed paradigm is rooted in constitutional law. By what right, Tonelson asks,

> can the President or the Congress make the decision to send our troops to alleviate suffering in dangerous situations in which they—the politicians—readily admit that there are no strategic stakes involved? As citizens of a republic, we authorize our elected leaders to take all sorts of actions . . . But we grant this authority because it is an American good that is advanced or defended—because the majority of members of the political community to which we belong will supposedly benefit.[7]

This nation-state argument (one can scarcely imagine it from the lips of a Napoleon) exposes one of the deep, though subterranean, fault lines within post–World War II American national security policy: much of the American security structure is "extended" to protect other states. There are complicated reasons for doing so that, in fact, support the conclusion that such policies confer important benefits on the American people, but these have seldom been fully argued to the public. Instead, while foreign policy elites have used the forward presence of American forces to anchor powerful allies—Germany and Japan—whose ultimate intentions were a source of concern, these policies have been sold to the American public as based on resistance to the Soviet Union. Thus, with the collapse of the Soviet Union, there has opened a hitherto unexposed crevasse between our deployments and the ostensible reason for those deployments. Before the Soviet collapse, as Christopher Layne and Benjamin Schwartz put it:

> In postwar Western Europe, American policy was spectacularly successful. Freed from looking nervously over their shoulders, the West Europeans were able to set aside their historical animosities and security fears and work together to achieve economic integration within Europe and economic interdependence between Europe and the United States. Because stability and reassurance were based on economic cooperation, it was at least as important for the United States to defend the Europeans from themselves as it was to protect them from the Soviet Union. Likewise, in East Asia, the U.S. reassurance against resurgent Japanese power enabled the region to concentrate on commerce rather than on power politics.

Since the aims of the preponderance strategy transcended the U.S.-Soviet rivalry, it is not surprising that the foreign policy community now seeks to employ the same approach after the Cold War. Indeed, the Soviet Union's disappearance has seemingly removed the last barrier between Washington and the complete attainment of its world order aspirations. The USSR's demise has also forced the American policy elite to be more candid in articulating the assumptions that underpin its view of American strategy.

The continuity in U.S. strategy was—and is—explained by the belief that preponderance prevents spiraling regional tensions by obviating the need for other powers to provide their own security. Removing the umbrella of U.S. protection would force other states to "renationalize" their foreign and security policies.[8]

Now the public asks, however: why do we need to spend so much money and run such risks if the foe is defeated?

In place of a "global pacification strategy," the anarchic paradigm of the New Nationalist accepts the condition of chaos as an irremediable feature of the state system. As de Gaulle remarked (and Palmerston before him), states have no permanent friends, they have only permanent interests. Rather than try to remake the nature of states, or human nature for that matter, proponents of the New Nationalism would operate within the natural, anarchic environment—preserving U.S. influence when a more ambitious agenda would dissipate it, strengthening our position by increasing our wealth rather than taking on ever-increasing expenses. Nor is this position confined to adherents from the Republican right wing. Paul Kennedy has eloquently presented a history of states whose power declined when strategic overreach impelled them to divert more and more of their resources into unproductive security investments as their global ambitions increased, and the need to protect peripheral assets became a policy imperative.[9]

The anarchic strategists go further and not only argue against strategic overcommitment but see opportunities in the very chaos of the international system that America's peculiar strengths would enable it to exploit. Unlike its potential competitors in Europe and Asia, the United States does not have powerful and threatening neighbors. That gives it less of a stake in the maintenance of a peaceful status quo, and allows for a comparative advantage should that system break down. Abandoning the task of underwriting a benign global political environment frees the United States to enjoy assets that are independent of that environment: the world's largest single market and the world's most secure geopolitical position. With such vast resources we can intervene when our own interests really are served, and pursue objectives that really are achievable. As Walter Lippmann wrote:

A mature great power will make measured and limited use of its power . . . will eschew the theory of global and universal duty which not only commits it to unending wars of intervention but intoxicates its thinking with the illusion that it is a crusader for righteousness. . . . I am in favor of learning to behave like a great power, of getting rid of the globalism which would not only entangle us everywhere but is based on the totally vain notion that if we do not set the world in order, no matter what the price, we cannot live in the world safely . . . We shall have to learn to live as a great power which defends itself and makes its way among the other great powers.[10]

In what does such a defense consist? There are three principal elements.

First, the defense of our economic strength and its growth. On this view, a national security establishment that, even in a period of record deficits and pronounced defense cutbacks, still takes about 29 percent of the national budget must rank as more of a threat to our long-term security than that posed by any particular state. Sizable and sustained tax cuts would be sought. Trade policies that are more geared to stabilizing the international trading system than winning advantages for U.S. companies and workers would be rejected. Military investment that is a drain on investment in infrastructure and innovation would be redirected.

Second, the avoidance of needlessly adding to the risks we would other-wise face. This means abstention from involvement in conflicts that would add to our burdens but do not actually threaten us. The state system will never be "in balance" because it is dynamic and historical. The relative positions of "one sub-Saharan state vis-à-vis another, or of Hungary vis-à-vis Romania, or of Serbia vis-à-vis Bosnia" pose no real threat to us. Indeed the many bitter conflicts in the world are largely focused on such dueling pairs, who would not turn their hostility against the United States unless we seek to insert ourselves, as the American involvement in the Middle East has shown.

Third, an assertive defense of our territory and freedom of action. This implies the abandonment of alliances, such as NATO, that have served their purposes but have no specifically American reason for being. This third element reinforces the demand for energy independence and a program of aggressive energy exploration and development. It implies a reconfiguration of the force structure: antimissile defenses ought to be developed that can shield the American homeland from the few, eccentric threats we might face as nuclear weapons proliferate to irresponsible but minor states like Iran or Libya. Without the obligation to defend Korea, Japan, or Western Europe, we would reshape our forces away from a large personnel base to fewer active-duty ground troops with greater readiness, fewer forward defense deployments, and greater sea- and airlift capability.

Such a proposed "paradigm" is far more tolerant of the proliferation of nuclear weapons to major states, because the latter (including the major state of Russia) do not pose geopolitical threats to the United States. At the same time, proponents of this view are more willing to hand over responsibility for regional security and regional trade to those states most closely affected. Far from feeling rebuffed by exclusion from a European Defense Community we should welcome it. If Ukraine had wished to retain nuclear weapons, we ought not to have ignored the advantages to the United States in having Russia checked by a regional nuclear power with its own considerable incentives to moderate Russian expansionism. In such a cacophony, the United States can prosper.

The New Nationalism represents a popular near-term option to remake American foreign policy. Some of its positions were adopted by Governor George W. Bush in his 2000 campaign for the U.S. presidency.* Such a program is the culmination of decades of change in which our attitudes have gone from "thinking like lawyers"—which gave us the collective security paradigm I will next discuss—to "thinking like economists." It is present in many forms in contemporary Western life and shapes and reflects our values to some degree in all our public (and a good many of our private) endeavors.

THE MULTICULTURAL SOCIETY AND THE NEW INTERNATIONALISM

"Fundamental shifts in the definition of security begin at the conceptual level and, through a process of interaction with historical circumstances and emerging political perceptions, gradually prompt realignments of practical policy." So wrote Janne Nolan and John Steinbrunner in *Global Enlargement: Cooperation and Security for the Twenty-first Century,* a report of the Brookings Institution and perhaps the most ambitious statement of the New Internationalism, the second proposed new national security paradigm of the United States. This proposal, in all its variants, relies on a structure of collective security. It is therefore a pole away from an autarkic, nationalist strategy. For our purposes it is important that the proponents of this view conceive it as a paradigm shift—whatever the philosophical merits of Nolan and Steinbrunner's (and Thomas Kuhn's) description of the process of shifts in paradigms.[11] The authors argue that "the major powers must completely reconcile their vaunted security strategies in this more multi-centric and unstable post-Cold War environment." Whereas the survivalist agenda of the New Nationalism focuses on the

---

*Though, as is to be expected, his policies in office have been more nuanced and varied. Even in the campaign, the governor supported NAFTA and NATO.

U.S. position alone, the goal of the New Internationalism is world peace. One might characterize the nationalist agenda as leading to an international society where it is "every man for himself," while the internationalist agenda is described as "all for one and one for all." "In the former case," a Carnegie Endowment for International Peace report says, "the enemy is another nation-state; in the latter, the enemy is war itself."

"Collective security" is an organizing strategic concept that seeks to marshal the resources of the group through institutionalized cooperation to achieve common goals. This perspective relies on the insight that the end of the Long War has globalized security needs in a way that only a global, collective response can cope with.

It is indisputable that the well-being of Americans is affected by the behavior of remote economic and political actors. How many American cities have substantial Vietnamese populations today, the internationalist asks, pointing to an obvious domestic consequence of foreign upheaval. Enthusiasts of collective security take this point to demonstrate that a nationalist agenda is therefore unrealistic and that the withdrawal of the United States from multilateral institutions is not really a viable alternative for policy. It has been estimated that, in 2001, more than a twelfth of the population of El Salvador and one-sixth of the population of Haiti was living in the United States. How, the internationalists ask, can a serene neglect of the troubles of others really protect the United States? That unfairly caricatures the nationalist approach, I think: its proponents are perfectly aware that the perceptions and policies of other states, and indeed actors that are not states, must be taken into account by U.S. security policy and, moreover, that the security problems America faces are global in nature. Rather, the nationalist believes that the most successful manipulation of those perceptions and policies lies in the bilateral dialogue of the United States vis-à-vis other states and actors, and not through the multilateral institutions that, necessarily, curb our freedom of action and reflect interests that are not our own. In any case, the nationalist argues, we cannot resolve civil conflicts in Viet Nam, El Salvador, Haiti, or anywhere else. If we had been more self-restrained in our policies to Southeast Asia, perhaps the Vietnamese would never have left in the first place. If refugee flows are the problem, then perhaps a stricter border regime is the answer. At least this lies within our control.

To this the multilateralist asserts two propositions: (1) that American leadership of multilateral collective institutions can multiply the weight of our own policies, giving them a legitimation (and a cost sharing) far beyond what the United States standing alone could achieve; (2) that the well-being of others is and should be treated as a fundamental national goal for Americans. Of course this last point is the sort of pulpit rhetoric that drives the nationalist wild, but there is more to it than simply a vague egalitarian altruism. As James Rosenau has pointed out, modern media make Americans conscious of the identity and conditions of people around the world, and this awareness changes and enlarges the objectives we care about.[12]

Nor should this difference about goals be overstated: many of the objectives sought to be achieved by the New Internationalism are the same as those of the New Nationalism: to deter attack on the United States, its armed forces and citizens; to maintain U.S. prosperity; to reduce the vulnerability of the United States to nuclear attack. The means chosen to accomplish these objectives simply are different. The internationalist believes that U.S. prosperity is best ensured by a general lowering of barriers to trade and that this can be achieved only through multilateral institutions, preferably global ones, like the GATT and the WTO. Regions important to our prosperity—East Asia, Europe, the Persian Gulf—must be kept out of the hands of hostile powers and this can be done at an acceptable cost only by sharing the burden of forward defense (as in the case of the Gulf War, which was fought largely by the United States but financed largely by others). The internationalist believes in stopping weapons proliferation much for the reasons her liberal counterpart believes in gun control on the domestic scene, and also in the necessity of economic development for all states in order to ensure civil stability much as those who promote jobs for the poor at home do so as a prophylactic for crime. The nationalist is more dubious about these means, but in any case, does not concede that international organizations, like the Nuclear Nonproliferation Treaty (NPT) regime or the World Bank and the IMF, have been or could be successful at achieving the ends that would be required of them by both internationalists and nationalists.

Some objectives, however, belong to the multilateralist alone. Ensuring that the basic needs of all peoples are met (whether or not they could conceivably pose a security threat to the United States even by migration); strengthening U.S. control over multinational corporations; maintaining equal terms of trade for all states; protecting the global environment; developing agreed-upon norms of international behavior in the resolution of conflict and the settlement of disputes. These ambitious goals are achievable, if they are achievable at all, only through multilateral institutions.

What are these institutions and how would they change? For some internationalists, NATO would be expanded both as to its mission and its membership. What have thus far been regarded as "out-of-area problems" beyond the scope of the North Atlantic Treaty, which set up NATO and commits its members to a collective defense of the European frontier, would henceforth be included within NATO's responsibilities. NATO forces fought the Gulf War, though no one much said so at the time. Now NATO's mission would be expanded to include not only the protection of the Gulf states, but other responsibilities as well. Article 43 of the United Nations Charter might finally be activated in order to provide armed forces to the U.N. which would take up the role in the Korean peninsula, for example, now filled by U.S. forces. The permanent membership of the U.N. Security Council would be expanded to include Germany and Japan and the most influential states from the southern tier, such as India, Brazil, and others, such as Indonesia and Nigeria. While NATO would be devoted to peacemaking, the U.N., with its own Article 43 forces, would be an active peacekeeper and intervenor to provide humanitarian relief. Multilateral institutions such as the G-8,* which is now confined to coordinating macroeconomic policy, or the Organization for Security and Cooperation in Europe (OSCE) would expand their missions to take on new roles including environmental protection, nonproliferation, counterterrorism, even the coordination of technology transfers. The IMF and the World Bank would be invested with greater funds to accomplish the mission of environmentally sustainable development in the Third World and in the former Second World of ex-communist states. GATT would be strengthened and extended to the equity and capital markets. Taken together, these institutions would act as a chorus, reminding the world of its possibilities and urging it on.

New Internationalists often hold, as James Chace does in his justly influential *The Consequences of the Peace*,[13] that economic stability is the precursor to international peace. Like the New Nationalists, Chace concedes that America's economic position does not enable it to either dominate the world economy or act as the world's policeman. But because international peace is the goal he wishes the United States to pursue, these concessions commit him not to a retrenched agenda of more or less autarkic objectives, but rather to reaching out to restructure international organizations to take up the role the United States is no longer able to play. Chace argues for a supranational central bank—Margaret Thatcher's worst nightmare—that could create and manage the money supply of a common global currency. He also envisions a parallel global organization vested with authority to manage international trade, pointing to the example of the E.U., which, unlike the GATT, has been able to abolish tariffs among the member states while maintaining their diverse tax and regulatory structures.

Like other New Internationalists, Chace supports an enlarged role for international security organizations, particularly the U.N. (although like Eugene Rostow, he points to Article 51 of the Charter as providing a reserve clause by which the United States can retain the power to act if the U.N. Security Council is stymied).

*As the Group of Seven (G-7) is known when Russia attends certain of the Group's meetings.

It is interesting to observe that multilateralists, like their nationalist counterparts, are inclined to believe that the day of the superpower is over. The United States's role as a debtor nation;[14] its comparatively low savings rates that make it hostage to the indulgence of those very competitors; and its lack of self-control regarding imports and consumption generally: these facts reflect and re-enforce the prospect of a diminished future. They are salient characteristics of our current situation for both the internationalist and the nationalist.

Precisely because no nation is self-sufficient, as Richard Rosencrance has argued,[15] and every economy is intertwined with others, either the United States must exploit the institutions that arise from this necessary interdependence or exploit the comparative advantages that may be ours in the disarray that would follow the collapse of those institutions. Depending on which of these alternatives one chooses, one counts oneself as an internationalist or nationalist respectively. And that choice in turn seems to depend on whether global peace or comparative American success is the principal objective of the policy.

Or does it? The New Internationalist counters that a stable international environment that the United States has a leading role in shaping will be less expensive over the long term than a volatile system drifting out of control. Moreover, the United States cannot shape a stable environment unilaterally, but it can use multilateral institutions to work its will and project its interests. Indeed it is hard to see how the United States could broker a deal wherein it offers its unique military assets as its contribution to international security, partly funded by others whose contribution is material but not military, in the absence of multilateral institutions. Without such a deal, however, U.S. forces become too expensive to use, possibly even to preserve. How can it make sense to liquidate those assets in the name of promoting the *national* interest? And how can it make sense to liquidate also the political capital of the West—the shared goals, values, habits of cooperation, and institutions that have emerged from the struggle of the Long War? It is precisely because, as former U.S. national security adviser Zbigniew Brzezinski suggests, America has neither the legitimacy to act as the world's policeman nor the liquidity to act as the world's banker that the northern-tier states must act together to preclude the re-emergence of the coercive, utopian-myth states that would arise in the vacuum created by our abdication of international leadership. Even the narrow goal of national survival is better served, he maintains, by collective security than by mercantile solitude.

Brzezinski argues that the American constitutional system has produced in the United States a policy of gridlock that prevents the institutions of government from dealing with our pervasive internal social problems.

Moreover, our reliance on legal institutions has replaced the moral consensus of the community with the technical substitute of the law: not right and wrong but legal and illegal are the standards by which behavior is measured. As a result, the United States, despite its military, economic, political, and cultural power, cannot sustain a position as international role model (as required by the New Evangelism) nor as the apotheosis of the New Nationalism (since the ethos of consumerism, not dour mercantilism, has replaced self-restraint with the "permissive cornucopia" of modern life), nor as arbiter of the balance of power, as called for by the New Realism (because our security problems do not arise from a competition among the great powers, but rather out of the seething underclass, domestically and in the Third World, that has been seduced by the cult of consumption at a time when the future dictated by its demographics moves this class ever farther from realizing its fantasies). By contrast, our constitutional structure and the dynamics of our political process make us "organically congenial" to multilateral, collective institutions. America's openness to outside participation in its own affairs—through foreign-sponsored lobbies, growing foreign ownership of its assets, and even some foreign participation in the definition of its domestic agenda—makes America both the exemplar and the harbinger of an increasingly internationalist state.[16]

Brzezinski believes that international society will sort itself into six power centers: America, Europe, East Asia, South Asia, the Muslim crescent, and a Eurasian black hole created by the breakup of the Soviet Union. Conflicts among these clusters are likely to be economic in nature, with violent conflict occurring within* some of the unstable clusters. A trilateral alliance of Japan, Europe, and the United States is the collective security arrangement he prefers, operating within the larger framework of a strengthened U.N., with a somewhat larger Security Council.

INTERNATIONAL SOCIETY IN BALANCE: THE NEW REALISM

The nationalist and internationalist models have ambitious goals for U.S. policy though they differ as to how these goals are to be accomplished. The New Nationalism seeks to improve the position of the United States vis-à-vis other states, by exploiting the natural advantages we enjoy in a chaotic environment; the New Internationalism seeks to improve the U.S. position absolutely (if not relatively), while improving the position of others also, so that U.S. dominance can be extended through multilateral institutions that provide security and prosperity to all.

---

*As opposed to violent clashes among the clusters as posited in Samuel P. Huntington, *The Clash of Civilizations* (Simon & Schuster, 1996).

Proponents of the compensating system, or balance of power, have no such illusions (as they regard them) about U.S. influence. The goal of these "New Realists" is less ambitious, or perhaps less starry-eyed. They aim merely to prevent the primacy of any other state. If the nationalist's fundamental objective is making the United States the fittest for survival, and the internationalist's the achievement of world peace, then the principal goal of the new realist is achieving world stability.

"Vital interests" are at the core of all these strategies, but what is really *vital* seems to vary with each perspective. The nationalist judges what is vital by its relationship to freedom of action, for only when the United States possesses such freedom can it use its power to protect itself from threats to its survival. The internationalist holds that the welfare of other states is vital, for only then will the world present a benign environment within which the United States can ultimately survive and prosper. Otherwise, the neglect of other states will turn the international environment into a cesspool of environmental and human rights degradation, out of which will emerge predators armed with weapons of mass destruction from whom there is, on our planet, no place to hide. New Realists—of whom former U.S. national security adviser and secretary of state Henry Kissinger is rightly the most celebrated—tend to define "vital interests" in terms of the stability of the state system. For the New Realist, our vital interests are only threatened when a state, or coalition of states, is powerful enough to successfully destabilize that system.

The differences among these varying definitions of the "vital," however, are largely apparent only, and can be attributed to differing attitudes about means, not ends. The balance-of-power realist simply doesn't believe that calls for peace and justice can unite the world community, or deter a predator (who perhaps has unfurled the banner "No Justice, No Peace" and believes the status quo to be fundamentally inequitable). Nor does the balance-of-power proponent quite believe the machismo rhetoric of the nationalist: it strikes him as adolescent, unrealistic, exaggerated. To maintain that one state—the United States—will be able to coerce all the others into participating in a system that perpetually keeps them at a disadvantage is wishful thinking. The international system may be chaotic, or anarchic, but even criminals can conspire.

Rather, the proponents of compensating balances believe that technique, rather than natural advantage or procedural perfection, will best ensure vital U.S. interests. It is a philosophy for the Talleyrand in every statesman, and it requires an adroitness and coolness of calculation, to say nothing of a dispassion toward the problems of other states, that the American public has seldom exhibited. A history written by such a realist is a history of great men, just as a history written by the Hobbesian chaoticist is a history of impersonal forces, and a history by the internationalist the account of treaties and resolutions and minutes of the meetings of multilateral institutions.

What are the elements of the New Realism, a paradigm that is based on a balance of power? If we assume that the goal of ensuring world stability is sought in order to achieve the same objectives as the various other paradigms—protecting American territory, armed forces, and citizens from attack or coercion, and providing for the continued growth and prosperity of the American market economy—how does this archetypal approach plan to achieve these objectives?

The New Realist takes a severe view of those threats that actually strike at our vital interests but is disinclined to see every atrocity as a threat to our security. Accordingly, a state (or alliance of states) would have to do more than simply kidnap an American citizen or massacre an African village in order to pose a mortal threat to the American state. The New Realist assumes that America's current position is both too weak to impose world peace and too strong to have to content itself with passively waiting for hostile forces outside our control to coalesce against us. In order to prevent a state from becoming powerful enough to menace us, the New Realist takes as the first imperative the prevention of the emergence of any state (or alliance of states) that could dominate the Eurasian landmass. This principle plays itself out differently with respect to different potential adversaries.

With regard to China, the United States should seek to encourage it to develop as a trading state, because this development is both salutary—in that it will, over time, loosen the grip of the totalitarian party and armed forces that currently rule the country and have in the past been tempted to seek hegemony in the region—and possible, because the United States represents a rich market for Chinese goods, one capable of improving the standard of living for hundreds of millions of persons.

With respect to the states of the former Soviet Union, the United States ought to encourage devolution and democratization, not so much because these are good in themselves, but because they are the best hedge against the re-emergence of a state with ambitions of world dominion. A broken-up Soviet Union is less likely to be able to mount a challenge against the United States; a democratized Russian state is less likely to threaten the other former republics, and also less likely to be able to re-emerge as a militant superpower.

The states posing the greatest potential threat, however, are not the collapsing red dwarfs of communism, the supernovas that are already imploding, but rather Germany and Japan and the productive countries that surround them in some anxiety. Whereas the New Internationalist seeks to extend the U.N.'s mission and NATO's to accomplish the agenda of a world order based on collective security, the New Realist wants to strengthen NATO to keep Germany anchored to the United States. The differing approaches imply different policies for the widening of NATO membership and the deepening of its portfolio of missions. NATO enlargement, to include Poland, the Czech Republic, Hungary, and perhaps the Baltic states, is the preferred realist proposal, not the expansion of NATO's missions out-of-area. While NATO remains the preferred institution for a German-American alliance, just as important is German membership in the E.U., which also ties German policy to its neighbors. Even a revived Western European Union (WEU)[17] would be preferable to a Germany looking eastward, with the potential to become a strategic superpower and the revived ambitions that would exploit that potential.

Japanese democracy is usually thought not to have achieved a very deep root structure, and thus to be even more at risk than the German democratic state. Moreover, Japan lies proximate to two potentially unstable, highly armed states—China and North Korea—and depends at present on U.S. forward forces and the U.S. nuclear deterrent for its safety. As I have written elsewhere, American policy to denuclearize North Korea or to induce respect for human rights in China must paramountly consider whether our steps are likely to bring the Japanese closer to nuclear and military self-reliance. It would be a tragedy for the world if, in order to extirpate a North Korean nuclear force with which Japan has learned to live, we plunged the Korean peninsula into a war that led to the mobilization of Japan's energy and wealth on behalf of its armed forces. Already the Japanese, with less than one and one-half percent of GNP, field the world's third largest defense establishment, and there is no NATO-like institution that links this establishment with the forces of surrounding states. It is probably far more important that the United States maintain forces in Korea than any other forward basing because Japan must be persuaded that the threats it faces—now that the Soviet Union is no longer among them—both require an alliance with the United States and yet will not lead to war owing to American unilateral action.

The New Nationalist strategy of closing American markets to East Asian competitors in a trade confrontation is precisely the sort of maladroit move that the New Realist seeks to avoid. Economic competition is doubtless the one area of interaction with the United States that could detonate Asian antagonism and anti-Western unity, particularly if it is sharpened by heightened trade exclusion on the part of the E.U. By treating each of the states of East Asia as a separate entrant into the U.S. market, the New Realist would balance one against another so that a coalition of East Asia states does not form, and no single state can dominate the others.

The same defensive posture dominates the New Realist calculus for American intervention: the United States should never intervene when its own vital interests are not at stake, and then only to prevent others from achieving a dominant position from which it can be threatened. Just as importantly, this principle should control our relationships with the internal forces at play within a foreign state. The Persian Gulf provides one example. The economic vitality of the G-7 states is linked to the flow of oil from the gulf; any state that controlled that flow would be in a dominant position vis-à-vis the United States, Japan, and Europe, who are all, to varying degrees, dependent on that oil. The states of this region to whom the United States gave security guarantees under the Carter Doctrine can be protected against local predators; the Gulf War and the earlier reflagging of Kuwaiti vessels showed as much. Accordingly the independence of the gulf states is of crucial importance and can and should be protected. It is far from clear, however, that these states are good bets for the long run. Modernization, democratization, and pan-Islamic movements stimulate internal threats that U.S. military intervention is powerless to deflect, and may even excite. Within such states the United States cannot afford to abandon the regimes on whose stability the economic life of the northern tier, postindustrial states of the world depends. But neither can the United States be so closely identified with those regimes that we, as well as they, become the target of revolution, as happened in Iran. This observation counsels that U.S. policy, perhaps through diplomatic or even clandestine contacts, must maintain a supple posture with respect to the internal dynamics at work in these states. Such a complex policy has strengths and weaknesses. It provides flexibility and avoids the rigid commitments of collective security that inevitably fail to reflect shifts in the politics and power relationships among and within states. It leverages American influence by linking it to coalitions of states that share America's interest in preventing a hegemonical threat from arising, rather than merely hoping to defeat such a threat once it becomes lethal. At the same time it is ineluctably linked to the status quo and thus makes the United States a locus of animosity among reformers whose values we may in fact share. Most important, it requires intimate knowledge of the political locale and a surefootedness in dealing with subtle and sometimes surprising shifts. It is one thing to muster the ruthlessness to abandon the Kurds in order to strengthen the shah of Iran for geopolitical reasons; it is quite another to predict the shah's replacement by the Ayatollah Khomeini, as so few analysts did. Yet without such accurate but difficult forecasting, the mere willingness to take cold-blooded decisions can amount to little more than a declarative pose.

Nationalists are inclined to downplay the proliferation of weapons of mass destruction. Most of these weapons, now that the Cold War has ended, are not trained on the United States—it is said—and, to the extent that they tie down our international competitors, relatively improve our position. So long as America is able to defend against the modest forces likely to be available to the current (and anticipated) generation of proliferatees, it is not crucial to us whether, for example, Iraq uses poison gas against Iran.[18] Internationalists, by contrast, seek a full court press against proliferation and even hope for cancellations of nuclear programs that have been pursued by states that are now willing to abandon them, for example, South Africa. With some exceptions, notably Kenneth Waltz,[19] internationalists tend to view any proliferation as inimical to world peace.

The realist view is more nuanced and more pessimistic. It seeks nonproliferation mainly of nuclear delivery systems, which are easier to detect and to destroy than fissile material. But the realist's position is essentially fatalistic and does not wish to waste diplomatic assets pursuing the fruitless goal of convincing Pakistan and India that nuclear weapons do not really enhance their security or that the threats each faces from the other are not mortal. Rather the realist accepts some proliferation as inevitable, and tries to mitigate its impact on the stability of the international system.

With respect to achieving American goals in the international economy, the balance-of-power approach shows the same watermark of maneuver and irony, and the same disdain for impractical programs (whether they spring from romantic idealism or sullen paranoia). This approach accepts that America's share of the world economic product has dramatically fallen since the end of the Second World War and is likely to fall still further as hitherto unproductive economies industrialize. Proponents of this view do not waste time lamenting this change or trying to recapture the past by withdrawing from these emerging states the markets they must have to thrive. But neither does the New Realism sacrifice American competitiveness simply to increase the world's wealth. Rather here, as with political competition, it seeks a certain relationship for the United States with other states that is relatively advantageous. Just as the New Realism seeks to prevent a situation whereby any state (or coalition) dominates the Eurasian landmass or crucial global sea lanes, so it seeks here to prevent the United States from slipping into an inferior position in the terms of trade with any state (or bloc of states) for much the same reason: in either case, the continued wealth and power of the United States become hostage to the policies of another state. For the New Internationalist, potato chip production is just as valuable as computer chip production: in a world market, the important thing is that every state produce what it has a comparative advantage in. This leads to the greatest efficiency and the maximization of international wealth. For the New Realist, however, this phenomenon is exactly what is to be deplored: the potato chip manufacturer, whose products have easy substitutes and for whom there is an infinite number of potential competitors because the human capital and the technology required for farm production are so modest and so widely distributed, will always be at the mercy of value-added products like the computer chip that enable so many other kinds of productivity, and can themselves only be made more efficient by the most sophisticated technology and the most competitive firms. Given a choice between a free market worldwide and a system that established favorable terms for trade for the United States, the New Realist would only smile: it is not a realistic choice. States will never permit a universal free market so long as they have the political power to engineer favorable terms for themselves through various anticompetitive tactics, including exploiting the free rider phenomenon,[20] and as long as domestic political groups can protect themselves from foreign competition at the expense of the larger society, as farmers have so successfully done in Japan, France, and elsewhere. Nor is any system that attempts to enshrine favorable terms of trade for the United States likely to endure for long, not least because the U.S. consumer would not tolerate the rise in prices such an imperial system would require. Competitiveness must be won. But through the adept use of retaliatory threats, state–private sector collaboration, and regional groupings like NAFTA that, for historic and cultural reasons, enshrine a favored U.S. position, it may be that the terms of trade can be successfully manipulated, at least to mitigate the effects of declining U.S competitiveness.

The New Realist is preoccupied with stability.* His forebears are those European intellectuals who attempted to tutor an unsophisticated and idealistic American policy elite in order to prevent a repetition of the catastrophe of Nazism that seemed to them as much a product of internationalist idealism and faith in the League of Nations as of the isolationism that characterized prewar U.S. policy. This group had little interest in the Third World; its successors do not either. There is nothing "vital" in American interests there, and the potential for costly diversion is limitless. Nor do the problems of transnationalism, the environment, refugee migration, epidemics, famine, and terrorism seem to concern the New Realist. He accepts the primacy of the nation-state, and at the same time realizes its existence cannot be successfully separated from that of the society of nation-states of which it is part, a member, so to speak, of an ensemble. Transnational problems, however, and the nongovernmental organizations that are increasingly the effective agents dealing with these problems, are difficult for the balance-of-power theorist to include within his frame of reference.

---

*See John Mearsheimer, *The Tragedy of Great Power Politics* (Norton, 2001).

THE DEMOCRATIC SOCIETY:
THE NEW EVANGELISM

In September 1993 the Clinton administration announced its policy of "democratic enlargement," a commitment to bring as many nations as possible into the fold of practicing free-market economies and limited-government democracies. This represented something of a change from the previous policy of "democratic engagement," by which the United States sought a dialogue with other states at varying stages of democratization to encourage them along that path. That subtle change turns on a key notion of democratic enlargement: the link between a nation's internal political order and its external orientation.

Whether by force following aborted elections (as in Haiti or Panama), or with economic aid after democratic revolutions (as in the former Soviet empire) or economic sanctions against existing parliamentary states (as against South Africa), Americans have acted alone and in concert with NATO allies or pursuant to U.N. resolutions to encourage democratic regimes. Establishing democratic regimes, however, is a far more ambitious agenda than simply encouraging them. For one thing, the former goal requires rewriting existing international legal norms because the nature of a state's political structure has usually been held to be an "internal" matter, for that state's determination alone. Observing that the state system was "built around the idea of sovereign equality and noninterference by foreign powers into a nation's internal affairs," the then director of policy planning for the State Department, James Steinberg, concluded, however, that "it seems clear that a rigid application of the concept of 'noninterference in internal affairs' is not enough. Neither balance of power nor collective security arrangements will be adequate. . . ."[21]

Steinberg, later a highly influential deputy national security advisor, further wrote that "the international community has begun to exercise the right, recognized in the U.N. Charter, to intervene in internal disputes when they pose a threat to international peace and security. And in practice, the international community is stretching the concept of a threat to internal peace and security to a broad range of cases where the internal conflict is serious, the humanitarian costs are large, but the external dimension is limited, as in Somalia."

Now suppose that, in addition to this appreciation of the changing transparency of sovereignty, we add the convictions that (1) democracies do not go to war against one another, and (2) a democracy crucially, if in part, consists in the security of basic human rights for its citizens, and (3) that free markets and democracy are mutually supportive and may even be indispensable to the longevity of either. We then have the "New Evangelist" position, which sees the U.S. role as one that, using international institutions wherever possible but acting alone if necessary, the United States should intervene to buttress, restore, or even establish democratic regimes where these are threatened or nonexistent, leading gradually to a world of like-minded communities sharing the universal values of liberty and freedom.

But are such values truly universal? George Kennan once wrote,

> I know of no evidence that "democracy" or what we picture to ourselves under that word is the natural state of most of mankind. It seems rather to be a form of government (and a difficult one, with many drawbacks at that) which evolved in the 18th and 19th centuries in northwestern Europe . . . and which was then carried into other parts of the world, including North America, where peoples from that northwestern European area appeared as settlers . . . Democracy has, in other words, a relatively narrow base both in time and in space, and the evidence has yet to be produced that it is the natural form of rule for peoples outside those narrow perimeters.[22]

Or, as Tony Smith put it in the *Washington Quarterly:*

> [Some realists ask]: Given the desperate condition of many African countries, how can the U.S. propose with confidence that if they follow its example they will find salvation? Can Americans realistically suppose that good relations with the Muslim world necessarily presuppose the conversion of these countries to liberal democratic government?[23]

The realist is content to offer limited help to struggling democracies, stressing that it is difficult to know what the right political system is for non-Western cultures and a mistake to identify too closely with every friendly regime. He doubts the premise that the security of human rights abroad is truly vital to American security. The nationalist, by contrast, is actually hostile to making the promotion of democracy a key American goal. He doubts the very underpinnings of the democratic evangelism, the belief that American security would be enhanced by a world of democracies because such states do not attack each other. France occupied the Ruhr in 1923 against the Weimar democracy; India attacked what was then East Pakistan when both states were thought to have generally democratic institutions; and Ecuador and Peru, Turkey and Greece have threatened recent hostilities. These and other examples may cast doubt on the theory, most eloquently argued in our day by the Princeton political scientist Michael Doyle, that democracies do not make war on one another. Moreover, the nationalist sees the New Evangelist as an impractical meddler, risking his own state's resources in a vain effort to reform everyone else. As Alexander Hamilton wrote:

> There are still to be found visionary, or designing, men who stand ready to advocate the paradox of perpetual peace between states. The genius of [democracy], they say is pacific; the spirit of commerce has a tendency to soften the manners of men and to extinguish those inflammable humors which has so often kindled wars. [Democracies] will never be disposed to waste themselves in ruinous contentions with each other. They will be governed by mutual interest, and will cultivate a spirit of mutual amity and concord.
>
> We may ask these projectors in politics, whether it is not the true interest of all nations to cultivate the same benevolent and philosophic spirit? If this be their true interest, have they in fact pursued it? Has it not, on the contrary, invariably been found that momentary passions and immediate interests have a more active and imperious control over human conduct than general or remote considerations of policy, utility and justice? Have democracies in fact been less addicted to war than monarchies? Are not the former administered by men as much as the latter? Are there not aversions, predilections, rivalships, and desires of unjust acquisition that affect nations as well as kings? Are not popular assemblies frequently subject to the impulses of rage, resentment, jealousy, avarice and other irregular and violent propensities?[24]

By contrast, the objection of the New Internationalist to the New Evangelist's proposed paradigm aims at a fundamentally different target: he questions the evangelist's emphasis on the importance of the internal. The internationalist strives for agreements to prevent the proliferation of weapons of mass destruction, ecological devastation, and world recession from a macroeconomic perspective; he is less concerned with the internal drama of party politics and microeconomic practices. Both approaches stress the importance of international institutions, but on closer inspection, the preferred organizations of the new evangelist are choirs composed of the converted—the G-7, for example, or NATO, not the United Nations or the Organization of African Unity.

The New Evangelist rejects the classic formulation that states have no permanent friends, only permanent interests. For the evangelist, the community of the faithful *is* permanent. Because they are chosen by the people, democratic governments regard each other's regimes as legitimate and deserving of respect. Because, domestically, they use civilized nonviolent means to resolve disputes, democracies tend to prefer the same methods internationally. The evangelist also downplays the fear of a hegemonic power or group of powers. Indeed, the Clinton administration was more enthusiastic about European integration than many of the members of the E.U. So long as the power is exercised by a democratic state, even nuclear proliferation, for example, to Israel, is acceptable.

Like each of the other competing paradigms, this view is linked to a perception of a particular threat that it regards as uniquely salient. For the New Evangelist, this threat arises from the resurgence of nationalism and violence in the hands of authoritarian states. To combat this threat to the United States, the New Evangelist proposes a kind of inoculation far more imaginative than anything envisaged by his competitors. Realists, nationalists, and internationalists all treat the world as relatively static. The Cold War has ended, but their prescriptions generally forecast more of the same. The New Evangelist has more dynamic developments in mind, and these lend support to his position: history seems to be moving in his direction (the number of democracies is increasing), at least in the short term, and he can mobilize democratic popular support on behalf of American democratic values in a way that more cynical or more abstract theorists cannot. A global democratic revolution has been going on since Prague Spring in 1968, and with considerably more success each decade. In 1975 the Portuguese overthrew their communist government with the help of the European democracies. In the 1980s Latin American states began to replace military regimes to an unprecedented degree on that continent such that by 2001, there were elected civilian governments in Argentina, Bolivia, Brazil, Ecuador, El Salvador, Guatemala, Honduras, Nicaragua, Peru, Panama, and Uruguay. In the 1990s, the transition from a racist, oligarchic state to a multiracial democracy in South Africa inspired the world community. In 2001, some 120 of the world's 192 states had democratic governments.

Unlike the other competing paradigms, the New Evangelism can call on these developments for inspiration and political support. Democratic ideology, it is said,[25] not weaponry, won the Cold War. "Ideas matter." We cannot ignore the role of values in shaping our security and our fate, nor should we. Being true to human rights, pluralism, freedom of conscience, and democratic governance is the only way we will be able to mobilize support at home for our policies and, if the New Evangelist is right, actually achieve a safer, more secure world. The end of the Cold War has freed us from having to support regimes that were hostile to our values. Now, as the sole remaining superpower, we can support those regimes with whom we have a true affinity.

It must be said that much of the enthusiasm behind this position does arise from our role as the sole superpower. The world is beset by enemies, many of them states that are the enemies of their own peoples. None really threaten us. If there was ever a time for the United States to assert its values, it must be now, for if not the United States, then who would do it, and if not now, when would we be in a better position to do so? And if no one asserts these values, isn't it just a matter of time before the fragile movement toward democracies is overtaken by the retrograde forces of jaded realists, reactionary nationalists, and relativist internationalists everywhere? In a period of *relative* American decline, doesn't our best insurance against the future lie in persuading other states to adopt a political system that is benign toward our state and congenial to our culture—a system, in other words, that is compatible with our strategic approach *and* our constitutional values?

Like all unipolar, or imperial, universal visions, however, the paradigm of the New Evangelist seems remarkably insensitive to the will of others. When a Clinton administration official proposed in an interview that "the U.S. must rebuild the Haitian economy and restructure its court system, its legislative system and its military system," a columnist replied, "What colonialist, racist nonsense. Haiti belongs to the Haitians to run as they see fit."[26] But isn't that the beauty of the democratic vision: that it alone of all the ideologies of modern government can lay a claim to truly recognizing the people's will in having a state of their own choosing? Only evangelism promises that, after conversion, one is empowered to do as one pleases.

The only major states in which democratic transplantation has been tried are Japan and Germany. These examples can be cited either way. Skeptics point out that the principal reason behind the alliance system was not to simply contain the USSR but to do so in a way that kept these new democracies from reverting to their old ways. This must reflect at least some nervousness about how entrenched the habits of democracy have become in those societies, even under the most propitious circumstances. Advocates point to the unblemished success of those two societies in peacefully transferring power (finally, in Japan) and in their nonthreatening international behavior. Perhaps the most salient point, however, is that it is no less important now to strengthen those democracies than it was before, and this, as before, is unlikely to happen in the absence of American commitment.

But what if a state is attacked that is not a fully functioning democracy, such as Kuwait? Or if a state threatens its neighbors even though it is a democracy, such as India? Or if the slow process of building democracies is too complicated and ponderous to treat emergencies such as occurred in Bosnia and Rwanda? In all these instances, democratic enlargement seems to have little of immediate relevance to say.

THE SOLE REMAINING SUPERPOWER:
THE NEW LEADERSHIP

Each of the preceding four proposed security paradigms shares an essential assumption about American power: that it is in relative decline and that the consequences of that decline will constrain the United States in its role as a world leader, a role to which it has become accustomed in the post–World War II period. One proposed paradigm, however, denies this assumption. This is the program I will call the "New Leadership." In the words of its most articulate spokesman, Charles Krauthammer,

> the true geopolitical structure of the post–Cold War world [is that of] a single pole of world power that consists of the United States at the apex of the industrial west . . . American preeminence is based on the fact that it is the only country with the military, diplomatic, political and economic assets to be a decisive player in any conflict in whatever part of the world it chooses to involve itself. . . . One can debate whether America is in true economic decline. [One should note, however, that] its percentage of world GNP is roughly where it has been throughout the 20th century (between 22% and 26%) excepting the aberration of the immediate post–World War II era.[27]

This point can be urged even more strongly: the United States, while in relative economic decline vis-à-vis the E.U. and Japan, whose percentages of world GNP were growing more rapidly (at least until the mid-1990s), has actually increased the measure of its geopolitical position by the defeat of its global adversary, the Soviet Union. As a result, as William Odom has written, "the configuration of power today is such that only the United States can launch the construction of a new system."[28] What sort of national security paradigm would enable the United States to play such a role?

Advocates of the New Leadership have something in common with each of the other competing schools: like the nationalists, they advocate a focus on U.S. vital interests and disdain charitable missions abroad, although they draw the line around such national interests far more expansively than other nationalists because they believe American interests to be global in nature and emphasize that American prosperity depends upon a stable international market; like the internationalists, they wish to strengthen NATO and various collective security schemes (such as the OSCE), but they conceive of these groups differently, believing them to be little more than a psychological fig leaf for the robust American assertion of power (and thus reserve a special contempt for the U.N.). As Krauthammer has put it:

There is much pious talk about a new multilateral world and the promise of the U.N. as guarantor of a new post–Cold War order. But this is
to mistake cause and effect, the U.S. and the U.N. The U.N. is guarantor
of nothing. . . . Collective security? In the Gulf, without the U.S. leading and prodding, bribing and blackmailing, no one would have stirred.
Nothing would have been done: no embargo, no Desert Shield, no
threat of force. The world would have written off Kuwait the way the
last body pledged to collective security, the League of Nations, wrote
off Abyssinia.[29]

Like the realists, advocates of American leadership place a strong
emphasis on bilateral ties and on preventing new hegemonies from arising,
but in contrast to the realists, leadership partisans focus more closely on
internal issues within the great power states and less on a grand ensemble
among them. Advocates of the New Leadership point out that balance of
power approaches are tone deaf, for example, to the importance of American values in U.S. foreign policy. Moreover, balance of power techniques
are considered outmoded from this point of view. As Odom puts it, "the
American concept for NATO at its creation was prevention of a return to
the old *Realpolitik* game in Western Europe, and although the alliance balanced Soviet power, it was created as much to solve Western Europe's
problem with Germany as it was to prevent Soviet expansion." Indeed
Odom stresses that Europe's security problems are "primarily ones of
internal instability and civil war, problems a balance of power approach
[with its purely external focus] will not solve."

One might say that, as opposed to the "democratic enlargement" of the
Clinton administration, the advocate of American leadership proposes
instead "selective engagement." But whereas conservative groups, such as
the Heritage Foundation, which coined this phrase, are strongly anti-
interventionist, the New Leadership would deploy selective American
engagement to achieve the global aims of American dominance. For example, this is the only paradigm that would, forthrightly, have counseled
significant NATO force against Serbia in 1991, in part because the failure
to do so amounted to an abdication of American leadership itself. If victory in the Gulf War may be thought of as symbolizing what might have
been the beginning of a new American century, then the collapse of Western will in Yugoslavia demonstrated what happens when the Americans
defer to the Europeans on such matters. If the unification of Germany represented a triumph of clear-sighted American diplomatic leadership in the
face of European confusion (and accordingly advanced American prestige) then the calamities in Bosnia give us some picture of what diplomacy
becomes in the absence of such leadership: impotence draped in cynicism.
In the end, the very Europeans who stalemated action in Yugoslavia will be

the ones who point to Bosnia as evidence of the futility of American leadership (and our prestige will suffer accordingly).

Advocates of the new leadership are, however, less eager to intervene in Somalia or Haiti, where the outcomes do not appear to affect American leadership one way or the other. Where they perceive future threats—such as those arising from the possession of weapons of mass destruction by terrorist states, such as Iran, Iraq, or North Korea—these advocates favor decisive action untempered by the effort to achieve consensus with our allies. President Clinton's role in negotiating a peaceful solution with North Korea was attacked just as much by partisans of the New Leadership, who favored a more robust response, as it was by the New Nationalists, who really had little to offer as an alternative.

As every leader instinctively knows, one's adversaries may present immediate problems, but preventing one's friends and colleagues from becoming successful rivals is the tricky part of the agenda of dominance. For this reason, New Leaders* and New Realists often appear to agree: both want to prevent the rise of a state, or collection of states, that would threaten the position of the United States. But whereas the realists wish to do so as a consequence of inevitable American relative decline, the leaders wish to preserve American hegemony at the top. Thus some New Realists would have demurred about intervention in the Gulf because Iraq is not a potential power of world-dominating ambitions, whereas for the New Leader, it was essential that the United States demonstrate it could act on behalf of the northern-tier states, from whose number a rival leader might emerge. While realists such as Jeane Kirkpatrick now suggest that "it is time to give up the dubious benefits of superpower status" so that we may aspire to be "a normal country in a normal time," the New Leader recognizes that we are still far from normal times.[30]

Above all, is not the New Leader the truly realistic one? For while others call for strengthening the democratic revolution, achieving a robust agenda of counterproliferation, and preventing hostile combinations from forming against us, only the New Leader actually plans to accomplish these goals by specific means within our control, as opposed to offering hortatory rhetoric and a sort of "you first" diplomacy. The probing question for the proponent of this paradigm: Can we afford it? Indeed there are some realists who claim that even attempting such an agenda is bound to weaken our geopolitical position, just as it did those of earlier superpowers who, having vanquished their opponents, found themselves increasingly unable to provide the economic infrastructure that would sustain their gains because they had diverted so great a portion of their resources to military budgets.

---

*I intend no allusion to the New Leader movement of the 1930s in Great Britain.

To this the New Leader retorts that whether or not our economic health can be improved through American hegemony, it certainly can't prosper without it. Moreover, the decline in American competitiveness is not, he argues, due to overspending on defense, but rather to those national characteristics that are the negative consequence of qualities whose positive effects far better suit us for world political leadership than for cutthroat trade wars in the game of geo-economics, a game that our rivals would be only too anxious to tempt us to play in lieu of the geopolitics where our overwhelming assets lie. Let me take up both these points, one at a time.

First, it is often assumed by many that the vast flow of international goods and information is a natural given and that any American resources spent to ensure international stability through defense expenditures are resources wasted because they are diverted from our economic well-being. How often are we treated to lectures by economists who claim that money spent on tanks is unproductive, while the same money spent on tractors contributes to our national wealth. In fact it took British expenditures well in excess of our own (as a percentage of GDP) to maintain the sea lanes on which British prosperity depended, and to prevent the competing hegemonies of those who would threaten her trade and later her industrial supremacy. It is open to question whether her relative decline began when the costs of empire overstretched her ability to maintain domestic investment, or when other states—Germany, for example, whose military expenditures were far greater than Great Britain's—overtook her and were manifestly willing to threaten the very international security on which complicated contemporary economic life depends. As Krauthammer puts it:

> It is a mistake to view America's exertions abroad as nothing but a drain on its economy. As can be seen in the Gulf, America's involvement abroad is in many ways an essential pillar of the American economy. The United States is, like Britain before it, a commercial, maritime, trading nation that needs an open, stable world environment in which to thrive. In a world of Saddams, if the U.S. were to shed its unique superpower role, its economy would be gravely wounded. Insecure sea lanes, impoverished trading partners, exorbitant oil prices . . . are only the more obvious risks of an American abdication . . . The cost of ensuring an open and safe world for American commerce—5.4% of GNP and falling—is hardly exorbitant.[31]

But, it is said, this is far more than, for example, the Japanese spend on defense (about 1.5 percent of GNP) and is a competitive drag on the U.S. economy. Surely Japan is as much in need of secure trade lanes as the U.S. and far more sensitive to oil prices. Wouldn't the United States be better off ceding some share of its responsibilities for international security to those states who, when they took up this burden, would thereby acquire a drag on their ascent and thus relatively improve our own competitive position? This is the second question suggested above, and it draws a distinct line between the purported paradigm of leadership and all others. For here the partisan of this approach denies the assumption on which the argument depends: geopolitical leadership, he argues, is not the same as geo-economic competition. "The notion that economic power inevitably translates into geopolitical influence," Krauthammer writes, "is a materialist illusion." Economic power is a necessary but not a sufficient condition for great power status, which also comprehends not simply military power, but the will to use it and the legitimacy to do so (so as not to arouse countervailing coalitions). Here the United States, in part because of its benign history toward the defeated states of World War II, is in a unique position. The moment for its aria has arrived.

It may appear that it is the imprimatur of the U.N. that conveys this legitimacy, but in fact this is only a reflection of the American desire not to appear hegemonical and thus to seek U.N. endorsements for its actions. A quick canvass of recent General Assembly resolutions would disabuse anyone who was tempted to think that the U.N. could, acting as an institution, convey legitimacy to any state act without the consent of the great powers.

Indeed the constitutional framework of the United States and its multinational state uniquely suit it to pursue the goals of world power without threatening its peers. The Long War was fought over issues of legitimacy; the resolution of that war in favor of the democratic republics has given us a postwar order over whose protection the United States is well placed to preside. To abandon this role will not only threaten that victory, it will inevitably invite the chaos that is most costly to a status quo power such as the United States. We have the most to lose by our own passivity and no other way to lose it.

PARADIGMS AND POLICIES

We have seen five proposals for a new strategic paradigm for the United States—the New Nationalism, the New Internationalism, the New Evangelism, the New Realism, the New Leadership. None has yet captured a consensus. This failure has prompted some to suggest that the world is simply too complicated now for a single paradigm.* "No doctrine,"

*Secretary of State Madeleine Albright concluded as much when she addressed the issue.

Richard Haass has written in a wittily titled article, "Paradigm Lost," "can hope to provide a lens through which to view most events."[32]

The first thing to be said about these proffered "new paradigms," however, is that they are not paradigms at all. In fact, the entire intellectual enterprise that has yielded these proposals has been triggered by a profound misunderstanding as to what has been lost and what can serve to replace it. The source of this misunderstanding may perhaps be traced, ironically, to the idea that the world inherited by U.S. administrations after the Long War is "a more complex place than what came before." According to this account presidents from Truman to Reagan had the comforting stability of the Cold War to provide a consistent and continuous context for foreign policy, but the aftermath of that war has not yet yielded a similar clarity. In the place of containment—the old "paradigm" through which all political events were mediated—there is only confusion, because the antinomies on which containment depended (the global competition of the West and the Soviet Union, the totalitarian ambition of communist ideology versus the pluralistic vision of the West) have also collapsed.[33] Perhaps until new threats against which the United States must contend are themselves clarified, its political class will be unable to decide what paradigm is to replace containment—or perhaps the threats are so diffuse that, as Haass suggests, no single paradigm will do.

What is wrong with this account? First, it confuses paradigms with policies. A paradigm is a worldview that members of a political community share; a policy is what some portion of them put into place in pursuit of the goals of that paradigm. Of course no single *policy* will do; indeed the history of the Cold War itself shows an enormous variation in policies, depending on the time, place, and manner of the campaign being waged. But without a shared paradigm, it's hard to know whether the proposed policy is effective when implemented. Without a shared paradigm, the United States is condemned to adopt that most seductive of strategies, the case-by-case approach. This approach is appealing to a powerful state because it obviates the need to make some crucial choices and comforts the decision maker that no precedent is created that will come back to embarrass him. The more powerful the state, the more appealing is this approach, because that state will always appear to prevail. It will always appear to get its way, if it is powerful enough to bring the other states into line. I say "appear to prevail" because it is not so clear what "way" the state, acting on a case-by-case basis, is actually getting when it gets its way. Any road seems like the right one if you don't know where you're going, because if you don't know where you're going, any road will take you there. So the United States may be said to have had its way when it persuaded the U.N. Security Council to adopt resolutions condemning the Serbs for war crimes, and when it led the Council in declining to prosecute those indicted, when it initially led humanitarian forces into Somalia *and* when it was the first to evacuate its own troops.

Second, the history of the account given above is saturated with presentism, the view that things have never been quite so much the way they are as they are right now. I doubt the world is, as is so often said, "more complicated, more complex," because the "world" in that sentence is not the teeming globe whose problems increase as our appreciation of them increases, but instead is the set of values that, problematically, collide in the attempt to allocate our power wisely. Such a world was hardly more complex for President George W. Bush, with vastly more resources, than it was for, say, John Quincy Adams, who was compelled to factor in the consequences of his foreign policy for the domestic crisis caused by slavery and also for our exceedingly precarious international position. President Bush's predecessor had to decide whether to intervene in Kosovo to halt a campaign of ethnic cleansing; Adams had to decide whether to give aid to the South American revolts against the Spanish empire. The decisions are no less complex in either case. Nor was the American position in the Cold War particularly simple either. As I wrote at the time:

> No effective American policy can be either pacifist or militaristic: for the U.S. must pursue an accommodation with the Russians in which we do not wholly believe, and at the same time, arm to prevent a conflict in which we do not truly wish to participate.[34]

Moreover, it is not the end of the Cold War that has transformed the world and left the United States without an objective. Our objective never was simply to defeat the Soviet Union. Georgiy Arbatov's cynical remark, "We have done our worst to you: we have deprived you of an enemy," is far more reflective of Soviet culture than American. Rather it is the end of the Long War, which was fought over the legitimacy of the democratic system itself and that of its competitors, that has quite appropriately left us with the slight puzzlement one feels after recovery from a long and life-threatening illness. What now?

Finally, it is not "containment" that is the paradigm that has been lost. Containment, composed of that set of policies that sought by defensive alliances to prevent the aggrandizement of the Soviet empire and, where possible, the avoidance of armed conflict in order to enable the internal contradictions of the communist system to manifest themselves and to be contrasted with the marked success of the Western states, was not a paradigm at all. Containment did not provide us with a way of understanding the conflict, but rather with a guiding set of tactics for winning it.

The paradigm by means of which Western statesmen and their publics have understood this century-long struggle is a picture of the State. That paradigm depicts the legitimate state as one that exists to better the welfare of its people. This paradigm distinguishes the nation-state from the state-nation that preceded it, the paradigm of which was a State that existed to mobilize the people for whom it was the sovereign; the state-nation was the state of empires. The nation-state is the state of nationalities.

For most of the twentieth century the picture shared by the American political community has been that of a State created by the self-determination of peoples. This paradigm has not been lost; indeed it is flourishing in many parts of the globe. It fails to provide guidance for U.S. policy because the problems that the American state faces now are not problems of the Long War, whose inception marked the beginning of the widespread transition to the modern nation-state. That paradigm continues to provide the requisite ability to see resemblances, to enable analogies, to structure consensus—if it didn't, then the fruits of the Long War would be incomprehensible to us. But as a consequence of that war, the American state has changed and is changing to reflect those innovations that brought victory. Part of that change, which is already well underway in the United States, will be a paradigm shift in our expectations of the State.

If the Wilsonian paradigm pictured a state that existed in order to better the welfare of its nation, the twenty-first century American state will exist to reflect, implement, inform, and diversify individual choice. It is tempting to say that this is a change from a democratic political matrix of ideas to a capitalist market matrix. But this would mistake the way we deal with problems for the problems themselves: there will always be a political and a market mechanism working in tandem because the kinds of problems states must solve cannot be wholly assimilated into one or the other approach.[35] Briefly put, systems for allocation that use political means (like the Selective Service Act) call on a different view of egalitarianism (one man, one vote, for example) than do market systems (like the All-Volunteer Force) with their distinctive view of equal treatment (to each according to his means and ability). One can never be wholly sacrificed to the other in a civilized society. Indeed one might go so far as to say that it is a distinguishing mark of a civilized society that it struggles to maintain many-valued forms of life despite the human condition of scarcity that compels choice among these forms.

What the proffered candidates for the "new paradigm" in fact offer are policies. Indeed they are the same policies we have more or less been recycling throughout the Cold War, and all sit quite comfortably within the Wilsonian paradigm for the nation-state. All five programs (the New Nationalism, the New Internationalism, etc.) have been, at various times, the implementing techniques for the Cold War policy of containment. Each has risen to temporary ascendancy at the time of a particular Cold

War crisis—the collapse of the Congo (internationalism), the Cuban Missile Crisis (nationalism), German unification (realism), the war in South Viet Nam (evangelism), the Arab-Israeli War in 1967 (leadership). The reason they are so very unhelpful—ask former President Clinton whether "the New Evangelism" actually helped him decide whether to use force to disarm North Korea's nuclear weapons capability or ask his successor, President Bush, whether "the New Nationalism" has helped him persuade our allies to support missile defense—is precisely because they are representative of a debate whose reason for being has ceased. If we are truly to imagine what a new paradigm might look like, we have to look at the State and the strategic challenges it faces, and determine how it itself has changed. Each of the current elements in the policy portfolio was once a paradigm of statecraft. When the sort of state for which it was essential changed, the paradigm ceased to have the force of a consensus worldview. Paradigms decay into policies.

The security paradigms—the worldviews of statecraft—of any particular era follow the constitutional makeup and outlook of the states of that era. As each form of the state underwent a transition from one constitutional order to another, it added an accompanying paradigmatic outlook. Thus we find in the political papers during the transition from the reign of feudal princes to that of the princely state, a refined and sophisticated development of the balance of power. Machiavelli speaks the idiom of realism. His city-state has his love, "more than his soul," he once wrote, not his ethnic group, which he seems to pity and even disdain. There is little, if anything, of nationalism in his papers, though he calls upon a "redeemer" for Italy. And there is nothing of praise for internationalist institutions—the Church—nor, of course, for democratic enlargement. The transition to the kingly state retains the concept of the balance of power among its lexicon of policies, but its outlook is one that we would associate today with hegemony. One does not negotiate the compensating system of balances when one hopes to overpower all the competing states. The count-duke Olivares wrote Philip IV:

> You should not be content to be king of Portugal, of Aragon and of Valencia and Count of Barcelona, but you should direct all your work and thought . . . to reduce the realms to the same order and legal systems as Castile. If your majesty succeeds in this you will be the most powerful prince in the world.[36]

Leadership and dominance are the language of Olivares and Richelieu, just as they are the animating ambitions of the Habsburg emperors, who shattered the princely states of Italy, and the French kings who, in turn, destroyed the hegemonical dreams of imperial Catholicism and whose model inspired Olivares. It would have been idle of Charles V or Maximilian to think in nationalist terms; what nation—Spanish, Austrian, Italian, Burgundian—would it have been? Nor did the great alliance structures of the period presage a system of collective security, precisely because these structures were not institutional in nature, and spawned no congresses or conventions that outlived the conflicts that gave them birth. Even shared religious allegiances could not create an alliance structure that outlasted a particular conflict and placed the security of the whole as its highest responsibility. In the Thirty Years' War, Catholic France proved Catholic Spain's decisive enemy.

It was the transition from kingly states to territorial states that introduced the paradigm of nationalism, as German princes became tied to particular peoples, in the slow working out of the consequences of the principle of *cuius regio eius religio*. Of course there persisted the continuing policies of the balance of power and of ideological hegemonism: the Treaty of Utrecht specifically cites the balance of power as its goal, and it was the thwarted ambitions of France to achieve hegemony that led to that treaty. But the "anarchic society" is a term one associates with Hobbes, not with his predecessors. It is he who insists that no individual is strong enough to guarantee his own security unaided, and that governments are required to do so in order to settle disputes that are not amenable to direct compromise or agreement among the parties. Conflict among states is the natural environment.

When Rousseau argues that moral rule, in order to be moral, must be self-imposed and thus that the State must originate in self-government, he writes words that to us suggest popular sovereignty, but to his contemporaries would have suggested the transition to the state-nation. For he also writes that the good of each citizen must be distinguished from his temporary desires. The permanent aim of the citizen—the product of his rational, true, higher self—is distinguished from his passing impulses. Thus obedience to the state is an act of allegiance to the true self-will; by this means, in Rousseau's word, "I am forced to be free." Because this higher good is the same for all rational citizens, their permanent selves are identical and can thus have a single will that is manifested in the State. Although it may shock us to think so, the view that would organize the powers of Europe on precisely the same bases that individual governments are constituted leads directly to Hegel and the deified State. For if states, collectively, are the only means of assuring security and concert, then is not the State the only vehicle for a realization of the nation, its protection and order?

Because these transitions occur in the nature of the State itself, it is hardly surprising that the paradigms of statecraft to which they give birth should reflect ideas about the legitimate constitutional makeup of the State.

Finally we come to the transition from state-nation to nation-state, which gave us the paradigm within which we currently strive. This may be stated thus: The State is constituted to improve the material well-being of the nation. Thus the nation-state bears within its legitimacy the problem of nationalities. Who can claim a state? What is a national people? Suppose the nation is itself divided—what means are permissible to coerce and legitimate unification? This is the program of the evangelist of democracy, and it is rightly associated with Lincoln and Wilson, but also with Otto von Bismarck and Adolf Hitler, Vladimir Lenin and Mikhail Gorbachev. Each of the three political philosophies that contested the Long War had a different answer to this issue, but for each it was *the* issue, whether it proposed submerging nationalism in the larger good owed to the international proletariat, or worshipping the nation as the authentic legatee of the *volk,* or placing at its disposal the procedures of legal process and representation. The United States has lived within a Wilsonian paradigm because that is the American understanding of the basis for the nation-state, but *all* the Great Powers lived within variations of the nation-state paradigm, whether Hitler's formulation or Stalin's. If, as I argued above, this paradigm has not withered away or been lost with the end of the Long War, why should we expect, much less search for, a new paradigm?

It could be that the vacillation of American foreign policy has no deeper cause than the poverty of its leadership; it may be that the prevailing paradigm is sturdy enough to provide a basis for choosing among competing policies in the various contexts that current affairs bring forth, if only leaders of a higher caliber were doing the choosing. I doubt this: the predecessor to the Clinton administration had no better answers to Haiti, North Korea, Somalia, Yugoslavia, or Ukraine, all of which it made modestly worse by not having a policy and bequeathing acute problems that became chronic to its successor. If, as I believe, President George Bush and Secretary of State James Baker will stand high in America's history for their contributions to unifying Germany and expelling Iraq from Kuwait, it can be seen already that the former was a problem in the endgame of the Long War, and that the latter did not even serve as a precedent for great power action a few months after Baghdad was surrounded when, for only the *second* time in the history of the U.N., a member state invaded another member state and annexed its territory. Virtually all of the Clinton administration's important achievements in foreign security policy—in China, Haiti, North Korea, Russia, Israel, Ireland, the former state of Yugoslavia—were at a tentative stage when the new Bush administration took office. The best that can be said of the Clinton initiatives is that they promised success even without a shared vision of the American role; the worst, that having lived by the expedient and the impromptu, we will find all these problems so much more troublesome when the arrangements that temporarily quieted them unravel.

I am inclined to believe, however, that it is not simply the absence of a structuring idea, a shared way of understanding the challenges we face, that pervades all the current proposals and disquieting performances, but rather the clinging to a paradigm that has lost its usefulness. The Wilsonian pledge—to make the world safe for democracy—and the Wilsonian understanding—that national democracies offered the best chance to benefit the people of the world—have not failed us; they have succeeded beyond what Wilson would have dared attempt in parts of the globe untouched by the Fourteen Points. They have succeeded in providing political principles that could guide our strategic policies during the Long War in which those principles were contested and sorely tried. Now, with the Long War over, we are so sunk in the habits of strategic thinking that we ceaselessly bat about alternative security policies at a time when we are unable to make the simplest decision when to use force. We have lived in a state of war for so long that, paradoxically, we are unable to make appropriate security plans for peace. The noteworthy feature of the policies that bid to succeed containment is that they, like that policy, assume a certain frame of reference for strategic conflict. Because the roles of history and law have been so well defined during the Long War—indeed they set its terms, because the establishment of legitimacy for state regimes after the collapse of the nineteenth century system was what the Long War sought, by strategic means, to determine—we have become accustomed to think within the context of that war.

In the next chapter I will offer some speculation as to what such a successor paradigm might look like, by examining current contexts analogous to those that provided paradigms to states in the past: the contexts of strategic innovation and constitutional change. Then it may be possible to answer the question posed in the Introduction: How ought the United States and its allies decide when to use force in the international arena?

Preliminarily, however, the first thing one ought to observe about a new archetype is that it will not be something wholly new in form. For the United States, for example, there will be no new constitution. Americans will still be called "Americans," though what image that word conjures up in their minds may not be the same as came to my father and his contemporaries. Indeed, perhaps the most serious impediment to creative thinking in this area has been our automatic impulse to assume that the next paradigm will involve something like a new kind of state, that is, a reiteration of the European state on a different scale. Articles such as "After the Nation-State, What?" capture this reaction, for they invariably posit a "superstate" or no state at all.[37] Moreover, because so many of the challenges facing the nation-state are supranational in character—environmental threats, mass migration, capital speculation, terrorism, and cyber interference, to name just five—and because supranational solutions will be required, many assume that delegations of sovereignty must and will occur. This is a profound misreading of how such integration as has occurred in Europe came about. It is American involvement in Europe, through NATO and the Marshall Plan, that has, paradoxically, provided Western Europe with such capacity as it currently possesses to act as a unified political entity. It is difficult to imagine Britain ever delegating such a role to the bureaucratic machinery of Brussels or to the one state capable of dominating that machinery by virtue of its military and economic potential, Germany. The unification of the German state has, for the foreseeable future, put an end to the unification of Western Europe by creating a power that is actually capable of managing an integrated E.U.

What critics writing in the security area have not contemplated is a change in the constitutional structures of the European (and other) states that does not surrender sovereignty to yet another state, but returns it even more radically to the people themselves.

CHAPTER TWELVE

Strategy and the Market-State

If we are to create historical art, it is not enough to look back on history; we must be able to live history, to take part in public life.

—Jacob Burckhardt, "Bericht uber die Kunstausstellung
zu Berlin im Herbste 1842."

MARKET-STATES:
MERCANTILE, ENTREPRENEURIAL, MANAGERIAL

The fundamental choice for every market-state is whether to be (1) a mercantile state—i.e., one that endeavors to improve its *relative* position vis-à-vis all other states by competitive means, or (2) an entrepreneurial state, one that attempts to improve its *absolute* position while mitigating the competitive values of the market through cooperative means, or (3) a managerial market-state, one that tries to maximize its position *both absolutely and relatively* by regional, formal means (trading blocs, etc.). This choice will have both constitutional and strategic implications.

The mercantile state seeks market share above all else, in order to gain relative dominance in the international market; the entrepreneurial state seeks leadership through the production of collective goods that the world's states want; the managerial state seeks power through its hegemony within a regional economic zone. One is not more moral or necessarily more benign than another. There are pitfalls in each position: the entrepreneurial state may be tempted to abdicate its leadership and initiative out of mingled pique and national self-absorption, as the American nation-state did after World War I; the managerial state always risks the dilution of responsibility that goes with cooperative systems—by just such means did the society of nation-states watch as genocidal campaigns proceeded in Libya, in Rwanda, in Cambodia, in Bosnia, in the Sudan; the mercantile state risks retributive reactions of the kind practiced by nation-states that so greatly worsened the depression of the 1930s. The entrepreneurial state may become so intoxicated with its own absolute position that it fails to prepare itself—by not deferring consumption in order to invest in infrastructure—for relative challenges from states whose competitive drive is masked by the improved wealth positions of all major players; by just such developments have great states routinely been displaced by hungrier antagonists. The mercantile state is subject to an analogous fate, however; Paul Kennedy's *The Rise and Fall of the Great Powers* is largely devoted to documenting the fall of mercantile states whose balance sheets between economic reinvestment and military expenditure tipped them into relative, and eventually absolute, decline. The mercantile state may also forgo the benefits of cultural and political cooperation that eras of peace can bring. Like the famous, faceless player in the Prisoner's Dilemma,[1] the mercantile state will routinely make suboptimal competitive choices out of the fear and suspicion that is conditioned in a society that has accustomed itself to long periods of conflict and is inept at collaboration. The managerial state will inevitably resort to re-regulation as a means of dampening conflict within its regional institutional group, and this is likely to lead to suboptimal economic performance.

One market-state already appears to have opted for the role of mercantile state: Japan. With its literate and educated people, largely devoid of ethnic conflict and possessing the most restrictive immigration laws of any major state, Japan is well placed to conduct a campaign of relative increase in enrichment at the expense of its trading partners. With a history of high savings rates, Japan can avoid some of the intergenerational conflict that otherwise accompanies state borrowing. Japan can also avoid the public order problems that seem to dog every multiethnic society, including the problems associated with immigration that are tolerated by societies that depend on a fresh source of cheap labor that Japan does not yet need owing to its practice of rigorous self-denial in personal consumption.* A mercantile trading policy depends on control of one's currency, which is supported by strictly enforced limits on public spending, and the presence of value-added industries that dominate the terms of trade. Japan has to a large degree been able to pursue such a policy. The difficulty with this course, as Japan's experience shows, is the rigidity and self-dealing that infest a mercantile state, transforming its markets by secretive, deceptive, and even corrupt practices. An entire banking sector run on the model of the military-industrial complex, for example, is unlikely to be the most efficient agent of domestic growth.

---

*Japan will, however, need more than 600,000 working-age immigrants annually to maintain its working-age population at year 2000 levels, and some 3.2 million annually to maintain its old-age-dependence ratio at 2000 levels. National Intelligence Council, *Growing Global Migration and Its Implications for the United States* (March 2001) NIE 2001-02D.

Is the mercantile role an appropriate choice for the United States? There is some doubt, in any case, whether the United States will be able to maintain a workforce capable of successfully operating in the high-technology industries that give a state favorable terms of trade. With the most relaxed immigration laws of any major state, the United States both adds to its welfare expenses and fragments its cultural unity.* Because of its decentralized social and political structures, the United States is unable to curtail individual consumption, leaving it with a high trade deficit (which results from lowering the costs of goods to the consumer through imports), a decade of high budget deficits (which results from lowering the costs of government to the taxpayer through borrowing), and a high national debt[3] that will have to be repaid even if, as some predict, the budget deficits might cease (the result of the interaction of the first two phenomena as money from imported capital and tax rebates fueled a period of rapid growth). There is little prospect for a change in course: indeed, if the market-state is constituted to enrich the opportunities of individuals (and not simply to enrich the people as a whole) why should a multicultural, multiethnic state like the United States impose austerity measures that address these problems? Most individuals, including especially the children of the poor, are far better off under current U.S. policies than they would be under taxes and monetary rules that penalized borrowing and importing. Only the children of the future are penalized, and multicultural market-states appear to feel somewhat less responsibility toward the unborn. In this way the market-state plays to American weaknesses as well as to our strengths.

In one respect, however, those particular weaknesses tend to undermine the maneuverability so crucial to the market-state. That weakness has to do with the "followership" traits of the American people at this time, traits that are indispensable to a successful mercantile state. An August 1995 poll of Americans revealed that 59 percent said that there was not a single elected official that they admired. Of the 36 percent who said they could think of one, the president was named by 6 percent, his then opponent the majority leader was named by 5 percent, and the new Speaker of the House by 4 percent.[4] Such coolness toward authority does not evidence the sort of social adhesion to the State that wins multistate conflicts.

But to say that the United States is not well situated, considered in the abstract, to be a mercantile state in the era of market-states, is not to say it

*"[In 1996] 21% of immigrants [were] receiving welfare payments, compared to 14% of citizens. Not only [was] there a higher percentage of immigrants on the welfare rolls, but they [received] more welfare dollars per person than citizens."[2] Immigrants currently account for about 65 percent of the growth in population in most developed countries, up from 45 percent during the 1990–95 period. The numbers for the United States are especially dramatic. Foreign-born persons—about 30 million—now account for nearly 11 percent of the U.S. population; this represents a doubling of the foreign-born population in the last twenty years.

could not prevail in this role. It need only be *relatively* well situated, vis-à-vis its competitors, and here the size of the American market, its role as currency provider for the developed world, and its abundant natural resources still ensure that, should it choose, it could dominate Japan or the E.U. or any other such competitor in a mercantile competition (so long as it could prevent the formation of an anti-American cartel, such as might occur between the E.U. and Japan). Precisely because we were so unsuccessful at developing exports—which account for less than 25 percent[5] of GNP—the United States has far less to suffer, in relative terms, from a decline in world trade and retaliation against American mercantile practices. We could be a successful mercantile state, as a market-state, as we were, despite our many shortcomings, a successful mercantile state as a state-nation.

That does not, however, decide the matter. Should the United States choose this option? What are the costs and benefits (for that is how the market-state will measure things) of being an entrepreneurial state? The entrepreneurial state would pursue the enhancement of universal opportunity through a nonmercantile, free-trade policy. An entrepreneurial state would allow for relatively free immigration so long as the costs imposed by immigrants did not significantly affect the wealth and wealth creation of those taxpayers already present. It would seek environmental protection and nuclear nonproliferation through any effective means, collective or unilateral—by force if necessary in extreme cases—because the general enrichment of mankind is a consequence of success, even if a single hostile state loses as a result. It would employ multilateral alliance systems, of which NATO is an example,[6] to expand collective security but be prepared to join ad hoc "coalitions of the willing"[7] when collective security institutions are stymied. Paradoxically, such a state would be more prone to intervention—in cases of ethnic cleansing, humanitarian relief, support for the peoples of hijacked democracies, the destruction of terror networks—than the mercantile state, which husbands its violence to pursue more directly mercantile goals. If being an entrepreneurial state leads to more absolute wealth, does it actually encourage reinvestment of that wealth, or is this wealth frittered away in various adventures? Even more important, can the entrepreneurial state avoid cataclysmic war more successfully because it can remain armed without the constant friction of strategic competition inherent in a system of mercantile states? Is the aggressive mercantile state in fact *more* likely to be weak militarily because it is so desperate to throw its resources into economic competition, while at the same time it fails to develop the cooperative practices that can ameliorate crises and conflicts? And if it is, and the choice of the mercantile option by other competitive states actually becomes a source of comparative advantage to the United States, should we continue to produce collective security goods, like the creation of the coalition that fought the Gulf War?

And what about the option of the managerial market-state? The United States is poorly situated geographically to lead a regional trading bloc. Canada represents a small market, Latin America an uncertain one, separated by language and culture from the United States. It is true that there is a large and rapidly growing Hispanic minority in the United States, but this pool of talented persons is not necessarily making the United States more congruent with the places they left. The day is far off when North Americans will grow up as bilingual as, say, people in Belgium or Denmark, where more than one ethnic community coexist.

And why, in the age of the Internet, should physical proximity dictate the boundaries of regional trading blocs whose trade will be mainly in nonphysical items? Suppose the United States were part of a "virtual" region, composed of the United Kingdom, Singapore, India, the Philippines, and Canada. This might make the managerial model more palatable. The real question then becomes: Should the United States take the fateful step of creating a second E.U.—an "Economic Union" like the European Union—knowing that by so doing it hardens the lines of world competition and forfeits its unique, even transcendent role? If, as appears likely, the world will have an E.U. for the indefinite future, having two seems to be a step in the wrong direction that we should only take if we are compelled to do so.

One proto-market-state that appears to be heading toward the role of managerial market-state is the new state of Germany. Although more truly multicultural than before, owing to the amalgamation of capitalist and socialist societies and the most open immigration policy of any E.U. member, Germany possesses a common language and a highly educated workforce. Germany's crucial roles in the E.U. and in NATO—linking economic and security interests, Atlantic and continental—give her the collaborative position that might have been Britain's (and under Tony Blair may still be). Unlike the United States, Germany has managed to maintain a strong currency and strong exports. Germany's venture into high debt is a model of imaginative investment in infrastructure because the proceeds of the borrowing went into the acquisition of East Germany and not into mere consumption. A collaborative foreign policy depends on refusing to tolerate or to become a free rider (that is, a mercantile state within a free trading system) *and* the willingness to use force to maintain world order and the ability to do so without exciting fear in other states. Germany has the self-discipline and the wealth to do both. Although Germany has been made the diplomatic scapegoat by her allies over Yugoslavia for her early recognition of Slovenia and Croatia, and although she has hitherto refused to take up security responsibilities outside the NATO area (as in Kuwait), it is noteworthy that she has since modified this policy and offered air force assets to protect the "safe areas" of Bosnia at a time when other NATO states were dithering. More recently, Germany offered military assistance to the coalition effort in Afghanistan. It remains to be seen whether Germany's wretched twentieth century history will be redeemed by her commitment to human rights in the twenty-first century or will cripple her altogether, making France's enforcer in Germany's more submissive periods and Eastern Europe's neocolonialist when German self-confidence asserts itself. NATO enlargement is one way the United States has encouraged the healthy development of the new German state.

Absent an acute threat to American survival, the United States may simply lack the sense of purpose to be an effective entrepreneurial state. Perhaps more than at any time since the civil rights revolution, the United States needs political leadership to re-establish a national history that reflects our strengths of character, our inventiveness, our talents for cooperation and our benign ambition, and above all, our confidence in a common enterprise.[8] President Clinton moved the United States far toward the market-state. President George W. Bush has entered office at a crucial time, and appears to be equally committed to this new constitutional order.

The very nature of the entrepreneurial state, however, with its decentralization, its economic evaluation of all policy, its meritocratic competitiveness, and, above all, its taste for irony and amusement, will not make either leading or following easy. It is, however, a sense of purpose that is most required by the entrepreneurial state, because only such a sense—cultural, intellectual, artistic, as well as political—can endow a national history sufficient to move our distracted people to take up the distant and abstract burdens of such a state. We usually imagine leadership to be concerned with the future, but in fact it is the shaping of the past in the crucible of the present that empowers leadership because it gives an identity and a common perspective to those who would follow. We must feel that we are the heirs to the responsibilities the entrepreneurial state would impose on us, that they are our natural inheritance. Only history can do this, for it unites strategy and law by telling a story that provides us with a basis for legitimacy, that is, with some other self-image than the one in the narcissistic mirror of the present.

Finally, we must determine which of these three choices, managerial, entrepreneurial, or mercantile, better reflects our role in the world, as it is and as we wish it to be. Which method of pursuing the goals we have embraced will evoke from our people those resources of will and unity and common enterprise that enabled us to prevail in the Long War? A mercantile state can unite us against a common foe and give us a central purpose, but it turns our people into an instrument. Education is undertaken for the enrichment of the business enterprise, not the intellect. Defense is bela-bored because it cannot show a bottom line, while our streets and our cities become more precarious than many theatres of war, and security itself becomes privatized by house alarms and psychiatrists. A movement toward a mercantile market-state by the United States will effect a decline in interstate cooperation at the very time when successfully opposing ter-rorism, international crime cartels, and the spread of weapons of mass destruction requires international collaboration.

On the other hand, an entrepreneurial state is not without its risks. Constitutionally, such an American state would reverse two of the impor-tant developments of late twentieth century American jurisprudence: the weakening of the executive and the decline of state and local government. An entrepreneurial state must have the executive authority to use force expeditiously and to keep its security secrets, two things an American president is hard-pressed to do today. The transparency in governmental affairs that is demanded by the citizens and the media of the market-state make its entrepreneurial form especially difficult to achieve. Yet such capabilities for secrecy are crucial for the entrepreneurial state because it is committed to enhancing world stability and thus even relatively abstract challenges—nuclear proliferation, ethnic cleansing in remote regions, international terrorism, environmental depredation—must never-theless be dealt with decisively, which often means without previous pub-lic exposure of operations and plans.

At the same time, the experimentation and innovation so dear to the market-state may thrive more abundantly under the federalism of the entrepreneurial state than under an omnicompetent government character-istic of managerial market-states. An entrepreneurial state might encour-age the locality as a laboratory and even tolerate wide variations in, for example, welfare benefits and criminal sanctions that would be inimical to the managerial state. But simply increasing the authority of local gov-ernments, which will be whipsawed by corporations demanding tax and environmental concessions, on the one hand, and special-interest groups attempting to heighten regulation, on the other, is no answer. The smaller the jurisdiction, the greater its vulnerability. Perhaps only a managerial, continent-sized state like the United States can withstand the alternating threats to relocate (by the corporation) or frustrate (by the special-interest groups). In an entrepreneurial state, invariably there will be wide differ-ences in local laws. In a country as tormented by race as ours, such varia-tions are bound to produce invidious inequalities and discrimination. Can we afford to sacrifice the unity that a managerial state provides, even in peacetime? An entrepreneurial state, which we have so richly earned, could be an era of renewal for the United States in which enrichment means more than positive trade flows. But it could also lead to the disintegration of the State into regional, quasi-racial, and religious enclaves, devoid of any sense of overarching identity.

Of course no state in the real world will embody 100 percent of any of these caricatures. Some states seem historically tilted toward one model: France, for example, appears to want to lead the E.U. into becoming a managerial superstate. Others, Britain and the United States for example, incline toward the entrepreneurial model. Still others, notably Japan and China, seem to have thrown their futures in with a more mercantile approach. Whatever choice we make, we will have to find a way to compensate for the market-state's inherent weaknesses—its lack of community, its extreme meritocracy, its essential materialism and indifference to heroism, spirituality, and tradition. The entrepreneurial state attempts to ameliorate the effects of the market through ad hoc institutions of maximum flexibility; the mercantile state compensates for the market by calling on national elements of competitiveness and achievement. The managerial state falls back on regulation to achieve stability and the ever-elusive "level playing field" so beloved of lobbyists who seek advantage, not neutrality, for their clients. All three models must cope with citizenries that are increasingly alienated from the State itself, indeed from the very societies that share the scope of the modern state—too large to comport with postmodern identities, too small to be viable on their own. There is a direct, although often obscured, line between the ever-presence of the threat of weapons of mass destruction (WMD), the immediacy of television images everywhere on the globe, and the very immanence of economic vulnerability, on the one hand, and the constitutional evolution of the State from a state focused on the people as a whole to one focused on persons, on the other.

This need not be a cause for despair. American society has much less invested in its identity as an ethnic group,* if indeed it has had such an identity since the Civil War; it has less to lose by shedding this constitutional form.† It is well placed to make the transition from nation-state to market-state. In the passage to a legitimacy conveyed by assuring opportunity—with its need for transparency in government operations, its enhanced possibilities for enrichment, its meritocratic egalitarianism—the

---

*In the United States, immigration by the year 2000 was at its highest absolute level ever—about 1.1 million. The neglect of the Jordan Commission Report that called for modest decreases in immigration must in part be attributed to the market-state's eagerness to recruit new workers. The Jordan Report was the product of a presidential commission chaired by the late Barbara Jordan, one of the United States's most distinguished public figures. The report called for long-term adjustments in U.S. immigration policy—including a greater focus on skills-based immigration and a narrower definition of "family" for the purposes of family unification—in order to create a more sustainable policy. Jordan's untimely death probably removed the one figure with the moral status to address this problem. The final 1997 report of the Commission on Immigration Reform can be found at www.utexas.edu/lbj/uscir/reports.html.

†For a contrary view, see the excellent essay by James Kurth discussing Samuel P. Huntington, "Clash of Civilizations: The Real Clash," *The National Interest,* 37 (1994): 3.

United States could develop a more responsive government, acting in fewer areas with greater confidence.

STRATEGY AND THE ENTREPRENEURIAL MARKET-STATE: A SECURITY PARADIGM FOR THE UNITED STATES

Many conflicts may lead states to war, but when these disputes implicate the basic legitimacy of states, we are led into the strategic whirlwinds that finally change the state system and its constituent constitutional archetypal orders. There are present in the current context three possibilities for this sort of conflict: wars between nation-states and market-states in which an exemplar of one of these forms challenges the other's assumptions about sovereignty, because these assumptions are not shared by the two orders; wars between one market-state and another, because the various forms of the market also differ with respect to fundamental ideas of sovereignty;* and war that spreads to the society of states from a civil war in one state where the partisans of the nation-state confront the partisans of the new market-state.

As an example of the first contingency, consider the possibility that a nation-state's nuclear testing program so endangered the global atmosphere that another state, a market-state or proto-market-state, assumed it had the right forcibly to halt the testing program, even though the tests were conducted solely on national territory. What is appropriate for the market-state—with its porous territorial concepts and its responsibility to preserve the opportunities for personal development, including, of course, access to a safe environment—seems to clash with the absolute sovereignty of a nation-state taking steps it alone can determine are necessary, within its territory, to protect the nation. Similarly, a war between the United States and China over Taiwan would present classic nation-state claims to territorial integrity and antisecession versus internationalist market-state claims that no state can be absorbed without its consent, and that its "national" ethnic basis is not conclusive as to statehood.

As an example of wars that might arise among or within market-states, consider three different sorts of such states—roughly characterized earlier as one working within traditions of individual rights, laissez-faire trading, and personal freedom, *versus* one coming from a tradition of group responsibility, state-managed trading, and rigid social stability, *versus* one within a communitarian tradition oriented to interest groups and social justice. Suppose these traditions came into conflict within a single great

*See Chapter 26.

market-state, precipitating a revolutionary situation? Analogously this happened to some degree in all the great nation-states, but especially of course in Russia and Germany. Or suppose great powers, representing these three different approaches to the market-state, found themselves in conflict over an as-yet-undecided great power's constitutional valence, that is, the sort of market-state to emerge there? This also happened to the great nation-states; indeed I argued earlier that the Cold War, the last phase of the Long War, was fought by great powers representing different ideological approaches to the nation-state, over the constitutional destiny of the divided states of World War II—Korea, Viet Nam, and supremely, Germany. Political ideology determined the valence of the nation-state; with the market state, the valence is determined by differing views of retained* sovereignty—that sovereignty reserved to the People that is not delegated to government. An analogous sort of conflict might occur in the twenty-first century between different forms of market-states over the future of a divided state—China or Russia, for example—whose orientation toward these forms was undecided.

One object of a security paradigm to accompany the constitutional archetype that will take us into the twenty-first century is to avoid such a cataclysm. If we are to avoid another world-rending war, then my hopes lie with the entrepreneurial state. Only it offers the chance, through constant and costly vigilance, steadily to release the pressures attendant in the shifting distributions of global power among competitive states. Such a model increases the likelihood that the United States will share its technology and information resources, and it is by sharing rather than hoarding that we stave off competition. On the other hand, it must be noted that a mercantile market-state offers a better chance of enduring such an apocalypse should it come, because such states cultivate self-sufficiency. And the managerial state promises the greatest likelihood of recovering from such a conflict, because it strengthens the institutional basis necessary for reconstitution.

Most important, however, the entrepreneurial model offers the United States the best chance of developing, marketing, and "selling" the collective goods that will maintain American influence in the world. We have been powerful and wealthy in eras past and have had little influence on world events; this might well be the case again should we decide for a mercantile market-state. I believe an entrepreneurial state can provide the structure and the new point of view we will need in order to prevent superpower nuclear proliferation (to states like Germany and Japan) and protect

---

*In contrast to the nation-state whose principal alternative archetypes differed radically as to delegated sovereignty, that is, the powers and responsibilities assigned to the State (to control the market, social relations, etc.).

the global environment (from states like Russia and China) and to avoid a coming cataclysm. If this is wishful thinking, let me put my conclusion another way: should the entrepreneurial state be unable to avoid such a cataclysm, the United States would have to shift its purposes entirely and concentrate on how to survive and prevail in such a terrible conflict. Mercantilism might offer a better chance of buying off conflict, at the expense of allies, than would cooperative, collective defense systems. Unlike the members of the great alliances forged by nation-states to win the Long War, market-states can act with greater tactical flexibility and the most (not the least) successful of them will do so, changing partners, bluffing, using nonstate actors as agents of compromise and deception, much as a contemporary corporation sometimes behaves. But for that reason, mercantile market-states will be vulnerable to the same sort of tactics that Napoleon trained on the coalitions of territorial states, picking each one off from the group and either coopting or destroying it. For most of us, except the most pessimistic, a safer ground surely lies in trying to avoid such a conflict, rather than in contorting our natural traditions in anticipation of such a catastrophe should it come.

If the United States, in the new context in which it finds itself, is to maintain its leadership in order to thrive as an entrepreneurial state, it will endeavor to do two things: to preserve its freedom of action abroad by limiting, to the greatest degree possible, the coercive harm other states can do to it; and to act consistently with its traditional moral aspirations but prudently within its means to "make the world available," that is, to maximize the degree to which the persons of the world are able to choose their own destinies. If the security paradigm for the American nation-state was to make the world safe for democracy, then the paradigm of the American market-state must be to make a world that is hospitable to the individual conscience, that is, *available*. Individual goods, like economic opportunity and freedom of religion, do not exist in the world without nurturing practices. They are linked to "collective goods," that is, things of benefit to the world as a whole.

STRATEGY AND THE ENTREPRENEURIAL MARKET-STATE: PROBLEMS

What security policies flow from this paradigm, in the way that intervention in World War I and containment in the Cold War flowed from Wilsonianism? This question can be broken down into four: (1) what technology should the U.S. exploit; (2) what force structure should we deploy; (3) what criteria do we apply to potential cases for intervention; and (4) to what threats do we give priority?

(1)

The superior U.S. technology that won the Gulf War and defeated the Serbian army and the Taliban is the fruit of a revolution in military affairs that has been underway for twenty years, and which was presciently anticipated by Marshal Ogarkov and played a decisive role in the Soviet military's support for Gorbachev's reforms. The U.S. military is currently pursuing what is sometimes termed "a military-technical revolution,"[9] an extrapolation of the computational, communications, and weapons innovations that won the Long War and brought us the market-state. These extrapolations would utilize various advanced technologies to enable the U.S. armed forces to see the entire battlefield[10] and transmit information quickly to commanders in order to guide attacks more precisely as well as to detect and respond quickly to attacks by an enemy.

> Further progress in the microminiaturization of electronics promise ever "smarter," meaning more autonomous and precise, weapons. . . . Exploited in combination, these technological advances hold the promise of replacing many of the functions that heretofore required the presence of human beings.[11]

The driver of change behind radically new military capabilities is the rapid advance in computers operating in coordination with communications technology and the equally rapid declining cost of their synergy.[12] The military-technical revolution promises a transparent battlefield, where commanders view operations on television screens and direct individual units (or nonmanned weapons) from remote locations and where helicopters launch missiles at tanks twenty miles away based on information from preplanted acoustic devices and airborne radar and satellite imagery, all operating in coordination.[13] Intelligent weapons would take real-time information and guide themselves to their targets. Miniaturized aerial weapons would replace fighter planes and tanks.

As previously noted, Marshal Nikolai Ogarkov anticipated much of this discussion when, as chief of the Soviet general staff, he warned of an imminent technology-driven revolution that would give conventional weapons a level of lethality comparable to that of tactical nuclear weapons. "Armor on the march might find itself detected and attacked by conventional missiles showering self-guided anti-tank weapons, in an operation conducted from a distance of several hundred miles and with as little as 30 minutes between detection and assault."[14] This was profoundly disquieting to the Soviets, as their strategic plans depended upon massed tank assaults across the central front in Germany. The arrival of parity between the superpowers in some central nuclear systems (long-range ballistic missiles) and the collapse of escalation dominance by NATO at the subcentral level had for the first time in three decades made a Soviet assault across the central front of Europe a plausible scenario in some circumstances.[15] There was always a significant chance that, no matter what the American rhetoric, Washington (and Bonn) would decline to "go nuclear" in a conventional war when doing so invited Soviet retaliation in kind. In the early 1980s this doubt may have crested; by the 1990s the rapid yet inexorable developments of high technology had brought about a nonnuclear stalemate in the field, and thus many years of Russian planning and expense were rendered pointless. Moreover, some Soviet leaders were well aware of the large gap between American and Russian computer development and the increasing speed with which developments were occurring in the West. In part because these developments were stimulated by research in the private sector, the Soviet Union was poorly placed to compete.

Reviewing this history, we now ask: What technology ought we to adopt presently to ensure victory twenty or thirty years hence? Another way of asking this: which revolution in military affairs (RMA) ought we to pursue, because there are several different possibilities.

One such option is basically the extension of current capabilities—stealth, precision guidance, advanced sensors, and reliance upon satellite systems. Extending this approach would rely on the information aspects of the RMA to inform long-range fire with more advanced target acquisition and more controlled execution. This option pursues the integration of advanced sensors, brilliant weapons, robotic craft, and simulation. This would allow the United States to destroy virtually any battlefield targets that possess a perceptible signature. Proponents of this approach hold that the pursuit and enhancement of these technical advantages will allow the United States to win large-scale, high-intensity conventional conflicts that are fought with large armored and mechanized forces.

If, however, one believes that the least likely eventuality in twenty years is that the United States will be forced to confront heavily armored and mechanized regional powers—like North Korea, Iraq, Iran—then one is compelled to rethink the RMA question. Jeffrey Cooper captures this well:

New opponents may decide ... to pose ... challenges that an RMA narrowly focused on the DESERT STORM scenario and based on technologies demonstrated in that conflict may be less capable of addressing. [O]ur next opponent [might try to prevent our force deployment—as Saddam Hussein did not—and] possess nuclear or other WMD and long range delivery systems capable of threatening not only U.S. forces but allies and third countries who control essential transit and staging facilities. .... Alternatively, an enemy may also decide to pursue a different set of strategic objectives—damage, disruption to civil society, or interference with key global links and use different strategic concepts—long range attack, clandestine forces, urban warfare . . . terrorism, or subornation and blackmail of civilian populations, using modern communications to bypass government itself.[16]

Current U.S. strategic planning largely ignores these possibilities in exploiting the RMA, in part because U.S. intervention doctrine is in such disarray. One question with which this book began—what are the appropriate criteria for the use of force—like the question "Which RMA?" cannot be answered in the absence of general strategic plan. The plan we currently employ is the product of a classic nation-state confrontation, the Gulf War that occurred just as the market-state was beginning to stir.

(2)

Since 1991, the United States has undertaken three major defense policy reviews: the Bush Base Force Review (1991), the Clinton administration's Bottom-Up Review (1993), and the congressionally mandated Quadrennial Defense Review (1997). Despite their advertising, these reviews were little more than budget drills, rationalizing an ever smaller force structure to the same roles and missions. The Bottom-Up Review, for example, postulated that the United States should focus on combat readiness to face threats of major regional conflicts such as those that might occur in Korea or the Persian Gulf. The Quadrennial Defense Review retained the two-major-regional-conflicts scenario, though adding the need to prepare for smaller scale contingencies (while cutting the total force by 115,000 uniformed personnel).[17] There was little in either report addressing the future absence of access to forward bases (or their vulnerability), critical infrastructure and computer attacks, attacks to space-based systems, urban operations, deep inland operations, or new forms of attack against the U.S. homeland.*

During the same period U.S. strategic planning for intervention moved from the well-defined but limited strictures of the Weinberger Doctrine to the somewhat muddier—but therefore less limiting—policies of the Clinton administration. If the Weinberger Doctrine can be said to have taken concrete shape with the U.S. experience in the Gulf War, then it is easy to see why it is harmoniously consistent with the two-major-regional-war strategy that governs U.S. force structure. On the other hand, because U.S. forces have been frequently deployed since the Gulf War in numerous non-traditional, interventionist roles, it is harder to explain why the Clinton administration neither changed its general concepts for the force structure nor articulated a new doctrine for intervention. Harder to explain, but not

---

*The Rumsfeld Top-Down Review in 2001 promised to redress these omissions and offer a broad reassessment. It quickly ran into formidable opposition from the services and from Congress.

impossible. The administration did make, as we shall see, several early efforts to redefine a doctrine for intervention that was better suited to the realities of 1990s conflicts; in the end, it was determined to maximize flexibility by simply not committing the United States to any particular doctrine. For much the same sort of reasons, the Clinton administration clung to the two-regional-war scenario because it believed it could perform smaller operations (like Bosnia and Kosovo) out of a force structure configured for but not limited to major operations.

(3)

Although Weinberger proposed his criteria for U.S. intervention following the debacle in Lebanon in 1982–1983, the six requirements of which it is composed more obviously reflect conventional criticism of the U.S. intervention in Viet Nam. Weinberger's requirements for intervention were (1) vital American interests were at stake; (2) there was a clear intention to seek military victory; (3) the intervention was in pursuit of precisely defined political and military objectives; (4) there was a reasonable assurance of support by Congress and the American people; (5) there was a continual reassessment of the relationship between objectives and the size, composition, and disposition of U.S. forces; and (6) force was only undertaken as a last resort. By the time the Congress pushed President Ford to abandon Viet Nam, the intervention there had indeed failed each of these criteria, as the Nixon and Ford administrations flailed about in their search for a mission statement that could be said to have been fulfilled and as the members of both parties in Congress coalesced around an account of the initial U.S. intervention that would justify their withdrawal of support. According to this agreed-upon account, the United States failed to consider other, nonmilitary alternatives to intervention in Viet Nam or (its twin criticism) did not truly seek military victory; nor was there a discernible national interest at stake; nor did the public and the Congress overwhelmingly perceive and verify that interest. Frankly, I do not believe the facts will sustain this characterization of our experience in Viet Nam, however frequently or tenaciously it is asserted.

Therefore, whether the Weinberger criteria would have prevented American intervention in Viet Nam is a debatable question. What is indisputable is that the Gulf War gave the doctrine a firm foundation because to many it showed that there were in fact some interventions that did fit the doctrine, and that success would rapidly follow if the criteria were met. General Colin Powell, who had been a young infantry officer in Viet Nam, endorsed the Weinberger Doctrine while serving as chairman of the Joint Chiefs of Staff. Indeed Powell gave an Army spin to the criteria Weinberger had offered, emphasizing that the clear intention of winning should be manifested by the use of overwhelming force and that Weinberger's precisely defined political and military objectives should be clearly linked.

The Clinton administration's first secretary of defense, Les Aspin, had been critical of the Weinberger Doctrine as a congressman. He and others complained that the criteria left the president with only two options: total force or nothing. And he argued that a more flexible doctrine, with more options, was required.[18] The new administration, however, was initially attracted to "assertive multilateralism" as a way of finessing the issue: acting through the United Nations and other formal institutions, the United States would avoid confronting the problem of unilateral intervention that must be justified on the basis of unilaterally determined interests. The widespread perception that the U.N. mission to Somalia was a failure, however, resulted in Presidential Decision Directive 25 in May 1994, which simply grafted the key criteria of the Weinberger Doctrine on to the decision of whether to support multilateral action.*

Nevertheless, PDD-25 has had little discernible impact on U.S. policy and its criteria have never been included in the National Security Strategy, nor did they appear to have been applied regarding U.S. missions to Haiti, Bosnia, or Kosovo. Aspin's successor, William Perry, was more influential when, also in 1994, he provided various criteria that have since rationalized U.S. action (and have been incorporated in every subsequent edition of the National Security Strategy).[19] Perry distinguished between three sorts of American interests—vital, important, and humanitarian—and argued that different uses of limited, not necessarily overwhelming, force were appropriate to protect those interests. The selective use of force was to be commensurate with limited objectives. This description was further elaborated by national security advisor Anthony Lake in a speech at George Washington University in 1996 in which he described seven broad circumstances that "may call for the use of our military forces."†

These general descriptions were intended to modify the exclusivity—amounting almost to a doctrine of massive retaliation in the intervention sphere—of the Weinberger ideas, but they did not accomplish the objective of actually telling anyone what criteria had to be met before American troops would be sent abroad. General Powell himself recognized both the feint in this direction as well as its vagueness when he stated just before retiring:

*Resulting in eight criteria for the United States to consider in deciding whether to support an intervention, an additional six restrictions for U.S. participation should American troops be involved, and a final three Weinberger criteria if there were a likelihood of combat.

†(1) Defend against direct attacks on the U.S., citizens and allies; (2) counter aggression; (3) defend key economic interests; (4) preserve, promote, and defend democracy; (5) prevent the spread of weapons of mass destruction, terrorism, international crime, and drug trafficking; (6) maintain our reliability as an ally; (7) humanitarian purposes. Anthony Lake, "Defining Missions, Setting Deadlines: Meeting New Security Challenges in the Post–Cold War World." Speech at George Washington University, March 6, 1996.

We can modify our doctrine, we can modify our strategy, we can modify our structure, our equipment, our training, our leadership techniques, everything else we do these other missions, but we never want to do it in such a way that we lose sight of the focus of why have armed forces—to fight and win the nation's wars.[20]

To some, Powell's words appear to assume a certain contingency for which we must prepare—the two-major-regional-war scenario—for if our strategic objectives were otherwise, fighting to achieve those objectives would compel, not guardedly permit, some important modifications. Conversely, we cannot bring about any effective modifications unless we have a clear idea of what sort of wars we expect to undertake.

(4)

In other words, we cannot decide which RMA to pursue, what force structure to provide, or what criteria to set for intervention until we have a clear idea of the threats we will face. Trying to answer these questions separately leads either to unstated assumptions that are not examined and debated or to ad hockery, where the decisions in each arena are taken as a matter of temporary expediency and a comprehensive strategy is replaced by rules sufficiently flexible always to permit citation but never to enable guidance. What is required is some explicit confrontation of what might be called the "ABC" problem.

"ABC" refers to the classification of potential competitors of the United States by a scheme that would be familiar to any society hostess. States belong to either an "A" list of peers such as Germany, Japan, France, or Russia, a "B" list that includes mid-level developing states with modernized conventional forces and primitive weapons of mass destruction such as Iraq, Iran, India, Pakistan, or North Korea, or a "C" list composed of militarily modest states—such as Libya, Serbia, Cuba—and nonstate actors, such as various terrorist, criminal, or insurgent groups that often pose threats to American national interests.[21] The ABC problem may be stated as follows: should the United States focus on outdistancing potential peer competitors to such a degree that the position we now enjoy—of having no hostile peers—can be indefinitely extended; or should we instead focus on those states and conflicts that might threaten our vital interests in theatres of traditional importance to us such as Europe, Pacific Asia, and the Persian Gulf; or realign our thinking to focus less on conflicts like the Gulf War and more on conflicts like that in Yugoslavia, as well as economic, developmental, and nontraditional threats including terrorism and disease. (That is, which threats should drive U.S. policies—A, B, or C?)

The choices appear rather stark, so much so that thinking about U.S.

policy in this way has inevitably tended to coalesce behind the "B" option on the theory that the forces required to defeat "B" list adversaries are so substantial that they can always be made available for "C" type expeditions while, through constant modernization, presenting an imposing threat to any ambitious peers. The B choice seems less a total commitment than the others, which almost seem reckless if their bets about the future turn out to be wrong.

For example, an "A" threat strategy seeks an innovative, high-tech military using all the potential of the RMA's systems of space-, sea-, air-, and ground-based networks of sensors. These sensors would identify, track, target, and destroy enemy forces, putting the United States so far in advance of other states technologically that cooperation from our peers is almost their only rational strategy. The money for all this comes from a downsized force structure and a degree of specialization that may make the military almost irrelevant to low-intensity conflicts, however.

But what if this implicit guess about the future—that current threats like those posed by North Korea or Iraq are diminishing—is wrong? Are we really prepared to scrap the reliance on battle platforms (aircraft carriers, fighter jets) and combat manpower that has thus far been supremely successful? Can we afford to decommission whole armies, collapse traditional service distinctions, and give up forward bases on an assumption about future technologies? And what if allies and multilateral institutions will not take up the slack in handling humanitarian and peace-keeping operations? Then the "A" list strategy begins to look exceedingly narrow, even disabling. As the historian T. R. Fehrenbach remarks, "You may fly over a land forever; you may bomb it, atomize it, pulverize it and wipe it clean of life—but if you desire to defend it, protect it, and keep it for civilization, you must do this on the ground, the way the Roman legions did, by putting your young men into the mud."[22]

To an even greater degree, a strategy that focuses primarily on "C" type threats is highly limiting. At the moment, none of the world's international institutions is capable of taking responsibility for world order, yet the threats to world order—as in Yugoslavia and Rwanda—typically arise within states, in contexts where the United States is loath to act alone. Moreover, "C" type threats are, by definition, those that least engage our national interest. To build an entire defense posture around them seems foolhardy.

So we muddle on, having settled on a strategy built around outdated concepts of conflict between nation-states, maintaining highly expensive conventional forces that are nevertheless not really capable of handling two major regional contingencies simultaneously, putting our resources into incremental modernization that increases readiness but does not really exploit the potential of the RMA, repeatedly stripping forces configured for major conventional conflicts in order to use them—very expensively—in low-intensity conflicts for which they are not trained or equipped, refusing to look ahead to the day when a peer competitor leapfrogs our current technological advantage while we sink more and more funds into refurbishing plant and equipment that soon will be obsolete.

Although one could say with much justification that our current strategy owes more to General Ulysses S. Grant than to General Colin Powell, let's go back and look at the Viet Nam and Gulf War conflicts that were so fruitful for current doctrine. I propose that the "lesson" of Viet Nam was not that the war effort was insufficiently supported, used too modest means, etc., but that the United States had difficulty fighting an opponent who was hard to isolate from the civilian population and therefore difficult to target and track, whose shoestring logistics were hard to interdict, and whose political elites were far more disciplined than our own (perhaps owing to the greater centrality of the conflict for them than for us). Suppose that is the lesson of Viet Nam.

And imagine, too, that there is a lesson from the Gulf War, but not one for us so much as for our adversaries. The lesson is this: On behalf of nakedly aggressive territorial seizure, do not attack the United States with conventional armies, invitingly massed for an assault from a force you have permitted to project itself many thousands of miles to your frontier. Do not fight the United States, in other words, without weapons of mass destruction, without plausible political pretexts, without disguised forces, and without maintaining the initiative.

If these are appropriate lessons from the Gulf and from Southeast Asia, then the strategic doctrines we have derived from our experiences there are almost precisely wrong. Not only are we untrained for low-intensity conflicts, and heedless of the necessity to maintain our current military dominance over potential peer competitors, we are not even well configured to fight the "B" list adversaries who will adopt tactics we are unprepared for and shun the tactics against which we train. On the other hand, if we drastically reduce our forces in pursuit of either "A" list or "C" list objectives, doesn't that send an inviting message to those states like North Korea and Iraq, which continue to put enormous funds into the maintenance of large conventional forces, that perhaps this time a conventional confrontation with the United States can be won?

Book I has argued that periodic revolutions in military affairs bring about changes in the constitutional order and that this relationship is mutually affecting, that is, innovations in the constitutional order can also bring changes in strategy. Perhaps if we focus on the nature of the market-state, we may find some guidance as to which strategy to pursue.

The characteristics of a market-state may make it possible for the United States to devise a strategy of long-term dominance over peer competitors that will enable it to prevail in conventional confrontations as well as to field expeditionary forces. In 1992 a U.S. Defense Planning Guidance was leaked[23] that called for the United States to prevent any military superpower from emerging anywhere in Eurasia. This objective—an "A" list strategy—was to be achieved through U.S.-led alliances and coalitions. Interestingly, the Guidance proposed that this could be accomplished with a Gulf War military, a highly dubious proposition.[24] But the Guidance also suggested that the United States should aggressively pursue the enabling technologies of the RMA as a political deterrent to the emergence of a peer challenger in the next two decades.

> Within this time frame, the United States may well face a challenger of significant economic, industrial, and technological potential, one that can also exploit the advantages of the information age for military purposes. A number of states are currently working in this direction, pursuing their own [military] revolutions based on, among other things, the acquisition and integration into their military establishments of long-range strike systems; weapons of mass destruction; space-based surveillance, targeting, and communications; and precision-strike munitions.[25]

The unique strategic demands of the market-state—especially its requirement to project overwhelming force without risking lives, and to exit dangerous involvements quickly—put a premium on the development of high technology as an arbitrageur of, and even a substitute for, human risk. This was clearly evident in NATO's air campaign in Kosovo, which could not have been executed successfully even a decade ago.* The pursuit of these enabling technologies will face two hurdles: the reluctance to put money into research and development while downsizing the force structure; and the inertial tendency to invest in technical fixes for the tactics and organization of the present.†

Instead, the United States should use the RMA as a basis for changing its forces' roles and missions, leveraging from the promise of technology a rational basis for reorganizing the services. The RMA should not be treated as merely a happy event that is useful to our current strategic plan-

---

*And evident also in the campaign against the Taliban.

†Fred Iklé, "The Next Lenin: On the Cusp of Truly Revolutionary Warfare," *The National Interest* 47 (1997): 9, 11. "Read any of the hundreds of Pentagon reports and scholarly articles on the coming Revolution in Military Affairs and you will find scarcely a thought about nuclear or other mass destruction weapons, save for a shy aside. To be sure, these writings contain fascinating points . . . about instrumented battlefields, where the commander can view on a television screen every piece of equipment belonging to friend or foe and give orders to every tank and foot soldier . . . Encouraged by the victory in the Gulf War, American strategists are now eagerly looking forward to the RMA—that is to say, their chosen RMA."

ning but rather as both a driver and a reflection of the broad period of change in strategy and the international order that we are now entering. As Jeffrey Cooper has written:

> The "Information Revolution" and the change to postindustrial econo-
> mies . . . presage significant changes not only for the means of warfare,
> but also for the objectives of war. Increasing near-real-time global
> telecommunications, the rise of centrifugal forces within the [State], all
> raise questions as to the future objectives of interstate conflict, the
> appropriate strategies for pursuing national objectives under these con-
> ditions, and the operational means for conducting war.[26]

The nation-state's strategic objectives of total war against the opposing nation, destroying its mass armies and its industrial base, terrorizing its civilian population, and forcing capitulation should give way to more precise and limited objectives. With the decreasing importance of territory and raw materials, and the increasing role of knowledge and computation/communications infrastructure, attacks will require more sophisticated weapons and forces and will aim at critical nodes—including leadership cadres—rather than the seizure and holding of territory. Indigenous mercenary forces can be used where ground action is necessary. At the same time, new peer competitors will be able to leapfrog the former superpowers tethered to vast, fixed, capital investments that require long periods of amortization, and instead more quickly acquire the power to strike with means that are more nimble and versatile.

This menacing fact also holds the most promise for an American RMA because it points the way to a solution to the underlying strategic dilemma. A forward-looking RMA can create the ability to strike at "C" list targets (as in the precision-bombing campaigns against terrorists like Osama bin Laden and states like Serbia) as well as "B" list forces because the "B" list competitors do not actually threaten the American homeland and therefore can be ceded the temporary territorial victories their large forces can seize while these forces are punished into political submission.

Some of the funds for this change can come from force downsizing. Once the two-major-regional-conflicts scenario is abandoned, it ought to be possible to maintain substantial forces abroad—100,000 in Europe, 100,000 in Asia, 20,000 in the Gulf—far more cheaply, while reducing the overall number of troops. Nevertheless, an RMA initiative (for these purposes) would probably augment the Pentagon's research and development funding by about 20 percent.[27]

The emergence of the market-state and the technology it has spawned can provide new incentives in international security affairs. These new incentives will, however, depend upon developing more effective means of power projection (in the absence of secure foreign bases, for example) and framework intervention forces.

STRATEGY AND THE ENTREPRENEURIAL MARKET-STATE: POLICIES

Just as the "revolution" in the constitutional order of the State will have an impact on national security policy, the RMA will bring changes in the operations and structure of states, in the mutual, two-way process we have observed in Part II.

The universal trend in market-states away from conscription toward a professionalized army (even if it sometimes exists side-by-side with a conscripted reserve force) is another feature of what is, in this case, misleadingly called "privatization" by the market-state.* The "short-service conscripts . . . equipped with the products of a high-volume military [industrial] manufacturing"[28] that were a notable innovation of the state-nation and whose use was intensified by the nation-state in the Long War are passing from the scene to be replaced with more educated, more highly trained professionals.

The market-state does not so clearly demark the military from the commercial as did the nation-state. In market-states around the world, government-owned defense industries are being sold, and tasks that were once the exclusive prerogative of military institutions are being privatized. Private contractors handled much of the logistical support for the U.S. interventions in Haiti and Somalia. Privately owned satellites are leased out for military and intelligence functions, to say nothing of the reliance of government on CNN and other news-gathering organizations. Today, almost all of U.S. Department of Defense communications go across the public switched network. The other side of this blurring of lines between the commercial and the governmental is that governments now can purchase weapons—perhaps fissile material, military expertise, and strategic planning—from a wide range of private sources, some of which, in a further blurring, are linked to corruption within governments. Thus the possibility exists that market-states that had been relegated to the second rank strategically by events in the Long War will be able to catapult into competition with the United States if they can generate the wealth to do so. Those market-states whose economies are technologically sophisticated will be able to quickly convert that sophistication into military power.[29]

The new market-states are transforming themselves by replacing

---

*I say misleadingly because the government retains the power of determining the use of such forces, as opposed to a true privatization, in which shareholders replace the government in the directing role.

economies and cultures that were formed by the Industrial Revolution with new forms arising from the Information Revolution. The latter promotes the creation and use of knowledge, just as industrial machines enhanced the use of physical power and production. Market-states provide ideas and services—ideas about society and the development and use of technology, and services like education, medical care, and investment allocation—to each other and to the rest of the world. The United States has already found itself, in the Gulf War, in the position of providing intelligence and information to other states and selling its services as a war-making state. If it can maintain its legitimacy as a provider of collective goods to the community of market-states; maintain its lead in the development of new strategic technologies and learn to apply these new techniques to the problems of international security; and, most important, enhance its reputation as a legitimate and benign broker of those services, it will provide the model that other states, in the mimetic way we have studied thus far in this volume, will copy or, if they cannot copy, will react against with innovations of their own. Such a state sets the terms of competition.

Innovative leadership, like that which brought us the Nunn-Lugar legislation in 1992, can deploy the techniques of the market-state in a strategically significant way. As of mid-1998, Nunn-Lugar funds had provided $2.4 billion to destroy or convert Soviet weaponry. More than 4,800 nuclear weapons have been eliminated; more than forty large engineering projects have been undertaken to safeguard or dismantle Soviet weapons.[30] Funds were provided to find new jobs for former Soviet nuclear scientists and engineers. Housing for former Soviet military personnel was subsidized so that they could oversee this effort. But while Nunn-Lugar is a shining example of what can be done, it is pathetically insufficient. Russia still possesses enough plutonium for 25,000 to 50,000 weapons and enough highly enriched uranium for 40,000 to 80,000 weapons,[31] to say nothing of its immense biological weapons stocks. What is needed is a vastly enlarged program that pays Russian officials to quarantine weapons under U.S.-Russian supervisory auspices. Congressional efforts to impose careful auditing procedures, to prevent graft or unlawful diversions, should not distract us from the main objective. The market-state can—relatively cheaply—have far more impact, far more quickly than arms control agreements. On the other hand, if the United States doesn't buy these goods, some other state may.

The American military structure, however, is at present poorly organized to fully innovate in the direction of the change in constitutional order experienced by the State. As Eliot Cohen observed:

> The United States may drive the revolution in military affairs, but only
> if it has a clear conception of what it wants military power for—which

it does not now have. Indeed when the Clinton administration formulated its defense policy in 1993 it came up with the Bottom-Up Review, which provided for a force capable of fighting simultaneously two regional wars assumed to resemble the Gulf War of 1991. By structuring this analysis around enemy forces similar to those of Iraq in that year—armor-heavy, with a relatively large conventional but third-rate air force—it guaranteed a conservatism in military thought . . .[32]

The current unwillingness of the United States to consider real challenges to its primacy from advanced market-states that may employ these strategic innovations is of course troubling. Current American deployments overseas are ludicrously low and in any case will be increasingly vulnerable to missile attack. They could not possibly serve any military function in a large conflict other than as a nuclear tripwire whose activation would immediately drive states within its theatre into major-state proliferation—that is, the proliferation of nuclear weapons to states such as Germany or Japan. The real function of such forces ought to be as expeditionary units configured for small scale, rapid interventions.

Should the United States direct the technological promise of an RMA to "A" list objectives? First, these new technologies may make possible the preemption of nascent programs of nuclear or other weapons of mass destruction. Precisely because the U.S. nuclear arsenal is effectively out of bounds for use, only very precise integration of intelligence and precision destruction could enable American conventional forces to destroy a hostile power's potential industrial development of chemical, biological, or nuclear weapons. Second, although we mustn't minimize the single terrorist attack sponsored by a state that disguises its role—imagine if the World Trade Center bombing had occurred with a nuclear device*—the threat to a benign world order or to U.S. primacy within it is unlikely to come from the "rogue" nations of the Third World, but from stiff competitors who have the technology, technocracy, wealth, and world-dominating ambitions of the most (not the least) successful states. Several states are at work on applying the technologies of the information revolution to military affairs, just as earlier generations applied the machines of the Industrial Revolution to the making of war. Third, the RMA can lead to a complete recasting of the force structure,† reshaping old forms of organization,

---

*On the threat of "asymmetrical" warfare, see the discussion in Chapter 27.

†"Large and slow-moving aircraft carriers would give way to submarines and other stealthier ships that would deliver much more than a carrier's worth of precision-guided munitions. F-22 aircraft meant for dogfights would give way to long-range bombers and to unmanned aircraft not limited by a human being in the cockpit. Large and cumbersome Army divisions full of tanks and artillery would give way to smaller, lighter, more lethal and more agile formations. All this force would be stitched together by real-time, space-based information systems and applied in new ways." (John Hillen, "Selling a New Armed Forces," August 24, 2001, *New York Times*, A21.)

using machines in place of men and women who currently perform strictly mechanical tasks (a holdover from conscription when commanders thought labor was cheap), and stimulating investment in research and development. Fourth, technology and tactics appropriate to "A" list objectives can be adapted, as was seen in Kosovo and Afghanistan, to "C" list wars, so long as the capability for the projection of a land force with close air support capabilities is not entirely scrapped.

The fruits of the information revolution, however, will not be automatically transferred from the private sector to the very different applications required by the security needs of the market-state. To realize their full potential, these technologies must be combined with new tactics executed by new organizational structures. A military establishment content to fine-tune existing operating strategies, enhancing them only with superaccurate weapons of somewhat greater range and making these weapons smaller, cheaper, and more manageable, will scarcely reap the benefits of the developments that are underway.[33]

Not every application of the RMA is suitable to a market-state strategy for the United States. As Richard Betts has pointed out, the RMA runs the risk of reinforcing a high-tech, large-unit way of thinking in the armed services that was given such impressive validation in the Gulf War but which is less useful in unconventional conflicts saturated with civilians, and which invites asymmetrical attack. Most terrifyingly, because the United States is so well placed to exploit a high-tech RMA, conflict with a power such as Russia (over a dispute in Eastern Europe or one of the states of the former Soviet Union) or China (over Taiwan)—that is, with a great power whose vital interests are at stake in a territorial conflict—invites resort to nuclear weapons on the part of the American adversary, because almost no other option would be effective against a United States armed with advanced twenty-first-century technology. Considerations such as these prompted Eliot Cohen to observe, "the revolution in military affairs may bring a kind of tactical clarity to the battlefield, but at the price of strategic obscurity."[34]

In the present, post–Cold War period, the enhanced power of conventional weapons—that is, nonnuclear weapons—will be of paramount importance, and indeed it is striking how little discussion there is in the RMA debate about the role of nuclear weapons. I believe this aversion to nuclear warfare has to do with the nature of the market-state and its evolution in response to the strategic innovations, including the use and threat of use of nuclear weapons, that won the Long War. We can anticipate that

> the post cold war era . . . is likely to put a political (and military) premium on such non-nuclear means. Only further progress in integrating

advanced technologies will provide the strategic reach, striking power, and maneuverability necessary to address the theater level of war without resort to nuclear weapons . . .[35]

The market-state, with its emphasis on efficiency and economy, demands that the military act within tight budgets, accept fewer casualties (even among enemy civilians), and not involve itself in potentially recriminative hostilities. Nuclear weapons haunt such a state because they are too devastating, and too imprecise; kill too many civilians; and, above all, because of their genetic and environmental consequences, make war into the state-destructive, revanchism-creating sort of conflict from which there is no return and, ironically in light of their lethality, no end. A state struck with nuclear weapons will never get over it, whereas the market-state wants to conduct a transaction and then to move on. The market-state depends upon bargaining, which an actual nuclear attack renders almost impossible. There is an apocalyptic savagery about a nuclear attack that calls forth all the atavistic bitterness that the cosmopolitan market-state wishes to be free of. These factors drive the market-state toward new technologies that promise an escape from the reliance on nuclear weapons.

Moreover, the market itself, from which much innovation derives, enhances the drive for technological advancement. While there is ample scope for U.S. defense expenditures on research, the market-state is nevertheless dependent on the private sector to create these technologies; this dependence will accelerate the pace of the RMA[36] because the marketplace will quickly make obsolete communications technologies for which the U.S. government is the only purchaser.

The arrival of the market-state has imposed severe budget restraints on defense expenditures. The result is that the United States is tempted to simply define away the problems of a large conflict (and of small interventions) in favor of conflicts with states that greatly resemble Iraq. One wonders how many defense intellectuals and planners are thinking about major-state competition and conflict.[37] If the United States is to sustain its competitive advantage, to put this in market-state terms, it will have to determine how best to reinvent a force structure that has hitherto been supremely successful—a difficult assignment. Yet this must be done in order to take advantage most efficiently of the options that new technology and the market are making available to that force structure and to its competitors. A radical restructuring of the armed forces may well prove to be our best means of sustaining its current primacy because the United States, as a culture, is relatively adaptable to change (even if the military subculture is less so). Doubtless it is also true that U.S.-led alliances and coalitions can prevent another military superpower from emerging in Europe or Asia, but it is unlikely that the United States will be called to such leadership unless it is clear that we are fitted by a wide margin, militarily and in other ways, for the role. In an era in which our marginal economic advantage may be increasing but our share of world GDP is declining, this will require astute strategic planning. It is the very antithesis of this planning to assume that our main competitors in the world are Iraq, Iran, North Korea, and Libya.

Many states will strive for primacy in their regions or in the world at large in the coming period. Some will do so pursuing the strategy of nation-states, like France, whose policies sometimes appear driven by a mixture of hauteur and reactionary anti-Americanism. Some will pursue the strategies of market-states, which can vary greatly. I believe the successful market-state strategy for the United States will be one that studiedly avoids both mercantile and managerial market approaches, which have the potential for alienating trading partners and heightening xenophobia, in favor of pursuing a goal of providing "collective goods" to the world. Joseph Joffe has prescribed this course with great insight:

> The United States must produce three types of collective goods: First, act as regional protector by underwriting the security of those potential rivals—Japan, China, Western Europe—who would otherwise have to produce security on their own by converting their economic strength into military assets; [s]econd, act as a regional pacifier; [t]hird, universalize [security] architecture [by which the United States acts with various regional players in concert against regional threats].[38]

> As long as the U.S. provides precious collective goods the Europeans or Asians cannot or will not produce for themselves—building coalitions and acting universally through regional cooperation, implementing anti-missile, anti-proliferation, and pro-environmental regimes, organizing humanitarian intervention—there will remain an important demand for U.S. leadership.[39]

Joffe contrasts this course favorably with a balance-of-power approach that I would be inclined to describe, in market terms, as a mixture of the managerial and the mercantile. These approaches are not well-suited to producing collective goods, such as mutual security, political unity within an alliance in the face of external threats, or stability in environmental and economic relations beyond the state or regional group. There is an intense debate within the United States, however, about whether the United States should become a more mercantile market-state and avoid some of the costs of producing collective goods. And there has always been a strong lobby in the United States for the beguiling prospects of burden sharing available to managerial market-states.

What would such a policy of producing collective goods look like? What programs serve that policy?

Consider the following seven possible programs to enhance the security of the United States in a world of market-states. These seven are analogous to the various programs that served the policy of containment (intervention in the Third World, nuclear deterrence at the central level, etc.) that applied the American paradigm in the context of the Soviet threat. They are examples of how, through the means of exercising leadership—for which the experience of the Long War has capitalized the United States with a reputation for relatively benign intent—the United States could be the principal provider of the most significant collective goods to the world community and in so doing, resolve its current intellectual stalemate over strategy.

(1)

The United States can take the lead in reforming NATO to give it a mission relevant to the twenty-first century. The North Atlantic Council, the decision-making body in NATO, would provide the framework within which intervention forces will be mustered. Former Secretary of Defense William Perry and Assistant Secretary Ashton Carter make this proposal:

> NATO's principal strategic and military purpose in the post–cold war era is to provide a mechanism for the rapid formation of militarily potent "coalitions of the willing" able to project power beyond [Europe. These] "coalitions of the willing" . . . will include some—but not necessarily all—NATO members, and will generally include nonmembers drawn from the Partnership for Peace [former Warsaw Pact states].[40]

This is not to suggest that NATO fundamentally change its national command protocols, but it does imply that member states would be able to organize peacekeeping forces without a unanimous vote in the North Atlantic Council. Perhaps the most promising objective of such a NATO-plus coalition is a low-intensity, high-intelligence war against international terrorism.

The United States should also take the lead in organizing G-8 activities that go beyond the mere conferencing of its members (e.g., providing aid to stricken countries, mustering coalition-supported U.S. forces to resist aggression and to halt campaigns of ethnic cleansing). In organizing "coalitions of the willing," the United States should place great emphasis on linking up with Russian forces. Joint professional activities with the Russian military should be given the highest priority. Russian units should be trained in NATO tactics, which include the use of nonlethal means for coping with contending local parties,[41] how to secure a town with a minimum use of force, how to man a checkpoint as part of a multinational force, even how to deal with the press.[42]* Russia has the potential to be a uniquely valuable security partner and, moreover, the experience of military-to-military cooperation in joint peacemaking enterprises could pay dividends in a more cooperative political relationship.

(2)

The United States could manage the world community's efforts to keep weapons of mass destruction out of the hands of hostile powers—either by maintaining nonhostile relations with those powers (like China) that have nuclear weapons, or by preventing hostile states (like Iraq) from acquiring them, or by inducing friendly states (like Japan and Germany) to rely on the United States rather than set in motion regional competitions to acquire nuclear arms, or by bribing hostile states (like North Korea) that have nuclear weapons programs to give them up. This role implies that the United States should not constantly reassess its demands for internal liberalization in China, but at the same time should continue to protect Taiwan, which will otherwise go nuclear itself, setting off chain reactions in Australia and Indonesia; and that it should take especial care to maintain the security guarantees with Japan and South Korea—and not press its trade disputes with these states so aggressively as to arm anti-U.S. parties in those states; that it should use intensified covert means to sabotage the weapons programs of "rogue states" and insist on the continuing sanctions against Iraqi rearmament (even while setting up generous infrastructure funds from the controlled sale of Iraqi oil to pay off Russian and French creditors and revive the Iraqi middle class); that it should proceed with NATO expansion as a way of maintaining the importance of the security guarantee to Germany; and purchase outright intact nuclear weapons from Russia, a more effective market-state method than the legally negotiated, treaty-mandated handover of dangerous and negotiable fissile material favored by nation-states; and fully implement the North Korean reactor exchange (to take a few contemporary examples).

(3)

The United States could organize a North Asia Security Council, anchored in Tokyo and including Japan, Russia, China, and South Korea. This Council would provide a forum for regional discussions, joint military exercises, and information sharing. It would emphasize that the United States is a Pacific power and offer a framework for our nonproliferation efforts. No two states have as great an interest in preventing the proliferation of weapons of mass destruction as do Russia and China. If the Chechens, for

---

*"The experience of working with Russia in Bosnia needs to be extended, deepened, and made part of the permanent security structure . . ."[43]

example, who have bloodied the Russian army with little more than small arms and antitank weapons, were to acquire such weapons, then surely the Tajiks and Azeris would not be far behind, with incalculable risks for the survival of the Russian state as it is now constituted. If Taiwan were to acquire nuclear weapons and thus force a stalemate, China would be hard pressed to maintain the threat that conventional force could mount a successful amphibious invasion. Yet without the incentive of this tacit threat, unification may be decades away. In these efforts the United States can find no more potentially helpful partner than China. China is a signatory of the Nuclear Nonproliferation Treaty (in 1992). It has signed the Comprehensive Test Ban Treaty (in 1996) and has affirmed (in 1992) and reaffirmed (in 1994) its commitment to abide by the Missile Technology Control Regime (MTCR). Yet there is ample evidence that China sold Pakistan ring magnets for use in a gas centrifuge to enrich uranium (for a nuclear weapon), and, despite the MTCR, transferred M-11 short-range missiles to Pakistan. There is further evidence that China has passed materials and equipment for uranium enrichment to Iran, as well as cruise missiles, ballistic missile technology, and chemical weapons precursors.[44] Why should we try to enlist such a partner?

China has more recently undertaken to halt this trade. More than any other state in the world, it has grounds for alarm at the proliferation of weapons of mass destruction. Only by enlisting U.S. cooperation in a nonproliferation regime can China ensure itself against this possibility. China is increasingly dependent on Middle East oil, and is at least partly responsible for provoking India's weaponizing its nuclear technology. Yet China ought to move to the forefront of enforcing a nonproliferation regime.

(4)

The United States might resist the regionalization of trade because it is a global power with global interests. No other power can speak for world trade cooperation with the legitimacy of the United States so long as the latter pursues free trade convincingly and exercises leadership in pursuit of international financial stability. This suggests that the United States should attempt to gain access to the markets of more than one regional trading pact; that it should resist efforts to have the euro replace or augment the dollar as the world's common currency; that it should tolerate wider swings in its currency than other states wish to permit; and, finally, that it should prefer virtual regional trading groups, which are united by cultural and business attitudes rather than by mere physical proximity. There is no reason why Sweden would not be a more appropriate partner in such a virtual union than, say, Guatemala. Proximity and contiguity should not be the decisive determinants of the perimeters of an economic union when the perimeters of economic life are unbounded on the World Wide Web. A nonexclusive free-trade zone between the United States and the United Kingdom makes far better sense than an anti-competitive hemispheric fortress for either state.

(5)

The United States could provide warranties for the security of important regional states vis-à-vis each other by offering an open bargain to aid any state that is attacked—bearing in mind, of course, that American assistance can take the many forms discussed above that are appropriate to a market-state—and to mediate any significant dispute. Warranties could even be brokered or factored by various state guarantors. This implies that the ongoing and costly role of American diplomacy in brokering foreign disputes is a good investment of time and energy. (For such a course to succeed, Congress would have to resist adopting measures like the Pressler Amendment, which embargoed Pakistani arms purchases, and the Glenn Amendment, which requires economic sanctions against a nuclear India, with no provision for a national security waiver. Taken together such laws can paralyze U.S. action on the subcontinent, to take one example.)

(6)

The United States could develop an action program of lease-hire security insurance, licensing some forms of defense technology and emphasizing the U.S. role in providing information, missile defense, and even intervention for hire.

> Consider, therefore, a vertical coalition in which the United States supplies intelligence and systems assistance to a beleaguered [state], which in turn, uses such help to organize its own sources of information, increase its battlespace illumination and support its own command-and-control, operational planning and rapid reaction . . . Vertical coalitions have several uses. In October 1994, Iraq massed its tanks looking southward to Kuwait, and the United States responded by shipping over 35,000 troops at a cost of nearly a billion dollars. What if Kuwait could have defended itself in the first crucial week with medium-range point-guided PGMs [precision-guided munitions] guided by the System (with in-place sensors) so that assault forces could be converted into real-time aimpoints? By revealing, for instance, precisely where opposing artillery is firing from, illumination could help one side (e.g., Bosnian Muslims) without risking American troops or impelling powerful countries to intervene on behalf of others (e.g., Bosnian Serbs). Border illumination could dissuade a U.S. ally from feeling the need to undertake problematic cross-border actions (e.g., Turkey's 1995 pursuit of Kurdish rebels into Iraq). Unlike a formal alliance, illumination could be offered

in finely graded doses depending on the degree of trust between the United States and others. Such applications could increase countries' confidence in their ability to see across their borders even without formal alliance commitments.[45]

Again, it must be emphasized that by sharing technology and information, the United States enhances its power; a failure to develop modalities of sharing will induce competitors to develop and provide similar services and products.[46]

(7)

Apart from these specific proposals, I will offer one suggestion that goes to the process of U.S. decision making. It is important that the United States, at the highest levels, create a strategic planning group analogous to the "vision teams" used by private industry. At this moment more than at any other time since Colonel E. M. House set up The Inquiry in 1918,* the United States needs to find the resources and commitment to engage in a strategic planning process.

As Keyes van der Heijden has recently observed,

[t]he need for efficient strategic thinking is most obvious in times of accelerated change when the reaction time of the organization becomes crucial to survival and growth. . . . The problem is that such periods of change alternate with periods of relative stability, when organizations often get stuck into established ways of doing things, making them ill-prepared for when the change comes.[47]

This is precisely the situation I have described with respect to the proposed "paradigms" for U.S. policy currently in play. But not just any process will do. One important element of such a process in an age of uncertainty is scenario planning.

The traditional approach [to planning] tries to eliminate uncertainty from the strategic equation, by the assumption of the existence of "experts" who have privileged knowledge about the "most likely future," and who can assess the probabilities of specific outcomes. [By contrast] [s]cenario planning assumes that there is irreducible uncertainty and ambiguity in any situation faced by the strategist, and that successful strategy can only be developed in full view of this. . . . The most fundamental aspect of introducing uncertainty in the strategic equation is that

*For a description of the work of The Inquiry, see Chapter 14.

it turns planning for the future from a once-off episodic activity into an ongoing learning proposition.[48]

Appropriate scenario planning can create an institutionalized learning system. I will have more to say about the scenario process in Chapter 26. For the time being, let me simply urge that a true strategic planning group be created linking the National Security Council, the National Intelligence Council, and the Policy Planning Staff and that a true "vision team" be simultaneously convened, in secret, encompassing a broad range of opinions to aid that planning group. Such a team, in contrast to House's Inquiry—which was composed mainly of lawyers and academics—should include business executives, not necessarily only American, as well as scientists, technologists, and editors from the news media. In other words, this team ought to be different in composition from the think tanks that are a prominent source of ideas in Washington.

It would be absurd to make long-term forecasts about future security environments that would aim to offer guidance for force planning, force sizing, and force structure. No one scenario about the future is certain enough to justify this. Rather, what I am urging is more thought about how our present decisions are likely to play out in bringing about different worlds. As Paul Bracken has written:

> It is not common to think about national security in such terms. Usually, policy goals are formulated and then force structure implications derived from them. History is not so clear in its causal relationships, however, and radically new improvements in military capacities can have their own impact on international relations.[49]

Let me be clear about the purpose of the seven proposals thus far canvassed. I am not proposing that the main force of the United States be converted from a large conventional army into a boutique force, capable only of high-tech special operations and humanitarian interventions. I strongly believe the greatest threats to American security in the early twenty-first century will come from powerful, technologically sophisticated states—not from "rogues," whether they be small states or large groups of bandits. And I believe that large defense budgets will be required to deter or, if necessary, meet these threats without resort to nuclear weapons. I have stressed the innovations just discussed rather as a way of coping with the fact that the United States is often ill equipped to act within the confines of the market-state, with its aversion to casualties and its sensitivity to events in remote theaters that do not impinge upon U.S. vital interests. The current U.S. force posture tends to lock it into a two-major-war contingency—the least likely of eventualities—and thus constrains the United States from using force appropriately in the battles it does fight.[50] And the U.S. emphasis on large platforms tends to lock in American budget commitments for decades at a time, precisely when new technological developments demand nimble, flexible procurement policies.

There are other proposals that would doubtless also serve this model—a robust debate within the parameters of the market-state will surely ensue. These seven are offered as exemplary only. What is important is that the United States adapt its leadership to the new society of market-states, and that it gradually abandon those attitudes and proposals (for a "new" Bretton Woods, or for a rapid reaction force for the U.N., or for enlarging the responsibilities of the World Trade Organization [WTO], to take three popular proposals) that arise from a mentality geared to the society of nation-states that is already decaying.

STRATEGY AND THE ENTREPRENEURIAL MARKET-STATE: PROGRAMS

Experienced diplomats and military leaders are creatures of the dominant strategic rules of the nation-state, but are soon to be called upon to make decisions in a world—and before the publics—of market-states. The demands upon these decision makers by their publics, who are sensitive to the sufferings of others and to those of their own armed forces in a way that is quite distinct from earlier generations, are met with a mixture of cynical deflection or perplexed frustration. The professionals knew, for example, that it would have taken at least 100,000 troops to pacify Bosnia, and they knew the public would never stand for such a massive deployment, but they were under great pressure from that public, and from politicians responsive to that public, to do something that would stop the ethnic cleansing in that region. So decisions oscillated between the public declaration of "safe areas" and private decisions to abandon their safety, between—to take another example—the highly publicized hunt for a Somali warlord and the humiliating scampering off when this hunt ended with the deaths of seventeen American soldiers. Two scholars writing in *International Security* summed up the Clinton administration's performance at this time by saying this:

> The accommodations that the Clinton administration strategy [of the first term] has made with the obstacles it has encountered have been incremental, rhetorical, disjointed, and incomplete. In theory, the inco-

herence of the current strategy could produce a series of new difficulties for the administration, and conceivably a disaster.[51]

And another writer asked, "What might explain this failure to define a grand strategy? . . . Is the failure due to Clinton, the person? Or to America, a society that is exceptional in its assets, aspirations and afflictions? Or to the post-bipolar setting?"[52]

This author concludes that it is all of the above; I think it is none. Rather, the Clinton administration, like its predecessor, was attempting to apply the policy tools of a mentality that was inappropriate to the context within which it had to operate. The Somalia misadventure provides a good example of this.

The Somalia intervention came to a sudden end after the bloody failure of a daring helicopter raid in true commando style—a normal occupational hazard of high-risk, high-payoff commando operations. But given the context at hand—a highly discretionary intervention in a country of the most marginal significance for American interests—any high-risk methods at all were completely inappropriate in principle.[53]

Many factors, including the immediacy and power of televised images, drastically lowered birth rates, the sense of heightened opportunities forgone by the wounded and killed, account for the public's increased sensitivity to humanitarian issues—including, of course, its sensitivity to casualties in the armed forces. But whatever its cause, the effect has been a drastic shift in the appropriateness of military means, accompanied, paradoxically, by increasing demands for its use as an instrument of humane intervention.

It is true that we can avoid flip-flops like the Somali embarrassment by setting criteria so confining that force is only used in situations that threaten our vital interests, have overwhelming public support, can be exited quickly, and so on, as former Defense Secretary Caspar Weinberger has proposed. But this is simply to apply the strategic mentality of the nation-state so thoroughly that problems with which it cannot deal are no longer to be treated as susceptible to the use of force at all. The Weinberger Doctrine is not so much a remedy as it is a symptom of the military's inability to deal with the shifted context.[54] There are casualties, however, attendant to this approach, too, among them the defense budget (for why should the public pay for a force structure that is so unresponsive to the public's perceived needs?) and the moral leadership of the world community (for why should the world defer to the richest and most powerful state in history when that state demands to sit passively by and expects other states to run the risks and bear the costs of humanitarian intervention?).

There are other alternatives. In an essay in *Foreign Affairs,* Edward Luttwak argued that the concept of war that governed American action had much to learn from the cabinet warfare of the territorial state. Eighteenth century wars, Luttwak noted, were characterized by

> [d]emonstrative maneuvers meant to induce enemy withdrawals without firing a shot [and were] readily called off if serious fighting ensued. Superior forces avoided battle if there was risk of heavy casualties even in victory. . . . [E]laborately prepared offensives had unambitious objectives, promising campaigns were interrupted by early retreats into winter quarters merely to avoid further losses, and offensive performance was routinely sacrificed to the overriding priority of avoiding casualties . . .[55]

Luttwak's essay is perhaps most helpful not as a recommendation that the strategic style of territorial states provides a model for use today, but rather as a reminder that that style was superseded when state-nations achieved ascendancy. Indeed Luttwak lamented that the current American military establishment is so thoroughly imbued with the nineteenth century Clausewitzian criticism of eighteenth century thought. It is the grip of such criticism—and its affirmative ideas about the overwhelming use of force, the necessity of great battles and decisive conflicts, etc.—that has made American power so helpless in the face of post–Long War crises both before and since the Gulf War.

Luttwak realizes that adapting to this new historical context will require not only a change in outlook as regards the means to be applied to military situations but also a greater modesty as to the objectives sought by these means. This insight is indispensable if we are not to dismiss some of the most useful of market-state military and nonmilitary strategic alternatives as merely ineffectual. By such alternatives, I have in mind economic sanctions, covert action, bribes and financial incentives, sustained campaigns of precision air strikes, novel military and political uses of intelligence products, information warfare, missile defense, simulation, the use of proxy forces, and the entire range of new technologies and tactics discussed earlier as the revolution in military affairs.

If economy in lives risked and efficiency in resources used to accomplish the goals of the public are the two guideposts of the market-state, then let us see how we might judge some of these seven programs.

(1)

Economic sanctions include a wide range of economic and financial measures—asset freezes, trade embargoes, expropriations, the withholding of credit, boycotts, and the like—that have become more difficult to maintain as the market has become globalized. Economic sanctions were not unknown to the state-nation—Napoleon's "continental system" is one famous example—but the sharp distinction between the operations of the market and the operations of government often made such sanctions hard to enforce. It was not thought unseemly that throughout the Napoleonic Wars, British bankers continued to finance French enterprises. The nation-state has not been so detached: with the coming of total war there arose also an intensified economic warfare against the civilian society.

The collective organizations of the society of nation-states have had a mixed record with such sanctions, however. The League of Nations was first called upon to apply economic sanctions to Japan following her invasion of Manchuria and the creation of the puppet state of Manchukuo. The League condemned Japan's actions as unlawful, but drew back from invoking economic sanctions for fear of provoking a Japanese attack on colonies in the Far East belonging to the League's European members. When Italy attacked Ethiopia, the League called for an embargo on arms, bans on loans and credits, the boycott of Italian imports, and an embargo on the export of key raw materials to Italy. All this failed to stop the Italian conquest, and when Ethiopia sued for peace, the sanctions were withdrawn. When Germany invaded Poland three years later, the Western powers simply declared war; the League's elaborate peacekeeping machinery, with its emphasis on economic sanctions, was completely bypassed.

Nor has the United Nations's record, until recently, been much better. As with the League, collective economic sanctions were given a key role in international peacekeeping, but because action by the Security Council requires a unanimous vote of the permanent members, such sanctions could never be invoked against a great power or against a protégé of such a power. Even when a great power allows the Council to condemn the actions of a friendly state, it usually vetoes economic sanctions, as the United States has done for Israel and the Soviet Union did for Iran. From 1945 to 1990, economic sanctions were invoked only once, against the white government of Rhodesia, which was in revolt against a permanent member of the Security Council, the United Kingdom.

The coming together of the great powers at the time of the Gulf War, however, allowed the U.N. to impose economic sanctions on Iraq. Oil exports have been barred, with limited exceptions to pay for Iraqi imports of food and medicines. Since 1990 these sanctions have been the principal means by which the coalition states that fought the Gulf War have controlled what would otherwise have been the rapid recovery of Iraq's military forces. It is estimated that during the first seven years following the Gulf War, sanctions have kept $110 billion out of the Iraqi treasury. Similarly, though less dramatically, the denial of Serbian imports and exports eroded the political base of the Serbian leader, Milosevic, and doubtless played an important role in his extradition to the War Crimes Tribunal in The Hague.

As in other matters at the time, this represented an Americanization of the U.N., though one of uncertain duration. For the Americans have relied on the economic weapon to a greater degree than any other state: since World War II, we have invoked economic sanctions against China, Cuba, Viet Nam, Iran, the Soviet Union, Libya, India, Pakistan, and Poland, among others. Indeed there has hardly been a time in which the United States was not applying economic sanctions against at least one foreign state. Partly this is owed to the important economic position of the United States in the world, and our crucial assets, a vast and lucrative market coupled with a self-sufficient economy. States that are vulnerable to retorsion are seldom enthusiasts for sanctions. Partly also the use of this instrument is a function of the gradual emergence in the United States of a market-state, and that sort of state's emphasis on market tools and its aversion to risking lives.

Despite this reliance, however, there is a consensus that economic sanctions do not "work," and they are seldom studied by military strategists. This conclusion is the result of a profound misunderstanding about the role of such sanctions. Economic sanctions are used precisely because they are unlikely to result in the kind of change of constitutional regime sought by nation-states in war. If such sanctions really could drive another state to total collapse, they would just as surely lead to armed conflict, and it is the avoidance of armed conflict that gave sanctions their unique role in the post–World War II environment. If the grain embargo imposed on the Soviet Union by the United States at the time of the invasion of Afghanistan really had starved Russia into famine, it would not have driven that country into political submission but rather into a war for food.[56] Sanctions are useful when conventional war is against one's own interests and therefore the relative costs of going to war, which are usually very high, must be kept high. Sanctions so powerful that they gravely weaken the opposing state quickly—as a decisive battle or military campaign can—would just as greatly lower the relative costs of war. It may be that this is what happened to the Japanese as a result of the U.S. oil embargo in 1941; the surprise attack on Pearl Harbor moved from being a clever theoretical possibility to a daring course of action acceptable to Japanese political authorities when the relative costs of war plummeted owing to the threatened imposition of a stringent oil embargo.[57]

Sanctions work by raising the cost of pursuing a particular political path—for both parties. (Thus they are especially useful to a rich power, like the United States, who can afford to play for "table stakes.") Sanctions can help to discredit a policy—again in both states, the applying and the applied-to—and are therefore most useful where there is an active oppo-

sition party in the state to which the sanctions are applied, and no powerful interest group that is forced to bear the cost in the applying state.
Even against a dictatorial government, sanctions can have a useful effect
because such regimes are no less rational for being authoritarian. The crucial points to bear in mind are that sanctions' true utility lies in the modesty
of their impact, a useful thing for the market-state that tries to shun warfare
where possible, and that only an internationally coordinated effort, as
exemplified by the sanctions against Iraq and Serbia, can be effective in an
era of globalized markets and transient capital.

(2)

The utility of the strategic alternative of *covert action* is also not widely
appreciated. Even sophisticated commentators persist in thinking that
covert action involves any clandestine action by a state's secret services. In
fact, "covert action" is a term of art in intelligence operations, referring to
those operations by a state that are intended to influence the politics and
policies of a target state without the hand of the acting state being disclosed. Thus covert action includes the training provided by the United
States to the Philippine anti-insurgency forces, requested by the Aquino
government but denied by both the United States and the Philippines at the
time; and the provision of radio transmitters to the mujahedin attempting
to destabilize the Iranian regime; and the cash contributions to the Christian Democratic Party in Italy after World War II, and the subsidies to
Encounter magazine at the same time. Covert action must therefore be distinguished from intelligence collection, counterespionage, and intelligence analysis and forecasting.

Of late, covert action has been generally held in low esteem in the
United States. Writing in *Foreign Affairs,* former American official Roger
Hilsman concluded that "covert political action is not only something the
United States can do without in the post–cold war world, it was something
the United States could well have done without during the cold war as
well."[58] Such an observation, whatever its historical merits, is a revealing
example of how disputes and positions taken during the Cold War tend to
hang over into the new market-state context. In this new context, however,
covert action is a far more viable and potentially useful tool. The most discrediting example of covert action—the Iran-Contra fiasco—was a fum-
bling attempt to privatize covert action, an objective consistent with the
methods of the emerging market-state. A brief study of that affair provides
an excellent object lesson in the home truth that all government acts must
be consistent, however, with the constitutional law of the State, regardless
of its constitutional order.

In the aftermath of the 1976 revelations of the Church Committee,
which had convened to investigate whether the CIA had been involved in

the Watergate Affair, various statutory and regulatory rules were promulgated that sought to limit U.S. covert action. The Reagan administration came into office in 1981 believing that the Carter and Ford administrations had been far too restrictive of CIA operations, and it wished to use covert action programs in Central America to challenge the new Sandinista regime in Nicaragua. A skeptical Congress cut back financing for such operations, and in 1983 adopted a complete ban on CIA operations against the Nicaraguan government. Moreover, throughout this period it had become increasingly difficult to plan and execute covert operations without their exposure to the press—sometimes, it was said, by members of the oversight committees in Congress that the post-Watergate statutes had put in place.

Thus in the early 1980s CIA operations in Central America were imperiled by a statutory cutoff in funding, and the Reagan Administration believed that it risked exposure of these operations and others by compliance with the statutory requirements to fully inform Congressional committees, some of whose members were hostile to the very idea of covert action. This picture was made more troubling by a rise in anti-American terrorism and the apparent inability of U.S. agents to penetrate and neutralize the groups responsible. Throughout 1984, the United States was the target of a wave of bombings, assassinations, hijackings, and kidnappings in Lebanon. The stateless chaos that reigned in that country provided the perfect milieu for such crimes because the traditional methods of counterterrorism depend upon careful and experienced police work backed by firm legal authority.

In this situation, the director of the CIA proposed the development of a quasi-private covert action agency. This scheme offered several important advantages to the administration: (1) using private persons as liaisons, the new agency could manage the Contra insurgency against the Sandinista government, providing the tactical and operational guidance that had been coming from CIA before its funding and participation were cut off by Congress; (2) it would avoid the unwelcome scrutiny of Congress because it would not be a government operation, dependent on government funding, and thus would not come within the provisions of various statutes that imposed congressional oversight; (3) a private agency could act more daringly, avoiding the legal prohibitions contained in prior Executive Orders (against assassination, for example) that it would have been embarrassing to repeal, and in defiance of international norms against violent reprisals; thus it was hoped the United States might recapture the initiative that seemed to have been surrendered to the terrorist groups; (4) because of the agency's dissociation with official government, it would provide the president with the option of "plausible denial" should the private agency's operations be exposed. Statutes adopted in the late 1970s had greatly increased the political costs of maintaining such presidential denials because these laws required that the chief executive actually sign a written verification of the necessity for each covert operation and report this "finding" to Congress; therefore there always hovered the possibility that such written authorization might be discovered by the press after an official denial had been made.

The plan of using a privately funded agency to provide, in the words of one of the conspirators, "a self-sustaining, stand-alone, off-the-shelf covert action capability" was a natural market response to the problem of overregulation. In many ways it resembles the legal schemes by which multinational corporations take their enterprises offshore to escape onerous regulations by the state in which their operations are resident. Major General Richard Secord, the chief operating officer of the new covert action entity, called it simply "the Enterprise," a very apt term. Although the public's understanding of this agency appears to be that it was created to manage the American arms-for-hostages deal with Iran, and then expanded its portfolio by diverting black-market profits from those arms deals to the Contras, in fact the chronology is the other way around. The agency was set up to manage the Contra account that Congress had taken away from the CIA; as the agency grew, it took up other accounts, conducting covert operations in the Caribbean, the Mediterranean, and the Near East. It was intended to be staffed and available for use for any covert operation that needed its special scope and freedom from legal restraints. Had "Enterprise" operations in Iran not been exposed by the Iranians themselves, its executives believed that it would have taken on further assignments, in Angola and elsewhere.

This agency ultimately collapsed because it was fundamentally incompatible with American constitutional law. The exposure of the "Enterprise," in a different political climate, could well have led to the impeachment of the U.S. president. Unlike other states—unlike even other representative democracies—the United States does not permit the private funding of federal operations because this would evade the legitimating check of representative government. Only when the persons for whom the electorate has voted require the taxpayers to pay money for government acts is there a direct link between voting and government operations. Otherwise, the framers thought, and our constitutional structure and practice reflect, the link between citizen responsibility and governmental authorization is broken. It is a very pleasing thing to have others pay for the operations of the State, but even gifts to the U.S. government cannot be accepted without statutory authorization. To do otherwise allows the government to undertake functions for which it has no authorization from the people.

But if the Iran-Contra Affair was a textbook case of how not to conduct a covert action, there is nevertheless an important role for such activity in the arsenal of the market-state. Usually such operations amount to the financial and technical support of local elements in foreign countries with whom the United States is in some sympathy, or at least with whom we are willing to cooperate for a common goal. Rarely, arms may be provided. Paramilitary forces may be supported by the provision of intelligence, logistical support, or financing. It is doubtful the Russian defeat in Afghanistan would have occurred absent U.S. support for the mujahedin. The key elements are strict accountability of funding; careful professionalism and planning; and setting achievable goals. With the multiplication of entities operating in the international environment, and the increasing sensitivity of most governments to public opinion, the potential usefulness of covert action increases with the emergence of the market state, as do the costs of exposure.

The Iran-Contra Affair was the result of a government that in some respects anticipated the new market-state and was eager to use its tools, but was insufficiently attentive to the rules of the American constitution into which the norms of the new constitutional order must be translated. Far from discrediting covert action, the affair should enable us to use this instrument with more care in the future by emphasizing the crucial role of the legal setting of the market-state. A deregulated state does not mean an unregulated state; indeed, the legal rules that remain after deregulation have an importance that is, if anything, more salient than under the ends-justify-the-means ideology of the nation-state. The Russian state has been imperiled by its involvement in black-market activities, precisely because it has been unable to heed this rule. Whether the United States can marshal the imagination and daring to execute significant covert actions in the new politically fraught context of the market-state remains to be seen.

(3)

Sustained precision bombing: In Operation Linebacker, conducted in Southeast Asia in 1972, some nine thousand laser-guided bombs were fruitlessly dropped near Hanoi and Haiphong over eleven days—roughly the same number as were dropped with far greater effect during the entire Gulf War. So-called surgical strikes are among the most desired, and most elusive, options in the military handbook. Three difficulties have thwarted their promise of low-risk, low-collateral damage and high destruction: (1) air crews are inevitably put at risk because precision bombing requires low-release altitudes, and the very technology that enables target acquisition and homing for the bombardier is also used by antiaircraft missiles with integral radar systems; enhancing bombing accuracy also usually means employing air crews more intensively—the "smartest" of smart weapons was, after all, the kamikaze; (2) precision-bombing campaigns require enormous quantities of real-time intelligence to locate targets and track them; this intelligence relies both on satellite tracking, which is only now becoming achievable, and on highly efficient collection methods; (3) such bombing campaigns require patience—which the publics of market-states, fed as they are by hyperbolic media and sensitized to the suffering of civilians who are harmed by the bombing, will seldom tolerate—and modest goals. Contradicting the promises of early strategic bombing theorists, like Douhet and Billy Mitchell, it is extremely difficult for strategic bombing alone to effect a constitutional change in a hostile regime.

All of these perceived shortcomings were in the minds of U.S. planners when they considered the problem of attempting to lift the Serbian siege of Sarajevo. Despite intense pressure from the public and Congress, senior military officials refused to carry out bombing raids against the Serbs in Bosnia on grounds that strikingly reflect the interplay between market-state constraints and nation-state military mentalities. These officials forcefully rejected any area-bombing campaign on the grounds that too many civilians would be killed, reports of which would horrify the American public, and they rejected precision bombing on the ground that the public would not tolerate a long-drawn-out campaign. Given the rugged terrain in Bosnia and the fact that Serbian mortars and even howitzers could be quickly moved and easily camouflaged, any air operation short of a long campaign or area carpet bombing would be ineffective. In any case, it was reasoned, air strikes alone could not resolve the political conflict in Bosnia, or even safeguard civilians from the campaign of massacres, rapes, and deportations. Indeed, any bombing by the United States risked retaliation by the Serbs, who might take hostages from locally deployed U.N. forces, which, if withdrawn, would only lead to a demand for American ground troops, something else the public would not support.[59]

In the end, it was the insistence by military and diplomatic officials in many countries that bombing could not be decisive that was itself decisive. Military moves that could win the war and force the Serbs to surrender their goals required tactics that the public would reject; anything else was futile and risky. In these two demands—the insistence by the public on quickly terminated action, and by security personnel on achieving total objectives—we see the intersection between market-state and nation-state, between, that is, the new role of media-driven public sensitivities and the military demand for definitive state action.

In the event, an extremely modest bombing campaign conducted over a series of days without any obvious stopping point in fact lifted the siege of Sarajevo—the longest siege of the century, longer than Verdun or Stalingrad. As the memoirs of the American negotiator Richard Holbrooke wholly demonstrate, it was in fact this open-ended bombing campaign— over the strenuous objections of the British and French—that brought the siege to an end and, with the Croatian ground campaign, brought the Serbs to the negotiating table.[60]

By contrast the NATO campaign against Serbia to force acceptance of an international protectorate for Kosovo relied on aerial bombing from the outset.[61] During the course of the campaign, nearly 40,000 sorties were flown with virtually no losses.[62] When Slobodan Milosevic acceded to alliance demands, delivered by Russian envoy Viktor Chernomyrdin and Finnish president and E.U. special representative Martti Ahtisaari on June 3, not a single NATO ground troop had entered Serbia.[63] How was this possible and what lessons are there for the future use of this arm for the market-state? Each of the three vulnerabilities of precision-guided attacks that had been used to forestall NATO action in Bosnia had been blunted. First, stealth aircraft—aircraft whose radar profiles are so attenu-ated as to render them invisible to radar-guided attack—had taken out anti-aircraft missile sites that would otherwise have posed lethal risks to American pilots. Second, new technology had allowed for more accurate target acquisition, and the targets themselves were not confined to tactical strikes against Serb forces but included strategic strikes against Belgrade and the Serbian infrastructure. Third, NATO's political objectives were sufficiently modest and did not require a change of regime in Belgrade.

More important for our study, each of these three potential shortenings of precision-guided attack is likely to be even further ameliorated. In the past, precision-guided munitions depended upon some sort of homing technology—relying on either guidance from a command operator, or using emissions from the munition itself, or homing in on energy bounced off the target by an external transmitter or energy emitted by the target. Currently, however, the United States has the capability to use radar onboard the munition to generate midcourse corrections for an inertial guidance system or to fly to a precise set of coordinates using a guidance system updated by a Global Positioning Satellite system. Naval vessels lying offshore or aircraft distant from the target can launch these pilotless munitions with an accuracy that even the kamikaze would be hard-pressed to match. This, plus the introduction of Stealth technology, can greatly lower the risk to pilots and the likelihood of collateral damage to civilians.

Just as significantly, however, the United States set modest, achievable goals in the Yugoslav campaigns. NATO was willing to settle for some-thing far less than victory; this did not prevent "ethnic cleansing," but it did enforce an end to the Serbian armed presence in the provinces where Serbs had conducted their ethnic campaigns.

(4)

The term *information warfare* usually* refers to the capacity both to penetrate and degrade an adversary's electronic communications and to protect one's own communications from interference. Such warfare played an important role in the Gulf War and doubtless will play an even larger role in future conflicts as electronic monitoring and control becomes more extensive, and the links to commanders more numerous.

This use of information technologies is potentially a highly valuable strategic option for the market-state. More important, however, the United States can also use information as a diplomatic and strategic commodity with which to create incentives and deterrents affecting the political behavior of other states. Of course it has long been true that the United States has shared information with allies—using satellites to aid Britain in the Falklands War, or forwarding decrypts to Stalin that revealed the impending Nazi invasion of the Soviet Union—but this was undertaken as an adjunct to military activities and not something that was pursued as a strategic alternative in itself. Now, however, dramatic developments in information technologies—the increased capabilities of intelligence gathering combined with the enormous synthesizing powers of computers—have made possible for the first time a truly global system of near-real-time monitoring.[64]

It is already the case that weather satellites, medium-resolution imaging systems, worldwide air traffic control networks, television links, and the like are being used by civilian corporations, while the U.S. military can rely on extensive photo reconnaissance abilities, infrared missile launch detectors, radar satellites, unmanned aerial sensors, remotely planted acoustic devices, and various military guidance tools. The United States could undertake to expand this technology in order to achieve a complete system of satellite sensors that would provide real-time monitoring on many wavelengths.[65] The architecture for such a space-based information system is new, but the necessary communications technology is already emerging from the private sector. The entire system, however, depends upon affordable space lift, and this is something the U.S. government must undertake.

Such a system would provide the United States with the ability to detect, identify, track, and engage far more targets with a higher degree of lethality and precision, over a global area, than ever before. Knowing which subset of targets to strike serves as an enormous force multiplier, greatly reducing the number of weapons and strikes necessary to prevail over an enemy force.[66] In addition, there are real benefits to the market-state to be

---

*Sometimes this term refers to the dissemination of propaganda; that is not how it is used here.

found in information sharing (and withholding) beyond what can be achieved by weapons strikes.

At Sandia National Laboratories, an experiment has been undertaken in which a cooperative monitoring center acted as a confidence-building measure in much the same way that negotiated troop positioning, missile constraints, and transparency were used during the Cold War between the United States and the Soviet Union. Mutual monitoring between two hostile states can reduce the chances of war by preventing successful preemption. Setting up such a center is an example of producing the collective goods that can maintain U.S. leadership. Indeed, as we shall see, the concept of collective goods is especially crucial to the market-state because the functions of that state do not replicate but supplement the market, which is astringently economical with public goods.

At present, the Global Positioning Satellite (GPS) network established by the United States is used by any country with the capability to access it. Foreign nations have previously utilized the GPS system to direct missile attacks against U.S. interests; indeed, GPS-guided weaponry could be used to destroy U.S. satellites in orbit.[67] Access to a truly global monitoring system, however, could be limited by the United States and bartered to licensee states either for fees or for political cooperation. In addition to its crucial contribution to warfare, such a system would be integral to weather control, asteroid defense, solar flare warnings, commodity planning, environmental monitoring, and the sustainable exploitation of natural resources, all *collective goods* for the society of states.

(5)

By providing licensed states with the protection of a *missile defense*[68] system, the United States could provide an effective and trustworthy strategic umbrella analogous to that it provided during the Cold War through extended nuclear deterrence. Moreover, without such defensive systems the vulnerability of U.S. forces to missile attack abroad will be an increasing deterrent to U.S. force projections in aid of allies or for humanitarian missions. Thus what positive effect still remains as a result of U.S. extended deterrence could be sharply eroded in the absence of a credible U.S. ballistic missile defense.

"Central deterrence" is a function of the threat to target a national homeland in order to protect the homeland of the threatening, deterring party.* For example, the U.S. central deterrent consisted of the threat to attack the Soviet homeland in order to protect the American homeland from attack. The term denotes a relationship between vital objectives whose very centrality to the State gives them the highest value to the deter-

---

*See the discussion of "central" versus "extended" deterrence in the Introduction.

rer and thus assures both the willingness to run the highest risks of retaliation or pre-emption and the will to inflict a level of harm commensurate
with the necessity to protect "central" objectives. "Extended deterrence,"
by contrast, projects nuclear deterrence beyond the absolutely central, into
other geographical, nonhomeland theatres or for other, nonvital interests.
Extended deterrence was the objective of the policy according to which the
United States promised to retaliate with nuclear weapons if the states of
Western Europe or Japan were attacked. Sometimes this threat of retaliation is called the nuclear "umbrella." Extended deterrence is the single
most effective instrument the United States has to prevent major-state proliferation because it permits these states to develop their economies without diverting vast resources to the nuclear arms competition, and yet
remain relatively safe from nuclear attack.

It would be a grave mistake to assume that the threat of missile attack
has receded worldwide as a result of the end of the Cold War. In the Gulf
War, Iraq launched almost ninety missiles against targets in Israel and
Saudi Arabia; 25 percent of all U.S. combat fatalities from that war were
the result of a single Scud missile strike. Moreover, missile technology is
quickly spreading to many states. North Korea, China, and other states
have played major roles in this export trade. When North Korea, Iran, Iraq,
and the North African countries ultimately possess the 1,300-kilometer-
range No-Dong I missile, or something like it, the capitals of Japan,
France, Turkey, Israel, Egypt, and Italy will all be within range of potentially hostile states.[69]

Since the end of the Cold War, the American program for ballistic missile defense (BMD) has been redirected away from the effort to achieve a
comprehensive shield against a massive Soviet attack and toward theatre
nuclear defense systems. The Clinton administration endorsed a program
that included an upgrade to the Patriot systems used in the Gulf War; a
Theater High Altitude Area Defense system that would supplement short-
range point-defense systems like Patriot; and a sea-based system using the
AEGIS ships.[70] The enthusiasm with which these systems have been pursued, however, has been diminished by the intellectual residue of the Cold
War: during the Soviet-American confrontation, many persons felt that
BMD was essentially destabilizing to the deterrence relationship because
it promised—a promise it could not possibly fulfill—to prevent the USSR
from being able to destroy the United States in a retaliatory strike, thus
potentially tempting both sides into pre-emptive moves.

It would reflect a considerable misunderstanding if these opinions,
whatever their merits in context of the Long War, were to prevent the most
rapid feasible deployment of BMD by the United States today. This
deployment would enable the United States to protect many countries—
perhaps for a fee—including states that would be hard-pressed to deploy

their own defensive systems and that therefore might otherwise be tempted to develop other, far cheaper, deterrent systems of mass destruction. Moreover, the deployment of a theater BMD system would cast doubt upon potentially preclusive moves by other states to prevent the United States from projecting power abroad through conventional forces. For example, the six-month buildup of coalition forces in the Saudi desert would have been far too risky for a market-state like the United States if Iraq had possessed adequate offensive missiles. Even for a nation-state acting to protect its survival, such a threat to an expeditionary force can be preclusive: with respect to the Normandy invasion, General Eisenhower wrote that "if the German had succeeded in perfecting and using [the V-1 and V-2 missiles] six months earlier than he did our invasion of Europe would have proved exceedingly difficult, perhaps impossible."[71] A theatre BMD might be able to rehabilitate future regional military operations similar to the coalition offensive in the Gulf War despite hostile missile proliferation that it is evident is very difficult for market-states to prevent. As an aside, I should add that it is not necessarily a decisive argument against BMD to say that it would be ineffectual against nuclear threats delivered by other means—the so-called suitcase bomb, for example. These devices are extremely difficult to manufacture and, more important, are as much a threat as an asset to an authoritarian state because, unlike missile systems, they do not require elaborate control procedures and technologies and are thus potential tools for insurrection.

(6)

As noted above, computer-assisted design and manufacturing, training simulators, and virtual-reality environments will doubtless shape the military planning process of the twenty-first century. *Simulation* might, however, play an even more ambitious role in the hands of a market-state arbiter, such as the United States, or an ad hoc group of such states. With global monitoring, it ought to be possible in principle to simulate battles and then assess costs and damages afterwards. No lives need be lost in such conflicts. The role of individual heroism, of unit esprit, and sheer good luck will be less perhaps in future wars where combat is mainly fought by machines against machines—or against defenseless persons once their machines fail. In a transparent environment without tactical surprise, it may well be possible to arbitrate disputes not so much on the basis of international law as on a simulated competition run by computers. Recalcitrant losers would face coercive measures as penalties. The American legal practice of plea bargaining is an analogous example of such simulation in a different context. Based on the likely assessment of what would happen if the defendant went to trial, the prosecution and the defense barter within a range of likely outcomes, each preferring to avoid the risks and costs of trial if possible.

(7)

Mercenary forces were once the dominant armed instrument of the State because they were an economical alternative to more expensive standing armies. In the future, the use of local proxy armies can offer a similar efficiency. Backed by the information and intelligence collection, the air power and the strategic direction of United States–led coalitions, such forces could provide the indispensable element of ground control without risking American lives to the same degree as U.S. ground forces. The risks attendant to the use of proxies—as Rome discovered—is that they are unreliable allies; the weapons and information they are provided must be carefully calibrated and the technological support given must be carefully weighed.

The present volume began with this question: why is it so difficult for contemporary leaders to determine when to use force in international affairs? Now, I believe, we are in a position to answer this question. If the American state—and many other states also—is in the midst of a transition from one form of constitutional order to another, then states are also in the midst of a change in their strategic relationships vis-à-vis one another that is related to this change in constitutional order. The difficulty lies in the fact that we have yet to appreciate the nature and implications of this transformation. We are quickly becoming a market-state. Yet we still cling to a strategic mentality that was formed within the constitutional order of the nation-state and its Long War for survival. It's not so much a matter of finding a new strategic paradigm as it is of acquiring the habits of thinking that are compatible with the character of the new constitutional order; then the paradigm will follow.

The United States's world role as protector of free states and our domestic constitutional institutions of liberty and equality are linked together by our history. Any set of rules that forbids the use of American force in virtually all the contexts in which the United States is likely to find itself moved by moral considerations in the current era will forfeit its claim on our moral sense. Then when those situations arise that do threaten our vital interests and call for a supreme national effort, we shall regret having ignored the cardinal historical lesson of American war making: that it is never done wholly on a moral or an expedient basis, but always and only when both are present. For two hundred years, U.S. foreign policy has been to offer assistance, where our assistance was sought and where it would be efficacious, to peoples who wanted free institutions and peaceful lives, and to oppose aggressors who threatened the constitutional way of life that is our greatest legacy to mankind. In service of the former objective we fought the warrior tribes of the Plains, the Mexican dictator Santa Anna, the German empire, the Spanish empire, and the Asian totalitarians Kim Il Sung, Mao Zedong, and Ho Chi Minh, and sent forces to many places around the world where the collapse of the legal order brought great suffering. To defend our constitutional form of life, we fought both Britain and France in the nineteenth century, and defeated fascism and communism in the twentieth. We have seldom sought territorial cessions by conquest and have largely grown our continental state by the wishes of the pioneer inhabitants of the territories we protected or purchased. This history must be qualified by the wrongs we have committed, including those against Native Americans and the preservation of slavery and the slave trade for half a century after it had been outlawed in Europe. Yet it is our history that gives us a consistent sense of our achievements *and* of our wrongdoings.

It is important for the United States and its leaders to remember that Thucydides concluded that the "truest reason" for the Peloponnesian War was Sparta's fear of the growing strength of Athens. Not simply increasing American power, but persuading others of our modesty, our benign intent, our deference to the preferences of other societies will be an indispensable element in maintaining peace. American references to "the sole, remaining superpower" are scarcely helpful but the label "hyperpower" comes from abroad.

For history is not made within the State alone. Indeed I have argued that the State depends upon conflict with other states—the object of strategy— in order to establish itself as the legitimate guardian of a legal order. What of the *society* of states? How does its constitutional order come about, and what legitimates that order? This is the subject of Book II.

> *All wars are so many attempts to bring about new relations among the states and to form new bodies by the break-up of the old states to the point where they cannot again maintain themselves alongside each other and must therefore suffer revolutions until finally, partly through the best possible arrangement of the civic constitution internally, and partly through common agreement and legislation externally, there is created a state that, like a civic commonwealth, can maintain itself automatically.*
>
> —Kant, *Idea for a Universal History with Cosmopolitan Intent* (1784)

CHAPTER THIRTEEN

The Wars of the Market-State: Conclusion to Book I

THE LONG WAR was an *epochal war.* Such wars are distinguished from other types not simply by their duration—which often spans lengthy periods of armistice—but mainly by their constitutional significance. Indeed such wars keep going precisely because they concern the fundamental legitimacy of the State. When revisionist historians suggest that the World War II Allies could have ended that war earlier by modifying the surrender terms offered the Japanese so as to guarantee the constitutional position of the emperor, these historians are reflecting their tacit understanding of the war itself. They think it was like other wars, mainly about the accretion of power or wealth. When we see World War II as but a part of a much longer constitutional conflict, however, such observations appear to miss the point.

Let me reiterate that the reasons epochal wars are begun are no different from those of any wars: they arise from clashing claims to power, from competing ideologies and religions, insistent ambition, the gamble for greater wealth, sympathy for kinsmen or hostility to foreigners, and so on. The reason epochal wars achieve, in retrospect, an historic importance is because however they may arise, they challenge and ultimately change the basic structure of the State, which is, after all, a war-making institution.

In studying past wars that came to be recategorized as mere engagements in longer, epochal conflicts, one repeatedly finds that basic issues persisted and were not resolved by the peaces that followed the cessation of overt belligerency. Because the very nature of the State is at stake in epochal wars, the consequence of such wars is the transformation of the State itself to cope with the strategic innovations that determine the outcome of the conflict. Thus, the transformations of the State into the various constitutional archetypes described in Part II are each associated with epochal wars.

The metamorphosis of the realms of princes into Renaissance princely states coincided with the Wars of the Italian Peninsula, begun by the French invasion of Italy in 1494. The modern state originates in the transition from the rule of princes to that of princely states that began there.

Of these new *princely states,* Machiavelli argued that their security and liberty were the prince's first concern and that all else depended on this.[1] The great princely states of Habsburg Spain, Valois France, and Tudor England were superseded by *kingly states* forged in the Thirty Years' War. On behalf of the kingly states, Bodin insisted that only a single sovereign embodying the ultimate authority of the State could prevent the religious rebellions that had repeatedly erupted during this epoch.[2] *Territorial* states in turn proved triumphant in the defeat of the greatest of the kingly states, in the wars of Louis XIV. Locke, whom we anachronistically associate with American democracy, in fact accepted a sovereign who singularly made all the laws, so long as this reflected a covenant between the governed and the governing. These regimes were in turn superseded by the great *state-nations,* of which Hume[3] is no less the prophet than Robespierre.* Burke famously said in 1774 that Parliament was not a congress of ambassadors from its various electoral constituencies, but "a deliberative assembly of one nation, with one interest, that of the whole."[4] The Napoleonic Wars accompanied the introduction of this constitutional archetype into the history of Europe, and their settlement at the Congress of Vienna enshrined this order for four generations. By contrast, the *nation-state* is associated with the Long War, a struggle that was fought over the moral and political orientation of that constitutional form in the twentieth century. Wilson and Lenin, Hitler and Roosevelt[5] all claimed that their systems would best benefit the material well-being of the people, a claim we have heard so much that it is hard for us to imagine a constitutional form that does not take its legitimacy on such a basis. Yet this was not always the case.

Legitimacy is what unites the problems of strategy and law at the heart of epochal war just as history supplies the answers to those problems. The axiom of legitimacy has changed as new constitutional archetypes have replaced their predecessors; it is invariably the consequence of epochal wars that new constitutional archetypes appear as the competing states

---

*See the essay by Peter Mancias in *State Formation and Political Legitimacy,* ed. Ronald Cohen and Judith D. Toland (Transaction Books, 1988), that observes of these remarks of Robespierre— "Democracy is a state in which the people as sovereign guided by laws of its own making, does for itself all that it can do well, and by its delegates what it cannot"—that it is "brilliantly ambiguous, of course, and allowed . . . that all effective power could be located in the ruling clique of the Committee on Public Safety." See also J. R. Pole, *Political Representation in England and the Origins of the American Republic,* (St. Martin's Press, 1966), 441.

involved in the conflict develop into more successful forms for managing the strategic innovations that win the war.

Civil wars and revolutions are characteristic of transitional periods between constitutional forms as the old constitutional archetypes struggle against the birth of the new,[6] whereas epochal wars are transformative. The Dutch Revolt of 1567, the English Civil War, the Fronde, the American Revolution, and the American Civil War all began periods that encompassed epochal conflicts and a shift in the constitutional order. Epochal wars often include, and indeed are often begun by, revolutions and civil wars. These revolutions determine the possibilities; epochal wars make the choices; history provides the rationale.

The link between the strategic and the constitutional is seldom drawn in contemporary affairs. There are notable exceptions to this: Michael Howard,[7] Geoffrey Parker,[8] Aaron Friedberg,[9] and Jeremy Black come to mind as military historians and analysts who have written with great sensitivity about the relationship between history and force; Anthony Giddens,[10] Peter Mancias,[11] and David Beetham[12] are political sociologists who are keenly interested in the relationship between legitimacy and violence, about which each has written with real insight. The problem seems to be that the two groups so seldom talk to each other. The contemporary debate over a future national security paradigm for the United States provides a good example of such missed opportunities. Although this debate is at the very center of current policy planning, and is being carried on by persons of great ability, it has as yet yielded little practical benefit to decision makers.

Why is it so difficult to decide when to use force today? Is it the nature of modern conflict with its nonstate actors, terrorism, transnational threats, and so on?[13] Or a more complex geopolitics perhaps, now that the Soviet Union has collapsed?* Or poor leadership? I think the difficulty is that before September 11, 2001, we didn't know what it was we were fighting for, and thus could not judge the appropriate costs. And that was because the market-state has not fully emerged or been fully realized and accepted by any society. So we did not yet agree on the fundamental constitutional order that we must secure. It was rather the attacks on this emerging order that gave it definition.

Without an understanding of the Long War as such, the current search for a new security paradigm is apt to confuse this endeavor with the search for policies; unless we understand the paradigm from which we have

---

*Charles Krauthammer, to the contrary, makes the excellent, and to my mind persuasive, point that things were not in fact so much easier during the Cold War, in his "The Greatest Cold War Myth of All," *Time* (November 29, 1993): 86.

emerged, we will not be able to free ourselves from the habit of thinking in its terms. And without an understanding of the constitutional source of war and the strategic basis for law, and, most important, the link between the two that has provided the choices that account for the transformations of the State over five centuries, we will be unprepared to understand the next transformation of the State and its strategic and constitutional consequences.

The history of warfare is often at the center of the study of the creation, character, and development of the modern state, but this centrality is frequently defined away as war is analyzed as a mere epiphenomenon of economics, ideology, or sociology. Strategic matters should have the same level of significance in such studies as that currently enjoyed by economic and social issues.[14] I hope the present work will help to revise the widespread assumption that economics and sociological conflict are the basis for all historical phenomena. A defining feature of any state is its ability to make war and keep peace. No state has ever *made* an economy or a class system.

The State is born in violence: only when it has achieved a legitimate monopoly on violence can it promulgate law; only when it is free of the coercive violence of other states can it pursue strategy. This history provides the reason why warfare—like law—is a key to understanding the development of the State for it connects the ever-present intrusion of international pressures (the outer) to the political anatomy of the State (the inner).

In the preceding chapters I have argued that the constitutional order of the State is undergoing a dramatic change. This, I believe, is not the first time such a profound shift has occurred either in our state or in other states, and therefore I disagree with the usual notion that the Westphalian consensus of 1648 produced the constitutional order of the nation-state within which we currently live. Instead, I have described a series of such orders, both before and after Westphalia. One such order, that of the market-state, is already superseding that of the nation-state, which can be seen to be only about a century old.

This change is taking place all across the society of states. The market-state manifests itself in three forms vis-à-vis the larger society of states:* the mercantile, managerial, and the entrepreneurial state. Mercantile market-states closely ally the state with national enterprises; they protect these industries with trade barriers, sometimes even using the national

---

*And in three constitutional variants, vis-à-vis each state's people. These are discussed in Chapter 26.

security apparatus on their behalf, and compete globally as if there were no distinction between the State and its corporations. Managerial market-states attempt to act as flywheels, using regional blocs as counterweights to national competition. Entrepreneurial states blur the distinctions between the welfare of the single state and that of the society of states, and seek the widest sharing of collective goods within that society.

In my view the United States ought to encourage the development of entrepreneurial states rather than other forms in order to avoid international conflict, including sabotage, industrial espionage, and even armed warfare. I speculate that leadership for this move is likelier to come from the leaders of multinational corporations and nongovernmental organizations (NGOs) than from leaders of the national security apparatus and the political establishment, but I concede that business leaders are generally not prepared for such a role today.

A market-state is not a market. There is an irreduceability of governing that cannot be assimilated into market operations. But governments must have a basis in legitimacy for them to exercise the powers of coercion that they alone possess. Business corporations cannot try people and jail them, or levy fines, and therefore they need not have any basis for legitimacy other than the voluntary consent of consumers. The State needs to produce public goods—which engender the qualities of reciprocity, justice, solidarity, empathy, and civility—because such goods are, by definition, what the market does not produce on its own. The mass protests that took place during the meetings of the G-7, the IMF, and the WTO remind us that unless there is a legitimate process by which public opinion, in all its shades, can be registered there is little reason not to take to the streets. The market (and new market-state institutions) do not provide these processes unaided by the State and its laws.

The State is not withering away, nor is it going to be replaced, but its form—its constitutional order—will undergo an historic change. In Book II we will study the impact of this new constitutional order on the society of states. There I will argue that the study of law must be at the center of the history of the society of states (as I have argued in Book I that the study of war is central to the history of the State) and that, contrary to our usual assumptions, international law is derived from the constitutional order.

At the end of the twentieth century, it is interesting to recall what persons at the end of the nineteenth century expected of the hundred years to come. There seems to have been widespread agreement on two expectations: that science and technology would make war impossible and that international law would govern the relationships among states.[15] In retrospect we might say that these expectations were direct extrapolations from the new prestige of applied science and from the successes of the Concert of Europe. It was, we are apt to conclude, rather naïve to believe that the constitutional order of the society of the great state-nations of the nineteenth century would proceed indefinitely toward perfection.

Today public expectations about the century to come are also likely to reflect our recent past. There is a widespread consensus that the future will be framed around conflicts,[16] and there is an unquestioned belief that governments will continue indefinitely to shape events in the international arena. In fact, governments are steadily being weakened with respect to their capacity to control international events, and the kind of security problems states will face in the twenty-first century are more likely to be about managing cooperation than triumphing through conflict. One can already see this in recent wars: the United States was not in direct conflict with Iraq or Serbia or Somalia or Haiti or Panama or even Afghanistan, though its armed forces attacked or occupied all of these states. Rather, the use of force was deployed through intervention to prevent "ethnic cleansing," to halt famine, to reverse the gains of aggression, to restore democracy, and to punish terrorism.

The great powers will repeatedly face five questions regarding the use of force in the twenty-first century, and none of them are usefully characterized in the zero-sum, conflictual way of strategic warfare. These questions are whether to intervene, when to do so, with what allies, with what military and nonmilitary tools, and for what goals.[17] Mass refugee migrations, international crimes, the proliferation of weapons of mass destruction, ethnic cleansing and other terrorist atrocities, environmental catastrophes—all will provide potential occasions for intervention. The great powers will be called upon to distribute help and re-establish order, not to secure raw materials and key ports as in the nineteenth century, nor to spread their ideology, as in the twentieth.

The market-state requires that we think in terms of global relations rather than international relations. The relations between governments will only partly determine events within the society of states. As a result NGOs (nongovernmental organizations), criminal conspiracies, terrorist groups, humanitarian philanthropies, and special-interest lobbies will all become significant participants in interstate affairs. It will therefore be crucial for the United States and other great powers to create global networks of nongovernmental resources they can draw on. It is already the case that NGOs like CARE, Amnesty International, and the major environmental funds have budgets and influence greater than those of many states. The same can be said of terrorism, which can now rely on an infrastructure that was previously only available to the secret agencies of states.

The difficulty in relying on private actors, however, is that their legitimacy as international agents is in question. Whom do they represent? Who appointed them? To whom are they responsible? The market-state attempts to solve this problem of accountability by a test that is, in its way, as characteristic of the market-state as the Montevideo Convention test for state recognition is characteristic of the nation-state. For the nation-state, controlling territory by the consent of the governed assured legitimacy. In the new information age that has brought about the market-state, institutions can exist and wield power in a nonterritorial space. Therefore the market-state's test of the accountability of the NGO is simply this: they are accredited if they can raise enough money to finance successful operations that do not violate international law. Thus in the market-state, there will be the problem of distinguishing crime from capitalism (the cocaine cartel claims, for example, that they ought to have the same legal status as the growers and marketers of tobacco), whereas for the nation-state the characteristic definitional problem was the distinction between the terrorist and the freedom fighter.

In this new era, looking at the world in terms of conflict—looking at the world, that is, from the perspective of the state of war—doesn't fully protect states because many highly dangerous threats don't come from adversaries but from systemic collapse. Power outages, epidemics, computer viruses, financial panics, overpopulation, deforestation, water pollution, and energy "famines" (so named because they arise from hoarding) might be exploited by our adversaries, but they will arise whether or not there is a mastermind behind them. Of course, peoples have always faced these or analogous threats; the plague of the fourteenth century, and the great famines of the Indian subcontinent in the twentieth century are examples. But these events rarely posed mortal threats to the state system. Today, however, because the system is both globalized and highly interdependent, nonmilitary events in remote regions as well as among nonstate actors can cascade, bringing states to the point of collapse.

The emergence of the market-state has not occurred in an instant but rather over a couple of decades. Within the most prominent market-states, the groundwork was laid by Margaret Thatcher and Ronald Reagan, who did so much to discredit the welfare rationale for the nation-state. The rationale that underpins the legitimacy of the market-state, by contrast, is that it maximizes opportunity. President Clinton was the leader who led the United States into this new constitutional order (just as Prime Minister Blair has done for Britain and Chancellor Schroeder has attempted to do for Germany).

A few representative quotations from President Clinton will suffice to illustrate the change:

The mission of this administration from day one has been to increase economic opportunity and maintain national security; to empower the individuals of this country to assume personal responsibility for their own futures.[18]

I do believe that the most important thing we can be doing today as a nation to create opportunity for our people is to give them the tools they need to succeed. In a global economy, the government cannot give anybody a guaranteed success story, but you can give people the tools to make the most of their own lives.[19]

I saw my job when I became President to create a structure of opportunity for the 21st century, so that every American would be able to make the most of their own lives.[20]

We must be committed to the pursuit of opportunity . . . And we must be committed to a new kind of Government, not to solve all our problems for us but to give our people, all our people, the tools they need to make the most of their own lives.[21]

As times change, so Government must change. We need a new Government for a new century, humble enough not to try to solve all our problems for us but strong enough to give us the tools to solve our problems for ourselves . . . Yet where it can stand up for our values and interests around the world, and where it can give Americans the power to make a real difference in their everyday lives, Government should do more, not less. The preeminent mission of our new government is to give all Americans an opportunity, not a guarantee but a real opportunity, to build better lives.[22]

Similar statements have been made by President George W. Bush:

The old way in Washington is to believe that the more you spend, the more you care. What mattered was the size of the line in the budget, not the effect of that line on real people's lives. My administration takes a new approach.*

Good jobs must be the aim of welfare reform. As we reauthorize these important reforms, we must always remember the goal is to reduce

---

*President discusses budget in radio address to the nation, August 25, 2001.

dependency on government and offer every American the dignity of a job . . . Government doesn't create jobs, but it can encourage an environment in which jobs are created.*

Government has a role, and an important one. Yet, too much government crowds out initiative and hard work, private charity and the private economy. Our new governing vision says government should be active, but limited; engaged, but not overbearing.†

Government has great responsibilities for public safety and public health, for civil rights and common schools. Yet compassion is the work of a nation, not just a government . . . America, at its best, is a place where personal responsibility is valued and expected.‡

The United States can benefit immensely from this shift because we are well placed to thrive in a globalized political economy. Indeed a globalized society of market-states plays into and enhances American strengths to such a degree that it worries some states that the United States will become so dominant that no other state will be able to catch up to it. In many quarters, globalization is so deeply identified with the United States that it is anxiously perceived as an American cultural export. Such anxiety is reflected in contemporary international relations on many issues: for example, the principal opponent of the hardly unreasonable U.S. position regarding landmines was Canada; the most sarcastic attacks on the rather sensible U.S. opposition to an International Criminal Court came from traditional allies. Moreover, these anti-American political reactions will, in a society of market-states, spill over to reactions against U.S. businesses, and vice versa. Offense given by McDonald's will be repaid by antipathy to the United States. Antiglobalization reactions will inevitably become attacks on U.S. policies.

When we look ahead we can see the market-state already forming. With it comes a new set of choices arising from the interplay between the strategic and the constitutional. Which way this new constitutional order will develop, constitutionally and strategically, is a matter of human decision.

The answer to how we will develop a calculus for the use of force in the present era depends on choices yet to be made. Either our rules for the use of force will re-enforce world order, which will require a readiness to

---

*State of the Union Address, January 29, 2002.
†Address of the President to the Joint Session of Congress, February 27, 2001.
‡Inaugural Adress, January 20, 2001.

undertake numerous, apparently endless small conflicts, or they will make larger wars more likely, risking the widening of small, seemingly irrelevant conflicts, or they will make a cataclysmic war inevitable when great regional blocs, with greatly differing views of their own sovereignty, find themselves the targets of events whose perpetrators they do not really know and cannot, even through harsh repression, really silence.

The calculus to be employed will become clear once we decide. The epochal war we are about to enter will either be a series of low-intensity, information-guided wars linked by a commitment to re-enforcing world order, or a gradually increasing anarchy that leads to intervention at a much costlier level or even a cataclysm of global proportions preceded by a period of relative if deceptive peace. It is ours to choose.

At the Bomb Testing Site

*At noon in the desert a panting lizard
waited for history, its elbows tense,
watching the curve of a particular road
as if something might happen.*

*It was looking at something farther off
than people could see, an important scene
acted in stone for little selves
at the flute end of consequences.*

*There was just a continent without much on it
under a sky that never cared less.
Ready for a change, the elbows waited.
The hands gripped hard on the desert.*

—William Stafford

Plates

PLATE I: THE CONSTITUTIONAL ORDERS

PLATE II: THE EPOCHAL WARS

PLATE III: THE INTERNATIONAL ORDERS

PLATE IV: BASES FOR LEGITIMACY

PLATE V: HISTORIC STRATEGIC
AND CONSTITUTIONAL INNOVATIONS

The following charts give a graphic if oversimplified representation of the six successive constitutional conventions of the international society of states. It will be immediately seen that these various periods correspond to those described in Book I: the eras of the princely state (1494 to 1620), the kingly state (1567 to 1702), the territorial state (1688 to 1792), the state-nation (1776 to 1914), the nation-state (1863 to 1991), and the emerging period of the market-state (1989). Each of these eras was defined by the triumph of one constitutional archetype for the State. The third chart shows the moment at which that dominant constitutional archetype was ratified by the society of states as the legitimate constitutional order: for example, this occurred with the Peace of Augsburg in 1555, which ratified the victory of the princely state and the defeat of a "universal" regime for Europe based on the premodern constitutional order of Christendom. It occurred again at Westphalia in 1648, where two peace treaties ended the Thirty Years' War and ratified the legitimacy of the secular, absolutist forms of the kingly state that had superseded the sectarian, dynastically plural forms of the princely state. The Peace of Utrecht in 1713 performed a similar constitutional function for the society of European states by enshrining a new security order in Europe based on the balance of power and recognizing the limited monarchies of the territorial state. The Congress of Vienna in 1815 ratified the success of one state-nation, Great

Britain, over another, the revolutionary Napoleonic Empire, and set up an international institutional system of the great powers with periodic congresses, while at the same time embracing the defeated French state-nation and integrating it into the new society. The Peace of Versailles performed the same function for the triumphant nation-state, which replaced the collapsing model of the imperial state-nation of the nineteenth century.

PLATE I: THE CONSTITUTIONAL ORDERS

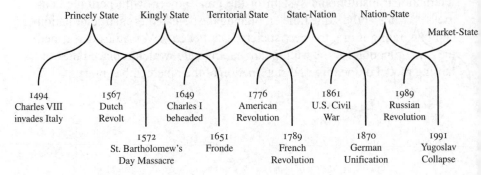

There have been six distinct constitutional orders of the State since it first emerged during the Renaissance.

PLATE II: THE EPOCHAL WARS

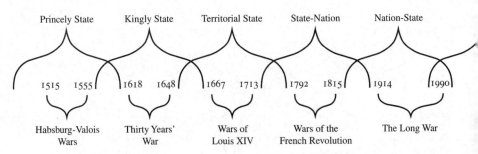

Each epochal war brought a particular constitutional order to primacy.

PLATE III: THE INTERNATIONAL ORDERS

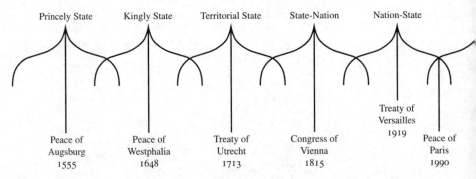

The peace treaties that end epochal wars ratify a particular constitutional order for the society of states.

PLATE IV: BASES FOR LEGITIMACY

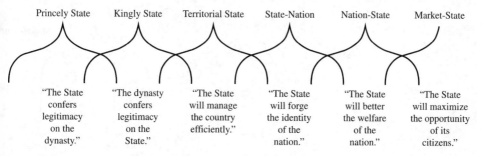

Princely State	Kingly State	Territorial State	State-Nation	Nation-State	Market-State
"The State confers legitimacy on the dynasty."	"The dynasty confers legitimacy on the State."	"The State will manage the country efficiently."	"The State will forge the identity of the nation."	"The State will better the welfare of the nation."	"The State will maximize the opportunity of its citizens."

Each constitutional order asserts a unique basis for legitimacy.

PLATE V: HISTORIC, STRATEGIC, AND CONSTITUTIONAL INNOVATIONS

Princely States	Kingly States	Territorial States	State-Nation	Nation-State
• Consistent Finance • Permanent Government	• Absolutism • Secularism	• Trade Control • Aristocratic Leadership	• Nationalism • Imperialism	• Nationalism • Ideology

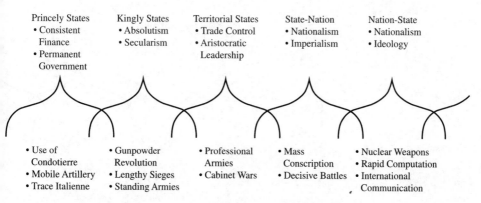

| • Use of Condotierre
• Mobile Artillery
• Trace Italienne | • Gunpowder Revolution
• Lengthy Sieges
• Standing Armies | • Professional Armies
• Cabinet Wars | • Mass Conscription
• Decisive Battles | • Nuclear Weapons
• Rapid Computation
• International Communication |

A constitutional order achieves dominance by best exploiting the strategic and constitutional innovations of its era.

BOOK II

STATES OF PEACE

Peace

When will you ever, Peace, wild wooddove, shy wings
   shut,
Your round me roaming end, and under be my boughs?
When, when, Peace, will you Peace? I'll not play
   hypocrite

To own my heart: I yield you do come sometimes; but
That piecemeal peace is poor peace. What pure peace
   allows
Alarms of wars, the daunting wars, the death of it?

O surely, reaving Peace, my Lord should leave in lieu
Some good! And so he does leave Patience exquisite,
That plumes to Peace thereafter. And when Peace here
   does house
He comes with work to do, he does not come to coo,
                    He comes to brood and sit.

—Gerard Manley Hopkins

Introduction:
The Origin of International Law
in the Constitutional Order

I.

When the Peace of 1990 burst on a world that did not expect it, there had been little thought given to what that world would look like when it was free of an institutionalized universal war. Virtually all our international institutions had been molded by the environment of global conflict, and even persons who did not shoulder a rifle or stand watch on a militarized border had found their expectations and attitudes so shaped by the environment of war that few could have said more than "peace is the absence of war" because war, not peace, was really all they had known.

This way of thinking treats states and their interests in much the same way that welfare economics treats the consumer: the decisions of states are, axiomatically, choices that define the interests of states, and, beginning from the positions of power in which they find themselves, states have the sole objective of maximizing that power.[1] But it is more than this. This way of thinking, which now seems as confined and airless as one realizes a closed room has felt only when one has left it, reflected a *strategic* approach to international relations. By "strategic" I do not mean simply "planned" or "economic," but rather an approach that focuses on the use of force as the principal arbiter of international affairs. Such an approach has been virtually exclusive of all other approaches in the context of a world war in which the very survival of the constitutional form of the State was at stake. One hardly needed to debate a threatened state's vital interests during the Long War; strategic requirements determined these interests.*

---

*Thus, for example, the protection of the South Korean regime became a vital interest of the United States.

When the war ended, however, this very lack of discussion underscored how ill-suited the methods of strategy are to determining national interests. As Stanley Hoffmann has written:

> Especially in a democracy the definition of the national interest is likely to be a matter of debate and to result at least as much from clashing partisan views as from the permanent necessities of geopolitical position or the unavoidable requirements of external conflicts.[2]

In war the calculus of strategy takes priority, because those states that ignore strategy cannot expect to prevail in an arena dominated by force. But, as Michael Howard foresaw, "A strategic approach may be necessary to produce conditions of stability which will make possible continuing peace; but other, more positive measures, are needed to create peace itself."[3]

Thus the first strategic consequence of the new peace is that strategy alone must be augmented. But with what? The approach to peace with which we must supplement strategy is that derived from law—the rule of law, as that phrase is understood in the context of constitutional law, but applied in the context of a new international law. We must, that is, develop an international system that treats states according to general, logical principles, regardless of the particular position of power of any state, but these principles must reflect a strategic appreciation of the relative positions of states' wealth and power. This amounts almost to a reversal of the present system of international law as reflected, for example, in the U.N. Charter, which provides the same universal principles for all states but privileges some to suspend those principles through the veto power or the collective action of the Security Council. Before a new, hybrid approach can be successful, however, perhaps before it can even be understood, we will have to change our ideas about international law, and the principles of this new international law will have to reflect the end of the Long War and the Peace of Paris. That is, these principles must reflect the emergence of a society of market-states in which law and strategy have begun to merge—where war often looks like crime and vice versa, where borders have less to do with defining the State than do more intangible perimeters like language and technological compatibility. One might say these new principles will be less about inter*national* law because the basis for the State will be less about nations and more about markets,* because these will have a greater role in defining the purpose of the State and its legitimacy.[4]

---

*Bearing in mind that there are markets in more than things, e.g., markets in time, information, education.

Now it is rare that strategic approaches to statecraft are combined, in any but the most cynical way, with those approaches associated with any sort of law. The definitive word on this subject, at least as regards international law, is presumed to have been given by Clausewitz, who dismissed the Grotian Law of Nations as "certain self-imposed, imperceptible limitations hardly worth mentioning, known as international law and custom."[5] To be fair, it must be recalled that Clausewitz was not writing about the conduct of statecraft but rather about the conduct of war. And although he was writing about war, he was living in a period of peace, in fact, a period of immense success for international law—that is, for the constitution of the society of state-nations known as the Concert of Europe.

Since Clausewitz, the disdain of statesmen for international law has come not in periods of peace but in that period I have called the Long War, largely in reaction to the international effort to restrain state behavior through law at the end of the First World War, memorialized in a series of disarmament treaties and the fatuous Kellogg-Briand Pact that was intended to "outlaw" war. The failure of the Wilsonian program, which sought to supplant an almost entirely strategic approach to world affairs with an almost entirely legal perspective, tended to alienate the two completely for the balance of the Long War. Only now can we perhaps see that even though we cannot prudently abandon a strategic approach to international relations, neither can we ignore that approach grounded in law because without it we have no real plans for how to conduct peace. When we lengthen our gaze, we will see more clearly that law and strategy have always been mutually excited switches on the same circuit, and that the State itself, as we have seen in Book I, is the mechanism of feedback.

Complicating this resort to law, however, is the fact that international law is itself in flux. Changes in the strategic environment inevitably produce changes in law, not simply because law tends to reflect the positions of power in a society—international society in this instance—but because law itself is composed of the practices of parties who will necessarily adjust their ambitions, their actions, and their doctrines to take account of changes in the strategic context. Had there been no Roman victory in the Punic Wars, can there have been a Roman law, *urbi et ubique* that lapped the Mediterranean as if it were a Roman lake? Without the American victory in the Revolutionary War, it is difficult to imagine a Monroe Doctrine, and without the Napoleonic challenge, it is difficult to imagine the British fleet enforcing the doctrine in the aftermath of that challenge. The international legal environment reflects the strategic environment, much as commercial law reflects the market, or the legislation of governments reflects events in politics.

This is not a one-way relationship, however. Suppose there had been no

Allied victory in Europe; would the doctrines of Nuremberg that are now a part of international law have come into being? It is a tempting irony to conclude simply that such trials would have been conducted in Manchester and London if the Nazis had won; this identifies law with power, a view that has many adherents. But why would the Nazis, of all people, have bothered with trials? And why did the Allies—at least one of whom had conducted a war crime of historic atrocity in the Katyn Forest three years before the tribunal met—feel the need to set a standard that might later embarrass them? The Allies not only sought to justify themselves by writing and applying these new rules; they sought to put into place practices that they could later rely upon to reinforce their own legitimacy as world leaders. By this means strategy and law were mediated by history.

Strategic outcomes affect international law, but international law—the rules of legitimate behavior for states—can affect the strategic, because it shapes the political goals that strategy is meant to serve. International law is thus among the first resources consulted in a crisis, and its treaties and treatises are among the last resources deployed when violence has ended and its consequences must be healed. This is not simply a matter of the victor enforcing his will; that too equates law with power alone in a kind of gross category mistake. Rather the will of the victor—what Saddam Hussein thought it reasonable to carry off from Kuwait (mainly German-made cars), and what Margaret Thatcher thought it reasonable to require of a defeated Argentina (mainly a dignified evacuation)—is formed by a particular view of law, and what law ought to be, and how it ought to be enforced. Every leadership of every state has such a view—self-interested, culturally idiosyncratic, haunted by historic threats, excited by historic visions—that is its own view of international law. The law thus viewed is an amalgam of the common practices of other states in an international context that reflects the collectivity of state views.

The coming of peace to the society of states has brought changes in international law, just as the war brought changes in constitutional law to the individual participants. These changes form the environment that has ultimately resulted from the end of the Long War. We eventually will have an international law that is based on the unwritten constitution of the new society of market-states.

II.

The international society we have today, manifested in the General Assembly of the United Nations and the various conferences of which virtually all states are members, has been shaped by the Long War. The U.N., like the League of Nations before it, was a product of one of the campaigns of that war, but this institution became universal only with the end of the Long War. The resignation of Germany from the league and the exclusion of the People's Republic of China from the U.N. were tacit concessions to the fact that universal rights and duties were not accepted by all states. Might we say, however, that a universal society nevertheless preceded the Long War (and was perhaps shattered by it)?

Hedley Bull concluded otherwise.

> [To be sure, the] expansion of Europe from the fifteenth century to the nineteenth . . . gradually brought into being an international system linking the various regional systems together, which by the middle of the nineteenth century was nearly universal. This did not mean, however, that there yet existed a universal international society. . . . [The states of the world] were not united by a perception of common interests, nor by a structure of generally agreed rules setting out their rights and duties in relation to one another, nor did they co-operate in the working of common international institutions.[6]

It is not thus mere ethnocentrism that leads the historian of the international system to focus, at least initially, on Europe. But if the predecessor of the international society of today was the European society of the nineteenth century (which had yet to be universalized), what was *its* predecessor? And what determines such a genealogy? We have to specify the trait we are tracing: in this case, it is the "perception of common interests [within] a structure of generally agreed rules setting out . . . rights and duties." It is the conceit of international lawyers and law professors that the fundamentals of international law have largely been the same for many centuries and that these arise from ancient Roman ideas of the interaction of foreign peoples with the empire. Thus there are almost no histories of international law, only historic claims of classical origin.

The Romans had a kind of international law—the *jus gentium*—that applied to matters between themselves and foreign entities. But this was not a reciprocal structure, that is, one that foreign entities also applied to Romans; it was simply the Roman assessment of what rules applied in dealing with others. "All nations," wrote Montesquieu in a famous, Gallic remark, "have a *droit des gens;* even the Iroquois, who eat their prisoners, have one."[7] But this sense of "otherness" is precisely what is not characteristic of a society and its law *among* its members; rather, it characterizes the law for *barbarians,* for those outside the society.[8] International law could have developed this way, from the outside in, as it were. We could have a law of nations that is constructed out of the accumulated and overlapping sums of how each state chooses to treat foreigners. But it did not happen that way. Instead, the law among nations developed from the inside out, that is, from within a society that gradually enlarged to encompass the world. This is what is meant by the definition of international law as

> the complex of rules that were developed by the sovereign states of Europe from the period of the Reformation and Renaissance onwards, which blossomed into . . . "classic" international law in the nineteenth century, and which, although challenged and remodeled in the period after 1918, is still discernible in the international law of today.[9]

This author is referring to "a specific kind of practice that emerged in history amongst a particular species of body politic,"[10] and he correctly dates its incidence as late as the Renaissance when the modern State first emerged, as described in Book I. The ideas that form the basis of international law today derive from European concepts of identity that were manifested when individual princes became the subjects of legal relations after the collapse of the Roman Empire. Understanding this origin is one important way of understanding international law because it focuses on the development of legal ideas rather than simply political events. As Adam Watson has wisely remarked:

> Power, not only between states, is a matter of great interest to academics. Much of their writing about states' systems has focused on power, and the struggle for power between states in a system, rather than on the working of international society . . . On the other hand, most practitioners, especially statesmen and professional diplomats [are] more keenly aware of the great limitations to which power in a society of states is now subject and of the opposition to the use of force or even inducement by the threat of it.[11]

These limitations derive from the constitutional order of the international society of states. We shall be looking at the history of international society from a legal perspective much as we analyzed the history of the individual State from a strategic point of view. Of course, the strategic, the legal, and the historical are closely intertwined. In the pages that now follow we shall explore the legal concepts that frame the exercise of political power, as these have been manifested and shaped throughout the history of the once small society of political entities that has become, so recently, the universal bearer of international law.

We will determine the content of the constitution of the international society of states by looking at the interplay between a changing constitutional order and the imperatives of international security. There have been many competing visions of that constitutional order that have risen, periodically, to a temporary ascendancy. One of these is the Wilsonian vision, within which much of the world has lived for most of this century.

This vision derives directly from an extrapolation from U.S. constitutional law—with its emphasis on national identity and constituency—to universal, international law. Once its origins in this extrapolation are appreciated, the idea of a universal international law can be better judged. In my view, this concept, which animates the U.N. Charter just as it did the League of Nations, is fundamentally destructive of both the society of states and of their security and for this reason will continue to frustrate the development of international law because statesmen, whatever their rhetoric, will always be unwilling to commit their fate to its dominion.

The Wilsonian idea arose out of the interplay between Wilson's constitutional ideas—self-determination and an idealistic, altruistic egalitarianism among nations—and the strategic ideas of his friend and adviser, Colonel E. M. House. This interplay resulted in the vision of universal law that is associated with Wilson's name.

Wilson's ultimate ideas, once this interaction had brought his views to maturity, can be easily described. First, they depend on constituency, the constitutional idea that the jurisdictional scope of a legal act is coextensive with the electoral franchise of its origin. Thus in the United States municipal law applies to the inhabitants of a city, county law to a somewhat larger domain, state law to all the counties within a state, federal law to all the states. Each legal jurisdiction deals with a certain subject matter, and where there is overlap it defers to the larger constituency within which it nests. One state cannot make law for another state, but the U.S. Congress can make law for all the people of the union of states. A universal constituency would give rise to a world law. It would be limited in subject matter to that which concerned all member states as states—that is, it would not deal with private civil matters, or crimes, but would confine itself to issues of maintaining peace, arbitrating trade and commercial disputes, and admitting new members to the society of states. Second, Wilson's concepts depend on national identity, by which is meant no more than the freely given decision of citizens to associate with one another. This, too, is a constitutional idea, and it also derives from the American experience, specifically the attempt at secession by the South. This idea, however, ignores the conundrum of minorities, for the self-determination of one group almost always isolates within the new state groups who might prefer a larger association or a state of their own. It goes almost without saying that this was the situation for many African-Americans in the South, and it is hardly surprising that Wilson's constitutional understanding of the Civil War virtually omitted the issue of slavery, just as the South after Reconstruction omitted African-Americans from its political society.

These two constitutional notions—nested constituencies, bounded by a freely chosen national sovereignty—were given universal scope when they encountered the idea of collective security propounded by House. *Collective security* along with the *balance of power* has for this century competed to provide a model for American leadership in foreign policy. Roughly speaking, collective security requires a state to pledge its national forces to defend the peace of an international (though not usually a universal) order; the *balance of power* requires a state to intervene only to maintain the equilibrium of an international order. Putting it this way shows that these two ideas are not incompatible, although the American debate tends to treat them as such. For example, the Congress of Vienna was a system of collective security devoted to maintaining the equilibrium of Europe. What has made the two concepts appear to be opposites has been the deployment of collective security on behalf of a universal order based on Wilson's constitutional conceptions (which are transcendently hostile to maintaining a balance of power, per se).

To this marriage of constitutional and strategic ideas we owe the League of Nations, and also the United Nations. House himself was a cold realist in foreign affairs and had no difficulty anchoring his policies in calculations of power and national self-interest. By contrast, Wilson did not believe that such motives could justify force; only altruism and the protection of the rights of the weak, only universalism (the very opposite of self-interest, which is necessarily particular) could permanently endow American foreign policy. As a result, the American debate over the U.S. role in international security has long been frozen in a fundamental disagreement about American purpose. This is often misleadingly characterized as arising from a difference of views about American exceptionalism, the idea that the United States has a unique historical role among states. In fact the proponent of U.S. self-interest may do so precisely because he believes it is America's mission to provide an example to the world (the early isolationists were such men), and the internationalist who strives for peace through world law may do so precisely because he does not believe the American purchase on virtue to be any greater than that of any other state. What really divides these two camps is the Wilsonian universalist proposition that actions based on self-interest alone cannot serve as a durable basis for policy because without a moral foundation for policy domestic support will inevitably erode.

Woodrow Wilson's views were taken up by Franklin Roosevelt. To appreciate this we have only to compare the structure of Wilson's League of Nations with Roosevelt's United Nations (although there are many other instances of this choice, for instance, FDR's hostility to European colonialism, his refusal to isolate the Soviet Union, and his insistence on unconditional surrender as a war aim). We are inclined to forget that the structure of the League mirrored that set up for the federal government by the U.S. Constitution and was faithfully replicated by the structure established by the U.N. Charter. The League of Nations was dominated by a Council of great powers whose acts required unanimity. There was also a General Assembly in which all countries were represented; a Secretariat was provided for, with an institutional residence, and a permanent court of international justice was set up. FDR's words in 1941—"our country must continue to play its great part . . . for the good of humanity . . . We believe that any nationality no matter how small, has the inherent right to its nationhood"—might have been spoken by Wilson in 1919. If anything, the measures in the Charter for U.N. military forces and the binding nature of Security Council decisions are even more universalistic than Wilson's proposals for the League.

The universal view of international law is flawed in two important respects (neither having much to do, however, with the common criticism that such universal scope must await a universal morality). First, it mixes the equality of states, a legal concept, with the decision to use force, a strategic concept, in a way that is fatal to both, and thus eerily recapitulates the early prehistory of the State, which was first constituted out of the separation of these two concepts. Thus it treats the society of states as if it were a society of individuals.

If all states are equal before the law, then every state can call upon the whole community for security assistance, just as the police protect every citizen. But the security interests of those states providing forces are not the same for all regions, much less for all states, even augmenting those interests with some concern for world stability. Bloodshed in Rwanda is just as terrible as bloodshed in Yugoslavia, but one is a humanitarian problem for the West, and the other a geostrategic crisis. Second, the universalist view assumes an all-encompassing jurisdiction that does not in fact derive from the constitutive nature of its institutions. Hitler, it will be recalled, took Germany out of the League of Nations (and Mussolini took Italy out). True, the U.N. Charter makes no concession to resignation. The decisions of the Security Council are everywhere binding. But the Council does not enfranchise all states. It can only be a matter of time before both these eventualities occur: resignation by some states who then dispute the legitimacy of U.N. jurisdiction; and calls for expanding the Security Council to include members elected by the General Assembly. The logic of universal law based on a constitutional extrapolation predicts, perhaps requires, this, but the contemporary reality is that of a world with an inceasing number of centers of power after the end of the alliance systems of the Long War.

The Wilsonian program has long been the subject of criticism by diplomats. George Kennan's *American Diplomacy 1900–1950* is largely an attack on the "legalistic-moralistic" preoccupations of American state-craft. Henry Kissinger's *Diplomacy* extends this critique by proposing a managed policy of equilibrium, relying on *Realpolitik* in the service of a balance of world power. Both writers stress the naïveté of Wilson. "A country that demands moral perfection of itself as a test of its foreign policy," Kissinger writes, "will achieve neither perfection nor security." But I wonder who is really the *naïf* here. A politician twice elected president from a minority party, who skillfully took his country from a stubborn isolationism to world leadership, is unlikely to have based his decisions on a childlike view of human nature. Moreover Kennan's and Kissinger's descriptions of the pernicious effects of law usually sound a little off-key to any lawyer; they tend to exaggerate the role of litigation and then substitute that rather limited role of law in resolving disputes before courts for the more pervasive and profound pull of legal grammar in a constitutional society like the United States.

What Wilson—and Roosevelt—understood quite clearly was the domestic wellspring of a sustainable foreign policy. They sought popular endorsement by playing the U.S. government's strongest card, the American commitment to constitutional ideas as law.* Both men attempted to universalize the American structure (with its three separate branches, its federalism, its separation of church and state) to apply not only to individual states but to the society of states as a whole. This vision is the subject of Part I of Book II, which follows.

In Part II of Book II, I will present the origins and development of international law according to the periods of the constitutional development of the State described in Part II of Book I. This development has been almost entirely a matter of European history. It is sometimes said, by Hans Kelsen among others, that constitutional law is derived from international law. And commentators today may draw erroneous support for this claim from the fact that international norms of human rights and supranational regional regulation have intruded as never before into state sovereignty. Once we understand, however, that international law derives from constitutional law—and thus follows the same periods of stability and revolutionary change charted in Book I—we will be able to appreciate that contemporary developments in limiting sovereignty are a consequence of the change in the constitutional order to a market-state, and are not imposed by international law, however flattering such an image may be to those who administer international institutions.

---

*Prior to the founding of the United States, sovereign governments were not bound by their laws. That is why the United States was the first modern state to have a written constitution.

In Part II I will argue that the great peace conferences that settled the epochal wars created the constitutions for the society of states. These constitutions will be described, and a similar attention given to their legal interpreters—lawyers and statesmen—as was given to the princes and generals of Book I.

In Part III, I will take up the emerging constitution of the new society of market-states. I will suggest that American principles of limited sovereignty better serve such a society than the European concepts that currently structure international law. I will imagine various constitutional orders of the society of market-states and conclude by arguing that, by varying the degree of sovereignty retained by the people, states will develop different forms of the market-state, yielding a more pluralistic constitution for international society. In some ways that constitution, and its international law, will resemble that of medieval society with its overlapping and complex system of jurisdictions (a society, in other words, that had no modern concept of state sovereignty based on the European model). In medieval Europe, a free city might owe legal duties to an ecclesiastical authority such as the local bishop, to a federal authority, and to a league of such cities, and even share certain legal responsibilities with local squires. The international law of the society of market-states will reflect an analogous complexity where multinational companies, NGOs, governments, and ad hoc coalitions share overlapping authority within a framework of universal commercial law but regionalized political rules.

Similar observations have led some commentators to suggest that the leading alternative to Wilsonian internationalism is a "new medievalism," which will follow the end of the nation-state. Power will shift away from the State to nonstate actors, who will replace the formal exercise of power by governments with a world order of nonstate actors. Sometimes this is expressed in the phrase that "global governance is 'governance without government.'"[12] This view, however, is more consistent with the conclusion that the State is evaporating than with the argument that the State is merely undergoing one of its periodic shifts in the constitutional order. The revolution in information technology that has so empowered nongovernmental actors will change—but not, I think, destroy—the State. On the contrary, at the center of both Books I and II is the conclusion that nongovernmental entities will play an important constitutional role in the operation of the market-state, not replace it. The most influential nongovernmental groups cannot function in a nonstate environment. Human rights groups depend upon courts; the Red Cross depends upon armies and at least minimal civil order; Morgan Stanley depends upon the Basel Committee of Central Bankers. It is the nation-state that is dying, not the State. With it will go much of the power and influence of the great international institutions of the society of nation-states, institutions like the World Bank, the United Nations, the International Court of Justice. This void will be filled by institutions and rules that reflect the new society of market-states because, as we shall see, international law and its structures arise from the constitutional order of states; when this order changes, as is now happening, the institutions of the society composed of states inevitably change also.

PART I

THE SOCIETY OF NATION-STATES

THESIS: THE SOCIETY OF NATION-STATES DEVELOPED A CONSTITUTION THAT ATTEMPTED TO TREAT STATES AS IF THEY WERE INDIVIDUALS IN A POLITICAL SOCIETY OF EQUAL, AUTONOMOUS, RIGHTS-BEARING CITIZENS.

In the society of nation-states, the most important right of a nation was the right of self-determination. This, however, posed a conundrum for that society: given the interpenetration of national peoples in multi-ethnic states, when did a nation get its own state? Was it when a majority of the people of the state agreed, or when a majority of a national group—which was usually a minority of the persons in the state as a whole—demanded it? And when one national group held power, what were the limits on its treatment of other national groups ("minorities" within the nation-state), given that one purpose of the nation-state order was to use law in furtherance of the cultural and moral values of the dominant national group? Confusion arising from this conundrum led to a diffusion of international responsibility, culminating in the Third Yugoslav War in Bosnia, which finally discredited the legitimacy of a society of states built on this constitutional order.

Departure

(Southampton Docks: October, 1899)

While the far farewell music thins and fails,
And the broad bottoms rip the bearing brine—
All smalling slowly to the gray sea-line—
And each significant red smoke-shaft pales,

Keen sense of severance everywhere prevails,
Which shapes the late long tramp of mounting men
To seeming words that ask and ask again:
"How long, O striving Teutons, Slavs and Gaels

Must your wroth reasonings trade on lives like these,
That are as puppets in a playing hand?—
When shall the saner softer polities
Whereof we dream, have sway in each proud land
And patriotism, grown Godlike, scorn to stand
Bondslave to realms, but circle earth and seas?"

—Thomas Hardy

CHAPTER FOURTEEN

Colonel House and a
World Made of Law

ONE AFTERNOON in the mild winter of 1991, several trustees of the university sat waiting in a Victorian parlor at Princeton. The parlor was on the second floor of "Prospect," the Italianate mansion on campus that formerly housed the university's presidents, until in the 1970s proximity to students became more dismaying than endearing.

In this room there were two paintings: over the fireplace a portrait of Woodrow Wilson, twenty-eighth president of the United States, tenth president of Princeton, the occupant of Prospect at the turn of the century. On the adjacent wall another oil portrait hung, apparently executed at about the same time by the same artist. Its subject had a singular face, quite unlike the handsome Presbyterian features of Wilson. This other man had more delicate, less open features: a carefully clipped white mustache, rather cold gray eyes, a small chin above a high, starched white collar. He wore a broad-brimmed buff-colored hat and a long pale duster. If Wilson's face was idealistic, virile, and Miltonian, this man's face was quiet, unflappable, the face of a rather shrewd baronet.

He had not matriculated at Princeton. Nor had he been a professor or university figure. The trustees, bored by waiting, wondered who he was. No one knew: not the editor-in-chief of *Time* magazine, nor the chairman of the Union Pacific Railroad, nor the U.S. Senator, nor the university president, a polymath whose interests were almost as broad as the curriculum. Someone read the nameplate, "E. M. House," and then some of the party recalled. "Colonel" House, as he was known to his contemporaries, had been the most famous American in the world in 1919, excepting only his ally and friend Woodrow Wilson. This fame was the result of a friendship unique in twentieth century American political history, for Wilson had devolved on the silent and mysterious Colonel the extensive powers of the U.S. presidency, though House never held any governmental office. His elusive figure was for seven years the alter ego of the president. House was often sent on missions to foreign governments though he was given no precise instructions save the president's assurance that he knew House would "do the right thing." House bypassed the Department of State entirely and communicated directly with Wilson by a private secret code. Indeed the two men seemed always to communicate with one another in a kind of mutual but exclusive sympathy. Yet in 1919 the two parted in Paris, never to meet again: Wilson to return to the defeat of the League of Nations and the rejection of American international involvement, of which House was the principal architect; House ultimately to vanish into the obscurity with which he had assiduously cloaked his achievements. House's story is the story of how America moved from being a marginal actor on the world scene to attempting to remake that scene on the basis of American constitutional ideas.

Edward Mandell House was born in Houston, Texas, on July 26, 1858. His father had come from England to make his fortune, first to New Orleans and then to Texas, where he fought in the Revolution. During the Civil War he was a blockade runner and there clings about Thomas House something of the Rhett Butler. Subsequently House became one of the leading citizens of Texas, a wealthy merchant, banker, and landowner. His son Edward idealized the West and its cowboy culture but he was small and after a childhood accident, rather frail. He was sent to Bath, England, for school and later to the Hopkins School in New Haven, Connecticut, to prepare for Yale. At Hopkins, House's roommate and closest friend was Oliver Morton (the son of Senator Morton of Indiana, Republican candidate for the nomination for president in 1876). When the nomination went to Hayes and the election resulted in a contested outcome, Senator Morton managed the Republican forces that won the White House. This was a constitutionally fraught period—in which the election was thrown into the House as the Constitution properly provides (they seemed to know better how to handle things in those days). The two teenage boys spent their time in Washington attending the sessions of the Electoral Commission on which Senator Morton was serving. This experience was a turning point for House. He became utterly absorbed by politics and he saw, he said later, that the system was actually run by a very few players in Washington.*

One of the boys failed his entrance exam to Yale; the two ended up at Cornell, where House remained until the beginning of his third year, when he left school to care for his father.

---

*"I saw that two or three men in the Senate and two or three in the House and the President ran the government. The others were merely figureheads . . . I had no ambition to hold office . . . because I felt . . . that I would fall short of the first place and nothing less than that would satisfy me."[1]

After Thomas House's death Edward married and went for a year-long honeymoon in Europe. His father had left him an independent income sufficient to ensure that he need never work, and so in 1885 he moved to Austin, the state capital, to bring himself closer to the political scene. As a youth, House had been brought close to national power, close enough to know that he wanted to surround himself with that distinctive, almost palpable aura of great things possible and great things attempted; but also close enough to realize how unlike the rest of the world such an environment is, and thus how rare and how very hard to achieve. He had been an observer on the national stage by chance. Could he now be a participant, by design?

Soon he had made his residence, invariably open to politicians, lobbyists, and journalists, into a focal point of the social and political life of the small city. House pinned his hopes on the key role Texas would play in the progressive wing of the Democratic party. For ten years, he studied Texas politics, and then in 1892 he ran the campaign of the progressive governor James Hogg.

Hogg was opposed by a coalition of railroad and corporate interests; every daily newspaper in the state was against him. When, despite this, he was re-elected, House's reputation as a campaign manager was assured. Thereafter he ran successful campaigns for the governorship in 1894, 1896, 1898, 1900, 1902, and 1904, becoming so powerful that when one incumbent attempted to stay on for another term in spite of House's advice, the sitting governor was turned out. Indeed, in each of these elections, House opposed potent political machines that he managed to overcome.

One aspect of his success is important to note. Texas at this time, like all the formerly Confederate states, was thoroughly committed to the Democratic Party. The Republicans were so identified with Reconstruction and the corrupt governments of that period that no legislature or gubernatorial office in the South was held by them for almost a century after the Civil War. This meant that once he had won the nomination (a process from which African American voters were effectively excluded), the Democratic candidate would inevitably win the general election. The successful nominee was chosen at a convention of delegates picked in local primary elections. In this way the state system actually mirrored the federal system, within which presidential candidates were elected by a college chosen on the basis of electoral victories in the states. Thus it had been possible for Tilden to win the popular vote nationwide in the 1876 election for the presidency but fail to achieve a majority in the electoral college. House's strategy of abandoning contests in constituencies that were committed to his opponents and focusing entirely on marginal contests was perfected in the Texas gubernatorial primary campaigns and would be the blueprint for electing Wilson to the presidency.

Like Theodore Roosevelt, House was attempting to put into place the policies that are the basic building blocks of the nation-state (less than a half century old at that point) in which it is assumed that the state's first duty is to benefit the mass of its people. In this his policies are to be distinguished from the old state-nation programs of the Southern Bourbons of the immediate postwar era, for this group conceived the purpose of the nation to be to serve the goals—moral, economic, or cultural—of the American state. What makes House interesting to us, however, is that he proposed an especially American constitutional vision of the nation-state to be the basis for the *society* of nation-states, an extrapolation that is only now basically complete just as it is about to become outmoded.

By 1908 House had grown thoroughly tired of his role in Texas politics. He had rebuffed overtures to run for governor himself in 1902 and for twelve years had bided his time as the Populist movement washed across the Democratic party. The nomination of William Jennings Bryan in 1896 and the adoption of a free silver monetary platform had doomed the Democratic party to minority status in the country at large. House waited.

In 1899 Bryan had sought a winter location in the South where he might bring his daughter, who had been ill. Hogg and House arranged for the Bryans to take a house virtually on the grounds of the House estate. As he did with so many politicians of this era, House captivated his guest with his mild manners and tough politics. Bryan was defeated for the U.S. presidency in 1900 and again in 1908, but his relationship with House grew stronger, despite the fact that House believed the Democrats had to be cleansed of the Bryan financial heresies before the party could regain the White House. Throughout this period, House cultivated the Bryans.

House had been spending his summers for some years in Magnolia, Massachusetts. Now he began spending more time in New York and, in 1910, came east to find a candidate for the presidency. Bryan had suggested Mayor Gaynor of New York City and so a dinner was arranged at the Lotos Club. But an embarrassing miscommunication between the two men involving a visit to Texas removed Gaynor from House's list.

He had decided that the nominee could not come from the South; that he must be an Eastern governor who would attract the Western vote by his liberalism. The new governor of New Jersey, Woodrow Wilson, had been touted to House by the editor of *Life* magazine. House began studying the speeches of the former university president, who was holding his first political office following a very public defeat at the hands of the Princeton trustees. Wilson had no political record and thus started with no political enemies; his troubles at Princeton had given him a national reputation as an opponent of aristocratic privilege. House went back to Texas having become convinced that he had found the right man.

Throughout the winter of 1910–1911 he began lining up political allies behind a Wilson candidacy. House returned to New York, where it was arranged that Governor Wilson would call on him at the Hotel Gotham.

Wilson was aware of House, because the latter—working through former Texas governor Charles Culberson, who was now a United States Senator—had skillfully deflected attacks on Wilson's party regularity that had threatened to end his candidacy even before it got off the ground. Wilson had been impressed by his reception at the time of an address to the Texas legislature, also orchestrated by House. The two had never met, however, and Wilson knew nothing of House's relationship with Bryan.

Wilson and House met in House's small hotel room on November 24, 1911, agreed to have dinner a few days later, and continued to meet alone at the Gotham as long as House remained in New York. House later wrote:

> The first hour we spent together proved to each of us that there was a sound basis for a fast friendship. We found ourselves in such complete sympathy, in so many ways, that we soon learned to know what each was thinking without either having expressed himself. A few weeks after we met and after we had exchanged confidences which men usually do not exchange except after years of friendship, I asked him if he realized we had only known one another for so short a time. He replied, "My dear friend, we have known one another always." And I think this is true.[2]

The next day House wrote his brother-in-law, Sidney Mezes, who was at the time the president of the University of Texas, "Never before have I found both the man and the opportunity." That same week House wrote Culberson, "[t]he more I see of Governor Wilson the better I like him, and I think he is going to be a man one can advise with some degree of satisfaction. This, you know, you could never do with Mr. Bryan."[3]

As if to test this proposition, House urged Wilson to attack the tariff and make free trade a centerpiece of his speeches. He had D. F. Houston, formerly the president of the University of Texas, at that time the chancellor of the University of Washington, come to New York to brief Wilson on tariff policy. Afterwards Houston wrote, "I can't tell you how much I enjoyed my visit with House . . . He has a vision. I should like to make him Dictator for a while." Wilson did refocus his campaign on tariff reduction. Despite his reputation in subsequent years, however, Wilson was no visionary; rather, he was a quick study of other men's ideas, an eloquent and passionate advocate, a sensitive and gifted performer.

In addition to positioning Wilson on the national stage, House had two crucial tactical objectives designed to win the Democratic nomination: to bring Bryan on board and to secure the Texas delegation. Neither would be easy: in a letter to a Princeton trustee Wilson had written, "Would that we could do something at once dignified and effective to knock Mr. Bryan once [and] for all into a cocked hat," and this letter had been leaked to the press by Wilson's opponents.

For months House had been nurturing Bryan's perception of Wilson, however. He pictured Wilson as opposed by the men who had opposed Bryan, and emphasized that the Hearst papers, who had made Bryan an object of ridicule for years, were for Champ Clark, the other liberal in the race and the other possible beneficiary of a Bryan endorsement. House depicted, accurately, the hostility Wall Street felt for Wilson and passed on stories to the populist Bryan that large slush funds were being collected to defeat Wilson. He urged Bryan's presence at a Washington banquet where Wilson praised Bryan, and he carefully maintained a separate correspondence with Mrs. Bryan, who was inclined toward the scholarly Wilson in preference to the professional politician, Clark. By June 7, he could write Wilson:

> Do you recall what I told you concerning the conversation I had with Mrs. B? I have a letter this morning from her containing this most significant sentence, "I found Mr. B well and quite in accord with the talk we had [that Clark was unacceptable]." It encourages me to believe that Mr. Clark will never receive that influence and that you will.[4]

In Texas the governor and the chairman of the Democratic State Executive Committee—and thirty of its thirty-one members—were opposed to Wilson. This was in December of 1911; by April of 1912 House had rounded up all of the Texas delegates to the convention for Wilson. These delegates, under House's tight control, were the key to his strategy. Nomination for the presidency at this time required a two-thirds vote at the convention. Wilson couldn't hope to go in with anything like this number, so House sought pledges from delegates committed to the front-runners for the first few ballots that these delegates would vote for Wilson if their candidates faltered. By the time of the convention, Wilson's forces had lined up commitments from delegates committed to candidates other than the leading front-runner, adding up to more than a third of the total number of delegates. This meant that the leading contender—Champ Clark, the Speaker of the House—could not win the nomination.

On June 20 House wrote Wilson from the Massachusetts shore expressing his regret that he could not be at the convention; he was, he said, "physically unequal to the effort" and he was leaving for two months in Europe. "However," he wrote, if "Clark's strength crumbles on the second and third ballot—which I hope may be the case—you will be nominated forthwith."

It was a near run thing. Clark almost got the two-thirds vote but eventually crested just short; the Texas delegates held firm. After numerous ballots that Clark led but could not win, those votes pledged to other candidates began to drift toward Wilson. In desperation the New York delegation, dominated by the Tammany Hall machine, attacked Wilson, which had the unintended effect of bringing Bryan onto the field with a Wilson endorsement. Bryan's intervention was decisive and Wilson was nominated on the forty-sixth ballot.

The United States had been governed by the Republicans since 1860, with the solitary exception of the Cleveland presidencies. It was a Republican country. The general election of 1912, however, would be dominated by the split in the Republican party between former President Theodore Roosevelt and his successor, President William H. Taft. House reasoned that Roosevelt's independent campaign would make him the lightning rod for conservative public opinion. Not only would Roosevelt cripple the Republican nominee by splitting the vote—this much was obvious to many—but he would, in House's view, legitimate the other progressive in the race, Woodrow Wilson, and make him the candidate of those who above all did not want to see a return of Roosevelt to the White House. The margin of Wilson's victory would be provided by lukewarm Taft supporters reacting to the ferocity of Roosevelt's attacks. So strong was this conviction that House did not bother to cut short his European tour and returned only at the end of the summer.

Then in October, only two weeks before the election, the country was stunned to learn that a would-be assassin had shot Roosevelt while the former president was campaigning. House immediately telephoned Wilson and persuaded him to cancel all further speaking engagements until Roosevelt recovered. Overruling the campaign committee, after some hesitation while House pressed for an immediate decision, Wilson abandoned his speaking tour for the balance of the campaign. House's appeal to Wilson's chivalry, coupled as it was with the shrewd insight of the true professional on whom Wilson could rely blindly, yielded an important public relations victory for the candidate at a crucial time. When the election returns came in on November 5, Wilson, though failing to gain a majority in the popular vote, had won an overwhelming victory in the electoral college, bringing with him large Democratic majorities in both houses of Congress. House immediately began planning to push through the legislative program to which he had long been committed: tariff reform, a Federal Reserve (opposed by both Wilson and Bryan), the federal income tax, and antitrust measures.

Before assuming the presidency, however, Wilson had to fill his cabinet. He had never held national office, never worked in Washington; indeed his only experience of politics was his single term as governor of New Jersey. His circle of experienced political office holders and administrators was limited. House persuaded Wilson to make Bryan secretary of state, on the grounds that this would prevent Bryan from opposing the Wilsonian legislative program. House himself resolutely refused to take any office— Wilson asked him to take any cabinet position save that to be offered Bryan—and urged instead that Wilson give Congressional leaders the largest say in appointments.

This accords with House's consistent counsel to Wilson during the latter's presidency: he repeatedly urged Wilson to pay more attention to congressional leaders, to give them a larger role in policy matters. Wilson, however, leavened the natural egocentricity of a public performer with the intellectual's contempt for politicians: of one senator he said that he "is the most comprehensively ignorant man I have ever met." Asked by someone whether he didn't think a particular statesman the "most selfish man in America," Wilson demurred, saying only, "I'm sorry but I am already committed to Senator ___."[5] When House did induce Wilson to invite members of Congress to the White House, they were dismayed never to be offered any alcohol to drink and not to be permitted to smoke.

House refused any appointment for himself because he knew that if he held administrative office he would be forced to take decisions that would, inevitably, be in advance of and occasionally at variance with the opinions of his chief. So long as he had no responsibility for making specific decisions he could defer to the president in conversation, avoiding committing himself until he and the president had come to mutual agreement. This freedom allowed him to be an ideal counselor, able to stimulate or soothe as required but never to be found in opposition once the president made up his mind. Moreover, House wanted the scope of the freelance, unconfined to any departmental duties. The historian Robert Hildebrand has written that:

> House's talents complemented Wilson perfectly. The president's greatest skills were rhetorical, House's were political . . . House willingly shouldered the burdens of the presidency that Wilson found most odious, making himself into a much-needed buffer between the president and the everyday world of politics. Above all, House was trustworthy; the value of both his advice and his friendship depended upon his complete lack of self-interest, which inspired Wilson's confidence and liberated his facility for emotional attachment.[6]

House had become Wilson's "man of confidence": anyone who wanted an appointment, who wished a change in policy, who sought a favor from the president, went to House. When the cabinet was complete, in addition to Bryan, two of House's closest associates from Texas—Burleson and Houston—were postmaster general and secretary of agriculture, while

Gregory, a third friend from Austin, ultimately replaced McReynolds as attorney general. "Mr. House is my second personality," Wilson replied when asked about his friend. "He is my independent self. His thoughts and mine are one. If I were in his place I would do just as he suggested . . . If anyone thinks he is reflecting my opinion by whatever action he takes, they are welcome to the conclusion."[7]

House's dream had been realized. But there was far more to this dream than mere access to power.

Immediately after the election of 1912 a novel entitled *Philip Dru: Administrator* was published in New York. This novel was dedicated to "the unhappy many who have lived and died lacking opportunity because, in the starting, the world-wide social structure was wrongly begun."

The novel tells the story of a young West Point graduate, Philip Dru, who is so moved by a public vision of the common good transcending the selfish demands of interest groups that he chivalrously champions the needs and hopes of the great mass of persons. It is a romantic novel, but Dru is far from a purely romantic figure: he is described as disappointing to look at, a "man of medium height, slender but toughly built and with a strong but homely face." He is taciturn in the extreme and never shares his plans. While in college his interest in politics is aroused by his connection to his roommate's family, who are influential members of New York financial and political circles. After leaving the army—though invalided he refuses a pension—Dru achieves instant fame when he wins a nationwide prize for solving a military problem. He uses this celebrity to become a syndicated writer, exposing the injustices of society and contributing proposals for their amelioration.

Unknown to Dru or the general public, a talented but corrupt political manipulator, Senator Selwyn, has conspired with the boss of the Credit Trust, John Thor, to control the government through the judicious use of a $10,000,000 slush fund. With the election of a few senators and an apparently progressive president who is his creature, Selwyn effectively delivers the federal government to the gilded plutocracy that has supplied the fund. A neglected dictograph, however, discloses a conversation between Selwyn and Thor that reveals the entire scheme. When leaked to the press, a recall of the president is demanded, and eventually a new civil war breaks out in the West in revulsion at these revelations. Dru becomes a leader in this rebellion and ultimately its general. After winning a bloody victory in the battle for the Midwest, he marches on Washington, forces the government—now overtly in the hands of Selwyn—to surrender peaceably and seizes authority. He then proceeds to rule by decree, successively reforming the constitutional structure along more parliamentary lines, ending lifetime tenure for federal judges, giving the states identical and much sub-ordinated constitutions, putting into place basic laws to protect union organizing and provide safe conditions of labor, and requiring government and labor representatives on corporate boards of directors. Dru institutes a graduated income tax and a federal inheritance tax; formulates a new banking law providing for a convertible currency administered by a federal central bank; introduces the corporate income tax, old-age pensions and unemployment insurance; abolishes tariff protection; and invigorates trust-busting. His reforms accomplished, he quits office, refuses to run in the elections he has organized, marries the love interest of the novel, and, quite literally, sails into the sunset to unknown destinations.

Philip Dru was written in the weeks before the Baltimore convention and published just after the election. "John Thor" was obviously a portrait of the financier J. P. Morgan; "Senator Selwyn" was just as obviously pat-terned on Senator Mark Hanna, the Ohio political boss who had engi-neered the election of McKinley. All this the reviewers and newspapers duly noted. But who was the author?

Philip Dru: Administrator was published with nothing to indicate the author's name. "Who Wrote 'Philip Dru'?" read an advertisement in the *New York Times*. "A forecast of the government of the United States after the Revolution. . . . [T]he story of the reforms he initiates is told well by one who knows politics from the inside." The publisher's prospectus, how-ever, listed the author only as "Anonymous." "There will be no attempt to make capital out of this anonymity," the press release read. "The fact is simply that it would be uncomfortable and unpleasant for the author to have his name known."[8]

The press release alluded to the sophistication of the author, in contrast to "most of the utopian, forecast, prophecy and reform novels that . . . are written by men who have little experience in the world of practical affairs,"[9] and this theme was picked up by the early reviews. The *Portland Evening Telegram,* for example, concluded:

> Although the name of the author of this book is withheld from the pub-lic, the reader can readily judge that whoever wrote the novel knows something of the "big business" of the country and the great forces which control the Nation's policies.[10]

The *Dallas Morning News* speculated that the author was "a man of great wealth, fine ideas and a desire to be of use in the world."[11] Others were not so sure. The Hartford paper wrote, "Somehow [this plea for anonymity] strikes one as weak and a suspicion arises as to this [author]. The political boss who, concealing his name, 'tells all he knows,' is pretty sure to tell a great deal more than he knows."[12] Similarly the Trenton news-paper suggested that "a lack of knowledge of the author offers doubt as to this authority."[13]

Generally, however, the press was enthralled. "Who wrote *Philip Dru?*" was the lead in the *Philadelphia Public Ledger*. "Men have endeavored to guess the author, but the fact that the latter makes no pretense to being a man of letters adds to the difficulty."[14] The *Los Angeles Times* wrote in February, that the "authorship of *Philip Dru* still remains a puzzle."[15] The *Cincinnati Inquirer* suggested, "Is the writer by any chance Bryan him-self"[16] but the *New York Times* retorted that the "style, with its slight rhetorical touch may well give rise to such a supposition but the schemes suggested for governmental benefit" do not.[17] The *Nashville Tennessean* proposed that "[a] strenuous person, brave and speechful, had a finger in the *Philip Dru: Administrator* pie," alluding to former president Theodore Roosevelt, the advocate of "the strenuous life," but to this suggestion the *Los Angeles Times* retorted that "if [Colonel Roosevelt] were trying his hand at fiction whatever its nature the world would not long have been left in doubt of it,"[18] and a Philadelphia paper concurred: "Surely the person-age referred to has not accustomed his public to anonymity, and to see in [Theodore Roosevelt] a retiring or timid author requires a flight of imagi-nation of which few will be found capable."[19]

Some papers hinted darkly at more sinister reasons for anonymity: "Even a casual survey of his pages will convince the reader that there are very good grounds for secrecy, for the plot hovers perilously near to revo-lutionary doctrines . . ."[20] All were curious: "If one wants to preach his po-litical creed through a novel, well and good. But *who is the author?*"[21] In March the *Los Angeles Times* could report that, according "to reliable sources, [*Philip Dru*] has been read by . . . the President and at least three members of his Cabinet" and that suggestions that Roosevelt or Bryan had written the book were incorrect; however, the *Times* went on, "it is un-likely that the writer's identity will be revealed."[22]

Few reviewers proposed that the book had much in the way of novelistic merit. "As a work of fiction the book is . . . stilted and often absurd,"[23] one wrote. Walter Lippmann concluded:

Now if the author is really a man of affairs, this is an extraordinarily interesting book. It shows how utterly juvenile a great man can be. If he is really an "insider" then we who are on the outside have very little to learn. If he is really an example of the far-seeing public man, then, in all sincerity, I say, God help this sunny land. The imagination is that of a romantic boy of 14 who dreams of what he would do if he had supreme power and nobody objected.[24]

The writing in *Philip Dru* is stilted, and its hero's expressions of chivalry do sound adolescent in parts. It is unlikely, however, that Lippmann had so little to learn from its author. For by the election of 1916 the following measures dreamt of by Dru had been adopted by the Congress and signed into law: the graduated income tax; a federal inheritance tax; the Federal Trade Commission; the Glass-Owen banking act; the parcel post; a maximum-working-hour law; a significant reduction in the tariff; the creation of a Federal Reserve Bank. If nothing else, the author had proved to be a political prophet. Lane, the secretary of the interior, wrote, "All that book has said should be comes about . . . The President comes to *Philip Dru* in the end."[25] One measure proposed by Philip Dru that had not been brought into being, and to which Lippmann may have most strongly objected, was the creation of a world federation of states bound to accept arbitration in lieu of force and subordinated to international rules based on "the Anglo-Saxon" rule of law.

Wilson believed, as Dru argued, that special interests had to be excluded from government because by their nature their point of view was selfish; that government must be ruled by a spirit of charity rather than the spirit of ruthless efficiency; and that the time had come when the State was responsible for reconciling the differences among classes, sexes, the economically, physically, or mentally strong and the weak, rather than exploiting those differences for the aggregated good of the State. Like House, Wilson had come of age in the defeated South and the two men shared a lack of faith in the discarded model of the state-nation that had collapsed. But Wilson was more like Dru in that he disdained political methods; in fact that was the principal reason he relied so heavily on House. House, ironically, had a large measure of the Selwyn in him—this made him valuable to Wilson—and this difference in attitude toward the world would ultimately be felt in the Versailles negotiations that ended their friendship and their political alliance. Dru could rule by decree. He did not need to court Congress or the interest groups that elected congressmen. Dru could conquer recalcitrant foreign countries; he did not need to parley with them. Above all, Dru did not need to compromise and thus had disdain for it. He sought a spiritual transformation of the society as the basis for a new politics. Compromise was certain to entrench the old ethos; only a constitutional metamorphosis could change it, and create a structure that would embody and reflect a new ethos.

But for our purposes, the most interesting aspect of *Philip Dru* is its international focus, and the extrapolation to the international arena of American domestic constitutional ideas of federalism and legitimacy derived from the consent of the governed.

The novel depicts a United States that, having conquered Mexico, allows it to develop its own constitutional institutions sheltered by an

American military and economic umbrella. All customs duties between
the two countries are abolished and Mexico retains her armed forces, flying the American flag alongside its own. Using this loose model, Mexico
then amalgamates with the states of Central America into one government,
though separate states are maintained.

Under Dru the United States absorbs Canada, undertakes with Great
Britain to protect the freedom of the seas, and negotiates a world federation committed to the maintenance of peace. Much of this is the standard
utopian fare of the early part of the twentieth century; what is more
intriguing about this dream-prophecy is its peculiar relation to the nation-
state. States are to assume, vis-à-vis the international order, a role similar
to that which the citizen plays in the domestic order. A constitution is
envisaged that will govern the society of states, as domestic constitutions
govern individual states. Each state is entitled to equality (in contrast to the
great-power hierarchies of the imperial state-nations) as each sits within a
kind of relaxed federalism, without "internal"—that is, international—tariffs or economic barriers. New states are encouraged to develop along their
own cultural lines by means of constitutional systems of popular representation and national self-determination.

In his illuminating and thoughtful book *On the Law of Nations,* former
senator Daniel Patrick Moynihan expresses the idea

> associated primarily with Woodrow Wilson . . . of a world ruled by law.
> It is probably fair to say that at the turn of the 20th century, most states-
> men in the West expected such a future for the World. It was part of the
> prevailing optimism of that time, closely associated with the confident
> expectation that liberal democracy—with its great emphasis on law as
> the arbiter of relations among citizens of equal rights—would become a
> near universal form of government.[26]

Philip Dru takes this expectation about the individual state and externalizes it to the society of states as a whole. When we speak of the New
World Order today, it is the World, not the Order, that is new. The collapse
of the Soviet empire and of European communism has made this a New
World. But the order, as Moynihan points out, is Woodrow Wilson's.

Or is it? For at some point Wilson had to be persuaded to abandon the
aloof, chaste isolationism with which he entered the White House and to
adopt the broad internationalism with which his name is associated in the
historical consciousness. We should remind ourselves that neither the tradition of the Democratic Party nor Wilson's background suggested any
interest in other than domestic matters. The Democratic platform of 1912
touched on foreign affairs only in a single reference to the Philippines,
and Wilson, in his first inaugural address, confined himself entirely to

questions of social and industrial domestic reform. Yet by 1917 Wilson had gone to Congress and stated:

> We have seen the last of neutrality. We are at the beginning of an age in which it will be insisted that the same standards of conduct and responsibility for wrongs done shall be observed among nations and their governments that are observed among individual citizens of civilized states.[27]

Wilson was not persuaded by a sentimental novel to abandon the convictions of a lifetime. What had happened? And what relation do those events have to do with the larger story of the development of a society of nation-states, a society within which a civil war was fought from 1914 to 1990?

After the hard winter of 1912–13, during which Colonel House devoted himself entirely to currency and banking reform and the achievement of the legislative measures described above, he went to Europe on his customary annual trip. He carried with him letters of introduction from the president authorizing House to mediate a dispute between the United States and Great Britain over the Panama Canal. According to the Hay-Paunceforte Treaty, all states were to pay equal fees for the use of the canal, but in a statute, the Panama Canal Act, Congress had directed that the United States be exempted from paying any tolls and this, according to U.S. law, superseded the treaty. Great Britain protested, but there was little the international community or the U.S. president could do.

At the same time, a rift had opened up between the United States and the United Kingdom over Mexican policy. The murder of the reformer-democrat Francisco Madero had horrified Wilson. Madero's successor, his enemy General Huerta, had not been recognized by Washington. London, on the other hand, was only too willing to settle for any end to the chaos that had plagued Mexico since the beginning of the revolution and believed that in Huerta they had a man "with whom we can do business." The end result of House's dialogue with Edward Grey, the British foreign secretary, was an agreement by the British to withdraw support for Huerta in exchange for American efforts to repeal the Panama Canal Act.[28] More important, House began a friendship with Grey that was to have historic consequences.

It had long been House's conviction that the Americans were uniquely suited to bringing about a period of détente, and even cooperation, between the British and the Germans. During a lunch with the German ambassador in Washington before House's departure for Europe, he had proposed that a sympathetic understanding between England, Germany, and the United States would be beneficial to all concerned. In his diary, House wrote that he told the German ambassador how

> together I thought they would be able to wield an influence for good throughout the world. They could ensure peace and the proper development of the waste places, besides maintaining an open door and equal opportunity to every one everywhere.[29]

House discussed this plan with the American ambassador to London during his summer visit to Europe in 1913. The basic scheme was to organize a system of arms reduction, followed by cooperative efforts to develop the hitherto undeveloped regions of the world,[30] diverting competitive energies into work for the benefit of both the developed and the undeveloped world. House waited, however, before presenting the plan to Grey.

Sir Edward Grey had become foreign secretary in 1905. His appointment was not in the Lansdowne-Salisbury tradition of great wealth and aesthetic or intellectual sophistication. Indeed he had been sent down from Oxford for idleness, spoke no German and little French, and during his first nine years as foreign minister did not once go abroad. Grey vastly preferred the company of the wildfowl on his country estate to that of diplomats and, possibly, to human interaction generally. His shyness, deep sense of honor, and lay evangelical background suggest comparison with Woodrow Wilson, and like Wilson, Grey also took an instant and deeply affectionate liking to Colonel House. Indeed Grey's biographer, G. M. Trevelyan, concluded that Grey's relations with House were his greatest personal contribution to the policy that won the war and founded the League of Nations.[31]

Grey's policy until the outbreak of war was founded on four principles: (1) to maintain the entente developed with Britain's two ancient enemies—by Lansdowne in 1904 with France, and by Grey himself in 1907 with Russia; (2) to ensure that neither of these friendly relationships, however, slipped into an alliance that would close the door to an amicable relationship with Germany; (3) to protect the relationship between the United States and the United Kingdom; and (4) to resurrect the Concert of Europe in order to guarantee European security against aggression in Europe. He pursued these objectives with courage and dexterity, but, as will be recalled from Book I, the pursuit of peace was doomed to fail. Germany, a protofascist nation-state, confronted France and Britain, two parliamentary state-nations, in a struggle to determine the grounds of legitimacy of the European state itself. There could be no Concert of Europe—the state-nation alliance of great powers—because Germany, a great power whose participation was crucial to any scheme of crisis management, was determined to destroy that Concert. Germany was too dynamic to intimidate, too ambitious to cooperate with. Inevitably, what began as an entente with France and Russia became an alliance once Germany determined on war through Belgium, whose territorial integrity was a British vital interest of long standing. German indifference to the creation of such an alliance against her is a measure of her determination to destroy the prevailing system; indeed, had Germany not attacked France through Belgium (in order to outflank French fortifications), it is unlikely that England would have intervened.

All this, however, was still to come when House contacted Grey's personal secretary in November 1913 to propose that House come to Europe on a mission of reconciliation. He hoped to achieve lower levels of armaments among the great powers in order to avert a potentially cataclysmic crisis. After wintering in Austin, House asked for Wilson's blessing for this mission and, receiving it, set out for Germany on May 16, 1914; he would be gone for two months.

On his arrival in Berlin, House was shocked and alarmed. "The situation is extraordinary," he wrote Wilson. "It is militarism run stark mad. Unless [we take the initiative] there is some day to be an awful cataclysm. No one in Europe can do it." After lengthy interviews with a hostile von Tirpitz, the architect of German naval growth, and a somewhat more sympathetic von Moltke—the nephew of the figure discussed in Book I— House was entertained by the kaiser. For over half an hour they spoke alone, with the Kaiser presenting a classic ethno-national, fascist argument: the Russians, as Slavs, and the French, as Latins, would never be suitable allies for the English. Only an English, American, and German alliance, based on their common Anglo-Saxon racial heritage, would withstand the challenges of the new century. German political strength, the kaiser said, lay in being always prepared for war at a second's notice.[32]

House correctly saw that Germany lived in an excited state of fear, something the other European powers, including Austria, neglected to appreciate. From Berlin, House went to Paris, where politics was paralyzed by a cabinet crisis and the shooting of an influential newspaper editor by the mistress of a disgraced minister. After a few fruitless days, House, who fully appreciated the impact of local politics on the ability of a government to focus its attention on international issues, simply retired to London. There he lunched with Grey and told him of his discussions with the kaiser. House proposed that Grey meet with the kaiser during a regatta at Kiel, but Grey demurred on the ground that the French and Russians would be alarmed. When House suggested that Germany be permitted to aid in the development of Persia, Grey replied that it might be a good move in order to play Germany against Russia. It is clear that, at this point at any rate, Grey and House are speaking on the basis of two completely different state "paradigms," Grey for the imperial state-nation and the balance of power on the one hand and House for the newly emerging nation-state and a scheme of collective security on the other. House later proposed a development bank funded by the United States, United Kingdom, France, and Germany to invest in underdeveloped areas of the globe, similar to the World Bank of our day. Grey expressed enthusiastic (if mercantile) interest, but explained that quick action would not be possible. The Irish question dominated the cabinet, Grey explained, and it would not turn its attention elsewhere for the time being. Indeed, when news came of the assassination of the Austrian archduke, no anxiety was expressed in London. Only on July 3 did Grey respond to House, telling him to let the kaiser know of the peaceable sentiments of the British in order to pursue negotiations along the lines suggested by House. On the 7th House wrote the kaiser, but by the time the note was delivered, Wilhelm II was at sea, from where he was recalled by the Austrian ultimatum to Serbia. Wilhelm later remarked that "the visit of Colonel House to Berlin and London in the spring of 1914 almost prevented World War I."[33] The most that can be made of this statement, however, is that House might have thrown off the timing[34] of the German general staff (as indeed the assassination did) had House been able to persuade the European powers that the new world of industrial warfare they were about to enter would mock their unrealistic ambitions. This was something, however, that even four years of horrific suffering could not do.

House sailed for Boston on July 21. As he was packing on the 20th a message arrived from Grey to the effect that the Serbian situation was now a source of grave concern. Despite this, and the fact that Mrs. Wilson was dying, House did not go to Washington but continued to the Massachusetts North Shore and waited to see Wilson until the latter came to New Hampshire after his wife's funeral. House's mission had been a failure owing to a lack of appreciation on all sides, including his own, of the nature of the conflict about to erupt. This failure to grasp the epochal nature of the conflict upon which the great powers were about to embark would persist throughout the next five deadly years and into the peace conference that followed. We can learn from House's vision, however, something of the world which we now inhabit at the end of that epochal war, when the conditions for that vision have finally been satisfied, even if, as will be seen, House's vision can no longer sustain the system it brought into being.

In November 1914, two months after the Battle of the Marne had claimed half a million casualties and blunted Germany's drive for a quick victory, House attempted to use the American continents as a model for the resolution of the European conflict. He presented a plan to Wilson by which

North and South American signatories were to (a) guarantee each other's territorial integrity and political independence under republican forms of governance; (b) commit to settling disputes peacefully through mediation; and (c) refrain from subversion or assistance to the enemies of any other signatory state. House was convinced that the outbreak of war in Europe had resulted "primarily from the lack of an organized system of international co-operation," which was perhaps true in a way: the competing constitutional paradigms of fascism, communism, and parliamentarianism could not coexist in a truly cooperative international security organization, as was later seen in both the League of Nations and the United Nations Security Council.

"It was my idea," House confided to his diary in December, "to formulate a plan, to be agreed upon by the republics of the two continents, which in itself would serve as a model for the European nations when peace is at last brought about."[35] House moved quickly, getting agreement in principle from the Argentine, Brazilian, and Chilean ambassadors to Washington. Already, however, he was making plans for an American mediation of the European war, and this forced him to turn over the Pan American negotiations to the State Department. This loss of momentum delayed the conference that was to produce the Pan American pact; without the pact in place, the United States lacked an international forum when Huerta's successor in Mexico was unable to prevent attacks on Texas by the Mexican partisan Pancho Villa. The U.S. intervention to capture Villa effectively killed the pact; no Latin American state could afford to be seen siding with the North Americans. In these circumstances the Chileans, who were least willing to join the U.S. initiative, pressed for further delays, and the American initiative came to nothing. The entire experience foreshadowed not only the substance of the American (as opposed to the European and especially the British) idea of a League of Nations, but also the essentially premature hopes of House and Wilson, dealing as they were with a new international order of states that had not yet resolved the issue of what, precisely, constituted a "republican" form of government, an international order that would always fall back on, and fall out because of, national rivalries and ambitions. The Pan American Pact thus sounded an overture for many of the discordant themes of the Versailles Treaty, to which House and Wilson were to some degree tone-deaf.

When Grey learned that House was proposing an American mediation of the European war on the basis of a system of mutual security guarantees, he cabled through the British ambassador to Washington:

[W]hile no peace negotiation could be undertaken before Germany's evacuation and restoration of Belgium and the humbling of Prussian militarism, a negotiated peace might be possible if the U.S. were prepared to join the European Great Powers in a mutual security system and to join in repressing by force whoever broke the treaty.[36]

Grey had long been familiar with the idea of a World League of Peace, which had been put forward in various manifestos, editorials, and monographs since the late nineteenth century. In March 1914 he had written that "fear will haunt our gates until we have organized an international system of security and order."[37] Such a system would commit the great powers to refrain from aggression, reduce armaments, and submit disputes to peaceful arbitration; if any power refused to abide by the results of the arbitral panel and chose to resort to violence instead, "the others would join forces against" that power. The Hague Conventions would be strengthened by providing that those becoming parties would bind themselves to uphold the conventions by force.[38]

Grey had in mind an extension, in the twentieth century, of the Congress system initiated by Castlereagh in the early nineteenth century. This system was managed by the great powers, dealt almost exclusively with security issues, and did not differentiate—despite Metternich's earnest efforts to the contrary—among states according to their internal forms of governance. House, by contrast, sought a system that embraced specifically "republican" states on the basis of equality, in which the great powers played a cooperative rather than balancing role. He thought that the most powerful states would realize that their interests were best served by maintaining the system as a whole, even when, on particular issues, that system gave preference to smaller and weaker states that could have been easily overborne by any of the powers acting alone. Thus House's vision more nearly accorded with the constitutional order of the nation-state, which was replacing that of the imperial state-nation and whose legitimacy was based on each state's embodying the principle of service to the nation it was supposed, by the self-determination of its people, to reflect. Neither sort of league could in fact have halted the Long War in its midst: a great power like Germany or Britain (or Russia) saw no reason to acquiesce in the constraint of its sovereignty; and there was as yet no consensus on what precisely constituted the "self-determination" of a nation in choosing its State.

On January 30, 1915, Colonel House sailed for Europe on the *Lusitania* with an offer to mediate the conflict. Two days before, an American merchant ship carrying wheat to England had been torpedoed by a German submarine, the first such attack against American commercial shipping. On February 4, Germany declared the waters around the British Isles a war zone, threatening all shipping that approached Britain.

At this time, both Germany and Britain menaced American shipping. The British, having control of the seas, were able to stop American ships and board them unlawfully, directing them to British ports if they were thought to contain "contraband," which included a wide range of nonlethal materials, including foodstuffs. Britain recognized that she could, over the long run, bring famine to Central Europe if she could blockade the ports to which the Germans had access. At the same time, Germany realized that her chief superiority lay in munitions. As a result, the Germans resorted to submarine attacks on all vessels bound for Britain that were thought to be transporting weapons and ammunition bound for the Allies. House's ostensible mission was to work out rules governing the compensation due to American merchants for British seizures. Actually he had been in negotiations for some months with the German and British ambassadors over American mediation of the war. The American proposal was to be based on the evacuation of Belgium by the Germans and a payment of reparations to that state; the French occupation of Lorraine, taken from France by Germany in 1870; and some guarantees against further aggression.

It is certainly open to question whether any of the European powers involved entered these talks in good faith. The Germans were anxious to separate Britain from France and Russia and doubtless hoped that effectively trilateral talks among the United States, the United Kingdom, and Germany would cause disquiet and even friction within the Allied group. The British were equally anxious to string the Americans along, presenting themselves as the most reasonable of the belligerents, shaping proposals they knew the Germans could not afford to accept, hoping to entangle the Americans into nonneutral cooperation or, better, belligerency.

Grey seems to have been largely free of this: his proposals for a League of Peace served both as an instrument for forging an Anglo-American entente as well as a sincere lever to encourage U.S. mediation. Upon House's arrival in London, Grey again questioned the American about the possibility of U.S. participation in a "general guaranty for world wide peace."

House was in London for a month and a half. He grew ever closer to Grey, writing in a memorandum in February, "If every belligerent nation had a Sir Edward Grey at the head of its affairs, there would be no war . . ."[39] But Grey did not think that House should go on to Berlin. German armies were at that hour attempting a vast envelopment against the Russians. Until the outcome of this maneuver was known, the Germans would not think seriously about peace. At the same time the American ambassador in Berlin was urging House to put forward new peace proposals. A German indemnity was out of the question, he wrote, and the German undersecretary for foreign affairs soon wrote to say that acceptance of American terms would mean the overthrow of the kaiser and the government.[40] Nevertheless, House pressed on, first to Paris then to Berlin.

In both capitals he found leaderships committed to wringing substantial territorial concessions from their enemies while insisting that peace guarantees were their ultimate objects. This was not necessarily as disingenuous as it may seem today. In both France and Germany domestic constitutional conflicts between Left and Right gave the state a constant sense of peril. It is altogether possible that sincere statesmen believed that success, the likelihood of which is usually overestimated by persons working to attain it, was the only alternative to a general settlement that no one—at least no one outside the United States—could envision. Indeed, these statesmen were entirely correct in this assessment, as the course of the Long War establishes. Only when the war aim of establishing a single legitimate form of the constitutional order was achieved—an aim that had to be a *war* aim because it could not be gained by negotiation as it implied the delegitimation of some of the negotiating states—could the crisis be finally resolved.

House returned on June 13 after the ruthless sinking of the *Lusitania* by a German submarine on May 7. From this point on, he seems to have regarded American involvement in the war as inevitable, and his various peace moves all began to take on a double-edged character, on the one side asserting a more dominant role vis-à-vis prospective allies regarding peace terms, and on the other maneuvering the German government into a position of contempt before the American public. On May 9 House had sent Wilson a cable, which the president read to his cabinet:

> It is now certain that a large number of American lives were lost [in the sinking] . . . America has come to a parting of the ways, when she must determine whether she stands for civilized . . . warfare. We can no longer remain neutral spectators. Our action in this crisis will determine the part we will play when peace is made, and how far we may influence a settlement for the lasting good of humanity.[41]

One cannot understand American policy in this period without appreciating that the deliberate determination to have a role in the design of the peace underlay every American decision. At this juncture, Wilson faced two alternatives: he could break relations with Germany on the ground that the submarine attack on an undefended ocean liner was a violation of international law and a crime against civilization itself; or he could demand an official disavowal and an assurance that such attacks would not be repeated. He chose the second course and on May 13 dispatched a diplomatic note to that effect. Wilson, as perhaps House of all most keenly appreciated, faced an uncomprehending public that would not support intervention, whatever view elite opinion might hold. Thus for the next two years House would search for peace proposals that, though they might conceivably end submarine warfare, probably had their greatest utility in uniting American opinion against the perpetrators of that warfare. While still in London, he had proposed a plan to the British cabinet by which the United Kingdom would lift its blockade if Germany abandoned submarine attacks; he suggested that it would be even better for Great Britain to propose such an initiative, putting Germany in the wrong in the eyes of the American public. The British demurred, and before the cabinet acted, the Germans replied with a refusal to consider the American proposal. House wrote that the Germans were absolutely convinced the United States would not enter the war under any circumstances and that this in his view would, ironically, ensure that an American intervention did ultimately happen. He now determined to return to America to work for that goal.

Bryan saw clearly where Wilson's policy was leading. The diplomatic note of May 13, though too timid for Theodore Roosevelt, who ridiculed it, was too aggressive for the pacifist Bryan, and he immediately resigned as secretary of state. Upon disembarkation in the United States, House was surrounded by reporters at the New York dock wanting to know if he would succeed Bryan. House took the occasion to publicly reject any possibility that he would serve as secretary of state; he rebuffed Wilson's proposal that he come to Washington, and instead retreated to Long Island, and then to the North Shore, where the President came to him on June 24.

On July 25 the American merchant ship *Leelanaw,* carrying flax, was sunk off the coast of Scotland by a German submarine. On August 13, the British passenger ship *Arabic* was sunk with Americans aboard. Wilson asked House's advice, and the latter proposed breaking off diplomatic relations with the Germans. Wilson, however, still hoped to avoid war, and before any more forceful American action was taken, Germany announced it was suspending operations against passenger liners. This was generally viewed in the United States as a triumph for Wilson and for moderation, but House knew the German policy could not hold for long. The submarine was Germany's only effective vessel to interdict the Atlantic sea lanes that her enemies controlled because the German fleet was bottled up in German ports and, except for the Battle of Jutland, played no important role in the war. While international law required belligerent ships to identify themselves in order to search neutral shipping, the lightly armored submarine was too vulnerable on the surface to risk this. Even the pledge to avoid passenger ships would have to be eventually sacrificed if the British stranglehold on German imports of foodstuffs was to be broken.

In the autumn, House came up with a new plan. The United States would propose a peace conference and fair terms for all participants. If any belligerent refused to attend, the United States would commit itself to joining that state's adversaries. It was a bold, if somewhat Machiavellian, maneuver. House moved carefully. First he wrote to Grey trying to flush out British peace terms. On September 22, 1915, Grey replied to House's inquiry whether a proposal to return to the status quo ante, followed by a broad reduction in armaments, would be welcome to the British government. Grey reported that "neither side is ready for such a proposal." But before Grey's reply could reach House, House appended to another letter this note: "Please do not take too seriously the suggestion I made in my last letter in regard to peace. It was merely to let you know the President holds himself in readiness at any time to do what is thought best. As far as I can see, and from all that I can hear from Germany, it is utterly hopeless to think in that direction now."[42]

But once House received Grey's reply, which can only be read as discouraging, he re-entered the game. Grey had added to his letter a long section devoted to postwar policy and this gave House the opening he sought. Grey asked: "Would the President propose that there should be a League of Nations binding themselves to side against any Power which broke a treaty; which broke certain rules of warfare on sea or land . . . or which refused, in case of dispute, to adopt some other method of settlement than that of war?"[43]

Now House wrote:

> It has occurred to me that the time may soon come when this Government should intervene between the belligerents and demand that peace parleys begin upon the broad basis of the elimination of militarism and navalism. . . . It is in my mind that after conferring with your Government I should proceed to Berlin and tell them that it was the President's purpose to intervene and stop this destructive war, provided the weight of the United States thrown on the side that accepted our proposal could do it. I would not let Berlin know, of course, of any understanding had with the Allies, but would rather lead them to think our proposal would be rejected by the Allies. This might induce Berlin to adopt the proposal, but if they did not do so, it would nevertheless be the purpose to intervene. If the Central Powers were still obdurate, it would probably be necessary for us to join the allies and force the issue.[44]

Grey replied: "What is the proposal of the elimination of militarism and navalism you contemplate? Is it that suggested in [my last letter, i.e., the League of Nations]?" and House replied, "Yes." Beneath House's copy of this note there is written in his hand, "Submitted for W's approval. Approved Nov. 11."

Now Grey faltered. Pointing out that the French and the Russians planned winter offensives in which they had great confidence, the British foreign secretary wrote, "[T]he situation at the moment and the feelings here and among the Allies, and in Germany so far as I know, do not justify me in urging you to come on the ground that your presence would have any practical result at the moment."

House was dejected. It seemed as if Grey did not appreciate what Britain was being offered—"the British," House commented at this juncture, "are in many ways dull."[45] In fact, Grey saw all too clearly what was involved. For the Allies, the American goal was a war aim scarcely worthy of the name. If the Allies committed to it they would have to abandon goals that they cherished and for which millions had died. But for the Americans, a League of Nations that would end war against the democracies and outlaw war in the future was a goal worth fighting for. If the United States did not take part in the war, however, she would not be able to direct the peace. What was for Grey merely a supplementary plan that might protect postwar British interests had become, for House and Wilson, the only justifiable reason to act.

House sailed for England on December 28. His mission has been variously misconstrued by those historians who cannot quite take seriously the uniqueness of House's and Wilson's war aims. "At best his behavior in these talks could be described as duplicitous; at worst he was dishonest in his dealings with both the British and Wilson. While House was reporting to the president that the allies were sincerely interested in mediation, he was presenting his plan to the British as little more than a pretext for entering the war against Germany."[46] Such criticism ignores Wilson's objective: whether by mediation on the basis of American terms, or by American participation in the war and thus also in the postwar settlement, Wilson sought to bring into being a system of enforceable law to prevent future conflicts. Mediation—now or later—was the American war aim. With *this* goal in mind, House's mission was rather cleverly but hardly duplicitously devised. It failed because neither the Allies nor the Central Powers wanted an evenhanded peace nor believed they, at that point, had to accept one.

After two weeks in England, House proceeded to Berlin and then to Paris for discussions; he then returned to London, where he and Grey initialed a memorandum two weeks later. This document, however, was never approved by the cabinet nor circulated to what doubtless would have been horrified allies. The belligerents saw what the Americans had in mind; they were in no mood to have purchased what were essentially American war goals, with the suffering of their populations and the deaths of their soldiers. House returned to the States.

In late March the British liner *Sussex* was torpedoed with twenty-five Americans aboard.[47] Throughout this period House was far more "hawkish" than Wilson, and more sensitive to the criticisms of former president Roosevelt. After the sinking of the *Sussex,* House rushed to Washington in order to prevent Wilson from sending a diplomatic note to the Germans that might have appeared insufficiently firm. On March 30 he spent a long afternoon meeting alone with the president, with the result that when Wilson emerged he threatened to break off diplomatic relations with Germany if submarine warfare continued. In the ensuing weeks, House undertook negotiations with the German ambassador, resulting in the May 4 "*Sussex* Pledge" by Germany that henceforth she would not use submarines in contravention of international law.

This success, though only temporary, as House expected, emboldened Wilson to try to resurrect the House-Grey Memorandum. The 1916 elections were approaching and Wilson was eager to bring peace to Europe lest the United States be drawn into war on terms, and for goals, that were unacceptable to the American public. The British were again cool to the Memorandum. The United States and the United Kingdom simply understood the war in different terms. For the United States, the world war was to be fought for the future of democracy. Not only would this ensure that wars did not occur—because the democracies would resort to nonviolent methods of resolving disputes—but this also meant that nation-states would derive their legitimacy from the consent of the national peoples they represented, which Wilson believed would result in a change in attitude toward war itself. Nor was Wilson naïve to believe this: when one recalls nineteenth century state-nation attitudes toward war—attitudes that exalted war, as was so passionately and eloquently done by Oliver Wendell Holmes, Jr., among others[48]—it is striking how much views have changed in the nation-state democracies.

For the United Kingdom and for France, both states in the midst of the transition from imperial state-nation to mass nation-state, the point of the Great War was rather different. For Premier Clemenceau, it was simply to prepare for the next war: that is, so long as there was a Germany, there would be a Franco-German conflict, and the point of the current conflict was to give the French the best position possible in the next one. For the British cabinet, the point of the war was to prevent a single continental power from dominating Europe, a war aim shared over the centuries with Pitt and Marlborough and Elizabeth's counselors. Both states—indeed, all European parties to the conflict, whether they were unreconstructed state-nations like Russia or the fascist nation-state of Germany—had war aims that sought to enhance each state's freedom of action and avoid any externally imposed constraint on that freedom. None of the European states conceived the goal of the war as achieving statehood for all national peoples, and some, like Russia and Austria, may have greatly feared this.

After refusing to become chairman of the Democratic National Committee, House put forward a strategy for the Wilson campaign that proved successful. In every political campaign in the United States of any complexity, there is always a decision to determine whether to concentrate on getting out the votes you are certain to get or whether to go after marginal "swing" votes (in the wooing of which you may alienate the loyalists). What made House's strategy for Wilson successful was his embedding this question in the idiosyncrasies of that unique American institution, the electoral college. House urged Wilson to concentrate his resources on swing districts of no more than a hundred thousand voters in those states that could likely go for either candidate—the marginal districts in the marginal states. Because the result in the electoral college is calculated by state and is indifferent to the magnitude of a winner's popular vote in any particular state, a narrow win in a large state is more helpful than a landslide in a smaller state. Wilson had been elected by a minority of the voters in 1912; if the Republicans could hold their own loyalists and pick up the Republican Progressives who had voted for Roosevelt, then Wilson would be resoundingly defeated. On the other hand, if Roosevelt were not in the race, Wilson could have a free run for the Progressive vote, attacking the Republican nominee on those issues that had made him acceptable to the Republican party where Theodore Roosevelt was not, while using the war issue to drive Progressives away from the Republican party. Thus Wilson would partly stress the progressive legislation he had sponsored and signed into law, and partly he would associate Roosevelt's call for American intervention with the Republicans. If the Republican nominee disassociated himself from Roosevelt, then Wilson would be the beneficiary of one group of progressives; if, on the other hand, he endorsed intervention in an effort to propitiate TR's supporters, then Wilson would gain Western Progressives who, in contrast to those from the East, were solidly for peace.

House's strategy exploited this narrow seam in Republican solidarity. To do this successfully, however, required four conditions: (1) Roosevelt must not be nominated; (2) House must be able to tell, with accuracy, how votes in the Progressive camp were shifting and where, so that Wilson could move to capitalize on these shifts; (3) the Democrats must hold the conservative, non-Progressive South; (4) the Republican nominee must not be allowed to move left, in a Progressive direction.

When Supreme Court Justice Charles Evans Hughes was nominated by the Republicans, the first of these conditions was satisfied; Hughes's campaign satisfied the fourth. As a compromise candidate between the Republican old guard and the Progressives, Hughes was entirely unwilling to take positions that threatened to alienate either wing. He thus became a kind of stationary target for Wilson, who ridiculed Hughes's unwillingness to endorse progressive legislation passed during the Wilson administration. Wilson was careful not to alienate the South, but these votes, as

House knew, had nowhere else to go, because the Republicans were so deeply identified with Reconstruction.

Everything then came down to House's strategy to organize districts of no more than one hundred thousand voters in those swing constituencies of the most important states. He thought that there were

> twelve states that were debatable, and upon whose votes the election would turn. He divided each of these states into ["the smallest possible units that could be arranged with available campaign funds"[49]] and began by eliminating all states he knew the opposition party would certainly carry . . . He also ignored the states where his side was sure to win. In this way he was free to give his entire thoughts to [a very few districts]. Of [a unit of] five thousand, he roughly calculated there would be two thousand voters that no kind of persuasion could turn from the national party and two thousand that could not be changed from the opposition. This would leave one thousand doubtful ones to win over. So he had a careful poll made in each unit, and eliminated the strictly unpersuadable party men, and got down to a complete analysis of the debatable one thousand. Information was obtained as to their race, religion, occupation, and former political predilection.[50]

This allowed House to track the reactions among swing voters and tailor Wilson's speeches and literature accordingly. By concentrating on so few districts, the campaign was able to field an intensive organizational effort. "We must run the President," House told Daniel C. Roper, the man in charge of organization, "for justice of the peace, and not for president; we need not consider the disposition of sixteen or seventeen million voters, but the disposition of the voters in individual precincts."[51]

House gave to the president a list of favorable states that House regarded as certain. This would give Wilson 230 of the 266 electoral votes needed to be elected. Thirty-six more had to be found. Never before had a president been elected without Connecticut, New York, New Jersey, Indiana, or Illinois,[52] but House's list proved accurate. Wilson narrowly won (277 to 254 for Hughes), the final tallies coming in the last hours with California's thirteen electoral votes. Wilson was the first Democratic president since Jackson to win a second consecutive term. Although today House's strategy might seem entirely routine given the techniques of snapshot polling and telephone banks, at the time it was considered highly risky and perhaps would not have been tried had Hughes not seemed so far ahead and so likely to win.

The election now over, Wilson and House turned their attention again to foreign affairs. Wilson had campaigned on a slogan, "He Kept Us Out of

War," though in truth he had been preparing for intervention for some months, should that ultimately become his chosen course. This did not trouble the pragmatic Colonel. Though acknowledging that he

> had himself advocated a plan which under certain conditions would have brought the country into the war, [s]ince the attitude of the Allies had prevented the execution of the plan, it would have been rather Quixotic to have disregarded the political advantages resulting from the Allies' refusal.[53]

A stronger case can be made that House's and Wilson's war aims were not entirely the same as Theodore Roosevelt's, who wished to enter the war unequivocally in support of the allies.*

In retrospect, the obvious question that the House-Wilson war policy raises is: for what? For what did the Americans need to send 1.5 million infantrymen into battle? Surely not for the technical violations of American neutrality; American-flagged ships were in fact being used to resupply and arm a belligerent, just as the Germans claimed. When the United States finally went to war, its disregard of the rights of neutral nations was as great as that previously exhibited by the Allies, to whom the United States was constantly protesting. The Germans could hardly be blamed for halting shipping in the only way the British Royal Navy permitted them, while the Royal Navy itself stopped U.S. ships illegally and simply seized them by virtue of its command of the ocean surface. Was it for the sinking of U.S. ships by German submarines, then, that the United States went to war? Surely the remedy for this, as for the attacks by terrorist states on American civilians, is retorsion. It can hardly be proportionate, or even rational, to decide that the death of innocent Americans requires a world war for just retaliation.

America went to war in 1917 in order to create a system of nation-states whose legitimacy would be based on democracy and self-determination. Within this system all states were to be legally equal, because Wilson and House believed that such a system would prevent future wars against the

---

*A similar election campaign occurred in 1964 when the incumbent, President Lyndon Johnson, ran against the Republican senator Barry Goldwater. Critics of the American intervention in Viet Nam have often claimed that they were misled by Johnson's claims to have kept America out of deeper involvement in Asia when he was, at the time of the election, already contemplating more extensive U.S. troop deployments there. Like so much else regarding Johnson's presidency, these criticisms have more to do with the pathology of the period than with Johnson's motives. No one can deny that Goldwater's war aims and tactics (including the use of nuclear weapons) were considerably more interventionist than Johnson's; nor that a responsible president must often prepare for war if he is to pursue peace. Wilson and Johnson each thought he could lead a nation into war by showing restraint, demonstrating that neither man desired war (which was in fact true). See Michael Beschloss, *Taking Charge: The Johnson White House Tapes 1963–1964* (Simon & Schuster, 1997). Once American troops were committed to combat, Wilson succeeded in uniting the country, as did Johnson for about the same period of time—and for no longer.

democracies. This system would reflect American conceptions of the relationship between nation and state and for that reason it could call upon an American commitment to intervene if necessary to protect the system. The establishment of the League of Nations came to be America's principal war aim because it gave an institutional structure to these ideas. A world order based on a German victory would not be one that was ultimately safe for the American democracy, but neither would an Allied victory that merely reinstated in Europe the state system that had collapsed in the first place. As Lord Devlin, a Wilson biographer, shrewdly observed, "Indeed [Wilson] never lost his distrust of Allied motives . . . The Allies did not, he believed, genuinely care about democracy and the right to self-government."[54]

And of course Wilson was right: the Allies, like the Central Powers they opposed, shared a European conception of sovereignty that held the State's authority to have come by descent from its predecessors, and not to arise directly from its people. Even democratic states like Britain and France held sovereignty to be distinct from elections; sovereignty was an attribute of the State. European states were not limited sovereigns. Because their peoples had wholly delegated their sovereignty to the State the nation could scarcely demand the creation of a new state by withholding sovereignty from that power that ruled them. Yet this was the reason America entered the Long War: to allow the democratic form to fulfill its role in creating the proper relation between a State and its nation. These are Wilson's words when he announced he was taking the United States to war:

> But the right is more precious than peace, and we shall fight for the things which we have carried nearest to our hearts—for democracy, for the right of those who submit to authority to have a voice in their own governments, for the rights and liberties of small nations, for a universal dominion of right by such a concert of free people as shall bring peace and safety to all nations and make the world itself at last free. . . . [T]he day has come when America is privileged to spend her blood and her might for the principles that gave her birth and happiness and the peace which she has treasured.[55]

This is Professor Wilson the constitutional scholar as well as President Wilson the statesman, for he was well aware that "the principles that gave [America] her birth and happiness" were the principles of the Declaration of Independence, that is, the assertion of limited state sovereignty, and not the constitutional structure of the mass democracy of the nation-state, which had had to wait almost a century to come into being. What Wilson sought required a world of law because his vision was universal, and because it rested on legal institutions that would enforce certain grounds of legitimacy (democracy) and justification (limited sovereignty). Yet even these conditions, though necessary, were not enough. If states stood toward one another under law in the same relation that individuals stood toward each other in society, they—like individuals—would still be animated by the same drives that had brought them to war in the first place. It was necessary that the state system generate a spiritual change in its composition. As Devlin noted, "It was almost, but not quite, as if he were trying to bring Christianity into public life."[56]

Wilson seems to have believed, with House, that truly democratic institutions that actually reflected the will of the people and made commensurate demands on their attention and contributions would yield just such a spiritual change in mankind. Certainly House did not believe that, absent such a transformation, these institutions could possibly prevail against the self-interests of the State and the powerful sectors that endowed the State, interests that sometimes led to war.

From 1916 on it began to be suggested that House was the author of *Philip Dru*.[57] One newspaper learned that House had given an autographed copy of the novel to Culberson.

> [O]fficial Washington is startled from its customary aplomb to find that the sphinx of Texas has treated it to a voluble discourse. Col. E. M. House, maker of governors and a President, the popularly accredited power behind the throne of the present Administration, the western Warwick, the silent Man of Mystery—and now *Philip Dru: Administrator*.

Most of the initial reaction tended to identify House with Dru: the newspaper that broke the news wrote, "Even the description of Dru in the novel is a description of House."

But it was not so simple. The 1916 election campaign had uncannily followed the prescriptions not of Dru, who ruled by decree, but of Selwyn, the corrupt political boss.[58] The entire organization of the campaign—the concentration on marginal states, the intense precinct focus on swing voters, the frequent polling and issue tracking—all were lifted from Selwyn's rules. Most important for our study, however, is Dru's exchange with his fiancée's wealthy and conservative father about the impossibility of the State actually serving the interests of the mass of its people by redistributing wealth. The father says:

> If we had pure socialism, we could never get the highest endeavor out of anyone, for it would seem not worth while to do more than the average. The race would then go backward instead of lifting itself higher by

the insistent desire to excel and to reap the rich reward that comes with success,

[to which Dru replies:] In the past . . . your contention would be unanswerable, but the moral tone and thought of the world is changing. You take it for granted that man must have in sight some material reward in order to achieve the best there is within him. I believe that mankind is awakening to the fact that material compensation is far less to be desired than spiritual compensation. This feeling will grow, and when it comes to full fruition, the world will find but little difficulty in attaining a certain measure of altruism. I agree with you that this much-to-be desired state of society cannot be altogether reached by laws, however drastic.[59]

House believed, like Hitler and Lenin, that his favored form of the nation-state would produce a spiritually renewed man, and a new society. For House, however, this would come about not through the creation and application of laws but in the private world outside law. House's new man grows from the earth of private life, not the concrete and steel of public life. That is what made House's vision uniquely American, marrying the American division between public and private, and its limitation of state sovereignty, to the parliamentary ideal of the nation-state. That is why Wilson's (and House's) League of Nations had to be a league of self-determination, of democracies, indeed, finally, of American democracies. *This* goal brought the United States into the world war.

House had persuaded Wilson that submarine warfare would inevitably draw the United States into the conflict and therefore the President now sought to press once more for mediation. Wilson wanted to begin by asking both sides to state their war aims, but House thought it was too late to act as an impartial broker; in the event, both the Allies and the Central Powers refused to state terms for mediation, probably on the grounds that if realistic terms were disclosed, the disclosure would endanger their war efforts. Wilson's proposal died stillborn.

On January 22 in a speech to Congress, Wilson called for a league of peace to enforce the peaceable resolution of state disputes, and he once again asked for the belligerent powers to state their terms. Then on January 31 the Germans did so, coupling their terms—which were expansive and provocative—with the announcement of the resumption of unrestricted submarine warfare. House went to Washington, and shortly thereafter, diplomatic relations with Germany were broken. Even now, however, Wilson did not agree with House that war was unavoidable, and left the next step to the Germans. Despite asking Congress for the power to arm merchant seamen on February 26, Wilson still maintained that no "overt act" had yet been committed. Actually that very day a German U-boat sank the liner *Laconia* without warning; twelve died, including two American women. Of even greater impact on the public was the sensational publication of an intercepted telegram between the German foreign office and the German minister in Mexico City instructing the latter, in case of war with the United States, to attempt to negotiate a Mexican-German alliance with the promise that Mexico would be assisted in the reconquest of New Mexico, Texas, and Arizona. On March 14, the American steamer *Algonquin* was sunk, again without warning. The next week, on March 19, three American ships were sunk within twenty-four hours by German submarines. Finally, on April 2, Wilson went before Congress, declaring that a state of war existed between Germany and the United States, though he was careful to discriminate between the hostile German state and its people. Wilson had written the pope, implying that the German regime was illegitimate and did not really represent its nation:

> The object of war is to deliver the fine peoples of the world from the menace and the actual power of a vast military establishment controlled by an irresponsible government. This power is not the German people but the masters of the German people.[60]

In October House sailed for Europe as head of the American mission and the U.S. representative on the inter-allied war committee. In August, he proposed to Wilson, and Wilson approved, the setting up of "The Inquiry," which would prepare for the peace settlement. The United States had gone to war not because she was attacked but to pursue specific international, political goals at the peace settlement. Now House had to prepare to achieve these goals, which were far more complex and difficult than the mere defeat of the German forces.

American war aims were outlined in the famous "Fourteen Points" first privately formulated by House and Wilson in early January of 1917. Throughout that year the two men worked to refine a settlement proposal embodying this model for internationalism, integrating the micro and the macro aspects, as it were, of a new world order. Now House and Wilson no longer had to attempt to persuade the warring states of Europe to accept American mediation. Rather they would use U.S. intervention in the war to pre-empt the allied states of their war aims, making agreement the price of alliance, while offering to Germany a more attractive settlement option than Britain and France would be willing to give. In the past House had played this two-track strategy: proffering American assistance to the Allies if they would back American war aims while enticing Germany to mediation with the threat of American intervention. This strategy had not worked. Neither side was willing to give up its national ambitions for the mere possibility of American intervention, which, in any event, might not prove decisive.

Now House had made this strategy more potent. By actually entering the conflict, the United States could replace its passive mediation objectives with war aims enforced by the American army. In order to do this, as Walter Lippmann later observed, House persuaded Wilson that by thus joining the war the United States could prevent future wars. He supplied Wilson "with the rationalizations by means of which Wilson was able to bow to a destiny that was overbearing him, and even ultimately to sow the seed of a triumph that may make him immortal."[61]

Lippmann was a member of The Inquiry, the secret project set up by House in the autumn of 1917 to collect the data that would provide the factual and analytical basis for an American-directed settlement. House chose his own brother-in-law Mezes, now president of the City College of New York, as the project's director. Although Judge Learned Hand, John Dewey, and Felix Frankfurter, among others, attempted to join the group once its existence became known—Hand asked whether he might leave the bench in order to work on the staff—appointments were tightly held, even as the group grew to 126 geographers, historians, economists, scientists, and lawyers. This group sought to determine what the map of Europe would look like based on American constitutional ideas of self-determination, and political objectives like a nonpunitive peace and an evenhanded system of free trade. No foreign ministry among the Allies—indeed, in the world—had prepared such briefs. In a letter to the secretary of war, Lippmann wrote that the American war effort was "the largest assembly of force for an entirely disinterested purpose ever known to history. The weapon is drawn by men who cannot worship it."[62] "We are fighting," he wrote House, "not so much to beat an enemy as to make the world safe for democracy."[63]

Secretary of State Robert Lansing and Secretary of War Newton Baker were entirely bypassed by Wilson, who made House his sole collaborator in the original drafting of the Fourteen Points.

"Saturday was a remarkable day," House wrote in his diary.

> I returned to the White House at a quarter past ten in order to get to work with the President. He was waiting for me. We got down to work and finished re-making the map of the world, as we would have it, at half-past twelve o'clock. We took it systematically, first outlining general terms, such as open diplomacy, freedom of the seas, removing of economic barriers, establishment of equality of trade conditions, guarantees for the reduction of national armaments, [a] general association of nations for the conservation of peace; (and of course) genuine self-government on democratic principles [for the various nationalities].[64]

House saw clearly that a great divide had opened up between the state-nations whose empires ruled the world before the war and the nation-states whose destinies were asserting themselves. He and Wilson also saw that parliamentary democracy was only one competing candidate for the constitutional order that the nation-state would come to embody. The Fourteen Points, which some historians have ranked with the Emancipation Proclamation in importance, proposed a world order of parliamentary nation-states that was significantly at variance with the order of state-nations but that also excluded fascist and communist nation-states.

Their vision was that of a universal constitution—the original draft of the Covenant of the League of Nations used the word *constitution*. This constitution rested on a universal common law and various explicit enforcement mechanisms. It simply replicated, at the supranational level, the processes of law making and law enforcement that Americans are accustomed to at the federal level. There was to be a body of legal rules that governed all states equally, regardless of their rank, and all nations, regardless of their power; there was to be a judicial institution of universal jurisdiction that applied these rules to controversies, and another institution of states that enforced these rules by sanctions, including violence if necessary. States were to be held, as Wilson ceaselessly put it, to the same processes as individual citizens had been.

Unless the uniquely *American* constitutional basis for this world constitution is appreciated, one cannot fully appreciate the intractable differences between the United States and her allies at the peace conference, and the difficulties faced by ratification of the Treaty that emerged from that conference once it went to the U.S. Senate. The customary criticisms of Wilson during this decisive period are that he failed to fight at Versailles for his ideals or was simply outwitted by Lloyd George and Clemenceau; and that he further ruined the chances for a stable peace by refusing to compromise with the Senate on various reservations to the treaty, thus keeping the United States out of the League of Nations and opening the door to the Second World War through a weakening of deterrence against Germany. These conclusions are partly based, however, on misunderstandings of Wilson's policy and the constitutional and strategic world within which it had to operate. Though widely held, these misunderstandings treat the political conflicts at Versailles and later in Washington as if they occurred in a constitutional vacuum, rather than in an environment structured by the Long War and a society of states with competing ideas of sovereignty.

The Fourteen Points were first presented to the Congress in an address by Wilson in January 1918. They can be reduced to the following six policies, each derived from some aspect of the U.S. Constitution: (1) open treaties, "openly arrived at"—a requirement that is absurdly quixotic unless one is committed by law to the American constitutional scheme of limited government and unalienable popular sovereignty, as a consequence of which no treaty that is secret from the People can be legally binding because treaty making requires the consent of the sovereign; (2) "absolute" freedom of the seas, such that in wartime neutral states could not be restricted in their commerce with belligerents beyond those customary rules of international law governing legitimate blockades, e.g., rules against contraband (weapons, munitions, and the like) and those rules protecting the civilians of neutral states against violence on the high seas; these rules have their parallel in the neglected original intent of the declaration of war clause in the U.S. Constitution;* (3) the removal of economic barriers among states—parallel to the abolition of internal tariffs that is found in Article IV of the American constitution; (4) arms reductions to the lowest point consistent with domestic safety—a qualification on sovereignty that is entirely inconsistent with the European idea of inalienable state sovereignty; (5) the impartial adjustment of colonial claims, according a weight to the interests of the national peoples concerned equal to whatever claims of title were to be asserted by the states who governed those people—an application of the idea that runs through the remaining nine points of the declaration that legitimate states are based on the self-determination of the peoples for whose benefit the state is constituted (parallel to the tenth and fourteenth amendments to the U.S. Constitution); thus the Fourteen Points specifically endorsed the creation of a Polish state, the independence of the Baltic states, and the readjustment of the frontiers of Italy "along clearly recognizable lines of nationality"; the people of Austria-Hungary were to be given "the freest opportunity of autonomous development."[65] And finally (6), in Point Fourteen, the creation of "a general association of nations [that] must be formed under specific covenants for the purpose of affording mutual guarantees of political independence and territorial integrity to great and small states alike"—the League of Nations, which in its structure replicates the federal and branch structures of the U.S. Constitution.

There is scarcely one of these war aims that was not as threatening to the Allies as to the Germans. If "open covenants" were to be an objective of Allied governments, what of the secret agreements they themselves had made among one another for a postwar division of the spoils? At least one state, Italy, had actually been induced to join the war on the basis of such undertakings. Great Britain had violated the well-recognized rules of international law governing free passage of neutral shipping in order to

---

*The original purpose of the Declaration of War clause was not, as is comonly assumed, to make Congress's adoption of a declaration a condition precedent for the United States to satisfy before it could enter into hostilities. Rather, the purpose of the clause was to enable the United States to *perfect* a belligerency, allowing the declarer to engage in unlimited warfare, as provided by international law.

starve Germany, and indeed would do so with such success once the armistice agreement finally stilled German submarine warfare, that famine became widespread across Central Europe. Trade barriers and national protection were the policies that defined "empire"—how could they be declared unlawful without disintegrating the system of imperial preferences? Self-determination presumably applied to the Irish as well as to the Indians, Algerians, and Indochinese. And, of course, a League of Nations whose security decisions would pre-empt those of its member states had yet to be willingly achieved between Britain and France even in the European Union of the late twentieth century. What made these aims so objectionable was not simply their astonishing scope, it was that at their very basis they presumed a relationship between the State and its people that was inconsistent with European ideas of sovereignty dating back to the origin of the modern State in the fifteenth century.

When informed of the president's address, Clemenceau reacted with derision. The Fourteen Points, he said, "bore me." "The Good Lord," he remarked mordantly, "only had ten." Lloyd George was in the midst of an election campaign in which he promised to make the Germans pay "the whole cost of the war." How could he possibly accept a statement of principles that confined a postwar settlement to an evenhanded treatment of victors and vanquished alike? The German reaction was also hostile. The German chancellor, Hertling, declared that "our military situation was never so favorable as it is now," and led the Reichstag in a rejection of the Fourteen Points.[66] Nevertheless, a month later the American president declared:

> There shall be no annexations, no contributions, no punitive damages. Self-determination is not a mere phrase . . . Every territorial settlement involved in this war must be made in the interest and for the benefit of the populations concerned, and not as a part of any mere adjustment or compromise of claims amongst rival states.[67]

There the matter lay for the early months of 1918, which the leaderships of all the European belligerents saw as absolutely decisive for the war as a whole.[68] After the slaughter of British forces at Passchendaele, the disintegration of the Russian army in the East, and the Italian debacle at Caporetto, the Allies braced for a fresh German offensive. By March 1918, the German army had a superiority of almost thirty divisions over the Anglo-French forces. If the German attack succeeded, Allied lines would be pierced and either the British forces surrounded by a sudden German move to the channel or Paris menaced by a drive on the French capital. The German high command mobilized all the resources of the state for this great gamble: if the offensive failed, German resources would be exhausted just at the time when the U.S. strength was growing from 300,000 troops at the front in April, when the attack began, to 1,200,000 in July.

By early June German forces had advanced to within thirty-seven miles of Paris and had inflicted enormous casualties on the Allies; their own losses, however, were just as staggering. By July, the Germans had lost about 973,000 men, and over a million more were listed as sick. On July 18, the Allies attacked at Soissons and Château-Thierry, with the Americans distinguishing themselves on the latter battleground. On August 8 an Allied offensive at Amiens achieved a breakthrough. In September, as if all at once, the German coalition collapsed. Austria-Hungary asked for a separate peace. The German High Command began pressing its government for an armistice. On October 3, a new German chancellor, von Baden, directly addressed the Americans, asking President Wilson for immediate negotiations on the basis of the Fourteen Points. Throughout the Central Powers, states were imploding, producing revolution and economic chaos.

In reply to the German plea, Wilson asked for a categorical acceptance of all the conditions laid down in the Fourteen Points. Colonel House was able to persuade Wilson to add an insistence on such military restraints as would "make the renewal of hostilities on the part of Germany impossible." The German government gave its assent on October 12, adding that "its object in entering into discussions would be only to agree upon practical details of the application of these terms."[69]

Wilson then turned to the Allies and found them far from receptive. After four years of awful slaughter, the American president who had once announced that he was "too proud to fight" now had arrived on the European scene with a peace plan, which he proposed to unilaterally negotiate with the enemy.[70]

On October 29, House met with the Allies. Point Seven had specified that Belgium should be evacuated and "restored"; Point Eight, that all "French territory should be freed and invaded portions restored." The Allies insisted, not unreasonably, that they understood the term *restoration* to mean that "compensation would be paid by Germany for all damage done to the civilian population of the Allies, and their property by the aggression of Germany . . ." Further, the British government announced a reservation to the requirement of freedom of the seas. On November 4, House cabled Wilson, who consented to an interpretation arrived at by House and the Allied leaders. Lansing informed Germany that the United States and the Allies were willing, subject to the reservations on reparations and freedom of the seas, to make peace on the basis of the Fourteen Points. "There can be little doubt that . . . by specifying 'damage done to the civilian population' [the Agreement] clearly excluded the costs of waging the war [however]."[71] An armistice was agreed to on the 11th of November.

While House was in Europe, Wilson made what House thought was the most disastrous speech of Wilson's career. It was an appeal to the public to elect Democratic congressmen and senators in the election of 1918 so as to help Wilson "win the peace." This speech shattered the wartime coalition between the parties, and effectively eliminated almost all existing Republican support for the treaty that would emerge from the Versailles conference. This insistence not only that he be right, but that others must play their role as "wrong" proved to be a fatal handicap to Wilson once he was no longer guided by House in his relations with Congress.

At Versailles, the Americans found themselves at odds with their allies over four issues: territorial adjustments in Europe (the French wished to dismember Germany, and all the continental Allies sought some territorial compensation); German colonies (sought by Great Britain); reparations; and making the League of Nations an integral part of the Treaty itself. The familiar account of the resolution of these differences holds that a naïve and wooden American president was simply bamboozled by more sophisticated Allied leaders into conceding the first three issues, in order to gain the fourth; and that he was betrayed by Colonel House, who made concessions in Wilson's absence on all four questions. Such an account obscures the historic constitutional and strategic struggle that did take place at Versailles and that set the terms for the Western approach to the Long War that persisted throughout the twentieth century.

One basis for this erroneous account can be found in the witty, acid rendering of the Versailles negotiations by John Maynard Keynes, economic adviser to the British delegation. It is too good not to quote, but it should be borne in mind that what really gave this narrative its devastating power in the United States was its reprinting by a feline Walter Lippmann in the pages of the American liberal magazine *The New Republic* and the use of Keynes's descriptions by Republican conservatives in order to destroy the prospects for treaty ratification in the Senate.* Keynes believed that the punitive nature of the treaty that ultimately emerged (he called it a "Carthaginian Peace") would drive Germany to bankruptcy and political ruin, and result in a fresh war of revenge. Lippmann and the American liberals believed this and more, that Wilson had failed to press hard enough for the ideals of the Fourteen Points and had thus betrayed his followers in the United States. The Republicans simply lifted the picture of an inept and slow-moving president being exploited by wily Europeans and used

---

*Lippmann later claimed that the decision to oppose the treaty was basically his editor's; "I followed him, though I was not then, and not now, convinced that it was the wise thing to do. If I had it to do over again, I should take the other side; we supplied [the Republican opposition to the treaty] with too much ammunition." Ronald Steel, *Walter Lippmann and the American Century* (Little, Brown, 1980), 166. See also Walter Lippmann, "The Intimate Papers of Colonel House," *Foreign Affairs* 4 (1962); and Walter Lippmann, "Notes for Biography," *New Republic*, July 16, 1930.

this portrayal to discredit the treaty. For the liberals, Wilson had been tricked into agreeing to an old-fashioned, great-power deal; for the conservatives, if Wilson had been tricked, it meant that he had mortgaged American national interests to European interests.

Here is Keynes's portrait of Wilson:

> The first impression of Mr. Wilson at close quarters was to impair some but not all of [our] illusions. His head and features were finely cut and exactly like his photographs, and the muscles of his neck and the carriage of his head were distinguished. But, like Odysseus, the President looked wiser when he was seated; and his hands, though capable and fairly strong, were wanting in sensitivity and finesse. But more serious than this, he was not only insensitive to his surroundings in the external sense, he was not sensitive to his environment at all. What chance could such a man have against Mr. Lloyd George's unerring, almost medium-like, sensibility to every one immediately round him? To see the British Prime Minister watching the company, with six or seven senses not available to ordinary men, judging character, motive, and subconscious impulse, perceiving what each was thinking and even what each was going to say next, and compounding with telepathic instinct the argument or appeal best suited to the vanity, weakness, or self-interest of his immediate auditor, was to realize that the poor President would be playing blind man's bluff in that party. Never could a man have stepped into the parlor a more perfect and predestined victim to the finished accomplishments of the Prime Minister. The Old World was tough in wickedness anyhow; the Old World's heart of stone might blunt the sharpest blade of the bravest knight-errant. But this blind and deaf Don Quixote was entering a cavern where the swift and glittering blade was in the hand of the adversary. . . .
>
> The President's slowness amongst the Europeans was noteworthy. He could not, all in a minute, take in what the rest were saying, size up the situation with a glance, frame a reply, and meet the case by a slight change of ground; and he was liable, therefore, to defeat by the mere swiftness, apprehension, and agility of Lloyd George. There can seldom have been a statesman of the first rank more incompetent than the President in the agilities of the council chamber. His mind was too slow and unresourceful to be ready with *any* alternatives. The President was capable of digging his toes in and refusing to budge, as he did over Fiume. But he had no other mode of defense, and it needed as a rule but little maneuvering by his opponents to prevent matters from coming to such a head until it was too late. By pleasantness and an appearance of conciliation, the President would be maneuvered off his ground, would

miss the moment for digging his toes in, and, before he knew where he had got to, it was too late.*

This is delightful writing, perhaps liberated by the biographical style of Keynes's Bloomsbury friend Lytton Strachey, but it is utterly blind to the constitutional basis of the struggle at Versailles and therefore places far too much emphasis on the purely personal elements in play.

The negotiations occurred in three crucial periods. The first culminated with Wilson's reading of the constitution of the League of Nations to the plenary session of delegates on February 14, 1919, and the adoption by that conference of the proposed League. Wilson then left for the United States in triumph, asking House to take his place until his return in mid-March.

In the second phase, during Wilson's absence, the French and British proposed a "preliminary" draft peace treaty that embodied the Allies' conditions concerning Germany's postwar military strength, frontiers, and reparations. This treaty, it was suggested, would allow a quick agreement and the more difficult question of the precise contours of League membership and operations could then be dealt with at leisure. House felt keenly that European political conditions would not tolerate for long a suspended state of settlement. An assassination attempt had been made on Clemenceau five days after Wilson's departure, and there were reports of incipient revolt in the French army which, however, couldn't be demobilized without the security assurances of the treaty. From every quarter in Europe there came fresh news of political turmoil: Bavaria had been seized by a communist putsch; soon Hungary was to follow. Poland had declared war on Russia, where a civil war raged between Whites and Reds. Throughout a Europe waiting on the treaty, famine stalked the civilian population. There was, also, the constant pressure from Allied military authorities to prevent any possibility that Germany would be able to renew hostilities, and at the same time resistance by the German army to completely abandon arms and positions in the absence of some guarantees about the eventual treaty.

Moreover, House was sensitive to the political positions of his partners: he knew that Lloyd George had a parliamentary majority that demanded far greater reparations, as the prime minister had led them to expect, than Germany could possibly fulfill. He knew that the Italian prime minister, Orlando, would not survive—as indeed he did not—without territorial accessions in the Adriatic for Italy. Above all, he knew that Clemenceau

*J. M. Keynes, *The Economic Consequences of the Peace* (Harcourt, Brace, and Howe, 1920), 39–44. Consider, however, that Keynes also described Lloyd George as "this goat-footed bard, this half-human visitor to our age from the hagridden magic and enchanted woods of antiquity." "Mr. Lloyd George: A Fragment," in John M. Keynes, *Essays in Biography* (Norton, 1963), 35.

could guarantee ratification only if it was widely perceived in France that Germany would not, for the third time in a half century, invade from the Rhineland. As soon as Wilson had departed, Lloyd George met with House and

> said that if I would help him out he would be extremely grateful. By "helping him out" he meant: to give a plausible reason to his people for having fooled them about the question of war costs, reparations and what not.[72]

It was now obvious that the treaty would not be based on the Fourteen Points. The European prime ministers made it clear that "if they yielded it would mean the overthrow of their governments."[73] House recognized that the Democratic defeats in the November elections constrained the U.S. delegation, and he closely followed the British elections and the vote of confidence sought by Clemenceau in the French Chamber of Deputies.*

It was perhaps true that "if the President should exert his influence among the liberals and laboring classes, he might possibly overthrow the governments"[74] of some of the Allies. But more chaos in Europe would scarcely strengthen Wilson at home in the United States, nor would it guarantee the stability required to make a New World Order actually function. Indeed, overthrowing Allied governments might very well lead to nation-states that did not share the parliamentary ideal. Wilson was forced to commit his hopes to the League of Nations because there was no alternative: the conference would not vote for a treaty based on the Fourteen Points. Subsequent modifications to the treaty and its ameliorative application by the League might, however, ultimately achieve Wilson's goals. If the United States left the conference without a treaty, Germany was scarcely likely to be more gently treated, yet leaving the conference was the only card Wilson had to play. If Wilson left he would get neither a more humane treaty nor the League.

When the third phase of the negotiations began with Wilson's return, his first reaction was fury at House for having made concessions on Allied military pensions (allowing their costs to be counted as part of the war) and for having entertained the possibility of a Rhenish republic, effectively creating a buffer zone for France. Wilson believed that he had completely secured the position of the League before leaving when he won a vote in favor of it at the plenary session of the conference. Now he thought he

---

*"House was well enough informed about French politics to be aware that failure to allay the well-founded French fears of a future German attack might result in the fall of Clemenceau and his replacement by a premier who would make impossible demands upon Germany in the name of security." Arthur Walworth, "Considerations on Woodrow Wilson and Edward M. House: An Essay Letter to the Editor," *Presidential Studies Quarterly* 24 (Winter 1994).

would return to bargain for the rest of the Fourteen Points. In fact, by putting the League issue first, he had delayed work on other issues so that now there was even greater pressure to resolve things quickly. Consent to the League could be used by the other Allies as a bargaining chip to be cast aside if the Americans were too obstreperous. Wilson's initial reaction is the source of Mrs. Wilson's oft-quoted memory of her husband's having said, "House has given away everything that I had won before we left Paris. He has compromised on every side, and so I have to start all over again."[75]

In fact, the two were soon in harness again as Wilson began to see what House already saw, the primacy of domestic politics in the new nation-state and the limited discretion it gave to political leadership. Wilson could indeed go over the heads of the delegations to their publics and possibly discredit them. He could expose the secret treaties the leaders denied having negotiated; he could make public their correspondence pleading for public support for provisions they conceded were irresponsible. Doing so, however, would not get him his League. Or he might use public opinion in a more channeled way, through the proceedings of the League. These, year by year, would build an international set of standards and practices against which the actions of states would be measured not simply by other states, but by the publics of the states concerned. This indeed was the ultimate function of the Helsinki Accords of 1975,[76] and their success is as surprising to their authors as understanding Wilson's not dissimilar program has proved elusive.[77]

In any case, the real issue was far more complex than a simple choice between a treaty with or without a League. The European states not only wanted, they demanded a League of Nations, by which they understood a permanent, institutionalized conference of great powers to interlock the security assurances of its members, drawing the United States into a guarantee against aggression. The United States—Wilson and House—wanted a League that would, over time, move the imperial state-nations toward the model of the nation-state, move socialist and militaristic nation-states toward parliamentary models, and move the State itself from a position of absolute sovereignty to an American model of limited sovereignty. Once rights were vested in nationalities, in "peoples," the State would be compelled to evolve in this direction by the force of public opinion.[78] In February, Wilson had described this process in these terms to the peace conference: ". . . throughout this instrument [the Covenant of the League of Nations] we are depending primarily and chiefly upon one great force, and that is the moral force of the public opinion of the world."[79]

Finally, both men were well aware that only a treaty that was actually ratified would be of any good to anyone and that the threats the treaty faced at the hands of European opponents, in their respective states, were the photo negative of those faced in the U.S. Senate, so that compromise in one theater jeopardized success in the other. Promising American intervention in case of aggression made the Treaty more attractive to European governments but less attractive to the U.S. Senate, for example.

For these reasons, House wrote on March 24[80] that he undertook to persuade Wilson to settle once and for all the persistent and vital question of inclusion of the Covenant in the peace treaty itself.

> I advised a showdown. I suggested that he tell them [Clemenceau and Lloyd George] that the Covenant for the League of Nations would either be written into the Treaty of Peace or we would have none of it; that the only excuse we could give for meddling in European or world affairs was a League of Nations through which we hope to prevent wars.[81]

In the end, the Americans negotiated the various compromises necessary to win consensus. Italy was denied Fiume, despite having been promised it by the Allies in the secret treaty that brought Italy into the war; Orlando left the conference in indignation and was promptly defeated at home. Alsace-Lorraine was returned to France, from whom it had been taken by war in 1871; the Saar was put under French control, though not annexed; ultimately Germany lost less than 4 percent of her territory, excluding Alsace-Lorraine. Poland, Czechoslovakia, Yugoslavia, and the Baltic states were created. A reparations bill was presented that was completely unrealistic but, Keynes's warnings notwithstanding, the final German payments were never more than five billion pounds, largely financed by the Allies. The political and human catastrophe that followed Versailles had, in fact, little to do with the actual economic impact of the treaty.

House understood the titanic forces that were carefully if precariously balanced by the Agreement.

> To those who are saying that the Treaty is bad and should never have been made and that it will involve Europe in infinite difficulties in its enforcement, I feel like admitting it. But I would also say in reply that empires cannot be shattered and new states raised upon their ruins without disturbance . . . The same forces that have been at work in the making of this peace would be at work to hinder the enforcement of a different kind of peace.[82]

There would be no final peace until nation-states had completely supplanted the state-nations that dominated the conference, until, that is, Wilson and Lenin and Hitler had destroyed the old state system, and, finally, until the new system had chosen among the three nation-state alternatives after three-quarters of a century of war.

Wilson and House had attempted to reform the deep structure of state sovereignty. Ironically, it was precisely the American system of limited sovereignty that crushed their plans, for it was the U.S. Senate's refusal to consent to the treaty that prevented ratification of the Versailles agreement and then thwarted U.S. participation in the League of Nations. The treaty came up for a vote twice, once in November 1919 and again in March 1920. The latter vote would surely have led to Senate consent had not the president instructed Democratic senators to vote against his own treaty because it was encumbered with a reservation to Article X of the provisions for the League (the Lodge Reservation). Article X empowered the League Council to advise member states to respond to aggression with sanctions and with armed force. The Lodge Reservation would have required that, in confronting a finding of aggression by the League Council, the United States could comply only if authorized to do so by Congress. As one of the members of The Inquiry had noted at Versailles, "[a treaty commitment to intervene] would be void . . . as Congress under the Constitution ha[s] the power to declare war. A war automatically arising upon a condition subsequent, pursuant to a treaty provision, is not a war declared by Congress."[83]

This misreading of the U.S. Constitution, which in fact contemplates several legitimate routes to war in addition to that of a formal declaration,[84] was used to decisive effect by the opponents of the treaty. House, however, was willing to accept something like the Lodge Reservation on the grounds that in practice the treaty, and the League, would be construed according to necessity. It was possible the other treaty partners would reject the Reservation; it was more likely that future presidents would not accept an unconstitutional restriction on their powers and would act within the treaty's confines unfettered by the Reservation. House, however, did not know the extent of the massive stroke that Wilson had suffered in September, nor did he know that presidential affairs were being conducted by Mrs. Wilson and the president's physician. He received no reply to his frantic entreaties about ratification and, indeed from the moment of Wilson's breakdown, was never again in close communication with the president. Once Wilson lost the one political adviser capable of steering him through the system he deeply revered but could not entirely navigate, his plans for enfolding the great powers within a similar system were dashed. Without his benign Mephistopheles, Wilson was returned to his Faustian study.

CHAPTER FIFTEEN

The Kitty Genovese Incident and the War in Bosnia

I.

ON MARCH 13, 1964, a little after 3 a.m., a twenty-eight-year-old woman named Catherine Genovese returned home to her apartment at 82–70 Austin Street in the Kew Gardens section of Queens in New York City. She was the night manager of a bar in a nearby community. Austin Street was a middle-class, tree-lined avenue flanked by apartment houses whose ground floors were given over to retail stores. The building where "Kitty" Genovese, as she was called by almost everyone in the neighborhood, lived was one such apartment house, a mock-Tudor structure with storefronts bordering the main street and separate entryways along the side and back to the apartments above. Adjacent to the apartment house was a suburban train station and commuter parking lot, which fronted on Austin Street.[1]

Kitty Genovese parked her car in the train station parking lot, turned off the car lights, locked the door, and started to walk the one hundred feet to her entryway. Apparently she noticed something that alarmed her, because she then turned away from the direction of her entryway and toward the street, walking rapidly up Austin Street, where a half block away there was a police call box. She got only as far as a streetlight in front of the neighborhood bookstore before a man caught up with her, grabbed her, struggled with her, and stabbed her. She screamed. Lights went on in the ten-story apartment house at 82–67 Austin Street that faced the bookstore. Kitty Genovese cried, "Oh my God, he stabbed me! Please help me, please help me."

From one of the upper windows in the apartment house, a man called down, "Let that girl alone." Other lights were turned on. The attacker fled back up Austin Street toward a white sedan parked in the commuter parking lot and he crouched there. No one from any of the apartment houses came down to the street. Kitty Genovese struggled to her feet and turned back, away from the call box, toward the side of the building by the parking lot beyond which her apartment lay. But before she could even get to the corner of the building, the assailant was on her again. She cried out, "I'm dying! I'm dying!" as he repeatedly stabbed her.

Windows were opened again and lights were turned on in many apartments. The attacker ran to his car, got in, and drove away. A city bus passed. It was 3:35 a.m. No one came to Kitty Genovese's aid from any of the buildings that overlooked Austin Street. She staggered to her feet, and again began to try to reach her apartment, which lay on the far side of the building from where she had been attacked. She was, however, now too weak to reach her entry. She made it about halfway, and unable to go further, she crawled under the stairs of another entry at 82–62 Austin Street, and tried to hide there. Her attacker, having circled the scene at a distance, then drove back again to the parking lot, got out of his car, and methodically searched the entryways until he found Kitty Genovese and fatally stabbed her. He returned to his car and departed. Still no one came to her assistance. Indeed it was not until almost 4 a.m. that a call was finally made to the police. Throughout the assault, not one person telephoned the police or any of the emergency services. The man who ultimately did call explained that he had only done so after much deliberation; in fact, he had asked a friend on Long Island for advice, and that person had persuaded him to call the police.

Over the next few days police took statements from thirty-eight persons who had witnessed the crime. The nation was stunned by the appalling account of so many bystanders doing nothing while such a brutal crime was committed. People groped for an explanation of what had happened. Why didn't her neighbors help Kitty Genovese? In 1964, many experts on human behavior were sought out to provide an explanation for the apparent apathy evident in the circumstances of the Genovese murder.

One psychiatrist attributed the tragedy to a constant feeling in New York that society was unjust. "It's in the air of all New York, the air of injustice . . . the feeling that you might get hurt if you act, whatever you do you will be the one to suffer." A sociologist at Barnard College offered an alternative view: it was an example of the "disaster syndrome." The result of witnessing a catastrophe such as a tornado or a murder destroyed the witnesses' feeling that the world was a rational place and resulted in an "affect denial" that caused them to withdraw psychologically from the event by ignoring it. Another psychiatrist proposed that it was the confusion of fantasy with reality, fed by the continual watching of television, that was responsible. "We underestimate the damage that these accumulated images do to the brain. The immediate effect can be delusional, equivalent to a post-hypnotic suggestion."

A psychiatrist suggested that the murderer vicariously gratified the sadistic impulses of those who witnessed the murder. "Persons with mature and well-integrated personalities would not have acted in this way."

Dr. Karl Menninger, the director of the Menninger Clinic, attributed the tragedy to "public apathy that is a manifestation of aggressiveness." And one theologian suggested that "de-personalizing in New York had gone further than we realized," to which he added, "Don't quote me."

One is inclined to be skeptical about such "explanations." They seem to provide, if they provide anything, a commentary on the world of the speaker more than the world of the event. And yet such shocking instances of bystander behavior are not uncommon, even if few of them are attended by the publicity of the Kitty Genovese murder. In January of 2000, a boy was beaten on a Boston bus while passengers looked on and did nothing.[2] In September of 2000, a woman was lured into a luxury apartment in a suburb of Fort Worth and murdered. Although all of the neighbors heard what one of them described as "piercing, gut-wrenching scream[s]" and listened for half an hour while the woman was murdered, nobody called the police.[3]

When such incidents occur, many explanations are put forward. "I would assign this to the effect of the megalopolis, which makes closeness very difficult," said one psychoanalyst at the time of the Genovese killing. "Apathy" was cited by many commentators as an explanation. Also, some referred to a "lack of concern for our fellow man." But the thirty-eight witnesses of Kitty Genovese's murder did not simply look at the scene once and then ignore it. Rather they continued to stare out their windows. One couple turned out their apartment lights to get a clearer view.

What does explain this? Some of the most fruitful psychological research into the subject of emergency intervention was undertaken as a consequence of the Genovese murder. Two psychologists, John Darley at Princeton University and Bibb Latane of Ohio State University, spent four years in a program of research into what determines bystander intervention in emergencies. In a remarkable series of experiments, staging "emergencies" in stores, offices, and laundromats, ranging from epileptic seizures to thefts and disorderly conduct, they managed to discredit virtually all the usual explanations. Darley and Latane hypothesized that the paralysis that seemed to grip bystanders resulted from what they called a "diffusion of responsibility" that occurred in situations as diverse as when a woman falls and sprains an ankle, smoke pours into a room through a ventilating system, or a cash register is robbed.

II.

Latane and Darley found that the crowd behavior in the Kitty Genovese case was very much like that of crowds in other emergency situations. Car accidents, drownings, fires, and attempted suicides all seem to attract bystanders who watched these dramas in helpless fascination. Riveted by the events, the bystanders were distressed and anxious, often full of remorse afterwards, but unwilling to act at the time. Their behavior was, as Latane and Darley put it, "[n]either helpful nor heroic; but it was not indifferent or apathetic either."

In general, people in nonemergency situations are quite willing to help when asked. Why aren't we even more willing in emergencies, in which the need for help is so much greater? Darley and Latane concluded that it was something about the nature of emergencies and not some pathology of the individuals who made up the crowd that accounted for the bewildering disassociation of bystanders in such situations. Emergencies, by their very nature, often involve actual harm or the threat of harm. An emergency can cost the life not only of the victim but of the intervenor, and the result even of a successful intervention rarely makes anyone better off afterwards than before the emergency event. Moreover, emergencies are, by definition, anomalous and rare events. Few individuals are prepared by training or practice to know how to handle such situations. Emergencies are unforeseen, and arise suddenly without warning. The bystander does not have time for consultation because the emergency, of all events, requires immediate, urgent action. Nor does the individual confronting an emergency come face-to-face simply with a single choice, but rather with a whole series of determinations, which he or she must usually make alone, even in the midst of a crowd.

The bystander must notice that something is happening, and then interpret the event as a real emergency. Further, he must decide that he has some personal responsibility for coping with it. At each stage of this process, the ambiguity of the event can paralyze a bystander, who is then forced to recycle through the entire process of decision. Is the event really an assault or just a noisy disagreement between two lovers? Are those screams of terror or peals of excited, nervous laughter? One witness to the Genovese murder said, "We thought it was a lovers' quarrel and I went back to bed." And if it is decided that the event really is an assault and some action ought to be taken, who should take it? Another witness to the events on Austin Street said, "I didn't want to get involved." It wasn't his job: it was for the police, or for Kitty Genovese's friends—he didn't know the woman—or perhaps for the woman herself to get out of the jam in which she found herself. To be "involved" meant taking on incalculable risks: suppose the man was arrested and tried; the person who called the police would have to testify; suppose the murderer was acquitted; might he then come after the witness? And finally, what exactly is the thing to be done: by the time most people had sorted out the salient facts, it was probably too late for the police to be contacted, arrive on the scene, and intervene in time to save the woman's life. Yet the middle-aged onlookers were scarcely in a position to tackle an armed killer themselves. They were not trained to act in such situations, had no experience of such horrors, and really had no idea what to do. Most people who saw the Genovese murder said simply, "I don't know—I don't know why I didn't do anything."

To summarize, we can say that there are five distinct stages through which the bystander must successively pass before effective action can be taken: (1) Notice: he must become aware that some unusual occurrence is taking place; (2) Recognition: he must be able to assess the event and define it as an emergency; (3) Decision: he must then decide that something must be done, that is, he must find a convincing reason for action to be taken; (4) Assignment: the bystander must then assign some person, himself or another, or some institution to be responsible for action; he must answer the question "who should act in these circumstances?" (5) Implementation: having decided what action should be taken, he must then see that it is actually done. If at any stage in this sequence a crucial ambiguity is introduced, then the whole process must begin again. The presence of ambiguity in urban life, not the callousness of urban dwellers, is precisely what makes emergency intervention in cities so problematic. In Johnson City, Texas, one is likely to know whether the man who has just slumped against the doorway is John, who recently had a coronary bypass, or Jack, the town drunk. In Queens, it is less likely that one knows, or that one can predict what will happen if one intervenes.

So it was with the horrifying events of the three years 1991–1994 in the former state of Yugoslavia: fascinated, frightened, appalled, the civilized world was anything but apathetic. And yet, like Kitty Genovese's murderer, the killers in Bosnia returned again and again, once the threat of outside intervention dissipated, leaving the rest of us as anguished bystanders.

Someday people will ask questions about the terrible crimes in Bosnia that are reminiscent of those asked after the murder of Kitty Genovese: How could the civilized, comfortable, and safe world have let those crimes happen? For much of the sequence of events in Bosnia has a parallel with the crimes on Austin Street, especially the pattern of aggression that falters when confronted but which returns when it is not suppressed, and also the pattern of rationalization that organizes our thinking, and prevents decisive action in emergencies. The results of Darley and Latane's research offer a key to understanding what went wrong for more than three years in Yugoslavia as well as what went wrong that night in Queens. And this understanding can yield insights into the nature of the society of nation-states, a society that was just as shaken by the horror it witnessed but did nothing to stop as was the small community of neighbors in Queens.

III.

When President Clinton said, mistakenly, that the current conflict in Bosnia-Herzegovina goes back to the eleventh century, he exposed more than a careless speechwriter of dubious erudition; rather he showed that he was unable to appreciate just what had happened.

The war in Bosnia was the culmination of a constitutional implosion that occurred in Yugoslavia as a result of the collapse of a one-party Communist dictatorship and its replacement by means of media-dominated multiparty elections. This implosion propelled Slobodan Milosevic into the leadership of the Serbian Communist Party and his reinvention of the Party as the nationalist champion of Serbs. His subsequent actions, when coupled with a system of free elections in the federated states of Yugoslavia, led to the rapid secession of Slovenia and Croatia, which in turn led, finally, to the dismemberment of Bosnia. Four wars were fought—in Slovenia, Croatia, Bosnia, and Kosovo—and four new states ultimately emerged from this constitutional and strategic process: Slovenia, Croatia, Serbia and Montenegro, and the Croatian-Bosnian Confederation.

There are two parts to this story. In the background is the history of the evolution of the Yugoslav state. In the foreground is the story of killers who came to Bosnia, at first timorously but murderously, and who were repeatedly frightened away by declarations on the part of the great powers, but who returned when these declarations proved to be mere threats. These killers returned, time and again, until 144,108 persons, including 16,795 children, had been murdered; 171,837 wounded (including 34,520 children), 12,290 disabled (including 1,879 children); in Sarajevo alone 10,436 were killed (of whom 1,592 were children). Not included are the statistics for the U.N.-declared "safe areas" of Srebrenica or Zepa, where the figures for massacres conducted by Serbian forces in the presence of U.N. peacekeepers were not complete as of this writing.[4] As will be seen, the constitutional metamorphoses that the Yugoslav state underwent are intimately connected to the slaughter and degradation of the Bosnian Muslims, leading finally to the discrediting of the United Nations and the Wilsonian system of international law.

But first we must acquaint ourselves with some background information: the history of the Yugoslav nation-state, its national composition, and then a more detailed year-by-year recitation of the events from 1991 to 1995.

The post-Versailles constitution of the Kingdom of Serbs, Croats, and Slovenes of 1921 provided for a parliamentary democracy. This state located its capital in Belgrade and was quickly dominated by Serbs, to the disadvantage of Croat political groups. In 1928 Stjepan Radich, the Croat political leader, was shot to death on the floor of the National Assembly. The following year King Alexander dissolved the parliament, suspended the constitution, and seized absolute power. In Croatia a separatist group was formed, the notorious Ustaša, which assassinated Alexander in 1934. When the Nazis invaded Yugoslavia in 1941, the Ustaša allied with the invaders and governed that portion of the country it was able to pacify. The Ustaša forced Orthodox Christians to convert to Roman Catholicism, rounded up Jews, and massacred about 400,000 Serbs. This post-Versailles, fascist campaign was the first occasion of a war between Serbs and Croats. It is not true that there is a long history of conflict between these native Balkan groups.

In addition to the claim that the recent wars in Yugoslavia are a continuation of an ancient conflict, it is often said that the war in Bosnia is an *ethnic* war. This too tends to obscure the issue, exaggerating the strangeness and the intractability of the conflict's sources. One way to appreciate the cultural history of the Balkans is to imagine three great cultural tectonic plates that come together there. To the west is the inheritance of Rome: the experience of the Renaissance, the Roman Catholic Church, the entire collection of attitudes that we think of as "Western." From the east, the legacy is Byzantine: Eastern Orthodox in religion, authoritarian in politics. From the south comes the Islamic tradition brought to Europe by the Turks.

These three cultural plates divide what is ethnically a single people, the Slavs of the southern peninsula. All the Yugoslav groups in the war—Croats, Serbians, and Muslims—speak the same language, have the same genetic characteristics, and are to a very large degree intermarried. Indeed, until the twentieth century Croats and Serbs collaborated to fight the Turks and to free themselves from the Austro-Hungarian empire. The Muslims, whom the Serbian terrorists are fond of calling "Turks," are in fact generally believed to be descendants of Bogomil Christians who suffered forcible conversion at the hands of the Ottoman Turks.

To say that this is an "ethnic conflict" is thus not quite right. There are no "ethnic Muslims" and in a strict sense there are really no ethnic Serbs or Croats, unless you think that Catholic Anglo-Canadians and Protestant Anglo-Americans are "ethnically" distinct. Catholic Croats, Orthodox Serbs, and Muslims in all of these states are all Slavs: indeed the word "Yugoslavia" means "the land of the South Slavs."

Serbian resistance to the Nazis and the Ustaša was initially led by Draza Mihailovic with military support by the British. This group was known as the Chetniks. After the invasion of the Soviet Union by Germany in the summer of 1941, a communist insurgency known as the Partisans arose. This force, led by Josip Broz, was more successful than the Chetniks against the Nazis and Croats. Eventually Broz's partisans were armed and supported by the British, despite the fact that the arms were often used against the former allies of the British—the Mihailovic forces—and were ultimately, and predictably, used to seize power for the Communists after the war.

Broz, whose partisan name was "Tito," ruled a brutal police state from 1945 until 1980. His conflicts with Stalin, however, and his position as a leader of the world nonaligned movement made him an attractive figure to many in the West. Moreover, because he was a Communist Croat, he seemed to bridge the conflicts of the Yugoslav experience in the Second World War. For these reasons, perhaps, the extent of his postwar domestic violence was greatly underappreciated by the international community.

Because Yugoslavia faced the virtual certainty of invasions by both the Warsaw Pact and NATO should war between those two alliances break out, Yugoslavia built up a well-equipped, well-supplied, modernized armored force. About half the federal budget of Yugoslavia went to the National Army (JNA). The officer corps was two-thirds Serbian, and the bureaucratic apparatus of the Communist Party and the organs of state were also dominated by Serbs.

Under Tito, Yugoslavia became again a federation of six republics. These boundaries roughly conformed to the ancient provinces that had existed in this region since the Middle Ages, but they did not strictly conform to any particular cultural division. Indeed, Serbia itself is only about 80 percent Serbian; Bosnia has no clear majority, being somewhat less than half Muslim. In 1974 Tito took constitutional steps to give more authority to the republics. It is this constitution that set the context for the conflict of the 1990s, because the controversial constitutional rearrangement of 1974 was in place when the shattering events of the late 1980s swept away the communist governments of Eastern and Central Europe. In addition to devolving power from Belgrade to the six capitals, the 1974 constitution granted autonomous authority to two provinces within Serbia itself. Kosovo (largely Albanian in makeup with a Serbian minority), and Vojvodina (largely Hungarian with a Serbian minority) border on Albania and Hungary, respectively. Granting them political autonomy was deeply resented by Serbia, and there were frequent reports in the Serbian media of mistreatment of the Serbian minorities in these two provinces.

In 1980 Tito died, and the federal presidency now circulated among the presidents of each of the six republics. Six years later, the Serbian Communist leader Slobodan Milosevic came to power in Belgrade. He saw that his future leadership and the future of Serbia lay not with the crumbling Communist powers in Central and Eastern Europe but rather, paradoxically, in the ethnically fraught province of Kosovo. It was in Kosovo that the Albanian majority, which is Muslim by religion, had been harassing Serbs and driving them out by various means. In 1987, Milosevic got control of the Serbian press, and he immediately made Kosovo the centerpiece of his campaign. The state-controlled press repeated a drumbeat of atrocity stories in which Albanian Muslims in Kosovo were reported to have terrorized minority Serbs. That same year Milosevic went to Kosovo and after an all-night mass meeting with Serbs in the province dramatically promised them that "nobody would ever beat the Serb again." During the next two years, Milosevic organized a pan-Serb movement and sponsored solidarity meetings throughout Yugoslavia on the pretext of helping the embattled Kosovo Serbs. In 1988 Milosevic was able to seize control of the Kosovo government and force the Albanian leaders to resign in the face of mob violence. Later these leaders were arrested. He then turned his attention to Vojvodina, where he was able to replicate his Kosovo campaign with an "antibureaucratic revolution" aimed at the provincial government.

In the spring of 1990, elections following the disintegration of the single-party system in Yugoslavia brought nationalists to power in Slovenia, Croatia, and Serbia. Thus by the time the Communist Party collapsed in 1990 Milosevic had been able to segue from his position as head of the Serbian Communist Party to a new role as the leader of the Serbian nation. In Croatia the Croatian extremist Franco Tudjman, formerly a henchman of Tito, came to power on a platform of secession from the Yugoslav state.

In May of 1991, Milosevic sent the JNA into Kosovo and Vojvodina, effectively ending their autonomous status and turning them into police states. These measures redeemed his pledge to reunite a Serbia divided by the 1974 constitution.[5] Public demonstrations staged by Milosevic had already ousted the Montenegrin party leadership in 1989 and installed a Milosevic ally in power there. Serbia now controlled four out of the eight votes governing the federal presidency. Milosevic then refused to permit the Croat president to rotate into the Yugoslav presidency, as provided by the constitution. All this had the effect of completely unsettling the populations in the other Yugoslav provinces. It appeared that Milosevic had hit upon an effective strategy for turning the Yugoslav constitution into an instrument by means of which he could create a Serbian state. That same month the Croatians voted overwhelmingly in favor of independence, as had Slovenia the preceding December. Initially the two republics had sought greater autonomy within Yugoslavia, but Milosevic had blocked this; now the experiences of Kosovo and Vojvodina gave fresh impetus to complete secession.

On June 25, 1991, Croatia and Slovenia declared their independence from the state of Yugoslavia. This set off a brief war between Slovenia and the JNA, and a protracted war in Croatia between the newly independent government of Croatia and the Serbian minority, supported by the JNA. The ten-day war in Slovenia ended in mid-July with the withdrawal of the JNA and the transfer of full-scale hostilities to Croatia. In August a Serbian revolt in Croatia broke out in Dalmatia and around Knin.

Serb minorities believed they faced real dangers in Croatia along the coast of the Adriatic, and above the northern tip of Bosnia, on the border between Serbia and Croatia, and in a land-locked enclave about seventy miles west of Serbia. Here the Serbs had experienced some of the worst atrocities of World War II, and here they now followed with apprehension the rabid nationalist campaigns of Tudjman. When war finally came to Croatia, it was largely owing to Milosevic's success in portraying his struggle for "Serb rights" as part of the constitutional campaign to preserve Yugoslavia. This brought the JNA into Croatia on the side of the Croatian Serbs. Local Serb tactics in Krajina, a Serbian enclave in Croatia, engaged Croat forces in armed conflict, thereby enabling the JNA to intervene, claiming to separate the parties, but in effect, protecting and arming the insurgent Serbs. In the midst of the Serbian/JNA campaign in Croatia, the Bosnian Serbs set up their own parliament. By August, one-third of Croatia had fallen to the Serbs and Croatia had been stripped of its federal weapons and munitions.

Thus the war in Croatia was significantly different from that in Slovenia. It was driven by Serb secessionists who wished to dismember Croatia, not by Croatian secessionists who wanted to leave Yugoslavia. Or, to put it differently, "[u]ltimately the war in Croatia, and later in Bosnia, was not so much a war of secession but a war provoked and waged by Serb nationalists and the Yugoslav army to establish a new Yugoslavia with new international borders."[6] It was a crucial mistake for the West to credit Milosevic's assertions that the state of Yugoslavia persisted at this point, allowing him to lay claim to the enormous magazines and matériel stationed in Slovenia on the northern border of Yugoslavia, where a Cold War invasion had been anticipated, and permitting him to return these stores to Serbia. But other European countries were pleased to have stopped the fighting in Slovenia through the Brioni Agreement and sympathized with Milosevic's protest that he had thereby lost a wealthy and important province. In fact, Milosevic was only too happy to see Slovenia go. This development now gave him a majority of 4–3 in the federal presidency, allowed him to quiet fears about German intervention on behalf of Slovenia, and permitted him to turn his attentions to Croatia. Unlike Slovenia, which had a small Serb minority, Croatia had about 600,000 Serbs living in four separated areas.

In the summer of 1991, following the end of the war in Slovenia, France, Germany, Italy, and the Netherlands proposed sending a ground force to Yugoslavia. Reports of atrocities in Slavonia and other parts of

Croatia were coming out of the now-collapsed state. Britain, however, resolutely opposed all efforts at sending troops and on September 19 was able to broker a statement on behalf of the European Community to the effect that no military intervention by E.C. states was contemplated. Within days, the Serbs unleashed massive attacks on various points in southern Croatia. The ancient and defenseless Adriatic city of Dubrovnik was shelled from the sea under the eyes of the U.S. Sixth Fleet, which duly reported each salvo but did not interfere. At the same time the Serbs began the siege of Vukovar, which was to prove a model for future campaigns. During the shelling of Dubrovnik, Serbian naval forces had been markedly anxious out of fear that the overwhelming power of the U.S. carrier task force that shadowed them might be used to destroy their attacking vessels. When nothing happened, the Serbs were emboldened. When the city of Vukovar surrendered in November, its inhabitants were massacred by Serb irregulars, and several hundred wounded Croatian soldiers were taken from a hospital in Vukovar, shot in a field, and buried in a mass grave. International forensic experts were subsequently denied access.[7]

In September the European Community sponsored a peace conference at The Hague. Lord Carrington was appointed by the European Union (as the E.C. became in November 1993), and in October he began efforts at mediation. This greatly respected figure saw the conflict as a reprise of the World War II Serb-Croat fighting. Both sides were equally culpable, and the trick was to contain the bloodshed through partition. That same month, Britain suggested to Serbia that it seek an arms embargo covering all the states of Yugoslavia. Perhaps it was thought in London that by this means any illusions about breaking away from Yugoslavia would be stilled in Bosnia, or at least that the parties would quickly come to terms with Serbia because without arms it would be futile to oppose the well-equipped JNA. In any event, in September the United Nations Security Council duly imposed an arms embargo against all the states of the former Yugoslavia.

In January 1992 the U.N. envoy Cyrus Vance achieved a negotiated cease-fire, and U.N. peacekeepers were stationed in Croatia to monitor compliance with the agreement. In accordance with the U.N. cease-fire, the JNA withdrew from Croatia. It proceeded to turn over its weapons* to the Bosnian Serbs, and Serbian/JNA heavy artillery took up positions around the Bosnian capital of Sarajevo. The former states of Yugoslavia now braced for the third Yugoslav war—in Bosnia, where the Serbs now had a

---

*These were used to attack Sarajevo in early 1992. The U.S. Air Force chief of staff recommended air strikes to relieve Sarajevo, and later testified that the artillery ringing the city in mountain batteries could have been destroyed from the air. This, however, was vetoed on the grounds that it might only prompt the Serbs to attack Sarajevo with ground troops. The siege of Sarajevo had begun.

monopoly on heavy and advanced weaponry, while the Bosnian government was constrained from obtaining arms by the international embargo.

Near the end of the previous year, Bosnia had been forced to confront the possibility that it would have to withdraw from the Yugoslav federation. The Bosnian president, the former anti-Communist dissident Izetbegovic, had traveled to Ljubljana and Zagreb on countless missions desperately trying to get the Slovenes and Croats to stay in the federation. The last thing the Bosnian leadership wanted was to face new independent states in Serbia and Croatia that could carry their war into Bosnia in order to incorporate areas with substantial Croat and Serb populations. The multicultural state of Bosnia could only survive within the umbrella of the Yugoslav federation. Milosevic, however, had methodically destroyed this option. The Hague peace conference had given an offer of E.C. recognition to any republic that met certain criteria for statehood; when Croatia and Slovenia prepared for independence, the Bosnians realized they could not remain in a federation virtually alone with Milosevic. Bosnia could not risk becoming the Kosovo or Vojvodina of the 1990s.

In January 1992 the E.C., after considerable debate and over Carrington's objections, recognized Croatian and Slovenian independence. The E.C. deferred action on Bosnia pending a referendum. Bosnia then held a referendum on independence in March. In an election boycotted by the Bosnian Serbs, 65 percent voted for statehood.

By April, there were reports of widespread shootings and bombings in Banja Luka and Mostar by Serb irregulars.[8] The JNA announced it was necessary to intervene in Bosnia to protect Serbs. In the first six weeks of the Bosnian war that ensued, Serb forces, using the JNA command structure and weapons, seized about 60 percent of Bosnia. Bosnian Croats took another 15 percent. The Bosnian army itself was without JNA weapons and, in an absurd gesture aimed at reducing tensions, had voluntarily given up its territorial arms.

On April 27, Milosevic declared a new Yugoslav state composed of Serbia and Montenegro. On May 22, Bosnia was admitted to the U.N. as a member state along with Yugoslavia, Slovenia, and Croatia. Milosevic declared that all federal troops had been withdrawn from Bosnia; in June a report of the Secretary General of the U.N. also claimed that there were no Serbian soldiers in Bosnia. While this may have been formally true—JNA soldiers were "released" to join the Bosnian Serb army—it was not the reality. Indeed as James Gow noted:

> The continuing presence in Bosnia after independence of the JNA, loyal to Belgrade, meant that although there were significant incursions across the River Drina between Serbia and Bosnia, there were also 80,000 troops already based in Bosnia.[9]

In 1992, the Bosnian Serbs set up a gulag of prison camps and detention facilities holding tens of thousands of Muslims and Croats. International investigators were denied access, though escapees described atrocities that they claimed were perpetrated in these camps. In the summer of 1992, an intrepid *Newsday* reporter penetrated one of the Serbian concentration camps, verifying these claims and exposing horrors that Europe had not seen since 1945. These exposés prompted Governor Bill Clinton to say on August 5, during his campaign for the presidency, "If the horrors of the Holocaust taught us anything, it is the high cost of remaining silent and paralyzed in the face of ethnic cleansing." The next day, asked what he proposed, he stated, "We cannot afford to ignore what appears to be a deliberate and systematic extermination of human beings based on their ethnic origin; I would start with air power against the Serbs."[10]

In response to mounting public outcry, the United Nations Security Council voted to send U.N. peacekeepers to Bosnia. Although it was estimated that 35,000 troops would be required for this mission, less than 7,000 were sent, largely drawn from British, French, Canadian, and Dutch forces. The arrival of U.N. troops was greeted with euphoria in Bosnia. Serb forces halted their attacks for a time in order to determine what effect the U.N. presence in Bosnia would have. These forces proved, along with the U.N. arms embargo, to be a fatal addition to the Bosnian equation. Now the Europeans—particularly the British—would be able to veto any actions against the Serbs on the grounds that U.N. or NATO armed action exposed their peacekeepers to reprisals.

In October 1992 Cyrus Vance, representing the U.N., and David Owen, who had replaced Lord Carrington for the E.C., proposed a new peacekeeping plan. It effectively recognized the ground gains by the Serbian forces and carved up Bosnia into various enclaves. The U.S. ceased supporting the no-fly zone which the British in December had argued against enforcing in any case—and which, though adopted by the Security Council in October 1992, would not actually be enforced until April 1993 by NATO—and began looking to the Vance-Owen Plan as offering a way out. Milosevic urged the Bosnian Serbs to accept the Vance-Owen Plan, and the United States strongly advised the Bosnian Muslims to agree, despite some misgivings over the Plan's apparent validation of Serbian territorial aggression.

In February 1993 the new American secretary of state, Warren Christopher, said that the "full weight of American diplomacy [would be brought] to bear" to win acceptance of the Vance-Owen peace plan that left the Bosnians only a fraction of their national territory. When the Bosnians were eventually coerced by the Americans into agreeing to the plan, the

Bosnian Serbs rejected it. The Serbs saw no reason to give up any of their gains. Indeed, now the killing began in earnest as Serbs tried to garner new territory that might be converted at the diplomatic table into legitimate possession by another international peace plan. A new term had entered the world's lexicon: "ethnic cleansing." This phrase was applied to the Serbian strategy of terrorizing the countryside in order to drive Muslims into surrounded and shelled cities. In this they were inadvertently encouraged by the United States, which had pressed for acceptance of a plan that ratified Serbian ground gains.

In May 1993, Christopher began referring to the conflict as a Yugoslav civil war, despite the fact that Bosnia had been a member of the U.N. for more than a year by that time. The U.S., downplaying allegations of Serbian atrocities, now said that all parties shared responsibility for human rights violations. The *New York Times* noted in April 1993 that the Clinton administration had "begun to talk about Bosnia differently, to cast the problem there less as a moral tragedy which would make American inaction immoral—and more as a tribal feud that no outsider could hope to settle." The president explained the difficulty of getting agreement on a peace plan by observing that "I would think these fights between the Serbs and the Bosnian Muslims and the Croats go back so many centuries, they have such powerful roots that it may be that it's more difficult for the people to make a change than for their leaders."

In May the Contact Group—formed by the United States, the United Kingdom, Germany, France, and Russia—proposed a plan of safe areas into which the fleeing Muslims could go for protection, and in June the Security Council agreed to secure these areas by "all necessary measures," including military force. The six "safe areas" announced by the U.N. Security Council were Sarajevo, Zepa, Bihac, Srebrenica, Tuzla, and Gorazde. Phillippe Morillon, the U.N. commander, negotiated an accord by which the Muslim defenders of Srebrenica handed over their weapons. He proclaimed that "an attack on Srebrenica now would be an attack on the whole world" and stated, "I will never leave you." For a brief period, attacks on Srebrenica, swollen with refugees driven into the town by Serb offensives in the countryside, halted. But on May 14, 1993, President Clinton stated that "[o]ur interest is in seeing, in my view at least, that the U.N. does not foreordain the outcome of a civil war," and Morillon withdrew to Sarajevo, where he was removed by the U.N. secretary-general, and was ultimately replaced by the more tractable British general, Michael Rose.

These events had the effect of encouraging the Serb forces in Bosnia to step up the violence and press their claims more aggressively, which puzzled and bewildered the rest of the world, including the United States. Although the Serbs seemed so unreasonable, in fact they were simply responding to the incentives offered by peace plans that recognized whatever they could take on the ground. No one seemed to appreciate that such encouragement was precisely what at least one state, the United Kingdom, actually had in mind because it believed that further resistance by the Bosnians was doomed and that the sooner the war was over and Bosnia partitioned along lines that recognized the military realities, the better for all concerned. Only the Americans appeared to have clung to the illusion that the Serbs would come around to the Vance-Owen Plan, or something like it, because the international community was united in proposing it and because the Serbs would not wish to defy the great powers indefinitely.

In one day in July 1993, 3,777 artillery shells fell on Sarajevo, a U.N.-designated "safe area" and part of the "heavy weapons exclusion zone" announced by the Contact Group.* President Clinton, in Asia for an economic summit, was enraged and asked his national security advisor to submit a plan to break the siege. But the Pentagon plan that resulted called for 80,000 troops, and this was thought politically unsupportable; the president had hoped perhaps 10,000 would be enough, and he dropped the idea. Then on October 20, 1993, he announced that "the conflict in Bosnia is ultimately for the parties to resolve" and repeated this later, saying: "Until these folks get tired of killing each other . . . bad things will continue to happen."

On February 4, 1994, a mortar attack on a Sarajevo market killed sixty-eight and injured another two hundred. Again public opinion was outraged by events—Sarajevo had been under siege for almost two years at this point—and again a weapons exclusion zone around Sarajevo was proclaimed. A small number of NATO air strikes occurred, and the Serbs actually turned over heavy weapons within the zone. For a period, the daily bombardment of Sarajevo ceased. Citizens of the besieged town could walk rather than run across streets raked by sniper fire. The Serbs regrouped to determine how to continue their siege without their heavy weapons. But the U.N. troops, lightly armed and dispersed, were effectively captives of the Serbs, and the U.N. commander, General Rose, could not bring himself to call on NATO for further support that might risk retaliation against his troops. U.S. proposals for the use of force against the Serbs were repeatedly vetoed by the U.N. Political Counselor, who reported to the U.N. Secretary-General, and the weapons turned over during this period were later simply reclaimed by the Serbs. In April, only two months later, Rose sent troops to Gorazde, one of the six safe areas, but was compelled to allow them to be disarmed by the Serbs. On April 23,

*A group including the United States and the most influential European powers, organized to deal with the Yugoslav crisis.

President Clinton demanded that the Serbs cease shelling Gorazde, stating that if this did not happen, NATO would conduct "massive air strikes," including "strategic targets."[11] The Serbs appear to have learned not to credit such threats and replied by taking U.N. peacekeepers hostage; when this occurred, NATO action was canceled. In May, Tuzla, another safe area, was shelled, killing seventy in a single day. On May 3, 1994, the President stated, obviously disheartened, and unable despite repeated efforts to move his allies, "I did the best I could. I moved as quickly as I could. I think we have shown a good deal of resolve."[12]

In the ensuing year, safe areas at Gorazde, Zepa, and Srebrenica were all isolated, bombarded, and put under siege, and a fourth safe area, Tuzla, was also again attacked. On June 5, 1995, an anguished president said, "It's tragic, it's terrible. But these enmities go back five hundred years. Do we have the capacity to impose a settlement on people who want to continue fighting? We cannot do that. So I believe we're doing the right thing." Then on July 11, 1995, 400 Dutch peacekeepers watched as Srebrenica, one of the "safe areas," was overrun and "sanitized" by occupying Serbs. Approximately 8,200 men and an undetermined number of women were trucked out by the Serbs and murdered, many within the hearing of the Dutch forces allegedly deployed to protect them. This left Sarajevo itself, Gorazde (which was now cut off from the outside), Bihac, and Zepa surrounded.

Finally in August of 1995 another mortar attack on the Sarajevo market galvanized public opinion. Seven shells fell within ten minutes, killing 37 persons and wounding 84. The next day U.N. peacekeepers deserted Gorazde, which ironically was a necessary step to true protection of the safe area. Rose's successor as commander, General Rupert Smith, asked for NATO air strikes, and following a two-week series of air and artillery strikes on Serb positions, the Serb campaign against Gorazde was halted and the siege of Sarajevo was finally lifted. Croatian forces entered the war in September and relieved the safe area at Bihac, driving about 100,000 civilian Serbs out of Croatia in a Croatian variant of ethnic cleansing. An agreement was forced upon the parties by the United States at an air force base in Dayton, Ohio. The agreement was subject to all the vagaries of hostilities in Bosnia and politics in the United States, but it soon became clear that the killing of Muslims had almost completely stopped as a result of the combined efforts of NATO Rapid Reaction Force shelling, the Croatian offensive, and U.S. air intervention. Despite some constitutional legerdemain on the part of U.S. negotiators, the country was effectively partitioned, owing to the unwillingness of the West to enforce the guarantees of the agreement that provide for repatriation of those systematically driven from their homes. The hardest days, diplomatically, lay ahead over communities like Brcko that link disparate enclaves of Serbs, and complications arising from the U.S.-contrived Croatian-Muslim federation. The murder of Muslim civilians with JNA heavy weapons, however, had been stopped by air and artillery strikes that took only about fourteen days and incurred not a single American casualty.

IV.

Darley and Latane's work can usefully be applied to the Bosnian emergency by examining the various stages that the bystander goes through before actually acting. With some slight reworking of their categories, I take there to be five stages: notice, definition, decision, assignment, and implementation. The bystander's attention must be forcibly drawn to the event so that she realizes something unusual is happening (notice); she must then recognize the event as an emergency, and not simply an ordinary event that appears to be an emergency (definition); she must then find conclusively good reasons for action (decision); and then determine who should act (assignment); and finally commit to some particular action and see that it is done (implementation). If an ambiguity is introduced at any stage—"Did I actually hear someone cry for help, or was that the sound of the television in the next room?"—the decision procedure is aborted and the cycle must begin all over again. This anxious cycling, not apathy, is what Darley and Latane found to be the state of mind of the persons who failed to intervene in the Kitty Genovese case. In the example of Bosnia, there were frequent efforts by government officials to *introduce* ambiguities into the debate, no doubt because these officials had real doubts themselves as to the true nature of the facts, but also because they wished to deflect public calls for action that they believed would be futile or counterproductive, while the Serbs maintained what might well be called a "strategy of ambiguity" in order to prevent Western intervention.

NOTICE: GETTING OUR ATTENTION

There are two parallel institutions, among others, that operate to bring the events of an emergency to our attention: the news media and the intelligence agencies. The latter's work is almost exclusively confined to alerting public officials, but the former, though they deal with the mass of the public, are no less powerful in moving official opinion, partly because officials must cope with public opinion shaped by the news media. Furthermore, there is some interplay between the intelligence product and the stories reported by journalists: intelligence reports can be leaked, or tailored to give a distorted picture to the press for political reasons.

American officials appear to have been well served by their intelligence agencies in having the looming crisis in Yugoslavia brought to their attention early on, and we may assume that the agencies of other states were also monitoring the situation. In 1990 the Central Intelligence Agency (CIA) correctly predicted the violent disintegration of Yugoslavia; at the beginning of 1992, with diplomatic attention focused on negotiations to achieve a cease-fire in the Second Yugoslav War (in Croatia), the CIA foresaw that the Third Yugoslav War (the war in Bosnia)[13] was about to begin. Moreover, the CIA also predicted that recognition of Bosnia might serve as a pretext for war against that state, absent some larger effort at containing or deterring the aggressive JNA and the Serbs. Finally, according to several former officials, the State Department was aware of the existence of Serbian detention centers for Bosnian Muslims as early as April of 1992, and by June had confirmed reports of torture and concentration camps.[14]

The American public and the publics of other concerned countries did not have access to these reports, of course, but they were nevertheless kept informed of events in Bosnia by televised and print journalism. There really can be no doubt that Cable News Network (CNN) was an influential factor in bringing the crisis to the attention of the public. This has also been the case in other emergencies: the spectacles of starvation in Somalia and mass slaughter in Rwanda are two recent examples of events that simply would not have been noticed in earlier periods. The "CNN Effect"— the jolt to public opinion given by televised attention to foreign crises—is now beyond question.* One can see this in the preoccupation of the public with events in Somalia, but not in the Sudan, in Haiti but not in Liberia, in Chechnya but not in Nagorno-Karabakh. In the first of each pair, the public was made to notice that something unusual and dramatic was happening; in the second, owing to the difficulty of getting televised coverage of events there, the public was not provided the same riveting and anguishing images, with the result that a great number of people simply never "noticed" those events.

In Bosnia this can be well illustrated by the televised accounts of three separate bombings of Sarajevo. In the course of the siege, more than 600,000 shells fell on a civilian capital with no significant military production. But it was three bombings of marketplaces that somehow stirred the public imagination.[15] In 1992 one such bombing led directly to U.N. eco-

*Former secretary of state Lawrence Eagleburger has observed that the Bush administration's decision to intervene in Somalia was strongly influenced by television coverage; others have concluded that the American decision to withdraw from Somalia was also precipitated by the media. Secretary of state Madeleine Albright told the Senate Foreign Relations Committee that "television's ability to bring graphic images of pain and outrage into our living rooms has heightened the pressure both of immediate engagement in areas of international crisis and immediate disengagement when events do not go according to plan." "Media and Information Technology," *Reinventing Diplomacy in the Information Age* (Center for Strategic and International Studies 1999), but see also Warren Sobel, "The CNN Effect," *American Journalism Review,* May 1996.

nomic sanctions against Serbia and Montenegro. In February 1994 a market bombing, which killed sixty-nine, prompted NATO to issue an ultimatum for Serbs to withdraw their heavy artillery. Finally, in August 1995, it was the bombing of a Sarajevo market by Serb mortars, which killed thirty-seven and wounded eighty-four, to which NATO responded with the bombing and artillery campaign that broke the siege of the city. One can only speculate about the reasons for such a reaction. After all, libraries, mosques, hospitals, and schools in Sarajevo had all been targeted and hit by the Serbs; what was it about the bombing of a market that seemed to hit a nerve in public opinion? Perhaps it had to do with the televised images such bombing provided. Unlike the scenes of bombed-out buildings, the photos of the market, with colorful clothes strewn among the vegetables and fruit stalls, the paving stones still wet and vivid with blood, provided disturbing yet compelling images. It was possible to televise such an atrocity only moments after it had occurred, with the shock still visible on the faces of the victims, and the wounded and dying bodies in disarray in what was otherwise a familiar and domestic setting. Shopping in an open-air market is so innocent and pleasant an act, so tied to bringing home food for a family, that its violent disruption is bound to capture our attention and shake our complacency.

While the effect of televised images is hard to overstate, I am inclined to believe that it was the print media that were most effective at bringing the public to a recognition that events in Bosnia demanded their attention. This was done in three ways: first, by deepening the significance of the televised images through the evocative writing of journalists pointing out the cultural and historic importance of ethnic cleansing; second, by exposing governments in acts that were designed to obscure public notice of these events; third, by casting doubt on the role of other media, especially the Milosevic-controlled Serb media organs.

On September 22, 1991, during the war in Croatia, the *New York Times* wrote in an editorial:

> Destruction on this scale has no precedent in Europe since Nazi Germany's vengeful "Baedeker" raids on English cathedral cities in 1942, and the Allied firebombing of Dresden . . . The loss of life in Yugoslavia is tragic. It piles horror upon horror to engage as well in cultural extermination.[16]

The *Washington Post* picked up this theme when the war in Bosnia began, publishing on October 16, 1992, this passage:

> The atrocity of ethnic cleansing in Bosnia is apparently an even more thorough business than the evidence of widespread murder,

deportations and brutality would indicate ... Serbian attacks ... have purposely and successfully targeted national libraries, museums and archives ... a kind of "ethnic cleansing" that adds a chilling new dimension to the atrocities that now dominate the news.[17]

Articles of this kind added depth to the CNN reporting by asking the public to notice a dimension of the emergency that is hard to picture on television, the cultural aspect of the ethnic cleansing of the Serbian campaigns.

The *New York Times* was also willing to expose efforts by the U.S. government to avoid notice. On August 27, 1992, the *Times** charged that the State Department had purposefully not tried to confirm reports of Serbian ethnic cleansing for fear of triggering the Genocide Convention. On December 20, 1992, the *Times* reported that, having received reports in the spring of concentration camps where Muslims were tortured and murdered, "Washington did not press for immediate investigation of the camps. Instead, it tried to keep the reports from becoming public." It was not until the summer of 1992 that a reporter was able to visit the camps and publish testimony of murders and atrocities. Even then, "the U.S. [merely] expressed concern and insisted that the Red Cross be allowed into the camps. It said nothing about freeing those imprisoned or punishing the perpetrators." *Le Monde* reported that the United Nations had attempted to suppress its own report for more than a year showing that "Serbs alone have pursued ethnic cleansing as a planned and systematic government policy."[18]

Finally, print media called attention to the role of the media itself in creating Serbian fanaticism and in attempting to prevent the world from noticing the crisis. The *Times* in an editorial published November 7, 1992, pointed out that when the JNA began the siege of Sarajevo one of the first targets of their bombardment was the television tower that allowed Bosnia's independent, multiethnic TV station to broadcast. Milosevic's media campaigns were widely noted, including the observation by the *Times* that "a climate of hate did not exist throughout Yugoslavia before warmongers created it, partly by manipulating the news."

At first, intelligence reporting and official reaction seemed to be in synch. As early as September 1991—three months after the outbreak of the First Yugoslav War (in Slovenia)—Secretary of State James Baker denounced the JNA for "actively supporting local Serbian forces ... causing the deaths of citizens it is constitutionally supposed to protect" and went before the U.N. Security Council to say that "the Serbian leadership"

*The following references are to the *New York Times; The Times* of London took a very different view.

and the JNA were "working in tandem [to] create a 'small Yugoslavia' or 'greater Serbia.'" But it simply wasn't clear that events in Yugoslavia, which had successfully been brought to the attention of world leaders and their publics, constituted a real emergency—a systematically organized mass killing—and should be understood that way. Instead, for a long time it appeared that preserving the Yugoslav state in its entirety could stave off a true emergency. As a result, some eight months after Slovenia made its first formal move toward secession, the United States and the E.C. member states, as well as the Conference on Security and Cooperation in Europe (CSCE), were still voicing continued support for a unified state under Belgrade. Baker asserted that the United States would not recognize the independence of Slovenia and Croatia "under any circumstances." When independence was declared by the two republics, "[b]oth the Bush administration, through the personal visit to Belgrade . . . of Secretary of State James Baker, and the members of the European Community . . . warned Slovenia and Croatia that they will find neither diplomatic recognition nor economic assistance following a unilateral decision on their part to quit the Yugoslav system and declare themselves independent."[19]

Thus it was obviously not enough to merely notice, as Baker clearly did. There also had to be a recognition of emergency, and this required an understanding of the situation that, for a long time, eluded the United States and its European allies.

DEFINITION: RECOGNIZING AS AN EMERGENCY

This recognition was long in coming. Indeed, several ideas were deployed, at different times, to effect what the *Washington Post* called "a flight from reality" and a condition of "denial."[20] Perhaps the most potent of these was that the conflict in Bosnia was a "civil war" and thus part of the normal evolution of state formation. Events worthy of notice were taking place, perhaps, but they did not constitute a true *emergency*. The appropriate use of the term "siege" was debated, with the inference that Sarajevo and other surrounded and bombarded cities were not really under siege because their citizens could have fled, quite consistently with the mission of the Serbs (who were more than happy to see them go), and were restrained from leaving either by fear or by actions of the Bosnian government that tried to keep its beleaguered citizens from deserting the capital. The Balkans were often described as a place with a long history of unfathomable violence, implying that war in Bosnia was really not so out of the ordinary. Finally, for a period there was doubt cast upon the persistent rumors of a network of Serb concentration camps, including specifically rape camps.

Henry Kissinger was among those who took the view that Bosnia was not "a true nation" and had no specific cultural identity; rather it was a kind of no-man's-land where rival ethnic groups vied for power. The war in

Bosnia "is a civil war," he wrote, "not an invasion of a sovereign country by a neighbor. Croatia and Serbia support their nationals inside Bosnia, though Serbian assistance is most flagrant."[21]

If it was a civil war, however, precisely against the government of what state were the insurgent forces fighting, Bosnia being no "true" nation-state?* A civil war pits the insurrectionary forces within a state against the government of that state or against other forces attempting to seize the power of the State; by definition, it postulates a "true" State, over whose government the war is being fought. Moreover, if the conflict in Bosnia were a civil war, how could the insurgent forces have been the "nationals" of other member states of the U.N.? Rebels are the nationals of the state whose government they wish to seize; if they are the nationals of some other state, which is "supporting" them, then they are an invasion force and not the partisans of a civil war. On Kissinger's view, whose nationals were the Bosnian Muslims? They couldn't have been nationals of Bosnia, because it was, on this view, not a true nation-state. Were they then the nationals of Croatia and Serbia? And if they were, then are we to understand that the murderous attacks on them by these states were engagements in a civil war against the governments of Croatia and Serbia by rebellious Muslims, and that this civil war simply happened to take place outside the territorial borders of both states?

The history of the four Yugoslav wars—in Slovenia (1991), Croatia (1991–1992), Bosnia (1992–1995), and Kosovo (1999)—invites confusion in characterizing the conflict, and in fact initially the United States and the European Community took the position that Slovenia and Croatia were illegal secessionists. That would have made the first two Yugoslav wars "civil" wars because there was only one state party to the war, Yugoslavia. This characterization, which eventually all parties—including even the Serbs—were forced to drop, might analogize the Belgrade regime in 1991 to that of Washington in 1861: a central federal government facing seceding states and struggling to hold the entire group together. Indeed Milosevic often made use of this analogy at the time, claiming among other things that the oppression of Serbs in the seceding states was like the practice of slavery by the American Southern states, against which federal troops had been used. Whatever the merits of this grotesque simile, it has little application to the war in Bosnia, owing to Belgrade's agreement in 1992 to recognize Bosnia as a separate state.

The reason that Secretary Baker and others initially characterized the war in Yugoslavia as a civil war between a central government in Belgrade and breakaway secessionist states with capitals in Ljubljana, Zagreb, and

---

*Presumably this argument does not apply to the conflict in Croatia, which is a true nation-state in that it is overwhelmingly the creature of a single cultural group, the Croats.

Sarajevo was simply that they believed that the breakup of Yugoslavia would lead to a bloodbath, which they of course wished to avoid. But this wholesome objective would not be served by such a characterization precisely because it was wholly contrived and had no relation to constitutional events within the state of Yugoslavia. Once Milosevic found himself able to manipulate the organs of a multinational federal state to effect a Serbian dictatorship, messages such as Baker's and the E.C.'s gave him a green light to use the JNA as ruthlessly as he wished[22] in pursuit of a constitutional arrangement that was itself really as much a new state as any of the others.

Perhaps what some had in mind was not that Bosnia was engaged in a civil war against Belgrade, but rather that the Bosnian Serbs and Croats, in their attempts to dismember Bosnia and amalgamate with their respective states across the border, were fighting a civil war against Sarajevo. The reason many persons held that Bosnia was not a "true" nation-state was that there is no single ethnic, "national" group that utterly dominates the state so that it becomes the engine of welfare for that group. It is disquieting that such an argument should be made in Europe today (it would disqualify many African and Asian states) because it so clearly calls to mind a precedent one would think that statesmen would shun. When Adolf Hitler wished to incorporate Czechoslovakia into the German Reich, he quite correctly pointed out that the Sudeten Germans were a large minority in Czechoslovakia (a more discrete and insular minority than the Serbs, one might add, who speak the same language as all other Bosnians), and that the Czechs themselves were not a majority national group (being about the same 44 percent that the Bosnian Muslims are in that state). Czechoslovakia was not a true nation-state, Hitler argued, with perhaps more justice than this can be said regarding Bosnia (which after all was the result of a national referendum and not of a great-power arrangement like the one at Versailles that created Czechoslovakia). On these grounds, Hitler argued that the Sudetenland ought to be amalgamated with Germany, just as Serbian leaders in Belgrade argued that Serbian areas of Bosnia should be detached from Bosnia and added to Serbia.

Civil wars are commonly held to be the bloodiest and most violent of wars. For our purposes, what is important about the characterization of a crisis as a "civil war" is that it blurs recognition of the crisis as an *emergency*. Though it makes the horrible reports coming in from the war no less horrible, they now conform to our expectations[23] and such a conflict will be resolved, presumably, in the usual way. The most frequently heard argument for enforcing the arms embargo against Bosnia—which Bosnia claimed to be a violation of that state's Article 51 right of self-defense under the U.N. Charter—was that to allow the Bosnians to be supplied with arms would merely prolong the war. That is, lifting the embargo would attenuate the natural course of such conflicts, increase the casualties and suffering, to no different end. Moreover, intervention in a civil war— like intervention in a marital dispute—is not only risky but officious. In the normal course of things the parties sort these matters out among themselves; there is no emergency, at least not for the society of states.

Against this view of the "normal" course of events, there intruded the insistent reports of Serb concentration camps. I believe there can be little doubt that, but for the suffering of Jews and others in the Nazi death camps in World War II, the news of Serb extermination and torture camps at Omarska,[24] Trnopolje, Susica, and elsewhere would not have had the same, sickening effect on public opinion.[25] Two heroic figures stand out in this reporting: Roy Gutman of the American newspaper *Newsday,* who managed to talk his way in August 1992 into the Omarska camp to confirm stories of torture and executions;[26] and Tadeusz Mazowiecki, the first non-Communist prime minister of Poland, who was appointed in August 1992 by the United Nations as special rapporteur on human rights abuses in the former Yugoslavia.

Mazowiecki filed a series of eighteen reports over the ensuing three years. In contrast to other U.N. reports which studiedly de-emphasized or obscured the facts of mass atrocities, Mazowiecki's are unflinching, carefully documented, and filled with gritty, factual detail. One documented 119 rape-induced pregnancies (from which it has been estimated a figure of 12,000 rapes in total can be statistically extrapolated).* One of his first reports described a Serb attack on Prijedor[27] the preceding May and gives a striking picture of the practice of ethnic cleansing. On the night of May 29, Serb tanks and infantry took up positions around Prijedor.

> When the attack began Serbs from the village guided the tanks to the homes of certain Muslims and the inhabitants were asked to come out and show their identity cards. Many of those who did were summarily executed. . . . Some 200 residents of Partisan Street were executed and a hundred homes were destroyed. During the [tank and artillery] attack the local radio continued to call for the surrender of arms, yet not one shot had been fired by the Muslims.

When the artillery barrage stopped around noon, Serb paramilitary moved in and slit the throats of Muslims. "The bodies of the dead were carried away by trucks, which left a trail of blood." Those not killed immediately were transferred to a convoy heading toward Omarska. Badly damaged

---

*The Bosnian government has assembled details of 13,000 rape victims. Noel Malcolm, *Bosnia: A Short History* (Macmillan, 1994), 295, n. 27.

houses were bulldozed, and their foundations covered with fresh earth. Five mosques were destroyed; the Muslim cemetery was razed.[28]

Mazowiecki's final report, from Srebrenica, gives a detailed summary. This account is taken from the Report:[29] On July 11 the Muslim "safe" enclave of Srebrenica fell to the Serbs. U.N. Dutch troops stood by while between 38,000 and 42,000 Muslims were expelled from the area. A group of mainly women, children, and elderly men were taken in trucks, some of which were driven by U.N. personnel, to U.N. headquarters at Potocari, where upon arrival they were forcibly seized by armed Serbs. Beatings, abductions of women, and acts of physical violence often resulting in death then occurred; witnesses reported executions. There were many reports of shots and screams in the nearby cornfield during the night.

A second group of about 15,000 draft-age Muslims and several women and children marched on foot out of Srebrenica toward Bosnian lines, consistent with earlier Serb campaigns of displacing Muslims. Most of this group were civilians, but between 3,000 and 4,000 may have been previously armed defenders of the city. This group was repeatedly shelled; these men who surrendered were physically assaulted, often fatally. Others were lined up against a wall and shot or were taken by the hair and their throats slit. The journey was fraught with chaos and violent attacks; thousands of persons in this group were executed by Serbs. Witnesses reported that some Serbs were disguised as U.N. officials (apparently with blue berets provided by the Dutch troops). Of this second group it is now believed that 7,500 were captured and murdered.*

In a summary section the Report drew several conclusions, including that credible direct and circumstantial evidence existed of mass executions, countless rapes and physical assaults, and the destruction of property by the Serbs. Ominously the report noted that still unaccounted for were thousands of Muslims who were removed from Srebrenica, and that the rapporteur had been unable to verify claims that they were in detention. In fact, they were not.

But the most startling element of the report, whose dispassion and repeated reliance on the credible "reports of international observers," gruesome detail, and evenhandedness are notable, was the letter that accompanied it. "Speaking of protecting human rights is meaningless in the context of the lack of consistency and courage on the part of the international community and its leaders," the letter read. The U.N.'s own leadership had

---

*Many Muslims, however, made it to Tuzla, where there were then reports of reprisal attacks by the displaced Muslims on Serbian civilians living there. Local authorities reported harassment and physical violence, and the robbery of several Serb houses, without police protection. Police reportedly watched as unknown persons killed a Serbian man. The mayor of Tuzla warned the police over this incident, and undertook to compensate Serbian citizens for damages thus incurred.

frustrated Mazowiecki's efforts to call attention to the "barbarous acts and terror on an enormous scale" that had occurred. He now resigned to protest U.N "hypocrisy" in "claiming to defend [Bosnia] but in fact abandoning it."

There were other figures,* including especially those conscientious young career foreign service officers who resigned their posts in protest over U.S. Bosnian policy, who enabled the world to understand that regardless of its juridical characterization, what was happening in Bosnia constituted a true emergency. By operating in tandem with the media, these officers were able to bring to the public information that otherwise was confined to diplomatic cable traffic. The *New York Times,* in an editorial on December 20, 1992, observed, "[T]he U.S. Government received the first unconfirmed reports from Bosnia that Serbs were setting up concentration camps in which Muslims were being tortured and killed. . . . Washington . . . tried to keep the reports from becoming public. If other countries received similar reports, they gave no public sign. . . . What did the world do?"

Even still, it was not enough to provide the world with clarifying ideas that defined the crisis as an emergency, that showed us why what was happening was so unusual. Once we realized that the reappearance of concentration camps, tank and artillery supplemented by organized paramilitaries, and international complacency in the face of these facts were the salient features of the crisis, we still required a reason to act. Events were now defined as an emergency, but this would not lead to intervention unless there were some decisive reason to intervene. Notice—the awareness that something dramatic is happening—and recognition that that "something" is an emergency—still waited on a decision to act. That could only come if the emergency was defined in terms that gave bystanders good and powerful reasons for action.

DECISION: DECIDING TO ACT

Pope John Paul II was one of those leaders who provided states with reasons to intervene in Bosnia. He issued a statement after the Mazowiecki report that read in part: "The news and pictures from Bosnia, particularly from Srebrenica and Zepa, testify to how Europe and humanity are still

---

*For example, Jon Western, a State Department analyst stated, after his resignation, "You can't read through the accounts of atrocities on a daily basis, add them up and see what's happening and not be overwhelmed," citing one cable—which he said was typical of the diplomatic traffic he received— that told of a nine-year-old Muslim girl who was raped by Serbian fighters and left in a pool of blood, and whose parents were forced to watch helplessly from behind a fence for two days as she died. A few days before Marshall Freeman Harris, another career U.S. foreign service officer, had resigned, calling attention to the U.S. administration's unacknowledged efforts to pressure Bosnia into accepting the Vance-Owen plan. These resignations and the public appearances of George Kenney, who resigned from his post as Yugoslav desk officer, gave credibility to the media's reports from the front, which otherwise tended to be discounted by diplomats and government officials.

collapsing into the abyss of degradation . . . They are crimes against humanity [which amount to] a defeat for civilization."[30]

Whose job is it to defend civilization, however? States have an interest in protecting the worth and value of civilized life. Achilles' shield depicts, it will be recalled, not only war and the law courts, but also religious ceremonies and wedding feasts. But what motivates states is not the same as what might move an individual or a nongovernmental organization or even a particular group of states, like an alliance, to intervene in an emergency. The case of the Iraqi invasion of Kuwait provides an instructive example.

It is frequently remarked that the reason the United States led a coalition of states in a campaign to expel an Iraqi occupation force from the state of Kuwait was because vast oil reserves lay within the territorial domain of Kuwait. Allowing these reserves to fall into hostile hands would have threatened the economic and military security of the West, of which the United States was the leader. If Iraq had invaded a state poor in resources, like the Kurdish section of Iran, the West would have done nothing, as indeed it did nothing during the Iraqi invasion of Iran.

This description of events is a kind of half-truth: it is true that the potential possession of crucial raw materials by an enemy gives a state a good reason to be sensitive to the actual seizure of those raw materials. With the vast new reserves Kuwait would have brought him, Saddam Hussein might have been able to raise oil prices to the economic detriment of many industrialized countries; certainly he was no counsel of oil-price restraint, as the Kuwaitis have been. Absent such a reason, it is quite possible that the United States and other powerful states would not have marshalled the enormous forces that won the Gulf War. But it is not true that the United States would have found such a threat to its prosperity a sufficient reason to intervene. Imagine, for example, what America would have done if, instead of simply invading and annexing Kuwait, Saddam Hussein had fomented a democratic uprising against the notably undemocratic Kuwaiti regime, and later contributed troops to aid a provisional government that had nominally maintained Kuwait's independent status but had overthrown its monarchy. It is highly implausible to imagine that the United States would have sent 400,000 men to the Arabian desert in such circumstances. What proved crucial in the Gulf conflict was the *combination* of both material reasons for intervention and the threat posed to the foundations of the states system. The Iraqi attack on Kuwait was the first time since the founding of the United Nations that one member state had invaded another, conquered, and annexed it. It was this intersection of interests, strategic and constitutional, that galvanized great power leadership.

Similarly, in Bosnia it was necessary for world leaders to recognize both the strategic reasons for acting and the legal imperatives to do so. Stopping a campaign of ethnic cleansing, which threatened the most basic human norms of decency, could provide one; the recognition of Bosnia as a true European state, with a right to exist, could afford the other.

For this reason, the answers to two apparently quite unconnected questions were both critical to moving the United States and other states to act: first, were the atrocities in Bosnia part of a systematic campaign of ethnic and cultural extermination against the Muslims or were the atrocities simply examples artfully chosen by the media of acts that had been in fact committed by all sides to the conflict? And second, were the borders of the Bosnian state worthy of legal respect or were they merely an arbitrary, anomalous hindrance to the recognition of the principle of self-determination by national groups? Dimitri Simes put these questions powerfully when he wrote, on March 10, 1993:

> It is hard to justify U.S. intervention on moral as well as geopolitical grounds. First, all sides in the war in Bosnia have committed atrocities, although the Serbs have committed more than the others, partly because their military advances gave them more opportunities. Paradoxically, because of Western insistence that the Serbian Army stay out of the confrontation, the fighting was assigned to the ill-disciplined Serbian militia in Bosnia, thereby increasing the likelihood for abuses. Second, do we really believe that the administrative borders in the ex-Yugoslavia—set up by Tito's Communist regime and based neither on history nor on current demography—should be treated as sacred?[31]

Simes may have been misinformed about the role of the Serbian army. In fact we know that Serbian irregulars (many of them members of the JNA who were detached from their regiments) were deliberately deployed in order to confuse the situation legally, disguise the role of Belgrade, and give the appearance of a Bosnian civil war rather than a Serbian invasion. Simes, however, was not alone, and with his customary insight, he had gone right to the heart of the matter: both of his questions had to be answered before a decision to act would be taken.

ETHNIC CLEANSING

On November 20, four months before Simes's article in the *New York Times,* Mazowiecki noted that particular attention should be drawn to the "appalling extent of persecution by 'ethnic cleansing' against those of Muslim ethnic origin [who are] threatened with extermination."[32] By contrast, in Simes's view, there is nothing unique about "ethnic cleansing": the atrocities committed by the Serbs were no different, though perhaps they were somewhat more numerous, than those committed by all the other parties to the Yugoslav conflict. To the extent that Serbian atrocities were more numerous, according to Simes this was partly because the JNA had not been an active party to the war, forcing Serbia to rely on irregular partisans, and partly a result of the large amounts of Bosnian territory under Serb control. To assess the truth of these observations, we might begin by asking: What is ethnic cleansing? Is it a random affair of irregular militias? Did all the parties to the Yugoslav conflict participate in such campaigns?

The forced resettlement of populations on the basis of their cultural identity is hardly novel or peculiar to the Balkans. Assyrian,[33] Greek, and Roman conquerors—to say nothing of the treatment of the American Indians—all provide precedents for such behavior.[34] Even the calculated destruction of an ethnic group and its culture, as was attempted by the Nazis against Jews, by the Turks against Armenians, by Australians against Tasmanian Aborigines, is hardly unique to Bosnia. What makes "ethnic cleansing" so odious is precisely the world's experience with it, especially in this century. The very term, with its eugenic overtones of extermination, repels and chills because it is not new—because, that is, it reminds us of precedents, of other horrors and other places.

The first English use of this term that I have been able to locate[35] occurred when a Reuters reporter in Belgrade quoted Croatia's Supreme Council as charging that "the aim of [a particular Serbian expulsion of Croats] is obviously the 'ethnic cleansing' of the critical areas to be annexed to Serbia."[36] One year later, a reporter writing in the *New York Times* in the summer of 1992, noted that "the precondition for [the creation of Greater Serbia] lies in the purging—'ethnic cleansing' in the perpetrators' lexicon—of wide areas of Bosnia of all but like-minded Serbs." Indeed what partly made the term so shocking was its casual use by the Serbs until the world community seized on this phrase. One scholar, Norman Cigar, has traced the phrase to the original program of the Serbian Chetnik leadership, issued on December 20, 1941. Two of the stated objectives of this program were

> to cleanse the state territory of all national minorities and anti-national elements . . . [and] to create a direct, continuous, border between Serbia and Montenegro, and between Serbia and Slovenia, by cleansing the Sandzak of the Muslim inhabitants and Bosnia of the Muslim and Croatian inhabitants.[37]

Why was this necessary? Why didn't ethnic dominance suffice in those areas where Serbs were in a majority? To understand the answer to this is to see why ethnic cleansing is a strategic and tactical set of ideas, and not just an emotive name for atrocities; it is also to see why the multiethnic state of Bosnia, unlike the states of Croatia and Serbia, is unlikely to have been a perpetrator of this strategy.

The biologists Stjepkp Golubic, Thomas Golubic, and Susan Campbell have published a demographic study of the Bosnian population that quantitatively demonstrates its essential indivisibility without mass resettlements.[38] Working from the 1991 census, they show that the districts in which various groups—Serb, Croatian, Muslim—were dominant prior to the war were neither homogeneous nor contiguous. Each of these areas in which a particular group had a dominant plurality also include a substantial percentage (between 22 percent and 43 percent) of another group. Moreover, each collection of dominant districts that was aggregated by contiguity amounted to only a fraction of the total population of the group, leaving between 35 percent and 68 percent of that group outside the area of its dominance.

Nor did dominance correlate with cultural purity: Bosnian Croats in the north of Bosnia, where they were the dominant group, lived with substantial minorities of Muslims, as they had (peacefully) for centuries. If statistical dominance does not correlate with cultural purity, and if the areas of dominance are not contiguous, then to achieve the dictatorship of one cultural group would require a use of force like ethnic cleansing. Moreover, the cultural patrimony of historic Bosnia would also have to be destroyed:

> Architecture . . . bridges [and] monuments built by the Ottomans were the most visible, most immediately tangible signs of Bosnia's "otherness." These became targets of relentless artillery bombardment or straightforward demolition. [L]ibraries housing rare books and priceless manuscripts were deliberately destroyed . . . Hundreds of delicately designed mosques, large and small, that had stood for centuries unharmed, untouched, disappeared overnight.[39]

One reason why the Vance-Owen Plan, which envisioned ten separate provinces, was criticized as a concession to Milosevic's program was that it was estimated that an additional two million persons would eventually be forced to leave their homes.[40]

Ethnic cleansing is more than simply a new name for forced resettlement, however. It is a calculated strategy that occurred when the political objectives of the parliamentary nation-states Serbia and Croatia (though they may have been led by communists or fascists) confronted the complex demography of the state of Bosnia.

> Just as the Krajina region of Croatia, for example, is now 91% Serb, though it was only half Serb before it was seized by Serbian military and paramilitary forces in 1991, so too in Bosnia, connecting a Greater Serbia called for cleaning non-Serbs from areas of Bosnia such as Prijedor, Srebrenica, Foca, Gorazde, and Brcko where Serbs had been a minority, as well as from Banja Luka, where they had been a majority.

In Zvornik, where Muslims once constituted 65% of the population, now . . . they are just a handful. In Prijedor, by September 1992 . . . Serb radio announced that the Serbs were now a majority and were ready for a referendum.[41]

Nor is ethnic cleansing only a strategy. It is also a well-defined system of military tactics, coordinating JNA and militia forces, involving a particular set of military maneuvers including artillery bombardment, encirclement, terrorism, and the maintenance of detention camps.

The tactics of ethnic cleansing are by now well known, though not always well appreciated. In the first stage, an operation commences with isolated terrorist attacks by Serb irregulars on rural populations of Muslims.* Thereafter, the role of armor and systematic shelling by heavy weapons is integral to its operations. The U.S. submission to the War Crimes Tribunal gives numerous accounts, of which I will excerpt an example:

A 27-year-old Bosnian Muslim witnessed the Bosnian Serb artillery bombardment of Biscani at about noon on July 20, 1992. Biscani was one of many Muslim villages in the Prijedor area and had a population of about 1,000 Muslims. Since May 1992, there had been Bosnian Serb soldiers and other officials in the town. From May to July, their activities had been limited to provoking the population by insults, residential searches, and general harassment. The primary targets of the provocations appeared to be the wealthier and more prominent citizens of the town, including doctors, lawyers, and business owners. Sometime between 2 pm and 3 pm on July 20, the artillery bombardment was lifted, and the town was assaulted by a force of Bosnian Serb infantry supported by one tank and one armored personnel carrier. Members of the attacking unit were Bosnian Serbs from the Prijedor area and from areas in the vicinity, such as Sanski Most and Banja Luka. The witness recognized several of the attacking soldiers as residents of the Prijedor area. All wore camouflage uniforms, red berets, and had the Serbian flag on one sleeve of their uniforms. Small groups of soldiers quickly occupied virtually every house in the village. After they had secured each house, they shot and killed most of the male residents in or immediately outside their homes. The women and children were rounded up and placed in a small number of houses so that they would be easier to watch. The witness observed the shooting through a window from

*One eyewitness report from the village of Zaklopca, where at least eighty-three men—virtually all the men of the village—were summarily executed by Serb irregulars, stated: "My brother in law was outside in front of the house when the Serbs appeared. They told him to give up his weapons. He told them that he did not have any weapons but that they could take his cows. Then one of them opened fire and killed him."

inside one of the houses. He saw two soldiers kill Vehid Duratovic and Sadik Causevic as they attempted to run away. He also saw seven Bosnian Serb soldiers assemble five male residents of the village in front of a wall of a house across the street where one of the Bosnian Serb soldiers shot and killed them. Four of the five victims were: Rifet Duratovic, Mirsad Kadiric, Ifed Karagic, and Ibrahim Kadiric. From July 20 to 27, the surviving local residents, mostly women and children, buried the victims' bodies in the local cemetery. On July 27, about 35 women and children and about 15 men were rounded up by Bosnian Serb soldiers. The witness believed that this group constituted all the remaining survivors of the village. This group was forced to walk to an unknown location near the entrance to the city of Prijedor where Serb soldiers had set up a roadblock. At about 8 pm, a bus arrived and transported the entire group to the Trnopolje detention camp. (Department of State).[42]

These tactics drove unarmed farmers and the residents of small villages away from their homes seeking protection. The refugees flooded into towns that swelled with their numbers. The "safe area" concept was actually quite consistent with the Serbian campaign of ethnic cleansing. It made towns like Tuzla and Zepa into concentration camps full of hungry and defenseless people without sanitation, without medicine, without effective weapons. And that brings us to the second stage of ethnic cleansing, the siege of cities that have been engorged by the arrival of rural refugees.

At this second stage, the Serbs, using JNA artillery, fired round after round into the surrounded city. When one sees the now familiar CNN film clip of a multistory apartment house in Sarajevo crashing down, one mustn't think that that is the result of isolated mortar fire. Rather, it is the result of artillery and heavy tanks in stable emplacements firing heavy caliber shells into the steel and concrete of the targeted building in a sustained bombardment.

In the third stage, the besieged city surrendered. When this occurred, the Serbs culled the men of military age. These were taken out of town and machine-gunned, and buried in mass graves. Then the tactical focus shifted to the remaining women. One element of ethnic cleansing has to do with the calculated policy of rape. This wasn't so much to eliminate the genes of Muslims (a kind of genocide), however, as it was to humiliate Muslim women so that they and their husbands would never want to return. Only when the men had been murdered and the women defiled did the buses arrive to take the remaining refugees to the humanitarian centers manned by the U.N. outside Serb territory. This explains the peculiar demographics of the refugee population, in which only the very old and the very young appear to be surviving when these are in fact the most vulnerable populations among refugees.

Ethnic cleansing is thus not merely a political goal. It is a coordinated set of tactics in service of a well-thought-out military strategy. Its success depended in part upon the nonenforcement of the U.N. Security Council resolutions that established the no-fly zone and banned JNA logistical support, upon the luring of refugees into the "safe areas" declared by the U.N. Security Council and upon the U.N. arms embargo that kept the Bosnians from effectively returning the fire that rained down upon them from artillery positions around their towns. Which is to say that "ethnic cleansing" depended upon the tacit cooperation of the U.N. Security Council, which studiedly and repeatedly confirmed all three of those supporting elements.

According to a Pentagon official, "[w]hen the Serbs began to move [against Sarajevo], we saw them executing the same strategy they had employed against other enclaves. They do not conduct a direct assault but surround the area and create an increasingly dire humanitarian situation." By using their control over access to the surrounded enclave, the Serbs could negotiate with the U.N., allowing humanitarian aid only to the extent that such negotiations enhanced the Serbian military position and compelled the U.N. forces (Unprofor) to become voluntary hostages. David Owen reflects this role as unwitting accomplice in his autobiographical memoir. "Living with the arms embargo," he writes, "for all its inconsistencies and evasions, was never an immoral position for it ensured the continuation of Unprofor's humanitarian mandate for the first few years, when it saved hundreds of thousands of lives."[43] He has a point, of course—but that point is enfolded within the Serbian tactics of ethnic cleansing, which carefully manipulated the "humanitarian mandate" to achieve its military goals.

One final element of this strategy must be touched upon.

The aim is not only to expel the ethnically "unclean" population from the desired territory but also to destroy all possibilities for their return—completely to dismantle the spiritual and material structure of the civilization of the unwanted population . . . [T]he expelled populations will stay away because they have no homes, mosques, schools, etc.—literally nothing to go back to. . . . [T]he real guarantee is fear: the knowledge that their neighbors remain in wait, should they try to go back. According to numerous testimonies, special military expeditions from Serbia and Montenegro have sought not only to slaughter and expel but also to inspire or force the indigenous Serbs to do the same. . . .[44]

Thus the strategy of ethnic cleansing is hardly a random affair managed by uncoordinated bands of irregulars. General Momcilo Perisic of the JNA has openly acknowledged the commanding role played by his army in the conquest of Bosnia.[45] Many facts, including logistical ones, support this finding of coordination, but some of the most telling of these facts are the most humble. International observers were at first puzzled to see rows of shoes neatly lined up on the edge of roadsides or forests where it was later determined that mass executions had taken place. Apparently the victims were instructed to remove their shoes before they were marched off to their execution sites. This small detail suggests a coordinated tactical plan that Serb commanders were instructed to follow, for it is unlikely that this would occur coincidentally at different sites.

All of this information was of course available to the states of the West—the United States and her European colleagues on the Security Council. What blurred these facts—just as Darley and Latane had predicted—was the introduction of a crucial ambiguity by the Serbs and others. High-ranking officials in the West repeatedly stated that *all* parties to the conflict were at fault, and implied that Muslims, Serbs, and Croats had all participated in such campaigns of "ethnic cleansing."

On May 18, 1993, Secretary Christopher, in preparation for testimony that day before Congress, asked the Balkan desk of the State Department to come up with examples of Muslim atrocities in the war in Bosnia. The desk officers angrily declined: they said that though there had been Muslim atrocities, they paled in comparison with those committed by the Serbs. Later that day, Christopher nevertheless stated in his testimony: "It's easy to analogize [Bosnia] to the Holocaust. But I never heard of any ethnic cleansing by the Jews against the German people." The acting assistant secretary for human rights later reminded Christopher, in a memo since disclosed, that, of the documented atrocities, only a handful (6 percent) could be attributed to Muslims, and that, in contrast with the Serbian and Croatian campaigns of ethnic cleansing, no evidence linked these isolated incidents to the central Bosnian army command or to the Bosnian government. In fact, the *New York Times* later reported, the State Department had for more than a year been reporting "complicity by the Milosevic regime and the Government of Croatia in atrocities of both regular and paramilitary forces."

Nevertheless, other officials testified before the House National Security Committee as late as November 1995 that all sides in the conflict shared the blame. "There are no white hats there" became something of a cliché among officials.[46] Similar sentiments were voiced by the U.N. secretary-general, who lamented that the conflict had "spared no one in its violence."

Indeed at the time one often heard, at first sotto voce, from senior officials that there was "evidence" that the Bosnians had shelled themselves on at least one occasion—the deadly mortar attack on the Sarajevo market on February 5, 1994—in an effort to kindle foreign intervention. Owen repeats this in his memoirs, unfortunately citing Tanjug news agency, a Belgrade government source; there is supposedly at least one U.N. report that attempted to make this claim, though later studies have been unable to confirm this. The most experienced and respected diplomats in the United States and the United Kingdom—Lawrence Eagleburger, a former ambassador to Yugoslavia and subsequently U.S. secretary of state, and Lord Carrington, a World War II veteran and former British foreign secretary—both quietly let it be known that to knowledgeable observers of the region all sides had a share in the responsibility for atrocities.

These perceptions, perhaps more than any other fact, introduced a pervasive ambiguity into the situation and slowed Western response. They are vaguely analogous to the perceptions on the part of the bystanders in Queens that Kitty Genovese was somehow mixed up in something that had led to the attack on her. Those who actually knew her (though slightly) were the very ones who knew that she worked in a bar, often came home late, was vivacious and outgoing.

This perception that "all sides are implicated" also fed the strict neutrality observed by the U.N. peacekeeping force. Observance of this neutrality had the perverse effect of making the Bosnians a constant irritant to the U.N. officials. Owen observes that the "prevailing view" of U.N. commanders was that "Unprofor's [United Nations Protection Force] worst problems were with the Muslims." When food convoys came to deliver humanitarian supplies to the enclaves, desperate crowds of Muslims would gather and try to keep the U.N. trucks from leaving. The British foreign secretary complained that the Bosnian Muslims were using Unprofor forces as a shield, as when Bosnian government forces would fire out from one of the "protected" but surrounded enclaves. General Rose repeatedly told observers that his governing rule was not to cross "the Mogadishu Line"—a phrase alluding to the U.N. experience in Somalia, when a mission that began as neutral peacekeeping led to involvement in a factional war, including a punitive search for a particular Somali warlord. The U.N. representative of the secretary-general, Yasushi Akashi, resolutely refused to authorize NATO air support when he believed this would amount to a partisan contribution to one side, exceeding the "mandate" provided by resolutions of the Security Council.*

Why did such experienced and distinguished diplomats as Eagleburger and Carrington, Owen and Douglas Hurd contribute so thoroughly to mud-

---

*UNSC Resolution 836 did, however, authorize U.N. forces to use "all means necessary" to protect the enclaves.

dying the waters, and clouding the otherwise clear perceptions of emergency and the necessity to act? And why did not the Muslims succumb to the sort of tactics that worked so effectively for the Croats and Serbs? Why *didn't* "all sides do it"? I think the answer to both questions is the same, and I hope it justifies the time spent on the description of ethnic cleansing in a book about the history and future of the modern State.

As we have seen, "ethnic cleansing" is more than simply the aggregate of countless individual atrocities. It encompasses a set of military tactics carefully designed to exploit the deep weaknesses in the *nation*-state. When Eagleburger and Carrington spoke about Yugoslavia, they spoke from broad experience and knowledge about the Serb-Croat nationalist struggles that, since the early part of this century, were saturated in the very sort of ethnic fanaticism that led to policies of "cleansing" territory of other ethnic groups. When these policies were deployed by former communist leaders like Tudjman and Milosevic to consolidate their own power in the aftermath of the collapse of communism, they led inevitably to the atrocities of the Bosnian theatre; the very intermixture of groups there insured that. Thus the war seemed merely like a continuation of the Serb-Croat struggle, which was the focus of their experience and insight. But it was also a brutal assault on Bosnian Muslims, and the media, which these statesmen so distrusted and despised, were making this assault into a defining hour for the society of nation-states. Could that society set legal standards for admission and defend those states that met those standards? Or was the conundrum of self-determination—when does an ethnic minority get its own state, thereby creating a new minority from the now-detached remnants of the formerly majority group—somehow bound up with the nation-state? Could tumors of nationalism grow and attack a modern state with a strategy, ethnic cleansing, that specifically arose from this conundrum, thus paralyzing the rest of the members of the society of states? To see the conflict as one that necessarily implicated "all sides" was to miss what was unique and defining—and yet seeing the parties in this way reflected how trapped these statesmen were in the paradigms of the nation-state. Experienced statesmen were slow to appreciate that action needed to be taken because they did not understand that the policy of ethnic cleansing posed a mortal, moral threat to the society of nation-states. Thus when these men were discredited by the horrors they did not prevent, the society of nation-states that they represented (as appointees of the U.N., the E.U., the OSCE*) was discredited also.

The Muslims were emphatically not the architects or perpetrators of ethnic cleansing because they did not see themselves as a separate national entity (rather more as a religious one) and few initially wished to have a

---

*The Organization for Security and Cooperation in Europe, the successor to the CSCE.

state whose legitimacy depended upon its championing a particular national or cultural group. This was dramatically demonstrated when an attempt by some Muslim elements to sequester Sarajevo Serbs in a football stadium was swiftly halted and roundly denounced. Bosnia was a multicultural state. Thus the helpful efforts of outside diplomats to partition the state (as was done in Ireland, India, and Cyprus) were perceived by the Bosnian government as an effort to destroy the fabric of their state, not simply take away territory. As Gow noted:

> The E.C. effort was essentially based on the adoption of an idea—ethnic territories or "cantons"—propounded by the Serbian camp. Understood by the E.C. negotiators as a means to propitiate the Serbs and avoid war, it was in reality a charter for "ethnic cleansing": ethnically designated cantons created the basis for ethnically pure territories.[47]

It is estimated that about a third of the marriages in Sarajevo are "mixed"—that is, multiethnic. Approximately one-third of the Bosnian government army is Serb. While there can be no doubt that Muslims have perpetrated atrocities (indeed, have been indicted by the War Crimes Tribunal[48]), the strategy of ethnic cleansing would have been antithetical to the constitutional ethos of their state when war broke out, though this ethos was sorely tested by events in the war, and there is at present a strong Muslim nationalist party.

ARBITRARY BORDERS

One other muddying characterization was offered up by Western statesmen. Whether or not they were able to persuade their publics that all parties to the conflict were equally culpable, there remained the idea that Bosnia's borders were essentially arbitrary ("set up by Tito . . . and based neither on history nor on current demography") and thus that the terrible events in Bosnia were part of a necessary adjustment: an event worth noticing, of course, an emergency even, but not an event that required any action by others. Thus, as U.S. Ambassador John Scanlan put it, "Two thousand years of imperial invasion and subjugation of the indigenous populations have imposed artificial borders which have left three million Serbs outside Serbia, two million Albanians outside of Albania, three million Hungarians outside of Hungary."[49] This makes any violation of Bosnian borders seem understandable and less reprehensible. It implies that certain adjustments ought to be made to correct territorial oversights on the political cartographer's map. In fact, the borders of Bosnia-Herzegovina have been virtually unchanged for almost five centuries.

The "stranded" Albanians, and Hungarians, and Serbs, and others have been in the provinces they currently inhabit for similar periods of time, much longer, it must be observed, than the Poles in what was once Germany, or the Russians in what was once Poland, borders that are perhaps better denominated as "artificial," but that few American ambassadors, I think, would suggest need adjustment.

In his memoir, Owen denigrates the "internal borders" of Yugoslavia that formed the state of Bosnia. "The unwarranted insistence on ruling out changes to what had been internal administrative borders within a sovereign state was a fatal flaw."[50] These borders were "arbitrary, " conceived by Tito's commanders "during a march" at the end of World War II. If Croatia and Bosnia had the right to secede, Owen argues, then surely the same right to self-determination should be extended to the Serb minorities living in those countries, and the borders adjusted accordingly.

There is some reason to doubt the factual basis for this argument. Historians generally agree that Bosnia was considered a distinct entity that maintained its identity throughout long periods in the Middle Ages until its conquest by the Ottoman Turks in 1463; the border between Croatia and Bosnia roughly corresponds with the extent of Ottoman penetration into Europe, and the border between Serbia and Bosnia, the Drina River, has not been breached since 1919. For our purposes, however, the greater significance of Owen's argument lies in his invocation of the paradox of self-determination. Why indeed should not the Serbs in Bosnia be allowed to secede? And then why not the majority Muslim populations in border towns along the Drina like Visegrad and Zvornik, whose peoples were slaughtered or made refugees? Why should not these have been allowed to remain and simply secede from the seceding Serbs? If, as Owen suggests, borders are arbitrary that do not correspond to the ethnic demographics of the local community, what precisely qualifies as the defining community? The IRA has long argued, for example, that the referendum to which the United Kingdom has agreed for the determination of the future of Northern Ireland must be based on an island-wide, rather than six-county, franchise. If they are wrong because Northern Ireland is in some way demographically distinct ("Protestant," for example), then what of the minority Catholics in the six counties? Shouldn't they be allowed to have a referendum limited to themselves on the same theory that allowed the Northern Irish to confine their referendum and exclude the Southern Irish?

This paradox of self-determination bedevils the nation-state. It is the original sin of this constitutional order, present at the creation of the American nation-state in 1861 and the German nation-state in 1871, the two first models of this archetypal form. The nation-state's "sin," if that is the way to put it, is that it promises to deploy a state on behalf of a nation when *nations* as such (cultural and ethnic groups) are a distinct categorical entity from *states* (legal and strategic structures). "All nations are entitled to their own states" is really a way of saying "all states must define and locate their nations," a lesson that Slobodan Milosevic, among others, clearly learned in his post-communist phase. The society of nation-states has no more significant responsibility than to manage this paradox. If every nation gets its own state, then who decides the territorial extent of the state when a national group is unevenly spread over many countries, dwelling within other national groups and encompassing other groups that dwell within it? Each nation-state develops its form of the State for strategic purposes— that is, it selects a legitimate form of the State that will serve as an effective military instrument to resist coercion; but if every nation gets its own state, then the strategic imperative of the State turns inward, to civil war, as each ethnic and cultural group attempts to assert itself, and the State endlessly divides and redivides along smaller and smaller sociological lines—or the strategic imperative of the State turns outward, to conquest, as each State collects its nationals and those territories important to their welfare, adding new members, subsuming them and then asserting their right to exist within a single state. This is more than a problem, it is a paradox because every nation-state also defines its "nation" for constitutional purposes—that is, it determines which cultural group on behalf of whose welfare the resources of the state will be deployed. But how can every nation get its own state when every state must choose its nation? Because of this paradox, the society of nation-states, rather than the single nation-state itself, sets limits on how a state may define its nation (representative democracy and human rights) and how the nation may define its state (the inviolability of borders).

The society of nation-states decides, either in peace conferences like those at Versailles and San Francisco, or in the ongoing institutions set up by these peace congresses—like the U.N.—what elements are required for self-determination. This could not have been clearer than in the example of Bosnia because the E.U. set up a special tribunal—the Badinter Commission—to set the criteria for international recognition of the new states being formed from the former communist countries of Eastern and Central Europe. Bosnia was recognized by the E.U. only after it had specifically satisfied the Badinter criteria, which included respect for the provisions of the Charter of the United Nations and the Charter of Paris, especially with regard to the rule of law, representative democracy, and human rights; guarantees for the rights of minorities; and respect for the inviolability of frontiers.[51]

By contrast, recognition of statehood on the basis of the criterion of *nationality* alone puts the ball in the court of the State itself. Nationality is very much a creation of culture and demographics, and therefore it is to some degree manipulable by the State, as Hitler showed. Thus to permit the transgression of Bosnia's borders by charging that they were merely "administrative" rather than sufficiently ethnic forfeits the society of states' ability to do anything other than partition—which plays into the paradox of self-determination rather than manages it. Such a step invites ethnic cleansing.*

The effect in the third Balkan war was to smudge the clarity of the situation, to make it far less clear that anything had to be done other than to recognize the ultimate demographic outcome of the war. Not only did this give a greater incentive to Serbian and Croatian aggression—and effectively doom the very "cantonizations" it was meant to support—it largely removed the society of states from the action. Doubtless for some statesmen, that is what it was designed to do. (This is perhaps why Gow characterized British policy as "pusillanimous realism.")[52]

Once we are clear of self-serving rationalizations, the true constitutional and political history of Bosnia and the former states of Yugoslavia has some troubling implications for this period in the history of the State, and the national idea of giving civil and political rights to minority groups as such. The coincidence of rights-based claims and ethnic identity is a policy born of the basic elements of the nation-state, and laden with peril for that constitutional form. Like an infection that uses the body's own nuclear material to attack the host, ethnic rights can be wasting, even fatal, to the nation-state. The wars in the Balkans represent the pathological endgame of the nation-state in which the constitution of a state is put into play whenever ethnic groups get on each other's nerves. Perhaps that is the real lesson of Yugoslavia. This conflict did not begin in 1350. It began in 1917 and took its crucial contemporary turn with the constitutional changes in 1974. In an effort to pacify one set of minorities—the Albanians and Hungarians—the 1974 Constitution created a new set of minorities: the Serbs within the Albanian and Hungarian enclaves. This peculiar political topology, the necessary creation of a new threatened group through the constitutional protection of an old one, propelled Milosevic out of the anteroom of Communist party hacks and onto the stadium stage of late twentieth century world political figures. Milosevic was able to capitalize on the techniques of modern media in order to mobilize around a twentieth century idea: because every "people" gets a state, the Serbian state should rightfully rule everywhere there were Serbs. By this means he was able to crush the constitutional position of Albanians within his state because there was a Serb minority within the Albanian minority and at the same time reach into other states like Croatia and Bosnia to aggrandize the Serbian state. The Serbian slogan was: "Why should I be a minority in your state when you can be a minority in mine? Why should I leave to join

*General Ratko Mladic, indicted for the massacre at Srebrenica, was determined to expel the refugees gathered there before any diplomatic settlement incorporated their right to live in the town and in the surrounding villages, like Zepa. Henry Porter, "Days of Shame," *The Guardian* (London), November 17, 1999.

Serbia, when you can simply leave and Greater Serbia will be the result?" The paradoxes of this topology fractured the confidence of the society of nation-states in a way that even its most senior and respected officials could neither repair nor quite keep from making worse.

In the end it was the sheer weight of horror, coupled with the unique and recent history of the European Holocaust, that persuaded states that action must be taken. The secretary-general of the United Nations never understood this. When asked why he did not return to New York when Mazowiecki resigned over the Srebrenica massacres, Boutros Boutros-Ghali replied, "Because if I do, all the African countries will tell the world that while there is ethnic cleansing in Africa—a million people have died in Rwanda—the Secretary General pays attention only to a village in Europe." This obtuse yet odious observation also in its way contributed to a stifling of action: after all, if there are genocidal campaigns underway all over the world, how can we act in all of them? Rather the secretary-general ought to have mobilized what public opinion there was for action, instead of lamenting that it was geographically misplaced, as, for example, in his famous harangue of the Security Council for its overattention to Yugoslavia ("a war of the rich," in Boutros Boutros-Ghali's much-reported outburst). Queens is not a dangerous place, and I imagine that at 3 a.m. there were more horrors underway in other districts of New York besides Kitty Genovese's stabbing.

When Lawrence Eagleburger met Elie Wiesel, Nobel laureate and chronicler of the Holocaust, in December 1992 the latter pressed him to take some action in the former Yugoslavia where crimes were being committed that he called ethnic cleansing. Eagleburger claimed that the State Department's lawyers* were strongly opposed to characterizing such actions as "ethnic cleansing." According to Eagleburger:

> Wiesel said: "Fine. Call them crimes against humanity then, but whatever you do, America can no longer remain silent about the atrocities being committed" . . . I relented. [Wiesel] made me look in the mirror and decide . . . [that we couldn't] stay silent.[53]

Four days later, Eagleburger spoke to a meeting of European foreign ministers in Geneva and urged a "second Nuremberg" to prosecute crimes committed in former Yugoslavia. "The fact of the matter is [the Serbs] were doing some things that were pretty . . . awful," Eagleburger later said. "And we ought to have been saying something about it. And we probably should have been saying something about it a lot sooner. [But] *I also knew it wasn't going to produce anything*."[54]

---

*Of whom I was one at the time, having been appointed the counselor on international law in 1990. This opinion did not, however, reflect my views, though it may possibly have reflected that of others.

Because once states had decided to act, it still remained for them to determine who should act and what should be done.

DETERMINATION: ASSIGNING SOMEONE TO ACT

Once these states had been brought to believe that something had to be done, opinion within the leading Western members of the society of states coalesced around four options as to who should act: it was either up to the parties to the conflict themselves, or a matter for the European powers, or for the U.N, or for the United States. As Darley and Latane might have predicted, each state's evaluation of these options depended upon its factual assessment of the situation. Thus those that believed the conflict was the result of ancient and implacable hatreds tended to conclude that there was little that outsiders could do, whereas those that believed that concerted multilateral diplomacy could effectively mediate the situation and then help monitor whatever settlement emerged, tended to emphasize a role for the U.N. (or the E.U.) unhindered by unilateral initiatives, in contrast to states that believed that decisive action depended upon the use of force. States in this last group were more likely to assign a leading role to the world's largest military power and the leader of NATO, the United States. It took some time, however, before a consensus formed around one of these options, if indeed it ever really did. In the meantime, as in the emergency situations studied by Darley and Latane, the sheer presence of so many potential intervenors tended to ensure that no one would act effectively.

A MATTER FOR THE PARTIES TO THE CONFLICT

Perhaps no characterization of the conflict was more widespread than that describing it as one going back centuries, reviving "ancient hatreds." In fact, the history of this struggle begins, as noted above, in 1917. The Corfu Declaration on July 20 of that year proposed a new nation-state that was to consist of Slovenia, Croatia, Serbia, Bosnia-Herzegovina, Montenegro, and Macedonia, that is, the six provinces that ultimately became the state of Yugoslavia (which would have included the various religious groups of the region, Catholics, Muslims, and Eastern Orthodox).

At this time Croats and Slovenes wished to join Serbia in order to become part of the winning side of World War I. The new Kingdom of Serbs, Croats, and Slovenes, as it was called, was not simply an artificial creation of the Versailles Conference, as is sometimes erroneously said; it actually embodied the national aspirations of the South Slavs. Like so many model marriages it began to fall apart almost as soon as it was consummated. The ensuing struggles were in sharp contrast to the historic cooperation between the various groups of southern Slavs against their imperial oppressors. Far from being an ancient ethnic conflict, the wars in Yugoslavia are very much a twentieth century nation-state affair.

Nevertheless, diplomats and politicians in the 1990s repeatedly referred to the wars in Yugoslavia as arising from primeval struggles. One French foreign ministry official declared, "They need to fight. They want to fight. They have hated each other for centuries."[55] When the Senate Armed Services Committee held hearings on Bosnia, a representative of the U.S. Joint Chiefs of Staff was asked by a member of the committee, "Why is it that they fall upon themselves periodically, and have done this for a thousand years?" The reply, even discounting for the obliging nature of such answers when questions are put to military personnel by senators, was remarkably inane: "Sir," the officer replied, "I wish I had the answer to your question . . . but there is certainly a history, going back, at least in my study of the problem, as far back as the 13th century, of constant ethnic and religious fighting among and between these groups."[56]

This description of the nature of the conflict was not merely an historical observation, however erroneous; rather, for many it became a highly purposeful characterization that compelled the inference that there was little that bystanders could do. As Charles Lane put it in the *Washington Monthly:*

> The most durable canard about the wars in the Balkans is that they are the consequence of ancient ethnic hatred, too complex and too deeply rooted to be fathomed, much less countered, by outside powers. This "analysis," which sounds sophisticated but is in fact intellectually lazy, became conventional wisdom—a kind of intellectual trump card—among all those who sought to forestall United States military intervention to stop the Serb drive in Bosnia.[57]

Not only officials but the public also made this link. Thus in a poll conducted by the *Boston Globe*,[58] a majority of persons were of the opinion that the United States should not be involved. A typical response: "The people in the Balkans have been killing each other for hundreds and hundreds of years. Putting our troops in there is not going to teach them how to get along with each other. If they are determined to kill each other, they're going to go right on doing it whether we're there or not. I don't want one American kid to die trying to teach them how to get along."[59]

Seeing the emergency as arising from intractable, atavistic behavior led almost inescapably to the conclusion that action would have to come from the parties themselves before anything else could be done. "Ultimately," the U.S. president said in 1994, "this conflict still must be settled by the parties themselves. They must choose peace."* And he asked rhetorically,

---

*Much to his credit, President Clinton later, in 1999, repudiated these remarks and publicly regretted them. Bill Nichols, "The More Policy Changes, the More It Seems the Same," *USA Today,* April 21, 1994, A4.

in June 1995: "Do we have the capacity to impose a settlement on people who want to continue fighting? We cannot do that there."[60] Even in July, after some of the worst shelling of Sarajevo and the other "safe areas," indeed after the fall of Srebrenica, President Clinton's remark that the Bosnian conflict "has roots in the 11th century," was quoted by a reporter who suggested that such an account of the conflict was designed to ward off pressure for the United States to intervene.[61]

This linkage was not hard to detect. As deputy assistant secretary of state Ralph Johnson put it:

> Many Americans are asking why we haven't done even more to resolve this crisis. That's an understandable question. It goes against all our instincts to see Yugoslavia descend into violence without stepping in to stop this tragic process. The bottom line in this crisis, however, is that the world community cannot stop Yugoslavs from killing one another so long as they are determined to do so. . . . [W]e cannot stop the violence or resolve this conflict. Only the peoples of Yugoslavia and their leaders can do that.[62]

Or, as Darley and Latane might have observed, even when bystanders notice a crisis and define it as such, and are persuaded some action must be taken, they will nevertheless assign that action to the parties involved depending on how those parties and their relationship are assessed. The *New York Times* columnist Thomas Friedman, in a passage that makes one wince, wrote at the time, "I don't give two cents about Bosnia. Not two cents. The people there have brought on their own troubles." The "ancient hatreds" argument implied that the relationship between the parties was one of feuding clans, rather than perpetrator and victim. No one would suggest that a rapist and his victim should be sequestered until they "work things out among themselves." The "ancient hatreds" gloss on the facts tended to denature the victims, making them more like co-dependents, to use a fashionable word, who could stop the ongoing antisocial behavior that was in crisis if only they would stop abetting it. These false assertions are similar to the ones made about Kitty Genovese. Like the facts about her—that she worked as the manager of a bar, that she was coming home at 3 a.m.—some of these facts about Bosnia were true. Like the implication that she was in part responsible for the attack on her, or at least might have been quarreling with a lover, the conclusions drawn were highly persuasive and prejudicial, though factually false. To the question "Who should act?" this approach implied: the parties themselves. Possibly someone on Austin Street in Queens said something like "I don't give two cents for that girl. She brought it on herself."

A MATTER FOR EUROPE

States, once they noticed that something was happening, and once they had interpreted that event as a true emergency for the international system, then had to decide what each state's responsibility was. Darley and Latane showed that the more persons who witness an emergency the less likely it becomes that any particular person will intervene. This seems at first paradoxical—isn't there safety in numbers? In fact, it is the diffusion of responsibility that paralyzes everyone. The person who comes upon a crowd standing around a fallen victim thinks, "Surely someone has called an ambulance." No previous crisis has been so flooded by helpful agencies: the European Union* appointed mediators, offered peace plans, convened conferences; the CSCE deployed its array of dispute resolution institutions; the U.N. was present to a degree that has, I believe, permanently damaged that institution; NATO was involved; and finally there was, of course, the Contact Group of the Great Powers. Rarely have so many institutions collaborated to produce so few satisfactory results, yet as Darley and Latane show, this should not surprise us. When Warren Christopher went to Europe for consultations in 1993, the very sincerity of his mission—that he genuinely sought consultations with our allies rather than trying to press them into line—doomed any conceivable effective action, because such consultations effectively paralyzed leadership by the United States.

This result was not, however, wholly unwelcome in Washington. Like the witnesses to Kitty Genovese's murder who said simply, "I didn't want to get involved," there were ample reasons for U.S. administrations from 1991 to 1995 to wish not to become parties to the conflict. Foremost among these were the political risks of introducing American ground forces into a shooting war in which American interests were highly attenuated in an election year (1992) and thereafter in a highly partisan atmosphere. Just what vital interest of the bystander is served when he intervenes—especially when there is some other bystander more proximate to the emergency?

Both President Bush[63] and President Clinton[64] referred to the situation in Bosnia as "a European problem." Deputy assistant secretary of state Johnson stated, "Why are we supporting the EC's efforts rather than taking the lead ourselves? [B]ecause we believe that Europe has the most at stake in this crisis." In a radio address on February 19, 1994, nearly two and a half years later, President Clinton said: "I want to be clear. Europe must bear most of the responsibility for solving this problem. . . ." The interesting aspect for our study, however, is the way in which assigning the

*As the European Community (E.C.) became in November 1993.

Bosnian emergency to Europe not only tended to remove the United States from taking action, but also diffused responsibility among Europeans so that thwarting intervention from *any* quarter ultimately became the effective policy of the society of states.

The European position, led by Britain and France, was anchored by three points: the European states would provide personnel for the U.N. force to protect U.N. humanitarian assistance (and in the event the majority of forces under U.N. command were actually European); they would not provide armed ground forces to enforce peace unless the warring parties agreed to a peace plan[65] and the United States also provided ground elements; finally, a diplomatic, rather than a military, solution was required. All of these points followed naturally from the premise that Bosnia was a "European" problem: Europe was responsible for providing forces to resolve the problem, and therefore could set the conditions under which these forces would operate, and the ultimate objectives for which they would fight.

In fact, however, these three points cannot be understood in isolation from the interplay with the various American proposals regarding Bosnia. The European position was artfully crafted, and withstood four years of assault in the press and by the Americans in NATO, precisely because it had been so carefully designed to fit with American diplomacy and presidential politics. By contributing small numbers of lightly armed troops to the U.N. peacekeeping mission the Europeans could veto any proposals for the use of NATO air power against the Serbs on the rationale that such attacks jeopardized European soldiers. By requiring advance agreement by the parties in Yugoslavia to a peace plan before being willing to commit ground forces, the Europeans effectively scotched any use of American ground forces to win such an agreement—because what U.S. president could justify sending American troops to a battleground in Europe from which European forces were conspicuously absent? Most interestingly, by stymieing any American initiatives, the Europeans thus took pressure off themselves from their publics: they were doing all they could, they said, in the face of vacillating and indecisive American leadership.

For so it did appear as the Americans made proposals that were rejected by the Europeans, which rejection was then made the excuse for withdrawing the proposals (which the Americans had only halfheartedly suggested in the first place). The characterization of the conflict as a "European problem" effectively meant that the least demanding course of action, essentially simply monitoring the war and waiting for a Serb victory to bring partition, became the de facto policy of the West. This also had the virtue, from the European point of view, of insulating European leaders from American criticism for inaction. On several occasions, European leaders made thinly veiled remarks about the right of those states with no forces at risk to criticize those states whose young men were actually in harm's way in Bosnia.

A case study in this exercise is the experience of the "Lift and Strike" policy. In early April 1993, the United States sent Reginald Bartholomew, one of its most experienced and capable diplomats, and Army Lieutenant General Barry McCaffrey, to London to suggest lifting the U.N. arms embargo that had throttled the grossly overmatched Bosnian government. The British rejected the idea, characterizing it as "pouring petrol on the fire"; but they countered with a proposal to launch NATO air strikes on the Serbs' largest artillery emplacements around Sarajevo. In Washington, the Joint Chiefs now balked: what was the "exit strategy"? How were we to know when the bombing should be stopped? More importantly, what if the Serbs retaliated by marching into Sarajevo? National security adviser Anthony Lake then offered a compromise plan, soon called "Lift and Strike." Lake countered that the arms embargo be lifted and air strikes be launched to hold the Serbs in check until the arms flow to the Bosnian army allowed it to defend its capital. This would provide the exit point and a prospect for relieving the siege.

In early May, Christopher returned to Europe with this plan. One day after his departure, the Bosnian Serb leader Radovan Karadzic announced that he had agreed to the Vance-Owen peace plan; the only remaining step was approval by the Bosnian Serb assembly. Christopher's mission was neatly thwarted. London and Paris rejected "Lift and Strike" and waited for approval by all parties of the Vance-Owen Plan. Four days into the trip, however, the Serbian assembly rejected the plan. Nevertheless, the Europeans now informed Christopher that "Lift and Strike" was dead as far as they were concerned. It would jeopardize their troops and abort whatever prospects remained for Vance-Owen. In Washington, the White House stuck to "Lift and Strike" but refused to go ahead without the concurrence of the Europeans. Removal of the threat of action against the Bosnian Serbs, however, had the effect of sinking Vance-Owen.

In mid-May Christopher testified that Bosnia was "a European problem" in which the United States could not act unilaterally. In June, to the question "Are people dying because the United States could do a lot more if we wanted to?" the undersecretary of state for political affairs, Peter Tarnoff, responded:

Yes . . . I am perfectly able to withstand criticism that we are abdicating power on this issue because I believe, and more importantly the President and the Secretary believe, that for major international issues of this sort, where other regional players have a great stake, we should make very clear that we will play a role, we will have a leadership role, but we are not going to be so far out in front as to allow them to defer to the

United States when it comes to making the very hard decisions on the commitment of men and women and resources.[66]

The Europeans meanwhile refused to put their own troops in further peril in the absence of American forces.

Thus the states of the West resolved Darley and Latane's question as to who should act by a complicated rondeau in which no one really had to take decisive action, but all were protected from public criticism by pointing at each other as the responsible party.

A MATTER FOR THE UNITED NATIONS

To many, the United Nations appeared to be the appropriate party to resolve the Bosnian emergency. The crimes against humanity perpetrated in Bosnia, the possibility of a wider war, and the flow of refugees fleeing the conflict—more than 500,000 fled to other European countries—provided ample reasons for U.N. action within the terms of the U.N. Charter. Moreover, the transnational consequences of the war did not directly threaten the vital interests of any one particular state outside Yugoslavia; for this reason too the U.N. must have seemed the right institution to act.

On June 15, 1993, at a news conference, President Clinton said, "Let me tell you something about Bosnia. On Bosnia I made a decision. The United Nations controls what happens in Bosnia." On July 6 he conceded "[w]hen it became obvious that I could not prevail upon the United Nations because of the opposition of some of the European nations, that's when things began to deteriorate again instead of move toward peace . . . [But] I *have* a policy."[67]

It is tempting to conclude that the decisions of the secretary-general and his appointees in Bosnia—the United Nations Protection Force (Unprofor) commanders, and the special political representative—were largely responsible for the debacle in that country because the U.N. was the institution that the society of states selected as the principal manager in the Third Yugoslav War. In March 1992, 14,000 troops—Unprofor, one of the largest U.N. peacekeeping forces ever constituted—arrived to monitor the Serbian and Croatian soldiers. Whatever the world may think now, it was once widely thought that this force was to protect civilians. The inability of Unprofor to defend the U.N.-declared "safe areas"—despite a Security Council resolution ordering them to do so with all necessary means—U.N. complicity in ethnic cleansing in the Serb depopulation of Muslim villages (even to the point of providing the transport),* the failure

---

*A January 1993 United States Agency for International Development Report concluded that 23 percent of U.N. relief supplies to the desperate refugees were in fact allocated to Serbian warlords. J.M.O. Sharp, *Bankrupt in the Balkans: British Policy in Bosnia* (Institute for Public Policy Research, 1993), 14.

to arrest war criminals even when these were indicted by a War Crimes Tribunal set up pursuant to a U.N. Security Council resolution, the refusal of the U.N. to permit NATO to enforce no-fly zones (also declared by the Security Council)—all provide a long list of failures for which critics will indict the United Nations.

Should we be persuaded by this indictment? It is true that all NATO air strikes had to be requested by U.N commanders and then approved by the political counselor representing the secretary-general before NATO could act, and that on many occasions the world witnessed awful slaughter because the responsible officials* could not be made to sign off on such strikes.[68] But who set up these rules? Not the secretary-general himself. In the Gulf War, although the Coalition was fighting with the authority of Security Council resolutions, there was never a suggestion that local commanders had to get the approval of U.N. personnel before acting to protect their troops. And why were Messrs. Akashi and Boutros-Ghali and generals Rose and Janvier so reluctant to use air strikes? Partly it was because, as they said at the time,[69] they were doubtful such air strikes would be effective. Partly it was also, I am inclined to believe, because the governments to whom the secretary-general reported did not really want air strikes if they *were* effective because these governments believed a weakened Serbian offensive would only prolong the war that was causing them such political embarrassment at home and presenting them with such difficult and risky choices abroad. Successful air strikes would only stiffen the spine of the Bosnian government to resist when the problem, as Boutros Boutros-Ghali repeatedly said, was that the parties did not "show the political will to end this terrible war."[70]

True, the local U.N. commanders were reluctant to risk retaliation against their own forces;† but who was responsible for the declaration of the "safe areas" policy in the first place—which accelerated ethnic cleansing by promising the fleeing Muslims safe refuge if they abandoned the countryside and their threatened villages—and for permitting artillery encirclements and sieges once the Muslims had been crowded into these city-camps? And who studiedly refused to provide enough troops and arms to carry out missions in Bosnia that were announced with such fanfare and resolve in New York? This was perhaps the most cynical of all the

---

*On July 10, 1995, Karremans, the Dutch commander of U.N. forces at Srebrenica, requested air support from the senior Unprofor officer, the French general Bertrand Janvier. These repeated requests were denied. When on July 11 Karremans desperately asked for NATO air strikes to relieve his position, Janvier declined to send the request forward, unbelievably, on the grounds that Karremans had used the wrong request form. The massacres occurred five days later.

†One doubts whether this justifies the actions of those Dutch soldiers who forced Muslim families out of the U.N. compound at one of the "safe areas" and then surrendered their U.N. helmets to the Serbs who used them to dupe Muslims who had fled to the hills into coming forward to their destruction. The real shame, however, lies with the political leaders who put these soldiers in such a position.

moves made in Yugoslavia because the European sponsors of Unprofor knew that once these troops were on the ground, they would effectively prevent any further action by the West. Because they were lightly armed and had no heavy armor, they could not protect themselves, and because they were vulnerable and present in so many dispersed locations, any forceful moves on their behalf threatened their lives. In effect, they were sent as hostages although they were dressed as peacekeepers.

The U.N. might have served as an open forum in which member states put the question of "Who is to act" to a public debate. Something like this was contemplated by the White House in June 1993 but rejected on the grounds that it would have embarrassed Allied leaders. "Christopher came back and the issue was, do we roll them and just say, 'OK, by God, we're going to the U.N. We're going to introduce a resolution. Veto it if you will,' " a senior White House official told reporters from six leading American newspapers. "European leaders called the White House after the visit by Mr. Christopher and argued that their reluctance to support air strikes and lift the arms embargo [Lift and Strike] was based on domestic political concerns." He said that "they pleaded that there be no destructive public recriminations. We concluded that then was not the moment to bring this into [an open debate]."[71]

Instead the U.N. was used by all parties as a cover for their own policies. The apparent answer to the question "Who is to act?" was the U.N., but this was only apparent. The actual answer was no one.

IMPLEMENTATION: WHAT IS TO BE DONE

The various policy options facing bystander states once they had decided to act can be grouped into several courses of action: (a) military responses; (b) neutrality; (c) economic sanctions; (d) humanitarian aid; and (e) political settlement. These courses of action were not mutually exclusive alternatives; they could be combined in different ways. Because each of these approaches also concealed various options—for example, precisely what military responses were appropriate: air strikes? ground attacks? monitoring by lightly armed observers?—they could be recombined in countless variations. Moreover, within each option the fundamental difference persisted between those who wished to intervene on behalf of the Muslims and those who did not. The result was that until one state actor, the United States, threatened to act unilaterally, the requirement of consensus largely frustrated any decisive action to bring the merciless suffering in Bosnia to a halt.

MILITARY RESPONSES

Consideration of the military option went through four phases that, like the more comprehensive Darley-Latane decision process, constantly recycled themselves, as decision makers searched restlessly for effective options, returning again and again to those that had been discarded when the ones that were chosen—usually various forms of inaction—proved disastrous.

The first phase was the consideration by the Pentagon of military action in the fall of 1991 when Dubrovnik was bombarded and Vukovar overrun. The chairman of the Joint Chiefs of Staff, General Colin Powell, expressed the view that nothing short of a massive deployment of ground troops for an indefinite period would be able to end the conflict. His view was by no means unanimously shared. Intelligence reports at the time disparaged the Serbian forces as undisciplined, poorly trained, and easily routed if confronted by regular armies. General John Galvin, at that time Supreme Allied Commander, Europe (SACEUR), urged the approval of air strikes that he believed would dispirit the Serbs, disrupt their steady supply of war matériel from Serbia, and remove the threat of heavy bombardment from Sarajevo. Powell's views, however, were far more sensitive to the political need, felt by all the member states of NATO in varying degrees, to avoid an open-ended commitment to a theatre of marginal political and strategic significance. Air power had been frequently oversold in the past; most governments realized that true pacification could come only with ground forces. Every government faced the same dilemma: the publics of the West were outraged by the horrific crimes in Bosnia but were united in opposition to sending ground troops to halt those crimes. As late as July 1995, Malcolm Rifkind, the British foreign secretary who succeeded Douglas Hurd, put it: "Britain hoped that the threat [of air strikes] would never have to be carried out. No one wishes to use air power, no one believes that that by itself will conclude the war in Bosnia."[72]

Moreover, the option of air strikes was intertwined with other, nonmilitary choices: the delivery of humanitarian aid to the besieged cities, for example, depended upon Serb cooperation. Once air strikes began, this cooperation ceased. Air strikes prejudiced the policy of neutrality toward all parties that was the posture of Unprofor, and it thus also jeopardized the safety of Unprofor forces who might be seized (as occurred in Pale after the air strikes in 1995) or fired upon.[73] When U.N resolutions authorized air strikes, the United States, Britain, France, and the Netherlands all sent planes to the region but no strikes occurred. Supported by the French, the U.N. secretary-general stipulated that strikes should be employed only if Serb tanks or artillery fired upon U.N. troops, and that the strikes should be limited to the sites from which the Serbs had fired. Only when U.N. peacekeepers were withdrawn and the secretary-general removed from the chain of command were effective air strikes really an option.

NEUTRALITY

One source of the paralysis that affected the assessment of options for action was the insistence of U.N. personnel that they remain neutral in the conflict. On such grounds, in September 1992, the secretary-general actually opposed enforcement of the no-fly zone despite a U.N. Security Council resolution to the contrary. In the spring of 1993, he reiterated instructions that U.N. peacekeepers were to remain neutral even when civilians were shelled inside U.N.-protected enclaves. In April of that year, he effected the recall of French General Philippe Morillon, who had personally led a convoy through Serb lines to relieve Srebrenica. In the fall of 1994, Boutros Boutros-Ghali requested the recall of a second French commander, General Jean Cot, who, he felt, had pressed too hard for air cover for his forces. Other U.N. officials said that strict neutrality should be maintained because the Serbs were no more guilty of aggression than the Croats and Muslims. In retrospect it can now be seen that the U.N. attempted to bolster its position of neutrality through the questionable suppression of information unfavorable to the Serbs: although the first press reports of Serbian concentration camps in Bosnia were published on August 2, 1992, U.N relief officials in Sarajevo admitted to having known about the camps for at least a month but having decided not to report this fact officially to New York. In any event, U.N. refugee officials in New York stated that action on the camps was an issue for the Red Cross, not for the U.N. David Owen points out in his memoir of this period that he "often stressed that the U.N. must not be seen as being at war with the Serbs."[74]

The difficulty with this position is that it was absurd in the Bosnian context: action (or inaction) by the U.N. inevitably helped one side in the war or the other. As James Steinberg has observed:

> The effort to maintain the U.N.'s "neutrality" in Bosnia face[d] an inherent contradiction: any effort to bring in humanitarian aid help[ed] the Bosnian forces in the struggle with the Serbs since the Serbs [were] attempting to use starvation and exposure to force the Bosnian government to capitulate. On the other hand, if Unprofor decline[d] to use force to overcome Serb barriers to the delivery of humanitarian aid, the U.N. [was] capitulating to the Serbs' strategy [and effectively aiding them because], in the guise of neutrality, the U.N. [would] neither guarantee the delivery of humanitarian aid nor allow the Bosnians to take their own effective measures.[75]

ECONOMIC SANCTIONS

Economic sanctions were widely applied in the Yugoslav conflict. Perhaps their most creative employment was the conditional sanctioning by the

E.U., which offered relief from economic sanctions following compliance with the human rights and other constitutional recommendations of the Badinter Commission. Sanctions were also applied to Serbia by the U.N. Security Council, initially in an effort to persuade Serbia to cease aiding the Bosnian Serbs. These sanctions seem to have had some effect: they are widely considered to have been the reason for the public distancing of Milosevic from the Pale government (the Bosnian Serbs), and for igniting anti-Milosevic opposition in Belgrade. The most controversial economic sanction, however, and the most far-reaching in its consequences, was the imposition and maintenance of an arms embargo on all the former states of Yugoslavia.

The arguments on this issue were partly strategic, partly legal, and partly moral. In military terms, it was clear that JNA weapons had made the material difference in the early seizure of 70 percent of Bosnian territory by Serb forces, but it was less clear that the Bosnian government would be able to hold on long enough to train its forces and equip them even if the embargo were lifted. Legally, the Bosnian government argued, the U.N. Security Council could neither institute a blockade (such as the one in the Adriatic that enforced the arms embargo) against, nor deny Article 51 rights of self-defense guaranteed under the U.N. Charter to, a member state that was plainly not an aggressor. The crucial argument, however, was moral: were the states of the West simply prolonging the suffering of the people of Bosnia by allowing arms to be brought in, or were they only giving the Bosnian government a fair chance to defend itself? To this last question the answer had to be "neither"—the words "simply" and "only" were not applicable in such a complex moral environment.

HUMANITARIAN AID

There was some shock in August 1992 when the former diplomat and columnist Leslie H. Gelb wrote in the *New York Times* that Western officials had told him their policy was to feed the Bosnian Muslims while "prompting them to surrender." "Let me be chillingly blunt about what Western officials told me regarding the Balkan crisis," he wrote. "They said that nothing they are doing or plan to do is at all likely to compel the Serbs to stop killing Muslims." Prior to this time it was not widely appreciated that the humanitarian mission to Bosnian Muslims was consistent with Serbian political objectives. In retrospect we can see that it couldn't have been any other way.

The supply of humanitarian assistance was made necessary in the first place by the Serb interdiction of utilities, water, medicine, and food to cities swollen with refugees fleeing Serbian attacks. These surrounded cities could not be resupplied by the U.N. without Serbian cooperation, which would be jeopardized by any Serb/U.N. confrontation. U.N. and

U.S. analysts have concluded that in any case only about one-quarter of the needed humanitarian supplies were reaching the target populations.[76] What did get through, however, depended upon negotiations with the Serbs who controlled access to the Muslim enclaves. This had the effect of pitting the officials of the humanitarian mission against any use of force against the Serbs, lest their relief routes be cut entirely. A senior U.N officer in Sarajevo was quoted by the *New York Times* as acknowledging that a newly proposed U.N. humanitarian relief plan for Sarajevo was not appreciably different than previous plans, all of which had failed. "But we felt we had to do something," said the officer with a *Bridge on the River Kwai* sort of logic, "or there would be no alternative to air strikes." Thus, despite a Security Council ban on all Serbian and other military flights in order to ensure "the safety of the delivery of humanitarian assistance," the U.N. actually resisted enforcement of the ban and limited itself to stationing monitors to observe infractions.[77]

Humanitarian aid provided a kind of camouflage to disguise inaction on other fronts. In 1992, the secretary-general stated, "I know that international public opinion is frustrated, they want to see quick results. But we believe it's important to avoid an escalation. . . . [The situation in former Yugoslavia] is not as difficult as it appears," he was reported as saying, pointing to the distribution of humanitarian aid.[78] By January 1994, Warren Zimmermann, the former U.S. ambassador to Yugoslavia who was running the refugee relief effort for the United States, quit in protest. "I had reached the conclusion," he said candidly, "that the humanitarian element for which I was responsible was being used as a cover for the lack of a real policy toward Bosnia."*

POLITICAL SETTLEMENT

Because the Serbs had been so successful in the Third Yugoslav War, any political settlement had to come to terms with their occupation of more than two-thirds of Bosnia, despite the fact that they constituted less than one-third of the population. This fact led to a series of proposed redivisions of the Bosnian state. Lord Carrington had initially suggested "cantonization" on the Swiss model. This was succeeded by the Vance-Owen Plan, which divided Bosnia into seven to ten largely autonomous regions with a limited central government. Owen himself worked hard to win acceptance of a Muslim mini-state on about a third of the territory of

---

*"As 1993 wore on, it became increasingly difficult for me to justify my personal participation in a policy whose tentative nature was being exploited by the Serbian aggressors. We were dealing fairly well with the humanitarian symptoms of the Bosnian war, the refugees and the displaced, but we weren't treating the causes. There was a tendency among administration officials to give public emphasis to the humanitarian issues as a way of disguising the lack of a consistent political approach. I sent several back-channel memos to Christopher suggesting variants of forceful responses but received no acknowledgement that they'd ever been read." Zimmermann, 226.

Bosnia. The Contact Group map, which was similar to the Dayton Agreement, provided for a Bosnia divided between Serbs and a Muslim-Croat federation.[79]

The difficulty with these various plans was that they violated the Statement of Principles agreed to by all parties at the London Conference in August 1992, which explicitly provided for the nonrecognition of territorial gains achieved by force and the restoration of the rights of persons driven from their homes. It may be, of course, that such objectives were simply unachievable in the face of a successful military conquest such as that by the Serbs, and that the authors of these plans were merely trying to put the best face on an unpleasant fact. But these proposed settlements, such as the Vance-Owen Plan, also were the product of the haunting notion that the Bosnian Serbs have some right, other than that earned by violence, to their own self-determination. If Bosnia had been allowed to secede from Yugoslavia with the consequence that its borders became the subject of international recognition and protection, then why wasn't this right also accorded to the Serbs within Bosnia, who had never wished to secede in the first place?

The answer to this is a complicated one. "Peoples" are entitled to self-determination, which is not the same thing as an entitlement to a state. Where there are adequate protections for minorities and fair and free electoral processes, a "people" has no right to secede absent the consent of the people with whom they share the right of citizenship. Bosnia was driven from a federation it wished to preserve by the violent transformation of that state into a Greater Serbia. There is no evidence that a similar fate awaited the Bosnian Serbs at the hands of the Sarajevo government.

Nevertheless, the recognition of Bosnian secession from Yugoslavia— pressed by Germany in the hope that recognition would provide some protection for Slovenia, Croatia, and Bosnia from Serbia—was unwelcome to most European states (and to the United States). In light of the breakup of the Soviet Union and secessionist movements in Spain, Northern Ireland, Italy, and elsewhere it is not hard to see why. Once the society of states accepted secession as a viable means of self-determination, something like "cantonization" became inevitable. Ironically, it was the military situation, which was presumed to have dictated this solution, that rendered the "solution" so objectionable. Whatever the advertising, most observers came to recognize that there would be no return for the displaced Muslims and that the Serbs had achieved by violence essentially what they sought.

The point isn't simply that deciding what action to take in Bosnia posed some hard questions. Security decisions that put lives at risk involve difficult choices. Rather it is that the difficulties arising from the Bosnian emergency are deep and problematic because their source lies in the origin of the nation-state in violence and ethnicity, and because the arrival of a new form, the market-state, with its universal media presence, exposes these deep conflicts to great and novel stress. Notice that the option of a military response was intimately connected to the provision of humanitarian assistance, which was also connected to institutional neutrality, which dictated the nature of both the economic sanctions imposed and the political solutions proposed.

In summary, as with the Darley-Latane description of bystander behavior in emergencies, it is the ambiguity of assessment that paralyzes action. Why didn't the great powers, and the United States, which purports to lead them, do more to stop the horrors in Bosnia? In Yugoslavia it was some time before the world noticed that something awful was happening; long before the massacres at Vukovar and Mostar the Serbian Communist leadership had embarked on a constitutional transformation of Yugoslavia that was accompanied by police terrorism and violent ethnic rhetoric. Once the world did notice, it wasn't altogether clear that the event was an emergency. There were many ambiguous interpretations that could be placed on events. Once the media had persuaded us that a true emergency was underway, it was very difficult to decide what to do as a consequence.[80]

These ambiguities went directly to the legitimacy of the nation-state. For example, is the war in Yugoslavia a civil war between a central government in Belgrade and breakaway secessionist states with capitals in Ljubljana, Zagreb, and Sarajevo? Or is it a series of civil wars between the Bosnian state and its Serbian and Croatian minorities and the Croatian state and its Serbian minority? Or is the entire affair simply the latest eruption of an intractable ancient conflict that was temporarily kept in check by the authoritarian regime that collapsed along with the other Communist states of Europe? Is what happened in Bosnia an example of ethnic cleansing or something else—a forced migration of the kind we have seen countless times before when new states are born?

V.

Of course the murder of Kitty Genovese under her blood-stained stairway in Queens is not the same, legally or strategically, as the ethnic cleansing of Muslims from the blood-soaked villages of Bosnia. If it were, then armed intervention (a strategic act) to protect the Muslims would be like police work (a law-governed act): that is, there would be no debate as to whether the benefit of enforcing the rules justifies the cost of their enforcement. Some international lawyers and diplomats behave as though there is a world order of nation-states that is analogous to the civil order of a society, and they argue that the international community must respond in the way that a domestic government responds to criminal behavior. This makes armed intervention into a kind of police work. If anyone still believed in this vision of world order in 1992, I don't see how that person could maintain such a view after Yugoslavia. One might say that the lifespan of the "New World Order" can be dated from its beginning in Kuwait City to its demise in Srebrenica. It would be more accurate to say that the society of nation-states that was forged in the Long War acted swiftly and with assuredness in Kuwait, where it offered a classic nation-state answer to a classic state problem of aggression to acquire resources; and that this sure-footedness vanished when that same society was faced with a more puzzling conundrum arising from its own identity: when does a "nation" get a state? What made this failure so significant—for it is hardly the first time this question has arisen—is that it occurred in the context of the emergence of the new market-states.

CHAPTER SIXTEEN

The Death of the Society
of Nation-States

THE LEGITIMACY of the society of nation-states will not long outlast the delegitimating acts of its leading members. Srebrenica represents the final discrediting of that society because there the great powers showed that, without the presence of the Long War, they were unable to organize timely resistance even against so minor a state as Serbia when Serbia threatened the rules and legitimacy of that society. By contrast, in Kosovo, a U.S.-led coalition attacked Serbia to vindicate *market-state* concepts of sovereignty—specifically, the novel* conviction that a state's refusal to grant rights to an internal minority renders that state liable to outside intervention. The U.N. was studiedly ignored in the Kosovo war—the Fourth Yugoslav War—and what failures there were, in an otherwise highly successful air campaign, can be largely attributed to the structure of NATO and the unanimity requirements of the North Atlantic Council.

In Bosnia, despite the presence of such mighty nation-state institutions as NATO, the U.N., the OSCE, and the E.U., states nevertheless did not dare risk the sacrifice of their soldiers on behalf of a cause whose relationship to the welfare of their own societies, and their citizens, was so attenuated. The Achilles' heel of the society of nation-states—the problem of self-determination for national peoples—provided the crucial ambiguity that invited the diffusion of responsibility that so consistently characterized the Third Yugoslav War. Armed with this ambiguity, the Serbs challenged the society of nation-states and humiliated it. But what had made that society more vulnerable than before? After all, the Italian attacks on Libya and Ethiopia and the Japanese attacks on Manchuria had been no less humiliating to the same society. Why was Bosnia of such great significance for the collectivity of *nation-states*?

---

*Novel, that is, for the society of nation-states. State-nations had no such restraints, as, for example, in the European coercion of the Ottoman Empire over the treatment of Christian minorities.

The globalization of (1) strategic threats (by virtue of nuclear and other weapons of mass destruction, which made states like the United States with no contiguous enemies nevertheless vulnerable to attack from anywhere on the globe), of (2) markets (owing to advances in computation, which permitted the rapid transience of capital), and of (3) culture (the result of a universal system of information that depends upon recent developments in telecommunications) put the nation-state under enormous pressure to enlarge. Only by expansion (such as NATO provided Western Europe by bringing the United States into the theatre of European security, or by means of the European Union, which broadened national markets into a single market of continental scope) could states hedge against the new risks imposed by globalization. China and Russia were compelled to open themselves to trade; North Korea did not, and starved. Yet lengthening the membrane that enclosed the State also meant thinning it, just as widening the membership of states in NATO and the E.U. put a stop to the deepening of political relationships among states within those organizations. Writing of the E.U., Charles Tilly cannily observed:

> Community-wide consumer protection, elimination of customs barriers, free movement of migrants, elimination of work permits for Community residents, participation of "foreigners" in municipal elections, transferability of university credits, Europeanization of driver's licenses and automobile standards, creation of a common currency, and establishment of Europe-wide television—all entailed by the Maastricht pact—will directly attack the capacity of any state to pursue a distinct and independent policy for employment, welfare, education, culture or military organization.[1]

As the nation-state increasingly loses its definition, the sharp cultural borders that, for example, made the Danes different from the Dutch, are losing legal and strategic significance. The nation-state is less able to deploy law (or strategy) on behalf of national cultural values, yet there is no "Euro-identity," for example, or similar transnational identity either. Instead, as Martin Wolf put it, globalization has undermined the collectivist values represented by the nation-state and turned attention to the benefit of individuals. Governments of nation-states are faced with the prospect of asserting national cultural identities against a fragmenting populace that takes its various identities from associational but largely non-national sensibilities. Indeed the nation-state may come to be seen as a kind of enemy of its people. Nation-states are too rigid, have too many rules for behavior (including economic behavior), have been captured by special interests whose welfare demands higher taxes with larger loopholes and more officious regulations (not limited to economic regulation but including also, for example, hate-speech laws, smoking bans, and the whole panoply of political correctness, as well as prohibitions against a wide variety of personal behavior).

The State has always depended on getting people to risk their lives for it. Each constitutional order found a way to do this. The nation-state persuaded people that a state whose mission was the improvement of their own welfare provided a valid justification for enduring personal jeopardy. If such a state is no longer able to enforce and sustain national cultural values ("family values" they were called in some states, "basics" in others), its claim on the sacrifice of its citizens weakens. Indeed, the new cultural values, precisely because they are so fragmented and promote such individuation, are not readily suitable to promotion by the State, which is too clumsy and moves too slowly and with too little discernment to shore them up. The popular sense of identity is becoming both too large for the nation-state (as with "Green" movements) and too small (as with breakaways like Catalonia or Lombardy or Guangdong). For nation-state conservatives, this means a nauseating loss of sovereignty to new transnational institutions (like the P8*); for nation-state liberals, this development threatens to remove the regulation of capital enterprises from the hands of states and surrender national life to the pitiless imperatives of the globalized market.

The shift to the market-state does not mean that states simply fade away, however. If the acquisition of more territory is less important than before to garnering wealth, the luring of people and capital by the most attractive state policies is absolutely crucial. For China, holding on to Tibet may someday become almost irrelevant, but incorporating Hong Kong increased Chinese GDP by 26 percent at a single stroke. Only a state could have done that. Assuring financial and legal stability, an educated workforce, and tax-friendly havens for investments are all state-governed activities, even when some of these operations are privatized by law. The real shift is simply from public purposes to private purposes, from a state that takes its legitimacy by assuring the common welfare to one that instead relies on providing the broadest possible opportunity for the satisfaction of individual interests.

In the face of such an historic shift in the constitutional order of states, the society of states also had to change. There is some movement—in Brussels, but also elsewhere—for larger, super-nation-states to cope with the challenges described above. In my view, this is a move in the utterly wrong direction. It would recapitulate on a continental or even global scale the transformation of the *Zollverein* (a nineteenth century German economic union) into the German nation-state at a time when the model

---

*The informal annual meeting of governments to discuss political topics that grew out of the G-7 (Group of Seven) economic summits.

itself—the nation-state—is less and less viable. Moreover, a super-nation-state, like the organizations of the society of nation-states, hypothesizes a world made of law that is incompatible with variations in sovereignty. Yet just such variations are the main method by which market-states will develop different forms in order to create a pluralistic society of states by some other means than simply granting states to desiring nations. The society of nation-states attempted to suppress such variations in sovereignty because of that society's basis in the equality of states. Its international law is universal and grows all the weaker because of this essential premise. Perhaps most telling of the impotence of the society of nation-states has been the fate of the United Nations.

The major institutional result of the idea of a world constitution of nation-states was the creation of the League of Nations. Among the most important of the many features of the League was the guarantee by member states of the political independence and territorial integrity of each member against aggression. This guarantee of sovereignty is repeated in the U.N. Charter. The Charter, like the Covenant of the League of Nations, assures states their independence and the undisturbed enjoyment of autonomy within their territory. This goal is built on a premise—the opacity of sovereignty—that will increasingly hobble the society of nation-states as that society attempts to deal with transnational threats to the environment, to its critical information infrastructure, and to its humanitarian ideals. The air war in Kosovo was a decisive step in recognition of this fact, and it was, in its way, just as deadly an event for the society of nation-states, which depends upon the premise of state sovereignty, as were the crimes at Srebrenica.

It is easy to see how the societies enmeshed in the immense agonies of the Long War would want to ensure international tranquility at all costs. Doubtless this desire lay behind the failure of the League to stop Mussolini's aggression against Ethiopia. It is difficult to forget the scene of the small Ethiopian emperor appealing in vain to the great powers for aid. But it seems to be equally difficult to remember the Italian aggression against defenseless Libyan tribes that occurred several years earlier. Then Italian planes strafed and waged, systematically if incompetently, a modern war of ethnic annihilation; this was when the first concentration camps were set up by a European power in the twentieth century.[2] Libya was, however, unlike Ethiopia, governed by Italy and thus these acts of aggression were veiled by the cloak of sovereignty. This failure to act by the society of nation-states was not simply a lapse of will, and so it is seldom associated with the League's other public failures. Rather such a failure was built into the idea of a world community composed of sovereign nation-states. The League was irrelevant to allegedly domestic disputes. Perhaps we should be grateful that Hitler invaded Poland, for otherwise we might have been treated to the spectacle of the society of states standing by while the Holocaust efficiently proceeded as an "internal matter."

Indeed the U.N. Charter under Article 2 (7) specifically precludes the organization from intervening "in matters which are essentially within the domestic jurisdiction of any state." Similarly, the Declaration on the Inadmissibility of Intervention into the Domestic Affairs of States and the Protection of Their Independence and Sovereignty provides that "[n]o State has the right to intervene, directly or indirectly for any reason whatever, in the internal or external affairs of any other State."

The U.N., a second generation of the League, has given us a second generation of such failures, that is, a new wave of crimes shielded by sovereignty.[3] Perhaps the most notorious is that of the Cambodian class crimes. The Khmer Rouge were the sovereign authority for purposes of international law; indeed the United States (and many states) voted to preserve their U.N. seat even when the Khmer Rouge abandoned Phnom Penh. Atrocities conducted within a state's borders are impervious to an international law built out of absolute sovereignty. Human catastrophes like the war in Mali simply never rise to the consciousness of the U.N., a majority of whose members could be counted on to keep it—as they long kept the Somali civil war[4]—off the international agenda. The same model of international law that has shaped the League of Nations and the United Nations has also created a certain sort of legal status for the State that actually enfeebles those international institutions with respect to a critical class of conflicts.

Nor can we say that these institutions have even succeeded in preventing or at least managing war, the goal for which their bargain with the State was struck regarding sovereignty. The story of the League's failure to prevent war, including World War II, is too familiar to recount. The U.N. was designed with precisely this failure in mind, and was given constitutional authority to arm itself and to wage war against aggressors who threatened the peace. It is instructive, however, to look closely at how the U.N. has actually managed to succeed when it has acted to wage war. It may surprise some to learn that its successes have come only because the ideal of a world covenant enforced by a world military force has been quickly, if quietly, abandoned.

Articles 42 and 43 of the U.N. Charter authorize the Security Council to use armed forces to maintain international peace and security. Article 43 provides for military agreements by which it was thought a U.N. force would be constituted from personnel contributed by the member states. This has never materialized. The temporary absence of the Soviet delegate in June 1950 permitted the Security Council to recommend that members repel the North Korean attack on South Korea and to authorize the U.S.-designated commander to use the U.N. flag. All U.S. forces, however, were under U.S. command and, save in name only, there was no significant U.N. force on the peninsula.[5] Absent the kinds of agreements envisaged under Article 43, the Security Council has no authority to command member states to commit their armed forces to a U.N. military enforcement action.

The consequence of this arrangement is that armed forces remain entirely the creatures of states. The recent coalition force arrayed against Iraq provides an example. With more justice, it might be said that this was a NATO force, with contributions from the Gulf region, rather than a U.N. force. There is nothing wrong with this; indeed I have suggested there is much right with such ad hoc coalitional forces. But we should not delude ourselves into thinking that they function as a U.N. enforcement arm. Whatever intentions the drafters in San Francisco may have had for a U.N. defense force, this force has never come into being. And it is notable that in the Fourth Yugoslav War, over Kosovo, the U.N. was bypassed entirely.

As if in tacit recognition of this fact, Article 2 (4), the heart of the U.N. Charter's security provisions, has been redefined *sub silentio*. Whereas it was once envisioned that the U.N. would have a monopoly on international violence—in a Wilsonian extrapolation to the global level of the individual state's own monopoly of violence within its domestic jurisdiction—this model has been long since abandoned. Article 2 (4) provides:

> All Members shall refrain in their international relations from the threat or use of force against the territorial integrity or political independence of any state, or in any other manner inconsistent with the Purposes of the United Nations.

During the first years of the U.N., there was general agreement on the construction of this provision if not its application. Clearly the Article outlaws aggression by one state against another. Apart from the collective action of the U.N. itself, the only lawful use of force by a state must come within the exception provided in Article 51 for self-defense against an armed attack. In time, however, the language of 2 (4) proved pliable to the realities of a society of states whose reason for being—nationhood—did not apply to the collectivity, but applied only to individual states. The whole, that is, was less than the sum of its parts.

For example, 2 (4) forbids the use of force against "the territorial integrity" of another state. Does this proscribe any use of force that momentarily penetrates a border or only attacks aimed at compromising the invaded state by occupying its territory and ultimately depriving it of land? Article 2 (4) forbids the use of force against the "political independence" of another state. But what about reprisals that do not seek to alter a regime? Exceptions such as these have sometimes been urged to justify the Entebbe and Tehran rescue missions, or the U.S. air attack on Libyan bases in retaliation for acts of terrorism. But such exceptions are of less help in rationalizing the U.S. intervention in the Dominican Republic, one of the most successful, pro-democracy acts of the period, to say nothing of U.S. intervention in Grenada, Haiti, or Panama.[6] Nor can 2 (4) be made to appear consistent with NATO intervention in Kosovo.

While 2 (4) was shrinking, Article 51 was expanding. This Article provides:

> Nothing in the present Charter shall impair the inherent right of individual or collective self-defense if an armed attack occurs against a Member of the United Nations, until the Security Council has taken the measures necessary to maintain international peace and security.

The original intent behind this provision seems clear: it is an exception to 2 (4), permitting a state that has been attacked to use force to defend itself and enlist others in its defense, *until* the Security Council has effectively acted. Because the Security Council was for a long time prevented from acting by the Soviet veto, however, and in any case cannot actually command member forces to provide assistance, this phrase has been subject to some interpretive pressure. First, the word *until* has acquired a Zeno-esque quality such that the Council's acts can be thought of as approaching but never quite arriving at international peace and security, thereby permitting the continuing use of armed force by the attacked party and its allies regardless of Security Council action. Second, it has been widely agreed that Article 51 merely recognizes but does not create or modify, the pre-existing right of every state to act in its own self-defense, which is an attribute of sovereignty. So it has been argued that the phrase *if an armed attack occurs* does not mean "*only* if an armed attack occurs." Therefore a state may employ force if it expects or fears an armed attack, as occurred in the Six-Day War. In any case, few influential states now argue that the U.N. has a monopoly on the use of force. As the background code for the law of war prevention, there is little evidence that the Charter has, in this regard, fulfilled the hopes of its framers and stopped aggression by making it unlawful.

Though the Charter, interpreted as a world covenant of superior law, has been of doubtful utility in preventing armed conflict, its most troublesome aspect may lie in peacetime. Very simply, it is not obvious that a universal law-creating system actually based on democratic majoritarianism and self-determination is either acceptable or desirable. Nor is the U.N. wholly consistent with such a system in any event, owing to the privileged role of the permanent, veto-bearing members of the Security Council. Yet a universal system that professes allegiance to the sources of authority of the parliamentary nation-state but denies them in fact is of doubtful legitimacy.

If the U.N. Charter were a universal superior law—as for example, the U.S. Constitution is superior to Texas laws—then it must take its legitimacy from a universal mandate. No doubt when House and Wilson thought of such a world, they envisioned something like the United States, composed of separate jurisdictions but bound together under one law. Such an institution might be the result of a world federation of states, or even an agglomerate of their populations; the United States Constitution was ratified by popular voting in individual state conventions, while the Charter was ratified by state parliaments and other state regimes. In either case, the reality is that such a world state would resemble Cold War South Africa more than the United States. A small group of ethnic minorities would own most of the valuable property and keep everyone else confined to "homelands." Surely the time is not far off when the large hostile majorities in the General Assembly that have denounced Israel will be deployed against the developed states, demanding economic concessions and constitutional reform consistent with a universal mandate. Whether the basis for a world sovereign is the majoritarianism of states or of the peoples of the various nations, the current constitutional framework is either contradictory (because it retains a superstructure inherited from the Concert of great powers) or fraught (because vast majorities can lay claim to its lawmaking power). When it is replaced by a constitution for a society of market-states, this problem will disappear because that constitution will resemble those of corporations, which allow for weighted voting based on wealth. But to adopt such a constitution, we will have to abandon the pretense of a world sovereign: corporations, after all, do not make law.

Abandoning the image of a world sovereign that stands behind international law will also help us to move toward the changes in sovereignty that are best suited to a society of market-states. And ridding ourselves of this image will clarify our security institutions. We are not going to have a world army,[7] as envisioned by the drafters of Article 42 and 43 of the Charter. Instead we will have a NATO force structure,[8] perhaps with forces committed to a defense component within the E.U. that can act in accord with but is not commanded by the Security Council. This, as the Gulf War showed, is both more practicable and more legitimating, using the organs of collective security and collective judgment in cooperation but not with the problematic pretense that one governs the other.

The United States has tabled, and all but one of the permanent members of the Security Council has accepted, a reform proposal for the International Court of Justice (ICJ) that would permit parties to submit to the Court's jurisdiction after electing a particular chamber—that is, after choosing a panel composed of judges acceptable to both parties. This proposal has stalled—despite the fact that it would bring Russia and China within ICJ jurisdiction for the first time—over whether the ICJ ought to have initial jurisdiction to determine whether exceptions to that jurisdiction on national security grounds are made in good faith. Now if you believe in a world common law—and compliance with ICJ decisions is considered a norm of customary international law—then it is perfectly natural to insist on this. Of course it is within the competence of the court. Its writ is universal. But if you see the ICJ as simply one more consensual method of resolving disputes, this insistence is perverse and counterproductive.

For these and other reasons I am inclined to conclude that the project of international law envisioned by House and Wilson and most commentators on the subject today can be regarded as a failure. Is the failure of this project a bad thing?

Former senator Daniel Patrick Moynihan has warned that the United States has commenced a general challenge to international law—a challenge, that is, to the project of a universal law—and he cites the U.S. invasion in Panama as Exhibit A. Former judge Robert Bork, on the other hand, has recently proposed that we frankly acknowledge the impracticality of the very idea of an international law and be done with it. What these thoughtful persons share is the idea that a binding world covenant is the basis for international law and vice versa. But as I suggested earlier and intend to show in the chapters to come, this has not always been so, and I will further claim it is not going to be so presently, either. The attitude that international law must be an overarching body of substantive, superior law is usually behind the criticism both of those who lament recent American practice and of U.S. officials, who deplore and resent the implicit reproaches of this ghostly law. But it may be that this widespread assumption is itself an error and that the "failure" of international law is neither good nor bad but only a way station in the process of change that the society of states is now undergoing.

In the months before war broke out in 1914, Colonel House went to each of the capitals of the great powers of Europe trying to persuade them to avoid war. His mission failed. The cataclysm came and, in one form or another, erupted, subsided, then erupted again and again throughout the suffering-saturated twentieth century.

House prepared the West to fight this Long War. As early as 1913 he was urging American engagement and rearmament, arguing that without these measures we could not persuade Europe to avoid war and that without our armies, even our successful persuasion would not survive the first recalculation of odds by the first General Staff or Cabinet meeting in a European chancellery. House urged a system of collective security that differed from previous alliance systems in these important respects: anyone could join, it was arrayed against no one in particular, and the United States was pledged to assist any state that was attacked. Most recently this pledge was redeemed in the Gulf War. That system ultimately triumphed after many failed attempts. Now the world's greatest powers are called on to fashion a new system of international security and respect for the rule of law that will withstand the stresses that are already pounding the barriers that House and his heirs built over a century of war.

In this, House cannot help us. We must put aside his vision of a world covenant of law, for this picture, which is so widely and tenaciously held, is actually destructive of international law as a legitimating force. To begin this effort, we must free ourselves from the assumption that international law is universal and that it must be the law of a society of nation-states. And we must see clearly what role violence and war have played, and will continue to play, in shaping that system.

Sarajevo

Now that a revolution is really needed, those who once
were fervent are quite cool.

While a country murdered and raped calls for help
from the Europe which it had trusted, they yawn.

While statesmen choose villainy and no voice is raised
to call it by name.

The rebellion of the young who called for a new earth
was a sham, and that generation has written the
verdict on itself,

Listening with indifference to the cries of those who
perish because they are after all just barbarians killing
each other

And the lives of the well-fed are worth more than the
lives of the starving.

It is revealed now that their Europe since the beginning
has been a deception, for its faith and its foundation is
nothingness.

And nothingness, as the prophets keep saying, brings
forth only nothingness, and they will be led once
again like cattle to slaughter.

Let them tremble and at the last moment comprehend
that the word Sarajevo will from now on mean the
destruction of their sons and the debasement of their
daughters.

They prepare it by repeating: "We at least are safe,"
unaware that what will strike them ripens in
themselves.

—Czesław Miłosz

PART II

A Brief History of the Society of States and the International Order

THESIS: MUCH AS EPOCHAL WARS HAVE SHAPED THE CONSTITUTIONAL ORDER OF INDIVIDUAL STATES, THE GREAT PEACE SETTLEMENTS OF THESE WARS HAVE SHAPED THE CONSTITUTIONAL ORDER OF THE SOCIETY OF STATES.

The international congresses that concluded peace treaties ending epochal wars produced the constitutions of the society of states for their respective eras. This process, beginning in Europe with the birth of a small society of states during the Renaissance, eventually expanded to encompass the globe. International law can be understood in terms of these constitutions and thus as having developed in several distinct periods. The study of this development provides a foundation for under-standing the next constitutional era for the society of states.

The Tenth Satire of Juvenal, Imitated

(excerpt from The Vanity of Human Wishes*)*

Let observation with extensive view,
Survey mankind, from China to Peru;
Remark each anxious toil, each eager strife
And watch the busy scenes of crowded life;
Then say hope and fear, desire and hate,
O'erspread with snares the clouded maze of fate,
Where wav'ring man, betray'd by vent'rous pride
To tread the dreary paths without a guide,
As treach'rous phantoms in the mist delude,
Shuns fancied ills, or chases airy good.
How rarely reason guides the stubborn choice,
Rules the bold hand, or prompts the suppliant voice,
How nations sink, by darling schemes oppress'd,
When vengeance listens to the fool's request.
Fate wings with ev'ry wish th' afflictive dart,
Each gift of nature, and each grace of art,
With fatal heat impetuous courage glows,
With fatal sweetness elocution flows,
Impeachment stops the speaker's pow'rful breath,
And restless fire precipitates on death.

But scarce observ'd the knowing and the bold,
Fall in the gen'ral massacre of gold;
Wide-wasting pest! That rages unconfin'd,
And crowds with crimes the records of mankind,
For gold his sword the hireling ruffian draws,
For gold the hireling judge distorts the laws;
Wealth heap'd on wealth, nor truth nor safety buys,
The dangers gather as the treasures rise.

Let hist'ry tell where rival kings command,
And dubious title shakes the madded land,
When statutes glean the refuse of the sword,
How much more safe the vassal than the lord,
Low sculks the hind beneath the rage of pow'r,
And leaves the wealthy traitor in the Tow'r,
Untouch'd his cottage, and his slumbers sound,
Tho' confiscation's vultures hover round.

—Samuel Johnson

CHAPTER SEVENTEEN

Peace and the International Order

COLONEL HOUSE and Kitty Genovese each lived during a particular era in the constitutional life of the State. House, his dapper appearance and his quiet manner, were made world famous by the Peace Conference at Versailles in 1919 that attempted to ratify—and set the rules for—the dominating constitutional order of the twentieth century, the parliamentary nation-state; Kitty Genovese, her bloody dress and her fruitless cries for help to her agonized neighbors, were symbols of an important political issue for the American nation-state because this particular constitutional order was held responsible for improving the safety and welfare of its people. A moral failure on the part of society was translated into a call for political action on the part of the State.

The massacre at Srebrenica will also mark an unexpungeable point in modern history, for it is one of the crucial events in the Yugoslav Wars that signify the end of the era of the nation-state. It is important to note that Srebrenica was a mass murder, a killing, and not a battlefield victory, which so often in the past has proved the turning point for a particular constitutional form. It was ethnic cleansing, not conventional warfare, that marked the end of the nation-state, perhaps because this form of the state purchases its political passion and sacrifice in warfare by emphasizing the sovereignty of peoples. Sovereignty that cloaks practices such as ethnic cleansing, however, cannot create borders that must be respected, especially at a time when borders are becoming so permeable for other reasons. The war against Serbia over the treatment of Kosovars *in Serbia* established this principle, but it would have come sooner or later in East Timor or Burundi or elsewhere.

In Book I, we have dealt with the relationship between constitutional change and strategic change, as this relationship affected the individual state. It has been argued that the constitutional orders, or archetypes, of the modern state were the product of the interaction between strategic and constitutional innovation: sometimes constitutional change posed a strategic

481

problem for the State that it had to solve if it was to survive. The French Revolution presented Napoleon with just such a problem. The Revolutionary regime could not rely on a highly professionalized army to execute the complex and rigorous maneuvers that Frederick the Great had institutionalized in Prussia and all others had copied. But the Revolution could produce great numbers of enthusiastic if untrained soldiers; the problem was to find a set of tactics that used ignorant but passionate troops effectively in battle.

Sometimes, however, the causal arrow ran the other way, and strategic innovation itself forced constitutional change on states.[1] The strategic challenge posed by the French invasion of Italy in 1494 was not successfully met by the Italian city-states until 1521, with Prospero Colonna's defense of Milan. The introduction of mobile artillery, skillfully employed, affected the entire conduct of campaigns, raising formidable problems of expense and organization. Only a constitutional transformation that augmented a prince with the logistical and taxing apparatus of the princely state would enable the besieged cities to survive. In place of campaigns that emphasized bravery and tactical skill, the prince had to master the art of creating the bastioned trace, the low, thick wall so humbling to cities that wished to retain their proud towers and high stone curtains. This meant that the prince needed money in vertiginous amounts and the organization to raise that money and use it effectively. Thus the constitutional order changed.

But states not only solve strategic and constitutional problems, they also create them in the first place. Thus the story had a dynamic and unpredictable character: no sooner had one constitutional form of the State been enshrined than a new form began to compete for dominance. Sometimes more than one such form pressed new challenges, and sometimes a form that ultimately failed seemed about to triumph over the others. Human choices determined which military and legal innovations were tried, as states moved through a series of prototypes in search of decisive strategic programs and stable constitutional forms. When one particular choice proved successful, other states were quick to copy it in a process Gibbon called "creative emulation." Sometimes the genetic inheritance of a state did not permit successful copying because the policies to be copied required material or cultural resources that the state did not possess and could not acquire. In those circumstances, the state was either compelled to innovate or to fall behind, becoming a mere relic of an earlier period. Some states did not survive and simply disappeared, and some constitutional forms never achieved universal legitimacy, their bases having been tried and found wanting in epochal wars that often lasted decades until a final decision was reached. Strategic success certified the constitutional form the winning state had adopted. History provided the legitimating characterization of the new order.

What provided legitimacy, however, for the *society* of states? When is a new constitution for the society of states adopted? How can we tell when an epochal war has truly ended and not simply paused, to be renewed when the parties have regained strength?

It is my premise that there is a constitution of the society of states as a whole; that it is proposed and ratified by the peace conferences that settle the epochal wars previously described, and amended in various peace settlements of lesser scope;[2] and that its function is to institutionalize an international order derived from the triumphant constitutional order of the war-winning state. Thus while violence and war initiate the process of change in the constitutional order, peace and law ratify the ultimate result. As Robert Randle has concluded:

> The settlement regimes established by the peace conference and the settlement documents constitute the new structure of the system. The multi-lateral war might have caused system transformation, but it is the *settlement* of war that creates a regime for the state system because it represents the signatories' acceptance of the norms or understanding embodied in the settlement documents.[3]

If we take this idea—the creation of a constitution for the society of states[4] from the settlement of an epochal war—in light of the relation between such wars and the constitutional order of states, then we can infer that international law arises from constitutional law. This is not merely a contemporary phenomenon; the relationship of constitutional law to international law has long been a constitutive one. It was the development of European states from the fifteenth century to the present that concomitantly brought to the world an ever-enlarging society of states formed by the perception of common ways of looking at government, and a structure of generally agreed-upon rules adopted in each century, setting out the rights of states and their duties in relation to one another and providing common international institutions.[5]

This society of states has a constitution; indeed, it has had at least five previous constitutions. As I have emphasized, every society has a constitution: to be a society is to be constituted in a particular way. What is distinctive about Europe is that, at the beginning of the sixteenth century, it produced a society of *states*. It is this society that has grown to encompass the globe. This is the society that the Americans joined in the early nineteenth century and attempted to reform in the twentieth, and to which the Yugoslav Muslims appealed for help in the early 1990s.

Each new period in the constitutional life of the State commenced with a revolution against an established domestic, constitutional order, though it is only with hindsight that one may say that a particular revolt led to the dominance of a particular constitutional form, because many such revolts have withered, or the forms to which they gave birth have contended with and been defeated by other forms that became dominant.[6] Each of these periods witnessed the eruption of a grand coalitional conflict that developed into an epochal war. Most important for our present purposes, each period was punctuated by agreements that emerged from the negotiations following an epochal conflict and reflected a constitutional consensus on the part of the participating states. These negotiations established a new constitution for the society of states, defining functions for states or allotting functions differently.[7] What war—and what peace—will someday be seen as having accomplished the same sort of fundamental change in the constitution of contemporary international society by legitimizing the market-state?

In the twentieth century we saw new functions allocated to the State— to enforce compliance with U.N. Security Council resolutions, for example—as well as functions allocated differently—for example, the shifting of state responsibilities to the International Monetary Fund or the International Court of Justice. Such rearrangements are not unique to the twentieth century. In Book II, we will look once again at the six periods we examined in Book I. Here, however, we will be looking at the effects of peace, rather than war, on the creation of the society of states, rather than on state formation per se.

What are the characteristics of a constitution for the society of states? Like other constitutions, this one sets up a structure for rule following; allocates the jurisdiction, duties, and rights of the institutions it recognizes; determines a method for its own amendment and revision; specifies procedures for coping with disputes arising from its implementation; and above all, legitimates those acts appropriately taken under its authority. Like other constitutions, written and unwritten, the constitution of the society of states relies upon the interpretive means by which it is to be applied. By providing legitimating modalities of interpretation, history enables law to reproduce itself. In the fifteenth century the constitution for the society of states provided rules for the conquest and annexation of territory and the colonization of the New World; it governed how nonstate actors, like the papacy and the Holy Roman Empire, were to interact with the society of states; it determined which territorial polities qualified as legitimate states and what rules governed dynastic succession; and, above all, it specified the relationship between the sectarian allegiance of the princely state and the religious practices of its people. Similarly, the constitution for the society of states in the twentieth century forbade the annexation of territory by conquest; provided for a process of decolonization; determined how the League of Nations and the Permanent International Court of Justice, or their successors, the United Nations and the World Court, are to interact with the society of nation-states; fixed what territorial polities are entitled to recognition within that society; determined what rules govern treaty succession; and, finally and most importantly, set the rules for the self-determination of national peoples. In other words, the constitution of the society of states will be different depending on whether its constituent parties are nation-states or princely states, but the fundamental functions of constitutions generally are largely the same although no two constitutions need share every function. Usually these functions will include the creation of rule-following procedures, and the provision of substantive rules of conduct that transcend single, one-time applications but provide instead frameworks for generating new rules within the constitution's general principles.

We shall be looking not only at particular strategic and constitutional periods whose international institutions were ratified by a general peace conference, but also at the international law of each period as described by its leading interpreters. These descriptions will give us some sense of the legal context within which these constitutions operated and which they also shaped. For no constitution, least of all one that governs different states, can determine its own interpretive context any more than a law can provide its own legitimacy. The epochal peace conferences and treaties, like the epochal wars they terminated, existed within a complex history that gave them meaning.

I do not wish to claim that the ideas of these historic figures in international law were unvaryingly decisive or even influential in their day, but rather that they reflect the changing international order that we seek to understand. They did not bring this order about (except in rare cases through their influence on a diplomat who was unlikely to have been moved by a reverence for international law but rather sought arguments and authority to bolster his case). To claim such influence on political developments is vain and, in any case, beside the point. We study these figures to understand their subject—international law—and not to exaggerate their roles. Though they did not bring the international order into being, they can help us understand it by understanding their responses to it.

CHAPTER EIGHTEEN

The Treaty of Augsburg

Medieval treatises on government dealt with what kings should do in order to be good. Commynes in his Memoires *(finished by 1498, first published 1524) and Machiavelli in his* Prince *(written in 1513, published 1532) tried to deal with something different, what kings found it most advantageous to do in order to be effective rulers.*[1]

THIS CHANGE in attitude on the part of monarchs and their counselors reflected the constitutional changes underway at the end of the fifteenth century.

The Hundred Years' War with the Lancastrian kings of England had required reforms in the Valois administration of France that greatly strengthened the French state. In particular, changes in finance and the organization of the army that had been introduced by Charles VII[2] to compete militarily with England had prepared the dynasty to make the transition from princes to princely state. Such reforms enabled France to organize the invasion of Italy in order to vindicate French claims to Naples and Milan. These dynastic claims assumed a greater importance under Charles VIII, when the imposition of permanent taxes in areas without provincial estates and the establishment of something like a standing army provided the foundation for the French attack at the end of the century. It is estimated that by 1494 the king of France had the largest army and the greatest annual revenue of any European monarch.[3] Moreover, political stability achieved through the strengthening of the apparatus of provincial government provided the conditions for civil peace necessary for agricultural improvement, the engine of economic prosperity. A generation of civil peace thus made possible the armed intervention in Italy, beginning the struggle that ended with the Peace of Augsburg.

THE CONSTITUTION OF 1555:
THE PEACE OF AUGSBURG

It was not the Treaty of Cateau-Cambrésis in 1559 that ended the Valois-Habsburg struggle, but rather the Peace of Augsburg four years earlier, which set the constitutional terms of the new society of states that emerged from this epochal war. Charles V's campaign for a single Christendom foundered not so much on French victories as on the advent and growing strength of the new princely states.

> Indeed at first sight, the phenomenon appears to be universal in Europe. One finds it spreading to Scandinavia, where the Reformation provided Danish and Swedish kings with the means of establishing strong rule; even in Russia, Ivan III and Ivan IV seem almost to duplicate the work of England's Henry VII and Henry VIII, of France's Louis XI and Francis I.[4]

What is sometimes less appreciated is that the principle that was the basis of Augsburg—the famous *cuius regio eius religio*—transformed this multilateral treaty into a constitution for the new society of princely states. This principle may be roughly translated as "he who rules, his is the religion"; it provides that the religion of a state is determined by the choice of the sovereign, with free immigration to all his subjects. It was an imaginative concept, although it had its roots in the prior practices of princes attempting to keep outside interference from complicating their relations with their subjects. Most significantly, *cuius regio eius religio* implied a "theory of sovereignty by the states of Europe that permitted no distinction in law between a Catholic and a Protestant country."[5] Thus the basis for a comprehensive society of states was formed.

The defeat of the Habsburg bid for empire[6] had destroyed Charles's hopes for a *Respublica Christiana;* the Peace of Augsburg ratified this failure and introduced instead the notion of individual state supremacy. Implicit in the principle of *cuius regio eius religio* is the territorial delimiting of sovereignty and the notion of state supremacy within that sovereignty. "There was thenceforth [after the Peace of Augsburg] to be no lord of the world, imperial or otherwise, for the simple reason that there was no single world. There were England, France, and Spain. The life of each was to be centralized within its ultimate sovereign."[7]

Medieval Christendom had known no society of politically distinct states.[8] After princely states first appeared in Italy,[9] they gradually spread throughout Europe, replacing the universal, overlapping structures of ecclesiastical, feudal society[10] with a discrete, territorial pattern of states. Latin, once learned by everyone in the learned classes, was replaced as the

bureaucratic language of officials by increasingly standardized vernacu-
lars. Adam Watson has observed that although at the time of the Peace of
Augsburg, "the principle of *cuius regio eius religio* applied formally only
to the Holy Roman Empire, . . . the practice quickly extended throughout
the Christian commonwealth of Europe. It carried, as a corollary, another
principle which rulers readily acknowledged and proclaimed though they
did not always scrupulously observe it: non-interference by one state in the
affairs of another."[11]

This doctrine of the essential separateness of the new states into which
Christendom was now divided was indeed the result of the principle of
Augsburg. This principle, which enshrined the legitimacy of state sovereignty, and denied the universal order of the *Respublica Christiana,*
replaced that order with the society of princely states whose horizontal
relationship indicated their mutual sovereignty. Thus the principle of
Augsburg not only excluded the imperial state sought by Charles, but gave
a constitutional foundation to the society of princely states.[12]

CONSTITUTIONAL INTERPRETATION: THE FIRST INTERNATIONAL LAWYERS

In August 1584 four Japanese emissaries arrived in Lisbon and immediately generated enormous excitement. In the following weeks they were
conducted to the court of Philip II and then to Pisa, Florence, Venice, and
finally Rome, where they were entertained by the Pope. At each of these
places the Japanese were greeted with enormous pomp and lavish ceremonies in which the visitors were presented to the public. Contemporary
accounts dwell on the great crowds that greeted them on their arrival in
each large city. In Rome, where the Japanese were preceded by the entire
papal cavalry, the Swiss guard, and musicians playing drums and trum-
pets, "the streets, the windows, the doors and even the piazze where they
had to pass were full of men of every type and condition."[13]

The visitors created a sensation, but these four young men were not the
first Japanese to come to Europe. Bernard of Kagoshima, one of Francis
Xavier's first Japanese converts, had visited in the 1550s. He, however, had
hardly caused a ripple of interest as he traveled through Portugal, Spain,
and Italy. Contemporary sources suggest that he was allowed to visit various well-placed officials, possibly even the pope, but no great crowds and
no retinues of bureaucrats and retainers greeted him; no state dinners honored him and no letters or treatises made him the subject of discussion
among large circles of Europeans.

"What had changed in the decades since Bernard's visit?" asked one
historian, and she concluded that it was

not that Europeans had become more curious about outsiders but that [politics] had changed. . . . In the 1550s the pope and emperor had been battling heretics within Europe. But after the Treaty of Cateau Cambresis, the Peace of Augsburg and the Council of Trent had drawn the confessional and political lines more clearly within Europe, both Philip II and the pope could turn their attention to extending their powers outside.[14]

And so it was: the definition of what counted as a possible solution to the problems of dynastic aggrandizement and religious counterrevolution, the same problems with which Charles V had had to deal, had fundamentally changed.

In the following section, we will examine the defining legal form of the new society of princely states in Europe by looking at the works of the first international lawyers. Had Charles V achieved his goals, had the Peace of Augsburg ratified an imperial constitutional form of the state instead of the archetype of the princely state, there would have been no international law (as we understand it) and no society of states predicated on the equality of state sovereignty. Every state has law, but only a society of states that recognizes the autonomy of its members can have the kind of legal rules that we call "international law." When states share a common commitment[15] to the maintenance of a common constitutional form that implies autonomy and equality, they have created a constitution for modern public international law.

The following discussion of modern international law belongs therefore to the very beginning of that subject. Four writers typify this period and are usually taken as laying the earliest foundations of the discipline: the Dominican theologian and law professor Francisco de Vitoria, writing on the eve of the Peace of Augsburg; the Jesuit counter-Reformationist Francisco Suarez, attempting to hold the theological line after Augsburg; the military figure Balthazar Ayala, who writes after the Dutch revolt in 1567, which began the movement toward the constitutional archetype of the kingly state, and who struggles to reinforce the princely state; and finally the magisterial Alberico Gentili, whose works already look forward to a new constitutional form and the new society of which it will be the constituent element.

VITORIA

Francisco de Vitoria was born sometime around 1483 in Burgos. He studied philosophy and theology in Paris from 1507 to 1522 and returned to Spain in 1523. Three years later he obtained a chair as professor of theology at Salamanca and remained there until his death in 1546. None of his lectures nor anything else of his work was published during his lifetime.

though he was an important advisor to the Spanish crown on public matters, including the divorce of Henry VIII and Spanish rights over the Indians of the Americas. But notes from his lectures were transcribed by devoted students, and in 1557, ten years after his death, the greatest part of his *Relectiones*—special lectures given by each professor annually—was published at Lyons. Two of these *relectiones* were of significant importance for the development of international law: the lecture on the American Indians (*de Indis*) and that on the law of war (*de jure belli*), both from 1539.

It is in some ways a misnomer to call Vitoria the "father of international law"[16] because he wrote in a period before the Peace of Augsburg, when an international society of princely states was just beginning to form. Perhaps "forefather" would be more apt. Certain ideas that do not seem to have been crucial to his thought—the change in the Gaian definition of *ius gentium* (the law of nations), the concept of *totus orbis* (a universal jurisdiction)—became crucial once a society had formed that could use these concepts. This accounts for the appearance (or illusion) of Vitoria's curiously modern ideas in the context of a rather conventionally Thomistic theology. Vitoria writes lucidly and provocatively of political communities that they are *perfected* when they can act independently of another political community, have their own laws, their own council, and their own bureaucracy (and thus may include pagan nations)—a very modern list of criteria for the legal recognition of states. At the same time, however, he makes the Church the arbiter of whether the conduct of a state is lawful, there being no society of states yet capable of making this judgment.

Verhoeven has written with insight that Vitoria's thought was structured by three facts: that it originated with issues arising from the discovery of America, that it was the work of a theologian-confessor, and that it had a single theme, war.[17] These three facts "set the stage," in Verhoeven's phrase, for the development of international law. This strikes me as precisely right: writing before Augsburg, Vitoria could do no more than anticipate international law, set the stage, as it were, but the peculiar collection of subjects he dealt with prompted him to proffer rules that would provide a structure for further development once the society of states got underway, because he was called upon to write on issues of strategy (war) and law (the rights of Indians and the legal obligations owed to them), and the relation between the two.

Vitoria was occupied with the question of the extent to which Spain could claim the resources of the Indians and subjugate them. The Dominicans had tried to protect the Indians from exploitation. The Dominican priest Bartholomew de las Casas (1474–1566), a contemporary of Vitoria's, was the principal early evangelist among the Indians and lobbied ceaselessly for their humane treatment.[18] Vitoria sought a solution in the doctrine of just war developed by the Dominican scholastic Thomas Aquinas. In order to apply this doctrine, Vitoria crafted an argument that, though in service to scholasticism, yielded elements we now regard as essential to international law. His argument had five steps.

First, Vitoria courageously rejected the claims of his king, Charles V, to global supremacy,[19] correctly observing that the political world was becoming one composed of separate princely states. Second, he shrewdly defined *ius gentium* (the law of nations) as the law *inter omnes gentes* (the law among all nations) as opposed to the construction provided by Gaius, whom Vitoria purported to be explicating, which held this law to be *inter omnes homines* (among all men). Third, thus armed, he was now able to bring Thomas Aquinas's doctrine of just war to bear on the problem, because this doctrine applied only among sovereigns, not among persons generally. Fourth, he associated natural law with the *ius gentium,* as Aquinas had held that the natural law was divinely inspired, in order that fifth, he might finally conclude that the Church was the ultimate arbiter of whether a war was just between two states. The Church, with its divine source of authority, would be the appropriate institution to apply international law (*ius gentium*).

Based on this argument, Vitoria could bring the Indians within the benign embrace of the Church by observing that they were distributed among states. As an almost inadvertent consequence, the fundamental ideas of a world composed of equal, separate sovereignties under law were laid out. Vitoria had expanded a law for a *society* (not an empire) composed of *states* (not princes).

Although Vitoria wished to treat the Indians humanely, his conclusions are hardly those of a humanist.[20] While holding that Spain had no right to the property of the Indians, he nevertheless justified Spanish violence against them on the grounds that the Indians had no right to reject commerce, nor to impede the travel of the Spaniards wherever they might wish to go or to develop commerce. The Spanish freedom to join in activities undertaken by the natives, like the mining of gold, or tilling the earth, was "violated" if the natives did not permit such foreign participation and amounted to a kind of "banishment" which, as a punishment only justifiable in case of crime, was therefore the basis for a just war against them. This brought the *conquistadores* within the Thomist rule: *"Unica est et sola iusta inferendi bellum, iniuria accepta."*[21]

SUAREZ

Vitoria's successor as the pre-eminent Spanish explicator of international law, Francisco Suarez, wrote after the Peace of Augsburg and therefore dealt with the reality of an international society and its law. Though he was scarcely sympathetic to this development, we can learn a good deal from his commentary about what his contemporaries regarded as the content of this law.

Suarez was born a Spanish aristocrat and became, like Vitoria, a professor of theology. In 1596, after the Spanish conquest of Portugal, Philip II arranged for the appointment of Suarez to the chair of theology at the Portuguese University of Coimbra. Unlike Vitoria in many respects, Suarez was a Jesuit, a prolific writer whose works in a nineteenth century edition fill twenty-eight volumes, and an aggressive polemicist. A great many biographies have been devoted to him, and his renown does not rest on his contributions to international law.*

His most famous work is the *Defense of the Faith against the Errors of the Anglican Sect* (1613), commissioned by Pope Paul V. In the course of arguing that the pope possesses powers that include the right to put a heretic king to death in order to protect the Catholic faith, Suarez offered a novel argument: because political power arises from the sociability of man and therefore resides originally in the people, it must be delegated to the prince by "human law"; if the prince turns out to be a tyrant, the pope may assert the rights of the people. Because the source of the pope's power is divine and does not come from the people, this theory gives papal authority a certain supremacy over lay rulers.

It is interesting to note that it is just this move, this particular argument, that constitutes Suarez's principal contribution to international law. He is the first writer to show clearly the ambiguity in the term *ius gentium,* an ambiguity that often bedevils the first-year student of international law who must confront Article 38 of the statute setting up the jurisdiction of the International Court of Justice, which provides in part that the court will apply general principles of law common to all states. This could reasonably be taken to mean either the universal principles of international law, which must necessarily be common to all states, or principles of domestic law that states happen to have in common (it is the latter).

Suarez saw that *ius gentium* might be given either of two meanings: in one sense it is the law that all peoples and nations (*populi et gentes*) observe in their mutual relations (*inter se*); in another sense, it is the law that various states (*civitates vel regna*) observe within themselves (*intra se*). The first concept is, for Suarez, the proper *ius gentium,* and this distinction, so important for the development of international law, also supports the international application of Suarez's deprecation of the power of princes within the princely state. (Note that the Peace of Augsburg, which was otherwise so offensive to the Catholic Church because it replaced the medieval paradigm of a single European polity, was nevertheless crucial to

*His celebrated and impressive (even to this day) Theory of Distinctions laid the basis for the philosophical analysis of identity and, importantly, for Descartes's argument for the separation of body and mind. I am indebted to Professor Mark Sagoff for this observation.

Suarez's argument: Augsburg's recognition of the status of the princely state allowed Suarez to distinguish between the power held by the prince in trust to the State, and his dynastic, personal power.)

In his most famous passage—and one frequently characterized as a hymn to international law[22]—Suarez sets out his view that the origin of international law lies in the society of states. If we read this passage carefully, however, and bear in mind his arguments in *The Defense of the Faith,* a somewhat less admiring view of the post-Augsburg world emerges than might at first appear.

> The human race, though divided into different nations and states, still has a certain unity, not only as a species but, as it were, politically and morally as is indicated by the precept of mutual love and charity which extends to all, even to strangers of any nation whatsoever. Therefore, though each perfect polity, republic or kingdom is in itself a perfect community, consisting of its members, nevertheless each of these communities, inasmuch as it is related to the human race, is in a sense also a member of this universal society. Never, indeed, are these communities, singly, so self-sufficient unto themselves as not to need a certain mutual aid and association and communication, sometimes for their welfare and advantage, sometimes because of a moral necessity or indigence, as experience shows. For this reason they need a law by which they are guided and rightly ordered in respect to communication and association. To a great extent this is done by natural reason but not so sufficiently and directly everywhere. Hence, special rules could be established by the customs of these nations.[23]

Rather than exalting a new "world made of law," in fact Suarez is eager to explain how natural law can account for legal events like the Peace of Augsburg, and the various practices of states that flow from their formal relationships. This enables him to demote, not exalt, the *ius gentium* (international law) as a mere supplement to natural law. The only treaties Suarez discusses are peace treaties: the observance of these he attributes to the law of nature because they (unlike the rest of international law) are the constitutional source of the law among states. Whether or not treaties are to be entered into in the first place Suarez carefully makes a mere matter of the *ius gentium*. By this characterization he ascribes the actions of the society of states to mere human law, and thus renders those actions susceptible to a superior theological judgment.

Thus so much of what is hailed in Suarez—and we must remember that his work in international law is a small part of the corpus of his writing—is truly important, but not quite in the way it is anachronistically praised.[24] Suarez's commentary reflects the dramatic change in European public affairs, not out of sympathy, however, but rather in an effort to contain and limit the significance of what has occurred.

This can be seen in Suarez's attitude toward what we would call today *humanitarian intervention*—the right of one state to use force to relieve the suffering inflicted on a people by its own state. Suarez clearly apprehends the new community of princely states and does not pretend that the medieval order of a single political jurisdiction still persists. Accordingly he writes that the "assertion made by some writers that sovereign kings have the power of avenging injuries done in any part of the world is entirely false, and throws into confusion all the orderly distinction of jurisdiction."[25] There is one situation, however, that does permit the prince to wage war without the pretext of an injury to his interests or an invitation from the state concerned and that is when "a state worshipping the one God inclines toward idolatry through the wickedness of its prince." In this we hear the spirit of the Counter-Reformation, of which Suarez was a notable leader, and which was to provoke the Dutch revolt that marked a decisive movement away from the princely state and toward the kingly state. This revolt gave rise to the interpretive work of Ayala.

AYALA

Balthazar Ayala was born in 1548 in Antwerp to a Spanish noble family. He served in the Spanish Netherlands during the Dutch rebellion and the savage repression of that rebellion by the Duke of Alba, and was auditor-general, a sort of military judge, in Philip II's armies. He published his book, *De Jure et Officis Bellicis et Disciplina Militaris,* in 1582; two years later he died, only thirty-six. Thus his entire adult life was spent in the service of Philip of Spain.

Philip II had effected the transition to the princely state, the most powerful in Europe, with deceptive ease. The abdication of his father, Charles V, amounted to the abandonment of the imperial constitutional model. Now Philip, with a dynastic state unencumbered by the Empire, with increasing revenues from the Americas and a dynamic military force, provided the model to which other princes looked. Ironically, the princely state was to receive mortal blows while in his hands, for he more than any other prince embodied two traits of that state that would be shed by the kingly state: first, even if the society of states no longer belonged to a particular sect, the princely state itself was intensely sectarian—that was the outcome of the settlement at Augsburg—and there was no constitutional state more sectarian than the Catholic regime in Madrid. Second, the princely state was dynastic, and although Charles's will had bifurcated the continental holdings of the Habsburgs, the realm inherited by Philip gave him responsibilities for a wealthy and self-confident territory with which he had no national identification. He was seen as a Castilian, not as a Burgundian,* and he governed with a bureaucracy sent from Madrid. Both of these shortcomings came into play when he decided to divide the four existing bishoprics in the Netherlands into eighteen in order to combat heresy.

Philip's father had adopted a series of heresy laws in the Netherlands covering practically every conceivable offense against orthodoxy. In the forty years before the Dutch revolt, some 1,300 heretics had been executed. Philip, however, was even more inflexible in religious matters than his father. He changed the pattern of prosecutions, replacing impoverished Anabaptists as targets for repression with well-to-do Calvinists, and equating the crime of heresy with that of treason, thus leading to the confiscation of property as well as execution. When Egmont, who had fought so triumphantly on behalf of Philip's crown, led a mission of nobles from the Low Countries to Madrid to petition for a relaxation of the heresy prosecutions, Philip replied by letter: "As for the Inquisition, it is my intention that it should be carried out." If, as Egmont argued, the executions merely created martyrs, then Philip advised that the executions should be carried out in secret. The velocity of the popular response to Philip's policies was proportionate to his attitude: it was total.

In Antwerp, Catholic images in churches were destroyed, and this practice spread to other cities. Revolt came the next year when two southern towns, Tournai and Valenciennes, were seized by Calvinists. At first Philip hesitated, but he eventually ordered a Spanish army under the Duke of Alba to suppress the insurrection. Alba instituted a reign of terror, immortalized by the Council of Blood set up five days after his arrival in Brussels in September 1567. That month Egmont himself was arrested, and the following June he was executed in the Brussels marketplace.† In the next six years, the tribunal condemned thousands of persons, of whom a significant number were executed. The citizens of besieged cities that surrendered to Alba were massacred. Then in 1574 the "Spanish Fury" occurred, when unpaid Spanish troops sacked Antwerp in a gruesome display that sickened Europe. Alba was recalled in 1576, but by then the Low Countries were in complete rebellion.

In this struggle, Ayala was a man committed to reinforcing the princely state. Unlike the theologians who were his predecessors, he fully accepted the Augsburg constitution of states and did not attempt to subordinate

---

*Much as his father had at first been seen as a Burgundian and not a Castilian—and had faced a Spanish revolt on that account. The key difference was that Augsburg had greatly enhanced the "territoriality" of the state, as Westphalia would do to an even greater degree, tying princes to specific places and increasing the importance of national identification with the ruler.

†Goethe's tragedy *Egmont* is based on this life, which also inspired Beethoven's *Egmont Overture*.

those states to the papacy. In Ayala we see for the first time the notion that a war may be just from the point of view of both sides, a thoroughly statist view of the matter. In Ayala's opinion, it was not appropriate to discuss the "equity of the cause of a war between sovereign princes." If such a war were lawfully conducted, it might be just from both perspectives.

In an interesting reversal of the events going on around him, Ayala maintained that treason could be likened to heresy, and thus could never provide the grounds for a just war. Rebellion was not only unlawful, it was unjust. Here Ayala broke new ground, for he considered the question of whether there could be an "unjust war," a point not elaborated on by his scholastic predecessors. Because rebels do not have the legitimacy of law under the princely state, they can be treated as pirates and criminals. They may be enslaved and their property taken. There is no duty to keep faith with agreements struck with them. A usurper of the power of the princely state may be slain by anyone; the laws of war do not apply in the context of rebellion. Thus the very man who thought a just war might possibly be waged by both states party to a conflict, denied that a competing prince— without a state—could *ever* wage a just war.

This is the first notable treatment after Augsburg of the problem of the civil war. When the prince was supplemented by the princely state, the rules against regicide, and for that matter parricide—the term used by Ayala—that had hitherto applied in the feudal context now came into play in the guise of treason against the State. Arthur Nussbaum observes that Ayala's analysis would justify the Spanish edict that offered 25,000 gold crowns and a grant of nobility to the assassin of Prince William I of Orange, the leader of the Dutch forces. Quite so.

The civil war is uniquely a problem of the State, because it is an attack upon the State, not upon the person of the crown. It is noteworthy that the commencement of every new period in the procession of constitutional archetypes can be marked by a civil war or revolution.[26] The State that ultimately emerged in the next century, the kingly state, differed from the princely state in its secular nature, among other things, and thus it is significant that the Dutch Revolt that began the era of the kingly state started out as a Calvinist-Catholic dispute.

GENTILI

Alberico Gentili may rightly be said to be the first secular interpreter of international law. Gentili, born in northern Italy in 1552, the son of a physician, studied law at the University of Perugia, where he took his doctorate. He began practice in his native country, the March of Ancona. But he and his father, having become Protestants, were forced to flee Italy in 1579 just ahead of the Inquisition, which sentenced them in absentia to penal servitude for life and confiscated their property. From Austria and

Germany, the Gentilis came to London in 1580, after which the son became a lecturer on civil law at Oxford University.

In 1584—the year of the assassination of William the Silent*—Gentili was asked for a legal opinion in the sensational case of Mendoza, the Spanish ambassador involved in the Throckmorton conspiracy to murder Queen Elizabeth. Contradicting the opinion of the Privy Council, Gentili held that Mendoza was protected by ambassadorial immunity and thus could not be tried by an English court. His conclusion, which defied public opinion of the day, was accepted by the government, and Mendoza was deported. With lawyerly economy, Gentili converted his memorandum into the treatise *On Embassies,* published in July 1585 and dedicated to his patron, Sir Philip Sidney.

Gentili left England the following year for Wittenberg but was recalled to Oxford to become Regius Professor of Civil Law, a post he held until 1600. For his inaugural lecture as professor in 1588, the year of the Armada, Gentili had chosen the timely subject: "Whether the subject of a prince whose religion is different from his may take up arms against a prince of his own creed, in other words whether a Catholic may legitimately fight against [a Catholic sovereign] in the service of his sovereign [Protestant] Queen."[27]

Gentili answered this question in the affirmative, in contrast to what might have been expected of the sectarian princely state. His lecture, the *Commentatio Prima* on the law of war, was followed by the *Commentatio Secunda* and *Tertia* in 1589, that, much revised, form the three books of the *De Jure Belli,* Gentili's masterpiece. In 1600 he began practice at Gray's Inn, ceasing to be a law professor. In 1605, he became counsel for the Spanish Embassy, defending Spain against claims made before the British Admiralty Bar by Holland, arising out of their war. This is sometimes thought paradoxical[28]—Gentili was, after all, a Protestant refugee—but it was entirely consistent with his approach to the role of international law.

Gentili recognized the arrival of the society of princely states that formed the basis of international law in the sixteenth century, and referred to the "general law of all kingdoms which comes into being with kingdoms themselves and, as it were, by the law of nations."[29] He defined war as a conflict between armed forces of a state, thus discarding the private wars of medieval princes. This view is especially evident in his treatment of treaties. In the medieval period, before the emergence of states, treaties were considered binding only during the lifetimes of the signatories. Gentili held that now treaties were binding on the successors of signatories, as well as upon the peoples of the parties to the treaty.

*The Spanish offer was successful.

Moreover, consider his treatment of the problem of duress in treaties. First, he argued that treaties are not the mere contracts of princes; they bind the State, and thus even the treaty made under duress is binding. A defeated prince cannot annul a peace treaty on the ground that he was compelled to agree to it.[30] Second, Gentili further distanced the State from the person of the prince by arguing that, even in the absence of coercion, an agreement made by a captive prince is not binding if it inflicts a severe injury on the State. Thus there are inherent limitations on the power of princes to alienate sovereignty.[31] And he goes further to recognize the society of states by asserting that there are common interests (*"commune ratione et pro aliis"*) that will serve as a legal basis for making war.[32]

Gentili's interest to us, however, lies not merely in his recognition of the post-Augsburg legal world as one in which a society of states has come into being, but also in his understanding of the shortcomings of that society and of its constituent elements, the princely states.

Princely states were ferociously sectarian and potentially incoherent (because they were composed by a kind of dynastic roulette and had no necessary national basis); they lacked a completely centralized authority (because they had not achieved financial independence from the various subparts of their holdings) and had so little juridical sense of themselves that the potential for international agreements to strengthen the State was limited to the advantages wrung by war and expressed in treaties of doubtful duration. Gentili's writing attempted to shore up the system of such states by addressing each of these difficulties.

Nussbaum calls Gentili the "originator of the secular school of thought in international law,"[33] and this is surely right. We have to see this in its context, however, to appreciate how Gentili sought to bring this about. He did not distinguish between *ius gentium* and *ius natural,* and indeed deliberately identified the *ius gentium* with the *ius natural,* both being an expression of divine will. Gentili was a devout Christian and could hardly have taken any other position. Rather, having accepted this substantive ontology, he then proceeded to distinguish those matters that were justiciable by lawyers and those that had to be referred to the clergy. Repeatedly he insists on the distinction between the respective jurisdictions of the *juris consulti* and the *theologi.** By this means he managed to narrow the scope of ecclesiastical decision to those matters concerning the first three of the Ten Commandments, and indeed largely stripped international law of the moralizing basis it had previously had, in favor of a juridical one.

---

*Thus, for example, he allocates the question of the lawfulness of duels between princes when their state is thereby jeopardized to theologians because it depends on a construction of the first three commands of the Decalogue. Similarly, concerning treaties concluded between men of different religions, Gentili delegates authority away from the lawyers. See Haggemacher, 171, who rather deprecates this move.

Perhaps his most famous remark is *"Silete theologi in munere alieno."** He excludes from the just causes of war opposition to the Christian faith or interference with proselytizing. He refuses to recognize any arbitral power of the pope, preferring instead to refer international arbitrations to "experienced judges."[34]

As is sometimes the case with the expatriate, Gentili was acutely sensitive to the ties of national culture and consanguinity. Arguing that a state, though not itself attacked, is obliged to aid an ally even beyond the terms of an existing alliance when the ally is unjustly attacked, Gentili goes even further and also urges that aid ought to be given to those states, whether or not they are allies, that are similar to the state in question with respect to race, blood, or religion. This invites moral relativism, of course, and Gentili does not shrink from this. He breaks decisively with the moral tradition of the scholastics by holding that a war may be just on both sides. Moreover, he concurs with Ayala that the just treatment of prisoners is not a matter of the justness of the war. By these moves, Gentili is able to argue for the humane treatment of prisoners on both sides of a conflict, i.e., whether or not the state of which they are subjects is at fault, and whether or not the oppressing state can be said to be just in its aggression. Taken together, these doctrines encourage the State and its subjects to more closely identify with each other.

The most important contribution of Gentili to the law of nations is his principle that a treaty is only binding so long as the conditions within which it is to operate have not fundamentally changed. This doctrine— *clausula rebus sic stantibus*—remains an important idea in international law. It is the complementary principle to the doctrine *pacta sunt servanda* (treaties are to be observed). One can see how these two fundamental ideas are given life by the society of modern states: the latter when treaty obligations are objectified and extended beyond the person of the prince or signatory; the former enabling states to behave according to their interests and not as a matter of personal, moral obligation. One can scarcely imagine recognition by the society of states of the *ragione di stato* of Machiavelli's princely state without something like the expediency of the *clausula*.

Gentili provided the society of princely states with an interpretation of its constitutional basis that addressed the weaknesses of that form of the State. Secularism, nationalism, and rationalism all were therapies much needed by the princely state. And in one more respect, Gentili sought to buttress that State. This was his adherence, which grew throughout his life, to greater forms of monarchical absolutism, anticipating (like the "therapies" just mentioned) the advent of the kingly state.

---

*Which means, roughly, "Theologians should be silent on matters beyond their province." *De Juris Belli*. I. xii. 92.

In his posthumously published *Pleas of a Spanish Advocate,* Gentili especially concentrates on subjects drawn from maritime disputes. He strongly advocates freedom of the seas and condemns states and nonstate actors who interfere with commerce in international waters. At the same time he reserves to the sovereign a dominion over the coastal waters extending to one hundred miles at a time when three miles—the range of a cannon—was the commonly accepted term. Nor was this an aberration. His service to Spain, which appeared to many so strange in the context of his personal history, seems less bizarre if it is remembered that Gentili sought, and was granted, permission to represent Spain from the English king James I, who himself was seeking greater absolutism in his own state.

It is sometimes said that Gentili and his predecessors, described in this chapter, were not discussing international law at all but were merely continuing the rich medieval genre of books about the laws of war. This seems to me to miss a profound point. The State is defined by law and by war: it is the State's monopoly on legitimate violence, within and without, that marks it as a State. Once a society of states comes into being, the laws of that society are perforce about war, just as the laws of a single state are about keeping the civil peace.

During Gentili's last years as an advocate, he was called upon to comment on whether there should be common-law judges sitting on appeals from the English Court of Admiralty. As one would expect of the former Regius Professor of Civil Law, Gentili wished to have the appeals bench consist solely of civil lawyers. The English common law, he argued, was not suited to lawsuits involving foreigners, whereas all parties would be perfectly satisfied "to be judged according to the *ius gentium* as found in the civil law." The king need only require the appellate judges to administer "the English civil law." This step—which makes international law the law of the sovereign, the "law of the land"—is no mere extension of feudal authority, but rather represents a journey to a new world. The State, only recently objectified, is now demanding recognition for itself *and* its counterparts. It is demanding recognition for an entire society of states.

CHAPTER NINETEEN

The Peace of Westphalia

THE SETTLEMENT of the Peace of Augsburg in 1555, which ratified the constitution of the society of princely states, was thrown into doubt in 1608 when Prince Maximilian of Bavaria annexed and re-Catholicized the Lutheran city of Donauworth. The Augsburg settlement had given sovereign princes the right to determine the religion of their subjects according to each prince's religion; and it had permitted free emigration in order to allow the transfer of Lutherans or Catholics to a sympathetic prince or city. The Treaty had also barred any Catholic bishopric or free city from converting to Lutheranism, and it had required that any spiritual prince— certain cardinals and bishops—give up his office and lands upon becoming a Lutheran.*

The treaty, however, had simply made no provision for the *seizure* of a city; it had fixed frontiers as they had been in 1552. Re-Catholicization jeopardized all the Protestant holdings that were the result of Church lands having been secularized after 1552: the return of these properties— bishoprics, abbeys, cloisters, and countless parishes—not only meant the loss of incomes from these holdings but also the enforced conversion, or expulsion, of the populations involved. The collapse of the Augsburg Constitution invited the carnage of the Thirty Years' War, which might be thought of as a civil war within the young society of states.

Out of the anarchy that characterized the final stages of the Thirty Years' War, there arose a stronger, more coherent society of states whose legal structure was redefined by a new constitution for that society. This constitution is the set of treaties known collectively as the Peace of Westphalia. At the apex of this society was the kingly state of France, which had displaced Spain, the leading princely state. Richelieu, who died in 1642, had never deviated from the strategic plan with which he began:[1] to cut the communications of the Spanish with their possessions in the

---

*It had expressly excluded Calvinists from the settlement.

Netherlands, and to obtain entry into the politics of the Empire. On his deathbed his confessor asked, "Do you forgive your enemies?" To which he replied, "I never had any, except those of the State."[2] For a man who was targeted for assassination by the king's brother, among others, this shows a remarkable degree of personal detachment and a deep identification with the State. Indeed, this remark is the administrator's equivalent of the classic formulation of the kingly state—"*L'état, c'est moi*"—the most famous utterance of the beneficiary of Richelieu's labors, who was four years old at the time of the cardinal's death.

Louis XIV, as the child became, continually asserted his own interpretations of the constitutional arrangements of the Peace of Westphalia and did his best to amend these arrangements by force. This raises two important points. First, "amendment" to an international constitution must be provided for or at least implicit in the constitution itself. The treaties of Westphalia accepted war as a legitimate means of changing the territorial settlement negotiated by the parties. Louis was not acting extraconstitutionally in his campaigns to expand his state and magnify his glory: the constitutional settlements that accompanied the subsequent wars of the seventeenth and eighteenth centuries invariably stated that they were merely partial renovations of the Westphalian agreements.[3]

Second, the domestic constitutional archetype of the State does not of itself determine the constitutional content of the international arrangement within which it sits; neither does the international constitutional form necessarily determine the domestic constitutional architecture. A kingly state may exist within a society dominated by princely states. An epochal settlement, like the Peace of Westphalia, however, recognizes and legitimates the dominant domestic constitutional order because that archetypal order has been forged in the conflicts that are composed by the peace settlement, and its triumph is reflected in the consensus that that triumph has wrung from the exhausted combatants.

THE CONSTITUTION OF 1648:
THE PEACE OF WESTPHALIA

"Peace was made at Münster and Osnabrück by a truly European Congress," wrote the historian E. A. Beller.[4] Such a Congress—a broad multilateral forum of parties—was required by the breadth of the conflict, which had involved many states, and by the scope of the constitutional consensus finally necessary to resolve the war. Westphalia provided the model for subsequent international constitutional conventions. In an important sense, Westphalia was to the states of Europe in 1648 what

Philadelphia became for the states of the American colonies in 1789: the birthplace of a new constitution for a small society of states.[5]

The Congress was convened on December 4, 1644, after six months of diplomatic wrangling, in two separate cities. Catholic estates, Spain, France and her ally the Dutch, representatives of the emperor, and a papal mediator met in Münster. Thirty miles away, at Osnabrück, Protestant estates met under the leadership of Sweden, with an imperial representative but without a mediator.[6] The negotiations ended with the signing on October 24, 1648, of a treaty of peace between the Empire and Sweden, and of a treaty between the Empire and France. A separate peace treaty between Spain and the Dutch States General was signed on January 30, 1648. The Peace of Westphalia—the 1648 constitution for the states of Europe*—was composed of these agreements.

At the outset, the Swedes and French insisted that they would only treat with the emperor if the Congress included the German estates. Eight months elapsed before the emperor agreed to this demand. This had the consequence of tying the imperial constitution to that of the international community: the provisions insisted on for the Empire in its relationship to the estates were made a part of the international constitution agreed to by all state parties.

The key negotiators were Count Maximilian von Trautmansdorff for the empire; Johan Oxenstierna and Johan Adler Salvius for Sweden; and Claude, Comte d'Avaux, and Abel Servien, Marquis de Sablé, representing France. All parties were acutely conscious of the ongoing fighting: Salvius, writing to Cardinal Mazarin, who had succeeded Richelieu, urged him to intensify the war effort—"the shield," he wrote, "is what the negotiation must rest on."[7] Similarly, the emperor, when things appeared to be going well for his forces, cautioned Trautmansdorff in October 1645 not to accept an armistice too quickly, and if one was agreed to, to make it for a short duration. Indeed it was not until early in 1646 that France and Sweden felt confident enough of their position in the field to put forward their negotiating terms.

It should not be concluded, however, that the insistence on military predominance was the only principle governing the timing of the settlement. Had this been the case, no agreement might ever have been concluded as each side hoped to better its position at precisely the moment the other side appeared willing to negotiate. There were strong motives for a peace settlement for its own sake in every camp, and these desires sometimes split the delegations. Thus Salvius kept up a backchannel to Christina, the

---

*This is so even though Russia, Poland, Britain, and other states were not parties; as late as the nineteenth century Burke was claiming that the partition of Poland was a breach of the Peace of Westphalia. *New Cambridge Modern History*, vol. 4, 358.

queen of Sweden, who, in order to win peace, favored making concessions beyond those thought prudent by her chancellor, Oxenstierna,* who happened to be the father of Salvius's co-negotiator. Three years into the Congress she had written to her ministers at Osnabrück, "I want you to be fully persuaded that above all I long for a secure and honorable peace. . . . [I]t is therefore my will that you . . . no longer dawdle. . . . Let not the fantasies of ambitious men detract you from this goal."[8]

As the situation grew more desperate, the emperor, too, urged his delegates not to delay. "To let the peace-making come to nothing . . . would, with regard to the beloved fatherland and the whole of Christendom, be irresponsible to us."[9] Even the French, whose forces were in the ascendant in the field, were willing to make concessions to achieve consensus. When the Swedes expressed anxiety over statements made by a French delegate, the French negotiator reassured his Swedish counterpart that he would exhort the Germans to be pragmatic and let the religious quarrel be decided in the next world.[10]

What were the elements of the consensus that had to be put into place for there to be peace? On the German side, Catholics and Protestants were united in their desire not to dismember the empire. This came as a shock to the French,[11] who assumed that the German princes would wish to separate into sovereign states, as had the Italians, in order to maximize the sovereignty and wealth of their domains. The French and the Swedes wanted a collective security system, but distrusted each other sufficiently that they were unable to achieve it, and so pressed instead for various key territorial cessions that might prove of strategic value later. Spain wished to renew her link with the Dutch provinces, even if this required an amicable divorce from her former possessions there. The emperor wanted a set of rules, agreed to by all parties, that would allow him an entirely free hand in his hereditary properties and would bind the imperial estates (and their foreign allies) to a more detailed version of the Peace of Augsburg, ending the interpretive battles over that covenant that had fractured Germany.[12] The critical common aspect of all these goals is that they depended on consensus: warfare alone could not gain some of them, and could gain others only temporarily. This is a lesson that the epochal war—because it is broken by false peaces—teaches the participants, and which each century seems to have to relearn. This requirement of consensus and the fundamental nature of the political objectives sought, together brought about the constitutional achievement at Westphalia. Randle was writing of the Peace of Westphalia when he concluded:

---

*This is the chancellor described in Book I who, defying pressure from the jittery regency council acting on behalf of the young queen, kept Sweden in the war after the death of Gustavus Adolphus. The son endeavored to reflect his father's policy.

The erection of a new order follows from the intention of the peacemakers to provide a systematic, revised basis for interstate relations, and to avoid the catastrophe of another multilateral war. Even apart from the intentions of the negotiators, the new constitution will arise . . . from the peace settlement itself. In the resolution of the multiplicity of issues of the war, particularly [those] which require the concurrence of many parties, . . . the peacemakers will be obliged to work toward a comprehensive settlement—one that will function to modify and order the relations of all the actors in the state system.[13]

When the settlement finally came, most of the territorial goals of the French and the Swedish were met. The Swedes had sought Pomerania, the Baltic port of Wismar, twenty million imperial dollars, the bishoprics that controlled the Weser and Elbe, and the province of Silesia. They got only a portion of Pomerania, but it was that crucial part containing the lucrative port at Stettin; Wismar; the bishoprics of Bremen and Verden; and five million dollars. These cessions were of critical strategic importance to Sweden and her Baltic trade. Because Pomerania was a possession of the Elector of Brandenburg, "compensation" was given him, of such an extent—Magdeburg, Minden, Halberstadt—that he emerged, after the Habsburgs, as the largest territorial prince in the Empire, a development that made possible the eventual emergence of Prussia and the territorial state in the next century.

The French demanded the fortresses of Metz, Toul, Verdun, Breisach, and Phillipsburg, as well as Breisgau, Alsace, and the four "forest cities" on the Rhine. All of these claims were met, excepting Breisgau and the four cities. In a complicated settlement, the French received certain rights in Alsace that the treaty language left ambiguous.

A fundamental constitutional arrangement was provided to the German estates that explicitly prevented the creation of a unified kingly state for Germany. More than three hundred effectively sovereign princes, free cities, and bishoprics, the treaty stated, had "territorial superiority in all matters ecclesiastical as well as political." They had the right to agree to and ratify treaties; they could declare war—indeed, war could not be declared by the empire without their consent. They could ratify peace treaties; they could levy taxes. The imperial diet was required to reach amicable agreement to settle all religious questions, rather than by majority vote. These provisions of the "Westphalian constitution . . . remained the fundamental constitutional law of the empire until its dissolution a century and a half later."[14]

With respect to the religious issues at stake in the war, Beller concluded that "[t]he solutions found . . . were essentially a broadening and a clarification of the Peace of Augsburg." This supports the view that the earlier

treaty was itself constitutional in nature, and that interpretive disputes arising with regard to the earlier treaty presaged the epochal character of the
Thirty Years' War.

Four important omissions, partisan provisions, and undetermined
points had haunted the Peace of Augsburg. Each was addressed at Westphalia. First, Westphalia officially recognized Calvinism. Second, the year
1624 was made the decisive date for the conversion of church properties.
Third, the "Ecclesiastical Reservation" was applied to both sects: if either
a Protestant or a Catholic bishop changed his faith, he would be forced to
resign. Fourth, the fundamental Augsburg constitutional principle—*cuius
regio eius religio,* subsumed in the Westphalian provision of "territorial
superiority in all matters ecclesiastical as well as political"—was elaborated by certain ameliorating additions: if the prince changed his faith, he
could not interfere with the religion of his subjects; rights of public worship, as of 1624, could not be changed by the conversion of the prince; and
the prince retained the right of expulsion, but with the important qualification of a five-year grace period during which property could be sold or
transported by the expelled parties.[15]

It is also important to see the Peace of Westphalia as a constitutional
renovation of the Peace of Augsburg, the first constitution of the European
society of states, because that is the way contemporaries saw it. It was
widely held among the delegates that

> the present war had been caused by the inadequacies of the 1555 reli-
> gious settlement, which had not clarified the rights of Protestant and
> Catholic estates with sufficient precision. A chief reason that the war
> had been so prolonged and acrimonious was that each party could con-
> vince itself that it was fighting for fundamental rights. . . . The convic-
> tion prevailed among the delegates that, provided the rights of each of
> the participating actors could be established definitively, no source of
> conflict would remain.[16]

With slight exceptions in Silesia and lower Austria, the emperor refused
to make any concessions to the Protestant subjects in his hereditary, Habsburg lands. Similarly, although Westphalia set the year 1618 as the date for
restitution and amnesty, the emperor refused to be bound by this in his own
hereditary realm, recognizing that the wholesale transfers of property after
the imperial victory at White Mountain would thus be undone. This concession by the Congress must be seen not as simply a peculiar artifact of
the negotiations, but as entirely consistent with the overall scheme by
which the emperor was reinforced in his dynastic role, but denied the unifying role he had sought with respect to the imperial, non-Habsburg lands.
Henceforth, the Habsburg emperors would focus their attentions on

Vienna; Brandenburg—the chief actor, with France, in the ensuing period—would dominate the affairs of central Germany. The controversies that had combined political and religious conflict were finally settled.

The pope strongly opposed Westphalia and denounced it in a bull. It is significant, however, that the treaty itself anticipated this objection and required all signatories, Catholic and Protestant, to bind themselves to ignore any ecclesiastical objections to it. Thus was the role of the Christian community of states replaced by the rule of state consent.[17]

Two new states were recognized: the United Provinces of the Netherlands and the Swiss Confederation. Their admission to the European society of states on the basis of provisions in the Westphalian Peace is yet another confirmation of the constitutional nature of the treaty. The great powers also claimed for themselves the authority to declare the public law of Europe. War was recognized as a legitimate form of resolving conflicts, hence the importance of the legal recognition the Peace accorded the strategic cessions of fortresses and ports sought by France and Sweden. The concept of the just war was nowhere mentioned. It had become irrelevant. No state was allowed to be destroyed, however, and compensation was to be awarded to those states that gave up strategically advantageous possessions.

This last rule is important to stress, as well as its corollary that mere possession was not equated with legitimacy. When Salvius discussed with some of the German delegates the proposal to compensate Brandenburg for part of Pomerania, which was being taken by Sweden, he completely dismissed the argument that Sweden could claim Pomerania by right of conquest and that, therefore, compensation was not required. Similarly, the port of Wismar was owned by the duke of Mecklenburg-Schwerin, who had been dispossessed by the emperor and restored by the Swedes. If Wismar was to go to Sweden, then the duke too had to be compensated because he held the legal right to Wismar, even though it was the Swedish conquest that restored him to possession.[18] Indeed Sweden took these territories as imperial fiefs, so that their cession to Sweden did not involve a loss of territory to the empire but an inclusion of Sweden among the various imperial estates, with accompanying duties owed to the emperor. From the outset, Sweden had maintained that it would only achieve its strategic objectives *"cum totius Imperii omniumque interessatorum consensu"*— with the consent of the whole Empire and of all of the interested parties. Even France ended up purchasing the Habsburg rights to the three fortresses it sought from the empire. The Treaty of Münster fixed the price at three million livres, a substantial sum, and to this the Treaty further added a French obligation to assume Habsburg debts.[19]

With such a mixture of principles, procedural rules, and jurisdictional allocations, it is hardly surprising that the "Westphalian settlement of 1648 was perceived as . . . a new constitution for the European state system. . . . [So it] struck the political actors of the day, as well as jurists and historians."[20]

In Book I's discussion of the development of the State, I dissented from the famous conclusion of the historian C. V. Wedgwood, who pronounced the Thirty Years' War "the outstanding example in European history of a meaningless conflict."[21] Her conclusion is even less defensible with respect to the society of states and the Peace that followed the War. The extension of the maxim *cuius regio eius religio* imposed common restrictions on states, adumbrating the emergence of a new society of states characterized by their sovereign equality. At the same time, the notion that the ruler of a state had the right to determine the religion of that territory the state controlled enhanced the movement toward absolutism in the member states of this new society.[22] "[T]he Thirty Years War was, after all, fought over the juridical definition of the position of the States and the Emperor,"[23] and, one might add, "of the legal position of all the states of Europe vis-à-vis one another." It is hard for us to recognize this from our current vantage point of cynicism about law and the prevailing view that law is a mere disguise for that power. This was not the view in early seventeenth century Europe, however, when law was the connecting bridge between politics and religion, and where the constitutional law of the Peace of Augsburg had set the terms of the geopolitical conflict. As Roelofsen reminds us, it was "only towards the end of the seventeenth century, with the famous 'partition treaties' between William II and Louis XIV, that considerations [of legal title] were seriously weakened in favour of more power-political *droit de convenance*."[24]

The idea of a juridical order without a higher political or ecclesiastical authority is so novel, and so far-reaching, that it has given immortality to the name with which it is mainly associated, that of the seventeenth century lawyer Hugo Grotius. His *De Jure Belli ac Pacis* is one of the cardinal books of European history[25] and he was regarded in his lifetime, as he is today, as one of the leading intellectual figures of the Baroque period. Gustavus Adolphus took *De Jure Belli ac Pacis* with him on his campaigns, and claimed to have based the political structure he sought for Europe on Grotian ideas. In our time, Grotius's fame has had a revival, and there is a good deal of literature on the "Grotian Tradition" and even the "Grotian Moment"[26]—that moment at which a new world order is put into place. In the following section, we will review briefly Grotius's rather disheartening biography; his views on international law, of which most commentators, perhaps too simply, regard him as the father; and the importance of these ideas for construing the international constitution of the period, the treaties that made up the Peace of Westphalia.

CONSTITUTIONAL INTERPRETATION: THE INTERNATIONAL LAWYERS

GROTIUS

Hugo Grotius[27] was born in Delft in 1583. His father was the chief city official of Delft, curator of the University at Leiden, and a close ally of the most dynamic Dutch political figure of the day, Johan van Oldenbarneveldt. Oldenbarneveldt was, at that time, Advocate for the States of Holland (which was the most important of the federal entities making up the United Provinces).

Grotius was a celebrated child prodigy: he wrote Latin elegies at the age of eight, entered the university at eleven, and is said to have converted his Catholic mother to Calvinism with irrefutable arguments when he was twelve. At fifteen he went with Oldenbarneveldt, now the grand pensionary of Holland, on a diplomatic mission to France where the king, Louis XIII, introduced the young Grotius as "the miracle of Holland." On this visit to Paris, Grotius determined to study law at Orleans. In 1598, at the age of fifteen, he emerged with his doctorate and returned in 1599 to practice law in The Hague.

At each important stage in Grotius's life, he was called upon to perform essentially professional duties as a lawyer that were of the greatest significance for his scholarly, philosophical work. Abstracting from a particular undertaking in a political, legal, or religious controversy, he found the underpinnings for his great jurisprudential essays, which cannot be usefully understood apart from these foundational ideas. These ideas might be stated as an epigram: history is the bridge between strategy and law; and law is the bridge between religion and politics. During his life, Grotius often suffered on account of his faith in these ideas, but had he lived somewhat longer, he would have been confirmed in their ultimate power.

In 1601 Grotius was appointed Latin historiographer for Holland. He undertook to provide an historical apologia for the United Provinces, comparable to other national histories produced by humanists of the sixteenth and seventeenth centuries. This history had an unusual significance for the Netherlands, however, owing to the Dutch revolt against Spanish rule. Most observers outside the Dutch Republic, and a considerable number within, entertained serious doubts about the legitimacy of the regime.* Foreign opinion was crucial to the Republic because the Dutch had had to rely on foreign intervention and assistance to resist Spain, the dominant military power of the era. In order to present the Dutch case in terms that

---

*Henry IV is recorded as having called the Dutch provinces *"libres, mais non pas souverains,"* in a conversation with the English ambassador. Roelofsen, 100, n. 23.

made sense to the European learned public, Grotius drew a line of continuity between the Batavian Republic of antiquity and the Holland of his own day. This work, published as *De Antiquitate* in 1610, provided a classical justification for the constitutional theory on which the Dutch Revolt was predicated. On this theory, the counts of Holland in the Batavian periods were not "monarchs" in the then-contemporary sense of the kingly state, but only hereditary executive officers. This history absolved the Dutch from the accusation of revolution against the king of Spain, who was not, in Grotius's view, their lawful dynastic ruler. This was the first important instance of Grotius's professional practice providing the impetus for his theoretical ideas.

A second significant example occurred in 1604. An admiral of the Dutch East India Company had taken a Portuguese carrack, the trading ship *Santa Catarina,* as a prize in the Straits of Malacca. This capture had offended the Mennonite shareholders of the company who regarded war as offensive to Christian beliefs. They threatened to withdraw from the company and set up a rival firm in France. The directors of the company, which had been founded by Oldenbarneveldt, turned to Grotius for a legal opinion evaluating the incident. In order to show that the prize taking was not an act of piracy, Grotius had to show why the war was lawful. Then as now, criminal acts of terrorism had to be carefully differentiated in law from acts of war. Grotius's essay, completed in 1606, is commonly known as *De Jure Praedae Commentarius* and was the basis for his masterpiece, *De Jure Belli ac Pacis.* The latter work represents a process of generalizing from the examples adduced in *De Jure Praedae.**

In 1607 Grotius was appointed Advocate, or attorney-general, of Holland. He was twenty-four. He was by now firmly associated with Oldenbarneveldt, who led one of the two great political movements in the United Provinces, and who was opposed by Prince Maurice.[28] Grotius's close ties with the Dutch East India Company brought him his first diplomatic mission as a member of a delegation to the Anglo-Dutch trade conference on Asian affairs in 1613. During these meetings Grotius was already well known enough to ask for, and be granted, a private meeting with King James I. Typically, however, the subject of this meeting was theology, not East Indian trade.

In Holland Oldenbarneveldt had become the champion of the Arminians, a liberal wing of the Calvinist church that attempted to soften the strict and pitiless doctrine of predestination. As with most religious conflicts of this period, this one played into international politics: the strict Calvinists,

---

*Only one part of *De Jure Praedae* was published in Grotius's lifetime (the book itself did not come to light until an auction in the nineteenth century); this was the celebrated *Mare Liberum,* arguing, as its title suggests, for freedom of the seas and against Portuguese claims to an Asian monopoly. The work of which it formed a part, however, dealt very largely with the legal basis for war.

or Anti-Remonstrants, accused the Arminians of being papists and idolaters. Oldenbarneveldt's party was linked to France, a Catholic state; Maurice's party was linked to Britain. Grotius, reflecting a lifelong conviction that the Reformed churches—Anglican, Lutheran, Calvinist, and others—should all unite, and eventually unite with the Roman Catholic, took his case to King James. The English king, a sophisticated intellect but utterly without a taste for attempting difficult political crusades, seems to have merely endured Grotius during a memorable interview. Grotius believed he had persuaded England to act as mediator between the Dutch factions, and even to favor the Arminians. This proved overoptimistic. The English did not intervene, and the king later recalled, "[Grotius] was some pedant, full of words and no great judgment."[29]

That same year, 1613, Grotius was chosen by Oldenbarneveldt to be pensionary for Rotterdam, making him Oldenbarneveldt's chief lieutenant in Holland. For the next five years he was deeply involved in attempting to heal the schism in the Dutch Reformed Church while asserting the independent federal status of the States of Holland. Grotius and Oldenbarneveldt apparently underestimated the mortal threat they posed to the centralizing goals of Prince Maurice of Nassau, who was, as we have seen in Book I, attempting to create in the Dutch provinces something like a kingly state with a unified church. The States of Holland and other states had resisted this effort and had persistently refused to accept the actions of the States-General, had refused to pay their share of national taxes, and had even raised a militia.

On August 29, 1618, Maurice struck. Oldenbarneveldt, Grotius, and the pensionary for Leiden were arrested. A special tribunal convicted Oldenbarneveldt and Grotius of high treason. Oldenbarneveldt was executed on May 13, 1619; Grotius was imprisoned for life at Loevenstein Castle. He was thirty-five. Like Machiavelli, he had risen as the brilliant protégé of a forceful and controversial leader, and had fallen with him; like Machiavelli he would spend the rest of his life writing and plotting his return to power; and like Machiavelli (and Thucydides), his ultimate fame would rest on the tracts he wrote while helplessly watching events in his native land in which he played no effective part.

In Loevenstein Castle Grotius was allowed to continue his studies. During this period he wrote a treatise on Dutch law (which treatise was used in South Africa well into the nineteenth century) and a widely published book on the truth of the Christian religion. Books were brought to him in large crates. Fittingly, for such a bookish person, he managed to escape by hiding in one of these library chests. He fled to Antwerp, then to Paris, where he was welcomed by Richelieu and given a pension. Because he was a Calvinist, however, he was denied any university post. It was in Paris that he wrote *De Jure Belli ac Pacis*.

This classic work is, one suspects, more cited than read. Martin Wight aptly speaks of "trying to pick a path once again through the baroque thickets of Grotius' work, where profound and potent principles lurk in the shade of forgotten arguments, and obsolete examples lie like violets beneath gigantic overgrown rhododendrons."[30] There is much to learn, however, from Grotius's *method,* which consists of abundantly collecting examples, usually from antiquity, to illustrate various points. This method is both the basis for and the consequence of his fundamental commitment to natural law, a subject that will be taken up presently.

For ten years Grotius tried to find a way back into Dutch politics. The death of Maurice in 1625 encouraged him, as did the support promised him in his correspondence with Frederick Henry, Maurice's heir. The city of Rotterdam had not dared to appoint another Pensionary because Grotius had been appointed for life. Finally, in 1631 he returned to the Dutch Republic, but in April the next year he was declared a fugitive by the States of Holland and he fled once again, this time to Hamburg.

Gustavus Adolphus's admiration for Grotius was well-known throughout Europe. After the Swedish king's death, Oxenstierna interviewed Grotius at Frankfurt-am-Main in 1634 and engaged him as the Swedish ambassador to the French court. This was a crucial period in French-Swedish relations: the Treaty of Compiègne, which brought France into the Thirty Years' War, was negotiated in 1635. Moreover, it was a difficult time for Sweden: after the Swedish defeat at Nördlingen, France became the dominant partner in the alliance and a competitor for postwar leadership.

Grotius served for ten years in Paris, despite repeated requests for his recall by Richelieu, who apparently detested him. It is usually said that Grotius was a failure as a diplomat, a "typical example of the intellectual in politics, lacking in political tact and common sense and more at home in the world of ideas."[31] Whether this was so, the French-Swedish relationship was not managed by Grotius. The real negotiations with France were carried on in Hamburg by Johan Adler Salvius and by Oxenstierna himself. When Grotius was finally dismissed, it was probably the result of his being caught between the queen's peace program, which offered a conciliatory attitude toward France, and Oxenstierna's less flexible policies.

It was Grotius's identification with the chancellor and the old guard in Swedish affairs that probably led to his dismissal. Incompetence is seldom a complete bar to diplomatic appointment, even for intellectuals, and Grotius was, and had been for a long time, a celebrated figure in the European republic of letters. During these years when he repeatedly angered the French over his refusals to accept French rules of precedence—rules that were to cause no little conflict at Westphalia—his main activity was not diplomacy but theology. His studies of the dogmatic disputes between the Protestant and Catholic churches favored unification, a position that brought forth abundant and wrathful tracts from Lutheran and Calvinist theologians.

Widely regarded as a failure in Paris, he was not included in the Swedish mission to Westphalia. He was, however, asked to be a member of the Swedish Council of State. This he declined, and began the journey back to Paris from Stockholm. A shipwreck cast him on the coast of Pomerania, the scene of Gustavus's great triumphs of 1630. There he died of exhaustion at Rostock. Three years later the Peace was signed and his immortality sealed, because the Peace presupposed the "juridical order without a higher political authority" of which he had been the most ardent and celebrated advocate. Hedley Bull concluded that the "idea of international society which Grotius propounded was given concrete expression in the Peace of Westphalia, and Grotius may be considered the intellectual father of this . . . general peace settlement. . . . [I]n their broad impact on the course of international history, the theory of Grotius and the practice of the Peace of Westphalia marched together."[32]

Grotius himself regretted his career. He frequently remarked that he ought not to have gone into law but stuck with literature, a frequent complaint of law professors with literary tastes. He sent his two sons into the army, not to the university as his father had sent him. And his last words are reported to have been "By undertaking many things, I have accomplished nothing."[33] Like other great men he seems to have forgotten that it takes an army of successors, often misinterpreting the great man's works or perverting them for their own reasons, to really accomplish something. Whether that posthumous army is summoned to any particular thinker's banner is usually not a matter of the great man's doing, as Oldenbarneveldt might ruefully have told him.

What is the "Grotian view," if by that question one asks "for what principles does Grotius's posthumous army fight?" Generally, a "Grotian view" is taken to mean the assertion of a duty on the part of the individual state to serve the interests of the society of states as a whole. A weaker version of this simply asserts that there are such interests; a stronger version claims that only such interests can justify certain activities of the State, such as war. Thus the Grotian view is to be distinguished from the Hobbesian view that international society can have no legal rules because there is no sovereign to organize and maintain the collaboration among states that might replace the constant struggle of each state against every other state. Although the Grotian society of states is perhaps anarchic, it does not exist in a naked state of nature. The rationale for the Grotian view is that there exists a great society of all mankind—*humani generis societas*—and

all human institutions are governed by the rules of that society. Thus the Grotian perspective is also quite different from the Kantian view that perpetual peace can only be achieved through the construction of suprastate institutions.

Six corollaries follow from the Grotian view: that natural law is a source (though not the only source) of the rules that govern states (because man is a creature of nature, and all his activities are governed thereby); that international society is universal and not merely limited to Christendom or the European states system; that individuals and nonstate actors can have a role in the application of the rules of international law; that the universal traits shared by all mankind can give rise to cooperative requirements, and these requirements can be a source of justice; that suprastate institutions are not necessary for the rule of law to be applied to states;[34] and that, being a source of law, the individual person is a bearer of rights.[35] Taken together, this infrastructure of ideas provides a surprisingly modern and surprisingly accurate description of international law as it actually is— universal yet pluralistic, occasionally the source of cooperation, functioning in the absence of a universal sovereign but difficult to enforce and rarely functioning very authoritatively, a discipline that embraces not only the relations among states, but also the human rights of individuals. Whether this intellectual infrastructure was actually supplied by Grotius, or is the invention of his highly capable and imaginative disciples, I am not certain. For our purposes it is enough to see that the constitutional aspects of the Peace of Westphalia are consistent with this vision of international law, though this may well be because it is a source of that vision rather than its product.

Of greater relevance to our study, however, is the Grotian method, and not simply the views advocated by those who are deemed "Grotians." This method supplies the ways of interpretation that are indispensable to a constitution. It was the absence of such accepted interpretive methods that had proved so destructive of the previous constitution, the Peace of Augsburg. Grotius's work is a milestone in human thought, a humanist achievement that links Erasmus and Adam Smith, but it lies not in the precepts of Grotius (the infrastructure so effectively and inspiringly described by Bull) but rather in the mundane and quotidian incidents of practice.

Our starting place must be this brilliant observation by Mattingly:

> [Grotius] was only trying, like most of his contemporaries, to justify what men were doing or thought they ought to be doing . . . But he was the first person to see, or to make clear that he saw, that, to be persuasive, the argument must be couched in the terms not of the interests of a single unitary commonwealth of which the princes and republics of Christendom were subordinate members, but in terms of the interest in

their own self-preservation of the independent, ego-centered, absolutely sovereign states whose aggregate composed the heterogeneous, pluralistic international society of western Europe. That was what the future was going to be like.[36]

In other words, Grotius linked his arguments to the newly emerging society of kingly states.

Grotius's method was to completely forgo the rich store of glosses, commentaries, opinions, and precedents of the immediate past—the past just preceding and following Augsburg—in favor of Cicero, Plutarch, and Livy. Biblical citations and classical references to the political behavior of the Greeks abound in Grotius; indeed the sheer assembly of all the classical instances that can be brought to bear on contemporary problems can be dazzling, even overwhelming. This is the method of the exemplary: finding and citing examples of previous state behavior, organized according to the principal problems facing the new state society of Europe. Nothing like this appears again until *The Federalist Papers,* which became for the American constitution a rich source of interpretive methods. Grotius did this for the European constitution.

Rousseau, with his customary eye for the corrupt and self-serving, saw through this method entirely. In *The Social Contract,* he wrote: "Grotius denies that all human government is established for the benefit of the governed and cites the example of slavery. His characteristic method of reasoning is always to offer fact as a proof of right. It is possible to imagine a more logical method, but not one more favorable to tyrants."[37]

But that was the point: Grotius's method—the exemplary, offering "fact as a proof of right"—enables law to act as an ameliorative bridge between religion and politics, channeling real and otherwise insoluble conflicts into more detached, legal terms. Rousseau's method, and that of the political philosophers who were his contemporaries, was instead to imagine a just rule and demand that the State adhere to it. Whatever the justice of Rousseau's method, and I think there is less than is commonly assumed, it is not a method that provides interpretive modalities. It is a pamphleteer's method, not a lawyer's. What the lawyers were trying to do, Mattingly reminds us, "was to rationalize the usual conduct of European governments, or justify the position of a client or patron in a dispute."[38] Precisely—and this is what gave Grotius his uncanny ability to anticipate what would be the course of the international society whose fate was being negotiated at Osnabrück and Münster as he lay dying in Rostock.

This is the true ground of Grotius's otherwise elusive concept of natural law. It is no more than the *way* things are done; not the substance of the law, not the things being done themselves—this Grotius called the "volitional law"—and not the divine law, but the ordinary, everyday methods of arguing and putting forward interpretations. Grotius appears to have believed that with this approach he might find a receptive audience for his ideas about uniting the conflicting theologies of post-Reformation Europe. Here he attempted too much: law might be a bridge between religion and politics, but not between religions. Only a true humanist could have thought otherwise.

Grotius's methods of interpretation, those that are implied by the "exemplary" approach to interpretation, are capable of embracing many sorts of problems. They allow for the destabilization of governments, the use of propaganda, the revoking of a pledged word by means of the *clausula,* the right of intervention—as much as they are a call to solidarity among states. Mainly these methods provide for the legitimacy of all civil authority, a rather useful idea when a new constitution for a society of new forms of the State is coming into being. Grotius defined sovereignty as that power "whose actions are not subject to the legal control of another, so that they cannot be rendered void by the operation of another human will." Thus when the State adopts the constitutional order of the kingly state— and has not only seized for itself a monopoly on violence, but admits no ecclesiastical superauthority (even as to ecclesiastical matters)—it has also achieved legitimacy. *De Jure Belli ac Pacis* is a compendium of methods by which the treaties and rules of Westphalia can be applied. It does not prescribe the content of those rules.

It is doubtless true that there was "little that guardians of *raison d'état* . . . in the class of Richelieu and Father Joseph could learn from Grotius. Yet their secret archives, diplomatic correspondence, sophisticated treaties . . . all attest to the competence . . . and the growing richness of the practice of European international law."[39] Richelieu and Gustavus Adolphus did not seek guidance (though Gustavus admired Grotius greatly). Their successors, however, needed interpretive methods to put into effect the system these leaders had designed and successfully fought for. Through the numerous editions and translations of *De Jure Belli ac Pacis* the idea of an international society of kingly states was chiefly spread.[40] In Grotius, the successors to Richelieu and Gustavus found ways to support the rights of kings to sovereignty, the denial of the supervening authority of the pope, the right to use force to vindicate the Westphalian system, the equal rights of Protestant and Catholic states, the rights of states to navigate the oceans and to conduct trade without the permission of other states, and the validity of agreements made with non-Christian powers. Most significantly for the Westphalian constitution, Grotius gave arguments for the use of war to uphold the general settlement.

The fact must also be recognized that kings, and those who possess rights equal to those kings, have the right of demanding punishments not only on account of injuries committed against themselves or their subjects, but also on account of injuries which do not directly affect them but excessively violate the law of nature or of nations . . . For liberty to serve the interests of human society through punishments, which originally, as we have said, rested with individuals, now, after the organization of states and courts of law, is in the hands of the highest authorities, not properly speaking, in so far as they rule over others but in so far as they are themselves subject to no one.[41]

Sovereignty thus implies rather than denies a duty owed to the society of sovereign states. Both Richelieu and Gustavus Adolphus had envisioned a collective security system that would emerge from the Thirty Years' War. Although both had died by the time of the congress, Richelieu's written instructions were followed unaltered. Minutes taken by the papal and Venetian envoys disclose that the French "proposed, for the safeguarding of the peace, a general league between all those concerned in this pacification . . . with the reciprocal obligation for each and any of them to take up arms against him or those who might infringe the present treaty."[42] Just such obligations are at the center of the Grotian rationale. In the end, the proposal foundered on Oxenstierna's suspicions of France, on the exclusion of the Franco-Spanish conflict, and on French hauteur. Grotius's moment was not complete.

Grotius had written in 1625,

I saw prevailing throughout the Christian world a license in making war of which even barbarous nations would have been ashamed; recourse was had to arms for slight reasons, or for no reason; and when arms were once taken up, all reverence for divine and human law was thrown away; just as if men were thenceforth authorized to commit all crimes without restraint.[43]

That is to say, strategy had been severed from law by war.

Grotius's reaction to this situation had been to persuade states that they had a common interest served by adherence to the rule of law, and that pursuing this interest would strengthen them as states. The Grotian ethos would serve states by giving them the means to agree upon rules of their own devising, rules that no state acting alone could enforce upon the others. The Westphalian congress was the perfect forum for developing such a consciousness: not only did it bring together the representative actors for a lengthy period of time, the work of the congress demanded consensus reduced to written law (the treaties of Osnabrück and Münster). This consensus was the result of the successful effort at defining a common interest.

Grotius believed that this common interest, which was the basis for law, arose from the inherent sociability of man. Nowadays we might say that human beings only become complete in association with one another, that every associational society has a constitution, and thus the nature of man gives rise to law. Men seek law naturally, as roses turn themselves to the sun, because law permits and enhances their development. Other philosophers, notably Thomas Hobbes, believed that man's inherent nature was for power and that the role of law was to prevent the savage competition to which man's nature would otherwise lead him. Thus men seek law to compensate for their natures, as wolves submit to the pack rather than starve singly. Either approach supported the legitimacy of the individual kingly state, but there were profound differences between these two views regarding the law of the society of such states. There being no sovereign, Hobbes denied that an international law could exist; by contrast, Grotius denied that there had to be a supreme sovereign for there to be a law of the society of kingly states or sovereigns, and he implied that kingly states could only achieve complete legitimacy as part of a society of sovereigns to whom they owed certain duties.

It is often said that Hobbes and later Spinoza extrapolated from the life of the individual human being to that of the State. If the natural condition of men was one of endless war, then the superimposition of an absolute ruler, the sovereign State—Leviathan—did not terminate the state of nature, but merely transferred it to another plane. States are enemies by nature. Agreements to cooperate will be preserved only so long as fear of the consequences of breaking agreements binds the parties. Grotius, by contrast, extrapolated from the lives of persons in a society to that of states in a society. The natural condition of a society is one of potential cooperation—no man is an island sufficient unto himself. Not fear but aspiration binds states to their agreements.

PUFENDORF

Grotius's successors responded to Hobbes and Spinoza by asserting that man's capacity for reason removes him from the anarchic condition of animals and permits him to choose freely to be bound by law. The State, precisely because it is a sovereign, will seek agreements and uphold them generally because it is rational to do so as a way of life for the State, whether or not upholding a particular agreement is to its advantage at a particular moment in time.[44] By means of this argument, Hobbes and Samuel von Pufendorf—the latter the most famous of Grotius's immediate followers—are brought into a measure of agreement: "Hobbes' opinion that the law of nature and the law of nations were the same was accepted by Pufendorf. He also accepted the assumption that separate states, having no common political superior, stood in the same relations to each other as men in a state of nature."[45]

Pufendorf, moreover, believed that the law of nature provided the only basis for international law, because there was no other source for law such as exists in a society with a sovereign. Indeed he went so far as to deny the key Grotian insight that international law arose from the customs and practices of states, maintaining instead that only those rules that are derived from universal reason were lawful, this being the means by which natural law was apprehended. The law of gravity governed heavenly bodies; the law of states was to be derived by much the same rational means.

This is not the place to dwell on the shortcomings of Pufendorf; Leibniz has done this definitively.[46] Nor is it necessary to complain about the habits of philosophers that addict them to imagining "states of nature" from which to extrapolate, heedless of the one natural state they know something about, namely the one they are in at the moment, which must be presumed to govern to some degree their speculations about other such environments. Indeed I think it equally likely that both Hobbes and Spinoza found their inspiration for the natural state of man in what they observed in the behavior of kingly states—Hobbes focusing on the domestic scene, Spinoza on the international—and reasoned back from this paradoxical interface of absolute domestic authority and apparent international anarchy to the nature of man, rather than the other way around.

However that may be, the political actors of the time confronted the problem of post-Westphalian law and order—namely, that in the absence of a universal sovereign every kingly state, which Westphalia had made the sole preserver of the liberty, authority, and even the life of the political society largely composed of such states, would attempt to aggrandize itself to the limit of its power. They solved this problem in a somewhat less reified, though no less abstract, way than the philosophers. Like the philosophers, the politicians and diplomats of this era were impressed by the power of reason to discover the principles of nature, and the power of rational systems to exploit those principles. This solution thus had much in common with the mathematics of the Age, but it was not achieved by or expressed in philosophical terms. Rather it was expressed in law, arrived at, as we shall see, by the legal means of a constitutional convention and the achievement of consensus at that congress.

CHAPTER TWENTY

The Treaty of Utrecht

THE WESTPHALIAN PROBLEM—that, absent an absolute and universal sovereign, every kingly state would attempt to aggrandize itself to the limit of its power—found its most threatening expression in the campaigns of Louis XIV that directly challenged the Westphalian settlement. The solution to this Problem was ultimately expressed in a series of eight treaties known as the Peace of Utrecht, which resolved the epochal war composed of Louis's campaigns.

France and Spain had signed the Peace of the Pyrenees in November 1659, ending the one remaining conflict left open by Westphalia, just as Cateau-Cambrésis finally ended the Valois-Habsburg wars four years after Augsburg. Louis XIV married the Spanish infanta in Bayonne and returned to Paris in triumph. France, after some years of turmoil following the death of Louis XIII, was now united.

Once Louis was liberated from internal challenges and the administrative despotism of a sophisticated kingly state was securely in place, he began to make war on the territorial settlements of Westphalia in order to become the arbiter of European affairs. During this period the French state was supreme on the continent. French became the language of diplomacy, French architecture and literature reached their zenith, and the French canons of manners and taste were accepted as the standard throughout Europe.

For seventeen years—from 1667, when he led an army into the Spanish Netherlands, until 1684 when the Truce of Ratisbon confirmed him in all his gains since 1678—Louis's ambition dominated European events. Louis attempted to compel the states of Europe to recognize Ratisbon as an amendment to the territorial dispositions of Westphalia. The design flaw of Westphalia was that it invited this limitless aggrandizement on the part of the prevailing kingly state. In the pursuit of his goal, Louis actually brought into being the coalition and the animating idea that would prove both his undoing and also the undoing of the kingly state itself.

In 1686 this coalition, the League of Augsburg, was formed between the emperor, the Dutch, the western German states, including the upper Rhine provinces, and, in the next year, Savoy. All were alarmed by French intentions and capabilities. Partly in reaction, partly in pursuit of his historic goals, Louis invaded Germany in 1688, burning Heidelberg and reducing the Rhine provinces to ruin. While Louis was thus engaged, William III of Orange landed in England, displaced Louis's ally James II, and took the English crown. Thus by the end of 1689, France faced the United Provinces, England, the Habsburg-led Empire, Spain, Savoy, and the principal German states. The Nine Years' War that ensued exhausted both sides, and in 1697 the Treaty of Ryswick brought a new armistice. Neither side was now able to penetrate the fortress line that divided them in the north. At this point Louis might have been content with his gains; he was certainly acutely aware of the forces arrayed against him. A diplomatic crisis developed, however, that ignited his dynastic ambition, ambition that drove the kingly state. This crisis, provoked by the death of Carlos of Spain in 1700, led to the final campaign of Louis's epochal war, the struggle over Spanish succession, in which Louis attempted to unite the French and Spanish kingdoms in the Bourbon line.

By 1709, however, Louis had withdrawn French forces from Spain and was fighting to preserve France itself. The battle of Malplaquet, near Mons, was a defeat for the French, though allied forces actually lost twice as many men. Now the allied campaign sank into a grinding, brutal, and expensive but indecisive struggle. Louis's efforts toward peace negotiations were consistently rebuffed.

Then in 1710 the Tory party resolved to end British participation in the war. The following year the emperor Joseph died—he had succeeded his father only six years before—and the Archduke Charles unexpectedly became emperor. Enthusiasm for continuing to fight in order to place this figure on the throne of Spain as well was hardly high in Britain. Bolingbroke, the new foreign secretary, argued that if Charles united the Habsburg possessions under a single crown, he would pose the same threat of hegemony that a Bourbon dynasty had created in uniting France and Spain. Thus Bolingbroke recast the purpose of the alliance as one organized to effect a balance of power (rather than to uphold the Treaty of London by recognizing the dynastic claims of the Archduke in opposition to Louis)—that is, replacing the war aims of a society of kingly states with those of a society of territorial states. By this means he provided the basis for a British about-face, as well as for the peace congress to follow.

Britain worked out a secret agreement with France. The British were to receive Gibraltar; Minorca; Nova Scotia, Newfoundland, and Hudson Bay in Canada; and, importantly, the *asiento*—the monopoly of the slave trade with the Spanish colonies—for twenty years. In return for these commitments, Britain forced the Dutch to agree to a general congress, threatening to make a separate peace if the Dutch refused. Thus the congress opened at Utrecht in January 1712, in a climate of mutual suspicion.

THE CONSTITUTION: THE PEACE OF UTRECHT

The British and French had hoped to conclude proceedings before the next year's military campaign got underway. When this failed to happen, owing to Imperial intransigence, Bolingbroke ordered British troops to withdraw from the alliance, and obligingly provided this news, along with the plan of the allied campaign, to the French. The resulting allied catastrophe at Denain on July 24, 1712, finally persuaded the emperor of the need for a peace.

The Peace of Utrecht consists of eleven separate bilateral treaties.[1] That it represented a constitutional convention of the kind that had met at Osnabrück and Münster was well recognized by the parties. In his correspondence during the treaty process, Bolingbroke repeatedly referred to negotiations about the *"système général des affaires de l'Europe"* and to a "system for a future settlement of Europe."[2] In fact, in the eighth of his "Letters on History," which deals with Utrecht, he writes that the object of the congress was to achieve a "constitution of Europe."[3]

There was a general distinction drawn by the statesmen at the congress between the "private" interests of the states involved in the negotiations and the "public" interests of the society of the states of Europe as a whole.[4] Bolingbroke wrote to Torcy, his French counterpart, that "[t]he queen's ministers are far from wishing that the king should act contrary to his word and his honour; but Sir . . . something must be done for the sake of the peace and the interest of one individual must yield to the general interest of Europe."[5]

The ability to put forward a state's arguments in terms of a society of territorial states—a society, that is, characterized by a concern for the territorial stability of the whole—bedeviled and eluded some of the actors at Utrecht. The emperor, for example, "showed little aptitude for putting his case persuasively, neglecting to couch it in the idiom of international consensus. . . . Charles was quite literally unable to communicate on the international level [and] found himself increasingly isolated."[6] The language of this new consensus was reflected in four striking contrasts with the idiom it superseded.

First, the language of "interests" replaced that of "rights." "Rights" were something that kings might assert against each other; "interests" were something that states might have in common. Whereas the Westphalian monarchs had been concerned to establish the rights of the kingly states—the legal status of dynastic descent; the absolute right of the king over his subjects, including especially control over the religious liberties of the persons within his realm; and the perfect sovereignty of each kingly state unfettered by any external authority—the society of territorial states was concerned instead with the mutual relationships among states, specifically with maintaining a balance of power within that society itself. At one point Bolingbroke observed explicitly that "enough has been said concerning right, which was in truth little regarded by any of the parties concerned . . . in the whole course of the proceedings. Particular interests were alone regarded."[7]

Second, aggrandizement—so integral to the stature of the kingly state—was replaced by the goal of secure "barriers" to such a degree that claims for new accessions were universally clothed in the language of defensive barriers. Aggrandizement per se was frowned upon and even regarded as illegitimate.

Third, the word *state* underwent a change.[8] A "state" became the name of a territory, not a people, as would occur later when state-nations began to appear, nor a dynastic house, as was the case at Westphalia. Bolingbroke, characteristically, swiftly picked up on the difference. When commenting on the dilemma facing Louis over Carlos's will, Bolingbroke wrote that "adhering to the partitions seemed the cause of France, [whereas] accepting the will [seemed] that of the House of Bourbon."[9]

Fourth, whereas the kingly states had seen a balance of power as little more than a temptation for hegemonic ambition to upset, the territorial states viewed the balance of power as the fundamental structure of the constitutional system itself. "The concept was no longer applied simply as a procedural rule ('counteract any power if and when it threatens to become dominant'), but as a device for controlling and planning—in advance, on this occasion—the structure of the system as a whole."[10]

At Utrecht, a new conception of the balance of power made its historic debut. Its novelty arose from the change the states of Europe were undergoing in their domestic constitutional orders. As the territorial state replaced the kingly state, the idea of the "balance of power" moved from providing the occasions for sovereign action to animating a constitutional structure for collective security itself. Consider this passage from one of the renunciation documents produced by the Congress and signed by Louis XIV's grandson, the Duke de Berry:

All the powers of Europe finding themselves almost ruined on account of the present wars, which have brought desolation to the frontiers, and several other parts of the richest monarchies among states, it has been agreed in the conferences and peace negotiations being held with Great Britain, to establish an equilibrium, and political limits between the kingdoms whose interests have been, and still are the sad subject of a bloody dispute; and to consider it to be the basic principle of the preservation of this peace that it must be ensured that the strength of these kingdoms give reasons neither for fear nor for any jealousies. It has been thought that the surest way of achieving this is to prevent them from expanding, and to maintain a certain proportion, in order that the weakest ones united might defend themselves against more powerful ones, and support one another against their equals.[11]

All of these developments are evident in the exchanges between the two principal negotiators at Utrecht, Bolingbroke and Torcy.

The immediate problem lay in persuading Philip V, king of Spain and prince of the French royal line, to give up one kingdom or the other in order to forestall the situation in which he, through a series of deaths in his family, might unite the two crowns in one person. This diplomatic objective underscored the preventive nature of the territorial states' concept of the balance of power, and the structural role of this concept. The issue was given new intensity in 1711–1712 by the deaths of three heirs to the throne of France. When in March 1712, Torcy told Bolingbroke of the death two days earlier of the Duke of Brittany, only his younger brother—a child of two who was suffering from the same disease as the little duke who had just died—stood between Philip and the French crown. There immediately ensued an exchange of proposals between Bolingbroke and Torcy that unmistakably disclose the changed world of the territorial state confronting the world of the kingly state that it would supplant.

Bolingbroke began by urging that Philip simply renounce his right of succession to the crown of France, and retain the kingdom of Spain he was at present governing. Torcy demurred; succession was a matter of divine will—a principle of the kingly state—and could not be lawfully altered. Torcy proposed that if Philip became king of France, he could at that point abdicate the throne of Spain in favor of his brother, the Duke of Berry, another of Louis's grandsons.

Bolingbroke took this counterproposal as evidence that a renunciation document *could* be effective: on the premise of Torcy's counterproposal, if Philip's "right to the crown of France comes to take place, he is not to enjoy both [crowns]; [but] how can he choose if he cannot renounce either? And can he renounce the crown of France, and not the right of it?"[12] Bolingbroke wrote Torcy:

We are happy to believe that you in France are persuaded that God alone can abolish the law upon which your right of succession is founded, but you will allow us to be persuaded in Great Britain that a prince can relinquish his right by a voluntary cession and that he, in favour of whom the renunciation is made, may be justly supported in his pretensions by the powers who become guarantors of the treaty.

In this passage are the characteristic markers of the society of territorial states: the downgrading of the dynastic principle; the willingness to subordinate the rights of sovereigns to the interests of the states involved; and the use of collective security guarantees to ensure the balance of power itself.

When Torcy countered with a proposal that Philip commit himself at Utrecht to renounce one crown or the other in the event of a potential union, Bolingbroke underlined this essentially structural goal, and its difference from the Westphalian model of intervention: "You will say, all the powers are guarantors of this agreement; such a guarantee may really form a powerful alliance to wage war against the prince who would violate this condition of the treaty; but our object is rather to find out the means to prevent, than to support, new wars . . ."[13]

Accordingly, Bolingbroke argued, Philip must make his renunciation now: then the guarantee of "the powers of Europe" only had to prevent Philip from reversing his word and seizing one of the two states, as opposed to forcing him to give up a state which he had already invested. Torcy replied: "A rapprochement is easily brought about . . . [Philip V] must remove the disquietude of Europe by an immediate declaration of the part he will take should the succession be ever open to him."

Torcy spoke from a perspective that sought to preserve the sovereign scope of action for Philip. All of his concessions amounted to promises to take a course of action in the event a certain situation arises; they were "promises to make a promise." By contrast, Bolingbroke sought a decision that would foreclose Philip's freedom of action. He justified this on the basis of an appeal to the balance of power and the good of the society of states. This difference in perspective—kingly versus territorial state—put the two men on different wavelengths. Bolingbroke at this point exasperatedly remarked:

The French have undoubtedly a great advantage in treating in their own language, and I can easily believe that some of the expressions in my letter to Monsieur de Torcy may have been either faint, improper or ambiguous; but surely the whole tenor of them makes it plain that we never intended to separate the option and the execution of the option.*

---

*H. St. John, 492, dated May 3, 1712 (1798). It may be that his constitutional perspective was so different from Bolingbroke's that Torcy misunderstood the nature of the British proposal. Or it may be, as I am inclined to believe, that Torcy "misunderstood on purpose," endeavoring to preserve the freedom of action of his sovereign.

Now the British put a new proposal on the table. Through a complicated set of contingencies, France was to receive Savoy and Piedmont if Philip agreed to stand down from the Spanish throne immediately, the Duke of Savoy replacing him. Having swapped titles with the duke, Philip would then carry Savoy with him when he inherited the French throne. If, on the other hand, Philip chose to remain king of Spain, he would renounce the French crown at once, and the House of Savoy, not Bourbon, would inherit the Spanish crown if Philip's line were to die out.

This scheme had the virtue of enlisting the energies of Louis because it promised an enlargement of his holdings. To this extent it was a Westphalian solution deployed for Utrechtian goals, as the balance of power would be maintained by separating the French and Spanish dynasties. Once he learned of the British offer, Louis pressed his grandson to give up Spain. Louis wrote Philip: "Should gratitude and affection for your [Spanish] subjects be strong inducements with you to adhere to them, I can tell you that you owe those same sentiments to me, to your family, and to [France] . . . I now call upon you to show me their effects."[14]

Philip complied, though he surprised his grandfather by choosing to renounce the throne of France and remain in Madrid. He had acquiesced to a plea from the old world of kingly states, but the effect was to ensure the success of the new world of territorial states. The treaty process now proceeded to a conclusion in the series of agreements known as the Peace of Utrecht. The elaborate French rituals of precedence that had so bedeviled sessions at Westphalia were dispensed with; it was agreed that the delegates would enter the meeting rooms in no fixed order and sit where they liked. As at Westphalia, the constitutional role of the congress was indicated by its power to recognize new states as members of the society of states. At Utrecht, Brandenburg appealed for such recognition and received it; henceforth the kingdom of Prussia was a member of the society of states, entirely apart from Brandenburg's role in the empire. The acquisition of defensive barriers[15] dominated the negotiations (in contrast to the rights to "compensations" at Westphalia). These arguments were necessarily clothed in the language of a systemic balance of power, even if the motives of the negotiators were sometimes indistinguishable from simple aggrandizement.

> The Utrecht settlement and the regime it created brought about a major transformation of the international system . . . After Utrecht—with its emphasis upon, and indeed development of, the "Public Law of Europe"—there was a greater collective concern for preserving stability. Policymakers were therefore functioning in a new decision-making environment after Utrecht, basing their policies upon assumptions and interests quite different from the years before 1713.[16]

This assessment reflects a consensus among historians about the significance of Utrecht; that this significance lies in its constitutional aspects is less generally emphasized.

CONSTITUTIONAL INTERPRETATION: THE INTERNATIONAL JURISTS

The balance of power was a constitutional concept for the society of European states, and also, as we saw in Book I, played a similar role in ordering the internal relationships of the states that composed that society. Indeed historians have only recently come to appreciate the complicated means by which the territorial states that were later characterized as the states of the ancien régime maintained the principles of an internal balance of power, in contrast to the absolutism that preceded them. But why did the balance of power, a concept long antedating the modern state,[17] achieve such a pervasive dominance in the society of territorial states?

Territorial states are so named owing to their preoccupation with the territory of the state. As part of the Treaty of Utrecht, the first agreements were introduced fixing customs duties levied at the state frontier and diminishing the role of internal customs duties. The "most favored nation" clause makes its appearance at Utrecht. This attentiveness to commercial matters—the peace was accompanied by an extensive series of commercial treaties among the signatories—is also characteristic of the territorial states. Rather than focusing on the communities and towns that defined the boundaries of the kingly state, the territorial state attempts to fix a frontier boundary, a line, that marks the jurisdiction of the state. These boundaries are crucial if bartering is to take place, and dynastic rights to be ignored, in maintaining the balance of power, so we may say that for this reason also the territorialism of the eighteenth century state favored a system of perfecting the balance of power among states—but why did these states seek such a system in the first place?

The territorial state aggrandizes itself by means of peace because peace is the most propitious climate for the growth of commerce. Maintaining the balance of power was believed to be the way to maintain peace; and in fact the so-called cabinet wars fought for strictly limited territorial objectives replaced the religious wars of the previous century that were potentially limitless in their destruction. As this new constitution took hold in Europe, a new international jurisprudence accompanied it. International law, which had, as we have seen, been influenced by Catholic theology in the period of the princely states and by Protestant theology in the time of kingly states, now found itself in the hands of deists, those empirico-rationalists who believed in a divine order that ordained and was constrained by the rules of reason. The most powerful and influential of the philosophers of this period, Berkeley and Leibniz, took a very different view of the human condition than had Hobbes and Spinoza. This new perspective, with its emphasis on human freedom and the role of human perception, was crucially influential in the work of the two writers who dominated international jurisprudence during the era of the territorial state: Christian Wolff and Emmerich de Vattel.

The political theories that supported absolutism, like those of Thomas Hobbes, were consistent with assumptions about the behavior of individuals: because, like the State, the individual sought only to preserve himself in a conflict over the resources necessary for self-preservation, and to aggrandize himself at the expense of others in order to better ensure his survival, he would unceasingly pose violent threats unless prevented from doing so by an even more powerful individual. Only an all-powerful person could bring order to the natural and otherwise inevitable and continual chaos of human conflict. These ideas were the intellectual basis for the kingly state; Grotian ideas of a society of states had to contend with the wilful elements of which that society was composed.

> The Westphalian settlement, which affirmed the absolute and mutual independence of all the sovereigns, created an uncivilized system. It encouraged war because differences between princes must be resolved by the right of the strongest. Insecurity reigned.[18]

In contrast, the settlement at Utrecht depended upon very different ideas about the nature of states, though these too were consistent with, perhaps even extrapolated from, assumptions about individuals. Leibniz held, for example, that the naturalistic view of human nature given by Hobbes was too fragmentary to be accurate. The key to human behavior was not compulsion and inevitability, but free will, and the society of free human beings was characterized not only by self-preservation, but by development. Leibniz opposed Hobbes's view that absolute sovereignty was essential to justice because Leibniz saw in human nature a will to cooperate that had its basis in the need for individual development. Law was not founded on the exercise of raw power, but rather it reflected practical arrangements that enabled the pursuit of human happiness. Thus the operation of reason, which Grotius saw as the unifying element in international law, was for Leibniz the tangible expression of this inner human desire for pursuing and nurturing happiness.

Much about the Grotian order appealed to Leibniz: he approved of the essential Grotian premise that there were deep principles of human nature that were reflected in experience but were independent of that experience. Moreover, he endorsed the most controversial of Grotius's positions, that natural law would be the same even if there were no God, a view that Pufendorf derided as "impious and idiotic." Actually, this position made good sense if, as I have argued, natural law for Grotius was not a set of substantive rules but rather the operation of reason itself, of *rule making*. But Grotius had agreed with his contemporaries about the need for a domestic absolutism; he was, after all, the international spokesman for the kingly state. Leibniz rejected this necessity (and the views of human nature on which it was founded) and replaced Grotius's deterministic account with concepts of free will. It was the paradox of free will, by which happiness was maximized but the possibility of error enshrined, that drove justice, according to Leibniz. Therefore there was no necessity for an overarching sovereign on an international scale. The division of the society of states into separate sovereignties was not fatal to international law because all the constituent members were moved to act in accord in order to develop; their very freedom to act, in which Hobbes saw the state's will to war, instead made possible the realization of peace and cooperation. True, it also made war possible, but there was no condition of international relations in which this was not the case, because the possibilities of free will always included the option of error, and even the pursuit of evil. For this reason, moral values were an inescapable part of the natural order—they played a role when men were free to choose.

WOLFF

Leibniz's most celebrated apostle was Christian Wolff, a German Enlightenment figure of polymath scope. Born in 1676, he ultimately became the principal apologist for the territorial state and came to regard Frederick the Great as the model of a "philosopher king." His sympathy for natural religion, a kind of deism, drew criticism from his colleagues at the University of Halle, and when, in a public address in 1719, he pointed to certain non-Christian rulers as exemplary, he caused a public sensation. In 1721 Frederick William I (the father of Frederick the Great) suddenly ordered Wolff into exile on pain of hanging, probably as a result of a campaign against him by the Protestant orthodoxy. Wolff immediately became a figure of European fame, a martyr for the Enlightenment. He took up a new post at Marburg and remained there for some years, despite the remorse of Frederick William and the latter's repeated efforts to bring Wolff back in honor. When Frederick the Great became king in 1740, one of his first acts was to extend to Wolff a generous and public invitation to return to Halle, which Wolff accepted, remaining there until his death in 1756.

Of the leading Enlightenment figures, only Wolff took a particular interest in the law of nations. In his writings, he followed Leibniz. Hobbes and Spinoza had taken the society of nations to be a kind of presocial jungle, replicating at the international level that world of human beings that had existed before the appearance of the absolute sovereign. Wolff accepted that society reflected nature—the nature of human beings. As Leibniz held, however, Wolff believed that it is in the nature of man not simply to preserve himself, but to seek to thrive and mature, to realize a potential to achieve harmony, a potential that is embedded in the possibilities of free will. Therefore the formation of states without a common sovereign, even if it did create a "state of nature" on the international scale, did not create a lawless jungle. Accordingly the interests of any state must include the promotion of this developmental aspect of human beings. In a concept remarkably characteristic of Frederick the Great and of the territorial state, Wolff held that states have fundamental interests derived from their obligation to themselves. These obligations include self-preservation *and* the development of the human resources of the state. This desire for harmony pre-exists the State and is residually existent also in the society of states. The obligations of one state to other states are nascent, "imperfect," until they are perfected through treaties.

Wolff expressed this underlying drive for peace in a legal fiction he termed the *Civitas Maxima*. This Latin neologism was meant to contrast with the term *Civitas,* which refers to the civil society of a single state. While the *Civitas Maxima* can be anachronistically misunderstood as a kind of precursor to the League of Nations, it is nevertheless strikingly modern in concept. It might be best explained as a collective unconscious that influences free, self-determining actions. The *Civitas Maxima* is composed of a body of rules derived from the promotion of the common good. These are not moral rules, but they are rather the source of our evaluation of all rules. Where Grotius thought the contents of natural law could be found in the received traditions of Western practices, Wolff believed that the logical implications of free will—which he saw as the foundation of truth—would provide guidance. These implications would show what states ought to do to enhance their interests, which include a common interest shared with other states. Nature has created a society of states, and the self-preservation of this society also forms an interest of the constituent members of that society.

The *Civitas Maxima* is a supreme state only in a metaphorical sense, composed of morally equal and free, self-determining states. The law of the "Great State" is composed of what the individual state ought to and would agree to, as well as what states have actually agreed to either by custom or treaty. Thus its laws are based, in every case, on consent, and genuine consent can only be given by free and independent actors. The sovereignty of states, which so bedevils analysts of international law who seek cooperation among states, is instead for Wolff a precondition for law based on cooperation.

Grotius saw in a just war the positive workings of international law: war decided disputes among sovereigns the way litigation decides disputes among citizens. Rights were vindicated by victory. Wolff maintained, instead, that because war could be considered just by both parties, each following his own free judgment, the point of war was the achievement of peace, not simply of justice. Only peace would vindicate the developmental interests of a state, and thus there is no automatic legal right to pursue war in the presence of peaceful alternatives. In domestic societies, not every dispute is solved by litigation, which is an expensive and chancy way to achieve harmony, and harmony after all is an essential element in justice. If, for Grotius and the Westphalian system, victory in war determined the rightness of a cause, for Wolff and the Utrechtian settlement, peace, not war, was the central element in determining rightness. A victor cannot acquire by force of arms a right unless a peace treaty ultimately ratifies that right; this underscores the fact that the assertion of interests, not rights, is the essential duty of the territorial state. Interests are best preserved by consensus, while rights can be vindicated in the costliest and most self-destructive of conflicts.

Toward the end of his life, the fame and drama of Wolff's early career faded. He drew fewer students. His public role had led him to style himself "professor *universi generis*," which was bound to invite ridicule. Eventually even Frederick began to avoid him, and on at least one occasion expressed displeasure at Wolff's prolixity. The enormous scope of his master, Leibniz, had degenerated in Wolff's hands into a systematic completeness that was pedantic. Wildebrand referred to him as a "schoolmaster" and pointed to Wolff's "ridiculous micrology." But though he could not save himself—his renown as a philosopher had vanished by the nineteenth century—he was saved by another, a shrewd and ironic diplomat. Emmerich de Vattel carried Wolff's name everywhere in the pages of Vattel's treatise, the most important and the most widely read essay on international law since Grotius's *De Jure Belli ac Pacis*.

VATTEL

Emmerich de Vattel was born in 1714. Like Pufendorf, he was the son of a Protestant minister, but here all similarities end. Baron Pufendorf regarded himself as principally a philosopher, although Leibniz seems to have had some doubts about this. There is a dogmatism about Pufendorf that one associates with persons who are certain not only of being right, but of being right for all the right reasons. Vattel seems to have been a more humane and engaging figure and one more attuned to reality at the same time.

He was born in the Swiss principality of Neuchâtel, which was by dynastic union connected with the Kingdom of Prussia. At age thirty-two he became a diplomat in the service of the Elector of Saxony, returning to Switzerland as ambassador three years later. In 1758 he was recalled to Dresden as the equivalent of a modern permanent undersecretary for foreign affairs. Vattel only returned to Neuchâtel in 1766 and died there the next year. Thus for most of his life, he was a practicing diplomat in the highly complex politics of post-Utrecht Germany.

Vattel was a man of letters. Before becoming a diplomat he had published his *Defense du système Leibnitzen* in 1741 and he thereafter wrote essays in a vein that recalls Montaigne, interspersing philosophical speculations with amusing and ironic observations about mankind. His fame, however, rests on one massive work. This was *Le droit des gens; ou Principes de la loi naturelle appliqués à la conduite et aux affaires des nations et des souverains,* published in 1758.

In this work, Vattel proposed to make Wolff's ideas on the law of nations accessible to "sovereigns and their ministers," translating Wolff's abstractions into practical and understandable propositions that could be applied to the circumstances of diplomatic life. Nussbaum, however, has concluded that, "in reality the *Book* is far more than a paraphrase of Wolff's treatise. It is the work of a modern-minded diplomat who, while leaning on Wolff, systematically sets forth his own opinions on the most diverse topics of international and constitutional law."[19]

The work met with instant and widespread success. It soon attained a circulation second only to Grotius's *De Jure Belli ac Pacis* and, in the first half of the nineteenth century, achieved oracular authority among diplomats.[20] It was immediately translated into English and German, the first editions appearing in 1760; it was in Benjamin Franklin's hands by 1775. By 1820 it had been cited by more American courts than Grotius and Pufendorf combined. By the time of Nussbaum's treatise in 1947, there had been twenty-one editions of the original French text and twenty-three translations into English (thirteen of them American).[21] Partly this was due to Vattel's style of reasoning, which provided for many exceptions to any general rule and was thus available to both sides of most disputes.[22] Partly, this was owing to Vattel's anticipation of the state-nation; this accounts for his popularity with American judges and political figures. But mainly it was because Vattel was reasonable and accessible, something hard-pressed politicians and diplomats appreciated and had scarcely found in the literature on international relations since Grotius, whether it was the violent narcissism of Rousseau or the detached abstraction of Wolff. Government officials needed resources to cope with the post-Utrechtian world; if there was a science of maintaining the balance of power, they wanted instruction in its principles and, more importantly, in the application of those principles.

Le droit des gens begins with a review of Grotius and faults him for postulating universal consent as the basis for international law. This is not entirely fair to Grotius, for the consent on which he held fundamental law to be based was not a consent to particular rules but to the method of rule creation. Nor is Vattel's criticism of Pufendorf—that the latter tried to give a theological explanation for the binding character of international law—quite just. In both cases, however, the criticisms are made to set the stage for Vattel's presentation of Wolff as a humanist who grounded the law of nations upon reason and thus fulfilled the project of Leibniz.

Like Wolff, Vattel saw the law of nations as a science of state interests. And like Wolff, he maintained a division between the natural, immutable law (which was the basis for the distinctions between just and unjust) and the acts of state (treaties and custom) that supplement this natural law. Whereas Grotius had maintained that the universal ground of law was legal method—the way in which legal rules were *created*—Wolff and Vattel held that the universal ground of law consisted in the way in which legal rules were *followed*. For example, it was part of the natural law that states are morally equal, each being able to apply the rules of law on the basis of the freedom to act, and thus what is lawful or unlawful for one state must be so for all. The universal ground, therefore, is the freedom to act, and this makes possible, as well as determines, the lawfulness or unlawfulness of a state's action (as when, for example, a state avails itself of a legal rule it would deny to other states). It follows that each state must be left to decide matters as the consciences of its leaders demand, and that each state owes to every other state what it owes to itself.

Following Wolff and Leibniz, Vattel wrote that the duties of a state toward itself determine what its conduct should be toward the larger society of states that nature has established. And what is that?

Each state must strive to develop, as well as to protect, its existence. Thus, like Wolff, Vattel gives primacy to national interests, not national rights. If states act to develop their interests, there will be more cooperation, not less:

> Nations would mutually exchange their products and their knowledge; profound peace would reign upon the earth and would enrich it with its precious fruits; industry and science and art would be devoted to our happiness no less than satisfying our needs. . . . The world would take on the appearance of a great Republic; all men would live together as brothers, and each would be a citizen of the universe . . . [23]

It is not surprising then that, for the author of such a passage,[24] the freedom of commerce is a common right of nations. Each state is free to trade as it wishes without accountability. An equilibrium of international trade will be achieved just as the unrestrained freedom of contract is supposed to achieve maximal economic results for a domestic society.

Neither Vattel nor Wolff believed war was endemic to international relations. Because some leaders despise justice and refuse to listen to reason, there will be wars, but such persons are not merely the enemies of the states they attack but the enemies of all mankind. This fits nicely with the ideology of the balance of power, which legitimates the acts of an individual state to achieve defensible borders and collective action in favor of the status quo but disdains intervention on Westphalian grounds, that is, to aggrandize the State.

Vattel and Wolff part, however, with respect to the *Civitas Maxima*. Ironically, Vattel rejects this legal fiction because he rejects the Hobbesian premise to which Wolff was responding. It had seemed to some commentators that Hobbes had posited a mortal counterargument to the Grotian system when he asserted that the one thing men had in common was a desire to take each other's property, not a charitable impulse to collaborate. Post-Westphalian Europe—indeed the entire history of the kingly state—appeared to support a Hobbesian rather than Grotian view. Pufendorf and Wolff responded in different ways to this perceived shortcoming in Grotius: countering that human beings had in common a moralistic perception (Pufendorf) and a rationalistic perception (Wolff), respectively, that inclined states toward collaboration. Accordingly, Wolff had postulated that international law would be as necessary to the survival and development of the individual state as domestic law was to the survival of the individual (even if the rational grounds for this necessity were far from Hobbesian), and Pufendorf had gone so far as to deny the usefulness of international law at all, since the laws of nature would bring about the same collaborative behavior as that sought by international law. It was Wolff's solution to the Grotian flaw that had led him to hypothesize the *Civitas Maxima,* a collective unconscious grounded in necessity.

Vattel argued, however, that

> it is true that men, seeing that the Laws of Nature were not being unvaryingly observed, have had recourse to political association . . . [b]ut it is clear that there is by no means the same necessity for a civil society among Nations as among individuals. It cannot be said, therefore, that nature recommends it to an equal degree, far less that it prescribes it. Individuals are so constituted that they could accomplish but little by themselves and could scarcely get on without the assistance of civil society and its laws. But as soon as a sufficient number have united under a government, they are able to provide for most of their needs,

and they find the help of [the society of states] not so necessary for them as the State itself is to individuals.[25]

Thus for Vattel it is not natural law but diplomacy exploiting the conditions of nature that is responsible for international law. There is a universal society, to be sure, and it is the result of man's interdependence. States that wish to develop themselves can best do so in cooperation with others. But there is no necessity about this; some states may well choose to shut themselves off, as did Japan in the eighteenth century. A legal fiction like the *Civitas Maxima* is not true to life.

In other respects, too, Vattel brings a fresh sense of realism to Wolff's ideas. Thus, where Wolff recognizes mere acquisition as achieving actual dominion over territory, Vattel more cautiously makes clear that possession is a prerequisite of effective occupation (and thus concludes that papal allotments of newly discovered territories are without legal force). Where Wolff places heavy reliance on the consensual effect of treaties, Vattel stresses the problems of treaty interpretation and perishability. He takes neutrality in war to be the legal effect of nonparticipation and thus dismisses Wolff's reliance on the neutrality treaties that had become obsolete by that time. Vattel takes up a number of practical problems—whether loans by a neutral to a belligerent compromise neutral status; the extent of the right of visit and search of neutral ships by belligerents to check for contraband; the sale of booty to neutrals—that have immense real-world significance but are ignored in Wolff's more philosophical treatise.

Vattel's most important departure from Wolff, however, lay elsewhere, for the Swiss diplomat was not only the patient recorder of the legal consequences of Utrecht, but also the harbinger of events that would burst upon the world in 1776 and begin the closing of the period of territorial states altogether. The law of nations for Grotius had encouraged the absolutism of the kingly state; international law, for Wolff, aimed at rules that would encourage the enlightened authoritarianism of the territorial state. Vattel took Leibniz's ideas about free will and the aggregation of free decisions one step further and sought to advance the arrival of the state-nation, where sovereignty lay in the people and not in the ruler. Vattel argued that rulers are merely representatives of the State who act in the national interest—Frederick the Great had already claimed as much—but inquired additionally, as to the content of the national interest, and by what right had the king acted in the name of the nation? Vattel's answers to these two questions show him to be a transitional figure, linking the rationality of the territorial state to the idealism of the state-nation.

If the national interest is determined by the duties the State owes itself—as Leibniz and Wolff had contended—then Vattel argued that first among these duties is the responsibility for the welfare of the State. The ruler, who represents the interests of the people, must sever his own personal desires and interests from those of the nation, in order that he might not sacrifice the latter to the former. "Where he personally may be inclined to forgive an injury, he may be obliged to uphold his nation's right."[26] But if the king's interest is not the same as the nation's, by what right does the king assert the nation's interests? Vattel concluded that rulers are merely representatives of the sovereign people: ultimate authority belongs to the nation, which authority is delegated to the State of which the king is the head. By this reasoning, the welfare of the State is the supreme duty of both the king (this was the rationale of the territorial state) and of the nation (the rationale of the state-nation). Sovereignty exists only when the nation governs itself; this much is clear from the argument from free will. If there is no choice but obedience, then no free decision to obey has been made, and no authority can be conveyed to the leadership. Furthermore, the personality of the State supersedes that of the king; this much is to be inferred from the contrast of the territorial state with the kingly state. Putting the two conclusions together, Vattel argued that sovereignty is delegated to the State, not to the king, and resides in the whole society, and that society can withdraw its consent from a despot because the welfare of the State is both the duty of the leader and of the nation. As will be recalled from Book I, this takes us to the very edge of the ideology of the state-nation.

Le droit des gens was published in French, the language of eighteenth century diplomacy, but it was not well received in France. The French had always been dubious about the role of international law. "They are all doctors," groaned d'Avaux at Westphalia, referring to the legalistic mentality of the German delegates[27] and expressing an attitude toward law that endures among diplomats to the present. There was something faintly ridiculous about a middle-aged Swiss bureaucrat from a second-rank German power declaring that the law ordained that sovereignty lay in the people and that the king was superseded by the State. Or so at least it seemed in 1758. Rather Vattel received his warmest reception in America. Citations to his great work appear frequently in the *Federalist Papers,* the most important interpretive document concerning the U.S. Constitution. Indeed the *Federalist Papers* take their legal significance from the fact that they were used to explain the Constitution to the American people and thus represent our best evidence of the understanding of the sovereign ratifiers as to what powers were to be conveyed to the new government. The importance of this fact lies in the idea of popular sovereignty; otherwise, why would it matter what the people were told in order to win their endorsement? Vattel appears in *McCulloch* v. *Maryland,* the foundation case for doctrinal argument in American constitutional law, as well as in *Gib-*

bons v. *Ogden,* the fundamental constitutional case construing U.S. federal power to regulate commerce.

Perhaps French antipathy lay in their suspicion of the Utrechtian constitution itself. Like Wolff, Vattel approved of the balance of power, and he shared the conviction embodied in the Peace of Utrecht that the rational application of the principles of equilibrium would assure European order. France, whose ambitions were checked at Utrecht, regarded this order as stacked against it. Though it came as a surprise to the states of Europe, it was not Prussia (which ruthlessly exploited the Utrechtian system) that shattered the constitutional consensus of Utrecht but France, which had never fully shared its goals.

When we read today, largely in the literature of welfare economics, about the canons of rationality, we are reading the legacy of Leibniz and the "science of interests." Grotius believed that the deep consensus among states derived from the way in which rules were made. Vattel asserted that this consensus arose from the way rules were followed. Both ideas are noticeably modern, which suggests that, like the archetypal forms of the State described in Book I, the jurisprudential approaches to the law of nations enter into history and remain, reappearing in an enlarged suite of choices as the society of states matures. For Wolff and Vattel natural law (what we would call the subject matter of the social sciences today) does not force man to obey certain rules, but is rather the ground of all rules, on the basis of which any particular rule is evaluated. The duties of the State toward itself are very much like the rationality that a "sovereign" consumer is thought to embody in making social and economic choices; out of an aggregation of such choices comes the most efficient system, by which is meant the system that maximizes the interests of the participants. Social choices are constrained by freedom—the freedom of the choices of others, whose choices affect our own—Leibniz might have told us. But what are the consequences for the society of states when the nation of a single state exercises its right of resistance and seizes the sovereignty it has delegated to a king? This Vattel did not say.

CHAPTER TWENTY-ONE

The Congress of Vienna

AT THE OUTBREAK of the French Revolution in 1789, the French army had profited from a series of reforms, discussed in Chapter 8. Nevertheless it was still the army of a territorial state: the officer corps numbered fewer than 10,000, of whom more than 85 percent were drawn from the nobility. Thus the Revolution initially faced a potential challenge from an army that might become the basis for counterrevolution. If the aristocratic officer corps of the army were suppressed, however, then France faced the prospect of an army without trained leaders. By the end of 1794, partly in reaction to a new military oath introduced in September 1791, replacing the old oath to the king, more than half the officers had fled. By 1799 less than 3 percent of the officer corps came from aristocratic backgrounds. In 1790 conscription had begun, and in August 1793 the National Convention introduced the *levée en masse* by a decree conscripting all French males into the nation's armies until the foreign enemies of the revolution had been defeated.

"All Frenchmen . . . are called by their country to defend liberty . . . From this moment until that when the enemy is driven from the territory of the republic, every Frenchman is commandeered for the needs of the armies." Thus the "nation in arms" was born. By the spring of 1794, France had more than 700,000 men in military service. While the armies of the territorial state were in place everywhere in Europe when the French Revolution broke out, soon, in Clausewitz's words, "such a force as no one had had any conception of made its appearance. War had suddenly become an affair of the people, and that of a people numbering thirty millions, every one of who regarded himself as a citizen of the state."[1]

The conventional account of the wars of the last decade of the eighteenth century and the first decade and a half of the nineteenth century stresses the ideological bases for the conflict: the war was fought by France to spread revolution to the rest of Europe, it is said, and this struggle to bring about a new order for each state was abruptly altered, in Napoleon's hands, to become a war to impose French norms generally—of culture, administration, rational statism—and to enhance the wealth and prestige of France itself. Opposed to France were reactionary governments of various kinds—parliamentary monarchies, petty princelings, ancient dynastic houses—who wished to restore the old order in the domestic arenas of politics and to restore the balance of power internationally.

In Book I, however, a somewhat different description has been given, one that suggests greater continuity between the revolutionary governments of France and the Napoleonic era, and a greater convergence between France and her adversaries. All the wars of France during this period were fought in order to obligate the mass of persons to the French state. Among this vast people various groups from the bourgeoisie were employed in the service of the state; for their members there were lower taxes and greater public expenditure owing in part to the enormous subsidies extracted by France from her conquered neighbors; working men found in the state an employer of last resort—the army (whose mass employment would not have been possible under the strategic and tactical constraints of the armies of the territorial state); and for every class a new meritocracy arose that measured status according to services rendered to the State.

The wars of 1792–1815 between France and various coalitions of other European powers were united, strategically and constitutionally, by the political program of the French Revolution. This program sought an end to the territorial-state autocracies and the replacement of these regimes by government in the name of the people, based on the people's political liberty and legal equality. If the people were the source of political legitimacy, then the people had a responsibility to defend their rights and powers against attack. The right of suffrage entailed the duty of military service. Conscripted armies replaced the small professional armies of the territorial state. Although France was ultimately defeated, the constitutional result of the epochal war waged from 1792 to 1815 was not to restore the ancien régimes of the territorial states.

The French innovations were soon carefully copied and more rigorously implemented in Prussia. The aristocratic, cruelly disciplined army of professional soldiers that Frederick the Great had developed was replaced by a "universality of responsibility for service in war, binding upon every class of civil society. Through this it will be possible to inculcate a proud warlike national character, to wage wearying wars of distant conquest and to withstand an overwhelming enemy attack with a national war."[2]

The Prussian military reforms from 1807 on were designed to effect this change. Here it is enough to say that the Prussian force that fought from 1813 onward waged war with the same patriotic motivation as that which inspired the French. As Clausewitz wrote, it was "a war of the people."

As with the wars of Queen Anne and the peace brokered by Bolingbroke, a new constitutional form of the State had arisen. When Louis

XVIII was set upon the throne of France by the victors in 1814 he was required to take an oath to the written constitution. Throughout Europe the regimes of the territorial states underwent seismic constitutional change, transforming themselves into state-nations, copying the constitutional form of their chief predator, France, and their chief defender, Britain. When the Congress of Vienna met to decide upon a new constitution for the society of states, it mandated that this new constitutional form be the essential element in determining a state's legitimacy.

The constitution of the state-nation system was embodied in a set of treaties that may for the sake of convenience be collectively referred to as the product of this Congress. These treaties restored (twice) the Bourbon dynasty to the throne of France, conditioned upon the acceptance by the king of a constitutional arrangement based on popular sovereignty; took the 300-odd pre-Napoleonic states, combined them into some thirty states and bound them into the German Confederation; recognized the state of Switzerland as a single state-nation and gave it neutral legal status in perpetuity; combined Belgium with the Netherlands and recognized a new state, the United Netherlands; re-created the state of Poland out of the Grand Duchy of Warsaw and effectively made it a colony of Russia; gave Britain Dutch colonial holdings in South Africa and Malta; made Finland a colony of Russia, and Norway a colony of Sweden; set up the congress system by which the member states of the international society of states would periodically meet to review implementation of, and decide cases arising from, the international constitution that had been agreed to at Vienna; elaborated an important constitutional human right* through the abolition of the slave trade; allocated to a directorate of the great powers the authority to maintain the new constitution; set up various procedural rules, including those governing diplomatic practice; prescribed the lawful use of international rivers by states; and, with respect to Austria and Prussia, extended the range of their state governance to adjacent, or previously held, territories as a means of strengthening those states. In other words, Vienna performed the constitutional functions for the nineteenth century society of states that Augsburg, Westphalia, and Utrecht had performed in earlier centuries. None of the key ideas associated with the Congress of Vienna—the maintenance of the balance of power, the insistent attention to legitimacy, the sensitivity to or dismissal of various national aspirations, and the institutionalization of the great power alliance—can be fully understood absent this constitutional perspective. Familiar terms of the past, such as the *balance of power* and *legitimacy,* take on a new meaning in the new constitutional context that is embodied in the acts of the Congress of Vienna; newer ideas, like nationalism and collective security, that

---

*As had earlier constitutions for previous societies of states, e.g., with respect to religious worship.

are familiar to us today were differently understood then in the historical context created by the new international constitution.

The Grand Coalition that defeated Napoleon, like the coalition that opposed Louis XIV, was not really fighting for the legitimist claims of a dead constitutional order, whatever these coalitions claimed. As Macaulay observed,

> the war of 1815 belongs to the same class of war with the war which the ministers of Anne carried on against the house of Bourbon [i.e., the wars of Louis XIV]. The claims of Louis XVIII were to the coalition of 1815 what the claims of the archduke were to the coalition of 1701—a means—and not an end.[3]

When those coalitions were victorious, they sought at Utrecht and, later, at Vienna the ratification of a new constitutional form. The mentality of the generation that met at Utrecht was in contrast to that which convened in Vienna, however. At Vienna, it was understood by all parties that international relations were developmental, organic, subject to change and human direction even at a fundamental, constitutional level. The American Revolution no less than the French Revolution (but no more than the Napoleonic legal reforms that spread to the territories conquered by the French) had shattered the idea so dear to the territorial state that custom and natural law were the sole sources of binding legal rules.

Metternich spoke for the rationalist, territorial state when he complained that civil and political "rights" existed, if they existed at all, in the nature of things; they could not be guaranteed by the adoption of rules. "Things which ought to be taken for granted lose their force when they emerge in the form of arbitrary pronouncements . . ."[4]

The new mentality was otherwise: human rights could be brought into being by political will—too many persons had seen it done to believe otherwise. Freedom could be expanded, or contracted, depending on the form of the regime. A novel political society that freed the classes had conquered Europe, and a secularized, comparatively meritocratic state that energized commerce and trade had just won the war. Representative institutions could claim a basis of legitimacy on account of their relation to the popular will. Law was the chosen instrument of fundamental change.

In this respect France was for other states a model of the new constitutional order, the state-nation. France was not the only model, however: both the United States (which had inspired France) and Great Britain, France's dogged opponent, presented to the world examples of this new and dynamic constitutional form. These states also sought ways in which to bind the mass of people to the interests of the State, and ways to represent the State as the creation and object of veneration of the nation. The importance of the state-nation, however, also lies in the kind of society of states it called forth. As one historian has observed, as "a result of revolutionary change in society, one can detect during the era of the Napoleonic wars the emergence of a public opinion to gauge actions of warring governments by the principles recognized in the teachings of international law."[5]

These principles awaited a constitutional convention to give them legal status. Thus, once again, war and constitutional change were followed by a peace settlement that took the form of a constitutional convention for the society of states, including even states that were not parties to the conflict. The new mentality—the mentality of the Congress of Vienna—brought issues to the fore that were quite distinct from those raised at Utrecht.

The state-nations that met at Vienna sought a special international arrangement that was not sought by the other states (of various constitutional forms) that came to the Congress, nor by the various constitutional entities that appeared at the Congress that were not themselves states.[6] The European state-nation powers, Britain and France, sought an international system that would strengthen them at home not by re-enforcing domestic coercion, but by providing an external consensus that would give international politics the stability and prestige of law and would ameliorate the international conflicts that had so recently threatened to polarize their domestic polities. The other great powers were not so well placed to become state-nations. After its adoption of French military reforms, Prussia was able to forge a state-nation, but it remained frustrated by the fragmentation of the German nation; Habsburg Austria seems never to have made the transition successfully. Unlike Prussia, whose embrace of the German nation was cramped by an older, narrower state form, Austria's embrace was too broad, encompassing so many nations that it could not persuade them that their magnification lay in the service they might render the state. Russia, like her quixotic nineteenth century rulers, oscillated between a passionate intoxication with the state-nation ideal, for which its popular institutions were hopelessly ill-suited, and a reactionary rejection of the threatening modernity the new forms embodied.

THE CONSTITUTIONAL CONVENTION: THE CONGRESS OF VIENNA

The constitution of the new international system was the Final Act of the Congress of Vienna, supplemented in time by various "amendments" ratified at subsequent congresses. The Congress was therefore the constitutional convention of Europe, and it was seen as such by the state-nations that brought it into being. This constitution represents a response to three points of acute sensitivity to the state-nation: the self-consciousness of the new constitutional form, which could not depend merely upon custom for its legitimacy and must therefore earn its right to govern through the studied design and implementation of its institutions; the role of public opinion, which had become so influential in this new order that it demanded recognition by politicians; and the requirement that government policy be justifiable on the basis of articulated principles that themselves were taken as legitimate (thus requiring that the judgment of legitimacy go well beyond merely assessing the head of state). With regard to international affairs, these three points of importance played out in the following way, respectively: there was a demand for a particular legal instrument, consciously designed to prevent future wars in Europe; when public opinion became engaged by matters abroad, there had to be a way for politicians to replace diplomats as the effective actors; and inherited principles regarding the "general interest" of all states, and of the "balance of power"—set forth in earlier international constitutions and enjoying the prestige and legitimacy of tradition—had to achieve a new consensus among the powers in order for the behavior of these states to seem principled yet these principles had to be updated and modified in order for them to be practical.

THE NEED FOR A NEW INSTRUMENT

The demand for an institution that was purposefully designed to deal with future conflicts arose in several ways. First, it was apparent that the Utrechtian system, which had succeeded in limiting war for a certain period, had been utterly unable to prevent a new sort of war, one that was so destructive that it had to be deterred in order to ensure the survival of states.[7] There was a fatal vulnerability in the elaborate conventions of the territorial states that became manifest once the energies of a state-nation were deployed against those conventions. Territorial states could not quite ever combine in a sustained coalition because they could so easily be bought off with territorial concessions at each other's expense. Enduring coalitions had not been necessary to fight the brief, limited wars of the territorial state system—indeed, there was a distinct value to that system in maintaining highly fluid relationships—but they were indispensable in the new era of conflict. Furthermore, the elites required to manage the elegant diplomacy of the ancien régimes had been replaced in some states by parties hostile to them. The Utrechtian system, however, as much as the territorial states that it comprised, depended upon an international elite. In any case, the prosecution of unlimited war took on a momentum owing to the national fervor that fueled it, regardless of who was in charge. Carefully calibrated restraint was scarcely possible in the face of popular passions.

Second, the mentality that arose with the state-nation could not passively accept an international system that seemed to depend upon etiquette for its operation. The state-nation was founded upon the claim (made notably by Hegel) that the State furnished the ideal vehicle for the realization of the nation; the nation could only be fulfilled through the self-conscious creation and enhancement of the State. During this period modern political parties came into being, as each offered to the nation a competing version of how best to fulfill the nation through the State. At Vienna, as at Augsburg, Osnabrück and Münster, and Utrecht, a program of international security was elaborated, but at Vienna, it had to be a program that was perceived to respond to the collective failure of the conventional, customary tradition that had hitherto provided an unquestioned context for events.

Third, state-nations claimed to rule on the basis of the consent of the governed. If an instrument were to be designed to govern the security affairs of Europe, it would have to be defended on the grounds that it too reflected the will of the peoples of Europe. The tsar is reported to have remarked that Napoleon was overthrown not by cabinets but by peoples, and that an outlet must be found for a new spirit in Europe that was at once constitutional, warlike, and national—a pretty good summation of the state-nation mentality.[8]

The multistate institution created by this legal instrument would have to be responsive to international opinion (in the way that the political institutions of the state-nation were responsive to domestic public opinion) in order to justify its decisions as ultimately based on consent; it would have to deter war rather than merely contain it; and finally it must be perceived by national publics as actually doing both these things. The solution arrived at was an ongoing international executive, composed of the five great powers, that would coordinate international security and summon periodic congresses, as necessary, to ratify the decisions taken by this directorate. This simply replicated in peacetime the pattern set up before Vienna: the Coalition allies had first agreed on a course of action, which was then presented for ratification to a congress of all states. In this way the Congress's apparent contradiction of the principle of consent—decisions by a few having been taken on behalf of the many—was resolved. The powers could rely on the common consensus for peace while asserting that only reliance on the few could keep the peace and thereby protect the many.

We can see this tactic at work in the opening weeks of the Congress of Vienna, when the allied powers were unable to reach a final decision before the date set for the Congress to open. Castlereagh drafted a declaration explaining the delay; in it he is at pains to show that the great powers are taking international opinion into account precisely with respect to a decision that the powers alone are in fact making. As he wrote in the draft declaration:

> The courts parties to the Treaty of Paris by which the present Congress has been set up, hold themselves to be obliged to submit for its consideration and approval the project of settlement which they judge to be most in accordance with the *principles* recognized as the necessary basis for the general system of Europe.[9]

The prototype for this arrangement is found in the First Treaty of Paris, Article I, which provides that "the high contracting parties shall make every effort to preserve, not only among themselves, but also as far as depends on them, among all the states of Europe, the good harmony and understanding that is so necessary for its repose," and in Article XVI,[10] which provides for the ratification of the provisions of the treaty by the upcoming congress.

By this means the directorate could claim broad-based consent for its decisions, relying on international opinion as well as deploying this opinion in dealings among themselves. This executive managed the Concert of Europe. Initially its members were confined to the parties to the Treaty of Chaumont; by 1818 France had been included in this executive and, as Kissinger has put it, "was admitted to the Congress system at periodic European congresses, which for half a century came close to constituting the government of Europe." Indeed, of the 170 million inhabitants of Europe (excluding those under Turkish rule), more than two-thirds were residents of states that were parties to the Treaty of Paris. As Book I elaborated, in an earlier era it had been possible for relatively small states like the Venetian Republic or later the Dutch Republic to be powerful geopolitical actors because they could fund formidable professional armies. The mass conscription of the era of the state-nation ended that possibility, ushering in a new sort of warfare, marginalizing many states, and making some large state-nations indispensable to any peace settlement. Not every leader understood this. In a letter to Castlereagh, Lord Liverpool phlegmatically wrote that "[a] war sometime hence, though an evil, need not be different in its character and its effects from any of those wars which occurred in the seventeenth and eighteenth centuries, before the commencement of the French Revolution."[11]

Castlereagh (and Wellington) knew better. The era of cabinet wars fought for limited objectives was over. In its place was a new age of national wars fought for national ideals—that is, massive armies deployed to pursue virtually continental, even global, goals. By comprising those states that were capable of fielding large armies, the system of collective security that the executive directorate administered made a virtue of what Kissinger identifies as the chief defect of such systems. Kissinger writes that "[t]he weakness of collective security is that interests are rarely uniform and that security is rarely seamless. Members of a general system of collective security are therefore more likely to agree on inaction than on joint action."[12]

In the case of the European executive, as with the domestic constitutional design of many of its members, inaction was exactly what was called for. All attempts by Metternich to convert the executive directorate into a roving commission to suppress democratic movements were frustrated, and no attempts were made by the great powers to assault one another until the Crimean War. It is not necessary that the interests of states be uniform for a system of collective security to function, only that these interests counsel the same course of action (or inaction). In the case of the directorate of the Concert of Europe, each member feared a new revolutionary upheaval and sought in foreign policy the prestige, legitimacy, and gravity that participation in the executive body conferred. When, in time, such upheavals came, they came not from a defecting state-nation member of the Concert but from states that had been excluded, Italy and Germany. The historian Bruun wrote that "[t]here is an element of historical irony in the fact that [Napoleon's] attempt to make France secure by extending French influence over Germany and Italy contributed to an opposite result."[13] How much more ironic that the attempt at Vienna to make the European society of states secure should ultimately founder on its failure to accord statehood to a great nation. It was a phenomenon, however, that state-nations encountered all over the globe, and it was perhaps inherent in this constitutional form. The very nationalism that energizes the armies and officials of the state-nation awakens the latent nationalism of their conquests and colonies. Though it is sometimes said that the Congress of Vienna ignored the matter of nationalism in its territorial settlements, this is only partly true: the Congress was extremely vigilant with regard to the national populations of the great powers. France was not dismembered, despite widespread sentiment to do so; German land earmarked for the English prince regent to be added to Hanover was instead given to Prussia, despite the fact that England was the chief architect of victory. Rather it was the national identities of those peoples without states that was sacrificed, and this says most about the state-nation itself and how it differs from the nation-state that is the source of our understanding of nationalism in state affairs today. The state-nation exalts the State and puts the nation at its service. The society of such states is therefore not concerned with promoting national identity per se, but rather with safeguarding the national identity of states. For this society, the Concert was an ideal institution.

THE NEED FOR A NEW POLITICS

The historian Webster in his study of the Congress of Vienna concluded that

> [it] cannot be said that [public opinion] affected the decisions of the statesmen to any material degree. The Polish-Saxon question [the most divisive issue among the coalition partners] was settled purely on grounds of expediency; and the populations of Germany were transferred from one monarch to another with scarcely the slightest reference to their wishes.[14]

This conclusion is overstated as it stands, and in any case it mistakes the role of public opinion in the state-nation for that within the society of state-nations. For the former, it is not the opinion of distant publics but the opinion of the nation which the state-nation represents that is crucial; for the latter, it is the way in which international opinion can be deployed by powers within the executive directorate that proves decisive, and this was even true, as we shall see, with the Polish-Saxon question. Osiander renders a better judgment when he observes instead that "what made [the Congress of Vienna] different . . . from earlier ones was the self-conscious way that public opinion was monitored by the peacemakers. The serene self-awareness of the Utrecht system was replaced at Vienna by anxious self-consciousness."[15] Obviously modern state-nations, whose governments hold power by virtue of some version of popular consent, are acutely attuned to public opinion. What is interesting, as Osiander notes, is that the *society* of such states should give a crucial role to public opinion in nondomestic affairs, not confining itself to the opinion of persons "back home" but carefully monitoring (and manipulating) the opinion in the various states with whom that society had to deal (as, for example, the opinion of French society regarding the provisions of the Treaty of Paris) and deploying arguments within the executive directorate based on international public opinion. Metternich, who carefully guided the public accounts of the Congress through Gentz, his protégé, wrote that "public opinion is the most powerful of all means; like religion, it penetrates the most hidden recesses, where administrative measures have no influence," and Gentz himself wrote that

> in the whole course of the latest events, the sovereigns of the coalition to destroy the ascendancy of Napoleon have regarded public opinion as one of their main supports, and . . . far from neglecting this opinion, they have rather laid themselves open to the accusation . . . to have listened to it too much . . . The Tsar . . . attaches the utmost importance to

it; whatever his political or personal ambitions, I am sure that he would rather sacrifice them than to be seen in the eyes of the public as unjust, ungrateful, or a disturber of the general peace . . . [16]

Talleyrand argued that this sensitivity was part of the new Age. In a letter to the French king, he wrote:

> Formerly, the secular power could derive support from the authority of religion; it can no longer do this, because religious indifference has penetrated all classes and become universal. The sovereign power, therefore, can only rely upon public opinion for support, and to obtain that it must seek to be at one with that opinion.[17]

Talleyrand was speaking of domestic opinion; Castlereagh extended this reliance to international public opinion. He wrote the tsar, regarding the Polish issue, that "if Your Imperial Majesty should leave public opinion behind you . . . I should despair of witnessing any just and stable order of things in Europe."

All these leaders had witnessed the destruction of the public stature of the French autocracy by journalists; each one knew that Napoleon's power, depending as it did on enormous public faith, derived at bottom from his place in the French imagination, a place he carefully nurtured in the bulletins he wrote. If religious tradition had underwritten the ancien régime, linking it with the dynastic past and imbuing it with the prestige of the mystical, then public opinion must underwrite the kind of state that depended on mass endorsement for its power and legitimacy. Perhaps Webster has in mind the form of the nation-state when, finding little sensitivity among the great powers to the national feelings of the publics whose states were being redrawn, he sees instead only expediency in the acts of state-nations.[18] The role of public opinion in the nation-state is to assess whether the welfare of the people is being attended to by the State, and it is true that there was little of this at Vienna. But the role of public opinion in the state-nation was to assess the character, fitness, and morality of the State as the apotheosis of, not the servant of, the nation. Thus, for example, one historian of the Congress has concluded that even the allocations of territories were not as important[19]

> in themselves as is often supposed. For Metternich, more than anything, the outcome of the redistribution talks mattered as an indicator of how successful Austria was at asserting herself. Austria was anxious to confirm its role as a principal international player. . . . [To] lose face in the German Confederation [would have been fatal to Austria's leadership of the new league]. This is not simply a matter of expediency, and it was

important, vitally important, to Austria what German and European opinion thought of it.[20]

Much the same case can be made even with respect to the autocratic tsar. The relation between a parliamentary leader like Castlereagh and the public opinion of his domestic constituency in a state-nation provides elements out of which the relation of a state-nation's leader to other peer leaders is created, and ultimately the relation of that state to other states. That relation too is compounded of prestige, reputation, and the stature that is conferred by being at one with public opinion, and therefore domestic and international public opinion are linked. The tsar wished to gain the respect of the European public in order to play a decisive role in the directorate, a body made up of leaders who themselves, in their domestic constituencies, had to be attentive to public opinion. The Vienna system could only successfully function if it were made sensitive to public opinion: the congresses and the directorate ensured this.

THE NEED FOR NEW PRINCIPLES

The most significant challenge facing the peacemakers, however, was neither instrumental nor political. This was the challenge posed by the loss of customary legitimacy by the ancien régime. In a previous work[21] Calabresi and I have suggested that one way to look at the different cultural institutions that societies use to address social issues is in terms of four paradigmatic allocation methods: economic, political, customary, and blind. These four methods function in part to resolve and in part to hide the conflicts in values that arise from contested allocations of resources and from the difficult choices among values that are thus forced on societies. Lottery (or "blind") systems share with customary systems the virtue of avoiding any overt consideration of the competing merits of different choices.[22] Dynastic legitimacy united these two paradigmatic methods, custom and chance, so that, unless the dynastic succession were unclear, societies did not have to expose the values they would have had to compromise in an open competition of preferences to choose a ruler. The civil wars that so often accompanied succession struggles are a testament to the divisions that are exposed when such a clash of values is brought into the open. Talleyrand believed that "the usual and almost inevitable consequence of an uncertain right of succession is to cause domestic or foreign wars and often both simultaneously."[23]

Succession by dynastic descent is a blind allocation system, a choice by the society not to actually choose. Like men drawing straws to see who will go on a perilous mission, it leaves the selection to fate. There is much to be said for such systems: juries; the Dalai Lama, whose time of death determines the time of the birth of his successor; and the holders of entailed wealth are all chosen in this blind way. If this method, however, is stripped of its reliance on divine intervention—the claim that lot systems, by their very randomness, allow God's will to be done without adulteration—then the blind system can appear irrational and the very mindlessness that originally commended the system discredits it.

What perpetuated the system of dynastic succession beyond the era of the kingly states and into the period of territorial states, which was dominated by rationalism, was the union of blind allocation with another archetypal allocative system, custom. Whether or not monarchies—leadership by a lottery among royals—would be perpetuated into the period of statenations depended upon whether they could call on resources of legitimacy that were sanctified by custom. Talleyrand here too saw absolutely clearly what was at stake:

> I speak of the legitimacy of governments in general, whatsoever be their form, and not only of those of kings, because it applies to all governments. A lawful government, be it monarchical or republican, hereditary or elective, aristocratic or democratic, is always one whose existence, form, and mode of action, have been consolidated and consecrated by a long succession of years, and I should say almost, by a secular prescription. The legitimacy of the sovereign power results from the ancient status of possession, just as, for private individuals, does the right of property.[24]

Denied the union of custom and chance that aided the territorial states, the Congress of Vienna invoked three crucial interlocking norms in order to confer legitimacy upon its undertakings. These norms were the balance of power, the general interest of the society of European states, and the special interests of the prevailing constitutional archetype.

THE BALANCE OF POWER

Because the Peace of Utrecht had enshrined the idea of a European equilibrium as the sine qua non of stability for the society of states, statesmen had for a century before Vienna repeatedly invoked this idea. It is open to doubt whether the Great Article of Utrecht in fact envisaged the same sort of distribution of power as was meant by the phrase "balance of power" in Europe a century later: for one thing, the indicia of power themselves had changed, with the sheer size of populations being of much greater importance than heretofore. There are other reasons for doubt: at Utrecht, the equilibrist idea seems to have meant achieving a mathematical, Newtonian "steady state" subject to minor fluctuations, an idea that was usefully augmented by the "barrier" concept used to define French borders.[25]

At Vienna two new ideas were present that modified the concept: first, that the balance of power was a dynamic, developmental situation that must be maintained and adjusted by the Concert of Europe (whereas at Utrecht such minor adjustments in territory as reflected the waxing and waning of state power were left to limited wars, waged in an appropriately confined manner); and second, that the maintenance of a balance of power was a matter of collective legitimacy as much as collective security. Maintaining the balance of power would become the chief business of the great power directorate. One member's delegation to Vienna confirmed its government's intention of maintaining "that system of equilibrium which [is] placed henceforth under the protection of the powers of the first order and shielded from all preponderance."[26]

The centrality of the balance was evident in the statement of all the chief actors at Vienna. Castlereagh wrote to his prime minister that he regarded his duty "to make the establishment of a just equilibrium in Europe the first object of my attention and to consider the assertion of minor points of interest as subordinate to this great end."[27] Talleyrand, in his final report from the Congress, repeated that its purpose, as recorded in the precursor Treaty of Paris, was "such as to establish in Europe a real and permanent balance of power."[28] The Declaration of Frankfurt, drawn up by Metternich as a statement of allied policy distribution, stated that the "allied powers . . . want a state of peace that, through a wise distribution of forces, through a just equilibrium, will henceforth preserve their peoples from the numberless calamities that, for twenty years, have burdened Europe."[29] The Congress convened a statistical committee to establish credible estimates of the number of persons in the various territories to be distributed, in order to facilitate a carefully balanced population because such a distribution was thought crucial to the Congress's work. Yet these statesmen were not so naïve as to believe that Europe could be carefully parceled into so many compensating weights. As Talleyrand wrote,

> [a]djacent to large territories belonging to a single power, there are territories of similar or of smaller size, divided up among a greater or lesser number of states . . . Such a situation only admits of a very artificial and precarious equilibrium which can only last for as long as some large states continue to be animated by a spirit of moderation and justice that will preserve it.[30]

What was required was not simply a careful division of resources, but also the will to maintain their division. That will could be animated by the state-nation's drive for legitimacy in the absence of those customs that had fortified the territorial state. Thus Talleyrand's insight links these two principles and lays the foundation for the ultimate resolution of the new difficulties posed by the post-Vienna world. By allocating the duty to

maintain the equilibrium to the directorate of great powers, the new constitution for the society of European states would both legitimate their role
and protect the peace from their disturbance of it.

THE GENERAL INTEREST

On the other hand, how was it to be determined precisely what distribution
was a "just balance"? Only a just balance (as opposed to the infinitely
many possible divisions of territory that might result in a theoretical "balance") could deliver legitimacy to the settlement. The application of the
principle of the balance of power could, in the context of legitimate dynastic states, direct the territorial augmentation (or diminution) of these states
strictly on equilibrist lines. This was the Utrechtian answer. But in the
absence of dynastic legitimacy, the principle could not determine what
states were legally entitled to receive territory. Even if every slice of pie
were made equal, how would one know how many slices there were to be?
To say of the great powers that they must be of equal weight does not
determine how heavy they are to be, or on what they are permitted to gorge
themselves.

As we shall see, four large questions preoccupied the peacemakers at
Vienna—the German and Italian Questions (which were the result of
Napoleon's erasure and redrawing of the German and Italian national
maps) and the Polish and Saxon Questions (which became interlocked
with each other). Of these four, the latter two became the most divisive
and, at one juncture, even threatened to lead to fresh hostilities among the
allies.

By the end of the war, Russian forces had occupied Poland and Saxony.
The Grand Duchy of Warsaw, carved out by Napoleon from Polish lands
partitioned to other powers in the eighteenth century, had no legitimate status, and the Saxon king had forfeited his status by abandoning his imperial
role and siding with Napoleon slightly but fatally longer than other powers
had felt it necessary to do. The Russian tsar therefore proposed creating
a new state of Poland, along state-nation colonial lines, with himself as
hereditary monarch. In exchange for Prussian support for this project, and
in compensation for Polish land hitherto granted to Prussia in the partitions and that would now be taken back, the tsar would see that Saxony
was granted to Prussia.

Such proposals were potentially highly damaging to the legitimacy of
the new international constitutional system. If Saxony, an ancient state
with a legitimate heir, could simply be absorbed by Prussia, then the right
of conquest had entered the world of the state-nation with all that state's
potential for ferocity and subjugation, a capacity unknown to the modest
cessions of the territorial state. If Poland could be re-created only to
become a colony of Russia, then the legitimate bases of state creation were

made a farce. The principle of the balance of power was of little help here. If anything, it could be argued that a larger Prussia would be a useful counterweight to France and that a Polish enlargement of Russia would pull Russia into European affairs, with salutary effects on Russian temperance and on the availability of Russian assistance in maintaining the balance of power in Europe generally. For Russia the point was moot: she had defeated an enemy at great cost and now deserved a reward. She asked for no more than that which she already, by force of arms, possessed.

Castlereagh wrote to the tsar of a "duty" owed by the great powers. The principle "of territorial compensation for expenses incurred in war, unless qualified in the strictest sense by its bearing upon the general system of Europe, cannot be too strongly condemned. . . . The peace of the world cannot coexist with such doctrines."[31] "Just" principles regarded the society of Europe as a whole. The great powers were given great responsibility, but it was not granted to them in order for them to embark on a "lawless scramble for power."[32]

The solution was to introduce a countervailing principle—the general welfare of the society of states, taken as a whole—and to comprehend within this principle the maintenance of the legitimacy of the new constitution. On the basis of this principle, Russia was persuaded to accept a further partition of Poland. Indeed, when the tsar ultimately agreed to this proposal, he told the Poles that he was unable to fulfill altogether their national hopes because the interest of Europe as a whole had to take precedence over their own.[33] More importantly, the Prussian attempt to annex Saxony was rebuffed. Each of the allies had been brought around to a position originally held only by Talleyrand, on the grounds that to decide otherwise would damage the legitimacy of the new system and thus imperil the legitimacy of all its territorial and financial allocations. The basis for this change in view was the consciousness of a "general system of Europe," and the "common interest of Europe as a whole" (*l'intérêt général*).

THE STATE-NATION

As we have seen, the Congress of Vienna was not the first such convention to define the legitimate constitutional form of government for member states, but it was by far the most intrusive. The state-nation—a constitutional entity based on the consent of the governed—was replacing the territorial states of the previous century, even though a coalition including territorial states had decisively defeated the most dynamic example of the new form. The third interlocking key to legitimacy lay in recognizing this development by specifying constitutional norms for individual states.

This had begun with the Bourbon restoration. The allies were careful to provide that the recall of the Bourbon dynasty was not an acknowledgment of pre-existing rights (as Pitt's original program might have been taken to mean). Rather Louis XVIII was required to grant a representative constitution (the *Charte*) and was placed on the throne only after an offer was forthcoming from the French Senate, an institution created by Napoleon. The states that defeated Napoleon essentially shared, or came to share, the state-nation constitutional form of which he was the main European architect. Though he despised Napoleon, Talleyrand appreciated this point. He wrote that

> however legitimate a power may be, its exercise nevertheless must vary according to the objects to which it is applied, and according to time and place. Now, the spirit of the present Age in great civilized states demands that supreme authority shall not be exercised except with the concurrence of representatives chosen by the people subject to it. . . . These opinions are no longer peculiar to any one country; they are shared by almost all. Accordingly, we see that the cry for constitutions is universal; everywhere the establishment of a constitution adapted to the more or less advanced state of society has become a necessity, and everywhere preparations for this purpose are in progress.[34]

The tsar had announced that he wished representative constitutions in all states,[35] and, as we shall see, the constitution for the German states, the Act of Confederation, included an obligation for all member states to enact constitutions providing for representative institutions. Some states resisted, of course, and some were unable to comply: Austria had no single nation from which it could forge a state-nation; indeed the nationality principle was lethal to its cohesion as a state. The most Austria could manage was to adopt the title favored by state-nations for the head of state; Francis had become "Emperor of Austria," as Napoleon had been "Emperor of the French," and as eventually Victoria of England was to become "Empress." Although Prussian representatives at Vienna had been among those who insisted on the provision for German representative institutions, Prussia too was hesitant. It was but a fragment of the German nation. Prussia could not support the creation of a German state-nation from which she was absent, but Austria and Russia could scarcely support a new German state of which Prussia was a part.

This concern for the domestic composition of constitutional regimes was tied to the issue of legitimacy and thence to stability. Wellington conceded that after the treaty France remained strong enough to overturn the rest of Europe—that, in other words, a balance had *not* been achieved—but rejected proposals to weaken her territorially through adverse cessions. Such cessions would delegitimate the French government. As Castlereagh put it, punitive reductions would leave "the [French] King no resource in the eyes of his own people but to disavow us; and once committed against us in sentiment, he will be obliged soon either to lead the nation into war himself, or possibly be set aside to make way for some more bold and enterprising competitor."[36] Wellington concurred:

> We must . . . if we [were to] take this large cession [crippling France's war-making power], consider the operations of the war as deferred till France shall find a suitable opportunity . . . to regain what she has lost . . . [W]e shall find [then] how little useful the cessions we have acquired will be against a national effort to regain them. Revolutionary France is more likely to distress the world than France, however strong her frontier, under a regular government; and that is the situation in which we ought to endeavor to place her.[37]

Thus we see intertwined the three issues of the balance of power, the general welfare of Europe, and the constitutional makeup of individual states, all bearing on the crucial matter of legitimacy. Only a Europe composed of stable states, managed by a directorate of the most powerful of these states, with a mandate to act in the interest of the society of states as a whole, would prevent a new outbreak of such cataclysmic war as Europe had experienced for twenty years. Otherwise, the collapse of legitimacy in one great power would provoke a new war, as had happened in France. The stability of the system thus depended upon the internal stability of its major states, and this domestic security could be ensured by attention to the security of the society of states generally. The one reinforced the other. Metternich and his allies in Berlin and St. Petersburg later attempted to deploy this insight in order to use the Vienna directorate as an engine for domestic repression. Be that as it may, the focus on the domestic constitutional structure of the member states represents a crucial step in the development of a constitution for the society of states.

THE CONSTITUTION: THE FINAL ACT AT VIENNA

Before Napoleon's fall, Metternich had persuaded the British ambassador to Vienna, Aberdeen, to join him in a peace overture that proposed terms that confined France to the Pyrenees, the Rhine, and the Alps. When learning of this, Castlereagh was horrified: the proposal violated the long-standing English principle of denying to any great power the Low Countries' approach to the English Channel. Thus appalled, he drew up his famous *Instructions* in his own hand and had them approved by the British cabinet. These he determined to take to the continent personally in an effort to hold the Coalition together for a peace of constitutional dimensions.

The *Instructions* envisioned the re-establishment of Holland (to include the former Habsburg Netherlands), Spain, Portugal, and Italy ("in security and independence"), Prussia brought west to the Rhine, the Bourbons restored in France to prewar borders—provided this dynasty could be shown to be acceptable to the French people—and above all, a consolidating and persisting international alliance. This alliance was "not to terminate with the war" but to remain as a deterrent to "an attack by France on the European dominions of any one of the contracting parties." Castlereagh then traveled to allied military headquarters in eastern France along with the advance. From there a "congress" convened at the village of Chatillon-sur-Seine in early February 1814. In an atmosphere of great tension owing to recent French victories in the field, acrimonious personal relations between Castlereagh and Metternich (and between Metternich and the tsar), Castlereagh persuaded the other powers to accept his plan for an alliance that would serve as the basis for a constitutional arrangement among the states of Europe to be worked out at a subsequent congress. This plan was adopted as the Treaty of Chaumont, signed March 9, 1814, and represents an historic moment in diplomacy. The treaty set precise conditions for the conduct of the coalition, provided for 150,000 troops to be contributed by each of the four powers, and required Britain to provide a subsidy of five million pounds to pursue the war. In Articles 5–16, the powers committed themselves to defend each other against any future French attack by contributing 60,000 men each to an international force to be commanded by the party requesting aid.

The Congress of Chatillon disbanded on March 19, and the allies took the bold decision to leave Napoleon in their rear and march directly on Paris. Paris fell on March 30, 1814. Talleyrand assumed leadership of the provisional government, convening the Senate on April 1 to approve guarantees of civil and political rights. These guarantees also gave assurances to officers, bondholders, and property owners who had profited during the Revolution and its aftermath. The government removed the requirement of loyalty to Napoleon and replaced it with a draft constitution which limited royal power and ratified both the revolution's seizure of émigré properties and the restraints it had placed on the Church. On April 6 the Senate summoned the Bourbon heir. Napoleon abdicated one week later and was conveyed to Elba, where he was given a minuscule island kingdom and an annuity of two million francs.

Thus the way was cleared for a treaty with a new regime in France. The result was the First Peace of Paris (so named because Napoleon's breakout in 1815 led to a second agreement between the powers and France), which has been rightly taken as a model for treaties of peace. It returned France, generally speaking, to the frontiers of 1792, when the epochal war had begun. It provided for no further occupation, no indemnifications, no confessions of wrongdoing—nothing that would humiliate the new king, Louis, in the eyes of his people, or give to future French leaders a means to incite popular indignation against foreign states. The treaty even permitted France to retain the looted works of art stolen from a number of continental capitals. Significantly, the treaty justified this extraordinary leniency by distinguishing the revolutionary regime of France from its people, thus emphasizing that the war that had just been waged was a war against Napoleon's government, not against the French people.

The Treaty settled matters between France and her adversaries, but it did nothing to sort out affairs for the rest of Europe. Vast territories were without government and the borders of many states were unsettled. Napoleon had swept away the old map and his defeat had now erased the new one as well. Armies of occupation roamed across vanished frontiers; rulers set on their thrones by Napoleon had fled (with the exception of Murat, who still reigned in Naples), but representatives of the old regimes Napoleon had replaced could not exercise authority without the mandate of the victorious coalition that had defeated him. Article 32 of the Peace provided for a new congress to be assembled in Vienna, to which invitations would be issued to all the powers engaged on either side of the conflict. Now Europe waited: its state system had been shattered—even the location and boundaries of most of its states lay undetermined—its commercial system had collapsed, the Holy Roman Empire had disappeared, and a new constitutional system for Germany had not been put in its place. All parties with interests in these events came to Vienna in September 1814. More than two hundred representatives of various entities arrived to press their claims for recognition and to advance their ideas for the new European order.

In a secret, unpublished article of the Treaty, the four victorious powers resolved to decide among themselves the ultimate direction of the Congress. By September 23, this general program had been refined. Proposals on all territorial matters would be decided upon first by the members of the Quadruple Alliance (the Grand Coalition of four great powers), then submitted to the French and Spanish for approval, and then forwarded to the Congress for ratification. The five chief German powers would draft their own plan for a German constitution. Britain, Russia, Prussia, and Austria, plus Spain and France, would determine procedural matters.

On that same day, Friday, September 23, 1814, His Serene Highness Charles-Maurice de Talleyrand-Périgord, Prince of Bénévent, formerly the bishop of the Revolution and Napoleon's foreign minister, arrived in Vienna. Within a week he had thrown the plans of the Coalition into complete disarray. Talleyrand—that "pattern of subtlety and finesse," "a creature of grandeur and guile," as the biographer Philip Ziegler refers to him—was not going to be content with the subordinate role the Four had assigned to France. He immediately objected to the exclusion of France from the directing role of the great powers. He took up the cause of all the excluded powers, arguing that the Four had no mandate to decide matters in advance of the convocation of the Congress, and in this he was supported by the Spanish representative, Don Pedro Labrador. After a meeting on September 30, a shaken Gentz, the secretary of the Congress, wrote in his diary: "The intervention of Talleyrand and Labrador has hopelessly ruined all our plans. They protested against the procedure we have adopted; they gave us a dressing-down which lasted for two hours; it is a scene I shall never forget."[38] Repeatedly Talleyrand threatened to take his case to the Congress as a whole.

Talleyrand even objected to the use of the word *allies*. He argued that the Quadruple Alliance had ended with the signing of the Treaty of Paris. The legal status of the Alliance existed only so long as hostilities remained unresolved; the four member states were legally bound as individual states simply to carry out the provisions of the Treaty, one of which was to convene the Congress—in its entirety—on October 1. The directing body of the Congress, insofar as it took its authority from the Treaty, must therefore consist of all eight powers who were parties to the Treaty, *if* their authority was confirmed by the whole Congress in plenary session.

Talleyrand's intervention was a tour de force. The defeated state had turned the ideology of the state-nation—its vulnerability to charges of illegitimacy, its ideology of consent, its sensitivity to public opinion, in short its entire superstructure of the man-made and thus the accountable—against the victors. On October 8 another meeting was held: Sweden, Portugal, Spain, and France would be added to the Four Powers, to make a "Preliminary Committee of the Eight." Four days later the Eight published their first declaration: the opening of the Congress would be postponed until November 1. This declaration expressed, perhaps a little defensively, the intention that all procedural issues would be resolved "in harmony with public law, the provisions of the [Treaty of Paris] and the expectations of the Age."[39]

The Committee of Eight handled most vital questions, often following meetings of the Four and, after January 9, the Five, France having finally been included in the smaller directing group. Ten special committees were set up to which various problems were allocated. The Congress, as such, only really came together in order to adopt the Final Act on June 9, 1815, when the assembled representatives with some exceptions (notably Spain) adhered to the findings of the committees, including those of the directorate of Eight.

Five particular questions bedeviled the peacemakers: the German Question (Napoleon had destroyed most of the three hundred kingdoms and principalities that composed the Holy Roman Empire, which in any case had been declared defunct in 1806); the Italian Question (Napoleon had driven Austria, the principal prewar power in Italy, from that entire country, stripped the Vatican of its temporalities, and imposed a usurper who still reigned in Naples); recognition and territorial problems associated with the new states of Switzerland, the United Netherlands, and with the Kingdom of Sweden, whose monarch was a former French marshal; and most intractably, the crucial issues of Poland and Saxony, described above, which pitted the policies of the prewar territorial states with respect to annexation, against those of the new state-nations and their quest for collective legitimacy.

It was widely assumed that because Prussia, a victor, could scarcely be expected to lose territories it held in 1805, the tsar and the King of Prussia must have concluded a secret compact by which Prussia would receive Saxony (still occupied by Russian troops) in order for Russia to create a new Polish kingdom that would incorporate Prussia's former Polish provinces. Initially both Britain and Austria supported Prussia in its bid for Saxony—Britain on grounds of improving the balance of power by bringing Prussia westward, Austria as part of a bribe to induce King Frederick William of Prussia to renege on his promises of support to Russia over Poland. By mid-October the British thought they had the makings of a compromise and proposed that Metternich present to the tsar a joint position on behalf of the other three powers: Poland could be wholly repartitioned, or given a genuinely independent status, or returned to its partial configuration as in 1791. On October 24, Metternich met with the tsar. The meeting was a disaster. Afterwards the tsar, joined by Frederick William, demanded that Emperor Francis replace Metternich. It was evident that an agreement among the coalition partners could not be achieved by the time of the proposed opening of the Congress.

Now the four powers faced a new dilemma: should they jeopardize the Congress itself by another postponement or should they risk throwing the settlement into the hands of an open constitutional convention? It was proposed that a three-man commission begin examining the credentials of the accredited representatives; that would buy time. The Committee of Eight would be convened when the credentialing process was complete, in order to discuss the organization of the Congress itself. Talleyrand began to speak sarcastically of "the Congress that [is] not a Congress."[40]

As public opinion began to turn against the annexation of Saxony (and as the tsar seemed intransigent regarding Poland), both Britain and Austria backed away from their support for Prussian ambitions. Castlereagh changed his position and advised the Prussians not to press the claim to all Saxony "against the general sentiment of Europe."[41] In reaction, the Prussians on November 7 informed the Austrians that they were breaking off all talks with Castlereagh over Saxony and Poland. That evening it was learned in Vienna that Russia had turned over the administration of Saxony to the Prussian army.

Now Austria played its German card: if Prussia wished to participate in the new German Confederation, it could not afford to alienate the other German states by consuming Saxony. Metternich sent Prussia a proposal to divide Saxony, giving some territory to Prussia but retaining Dresden and Leipzig in an independent kingdom ruled by the hereditary heir. For the first time, these proposals were sent to Talleyrand.

In a state paper of December 19, Talleyrand argued that the important issue raised by Saxony was one of legitimacy, not merely one of territorial compensation or the balance of power. An established heir could not be deposed simply because other sovereigns coveted his lands, as Frederick the Great had coveted Silesia. In the new world of the state-nation, the right of marginal conquest so dear to the territorial state had to give way to the claims of legitimacy. It was "contrary to justice and reason," Talleyrand wrote, for Prussia to demand territory; it was a matter for the lawful monarch, the king of Saxony, to decide what he was prepared to yield to the Prussians, and in any case, he could not yield the state itself because it was impossible on legitimate grounds for him to do so. Saxony belonged to its people, not to its king.

In October Castlereagh had had a similar exchange with the tsar. The Russian emperor had angrily pointed out that he had 200,000 troops in Poland, and occupied every city and village. Castlereagh had replied:

> It is very true, His Imperial Majesty [is] in possession and he must know that no one [is] less disposed than myself hostilely to dispute that possession, but I [am] sure His Imperial Majesty would not feel satisfied to rest his pretensions on a title of conquest in opposition to the general sentiment of Europe.[42]

Now, in the last two weeks of December, Metternich and Castlereagh brought Talleyrand increasingly into their confidence. In January a secret defensive alliance was concluded among France, Britain, and Austria in case negotiations broke down completely. Historians disagree whether this move had any impact on the other members of the coalition, but in any case within two days Castlereagh was writing to London that "the alarm is over." Poland was once more partitioned; Austria retained Galicia and Tarnopol; Prussia got back Poznania; and the rest of Napoleon's Grand Duchy of Warsaw became a Kingdom of Poland ruled by the tsar. Cracow became a Free City. Three-fifths of Saxony was restored to the king, the remainder going to Prussia.

Other matters were more easily settled. Prussia was given territories in the Rhineland that, with her Saxon acquisition, doubled her population; Austria ceded Belgium to the Netherlands. Austria received Dalmatia and territories in northern Italy from which she had been driven by Napoleon, including Lombardy and Milan, and various possessions of Venice. Events now took an unexpected turn that not only resolved the remnants of the Italian Question but also solidified the former coalition that had begun to show strains at the peace conference.

On the evening of Monday, March 8, Talleyrand, Wellington (who had replaced Castlereagh in February), the Prussian chancellor Hardenberg and the tsar's chief foreign minister, Nesselrode, met with Metternich at his official residence to discuss their trip the next day to inform the king of Saxony of the outcome of the debates over his future. At 3 a.m., the meeting finally broke up and Metternich went to bed, to be awakened at 6 a.m. by an urgent dispatch from the Austrian consul at Genoa. Metternich ignored this, but at 7:30 a.m., nagged by the presence of the message, he opened the envelope and learned that Napoleon had disappeared from Elba.

Within half an hour he was at the side of the emperor Francis; at 8:15 he saw the tsar; at 8:30 the king of Prussia. By 10:00 a.m. the ministers of the great powers were gathered in Metternich's study, and couriers were dispatched to the armies of each of the allies. Austrian forces were concentrated in northern Italy, the Prussians in Saxony, the Russians in Poland, and the British in Belgium. For some days these forces were kept on the alert as all Europe waited to see what Napoleon would do. Would he make for the Italian coast, as Wellington and Talleyrand thought, or go directly to France? Not until March 11 was it known that Napoleon had landed near Cannes on March 1. His first words on landing on French soil were reported to have been, "*Le Congrès est dissous.*"*

Napoleon had headed directly for Lyons, where he arrived on March 10. By the 17th he was in Auxerre.

It was not a campaign, but a procession. Troops were sent against him—and joined him. Ney, who was to bring him to Paris in an iron cage, fell on his neck. The peasants whose lands were threatened, the ex-soldiers who had lost their livelihood, the serving soldiers who had been given strange and dandified officers, the ordinary Frenchmen, who disliked the *émigrés,* remembered the victories and forgot the wounds—all rallied to his support.[43]

*"The Congress is dissolved."

On the 13th, the Committee of Eight met and issued a declaration indicting Bonaparte as an outlaw and the "disturber of world repose." He had placed himself, they declared, "outside the pale of civil and social relations." Reports were received that French regiments, sent by the king to arrest Napoleon, were defecting to their former commander as he proceeded toward Paris. Rumors began to circulate that he had already taken Paris and although these were premature, Napoleon did in fact triumphantly invest the capital on March 20. Louis, who on the 16th had put on the rosette of the Legion of Honor and promised the Chambers that he would die in their defense, fled in a closed carriage on March 19. *"Mon chèr,"* Napoleon is reported to have said to Mollien, as he passed through the colonnades of blazing torches and the exhilarated crowds, and into the throne room at the Tuileries, "the people have let me come, as they have let the others go."

At Vienna, work began on creating a new coalition; a treaty of grand alliance was presented on March 25. The four allies would contribute 150,000 men each to defend the frontiers they had drawn. They promised not to lay down their arms until Napoleon had been defeated. Louis and the other powers were invited to associate themselves with the campaign. For the congress, or rather for its directorate, the negotiations over a constitution for Europe continued; indeed, great progress was made during the Hundred Days of Napoleon's brief resurgence, doubtless because this new threat united all parties and imbued the Congress with a sense of urgency.

At the end of March a message was received by the tsar from Napoleon. It contained conciliatory words and a copy of the secret alliance against Russia agreed to by Metternich, Talleyrand, and Castlereagh in January during the Polish dispute. It had apparently been left behind in Paris when Louis fled. There are differing accounts* of Alexander's reaction—some have him flinging the document into the fire in Metternich's presence; one eyewitness reported that the tsar merely presented Metternich with the treaty and said, "Let us never mention this incident again and let us attend to more serious matters."[44]

The Committee of Eight now finally set the boundaries of the new Kingdom of the Netherlands and accepted the constitution of the new confederation of Swiss cantons. Formal treaties ratifying the Polish settlement, including a constitution for the Republic of Cracow, were presented. The Committee set to work with twenty-five secretaries to draft a Final Act, which would be presented to the entire Congress. Agreement was reached over the abolition of the slave trade (the movement for which gained momentum when Napoleon announced his own declaration of abo-

---

*"Let us kiss and let all be forgotten" was Metternich's own account of the tsar's words.

lition) and over the human rights of Jews in Germany. By early May, committee reports were finalized on the navigation of international rivers and on the protocols for diplomatic rank. Only the question of the German constitution and the residue of the Italian Question remained.

On April 7 the entire mosaic of northern Italy fell into place with the creation of the Lombardo-Venetian kingdom. The Habsburgs were returned to the principalities of Parma, Modena, and Tuscany. The Papal States were restored to the Vatican. But there remained the question of Naples.

Austria had concluded a secret treaty before the Treaty of Paris, supporting the former Napoleonic marshal, Murat, in his claim to Naples in return for which the latter had agreed to restore the Bourbon heir to the Kingdom of Sicily. This treaty violated all the principles of legitimacy the Congress was asserting, and though the allies had tacitly accepted this settlement, the Italian Question could not be resolved until a consensus was achieved regarding Naples. It was widely thought that Murat would be difficult to dislodge, as he had an 80,000-man force at his disposal (although the previous monarch had said of this army, "You may dress it in blue, or in green or in red [that is, in the colors of France, Austria or Britain] but, whichever you do, it will run"[45]).

By an ill-fated coincidence, Murat chose this moment to attempt a general Italian uprising. Ten days after Napoleon entered Fontainebleau, Murat issued an appeal from Rimini calling on the Italian people to rise against Austria. Fighting broke out between Austrian units in central Italy and Murat's Neapolitan army. The allies now denounced the treaty with Murat, and on April 18 war was declared by Austria. The campaign was over in a month. This cleared the way for the restoration of the Bourbon king, Ferdinand, to the throne of the Two Sicilies, and now there remained only the German Question.

The committee appointed to draft proposals on this issue faced opposition from three quarters: liberal nationalists, who wanted a state-nation for all Germany; dispossessed princes and kings who wanted the return of the territorial states they had held before being turned out by Napoleon; and those lingering dynasties—like Saxony—that feared the action of the Congress would terminate their sovereignty, or at least greatly compromise it. Finally, in the third week in May, the Committee adopted a plan jointly submitted by Austria and Prussia, the ninth constitutional draft to be discussed in five months. This provided for a federal parliament at Frankfurt, under an Austrian presidency. The sovereign rights of the members of the federation were limited in two respects only: by restraints on foreign alliances and by a requirement that each member state grant a constitution to its citizens based on popular representation.[46] Thus a common constitutional system was provided for the German states derived from state-nation principles, even if a German state-nation was not achieved.

On June 9 the Final Act of the Congress, embodying its schemes for the reconstruction of the frontiers of Europe, for the provision of constitutions for numerous states, and above all, for a constitution for Europe itself, was presented. The document contained 121 articles. Of the eight powers, all signed except Spain (though Sweden consented subject to reservations). On June 18 Napoleon was defeated at Waterloo. On June 19, the entire Congress was convened again for signing by the smaller powers.

CONSTITUTIONAL INTERPRETATION: THE LAW PROFESSORS

> We [hoped] . . . that the Congress would crown its labors, by substituting for [the territorial state's] fleeting alliances (the result of necessities and momentary calculations) a permanent system of universal guarantees and general equilibrium . . . [T]he order established in Europe would be placed under the perpetual protection of all the parties interested, who by wisely concerted plans, or by sincerely united efforts, would crush at the outset, any attempt to compromise it.[47]

The constitutional order created by the five powers and ratified by the Congress embraced several treaties: the Treaty of Chaumont—which, by binding the parties to pursue victory despite tempting French offers of advantageous individual peace settlements, was the key to all that followed—the first Treaty of Paris, the second Treaty of Paris (which followed Napoleon's defeat at Waterloo), and the Final Act at Vienna. Pursuant to that system, further treaties were made—notably the Holy Alliance and the Quadruple Alliance—and further congresses were held, at Aix-la-Chapelle (1818), Troppau (1820), Laibach (1820), and Verona (1822), which attempted to apply the arrangements earlier agreed upon. This system of congresses soon proved logistically cumbersome, however, and for most of the life of the Constitution of Vienna, informal meetings of the directorate replaced grand convocations. This directorate, acting on behalf of the Concert of Europe, set frontiers, recognized states, resolved crises, and declared new rules of international law. If the role of the ratifying congresses was erased, however, what gave the great powers the right to promulgate new law?

Two answers were given by remarkable nineteenth century figures whose contributions to jurisprudence have left an important legacy, even if the international form with which they were concerned—the society of state-nations—has disappeared. Both men were law professors, but otherwise the careers of John Austin and Johann Bluntschli could not have been more different.

AUSTIN

Austin's life (1790–1859) was one of repeated disappointments. He began the study of law in 1812 after five years in the army. For a dozen years he then practiced, unsuccessfully, at the chancery bar. In 1826 he was appointed the first professor of jurisprudence at University College, the University of London. This career, too, ended in fiasco: he resigned his chair in 1832, having failed to attract students to his lectures. For a while he served on the Criminal Law Commission and then, in 1836, on the Malta Commission. He moved to Paris and lived there until the upheavals of 1848. He then went to Surrey, where he died ten years later. He had published his fundamental views in 1832, the year he was forced to abandon his professorship, but these were given little attention during his lifetime. His lectures on jurisprudence were only published posthumously.

Austin's answer to the problem of consent posed by the great-power directorate was to deny that the relations among nations were governed by law at all. Austin did not deny that there were international rules of behavior; indeed the source of these posed the problem to be addressed. Nor did he deny their efficacy and power. Rather he attributed these rules, which were an important factor in international relations, to custom. International law "consists of the opinions and sentiments current among nations generally," he wrote. It is "a law in name only," because there is no sovereign governing the states who are supposed to obey these rules.

"In order to [provide] an explanation of the marks which distinguish positive law, I shall analyze the expression 'sovereignty,'" he began. Austin then proceeded to define law as the commands of a sovereign addressed to political inferiors, backed by threats of harm in the event of disobedience. "The generality of the given society must be in the habit of obedience to a determinate and common superior: whilst that determinate person, or determinate body of persons, must not be habitually obedient to a determinate person or body," i.e., must itself be sovereign. Thus obedience is not a rational matter, as for Hobbes, nor a consensual one, as for Rousseau, but merely a fact. Whether it is justified is not a matter for the lawyer, who confines himself simply to analyzing what is. This distinction between legitimacy (a matter of habit) and justification (a matter of morality) tracks a similar distinction made by the architects of the Vienna settlement.

Notice that *positivism,* as Austin's doctrines are known, does away with two of the core ideas that had shaped international law from its inception at the time of the birth of the modern state: natural law and the theory of the just war. Natural law, whatever its content—and the positivists took some pleasure in pointing out that, unlike other observable phenomena in nature, no one could agree on the content of allegedly "natural" law—became an irrelevancy. If a provision was enacted into law by the sovereign, then that act made that provision law, whatever its origin; and if the sovereign denied authority to a "natural" law, it ceased to have any legal effect. As to the just war, its "justice" was a matter of morality, not of law. Whether a war was lawful was a matter of the sovereign's rules. For example, if the constitutional law of the United States were scrupulously followed, the fact that the United States manufactured an incident that provoked an attack (as, it is claimed, was the case in the Mexican-American War) while relevant to the moral judgment of the acts of the United States, was scarcely material regarding the legality of those acts. A war might be lawful but unjust, or just but unlawful; there was no necessary correlation. To the problem of whether more than one belligerent might prosecute a just war, the positivist would reply, "That's not my department; consult the clergy or perhaps (today) the psychoanalyst," for positivists tended to treat moral judgments as projections of the emotions of the persons declaring moral rules. These concepts form the core of the jurisprudential doctrine of positivism, which, crucially, distinguishes law from morality. Although law might well be derived from moral precepts, such precepts become law only when commanded by a sovereign.

This approach to law perfectly suited the Vienna system. That system was of course a product (and key determinant) of its Age. A self-consciously designed constitutional system, it reflected the idealism of the late eighteenth century, just as the system of Utrecht had reflected (and contributed to) the rationalism of the Enlightenment. Like the Vienna system itself, positivism reflects the self-consciousness, attention to public behavior, and sensitivity to the bases for legitimacy that characterized the state-nation. It raised, however, a fundamental question for this form of the State: is sovereignty defined in terms of domestic law or international law? It must be one or the other, because only de jure sovereignty, as opposed to de facto sovereignty, could serve as the fount of law. But if, as Austin claimed, international law was non-law—that is, it was only the positive (as opposed to natural) morality imposed by the opinion of the society of states—then international law could not confer a de jure status on the states it recognized as sovereign. On the other hand, if de jure sovereignty were a matter of domestic law only, then—at least outside the club of like-minded European state-nations with consistent customs—there was no consistent basis on which it might be identified. Sovereignty then became merely a matter of de facto control, and this the sovereigns of the directorate were at pains to deny, believing as they did that domestic revolution—which seizes sovereignty—was a real source of potential destruction for their international constitutional system.

BLUNTSCHLI

This paradox was taken up by Johann Bluntschli (1808–1881), a Swiss jurist whose life was as studded with success as Austin's was with disappointment and failure. Bluntschli presents the remarkable case of a law professor who achieved enviable mastery in two societies: after a successful scholarly and political career in Switzerland, he emigrated first to Munich in 1848, and then to Heidelberg, where he remained for the last twenty years of his life as the most prominent international lawyer in Bismarck's Germany. In 1873, he founded the Institute of International Law, which continues to flourish, and his name was well enough known to have been appropriated by George Bernard Shaw for the main character in his play *Arms and the Man*.

In 1866, Bluntschli published *Das moderne Kriegsrecht,* which became the basis for the codification of the laws of war enacted by the Hague Conferences of 1899 and 1907.[48] In 1868, there followed *Das moderne Völkerrecht,* which presented an apparently comprehensive system of international law in the form of a tersely worded codification with explanatory notes. It was immediately translated into several languages and quickly became the standard reference work for diplomats. In 1885, the author Pradier-Fodere wrote with some asperity that Bluntschi's book "is almost the only one which is today consulted by diplomats and all those obligated by their profession to possess some notion of international law."[49]

Das moderne Völkerrecht appeared when Bluntschli was sixty. He was already known as a figure of unusual stature—a statesman and religious leader of liberal and cosmopolitan views, a "good European." The book was received as his masterpiece, the mature expression of a humane and cultivated mind. Nonetheless, the book was sharply criticized for one notable departure from the style of previous treatises.

> While there had been earlier private attempts at codification of international law, that of Bluntschli was marked by a rather puzzling peculiarity: in view of the imperfection of the law of nations, he deliberately filled the gap by what he considered the commendable view, without drawing the necessary line of demarcation between law and proposal.[50]

When we understand Bluntschli's project, however, this aspect of the book will appear more dazzling than puzzling.

Indeed, to Americans familiar with the *Restatements* of the American Law Institute (ALI), Bluntschli's *Handbook* will seem comfortingly familiar. Like the ALI, Bluntschli dealt with a mass of instances, "cases" decided by governments, though not, as with the *Restatements,* cases decided by courts, for "[t]he preservation of the peace of nations did not depend upon the resolution of lawsuits."[51] Bluntschli dealt with examples of state behavior as these established "customary" international law. Not all this behavior could be rationalized as following the same rule, and thus, in discordant cases, Bluntschli stated (or "restated") the "better rule" as the rule of law.

For our purposes, the importance of this approach is the basis in law it gave to the acts of the Concert of Europe. Because the directorate was composed of the great powers, and because customary international law is principally determined by the acts of the most influential states, the acts of the directorate—so long as they rationally followed a consistent and principled course—created law, an international common law, as it were. The conundrum of the positivist was thus solved: sovereignty is bestowed by the international community, but that community's rules are the consequence of combining many cases of individual behavior by those states already acknowledged as sovereign. The acts of states, therefore, not those of the international community (which has no sovereign), can be amalgamated to give de jure status to the acts of any one state.

Like the debates and actions of the ALI, such an approach works best within a community of very similar actors. This makes such an institution vulnerable to "an attack upon its myths," those fundamental assaults that proceed by disagreeing with the basic premises of the system on perspectival grounds, allegedly demonstrating the arbitrariness and self-serving nature of fundamental assumptions. Moreover, there is no mechanism to resolve disputes among the sovereigns themselves because for the Concert there was no ratifying congress. When these two vulnerabilities were seized upon by imperial Germany, a state that rejected the constitutional premises of the state-nation and embarked upon the brinkmanship by which Alsace-Lorraine was annexed and Europe was intimidated, the constitutional system established by Vienna collapsed.

The Vienna constitution had sought to reconcile the general interests of Europe as a whole with the individual interests of the European states. In a protocol to the Belgian Conference of 1831, this passage occurs: *"Chaque nation à ses droits particuliers; mais l'Europe aussi à son droit. C'est l'ordre social qui le lui a donne."*[52]*

Bluntschli had hoped that a European confederation would develop in order to provide just the check he foresaw was needed in case of a breakout by one great power. In his last major work, *Lehre vom modernen Staat,* written four years after Bismarck had refused great-power mediation in the Franco-Prussian conflict, Bluntschli argued that as states experienced greater security, they were able gradually to turn away from preparations

---

*"Each nation has its particular laws; but Europe has its law too. It is the constitutional order that provided it."

for war and be more inclined to pursue peaceful cooperation. He doesn't seem to have appreciated that, for the new nation-state, the enhancement of the security of the state would be transformed into the enhancement of the security of the people, and that this goal created new ambition, new hungers. After the Franco-Prussian War, which may in some senses have enhanced the security of both states, Germany nevertheless was fearful of French revenge, and France was eager to recoup her lost provinces; their arms competition became all Europe's.

> . . . Europe was in peace, the Armed Peace, which like the German Empire is a thing unique in history. Never before had the state of the world been fully armed or on a war-footing without war breaking out. This was the condition of Europe from 1871 to 1914. It was organized for war. Every continental Great Power was a state or nation in arms, ordered, equipped, instructed, and ready for instantaneous war. The peoples lived under perpetual danger of destruction, but they discounted the fear, as is the way of mankind when the danger is permanent, just as they discount the fear of death from traveling by train. Nevertheless the danger was always present . . . after 1871, with universal conscription, the standing armies were always on a war-footing . . . the front-line fighting army was always mobilized, always in being, in time of peace as much as in time of war.[53]

Like the American Law Institute, the Concert of Europe "presupposed a certain harmony."[54] Following the creation of the German nation-state, Bismarck labored, as we have seen, to restore the credibility of the institution he had done so much to destroy. The Congress of Berlin and the Berlin Conference of 1884 were convened as a result of his advocacy. In 1878, Bismarck's mediation prevented a war between Great Britain and Russia.

The Concert, however, had ceased to function as an institution of European politics. It had become, instead, an instrument of German foreign policy. For Bismarck, "Europe was nothing more than a geographic reality."[55] After all, what "nation" did Europe answer to? The state-nation asks only that the state represent the nation; the nation-state is a more demanding mistress.

CHAPTER TWENTY-TWO

The Versailles Treaty

IN 1883, as Bismarck was completing the transition from Prussian state-nation to German nation-state, Friedrich Nietzsche wrote:

> Somewhere there are still peoples and herds, but not where we live, my brothers: here there are states. State? What is that? Well then, open your ears to me, for now I shall speak to you about the death of peoples. State is the name of the coldest of all cold monsters. Coldly it tells lies too; and this lie crawls out of its mouth: "I, the state, am the people." This is a lie! . . . This sign I give you: every people speaks its language of good and evil, which the neighbor does not understand. It has invented its own language of customs and rights. But the state tells lies in all the languages of good and evil; and whatever it says, it lies—and whatever it has it has stolen.[1]

Here are heard many of the complaints against the imperial state-nation: that it acts in solidarity with other state-nations, rather than representing the nation; that it claims to be the nation when in fact it is acting to perpetuate and serve its own interests; that it is indifferent to—cold, shares no sentiment with—the people who alone are the source of its authority and wealth.

It is a common error to say that the imperial states defied nationalism. On the contrary, these states exalted nationalism and claimed it for themselves. Imperialism, in the words of one of its greatest historians, William Langer, was "a projection of nationalism beyond the boundaries of Europe."[2] It was the co-opting of nationalism by the state-nation that so infuriated Nietzsche: the state-nation had subordinated the nation to itself. "Ask not what your country can do for you, but what you can do for your country" might well have been spoken by the leader of a state-nation.

By contrast, the nation-state replies, "Go ahead: ask! Let's see what we can do for you!"* For this reason, the nation-state provided social security, free public mass education, universal suffrage, and redistributive taxation. The nation-state sought its legitimacy in the betterment of the welfare of its people. This, however, brought forth a shadow for every variation of its constitutional form. The shadow of the nation-state is its ideology: by setting the standards by which well-being is judged, ideology explains how the State is to better the welfare of the nation. Whereas the state-nation had studiedly contrived to legitimate itself through the creation of a certifying club of other state-nations, admission to which stamped the state as the representative of the nation in whose name it ruled, the nation-state could not resort to this method. It tried this tactic, as we shall see. At Versailles in 1919, and still later at San Francisco in 1945, the great powers tried to reproduce the authorizing society that would legitimate their claim to rule, as their predecessors had done at Vienna. But this could not succeed, because three different kinds of such states presented themselves as best at serving their peoples. Until the debate among fascism, communism, and parliamentarianism could be settled, the nation-states could not form a legitimating society, because it was the legitimacy of their competitors that each ideology attacked.

A number of historical conclusions follow from this: first, that the war that began in 1914 must properly be seen as having continued until 1990, at which time a legitimate constitutional form of the State achieved a consensus among the great powers; second, that the constitutional mandate sought by the parties at Versailles was therefore premature, and could only come when the ideological conflict among the great powers was settled; and third, that the so-called failure of Versailles was to a very great degree preordained, and perhaps could not ultimately have been avoided. In Book I, we took up the first of these conclusions. Here we shall take up the second and third.

Although the Versailles agreement might have been a constitution for the society of states in the way that the peace agreements at Westphalia and Vienna may be said to be, it can be quickly shown that this was not quite the case.[†]

The Treaty of Versailles and the various other treaties that together form the Peace of Paris of 1919 did not constitute a settlement consensually agreed to by the great powers who fought the war. The treaty terms of Versailles were imposed upon Germany, while hostile military action—a

---

*And the market-state says: "Don't bother asking. You're on your own now."
[†]This suggests that the peace settlement in 1919 did not come at the end of an epochal war.

blockade that starved thousands to death during the pendency of the Peace Conference—was still underway. A single state's constitution can of course be imposed by war, but a constitution for the society of states requires consensus because it depends upon the vanquished state playing by the rules once the war is over. Moreover, the United States refused to ratify the treaty that emerged from the Peace Conference, and the Soviet Union was excluded altogether. No constitutive agreement can emerge when so many great powers are absent or alienated.

To be sure, there were many similarities between the Paris Peace Conference and the Congress of Vienna. Seventy plenipotentiaries from thirty-two countries came to Paris. There were 1,000 delegates. New states—Finland, Estonia, Latvia, Lithuania, Poland, Czechoslovakia, Yugoslavia—were created or legitimated, and the conference assumed the legal authority to abrogate pre-existing treaties, most important, the Russo-German treaty of Brest-Litovsk. Like the Vienna Congress, all the important decisions were made by a directorate of powers, which then presented the outcome to the general convocation. The Council of Four took the decisions, in secret, that determined the content of the peace treaty, just as the Committee of Four had attempted to determine the outcome of the deliberations at Vienna a century before. The draft peace treaty was presented to the Conference on May 6, 1919, just one day before it was to go to the German delegates.

The critical difference was that the states themselves were different: they were becoming nation-states. As Osiander insightfully points out, in "order to enhance their domestic legitimacy, increasingly governments gave up their solidarity with one another on which the Vienna system had been based."[3] This development can be attributed to the different basis of legitimacy claimed by these two different state archetypes.

The nation-state pursued a new bargain with the nation: in exchange for the release of enormous national energy, the State harnessed itself to the nation, promising more than simply its own aggrandizement and glory; it promised actual improvement in the material well-being of its citizens. Because the lot of all the citizens of a state can seldom be simultaneously improved, and because most governmental decisions produce losers as well as winners, such a task inevitably brought divisive pressures to bear within the State. In the parliamentary democracies, if they were lucky, this meant a restless changing of governments as the discontented accumulated with each decision; for the fascist states it encouraged an effort to divide the domestic polity into citizens and scapegoats, and to find foreign countries that could be frankly exploited to benefit the citizenry; for the socialist states, it invited a relentless program of class warfare, exalting one part of the citizenry at the expense of the other. None of these ideological forms, however, gained in prestige or sentiment by identification with the society of states as a whole or with the state-nation heritage of Vienna. The leaders of nation-states distanced themselves from the society of states because they simply had no choice. War itself was blamed on the society of state-nations.[4] Speaking of the war that had just ended, Woodrow Wilson said: "It was a war determined upon as wars used to be determined upon in the old, unhappy days when peoples were nowhere consulted by their rulers and wars were provoked and waged in the interest of dynasties or little groups of ambitious men who were accustomed to use their fellowmen as pawns and tools."[5]

Wilson insisted that there be "no odor of the Vienna settlement" at Paris.[6] Insofar as the nation-state tolerated a supranational presence, it was that of all peoples, not merely governments. As Wilson put it, "there is a great voice of humanity . . . in the world . . . which he who cannot hear is deaf . . . We are not obeying the mandate of parties or of politics. We are obeying the mandate of humanity."*

Such a view of the role of peoples, of course, is not incompatible with a constitution. Indeed it is the basis of most nation-state constitutions, including that of the United States. And it is true that the U.S. constitution provided the basis for the structure and ideology of the Versailles Treaty and the League of Nations. But before these provisions could be adopted as a constitution for the society of states a consensus was necessary on the ideological valence of the nation-state, which among other matters determines just how the public's mandate is to be ascertained. The United States was lucky to have achieved a domestic consensus on this matter early on, having fought a terrible civil war to determine its terms for the nation-state; this consensus was one the other great powers of the twentieth century did not share.

It is commonly held that the principal blunder of the peacemakers at Paris was their harsh treatment of defeated Germany. The Allies rejected the example of the victors at Vienna, which had embraced the new French government on the grounds that France had replaced the Napoleonic adversary and was now again a legitimate member of the society of states. Instead, the victors at Versailles rejected the proposal of Colonel House that the German delegates take part in the Conference, as provided in the U.S.-German exchange of notes on November 11, 1918, and refused to permit even oral discussions with the German representatives prior to presenting them with a draft treaty that the Germans were coerced into accepting by threats of further war and by the ongoing Allied blockade that had brought famine to Germany.

---

*A History of the Peace Conference of Paris, vol. 3, ed. Harold Temperley (1920), 59. Not every leader of a nation-state saw the force of humanity as so constructive. As Bismarck put it, "One can ride the wave, but one cannot steer it." Ibid., 250.

This situation was largely due to the unusual way in which the war had ended. Germany had agreed to an armistice on the basis of the famous Fourteen Points, a paper presented by Wilson that was in important ways inconsistent with the war aims of the other allies.[7] This paper was given a gloss to hold the Allies together, but this interpretation was not communicated to the Germans.[8] In fact, the Allies differed among themselves on major issues and were therefore unable to present Germany with comprehensive terms prior to the convocation of the Paris Conference.[9] Thus the Conference itself became the forum for hashing out terms for Germany among the contentious Allies, terms that were exaggerated in order to allow for concessions that, owing to public expectations inflated by these very exaggerations, could scarcely in fact be made. The Germans were not invited to participate because no decision was ever taken by the Allies whether the Paris Conference was a meeting to draft preliminary terms that, once negotiated with the Germans, would give way to a Congress of all parties, or a meeting to agree on a final settlement. In the event the "preliminary" agreement was so precarious among the Allies themselves that the Germans were not permitted to discuss its terms, and it metamorphosed into a final settlement driven by Allied fear that their domestic publics had lost patience.

The German response to the treaty with which they were confronted was one of bitter dejection. In the "Observations of the German Delegation on the Conditions of Peace," the German government expressed dismay that Germany's new constitutional arrangements—which had replaced the Kaiserreich with a parliamentary republic—had not been taken into account by the Allies. Furthermore, "[n]o recognition of [Wilson's] principles can be traced in the peace document laid before us," they wrote.

The Allied reply to this paper was brutal:

> The Allied and Associated Powers believe that they will be false to those who have given their all to save the freedom of the world if they consent to treat this war on any other basis than as a crime against humanity ... Justice is what the German delegation asks for and ... justice is what Germany shall have ... Somebody must suffer for the consequences of the war. Is it to be Germany, or only the people she has wronged?

Article 231 of the Treaty included a "war-guilt" clause by which Germany took responsibility for the war. This too was a break with earlier general settlements: Westphalia, Utrecht, and Vienna had all included amnesty clauses, deliberately omitting any distinction between victors and vanquished.[10] The Versailles Treaty instead provided for the extradition and trial of the kaiser.

Of course the Allies' charges were perfectly right: Germany had caused the war, Bethmann Hollweg's celebrated remark ("How did it all happen?") to the contrary notwithstanding. Yet the failure to discriminate between the regime that had prosecuted the war and the Weimar Republic that now ruled in Germany seems an obvious and gratuitous mistake. Had European statesmen already forgotten the counsel of Castlereagh that punitive reparations would drive the former enemy's successor regime either into disrepute with its own people or into fresh aggressions? Wilson himself had said, on January 22, 1917:

Victory would mean peace forced upon the loser, a victor's terms imposed upon the vanquished. It would be accepted in humiliation, under duress, at an intolerable sacrifice, and would leave a sting, a resentment, a bitter memory upon which terms of peace would rest, not permanently, but only as upon a quicksand.[11]

It seems clear that the victors had lost sight of the fact that they were framing a constitution for the society of states and behaved instead as though they were drafting a bill to be paid. Only Wilson saw the work of the Conference as constitutional in nature, and he contented himself with providing the procedural provisions for such a constitution, neglecting the political consensus that had to be its foundation. By eliminating Germany from this consensus, and having excluded Russia at the outset, any constitutional program, such as the kind that came out of Vienna, or Westphalia, or Utrecht or Augsburg, was doomed. But was it doomed anyway?

We have observed that the end of an epochal war provides the opportunity for creating "constitutions in the usual sense of that word because they . . . [establish] diplomatic and legal rules for international relations and [determine] the nature of future conflicts, not only among the former belligerents, but of other states in the state system as well."[12] Yet, with a hostile Bolshevik regime in Russia, and an undiscredited, popular fascist movement in Germany, the epochal war that began in 1914 was far from over. It was an obvious mistake—one that was clear to virtually all the contemporaries—not to try to shore up the Weimar Republic by a generous peace and to enlist its participation in the drafting of an international constitution under which it would have to live and whose support it would depend upon. Instead, Germany was not even permitted to join the League of Nations at its founding. But too little was settled by 1919 for us to conclude that the epochal war of this century had ended, and if there was no end to the war, there can have been no beginning to the constitutional peace that was to follow it.

As a result, the Allied leaders were sharply divided between pressing for a strategic advantage over the Germans—bearing in mind always the potential for a war with Russia as well—or ratifying a conciliatory peace that would, perforce, leave Germany in a formidable military position. This accounts for the curious schizophrenia of the peace agreement, which neither reconciled Germany nor crushed her strategic power. It also accounts for the odd combination of self-determination for some nationalities and a ruthless, pawnlike treatment of others that would have bemused even the most cynical peacemakers at Vienna. Two new states, Poland and Czechoslovakia, were created on the grounds that the Polish and the Czech nations were each entitled to a nation-state, but both these new states included a substantial number of ethnic Germans who, presumably, were no less entitled to their own state. Indeed it was perfectly plain that these new countries were purposely being created with an endowment that would make them enemies to the states from which these lands were taken, Germany and Russia. That was the victors' point: to create new allies for a future war, and to weaken the adversaries they might face in such a war. Germany and Austria were prevented from amalgamating with the Sudetenland, Alsace-Lorraine, and each other, for the treaty forbade them to unify, despite the fact that, of all the peoples of Central Europe, the Germans had the clearest claim to a single state on the grounds of national self-determination.

Georges Clemenceau is the dark figure who is blamed for injecting a venomous revanchism into the peace agreement, abetted by David Lloyd George, largely on the grounds of campaign promises made to British voters that the Germans would pay Britain's war debt (and perhaps more), and only slightly diverted by a hopelessly naïve and ineffectual Woodrow Wilson. This was Keynes's famous portrait of the world's leaders at any rate, and it has been adopted generally by historians and politicians (it is quoted in Chapter 14).

There was, of course, merit in Keynes's analysis that the reparations burden placed on Germany could not possibly have been fully liquidated, and the peace agreement generally was a punitive one. Perhaps when World War II came, as Keynes* predicted it would, he felt that this analysis had been vindicated. However that may be, the attitude that Germany had been treated unjustly, widespread among intellectuals and journalists of the period, had much to do with the feckless appeasement of the interwar years after the Nazis came to power, and the refusal by the Allies to enforce the terms of Versailles when these were contemptuously violated by Germany. The Versailles terms gave Hitler a rhetorical stick with which

---

*It is likely that the most important service performed by Keynes in 1919—he was the Treasury's representative on the British team—was to take a short manuscript from a prison camp at Monte Cassino via his diplomatic pouch to Bertrand Russell in Cambridge. This was the immortal *Tractatus Logico-Philosophicus,* written by Ludwig Wittgenstein in notebooks he carried during the war. Wittgenstein had enlisted in the Austrian army at the outset of the war, served on the eastern front and in the Tyrol as an artilleryman, and been taken prisoner by the Italians in November of 1918.

to beat the Weimar Republic: either the republic's politicians could attempt to comply with the agreement or negotiate a reduction in its terms—in either case they would be groveling supplicants to their oppressors and traitors to the German people—or they could rebel. But if they rebelled, they sacrificed the one link that gave parliamentary governance legitimacy in Germany, namely its connection to the other parliamentary states. As the German delegates had petitioned the Peace Conference in 1919: "In view of the inter-connection which exists today between conditions throughout the world no people can, however, stand alone in its development but each one, if it is to be an efficient and trustworthy member of the family of nations, needs the support of its neighbors . . ."[13] And in any case, if the German people wished to rebel against the society of states, they would not turn to the politicians of Weimar to lead such a revolution.

But was Keynes right to imply that a more generous peace would have lasted? Was Clemenceau so obviously wrong? For all of his ridicule of Wilson, it is Keynes who sounds disturbingly naïve in imagining that a reduction in reparations debts—which in the event were, in fact, dramatically reduced, as Lloyd George and others fully expected—would reconcile the German public to its defeat. It is Keynes, not Clemenceau, who treated the German and British states as if they were fungible, and who ignored the ideological strife going on with deadly earnestness in Germany and on the continent. It can surely be argued that a more generous settlement and a refusal to take territory from Germany or prevent its national consolidation would have merely made a stronger Third Reich. This point was pressed by Clemenceau in this exchange with Wilson.

WILSON: I trust that, in principle, you are agreed with Mr. Lloyd George as to the moderation which must be shown toward Germany. We do not want to destroy Germany and we could not do so: our greatest mistake would be to furnish her with powerful reasons for seeking revenge at some future time. . . . We must not give our enemies even an impression of injustice.

CLEMENCEAU: My principles are the same as yours; I am considering only their application . . . [W]hat we regard as just here in this room will not necessarily be accepted as such by the Germans . . . Their idea of justice, I assure you, is not ours . . . Shortly before he died Napoleon said, "Nothing permanent is founded on force." I am not so sure . . . You wish to do justice to the Germans. Do not believe that they will ever forgive us; they will only seek the chance for revenge.[14]

I am inclined to believe that German war resurgence had less to do with the eternal German spirit, as Clemenceau claimed to believe, than with the unsettled constitution of the German nation-state, the legitimacy of which was very much contested. It was not simply revenge that drove German politics, but the strife that resulted from three closely matched ideological candidates for control of the nation-state. Until this competition was settled, Germany could not have been a competent partner to a new constitution for the society of states. This can be seen clearly in the example of Italy, which neither suffered the loser's dismemberment nor manifested an especially warlike spirit.

Indeed Italy had been a member of the victorious alliance. Its premier, Orlando, was included in the Council of Four. On a visit to Italy in January 1919, Wilson had given his support to Italy's claim to the strategic Brenner Pass. This meant an extension of Italian rule to a large ethnically German population and was in direct contradiction to Point Nine of the Fourteen Points, which provided that a "readjustment of the frontiers of Italy should be effected along clearly recognizable lines of nationality." When the Peace Conference later convened and Italy pressed for more territorial concessions at the expense of Yugoslavia, Wilson balked and effectively checked Italian claims. The consequence was the dramatic abandonment of the Conference by Orlando, a wounded refusal to sign the Treaty, and a persistent claim for aggrandizement that the Italian fascists could exploit. It was the weakness of Orlando's domestic position and the strength of Italian fascism that allowed such a claim to become a passionate and effective means of tormenting the Italian parliamentary government in Rome. So long as the new nation-state did not have a sure ground of legitimacy, the Peace Conference could only offer opportunities for further political struggle. It could not end the domestic political conflict. Yet without ending such conflicts, the Conference itself could not produce a consensual constitution: there were not sufficient legitimate regimes that would ratify it, whatever its content.

What was wanted was a way to hedge against the strategic assets that might end up in the hands of a hostile fascist or communist state, and at the same time to shore up the fragile parliamentary regimes who would be accused by their domestic opponents of selling out the nation's strategic interests. House and Wilson thought this might be done by getting states to participate in a system of legal adjustments of political disputes: this process would tend to legitimate the governments of the participating states with their domestic publics, while defusing strategic crises. I very much doubt such reliance upon legal systems would have been feasible. That reliance depends upon an idea about law, and its power, that was far from a natural assumption for the states of the world where the basic legitimacy of the regime was a contested notion. In such environments, the political resolution provided by the operation of law does not reinforce legitimacy but only puts it in play. Law is dragged into the most intense political disputes and "exposed" as a mere façade for political action.

The settlement that finally emerged at Versailles was on the scale of, but did not share the transforming finality of, earlier constitutional settlements. The state-nation form had already been abandoned in Russia, Germany, Austria, Hungary, and Turkey, and even before the war in Portugal and China. Norway had seceded from Sweden, without the benefit of a blessing by the Conference, just as Ireland would break away four years later from Britain. Moreover, wars arising from this transition from state-nation to nation-state outlasted the "peace" of Versailles: the Greco-Turkish war began in 1920 and lingered until 1923; the Russian wars continued until 1922, involving Britain, the United States, Japan, and France in various parts of Russia;[15] the Russo-Polish War broke out in 1920 and lasted until the next year, supplanted in part by the Polish-Lithuanian War that continued until 1923.

There was widespread disillusion with the Treaty. The American Secretary of State, Lansing, noted that "the impression made of it is one of disappointment, of regret, and of depression."[16] Harold Nicolson recorded in his letters, "The more I read [the Treaty draft] the sicker it makes me . . . There is not a single person among the younger people here who is not unhappy and disappointed at the terms."[17] This disappointment, though profound, cannot simply be attributed to the failure to live up to the magnanimous peace promised by Wilson's Fourteen Points. Rather it reflected, especially among the younger persons present, the conviction that another war would soon come. The Congress model, faithfully reproduced at Versailles and sought to be institutionalized in a League of Nations, became globalized with the 1919 Conference. The society of states had expanded beyond Europe, and its peculiar pattern of war and constitution making had also spread. What was missing—and what would remain missing after World War II, whose victors did not even attempt a general peace treaty— was the political, constitutional basis *within* each of the great powers that would make a general constitution for their society possible.

To make this point, let us examine the constitutional situation of the crucial parliamentary nation-state of Germany and, following this, focus the discussion on its legal interpreters of Versailles to make the constitutional conflicts of the Weimar Republic more vivid and comprehensible.

WEIMAR

At the congresses both of Westphalia in 1648 and of Vienna in 1815, the great powers had approved a constitution for Germany. At the Peace Conference of Paris in 1919, however, this was not done, and indeed might have been thought improper in some quarters because the Versailles powers' commitment to self-determination, a principle of the nation-state, also committed them to letting each state choose its own constitution. Nevertheless, the constitution that governed postwar Germany was very much in accord with Allied political views.

In the waning days of World War I, revolution had broken out in Germany. A new government was created virtually simultaneously with the deliberations at Versailles. The day the kaiser abdicated and fled, the chancellorship was given to the Social Democrat Friedrich Ebert; the German delegates to the Paris Conference had already left Berlin by this time. After the suppression of a violent left-wing revolt, elections for a constituent assembly were held in mid-January while the Peace Conference was underway. A new national assembly met on February 6, 1919, at Weimar, a German city associated with the liberal heritage of Goethe and Schiller, which was distant in a great many ways from the Prussian capital, Berlin. There a new constitution was promulgated in August providing for a legislative body, the Reichstag, to be chosen by a system of proportional representation based on universal suffrage. This is characteristic of democracies that came of age in the era of the nation-state (whereas proportional representation is rare in democracies that originated in the state-nation period). The new constitution was made easy to amend: as little as four-ninths of the membership of the Reichstag could change the fundamental law by a constitutional convention or by referendum without any requirement of subsequent ratification by the federal states.

Under this constitution, the chief executive was given unusually broad powers: elected by a national vote to a seven-year term and eligible for re-election, he could dissolve the Reichstag and submit any law enacted by it to a public referendum. Most significantly, under the notorious Article 48, the president could suspend civil liberties in case of an emergency and rule by decree.

This constitution and the "Weimar" Republic it established were barely in place when the Allies presented their draft treaty proposals on May 7, 1919. The new German republic earnestly exemplified the parliamentary form of the nation-state,[18] whose advocates had contended in German politics since their break with Bismarck in 1878–1879. Nevertheless, the treaty terms were harsh. In addition to the various European cessions extracted from Germany—Upper Silesia, most of Posen, and what is now Pomerania all went to Poland; North Schleswig went to Denmark; three small frontier districts went to Belgium; Memel went to Lithuania; Alsace-Lorraine and the subsoil rights to the mines of the Saar went to France—all German colonies were handed over to the Allies, who were also to occupy the west bank of the Rhine for an unspecified period between five and fifteen years, a period during which France was to administer the Saar, whose ultimate future would be determined by plebiscite. The German army was to be limited to 100,000 troops (no more than 4,000 of whom could be officers); the navy was similarly reduced; the German general staff was dissolved; no military aircraft were allowed; artillery was limited to 105 mm guns;* and vast quantities of war matériel were handed over to the Allies.

Although the treaty made no final determination of reparations, Germany was to make an initial down payment of twenty billion gold marks. German assets abroad were confiscated, and the German merchant fleet was reduced by 90 percent.

There was a widespread reaction among Germans, shared by all parties including the Left, that Germany had been tricked into an armistice by the inducement of the Fourteen Points and then presented with a punitive settlement agreement once it had sacrificed any defensible military position. In June the Allies presented an ultimatum. The Weimar chancellor, Schneidermann, who opposed ratification, was forced to resign. On June 23, with Germany facing famine and there really being no alternative, the Reichstag voted to accept the treaty terms.

The Weimar coalition of Social Democrats and two center parties continued to govern until the elections of June 1920, when parties to the left and right of the coalition gained strength. A new chancellor formed a coalition with the center parties, joined by a right-wing populist party and without the Social Democrats.

A right-wing coup d'état was attempted in March 1920, but it failed. There were left-wing armed revolts in 1920 and again in 1921, but gradually the republic stabilized. On April 27, 1921, the Allied Reparation Commission fixed the amount to be paid by Germany at 132 billion gold marks. The German government immediately fell, but the new chancellor nevertheless managed to secure a pointless acceptance by the Reichstag—the sum was far in excess of Germany's ability to pay. When a technical default in timber deliveries occurred, the French used this as a pretext for occupying the industrial Ruhr Valley. The value of the German mark deteriorated steadily, partly owing to reparations transfers and partly to the result of monetary expansion to cover budget deficits. Inflation flared wildly. In 1922, the value of the mark fell from 162 marks per U.S. dollar to more than 7,000.

This situation was considerably exacerbated by France's seizure of the Ruhr, to which the German government responded by organizing a campaign of passive resistance. French occupation forces replied with mass arrests, and with an economic blockade that cut off the greater part of the

---

*Which had the unintended effect of precipitating the rapid development of German rocketry. William B. Breuer, *Race to the Moon: America's Duel with the Soviets* (Praeger, 1993), 10.

occupied Rhineland from the rest of Germany. By July 1, the mark had fallen to 160,000 to the dollar (the prewar figure had been 4.2 marks to the dollar); by November 20, to 4.2 trillion to the dollar. Barter replaced currency; food riots broke out; savings and pensions were erased.

The extreme parties gained by this situation, their ranks swollen by veterans who formed paramilitary groups attached to left-wing and right-wing movements. The communists attempted a revolt in Hamburg in October 1923; the fascists attempted a coup in Munich on November 8 of the same year. A new chancellor, however, Gustav Stresemann, canceled the campaign of passive resistance, resumed reparation deliveries, simultaneously declaring an emergency and using the army to suppress the uprisings. Gradually, better relations were established with the Allies. Inflation was brought down by the issuance of a new mark, supported by mortgages on the entire industrial and agricultural resources of the country. Foreign investment began to flow back into Germany, and production, as well as employment, boomed. A new reparations agreement, the Dawes Plan, restructured the reparations schedule and provided for foreign loans; eventually the total amount was set at 121 billion marks, to be paid over a period of sixty years.

Throughout this period, Germany's relations with the international community were a principal domestic political issue. Stresemann, now foreign minister, pledged to fulfill German treaty obligations, which had the effect of securing substantial Allied concessions, and restoring Germany's international stature; but his policies were violently attacked within the country. In return for German acceptance of the Dawes figures, Stresemann won the withdrawal of French troops from the Ruhr in 1924. In return for a renunciation of claims on Alsace-Lorraine and guarantees of the Versailles borders, Germany gained the Allies' evacuation of the Cologne zone of the occupied Rhineland, and entry into the League of Nations in 1926.

These links to the international community were largely responsible for Germany's recovery and Stresemann has been rightly honored for forging them, but they also meant that German prosperity was dependent on foreign credit so that when the worldwide depression caused a contraction of liquidity and a sharp reduction in overseas Allied investment, Germany was particularly vulnerable. Moreover, the actions of foreign governments—like the blocking of a customs union between Austria and Germany by French and Italian opposition—were viewed in Germany, not unreasonably, as impeding any economic rebound.

Through all this, Hitler rose to power. He made his first public impression, and he continued to draw audiences, and hold and augment them, by delivering the same speech over and over again: a vitriolic speech entitled, *The Treaty of Versailles*.[19]

Notice that this is an example of an inner constitutional movement—the fascist attempt to seize the German nation-state—in reaction to an external constitutional movement—the attempt by the society of nation-states to impose a parliamentary form on Germany. Hitler saw this relationship and we must not miss it.

In early 1932, the number of unemployed reached six million, or about one-third of the workforce. The Nazi Party, which had come into being out of hostility to the Versailles Treaty,* became the largest party in the legislature of Prussia, the largest of the German states. Adolf Hitler, the party leader, came in second in the national presidential election to the incumbent, the venerated World War I general Paul von Hindenburg. After the election, a new chancellor was named, Franz von Papen, who negotiated the virtual abolition of reparations at a conference in Lausanne in June 1932; a lump-sum payment of three billion marks was to be made into a fund for European conservation.

Nevertheless, elections in July gave the Nazis 230 out of 647 seats in the Reichstag. They immediately brought down von Papen when the parliamentary session began, and he then dissolved the Reichstag and began to govern by decree, as provided by the constitution. Fresh elections were held in November; a new chancellor was named, General Kurt von Schleicher, but he too was unable to put together a governing coalition. This time Hindenburg refused to permit the Reichstag to be dissolved. In this crisis, von Papen brokered a deal whereby the Nazi Party would be brought into a governing coalition. The Nazi ministers would be heavily outnumbered in the cabinet and would hold no key posts, but the chancellorship would go to Hitler. On January 30, 1933, he was given the seals of office.

Hitler immediately pressed for fresh elections, reassuring the cabinet that the composition of the coalition would remain unchanged. The election day was set for March 5. On the night of February 27, however, the Reichstag building was destroyed by arson. On the plausible pretext that this event presaged a Communist coup, Hitler assumed emergency powers. In the election, the Nazis increased their numbers to 288 and with the 52 conservative Nationalist members achieved a working majority.

Now Hitler proposed the Enabling Act, which would allow the government to rule by decree independently of the Reichstag or the president.

---

*Nor was this a unique reaction. We should bear in mind that in 1919, student protests against the Chinese government's negotiations at Versailles led to the May 4 movement from which the Chinese Communist Party eventually emerged. And Lenin said in Moscow on October 8, 1920, that by attacking Poland "we are destroying the Versailles settlement."

Such a step required a two-thirds majority, but this was achieved once Hitler was able to persuade the center party to support the measure. The Enabling Act remained the statutory basis for Hitler's dictatorship throughout the Third Reich. Prior to this, the Weimar constitution had permitted several chancellors to stay in office even after the president had dissolved the parliament in which the chancellor had held his majority; these chancellors had continued to govern through the use of presidential emergency powers, and by legislating on the basis of powers previously delegated to them by the Reichstag.[20] The Enabling Act was a more extreme step in the direction of making the *emergency* state a continuous constitutional one.

CONSTITUTIONAL INTERPRETATION: THE LEGAL PHILOSPHERS

Weimar presents a drama that illuminates the constitutional difficulty that faced the peacemakers at Versailles, for in Weimar[21] the constitutional problems that led to and extenuated the Long War were conspicuously acute. We can usefully link these problems with the important legal interpreters who addressed them, and gain an understanding of the moral choices facing constitutional decision makers at this historic juncture.

First, there was the transition from the state-nation to the nation-state, which required a complete rethinking about the sources of state legitimacy; the legal figure most associated with this rethinking in Germany was Georg Jellinek. Second, there was the unresolved ideological conflict among liberals, fascists, and communists, a conflict that reflected in miniature the worldwide struggle that would last until the end of the 1980s. Two emblematic Weimar figures symbolized for their contemporaries the liberal and fascist approaches to the bases for law: Hans Kelsen and Carl Schmitt; to them should be added the leading members of the Marxist Frankfurt School. Their three approaches to the construction of constitutional jurisprudence were fundamentally incompatible; there was no mediating approach that could reconcile them. In such circumstances, Germany—and the world for which Germany provided a stage for this struggle—had to resolve the conflict by the triumph of one approach and the destruction of the others before a constitution for Germany (or for Europe) could endure.

JELLINEK

Georg Jellinek was born in Leipzig in 1851, the child of a highly distinguished Moravian Jewish family.[22] Like many of his contemporaries,

Georg Jellinek converted to Christianity, perhaps to remove any legal disabilities that were attached to Jews.

Jellinek taught in Vienna for ten years (1879–1889), briefly at Basel (1890–1891), and for the last twenty years at Heidelberg (1891–1911). He achieved international fame with *Die Erklärung der Menschen- und Bürgerrechte* (1895), which was translated in 1901 into English as *The Declaration of the Rights of Man and of Citizens*. This book presented the thesis that the French Declaration of the Rights of Man was derived not so much from the thought of Rousseau, as was (and is today) generally believed, but largely from the Anglo-American theories used to support the American Revolution. Book I of the present work suggested a similar relationship.

The State, Jellinek held, is a psychological mass-function. It has no reality apart from its human constituents, who associate in order to form a community of purpose. This emphasis on the nation's role in endowing the State with meaning is the nation-state's reversal of the ideology of the state-nation, which held that it was the State that endowed the nation with meaning.[23] Jellinek saw that the legitimacy of the State itself was at stake whenever it changed constitutional form. "To think of the sovereign as a 'determinate human superior' without qualifications concerning the legitimacy of this superior's position . . . is a misunderstanding derived from the days of autocratic monarchy."[24]

Jellinek analyzed law through two overlays: sociological and normative. These two are in some tension, for according to the former analysis, a legal rule earns the status of law to the degree it is accepted, as reflected in popular behavior; whereas for the latter approach, a legal rule retains the status of law even if it is disobeyed. Reconciling the two perspectives is critical to Jellinek's overall view.

On that view, only a valid law is part of the legal order; the test of that validity is the ability of a norm to motivate compliance by engendering a sense of obligation, and because we only feel a sense of obligation to those laws we believe are valid, Jellinek's characterization is refreshingly non-foundational.* A valid law is simply one that is accepted as valid.

It seems generally true of human nature that it regards that which is seen to exist in fact, especially over a period of time, as normal, i.e., as establishing a norm. To find a reasonable justification for this normative power of facts would be wrong; whatever actually exists can be rationalized later; its immediate normative significance lies in the irrational acceptance of what is known and practiced as being right.[25]

---

*In contrast to the legal philosophers of earlier periods who sought an external validation, e.g., the command of the sovereign (Austin) or natural law (Pufendorf).

In contrast to Austin, Jellinek rejected the idea that coercion can render a law valid: if coercion were the validating element, then any legal rule could be law, whereas we know that actual laws are constrained by real conditions. Moreover, any positivistic rule that postulates the existence of the State prior to law and postulates the State as the only source of law will be unable to account for the validity of international law. On the other hand, Jellinek conceded that there is no *Volk,* no nation, that validates international law by virtue of its traditions and culture.

This argument led Jellinek to his most famous formulation, the idea of autolimitation. It is a crucial notion for the nation-state, because the State is held to derive its authority from the nation. If the State promulgates law, how can it bind itself? If the nation is the source of authority, how can it be bound? Jellinek concludes that the State is bound by norms, the content of which it controls to this extent: the nation authorizes the State to act according to the norms the nation recognizes; the State chooses those norms that serve as the substantive content of the law it enacts. This means the State must agree to limit itself according to the norms it serves. And this also accounts for international law: not just the will of a single state, but rather the collective autolimitation of a number of states acting in accord produces international law. One consequence of this view was the discrediting of the former state-nation structure of the German Confederation, which the Congress of Vienna had set up, because the confederation form was backed solely by international law and thus was a weak and ineffectual structure, having no roots in a national society to supply a sense of obligation.

Jellinek's views are a good summary of the jurisprudence available to the statesmen who took the nation-state of the Kaiserreich into the nation-state of the Weimar Republic. That Jellinek's fundamental postulates—the normativity and theoretically independent validity of law, and its dependence in fact on the real existence of the politically organized *Volk*— would prove incompatible was quickly evident in the new state. In the first direction went the liberals, who maintained the integrity of the law above politics; in the second direction went the fascists and the communists, who demonstrated that law could not function in an atmosphere of violent political discord.

KELSEN

The leading figure of twentieth century jurisprudence was Hans Kelsen. Born in Prague in 1881, Kelsen was a professor of law at the University of Vienna in October 1918 when the Emperor Karl restructured the Austro-Hungarian empire. Later Kelsen became an important drafter of the post-war Austrian constitution, which, like that of Weimar, was organized according to parliamentary nation-state ideas. His principal contribution to this effort was the shaping of the Constitutional Court, to which he was named justice and general rapporteur, a post he held until he was deposed in 1929.[26] In 1930 he became a professor at the University of Cologne. After emigrating to the United States in 1940 he taught at Harvard and then at Berkeley.

Jellinek and others recognized that law is normative (that it sets a standard) and therefore different from social facts (which are as they are, not necessarily as they should be). Kelsen's fundamental insight was that the full significance of this distinction had not been appreciated. This led him to two postulates: (1) the relative nature of law, and (2) the essential criterion of formality. Kelsen's working out of these two principles led him to a third, (3) the primacy of international law.

Jellinek conceded that law asserts norms, and he acknowledged that juristic concepts do not decide natural facts,[27] but he made law depend upon the psychological fact of acceptance. For Jellinek, the normative power of a legal rule depends upon its motivating power; its validity is a matter of its effectiveness. This introduces the world of causality, which is a feature peculiar to the world of natural reality. This move, in Kelsen's words, overlooks the fundamental characteristic of any norm: "that it is a rule not of but for human behavior."[28]

No idea of Kelsen's is more celebrated or more misapprehended than this distinction between norm and fact. Relying on the Kantian idea that the categories of a field constitute its facts for it, Kelsen rejected Jellinek's assumption that sociology and jurisprudence have the same subject matter. This move led to Kelsen's description of the relative nature of law and not, as is usually asserted, the absolute nature of law, isolated from all culture.

Consider the neo-Kantian distinction between a *practical* and a *theoretical* science. A practical science (like Kant's practical reason) tries to bring about factual conditions in accordance with some desired standard; this standard is the normative. Every practicing politician, no less than every minister delivering a sermon, reflects such practical reason in his or her program. By contrast, a theoretical science determines the object of its discipline and explains and unifies the data that are factual for it. Every theoretical physicist, no less than every historian, must collect and attempt to explain the facts of his or her study.

Jellinek too had distinguished between theoretical and practical science by claiming that a theory is explanatory, while a practice is applied. Kelsen, however, contended that the distinction between theory and practice is a relative one, and that it depends upon the further distinction between fact and norm. The relevant facts for a theoretical science are different from those of a practical science, though both must deal with facts.

The real difference between theory and practice is that each deals with different facts and has a different role for norms. This is the key to law's relativity. Vis-à-vis the social sciences, law is practical and has a normative aspect, whereas social sciences deal in social facts as they are; in such a context, law is a norm. But vis-à-vis politics, morality, ethics, and philosophy, jurisprudence is theoretical and in this context law is only a fact. Whether a law is wise or just or cruel is an important question, but not one for jurisprudence; whether studies show us that most French citizens do not report all their earned income does not bear on whether the French income tax law provides that such income is reportable.

Kelsen's first postulate then was that law has a Janus face; to ignore either of its visages is to assimilate it into a different discipline and thereby distort its true subject. The sociology of law, for example, is desirable as a guide to the development of new law, but such studies do not make up jurisprudence because they treat law not as a norm, but as a causal factor. Such efforts, in their "desire to explain how law 'actually happens[,]' [try] to put legal norms on the level with laws of nature." Unlike the law of gravity, however, a legal norm is not always obeyed; indeed, there must be the possibility of disobedience or the rule would not embody a norm. For this reason, Kelsen disagrees with Oliver Wendell Holmes, Jr.: jurisprudence is not a prediction of what courts will in fact do, as Holmes concluded, but an assertion of what they ought to do.

At the same time, however, the norms of law are not those of justice. If law reveals its normative face in the presence of social science, it is a mistake to conclude that the standards of normative disciplines—ethics and morality, for example—are coextensive with those of law. This is hard to accept because, Kelsen wrote, we are inclined to identify law with justice in order to justify a given social order. There seems to be an irresistible urge to use jurisprudence as a means of attacking a particular social system (or promoting one). This, however, is beyond the cognition of legal science. To decide whether a norm is law, one must look to the presence of certain formal elements. After all, there are many wholesome rules of life that are not adopted by the legislature and enforced in actions before courts. Moeover, to decide whether a law is just, one cannot look to any criteria in the law itself, for both just and unjust rules can be (and are) embodied in valid laws.

This brings up the question: when is a law valid, if it is not when it is just? Kelsen's answer is that a valid law is one that follows that logical form* that is unique to the discipline of law. That particular logical form reflects the internal order of the law itself: law is a specific technique for

---

*For the philosophically inclined reader, Kelsen's rendering will be strikingly reminiscent of Ludwig Wittgenstein's *Tractatus Logico-Philosophicus*.

social control that, unlike such other techniques as religion or morality, which also offer forms of ordering relations, depends upon the invocation of a particular coercive sanction by an enforcing official as the consequence of an unlawful act. This internal logic is therefore the logic of the hypothetical: if X occurs, then Y ought to follow. Therefore, Kelsen argued, the logical form of a legal proposition must also be that of a hypothetical: if an act is performed (or fails to be performed) such that an event ensues, then enforcement by an official of a sanction against the actor responsible for the event can result. This hypothetical states the fundamental logical form of the legal proposition.[29] If the advocacy of a crime actually produces that crime, then the police can arrest the advocate; if the failure to maintain proper brakes actually results in an accident, then the magistrate can hold the automobile owner liable for the damages resulting from the accident; if the parties to a contract agree to perform certain acts, and the execution of a contract memorializes this agreement, then a court can enforce the agreement against the parties; and so on.

This view—which Kelsen called the "Pure Theory" of law—has significant implications for the various views it is attempting to displace. For example, one familiar answer to the question how we know when a law is valid is whether the positive law in question corresponds with natural law. On Kelsen's view, however, positive and natural law can't both be law at the same time. If they are the same, then one scarcely needs positive law;[30] if they are different, then one formulation or the other is not law because both can't correspond to the formal expression indicated and be noncontradictory if they are not the same.

Similarly, Kelsen dismisses Jellinek's proposal that it is the efficacy of law that makes it valid; there is no term for efficacy in the formal proposition. Even an ineffective law would still be law if it corresponded to the formal expression that is inherent in legal rules. Even if, that is, an official were bribed and did not enforce a law, it would still be law—and why not, because if it weren't still law, there would be no need to bribe the official. Indeed one might say that, according to Kelsen's view, law takes place precisely when its exhortations are not wholly effective, i.e., when it has failed to be followed, and an organ of the State is therefore engaged to render a sanction in order to bring about compliance.

Notice that Kelsen's formulation directs the rule to an organ of the State and not to the subject of the rule. This has the effect of doing away with fictions like *the will of the people* or the *intention of the legislature* and other metaphysical entities like *the sovereign*. All the elements in Kelsen's formula are observable statements of fact (though again it must be said that they are facts about norms—otherwise one runs the risk of confusing Kelsen with the behaviorists). There is no need for Austin's fictional *command.*

But if we give up Austin's sovereign, what legitimates a legal rule? The answer is found in Kelsen's description of a legal order as a hierarchy of norms.

> To the question why a certain act of coercion . . . is a legal act, the answer is: because it has been prescribed by an individual norm, a judicial decision. To the question why this individual norm is valid . . . the answer is: because it has been created in conformity with a criminal statute. This statute, finally, receives its validity from the constitution, since it has been established by the competent organ in the way the constitution prescribes.[31]

What then legitimates the constitution? It is its correspondence with what Kelsen chooses to call "the basic norm" (*Grundnorm*). The basic norm "may state that the will of the king shall constitute law because he holds his authority by the grace of God, or it may say that what the medicine man declares taboo ought to be avoided because he has communion with the spirits."

Of this basic norm many things can be said; indeed Book I of the present work is in part a history of the morphogenesis of such norms. But these things cannot be said within the discipline of jurisprudence, for which the basic norm is a fundamental datum that simply must be taken as it is. For jurisprudence the basic norm is a necessary condition, but not a cause. It will be evident from this description that while he provides an account of the legitimacy of a state's constitution, Kelsen does not provide for the legitimacy of the State itself.

For Jellinek the State had been a sociological fact, a thought-content common to a group of people; that it could also be the subject of a juristic account posed no problems for him. Jellinek held that the same object can be a datum for different realms of cognition, as a symphony can be described both according to aesthetics and according to physics. Kelsen strongly disputed this. Indeed he took Jellinek's example, the symphony, and turned it against him: the mere physical description of sounds might be called many things, but not a symphony.[32] The State is a juristic phenomenon. The sociologist has to presuppose a legal order so that he or she may then describe the State. Therefore no sociological account can provide for the legitimate basis of the State.

The world is made up of facts.[33] Statements that evaluate rules can do so on a factual basis (for example, a change in tort liability might lead to a more or less efficient outcome), but if these statements purport to do so on a normative basis (a more efficient tort rule is a better tort rule), they do not state facts. A thought is a fact; the totality of true thoughts would be a representation of the world. By contrast, all human institutions are nothing more than various orders, sets of rules, and thus they are normative. Institutions, therefore, have no real existence. The legitimation of the State cannot come from the fact of the law because a fact cannot legitimate, cannot provide a normative outcome. The mere presence of a constitution cannot legitimate a state. Nor can this legitimation come from the normative dimension of constitutional law because the State is merely the juridical employee of constitutional law. Some *other* normative order must legitimate the State.

The State has the juridical status of a corporation: it exists by virtue of a superior legal order that endows it with validity. Because the validity of a legal order is a matter of its correspondence with a norm, it follows that a state can be legitimated by its correspondence to those rules that are the product of interstate norms. In other words, the state is legitimated by the norms of international law, not constitutional law.

> . . . All legal formations may be arranged as a continuous line of formations gradually passing into one another. This continuous line starts with the contractual community of private law, leads to the association, the municipality, the country, the member-state, the federal state, the unitary state, unions of states, and treaty communities of international law, and ends in the universal international community.[34]

Kelsen's argument for the primacy of international law can be summarized as follows: only one normative system can be valid at one time; if the State was the creator of its own total legal order, these various orders would have to be consistent in order for there to be international law; there is an international legal order because its propositions can be stated in terms of the fundamental legal sentence formalized above; therefore, while it is possible that international law is delegated from the various states, if there is an international legal order—and Kelsen analogizes it to a primitive legal order where self-help is the principal law-enforcement regime—then it is reasonable to conclude that national authority is delegated from international authority, not the reverse.

A number of interesting conclusions may be drawn from Kelsen's views. First, the State simply drops out as a real entity. In Kelsen's words, the State "plays the same role as that of God in metaphysics and gave rise to the same problem, the reconciliation of sovereignty and legal limitation," the problem that Jellinek sought to solve by autolimitation, the problem that theologians struggle with when they undertake to reconcile the existence of free will in the world where there is an omnipotent god. The State is a kind of ghost in the machinery of official acts, which correct analysis can eliminate the way analytical psychology eliminates the soul.

Second, the status of revolutionary states that challenge the international status quo is delegitimated, whereas otherwise the different moral and political qualities of states are treated relativistically. That is, each is derived from a broad legitimacy and differs from every other insofar as some fundamental, local social norm is being followed, the evaluation of which is beyond the scope of law.

Third, there is a strong implication that "political theology"—the focus on value-laden dogma and dialectic—unnecessarily makes the achievement of an harmonious legal order more difficult.

Fourth, the emphasis on the application, rather than the creation, of norms suggests a constitutional emphasis on the judiciary rather than on the executive or legislative.

In sum, Kelsen's is the jurisprudence of Versailles and Weimar, and as such it was at the epicenter of the political hurricane building in Germany in the 1920s and 1930s.

SCHMITT

Kelsen sought a jurisprudence that would support "a government of laws, not of men." Lawfulness is the measure of legality. Such a jurisprudence is stifling, however, when it confronts a treaty that though lawfully ratified is believed to be the instrument of oppression, or when it encounters parliamentary maneuverings that though procedurally correct are the subject of universal contempt. Hans Linde has written:

> It was inevitable that a theory which thought it beyond the competence
> of legal science to attempt a solution of, or even to recognize, the social
> and economic problems foremost in the contemporary public con-
> sciousness would meet with considerable opposition.*

Many Germans sought a jurisprudence that would locate the criteria of legality in the substantive content and real-world effects of the law.

This movement included Marxists, pragmatists, nationalists, sociologists, and others, who all agreed that law was first and foremost an element in human culture and therefore that it must be understood in its relation to the totality of the cultural milieu. Whereas the neo-Kantians, of whom Kelsen was the most prominent, held that the test of legality lay in the correspondence between the legal rule and the formal requirements of a legal proposition, these neo-Hegelians believed that legality was derived from a correspondence between the legal rule and the cultural needs and identity

---

*Linde, 99. It is interesting that logical positivism—which renounced any possible philosophical contribution to moral and political debate and indeed held that all metaphysical statements are nonsense—also reached its zenith of influence at this morally and politically fraught time.

of the society. It was the duty of the neo-Hegelians to expose the derivative nature of legalization, and to show how cultural institutions tended to serve certain interests. Such a view tended to legitimate change (as the needs of the culture changed) instead of reinforcing stasis.

The most forceful critic of Kelsen and the legal order of Versailles and Weimar was undoubtedly Carl Schmitt. His early reputation in the 1920s was built upon his savage criticism of liberal ideas and institutions. His "debunking of parliamentary government and his exposes of liberal hypocrisy remain influential,"[35] particularly on the Left, although Schmitt himself was an ardent fascist. The enduring interest in this figure must be attributed partly to the Nietzschean glamour of his aphoristic prose, but also partly to his role as the chief juristic apologist for the Nazi regime. He was, Herbert Marcuse said, the most brilliant of all the Nazis, and this alone would lend a certain fascinating horror to his writing.

The Versailles settlement meant that Schmitt could not receive a post at the university where he had qualified as a law professor because Strasbourg was now a part of France.[36] Instead he found a lectureship at the Business School in Munich and began a prolific career as a scholar and polemicist.[37] In 1921, Schmitt moved to the University of Bonn and began the work for which he is best known today.

In 1922, his small booklet *Political Theology*[38] appeared, which began with the famous sentence "Sovereign is he who decides on the state of exception." This electrifying expression was strikingly unconventional because, unlike Jellinek's and Kelsen's, its definition of sovereignty addressed the power structure of the State instead of its legal framework. In a single sentence, it captures the essential idea of the "Führer," a leader embodying sovereignty who can thus decide when the rules of law can be suspended, and it unites this idea with the most profound identity of the State. The State is not driven by law: rather law is the State's creature, to be used as the State determines. The following year he published *The Crisis of Parliamentary Democracy,*[39] which attacked liberal parliamentarianism and drew a sharp distinction between democracy and representative government. Then came *The Concept of the Political,*[40] which introduced the friend/enemy distinction as the basis for all politics, the idea for which Schmitt is best known.

In 1933 Schmitt accepted an offer from the University of Cologne. He had previously visited the most renowned member of that faculty, Kelsen, and asked his support for the appointment despite their controversies in the past. Kelsen had obliged. On March 23 of that year, the Reichstag adopted the Enabling Act, empowering Hitler to rule by decree. In April, Jews were banned from university posts; Schmitt was the only law professor at Cologne not to sign a petition on behalf of Kelsen, who was removed. On May 1, Schmitt became a member of the Nazi Party.

In November Schmitt became the head of the professors' branch of the Nazi legal organization; in June 1934 he was made editor-in-chief of the leading law journal. He was given a chair at his alma mater, the most prestigious German university, the Royal Friedrich-Wilhelms in Berlin.

After the war he was interrogated at Nuremberg, but was not prosecuted. He never held another university post.

Schmitt lived on in West Germany until his death in 1985. He maintained always that he had been the victim of the Nazis, forced into collaboration by the politicians who voted for the Enabling Act. He called his house San Casciano, in an allusion to the place where Machiavelli spent his exile writing the *Discorsi* and the *Principe*. Schmitt described himself as a kind of Benito Cereno—the character in a Melville novel who, as captain of a slave ship taken over by slaves in a revolt, is forced to sail to Senegal. His peculiar behavior and unusual activities on board the ship are observed by the captain of an American boat who does not really appreciate what is going on; only later, when Cereno escapes to the American vessel, is everything explained.

Schmitt's jurisprudence reflects four notable ideas: (1) that the crisis in Weimar Germany can be traced to its constitutional order—liberal parliamentarianism—and that this order was imposed on Germany by the Versailles Conference, whose directorate attempted to compose a society of states with similar liberal parliamentary constitutional orders; (2) that the State defines itself by the distinction it draws between friend and enemy, and that it achieves unity and makes homogeneity possible (without which unity is impossible) through its reliance on this distinction;[41] (3) that sovereignty is the power to determine when an emergency situation exists and thus when the legal rules that ordinarily govern should be suspended; (4) the relationship Schmitt draws between rule, order, and decision that is sometimes labeled "decisionism," including his distinction between the commissarial and sovereign dictatorships—between, that is, a dictator who suspends the constitution in a case of emergency in order to protect the substance of the constitution, and the dictator whose intention is to produce an entirely new constitution by abrogating the present constitution.

Schmitt despised the Weimar regime and also the parliamentary democracies of which it was a copy, which had forced the Versailles agreement on Germany. All of these elements were interlocked in Schmitt's thought: that the parliamentary democracies represented only one version of a new constitutional order, the nation-state; that their victory in the war prompted the Germans to copy their constitutional form at Weimar; that the Peace Conference composed of the society of such states then ratified its consensus on this form, and imposed this form on the states of Europe and much of the world. For this reason, it is sometimes hard to see whether the basis of Schmitt's views lies in his hostility to Versailles or to Weimar.

According to Schmitt, parliamentarianism—which he called "government by discussion"—is an ineffectual and ultimately self-destructive guardian of the State, and thus was unable to protect German interests abroad or even to bring about stability at home. Moreover, parliamentarianism's claim to democracy is a fraudulent one; it is merely a ruse to allow government by an intellectual and liberal hierarchy. True democracy relies on the principle that equals are treated equally and, just as importantly, that unequals are not treated equally. Thus true democracy requires homogeneity—the assemblage of equals—and, sometimes, the eradication of heterogeneity.* In Schmitt's view, a democracy can only maintain itself by protecting its homogeneity. But parliamentarianism, because it depends on a pluralistic coalition of interest groups and because it is too weak to take decisions, will never be able to secure homogeneity. Immigration of minority groups will be unimpeded, and thus increase the fragmentation of the society. In the weak parliament that results, special interests will be able to tie up legislative action and thus frustrate true democracy.

For Schmitt, parliamentarianism is that constitutional system that serves the bourgeois interests that support liberalism. First, it subordinates the monarchy and aristocracy and thereby elevates the middle class to a position of governance; at the same time, it co-opts democracy by channeling the power of the more numerous working class into stalemated parliamentary maneuvers and into the separated, and therefore powerless, branches of government. Second, parliamentarianism establishes a normative order that secures the structure of a market economy, restricting the taking of property by the government and using public power to enforce private agreements. Third, parliamentarianism enshrines civil liberties that are of the greatest value to the professional and merchant classes and thereby gives the imprimatur of legitimacy to the tools of political dominance of one class.

Every legal order, according to Schmitt, is the reflection of a concrete social and political order in which some individuals or groups rule over others; the unusual thing about liberal parliamentarianism is that it seeks to conceal the dominance of the bourgeoisie behind a façade of legal procedures. Parliaments are useful in order to let certain measures through when these benefit private interest groups (claiming that these reflect the will of the majority and therefore must become law) and to bottle others up when they would undermine the interests of the bourgeoisie. In either case the clash of values that lies at the heart of politics, the resolution of which is the purpose of politics, is buried or even denied in the larger allegiance to the law and to lawful procedures.

*Schmitt cited both the Turkish democracy's expulsion of Greeks and the Australian provisions for restricted immigration by Asians as examples.

Kelsen and Schmitt agree that we live in an age of relativity, that is, an age without a single overarching, governing norm. Liberalism's solution to this vacuum of received authority is rationality. Let people believe what they wish; all people are rational and seek self-preservation; governments exist because it makes sense for them to exist from the point of view of the individual who seeks protection—no matter what other views he or she may have. By stripping the State of any particular legitimating myth, however, Schmitt thinks that liberalism perpetuates the greatest myth of all, the depersonalized, rational, mechanistic operation of the law. "Eventually, as part of the logic of the process, all that will matter is that the machinery functions, on the one condition that the subjects continue to enjoy protection so they can go about their own lives."

By thus making civil society the field of competition for numberless private myths, the State sows the seeds of its own destruction because it has become marginal to the production of meaning, while private interest groups, each organized around its own myth, try to capture the machine of government. Meanwhile the lives of its citizens dissolve into consumerism, hedonism, and an attraction to cults.

The change in the constitutional role of the individual conscience, from something wholly marginal in Hobbes to something so central that it is the justification for the State's existence, is (according to Schmitt) the work of Jewish philosophers such as Spinoza and Moses Mendelssohn, who wished to cripple the state out of self-interest, and whose intellectual descendant is Hans Kelsen. This change leads to the gradual abolition of politics; indeed Schmitt takes liberals as attempting to reduce as far as possible the necessity of politics by establishing the supremacy of impersonal law. Such a world would lack the ambiance that can exist only when there is the possibility of sacrifice on behalf of a common ideal. This is, as Schmitt concluded in a lecture in 1929, "the loss of all that is noble and worthwhile; it is the loss of life itself."[42] For Schmitt as for modern-day communitarians, "[s]omething more than the economic hedonism of a crude liberal individualism, some idea of belonging to a well-defined community, is needed to impart worth to individual lives."[43] "[T]he value of life stems not from reasoning," Schmitt wrote, "it emerges in a state of war where men inspirited by myths do battle."

For Schmitt[44] all concepts of law are fundamentally political. Indeed, "[e]very form of political life stands in an immediate, reciprocal structural relationship with its specific modality of legal argumentation and thought."[45] Because the standard modalities of liberal parliamentarian legal thought are not hierarchical—because the liberal claims to be neutral among the forms of legal argument—there is no rational way to resolve conflicts among them.[46] Hence liberalism's claim to rely on rationality is either a fraud and masks the effort of the bourgeoisie to maximize their power, or an impossibility, which will necessarily give way to defeat by specific interest groups that can impose an agenda that ranks legal choices rationally according to how their interests are served. The judge, not the norm, decides; the politician, not the process, picks the judge; the legislator, not the law, determines the jurisdiction of the court; the constitutional authority, not the constitution, grants the power to legislate. Thus the liberal legal order is doomed to undermine itself because when it finally does act, it exposes the parliamentary order to be the acts of men, not of laws.

Finally, liberal democracy finds its ideal in eternal discussion and compromise, whereas great political issues admit of no compromise. Just as "[b]etween Catholicism and atheism there is no compromise," so between dictatorship and anarchy there is no mediator.

The Concept of the Political (1928) begins with the sentence "The concept of the State presupposes the concept of the political." The political, in turn, depends upon Schmitt's famous distinction between enemies and friends.

> The specific political distinction that is the basis for all political activity and impulses is the distinction between friend and enemy . . . The point of the distinction between friend and enemy is to denote the highest possible intensity of a union or separation, of an association or disassociation. . . . The political enemy need not be morally evil or aesthetically ugly; he does not have to make an appearance as an economic competitor, and it can even be advantageous to do business with him. However, he is the other, the stranger. It suffices for his being that he is in some specially intensive sense something existentially different and strange, so that in the extreme case conflicts with him are possible which cannot be decided by some predetermined general norm or by the pronouncement of some "disinterested" and thus "unpartisan" third party.

Schmitt's choice of the word *enemy* is not mere hyperbole:

> the friend and enemy concepts are to be understood in their concrete and existential sense, not as metaphors or symbols[47] . . . To the enemy concept belongs the ever-present possibility of combat. . . . The friend, enemy, and combat concepts receive their real meaning precisely because they refer to the real possibility of physical killing . . .[48] What makes politics special, what lends it its "specific political tension," is the shadow of violent personal extinction cast over all genuinely political action. "The political" lofts citizens above the "economic" by confronting them with a mortal enemy, with the threat of violent death at the hands of a hostile group.[49]

Many conclusions are drawn from this vivid, even harrowing idea. A constitution depends on an act of sovereign decision; sovereignty is created by the political decision to constitute the political unity of a people—that is, the institutionalization of a particular friend/enemy distinction. Only when the criteria for being a fellow member of a homogeneous nation have been determined—an existential matter—is the authority created not only for politics but, a fortiori, for law.

Schmitt is able to draw sharp criticisms of parliamentarianism and socialism from this distinction. According to Schmitt, the parliamentarians usually divide conflict into three types—conflicts of interest, ideas, and ultimate values—and deal with these by means of negotiation and compromise, rational debate and voting, and the privatization of the spiritual, respectively. Socialists reduce all conflict to class conflict, which will ultimately end with the victory of those who are morally superior, the members of the working class. But neither of these ideologies accounts for the sort of conflicts one currently sees in Lebanon, Northern Ireland, the former state of Yugoslavia, Kashmir, Rwanda, and elsewhere. Rather noneconomic divisions arising from religion, ethnicity, and race are peculiarly insensitive to treatment by rational debate and negotiation, because such conflicts are defined by the confrontation of absolutes and by absolute commitment to that confrontation. The parliamentarian can't face this reality. The socialist merely brings it home and, by making the enemy a class within the nation, turns the fact of conflict into civil war.

Most importantly, the friend/enemy distinction provides the basis for Schmitt's theory of law and the significance of law. *"Der Feind ist unsere eigene Frage als Gestalt."* ("The enemy is our own question in visible form.") The basis for the crucial distinction between friend and enemy is a cultural matter, and because the legal order depends upon the State's decision in making this distinction, the cultural order is prior to the legal order. Kelsen had assumed, like Hobbes, that the condition prior to law was complete anarchy and that a legal order permitted a cultural order to develop; Kant gave the example of the cultural phenomenon of marriage arising from a legally recognized contract for mutual sexual relations.

Schmitt, however, argued that cultural institutions are not created by law, nor can their peculiarities be reduced to legal norms; cultural customs and practices carry their own concepts of what is lawful and what is normal. Law is forced to accept these cultural standards. If legal rules conflict with cultural norms, the legal rules will not function as a norm. By identifying the role of the friend/enemy distinction, Schmitt hoped to repoliticize theories of law and link them to the existential facts of a national culture.

"The normal," Schmitt wrote, "proves nothing, the exception proves everything; not only does it validate the rule, the rule above all lives off the exception. In virtue of the exception, the force of actual life breaks through the crust of a mechanics grown listless by repetition."[50] The resolution of fundamental clashes of values, which underlie conflicts in law, cannot come by negotiation or procrastinating compromises and half measures. Rather this resolution will occur when the sovereign makes a genuine political decision by invoking a condition of exception. "And the struggle for sovereignty, the struggle to be the one who decides, will be won not in the reasoned debates of parliamentary politics, but in the battle of the politics of identity."[51]

Why does law bind the sovereign, if the sovereign is the source of the political authority for law? And if law does not bind the sovereign, how is it possible to operate in normal times when a fresh decision by the sovereign is not necessary (or possible) in every instance of the law's application? The answer is to reserve to the sovereign the decision of when to suspend the normal operation of law; indeed, this can be the only answer that is consistent with both the concept of sovereignty and the existential basis of law.

Liberalism attempts to cabin such situations by specifying in advance the conditions for declaring a state of exception (for example, the provision in the U.S. Constitution for the suspension of habeas corpus) and the method of resolving the crisis. Kelsen, as we have seen, solves this problem by eliminating sovereignty altogether as a kind of epiphenomenon of law, a concept that has no independent existence outside law, a mere personification of the legal order. Schmitt, however, sees that the death of an external sovereign, like the death of God, does not lead to the triumph of science—even legal science—but to the war of gods, the conflict of interest groups each animated by its own myth. As a description of Weimar Germany, one would have to say that Schmitt's account, not Kelsen's, was closer to reality.

It must be emphasized that Schmitt is not antidemocratic. On the contrary, he holds that only an appeal to popular sovereignty can legitimate modern political authority. Like Kelsen, he is a partisan of the nation-state. He rejects claims of legitimacy based on tradition, but he also rejects the claims of parliamentarianism that base legitimacy on rationality, because rationality inevitably subverts authority and thus indirectly subverts democracy.

Recognizing politics' need for a myth, Schmitt wishes to replace the procedural myth of Kelsen with a myth of substantive content. In Schmitt's view, this means a vision on behalf of which persons will be willing to sacrifice their lives. Indeed he holds that one's life is worthless unless one has a purpose for which one is prepared to die. Liberalism cannot ask for such sacrifice from individuals because it exalts the ultimate worth of the individual life.

Schmitt relies on two concepts—the state of exception and the friend/ enemy distinction—to draw one fundamental conclusion: the critical need for a decision.[52] The constitution of a State is the result of an act by the nation that determines the form in which its will is to be expressed: that act, whether it is the foundational act of creating the friend/enemy distinction or the amending act of the state of exception, is the crucial act of decision.

By contrast, for liberal parliamentarians invoking a state of exception meant a ceasing of the operation of law. If, as Kelsen held, law is equivalent to the norms contained in the positive law of a valid legal order, then the cessation of the operation of law also meant a collapse of the legal order. Gerhard Anschütz, Weimar's most distinguished constitutional lawyer, said of Article 48—the provision for emergency powers in the Weimar constitution—"[h]ere the law of the State stops short." Schmitt found this a telling remark, the inadvertent but unavoidable consequence of liberalism's effort to remove politics from law. Such a moment of supreme political importance was to occur in a legal vacuum. On the contrary, Schmitt argued, all legal orders are founded on an existential decision, and not on a norm. As a result, even in the state of exception where the positive law recedes, the State—the legal order—remains.

Democracy, Schmitt writes, is defined as the mutual psychological identification of rulers with ruled. While the parliamentary democracies divide the public will through organized dissent, opposition parties, pressure groups organized around particular issues, a critical free press, minority protests, and even the secret ballot—which effectively prevents a union of wills in one public acclamation—the dictatorships provide an opportunity for the coming together of a people and a forum for the expression of their unity. The public will is not parceled out and diluted by elections, but rather focused in the way that only the will of a substantively homogeneous group can be.

Perhaps at one time the myth of parliamentarianism—the picture of independent representatives of the people engaged in a rational search for consensus on the best policy for the society—could obscure the reality of parliament as an auction house for bargaining among interest groups. But the rise of mass parties, highly effective interest groups, expensive political campaigns, a broad-based electoral franchise to whom advertising is as important as it is to a broad-based consumer population, and, above all, a free press to expose parliament as little more than the display case of speeches made on behalf of clients—these developments have exploded the myth of liberal parliamentarianism. In its place is the movement and its leader: a state defined by values evoked by a decision, and ratified by ecstatic mass acclamation.

The dictator is required to act not only in the constituitive moment but at all times. He gives voice to the sovereign people, the nation.

The norm does not exist which can be applied in chaos. The order has to be established, so that the legal order must have meaning. A normal situation has to be created and sovereign is he who definitively decides whether this normal state actually obtains. All law is "situation law." The sovereign creates and guarantees the situation as a whole in its totality. He has the monopoly on this ultimate decision.[53]

All this was very congenial to the Nazi state. Even though this state was stratified into many different groups, it was not a pluralistic state, because it sought a total unity of order arising from the führer's decisions. Moreover, there was an enormous increase in discretion, even to the point of passing ex post facto laws applying new rules to legal situations that arose prior to the rules. This arbitrary discretion was rationalized by invoking the nation-state legitimacy conferred by the führer as the apotheosis of the popular will, or as Mussolini put it (speaking of himself): *"Duce sei tutti noi!"*[54]

In summary, "decisionism" did not merely exalt the role of the decision. Where Kelsen, beginning with the logical form of the legal proposition, looked behind each legal act for the norm validating it and attempted to show that the basis for establishing the legality of a decision stood prior even to the constituent authority, Schmitt saw each legal act as a decision. Like his opponents in the Frankfurt School, he saw law as indeterminate, requiring fresh decisions inevitably and ubiquitously. He therefore substituted a hierarchy of men for the hierarchy of norms, finding the basis for legal validity in the correspondence between law and the actual social and political situation.

THE FRANKFURT SCHOOL
AND OTTO KIRCHHEIMER

Schmitt and the German fascists were impressed by what was happening in Rome in the 1920s, but other intellectuals looked to Moscow. The Versailles settlement was no less an anathema to these persons, and Weimar, which they too saw as the creature of Versailles, was no less contemptible. Indeed the ideological alternatives that made their capitals in London, Rome, and Moscow were precisely mirrored in Weimar political society and thus the constitutional turmoil of that society is an excellent subject for our study of the constitutional situation of the larger society of nation-states.

"The Frankfurt School" is the name given to the writers and their works that came out of the Institute for Social Research founded in 1924 and attached to the university of Frankfurt. Its members were driven from Germany by the Nazis; some emigrated to Paris, to New York (where they became attached to Columbia University), and to Los Angeles, and their most prominent leaders then astonishingly returned to Germany after World War II. The romantic aura that still surrounds the Frankfurt School arises perhaps from this saga of a persecuted community of intellectuals, hounded into exile, courageously defending their vision against a malignant, or in some cases benign but apathetic, bureaucratized world.

This saga began when Felix Weil, the son of a millionaire who had made a fortune in South America, set up a trust fund to found an institute for Marxism, hoping one day that it would be handed over to a triumphant German Marxist state. Under the Institute for Social Research's first director, Carl Grunberg (1924–1928), the focus of research was largely Marxist orthodoxy. In addition to Weil's funds, the Institute sought financial support from the Prussian Ministry of Culture (Frankfurt was situated within the state of Prussia) and an affiliation with the University of Frankfurt. Despite the open breach between communists and democratic socialists, the Prussian state government, which was controlled by the Social Democratic Party (SPD), nevertheless supported the Institute and a university affiliation was procured.

The members of the Frankfurt School from 1923 to roughly 1950 were Marxist intellectuals of a specific sort.[55] In his important collection of essays, published the year of the founding of the Institute, György Lukács wrote:

> Orthodox Marxism . . . does not imply the uncritical acceptance of the results of Marx's investigations . . . It is not the "belief" in this or that thesis, nor the exegesis of a "sacred" book. On the contrary, orthodoxy refers exclusively to *method*. It is the scientific conviction that dialectical materialism is the road to truth and that its method can be developed, expanded and defended only along the lines laid down by its founders.[56]

In this sense, the members of the Frankfurt School were orthodox Marxist theoreticians, but their aim was to broaden the Marxist critique that hitherto treated philosophy, politics, and society as mere symptoms of the class economic struggle. Throughout their careers, the members of the School defined themselves in opposition to what they took to be empiricism and positivism. The verifiable theories of positivism would only confirm the surface phenomena of society; what was needed was critical insight to expose the façade that mesmerized the positivist.

By 1930 the focus had shifted to this project, the broadening of the Marxist critique, under a new director, Max Horkheimer. By supplementing the Marxist material and economic analysis with the cultural and psychological criticism of society the theorists of the Institute sought to account for the failure of the communist revolution despite the crises in capitalism of the First World War and the Great Depression. To explain the proletariat's failure to assume its historical role, Lukács had proposed the notion of class consciousness in the subjunctive mode, as it were.

> Proletarian class consciousness is not the empirical consciousness of individuals or groups but rather what that consciousness of the proletariat would be if it could grasp its class interest and its historic role. The absence of proletarian class consciousness is blamed on the reification of consciousness.[57]

The central theme of the work of the Institute became the elucidation of the Marxist theory of alienation, based on the notion of reification—the idea that within capitalist societies, the relationships among human beings had taken on the form of the relations among things. This elucidation was embodied in a total cultural critique of the superstructure of society, encompassing art, music, psychology. It is sometimes said that the Frankfurt School, along with György Lukács, attempted a kind of Reformation of Marxist theology.

In addition to Horkheimer—an autocratic and tactically adept administrator—the other driving intellectual force was his close friend, Theodor Adorno, brilliant, immensely prolific, and a passionate critic of modern art and music (especially jazz) as well as of politics. Associated with these two, at various times, were Walter Benjamin, Erich Fromm, Herbert Marcuse, Franz Neumann, Friedrich Pollock, and Otto Kirchheimer. Although the Jewish background of each of these varied, some elements of traditional Judaic thought—a commitment to social justice; a utopian messianism and attachment to a vision of a world emancipated from the bondage of law; and a self-conscious affinity for ethical concerns—figure in virtually all the work of the School.[58] Assimilated and yet marginalized in German society, saturated in high German culture and yet genuinely cosmopolitan, Marxist-Leninist in orientation and yet acutely aware that fascism was swelling with mass proletarian support, these writers provided a serious intellectual underpinning to Weimar revolutionary theory and brought this theory within the sheltering respectability of one of Germany's most prestigious universities. Their members were prominent targets for the Nazis, who closed the Institute in March 1933. Benjamin went to Paris, and probably committed suicide in 1940 after a failed attempt to emigrate. Neumann went to London.[59] But most went to the United States.

In America, the school's most powerful members, Horkheimer and Adorno, were shrewd as well as committed; for the word *Marxism* they had invented the term *critical theory;* in place of *capitalism* they used the phrase *forces of domination* with such success that in 1934, Nicholas Murray Butler, the far-from-radical president of Columbia University, agreed to support the affiliation of the Institute with the University and to locate it in a Columbia building. Horkheimer and his colleagues were, Butler was told, "on the liberal-radical side." Indeed they were: in 1939, Horkheimer wrote, "no one can ask the émigrés to hold a mirror up to the world that has produced fascism in the very place in which they are being offered asylum. But those who do not wish to speak of capitalism should be silent about fascism," a piece of advice that we can be thankful was ignored by Franklin Roosevelt.

After the war, Horkheimer and Adorno returned to Germany. In the fall of 1951, the Institute for Social Research was reopened in Frankfurt, and in that year Horkheimer was also appointed rector of the University there. Adorno went back to Frankfurt in 1953 and was appointed to a chair in philosophy and sociology established as compensation for the expulsion of scholars by the Nazis. He never returned to the United States, and in 1955 he became a German citizen again.

Today the legacy of the early Frankfurt School is in evidence as much in the work of the American critical legal studies group as in the Institute's leading contemporary philosopher, Jürgen Habermas (who has recently been at pains to repudiate the critical legal studies movement).[60] Whereas Habermas tends to emphasize Horkheimer and Adorno's arguments about individual autonomy in a conformist society, the ambivalent inheritance of the Enlightenment and its instrumental rationality, as well as the Americanization of German culture that has occurred since the first period of the Frankfurt School's work, the American critical theorists appear more attracted by the Frankfurt School's blending of psychoanalysis and sociological Marxism, which produces a "total social critique" that unmasks the law as a tool for capitalist and elite domination, and exposes, so we are told, the vast self-deception of liberal political society.

The Frankfurt School, however, did not attempt a Reformation with respect to the Marxist view of law; indeed, with the exception of Franz Neumann and Otto Kirchheimer the School showed little interest in questions of jurisprudence. For the members of the School, as for the communists of Weimar, law was a simple mask for domination, a by-product of the class struggle.[61] This orthodox legal nihilism was largely accepted by otherwise reform-minded Marxists of the School.[62] By unequivocally equating the formalistic, coercive character of the law with bourgeois class interests and bureaucratic authoritarian rule, the Frankfurt School was unprepared for the Nazis' abandonment of rigid legal protocols in favor of undefined, "soft" discretionary rules. Kirchheimer speaks best for this attitude, which may be said to present the third alternative approach to jurisprudence in the Weimar Republic, opposed to parliamentarianism and fascism.

In Kirchheimer's "The Socialist and Bolshevik Theory of the State" (1928), one reads a ferocious Marxist attack on Weimar parliamentary ideology that is nevertheless thoroughly redolent of Carl Schmitt's thought.[63] Kirchheimer had been a student of Schmitt's; indeed "The Socialist and Bolshevik Theory of the State" was originally part of Kirchheimer's dissertation, written under Schmitt. The basic flaw with liberal democracy, Kirchheimer writes, is its refusal "to decide"; by compromising with its bourgeois political foes, the social democrats of the Weimar state blur the true nature of politics, which is class conflict. Weimar is unable to act ruthlessly, in pathetic contrast to the Bolshevik liquidation of class enemies in Russia. In Kirchheimer, Schmitt's friend/enemy distinction is applied to the conflict between working class and capitalist class. The refusal to write this basic enmity into law reflects Weimar's greatest error. Lenin is lavishly praised for "a doctrine of unmitigated, all embracing struggle." By contrast, Weimar is "a shell of a state . . . something less than itself" because it continues to tolerate, and even debate with, its enemies.

Kirchheimer emphasizes three other points: first, "[o]f fundamental importance for every political theory. . . is to what extent it takes account of, and admits into its texture the principle of emergency."[64]

> Soviet strategists understand the centrality of the emergency and, faced with internal and external threats, are ready to act ruthlessly against their enemies without qualms about establishing a dictatorial regime as a way of undertaking the crucial task of integrating their supporters according to a set of far-reaching shared ideals.[65]

Second, the Bolsheviks have been able to portray convincingly the myth of world revolution, which both inspires the working class and clarifies the nature of the struggle. Soviet myth making is far more effective than parliamentarianism's "medley of economic development and democracy, of majority vote and humanitarianism."[66] Finally, revolution is the existential decision, the defining constitutional moment. Revolutionary societies have the right to depict their opponents as "alien" and as "infidels" who must be destroyed. Kirchheimer admires Lenin for emphasizing the necessity of an ultimate and annihilating battle between socialism and capitalism. In this essay,[67] as well as the later "Weimar—And What Then?"[68] he fairly pants with praise for the Soviets who crush their enemies instead of arguing with them.[69]

Kelsen is also a target for Kirchheimer. When Kirchheimer berates the

Weimar constitution because it sacrifices its *will* and *substance* in favor of *formalistic institutions,* when he claims that the parliamentary state "tends to disappear behind its own legal mechanism,"[70] he is faulting Weimar for achieving precisely the goals Kelsen sets for the State. Because Kelsen treated sovereignty as a ghost, the politics of class compromise result in the "impossibility to find, in our age of formally democratic structures aiming at social equilibrium, a satisfactory answer to the question of who is the wielder of sovereignty, that is, who makes the actual decision in the conflict situation." Whereas parliamentary democrats take it as a major achievement of their ideology that it can transmute difficult and potentially deadly political disputes into peacefully resolved legal ones, Kirchheimer contemptuously calls this an attempt to "juridify" conflict. A writer so attracted to violent and final conflict doubtless hoped that the emergency that he believed Weimar to be incapable of handling would be one, at least in part, of his own making.

Far from pluralism, Kirchheimer yearns for a purifying solidarity that has found expression in our own times in the Khmer Rouge campaigns in Cambodia and the Cultural Revolution in China. For Kirchheimer, the cultural ethos becomes the constitutional ethos. As there must be a commonly shared cultural ethos in order for the State to achieve unity, so the constitutional ethos spreads to every aspect of cultural life. The consensus that emerges from the defining decision of revolution (Kirchheimer calls it the "creative act of revolution") not only determines the fundamental law of the State, but also specifies policy choices and even the form of much everyday life. Because values correspond to the social context, a truly homogeneous social order will result in a cultural, moral, and social homogeneity. Only this conformity is capable of producing the necessary strength to deal with the emergency situation.

Kirchheimer praises the Bolsheviks for seeing and, unlike the liberal parliamentarians, for saying that law is no more than a political instrument to be used to discipline those who have yet to accept the values of the community. Because the decisions taken on behalf of that community must, in the case of the exception, be normless, the distinction between enforcing the values of the community and mere physical coercion is erased. Even compliance cannot be anticipated when the dictatorship governs according to exigency only. Law and force become the same thing. Lenin puts this forthrightly: "The court is not to abolish terror . . . but it should make it understandable and should elevate it to a legal rule, as a matter of principle, clear-cut, without hypocrisy and without embellishments."[71]

Because legality equals social justice, there is no distinction between the legitimacy and the justification of a legal rule. The arbitrariness and radical discretion imposed by the exigency—which amounts to what can be justified by events—becomes the rule. In Kirchheimer's description of an authoritarian socialist alternative, the rule of law is reduced to nothing more than what those with power decide. "The Socialist and Bolshevik Theory of the State" argues

> that whereas the explosion of legal instruments (in the form of new labor and social welfare courts, for example) in the West is expressive of democracy's anti-political refusal to make a decision in favor of a set of common interests and values . . . [l]aw in the Soviet Union is directly linked to the Communist Party's program and is made, as Lenin notes, "an instrument for education and for imparting discipline" . . . [Thus] the Bolshevik legal system is based on ever-changing "temporary law."[72]

Kirchheimer approvingly reports that in the Soviet Union law had become "so dependent on the government objectives at any given time that the suggestion even was made to limit the validity of the new Soviet Civil Code to only two years."[73] In any case, what such a system aims at is not the application of formal law, but rather a judicial system of the appropriate revolutionary consciousness so that each situation is treated in a way that is plainly adapted to the mores of the socialist community.

This union of cultural and constitutional ethos divided fascism and communism from parliamentarianism. In 1939 Kircheimer bewilderedly wrote that "the attempt of the [fascist] legislature and the judiciary to use the criminal law to raise the moral standards of the community appears, when measured by the results achieved, as a premature excursion by fascism into the field reserved for a [socialist] society."[74] But by 1941, he conceded that the Nazis had "closed the gap which, under the liberal era, had separated the provinces of law and morality."[75] We are inclined to forget that, until the mid-1930s, liberal parliamentarianism, not fascism, was the principal target of communists. In the chapter "Elements of Anti-Semitism," for example, in the *Dialectic of Enlightenment* by Adorno and Horkheimer, the authors had even concluded that "the German fascists were not anti-Semitic but were liberals who wanted to assert their anti-liberal opinions."[76]

The brief Weimar period from 1919 to 1933 has often been studied as a textbook case of state formation in times of economic and political crisis. This discussion of various law professors active in that period has aimed to provide a survey of the three principal alternatives in play at the time. All of those persons discussed above were, in one way or another, concerned with the problem of how to achieve legitimacy for the new German state. So long as the ideological valence of the new nation-state form lay undecided, in any state where these alternatives contended on roughly equal terms there could be no stable constitutionalism for the State. Unlike the forms of the State in earlier periods, the nation-state requires an ideological shadow before it can come to life. When it acquires this shadow, it is a formidable strategic archetype, as the Nazis and the Soviets, no less than the liberal democracies, demonstrated.

The Weimar experience thus provides a national microcosm of an international phenomenon, the unstable competition among ideological forms of the nation-state that occurred in the aftermath of Versailles. Parliamentarianism, fascism, and communism contended in every major state, although in none were these forces so finely balanced as in Germany. Just as there could be no peace within Germany until this competition of values was settled for the German state, so also there could be no peace among states until the same question was answered for the society of states. It was necessary to determine which of the three putative ideologies of the nation-state would achieve legitimacy because each of these ideologies contended on the level of legitimacy: that is, each offered a standard by which the promise of the nation-state to enhance the welfare of the nation would be judged. Each form attacked not merely the policies of its competitors but their very right to govern, even to participate in political life. Normal politics could not take place until this fundamental question was resolved.

Many readers will recall that when Hitler accepted the surrender of France in 1940, he insisted that the signing of the articles take place at Compiègne, in the same railroad car where German generals had been forced to surrender in 1919. But few are likely to remember that in 1919, at Clemenceau's insistence, the Treaty of Versailles was signed in the Hall of Mirrors because this was the place where, in 1871, Bismarck had had William I proclaimed ruler of Germany, the first nation-state in Europe.

CHAPTER TWENTY-THREE

The Peace of Paris

THE PEACE OF VERSAILLES did not bring closure to the epochal conflict that had begun in August 1914. Like earlier international constitutional conventions, Versailles enshrined a new constitutional order, which was the nation-state. But the nature of this form of the state required a further decision among ideologies, and with respect to this decision, Versailles was premature.

Versailles did attempt to certify one ideological variant of the constitutional order, but this variant was not accepted by two important states, Germany and the Soviet Union. The ideological option endorsed by Versailles, the parliamentary nation-state, accepted the legitimating premise of the nation-state that it was based on the will of the people and was constituted for their material benefit. Parliamentary ideology went on, however, to specify free, fair, regular, and open elections as the means of determining the popular will. The parliamentary nation-state made voting publics the judges of whether their governments were in fact maintaining and enhancing the welfare of the nation. Moreover, this type of constitutional form required governments to comply with their own laws and to administer law impartially. Accountability to the electorate provided the ultimate check on whether such respect for the rule of law was forthcoming from the State.

The parliamentary nation-state, however, was by no means congenial to many persons in Germany, on whom it was pressed by the Versailles victors, nor to the new state of the Soviet Union, which proffered to the world its own variant of the archetype of the nation-state. Until the fascist and communist alternatives to the parliamentary nation-state were discredited in the eyes of the German and Russian people, the Long War could not end, for this war, like other epochal wars, continued precisely because it had become a struggle over alternative constitutional orders and thus the State itself was at stake.

In time both the fascist and communist Great Powers were defeated and their constitutional forms discarded. Nazism, with its claims of militaristic racial superiority, was thoroughly beaten by an alliance that included the multiethnic United States and the Slavic Soviet Union. Most damning, however, to German fascism was the disclosure of the death camps, a logical culmination of fascist ideas about racism and the State. The disgust and horror experienced by civilized people everywhere effectively removed fascism from the list of possible choices that nations might consider in forming states and marginalized it forever to the dormitory rooms of misfits. At least one cannot add futility to the cruelties suffered by the victims of Nazi concentration camps, for these victims did not die in vain. They defeated fascism just as surely as did the victorious soldiers at Normandy or Kursk, because the crimes committed against them rendered fascism odious. The discrediting of communism came in a different way—though the exposure of the murder of millions of innocents played a similar role. In this chapter we will discuss how this delegitimation came about in the Soviet Union and in the Warsaw Pact countries, and how this led to the Peace of Paris that completed the work of Versailles in 1990.

THE END OF THE LONG WAR

What brought about the end of the Long War and the adoption of the parliamentary nation-state by Russia and a united Germany? At present, most accounts of these extraordinary events can be grouped in two general categories: those that argue that economic pressures—perhaps intensified by the defense policies and diplomacy of the Reagan administration—forced the Soviet state to buckle;[1] and those accounts that argue that it was Mikhail Gorbachev's drive for domestic reform that opened up the path that led eventually to Paris.[2] To the extent that they recognize the interconnection between domestic and international events, either approach might provide a satisfactory account: if the Soviet regime was compelled to adopt market methods in order to compete strategically, it may be that these reforms led to an unraveling of the command ideology even though they were merely intended to modify the command economy (as is often prophesied for China); if *glasnost* and *perestroika* (policies we may roughly translate as *transparency* or *openness* as applied to government and *restructuring* as applied to the economy) loosened the grip of the police state, this made it harder to crack down on secessionists in Eastern Europe and in the Soviet republics. And, of course, these approaches might be seen as complementary, or even as mutually reinforcing. Perhaps Gorbachev's domestic policies of liberalization were intensified by a sense of strategic desperation, or perhaps his conciliatory posture towards the West reflected the more humane norms of his efforts at domestic reconstruction.

I propose, however, to offer a somewhat different account. The two approaches I have thus far described are the consequence of separating strategy and law. The former treats international relations as driven by the strategic requirements of force and the relative comparison of capabilities alone. As the Athenians told the Melians, the strong do what they wish, the weak suffer what they can. From this point of view, the bipolar world should have continued even after the constitutional changes brought about by *glasnost* and *perestroika,* because these did not significantly affect the correlation of forces between the superpowers.* I do not believe the facts will bear out any abrupt shift in the force capabilities between the super-powers that would have compelled the change in Soviet policies that occurred in the late 1980s (although significant changes did occur thereafter). Yet while the relative capabilities of the United States and the USSR did not change very much during the years from Gorbachev's accession to power in 1985 until 1989, international relations were fundamentally transformed during that one year. In any case, such an account does not tell us why the Soviets reacted to their dilemma in the way they did (rather than by heightening tensions, as Andropov chose to do when confronted by Reagan's adversarial posture, or by simply grafting market mechanisms onto the party state, as the Chinese have chosen to do).[3]

The second approach treats constitutional developments as causing, but not caused by, international change. In this view, Gorbachev's domestic reforms led to the collapse of the communist system because he sought to dismantle a totalitarian system that had previously held the states of Eastern Europe and the Soviet republics in thrall. I am skeptical, however, that Gorbachev came to power committed to parliamentarianism and determined to effectuate its triumph over communism. Nor do I believe that he was willing to permit the subordination of the Soviet position internationally in order to achieve domestic reform, nor that he was foolish enough to believe that he could delegitimate the communist system without placing increased strains on his ability to restrain defections from the Warsaw Pact, including the option to use force. Nor does this account tell us why Soviet reformers did not embark upon political liberalization coupled with a demand for international concessions, that is, a radical extension of the Brezhnev/Helsinki policies or any of the other plausible programs of domestic constitutional reform that did not entail a strategic retrenchment.

The Long War ended when General Secretary Gorbachev—as he was before he sought a new constitution that styled him president—attempted

---

*And indeed some of the most sophisticated commentators continued to maintain that nothing had really changed in the bipolar relationship even after Gorbachev introduced *perestroika* and *glasnost* and the "new thinking," because nothing much *had* changed with respect to the comparison of forces and nuclear arms. These persons were highly dubious of Gorbachev's international proposals. William G. Hyland, *The Cold War Is Over* (Time Books / Random House, 1990).

to mimic the strategies of the West in order to compete more successfully internationally, and this mimicry led, unintentionally, to constitutional changes he was unable to control. These changes, in turn, prevented him from falling back on the old strategy of international coercion and he was forced irresistibly into an ardent effort to join the community of parliamentary states—the Versailles/San Francisco community—as the only way of saving the geopolitical position of the USSR, which his own policies had jeopardized. The political problem for the West, without a satisfactory solution to which the Peace of Paris would not have been possible, was to keep Germany from succumbing to the temptations of neutrality during the process of Soviet change, without so alienating Germany that it would go off by itself when that process was complete. This required the United States not only to persuade President Gorbachev that he should urge that the United States stay in Europe—a complete reversal of Soviet policy hitherto—but also to concert American allies in the acceptance of a stronger, unified Germany. If the principal character in this account is Gorbachev, the figures of the American secretary of state, James Baker, and his Soviet counterpart, Eduard Shevardnadze—both, like Bismarck and Castlereagh, political party men and not professional diplomats—and the U.S. president, George H. W. Bush, were equally crucial.

Thus the Soviet Union under Gorbachev followed the historical pattern of states mimicking their successful competitors.[4] This brought about the loss of legitimacy experienced by the Communist Party in the Soviet Union and in Eastern Europe. Eventually the history of Communism came to be seen as one of moral and physical impoverishment. The communist state became detached from the legitimating basis of the nation-state, the mission to better the welfare of its people.[5]

Gorbachev did not set out to dismantle communism or the Soviet state; rather he was a committed communist who frequently reaffirmed that commitment. "We are looking within socialism," he declared, "rather than outside it, for the answers to all the questions that arise." In his devotion to the socialist alternative he was no less committed than Deng Xiaopeng, the other pivotal figure in the communist world during this period. As Adam Michnik acutely observed in 1987, Gorbachev's reforms should not be interpreted as advancing liberal democracy but instead as efforts on behalf of the "socialist counter-reformation."

> Essentially Gorbachev attempted to retain control over [the Soviet empire] through allowing, and then even encouraging, reform of communism domestically with the expectation that his own model of *perestroika* would prevail and bring to power similarly minded leaders in the Soviet bloc. The need for Gorbachev's counter-reformation was provoked by the legitimation crisis of the Communist party . . .[6]

I believe it can be shown that the strategy of counter-reformation was not the result of an economic decline in the Soviet Union in the years leading up to Gorbachev's accession to power. In the four years following Gorbachev's election as general secretary in 1985, however, the consequences of his mimesis of the West—the attempt to graft market management techniques* of decentralization onto socialist planning—drove the Soviet leader into increasingly desperate maneuvers until, in 1989, admission to the society of parliamentary nation-states was the only way left to preserve a role for himself and unity for the Soviet Union. Even this failed him, but it is important to see this development as a culmination in tactics that resulted in the astonishing decisions to combine international conciliation with pro-market and pro-democracy domestic policies. Indeed, only if we appreciate that the need for legitimation was driving Gorbachev's improvisations once the program of radical reform of the economy failed, with each new maneuver further sapping the stature of the Party in the Eastern bloc as well as in the Soviet Union, can we appreciate how unilateral concessions to the West were a rational response by a leader anxious to preserve a bipolar world. The Soviet Union was no weaker militarily, and the United States no stronger, in 1989 than in 1985, yet

[f]or Gorbachev and those closest to him the game in world politics had changed profoundly in the four years that separated his elections as CPSU general secretary and the collapse of Soviet power in Europe; if prior to 1985 the overarching object of Soviet foreign policy had been to strengthen the "positions of socialism" at the expense of the West, by 1989 a new goal—to secure Soviet admission to the elaborate collection of institutions that constituted the Western economic and political system—had arisen to take its place.[7]

This change in strategic objectives had come about as a result of the interplay between the international and the domestic, between strategic and constitutional change. It was Stalin's insistence on transforming the constitutional order of the states of Eastern Europe and the West's refusal to permit Germany to join this order, that kept the war going after World War II. As he told Milovan Djilas in the spring of 1945, "[w]hoever occupies a territory also imposes on it his own social system. Everyone imposes his own system as far as his army can reach. It cannot be otherwise." Just as Napoleon had taken the tactics of artillery siege and broadened these, first to battle itself, and then to war against other states, so Stalin took the tactics of interstate conflict—the internationalized civil war

---

*To be distinguished from the Chinese strategy of actually introducing markets.

of classes—and turned these tactics against the peoples of his own state and those he conquered.

This transposition was at the heart of the Long War, and it was no different in its way for liberal parliamentarians or for fascists. Each ideology sought to use its military victories against other nations as a means of imposing that variant of the nation-state that it championed. Thus, speaking of Poland's twentieth century conquerors, Michnik wrote:

> In contrast to the Nazis, the Soviets imposed their own organizational structures on the Poles. [The Nazis] could not be bothered to create political organizations for the conquered people, whom they wanted to transform into a race of slaves [to serve the German nation]. The Soviet[s] systematically destroyed all social ties, political and cultural organizations, sports associations, and professional guilds, and abrogated civil rights and confiscated private property.[8]

And, it should be added, after the Japanese defeat the Americans rewrote the Japanese constitution, instituted a multiparty bicameral legislature and the Australian ballot, and provided for an independent judiciary.[9]

The real difference with respect to such forced conversions is between the nation-state, of whatever variant, and its state-nation predecessor. The imperial states of the nineteenth century were largely indifferent to the domestic social structures of their colonies so long as they were compliant. This point is ignored by those who claim that the Soviet Union was no more than a contemporary manifestation of historic Russian barbarity in politics. As John Gray noted in 1987,

> this [claim] neglects the role of Marxian theory in constituting and reproducing the Soviet system and the relentless hostility of both to the traditions and achievements of the Russian people. [It fails] to grasp the radical modernity of the Soviet totalitarian system . . .[10]

This is the system that Gorbachev inherited: one that was preoccupied with the control of domestic society, which preoccupation was highly sensitive to global politics because international events had a profound effect on the legitimacy of the domestic regime. When Gorbachev attempted to transform Soviet and Eastern European domestic societies, it was with the goal of enhancing communism as a strategic actor; when this transformation only succeeded in delegitimating the socialist system itself, there were important consequences for Soviet international operations.

This process was begun by Gorbachev's adoption of the "revolutionary" methods of his predecessors, altered in content by the generational change which Gorbachev reflected and which was characterized by an attraction to some Western methods. Roughly speaking, Gorbachev went through three periods of cultural and political revolution: from 1986 to 1988, he attempted to renovate the domestic economy—not to prevent an imminent collapse, as sometimes appears in retrospect, but to make the socialist model more competitive internationally. In 1988 he broadened this agenda by introducing Western political reforms into the Warsaw Pact states (including the Soviet Union), though for different reasons abroad than at home. By 1989 he faced an unmanageable revolt in Eastern Europe, and economic and political disintegration in the Soviet Union, and he turned to the society of Western states for integration.

Radical economic upheaval was a periodic tactic of political reform in communist systems.[11] Stalin's "Second Revolution" discredited the NEP,* reversed Lenin's own reversals of his original program, and campaigned against the Old Bolsheviks. Gorbachev's program of *perestroika* was the last of such revolutions, and even its most memorable phrases were repetitions of slogans that originated with the Second Revolution, had lain dormant, and had been picked up again during the period of Khrushchev's radical populism.[12] From 1929, the beginning of the Second Revolution, to 1938 fourteen books used the word *perestroika* in their titles, but only two between 1939 and 1956. During the period of Khrushchev's radicalism, the term reappeared and nineteen such titles were published.

Gorbachev was a generation younger than the other members of the Brezhnev politburo of which he became a full member in 1980. His colleagues at that stage had lived through, and perhaps been formed by, the Stalinist "revolutions," including the attacks on "left revolutionaries" and the adoption of "Socialism in One Country" that had subordinated international socialism to the improvement of the USSR. By contrast Gorbachev and his contemporaries described themselves as "children of the Twentieth Party Congress," the congress at which Khrushchev had attacked Stalin and attempted to liberalize Soviet politics. If we may say that Brezhnev brought stability and predictability to a state that had been repeatedly jarred by Khrushchev, then we might also say that Gorbachev was eager to bring energy and innovation to a state that was widely perceived to have become sclerotic.

It was not a state, however, that was in deep economic difficulties or that was unable to hold its own in the superpower confrontation with the United States. Gorbachev's response to Reagan's challenge had more to do with his own dynamism and desire for innovation than with any particular difficulties imposed by the United States on the Soviet position. One can see this by simply comparing Gorbachev's response to American strategic initiatives in the world with those of Andropov and Chernenko, who

---

*Lenin's relatively liberal New Economic Policy, described in Chapter 2.

worked in the early 1980s with virtually the same economic resources that Gorbachev had in 1985. When NATO refused to cancel its long-range theatre nuclear force deployments in Europe, Andropov abruptly withdrew from the Intermediate-range Nuclear Forces (INF) talks rather than bargain away the SS-20 forces that had prompted the NATO deployments in the first place. When Chernenko agreed to return to the talks, he offered a proposal—the so-called "zero option"—that eventually was accepted by the United States after Gorbachev had come to power. There was no noticeable difference in the strategic or economic conditions faced by the Soviet leadership under any of these men prior to 1988. The economy, which had grown at rates of 5 percent in the early 1970s, was, according to official estimates, slowing down to a rate of 2.5 percent by 1984, but this decrease was hardly unique to the Soviet Union. Growth in the United States, which had been at an average rate of 4 percent throughout the 1960s, had declined to about 2.7 percent in the 1970s and 1980s. Most Western European economies, already lagging behind the United States in per capita income, also experienced slower growth during the 1980s than the United States.

What did occur was a contraction of absolute growth in 1979–1982, but this was in part caused by a series of poor harvests and a drop in the utilization of industrial capacity, both temporary. In fact, grain yields rapidly improved from 1981 to 1986, apparently due to the adoption of improved agricultural technologies. Andropov's program of enhanced discipline also seems to have had a positive effect: industrial growth rebounded in early 1983. If the "core legitimation of Soviet rule was provided by the Marxist thesis that public ownership of the means of production, and the unified direction of production toward public objectives, would make a socialist economy more efficient than a capitalist one"[13] and thereby enable the state better to provide for the welfare of the nation, then the contractions of the late seventies and early eighties were cause for some concern. After a long period in which the much poorer Soviet economy had grown at a faster rate than that of the richer and more developed West, it now appeared to be slowing down. This occurred, however, for so short a period and at so slight a rate that it is difficult to believe that it was in fact the source of the legitimation crisis that Gorbachev eventually found himself forced to confront. Rather, it was when Gorbachev sought to streamline the Soviet economy in order to make it more competitive strategically that his efforts inadvertently threw the Soviet state into a crisis in which his increasingly desperate measures—all efforts to copy successful Western programs to some degree—only furthered ensnared him. Partly this occurred because the piecemeal adoption of Western practices was counterproductive; partly because championing Western methods tended to enhance the prestige of the West at Soviet expense; but mainly because

Gorbachev himself attempted to delegitimate Soviet practices in order to win support for his reforms—in much the same way that earlier internal revolutions had been conducted by Soviet leaders. When his program of economic reform failed, however, he himself had too greatly weakened the state apparatus for it to recover, and there was left only the residue of the delegitimation campaign he had all too successfully conducted. This climactic story began, it must be recalled, not with a Soviet program of conciliatory rapprochement with Western states, but with a pulsating ambition to compete with them.

Even before his election as general secretary, Gorbachev had warned that "[o]nly an intensive, fast-developing economy can ensure the strengthening of the country's position in the international arena, enabling it to enter the new millennium appropriately as a great and prosperous power." When Chernenko died in 1985, Gorbachev became general secretary of the Communist Party. In one of his first speeches after assuming the leadership, he asserted that "the fate of the country and the place of socialism in the world" depended upon the Soviet Union reaching its economic objectives.

Gorbachev's first major announcement was the initiation of a strategy he termed the "acceleration" of economic growth, to be achieved by a quantum shift of resources into the machine-tools sector. This sector was directed to increase innovation and the share of new products in its output. Abrupt shifts of investment, which are characteristic of command economies, can bring about serious sectoral imbalances, slow growth, and cause inflation in the short term, but if the leading sector has been correctly identified, such investment strategies can bring competitive benefits. The Japanese approach of encouraging investment in certain identified sectors has, on the whole, been a success. And indeed the main feature of the Soviet 1986–1990 Five-Year Plan was a tremendous shift of investment into high technology.

For the USSR, however, the payoff of a stronger machine-tools industry never arrived because the government abruptly switched strategies. In 1987, barely two years after its adoption, the "acceleration" strategy was abandoned to the accompaniment of harsh attacks by Gorbachev on the command economy ideology that had produced such a policy. An alternative strategy of "radical economic reform" was announced. It is worth emphasizing that "radical economic reform," far from implying a step toward a noncommunist program, was actually intrinsic to the communist system. Because the state was in charge of central planning for the economy—setting prices, allocating production targets, enforcing managerial discipline—any changes came from the top where advances in knowledge were expected to be reflected in refinements in policy. "Reforms reflected confidence in the strength of the system and its potential for improvement, and the revealing expression 'further perfecting' was a standard part of reform decree titles. Some of the most sweeping economic reforms had been announced in the later 1950s, the golden age of Soviet society . . . when national income grew by more than 7 percent per year."[14]

Gorbachev's new economic reforms consisted of attempts to graft market practices on to the centrally planned Soviet economy. Profit incentives were introduced and output targets deprecated. These reforms tended to undermine the authority of the command economy without actually producing the benefits of the market because they operated in isolation, without the background of the market and its free flow of labor, decentralized transactions, and demand pricing. In the Soviet environment, partial market practices either were of little effect or operated in perverse ways, as if to vindicate the microeconomic "theory of the second best."[15] Gorbachev's radical reforms brought about this contradictory environment: output targets were abolished but the state retained the right to requisition products at levels that encompassed most of enterprise output; the state renounced liability for enterprise debt but if losses were incurred, the ministry was the creditor of last resort; the ministry could no longer direct particular enterprises but was responsible for their overall performance; the "Law of the Enterprise," which was supposed to give managers more discretion, stipulated managerial duties down to minute details.[16] The economist Vladimir Kontorovich concluded of this reform agenda that

> it could not work. Three elements of reform proved to be most destructive: managerial discretion over the output in excess of the state order, flexibility in wage and price setting, and strong incentives to earn above planned profit. Taken together, they frequently allowed the managers to raise prices of their products and the wages of their employees while cutting output.[17]

The effect was to increase inflation, which, in a command economy where prices were fixed, was reflected in worsening shortages of consumer goods. The actual economic contraction brought about by these reforms, however, was far less visible than the empty store shelves of which consumers complained.

During a series of addresses in 1986–1988, Gorbachev ridiculed central planning and the methods of the command economy, and called for "unleashing" the creativity of individuals, freeing them from overregulation and control and giving them a share in ownership. Compensation was to be tied to performance, not to a lock-step system that discouraged initiative. Part of the radical reform plan of 1987 provided for the election of enterprise managers by their employees. Nor was this delegitimation campaign confined to the shop floor:

The destruction of authority had actually started in 1986 with media criticism of managers, officials, and bureaucrats. This was a vintage communist campaign: high pitch, unrelenting, blanket demagogy.... The de-legitimation of authority and demoralization of those who wielded it swiftly led to an erosion of discipline. [By] 1988 it was becoming difficult to get workers for night or weekend shifts. Relations between suppliers and users, previously moderated by local Party committees, became more chaotic. Personnel cuts led to fewer and less coherent commands.[18]

More players moved into the vacuum thus created: miners went on strike, chemical and power plants were shut by environmental protests, and local authorities began to assert more independent control. The election of managers proved so costly to management control that it had to be reversed in 1990, but the collapse of managerial authority could not now be reversed.

Soviet statistics estimated the growth in national income in 1988 at 4.4 percent and in GNP at 5.5 percent (although the CIA estimated GNP growth at 2.2 percent). By 1989 there was widespread recognition that the reform agenda had failed. Most of Gorbachev's original policies had been reversed or abandoned; "acceleration" and "radical reform" were scrapped. Investment in high technology was frozen, and steps were taken to propitiate new players, the consumers and the workers. The Soviet Union had suffered other similar periods of recession but what now occurred was unprecedented: in the attempted reversal of the "acceleration" program and the "radical reform" program, it soon became clear that decrees to roll back these policies were simply being ignored and that the government in 1989 had lost control of the Soviet economy. By his attacks on the legitimacy of the system of central planning, Gorbachev had crippled the mechanisms that might have allowed him to halt the recession.

Broad public awareness of the impact of the reforms only came in 1990 when official statistics showed actual declines in GNP of 2 percent and 4 percent in national income. In 1990 military expenditures began to decline and higher priority was given to the production of consumer goods. By 1991 official data showed an extraordinary contraction of 15–17 percent, and the following year the rate of decline exceeded 20 percent.

There can be no doubt that the general secretary of the Communist Party played a decisive role in the collapse of the Communist system,[19] as did the United States president, but these roles are often distorted. President Reagan's confrontational anti-Soviet scheme, his increase in U.S. defense expenditures—particularly on missile defense—and his program of denying the Soviet Union hard currency (by holding oil prices down and thwarting the completion of a European pipeline) and high technology (by enforcing export controls) did not force the Soviet Union into an economic collapse. But these measures did focus attention on the superpower confrontation and challenged the complacent Soviet leadership, accustomed to détente in the Brezhnev years, to take up that challenge. This was enthusiastically done by the dynamic Gorbachev, who proceeded to mimic what he took to be the most successful strategic innovations of the West. This policy of partial strategic adaptation proved to be an economic mistake, but it only became an economic disaster when the political underpinnings of that adaptation began to be felt, because these disabled the Soviet Union from making the midcourse corrections that would have allowed it to stabilize and avoid the catastrophic economic events of 1990–1991. Moreover, the process of delegitimation used to win domestic support for these adaptations set in motion events on the international front—particularly in Eastern Europe—that ultimately played back into the constitutional politics of the Soviet republics and triggered the final collapse. All of these events followed the pattern of mutually affecting strategic and constitutional change described in Book I.

The Gorbachev of 1986 was hailed in many Western quarters as a conciliatory international leader; with the events of 1989 (including the acquiescence of the Soviet Union in German unification and Eastern European autonomy) and 1990 (especially the signing of the Charter of Paris) this view became the general opinion. Nevertheless, a less anachronistic description is probably closer to the truth.

For the confident Gorbachev of 1986 was by no means the supplicant of 1989. Two moves on the international scene won for him a wide following in liberal circles in the United States, Germany, and elsewhere: the surprise proposal made at Reykjavik in October 1986 to scrap nuclear weapons and the INF agreement signed in Washington in December 1987. I am inclined to believe that neither of these events justifies the conclusion that Gorbachev had abandoned, with these proposals, the Soviet aim to win decisive strategic advantages over the United States. On the contrary, both measures struck at the vitality of U.S. extended deterrence.

It is easy to lose sight of what was at stake in these dramatic negotiations, yet only if these stakes are kept firmly in mind can we make sense of the course of the talks. Very briefly, it can be said that the United States wished to treat Western Europe as part of its homeland (NATO having arisen in the period when there was only *central* deterrence), despite the reality of the end of deterrence identity between the United States and Europe (owing to U.S. homeland vulnerability to Soviet nuclear systems and the resulting birth of *extended* deterrence). At the same time, however, the USSR wished to treat Western Europe as a mere launching platform for the United States, not as a superpower in itself nor as a part of a superpower's homeland (because a threat against it was manifestly not as force-ful as a threat against the U.S. homeland), despite French and British inde-pendent nuclear deterrents and the presence of American troops defended by nuclear weapons. Unwilling to concede the identity of security interests between the United States and Europe, the USSR could not, however, insist on wholly separate treatment either because to do so would have jeopardized the Russian insistence that its position as a superpower en-titled it to parity with "the other half," the rest of the developed world, then largely arrayed against it. This explained the constant Russian pressure on Western Europe to identify itself as distinct from U.S. interests, coupled with the contradictory refusal to treat Western European security concerns as on a par with those of the United States and the USSR.

One might draw the comparison in this way. For the Soviet Union, a superpower was entitled to pose threats (deployments) equal to the threats it faced from all sources; a *balance* existed when each superpower faced equivalent threats. For the United States, a superpower was entitled to pose threats equal to the threats posed by the other superpower; a *balance* existed when each superpower faced threats equal to those it posed. These paradigms are derived directly from the respective superpower relation-ships to Western Europe, one threatening, as it had to if its empire in East-ern Europe was ever to be truly secure, the other protecting, as it had to if its political and philosophical positions were not to be isolated in the world.*

There are two reasons why Gorbachev's strategic proposals have been regarded as evidence of his transcendence of previous Soviet thinking. First, many Western observers were themselves supporters of the aban-donment of U.S. extended deterrence, that is, the abandonment of the protection of Europe by American nuclear weapons. Just as Soviet market-oriented reforms were applauded because they were associated in the West with economic efficiency and seemed likely to bring political liberaliza-tion, so dramatic cuts in nuclear weapons were also hailed as evidence of a reasonableness that heralded progressive political evolution. Second, later events did in fact lead Gorbachev to make significant concessions, and these—like the later economic collapse—imperceptibly color the way we see his earlier actions. Principal among these was his decision not to

---

*This fundamental paradigm applied in the conventional, nonnuclear arena as well. The late Johann Holst noted that "Soviet negotiators have attempted to structure the geographical parameters for arms control regimes in Europe in a manner which will preserve for Soviet territory that privileged status of being exterior to the regime in question. The definition of the reduction zone in MBFR [mutual balanced force reductions] and the refusal to include anything more than a narrow zone of 250 km of the Soviet Union in the CSCE/CBM [Conference on Security in Europe/Confidence Building Measures] regime, indicate the way in which Moscow approaches arms control as a means for struc-turing the broader context of the political order." Johann Holst, "The NATO–Warsaw Pact Relation-ship?" in *New Directions in Strategic Thinking,* ed. Robert O'Neill and D. M. Horner (Allen & Unwin, 1981), 93.

intervene to shore up the Communist regimes in Central and Eastern Europe. This was, I think it can be shown, a decision, as Gorbachev's admirers assert, dictated by his vision and not, at least at first, by necessity. That vision, however, was not one of a pluralistic Central Europe, independent of Soviet control. Rather it was a strategic vision, animated by a rather daring innovation: he would make the Warsaw Pact over in the image of NATO in order to protect it from the buffeting of developments in the domestic politics of its members, remove the stain of the Prague intervention when the Pact had been turned against one of its members, and use the alliance as a lever to pry away older leaders with whom he had little sympathy and replace them with younger ones who shared his dynamism and zest for innovation.

Throughout the 1980s various political and human rights movements in Eastern Europe had exploited the Helsinki Final Act declarations in order to develop civil institutions within socialist constraints. In Poland, Hungary, and Czechoslovakia there arose movements that anticipated the market state by bypassing state institutions and creating a sphere of private, associational action within which democratic methods and ideals prevailed. This was a daring intellectual leap, because it reversed the Marxist notion that materiality determines human consciousness. By simply creating a space where persons could speak the truth, recount their memories without self-conscious editing, and cooperate to perform nonpolitical tasks, these movements struck at the passivity that underlay the grip of Communism on Eastern Europe since its crushing of the popular revolts of the 1950s and 1960s.[20] The military strength of Soviet forces was no less in 1989, however, than it had been in 1968 when Warsaw Pact troops invaded and quickly overwhelmed Czechoslovakia. What had changed was not Soviet military dominance in Eastern Europe but the growth of an organized civil society there—as well as a different mood in the Soviet Union itself as a result of *perestroika* and *glasnost*. This new consciousness was reflected in literary works[21] and philosophical essays,[22] but it found its most powerful institutional instrument in the Polish labor coalition *Solidarnosc* (Solidarity). Eventually this group embraced 90 percent of Polish workers; it assumed responsibility for managing production, settling trade disputes, and wage bargaining, thus bypassing communist institutions and rendering them obsolete by informally assuming their functions. When General Jaruzelski felt compelled to seize control of the country in 1981—in order to pre-empt Russian troops poised to cross the Soviet-Polish border—it was a tacit admission that the communist state had failed to legitimate itself with its principal constituency, the mass of industrial workers.

The Jaruzelski crackdown and the subsequent imposition of martial law were closely studied by the new Soviet leadership that came to power four years later. Shevardnadze concluded that imposing martial law had stimulated rather than silenced the noncommunist opposition. "So there is no reason," he asserted, "to hiss at *perestroika* and cheer for military force. It would not be a bad idea for us to learn the lesson of martial law in Poland for ourselves." Instead of opting for force—and here Shevardnadze and Gorbachev may have made an error by not distinguishing between Polish and Soviet force—the new Soviet leadership chose a strategy of counter-reformation, disclaiming the Brezhnev Doctrine and attempting to distance itself from the traditional communist leaderships in the other Warsaw Pact states, while striking the pose (which Gorbachev believed would be alluring) of a new, more humane socialism. This was certainly no mere miscalculation. Gorbachev was well aware that popular revolts had broken out in the Central European states whenever a Soviet leader had signaled the advent of a program of liberalization. This had occurred in Germany in 1953 after Stalin's death when Georgy Malenkov had briefly appeared to be contemplating a less restrictive relationship between the USSR and her allies; and again in Hungary and Poland in 1956 following the distribution of Khrushchev's secret speech denouncing Stalin.

Moreover, Gorbachev was also aware that the regimes which these revolts had briefly brought to power in Hungary and Poland had announced their intention to withdraw from the Warsaw Pact. Gorbachev was eager, however, to discredit the prevailing communist leaders in Eastern Europe in order to rally support for his own policies in the Soviet Union. If he were ever forced to order troops to fire on workers, the delegitimation crisis would grow even worse for communism in both places. He had to avoid being lumped with the leadership of a past generation, for whom (with the exception of Andropov) he had no great regard, and also thwart popular movements that might defect from the Warsaw Pact military alliance if these movements took power. A misstep in either direction would risk destroying the Warsaw Pact, as the inevitable domestic turmoil accompanying Gorbachev's liberalizations erupted in the member states.

If, instead, he could decouple domestic politics from membership in the Pact—as NATO had successfully managed to do—he might also be able to use the prestige and power of his role in the Warsaw alliance to improve his position at home without being dragged into embarrassing positions vis-à-vis the Soviet client states of Europe. If the communist governments could no longer maintain, let alone improve, the welfare of the populations they ruled in exchange for passive political and social compliance, it might nevertheless be possible to give responsibility for the economic problems with which these leaders had to deal to persons less tightly linked to the Soviet apparatus. Gorbachev thought he had found a way to detach the Warsaw Pact from the vulnerability of the Party, and even to strengthen his own control when like-minded leaders came to power in the associated states. The opportunity to test these ideas first presented itself in Poland.

A new round of strikes in 1988 forced the Polish regime to negotiate with Solidarity. Two outcomes of these negotiations were the acceptance of free associations—the cornerstone of the civil society developed in Poland and indeed the basic idea of Solidarity itself—and an agreement to hold partially free elections in June of 1989. Solidarity candidates proceeded to win virtually every seat for which they were allowed to compete, preventing Jaruzelski from forming a communist government. He then asked Solidarity to come into the government as a coalition partner. When Polish Communist Party leader Mieczyslaw Rakowski balked at this, Gorbachev telephoned him on August 22, 1989, and directed him to go along. In exchange, Solidarity promised to remain within the Warsaw Pact and to preserve communist control over the state organs of security. Jaruzelski would become president and chief of the armed forces; the Ministry of Defense would remain in communist hands. Now, Gorbachev calculated, the economic crisis triggered by the accumulation of debt from the previous communist regime would have to be dealt with by Solidarity. The Warsaw Pact was, if anything, stronger than before and promised to survive the domestic upheavals that seemed to be spreading throughout its membership.

This perception was flawed in two respects. First, to the Poles and to others in Central Europe, Gorbachev's policies reflected Soviet doubt about the effectiveness of coercion. This tended to embolden the non-Communist opposition. Second, events in the Central European states inevitably reverberated in the Soviet Union itself. To Soviet citizens what was happening in Central Europe was unsettling, and made the communist alternative appear to be shunned by peoples thought to be fraternal allies.

The next opportunity to test Gorbachev's plans came in East Germany. When thousands of East Germans began packing the embassies of sympathetic Warsaw Pact states in an effort to expatriate to the West, Gorbachev gave approval to the Hungarian regime's proposal to open its border with Austria, permitting East Germans to flee. This triggered a mass exodus from East Germany and began the political crisis there that toppled the Honecker regime. As Michael Beschloss and Strobe Talbott wrote:

> The Hungarian government had obtained the Kremlin's tacit consent in advance. . . . [Gorbachev] privately told his aides that Honecker would have to go, as soon as possible. "The East German leadership can't stay in control." He ordered his General Staff to make sure that Soviet troops stationed in East Germany did not get involved in the strife that was sure to envelop the country.[23]

After letting some nine hundred Germans escape in August, Hungary opened its borders in September. In October, Gorbachev met with Honecker in East Berlin and urged him to adopt "reforms"; twelve days later Honecker was removed from power and replaced by Egon Krenz. On November 9 the East German government opened up the Berlin Wall. Krenz announced that he was planning free, democratic, and secret elections. These elections removed him from power.

As Fyodor Burlatsky has put it, Gorbachev's original hope was to have "mini-Gorbachevs" come to power. As is now clear, he overestimated the degree of legitimacy of communist reformers in Eastern Europe. While his counterreformation might have worked in 1968, communist revisionism was long dead by 1989. A civil society had developed and with it, legitimate leaders had emerged [who] could demand greater concessions from the revisionist communists who were espousing the *perestroika* line.[24]

Because these concessions were constitutional in nature they ultimately worked to defeat Gorbachev's strategic plan by destroying the Warsaw Pact.

On November 17, enormous spontaneous demonstrations erupted in Prague. Within one week the communist party leaders had resigned and a new government was formed. Now the process of constitutional mimicry began to operate against Gorbachev. Czechoslovakia and Hungary eliminated the leading role of the Communist Party from their constitutions in the fall of 1989, something hardly contemplated by *perestroika*. This quickly led to Czechoslovakia's decision to assert an independent foreign policy and to demand the removal of Soviet troops from Czech soil. On December 14, Poland announced that the agreement by which the Soviet Union had stationed troops in Poland was no longer valid. As Koslowski and Kratochwill concluded,

by allowing the eclipse of the leading role of the Communist Party within the bloc and at home, Gorbachev, probably unwittingly . . . defeated the rationale for the very existence of the bloc and its domestic institutions. When socialism was not automatically accorded a privileged position in the constitutions of any bloc state, the Warsaw Pact had lost one of its fundamental reasons for existence, making its continuation as an effective alliance less likely.[25]

In February 1990 Gorbachev took two fateful decisions: He agreed to a plan for German unification and he essentially jettisoned the Communist

Party as the vehicle for guiding the Soviet state. In that month he engineered the decision by the Central Committee to give up the Party's monopoly on power and allow a multiparty system. This move was completed when in March, Article 6 of the Soviet Constitution was abolished, thus legitimating opposition parties, and at the Twenty-eighth Party Congress in July, when the Party voted to give up its supervision of government by removing all government officials (except Gorbachev) from the Politburo.

But the Czech, German, and Polish revolutions in which Gorbachev had collaborated had encouraged rebellions in the Soviet republics. Widespread noncompliance with Soviet draft calls swept the country in 1990. The republics attempted to enhance their own legitimacy by declaring their separateness from Moscow, and assuring their publics that troops would not be used to suppress national movements. Boris Yeltsin, then the president of the Russian Republic, instructed Russian soldiers not to use force during the Lithuanian revolt, which occurred when the Baltic states asserted their independence from the USSR.

Gorbachev was no longer attempting to forge a more powerful and competitive Soviet Union; it was now a matter of simply preserving the Soviet state. This he decided could only be accomplished by joining the West. The vehicle for this partnership was collaboration in German unification. Such a partnership would offer him two advantages: it would enhance his personal political prestige as he would now be allied with the desirable West rather than the crumbling Party, and it would offer him access to financial support with which he might halt the Soviet state's quickening slide into bankruptcy.

This collaboration ended the Cold War. First fascism and then communism had been discredited, strategically and then constitutionally in the case of fascism, in the reverse order in the case of communism. Gorbachev's attempts to create a more strategically dynamic Soviet Union through constitutional innovation had in fact engineered a strategic collapse. In the wake of that collapse, legitimacy deserted the Soviet state.

A CONSTITUTIONAL AMENDMENT:
THE PEACE OF PARIS

The focus now shifted to Washington, where an exceedingly complex set of problems presented themselves. While for many persons the chief American figure in the collapse of the Soviet Union was Ronald Reagan, a better case can be made for the team of George Bush and James Baker, who in 1990 faced a delicate and dangerous set of issues they managed to resolve with consummate skill. The fact that the Soviet Union collapsed on their watch did not, of itself, assure them a secure status in the pantheon of Western statesmen; to the contrary, had they pressed too hard in an effort to exploit the vulnerabilities of the Soviet position they might very easily have cast away the winnings earned by several generations of Allied leaders. Nothing could be more misleading than the cliché that the Bush administration "presided" over the demise of the Soviet Union.

George Bush and James Baker had formed their friendship in Texas. Bush's father had been an investment banker and later U.S. Senator from Connecticut; the son had come to West Texas to make his fortune in the oil business, and he had succeeded. Like the father, he now turned to public service. In Houston he met Baker; the two families soon became friends. Their backgrounds were not dissimilar: Bush had gone to Andover, then to Yale, where he studied economics and was tapped by Skull and Bones. Baker had gone to Lawrenceville, then to Princeton, where he studied politics and was bickered into the Ivy Club. Bush had joined the Navy after college and seen action in the South Pacific; Baker had joined the Marines during the Korean War. Baker had returned to Texas to go to law school and then had gone back to Houston, where his grandfather's firm was one of the largest and most successful in the country. Bush had moved to Houston to enter politics. When Baker was becoming the managing partner at a prominent Houston law firm, Bush was being elected the first Republican congressman from Houston in almost a century. The two men were tennis partners at the local country club. They had similar political views though one was a Republican by inheritance and the other a Democrat for much the same reason; both were centrist, mildly conservative, and rather nonideological. When Baker's first wife died after an agonizing illness, Bush persuaded his friend to manage the Bush campaign for the Senate. Baker changed his registration and discovered a flair for politics that might have appalled his grandfather. Both men lost statewide races in Texas—Bush when he was defeated for the Senate in 1970, Baker when he ran for Attorney General in 1978. Neither man was a natural candidate. Indeed, excepting Bush's one successful race for the presidency (which Baker ran), neither has held public office by winning an election on his own since their defeats in Texas. Instead they flourished in high-level appointments in Washington, Baker first coming into the Ford administration as undersecretary of commerce, Bush having served Presidents Nixon and Ford in a series of senior posts (ambassador to the United Nations, director of Central Intelligence, envoy to the People's Republic of China). Bush arranged Baker's appointment at Commerce, and it was Baker who orchestrated Bush's most pivotal appointment, as running mate to Ronald Reagan in 1980. Baker managed the second Reagan-Bush campaign that assured Bush's primacy for the 1988 nomination.

Yet it was Ronald Reagan, who *was* a natural politician and had none of the awkwardness and self-consciousness of the privileged when they take up politics in a democracy, who brought both men to real power. He, and not they, had caught the wave of reaction that swept the United States in the late seventies and eighties. He made Bush vice president and then, to general surprise and some consternation among conservatives, chose Baker as his chief of staff. In Reagan's second term, Baker became secretary of treasury (having been blocked by conservatives from becoming national security adviser).

When Bush was elected, Baker was promptly named secretary of state. The Treasury portfolio is an ideal post, in the current era, to prepare for the State Department. It commands far less media attention and less competition from other players trying to usurp its role than the top jobs at State. By all accounts Baker was an effective treasury secretary, was partly responsible for the creation of NAFTA, successfully talked the dollar down in a tour de force of media and market psychology, and gained a reputation as a skillful negotiator. The Baker Plan to relieve Third World debt, however, never quite succeeded. Baker took to the Department of Treasury a team he had worked with at the White House, and these—Kimmitt, Zoellick, Ross, and Baker's spokeswoman Tutweiler—along with others he subsequently took to the Department of State. Thus by the time Baker went to State he had had eight years at the highest levels of government, in concert with a highly respected staff with whom he knew he could work effectively.

For several reasons Baker was better prepared for the role of secretary of state than any appointee since Dean Acheson. Like Acheson, he had served at the Treasury and had conducted negotiations with foreign states at the highest levels; like Acheson he had been a successful lawyer and thus blended a sense of practical affairs with the ability to interpret and formulate messsages; like Acheson he had cultivated with success members of Congress and the media, the two most powerful constitutional entities in Washington; like Acheson, he had served a charismatic president but had reserved his trust and intimacy for that man's less glamorous successor. But above all, like Colonel House, he had engineered the nomination and election of a man who regarded him as a trustworthy and intimate friend.

Beginning in late 1989—as Gorbachev changed direction and began aggressively seeking a cooperative relationship with the West—Baker developed an intense collaboration with his Soviet counterpart, Shevardnadze. From the following February, Baker and Shevardnadze met every single month (with one exception) until the signing of the Paris Charter.*

---

*Consider the calendar of that fateful year which led up to the Peace of Paris. After Gorbachev accepted the Hungarian government's decision to allow independent political parties (February 1989) and the Polish roundtable agreement (April), Bush responded in May by stating that it was "time to move beyond containment" and to "seek the integration of the Soviet Union into the community of

There were of course many issues to be thrashed out in this breathtaking schedule of meetings, but two particular objectives dominated all others. First, the Soviet Union had to be moved along a path that would transform it from a communist to a parliamentary state. Second, the incorporation of a unified Germany into the Alliance that had in one coalitional form or another fought the Long War, had to be accomplished. Of course these two goals were to a large extent intertwined, and this added to the complexity and difficulty of the diplomacy by which they were achieved. If either objective had failed, that failure could have sunk the other. For example, at the Twenty-eighth Party Congress in July 1990, anti-Gorbachev elements counted on the spectre of German unification to rally opposition against the government. If West Germany (the FRG) had appeared more threatening—less linked to NATO's essentially defensive posture, more likely to acquire nuclear weapons—the result could well have been increased support in the balloting for Yegor Ligachev, who had become the leader of the anti-Gorbachev forces. The prospect of removing the most critical state, East Germany (the GDR) from the Warsaw Pact and simply handing it over to the stronger FRG—a conquest without cost—ought to have been frightening enough to threaten Gorbachev's hold on power. The United States, however, had proved itself a supportive and sympathetic partner since the Malta summit and NATO at its London meeting the same month had publicly agreed to "eliminate the last vestiges of the Cold War." Gorbachev was able to defend his policies by saying that the "context" provided by the Americans supplied the reassurance that enabled further agreements. Or to take a different counter-factual, if a more confrontational regime had replaced Gorbachev in Moscow, the German objective of reunification would not have simply vanished—it had achieved far too much momentum. Rather it would have been pursued by other methods, perhaps including the move toward neutrality with which the Soviet Union had so often tempted the FRG in the past. Bush and Baker thus had always to so maneuver in one dimension, the Soviet relationship, that they could use positive developments there to achieve results in the other dimension, Germany—and vice versa—when the historic relationship between the two states suggested just the opposite, namely that strengthening either society would alarm the other.

nations." He set, as a precondition for this integration, "a significant shift in the Soviet Union" and a "lightening-up on the control in Eastern Europe [that would allow those states] to move down the democratic path." In July, Bush secretly invited Gorbachev to meet in December—in advance of the scheduled summit planned for March. Gorbachev responded with alacrity and publicly acclaimed the invitation to "join the community of nations" by sending a letter to the members of the G-7 meeting at Paris. On September 21–23, Baker and Shevardnadze met at Baker's ranch in Wyoming and released a detailed joint statement covering the full range of U.S.–Soviet issues. On December 2–3 Bush and Baker, Gorbachev, and Shevardnadze met on shipboard for a wide-ranging discussion. The Americans proposed negotiating a trade agreement that would lift the restrictions on most favored nation status for the Soviet Union.

The most important steps that Bush and Baker could take to keep Gorbachev on the path toward assimilation into the society of parliamentary states had to do with protecting the increasingly hollowed-out shell of the Soviet state. So long as that state existed and so long as Gorbachev was its dictator—he had managed to ram through decisions when most of the Politburo opposed them, even in the case of the decision to remove the Communist Party's leading role in government—the Soviet Union would become increasingly parliamentary. Gorbachev was now careening along a course that could have almost no other desirable terminus for him than the embrace of Western economic and political multilateral institutions. Only a coup d'état would interrupt this trajectory. If the state collapsed altogether, however, Gorbachev lost the reason for which he had turned to the West, which was the survival of the state. In such chaos, it was not clear in 1989 what leaders would succeed Gorbachev and what their policies might be. It may have appeared that the Soviet Union was unworkable and that it was disintegrating under its own, entropic forces, but in actuality the Soviet economy was

> a workable system [though] decidedly inferior to capitalist economies. [I]t was compatible with modern industrial society and capable of technological change, increasing consumption, and taking on the rest of the world in military [and space] hardware.[26]

Indeed it still possessed the world's largest arsenal of nuclear weapons. It was therefore imperative that Bush and Baker take every opportunity to insulate Gorbachev from the consequences of the ideological and political collapse of communism and to avoid appearing to exploit his troubles. After so long a struggle it would have been tempting to destabilize the Soviet system, covertly giving arms to the breakaway republics, flying into Eastern European capitals to make dramatic declarations on the order of Charles de Gaulle's "Quebec Libre!" speech, accelerating interest-payment schedules in order to increase pressure on the regime, and so on.*

From the West's point of view, however, the Soviet Union in some ways presented a more tractable set of problems than did the issue of German unification. Chancellor Kohl, who had often been derided as an unimaginative, plodding leader in comparison to his more glamorous (and rather more vain) predecessors Brandt and Schmidt, had seized the unification issue with an energy that surprised everyone, not least of all his allies. Legally, however, it was not an issue that was Kohl's to decide. The Four Power Agreement that originally divided Germany gave no sovereign status to either the GDR or the FRG. Unification would have to come about as

---

*Which would have played well with the right wing in U.S. politics that distrusted Bush and Baker.

a result of negotiations and agreement among the signatories to that agreement, namely France, Britain, the United States, and the USSR. Each of these great states had substantial interests in the outcome of German unification. Britain, France, and the Soviet Union were far from eager to see a resurgent, single German state in the heart of Europe, united only by a shared sense of German nationalism. Each state looked to use its role as one of the Four Powers to protect itself by managing the course of any unification. This arrangement, however, would deny Kohl the leading role as architect of unification and inevitably pit the Soviets (and possibly the French) against the United States and the United Kingdom over German membership in NATO and the continued presence of U.S. troops on German soil. Yet only Kohl was capable of keeping the new Germany in NATO; the Social Democrats in both Germanys had just agreed that a united Germany should not belong to any military alliance. The United States would have to find a way to reassure its allies that unification should proceed on Kohl's timetable and largely under his direction, and at the same time trust that Kohl would not compromise on the Alliance issue even though he would be subjected to enormous pressures to do so. These pressures would come from two sources: first, Gorbachev might make renunciation of NATO membership the price of Soviet consent to unification, and second, Kohl would soon face a pan-German election in which a large part of the electorate would have recently been at least nominal communists while Kohl's own coalition held a bare majority in the West German Bundestag.

Baker and his team handled both sets of problems with such effectiveness that it can be argued that their ultimate resolution in Paris ranks in significance with House's bringing the United States into World War I and Acheson's skillful creation of NATO and the Marshall Plan after World War II. Of course everything depended upon the president in each of these instances. George Bush possessed the personal modesty not to showboat at Gorbachev's expense and the patience to let the Soviet Union metamorphose internationally according to its own inner dynamic. Bush had cultivated good relationships with Allied leaders and was trusted by them. Perhaps most importantly, he deeply believed in the goals of the Long War. Every president has in his mind a predecessor who sets the mold for how he thinks the presidency should be conducted. For Franklin Roosevelt it was Wilson; for Lyndon Johnson it was FDR; for George Bush it was Dwight Eisenhower; for Bill Clinton it was John Kennedy. And for every presidency this mental model eventually causes great difficulties. President Bush was criticized for not having a domestic vision because he basically held, with Eisenhower, that the domestic sector would take care of itself if left alone by government. Bush was praised for his Gulf War leadership in part because, like Eisenhower, he proved to be an excellent coalitional war leader, sensitive to the political dimensions of alliance war-fare. Eisenhower's life had spanned the Long War, and he held a crusader's view of its goals, expressed in the flat rhetoric of a centrist Republican. Bush was ideally suited to bring the Long War to a close, but he needed a foreign secretary who could devote himself almost wholly to this problem and devise and execute a set of negotiating tactics through the thicket I have described above, confronting and persuading three difficult parties: the Soviets, the Allies, and the U.S. Congress.

Instead of exploiting the increasing disarray within the Soviet bloc, the United States extended to the Soviet Union access to several multilateral institutions, offered financial aid and technical assistance for economic reform, and most importantly supported Gorbachev's obviously doomed efforts to hold the Soviet state together. Gorbachev's strategy now was to secure financial support for the Union, hoping that the republics would not wish to abandon a state that was their lifeline to economic assistance.*

During this period, Baker and his team devised a plan for effecting the reunification of Germany that had two important features: first, the Four Power Agreement would be used to create a "Two-plus-Four" negotiating framework, thus breaking out the two Germanys to negotiate with each other, and then presenting the results to the Four Powers, France, the United Kingdom, the United States, and the Soviet Union; second, Soviet consent would be sought for a new Germany within NATO. Both of these notions were highly controversial and there was strong opposition, within the Alliance and in Moscow, respectively, to both ideas. Baker, however, linked the two, realizing that by strengthening Kohl's position *and* Gor-bachev's the United States stood the best chance of achieving its Long War goals—that is, of anchoring German democracy to the West and bringing the Soviet Union into the society of parliamentary states.

Initially, British, French, and Soviet foreign ministers rejected the Two-plus-Four plan, preferring what might be called "Four-plus-Zero" instead. This would have provided that the four powers agree among themselves on a program for reunification and then present it to the FRG and the GDR. This would have posed an insurmountable problem of what is sometimes called "path dependence," the idea that the order in which decisions are

---

*With the Central and Eastern European countries, the United States was studiedly circumspect. The Bush administration responded to the East German revolt by sending Baker to meet with the com-munist premier and to offer economic assistance to the GDR. When violence broke out in Romania after the revolt against the dictator Ceaușescu, Baker announced that he would not oppose Soviet inter-vention, even though until recently Romania had enjoyed privileged status in the West owing to its independent line from Moscow. In response to the Lithuanian declaration of independence in May 1990, Baker refused to recognize the new government even though the United States had long main-tained that the Soviet annexation of the Baltics was illegal. Even as late as six weeks before the anti-Gorbachev coup, Bush went to Moscow to sign the Strategic Arms Reduction Treaty (START) and then stopped in Kiev to warn the Ukrainians of the dangers of independence.

taken affects their outcome. If an initial consensus among the Four Powers were required, the Soviet Union would be in a position to insist on a non-NATO Germany. But if the two Germanys themselves could reach consensus on a unification plan that permitted NATO membership, then the chancellor could bargain directly with Gorbachev and perhaps find a price for Soviet consent.* Moreover, "Four-plus-Zero" was a reprise of what had happened at Versailles—the imposition of a constitutional order without first achieving a consensus that included the German leadership.

In December 1989, President Mitterand and Prime Minister Thatcher met privately to share their misgivings about German unification. Earlier Mrs. Thatcher had emphasized that German unification was, after all, "more than a matter of the sensitivities of the German states." She stressed that "the feelings and interests of other European countries" had to be taken into account. In Paris a debate began about whether a reunified Germany would kill the European Union. The diplomatic commentator, Pierre Lelloche, wrote at the time that "[t]he French are beginning to realize that post-Yalta Europe may well signal the end of French dreams of grandeur and French-controlled European 'federation.'"[27] Baker, however, was able to persuade the British that "Four-plus-Zero" meant unacceptable delay and risked German unification by fait accompli. Without the British, the French could not afford to alienate German sensibilities by being the sole objector; in March the French Foreign Minister announced that France would not insist on a purely Four-Power agreement. In Ottawa on February 13, 1990, representatives of the Four Powers agreed on the "Two-plus-Four" plan.

Delivering "Two-plus-Four" cemented the U.S. relationship with Kohl, and in turn "enabled Kohl's government to persuade the Germans that a united Germany should stay loyal to NATO."[28] Now Baker turned to winning the approval of Gorbachev for German membership in the Atlantic alliance. If this could be accomplished, then any residual German doubts about the wisdom of remaining in NATO would be quieted. At the same time, Baker sought to couple Soviet consent with approval of the Conventional Forces in Europe (CFE) Treaty, making drastic cuts in troop levels and armaments deployed across the Central Front of divided Europe. The vast size of the Soviet forces would be dramatically reduced and a system of international inspections put in place to ensure transparency—a confidence-building measure by which strategic surprise and an unintended chain reaction of mobilization and even pre-emption are sought to be avoided. The NATO fear of a massed tank attack that only the use of

---

*Although it was not much commented on at the time, a not dissimilar consideration operated with respect to France, which might not have been entirely averse to seeing U.S. troops expelled from Germany and to having the WEU, of which the United States is not a member, supplant NATO.

nuclear weapons could stop was abating. If Soviet consent could be won for "Two-plus-Four" *and* CFE, two parts of the three-part Paris Charter would be in place.

Chancellor Kohl now left for a hastily arranged meeting in the Caucasus with Gorbachev. About 3,000 East Germans were emigrating daily in addition to the 344,000 who had gone west in 1989. Kohl claimed that monetary union with the East was the only way of avoiding a complete East German collapse and a flood of refugees numbering in the millions. Gorbachev had continued to insist that a unified Germany would either have to be neutral or at least free of any foreign troops. The week of Kohl's visit, Yakovlev, Gorbachev's closest ally in the Politburo, asserted that Soviet troops would leave East Germany only when NATO left West Germany.

Three events beyond the Soviet Union, however, combined to change the Soviet position. First, at the Camp David summit in June Gorbachev had stressed his view that an American troop presence in Europe was a factor for stability. "I want you to know that I regard this as in your interest and in our interest," he is reported to have told Bush, providing one more example of Gorbachev's increasing desire to become a part of a Europe-wide security system (within which, as many realized, Germany would sit uneasily as a nonnuclear power if the Soviet Union and not the United States were part of that system). Gorbachev had to be persuaded that the Soviet goal of a de-Americanized, denuclearized Germany was potentially catastrophic for Soviet interests: so long as Germany did not have nuclear weapons, the Americans would have to be present in Europe to provide a link to extended deterrence; if the Americans left, Germany was likely to acquire nuclear weapons for herself. Not two superpowers, half a globe apart, but the two largest armies in Europe would face each other, separated only by the Polish plain.

Then the Americans had proposed at the London NATO Council meeting on July 6 that the Soviet Union no longer be treated as an "enemy and that NATO should be transformed from a primarily military alliance to a primarily political institution." Bush wrote to Gorbachev, "I want you to know that [the London Declaration] was written with you importantly in mind." Having floated this offer scarcely a week in advance of the Kohl-Gorbachev meeting, the Americans waited anxiously for a reply.[29] Finally, on the day before Kohl left for Moscow, the West Germans announced they were sending the Russians food aid worth about $130 million. Against the background of these three events, on July 15 it was announced that Gorbachev and Kohl had agreed to a cut in German armed forces, a German subsidy to Soviet troops during the period of transition, and a Soviet undertaking to renounce all restrictions on the exercise of German sovereignty, including Germany's right to choose its own alliances. Kohl promised a broad program of economic assistance to the Soviet Union.

The Soviets had abandoned their long-standing policy of forcing a German choice between unification with neutrality or continued German division with West German membership in NATO.[30]

While Gorbachev and Kohl were celebrating their agreement, Ukraine became the seventh Soviet republic to declare its sovereignty. Like the Russian Federation, it chose for the moment to remain within the Union but it revoked the right of Soviet troops to remain on Ukrainian territory. Now the Soviets could hardly refuse to sign the CFE Treaty: in promising to remove troops from forward areas they were only conceding what would soon be forced on them. From the U.S. point of view, however, CFE established a precedent that would subsequently be used to govern agreements with Ukraine, Belarus, and the Russian Federation. There remained only the final piece, the commitment to parliamentarianism itself.

On September 3 Baker gave a summary of his goals: "to cast our vision beyond the prevention of war . . . to the actual building of peace. To prevent war, we must continue to deter aggression . . . To build the peace, however, America's role must go beyond balancing itself against remaining Soviet power."

The "first task" on this agenda, he said, was

> fostering legitimacy—or, to put it plainly, government selected by the people and responsible to them. After sweeping away the dictators of the past, the peoples of Central and Eastern Europe are working to build legitimate political orders that can endure. America must continue to stand with them, reassuring them of our commitment to their new democracies.[31]

He then proposed free elections as the qualifying standard for every state, and outlined a CSCE (Conference on Security and Cooperation in Europe) process to monitor such elections. This proposal was formalized in the Copenhagen Declaration, which was then ratified by the Charter of Paris and formed one of the crucial documentary elements of the Peace of Paris. When Gorbachev was temporarily overthrown in a coup d'état, this provision was given such dramatic emphasis that the subsequent Moscow Declaration, the final document in the Peace of Paris suite, explicitly provided that democratic regimes were to be guaranteed by the state system and that the sovereignty of any state was forfeited if it failed to uphold the parliamentary model. The Long War was ending, and a new constitution for the society of states was being put in place.

In form, the Charter of Paris is more or less explicitly an amendment and extension of the Charter of the United Nations, which is reaffirmed in the text of the Charter of Paris. Indeed the Peace of Paris, which includes the Charter of Paris, can be seen as an amendment to Versailles (and San

Francisco, which had promulgated the United Nations Charter). The final amendments to the Versailles/San Francisco system include the series of political agreements made by the participating states of the CSCE, beginning with the Helsinki Final Act in 1975, the Charter of Paris in 1990,* as well as the Copenhagen and Moscow Documents, which bracketed that Charter. These signified the end of the Long War by recognizing Germany, and created the instruments by which Russia was formally admitted to the society of parliamentary nation-states. Taken together, these agreements provide the texts of the constitution of the society of nation-states. As Judge Thomas Buergenthal wrote in 1992, the process I have called the Peace of Paris "has transformed into a new order for the world."[32]

For three days in Paris in late November 1990, the heads of state or government from thirty-four nation-states—including the Soviet Union, the United States, Great Britain, Germany, and France—met for the second time since the signing of the Helsinki Final Act in 1975. The Paris summit was neither one of the follow-up meetings contemplated by the Helsinki Final Act, however, nor one of the minor meetings provided for on specific subjects. Indeed a "summit of this nature was, in fact, not envisaged by previous CSCE decisions."[33] Gorbachev proposed this reconvening of the parties that had first met at Helsinki in order to give the blessing of the society of European states to the "Two-plus-Four" agreements that unified Germany.[34] It was also felt that such a forum might encompass the signing of the CFE Treaty among twenty-two of the CSCE members, confirming for the entire European community an arms control agreement to which only some members were parties. Finally, the meeting in Paris would formalize the adoption of free elections in all member countries. The linking of these three subjects is significant for our study. Only when one variant of the nation-state had achieved consensus could the Long War end, unifying Germany and demilitarizing the central front. The commitment to parliamentary forms of election was thus a precondition, not a consequence, of the success of the other two issues to which it was joined in Paris.

The core provisions of the Charter of Paris that issued from this congress are contained in its first chapter, "A New Era of Democracy, Peace and Unity." It declares that

---

*The Helsinki Final Act was signed by almost all the principal European leaders of the time. It was the product of an intensive effort by the Soviet Union and its allies to obtain recognition for the strategic division of Europe. In exchange for this recognition, the West obtained various paper concessions from the Soviets in the area of human rights. Somewhat unexpectedly, Eastern Europeans and later Russians used these concessions to delegitimate the communist party regimes then prevailing such that once the Berlin Wall came down, the CSCE process set up at Helsinki quickened. Between January 19, 1989, and October 3, 1991, the Vienna Conference was concluded and followed six months later by the Paris Conference, which was in turn followed one year later by the Copenhagen Conference, and then by the Moscow Conference—all children of Helsinki.

Europe is liberating itself from the legacy of the past. The courage of men and women, the strength of the will of the peoples and the power of the ideas of the Helsinki Final Act have opened a new era of democracy, peace and unity . . . *We undertake to build, consolidate and strengthen democracy as the only system of government of our nations.* In this endeavor, we will abide by the following: Human rights and fundamental freedoms are the birthright of all human beings, are inalienable and are guaranteed by law. Their protection and promotion is the first responsibility of government. Respect for them is an essential safeguard against an over-mighty State . . . Democratic government is based on the will of the people, expressed regularly through free and fair elections. Democracy has as its foundation, respect for the human person and the rule of law. Democracy is the best safeguard of freedom of expression, tolerance of all groups of society, and equality of opportunity for each person. Democracy, with its representative and pluralist character, entails accountability to the electorate, [and] the obligation of public authorities to comply with the law and justice administered impartially . . .[35]

This charter then affirms the principles of the Helsinki Final Act, welcomes the new CFE Treaty, and concludes with an explicit approval of the Treaty on the Final Settlement with Respect to Germany signed in Moscow on September 12, 1990, which united Germany. Thus the title of the chapter: "Democracy [the provision for free elections and human rights], Peace [the endorsement of CFE], and Unity [the recognition of Germany]."[36]

Other commentators likened the summit meeting to "the historic Congress of Vienna."[37] In a perhaps unwitting reprise of Woodrow Wilson's remarks about the Versailles Conference,[38] President Mitterand emphasized, however, that the Paris "Summit was the 'anti-Congress of Vienna' because on the previous occasion the victorious powers remodeled the map of Europe without much regard for the aspirations of the peoples while the [Paris] Summit was the exact antithesis of such an approach."[39]

Perhaps most interesting for our study, however, is Mrs. Thatcher's characterization of the Charter of Paris as "a new Magna Carta."[40] What the British prime minister had in mind by this description is the Charter's emphasis on the provision of human rights. This observation underscores the role of the Peace of Paris as a constitution. Earlier constitutions, particularly Augsburg and Westphalia, had intertwined human rights—religious freedom in particular, but also the right of immigration—with the powers of states, just as domestic constitutions do. In contrast to the U.S. Bill of Rights, which might be said to describe a structure wherein every power not granted to the government is retained as a human right by the people, Magna Carta is best described as *granting* rights. In the case of sovereign states, such as those that convened in Paris, their promises to secure human rights are indeed very similar to those of Magna Carta. The Charter of Paris provides that states "affirm that, without discrimination, every individual has the right to freedom of thought, conscience, religion or belief, freedom of expression, freedom of association and peaceful assembly, freedom of movement [and that] no one will be subject to arbitrary arrest or detention, subject to torture or other cruel, inhuman or degrading treatment or punishment . . ." This language is further evidence of the constitutional nature of the Long War—the struggle to define the source of legitimacy for the State from which the division of rights and powers arises—intertwining the domestic and international, the legal and strategic. "It is clear that states which adopt ideologies incompatible with the new . . . democratic public order must henceforth be considered in violation of their [legal] commitments."[41] Strikingly the Moscow declaration, the final element in the Peace, states, "the commitments undertaken in the field of the human dimension . . . are matters of direct and legitimate concern to all participating States and do not belong exclusively to the internal affairs of the State concerned."[42]

The Peace of Paris provides the source of an overarching constitutional order that sets the standard to which all national legal and political institutions must conform. In Buergenthal's insightful words,

> [t]hese constitution[al documents] articulate national political, social, economic and sometimes even moral values; they set various priorities for the nation; they establish or call for the establishment of governmental institutions; and they lay down the framework for the evolution of the political process. In short, they shape and are the ideological and political source of the nation's constitutional order. . . . *The nation's law and legal institutions derive their legitimacy from these constitutions.*[43]

The Peace of Paris ended the Long War, amended the agreements at Versailles and San Francisco, and completed the process of formally globalizing the European nation-state through a universal international law. The Peace of Paris also, however, has elements of a transitional document about it for it gives a glimpse of the new constitutional order that is emerging and that has yet to suffer *its* epochal war.

These harbingers of the market-state include a change in the definition of sovereignty that allows human rights to become an enforceable part of international law, as was most recently seen in Kosovo, where Serbian sovereignty was abrogated; an effort to give formal recognition to nonstate institutions, like the media of journalism and the multinational corporation, and to give them a constitutional role in the life of the State according to consumer, not voter, preferences; to ensure for the market-state and its consumers free and open markets (just as Versailles had attempted to ensure free and open democracies for self-determining voters). All of these portentous changes were largely ignored at the time but each is highly controversial and likely to be the source of conflict in the future. Slobodan Milosevic is not the last leader to deny vital human rights to a group of his citizens—as the Dalai Lama might have reminded us. Some twenty states still attempt to censor or strictly control access to the Internet, and Malaysia has been successful—for the time being—in imposing capital flow controls to regain some measure of power over its currency. Most important, there are deep divisions—described in the scenarios in Chapter 25—among the three emerging versions of the market-state and their respective attitudes toward sovereignty and the relationship of sovereignty to human rights.

CONSTITUTIONAL INTERPRETATION: THE LEGAL SCHOOLS

In 1922 Maxim Litvinov, the Soviet foreign minister, said that "it was necessary to face the fact that there was not one world but two" and "there was no [other] world to arbitrate [between them]." In 1990, however, Gorbachev proposed, in a speech to the United Nations,

> to expand the Soviet Union's participation in the controlling mechanisms of human rights under the aegis of the U.N. and within the framework of the European process. We think that the jurisdiction of the International Court in the Hague with regard to the interpretation and application of agreements on human rights must be binding on all states.[44]

What developments had occurred in international law that reflect this enormous journey?

The international law that led to the Peace of Paris was a reaction to the failure of both Weimar and Versailles: that is, it was a reaction to the domestic consequences of the collapse of a legally constructed state and to the international consequences of the continuation of the Long War precipitated by that collapse. Not simply the laws, but the very state itself of Weimar* was purpose-built, and this obvious fabrication was inevitably

---

*The capital of unified Germany has been returned to Berlin.

contrasted unfavorably with the sentimental, allegedly ancient, customary state of the Wilhelmine Reich (though both were of a very recent constitutional order, the nation-state). The Weimar state was discredited by Versailles, which imposed a parliamentary form on Germany; and the failure of Weimar in turn was soon also to discredit Versailles, as it became apparent that the peace settlement had failed and that the war that began in 1914 had persisted beyond 1919.

It has rightly been observed that the international law of the period before the Long War

> [saw] intergovernmental and non-governmental organizations playing relatively a minor role on the global stage. Customary law and state practice formed the primary sources of international law which served a largely interstitial *laissez-faire* function, reflecting vested national interests and leaving large realms of unregulated state activity.[45]

The Long War, however, introduced a new era, which has been characterized as that of international *institutions* rather than international *law*.[46] The customary practices of the great state-nations gave way to the codifications of the nation-state, which created the League of Nations and the Permanent International Court of Justice. These products of Versailles reflected the nation-state's characteristic reliance on law. In the most public and historic way possible, however, the League and the PICJ soon proved to be failures.

The San Francisco replay of Versailles had intensified the move toward institutionalizing international law, with not much better results. Harold Koh puts this well:

> Following World War II, the architects of the postwar . . . system posited [a] complex positive law framework of charters, treaties, and formal agreements, [an] intensely regulatory, global framework. . . . Almost immediately, however, the Cold War era and the intense bipolarity and political realism it fostered rendered this positivistic vision a Potemkin Village.[47]

The irrelevance of international law to the global, epochal conflict then raging was compounded by changing attitudes toward law itself. Dean Acheson wrote dryly that "[t]hose who devote themselves to international relations . . . are understandably reticent about the role of law." They knew, Acheson said, that law was what government officials said it was— no more—and that the study of law was the assessment of what, in fact, authoritative legal decision makers would do when law was invoked as a basis for decision making.* This was hardly welcome news to those international lawyers who hoped to restrain power through law; if law was only what the powerful said it was, how could international law compel a state to do anything that was not in that state's interest? And if that was the limit of the law, what did it contribute beyond the rational assessment of self-interest that would take place anyway?

Out of this intellectual and moral abyss, a half dozen schools of thought emerged, each trying to establish a justifiable yet realistic basis for international law. They began with the classic approaches that had originated with Vitoria and Suarez at the birth of the modern state, but these schools transmuted those inherited approaches in light of the challenge of the Long War and the death of the idea of a jurisprudence that was distinguishable from politics, a jurisprudence that could be *found,* rather than made (up).

The fundamental approaches that divided thinkers about international law before the twentieth century can be roughly characterized as formalism and naturalism. Formalism focuses on the extent to which legal truths are the result of following arbitrary rules, that is, rules that have no necessary relation to any particular content. The formalist in international law, like Suarez[48] or Austin (or Leibniz), derives the truth or falsity of a legal proposition from a fact unrelated to its content. The international law governing, for example, the extraction of minerals from the sea may change its content over time but so long as it is generally recognized by the society of states, it has the status of law. Any particular proposition of law (e.g., states are entitled to the minerals in their littoral waters) is true if the test of general recognition is met. By contrast, the naturalist in international law, like Grotius[49] or Bluntschli (or Hume), holds that the relationship between the content of legal rules and the world accounts for their truth or falsity. Legal rules must be in accord with the nature of man, which is part of the nature of the universe. For example, one of the doctrines of *jus cogens*† holds that slavery is a violation of international law. If a state were to deny this was the case—indeed if two states were to deny this proposition in a treaty between them—the proposition that slavery is against the law would still be true, because it is in accord with the most fundamental human rights that arise from man's capacity for free will. In the case of both naturalism and formalism, the truth of a legal rule is tied to something in the world, but in one case (naturalism) that *something* has to do with the content of

---

*Acheson's successor, John Foster Dulles, declared, "I confess to being one of those lawyers who do not regard international law as law at all." Anthony Arend, *Pursuing a Just and Durable Peace: John Foster Dulles and International Organization* (Greenwood Press, 1988), 57.

†"Jus cogens norms, which are nonderogable and peremptory, enjoy highest status within customary international law, are binding on all nations, and cannot be preempted by treaty . . . [They include] torture, murder, genocide, and slavery" *U.S.* v. *Matta-Ballesteros,* 71 F. 3d 754 (1995).

the legal rule, and in the other (formalism) that *something* has to do with the status of the rule as law, irrespective of its content.[50]

In the early twentieth century, principally in the United States, the foundations of these two traditions were shaken by a new movement, Legal Realism. One of its founders, Karl Llewellyn, had written in 1930, "What these officials [judges, sheriffs, clerks, lawyers, presidents] do about disputes is, to my mind, law itself."[51] Llewellyn and others then set about showing that it was virtually impossible to account for past decisions by reference to the body of legal rules alone, let alone to predict what officials would in fact do in actual cases in the future. When the move to a society of nation-states took international law away from a small coterie of sophisticated specialists and put it in the hands of mass propagandists seeking justifications for their foreign policies, international law became vulnerable to the disenchantment that arose from the Realist critique of law generally. It was obvious that international law was manipulated to rationalize rules rather than to determine them, that sometimes it was ignored in deference to powerful interests, and that it even appeared indeterminate, leaving its commands to be decided by the changing needs of foreign policy.

Formalism and Naturalism in international law played out in various different attempts to meet the challenge of Legal Realism. Formalism became the source of three schools of thought: Legal Process, Nominalism, and Consensualism. Naturalism served as the source of the New Haven School, Neo-Realism, and what might be called *Perspectivism*. These families of thought about the basis for international law have, as families do, overlapping memberships, black sheep, father figures, deeply held prejudices about each other, relationships deriving from birth order, inherited traits, exaggerated genealogies, and so on. The distinctions among them have to do with their answers to the two shattering twentieth century questions about international law: if the body of international legal rules cannot uniquely determine the legality of a particular act by the parties it is supposed to govern, how can it be law? And if international law is law, why doesn't it seem to have any effect? Indeed these two challenges, arising from developments in law (the claims of Legal Realism) and strategy (the persistence of the Long War), might be put in a single question: would the history of the twentieth century have been any different if there had been no international law?

LEGAL PROCESS

The advocates of the International Legal Process School begin with the answer to the Legal Realist challenge given by Henry Hart, whose influential work, *The Legal Process* (with Albert Sacks), initiated an entire movement in American jurisprudence. Hart sought to change the focus of jurisprudence from the substantive rule finding so much in evidence in nineteenth century treatises on law to the process of creating precedent. It's not what judges do, Hart told us; it is how they do it. Granting the Legal Realist's argument that assessing the substantive fairness of a particular outcome is a matter of ideology, Hart's approach holds that fairness will nevertheless result if methods of legal decision making that all parties concede to be fair are scrupulously adhered to. That adherence, not the substantive fairness of the rules, will in turn deliver legitimacy, and legitimacy will bring about compliance. Thus the International Legal Process School denies that law is altogether manipulable by the parties—and thus it retains its distinction from politics—because the legal process is distinct unto itself,* and is assessed by legal, not political, standards.

The Hart and Sacks materials that dealt with U.S. domestic law had emphasized the interaction of institutions and procedures. When Abram Chayes, Thomas Ehrlich, and Andreas Lowenfeld published a set of case materials on international law, these were self-consciously styled on the Hart and Sacks work. Like the earlier case materials, they cut across doctrinal lines, including case studies drawn from international business as well as public international law and those arising from the acts of international organizations as well as the acts of states. The authors met the Legal Realist attack on international law head-on: they explicitly asked, "How and how far do law and lawyers and legal institutions operate to affect the course of international affairs?" and, anticipating their own answer to this question, they added, "What is the *legal process* by which interests are adjusted and decisions are reached on the international scene?"[52]

Hart's jurisprudence, however, was highly court-centered. The legal process was legitimate because the conscientious work of judges, rendering dispassionate judgments based on neutral, general principles derived from precedent, seemed to provide an answer to the Legal Realist's insight that the substance of the principles themselves could not be explained on a neutral basis, nor the scope of their application—their generality— justified on distinctly legal grounds. The role of courts and the availability of sanctions that render courts powerful were, however, far less in evidence on the international scene. Here, the International Legal Process advocates offered a startling defense of the analogy of their subject to that of Hart and Sacks: domestic law was not, in fact, as court-driven as it might appear. Much constitutional law was, for example, not reviewable

---

*Thomas Franck writes, "Legitimacy is a property of a rule or rule-making institution which itself exerts a pull towards compliance on those addressed normatively because those addressed believe that the rule or institution has come into being and operates in accordance with generally accepted principles of right process." The legitimacy of a norm in international law is indicated by four facts: its determinacy or clarity; its symbolic validation by diplomatic rituals and formalities; its conceptual coherence; and the development and maintenance by "right process." Thomas M. Franck, *The Power of Legitimacy among Nations* (Oxford University Press, 1990), 24.

by courts[53] and therefore the near-absence of judicial process in the international arena was not fatal to the Legal Process theory. Analogous institutional methods of constraining power by professionalizing the habits of officials were at work in both systems, domestic and international. Diplomats and senior officials also profited from the legitimacy conferred by well-understood rules, dispassionately applied.

But if the practical benefits of compliance with international law—predictability, mutuality, inertial continuity—were the basis for its operation, then presumably adherence to law would be abandoned when even greater benefits ran in the opposite direction, that is, toward noncompliance. That made legitimacy nothing more than a by-product of convenience. The international wing of the Legal Process School, by stressing the real-world forces making for coherence in and accommodation to law, sacrificed Hart's claim that legal process was fair not because it was efficient and effective but because it treated parties equally. By contrast, in the real world of international affairs, the relative weight and influence of the parties was supposed to be a determinative factor: that's what made the real world "real."

CONSENSUALISM

Outside the United States, one school of thought overwhelmingly dominates international law. I have chosen to call that school—which to most of its adherents seems so authoritative, so indisputable, that the term *school* seems inappropriately sectarian—*consensualism* because it holds that the content of international law depends wholly (or almost entirely) on the consent of states. Because states are the only entities capable of endowing international law with authority (on this view), only law created by states can legitimately bind them; and because states are sovereign, they can only be bound by that law to which they consent. To the challenge posed by the Legal Realists, the Consensualist replies that the entire approach of Legal Realism is parochial. *Of course* international law does not have the structures of compliance that domestic law does and therefore to the provincial mind might appear not to be *law,* just as snails or sweetbreads might not appear to be food to someone accustomed to the sort of cuisine found at McDonald's.

> A system of law designed primarily for the external relations of states does not work like any internal legal system of a state . . . As regards [the question of] international law as "law," the arguments of the critics [seize] upon . . . the topic of sanctions and compliance without recognizing the historical, structural and functional differences between legal systems within states and the international legal system as the necessary starting point of analysis. After all, there is no reason to assume

that the international legal system must, or should, follow the historical models of centralized systems of national law . . . A horizontal system [like that of international law] operates in a different manner from a centralized one . . .[54]

To the critic's point about the apparent failure of compliance with the legal order, the Consensualist has a suave and disarming reply. Because the international legal order is solely composed of those rules consented to by states, it is, ipso facto, usually complied with although its domain is more modest than those persons might wish who seek to use international law to reform states or coerce them into adopting particular policies. In any event, "spectacular cases of violation of international law, which attract the attention of the media more than regular conduct, are exceptional and should not be confused with the ordinary course of business between states."[55]

Consensualists share a fundamental premise: because international law is made and implemented by states, the consent of states, as manifested in their original intentions memorialized in explicit or implicit agreements, is the only basis on which rules may legitimately be said to govern state behavior.

Both parts of this premise, however, are under intense attack: the first because it seems to fly in the face of the increasing role of international organizations and the development of doctrines of human rights in international law that accord a legal role to the individual; the second, because the current behavior of states is a much surer guide to their attitudes about the propriety of governmental acts than an hypothesized "original" intention at some earlier time, even if that intention could be determined with accuracy (which is seldom the case).

There are answers to these objections. To the first, it might be observed that international organizations are to a large extent dependent upon the territorial entities—states—that fund them, carry out their mandates, and permit them to operate within their jurisdictions; this goes for the NGOs (nongovernmental organizations) as well, who exist at the sufferance of states, despite the occasional press release of the NGO that appears to suggest that it is the other way around. After all,

[o]nly states can be members of the United Nations, only states are entitled to call upon the U.N. Security Council if there is a threat to international peace and security, only states may appear in contentious proceedings before the International Court of Justice, and only states can present a claim on behalf of a national who has been injured by another state if there is no treaty [an agreement confined to states] to the contrary.[56]

To the second objection, the Consensualist replies with alarm that to abandon the edifice of the law in favor of chasing after the current political practices of states is to abandon what is useful and distinctive about the law: that it provides a standard by which current state practices are to be judged. A constant revision of these standards in order to bring them into congruence with discrepant behavior sacrifices this role; it allows "acts that would otherwise appear delinquent [to be] alchemized into harbingers of revised standards."[57]

The risk incurred, however, is that political actors will simply ignore a body of doctrine that increasingly departs from their interests. The Consensualist accepts this risk, underscoring the difference in mission between the Consensualist and other post–Legal Realist thinkers: the former does not seek to be a political adviser; rather he wishes to "preserve law's contribution to order by protecting its autonomy from ephemeral shifts in power and interests,"[58] even if it means appearing irrelevant. The Consensualist has one powerful arrow in his quiver—the ability to make governments squirm, to embarrass them, to require them to play the hypocrite before their publics—and he is reluctant to give up this high moral ground. The Legal Realist's reply concedes that, as la Rochefoucauld said, "hypocrisy is the compliment that vice pays to virtue,"[59] but asks "what good are compliments"?

There are, however, also very practical reasons why this particular school, so much ridiculed in the United States, is far and away the most dominant form in the world generally. One reason why the Consensualist position appears so unrealistic is that it treats the consent of all states equally, ignoring their relative positions of influence. This has the consequence of requiring a breadth of consensus to change international law that is very difficult to achieve and that gives marginally less powerful states a more influential role than those schools of international law that look to the behavior of the most powerful state as determining the content of legal rules. I think this in part accounts for the fact that outside the United States much of what Legal Realism regards as the "basic legal myth" still flourishes in international law. Not only European scholars[60] in international law, but also Asian scholars and commentators have been reluctant to depart from the traditional, Consensualist view of international law as located and determined rather than decided upon.[61]

NOMINALISM

The original intention of the states who are parties to a treaty or to a tacit understanding (as with custom) is binding in international law because that intention represents the scope of the states' consent. This is the basis for consensualism. But to what precisely did the parties consent? Not to their *intentions*, for states seldom have precisely the same intentions.

Rather like partners in a marriage of convenience they share the same bed but dream different dreams. The parties consent to a *text,* however, regardless of what intentions, if any, they may have shared. Indeed as a predictor of behavior, the original intentions of the parties begin to decay as soon as the moment of consummation has passed. If international law is extrapolated from the behavior of states, then their once-consensual agreement on a matter must be counted an increasing irrelevancy because "original intention has no intrinsic authority"[62] save what states choose to endow it with. Because the society of states is still in session, if intentions are to govern there is no reason to deny that society the authority to determine the propriety of a state's acts and omissions according to the present intentions of that society. But to do that is to accept that international law is no more than what states at any moment wish it to be.

A different approach to the problems posed by Legal Realism avoids the pitfalls of intentionalism by directing us to the text—for that is what the parties have agreed to, regardless of their intentions or their subsequent regrets. This approach can be termed *nominalism.*

The creed of the Nominalist might be put this way: Statecraft, long before there were written constitutions, found a role for written agreements.[63] Texts do not replace the networks of norms, conventions, and institutions that help to manage international relations and are so prized by legal process theorists, but formal writing in the diplomatic idiom does provide an economical and relatively unambiguous way for political leaders to commit themselves and their posterity, a necessity precisely because intentions may change. Besides this, written commitments catalyze a public dialogue over proposed commitments by the state. Such a dialogue can coalesce the public and its leadership around these commitments or prevent the state from making undertakings it cannot or should not fulfill.

It is true that "international law, like all law, involves the pursuit of social ends through the exercise of legitimated power and that in this sense it is reasonable to consider it as an aspect of the broader political process influenced by the factors that operate in politics generally."[64] But law is not the same as politics, for the set of rules that law comprises is binding on the political process, that is, accepted "as a means of independent control that effectively limits the conduct of the entities subject to the law."[65] Thus Oscar Schachter, a leading Nominalist in international law, rejects the Legal Realist's conclusion that international law is simply what states do. If we were to accept that state practice, and not the substance of legal rules, legitimates state action, then we would have sacrificed the binding, normative element of law. It seems as though we must then either put this element back in (as do the New Haven School personalities with whom Schachter was once associated) by empirically locating the normative nature of legal rules in a survey of the universally shared norms of the world's political cultures, or do without it, thus rendering law no more than an eccentric garnish,[66] like a classical allusion in a modernist poem. The Nominalist, however, locates this normative element in texts, and supports his position by pointing to the empirical fact that states are indeed most likely to restrain themselves when bound by specific treaty language. This is the Nominalist cosmology—a universe in which legal rules can be distinguished from both statements about the world (e.g., states happen to observe the three-mile limit) and moral statements (e.g., for the good of all, states ought to observe the three-mile limit). While there are areas of the law—including the regulation of force, the right to self-determination, the economic rights and duties of states, and extraterritorial jurisdiction— where "the ratio of specific rules to general principles is low," these are areas largely bereft of binding texts and, for this reason, are appropriate for the admixture of policies and practices.[67]

One example of this approach can be found in the debate over the legal parameters of armed intervention. The United States has argued that because sovereignty arises from the people, states that repudiate that popular basis—by denying democratic forms, or by practicing terror against their own populations—forfeit their claims of sovereignty and are therefore subject to lawful intervention by other states. Both the Haitian and Panamanian interventions* can be legitimated on this basis. Yet the texts of the U.N. Charter, numerous treaties, and U.N. resolutions explicitly proclaim the territorial integrity of states and their right of independence without qualification. For Schachter, the idea that "wars washed in a good cause such as democracy and human rights" do not violate these explicit textual prohibitions demands "an Orwellian construction of those terms."[68]

Text-based Nominalism is to be distinguished from the Legal Process School by its recognition that the normative force of the law is not to be found in legal procedures, but in the creation and application of substantive legal rules that "necessarily involve conditions, determinants and values that fall outside the law." At the same time, Nominalism is also quite different from Consensualism. For example, in the dispute over whether the special military agreements contemplated by Article 43 of the U.N. Charter are a precondition to the forming of military forces for missions endorsed by the U.N. Security Council—a dispute that arose over Desert Storm operations against Iraq—the two approaches came to different conclusions. An historical, consensualist account, reflecting the intentions of the framers and ratifiers of the Charter, would appear to require such agreements.[69] Schachter concluded, however, that the fact that there is "*no explicit language* in Article 42 or Article 43 . . . preclud[ing] states from voluntarily making armed forces available to carry out the resolutions of

*And the NATO action in Yugoslavia over Kosovo.

the Council [validly] adopted under Chapter VII" permitted the use of these forces.[70]

THE NEW HAVEN SCHOOL

Oscar Schachter posits this hypothetical: Suppose the U.N. Charter's unanimity rule for action by the Security Council were to be challenged on the ground that this rule was not, after all, compatible with the higher values of peace and security, as was shown countless times during the Cold War when the Soviet veto thwarted action by the Security Council. Suppose the network of treaties making up the Law of the Seas were to be held inconsistent with the fundamental goal of the freedom of the sea. Or imagine that one were to attack the decision of the International Court condemning Iran in the Tehran hostage case as invalid "by asserting it gives effect to diplomatic immunity, a 'secondary' international policy rather than to national sovereignty, a 'fundamental' goal." There is no treaty, no legal rule, no precedent that cannot be unseated by an appeal to higher values— which is a way of saying that law is replaced in such analysis by policy. The object of this hypothetical exercise[71] is to ridicule gently the New Haven School,[72] which exalts the fundamental values of world order as the indispensable guide to determining and applying international law.

The New Haven School is an informal collegium that resulted from the remarkable collaboration between Harold Lasswell, a polymath social scientist, and Myres McDougal, a Legal Realist law professor at the Yale Law School and academic empire builder of whom Clive would have been envious.

By the mid-1930s Legal Realism had successfully discredited the image of lawyers and judges mechanically finding the law and unreflectively applying it. The result was a widespread disillusionment with legal institutions as they came to be seen as more politicized and therefore less detached than had hitherto been believed. But whereas the three schools previously discussed each attempted to restore legitimacy to law and deflect the Legal Realist's indictment through a series of avoidance maneuvers, the New Haven School robustly embraced the fundamental insights of Legal Realism.

To the Legal Realists, law was "too filled with conflict . . . leaves too much open . . . too much to be decided" for legal rules to completely control a decision.[73] Yet it was this mechanistic, formulaic image that had sustained the law's prestige in the era of the state-nation. If there were *choices* to be made—inevitable, ineluctable, inescapable choices—then axiomatic legitimacy could not be accorded whatever decision was made.

As Michael Reisman, the scion of the New Haven School dynasty,[74] put it, McDougal and Lasswell—the School's patriarchs—undertook a "constructive operation . . . in the world community shattered by World War II precisely because the classical system [of world order] and the classic legal tradition were not working."[75] Richard Falk, the Absalom figure in this drama and another second-generation spokesman for the New Haven School, noted:

> The McDougal and Lasswell undertaking can be regarded as converting the core insight of legal realism into a comprehensive framework of inquiry, including the provision of a normative rudder . . . dedicated to the promotion of human dignity—by which to assess the relative merits of opposing lines of argument . . . [76]

But of course Legal Realism did not simply fail to provide "a normative rudder"—it denied the very possibility of one, apart from one arbitrarily chosen (or unconsciously adopted). As a result, the New Haven School's helpful proposal of a golden rule by which to assess all other rules has proved to be the most controversial part of its program. That program does indeed co-opt, as Falk argues, the core insight of Legal Realism: that law is more than a collection of rules and that it is a continuous process of "authoritative decisonmaking."* But in addition to its descriptive dimension (which is wholly consistent with the program of the Legal Realists) the New Haven School has a prescriptive dimension (which breaks new ground). The latter reflects the ethical norms of the parliamentary nation-state, not the scientistic ethical detachment of Legal Realism (even though it sometimes, unfortunately, adopts its locutions).

The New Haven School descriptive program depicts a process of law creation and application that aims to clarify the choices made by decision makers. Lawyers are assigned the role of "experts in making and helping others to make rational choices about law."[77] Instead of merely summarizing the available precedent, the New Haven School attempts to analyze the factors that led to particular precedents and to posit various alternatives, using empirical studies where possible. The purpose of any process of legal decison making is to allocate resources according to the values of the community. The objective of the New Haven School analysis is to allow the decision maker to maximize the degree to which these desired values are in fact reflected in the ultimate allocations.

So far we have the program of the Legal Realists: to enable decision makers to maximize social values,[78] going beyond the casual assemblage of anecdotal evidence confirmed by precedent and aiming instead at a sys-

---

*Decisions are not law unless they possess both *authority*—"the participation in decision in accordance with community perspectives about who is to make what decisions with what criteria"—and *control*—defined as "effective participation in [decision making] and execution." McDougal and Lasswell, 384. "When decisions are authoritative but not controlling, they are not law but pretense; when decisions are controlling but not authoritative, they are not law but naked power." Ibid.

tematic assessment of the empirical bases for all policy alternatives. McDougal, however, wished to ground this assessment in a particular set of values: specifically he wanted to measure all international law against the goal of promoting a world order founded on the fundamental principles of human dignity. This is the prescriptive side of the New Haven School program. McDougal subtly insinuated this prescription into the Realist program by claiming to have empirically determined the expectations of the community whose values law is supposed to promote.

For international law, McDougal held that the relevant community is that of the entire "earth-space" in which people interact. Far from concluding that such a space includes communities of incompatible value systems,[79] the New Haven School identifies a common goal, human dignity. The realization of this common goal requires, as a practical matter we are told, a free, democratic, parliamentary nation-state.

Schachter is wittily dubious about this "empiricism" and attempts to turn the argument, as we shall see, into a textual one. He writes:

> But how does one discover the values that some four billion people actually hold? McDougal has no great difficulty. He finds without any research but quite plausibly that the "overwhelming numbers of people of the world" want peace, security, respect, the right to determine their own destinies. These aspirations are summed up as the values of human dignity . . . A cynical critic may question the assumption that these values are universally shared. It is not only that they are rejected by many repressive regimes; it is also evident that peoples everywhere manifest aggressive tendencies, show contempt for different faiths and cultures, seek to dominate and coerce others. Can we say on a purely empirical basis that respect for the worth of an individual is a value held by most peoples? . . . The important fact for law and international politics is that these "higher" values have been accorded normative status by their inclusion in *authoritative instruments* [the texts of treaties, conventions, declarations, etc.] that have been accepted by virtually all of the world's governments . . . Their normativity also has a legal character inasmuch as they are embodied in legal principles expressed in such authoritative instruments as the U.N. Charter and other major treaties.[80]

It is easy to see the distinction between Schachter's reliance on texts and McDougal's program. McDougal, too, realized that the values of human dignity can "be found in expressions in the U.N. Charter, the Universal Declaration of Human Rights," and other documents. But while for Schachter this is what gives humane values their legal authority, for McDougal their presence in legal documents was merely evidence of the ethos of humanity underlying those documents. "The 'precedents, treaties, and established legal concepts' to which Professor Schachter refers are of course relevant, but they are relevant only for the policies they express."[81]

McDougal maintained that there was an ethos present in the society of states—the drive to win and secure human dignity—and this proved a decisive insight in the Long War between the parliamentary nation-state and its Communist foes. He correctly saw that there was no middle ground.

History is encoded in our institutions. McDougal sought to read that code by means of his meticulous if sometimes tedious lists. The history he read there united the basis of the legitimacy of the parliamentary nation-state (its commitment to individual dignity) with its strategy (to achieve a world order in which this commitment was not under mortal threat). But this position was not "compelled" by legal argument, no matter how passionately McDougal adhered to it.

The New Haven School has been controversial throughout this era. Thomas Franck has disparagingly written of "vogue-ish legal thinking, dominated by the school of policy science, [which] has professed its normativity even while advancing a theory of creative interpretation of positive law that is nihilist in all but name, thus pitting the descriptive and prescriptive aspects of the School against each other."[82] Louis Henkin has criticized the School's view of law as a policy process by noting that it is a view of law "not as is but always as becoming . . . The law is what God, or the United Nations, or History . . . will say—later—in judging what nations had done in the light of context and consequences."[83] But no criticism was quite as furious as that which came from the staunch anti-Communist Dean Acheson.

NEOREALISM

Pollack concluded in 1987 that

> American legal realism reached the zenith of its popularity in the first half of the twentieth century. Its supporters included many of the leaders in legal education, the judiciary, and the bar. This popularity, however, declined rapidly, and today the theory is without important representation.[84]

This statement can only be true if the author intended to exclude virtually all senior officials working in the U.S. national security establishment. As Acheson put it in a scathing attack on McDougal:

> Those who devote themselves to international relations in foreign offices at what is disparagingly called "the working level" are understandably and wisely reticent about the role of law. This, however, is not true of academicians who write about it and teach it. . . . When former

Justice ... Hughes bluntly ... said that the Constitution is what the Supreme Court says it is, the lawyers were not too shocked, although they pretended that they were.[85]

Acheson was referring to one of the sacred texts of Legal Realism, the remark[86] by Chief Justice Charles Evans Hughes—also a former Secretary of State—that appeared to concede Karl Llewellyn's point that law is a matter of what decision makers decided it to be. Moreover, Acheson accurately (I believe) represented the attitudes of many diplomats and officials that international law is little more than a pretentious irrelevance. George Kennan, whom we may take to speak for the career foreign service and other military and intelligence professionals, shared this view. I will not quote at length Kennan's celebrated attack on international law, because Acheson is a more influential figure in this matter, perhaps because Acheson, unlike Kennan, was trained as a lawyer and became a distinguished partner at Covington and Burling. More importantly, he was "present at the creation" not only of the doctrine of containment, NATO and the Marshall Plan like Kennan, but also of Legal Realism. A protégé of then-professor Felix Frankfurter at the Harvard Law School, Acheson was selected by Frankfurter, a leading Realist, to become law clerk to Supreme Court Justice Louis Brandeis, a leading icon to Legal Realists. Brandeis, Acheson would later say, "had taught him to be both a pragmatist and an empiricist," the prescriptive and descriptive embodiments of Legal Realism.

In 1949, President Truman appointed Acheson secretary of state. His immediate task was to complete the process of bringing Germany and Japan into the society of states. In both cases, Acheson worked to qualify the sovereignty of the formerly fascist states where he ardently sought the development of democratic institutions. He was apparently heedless of the arguments from international law that these states had the right to develop their own security structures as they saw fit by virtue of their sovereignty, arguing instead that "world structure and order" demanded these invasive restraints. Because it was a matter of the stakes at risk in the Long War, which went to the heart of the constitutional existence of the parliamentary nation-state, Acheson believed American action on these questions could not be governed by any international legal rule. After all, the society of states that created such rules takes its legitimacy from its constituent states; how therefore could that society insist on the application of rules that might be fatal to its leading members? He later wrote:

I cannot believe that there are principles of law that say we must accept destruction of our way of life ... [when] the power, position and prestige of the United States ha[s] been challenged by another state ... [L]aw simply does not deal with such questions of ultimate power ...

No [international] law can destroy the state creating the law. The survival of states is not a matter of law.[87]

Note the *structural* basis for this argument—that international law is
created by a society of states that draws its constitutional power from its
constituent members, and thus cannot impose legal rules that undermine
the constitutional vitality and survival of the states themselves. It is important to distinguish this form of argument from the merely prudential—that
it is simply wiser not to follow such legal rules—because although structural arguments have a prudential component, their terms basically are set
by a constitutional structure and the inference that any legal rules thus
derived must cohere with that structure. This principle provides the goal
against which the prudence of any particular means is measured.*

The Neo-Realist finds something in the structure of international relations—its organization around states, their drive for power, their varying
and often conflicting national aspirations, the differences in strength
among them, the lack of a common morality—from which, given certain
commonsense assumptions about strategic behavior, legal rules can be
inferred. For example, consider the syllogism: (1) the constitution of the
society of states provides for the sovereignty of all members; (2) thus there
must be at least one thing that a state alone can decide for itself (there may
be more) or states would not be sovereign; (3) determining one's vital
interests is one item that must be for the state alone to decide because, as a
practical matter, if this determination were in other hands the state would
cease to be sovereign as all its other decisions could be manipulated or dictated. From this argument a legal rule regarding the admissibility of self-
defense can be inferred—"A state always has the right to act on behalf
of its vital interests—that is, those interests without which it would cease
to be able to perpetuate its society's way of life." This is in contrast to an
argument that adduces reasons extrinsic to the structure of the society of
states, either drawn from morality ("Some means of defending vital interests are inherently immoral and thus legally indefensible, for example, the
use of nuclear weapons") or from efficiency ("An arms embargo can
legally be imposed on a state—like Bosnia—despite its sovereignty if the
import of arms would only prolong a war whose outcome is foreor-
dained") or from some other, nonlegal parameter.

It was Acheson who brought Paul Nitze to the State Department. As
director for policy planning, Nitze became the principal author of NSC-68,
which firmly established a version of the doctrine of containment for

---

*As Paul Porter—another celebrated Washington lawyer—is said to have remarked, "If the ends
don't justify the means, I'd like to know what the hell does!"

which Kennan's famous Long Telegram* was, in retrospect, an overture. NSC-68[†] contained as its centerpiece a quotation from the *Federalist Papers* (#28), the most important legal document construing the U.S. Constitution and itself a rich mine of structural arguments about the relation between constitutional law and strategy.

There continues to be a debate, much of it revolving around NSC-68, about which country, the United States or the USSR, was responsible for the Cold War.[88] From the perspective of the present work, the two sides in this debate both manage to be wrong, claiming, respectively, that the United States started the war or that the Soviet Union did. The Cold War didn't "start"; rather the Long War never stopped. The United States bears responsibility for this, because the U.S. made "the move to war," continuing the Long War, when it refused to acquiesce in Soviet expansionism. The key event was the invasion of South Korea, which was part of a general Soviet strategy.[‡]

In June 1946, Litvinov told an American correspondent that if the West granted all of Stalin's demands, "it would lead to the West being faced, after a more or less short time, with the next series of demands . . ." owing to "the ideological conception prevailing here that conflict between the Communist and capitalist worlds is inevitable."[91] There was "nothing" the United States could do to satisfy the Soviet Union, he told Averell Harriman. Until North Korea invaded the South, however, Truman refused to endorse NSC-68 and to increase military spending. In 1948, the administration had limited defense expenditures to $15 billion for 1950 and beyond, whereas NSC-68 had called for budgets more than twice that size. After the Korean invasion, the defense budget leaped from 5 percent to 12 percent of U.S. GNP. Acheson was the figure who made the strategy of NSC-68 into reality, orchestrating the effort to persuade the U.S. Congress to fund the military buildup and the Marshall Plan.

---

*This cable, sent from Moscow where Kennan was serving as deputy to the U.S. Ambassador, alerted official Washington to the intractability of the Soviet position and advised in favor of "containing" Communist expansion.

†See Chapter 4.

‡As Goncharov, Lewis, and Xue Litai show on the basis of archival research and interviews with Korean, Chinese, and Russian participants, "the invasion of June 25, 1950 was pre-planned, [approved] and directly assisted by Stalin and his generals, and reluctantly backed by Mao at Stalin's insistence." These archives reveal that Stalin, beginning in 1949, launched an immense arms buildup, believing that Korea would serve as a springboard for the invasion of Japan and that a Chinese-backed revolutionary struggle in Viet Nam and Southeast Asia would force the United States to divert critical forces from Western Europe. Consistently with our study, Stalin's moves, as Jacob Heilbrun astutely observes,[89] had their "origins not in economic fears of American expansionism but in the need to restore his party's grip on his [own] society . . ." Soviet occupation abroad even replicated the tactics Stalin had used to consolidate power in the USSR before the war. In Stalin's case, the constitutional imperatives of communism not only determined Soviet strategy abroad but also its tactics in the Long War.[90]

Yet Acheson was not a popular figure in Congress or in the country. Partly it was his habit of speaking too sharply (and too epigramatically) about his contemporaries. Adlai Stevenson, Acheson remarked, "had a third-rate mind that he can't make up."[92] The years Chester Bowles had spent doing advertising had created in him "a permanent deformity like the Chinese habit of footbinding."[93] The people Dulles brought to the State Department when he succeeded Acheson as secretary "always seemed to me," Acheson said, "like Cossacks quartered in some grand city hall, burning the paneling to cook with." Partly it was his demeanor: great success in law school often conveys to young men who achieve it a certain haughtiness owing to their discovery that they are easily measured as superior to other brilliant young men at a way of thinking that is supposed to encompass all human endeavor.[94] Acheson's trans-Atlantic accent sounded like a phony affectation to Midwestern ears, an image enhanced by his waxed mustache and his tweeds. Perhaps the most famous remark about Acheson was made not by his mentors Brandeis and Frankfurter, but by Senator Hugh Butler of Nebraska, who said, "I look at that fellow, I watch his smart-aleck manner and his British clothes and that New Dealism in everything he says and does, and I want to shout, 'Get out! Get out! You stand for everything that has been wrong in the United States for years.'"[95]

No one would have said that about Myres McDougal, with his large bearlike figure and green eyeshade, more reminiscent of Roscoe Pound and the country store than of the Metropolitan Club. Though in fact McDougal's politics—with their redistributionary objectives, goals of racial equality, and statist definitions of property—were well to the left of Acheson's, McDougal's genuine warmth and affection for people made him less a target of personal attack than did Acheson's imperious manner. When Acheson attacked McDougal over U.N. sanctions against Rhodesia (Acheson had called the U.N. an "international orphan asylum"), the tone of his assault makes one wince, and although he accused McDougal of being "intoxicated by the exuberance of his own verbosity,"[96] it is a charge that more closely fits the attacker than the attacked. Acheson claimed that McDougal, in calling for economic sanctions against the white supremacist government of Rhodesia, "would impose upon states in the name of law [his] own subjective conceptions of justice." In a later memorandum to the Nixon White House, Acheson railed against the "subjugation of Rhodesia to majority rule."[97] "Conscience used to be an inner voice of self-discipline; now it is a clarion urge to discipline others."[98] These remarks illustrate the difference between structural, Neo-Realist perspectives that tend to subordinate all issues to strategic matters (Rhodesia was a functioning, anti-Communist state), and ethical, New Haven School approaches that have the virtue (or the shortcoming) of treating the human rights of every person as equally valuable. Both approaches are to be sharply distinguished from what I will call Perspectivism—the adduction of extrinsic facts about the world, that is, facts not confined to the constitutional ethos of the society of states, nor to its constitutional structure—in order to resolve the Legal Realist's dilemma. That dilemma may be expressed thus: how do we restore legitimacy to law when it is subject to everyone's interpretation, and especially that of the deciders who create it and demand that the rest of us obey? The hard-working practitioners of American diplomacy, like their counterparts in law firms, may have an answer to this dilemma: they embrace it, and relish the fact they happen to be the deciders, but this is not a welcome solution to everyone else, and certainly not to Perspectivists.

PERSPECTIVISM

There are fundamental goals of the society of parliamentary nation-states that are often in conflict: sovereignty, democracy, human rights, and self-determination are examples. A state that denies human rights to its citizens can be subject to humanitarian intervention by other states in order to vindicate those rights, but this compromises sovereignty; a state that promotes democracy can, through the democratic operation of majoritarian elections and legislative action, end up denying rights to minorities; a national people that is permitted to create a state inevitably entraps persons who would have been in a majority in a differently drawn territory, or who become permanent, insular minorities in the one that actually comes about. McDougal refers to certain goals in conflict—such as peace *versus* justice, or freedom *versus* order—as antinomies that are in fact complementary and can be harmonized by reference to the overriding ethos of the constitutional order of the society of parliamentary nation-states, the dignity of man. But he appears unwilling to recognize that in some cases—perhaps the most important cases—there are other goals (such as the four mentioned above) that can never be wholly satisfied in the natural world of scarcity.[99] Like McDougal, Acheson recognizes the rueful truth of Llewellyn's claim[100] that for every legal maxim a countermaxim can be found, but also like McDougal, he has a preferred value, strategic security, that overrides all others, and that can be derived from the constitutional structure of the society of states within which international law must operate.

Perspectivists attempt to overcome what they believe to be the inherent cultural, class, and other biases in such overriding approaches, whether they are McDougal's or Acheson's, noting that these biases are especially evident in international law

> when the higher goals are determined by the particular policies of a national state. . . . That [national elites] tend to regard their national

state's conduct and policies as more conducive to achieving universal ideals is understandable. Sentiments, education, information sources and deeply rooted affinities are likely to prevail over the claims of distant, uncongenial societies.[101]

One might argue that the post-Versailles order is actually designed to give expression to such biases: by transposing to the international level the respect for the individual that structures the liberal, parliamentary domestic order, the system denies an external standard by which it is to be judged, regardless of whether this standard arises from the states themselves. Like the liberal constitutions of parliamentary nation-states that seek to allow each person to pursue his or her own path to happiness and fulfillment, international law in the current era, as Louis Henkin has observed, "is designed to further each state's realization of its own notion of the Good."

The agnosticism of such a system toward particular substantive values is irksome to some. While they frankly concede the Legal Realist's argument that legal rules are indeterminate, they wish to bring external, nonlegal preferences to bear in order to resolve the indeterminacy problem. I will mention three prominent alternatives, but they are treated very cursorily because their impact on the international law of the society of nation-states has thus far been quite marginal. These alternative views are offered as exemplars of how an external standard, located in the world but not in law, might be applied.

One such option is feminism. A central feminist argument is that the international legal system is patriarchal, hierarchical, militarized, and masculinized. It has been urged[102] that the practices of warfare favor men's lives over women's because the rules for combatants, who are almost exclusively men, tend to be better developed and better enforced than the rules governing the use of air power, which is often directed against civilian targets. The crucial dichotomy in law between the public and private that, on the level of the individual state, tends to cloak violence against women by privatizing it, on the international level protects the denial of human rights when these abuses are committed by nonstate, "private" actors.[103] There is some doubt as to whether feminists from different societies share the American feminist agenda, but there can be little doubt that violence against women, their suppression as political actors, and their economic subordination are phenomena found in every society, and that, moreover, issues relating to the family and children are largely neglected in international law.

Another external standard comes from Islamic fundamentalists who have been outspoken in their condemnation of Western values, explicitly including international law. Perhaps because the world of Wilson and House sought to project onto the globe a legal system in which states bore the same relation to international law as individuals did in the United States to domestic law, considerations of religion were excluded from international law.[104] This is not to say that Islamic notions of international legal rules have been excluded; during the International Court of Justice litigation over the Western Sahara, Islamic legal arguments were presented to the effect that the Polisaro insurgents in Morocco constituted a lawful state according to Islamic rules and that they therefore were entitled to self-determination. Rather it is that the basic supposition of international law in the era of the nation-state has been that shared substantive religious belief is not a prerequisite to common understanding. All nation-states, regardless of their religions, are equally bound to the international order.

> Islamic scholars, who locate legal authority with God, cannot so easily separate law and belief. The public international law solution of order without shared belief is not available to [them] insofar as their work is informed by Islam. The arguments they make within Western categories are not authoritative to a Muslim. The arguments they make from Islamic authority do not confront the political organization of the contemporary world.[105]

Yet law *is* argument—or, to put it another way, the modalities of legal argument determine how legal propositions are deemed true or false; to be outside these modalities is to be beyond legal discourse. That, of course, is what all externalist projects have in mind: to find a perspective outside the law from which to evaluate it and thereby to justify it when it corresponds to the preferences of that perspective.

A third alternative is proposed by the "critical analysis" school of jurisprudence. The title of Martii Koskenniemi's essay "From Apology to Utopia: The Structure of International Legal Argument" is suggestive of this approach.[106] International law, in this view, either amounts to an apology for state acts (legitimating international behavior) or it dissolves into utopianism (which is "incapable of providing a convincing argument on the legitimacy of any practices"). In either case, international law is "singularly useless as a means of justifying or criticizing international behavior." This charge is certainly true. Indeed law itself, though it can legitimate, cannot justify its practices.[107] Koskenniemi argues that an international lawyer should be "committed to reaching the most just solution in the particular disputes he is faced with." This will require "sociological enquiries into causal relationships and political enquiry into acceptable forms of containing power."

Whether or not such a program rests on inquiries in which one can have supreme confidence,[108] one can hardly be insensitive to the hunger for an external standard by which to assess the justice of our acts.

There are of course several other options in the Perspectivist portfolio. I have not mentioned the law and economics movement,[109] communitarianism,[110] or the theories and terminologies of Ronald Dworkin,[111] John Rawls,[112] or Jürgen Habermas,[113] which have been so fruitful for jurisprudence at the noninternational level. I have only tried to give a sample of what a Perspectivist sort of approach is like.

As a postscript to this *tour d'horizon* of the post–Legal Realist approaches to interpreting and applying the law of the society of parliamentary nation-states, I would make two observations. The first, which I indicated at the beginning of this section, is that these six alternatives are simply contemporary versions of Formalism and Natural Law. The Legal Process, Nominalist, and Consensualist schools have in common the belief that, as Brierly put it, "[n]othing can be law to which states have not consented,"[114] although they differ in precisely how to determine that to which states have in fact agreed. Their primary jurisprudential task is the identification of what must be obeyed; hence their concern with locating the legitimate sources of law. The New Haven School, Neo-Realists, and Perspectivists all find something in the world, outside law itself, that validates international law, though they strongly differ as to what that something is, and what relation it must have to law in order for a legal rule to be legitimate. Their primary concern is the problem of making political choices;[115] hence their attention to facts extrinsic to the law that prompts, but does not decide, such choices. All these approaches are efforts to respond to the challenge of the Legal Realist, and none is necessarily the captive of the Left or the Right.[116]

My second concluding note is perhaps somewhat more novel, but it is in accord, as will be obvious, with the entire history portrayed in Book II. These six schools of international law track the six modalities of U.S. constitutional law, for as we have seen, international law is built out of the constitutional law of states and the international constitutional order of this period has been in part the work of American leaders, from Colonel House to Dean Acheson, who seized world leadership from the society of state-nations and then created, with the leaders of the other parliamentary nation-states, the coalition that fought and won the Long War.

The "modalities" of American constitutional law are the ways in which we characterize a proposition of that law as true or false. The six modalities of constitutional interpretation in the United States are (1) historical (relying on the intentions of the ratifiers of the Constitution); (2) textual (looking to the meaning of the actual terms of the constitutional text as these would be understood by the contemporary "man in the street"); (3) structural (inferring rules from the relationships that the Constitution mandates among its structures—federalism, the three branches of the federal government, etc.); (4) doctrinal (applying rules generated by precedent); (5) ethical (deriving rules from the ethos of the Constitution, described in the Declaration of Independence and elsewhere); and (6) prudential (seeking to balance the costs and benefits of a particular rule according to a parameter—economic, political, or otherwise—extrinsic to the Constitution).[117] Other states may use different modal forms of argument—in Iran, religious argument and the *sharia,* for example, which would not be admissible in the United States forum—and even the modalities currently in use in the United States will change and develop through time.

It will be easily seen that each of the schools of international law discussed can be paired with its constitutional modality: consensual/historical; nominalist/textual; Neo-Realist/structural; Legal Process/doctrinal; New Haven School/ethical; Perspectivist/prudential. One sees these pairings in the willingness of the Consensualist to consult the *travaux préparatoires* and the constitutional originalist's desire to invoke the *Federalist* papers; the struggle of Henry Hart and his colleagues to formulate the Legal Process ideology to save doctrinalism in the face of Legal Realism; the efforts of McDougal to identify a universal *ethos,* the dignity of man, and so on.

The market-state described in Book I will also strive to make its constitutional form the template for a constitution for the society of states. How this struggle will play out remains to be seen. Whether we will face another epochal war on the scale of the Long War, I cannot say. But mustn't we try to anticipate what such a constitution would look like and how it might be reconciled to the society of states without a cataclysmic or critically disabling conflict? These issues are the subject of Part III.

In the winter of 1917, an observer standing on the corner of Fifth Avenue and 42nd Street in New York, and watching the persons hurrying up the broad stone steps of the neoclassical public library, would have observed five men who arrived separately but at about the same time each day. Only one man of this group, if any, would have been known to the public; that man was the president of City College, and more importantly, he was the brother-in-law of Colonel House, the most powerful political figure in America outside his alter ego and closest friend, Woodrow Wilson. The other men were also chosen by House: an historian from Columbia University; a rising young journalist from the *New Republic* magazine; a law partner of House's son-in-law; the director of the American Geographical Society. These five were the inner core of a secret group, code-named The Inquiry, set up on Wilson's orders to bypass the State Department and formulate America's plans for the postwar world. Before the United States ever entered the First World War House had suggested to Wilson that a body of experts be convened to supply American delegates to the future peace conference with the information they would need.

The staff of The Inquiry was ultimately frustrated in its role. At the Versailles Peace Conference the group was marginalized by the president's isolation and the primacy of more institutional players. In any case, the advice of academics, journalists, and lawyers could hardly have averted the political catastrophe that befell their hopes at the Conference. When Wilson broke with House at the Conference, more was shattered than a remarkable friendship: the American dreams of a nonpunitive peace, of a postwar world order guaranteed by the great powers and built out of the self-determination of national peoples, an economic environment of nondiscriminatory trade practices, a political environment "safe for democracy"—none of this came to pass, in part, but only in part, because the Americans were unable to overcome the mercantile and strategic ambitions of their allies abroad and isolationism and ignorance at home. House wrote, when it was all past, "I wish we had taken the other road . . . [the peace settlement promised by Wilson to the Germans and to the public]." When the German representatives signed the treaty, the British diplomat Harold Nicholson wrote in his diary, "To bed, sick of life." Even Lloyd George acknowledged that it was "all a great pity. We shall have to do the same thing all over again [we shall have to fight another world war] in twenty-five years at three times the cost." John Maynard Keynes, who had been attached to the British delegation, wrote to his mother, "I've never been so miserable . . . [T]he peace is outrageous and impossible and can bring nothing but misfortune." The American secretary of state, Lansing, noted his first reactions to the treaty document: "disappointment, regret, depression."

By contrast, when the Peace of 1990 came to the world all of the great powers knew what must be done. James Baker, who in some ways played the role of Colonel House in a later era as the president's political manager, personal intimate, and international representative, did not need to convene a new version of The Inquiry to determine what the postwar program should be, because it had not essentially changed since Wilson's day. Chastened by another world war, the Cold War, and the nuclear annihilation that threatened them all, the Allies this time did not try to ruin their adversary but endeavored instead to include him in a New World Order. Unlike Lansing, Baker exhilaratedly wrote when he returned from his journey to Paris, "The very nature of the international system as we know it [has been] transformed."[118]

With the Peace of Paris, a door closed in human history. The East/West global struggle had divided the whole world as sharply and carefully as Gregory XIII divided the then–New World of the sixteenth century. Now there are many able academics and civil servants working hard on the issue of what sort of new world the twenty-first century will bring into being, and how it will be divided. Surely we need a New Inquiry, for what we need to know is not simply where we are going, but where we are, and, then, where we *can* go. Governments everywhere are floundering with regard to their security policies. Some have pursued consistent policies, only to find that it has been a relentless pursuit of failure, enhanced by an inability to rethink, but when governments have been inconsistent—and no governments have been more so than the United States and Britain— these governments did not find their way to fresh insights, unless it was the insight that the policy that they have just adopted was one they had recently abandoned.

Does this matter? We are in a time of crisis, and must turn our attention to international terrorism. Why should we pursue thought when action is required? Colonel House had to have answers before his war ended; he didn't know it would continue for seventy more years. Now that the Long War is over, and the Peace of Paris signed, and the possibility of a new war looming, why must we urgently undertake a New Inquiry? Be- cause we are daily making decisions that will structure the kinds of oppor- tunities available to us in the future. "Once in a while a door opens," wrote Graham Greene, "and lets the future in." This is such a moment.

From Mythology

First there was a god of night and tempest, a black idol without eyes, before whom they leaped, naked and smeared with blood. Later on, in the times of the republic, there were many gods with wives, children, creaking beds, and harmlessly exploding thunderbolts. At the end only superstitious neurotics carried in their pockets little statues of salt, representing the god of irony. There was no greater god at that time.

Then came the barbarians. They too valued highly the little god of irony. They would crush it under their heels and add it to their dishes.

—Zbigniew Herbert
(translated by Czesław Miłosz)

PART III

THE SOCIETY OF MARKET-STATES

THESIS: A NEW SOCIETY OF MARKET-STATES IS BEING BORN.

The challenges facing the society of states are a direct consequence of the strategic innovations that won the Long War. The ways in which the various basic forms of the market-state cope with these challenges will structure the conflicts of a new society. We must act with this development in mind, accepting conflict where it is necessary to avoid cataclysmic war or the breakdown of the global superinfrastructure, and creating institutions that will legitimate the new society of market-states.

The Terrorist, He's Watching

The bomb in the bar will explode at thirteen twenty.
Now it's just thirteen sixteen.
There's still time for some to go in,
And some to come out.

The terrorist has already crossed the street.
The distance keeps him out of danger,
And what a view—just like the movies.

A woman in a yellow jacket, she's going in.
A man in dark glasses, he's coming out.
Teen-agers in jeans, they're talking.
Thirteen seventeen and four seconds.
The short one, he's lucky, he's getting on a scooter,
But the tall one, he's going in.

Thirteen seventeen and forty seconds.
That girl, she's walking along with a green ribbon in her hair.
But then a bus suddenly pulls in front of her.
Thirteen eighteen.
The girl's gone.
Was she that dumb, did she go in or not,
We'll see when they carry them out.

Thirteen nineteen.
Somehow no one's going in.
Another guy, fat, bald, is leaving, though.
Wait a second, looks like he's looking
For something in his pockets and
At thirteen twenty minus ten seconds
He goes back in for his crummy gloves.

Thirteen twenty exactly.
This waiting, it's taking forever.
Any second now.
No, not yet.
Yes, now.
The bomb, it explodes.

—Wisława Szymborska

CHAPTER TWENTY-FOUR

Challenges to the New International Order

THE ECONOMIC ORTHODOXY of nation-states counseled state intervention in the national economy as a necessary means of achieving growth and other goals. Economic regulation was part of this orthodoxy and fitted the ethos of nation-states that relied so heavily on law. Market-states will have their own economic orthodoxy and their own distinctive tools.

Eventually, all the leading members of the society of market-states may come to accept views similar to these: that capital markets have to become less regulated in order to attract capital investment and that capital has to become more global in order to achieve the maximum returns on investment; that labor markets have to become more flexible in order to compete with other, foreign labor markets and to keep jobs at home that depend upon producing products at a cost that can compete with the products of states that have lower labor costs; that if the world economy is to grow, access to all markets has to be assured and trade has to become less regulated; that a state's trade policy will have to become more free if that state's goods are to be able to penetrate foreign markets and thus participate in this growth; that government subsidies, spending, and welfare programs have to be managed in order to permit more investment in infrastructure and to allow greater private saving (which will lower the cost of investment); and that tax policy has to provide incentives for growth in order to attract enterprise and to maximize innovation and entrepreneurship. Early in the twenty-first century, it seems not unlikely that virtually all major states will accept for themselves the fundamental assumptions that Margaret Thatcher and Tony Blair urged for Britain and that Bill Clinton and George W. Bush urged for the United States, and furthermore that they will accept that if these states do not heed those recommendations, the United States, the United Kingdom, and other states will gain a decisive advantage over them.

If a market-state fails to provide tax incentives for capital formation and capital retention, domestic investment will either not take place or will flee along with foreign investment; if investment goes elsewhere, then innovation and productivity gains will go with it, so that the products that are its result will be cheaper and better than those produced at home; if the products of other states are more competitive, then jobs will be lost to those states; if jobs are lost, then tax revenues will fall, and unemployment and welfare costs will become unsupportable. Ever higher taxes will produce ever lower revenues. The state that resists liberalizing its labor markets in order to protect high-wage jobs will end up with no jobs to protect; the state that resists cutting back on welfare will find it has to cut back anyway when revenues fall and that it now has even larger welfare bills to pay as unemployment climbs; the state that attempts to protect its domestic industries by refusing to liberalize its trade policy will find that those industries are locked out of other markets and in any case are uncompetitive, so that domestic prices stay high and the domestic standard of living falls; the state that tries to restrict capital flight will be shunned, and the state that inhibits capital imports will be ignored. That too will raise the cost of production and depress the standard of living in another turn of this vicious circle. If Mikhail Gorbachev could get this message in the 1980s— the secure leader of the richest and most powerful socialist nation in the world—it will not be lost on anyone else.

Moreover, the market-state promises a "virtuous" circle to those states that copy its form and obey its strictures. The privatization of state-owned firms brings immense capital gains to the state as it liquidates vast monopolies; this windfall supplements the savings from cuts in welfare programs and thus lowers deficits, which leads to less inflation, which attracts capital and lowers the borrowing costs required to finance deficits, which in turn lowers the deficits still further, which permits lower taxes, which can produce more savings, which can enable more investment, which produces more funds for research and development, which enhances productivity, which lowers prices thus making exports more competitive, which creates jobs while lowering the cost of living for the consuming public. In the underdeveloped world, such policies mean higher growth owing to comparative wage advantages, which growth leads to a more educated population, which brings more women into the workplace, which leads to lower birth rates, which enhances political stability, which means greater macroeconomic prudence, which leads to more foreign investment, which finances still more growth, which tends to liberalize authoritarianism, which encourages personal autonomy.

The new orthodoxy of the market-state will surely play out in several competing formulations. In the following pages I will speculate about these different versions and describe what they might look like in the future. Like different race cars, they all compete in the same race, meet roughly the same specifications, and are governed by the same rules, but they approach the common competition with different drivers who use different tactics.

In Washington, for example, state intervention is anathema. The state can never adjust prices as quickly and as efficiently as the market, and every state intervention skews the price function to some degree. Moreover, the democratic, representative, deliberative state is slow-moving and cumbersome—just the sort of institution one wants where human rights are at stake or in a society where it is difficult to achieve consensus across many cultural communities but one that is deadly to innovation and the nimble reactions required to take advantage of changes in the marketplace. All market-states take as their legitimating charter that they are responsible for maximizing the opportunities of their citizens. In Washington, this means providing infrastructure (including intangible infrastructure like education and the means of enforcing agreements) and relying on private enterprise to maximize the abundance of consumer choice and minimize the costs to the consumer of exercising choice.

In Tokyo, by contrast, maximizing opportunity means protecting domestic industries so that future generations will have a full array of employment opportunities, subsidizing research and development so that future opportunities for innovation will be practicably exploitable, and restricting the import of capital so that the government remains in control of its capital allocation.

In Berlin, maximizing opportunity means ensuring social and economic equality among citizens, using the corporation as a stakeholder for the public interest so that the opportunities available to communities, workers, and future generations are maximized rather than maximizing the short-term profits of shareholders.

Because the market-state secures political legitimacy through the active pursuit of opportunity for its citizens but declines to specify the goals for which opportunity is to be used, there will be different models whose advocates can plausibly maintain that their constitutional strategy best maximizes opportunity. For example, consider these contrasts between the Tokyo and Berlin models: education financed privately *versus* public education; high savings rates *versus* low savings; low currency values *versus* high currency values; low interest rates *versus* high interest rates on corporate borrowing; high interest rates *versus* low interest rates on consumer loans; personal sacrifice *versus* a higher quality of life; long working hours *versus* leisure consumption. Either set of choices can plausibly be said to maximize opportunity, depending on what that opportunity is for and what it consists in. What is more difficult to maintain is a set of choices that skips around, pairing high leisure consumption (which maximizes the freedom of choice for one's pleasure) with personal sacrifice (which maximizes the freedom of the society as a whole). So these choices tend to fall into discrete sets.

THE ENTREPRENEURIAL MARKET-STATE

Labor relations under this model are confrontational as well as sectoral—a new experience for market-states such as China that have not previously permitted voluntary and competitive labor organizations. Because wages are low and because the relocation of investment is entirely unfettered, labor unions are weak. Job creation is achieved at the cost of job security. Local industries are largely unprotected from foreign competition, which tends to make the firms that survive hardy, agile, and attractive to foreign capital. Interest rates are maintained at a relatively high level in order to encourage foreign investment and to suppress inflation. Considerable income disparities are tolerated on the grounds that everyone is richer owing to the booming economy that such freewheeling competition can provide, and it is certainly true that, in terms of personal consumption and standard of living, the entrepreneurial market-states outperform all comparable states (that is, they exceed the improvement in consumer standards of living achieved by states that began with comparable levels of development).

Immigration is robust under the Entrepreneurial Model because it freely imports highly paid talent as well as low-wage workers, which tends to suppress labor costs and keep capital from going abroad. By contrast the Mercantile Model shuns immigration; indeed cultural homogeneity is almost a prerequisite for its successful operation. The Managerial Model is ambivalent: open to "guest workers" but hostile to new citizens. The Entrepreneurial Model tends to loosen the identification that citizens feel with the larger polity: autonomy and individual achievement are so prized and the consumption of particular goods so meaningful an act of self-definition that the citizens of these states "invent" their citizenships, identifying themselves with those subgroups within the state with whom they share a consumption pattern. This exacerbates the problems of social cohesion that every market-state faces. These effects are acutely felt in the entrepreneurial states that have all-volunteer military forces, federal political structures, strictly meritocratic promotion ladders, and multicultural media. Both the mercantile and managerial states, by contrast, retain conscription for military service (though with force levels vastly reduced from those of the twentieth century), affirmative action for certain social groups, and varying degrees of state control of the media.

The basic ethos of the Entrepreneurial Model is libertarian: the conviction that it is the role of society to set individuals free to make their own decisions. This ethos counsels minimal state intervention in the economy as well as in the private lives of its citizens. Privatized health care, housing, pensions, and education as well as low taxes and low welfare benefits all characterize such states. Regulation on behalf of special interests is discouraged. Indeed, responsibility for regulation of any kind is largely abdicated in favor of policing by the market, which responds with extensive information to the consumer, who is expected to look out for himself. That doesn't necessarily mean that the environment is not protected or that labor is exploited: companies soon discover that they will be rewarded for "green" policies and penalized if they are discovered to have engaged in exploitative labor practices. It simply means that the role of government in protecting the public has to some extent been taken over by the media and by private groups acting on the information from, and in concert with, the media.

THE MERCANTILE MARKET-STATE

This model relies upon a strong central government to protect national industries, subsidize crucial research and development, and steer certain important enterprises toward success. Artificially low prices are set for export goods and artificially low interest rates are maintained that depress currency values. This would lead to capital flight except that capital flows are also regulated by governments and forced savings are extracted from all incomes. Under the Mercantile Model, the opportunities available to the consumer, which have been exalted under the Entrepreneurial Model, are sacrificed to the long-term opportunities of the society. These societies are able to maintain social cohesion—to a far greater degree than entrepreneurial market-states—in part because income disparities are suppressed, variations in take-home pay between manufacturing workers and service workers are rationalized, and elaborate social welfare subsidy systems, including public housing and access to education, are put in place for those—this must be emphasized—who are eager to work. It is important for the states that follow this model to monitor the collusion between the large corporate structures endemic to this model and their bureaucratic allies. Otherwise, the predictability sought and prized by this model will also bring potentially crippling inefficiencies and even corruption. Educational curricula must be tempered by some sense of the demands of the market; otherwise far too few persons will emerge from the educational system with the skills that fit them for employment (a problem that plagues the Managerial Model as well, though the latter's difficulties stem not from a refusal to give technical training so much as a willingness to underwrite costly studies with no professional future).

Mercantile market-states have achieved impressive growth rates: Singapore and Hong Kong have higher living standards than the United Kingdom. But this has not been accomplished through the efficient use of scarce resources. In terms of sheer efficiency, Taiwan, South Korea, and Hong Kong are in about the same productivity class as Egypt, Greece, Syria, and Cameroon. Rather, the mercantile states have succeeded by mobilizing the labor of the total society, and by encouraging very high accumulations of capital. Investment is subsidized and promoted in these states, and although exports generate considerable revenue for investment, it is savings by individuals, corporations, and governments that account for the high levels of investment in Taiwan, South Korea, Singapore, and Japan. Thus although this model may attract adherents because of its historic record of high growth, there is a limit to the performance a state can wring from increased inputs of capital and labor without increased efficiency.

There are several challenges that face this model wherever it has been adopted: opening up domestic markets to foreign competition; reforming the banking sector to bring greater scrutiny to credit transactions; allowing access to cheaper credit for smaller firms that are usually restricted to relatively high priced domestic finance and letting the cost of capital to the few dominant firms rise.

All of these challenges confront the inefficiencies of concentrated economic power that is a notable feature of the Mercantile Model. For example, the Korean version is characterized by the concentration of power in four great companies (Samsung, Hyundai, Lucky-Goldstar, and Daewoo) that together account for over half of that country's exports and a third of its sales. These companies are both the instruments of and the beneficiaries of government policy. Yet between 50 percent and 60 percent of the equity of the top thirty companies in Korea is held by the founding families. In Japan, the largest six great companies account for over half the total assets of all listed enterprises. Furthermore, some three-quarters of all shares are mutually held between companies and their financial institutions.

THE MANAGERIAL MARKET-STATE

This form of the market-state (often called the *Soziale Marktwirtschaft*) consists of three basic elements: free and open markets within a regional trading framework, a government that provides a social safety net and manages a stringent monetary policy, and a socially cohesive society. Private property and private enterprise are valued, but their constitutional status is dependent upon their contribution to the public good. Labor relations are broad and participatory. Workers sit on corporate boards. Strong national unions negotiate contracts across whole sectors of the economy rather than by individual company or factory. They bargain with all-encompassing owner federations that are empowered by law to hold their member companies to the terms of the deals that are struck, overriding shareholder objections. Multinational corporations are required to share their strategic plans with elected workers' councils. Regulations require companies to consult labor on all major decisions. This tends to pacify workers who in other societies have rebelled when low-wage jobs were exported because workers expect that the profits from offshore production will eventually be repatriated to finance high-wage jobs at home, making exports more competitive.

The "stakeholder company," a key concept in this model, seeks to reflect the priorities of workers, managers, communities, vendors, and environmentalists on something like parity with the interests of shareholders. Corporate ownership is closely held in the largest and most important industries, usually through a centralized commercial bank. As the largest holder of both equity and debt in such a company, the bank can exercise a close scrutiny over corporate decisions and can afford to take a long view of corporate strategies, in contrast to those companies that raise money in the equity markets. This enables corporations operating within this model to garner the so-called patient capital necessary for long-range success. Publicly financed institutions promote the transfer of technology from defense research and development to the private sector. Technology diffusion is further encouraged within the regional trading organizations on which this model greatly depends.

If the object of the mercantile state is to ensure social stability, the goal of the managerial state is to achieve social equality. The class divisions that wracked the state-nations of Europe and gave birth to fascism and communism within the nation-state are suppressed by every legal instrument that can be brought to bear by this form of the market-state. Private and sectarian schools are often outlawed; estate taxes at death approach the confiscatory; modern versions of the eighteenth century "window tax" are reintroduced to discourage opulence.

Government intervention in the economy under the Managerial Model tends to occur on the labor side to a greater extent than on the capital side, in contrast to the Mercantile Model. Training and retraining programs often take as much as 2 percent of GDP (as compared with .25 percent under the Entrepreneurial Model).

Taxes for such states are high, sometimes peaking at over 70 percent of GDP (40 percent payroll taxes were not uncommon), and there are sizable value-added taxes (VAT) and consumption taxes, though these vary considerably. Not many of the world's states can afford generous welfare provisions, although it should be pointed out that, just as mercantilism is not confined to Asian societies, managerialism is not confined to the wealthy continent of Europe. India—whose subcontinent has the largest concentration of poverty and illiteracy in the world—is attempting a decisive move toward the Managerial Model of the market-state. A complex system of entitlements, including free rural electricity, subsidized fertilizers, cheap water irrigation schemes, subsidized university education, and cheap food, as well as a bewilderingly complex system of ethnic and class preferences on behalf of certain minorities and lower castes, all incline India toward this model. Turkey and Egypt may also be considered candidates for this model that lie outside the central zone of European prosperity.

To a far greater degree than the other two models of the market-state, managerialism uses legal regulation to enforce standards of conduct, including the use of potentially heavy fines. Liability rules, as well as the social safety net levels of the late twentieth century, are difficult for the managerial market-state to modify. Interest groups, such as pensioners, consumers, lawyers, and advocates for the beneficiaries of welfare subsidies, make any ratcheting down of these benefits hard to achieve. As a result, innovation is slowed—even in areas, like Europe, where technological innovation ought to be at its greatest.

Advocates of the Managerial Model are not economically naïve. Rather they recognize that all-out economic competition tends to leave some persons behind and that this alienation from the economic system breeds crime, family breakdown, alcoholism and drug addiction, even illness on the job. These advocates calculate that it is cheaper to prevent the costs of these maladies than to try to compensate for them after they have manifested themselves. This attitude of giving priority to social cohesion is shared by those who favor mercantilism but with this difference: while mercantile states try to guarantee a job for every person (or at least every male) and provide little in the way of welfare programs, managerial states provide jobs only for the most productive workers—at good pay—and generous welfare for the rest.

Thus, even though the United States has been more successful at creating new jobs (maintaining an unemployment rate at about half that of the E.U.), this has been achieved at the expense of real wage levels. Accordingly, each model must contend with its own sort of alienation: the lowest paid workers in the United States are vastly worse off than high wage earners, while the unemployed in Europe can get by on welfare benefits alone but have little prospect of a job. By contrast, the Mercantile Model maintains artificially high employment rates, at wages that reflect far less disparity between the highest and lowest paid. The unavoidable cost is in productivity and efficiency, which sets the stage for a new kind of alienation, that of the young from the old.

With its appeal to universal hedonism, the Entrepreneurial Model appears almost acultural, particularly in contrast to the family-oriented, hierarchy-honoring Mercantile Model, and even in contrast to the larger, transnational bureaucratic zones of the Managerial Model that prize human rights to a greater degree. The Entrepreneurial Model claims to be pluralistic, nonjudgmental, and open to many cultural forms, and indeed states as diverse as Thailand and Peru are pursuing this model. But it does hold that every such state must guarantee human rights—by which it means the opportunity to express essentially individual values—a free press, an unfettered political opposition, even the secret ballot (which may perhaps be said to be a Protestant, that is, individualist, form of confession). Adherents to mercantilism maintain that its human rights are communitarian rather than individualistic; that its political system seeks harmony rather than division—that respect and reverence are a truer expression of its cultural values—and therefore these states attempt to minimize the public expression of opposition.

At the beginning of the twenty-first century, it is to be hoped that informal private networks that cross international lines—for example, the large multinational corporations developed in the twentieth century, or the extensive social networks developed by overseas Chinese in East Asia and the United States, or global nongovernmental organizations—will supply the links necessary to prevent the growing divergence of the three models of the market-state. Because divergence is principally a function of domestic politics, it tends to accelerate, however, when national leaders take unpopular steps in order to enhance international cooperation or when they blame competing models for "keeping interest rates high" (the Managerial Model) or "failing to get control of consumption and thus exporting inflation" (the Entrepreneurial Model) or "exploiting foreign markets while closing their own" (the Mercantile Model).

Each of these versions of the market-state claims to be the unique and final expression of the constitutional archetype of the market-state. In this way, these claims are reminiscent of the three ideological forms of the nation-state (parliamentarianism, communism, and fascism) that competed during the Long War. For just this reason, leaders ought to be wary of domestic conflicts that threaten to become crises of legitimation. At present these conflicts chiefly arise from the debate surrounding globalization. As with the twentieth century, such domestic crises can move the champions of each form to seek a universal international adherence.

The Long War ended in 1990. Like the other great epochal wars whose true identity and shape only became apparent in retrospect, the Long War followed a period of constitutional stability in the relations among the various states of the great powers. A single constitutional archetype dominated that stable period, the form of the imperial, patriotic state-nation. This was the constitutional model of Napoleon no less than of Castlereagh, and of George Washington no less than of Tsar Alexander III. Axiomatic legitimacy accrued to any state that followed this model. But when a new archetype arose—the nation-state of Lincoln, Bismarck, and Cavour—constitutional conflicts within all states began to arise, culminating in the seventy-six-year struggle I have called the Long War. Like other epochal wars, even those that antedate the modern state like the Augustan War, the Long War was a struggle that determined what form of constitutional government would succeed to the legitimacy of the dying archetype. The Charter of Paris in 1990, signed by the United States, the United Kingdom, France, Germany, and the Soviet Union, and obligating the signatories to maintain democratic, representative institutions, marked the beginning of the peace that the Treaty of Versailles had been unable to deliver.

This Charter also obligated its signatories to adopt market methods of allocation and thus this international constitution contained within it the seeds of a new international order.

The strategic innovations that won the Long War and culminated in the Peace of Paris have set in motion constitutional changes that will move states away from the archetypal form of the nation-state that emerged in the second half of the nineteenth century toward the market-state that is today emerging in the United States, the European Union, East Asia, and elsewhere. This new archetype will manifest itself in several actual forms, none of which is yet fully realized. Following the pattern of the earlier periods chronicled in Part II, we want to ask: Can we study the strategic innovations that won the Long War (nuclear weapons, international communications, and electronic computation) in order to gauge their effect on the constitutional development of this new society of states? Or, to put it in broader terms, how will developments in weapons technology, the globalization of culture, and the liberalization of trade and finance challenge the society of market-states?

WEAPONS OF MASS DESTRUCTION

NUCLEAR PROLIFERATION

Usually nuclear proliferation is discussed as a threat to one nation, or to a group of nations that are allies. In this section we shall be concerned with the *systemic* consequences of proliferation, just as we earlier discussed the systemic effects of other strategic innovations in other eras. But perhaps initially one ought to question whether nuclear weapons did in fact play a decisive role in winning the Long War.

It is evident that the German surrender in 1918 did not destroy fascism. Indeed, owing to the infirmities of the Versailles process, fascism may have been inflamed by the false peace of 1918. What was required was the discrediting of this alternative in the eyes of its most dynamic advocates, Germany and Japan. In Germany's case, nuclear weapons played an important delegitimating role because they were *not* acquired by the Nazi state. Had the V2s that landed on London in the last year of the European battle been available earlier, none of the decisive engagements in Europe—the Normandy invasion, the tank battle at Kursk, the removal of the Nazis from North Africa and proximity to the Near East—could have taken place. Had they carried nuclear weapons the outcome of the war would surely have been different. Germany had the technical expertise and the technocracy to pursue the development of such weapons and faced the necessity to do so. But Germany lacked capital to divert to nuclear development on the scale of the U.S. Manhattan Project, and its political establishment was unwilling to entrust to non-Party scientists such a commitment of resources and decision making, even if those resources could have been found. When the war in Europe ended, Allied investigators determined that the Germans were still four or five years away from a testable fission weapon. That Germany could be so thoroughly defeated by "races" that were inferior to the warrior *Volk* of Teutons, and that this defeat could be sealed by the technical achievement of American invention and engineering that exploded over the fascist state of Japan: these facts made the pretensions of fascism seem pathetically inadequate. Had Germany acquired nuclear weapons, the pathos would have lain elsewhere.

In the case of Japan, the issue of the role of nuclear weapons in ending the conflict is still much debated.[1] At this remove we are inclined to forget that Japan's land forces were still largely intact in 1945. The bulk of these forces were in China and had never been defeated. A negotiated peace before the atomic attacks, conceding a postwar role to the emperor, would have had the same effect as the German surrender in 1919: infecting the society with the historical claim of a "stab in the back" by politicians and diplomats who betrayed the armed forces, and encouraging a revanchist movement that alone could lay legitimate claim to Japanese nationalism.

Whether one believes that credible peace offers were actually available to the United States before the atomic attacks on both Hiroshima and Nagasaki, one must consider the strategic goals of the Long War to determine whether such a negotiated surrender would have brought peace. The Japanese people had been bombed on an horrific scale for months. They remained disciplined and intensely loyal to their regime, and showed no signs of giving up. Far from there being any significant political opposition to continuing the war, the only evidence of an internal revolt came after the atomic attacks, when a military coup was attempted to *reverse* the Japanese offer of surrender. What was required, and what only the second atomic attack seems to have delivered, was the complete discrediting of the regime's promises to win a negotiated peace through stiff resistance to an American invasion. I have never been persuaded of the moral position of those who would have urged continued nonnuclear bombing of the Japanese people for an extended period of months, accepting also the American casualties that would have ensued in an invasion, as preferable to the atomic attacks on the two Japanese cities. The only alternative to this carnage would have been a half-life for fascism, in a kind of negotiated twilight. And that is precisely what the Long War was fought to eliminate.*

In the case of the Soviet Union and the defeat of European communism, nuclear weapons were also decisive. First, American nuclear weapons neutralized the effect of the Red Army in Europe and the geopolitical fact that Europe's strongest ally was an ocean away. Whether or not the USSR would have invaded West Germany—and without the U.S.-backed guarantee of West Germany's defense, one can think of many occasions on which this option might have proved attractive to the Soviet bloc—the fact that this invasion was made unlikely gave the Western states of Europe the time to solidify parliamentary institutions, build prosperous market economies, and unite among themselves rather than renew their traditional conflicts as one state after another was picked off by neutralist, socialist movements. Second, nuclear weapons ultimately created the superpower context of mutual vulnerability, which rendered continuing competition both highly expensive and militarily fraught. This military stalemate gave the political systems of the Warsaw Pact states time to collapse of their own inner inefficiency and self-disgust. These systems would have been far less scrutinized by their publics in the context of warfighting. Third, the nuclear dimension of the conflict kept the United States engaged in Europe, and this engagement provided the engine that drove changes in U.S. strategy in this era, always keeping pressure on the Soviet state and innovating as the Soviet threat changed. But for the vulnerability of the United States to

---

*Nor can one adequately imagine the peril if the Long War after 1945 had triangulated among the USSR, the United States, and Japan, all with nuclear weapons.

Soviet nuclear weapons, it would have been too tempting to seek refuge in the isolationism that is so much a part of the American political tradition. In the nuclear era, there was nowhere to hide.

Thus I think it can be demonstrated that the strategic innovation represented by the development and deployment of nuclear weapons played a decisive role in ending the Long War and that, as we saw in Book I, this will have important constitutional effects on each of the states that fought that war. For the *society* composed of these states, the most profound impact is the restructuring required to deal with such weapons, for they cannot now be uninvented.

The problems that nuclear proliferation pose for the society of market-states arise from this question: is the possession of whatever weapons a state can acquire and deploy an attribute of sovereignty? For if it is not, then by what right do certain states possess weapons of such awful magnitude? And if it is, how can there ever be measures both appropriate and practical to limit the deployment of such weapons? And finally, even if having a nuclear weapons capability is a condition to which any state may aspire, does the possibility of a widespread nuclear proliferation pose such a threat to the peace and survival of the society of states that what hitherto was a state's sovereign right—the right to deploy the weapons of its own choosing—must now be rethought?

Nuclear weapons made a decisive contribution to the end of the Long War because their staggering ratio of destruction to attrition makes them virtually impossible to defend against. There are some targets of nuclear attack that can be defended against ballistic missiles—missile silos or underwater vessels, for example—but the nuclear weapon itself is so devastating that thus far methods of defense against its delivery to most targets are rendered absurd. Thermonuclear weapons can inflict such damage that even if virtually all the delivery systems used in an attack on a city were deflected, a single warhead arriving at its target would make further defense pointless. The enormity of this threat has obvious implications for individual states: the security of the United States is, on the one hand, at an all-time high, given its dominant economy and the pre-eminence of its armed forces, and on the other hand, at an historic low because the detonation of a handful of weapons launched from anywhere on the globe could utterly destroy it. "Counterproliferation" is at the top of the U.S. security agenda today, having moved from the periphery of the national security consciousness, along with the protection of the environment and of human rights, to the center of American concerns. What, however, is the importance of counterproliferation to the *society of states,* when some members may gain from acquiring such weapons, and none currently possessing such technology seem eager to give those weapons up?

A state's deployment of nuclear weapons can be either stabilizing or destabilizing for the international system. This is largely a function of the mechanics of deterrence, and thus it ought to be the policy of the international state system to deny nuclear weapons to some states, just as certain unstable geological regions are unsuitable for nuclear reactors. A nuclear weapons state can be reinforcing for the security of the society of states when its *capabilities* do not introduce multipolarity into the system, when its *intentions* do not threaten the legitimate constitutional sovereignty of other states* (unless it is attacked), and when its political *culture* is stable enough to ensure the endurance of such benign intentions. A nuclear weapons state imposes unacceptable risks on the system of deterrence when it threatens to make other states nuclear targets for geopolitical objectives that are incompatible with the maintenance of the current state system† or for geostrategic goals that are incompatible with the stability of the system of nuclear deterrence.‡ In either case, the unpredictability of nuclear attack increases, with potentially devastating consequences for populations and states.

This observation helps us answer the sovereignty question: no state that does not derive its authority from representative institutions that coexist with fundamental human rights can legitimately argue that it can subject its own people to the threat of nuclear pre-emption or retaliation on the basis of its alleged rights of sovereignty because the people it thus makes into nuclear targets have not consented to bear such risks. At a minimum, the Peace of Paris stands for this. One inference from this rule is that no such state therefore has a *sovereign* right to impose such threats on other peoples either.

For the same reason, such a state has no sovereign right to develop weapons of mass destruction generally. This argument turns around the usual rationale for the acquisition of nuclear weapons. States claim that they must deploy these weapons in order to deter attacks on their peoples. And there is a good deal of truth to this: the United States would doubtless not have bombed Japan with nuclear weapons if Tokyo could have retaliated in kind. But the acquisition of nuclear weapons also increases the risk of attack by pre-emption or by a disguised attack (so that the threat of retaliation cannot successfully deter). Each state must decide for itself how

---

*I am aware that in some quarters the United States is believed to be just such a state—interfering in the constitutional makeup of states like Grenada or Panama, and changing the boundaries of Serbia and Iraq. The Peace of Paris ought to settle this constitutional question for the society of states: no state's sovereignty is unimpeachable if it studiedly spurns legitimating parliamentary institutions and human rights protections. The greater the rejection of these institutions—which are the means by which sovereignty is conveyed by societies to their governments—the more sharply curtailed is the cloak of sovereignty that would otherwise protect governments from interference by their peers. U.S. action against the sovereignty of Iraq, for example, must be evaluated in this light.

†In order to conquer and annex another state against its will, for example.

‡In order to bring about nuclear multipolarity or acquire clandestine nuclear weapons, either of which would destabilize the system of deterrence, for example.

to resolve this calculus of risks. A state without representative institutions and effective guarantees of basic human rights has no way to win consent to such a decision.

A state that derives its legitimacy from representative institutions free of coercion can demand that other states recognize its right to acquire nuclear weapons, but though a state has this right, it ought to be dissuaded from acquiring these weapons when their deployment is destabilizing for the international system. When does this occur, and just how can this dissuasion be accomplished?

Thus far I have implied a link between proliferation and deterrence, suggesting that the society of states as a whole can determine when proliferation poses a *systemic* threat by asking whether a state's acquisition of nuclear weapons strengthens or weakens the prevailing system of nuclear deterrence. That system is currently underpinned by United States nuclear forces. It rests on the assumption that the United States will not use nuclear weapons as a means of aggression, but that it will actually destroy another state if that state cannot be otherwise dissuaded from attacking a state protected by the American nuclear deterrent. If the United States were to change its policies in either aspect, the current system of deterrence would be difficult to sustain, as formerly protected states raced to arm themselves and formerly deterred states began to explore the rewards of coercion.

This present system would be gravely undermined by multipolarity—the acquisition of a third superpower nuclear arsenal—for two reasons. First, multipolarity introduces a complexity that tends to weaken American commitments by blurring the identity of the states to be deterred: in a tripolar or n-polar world, responsibility is diffused. The persuasiveness of the argument, often heard in the United States during the Cold War, that the United States must act to suppress international violence or parry aggression, because if the United States doesn't, no one else will, fades in a multipolar world. The sheer complexity of deterrence in a multipolar world, coupled with an understandable American willingness to let other powers take up burdens long carried by the United States, creates a situation similar to that of the paralyzed crowds that attend emergencies. Second, the system of deterrence is stressed whenever a crisis triggers the threat of the use of nuclear weapons to deter aggression: such crises call the American bluff and require the United States to run potentially fatal risks to enforce dissuasion. Multipolarity can only increase, perhaps exponentially, the number of nuclear crises. We could have had another system of nuclear deterrence, perhaps managed by other powers, but this is the one we have, and this is the system bequeathed us by the Long War.

The link between nuclear proliferation and nuclear deterrence is too seldom drawn. In part this is a sociological phenomenon: the deterrence theorists tend to be interested in strategic studies and are often from military backgrounds; they are more curious about targeting and weapons development, and more informed about the formerly "central" balance between the superpowers than about "weapons of mass destruction" per se. The nonproliferation experts tend to be more interested in arms control than in strategic options, more conversant with the design of nuclear reactors and the processes of the nuclear fuel cycle than with the design of missiles and nuclear delivery systems, more global in orientation. In part, this disjunction is an intellectual phenomenon: the categories of thought are put in different terms, have different vocabularies. Theories of deterrence do not tell us which restraint agreements, like the Nonproliferation Treaty (NPT), will slow down proliferation; nonproliferation theories, on the other hand, more or less assume that any deployment of nuclear weapons is necessarily an evil, and that their use can never be justified. This largely unbridged chasm is a costly one because the strategic issues brought to the fore by the end of the Long War are pre-eminently questions of voluntary restraint, and thus the advocates of environmental protection and arms reduction can, perhaps for the first time in this era, realistically expect cooperation from the strategic sector.

Or should one say it is the second time? For there is an historic link between proliferation and the prevailing system of deterrence, and it is this link that principally accounts for the enormous success of nonproliferation efforts since the coming of nuclear weapons. The most important thing to be said about nuclear proliferation is not that it did happen in Israel, or India, or even France, but rather that it didn't happen in Japan or Germany; and the main reason it failed to take place in those two states was that the American nuclear guarantee to those countries provided a measure of deterrence sufficient to make it unnecessary for them to deter other states.

This is a controversial assertion. Sometimes it is claimed that Japan, because it had been the subject of nuclear attack, would never acquire such weapons. This may be, but it is equally possible that, precisely because it felt aggrieved over the Hiroshima and Nagasaki bombings, Japan might consider itself uniquely privileged to deploy the one weapon that would best ensure that this would never happen again. From time to time Japan has confirmed its pledge to forgo the development of nuclear weapons; the Japan Defense Agency has steadfastly maintained, however, that the bar against aggression in the Japanese constitution does not proscribe nuclear weapons so long as these do not exceed the minimum needed for defense.[2] The Indians have shown the world how a single election can quickly be translated into a policy of nuclear weapons acquisition and deployment. The election in Japan of a similarly nationalistic party could have similarly fateful consequences.

The Germans are also said to be unlikely candidates for nuclear proliferation. They, like the Japanese, are supposed to be acutely sensitive to the anxieties they arouse in their neighbors, and it is true that, in the late 1950s, when the Germans discussed the option of a nuclear weapons program, French and British sensitivities were sufficiently aroused to head off this idea. It was ultimately the American role in German defense that dissuaded the Germans, however, who doubtless appreciated the fact that French and British forces in Germany could hardly have withstood a Warsaw Pact assault *without* using nuclear weapons. Absent the American nuclear guarantee, it is even doubtful that West Germany would have remained in the Western Alliance, with consequences that we can easily imagine.

What has kept Japan and Germany from going nuclear, when proximate states like China and France did so; when they possessed the wealth, ambition, and skill to do so; when they faced the threat of mortal attack on the front lines of the Cold War? It was the assurance provided by the American nuclear umbrella and the positioning of American troops in forward bases such that any invasion would quickly engage them and thus would immediately commit the United States and in all likelihood involve the use of nuclear weapons to protect her forces. Reviewing the period since 1945, Lawrence Freedman has concluded that "the critical variable [that accounts for nonproliferation to Germany and Japan and the acquisition of weapons by India, China and France] is the prevailing alliance structure . . . Drawing on the deterrent power of another may carry fewer risks as well as lower costs than a drive for a national capability. The incentives for proliferation grow with the lack of a reliable superpower protector."[3] How can this lesson be applied to stem the proliferation of these weapons in the era we are now entering?

If deterrence is a key to nonproliferation, then what regime of weapons deployment might lend the most stability to the international system? Perhaps the most famous proposal that links deterrence to proliferation was made by Kenneth Waltz. In "The Spread of Nuclear Weapons: More May Be Better" Waltz suggested that widespread nuclear proliferation would in fact enhance stability, as various nuclear armed states paired off, just as the United States and the USSR had done.[4] This would result in a profusion of bipolar systems—India/Pakistan, Israel/Iraq, Ukraine/Russia—rather than a multipolar world. Waltz well recognized the acute danger posed by multipolarity. In "a *multipolar* world there are too many powers to permit any of them to draw clear and fixed lines between allies and adversaries" while at the same time there are so few (not every state can afford a superpower's arsenal) that the action of any single power is likely to engage the security of others. In a world of dancing partners, each conflict twirling around the international ballroom, however, it is perfectly clear who is to be embraced and who ignored. Multipolarity is neatly avoided.

But is this description entirely plausible? If it is true for India/Pakistan, what about India/China/Pakistan? Or Israel/Iraq/Iran? Or even Japan/Russia/China? Waltz must assume that each new nuclear state has but a single nuclear-armed adversary, and also that each such state actually has such an adversary, because otherwise the temptation to coerce nonnuclear states would potentially upset the stability of the proliferated international regime. And if Waltz is proved wrong (once we have brought a heavily dispersed and proliferated nuclear world into being), how would we go back to the position we are in today, which might then appear to have been a golden age?

A second suggestion follows directly from Freedman's observation that "nuclear proliferation is most likely to occur where external guarantees have come to be doubted, as in the Middle East, or barely exist, as in South Asia. Acquiring a nuclear capability is a statement of a lack of confidence in all alternative security arrangements."[5] Recognizing this, some commentators have proposed extending the U.S. nuclear guarantee to those former states of the Soviet Union, or former members of the Warsaw Pact, that might otherwise become nuclear powers. In the absence of such a guarantee these states might acquire nuclear weapons in response to the Russian nuclear capability, and then, in response to each other, much as Pakistan developed weapons in response to India, once India had itself responded to the nuclear weapons of China, which initially was reacting to the nuclear capability of the United States and the USSR.

Such proposals have an air of unreality to those of us who lived through the "decoupling" debates that periodically seized the Atlantic Alliance from the late 1950s until the late 1980s. Briefly, these debates arose from European skepticism that the United States, in the event of an attack on its European allies, really would risk nuclear retaliation directed at the American homeland by fulfilling its nuclear pledges to its allies. The European theatre, it was feared, would be "decoupled" from the continental United States if the United States reneged on its promises, or "uncoupled" if those pledges were fulfilled, making Europe a nuclear battleground, while the American and Soviet homelands were kept as tacitly (or even explicitly) agreed-upon sanctuaries. Regardless of the grounds for such doubt—and one may recall Sir Michael Howard's witty observation that, where nuclear risks are concerned, it takes a great deal more to reassure an ally than to deter an adversary*—if these doubts were enough to move France to develop its own deterrent, how could they possibly not assail Ukraine or Belarus? Even if the United States could be induced to make such pledges,

*See the discussion of reassurance in the introduction to Book I.

how could they be believed in the absence of the kind of American ground forces that underwrote the U.S. pledge to West Germany? And what, in such an event, would be the likely reaction of Russia, whose nuclear attitude remains vastly more significant than even that of the most ambitious potential proliferatee?

Yet a third approach comes from Margaret Thatcher. At a speech in Fulton, Missouri, commemorating Winston Churchill's famous Iron Curtain address there, Lady Thatcher said:

> The Soviet collapse has aggravated the single most awesome threat of modern times: the proliferation of weapons of mass destruction. . . . If America and its allies cannot deal with the problem directly by pre-emptive military means, they must at least diminish the incentives for [rogue states] to acquire new weapons in the first place. That means the West must install effective ballistic missile defences that would protect us and our armed forces, reduce or even nullify the rogue state's arsenal, and enable us to retaliate.[6]

I think we may assume, with Thatcher, that "it is probably unrealistic to expect military intervention to remove" those weapons of mass destruction that are in hostile hands. What, then, about missile defense as a parrying technology to nuclear proliferation? Is it really sensible to think that providing the great states of the West with ballistic missile defenses would actually discourage a "rogue state" to a greater degree than the assurance of nuclear annihilation that would surely follow such an attack already deters them today? To believe this assumes a psychological hypersensitivity to the mere possibility of failure on the part of the leaderships of Iraq, Iran, and North Korea that seems incompatible with their characters, insofar as we know them, and an indifference to survival that these leaders, though they may seek it in their recruits, do not prominently display themselves. To the contrary, Martin van Creveld, in his study *Nuclear Proliferation and the Future of Conflict,* concludes:

> There seems to be no factual basis for the claims that regional leaders do not understand the nature and implications of nuclear weapons; or that their attitudes to those weapons are governed by some peculiar cultural biases which make them incapable of rational thought; or that they are more adventurous and less responsible in handling them than anybody else.[7]

The real strength of Thatcher's proposal lies, as the last sentence in the passage quoted from her speech discloses, in the hope that a sound defense would *enable* retaliation, thus removing the possibility of successful extortion by the rogue states. Yet the day in which any states vying for "rogue" status could *disable* retaliation through accurate preemption is, thankfully, far off.

An alternative approach was reflected in the Clinton administration's efforts at "counterproliferation." This was a multifaceted policy whose central method combined U.S. pledges not to use nuclear weapons with various arms control schemes like the Nuclear Nonproliferation Treaty, renewed with great effort, and the Missile Control Technology Regime (MCTR), whose enforcement has so bedeviled American relations with China and other states.

If I am correct in arguing that deterrence is crucial to the successful pursuit of nonproliferation, then the administration's policy could have been at most a partial success. A sincere pledge of no-first-use of nuclear weapons would scarcely reassure those states that feel the need to acquire nuclear weapons to protect themselves *from* us (as to which Iraq's recent experience with American conventional arms is exemplary) nor buck up those states who fear such attacks from others and look *to* us for protection. Israel, to take one case, can hardly be expected to renounce her nuclear weapons in light of a pledge by the American president not to use nuclear weapons first to protect it. Counterproliferation is, rather, the response of a political community that seems to have only the ideas that were in play before the end of the Long War; in that respect, the Clinton administration's nonproliferation strategies were no worse than those of its immediate predecessor.

Let us return to the criteria proposed to enable the international community to determine when nuclear proliferation is unacceptable. Then perhaps we can see which of these proposals, or others, might successfully enforce the rules implicit in those criteria. The first proscription was against multipolarity. This suggests that a principal task of any nonproliferation regime must be to prevent Germany and Japan from "going nuclear." The second proscription was against the aggressive use of nuclear weapons, and the third, against proliferation to states so unstable that aggression might suddenly become attractive as a means of consolidating domestic power. These suggestions imply that states recently or currently engaged in aggression or threats of aggression against others are unwholesome candidates for the possession of nuclear arsenals—such states as Syria, Iraq, Libya, and North Korea. And states like Indonesia, owing to its political instability, ought to be on a watch list. As to others, there may be strong reasons to discourage their acquisition of nuclear weapons, but proliferation to such states is not necessarily critical to the system as a whole. It may be unsettling for Peru if Chile begins a nuclear program, or for Turkey if the Greeks do. But these developments do not threaten a systemic collapse of deterrence, even if they are cause to activate the diplomatic efforts of states that have influence in those regions.

For Germany and Japan the question of reassurance is more problematic in some ways now than it was before the end of the Long War. For the Japanese, the prospect of a North Korean nuclear device is no more threatening than a Chinese nuclear capability, with which they have lived for some time. The real anxiety arises from what might ensue if the Americans confronted either North Korea or China. Thus the Americans are in the paradoxical position of having to tread softly where northeast Asian nuclear proliferation is concerned, precisely to avoid a far more dangerous proliferation should the Japanese become alarmed by a turn of events toward crisis. In the case of Germany, the problem is exacerbated by the prospect of an E.U. nuclear capability. If NATO should falter, then such a capability could repolarize the nuclear world—the second Rome, as it were,* that seems so dear to the hearts of many in Brussels and Paris. Here the American role is not the decisive one. Rather it depends upon E.U. members, especially the British and French, to argue for, paradoxically, the maintenance of independent but modest proliferated deterrents, such as France and the United Kingdom currently deploy, rather than for a specifically E.U. nuclear force. These examples of nuclear proliferation can act as inoculations against an E.U. nuclear virus. French behavior on this matter has thus far not been entirely encouraging. There have been many reports of French efforts, at present quiescent, to seduce the Germans into a nuclear partnership.

For both Germany and Japan, the utility of antiballistic missile defenses can be very high, both as a hedge against nuclear attacks (or missile attacks with other warheads of mass destruction) and, just as important, as a means of reassuring their respective publics that a national deterrent is not necessary. Thatcher's program of ballistic missile defense development makes a great deal more sense in this antiproliferation role, than as a force for states already possessing nuclear weapons. To the extent that the United States supplies technical assistance for such defenses, this will require a modification of the Antiballistic Missile (ABM) treaty. This is, I believe, well worth the diplomatic cost.[8]

The contribution of international law to preventing major-state proliferation is limited. Germany and Japan are states with representative institutions that can legitimately claim the rights of sovereignty to choose the means of their own protection. Insofar as the peace and stability of the entire international system is jeopardized by the multipolarity such proliferation brings in its wake, there are grounds for condemnation and perhaps even some sort of sanctions, but these are the sort of steps that isolate

*A reference to the Avignon papacy.

rather than reassure a state and thus tend to radicalize the domestic politics of a democratic state with problematic consequences for its security policy. Rather the role of international society, and its rules, is as a benchmark: it tells us what steps are disfavored, but it does not tell us what to do once these fateful steps have been taken. The renewal of the prophylactic Nonproliferation Treaty (NPT) must be taken as an important accomplishment, although the treaty doesn't specify effective remedies for its violation. Both Japan and Germany are signatories, and despite hard bargaining to the contrary, no new American nuclear guarantees to other states were extracted as a price for the agreement. Such guarantees—particularly to the former Warsaw Pact states and the states of the former Soviet Union—would have run the risk of undermining the tie that binds Germany to the West, because these guarantees put Germany in the position of an unwilling, and unarmed, co-guarantor who might be dragged into a nuclear conflict. We should not want to put Germany in the situation that Japan now finds itself in with respect to the American guarantee to South Korea.

Major-state proliferation that risks multipolarity is the most important, but not the most intractable, part of a nonproliferation agenda for the society of states. That dubious status is reserved for the medium-size state that is a party to a long-standing dispute and feels the necessity of acquiring nuclear weapons, either for an advantage in that dispute or to protect against its adversary's gaining an advantage by a timely nuclear deployment of its own. India and Pakistan, Israel and Iraq, Brazil and Argentina, China and Taiwan, Iran and its several targets—all either have nuclear weapons or have at one time had active programs to acquire such weapons. Insofar as such states develop a capacity to deter Western intervention, they check the West's power to enforce international norms, as we saw in the Gulf War. This, too, is a threat to the society of states, because the West—and particularly the United States—underwrites the stability of that society.

There are two ways we might approach such a problem: we could expect the great market-state powers to choose sides in each potential conflict, ad hoc, and give those great powers a free hand to resolve matters by mediation or force; or we could set up rules that specify sanctions (including force) whenever the acquisition of nuclear weapons violates international understandings like the NPT and the MTCR, or is done in contemplation of international aggression. The successful Gulf War action was an amalgam of both approaches, but so was the Bosnian debacle. The latter experience suggests that relying on the West to act forcibly outside immediate threats to its well-being is impractical, even when it is clear that such inaction can ultimately reduce the West's ability to deter or to act.

To date, the only successful examples of active counterproliferation are the Israeli and coalition attacks on Iraq in 1981 and 1991, respectively. These can hardly provide a precedent for action generally. It is more likely that the buyout of North Korean nuclear capacity, should it prove successful, will provide a model for the future. Certainly the South African renunciation of its nuclear program seems to fit within a market-state paradigm—exchanging military power of dubious utility for economic relationships that promise development and investment. But what of the "rogue state"? Is it realistic to think that radical states can be bought off?

Perhaps not. But in such cases, who is really at risk? Is the system at risk? Libya threatens Chad; it does not really threaten Italy, which is a member of NATO, or the United States, which has evidenced its willingness to retaliate and whose means, which once deterred the Soviet Union, ought to be adequate to deter Libya. Iran threatens Israel, Iraq, and Saudi Arabia—but Israel and Saudi Arabia are protected by U.S. weapons, including nuclear weapons, which the U.S. administration has stated were in readiness during the Gulf War in case Saddam Hussein resorted to weapons of mass destruction. Only North Korea poses a challenge to the international system as a whole, not because it threatens South Korea—which is also protected by the U.S. nuclear deterrent—but for the ironic reason that it can provoke the United States to reactions that will themselves destabilize the system of deterrence, by overreacting or by withdrawing, either of which could propel Japan into developing its own nuclear option. No set of legal rules can help much here: it is a matter of prudence and wisdom in the formation and execution of policy. Nor can the international society of states do much as a group because so much turns on the policies of one state, the United States, which, after all, committed the first act of nuclear proliferation at Alamogordo.

Perhaps the best argument for a credible, if limited, ballistic missile defense lies not in its impact on "rogue states" so much as in its reassurance to potential proliferatees that fear attacks from such states. Such defenses reduce the extortion value of nuclear threats. The actual operation of missile defense systems, however, will bring new and complex problems of international coordination. These can be greatly eased by the sharing of U.S. air surveillance and early warning capabilities. *Indeed, the provision of information by the United States in order to enable missile defense may play as large a role in the twenty-first century as the provision of extended deterrence did in the twentieth.* What is needed is an institutional mechanism for sharing and protecting this information.

That brings us to the two other acute threats to a stable security system of market-states, Russia and China. They pose the most signficant concerns in the immediate future precisely because their own constitutional forms are still at issue and because they are both nuclear powers. Insofar as the society of market-states can help bring about a domestic transformation in the constitutional form of these states, it ameliorates the nuclear problem. In the meantime, these proto-market-states are likely to be among the most serious violators of the bans on the sale of missile technology and fissile material. Financial and political assistance to domestic parties in these states that wish to pursue admission and acceptance into the society of market-states is an apt investment for that society.

The market-state will face nuclear threats that are as novel and as market-driven and decentralized as it is. Nuclear terrorism, both on a large scale, involving attacks or threatened extortion against nuclear reactors, and on a micro level, using the nuclear materials commonly found in hospitals, universities, and laboratories, is more likely than an attack using a nuclear warhead. Still, the active international trade in weapons delivery systems and even fissile material will experience the same heady change in the scope of its markets, the speed of its transactions, and the astounding return on investment that the international market has provided other commodities, especially illicit ones. At some point it will simply be impossible to keep up with the nuclear weapons trade, which is at once lucrative and easily concealed. We missed a chance to slow this down when the United States failed to take up a suggestion that Soviet missiles simply be bought intact and destroyed rather than dismantled. This failure led to new opportunities for the diversion of nuclear fissile material, but some dispersion would have taken place at some time in any case. This is a proliferation of a different kind, less statist and all the more difficult to manage for that reason. The society of market-states will find it difficult to police such proliferation because intelligence sharing is as politically and strategically fraught for the market-state at peace as it was for the nation-state at war.

Deterrence and reassurance are the keys to the prevention of nuclear proliferation to states; they offer little in the way of help vis-à-vis transnational, stateless aggressors. This is the most difficult part of a nonproliferation agenda. If such organizations can be denied a state sanctuary, however, it will be difficult for them to assemble and deploy nuclear weapons on any scale that might disturb the system of stable deterrence, though they may be able to wreak a terrible destruction nevertheless. There may be a useful analogy, however: if the contribution of deterrence to nonproliferation is primarily that of reassurance, then the entire battery of market-state mechanisms for reassurance—surveillance, missile defense, redundancy of critical infrastructure, even market programs as mundane as insurance—should prove helpful. Ultimately only a global coalition that shares intelligence and information can hope to forestall terrorist attacks using nuclear weapons. We are in a race against time: can the new society of market-states develop technologies of information collection—like nanosensors, for example, that detect nuclear traces—*and* habits of cooperation before terrorists deploy nuclear devices in an attack?

CHEMICAL WEAPONS

The materials needed in order to create chemical weapons are far more widely available than those required for nuclear devices and the techniques of manufacture are vastly simpler. For these reasons, chemical weapons are often called the "poor man's nuclear weapons." As with so many substitutes imposed by poverty, however, the "poor man's alternative" provides nothing like the satisfaction of the real thing. Although chemical weapons are ritually referred to as weapons of mass destruction, the lethality they bear is not all that "mass." Chemical weapons would cause a small fraction of the deaths caused by nuclear or biological weapons. To take a single example: 100 kilograms of anthrax distributed in an aerosolized weapon by a cruising airplane would cause 300 times the fatalities that would occur if the same plane carried 1,000 kilograms of sarin gas.

Insofar as treaty regimes are useful in achieving the goals of nonproliferation, the ratification of the Chemical Weapons Convention provides a heartening case of politics in the market-state. Large chemical companies, concerned about the impact of the treaty on their enterprises if the United States stayed outside the treaty regime, were able to bridge the partisan gap in the U.S. Senate that has stymied so many other measures. On the other hand, it must be recognized that renouncing chemical weapons makes U.S. reliance on nuclear weapons that much greater[9] and the consequence of this enhanced reliance could be a contraction of the willingness of other states—potential proliferatees—to rely on American security guarantees. Suppose for example that chemical weapons were used against a state that the United States had pledged itself to protect. The previous American position, no first use of chemical weapons, would have at least permitted retaliation in kind. Once the Chemical Weapons Convention came into force, requiring the destruction of American stockpiles and proscribing their use, however, retaliation (and hence deterrence) have depended upon a commitment of American conventional forces or nuclear attacks, as to both of which potential allies might have some skepticism. As is so often the case with respect to arms-control agreements—the landmines movement comes to mind—the United States is simply not in the same position as other states, at least as long as it continues to assume global security responsibilities, and therefore should not be shamed by charges of hypocrisy when it fails to adopt regimes that it urges on others.

BIOLOGICAL WEAPONS

The tactical use of microorganisms and toxins as weapons has been attempted by many warring parties, including aboriginal Americans who tipped their arrows in amphibian-derived poisons. Fomites—entities that harbor and transmit disease—have been used to spread infection since antiquity. During the fourteenth century siege of Kaffa, a Genoese cathedral city on the Black Sea, the attacking Tatar force was struck by plague. They catapulted their diseased cadavers into the besieged city in an attempt to start an epidemic in 1347—or perhaps to trigger a collapse of morale within the city walls. An outbreak of plague did ensue and Kaffa fell. Ships carrying refugees from Kaffa are thought to have begun the second plague pandemic in Europe.

Smallpox was deployed as a weapon against Native Americans by the British in the eighteenth century.[10] During the French and Indian War, Sir Jeffrey Amherst proposed the use of this weapon in order to reduce the tribes hostile to the British. When smallpox broke out at Fort Pitt in 1763, a Captain Ecuyer gave blankets and a handkerchief from the smallpox hospital to Indians and recorded in his journal, "I hope it will have the desired effect." A smallpox epidemic did follow, although it is impossible to isolate the cause.[11]

The formulation of Koch's postulates[12] and the development of modern microbiology in the nineteenth century led to the isolation and production of specific pathogens. In the ensuing years, many states attempted to develop pathogens and weaponize them. In World War I, Germany pursued an ambitious program using attacks on livestock in neutral countries and poisoning animal feed for export.

Japan conducted biological warfare research from 1932 onwards in occupied Manchuria. Prisoners were injected with anthrax, meningitis, cholera, and plague. At least 10,000 are said to have died. Eleven Chinese cities were attacked using contaminated water and food supplies. Pathogen cultures were also sprayed from airplanes. Plague was developed by allowing laboratory fleas to feed on plague-infected rats; these fleas were then harvested and were released by aircraft over Chinese cities. Fifteen million fleas are reported to have been released per attack.

During the same period, the British experimented with weaponized anthrax off the coast of Scotland. It was the discovery of the Japanese program at the end of World War II, however, that galvanized research in the United Kingdom, the United States, and the USSR. Japanese scientists were granted immunity from war crimes prosecution in exchange for extensive debriefings. During the Korean War the U.S. program expanded, and full-scale production of pathogens for weapons began in 1954. As part of a biological countermeasures program, American cities like New York and San Francisco were surreptitiously used as laboratories to test aerosolization. The offensive program was unilaterally terminated by President Nixon in 1969, and in 1975 the United States ratified the Biological and Toxic Weapons Convention. This treaty prohibits the development, production, and retention of microbial or other biological stockpiles in quantities that have no justification for prophylactic purposes.

Unlike the Chemical Weapons Convention, however, the Biological and Toxic Weapons Convention has no provisions for verifying compliance. It is now widely conceded that several signatories have violated the Convention's provisions. For example, the KGB weaponized the lethal toxin ricin by producing small metallic pellets that were cross-drilled, filled with the poison, then sealed with wax that would melt at body temperature. The pellets were discharged by a spring-loaded weapon disguised as an umbrella. By this means the Bulgarian dissident Georgi Markov was assassinated in London in 1978 and at least six other persons were murdered. In 1992 President Yeltsin disclosed that the Soviet Union had pursued its biological warfare program in violation of the Convention and confirmed that an outbreak of anthrax in 1979 had been caused by an accidental release of spores from a biological weapons facility.

The scope of the Soviet program, as described by a defector,[13] embraced more than 55,000 scientists and technicians. Yeltsin promised to suspend these activities; a 1995 report, however, concluded that between 25,000 and 30,000 persons were still engaged in various related programs.

The Iraqi program, while on a different scale, is known to have been extensive, and may have produced up to ten billion doses of anthrax, botulinum toxin, and aflatoxin. UNSCOM, the UN agency set up after the Gulf War to discover and dismantle Iraq's programs of weapons of mass destruction, concluded that biological agents had been weaponized in considerable variety, including 155 mm artillery shells, 122 mm rockets, aircraft bombs, missile warheads, and aerosol tanks. UNSCOM was unable to determine, however, whether these weapons had been destroyed.

Today, it is thought that China, Egypt, Iran, Libya, Taiwan, Israel, and North Korea have active biological weapons programs.[14] Public sources have estimated that between 10 and 25 countries possess or are seeking biological weapons. Unlike nuclear and chemical weapons, biological agents are easy to make and conceal and they are inexpensive. They can be produced in facilities that are also involved in legitimate scientific and pharmaceutical activities. These programs can flourish despite rigorous export control regulations because the same agents that furnish lethal weapons are also naturally occurring microorganisms and toxins. Similarly, the dual nature of biological agents makes verification of treaty commitments against weaponizing these agents virtually impossible. Finally, the advanced nature of the Soviet program and the temptation to market its fruits to other states presents a scenario every bit as disturbing as that involving Russian nuclear devices.

This duality of use—biology as medical science/war weapon—that so bedevils control regimes also, however, holds the possibility for at least tempering the problem. The Soviet program turns out to be readily convertible to peaceful uses, in a way that its nuclear weapons program is not. One commentator has asserted that many of the Russian biological weapons facilities can be readily converted to biomedical research work and vaccine production, providing employment to a large number of scientists and technicians.[15] In a highly creative approach, another commentator has argued that trade regimes and nonproliferation regimes can be carefully crafted in order to attract and enmesh a new tier of states that have been recently endowed with advanced technological capabilities, including the capacity to manufacture weapons of mass destruction.[16] This approach plays on the new market-state and its intertwining of security and commercial links among states such that the transparency so crucial for market development can also be used to prevent clandestine military development.

At present, however, it is hard to get security analysts to pay much attention to biological weapons. To persuade them to pay more, we must first answer the question: if these weapons are so easy to deploy and so lethal,[17] why haven't we seen more of their use?*

The two sets of consumers for such weapons are military commanders and terrorists. For commanders, biological weapons are too slow to affect operations at the front (it may take days or weeks for an enemy soldier to sicken, during which he can do a lot of damage) and too unpredictable[18] (because the wide diffusion of virulent agents can infect one's own troops).† For terrorists, the same features of biological weapons cut the other way: delay allows perpetrators time for escape, and an agent like smallpox is terrifying to the public because it is unpredictable owing to the fact that it is communicable. Communicability poses its own threats, however; it may be some time before the terrorists know whether they are themselves infected and are infecting others (their colleagues, for example) unintentionally. Accordingly, many biological weapons programs have mainly focused on anthrax spores that enter the lungs and hatch bacteria that multiply rapidly within the body but don't infect anyone else.

Genetic engineering, however, may be able to make biological weapons far more useful to both the commander and the terrorist. It should be possible to design a virus that would disproportionately afflict members of a particular ethnic group, giving safety to attackers from a different group.[19] Genetic engineering could also match a particular virus with an effective

---

*Even the anthrax attacks in 2001 in the United States, alarming as they were, did not cause mass casualties.

†Indeed the German army in World War II avoided areas with typhus outbreaks, prompting one community to vaccinate its citizens in order to register false positives on the Weil-Felix diagnostic test. This saved the residents from deportation to concentration camps. E. S. Lazowski and S. Matulewicz, "Serendipitous Discovery of Artificial Weil-Felix Reaction Used in Private Immunological War," *ASM News* 43 (1977): 300–302.

vaccine so that the aggressor would be immunized; or piggyback two agents, one quick and confined and the other latent and communicable. This sort of engineering will allow for the cloning of vast quantities of both traditional pathogens and new designer agents; these could be created quickly and cheaply, while their antidotes might take decades to develop. Such frightening prospects also hold within them some hope: the revolution in genetics might also provide framework vaccines and antidotes that can be quickly modified and rapidly produced.

If biological weapons were used today against a civilian population, the public health systems of any of the major countries would be quickly overwhelmed. Our best strategy lies in recognizing the new and distinct nature of this threat and strengthening the public health surveillance systems,* as well as the intelligence collection capabilities, that can quickly detect and possibly thwart such attacks.

IMMIGRATION AND HUMAN RIGHTS

THE GLOBALIZATION OF CULTURE

Progress in international communications that occurred during the Long War—beginning with the radio and culminating in the satellite-borne signals of global television—was decisive for that war. It may be unlikely that forces of the size that invaded Normandy, vastly larger than anything in the past, will ever be marshaled in an amphibious assault in the future, but it is also clear that only modern telecommunications could have made such an enterprise possible. The great naval campaigns of the Pacific were enabled by a communications network of staggering complexity, involving the coordination of distant fleets, air assaults, and landings combining all arms of the American forces. And, too, it is difficult to overestimate the role of Churchill's stirring addresses to the British public or Roosevelt's Fireside Chats in rallying public opinion, which is a crucial element in mobilizing the popular resources of the nation-state necessary to execute strategies of mass warfare and to withstand mass civilian suffering. The most critical role played by these technologies, however, came at the endgame of the Long War. It was the irrefutable comparison between life in the West and in the Soviet bloc, made possible by modern communications, that utterly demoralized the communist leaderships and so alienated their peoples.†

---

*It is a mistake to assume that the victim of a biological attack will automatically seek assistance or that he would be correctly diagnosed in any event. Some victims would wait until it was too late for effective treatment; some doctors might not recognize unfamiliar symptoms. In the case of infectious diseases such delay could be costly.

†It is alleged that Leon Trotsky proposed at one time a modern telephone system for the new Soviet state, and that Stalin vetoed this idea with the remark that he could imagine no greater instrument of counterrevolution.

Nor did this communication go in one direction only. Dissident groups in Poland, Czechoslovakia, and elsewhere were able constantly to expose the actions of the police states under which they labored. The Helsinki Accords gave dissidents an international standard of human rights against which to measure the acts of the Soviet bloc; modern communications made it possible to report these evaluations. An equally important line of communication was the limited travel to the West accorded citizens of the Warsaw Pact states. The bloc actually began to hemorrhage with a mass migration of German citizens through Hungary in 1989.

These two phenomena—immigration and human rights—that are connected to innovations in communication also pose two major challenges to the society of market-states. Immigration on a scale never hitherto seen in peacetime bears a relationship to the market-state different from that it bore to the nation-state. The nation-state could effectively seal its borders because it had the duty of protecting the ethnic nation for whose benefit it was constituted.[20] The market-state is more ambivalent about such matters because it can so usefully employ the lower-cost labor of new immigrants to increase the productivity of the society. Moreover, in its multicultural form—like the United States—the market-state must deal with new immigrants who can call upon political groups to whom they are ethnically allied, as well as upon an American political consciousness that is wary of policies favoring exclusion.

It is global communication, both logistically and in images, that drives this immigration. As the market-states of the developed world increase their wealth, they become the target of immigration for peoples of the Third World whose demographic dynamics could quickly overwhelm the capacity of any state to assimilate them. Furthermore, the abandonment of the integrative function of the nation-state, which sought to transform immigrants into versions of the pre-existing national group of the country to which they had come, means that large, unassimilated ethnic groups are now without the resources of the State that would enable them to be assimilated. Maximizing the opportunities of its citizens means that the market-state must leave it to those citizens to determine what cultural attachments they wish to form. Even market-states that do not embrace the multicultural variation chosen by the United States may still face the reality of large knots of unassimilated immigrant communities within their midst, and thus face also the choice of according them full democratic privileges—and risking the loss of civil cohesion—or denying them the right of equal democratic status.

Thus again the ironic intertwining of immigration and human rights: the communications media that bring glamorous images of the developed states to those living in wretchedness also bring to those in comfort images of the suffering and cruelty visited on the less fortunate. Perhaps this latter development is really a benefit: the states of the developed world must welcome the opportunity to deploy their resources in ways that benefit the oppressed and the poor—this, after all, can justify our good fortune. But polities that are emotionally whipsawed by the most affecting shows of suffering are ill-equipped to devise long-term policies to help anyone. One month's poster child gives way to another. The Kurds had languished under oppressive and genocidal rule since the seventh century until CNN* brought attention to their plight in Iraq, but soon thereafter attention shifted to the suffering of Muslims in Bosnia.

Lacking the political focus that enables sustained attention to a problem, the publics of the developed states must soon grow disillusioned with humanitarian efforts altogether. Sooner or later there will be analysts who will explain that any help will create dependency, that aid, however well intentioned, actually makes things worse, and so on. In a world of suffering, the dimensions of which are necessarily beyond complete cure because they are essentially comparative, fed by international communications that so vividly and increasingly display the contrast between rich and poor, the society of market-states is ill-suited for helping. Each state is, after all, competing for the skills of learned castes who, unlike the individual bearers of capital under the nation-state, can take their knowledge with them (or withhold it). To become either the most welcoming refuge for the poorest or the chief ministering angel to the Third World is to consign one's state to a steadily degenerating competitive position vis-à-vis other market-states. We can expect moves among some members of the society of market-states to require others to take immigrants, provide aid, or change their human rights policies, thus breeding conflicts among states.

To simply ignore suffering and the denial of human rights in other states, however, is also destructive, depriving states of their moral basis. Of course it may be that the citizens of such states will wall themselves off psychologically, in much the way they can wall themselves off architecturally, from the unassimilated poor in their own countries. This renders the market-state an attractive target, however, to civil disorder as well as to international terrorism.

There are many other problems created for the State by the explosion in communications technology: the privacy interests of individuals and the protection of the family from offensive intrusion are examples. Immigration and human rights, however, are different because they do not admit of single-state solutions. Only coordinated action within the society of states can treat these particular problems effectively and with an attention to their interconnection. These problems bring unusual strains to market-states

---

*I am indebted to Ashbel Green for pointing out that the revolt in the Ivory Coast was at least in part inspired by what its citizens saw happening on TV to Milosevic. What has been called the "CNN effect" apparently has consequences for repressive regimes too.

because they are called upon to devise cooperative solutions even though the salience of the market—which is indifferent to such concerns and hostile to the transaction costs such solutions impose—is especially high within such states.

THE LIBERALIZATION OF TRADE AND FINANCE

ECONOMIC DEVELOPMENT AND THE ENVIRONMENT

The introduction of the computer[21] and the mathematics on which high-speed computation is based played a decisive role in defeating fascism and communism in the Long War. No history of the Second World War can give anything like an accurate account if it was written before the revelations about Allied code breaking that began to appear in the 1970s. Nor can any political history of the Cold War omit the phenomenal growth of the developed economies, especially Japan and the United States, that occurred as a result of the introduction of microchip technology. Although, as observed above, the percentage of the American workforce devoted to manufacturing has dropped with the precipitousness that earlier occurred with respect to agricultural workers, the percentage of U.S. GDP contributed by manufacturing has not changed in a significant way. The enormous growth in productivity that accounts for this fact can be largely attributed to the products of the computer revolution. It is not that computer operators have replaced clerk-typists, or even that new computer-based products have given a shot of adrenaline to consumer demand comparable to that of the automobile in an earlier period. Rather it is that a new source of wealth has been discovered: the application of vast amounts of information rapidly applied to the tasks of work. Not only did this greatly enrich the United States and Japan, but it created explosive markets for the products of an entirely new list of economic players on the world scene—Korea and Taiwan, among others—as well as enabling the renovation of the Western European infrastructure that had begun the Industrial Age.

The introduction of the computer was a strategic innovation* that was productively married to the American doctrine of containment. This doctrine proposed that communism would collapse of its own steadily increasing deterioration if it could be prevented from actually seizing other states (by invasion or subversion). This required that the noncommunist states be made strong through increasing prosperity and effective alliances. It proved to be an effective strategy for the noncommunist society

*See Chapter 10.

of nation-states, and yet some of the innovations that made it succeed were ultimately destructive of the power of the nation-state itself. But for the development of the computer, George Orwell might well have been right about the power of communications technology to observe and control national populations. Instead, this technology decentralized the power of institutions, including the State, so that the objects of control slipped out of the hands of governments altogether. George Gilder gives this example:

> A steel mill, the exemplary industry of the industrial age, lends itself to control by governments. Its massive output is easily measured and regulated at every point by government. By contrast, the typical means of production in the new epoch is a man at a computer work station, designing microchips comparable in complexity to the entire steel facility, to be manufactured from software programs comprising a coded sequence of electronic pulses that can elude every export control and run a production line anywhere in the world.[22]

Regulation by law—the characteristic method of the nation-state—is both losing its effectiveness because of this technology and becoming more costly because the technology of computers has conferred greater value on intellectual capital, which flees from regulation wherever possible.

Indeed some of the core concepts that enabled the nation-state to attempt to manipulate its economy through regulation have become vacuous under the pressure of the mobility made possible by computing technology. The notion of the *trade balance* that has long been held to be crucial to the nation-state depends upon our being able to value the goods and services exchanged in international trade and to assign these values to a particular state. Where the most valuable good is information, which is highly mobile and cannot be measured in these terms, however, it is fruitless to measure trade balances precisely because they are limited to the measurable. One example is the printed book: for a publisher in one nation-state, "foreign earnings" from such a book in another state may account for a large share of total revenue, even though no actual books are exported. This is because it is more profitable for the publisher to sell derivative copyright licenses than to ship books abroad. As Peter Drucker points out, "the most profitable computer 'export sales' may actually show up in trade statistics as an 'import.' This is the fee some of the world's leading banks, multinationals and Japanese trading companies get for processing in their home office data arriving electronically from their branches and customers around the world."[23]

Moreover, computing technologies have made possible the complex logistics of transnational value-adding production.

The dress a customer purchases at a smart store in San Francisco may have originated with cloth woven in Korea, finished in Taiwan, and cut and sewed in India according to an American design. Of course a brief stop in Milan, to pick up a "Made in Italy" label, and leave off a substantial licensing fee is *de rigueur* before the final journey to New York.[24]

In such circumstances, what sense does it really make to consider this an Italian export? We accept, conventionally, that it matters if the company exporting from Milan is U.S.-owned; the company's earnings will be repatriated and can be measured. But suppose it simply can't be determined what country's investors own the exporting company, and to what degree the country that finally exports a product to the United States is the source of value? This casts doubt on the very notion that the world can be subdivided into national economies. And if this is so, then monitoring one of the key functions of the nation-state is erased to nothingness.

Walter Wriston asks:

How does a national government measure capital formation, when much new capital is intellectual? How does it measure the productivity of knowledge workers whose product cannot be counted on our fingers? If it cannot do that, how can it track productivity growth? How does it track or control the money supply when the financial markets create new financial instruments faster than the regulators can keep track of them? And if it cannot do any of these things with the relative precision of simpler times, what becomes of the great mission of modern governments: controlling and manipulating the national economy?[25]

Monetary and fiscal policy are the two great levers available to the State to manage its national economy. By manipulating the value of its currency, a state can raise or lower interest rates, stimulate or suppress growth, increase exports or imports. In a world of floating exchange rates, however, states do not set the value of their currencies with respect to an external standard—such as the gold standard, or a basket of values related to interstate economic comparisons like the European Monetary Standard—but rather are judged by the market as if currency were any other commodity, like soybeans or petroleum.* In such an environment, the computer has made possible the instantaneous judgment by the market as to the value of any particular currency because it allows hundreds of thousands of investors to voice their demand decisions through computer-assisted trans-

---

*A development in economics analogous in my view to the transformation of time, in physics, from an invariant measuring standard to a concomitant element of the dimension of space.

actions vastly in excess of the demand for money required by purchases of goods and services. As Wriston, the former head of one of the world's largest banks, noted, "[u]nlike all prior arrangements, the new system was not built by politicians, economists, central bankers or finance ministers. No high level international conference produced a master plan. The new system was built by technology."[26] As of this writing, the amount of dollars trading per day exceeds the total GDP of the American economy annually; only a tiny fraction of this is available to central banks trying to manipulate this trading.

Wriston asked, "What becomes of the great mission of modern governments?" The reply must be: the mission changes. The market-state ceases to base its legitimacy on improving the welfare of its people, and begins instead to attempt to enable individuals to maximize the value of their talents by providing them with the most opportunity to do so. "Be everything you can be" replaces "A chicken in every pot."[27]

The market-state has shifted its mission to respond to the new circumstances in which the nation-state found itself. Market-states composing a society of such states reflect the consequences of the strategic changes that won the Long War; with respect to rapid computation, two kinds of challenges arising from this history are paramount: (a) the possibility of a trade war among the developed northern-tier states and/or a trade collapse between North and South, and (b) the transnational problems of protecting the environment. Both of these challenges to the society of market-states are attributable to the revolution in information technology—North-South discrepancies in wealth resulting from a dramatic change in the terms of trade have been further accentuated by it—and yet both problems can benefit from this technology.

CONFLICTS ARISING FROM INTERNATIONAL TRADE

TRADE WARS

The society of market-states will be dominated by three important actors, much as the Cold War was dominated by two. Europe will be the world's largest market and the largest trader; Japan will be the world's largest creditor, as it is now, with a GDP that approaches that of the United States; the United States will remain the world's most powerful single economic state, the possessor of the world's reserve currency,* and the market with the largest GDP.

Since the end of World War II, economic relations among these three actors have been largely guided by the Long War objectives they shared and the security alliances that served those objectives. Indeed there was

---

*This speculation assumes that the euro does not displace the dollar—a guess that, thus far, seems plausible.

relatively little direct collaboration between Japan and Europe, as both saw their futures as linked directly to Washington. German redevelopment occurred, perhaps could only have occurred, within the nuclear and conventional strategic guarantee of NATO. This relationship tempered economic competition in both directions: the Americans were anxious to develop a strong ally as a bulwark against communism; the Germans were eager not to alienate the Americans and be abandoned in the center of Europe, astride the division between East and West. Germany realized that its long-term goal of reunification could only take place under American sponsorship; America understood that a neutral West Germany would not only demoralize the remaining noncommunist European states, but would cease to be the driving economic engine of European recovery within what was then the European Economic Community (EEC). The EEC itself was strongly endorsed by the United States as offering the best prospect for European growth and stability.

With respect to Japan, the intertwining of economic development and security guarantees was even tighter. Japan faced at least three potentially lethal adversaries in the western Pacific and was largely unarmed; she therefore depended upon the United States to underwrite her survival as an independent state. At the same time, the United States was an avid mentor, encouraging economic development. Here too Washington believed that its own struggle against communism would be best served by a dynamic, capitalist economy in an allied state. For its part, Japan attempted to pacify U.S. alarm over growing American trade deficits, in order not to upset existing security arrangements. As C. Fred Bergsten observes:

> The United States and its allies . . . frequently made economic concessions to avoid jeopardizing their global security structures. Cold War politics in fact sheltered the economic recoveries of Europe and Japan, and America's support for them. The United States seldom employed its security leverage directly in pursuit of its economic goals; indeed, security and economic issues remained largely compartmentalized in all of the industrial democracies.[28]

Bergsten concludes that the end of the Cold War will "sharply heighten the prospect of a trade war"[29] among these three northern-tier communities. For each of the world's principal market-state actors, the overriding security concerns that muted its economic conflicts have receded, and there are substantial incentives to play a rougher game. In Europe, efforts to deepen the European Union (bringing about greater political centralization within the E.U.) and widen it (expanding E.U. membership to Central and Eastern European states) mean that imports to the European market are likely to decline. Preferential access to markets within the E.U. will act to deliberalize global trade. Even with Great Britain within the E.U., the historically mercantile trading policies of France and the consistent German demand for a strong euro—with all this entails for the other E.U. members' monetary policies in a single currency environment—will drive the demand for strong external barriers against the United States and Japan. A strong euro makes German exports less marketable and makes foreign imports more threatening; if the other E.U. states are required to adopt deflationary monetary policies, then it is difficult to see how they could maintain liberal trading policies with either Japan or the United States.

For their part, the United States and Japan are locked in a kind of co-dependency. The Japanese have a large investment in American firms* and hold a large amount of American external debt.[30] Indeed Japan can be said to have financed the U.S. budget deficit for over a decade. Without this ready buyer of American debt—Japan is now the world's largest creditor state and holds between one-quarter and one-half of all U.S. debt to foreigners—interest rates in the United States would have increased, choking off growth. The alternative, a rapid and precipitous tax increase, would have had the same effect, drawing liquidity out of the American economy at a vertiginous rate. There was, in reality, no other short-term alternative. At the same time, Japan has been dependent on the vast American market to supplement consumer demand at home. Only this fertile opportunity has permitted Japan to maintain full employment despite a sluggish domestic economy that has failed to generate new jobs. Without exports to the United States, Japan would have unemployment rates similar to those of Western Europe—9 percent to 11 percent at this writing—and higher in the politically sensitive smokestack industries that are facing ruthless competition from states such as South Korea.[31] Like two persons trapped in a bad marriage, the United States and Japan have grown increasingly hostile to one another precisely because each blames the other's unwillingness to reform for its own troubles. There are powerful political voices in both countries that find popular support in bashing the other. Any significant recession in either state would result in calls for an aggressive protectionism—but against whom?

Strategic studies in history, as well as contemporary game theory, suggest that a multipolar system is an unstable configuration.[32] Two parties will inevitably coalesce, leaving the third in a highly threatened position. The incentive that drives war is usually the desire to prevent a steadily worsening position. In such circumstances it hardly matters to the society

---

*Though, according to Japan's External Trade Organization, the Japanese slump in the 1990s has reduced Japanese direct investment in the United States from $32 billion to about $12 billion. These figures are very difficult to compute, owing to differences in definition and the lack of consensus on technology transfer numbers. See *Trends in Japan's Foreign Investment Outflow,* Table 9, March 23, 2001, JETRO website.

of states which coalition forms—there are plausible scenarios for all three possibilities. Europeans and Americans have strong cultural bonds; the United States and Japan have, as we have observed, strong economic links that are acutely sensitive to severance; Japan and Europe have similar protectionist attitudes, and similar models of close cooperation between banks and industries with government planning and support.

Nor would a trade war necessarily take on the overt, violent manifestations of previous wars. If that were so, then perhaps the underlying strategic strength of the United States would assert itself toward harmony (though it is just as possible that Germany and Japan would react by developing nuclear weapons). Rather it is more likely that trade conflicts in the twenty-first century will be fought with covert means for which governments could deny responsibility. So-called logic bombs, which are planted in computer software, could disrupt and even cripple the economic behavior of any of the advanced states. The "choke points" so beloved of strategists from Mahan onwards, the closing of which could interdict sea-borne supplies, may now take on a less geostrategic and more cyberstrategic aspect. In a tripolar world of disguised, privatized attacks, against whom does one retaliate? And if retaliation becomes uncertain, of what real significance is it that a state has the power to retaliate, this power having lost any deterrent effect?

The nation-state is peculiarly vulnerable to such attacks because they appear to come from the private sector and not directly from a rival state. With its sharp division between state activities and private ventures, nation-states have difficulty—as we have seen in the case of covert state-sponsored terrorism—dealing with threats that do not obviously come from other states. A society of market-states could better cope with such attempts at extortion. The emergence of the intense economic competition that characterizes market-states, however, might also combine with another strategic innovation of the Long War, the development of weapons of mass destruction, in a particularly threatening mode.

Consider, for example, the possibility of using biological (and possibly chemical) weapons not against the military targets of the nation-state, but against the economic targets of the market-state. Suppose an adversary raw materials producer—say China—attempted to gain market share in corn exports by dramatically weakening U.S. corn production. There are corn-seed blights, such as *fusarium graminearum,* that could be clandestinely sprayed over the U.S. Midwest from commercial airliners flying the polar route from Beijing to Chicago or St. Louis.[33] If this hardy spore were disseminated in winter, the blight would be present in the soil at the time for spring planting. The resulting corn-seed blight would crush the U.S. crop. Hogs and cattle would become too expensive for many farmers to feed. The United States would be forced to import corn for the first time in its history. Food prices would skyrocket with immense profits to those states that could still produce. If, as Shintaro Ishihara predicts, "the twenty-first century will be a century of economic warfare," the means of prosecuting such warfare will arise from the innovations that won the Long War.

Information technologies are the product of the synergy evident in two of the Long War's strategic innovations, international communications and rapid computation. These technologies enable private companies to elude and even punish nationalist attempts by governments at controlling the market. As a result, market-states are compelled to avoid measures that are anticompetitive if these states are to maintain the basis for their legitimacy, because only the most efficient responses to the demands of the international market will maximize the opportunities available to consumers and producers. Patently "protectionist" moves to manipulate that market—as Japan, Europe, and the United States have all attempted—are, in fact, counterproductive because the information technology available to the private sector can easily counterbalance any national efforts to govern the market. Two examples will suffice.

In order to stimulate exports, Japan has manipulated the yen, depressing its value. The domestic Japanese economy, however, has not responded to this stimulus, even at interest rates that are at historic lows. With a huge dollar surplus, the Japanese have been forced to overinvest in United States assets even though Japanese financial experts, and the Central Bank, knew these assets were overvalued and would have to be marked down. The United States attempted a similar effort to boost exports in the late 1970s by depressing the value of the dollar. American exports rose sharply, but here too the domestic economy failed to pick up. Indeed it fell into a recession, producing high unemployment figures and high inflation. In both cases international markets in the yen and the dollar absorbed the manipulative efforts of governments, without producing a domestic stimulus.

Only economic activity that actually enhances wealth—as judged by its contribution to the valid information devoured by the market—produces growth. Neither the Japanese nor the U.S. model for economic management is necessarily better (despite current appearances to the contrary), as we will see in the next chapter, because each must be measured not only in terms of economic performance but also with respect to the culturally idiosyncratic needs of very different societies. Neither a mercantilist, export-driven policy with an emphasis on capital formation and protection nor a free-trade, consumer-oriented, debt-financed policy is a priori superior. Either policy can succeed—and has—so long as it does not defy the source of wealth within the society of market-states, valid information, by attempting to manipulate that information through regulatory, fiscal, and monetary policies. Corruption and cronyism, on the one hand, and concern for the disruptive effects of free trade on workers or protected sectors like farming, on the other, can motivate states to perpetrate such distortions.

Enhanced technologies of computation and communications will further accelerate the shift to the market-state that maximizes opportunity (which is an information good) and the shift away from the nation-state that maximizes welfare. This movement, however, may provide the best inoculation against trade wars. A nation-state only wishes to improve its relative position, in order to be able to control its environment and thus bring a better life to its people than its ideological competition; a market-state attempts to improve its absolute position, because only in so doing can it maximize the opportunities available to its citizens. For this reason, nation-states were actually more likely to wage trade wars and market-states more likely to concentrate their energies on more aggressive competition—though we must bear in mind that the two strategies are by no means mutually exclusive.

NORTH-SOUTH CONFLICTS

The long-term decline in the demand for raw materials that began in the late 1970s has inevitably had important effects for the states of what was once called the Third World. If, for example, raw-materials prices had not collapsed in these years, Brazil would have had an export surplus almost 50 percent higher and would have had little difficulty in meeting the interest payments on its foreign debt. Indeed, if raw-materials prices had remained at 1973 or even 1979 levels, there would have been no debt crisis for most debtor countries, especially in Latin America.[34] More important, the terms of trade—the ratio between the prices of manufactured goods and services and the prices of raw materials—are at present as unfavorable to the underdeveloped, raw-material-producing states as they were in the deflationary period of the Great Depression.

This is partly the result of abundant harvests and greater efficiencies in producing raw materials. It is also the result of the smaller—and shrinking—component that raw materials make up of finished products. An IMF study concludes that the amount of raw material needed for a given unit of economic output has been declining at the rate of $1\frac{1}{4}$ percent per year since 1900.[35] In 1984 Japan consumed only 60 percent of the raw materials consumed for the same volume of industrial production in 1973.[36]

Several factors are responsible for this change. Industrial production is switching away from products like automobiles (40 percent of whose cost is in raw materials) to microchips (1 percent to 3 percent). Automobiles and other traditional goods are themselves using cheaper, artificial materials (steel is being replaced by plastics made of raw materials with half the cost of steel); fiberglass cables can transmit as many messages over 50–100 pounds of cable as are carried by one ton of copper wire.

Additionally the comparative advantage of low labor costs in the under-developed world is increasingly of less significance as labor costs them-selves amount to a smaller percentage of total manufacturing costs. Partly this is due to increasing automation and the replacement of manual labor by machines, including robots. But this change in the components of pro-duction costs is also due to the shift from industries that were labor-intensive to those that are information- or knowledge-intensive. The manufacturing costs of the semiconductor microchip are estimated to be about 70 percent intellectual (research, development, testing, marketing) and less than 12 percent labor. About the same figures obtain for pharma-ceuticals, whereas even the most highly robotized automobile plant would still find about 20–25 percent of its costs consumed by labor. Because raw-materials earnings and profits from labor-intensive industries are used to provide the capital for industrialization, one can wonder on what basis development can take place in the Third World when these avenues are denied them. Peter Drucker notes:

> In the rapid industrialization of the nineteenth century, one country, Japan, developed by exporting raw materials, mainly silk and tea, at steadily rising prices. Another, Germany, developed by leap-frogging into the "high-tech" industries of its time, mainly electricity, chemicals, and optics. A third, the United States, did both. Both routes are blocked for today's rapidly industrializing countries—the first because of the deterioration of the terms of trade . . . the second because it requires an infrastructure of knowledge and education far beyond the reach of a poor country . . . Competition based on lower labor costs seemed to be the only alternative; is this also going to be blocked?[37]

The potential consequence for the society of states is a disjunction between one group composed of market-states and a second group of states whose underdevelopment hampers their making a constitutional transition to the new form. Of course, at any moment in the story of consti-tutional change, there are always examples of different models being simultaneously pursued. Many Third World states (such as Taiwan, Jor-dan, or Guatemala) did not become nation-states until almost the end of the era of the nation-state itself, but most had long been nation-states (though some, such as Saudi Arabia and Brunei, resemble much earlier constitutional forms).

The consequence for the society of states can be profound, however, because the unassimilated states will be unable to participate effectively in the multistate institutions and practices that this new constitutional form creates. The relationship between the G-7 and the Group of 100 (proto-market-state institutions) scarcely parallels that which exists between the U.N. Security Council and the General Assembly (with regard to nation-states). Unlike nation-state institutions with virtually universal membership based on the political equality of states, there is a price of admission to the society of market-states (though there may be "scholarships" for some). Some states will be left behind. With no stake in the system as a whole, and following a different archetype for the very basis of legitimacy of the State, these unassimilated states may form a competing, retrograde society, or simply become solipsistic, venomous states, alternately dedicated to isolation from the rest of the world and to its destruction.

TRANSNATIONAL PROBLEMS OF THE ENVIRONMENT

So much important work has been done to bring to the attention of the public the inherently transnational nature of environmental problems that it hardly seems necessary to stress that the society of market-states, like that of nation-states before it, will have to devise ways of coping, as a collectivity, with these matters. Here I want only to discuss two issues: environmental problems that have the potential for *disconcerting* the society of states, and the contribution that rapid computation, perhaps in conjunction with telecommunications, can make to the resolution of these problems.

Three major environmental events have occurred since 1970 that manifested this potential to bring about rapid and profound disquiet: the AIDS epidemic, the nuclear core accident at Chernobyl, and the scientific confirmation that the earth's ozone layer is being destroyed. Each of these events arose as a function of the interactions among the states of the new global economy, the mass movement of peoples and products, the transfer of previously familiar technologies to new settings, and the development of new technologies and materials.[38] Part of what is disconcerting about these three events is precisely their links to this new world; the eruption of Mount Saint Helens perhaps had a greater environmental consequence than any of the three, but it did not have their unsettling quality.

Acquired Immunodeficiency Syndrome (AIDS)

AIDS is the physical condition of malaise leading to death that occurs as a consequence of an attack on a human being's immune system by the human immunodeficiency virus (HIV). Its origin remains obscure, but it seems to have bridged the gap of space and culture from West Africa to the developed states in the late 1970s. One plausible explanation is that it was the result of the transfer to human beings of a retrovirus previously found in monkeys, through the use of hypodermic needles that were employed to inject monkey blood and plasma into human beings as part of a cultural ritual. This theory of origin, if true, places AIDS among those other diseases with a technological component, such as toxic shock syndrome (caused by the superabsorbency of a tampon) and Lyme disease (caused by the changing ecology of suburban growth, reforestation, and the altered demographics of deer populations), the Hanta virus, the zebra mussel contamination in the Great Lakes, and the discovery of radon in homes.

Other infectious diseases have exposed residents of the temperate zones to tropical infections owing to increased travel in both regions, the global sources of the food supply, and the ever-increasing number of human hosts within which viruses may proliferate. Whatever its origin, AIDS has been widely spread among heterosexuals in the developed world by the use of hypodermics, and by sexual practices among both heterosexuals, mainly in underdeveloped states, and homosexuals in all states.

Its disconcerting nature has to do with at least three factors: first, such epidemics were widely believed to have been relegated to the past by modern antibiotics; second, AIDS has been invariably fatal, striking the young and otherwise healthy with a grim inexorability; third, although AIDS has been largely confined to groups that, for differing reasons, can be marginalized from the mainstream culture of the developed states, yet it has the potential to overwhelm the populations of those mainstream cultures. AIDS is now the leading cause of death among Americans under the age of twenty-one.

In 1976, the historian William McNeill, writing about the role of plagues in the past, presciently observed that

> it now requires an act of imagination to understand what infectious disease formerly meant to humankind, or even to our grandfathers. Yet as is to be expected when human beings learn new ways of tampering with complex ecological relationships, the control over microparasites that medical research has achieved since the 1880s has also created a number of unexpected byproducts and new crises.[39]

Thus AIDS is probably not the last of such disconcerting diseases. Unexpected outcomes of recombinant DNA activities, toxins developed for the purposes of biological warfare, obscure parasites sprung from their remote geographical niches, or even familiar viruses that have developed strains resistant to modern antibiotics are all candidates for the plagues of the twenty-first century. They pose a unique challenge for the society of market-states, as threatening in its way as the challenge posed to Christian faith by the bubonic plagues of Europe because developments in molecular biology—fueled by abundant investment made possible by the financial liberalizations of the market-state—have given many persons a faith in technology and in its ability to grant something like immortality to human beings.

The society of market-states will have to confront its fundamental ordering principle, the market, at a juncture where the market works poorly, the decision to whom to give life-saving medical care. If each state decides on its own, in the manner of current states, then some persons will be excluded from care because they are not members of the preferred groups of recipients, while others will be excluded for lack of personal or institutional resources. If, on the other hand, some multinational market is set up, then the wealthy from one country will sop up the health resources of others, as in the example of richer persons buying kidneys and other organs from impoverished donors.[40]

The encouraging fact is that a society of market-states will be better prepared to evaluate, analyze, and treat such diseases because it will most efficiently allocate resources to the task and have a worldwide charter to do so. The mere fact of a state boundary will not stand in the way of ad hoc groups, authorized by the society of such states, who act to protect the world from an apocalyptic pestilence. But this too will test the legitimacy of that system, as it assumes authority—by what right?—that the peoples of the world have not given it by any recognizable plebiscite, or other method approved by the nation-state. Moreover, actions by a society of market-states will inevitably bring the values of the market to bear—especially pricing—on goods (such as life itself) that we have tried to treat as priceless.*

Chernobyl

Chernobyl was not the first such health event to result from the introduction of dangerous technologies into contemporary life. The nuclear release at Three Mile Island; the chemical releases at Seveso, Italy; the explosion at Bhopal, India; and the pollution of the water table at Love Canal in the United States all come to mind.

The disturbing nature of these events is traceable to their origin in the malfunctions of human-designed and -maintained machines. Unlike the infectious retrovirus, the operations of a nuclear reactor are well understood. Similarly, the effects of the toxic gas used in the production of pesticides at Bhopal were perfectly predictable. In such cases, a series of human errors and equipment failures combined to bring about the disaster. At both Chernobyl and Bhopal there was little oversight or effective regulation. Mandated safety standards by the state were ignored owing partly to a lack of the technical and institutional resources necessary to achieve compliance.

---

*The decision by U.S. trade authorities not to protect American pharmaceutical patents from Third World unauthorized production in states gravely threatened by AIDS is a hopeful sign. This decision led directly to the collaboration between pharmaceutical companies and Third World states to reduce the cost of treatment.

This sort of crisis strikes at a weak point in the political superstructure of the society of market-states, its moral vulnerability. At Bhopal, Chernobyl, and elsewhere, the lives of persons whose economic worth was negligible were put at risk in order to provide cheap chemicals to agriculture or cheap power to electricity consumers. So long as it is profitable to do so, we can expect multinational corporations to draw the calculus of safety no more expensively than the global possibilities of relocation demand, and we can expect state enterprises to do the same (because even though they cannot relocate, they must compete against the global multinationals).

Here too, however, there is hope. Chernobyl was a national failure, prompted as much by the shortcomings of Russian technology as by the inevitability of accidents. The society of market-states would be able in principle to deploy technicians within a global market, denying dangerous technologies to those states that do not provide adequate safeguards and helping poorer states to maintain the complex equipment that may be located there.

Chlorofluorocarbons

Chlorofluorocarbons (CFCs) are synthetic chemical compounds first developed in 1928 to replace the hazardous refrigerants, such as ammonia, methyl chloride, and sulfur dioxide then in use.[41] By the 1970s CFCs—nontoxic, nonflammable—had completely transformed the refrigeration industry, replacing chemicals in refrigerators and launching the fledgling air-conditioning industry. Eventually CFCs were adopted as propellants in ubiquitous aerosol spray cans for everything from whipped cream to hair spray.

When, in 1974, two scientists published a technical paper suggesting that CFCs might threaten the environment, the world was producing almost a billion kilograms of CFCs a year, with the amount doubling every five years. These scientists hypothesized that CFCs were slowly drifting upward into the stratosphere where, having broken down molecularly, they were releasing chlorine atoms that destroy stratospheric ozone, causing higher levels of ultraviolet radiation to reach the surface of the Earth. This might lead to a deadly rise in the occurrence of skin cancers.

Robert Kates picks up the story here and sketches the ironic turn of events that ensued:

> Urged on by activist scientists and a concerned Congress, U.S. media took the lead in spreading the alarm. They devoted an extraordinary amount of coverage to CFCs in 1975 and helped to fix inexorably in the public mind the image of frivolous spray cans blasting holes in the sky. The prospect of increased cancer risk lurked just offstage. Local political action and consumer boycotts against products containing CFC

propellant spread rapidly. By the time the U.S. government officially banned CFC propellants in 1978 the action was virtually superfluous: Domestic use had already fallen precipitously, solely on the basis of an as yet unproved hypothesis. . . . A decade after the initial surprise, the threat of ozone depletion had been all but forgotten by the media, politicians and the public. After dropping somewhat, worldwide CFC production climbed back above its 1974 level. [It was only] the discovery of a . . . hole in the ozone layer in 1985 [that] put the issue back onto the public agenda.[42]

The unnerving aspect of the ozone case lies in its grotesque transformation of something ordinary and benignly mundane into something unexpectedly malignant. Similar shifts have occurred with respect to cigarette smoke, asbestos fibers, and lead in paint and gasoline. In the market-state, there are powerful lobbies with a stake in persuading the public and public officials that there is really nothing to worry about, and a no less powerful media and public interest alliance anxious to detect an alarming new crisis as frequently as possible. The lobbies depend upon companies whose sale of the dubious substance is threatened, but the media and public-interest groups also have a material stake in the matter, because the market-state requires that they make their way on the basis of public contributions,* which requires an ever-escalating hyperbole to stimulate giving. In the ozone-depletion case, public reaction first outran and then lagged behind the science of the matter.

The society of market-states is vulnerable to such threats to the environment and yet in some ways better equipped than the society of nation-states to deal with them. This new society is vulnerable because it places such a high value on the autonomy of the market. CFCs are, after all, a cheap and otherwise safe method of refrigeration and vapor propulsion; there will be some countries that choose to continue their use, noting along the way that because their impact is so minor compared to that of market giants like the United States, little harm will result to the atmosphere. Global marketing will allow the transfer of such products to those countries whose publics are not so sensitive (or who feel they cannot afford to be sensitive) to charges of environmental degradation.

At the same time, the global corporation is itself vulnerable to reports in its major markets disclosing practices it would like to confine to marginal markets. Boycotts, not laws, led to the original decline in CFC use in the United States. The problem is how to organize the actions of the society of market-states in much the way nation-states were able to mobilize multi-

---

*The idea of a state-owned press or television, while the norm in the nation-states of the past, is becoming a rarity in the market-states of the present.

lateral legal regulation. Law will continue to be a resource available to state but it will occupy a very different role in the world of market-states than it did in the world of nation-states.

The Long War was won by strategic innovations that we might nowadays call the development of weapons of mass destruction, the globalization of communications, and the international integration of finance and trade. These strategic innovations have brought with them new challenges that now face the society of states that the end of the Long War is bringing into being. Three fundamental choices confront the society of market-states with respect to each of these challenges. Until they have been made, we will live in a period of transition.

These choices are (1) regarding weapons of mass destruction: (a) whether to attempt affirmatively to check the proliferation of such weapons, through extended deterrence, and to suppress proliferation through ad hoc intervention, or (b) whether to rely on multilateral arms-control agreements, accepting as inevitable that some proliferation will occur outside these agreements, or (c) whether to rely on the wholesome effects of internal liberalization through economic growth and mutual deterrence to contain this proliferation; (2) with respect to the globalization of communications: (a) whether to address the linked issues of immigration and human rights by encouraging a global network of economic growth premised on the transparency of sovereignty, or (b) whether to cultivate the fragmentation of states within "umbrella" megastates, or (c) whether to strengthen the protection of national cultures and the regionalization of international law; (3) with regard to the international integration of finance and trade: (a) whether to increase the absolute wealth of the society of market-states, taken as a whole, without regard for distributional effects, or (b) whether to manage growth with an eye to short- and medium-term distributional effects, or (c) whether to encourage economic stability through growth tempered by a regard for long-term balance.

Some market-states will doubtless attempt to mix and match these alternative policies but as a general matter one or another set of mutually supporting policies—(a/a/a) or (b/b/b) or (c/c/c)—will rise to dominance in each state because these options reflect different views of state sovereignty. A state that relies on pre-emption to thwart nuclear proliferation is all the more likely to support transparency in sovereignty when it comes to human-rights violations. A state that is anxious to preserve the cultural integrity of its minority groups is unlikely to pursue economic strategies that shred the social contract. Inevitably, one of these sets of approaches—entrepreneurial, managerial, or mercantile—will dominate the constitution of the society of market-states, because a society of states that pursued policies that were inconsistent with respect to state sovereignty would produce an incoherent and unstable constitution.

Which model of the market-state is best? I would answer by recalling the moving scene* in Act III of Gotthold Lessing's dramatic poem, "Nathan the Wise." Lessing was a German author of the Enlightenment;† the play is his last major work.

Nathan, a Jew, is summoned before Saladin, the great Muslim warrior. Saladin asks him which religion is the true one—Islam, Christianity, or Judaism—hoping to trap Nathan into either denying his own faith or insulting Islam by implication, in which case his property will be confiscated.

In reply, Nathan narrates the parable of the Three Rings.‡ A wise king possessed a ring, the wearer of which was said to be beloved of God and man. He had three sons, to each of whom he promised the ring. When the king died, each heir was given a ring, and all three rings appeared to be identical to that of the old king. When the sons went to the royal judge and demanded to know which ring was the real one, the judge said to them:

> Your father, the king, wore a ring of which it was said that the wearer would be beloved of God and man. Each of you has been given a ring. Wear your rings. Do your best to be beloved of God and man. Let your rings descend to your heirs. Then someday, some future judge will assess your work and know whether you had the right ring.§43

While it is likely, as we will see in the following chapter, that states may choose different forms of the market-state—and experiment with hybrid forms—each state must decide on the basis of the constraints on its resources, its heritage, and its destiny what archetypal form best confers legitimacy.

---

*Scene 5.
†He also wrote an essay on the shield of Achilles.
‡This story is drawn from Boccaccio's *Decameron*.
§I have simplified this enchanting parable considerably. Please consult the endnotes for a fuller text.

CHAPTER TWENTY-FIVE

Possible Worlds

By considering alternative futures, we begin to see that the future is shaped not only by the past but by what we think is possible and by the choices we make.

—Shell International Petroleum Company, 1992

I WILL NOW take up the question of how the society of market-states might respond to the challenges just surveyed. But rather than prescribe a single set of solutions to these challenges, I will describe alternative approaches, whole worldviews that, if they govern action, will bring into being radically different worlds. I choose this approach for four reasons: first, because simple forecasting—on which a prescriptive analysis must be based—is inadequate at a time when fundamental change in the constitutional order of states is occurring; second, my method can be used independently by readers whose values and preferences may not coincide with mine; third, this sort of presentation can clarify the moral choices we must make in the coming decades—having to do with what kind of world we want to live in and what we are willing to do to achieve it—rather than submerge those choices in the seductive calculus of efficiency; fourth, the implementation of the choices that are ultimately made will have less to do, in a market-state environment, with codified proscriptions and more to do with shared understandings, goals, and expectations.

Imagine unexpected, gravely unsettling events that happen to the world in the next few years: suppose an asteroid struck the Earth, setting in motion changes in the atmospheric climate; suppose a continental crisis in the groundwater table appeared, caused by saline-freshwater mixing zones that spread across numerous states; suppose a state embarked on a radical program of mass eugenics using genetic engineering on its own population; suppose infectious diseases appeared on a pandemic scale that could not be vaccinated against or eradicated, but that could be successfully treated by very expensive drugs; suppose a civil war broke out within a single state, leading to the use by one of the parties of biological weapons; suppose earthquakes triggered a deep worldwide economic depression.

Is the General Assembly of the United Nations the place to address the problems that would arise as consequence of these events? If not, is the U.N. Security Council endowed by the rest of the world with the political and moral authority to cope with these shattering events? Can we assume that the United States, or any other single power, could solve them alone? As we faced the year 2000 computer problem, who actually believed that the U.N. or NATO or the Council of Europe or the OAS was the institution that could solve it? This simple thought experiment shows how far we have already come from the society of nation-states and its constitution toward the society of market-states. Nor do I believe that international law—at least insofar as it may be invoked to prohibit state acts like tampering with the human genome, for example, or the use of biological weapons—is the resource we would turn to for resolution, nor that the International Court of Justice is the place we would go.

In the election of 1992, George Bush was taxed with lacking, as he himself put it, "the vision thing"—a vision of the future toward which he proposed to lead the nation with his policies. This was obviously not something Ronald Reagan had lacked, nor Jimmy Carter and certainly not Lyndon Johnson. All had clearly definable views of the future state of the union that they wished to bring about. Yet those writing speeches for George Bush and the senior officials of his administration were to a large degree the same persons who had done those jobs for President Reagan. What had changed was not simply the personality of the president: *everything* had changed, although things looked pretty much the same.

Before the sea change from nation-state to market-state, "vision" was simply a matter of looking ahead, extrapolating from the present. Realizing that vision was a matter of strategic planning. President Clinton's health care proposals would have fit into President Truman's Fair Deal; President Bush's START II treaty was a continuation of President Reagan's arms-control agenda. Suddenly in the 1990s, no one really had a "vision" of the future because the future was going to be so unlike the past. What was required was not lacerating self-criticism over our failures to foresee the collapse of the Soviet Union, the Gulf War, the disintegration of Yugoslavia, and the mass migrations in East Africa. Rather we needed to approach the future with an acceptance that simple forecasting was not going to be useful to us for a while, that no one had any clear view of what was coming and therefore no one could be confident that he or she was offering a realistic vision of the future. Instead we had to sharpen our skills at imagining different futures so that we had some idea of what was at stake when the choices the future presented were actually upon us.

To say this is to contrast "strategic planning" with "scenario planning." Both rely on intelligence estimates that are based on the careful analysis of immense amounts of information, sorting out the true from the false, assigning probabilities to information that might be either true or false, guessing what the future would be like if all the relevant facts were available to the analyst.[1] The problem for estimative intelligence in the current environment is that it depends upon a relatively stable world from which to extrapolate. No one has grasped this better than Joseph Nye, the former head of the National Intelligence Council at the CIA, who wrote:

> Greater complexity in the structure of power means greater uncertainty in estimating the future. Polities often undergo nonlinear change, but such changes have become much more frequent than during the Cold War. In the 1980s, for example, if one were estimating the number of nuclear weapons South Africa would have in the 1990s, one would have calculated what their uranium enrichment plant could produce and answered "six or seven." But the correct answer today turns out to be zero because of radical political discontinuities associated with the transition to majority rule and the end of the Cold War. Similarly, if one were to estimate today how many nuclear weapons a country with no nuclear facilities might have in five years, the linear answer would be zero. But that would change if the country were able to purchase stolen nuclear weapons on the transnational black market.[2]

This is precisely the problem, and Nye's recommendation—the construction of alternative scenarios rather than single-point predictions in order not so much to predict the future as to help policy makers think about the future—is precisely the solution. But scenario planning is not widely practiced in governments, as opposed to corporations, and it is easily confused with strategic planning.

Scenario planning relies on the creation of hypothetical, alternative stories about the future that share certain factual assumptions but differ based on decisions made within each scenario; strategic planning is a formalized procedure that aims to produce an integrated system of decisions based on predetermined goals. That is, strategic planning assumes an answer to the question that scenario planning poses: what sort of future do we want? The time horizon for scenario planning is typically from five to more than twenty-five years; strategic plans usually go no further out than one to three years. Inputs to scenario planning are more qualitative, that is, they share certain factual estimates about the future but emphasize economic, technological, resource, and cultural trends. Inputs to strategic planning tend to be more quantitative, looking to past performance, forecasts, and probabilities. Thus scenario planning exploits uncertainties, allowing the creation of alternative futures; strategic planning attempts to minimize uncertainty. The results of scenario planning are multiple alternative outcomes versus the quantified single outcome based on the likeliest scenario that is the setting for strategic planning.[3]

The difficulty with implementing Nye's proposed solution is that such scenario construction depends upon a dialogue with decision makers at many levels in order to create a culture that is sensitive to the implications of change and alert to opportunities to create favorable conditions for change. Members of this culture produce the raw material on which scenarios are based; intensive briefings with them, once the scenarios are written, are as important to the process as the written product. But the National Intelligence Council cannot spend the time with the president and the senior members of his National Security Council, nor is it willing to disclose its estimates to the many hundreds of other less senior officials who, together, could bring such a culture into being. High-impact but low-probability contingencies, which are crucial to the imaginative dialogue of the scenario process, are of little interest to busy politicians. Competing scenarios, in the absence of a culture of dialogue animated by a sense of rapport with leaders at the top, are anathema to bureaucrats whose careers are risked by answering questions like "What would it take for this estimate to be dramatically wrong? What could cause a radically different outcome?" which translates to "What arguments can you give me that undermine your recommendations?"

Things are easier for the business corporation. In the early 1970s Royal Dutch Shell was regarded as the weakest of the great multinational oil companies, known as the "Seven Sisters." At that time Shell began a series of scenario studies that are credited with assisting that corporation's remarkable rise since then. As early as 1972, one of Shell's scenarios envisaged the formation of OPEC and the sudden rise in oil prices that hit the world in the winter of 1973–74; and a subsequent scenario correctly described the equally dramatic drop in oil prices that began in early 1986. In 1984, a Shell scenario (called "The Greening of Russia") described the possible breakup of the Soviet Union and the ensuing chaotic conditions in Eastern Europe. But to depict these descriptions, which turned out to be accurate, as validating the scenario process is to misunderstand its significance completely. After all, if a corporation is doing more than one "estimate," it will often be able to predict a rise (or fall) that turns out to be true. What the scenario process did was to make some futures appear less plausible that had more or less been taken for granted, and to prepare managers to look for signs of likewise unexpected futures. In the absence of this preparation, managers are inclined to shoehorn events into their settled expectations or to ignore altogether outlying facts.

Since Shell's highly publicized success with scenario planning in the

1970s and 1980s, many corporations have attempted to employ this tool with the hope of achieving similar dramatic results. The Corporate Executive Board reports, however, that there has been some disillusion with the scenario-planning process. "Perhaps the single greatest driver of this dissatisfaction," the Board has concluded, "is a widely held yet misguided expectation that scenario planning readily and directly improves strategic decision making; misconceptions rooted in scenario planning's history promote this expectation . . ."[4] The problem is that Shell's successes are inevitably laid to having correctly predicted the future, rather than having enabled its decision makers to cope better with that future as it, unpredictably, unfolded. Prepared by their *alternative* scenarios, Shell executives were able to see a pattern in events—a story—that their competitors experienced as mere noise, a chaotic departure from conventional expectations.

Instead of simply relying on forecasts, the Shell Group does its planning for the future through a complex process of consultation, the drafting of alternative decision scenarios, and a thorough debriefing process around the world with its managers. The object is to use scenario planning as a means of stimulating institutional learning; what is being learned is a way of assimilating new events through the incorporation in (or the destruction of) the ostensive, simple stories of the scenarios. However sophisticated the tools, if there is no significant effect on exposing assumptions and heightening the focus on values, people will quickly fall back into the old habit of asking, "Tell me what will happen."[5]

The managers of every corporation operate according to conventional expectations, usually unarticulated and seldom fully tested against alternatives. The scenario process externalizes these stories, tests them against known facts, and then uses them to provide a basis for further reaction by managers as events fit (or don't fit) the story. Following extensive interviews with fifty or so top managers at the Shell Group and with a large network of academic, political, business, and cultural figures around the globe, a team synthesizes the information drawn from these conversations into two or more competing scenarios. Thus about every three years a book of these scenarios—global, regional, country, and topical—is produced, and extensive briefings are done on its basis.[6] According to Shell, the most important aspect of this process is that "[b]y considering alternative futures, we begin to see that the future is shaped not only by the past but by what we think is possible and by the choices we make."[7] Let us apply this analytical process to the problem of meeting the challenges to the society of market-states described in the preceding chapter.

Initially, one must determine the fundamental choices facing states. With respect to security issues, the first set of choices derive from the military innovations that won the Long War. These have given birth to new sets of problems with regard to intervention, the proliferation of weapons of mass destruction, and the development of new technologies like ballistic missile defense. For example, the society of states must decide whether the most powerful members of that society ought to intervene in order to maintain democratic regimes and protect human rights, or whether that society should rely on regional security organizations in these matters, or whether the wisest course lies in permitting states to sort out their own internal affairs. Similar sets of alternatives exist for each of the new security challenges described in Chapter 24, particularly the challenge posed by international terrorism.

Another set of choices focuses principally on the cultural consequences of globalization, which are the consequences in the twenty-first century of the revolution in telecommunications that occurred in the twentieth, especially the interconnection between immigration and human rights. Just as each market-state must find for itself the right balance among a reverence for cultural tradition, a tolerance for individual conscience, and a respect for different groups, so the society of states will confront choices that inescapably will structure this balance. These choices center on the inequalities of opportunity and self-respect generated by meritocratic, dynamic capitalism; the intergenerational conflicts that are exacerbated both by rapid change and by the holdover of programs from the decaying nation-state; and lastly the threats posed to traditional cultures by the liberating but penetrating media of twenty-first century entertainment, information, and education.

A final set of alternatives deals with the consequences of the revolutionary liberalization of trade and finance that occurred as a result of the development of high-speed computation, producing conflicts in the areas of development, trade, and the protection of the environment. The states in these scenarios will experience the same stock market crashes, the same droughts and epidemics, the same high-tech breakthroughs. But they must decide to what degree the market will govern the market-state in the pursuit of economic growth, social stability, and long-term prosperity.

Next, one must select the key influences, or "drivers" in planning jargon, that will structure the decisional environment within which these choices are made.

These drivers include demographic developments, the availability of and access to resources (especially energy and water), innovations in technology and its diffusion, events in the new economy of market-states, and of course the synergy among these drivers. There is one other key driver, however, that is also the consequence of the outcome of the Long War and on which each of the scenarios greatly depends: this is the role of the United States. For if, in the past, only an epochal war could produce the consensus that created a constitution for the society of states, it may be that now we are entering a period in which conflict itself may take an unprecedented form and that actions of one very powerful and influential state might bring about that "creative emulation" described in Book I when states copy the triumphant winner of an epochal war. There are several ways to describe this: it may be that market-states will be led to adopt that form of the new constitutional order that is chosen by the state most dominant in the new globalized market; or it may be that a "chosen" epochal war will be a product of that state's decisions—to intervene in a long-running series of low-intensity conflicts, or to check regional actors with predatory pretensions, or to deflect (or even defeat) any peer challenges to the diffident hegemony that at present appears likely to continue for the foreseeable future; or it may be that the new, irresistible world culture will insinuate more than dominate, carrying states along a path strewn with Big Mac wrappers and universally accessible websites (in English) so that, like habits generally, the bonds of adherence will be too mild to be felt until they are too strong to be resisted. However it may be, in the following scenarios one driver partly determining which of the three general models of the market-state sweeps through the society of such states is the actions and attitude of the United States. As the U.S. National Intelligence Council put it in 2001:

> U.S. global economic, technological, military and diplomatic influence will be unparalleled among national as well as regional and international organizations in 2015. This power not only will ensure America's preeminence, but also will cast the United States as the key driver of the international system.[8]

Finally, two or more alternative and internally consistent narratives must be constructed for each driver, which are then combined to produce alternate scenarios.

The following pages offer three general scenarios, constructed by assembling the elements of possible worlds that are brought into being by crucial, fundamentally moral choices that might face states—choices that could plausibly be made in a number of ways. These are only very simple stories. Because they do not attempt to capture the full richness of reality, they can make our basic assumptions stand out in a way that fate, culture, and history seldom afford.

What might the world might look like if one of the three constitutional models of the market-state dominates the society of such states? I will call these three worlds "The Meadow," "The Park," and "The Garden."

The world of *The Meadow* is that of a society of states in which the entrepreneurial market-state has become predominant. In this world, success comes to those who nimbly exploit the fast-moving, evanescent opportunities brought about by high technology and the global market-place. Such a world provides an environment for the fullest expression of individual creativity; it rewards those who innovate and who can deal with, indeed who relish, impermanence. There are no fixed rules or taboos. Competition is the great god that sorts out the quick and the dead.

The world view portrayed in *The Park* is quite different, and it reflects a society in which the values and attitudes of the managerial market-state have prevailed. Governments play a far larger role in defining the common interest and using the political power of government to assert that interest. Minority rights are more carefully husbanded; international institutions are maintained; protection of the environment is given a priority. In short, there is a sincere effort to afford respect to the mores of many different groups, accepting that this can be a costly strategy.

Finally, *The Garden* describes an approach associated with the mercantile market-state. In this set of scenarios, governments also play a large role but that role is less a regulatory and more a supportive one. Here governments provide long-range strategic planning based on the good of society taken as a whole—not the sum of its interest groups. Unlike the regional groupings fostered by The Park, the states of The Garden have become more and more ethnocentric, and more and more protective of their respective cultures.

In a meadow all is profusion, randomness, variety. A park is for the most part publicly maintained, highly regulated with different sectors for different uses. A garden is smaller, more inwardly turned—it aims for the sublime, not the efficient or the just.

DRIVERS AND TRENDS

(These conditions are assumed for all three scenarios.)

POPULATION

Despite a substantial fall in fertility rates, especially in developed countries, and a continuing decline in global population growth rates, the momentum of the existing population will increase the world's numbers from 6.1 billion to over 7 billion by 2015. Ninety-five percent of this growth will take place in the Third World, where most of the world's largest cities will contain about half the world's population. In many developing countries, particularly in sub-Saharan Africa, the Middle East, and parts of South Asia, the rapidly increasing number of persons between the ages of fifteen and twenty-four will strain educational systems, infrastructure, and job markets. At the same time, the population of the northern tier states will markedly age. Increasingly, the needs of older persons will impose enormous economic burdens on shrinking workforces. Facing labor shortages, some industrial countries will encourage immigration of both skilled and unskilled labor, as the United States has done. Other countries may prefer to substitute technology for labor or to outsource their labor requirements overseas. Russia's population is likely to decrease substantially, as a result of poor health care and declining birth rates. Russian life expectancy is expected to continue to decline.

Some developing countries will not experience net population growth; despite high birth rates, some African countries that are heavily infected with HIV and other diseases will have stable or even declining populations. Infectious diseases will pose a growing threat fueled by population growth, urbanization, and migration, as well as other factors such as microbial resistance. At the same time that progress is being made with respect to some diseases—such as polio and measles—diseases such as tuberculosis and malaria are re-emerging in deadlier, drug-resistant variations while new infectious diseases appear. It is estimated that at least thirty previously unknown diseases have appeared globally since 1973, including the incurable HIV, hepatitis C, Ebola hemorrhagic fever, and encephalitis-related Nipah. Asia is likely to witness a major increase in infectious disease deaths, replacing Africa as the epicenter of HIV by 2015.

RESOURCES

World food stocks are projected to be sufficient to meet overall global needs through 2015. Problems with distributing food to the world's poorest as well as those displaced by internal conflicts will, however, persist. North Korea will continue to be vulnerable to nationwide famine, possibly exacerbated by natural disasters. Famines will continue to occur in countries such as Sudan and Somalia, which are also subject to natural disasters.

Fresh water, while globally abundant, will become a critical resource issue. It is estimated that by 2025, 40 percent of the world's population will live in countries, most of them in Africa and South Asia, that are water-stressed. This represents a sixfold increase since 1995. These countries will be unable to provide sufficient water for agricultural, industrial, and household needs. This will be especially true in northern China, the Middle East, South Asia, and parts of Africa. There will be serious risks of water wars between states proximate to large rivers and seas.

ENERGY

Even if fuel cell technology progresses as hoped, it is projected that by 2010 worldwide demand, driven by growing populations and increases in per capita income, will require added production of energy on the order of what OPEC states now produce in toto. Assuming a fairly robust annual global per capita income growth of 2 percent through 2015, the demand for primary energy will increase by 60 percent over present levels.

The market will be able to make available vast reserves—their location is already known—but the fragility of the pipeline and distribution network will increase. Technological innovations will continue to expand access to oil fields, lowering the cost of developing new wells, and improving efficiencies in automotive transport. The most exploited oil deposits will remain in the Persian Gulf and Venezuela, with new areas coming online in the West African basin and the Caspian Sea. The global shift to natural gas, with its fixed installations for fuel delivery, could establish long-lasting energy dependencies, making neighboring countries increasingly reliant on natural gas supplies from Russia, Algeria, and Central Asia. Improvements in the efficiency of solar cells and batteries, though they will result in a greater use of these and other renewable energy resources, are unlikely to significantly affect world reliance on fossil fuels in the next twenty-five years.

ECONOMIC GROWTH

The globalization of financial transactions and the rapid increase in the volume of the money supply in global financial markets will create a new global vulnerability to periodic financial crises. Notwithstanding this concern, it is anticipated that accelerating global trade, the growing integration of capital markets, and efficiencies gained from the increasing use of information technology will lead to a real growth in per capita income of about 2 percent annually.

Global economic influence and power will spread from the current G-7 countries of North America, Europe, and Japan to a more multipolar global economic system in which Brazil, India, China, and South Korea will become economic centers. Output from non-OECD countries will rise from 45 percent to about 60 percent of global GDP by 2015. Nevertheless, the inclusion of these countries—the "have-nots"—in the global economy will be marred and slow-paced. The division between the "haves" and "have-nots" could spark a backlash against globalization, reversing the trends of openness to foreign investment and trade that have been driving global economic growth. Those countries with active internal conflicts will tend to fall further behind. In virtually all countries, the disparities within societies will increase. The wealthy and well-educated will get richer, while the poor will get relatively poorer with the middle classes dividing toward one or the other group.

All states will become more vulnerable to the shocks and disruptions that are a major downside of global economic integration. The world economy is highly dependent on the United States. A major U.S. stock market correction could have a significant impact on the world economy. So could a major disruption in global energy markets arising from political instability in the Persian Gulf. Finally, weak domestic financial institutions in emerging countries could trigger a major financial crisis, crippling future financial flows. The strength of financial institutions in many countries has not kept pace with the volume of financial flows.

TECHNOLOGY

International affairs will increasingly involve the use of information networks, and information technology will not be owned by any single country. Nor can this technology and the information it conveys be easily contained. Information and communications technologies will continue to advance and diffuse rapidly, becoming so inexpensive that most countries will be able to connect to the global information infrastructure.

The United States and other developed countries will face an increasing challenge to maintain its critical infrastructure—the networks that will increasingly unite the hitherto separate sectors of banking and finance, energy, transportation, communications, and government services. Cyber threats to this infrastructure will become a major defense issue by 2015.

Rigid and authoritarian governments that resist the flow of information and attempt to restrict openness and ease of connectivity, will fall further behind economically and politically. The problem of "haves" versus "have-nots" will become increasingly related to information sharing and the diffusion of information technology.

The biological sciences will grow in importance for their applications to medicine and agriculture. Advances in basic biology will allow us to diagnose and cure diseases on a broad scale; but most biomedical advances will remain expensive, benefiting only those who are relatively well-off, most of whom will live in developed countries.

The capability to purchase, copy, or steal existing technologies rather than develop new ones offers significant catch-up opportunities for less developed countries and also for nonstate actors, including terrorists and criminal organizations. Among these technologies must be included weapons of mass destruction. Information technology will allow widely dispersed but globally connected groups such as terrorists, criminal organizations, and narcotics cartels to create far-flung networks and alliances. In some countries, these groups will be better armed than their governments and may control significant portions of territory.

It is projected that during the period 2000–2015, the United States will face ICBM threats from Russia, China, North Korea, Iran, and possibly Iraq.[9] The arsenals of the new missile powers will be dramatically smaller, less reliable, and less accurate than those of Russia and China. European nuclear arsenals with a global reach will remain; the nuclear weaponry of

Israel, India, and Pakistan will be regional in scope, however. Precisely because nuclear weapons delivered to missile technology is likely to remain a state-centered enterprise, and its use therefore subject to deterrence and retaliation, new weapons of mass destruction that exploit an ambiguity of origin will come into being. States that intervene abroad will find themselves the target of unnamed groups with the ability to do substantial damage through violent and nonviolent means.

EVENTS

(These facts are assumed to be possible for all scenarios, but vary from scenario to scenario, depending on the decisions taken by states.)

SECURITY

Suppose—

- The Balkans degenerate into another regional war.
- The Koreas collapse into a peninsular conflict.
- China does not peacefully resolve its differences with Taiwan.
- A pre-emptive strike occurs against a developing nuclear state in Central Asia.
- A government unfriendly to the United States develops miniaturized nuclear devices.
- Japan rearms with weapons of mass destruction.
- Russia takes a turn toward authoritarianism domestically and asserts itself internationally with threats of violence.
- Successful ballistic missile defenses are developed.
- Nuclear conflict occurs in South Asia.
- An attack on the critical infrastructure of the developed states brings major sectors of the global economy to a halt.
- Ethnic cleansing and genocide erupt in Latin America or sub-Saharan Africa or South Asia.
- Nuclear proliferation to Iran or to an Arab state occurs.

CULTURE

What if—

- Unprecedented immigration follows a nuclear accident or a Mexican or Turkish Revolution.
- Europe and Japan fail to manage their demographic challenges, aging rapidly yet unable to replace 110 million lost workers by 2015.

- A cheap technology for universal, wireless communication via voice/text/image becomes available.
- Weather epidemics—the health consequence of rapidly changing weather patterns—strike.
- A new incurable but highly infectious virus emerges.
- Rapid advances in, and the diffusion of, biotechnology, nanotechnology, and the materials sciences extend life and expand the quality of that life, while also adding to the bioterrorist arsenal.
- China disintegrates, with a new state emerging composed of the Guangdong region, Hong Kong, and Taiwan.
- The United States (or the European Union) loosens the human rights restraints on federalism, giving far greater autonomy to its constituent states.
- A cultural incident inflames Muslim opinion, leading to anti-Western terrorism.
- Criminal conspiracies flourish, trafficking in illegal immigration, money laundering, narcotics, and illegal arms trade.
- The emergence of enlightened business leaders creates a climate of international cooperation.
- New international institutions emerge to manage the effects of globalization.

ECONOMICS

Imagine—

- The U.S. economy suffers a sustained downturn following a dramatic stock market crash.
- China and/or India fail to sustain high growth rates.
- Chemical etching for integrated circuits yields dramatically cheaper and more powerful computation.
- Hybrid fuels greatly lower energy costs, bringing the price of oil to record lows.
- Green tariffs are widely used by the developed states in order to protect the global environment, including punishment for the "environmental rogue state," the United States.
- Japan fails in the structural reform of its financial institutions and triggers an Asian currency collapse.
- An antiglobalization movement, the New Luddites, emerges using laptop computers, websites, and sophisticated encryption to conduct a worldwide campaign of anarchy.
- Exports surge to 50 percent of global product.
- Global energy supplies are disrupted in a major way.

- Major Asian countries establish an Asian Monetary Fund and/or an Asian Trade Organization, triggering a European reply in kind and undermining the IMF and the WTO.
- Owing to escalating trade disputes, the U.S./European alliance collapses.
- The euro becomes an alternative reserve currency with the dollar.

DECISIONS

Although each of the scenarios assumes the same factual premises, the events in each may vary depending on decisions that are taken within the scenarios to cope with unanticipated matters. I have italicized those critical decisions in order that the reader may ponder them in a way that would not necessarily be available to the decision makers. Some are defining moments, some are turning points, some illuminate one future while casting other possible worlds into the shadows. Yet each may come accompanied by such urgency and such noise that its true significance is not apparent (the decision in the early 1970s to float the dollar is an example). Or it may come so gradually that only when one looks back can one see that a great turning has occurred and the past is no longer visible (as occurred with American immigration policy after the mid-1960s). Or dominant ways of looking at the world may assimilate a new development for a while obscuring its power to change the way we look at things (the decision to use nuclear weapons against Japan in the mid-1940s was just such a decision, taken more or less routinely as an orderly continuation of the campaign of strategic bombing). All these decisional environments are present in the scenarios that follow.

Taken together the italicized decisions in each scenario make up the unique style of that particular world: The Meadow with its impatient and ruthless naturalism, The Park with its bureaucratic Cartesianism, The Garden with its understated but iron insistence on harmony. Taken individually, these decisions show how essential human agency is to any account of history (even an historical account of the future) and yet how confined our choices can become as a consequence of precedent-setting decisions taken on matters that seemed, at the time, not to present much difficulty. Each scenario suite that follows will comprise three subject areas: security, culture, and economics.

THE SCENARIOS

THE MEADOW

SECURITY

In September of the first year of the new millennium, the United States was struck by a terrorist atrocity on a scale that dwarfed previous attacks. Perhaps as many as six teams of airplane hijackers attempted to take over commercial aircraft and fly them into a set of targets that included the World Trade Center towers in New York and the Pentagon in Washington; three teams succeeded. A death toll in the thousands was the result.

The terrorist teams were linked to a shadowy Arab leader who was believed to control a mercenary and religious network of zealots in many countries, but was based in the state of Afghanistan, which had, for four years, been controlled by a fundamentalist movement known as the Taliban. Allied to this movement, this charismatic leader trained thousands of terrorist fighters in Afghan camps. *Now the United States demanded that the Taliban dismantle the camps and turn over the terrorist leadership.*

For the first time in its history, NATO invoked Article Five of its founding charter, declaring that the atrocities were an attack on the alliance. The United Nations' Security Council adopted a resolution authorizing states to employ "all necessary means" to prevent future terrorist acts. Despite these moves, the United States chose to assemble a multistate coalition not limited to NATO nor acting under U.N. authority. At the center of this coalition are the American president, the British prime minister, and the Russian president.

The first week in the following October the coalition began its attacks on Afghanistan, largely using American air assets to conduct a bombing campaign and relying on indigenous Afghan forces to defeat the Taliban on the ground. That same week a Russian airliner flying from Israel to Siberia exploded in mid-air and crashed into the Black Sea. The next week a letter seeded with anthrax arrived at the office of the U.S. Senate's majority leader. Similar letters were found in various offices, including those of other senators, media outlets, and postal sorting centers. In mid-November an American passenger jet crashed into a residential neighborhood in New York City. None of these events—the airliner crashes or the anthrax mailings—were ever conclusively tied to the militant Muslim conspiracy but nor were they definitively investigated.

By December Taliban forces had disintegrated and some of the senior leadership of the terrorist network had been eliminated. There remained, however, a decade of warfare ahead. During this period the Holland and Lincoln Tunnels into New York City, as well as the Chunnel connecting France and the United Kingdom, were attacked with explosives and collapsed. The National Cathedral in Washington, the Central Synagogue in New York, the John the Baptist site on the Jordan River, and the gothic cathedral at Chartres were all targets of attacks or attempted attacks by terrorists.

International civil aviation was renationalized and taken over by governments when it became impossible to maintain profitably. This was the result of repeated bombings on aircraft and at airports, including London's Heathrow and the Los Angeles terminal known as LAX and the destruction of a Concorde after takeoff from Charles de Gaulle.

The consequence of these horrors on the law of the countries struck was relatively consistent in The Meadow. *Thousands of persons were arrested and detained without charge; some were tortured and beaten to extract information. Nonjudicial tribunals were sometimes used to convict those arrested* when it appeared that they might go free under traditional rules of criminal procedure or when it was feared the ongoing threat posed by their co-conspirators was too great to risk the exposure of intelligence assets required for a successful prosecution.

Nothing seems to work to stop these attacks until two developments, one political, one technological, converge. For three decades the leaders of the most influential economies have been meeting informally, at first to discuss particular crises, and later to seek consensus on the development of the society of the market-states. Originally called the Group of Seven (G-7) by the press, the membership of this group had changed eventually to encompass a political group (the United States, United Kingdom, France, Canada, Japan, German, Russia) and an economic group (adding China).

At the G-9 (P8) meeting, the U.S. president proposed an ad hoc intelligence coalition to be financed by voluntary subscriptions by members of the society of states, and empowered to share information on a global scale. The G-9 (P8) meeting was no more than a forum; it took no position as a group on the president's proposal. In the case of anti-Western terrorism, funding for this intelligence institution was initially contributed by Saudi Arabia, Japan, Russia, Turkey, Germany, Britain, and the United States. *For the first time, cooperation among the world's financial institutions (prompted by the solidarity shown among finance ministers and central bankers) yielded substantial progress in tracking and interdicting the financing of terrorism.*

Careful investigative work by units of this institution was responsible for uncovering an Iraqi attempt to use the terrorist network for a nuclear attack—actually a conventional explosive that would disseminate radioactive materials, the so-called dirty bomb—against the city of Washington in 2007. But the G-9 successes were marred by an attack that used a device apparently loaded onto a container ship in Antwerp, off-loaded in

Canada, and detonated by satellite signal while on a train that passes through Chicago. No one ever really determined the source of this attack. The terrorist network denied responsibility, but then they had adopted the tactic of denial sometime past. Ultimately Iraq is blamed and this provided the decisive impetus for an invasion. A slightly different coalition was organized to provide an expeditionary force.

The former Iraqi leader, Saddam Hussein, had been removed by 2004 but his successor, a Baath party functionary of Iranian descent, had continued the predatory policies of his predecessor. The new expeditionary force, composed of troops hitherto delegated to NATO commands by the United States, Germany, and the United Kingdom, launched an airborne assault, seizing Baghdad, and meeting up with an amphibious offensive from the Persian Gulf, joined by overland elements of the same force from Kuwait.

Only, however, when the G-9 coalitions were aided by technological breakthroughs in nanosensors—which could detect the molecular presence of weapons of mass destruction—and in global surveillance systems did terrorism on a catastrophic scale finally abate in 2015.

The success of this innovative coalitional arrangement against terrorism led to several structural reforms: *first the G-9 (P8) members announced a series of rules for intervention, including commitments to deliver humanitarian assistance.* In every situation, a G-9 (P8) member had to propose an intervention and raise the funds for the operation, provided only that a simple majority of the Group endorse the effort. The actual forces used are contributed on a cost-plus basis, and are placed under the unified command of the state organizing the intervention. Relying on the widespread belief that democratic regimes do not wage aggression, the G-9 (P8) is in effect offering a substantial security subsidy—through a kind of extended deterrence, that is, the promise of protection against aggression—to those states that adopt and maintain democratic regimes. At the same time, by promising to intervene against international terrorism and ethnic cleansing, and to treat epidemics and famine, the G-9 (P8) linked human rights to liberal constitutionalism, regardless of the democratic nature of the affected regime, thus reserving to itself the right to compromise the sovereignty of any state when it is unwilling, or unable, to protect a group of its own citizens from mass depredations.

This policy was tested over the next decade and a half in regions as diverse as South Asia (where a Sri Lankan revolutionary regime attempted to slaughter ethnic Hindus), *South Africa* (where a democratic government was temporarily deposed by a coalition of white supremacists and African separatists), *and Latin America* (where a Guyanese dictator refused to permit humanitarian aid to stem a smallpox epidemic). It may be judged a success in retrospect, but it did not operate in isolation. The G-9 (P8) directorate was greatly aided by three factors that tended to stabilize and enhance its impact.

First, the war against terrorism was a conflict all the great powers could unite on. Each faced the threat of attacks on its own modernity and the secular nature of its state. *Thus Russia and China were no less willing to join the coalition against terrorism than were France and Japan.*

Second, as they developed increasing confidence in the G-9 (P8) plan, most *states were able to divert more funds away from military expenditures in their own budgets,* thus accelerating their economic growth and allowing for higher payments to fund G-9 (P8) expeditionary forces. Failure to do so meant effective exclusion from the decision making process of the world's leadership.

Third, the G-9 (P8) states were able to develop a comprehensive system of nanosensors, satellite surveillance, and ballistic missile defense that provided a limited shield against weapons of mass destruction. The sheer investment required by such an effort could only have been feasible by a multinational consortium; when finally deployed, this system had the additional effect of rendering the G-9 (P8) more credible, because, at least for a time, it seemed impossible to threaten G-9 (P8) states (as Iraq had threatened Israel at the time of the Gulf War) with long range retaliation by modest or disguised forces. This tended to quiet various regional enmities (like that of China, India, and Pakistan) where states had "gone nuclear."

Russian participation in the G-9 (P8) force structure had the wholesome effect of tying the new Russian state to the world's most influential economies. This had a stabilizing effect on politics within Russia, and enhanced Russia's prestige vis-à-vis the bordering states of the former Soviet Union. At the same time that Russian forces were ever willing to join ad hoc expeditions (for which they were well paid), the Kremlin was also more willing to resort to G-9 (P8) mediation over the autonomy campaigns of the Chechens and others.

On the other hand, this informal system had the effect of weakening the U.N. and its associated peacekeeping institutions to the vanishing point. *Gradually, the United States reduced its funding to about 10 percent of the total budget, an 80 percent cut.* Other multilateral security institutions adapted: *NATO, for example, jettisoned its unanimity rule for the North Atlantic Council and transformed itself into a rapid reaction force for hire.*

This ad hoc system was sorely tested, however, in 2018. The South Korean government was in the final stages of negotiation with North Korea over a federal reunification plan, to be financed by a huge South Korean subsidy, when labor unrest in the South broke into mass riots against the government. Although the riots initially erupted in Seoul, they soon spread to other cities and were most violent in the southern port of Pusan. Here a provisional government led by a workers' party proclaimed its independence in May, after six weeks of revolt; this government called upon the North for aid when it was reported that troops from Seoul were bound for Pusan to quell the insurrection. The North responded with such alacrity that it is clear that some sort of collusion with the rioters was already in place. Northern troops poured across the border in two columns, advancing down the Chorwan Valley and the Kaesong-Murasan Approach against Seoul. Intelligence sources indicated that, as had been expected since the 1960s, this was to be a direct strike against Seoul, but in fact the city was partly encircled and then bypassed as the Northern forces split, one group streaking south toward Pusan, the other army group attempting to trap some 15,000 U.S. troops outside Taegu. *These U.S. forces were the last remnant of the American post–Cold War force stationed on the Asian mainland; they had been stripped of their tactical nuclear weapons in 1991.* When the American forces were virtually surrounded, and the North Korean main force had entered Pusan, the Pusan provisional regime contacted Washington, offering to barter a peaceful withdrawal of American forces. Washington faced a dilemma: either it would risk the annihilation of its forces in an attempt to intervene to save them and to shore up the Seoul government, or it would shatter its security commitments in an ignominious evacuation. Intervention would require the reintroduction of nuclear weapons, a move strongly opposed by Japan, where the only other American forces in the area were stationed, *the U.S. base at Okinawa having reverted to Japanese sovereignty.*

It was never imagined that the G-9 (P8) ad hoc forces would confront a challenge of this magnitude; they were mainly expeditionary in nature. In any case, *Japan blocked G-9 (P8) action* by successful lobbying, out of concern that nuclear weapons might ultimately be used in the Korean peninsula with incalculable consequences for Japan. *U.S. appeals to China for diplomatic mediation were rebuffed,* partly, it was surmised, because China wished to remove Korean economic competition from its own export markets. In any case, *China vetoed a resolution in the U.N. Security Council condemning the Northern invasion.*

It remained unclear for some weeks whether North Korea had produced its own nuclear weapons, using reactors it had been given in the 1990s to replace the heavy-water reactors it was then relying on. Although the replacement reactors were less useful in producing fissile material for weapons, they could have served this role and there were no definitive sources of intelligence either way. This possibility added to the complexity of the American position.

On June 1, *American airborne troops attempted to reinforce the Taegu force* in preparation for a breakout. Cruise missiles with conventional warheads hit targets in the North but refrained from striking Pusan. Despite the fact that U.S. troops were prepared for a chemical attack by North

Korean forces, Washington seems to have been surprised when a large-scale chemical assault on Seoul was carried out by infiltrators the night of June 2, allegedly in retaliation for civilian casualties in the North resulting from American air strikes. In the aftermath of this horrifying event, a *joint Chinese-Japanese proposal was put forward by the terms of which the American troops were evacuated,* and emergency medical aid was sent to Seoul. Following the negotiated withdrawal of American troops, the Seoul government capitulated and Korea was ultimately united not under a federal plan as previously negotiated, but under central control from Pyongyang.

After these traumatic events, *the society of market-states rallied and augmented its announced rules of international security policy.* Henceforth, all ballistic missile systems capable of delivering nuclear, chemical, and biological weapons, were to be placed in escrow—held in protected sites under the authority of a multinational, quasi-private consortium—and no future development of such systems was to be tolerated, on pain of pre-emption. *The first pre-emptive strike by an ad hoc coalition occurred against a Central Asian state in 2020.* Russia and the United States both contributed large numbers of ballistic systems to these cantonments, although the actual effect of this isolation was muted by the widespread deployment of cruise missiles by many states.

The evolution of international law in this period took its direction from the doctrine of "the new sovereignty," on the basis of which the United States, and later NATO, had intervened in Panama in 1990 and in Kosovo nine years later. This doctrine held that a state's sovereignty was only valid so long as various criteria were met. *Based on this doctrine, the United States and allied Caribbean forces overturned the "drug states" of New Grenada and New San Martin, where narcotics organizations had seized power.* But faced with widespread calls for intervention to redress human-rights violations in many parts of the globe, the G-9 (P8) states also found fewer and fewer of their citizens were willing to serve in the armed forces necessary to mount such interventions. This meant that intervention forces had to rely on what were effectively nonnational mercenaries. *Proposals to reintroduce the draft in the United States and France were greeted with widespread protests and were quickly shelved.* When a breakaway state in the Congo Republic massacred 250,000 of its citizens, there was no political consensus on the part of any G-9 (P-8) states—though some, notably the United States, were more willing to intervene than others—to fund or support an intervention.

By 2020 the experiment of the G-9 (P-8) ad hoc forces had been re-structured. All-volunteer forces—essentially multinational mercenary groups—eliminated the need for the G-9 (P-8) states to rely on the troops of member states. Such forces were successfully used by the British in

Sierra Leone, by the United States in Haiti, by deBeers in southern Africa, and by Singapore in Irian Jaya. Though buffeted by many calls on its resources the G-9 (P-8) was eventually able to concentrate on those crises that were economically and strategically significant to the wealthiest states, which included some, but by no means all, human-rights crises. The G-9 (P-8) developed patterns of cooperation over time—including intelligence sharing, joint exercises, interoperable equipment, consolidated training—that brought defense costs down and muted great power conflicts.

In The Meadow security was commoditized. Market mechanisms were hitched to geostrategic objectives. Political discontent with the prevailing system was equated with crime. Still, states were able to cooperate to cope with a variety of crises.

CULTURE

In the West, the growing inequalities of wealth and personal safety were dissolving the bonds of civil society in state after state. Riots, kidnappings of wealthy persons, the anticomputer terrorism of the technically sophisticated New Luddites, the green terrorism of the "Boy Scout" movement (no relation to the twentieth century group of child explorers), begging in the streets of the wealthiest capitals, and anarchy in the poorest ones—all these were accepted as the inevitable costs of rapid growth and rapid change. There even came a point, during the worst of the terror attacks on the United States, when it appeared that New York and Washington would be depopulated like Rome during the plague, but this did not happen.

Globalization—and its terrors—were of necessity an engine of change, and the resulting dislocations were taken to be unavoidable. The bottom line was that even after an American stock market collapse in 2005 and a worldwide recession that had lasted throughout 2007, most persons were wealthier (had more consumer goods, more leisure time), healthier (owing to computer-enabled methods of preventive medicine that earmarked individual vulnerabilities before they became acute), and better educated (again owing to computer innovations that gave every child several hours of individual instruction daily for fifteen years and provided access to an almost infinite amount of information) than ever before. Led by the United States, virtually every state in the developed world and many outside it adopted a hands-off attitude toward popular culture and behavior. *Affirmative action, anti-abortion laws, narcotics and prostitution prosecutions, and subsidies for the arts all vanished.* The withdrawal of the state from enforcing particular sectarian views did not mean that pressure groups declined.

On the contrary, by 2010 everyone in the former First World seemed to believe in something—often so intensely and parochially that political systems all across the developed world were deadlocked. NGOs, however, flourished. These began reaching out to the Third World. In Africa and Latin America, philanthropic groups supported both Christianization and de-Christianization, attempting to change people's religion either to some form of Christianity (including Mormonism) or to some "indigenous" sect thought to have been threatened by Christianity (including animism). To these causes were added Green concerns (reforestation, restoration of species, soil depletion headed the list), inoculation against infectious diseases, and famine relief.

Indeed the proliferation and profusion of NGOs in the developed world led a large number of countries in the developing parts of the world to devise cultural policies catering to First World interests. *Some countries legalized assisted suicide; some instituted Islamic legal and cultural rules; some hosted genetic engineering projects ranging from modified crops to organ harvesting; some virtually became theme parks.*

NGOs also led the movement to improve health in the developing world. In many countries, rapid urbanization had outrun the capacity of the urban infrastructure and social services to cope, leaving cities to incubate disease and without adequate sewage or health facilities. *NGOs organized treatment centers, and in some states governments virtually ceded their health policies to these organizations,* which had the resources to alleviate disease but not the legitimate power to resolve the underlying problems that had created the crisis.

By 2025 the world's population had increased by 50 percent since the year 2000, to a level of about 7.5 billion. The most dramatic demographic event in the first quarter century, however, was a precipitous drop in population growth. This drop did not occur uniformly. The states of the developed world lost population share, going from 21 percent to 12 percent—since 1650 it had hovered between 34 percent and 26 percent—and aged at a faster rate than any other group of states. Within the group of developed states, however, there were significant differences. Japan and Italy, whose low population growth was a source of anxiety at the turn of the century, aged rapidly, Japan overtaking Italy. Except for Poland and Moldova, the European populations of the former Warsaw Pact uniformly declined. In 2020, Britain and France had a high average age among industrial countries; that same year the United States had the youngest average age. And even within a single state, there were large variations: *the relative youth of the American population derived from a high rate of immigration.*

In this period *a number of less developed states stabilized their populations*—China, Taiwan, Korea, Algeria—and their birth rates actually began to decline. Other states—India, Pakistan, Mexico, Brazil—continued to grow and then leveled off in the 2030s and 2040s. Some states—Nigeria, Zaire, Ethiopia, Rwanda—experienced a largely unchanged, high fertility rate, but their population levels suffered owing to various catastrophic events.

These population variables set the terms of the differential growth rates that occurred in the first part of the twenty-first century, as the world in 2025 saw a falling population for the first time in four centuries. In the northern-tier developed states, the demand for consumer goods was faltering as the population aged; in the less developed southern-tier states, increasing population pressures drove up the price of foodstuffs. Nevertheless both sectors—with the exception of some African states—were linked by multinational commerce, opening up vast consumer markets in the South, to which genetically engineered grains and proteins were ultimately exported. By 2020, 70 percent of the world economy was in the former Third World and China.

There were some unattractive aspects to this flourishing trade. For example, *organ farms (really "hospitals" that removed organs from paid donors) arose in Pakistan, the Philippines, and various other states to supply First World demand for transplants,* though these were ultimately replaced by transgenic methods using animals. *Some states acquired needed capital by locating nuclear waste sites on their national territory* and by *permitting mineral-extraction methods that were outlawed elsewhere.* Russia for a time in the 2020s was taken over by a raw-materials development company that employed political prisoners as workers in mines and wholly corrupted the Duma by giving members "derivative" subsoil rights to the petroleum and minerals beneath Siberia. *In Russia at this time, a new form of civil right was introduced, permitting any citizen or registered company to buy shares in the state, thus giving weighted voting according to the number of shares purchased.* Unsavory as this sounds, it did have the result of efficiently extracting the abundant raw materials of the Russian state, which had hitherto frustrated most attempts at development. Moreover, the privatization of the state brought sufficient capital to the country through foreign investment that perennial Russian agricultural shortfalls were finally halted through a program of genetically engineered hybridization.

Pakistan and India joined in a free trade area in 2010, providing the crucial momentum that made India the world's largest single market by 2025. Other, intermediary states flourished in the new environment of general free trade: Turkey, Indonesia, South Africa, Mexico, Iran, Algeria. A global hiring program operated on the Internet allowed anyone anywhere to access job opportunities worldwide and to receive a one-year "green card" once employment was assured, as part of a universal reciprocity regime for jobs. By 2040, the number of nominal citizens and resident citizens combined of the top fifteen formerly Third World countries surpassed year 2000 levels of GDP per capita for First World countries.[10]

In these rapidly developing countries, the proportions of GDP derived from industry and manufacturing hit the conventional maxima for a developed, postindustrial state, giving way to the relative rise in services that seems characteristic of affluence.[11] Successful economic reforms in these states—especially the *free trade areas of India-Pakistan, China-Taiwan, Korea-Japan, and Singapore-Malaysia-Indonesia-Thailand*—prompted the election of politicians committed to economic reform. Increases in successful free-market reform yielded increases in individual freedom. Third World development spurred demand for First World products that became, as the century wore on, ever cheaper.

By contrast, per-capita consumption in the First World shifted as more emphasis was placed on quality-improving investments such as child safety, preventive medical care, and lifelong education. *Environmental quality was monitored and protected by licensed entrepreneurs who held various resources (for example, air quality) in trust for the state.* The 2020s also saw a number of innovations in civil society: *violence-prone adolescents—identified by genetic screening at birth—were monitored when convicted of violent crimes, and their activities circumscribed through various electronic means;* the most serious offenders were exiled to other countries in exchange for cash payments, and there typically turned to agricultural or military duties. In some countries, *medical and education vouchers were earned through the avoidance of legal "demerits"* so that citizens with a record of infractions were barred from schooling beyond high school and from all but some inexpensive forms of acute care, unless they were able to secure a source of funds of their own. This rather draconian system was to some extent mitigated by *a system of behavior bribes whereby nonviolent offenders were paroled to specialized private corporations where they were maintained as wards of the market,* in comfortable circumstances performing menial tasks, so long as they refrained from further offenses. *Drug offenders were either exported to states that had legalized drug use, or confined to privately run "Virtual Holiday" camps* where nonlethal drug use was permitted. By these various means, prison populations were dramatically reduced (though some increased crime did inevitably accompany this reduction).

The universal communications made possible by the ubiquitous (and cheap) handheld wireless computer/telephone/television tied the world's cultures together as never before. The reach of a single language—English—embraced 60 percent of the world's inhabitants by 2040. Only one region seemed impervious to the general economic upturn, and from that continent came the horrors that haunted the society of market-states.

In Africa, the greatest increase in population during this period occurred, from 642 million persons in 1990 to 2.25 billion in 2050, an absolute increase of more than 1.5 billion and a percentage growth (253 percent) that was more than twice as great as the rise in total population of the underdeveloped countries (including China and India) taken as a whole (109 percent). This growth was uneven, largely owing to AIDS deaths in some sub-Saharan states. Nevertheless Nigeria alone exceeded 500 million people at the end of this period. This enormous influx of population into the ecosystem of the African states accelerated the process of deforestation that was already well underway in the 1990s. One result of this deforestation was the triggering of the first twenty-year drought, which began in 2007–08. This drought brought about a shortage of fresh water that was so severe that even the development of genetically modified hybrid strains of sorghum and cassava were unable to alleviate Africa's grain shortfalls. Indeed, the availability of water proved to be the principal bottleneck to agricultural progress in many areas of the globe in the first two decades of the twenty-first century before laser-fusion technology made desalinization practicable. By that time, Africa had been struck with a new plague, the so-called weather epidemics of the mid-2020s.

"Weather epidemics" are so named owing to illnesses that appear to arise from unusual disturbances in the weather patterns of a given ecosystem. It is still not clear whether the bizarre weather conditions that began in the winter of 2026 were the result of covert experiments by private companies that went awry, or were another consequence of deforestation or of the *intense development without environmental quality restraints that took place on the west coast of Africa in the beginning of the century,* or of some combination of many unknown causes. In any event, a general malaise leading to extreme enervation, but usually not death if dehydration and starvation were treated, struck the African continent below the 10th parallel. Although there were deaths in the tens of thousands, the worst consequences of the weather epidemics, like those of the twenty-year droughts, were avoided by *a voluntary system of secular tithing in the developed world, stimulated by advertising campaigns and administered through various NGOs, including the Red Cross.* The ability to transmit worldwide the images of starving African children through wireless hand-held communicators, enabling First World individuals to "adopt" and monitor particular children in the refugee camps, stimulated a response from the international public that dwarfed anything that governments were prepared to do. The money thus raised was used to bring food, medicine, and water to the dyshygenic new cities of West Africa, and to the swollen refugee camps of Central and East Africa.

Medical historians now believe, however, that it was an indirect consequence of this inspiring outpouring that led to the third and most lethal of the plagues to strike Africa. There is an emerging consensus that it was the pirating of portable X-ray machines from the Red Cross facility at Kinshasa and their subsequent misuse that resulted in the mutated virus known as OOA-V. Like HIV, this virus can be transmitted through sexual contact and thus spread quickly through the polygamous societies of Africa, before leaping the Atlantic and turning up in the Caribbean. But this time, *unlike the HIV crisis of the late twentieth century, the disease had been identified and definitively traced.* Simple *sputum tests were given to passengers of air or ocean craft; whole countries were quarantined* (Equatorial Guinea being the first). The medical infrastructure of the African states, still reeling from the weather epidemics, was completely overwhelmed. This time, there was no commensurate outpouring of aid from the northern-tier states. *Such funds as their people were willing to spend on the problem were spent on prevention and quarantine measures.* By the end of the decade—2049—OOA-V had claimed, directly or collaterally, something approaching twenty-six million lives and it appeared still unchecked.

There was a pervasive sense that an international society that could be so rich and at the same time couldn't be bothered to alleviate, much less prevent, a human catastrophe on this scale had much to answer for. Sheer materialism had become more glamorous, more accessible, and yet more alienating. Not everyone was well positioned to succeed in the Meadow's meritocratic competitions. Some were poorly educated, some were ill at ease with technology, some simply not sufficiently motivated. Marx had used the term "alienation" to describe a psychological loss of self-worth, and this perhaps was the most disturbing aspect of The Meadow. Far from creating revolutionaries and criminals, its unemployed and underemployed persons felt themselves to be at fault and punished themselves through absorption in games and drugs of many kinds. The so-called helping professions—nursing, teaching—made a comeback as people yearned for a sense of community and common purpose. But there was really nowhere to go to find such a community: The Meadow was globally pervasive.

ECONOMICS

Although the path was difficult, states in The Meadow were best able to cope with the recession of 2005. Their recovery, however, was volatile and erratic, causing vast inequalities in distribution. As one commentator put it at the time, "it seemed that every tip of the boat during the hectic years from 2003 to 2009 resulted in a new class of millionaires, mostly entrepreneurs, investors, and currency speculators, in one part of the world and a new class of recently impoverished in another."[12]

The United States was identified throughout the world as the leading proponent and beneficiary of globalization. Yet the entrepreneurial market-state was by no means limited in its appeal to *the United States, which had led the movement to adopt this model, even to the extent of per-*

suading Germany to abandon its corporatist policies. At different times in the first half of the twenty-first century, this model was chosen by Britain, Germany, Japan, the Baltic states, Russia, Spain, Mexico, Chile, Indonesia, Nigeria, Switzerland, Thailand, and Singapore, among others. Each sought a weak, minimal central government with low taxes; each tolerated in some economic sectors a functioning anarchy loosely governed by largely deregulated markets and some degree of persistent corruption. Each developed a high degree of privatization embracing pension plans, power utilities, and, in some states, education and relied to a great degree on local ad hoc action-oriented groups to solve political problems.

The global society—The Meadow—led by such states proved to be a phenomenal engine of innovation. The Park and The Garden eventually developed the chemical etching procedure for integrated circuits that broke the silicon barrier and multiplied the speed of computers by a factor of 100 billion, but it took so much longer and the finished cost was so much higher than in The Meadow that its benefits were confined to supercomputers in those worlds. Hybrid fuel vehicles (which cushioned The Meadow from the oil shocks of the 2010–2015 period and brought forth $10-a-barrel oil for the rest of the scenario period), domestic and agricultural robots, nanodevices for the diagnosis of diseases and stem cell techniques for DNA repair and immune system regeneration, genetic mapping, the ubiquitous handheld wireless computer/television/telephone nanosensors to detect the presence or transport of weapons of mass destruction: all these devices were the offspring of The Meadow. Indeed even though the first computers were developed for military purposes driven by the Long War, it was the commercial success of the first Apple and then IBM personal computers that provided the impetus for the miraculous developments of the early twenty-first century. The difficulty was that The Meadow was not the best place to make these marvels available to the peoples of the world because it invited—perhaps required—severe distributional effects and these eventually dampened demand.

The Meadow's global economy led to lower wages, as deregulated capital sought cheaper and cheaper costs of production. At the same time, new technologies had enhanced worker productivity, so that for the first time the world began to see both increases in worker productivity and falling wages. Liberalization of markets had led to lower prices. As a result of these three factors, the supply of finished goods increasingly exceeded world demand, and prices fell still lower. Workers were too poor to buy new products, and wealthier citizens tended to invest rather than consume, shifting the prices of financial goods higher and the prices of products lower.

The Meadow ignored and thus weakened international institutions. For example, the *IMF did not have sufficient resources to counter the Asian currency crises that struck in 2003.* Japan's economy failed to revive, despite generous fiscal stimuli and real if grudging banking reform. *When Japan finally liberalized its financial services industry in 2004, allowing ordinary savers to invest in financial instruments abroad, the government faced a choice: it could either raise interest rates to coax investment back into the economy or it could increase the money supply. Following the precepts of the Meadow, Japan did both.* The yen fell calamitously and the Japanese trade surplus rocketed up.

These events occurred contemporaneously with a deep cyclical downturn in the U.S. economy in 2005 that was powered by the *contractions in the money supply that were the Federal Reserve's response to its overreaction to terrorist attacks on the U.S. banking and transportation systems.* The Dow Industrial Average fell to 6,000 points from a high of over 14,000. *The Federal Reserve then took measures that increased liquidity.* These steps weakened the dollar and sent investors to the euro. But the rising euro further dampened U.S. demand, and European exports collapsed. The slower European growth that followed resulted in lower tax revenues and higher claims for unemployment benefits. This caused the *European Central Bank to tighten credit. When Japan and the United States felt forced to follow suit in 2006,* the resulting tight money policies triggered a world recession. European, Japanese, and U.S. output suffered losses of 1–2 percent for the next three years in a row. During this period world growth hovered around zero. The recovery only began when *the United States took on considerable debt, ran a series of sharpening deficits, and increased the global money supply.*

This was the situation when a new American administration took office in 2009, stunned by the economic slowdown that, beginning in 2004, had for four years ruined the optimistic projections of the preceding eight years. The terrorist attacks that had struck The Meadow since the World Trade Center atrocity in 2001 had had a harsh effect on the economies of the developed states. Despite repeated interest rate cuts by central banks, the equities markets never regained their pre-2001 highs, and several industries, notably the airlines, were crushed.

The recovery from this recession had been enormously expensive and the new administration was committed to drastically reducing U.S. government debt, which at that time totaled $3 trillion (in a $9 trillion economy). *Several steps were taken by the new administration, including some modest tax increases and even more modest cuts in entitlement spending, but the most dramatic tactic was the devaluation of the dollar,* allowing the United States to pay off Treasury obligations with cheap dollars and boosting exports to unprecedented levels. Within ten months the hitherto chronic trade deficit of the United States had been largely erased, but inflation levels soared. As if by implicit collusion, *once the greater part of the*

U.S. debt had been retired, the Federal Reserve tightened interest rates to halt inflation. A second stock market crash—over 1,000 points in a single day—was only a symptom, but a significant one, of the deflation to come. Stock equities composed a far smaller share of U.S. capital than in the 1930s, and so a sharp contraction in the stock market did not itself bring about a catastrophe. The borrowing that would ordinarily replace such lost liquidity, however, had been dried up by the deflation and the flight of foreign capital from Treasury instruments.

This one-two punch had shattering consequences around the world. Having seen its U.S. financial assets written down by its principal debtor, Japan then saw its export market to America evaporate. By the time the U.S. Federal Reserve acted, a full-scale depression had begun in East Asia. The Fed's action only made things radically worse by depressing American demand just at the time that imports were returning to competitive prices. In Europe, the Eurodollar market had caused European Union currency—the "euro"—to skyrocket, driving up European interest rates and choking off consumer purchasing power. *The hitherto willing labor forces in Europe that had accepted tight money policies in exchange for a social contract now demanded higher wages to keep up with the increased cost of living.* In 2010 the European Central Bank was repopulated by reformers, appointed by a new coalition of environmental and consumer parties. In the United Kingdom, mysterious groups of cyberterrorists, calling themselves the "New Luddites," began attacking the computer systems that operated electronic banking and financial infrastructures. The computer plagues that followed may have been a consequence of these attacks, but this was never determined.

Especially hard hit during this period was the Asian subcontinent. In 1950 the population of India was less than half the 900 million it had reached by 2000; by 2025 this had grown to 1.5 billion. The celebrated Green Revolution that had, for a time, made India a net exporter of grains had been achieved through intensive overplanting, which had depleted both soils and the watershed. In retrospect it appears that the Indians of the late twentieth century were feeding themselves on the food sources of their children in the twenty-first century.

Nevertheless, the policies of The Meadow allowed India and Pakistan to recover. The water wars predicted by many analysts never materialized and the food shortage that followed the great drought of 2020, which might have triggered such wars, was ameliorated by ample U.S. investment in drought-resistant grains. The widespread use of English, computer skills that were learned during the course of Y2K remediation (most of which was done in India), and the reluctant adoption of the entrepreneurial state model by both countries meant that when the world economy recovered, South Asia was poised to take advantage of it.

The entrepreneurial market-state—and The Meadow, which is its extrapolation by the society of states—is profoundly indifferent to sex, class, religion, and ethnicity and these were precisely the prejudices that had held South Asia back. Relying on its highly developed merchant class, a skilled labor pool of many millions of scientists and technicians, a British legal system of property rights, and a large domestic market, Indian growth rose from 6 percent in 2000, before the first world recession, to 9 percent in 2010. The Indian middle class, which already numbered 150 million in 2000, doubled by 2015. The discrediting of socialism led to the weakening of unions, and this permitted a restructuring of industry that lured foreign investment. The environment was essentially for sale: *multinationals were allowed to use methods in South Asia that were permitted in few other places.* The sorts of planning required to modify a pure market approach—developing markets in risks, for example, to spread the impact of foreseeable events—require institutions strong enough and practiced enough to make such an approach work. Yet the very development of highly competitive practices rendered the creation and maintenance of such institutions problematic. The aggressive free-trade intrusions of entrepreneurial market-states made other states wary of cooperation, lest they be co-opted. With weak international institutions and weak allegiances to those institutions on the part of market-states, the *political leaders of each state were led to lay blame on the other models for the imperfections of the market-state model each had chosen,* rather than to persuade domestic constituencies to accept the costs of modifying the operations of the market. Such adjustments would have met fierce resistance within their respective states, and no government was willing to confront such opposition. The difficulty with the modified market approach of The Meadow is that market-states are less able to muster the political strength to mitigate the operations of the market (just as nation-states had difficulty assembling the political will to overcome the vested interests that grew up around regulation). The problem really was that the United States—of all the market-states—had fixatedly followed the entrepreneurial market-state model, and without U.S. leadership to find common economic interests, the society of market-states could prosper but not thrive. This failure of leadership was exacerbated by the common perception among the other states that world events—in genetic engineering, in currency flows, in computer innovation, all with incalculable consequences—were in the hands of the reckless and self-absorbed Americans.

THE PARK

SECURITY

Perhaps more than any other driver, it was the implicit erosion of confidence in U.S. nuclear extended deterrence following the terrorist attacks on the United States that began in earnest in September 2001 that brought the world of The Park into being. Once the hitherto protected states of *Japan and Germany sought their own weapons of mass destruction, regional security alliances developed that excluded the United States from North Asia, Western Europe, and elsewhere,* with important consequences for nuclear proliferation.

The Korean crisis that bedeviled the Meadow in 2010 never occurred in the Park because *South Korea had earlier acquired nuclear weapons* and the North was unwilling to test Southern resolve to use these weapons, even against other Koreans. *Japan's leapfrogging of nuclear technology* had set in motion nuclear proliferation to Korea, and this had the ironic effect of pushing U.S. forces (some would say releasing them) from the Korean peninsula. Once the *Japanese navy went postnuclear, the Koreans demanded an American nuclear guarantee against Japan. This the Americans were unwilling to give,* though various other assurances were offered, including the continued forward positioning of U.S. troops as a kind of hostage to Japanese intentions. The Koreans, however, determined to deploy nuclear weapons on their own—they faced potential adversaries on every frontier (China, Russia, North Korea, Japan)—and, after lengthy but failed bargaining, went ahead with these deployments, as a result of which the *American forces, as well as their nuclear umbrella, were withdrawn.*

The South Koreans had the wealth and the technocracy to deploy these weapons, but the world was surprised at the speed with which the necessary advanced technology found its way to South Korea, whose nuclear reactors had a spotless International Atomic Energy Agency (IAEA) inspection record. In the summer of 2010 an event took place at the Indian port of Kandla that led to an unraveling of the true history of the Korean program. At Kandla, Indian customs officials acting on a tip demanded to examine the hold of a Korean ship unloading a cargo of sugar. Inside the 9,600-ton steamer they found 150 containers listed on the cargo manifest as "water purification machinery" destined for Malta. These containers in fact held warhead components. In time it was revealed that a *lucrative partnership in nuclear delivery systems (China), fissile material (Russia), and warhead design and computer simulation (Israel) had loosely cooperated to arm,* or partially arm, a number of wealthy but otherwise unlikely states. By this means, *Iran acquired nuclear weapons,* one of which was detonated in an underground test in 2012. Pakistan and India had weaponized their own nuclear materials as far back as 1998. *Now two consortia of states—Iraq, Russia, and India on the one hand; China, Pakistan, and North Korea on the other—competed as suppliers in the burgeoning trade in nuclear weapons technology and delivery systems. When Indonesia acquired MRBMs in 2011, Australia pulled out of the ANZUS pact and began to develop weapons of its own.* This in turn prompted a rush for weapons by Malaysia and Tokyo; in the region, only Taiwan held back, at least overtly, from nuclear or postnuclear weapons of mass destruction, and clung to the American security guarantee.

The American guarantee was abrogated when evidence was laid before the press showing that *Taiwan had approached two Italian suppliers for technology* whose only practical use could have been to develop chemical and biological weapons delivered by medium-range ballistic missiles. These disclosures confirmed what had long been suspected: that the states of the European Union were violating treaty restrictions on the export of nuclear and missile technology. *France had aided Iraq by providing crucial technology at about the same time German companies helped bring Iran into the nuclear club.* When international terrorism repeatedly hit the United States but not the European mainland, American alienation increased.

The public outcry in the United States at these revelations may have hastened the inevitable shift from a European security pillar within NATO to a separate E.U. community-wide defense system. After some modest progress toward political union in the late 1990s, the *European Union now attempted to create a common defense policy* under the umbrella of a European Defense Community (to which particular weapons and units were assigned) within the Western European Union (which largely replaced the role of NATO and from which the United States was excluded). *U.S. troops were entirely withdrawn from the continental landmass of Europe,* though they continued to conduct joint naval exercises with Britain.

The Fifth Yugoslav War never occurred because *NATO forces were withdrawn from the Balkans in 2005 as a result of U.S. retrenchment.* Serbia and Croatia quickly partitioned Bosnia with tacit European support and Serbian forces retook Kosovo the following year. This returned the province to the legal status quo ante the NATO intervention of 1999, with some residual terrorism by the Kosovo Liberation Army (KLA) but with less depredation by Belgrade.

British and French nuclear weapons were assigned to the EDC, for use under EDC/WEU commands, on a dual key basis—that is, both the French or British commander and his EDC/WEU counterpart had to concur before any weapons could actually be used. Two developments soon cast doubt on this arrangement: first, the French refused to participate in planning that would target any of the states of Eastern Europe or the former Soviet Union, even after it was learned that Ukraine had deployed weapons thought to have been turned over in 1996 to Russia; second, the United Kingdom refused to take part in planning that would target the United States. *The result of this dissension was the so-called Multilayered Concord, which delegated some weapons to the EDC for "all-azimuth planning" but not actual targeting,* and provided some rather general rules for WEU engagement. *After Russia's amalgamation with Belarus, Poland acquired a limited number of postnuclear weapons* (possibly with French commercial collusion), putting the accord in question and generating inevitable pressures in Germany for that state to acquire her own nuclear and postnuclear arsenal. Concern for reassuring Russia, however, checked any German moves in this direction and, by 2015 EDC nuclearization, including the Multilayered Concord, still held. German access to a nuclear trigger continued to depend on British or French concurrence. *That year Slovakia and Ukraine were made associate members of the E.U.* (Slovenia and Croatia having previously achieved this status along with Poland, Hungary, and the Czech Republic) and *atomic demolition mines were deployed in the High Tatras of Slovakia.*

Europe had set a pattern for the development of regional security associations that now sprang up all across the society of market-states. Authorized by the U.N. Charter and created pursuant to Security Council resolutions, these associations were created to deal with the sort of problem that the U.N. and the E.U. had ducked in 2004 when the Balkan crisis had erupted. Principal among these were the *North Asia Security Group* (including South Korea, Japan, and China), the *West African Organization for Peace* (Nigeria, Cameroon, Ghana, and Cote d'Ivoire), the *South Pacific Treaty Association* (Malaysia, Singapore, the Philippines, Indonesia, and Viet Nam), the *Caspian Sea Security Arrangement* (Georgia, Azerbaijan, Kazakhstan, and Turkmenistan), and others.

These regional arrangements were a force for stability, but they were not without shortcomings. First, they tended to be relatively passive because, even following Security Council reform, it was still easy to block any U.N. endorsement of action. Various horrors in South Asia, South Africa, and Guyana had failed to prompt armed intervention. Second, *key states with respect to a particular regional group—like Russia and the Caspian Sea Security Arrangement, or China and the South Pacific Treaty Association—were disinclined to participate,* fearing their pockets would be picked by the other members who would rely on them for funding. Third, the true security interests of market-states were not especially regional, being connected instead through an abstract archipelago of shared economic and cultural interests.

All of these factors were in play when *China seized Taiwan* in a series of shrewdly planned, if brutal moves. China's navy and air forces were large, but consisted mainly of small coastal craft, antiquated Soviet submarines, and obsolete fighter aircraft. There was little fear that China could conduct a successful amphibious assault against the island. Moreover, China's nuclear weapons were scarcely suited to reuniting a related but recalcitrant province. It was rather *China's acquisition of neutron bomb technology* (aided perhaps by espionage) that proved the key to the takeover. In an assault that was murderous but highly confined, China attacked military targets with ballistic weapons that were conventionally armed and, hours later, irradiated the largely Formosan city of Tainan, one of the centers of the independence movement. It is estimated a quarter of a million persons died in the brief, two-week campaign. *The United States no longer perceived itself as a protector of Taiwan. The regional group did not want to get involved. Action by the U.N. was stopped by the Chinese who treated the entire affair as an internal matter.*

This event again focused attention on the U.N. and its provisions for regional security organizations. *Security Council reform had already changed the membership of that body*: the European members (France and the United Kingdom) had been replaced by a single E.U. representative. Representatives of India, the Southern Cone Common Market (Mercosur), and the Association of Southeast Asian Nations (ASEAN) also sat as permanent members of the Council. Moreover, the veto power vested in permanent members was modified to prevent a veto that would trump action recommended by a unanimous regional group, which is simply to say that nonregional permanent members could not stop action outside their own immediate regions. By 2020, however, regional forces had completely replaced any "blue-hatted" U.N. peacekeepers just as NGOs had replaced the U.N.'s humanitarian arm, though it must be conceded that these regional forces were used chiefly to suppress separatist movements at the behest of various states. This paved the way for a universal consensus around a concept of sovereignty that would have been familiar to international lawyers of the second half of the twentieth century. One might call it "sovereignty with exceptions," meaning that the classic view of impermeable sovereignty was qualified only to the extent that the U.N. Charter was held to endorse such limitations. This satisfied both large states—that wished to avoid being drawn into local conflicts—and small states that feared intervention. The state leaders of The Park considered themselves worldly wise: they did not chase after humanitarian crises; they were willing to accommodate the facts of life; above all, they sought reassurance in alliances with those to whom they were historically bound. This set the stage for great power confrontation among the three great blocs—Asian, American, and European.

CULTURE

In the uncertain economic environment following the American recession, a new destabilizing element appeared: the shift in the ratio between young and old. In 2003, Italy's population of persons sixty-five years of age and over passed 20 percent of the total; Japan followed in 2005 and Germany in 2006. France and Britain arrived at this figure in 2015. At the same time, global life expectancy was rapidly growing. As life spans increased, fertility rates in the developed world plummeted. As recently as the 1960s, the worldwide fertility rate (the average number of lifetime births per woman) was at 5.0. By 2000 it stood at 2.7—a figure fast approaching the replacement rate of 2.1. In the developed world, the average fertility rate declined to 1.6. By 2000, Japan was projecting a population decline of 20 percent in the ensuing two and a half decades. In Germany, where the rate had fallen to 1.3 by 2000, fewer babies had been born each year in the 1990s than in Nepal. In the United States this development had been masked by large numbers of immigrants, who included families with higher fertility rates than those of native-born Americans. The looming demographic crisis pitted young unemployed persons against taxpaying workers against pensioners. As a result of this tricornered struggle, by 2010 the politics of social security reform became effectively paralyzed. Governments were forced to make severe cuts in defense spending, infrastructure maintenance, and finally in health benefits.

These developments—unemployment, social tensions among groups, and a recession that followed government cutbacks—brought to power a number of reform-minded governments determined to protect the youth who had elected them. To invigorate their economies—and mindful that falling population rates could not be made up by productivity gains—*states in the developed world followed the U.S. example and began loosening their immigration rules.* These immigrants brought with them higher fertility rates and lower labor costs, forcing a revision of state-regulated employment practices that had stifled growth. In Germany, foreign workers rose to 40 percent of the workforce by 2025 and dominated cities like Munich and Frankfurt. At the same time, *governments began encouraging higher fertility rates and investing more in the education and the productivity of future workers.* In the high-tax states that followed the managerial market-state model *tax credits were offered for taking intergenerational responsibility within families, including home day care for the young and residence care for the elderly.* Because these popular measures directly attacked the existing social contract and affronted entrenched ideologies and interests, they opened up the politics of these states to reform; and because such policies brought youth into the reform camp, the parties of the past with their addiction to state ownership withered away.

The economic turmoil leading up to this revision and the demographic crisis that brought it to a head were certainly critical factors; so also was the growth in knowledge about how other people live and how other social systems function, which fueled immigration. The core E.U. was now powered by two late twentieth century developments that had appeared to be a drain on the E.U.: the takeover of East Germany, bringing a well-educated workforce into the capital system, and the proximity of Poland, Hungary, the Czech Republic, Slovenia, the Baltic states, and Ukraine, which enlarged the E.U. and provided cheaper labor and a vast new market for consumer goods once they were assured that their national cultures would be respected. Indeed it was the ability of the managerial market-states to recognize the rights of cultural minorities—including the United States with its decentralized constitutional system of federalism—that ultimately provided a key to success.

One important constitutional tool in the institutionalization of this respect for minorities was the relative ease with which devolved partial states were created. *Regions in Italy (the northern industrialized region centering on Milan and Lombardy), Spain (Catalonia and the Basque region), Canada (Quebec and the city-state of Vancouver), and the United Kingdom (Wales and Scotland) all "devolved" into new states* with varying defense and trade relations to their parent states or, like the *two partial states that emerged from the breakup of Belgium, sheltered within the economic and defense community of the E.U.* The results were generally positive: the new states retained the role of reinforcing the historic culture of their peoples (something the market-state had been in danger of losing as it became more meritocratic, more multicultural, and more secular). As one observer noted:

> In social policy terms, regional organizations allowed different ethnic groups to choose their own cultural policy. In Europe, for example, demands for Basque language schools subsided as it became apparent that, while the Basques were not happy to be schooled in Spanish, they were perfectly happy to be schooled in English with Basque as their second language. By 2025 all of Europe and much of Asia had accepted the policy of "English plus two," meaning that primary and secondary school students were taught in English and two other languages, usually their native language and one foreign language.[13]

In the United States, cultural groups were allowed, by constitutional amendments that altered the application of the 14th Amendment, to transform states to their own liking. This led to considerable migration within the United States as its citizens sought congenial states that catered to religious, ethnic, and political preferences. *All these new "states" retained an open trade relation with the rest of the United States much like the one that prevailed in Europe within the E.U., and all adhered to a common defense policy with the rest of the United States under a much-shrunken defense establishment. Only their state constitutions were radically different: some permitted a union of church and state; some allowed the prosecution of "hate speech" and forbade books and movies that reinforced racial or gender stereotypes; some reintroduced corporal punishment, while others forbade capital punishment. There were feminist states where women were given certain affirmative benefits, including requirements that a certain number of officeholders and corporate board members be women; there were religious fundamentalist states that forbade commercial transactions on the Sabbath, required prayer in schools, and outlawed the sale of alcohol; there were ethnic states where English was a second language;* and so on. In short, the new states permitted a closer match between the values of a certain polity and its legal rules—a reaction, it may be said, to the market-state's indifference to cultural values.

This ability to decentralize not only liberated the political evolution of the highly developed states; it also led to a recognition of the economic, social, and environmental interdependence of states. *Green tariffs*—which penalized imports from states that did not obey Kyoto standards for environmental protection—date from this period. States in The Park were well-positioned to create the *World Environmental Organization* in 2008 as a follow-up to the Rio de Janeiro initiatives of the late 1990s. States were able to agree, as they were not at Rio, on principles of allocating environmental property rights. *The WEO administered these rights, sometimes arbitrating, sometimes auctioning off rights.* The largest step forward occurred in 2012 when the *WEO won agreement on rules for tradable licenses to water, fishing, and emissions rights. The introduction of fungible carbon dioxide emission rights had come somewhat earlier.* Thus different regions were able to achieve environmental targets in different ways, while bartering development and pollution rights globally.

The creation of other multinational institutions followed: the World Commission on Biotechnology in 2010 and the World Commission on Internet Privacy in 2013. In some quarters, these commissions were viewed as high-handed and stifling of innovation, but the general view was that the society of states was better able to manage a new generation of multinational institutions in The Park than under other global approaches.

Finally, though total wages grew more slowly than in The Meadow, wage disparities within the states of The Park were far less. Indeed, the relatively high wages in the developed world tended to encourage growth in the developing world. The Asian Industrial Prosperity Conference and the North American Free Trade Association were able to raise wages to such a degree that *multinational corporations looked to Africa to reduce their labor costs.* This resulted in a slowing of migration to African cities as *factory complexes were sited beyond the supercities.* This allowed Africa to avoid the flight to the coastal cities that plagued The Meadow, with the consequence that hygiene and sanitation were sufficient to mitigate the health threats that had haunted Africa.

ECONOMICS

The Park was characterized by three great blocs of states whose leading members had chosen some form of the *Soziale Marktwirtschaft*. The decisive step had been taken in 2005 by the *United States when it rejected a British proposal for a "virtual" regional free trade alliance that would have included Japan, and decided instead to pursue a larger NAFTA*. The result was a hardening of regional lines and a surge of regional protectionism.

Within three blocs—led by Germany, Japan, and the United States respectively—trade flourished. By the year 2025, market-states within these groupings were exporting 50 percent of their production, even though most of this product was, at some point, made in other states. By adding value at the high end, and *by erecting a forbidding tariff wall around the trading bloc*, individual member states were able to maintain a large share of global profits through repatriation. At the same time, the protectionism of the regional blocs tended to retard the advance and diffusion of technology, and to reduce economies of scale. Conflicts over market openings for high technology became endemic, with charges of pirating and predatory pricing being frequently and acrimoniously exchanged.

Unemployment was relatively high within these blocs, usually above 10 percent in the years between 2000 and 2025 in the Americas, almost 20 percent in Europe—but a jobless worker with a family could draw benefits equal to almost 70 percent of his former net earnings (somewhat less in the Asian countries). There were generous child allowances, substantially larger for poorer families, to the age of seventeen—or twenty-one if the child elected to go to college or state-sponsored vocational training. Parents drew child-rearing benefits for up to two years if they chose to take work leaves in order to stay home with children; job rights for those taking parental leaves were protected for three years.[14] Periodic efforts to change provisions like these in order to curtail government expenditure collided with the fundamental sense of fairness that pervaded states in The Park. True, innovations like domestic robots were more expensive than they might otherwise have been and the most efficient hybrid fuel vehicles were beyond the reach of most—a painful fact as governments began to enforce more and more stringent air-quality controls—but the price of these items eventually came down. Innovation occurred, but at a far slower pace and with more expensive development costs than would otherwise have been the case.

The principal external effect of the dominance of these three great groups of states was to restrict growth in the Third World by shifting the terms of trade sharply against raw-materials producers, though wages did rise in the developing world as corporations fled the high-wage blocs.

Within the blocs, the main result was to delay innovation and increase costs to the consumer. Both internally and externally, the Park encouraged state fragmentation within the umbrellas of its larger groups and beneath the sheltering international institutions that it excelled at creating and maintaining.

While many persons feared a Y2K crisis over New Year's Day 2000, this never materialized. What came later, however, was an infrastructure overload that cascaded through interconnected systems, apparently coincidentally, on New Year's Day 2005. Many analysts now believe this event triggered the stock market crash in 2005. The flight to the euro resulted in a 40 percent appreciation against the dollar, effectively destroying European exports. When the world recession struck in 2006, growth in The Park, which had been sluggish, turned sharply negative.

The Park was hampered in its recovery by a problem that, though hardly unique to this particular society of states, was characteristic of it. This was the phenomenon of "moral hazard"—overaggressive risk taking pursued in the confidence that market-state governments would not permit truly large enterprises—or interest groups—to fail. It was evident, for example, that the *Federal Deposit Insurance Corporation provisions in the United States induced many savers to make deposits in bankrupt banks and savings institutions* because these desperate enterprises were offering the highest rates on short-term deposits. American savers correctly calculated that the government would bail them out when the crash came. Similarly, the difficulty for states in The Park was that, by removing risk from some investments, these states crippled the ability of the market to discipline investment and brought about costly misallocations. Although the hardest hit economies in The Park were India, Nigeria, and Brazil, all economies suffered from this phenomenon because the social safety nets of The Park created perverse incentives by distorting true market risks. Furthermore, the high trading walls of the three great blocs prevented the development of a truly global system of reinsurance that would have cushioned the setbacks of this decade.

Instead, states of The Park turned to the creation of new international financial institutions. In 2006, *a conference in Paris resulted in the transfer of the functions of the IMF to new institutions,* more market-state than nation-state in their orientation (and located outside of Washington). First, the *Commission on Monetary Stability was given authority to combat speculation not by trying to outbid speculators, but by negotiating complicated baskets* that bundled various currencies together and stabilized Third World monies by tying them to the dollar, the yen, or the euro. This commission was sometimes referred to as a New Bretton Woods, but its methods were decidedly those of the market-state. Second, *the International Banking Board was created in order to oversee the capital adequacy of banks* and their provisions for bad loans—not by mandating certain ratios but by publicizing the prevailing ratios and permitting shareholders to do the enforcing—and to prevent money laundering by much the same methods of transparency and public revelation. Third, *the Agency on International Transactions attempted to prevent e-commerce from evading national value-added and sales taxes* by licensing only certain firms on the Internet. It also aimed to create exceptions to sovereignty in order to prevent tax havens in the Caribbean, the Pacific, and elsewhere and to employ electronic monitoring to track liquid capital. It must be said that these efforts were not entirely successful, owing in part to corruption within some of the agencies created. Finally, *the mission of the World Bank was changed from a lender-for-development to the Third World to a lender-of-last-resort* for countries who could persuade the bank that avoiding default was to the economic benefit of the entire society of states, and not simply for the sake of the potentially defaulting state.

These institutional measures were of some benefit to the northern-tier blocs, but they did little to cushion the main effect of The Park, which was the rupture of North-South economic relations. Writing in 2020 and looking back on this period, one commentator observed:

> This age of fragmentation and regrouping within the society of market-states took place on account of the rupture of trade and interdependence between North and South. When the developed states looked to the South they saw refugees pounding on their golden doors, driven northward by the squalor, crime, disease, and environmental degradation that seemed immune to human ingenuity once a certain level of population growth and resource exhaustion had occurred. When the undeveloped states of the South looked to the North for investment and assistance, they believed they received instead cultural viruses of secularism, materialism, racism, and neocolonialism. In both cases, the result was an increase in regional capitalism enforced by protectionist barriers to the import of investment or goods.[15]

Without growth in the underdeveloped states, the northern-tier economies stagnated for a lack of new markets. With their aging populations, savings rates in these countries plummeted and, along with them, the rate of new investment. In each of the principal states of the former First World, government deficits burgeoned as older populations demanded more and more services that had become more and more expensive (including costly anti-aging genomic treatments). The fragmentation of the polities of these states along cultural and ideological lines—the creation of interest groups willing and able to block legislation that did not buy off their constituents—paralyzed the adoption of the fiscal policies necessary to cope with these demands. This paralysis was worsened by *the adoption, first in the United Kingdom, but later in the United States* and elsewhere, *of a system of proportional representation in parliament and Congress.* The revenue base of governments eroded as capital moved abroad beyond the reach of tax collection. Many wealthy persons ceased to think of themselves in national terms and adopted tax residences in state havens abroad where their income could be sheltered.

Concern about the environment led to costly regulations, which had the effect of imposing ever higher barriers on the products of the undeveloped world. *States like China and India that refused to reduce emissions* found their products barred from entry to lucrative First World markets. Agreement to reduce emissions, however, meant imposing lower standards of living on local populations and immense capital costs on producers. Either way, the effect was to close the markets of the developed world, just as *concern about genetically engineered foods had closed the E.U. to American exports,* or *concern about child labor had closed the United States to Asian exports.* Interest groups in the Park struck alliances that invariably proved costly to economic vitality.

With export-driven growth cut off and without investment inflows from the developed states, the economic situation of the underdeveloped states grew worse. Overpopulation led to resource scarcity; resource scarcity led to deforestation and desertification, which led in turn to water shortages and migrations to cities that were plagued with disease, crime, and a breakdown in political authority. Except in search of lower wages multinational corporations were reluctant to be lured to these countries, even when enticed with large tax incentives. The other such incentive—relaxed regulations—had backfired in the face of so-called *green tariffs imposed at the behest of an alliance between environmental groups and First World companies* saddled with expensive environmental regulations. These provisions kept the products of poorer countries without environmental safeguards out of First World markets. Thus the opportunity to garner capital for infrastructure from exports wilted.

The effects of these policies can be seen in India's experience in The Park at this period. Owing to resistance from various interest groups— civil servants, workers in long-protected domestic industries, political allies of the ruling government, even religious and ethnic groups that had been subsidized—it was difficult for reform regimes to modernize the Indian economy. The socialist policies of the Indian nation-state were largely dismantled and domestic competition thrived, but truly radical reforms that would make products export-worthy were harder to bring about. Secessionist movements not only in Kashmir and Punjab but in literally dozens of smaller areas were a constant threat to the central government.

The consequences of falling water tables served as the flash point between the Muslim and Hindu populations relying on irrigation in the Indus River Basin. Pakistan had not participated in the growth experienced by India. With 65 percent of its land dependent on intensive irrigation, with widespread deforestation and a yearly population growth of 2.7 percent, Pakistan had no margin for failure when crop yields began to plummet in 2015. *Neither the Indian nor the Pakistani government was strong enough to enforce restrictions on water use;* neither had the legitimacy among its starving citizens to get them to refrain from attempting to drive away their neighbors in order to cultivate more land. The Water Wars of the Indus that began in 2017 lasted ten years. By the end of this period, 140 million people had starved or been driven from their homes by violence. (This dwarfed the 1960 famine in China, in which thirty million are supposed to have died.) *International attempts at mediation—even the supply of emergency food relief—were rebuffed by officials on grounds of "Indian dignity."* The arrival of partial laser-fusion eventually would reverse the draining of the water supply by providing power to tap freshwater sources in the Himalayas, but this technology required capital investments on such a huge scale that only very large, wealthy states could afford it, and there were no such states remaining on the subcontinent. Pakistan had devolved into a patchwork of ethnic states of which Pakhtunistan was the largest and throughout which a strict Islamic code prevailed; India had fragmented into a loose congress of more than fifty states—largely organized along linguistic and religious lines. If these devolved states were too weak to enforce population growth control or environmental protection, and too contentious to ally in order to accumulate capital, they were also too feeble to wage war on a continental scale. One of the remarkable facts about *the Water Wars is that neither side used nuclear weapons,* though both possessed them, perhaps, one may speculate, because the small size of their respective arsenals encouraged them to husband such weapons. As a result, the soils of the subcontinent, though depleted, were not irradiated, and began slowly to recover as new genetically modified grains came into being, and population rates leveled off and then fell.

The lesson learned by the states of The Park was that regional protectionism tended to lock in high unemployment rates and slow growth in part because it locked out global capital flows and the rapid diffusion of new technology. Coping with these problems gave a new lease on life to government agencies that might otherwise have died with the nation-state but that remained and further hampered economic efficiency.

THE GARDEN

SECURITY

The U.S elections of 2008, it can be seen in retrospect, were a watershed in American politics, not so much for the new leaders in both Congress and the White House who were brought to the world stage as for the consensus reflected in the election results that the governance of the preceding years—both Democratic and Republican—had been misguided. The slow recovery from the recession encouraged protectionist barriers to trade; these further constrained the global recovery and invited foreign criticism that Americans found irksome. American pre-eminence in many arenas was perceived abroad as hegemony and contributed to a U.S./European estrangement. Traditional ethnocentrism in Asia coupled with mercantile trade policies intensified the sense of mutual alienation that arose between Americans and Asians.

In a stunning repudiation of previous policy, a public consensus in the United States emerged that the multilateral interventions of the previous twelve years had been a mistake. The steady, unpredictable terrorist attacks (and, it must be said the harrowing but fruitless "alerts") left the United States demoralized. Many believed that, but for American involvement abroad, the terror campaigns would never have happened. The collapse of Haitian democracy; the televised melees in the refugee camps of Burundi and Rwanda, in which Western aid workers were set on fire; and the much-publicized case of a French commander at NATO headquarters in Brussels, apparently part of a vast network of agents, who had been stealing high-tech American industrial secrets in order to aid French companies— all these had the effect of extinguishing the enthusiasm of the U.S. public for foreign cooperation. Undoubtedly the decisive event, however, was the discovery that, through a complicated system of loans guaranteed by foreign government bonds, *both U.S. political parties had unwittingly accepted huge sums of money from foreign governments* whose role was hidden by the use of intermediaries. Disillusionment and disgust swept across the entire landscape of foreign policy engagement: *U.S. support for the U.N., which then stood at 25 percent of the U.N. annual budget, was reduced to 10 percent* by a joint resolution of Congress on the technical ground that the U.N. was not permitted to acquire debt without the express permission of the Security Council (debt that had in fact accumulated as a result of a U.S. refusal to pay its dues). *U.S. foreign aid, which had stabilized at a meager $10 billion, was slashed by 30 percent with a proviso that it was to be phased out altogether over a ten-year period; funds originally earmarked for Russia to assist with denuclearization were cut completely* when comptroller reports disclosed widespread skimming by Russian officials. For roughly similar reasons, *U.S. support for drug* *eradication in other countries, largely Latin American and Asian, was simply stopped.* After a fruitless effort to get NATO to intervene in the renewed Balkan conflict, the United States had allowed the North Atlantic Council to fall into desuetude, and at this time the top three NATO commanders were all non-American. But the most dramatic breaks in policy occurred with those states who had been caught in the campaign finance scheme: Israel, China, and the Gulf States.

The United States had played a pivotal role in the Middle East since 1948. The disclosure of covert campaign assistance by Middle Eastern governments to both American political parties coincided with widely televised, violent Israeli repression of Palestinian marches for suffrage in the occupied areas still under Israeli control, and the savage suppression of a "pro-democracy" movement in Kuwait (including allegations of beheadings). Many Americans suspected, although probably without foundation, that the campaign finance loans by foreign governments had effectively bought U.S. military assistance to both states. The result was *the withdrawal of U.S. naval forces in the region and a sharp scaling back in security assistance.* The continuous fall in world energy prices had reduced the importance of the region to American interests, but it was at least as significant that, after sixty years, the regional conflict in that area seemed no closer to resolution. *The United States virtually withdrew from any high-profile leadership in the area, taking with it $3 billion in direct aid to Israel and about $2 billion in aid to Egypt.*

In Asia, once the Chinese regime had been listed as a "human rights abuser" by the United States in 2004, *U.S. statutory restrictions kicked in that had the effect of virtually ceding Chinese markets to European, Korean, and Japanese exports.* When Chinese covert campaign assistance came to light, it appeared that the Chinese were trying to reverse this "decertification" process by corrupt means. There was some evidence that members of Congress and the administration had made promises to Chinese intermediaries that were embarrassing, and that they had made public statements that were plainly at variance with the known facts about Chinese human rights policies. It appeared that in many places—Panama and Haiti, Israel and the Gulf, China and Russia—American meddling had been expensive and counterproductive; now this appearance was acutely enhanced by the fact of foreign meddling in American affairs, suggesting to some that hidden forces were manipulating U.S. policy.

Perhaps no line received as much applause at the Inauguration as when on January 20, 2009, the new American president said,

> No one can see the future. But the recent past has taught us that we must let every nation develop in its own way, making its own mistakes perhaps but living and growing according to its own lights. To do otherwise

encourages dependency in the weak and the constant drain of resources from the strong, and above all, interference in other people's business. No one—and no organization—is anointed to decide which nations shall survive and which shall be left to fail. We shall tend our own garden.

When the Sri Lankan massacres occurred, when the South African coup took place—even when the situation in Guyana potentially threatened a renewal of the boat people crises of the 1990s (only worse, because these refugees were laden with disease), even then the *United States studiously did not intervene*. Other states were in much the same mood. In Japan, the Liberal Democratic government had fallen over its insistence on observing the U.S./Japan Status of Forces Agreement's provision that American servicemen indicted for crimes in Japan be tried in the United States. A brutal rape by a group of American sailors based in Yokohama had become a cause célèbre; in the elections that followed, a coalition came to power pledged to terminate the treaty and to demand the withdrawal of all U.S. forces from Japan. "The Occupation Is Over"—*Senryou Teppai!*—was the campaign slogan of the victorious candidates. The new government's pledge to increase self-reliance struck a welcome chord with the Japanese public. Few voices of dissent were raised when *the Japanese defense budget—since 1989 the third largest in the world—was raised by 15 percent* to develop and procure a new generation of cyber weapons, leapfrogging the delivery systems of the late twentieth century. These weapons primarily targeted information centers and networks rather than conventional military bases, harbors, and railway centers. With respect to these latter targets, the Japanese nuclear-powered submarines that had flourished in the late twentieth century took over as platforms for a new generation of smaller but equally lethal postnuclear warheads. The accuracy of these systems, directed by Japanese "black"—undetectable—satellites, permitted the Japanese to continue their adherence to the Nuclear Nonproliferation Treaty while advancing to a newer generation of weapons of mass destruction that the United States had yet to deploy. Japanese rearmament was sufficient to check North Korean ambitions on the peninsula, but this had the unintended and undesired consequence—from the Japanese point of view—of bringing about a closer relationship between the two Koreas.

These events led to what became commonly known as the Iron Triangles, a series of interlocking deterrence relationships around the world in which, it was believed, a mutual stability was achieved through nuclear proliferation among regional adversaries. China-Korea-Japan; Germany-Russia-Ukraine; India-Pakistan-China; Iran-Israel-Iraq; Australia-Indonesia-Malaysia; Chile-Argentina-Brazil: these were the main Iron Triangles, with subsidiary triangles such as Singapore–China–Viet Nam, Germany-Poland-Russia, France–Germany–Great Britain.

The intense trade in weapons and delivery systems was responsible, as much as any other single factor, for the surge in capital growth in Russia and the liberalization of the Chinese regime once it effectively merged with the now-compliant island of Taiwan. Unable to either acquire nuclear weapons (for fear of Chinese pre-emption) or hold on to a U.S. defense commitment, *Taiwan had been forced to negotiate a union with the mainland*. With the Hong Kong Chinese and the Shenzhen, the Taiwanese had effectively bought their way into influence with the army with the promise of larger defense budgets and had managed to significantly liberalize the Chinese political environment. In 2018 the *Chinese capital was moved to Shanghai,* and *Tibet was allowed limited autonomy as a theocratic state.*

Only two states stood aloof from this rapidly replicating system of mutual deterrence relationships: South Africa and the United States. *South Africa renounced all weapons of mass destruction* and became a haven for persons everywhere seeking refuge from the terror of nuclear war. *The United States, having no obvious proximate adversaries, devoted its attention to developing ballistic missile and anti-aircraft defenses* that, by the year 2020, were confidently thought to be effective against the sort of proliferated delivery systems that most states were now acquiring. The preceding period of arms control and reduction was now seen by most commentators as one of intense danger in which the United States and other powerful states had unsuccessfully attempted, through the Nuclear Nonproliferation Treaty and the Missile Technology Control Regime, to determine what states would be allowed to have the weapons of survival. This had been replaced by a more stable international environment, it was usually said. Terrorism had steadily abated during this period.

At least this was the common opinion when, on May 1, 2021, the *Russian government announced that it was the subject of an extortion demand and asked for financial support from the international community.* This demand came from a shadowy group that claimed to have control over a biological/computer virus that could spread a debilitating influenza through the Internet. This threat struck directly at the weakness of international institutions during this period—for who was there to broker such financial support? Or to determine whether elements of the Russian government itself were behind the scheme?

The Russian government had promised to bring prosperity by relying on unique Russian capabilities in two areas: natural resources and the arms trade. The energy sector had been nominally privatized but in fact was part of a cooperative complex that included not only the large energy firms that had succeeded Gazprom, but also the principal banks and the armed forces. This system was highly popular with the public because it promised growth after years of economic stagnation. Arms deals flourished and Russian exports soared. Few realized, however, that Russian weapons development would include biological weapons or that it might be possible to create a "doomsday" machine that could spread biological agents electronically.

The classic view of sovereignty dominated this period and reinforced Russia in its assertions that its internal affairs—especially how to investigate and prosecute crimes—were finally a matter for its own determination. Nevertheless *there were calls from many countries, including the United States, for an international investigation*—even intervention—in order to head off the possibility that this virtual machine would be turned on other countries. For the first time since the fall of the Berlin Wall, a superpower crisis occurred that had the potential to lead to a cataclysm. The United States, which had withdrawn from Eurasian affairs, now seemed prepared to reassert itself in an environment fraught with peril. Highly threatening messages were exchanged over a hotline (a satellite system that sends only written, coded text) that had not been used for decades. U.S. nuclear warheads targeted a laboratory beneath a mountain in the Caucasus where it was believed the conspirators were working; no other weapon was powerful enough to guarantee destruction of the lab.

In the event, Russian police work—using methods that were not for the squeamish—successfully ended the crisis. By resolving matters without resorting to intervention, the society of states had strengthened the shared confidence that its members would be allowed to develop in their ways. The *doomsday virtual machine was "dismantled" and handed over to a consortium of states that agreed to provide long-term credits to Russia.*

This period had enshrined, as never before, the absolute equality of states to determine their own security needs. In so doing, the society of market-states bore unavoidable responsibility for refusing to protect some (such as Taiwan or the many states of the Third World like Sri Lanka who became de facto provinces of their nuclear neighbors) or to shore up the positions of those states least likely to engage in aggression (like the United States). "Let many flowers bloom" was a popular political slogan during this era, but gardens take cultivation and selection, whereas the society of states resolutely refused to prefer one regime to another, leaving it to fate to determine which one would find itself outside the stability-conferring systems of terror and technology. The Garden also brought the world closer to a nuclear cataclysm between the United States and Russia than it had been since the end of the Cold War.

CULTURE

The enormous wealth made possible by the technological breakthroughs of this period, especially laser-fusion, fueled the recovery from the

2005–2009 recession, but it was simply not enough to paper over the cultural chasms that opened up among states. These chasms were in part the result of the dizzying growth in the knowledge about how other people live and how other societies' systems work. A deep alienation arose between the states of the developed North and the underdeveloped South and also even within states, leading to a fragmentation of the world trading system and the creation of the first new states since the collapse of the Soviet Union and of Yugoslavia in the 1990s. In some parts of the world, the terrifying appearance of the weather epidemics followed by the OOA-V plague raised suspicions that government agencies in the developed world—the CIA was often mentioned—were deliberately trying to depopulate the Third World.

In the 1990s, an analyst from the policy planning staff of the U.S. Department of State had concluded that the "unfolding of modern natural science has had a uniform effect on all societies that have experienced it. . . . This process guarantees an increasing homogenization of all human societies, regardless of their historical origins or cultural inheritances."[16] He further concluded that these forces "have a powerful effect in undermining traditional social groups like tribes, clans, extended families, religious sects, and so on,"[17] and predicted "something like a Universal History of mankind in the direction of liberal democracy"[18] which actually seemed about to come true in the wake of the commitments of the Peace of Paris. In retrospect we can see, however, that the disruption of traditional societies and values had exactly the opposite effect, rendering the South suspicious and insular, and ultimately fractionating the progressive states of the North. Moreover, one of the consequences of modern science, advancing automation, deprived the South of the capital benefits of cheap labor that would otherwise have resulted from globalization. With hostility and fear toward the messages that advanced telecommunications would bring, and without the capital to build the telecommunications infrastructure needed to exploit that technology for their own benefit, the states of the South gradually sank into a kind of silence, but not before they had received pictures, and been pictured, in ways that deeply alienated the two parts of the globe from each other.

Emblematic of this mutual misunderstanding was the massacre at Times Square in 2005, only one year after the final collapse of the remnants of the Al Qaeda network that had savagely attacked the United States in 2001. The movie version of the novel *Mahomet* depicted the prophet as a young man in defiance of the Islamic injunction not to portray his face. Perhaps because the script had been the subject of worldwide protests, large crowds were gathered on the evening of the premiere at a theatre on 42nd Street in Manhattan. *The movie's principal actors, as well as about two hundred persons, including many adolescents, were attacked with automatic weapons by a militant Islamicist group.* More than fifty were killed. The pictures of the massacre—the entire scene was captured on video—were repeatedly played across the world and, to the growing consternation of many, produced diametrically opposed opinions in different countries. In the West there was outrage at the killing; in many Islamic states, the terrorists were regarded as heroes. *When their release was achieved through a bombing campaign against movie theatres* that threatened to shut down the film industry, *the West embargoed oil sales from Iran* (where the terrorists had turned up to a tumultuous welcome). *This proved to be the first in a series of economic reprisals against various oil-producing states in the Middle East,* which had the unfortunate effect of raising oil prices and slowing growth early in the century. There seemed to come from the Islamic world a surge of hatred that distressed, alarmed, and above all baffled[19] persons in the West. In retrospect this should not have come as a surprise.[20]

In the opening decades of the twenty-first century, Muslims had suffered successive stages of humiliation at the hands of the West. The first was their loss of a leading role in the world economy as other energy sources—principally owing to laser-fusion technology, which brought the long-sought "hydrogen economy" into being—finally lessened reliance on the fossil fuels that were the source of wealth for many Muslim states. The second was the undermining of Muslim authority in Palestine through the economic renaissance of the Israeli state in the very midst of one of Islam's holiest lands, and *the refusal of the United States and other powers to play a part in Mideast negotiations with Israel.* The third was the challenge to Muslim cultural traditions, from emancipated women to rebellious children, as the presence of the new handheld television/computer/telephones—loaded with "edutainment" software that combined educational materials with entertainment formats—began to sweep the world. The main effect of the efforts of *various Islamic governments that undertook spectrum jamming in an effort to disrupt the signals on which such technology depended,* was to remove large sections of the globe from the international communications architecture. The Muslim world was the first to turn its back on the West and the ethos of consumerism, secularism, and libertarianism that was the engine of economic growth of this era. Not all Muslims were reconciled to the ignominious defeat of the Taliban in 2001, nor to the death of their terrorist collaborator. One consequence of the World Trade Center attacks had been a mutual suspicion between Islamic and non-Islamic cultures.

At almost the same time, the meltdown of a nuclear reactor in Belarus (of the same design as the one that curdled at Chernobyl in 1988) caused a flood of refugees from Russia, Ukraine, and Poland to storm barricades hastily erected at the German border. In the next two and a half months, more than 1.5 million persons tried to enter Germany, *where eventually they were housed in camps.* Unable to return to their poisoned homelands, *these persons were not allowed to move further west into Germany and were strictly confined.* A wall, unfortunately reminiscent in some ways of the Berlin Wall, was ultimately erected around the perimeter of the camps.

Then, as if to show that no area would go unscathed, *an indigenous revolution in the southern states of Mexico* ignited a popular uprising in the economically depressed north. This touched off another mass migration, with eventually more than five million Mexican nationals pouring into southern Texas and California. Scenes of vigilante violence against the illegal aliens shocked the country, and perhaps more ominously angered and repelled the Hispanic community in the United States. *In both Texas and California there were reprisals; armed Mexican Americans volunteered to protect the refugees;* for some months there was a lawless state of affairs along the border. Throughout the nation, there was a mood of mutual disgust: non–Mexican Americans felt betrayed by those who sheltered and hid illegal aliens. Hispanic Americans, in numbers well beyond those of Mexican heritage, felt contempt for their fellow Anglo citizens who had appeared indifferent to Mexican suffering.

In 2015, a teenage gang led by a former Army officer known to the world only as "Prince" seized power in the area around Monrovia, in Liberia. There were at that time about one million persons living in this city without potable water and without electricity. Using automatic weapons and often accompanied by handheld minicams, soldiers from this force engaged throughout the next months in a campaign of terror and depravity that was filmed and sold to distributors in the West. An outcry arose in the United States in particular urging intervention to restore order. There was no G-9 (P8) or U.N. force available to intervene. The advocates of a policy of intervention captured the imagination of the African American community—Liberia had been founded by former American slaves—who detected an unspoken racism behind the president's reluctance to intervene. Many Americans, however, saw the matter differently: the problems of poverty, political instability, and what were widely perceived as "tribal" conflicts were thought to be beyond solution. Indeed events in Africa tended to harden the worst racial stereotypes in the developed world. *A divisive and intemperate debate in the Congress over whether to send humanitarian aid ended by failing to provide any funds for such a measure.* Rioting broke out in Washington, D.C., where an Afrocentric curriculum had long been mandated in the public schools.

These developments seemed to exhaust the global community, which had struggled with the immediate but attenuated empathy that instant communications seemed to evoke. In reaction, states of The Garden turned inward, and groups within those states ceased striving for cultural homogeneity and celebrated differences instead.

Ironically, it was the multicultural aspects of the developed states that fostered this mutual distancing. By creating a culture in which the international media and entertainment industry had more influence than the national political class of any state, the market-states of the early twenty-first century had also created a powerful weapon that destabilized other societies and, even in their own societies, brought forth violent reactions that sought to restore the cultural values that were apparently being cast away. International communications at first made famines in faraway countries moving and tragic; eventually, these events seemed tiresome and inevitable. International communications initially made the prosperity and liberty of the developed states alluring; eventually these qualities came to seem vulgar and addictive. The national political class was powerless to either lead a state's people toward compassion or insulate a state from cultural invasion. The fragmentation that then occurred in these developed states was only an inner reflection of the alienation their peoples felt toward the outer, foreign world: the contact with other cultures had reinforced the intractability of cultural differences and the felt need to avoid the frustration and danger of such encounters.

As a result, the market-states of this era were thrown back on custom. Customary approaches to allocations are not concerned with optimizing output or increasing the productivity of the individual. Many of the steps taken by the states in this era were irrational, if by that is meant the adoption of policies that cannot in the long run strengthen the economic opportunities of the society on whose behalf such policies are undertaken. Openness and candor are often sacrificed by relying on customary approaches, but openness and candor are not absolutes and there are other values—the preservation of a way of life, religious values that range from the sanctity of life to the protection of a certain structure of the family—that were protected. By mid-century languages that were almost dead in 2000 were flourishing. Art and architecture ceased to be dominated by the West and experienced a new renaissance. Educated persons played more musical instruments, performed more plays, and made more art now that technology brought down the skill levels required for these tasks. The Garden, by subordinating the value of the race for wealth, evoked the value of artistic expression in many cultures that had almost nothing else in common.

ECONOMICS

During this period of increasing surpluses in finished products, little attention was paid to stable or slightly falling levels of food production. Grain stockpiles had been reduced during the middle teens of the century, but as population seemed to be leveling off, there seemed to be no cause for alarm. When in the summer of 2020, a drought struck the United States there were ample world reserves of foodstuffs.

But the following year the drought expanded, and by 2022 it was clear that the world might be entering a period of food shortages. As world stocks of grain became depleted, *China and Japan began buying rice in large quantities; Russia attempted to purchase virtually the entire U.S. wheat export crop,* which had been cut by a third by the drought. Prices started to rise aggressively: wheat went to $10 a bushel; soybeans hit $15, while corn topped $9 for the first time in history.[21]

Weather patterns around the world intensified the drought that gripped the United States and Canada: records for the severity and duration of winter were set in Russia, Poland, and Germany; dramatically uneven precipitation caused flash floods in China and Southeast Asia, bursting dike systems and polluting rice fields. The price of wheat doubled to more than $20 per bushel; a loaf of bread in an American supermarket cost $4; the price of a quart of cooking oil went to $8. Hoarding began to spread across the developed world, as images of starvation in India, Bangladesh, and Central Africa filled television screens.

There was, in fact, plenty of food for the world's population, although its availability—particularly that of proteins—was sharply constricted by hoarding in the wealthier states. The real difficulty was distribution, and here the collapse of international cooperation proved highly destructive. Nation-state institutions like the IMF and the World Bank had been discredited (the IMF by its doctrinaire adherence to the Washington Consensus, the bank by its perceived reluctance to follow that Consensus) and had fallen into disuse. The OECD had become a forum for high-profile quarreling and finger-pointing. There were literally no international institutions that might have stepped in to organize a worldwide, rational distribution system for food, and in any case there was no legal authority to do so. When in 2024 *Viet Nam announced that it was joining a food cartel organized by Japan, China mobilized its armed forces and with some difficulty occupied Hanoi. The following year Russia massed troops on the Ukraine border and virtually coerced an economic union between the two countries to get access to Ukrainian crops.* So things stood in 2025 when weather patterns began to ease.

The mercantile model had been adopted by many market-states—and sometimes by states that had tried, and abandoned, the entrepreneurial model, such as the United States. States as varied as Canada, France, Japan, Tanzania, Korea, Kazakhstan, Indonesia, Ecuador, Iran, and even Norway all pursued this method of achieving market success. The mercantile market-state stressed the need for harmony among different market actors. On average, in market-states that adopted the mercantile model the incomes received by the highest 20 percent of the population amounted to no more than four times the incomes of the lowest 20 percent; in entrepreneurial market-states the ratio had often been more than 15 to 1. By sharing the benefits of growth widely among its citizens, a state following this model was able to justify subsidies to certain sectors and to maintain political stability. To be sure, some states without an almost exclusive ethnic and cultural homogeneity that attempted this model—Brazil did so in the early teens of the twenty-first century, for example—faced widespread consumer-led revolts. Still, states following this model seemed to be able to avoid the problems of organized crime and of street crime that plagued other market-states, though whether this was a result of their more homogeneous societies or (as in the United States) other factors cannot easily be determined.

Initially, The Garden was an inhospitable environment for the society of states, because it stressed the mercantile, competitive relations of nonhomogeneous groups like a society of states. What was required was an international system that could generalize to the society of states itself the self-consciously stable and equitable obligations of the mercantile market-state. Because such an approach depends on complex systems of mutual obligation and trust, it may be that this could never have come into being without the famines and food crises of the early twenty-first century, which ultimately discredited mercantilist attitudes.

Prior to the famines, Asian business combines of hitherto unimagined size dwarfed all other enterprises in other countries. The largest twenty banks, the largest seventy-five corporations, the largest fifty trading companies were all Asian. This figure hid the fact, however, that intra-Asian competition was more cutthroat than ever before, with savage competitive tactics that, in an effort to gain market share in the consuming West, had led to falling living standards in Asia despite the fact that these had been the fastest-growing economies in the world. *The intensely aggressive policies of these states—ruthless market penetration through price-cutting combined with heavily regulated imports of capital and goods—gave them trade surpluses and made them creditors but did not raise living standards.* Child labor appeared more broadly in the world, moving into the developed states, which had not seen such practices since the early decades of the previous century. Moreover, *greater investment was being diverted into military uses,* as each of these states began to fear domination by one of the others when tensions rose out of fierce economic competition.

Among world business leaders, there emerged a consensus that would have surprised many of the businessmen of the twentieth century: all three state models were rejected on essentially ethical rather than economic grounds. The entrepreneurial model, because it emphasized personal rights at the expense of personal responsibilities, led to a kind of libertarian anarchy. The managerial model induced in the peoples of the countries in which it reigned a torpor and dependence on the welfare state that produced a youth culture of drug abuse, birth rates so low as to be practically nonexistent, and ubiquitous vandalism. The mercantile model had proved too competitive, too national to apply even to a handful of states in the same region—much less to all the developed and developing states. This model turned out to work best when it took advantage of a stable international set of rules on which it could act as a free rider, but it had had the effect of dissipating the very system on which it was parasitic.

In the year 2004, the chairman of the largest of the American investment banks gave an address to a group of international executives. It was widely reported and eventually took on an iconic status, though at first its impact was largely owing to the novelty of an American executive thoughtfully comparing the entrepreneurial and the mercantile market-state models. He said:

> For the past fifteen years I have been calling for the establishment of an ethical state with a concrete plan for change. The policies pursued by Japan and others have succeeded in achieving the objective of social prosperity; this sense of cohesion is something we seem to lack here in the multicultural United States. We have learned, however, to live and let live in our society, even if this has meant a little distance sometimes. Now we must adopt a principle of "kyosei"—of living together in harmony and interdependence with the other peoples of the world—and commit ourselves wholeheartedly to this purpose . . . We have learned that governments matter, not as a source of welfare benefits, but as the provider of key elements of infrastructure such as education and primary scientific research, and the enabler of societal changes necessary to take maximum advantage of new opportunities. Now we are learning that government also matters as the legitimate arbiter of those decisions we are unwilling to leave to the market, decisions which those new opportunities have set before us.[22]

This criticism of the entrepreneurial model from one of its most successful advocates stirred many. That same year the first of the gene-tech scandals occurred: a series of gene manipulations by computer-assisted technology that went awry and produced horrifying birth defects. When serious weather-induced food shortages began to appear the following year, there was widespread suspicion that these too were the result of corporate experiments with computer-guided weather control systems that had misfired. Although this was never actually determined to be the case, the public's outrage and fear gave immense momentum to movements that sought to reinvigorate the political dimensions of the state. The speech was thought to have prophesied something of what had happened and its call for an "ethical state" was renewed.

One unusual element of that speech was the call for a greater role for the corporation and for business leadership generally. "Today," this corporate leader had said, "there is only one entity whose effort to create stability in the world matches its self-interest. That entity is a corporation acting globally. In the increasingly borderless world created by the microchip, politicians and bureaucrats will not be the ones to turn to for guidance. It is in the nature of politicians and bureaucrats to serve one country. But global corporations can only do business in a peaceful and stable world."[23]

This might have been the most controversial part of the speech; after all, the "gene-tech" scandals and weather-induced famines had called into question the accountability of global corporations. Some corporate leaders might truly act on the assumption that their business enterprises were responsible to their "customers, their employees, and society," but most thought they were solely responsible to their shareholders. In fact, it wasn't clear that most managers would know what to do if such a broad social responsibility were given to them. They were not politicians or lawyers. Government leaders only knew one way—the way of the nation-state—to make corporations accountable: this was through law and close regulation. Corporations that could pollute the gene pool and precipitate mass migrations by manipulating the weather were hardly to be trusted. On the other hand, absent a culture of trust, there could never develop the long-term relationships of stability and responsibility that seemed so lacking in the states of this period.

In many countries there were riots against the offices of multinational corporations; some firms hired private security forces that grew until they were private militias. Most states were too weak to prevent this development; *others had already privatized police and even core military functions,* so that the line between the security force protecting the corporate headquarters and that protecting the seat of government was blurred.

The principal transforming event, however, was the famine. The collapse of an international effort by governments to save the worst-hit areas from mass starvation—evoking the disillusionment of citizens in relatively prosperous areas who began to fear for their own well-being—was replaced by *an international consortium of business firms who levied a kind of tax on their customers*—really a price surcharge on their products—to finance food aid. *This consortium turned over its operations to government agencies when the crisis had passed.* There is little question that millions of lives were saved. This enhanced the credibility of multinational corporations generally, even though suspicions persisted in some

circles that the weather changes had been artificially induced. Nevertheless, investigations, including an antitrust prosecution for the price fixing
by which the famine funds had been raised, proved fruitless and were
widely unpopular.

When *the United States and the E.U. were able to negotiate a huge
revaluation of the yen* in order to improve their trade deficits, they found
that the purchasing power of Japanese multinationals had skyrocketed and
that the largest corporate taxpayers, as well as the largest equity holders,
were now Asian companies. It was as if these companies had bought the
real assets of European and American states through a kind of novel lease-
purchase—lending to finance trade deficits and then, through the revaluation, converting those liens to ownership. This too, however, had the effect
of strengthening the move to give a political role to the multinational
corporation.

By 2025 an informal code of conduct was developing between international business and market-state governments. Those governments that
were able to enhance stability while maintaining an open intellectual environment became magnets for investment. *Measures such as income supplements to enable families to care for their elderly relatives, property tax
breaks to encourage longer periods of residence in a single community,
and invigorated libel and consumer protection laws* all tended to impede
market growth; but they also contributed to the citizen's sense of well-
being, his sense of place in the environment, and his growing assumption
of responsibility. These factors tended to increase trust, which lowered the
burden of legal regulation—greater delegation and discretion replaced rule
making and litigation—and thus enhanced market growth by lessening
transaction costs. Here the computer was indispensable, because *informal
networks alerted consumers to the activities of responsible corporations* as
well as facilitating ad hoc "communities" centered on common problems.
These developments tended to raise citizen confidence that the society was
able to respond to social problems and that society's members were willing to take responsibility for addressing these problems.

These structural adjustments did much to ameliorate the worst excesses
of the market. *Informal business codes enabled corporations to isolate
and shun other businesses that failed to act in the long-term interests of the
communities they served* (including large wage differentials between managers and workers) and the instant information provided by computer
linkups gave consumers an enforcement mechanism to supplement business pressure. But these adjustments did little to resolve issues of social
justice and group identity. Many persons felt stifled in The Garden that
emerged from this process of business-led harmony. While crime as a
whole lessened in the developed market-states, partly for demographic
reasons, the lethality and intensity of criminal acts increased. Millennial

cults grew up even though the millennium had passed, and in 2030 the first of a series of computer plagues struck the infrastructure of the developed world. The world saw the first hostile use of a nuclear weapon since 1945 when an Indian religious cult devastated the financial center at Bombay by poisoning its water supply with radioactive isotopes stolen from a lab.

At the same time, corporate-led international policy was more successful in the developing world where its *innovative system of institutional "tithing" was coupled with the business codes' emphases on environmental protection as a basis for developmental aid*. Corporations could direct capital investment to those states committed to sustainable development and deny capital and expertise to states determined to despoil their own environments in an effort at too-rapid growth. What was lacking, as evidenced by the soaring levels of crime in these countries, was the mechanism for political cohesion. The market-state had survived by bringing international business leadership to bear on interstate problems and the society of such states was stronger for this move. But the State still had difficulty regaining its position as legitimate social arbiter of those moral and political questions to which business was indifferent, and for which an international institution, like the multinational corporation, was too acultural, too ahistorical to replace the State.

Nevertheless the new market-states of this era—roughly 2012–2030—had successfully used the business corporation to introduce decentralization and individuation into government, supplementing the role of citizens, who could only act in groups, with that of individual consumers, who acted individually and instantly. Historians looking back on the period between 2000 and 2050 will surely debate which of several factors was responsible for the sustained worldwide economic growth of this period: the technological breakthroughs of superconductivity and laser-fusion and gene modification; the spread of new and successful managerial techniques for both firms and countries; falling populations and a fall in the price of raw materials; a changing leadership that moved multinational corporations into a higher profile in providing transnational political direction; unexpected and heartrending events that exposed the lack of common ground among groups in the pitiless market-state. Much of the credit, however, must go to The Garden itself, which brought forth business leadership at a crucial time.

CONCLUSION: THE THREE SCENARIO SUITES

It is tempting to read these small narratives and conclude that there is an optimum course for the society of market-states to pursue. On the contrary, these scenarios reveal instead that any choice burdens our values, for these values are both contradictory and incommensurable.*

In The Meadow pressures from population growth were mitigated by high average annual economic growth. Cities, however, became scarcely livable. Elites thrived but the majority of persons were not better off and their prospects for social and economic security were constantly threatened. High migration was beneficial for both the sending and the receiving states, but ethnic heterogeneity threatened the cohesion of some states and communal violence escalated accordingly. The advanced countries largely solved their resource problems but they stressed ecosystems causing increased CO_2 pollution, deforestation, the loss of species, and widespread soil degradation through their dietary demands for animal protein. The Meadow was an hospitable place for technological innovation, the diffusion and implementation of information technology, biotechnology, and smart materials. But most countries fell further behind because they lacked the education levels, infrastructure, and governance systems to exploit these technologies. And new technologies could also be destabilizing, empowering terrorists and criminals and accelerating the proliferation of weapons of mass destruction. As the chief advocate and beneficiary of globalization, the United States assumed world leadership in The Meadow, but a U.S. economic downturn sent other states into a tailspin, ultimately eroding support for the United States. The Meadow managed low-intensity interventions with characteristic inventiveness, but the risk of regional conflict in Asia rose substantially.

In The Park regional integration increased rapidly, bringing robust initial growth. This growth was eventually diminished, however, by the effects of regionalism and protectionism. Growth within the developed states of The Park was less volatile than in The Meadow, and therefore more sustainable; furthermore, the benefits were more widely distributed within the leading societies of The Park, enhancing the quality of life for more persons. Nevertheless, increased regionalism resulted in irrefragable positions about markets, investment flows, intellectual property rights, and natural resources. The United States was confined to a single regional grouping, the Americas, which was neither in its interest nor that of the world, with which it ought to have had broader economic intercourse. International collaboration was reduced regarding terrorism, crime, cross-border conflicts, humanitarian interventions, and the proliferation of weapons of mass destruction, yet some national and international—though not global—institutions that had atrophied in The Meadow thrived in The Park. Regional identities sharpened political resistance to the United

*Though not incomparable; see Mathew Adler, "Review of Incommensurability, Incomparability and Practical Reason," XIX *Philosophy in Review* 3 (June 1999): 168.

States and to U.S.-led globalization in The Park; this was reflected in the uneven absorption of new techniques in biotechnology. So long as the United States continued to develop cutting-edge military technology, there was no prospect of great power conflict in The Park, but there were far higher levels of internal and crossborder conflicts in developing countries. Diversity (through federalism) thrived, but true multiculturalism shrank.

In The Garden, the seductive melody of withdrawal, almost isolation, contributed to U.S. disengagement in the world. Traditional national identities asserted themselves. Mercantilist competition strengthened the state while weakening global and regional intergovernmental institutions. As the United States withdrew its presence in Europe and Asia, China drove toward regional dominance, Japan rearmed, and the risk of great power conflict for the first time since the end of the Long War increased when the United States sought to reassert itself in Asia. Nevertheless, Korea was able to achieve normalization and unification. The cultures of emerging market-states were able to protect themselves from historical annihilation. The need for community, felt but ignored in The Meadow, was addressed in The Garden. Most important, the ability to develop business leaders who would take up the moral and political challenges abandoned by states was nurtured in The Garden, though scarcely tolerated in The Park and out of place in the entrepreneurial Meadow.

Think of The Meadow as "A," The Park as "B," and The Garden as "C." If we rank these approaches with respect to the security decisions taken in each scenario, A is preferred to B, which is preferred to C. That is, peace with some justice (the protection of nonaggressors, for example) is to be preferred to simple peace (bought at the price of sacrificing innocent peoples), which is still preferable to a cataclysm that would destroy the innocent and guilty alike. Or perhaps we get B/A/C—no conflict is preferred to frustrating low-intensity conflict, which is still preferable to a high risk of cataclysm. In any case, we can agree that C (The Garden) presents the worst option for satisfying the world's security needs. But if we do the same sort of exercise with respect to the issues raised by the "culture" scenarios, preferring genuine pluralism to mere cultural protectionism, and yet preferring the protection of minorities to their marginalization, we get B/C/A. Or at least we get C/B/A, for some will feel that the protection of sanctified ways of life trumps pluralism. In any case, we can agree that A—The Meadow—is an inhospitable place for the serenity, continuity, and community that protect cultures. And if we conduct this same exercise with respect to the scenarios devoted to economic issues, ranking sustainable growth ahead of recovery, which is still preferable to stagnation, we get C/A/B. Or, if growth alone is our objective, we get A/C/B: the insatiable but impressive engine of dynamic, innovative risk taking is preferred to the methods of mercantilist competition. In any case we must concede that regional protectionism—the world created in the Park—is a sure route to high unemployment, slow growth, and the costliness (and uneven diffusion) of new technology.

Moreover, we are unwilling, or we should be, to trade off our economic or cultural or strategic well-being because these interests are in fact so bound up with one another. Even survival is not an ultimate value, for there are conditions of life that are intolerable. So we have this unstable *contredanse*, ABC/BCA/CAB, or BAC/CBA/ACB, contrived—of course—to make this point: that an optimal constitutional arrangement is one that permits peaceful change as states shift from one approach to another over time and as these shifts impose stresses on international society that mirror the stresses felt within states. In the stories, as I have written them, it is that constitutional arrangement that allows a society—even a society of states—to transcend its prevailing approach that proves most successful. It is human agency that avoids the plausible futures that on examination seem so intolerable.

We choose which questions to answer in life just as studiedly as we choose our answers. Societies are creatures of their decisions to treat certain issues as problems, because such decisions enable societies to respond to those problems. Because there is at this moment a growing confusion in our understanding of the role of the State, our usual habits of choosing certain problems and creating our history by means of crafting solutions to those problems is at present ill-formed and confused. We know the old rules—to uphold the international law of nation-states—no longer command us. Yet we are unclear about the choices we are making in the new society of market-states when we decide cases whose ultimate significance is still hidden from us. In the scenarios just described, we can get some picture of the problems and opportunities that may arise as a result of our choosing different paths for this society.

We do scenarios to help us define what kind of world we really want, among many possible worlds, to clarify how decisions taken today will effect large-scale results later, and to make us more alert to the meaning of unfolding events. Thus scenario-based planning is not about solving the hypothetical problems of some distant tomorrow, but about making decisions wisely today. To take one example from the scenario exercise above: the first decades of the twenty-first century will witness the acceleration of two trends already evident at the end of the twentieth: the withdrawal of governments from the task of providing for the ultimate welfare of their citizens and the increasing assumption of this responsibility by the private sector. All across the postindustrial world, governments will have to learn from the experience and knowledge of the private sector how to create opportunity, and business leaders will have to learn how to manage with an eye to the public acceptance of their actions. Business leaders are wholly unprepared to take up the moral and political responsibilities that governments are busily casting off, and politicians and bureaucrats are seldom well situated to make the long-term investments in infrastructure that create opportunity. Yet how many business schools, law schools, and public policy institutes will plan this next semester's curriculum with these shortfalls in mind? How many are even aware that they are contributing to these mounting intellectual deficits?

This chapter, "Possible Worlds," is not the last chapter in this book because it is not really about the future. It is not a coda. It is not futurology. It is about current choices, as these can be illuminated by the imagination.

CHAPTER TWENTY-SIX

The Coming Age
of War and Peace

EVERY MARKET-STATE will make historic choices among the models described in Chapter 24, and perhaps among other models that are yet to be developed. These choices will do much to shape the constitution of the society of states, and it may be that, as described in Chapter 25, one model will predominate. But suppose this does not happen? Suppose these three models—or others—all seek an international order reflecting their priorities but none succeed?

The Peace of Paris suggests some common elements among the various versions of the market-state. The treaties that compose that Peace specifically refer to the necessity for market economies and for the human right to possess property as well as the requirement for parliamentary, democratic, and judicial processes. The Peace of Paris, however, does not resolve the tensions among the alternative forms of the market-state, tensions that mainly lie in the varying degrees of sovereignty retained by the people of a market-state. Instead, by ending the Long War and incorporating the agreements reached in San Francisco and at Versailles, the Peace of Paris completed the process of globalizing a certain form of the nation-state while universalizing international law—achievements that are to some degree incompatible with the market-state. Indeed, many of the international institutions of the last fifty years—the United Nations, the World Health Organization, the World Bank, the European Union, the North Atlantic Treaty Organization, the Organization on Security and Cooperation in Europe, to take but a few notable examples—will either have to be radically transformed or will decay into obstructive irrelevance. The U.N. Security Council is obviously a Long War creation: who would choose those particular five states to manage international security today? Our recent experience in Bosnia suggests that NATO might be able to make this transition while the U.N. might not, while our even more recent experience in Kosovo suggests that NATO can perhaps enable the U.N. to act effectively in the new era.* This example of the regional enabling the universal mirrors the phenomenon of the market-state in which devolution goes hand in hand with more unified markets. Perhaps neither could exist without the other: Lombardy may be too small to be economically viable while the European Union may be too large to command the cultural allegiance of Lombards. Together, these new models for state organization reinforce each other.

We will seek a new constitutional order for the society of states in order to cope with the novel challenges presented in Chapter 24. The bureaucratized nation-states struggling to satisfy the ever-escalating requirements of providing for the welfare of their aging publics are increasingly being denied their axiomatic legitimacy by those very publics. Those publics are beginning to look to transnational entities, like the multinational corporation (whose shares they hold), and subnational institutions, like particular interest groups (whose fund-raising they support), to provide for their tangible well-being. So long as the State's legitimacy is a matter of ensuring the welfare of its citizens, then the globalization and interdependence of its economy, the vulnerability and transparency of its security, and the accessibility and fragility of its cultural institutions will increasingly deny the State that legitimacy. As a result, individual states will change—they are already changing—to reacquire legitimacy by creating a new basis on which they may claim it. A change in the constitutional order of states will eventually recreate the nature of the society of states and *its* constitutional order.

Before we can create such a new order, however, we must establish a consensus; that is to say, before we can have a new constitution for the society of states, we must have a constitutional convention. In order to have a constitutional convention for this society there must be a congress of the kind that met at Augsburg, Westphalia, Utrecht, and Vienna. This congress need never meet; it need never produce a single document: the only necessary element it must possess that it shares with the great congresses of the past is consensus. War provided the means by which consensus was achieved in the past. Peace resolves issues that war has defined, winnowed, and presented in a way that is ripe for resolution. The great peace congresses that ended epochal wars were constitutional conventions for the society of states, convened to resolve matters tried by state violence.

It is worth remembering that neither changes in the constitutional order nor innovations in strategy *cause* wars. Wars are fought over the usual mix of ambition and fear that has characterized state conflict from the time states began. The causes of epochal wars are no different from the causes

---

*And the most recent experience, as of this writing, in Afghanistan suggests that while NATO and the U.N. have important political roles, the actual management of crises in international society will fall, as predicted, to ad hoc coalitions.

of war generally. What marks these conflicts as "epochal" has to do not only with their duration and scope, but also with the fact that epochal war encompasses fundamental constitutional issues that must be resolved for peace to take hold. Regardless of what caused it, the epochal war has the consequence of changing the constitutional order of the states that fought; the peace conference that follows such a war marks the acceptance of a new constitutional order for the society of states.

Virtually no one, apart from a few apocalyptic millennialists, is concerned about the possibility of large-scale war at the present time. The assessment of the strategic threats facing the world that is given in the U.S.'s 1997 Quadrennial Defense Review (QDR) concluded that the international community has barely commenced a ten-year strategic lull. In late 2000, the U.S. intelligence community concluded that the risk of war among developed countries will be low through at least 2015.[1] This sense of peace "as far as the eye can see" is widely shared.[2] Yet there is also a sense in the QDR and elsewhere of uneasiness, a sense that the future is likely to be dangerous in new ways—even a sense that we will look back on the Cold War as a golden age.[3] For the reasons given in the preceding chapters, I think this sense of foreboding is justified, and that the new ways in which the world will be threatened are exquisitely connected to the old ways in which the Long War was finally silenced. If the bombing of Hiroshima and Nagasaki was the apogee of the nation-state—for what other political entity could possibly have financed and manned such an undertaking as the Manhattan Project, let alone World Wars I and II—then that moment was also the birth of the universal vulnerability of the nation-state. If the development of high-speed computing was critically important to ending the Long War without armed conflict between the superpowers, this development has also made possible asymmetric warfare by individuals and small groups that are otherwise powerless. If the creation of the international telecommunications system crushed the pretensions of the nonparliamentary nation-states, it also made the very notion of creating a state in the image of a nation seem vain and insular. These are the new ways—the proliferation of weapons of mass destruction, asymmetric warfare by means of attacks on critical infrastructure, and the transnational environmental and epidemiological plagues of the future—in which threats will be manifested. These new ways must be added to the more conventional threats to states, which, if they have in some theatres receded, have not vanished.

But even if this sense of foreboding is not without foundation because these new tools lower the costs to an aggressor of waging war, why should we prepare for a new *epochal* war? What is it about our current situation that would justify such apprehensions, and if they are justified, what precisely should we do about it?

The three new forms of the market-state that are currently emerging are marked by radically different views of sovereignty. The entrepreneurial market-state holds that state sovereignty is transparent: other states are entitled to pierce the veil of sovereignty if the target state has forfeited its claim to legitimacy, even by its internal acts. Managerial market-states hold, by contrast, that sovereignty can be penetrated only with the endorsement of the United Nations, or at least the ratification by a regional security organization that is itself endorsed by the U.N. Mercantile market-states hold that sovereignty is opaque and cannot be breached on the basis of a state's internal behavior.

When the United States and other entrepreneurial market-states intervene abroad, other states—with different views of sovereignty—are threatened. The use of force against an international terrorist network, for example, might involve interventions in Somalia (where there is at present no effective government), the Philippines (where the government has solicited assistance against Abu Sayyaf), Colombia (where the government is fighting terrorists unsuccessfully), or Iraq. If prolonged hostilities on a global scale result, the conflict could put in play the very bases of the constitutional order itself. This, of course, is the watermark of the epochal war.

Then why not simply renounce foreign intervention for the domestic acts of other states? What's wrong with a little modest circumspection? First, we forfeit the chance to build collaborative relationships with other peer competitors through the management of joint interventions. Second, such a renunciation saps the moral role of the State as a protector at a time when its constitutional order, that of the market-state, is particularly vulnerable to the charge of amorality. This makes the State a likelier target for civil disorder and even civil war on the basis of one of the other competing constitutional forms (including nation-state versus market-state). Third, and most important, if one group of states renounces intervention—for whatever reason—it is by no means obvious that all states will do so. China can consistently hold that sovereignty is opaque and still invade Taiwan; the same thing can be said of the Koreas and other divided states. Nor should we rely on consistency: hypocrisy is not unknown in world affairs.

The alternative to abandoning intervention as an instrument of the State is to set clearly articulated standards for intervention so that other states do not become threatened by interventions in remote regions that do not, in themselves, threaten the vital interests of anyone other than the targeted state. China must know that an intervention to rescue Hutu civilians in Burundi or to trap Al Qaeda leaders in Afghanistan is not preparation for intervention on behalf of Tibetans.

This suggests "epochal war" might come in alternative forms. It might come in the guise of a series of asymmetrical low-intensity conflicts like the war against terrorism; or it might resemble the great continent-spanning coalitional, high-intensity wars of the past; or First World peer competitors might fight a largely nonexplosive technologically sophisticated war by attempting to bring about unattributed disruption through stealth.[4] I will term these three possibilities the "chronic," the "cataclysmic," and the "critical" respectively.

We must choose which sort of war we will fight, regardless of what are its causes, to set the terms of the peace we want. To many, such a sentence must sound like courting war. Shouldn't the avoidance of war be our objective? The avoidance of war per se, however, is not an objective; it is a policy. And I fear it is a policy that can mask the approach of cataclysmic war because it counsels against the preparations for war that might avert massive, carefully planned, large-scale attacks by one state on another, and because it actually invites low-intensity conflicts once aggressors can rest assured they can find sanctuaries where they will not be troubled by outsiders.

There is a widespread view that war is simply a pathology of the State, that healthy states will not fight wars. This view ignores the role strategy plays in the formation and continuance of states. War, like law, sustains the State by giving it the means to carry out its purposes of protection, preservation, and defense. This view that the State can be permanently separated from the historic occurrence of war also mistakes the sources of peace. Peaces, when they are constitutions, contain within them unresolved challenges to the orders they establish. Consensus does not mean stasis.

Divided nations seeking nation-states present the greatest threat to the society of states. The two Koreas, China and Taiwan, the states of the former Palestine, the states of the former Soviet Union and the former Yugoslavia, and the states of the subcontinent, India, Pakistan, and Bangladesh—all present lethally inviting venues for war that could become cataclysmic. The partition of states along national lines was the constitutional surgery of choice for the society of nation-states; reintegrating these fragments of a whole will present a formidable challenge to the society of market-states that has inherited the consequences of these diplomatic fixes. If we wish to ensure that the new states that emerge are market-states rather than chronically violent nation-states it may be that only war on a very great scale could produce the necessary consensus. We should not exclude the democracies from idealistic ambitions that could lead to conflicts on such a scale. It is often said that democracies do not attack other states. Actually, the historical record tends to support the narrower assertion that democracies do not attack each other[5] (and even this assertion has been challenged).[6] Such states have shown themselves quite ruthless in conflicts with states that are nondemocratic or against groups that were perceived as threatening the stability of the democratic state.[7]

Cataclysmic war is a real possibility in Asia. India, Russia, and China all face nationalist challenges to the development of a market-state. Each could provide the theatre for war. China possesses a potential for civil war that is the product of the attraction and repulsion the market-state holds for Chinese society. For this reason a weak and unstable China is far more dangerous than a strong China. Russia is experiencing a Weimar situation at least as painful as anything Germany endured. What other state today combines a nuclear arsenal with surging mortality *and* plunging fertility tables? Both Russia and China—because of their weakness—find themselves intertwined with criminal conspiracies that could lead to external conflict. China has been an unacknowledged partner of the East Asian sea pirate networks; in Russia, there is "such extraordinary interpenetration of the intelligence services, organized crime, and business that it is very difficult to tell with whom one is dealing in almost any circumstance."[8] These criminal involvements pose two potential problems: first, they may launch irritating, sometimes deadly, probes to which other states may react with violence and the intent to pierce Russian or Chinese sovereignty. Second, the involvement of criminal conspiracies raises the possibility of theft from their respective military industrial complexes, including fissionable material, biological weapons, guidance systems, and other deadly exports. Like Russia and China, India is a nuclear power—though a modest one—with a high potential for dissolution, and thus a domestic appetite for international adventure. In any of these countries, the outbreak of civil war could be succeeded by predation on neighbors. Great powers that sat by during the first phase of conflict might be drawn into the second.

There is no certainty, however, that even a pluralism of constitutional forms of the market-state can exist without violence. The three versions of the nation-state that competed in the Long War had to externalize to make themselves secure at home. Parliamentarianism, fascism, and communism in every state rose and fell with their fortunes abroad. By contrast, the three versions of the market-state have to be internalized to become secure abroad. The entrepreneurial, mercantile, and managerial alternatives will rise—or fall—in popularity depending on the success and cohesion each is able to achieve domestically. Inevitably this will mean a rise in domestic coercion in some states. When this happens, threatened local groups will call on their allies in states abroad. Then, as before, law and strategy, the inner and the outer faces of the State, will be united. Civil disobedience and civil strife will become more widespread, and more threatening. This could mean a silent war, fought with largely covert means because overt conflict is too risky and too discrediting. Such a war would be fought principally with defensive weapons—redundancy, deception, missile defenses, information, and ever-advancing technology, including genomics—against undefined adversaries supported by rival states.

A third kind of war whose duration and consequences might prove epochal is an endless, low-intensity conflict with some states and nonstate groups whose plights are the consequence of an evolving pluralist society of market-states. It is obvious, I suppose, that some of these groups are drawn from those who oppose the emergence of the market-state in the first place: states that have been destroyed by globalization and cultural groups that are threatened by universal communications and migration. It is perhaps less obvious that there are other groups spawned by this development that actually thrive in the new environment but that are no less dangerous—criminal conspiracies, anarchic movements, transnational and subnational terrorists of many varying motivations. Finally, it is least obvious that the society of market-states is the target of national groups that are still in thrall to the romance of the nation-state: French Canadians in Quebec; Kurds in Turkey, Iraq, and Iran; Sikhs in the Punjab; Basques and Catalans in Spain; Indians in the Central American states, and others. One would imagine that the society of market-states, with its many varying territorial forms, would make a diffuse target for such unfashionable and passionate dreams. For the society of market-states there is no essential difference between umbrella states like the European Union or the Asian Pacific Economic Council, and leagues of great scope (like NAFTA) or small compass (like Italy's Northern League) or even nonterritorial entities like CNN, the Shell Oil Group, the Medellín Cartel, or Hamas. But this agnosticism does not make it any easier to satisfy the ambitions of irredentist nationalities: the drive of stranded nations like the Kurds for a state makes them hard to bribe, in the economic sense of that term, because they have a single, nonnegotiable demand that, by the nature of the new society of states, it is very difficult for them to achieve. Unlike Wilson and House, the leaders of market-states do not create nation-states. Yet the indifference of the market-states to such demands can provoke efforts to get their attention.

If we wish to avoid cataclysmic war and invisible, silent war, we shall have to learn how to wage wars like the ones in Yugoslavia and Afghanistan, using the tactics of relentless airstrikes, special forces teams, and indigenous allies. This means, pre-eminently, that we shall have to develop rules for intervention.[9] Out of this new epochal conflict can come, some day, the consensus that will provide the basis for a constitution for the society of the new form of the state.

In the meantime, we shall have to reorient our concerns to cope with the changes brought about by the emergence of the market-states. Let me give seven examples of this reorientation, the fifth of which (critical infrastructure) I will discuss in somewhat greater detail. In each of these cases the difficulty arises along the seam between the nation-state and the market-state. The nation-state is oblivious to these issues because it treats them from a perspective that is indifferent to the externalities they impose on other states. What does it matter, for example, if the state of Colombia is ruined by U.S. drug consumption; that is, after all, Colombia's affair. The U.S. is doing everything in its power to stop such consumption—except, of course, compromising on our deeply held value that the state should protect its citizens from toxic substances.

At the same time, each of these cases is an example of market failure: that is, the market acting alone in the absence of state regulation is indifferent to these issues. What does it matter to the market, for example, whether there are international rules for access to technology? If an economic profit can be made by sales of high-speed computers to Iran, or missile parts to Iraq, or fissile material to North Korea, that is surely all that is of interest to the market.

(1)

The role of the news media has changed, constitutionally speaking, in the last three periods of the state.[10] In the era of the state-nation the constitutional role of the press was foremost to transmit the political leadership's views. This often amounted to functioning as an organ to shape public opinion. Napoleon's bulletins provide a good example.* So do the *Federalist Papers,* first published as essentially op-ed pieces, and the journalism that powered the French Revolution. In the nation-state period, to this role was added the function of informing leaders about the public reaction as the public spoke back to government through the media. William Randolph Hearst's famous remark ("You provide the pictures, I'll provide the war") showed a shrewd appreciation of this. The pivotal role played by the *New York Times* in opposing the War in Viet Nam that it had so heartily supported and the *Washington Post*'s crucial exposure of Watergate

---

*"Bonaparte's victory bulletin was typical in every respect of the many hundreds that were to follow in the course of the next thirteen years—the eagerly awaited bulletins, from Germany, from Austria, from Poland, from Russia, from Spain; the bulletins that set the imagination of young boys on fire and whose memory made the postwar years seem so drab and dull to them; the bulletins that old couples and young wives and mistresses and sisters would pore over, wondering whether the digits and the ciphers representing the crippled and the dead, the brave who were immortalized in an anonymous glory, included those they loved; the bulletins to which there seemed to be no end, as if henceforth the purpose of men's lives would be forever the gain of honor at the price of death; the bulletins that spoke, in lapidary yet incandescent prose, of the beauty of battlefields, the splendor of cities aflame; the glorious, hateful bulletins, with their exhilarating statistics of captured flags and guns, of enemies killed and wounded, of individual acts of bravery, that form the stanzas of the epic of Napoleon." J. C. Herold, *The Age of Napoleon* (American Heritage, 1963); "To lie like a bulletin" was a proverbial expression in Napoleon's army, Ibid., 408. See also Louis-Leopold Boilly's painting of the French family poring over one of these bulletins.

felonies both showed the press not only leading the public but also constantly reporting trends in public opinion on the same issues. Editorial opinion and its counterparts in the electronic media eventually stood for public opinion. When the CBS anchorman Walter Cronkite turned against the Viet Nam War, President Johnson is reported to have concluded that his war policies no longer had the confidence of the public.[11]

In the market-state, the media have begun to act in direct competition with the government of the day. The media are well situated to succeed in this competition because they are trained to work in the marketplace, are more nimble than bureaucrats hampered by procedural rules, are quick to spot public trends, can call on huge capitalizations, can rely on sophisticated managers and technocrats, and are the most capable users—far outpacing politicians—of the contemporary techniques of advertising and public relations. Finally the media, protected in many countries by statutes and constitutional amendments, are free of many of the legal and political restraints that bind government officials.

The changing role of the media as it enters the era of the market-state is felt in many quarters. David Anderson, a law professor and former journalist, has observed that the constitutional protections surrounding libel defendants have been transformed from protection for the lonely, vilified civil libertarian to an insurance policy for media multinationals.[12] To take another example, one aspect of President Clinton's difficulties in persuading the public that the campaign of vilification directed against him came from a "right-wing conspiracy" is that some of its most avid adherents were liberal journalists. They were not conspirators—at least not of the right-wing variety—so much as soldiers in an historic struggle to wrest power from the presidency, and to gain even greater control over the electoral process than the media now enjoys.

Indeed the competitive, critical function of the media in the market-state is similar to that of the political parties of the Left in the nation-state: the Left was always a *critical* organ in government, reproving, harassing, questioning the status quo; it sought a governing role even though whenever Left parties held office, they quickly moved to the center, co-opting (or being co-opted by) the Right. Now with the discrediting of the Left in the market-state, this competitive critical function has been taken up by the media.*

The media are completely untrained in this task—ethically or politically. Much the same can be said for the leadership of the great multinational corporations (of whom the media empires form a subset). Nor can

---

*Which is not to say that political partisanship is dead. It thrives in the transitional environment from one constitutional order to another. But this partisanship is programmatic (it *is* a right-wing conspiracy, or left-wing, or some other) whereas press opposition is nonsubstantive, in the sense that it *objects,* period. It poses no alternatives.

these institutions expect much guidance from the political class that has so enslaved itself to the market via its reliance on campaign contributions.

Relations between the media and the other organs of government are further exacerbated by the fact that in the market-state the public's attitude toward what can be accomplished by government changes (and thus also changes with respect to the scope of personal responsibility). Now it is up to the individual to avoid problems, not up to the state to fix them. If there are unsafe areas of town, the citizen is best advised not to go there, rather than expect the police to ensure a safe environment. If a person becomes a politician or seeks fame, he will get little sympathy if he is badly treated thereafter: he sought the role, and therefore he bought into a bargain that includes loss of privacy, jeopardy to reputation, loss of earnings. The market is inherently unpredictable, so persons become more fatalistic; the nation-state, based on the operations of law rather than the market, gave a sense, perhaps illusory, that expectations would be fulfilled through policy.

In the transition, the nation-state will appear to be doing even worse than it is. Popular appreciation will plummet because the public has been persuaded that the government cannot accomplish anything positive of note. This is partly due to the switch in roles by the media, which retain the credibility of reportage but now also have the mission of opposition. Business activities—and the activities of business leaders—are replacing politics as the central source of news about the welfare of the people.

Absent the threat of war, it is very difficult to believe that the publics will be eager to follow the urgings of their political leaderships to make the sacrifices that states often require. This development will strain the political structures of the great powers to their utmost, making them vulnerable to delegitimation in a crisis. Political leaders may find they are able to inspire a sense of mission only through the shrewd manipulation of the media, a short-lived tactic that ultimately must invite contempt. At the same time, some sectors of the public will become more credulous, more willing to believe preposterous stories about government cover-ups.

(2)

At present when we consider environmental threats to the collectivity of mankind, we have tended to concentrate our concerns on cumulative threats like global warming and the destruction of the ozone layer. When we think about environmental events that threaten a single state, we focus on oil spills, desertification, and deforestation. We have neglected events relating to the environment that bring about conflict among the members of the society of states. Crises like those provoked by the meltdown of a nuclear reactor, the incubation of an infectious disease, the migration of industrial pollutants or water-table contaminants, genetic interventions with unanticipated consequences all will put stress on an international system that is steadily divesting itself of legitimate universal legal institutions, even as it is creating new global economic ones. During much of the period in which the particulate ash and smoke from the fires in northern Mexico blanketed Texas in 1998, Mexico refused U.S. assistance in putting the fires out. When a Russian submarine with a nuclear reactor aboard was crippled in 2000, Russia similarly refused assistance until it was too late to rescue its crew. The president of South Africa once took the view that AIDS was not related to HIV and could have, had he persisted, greatly worsened a transnational epidemic. These incidents may be harbingers of the sorts of environmental problems that can easily lead to conflict.

Nation-states tend to treat epidemiological matters in nonsecurity terms. Air travelers, for example, are routinely screened for carrying weapons across national borders; they are seldom required to demonstrate that they are free of lethal communicable infections. By viewing such matters as international security issues, the market-state sets the stage for strategic conflict over their resolution.

(3)

Nation-states continue to think in terms of maintaining control of conventional agricultural and industrial raw materials (like food and oil) by encompassing them within their territories, neglecting to put in place rules of behavior that will govern the distribution of goods like water and technology when these are at least as likely to be the source of interstate conflict in the future. Hitherto restrictions on technology transfers—like those governing the export of high-speed computers that can be used in missile telemetry—arose from state conflicts like the Cold War. In the future such restrictions may themselves be the cause of conflict.

(4)

Nation-states tend to treat crime and corruption in terms of the laws of a single state, using suppression to its fullest effect. This overlooks the destructive economic and political effects in other societies of the markets in illegal enterprises created by such national suppression. The inadvertent consequences of the United States's attempted suppression of cocaine consumption has perhaps done more harm to the polities of many Third World governments than meddling and intervention ever did.

(5)

The next example of the historic juxtaposition of these two archetypal forms of the State is potentially the most disturbing. This is the set of issues that is becoming known as the problem of "critical infrastructure." A society's critical infrastructure is composed of those elements—telecommunications, energy, banking and finance, transportation, government services—that undergird modern life such that their extended interdiction would have consequences for the sustainability of that way of life. Historically, these elements were confined to national territories. Moreover, these individual elements of the infrastructure were physically and conceptually separate systems that had little interdependence. Generation of electricity by the local power company did not depend, in any immediate way, on the operations of the local phone company or the local bank; the German phone company did not depend on the British phone system, nor did the Japanese banking system depend on the day-to-day operations of the Italian banking system. Beginning in the mid-eighties, however, the interplay among a number of factors created a new largely intangible infrastructure, the international superinfrastructure, that is critically essential to, yet also critically dependent upon, each of the traditionally recognized infrastructures. The factors bringing about the emergence of this superinfrastructure include the many developments in information and communications technology, but also, crucially, a change in attitude among the most highly developed members of the society of states about the role of government and the market. This change in values within many states—which is encapsulated by the claim that we are moving from the era of the nation-state to that of the market-state—has had two effects that are relevant to this problem. First, it has vastly enhanced the vulnerability of the critical infrastructure of states because the reshaping of the various sectors mentioned above (banking, energy, and so on) has taken the path of greater efficiency rather than greater national security. Deregulation and greater competition have meant that there are now more competing operators with access to critical systems, and that operators are no longer monopolists with annual profits guaranteed by the State with which they can be relied upon to cooperate in matters of national interest. The new players have a different attitude toward their responsibilities to the society in which they operate.

Second, each government's role in protecting its state's infrastructure has become bewilderingly complex, even paralyzing. Two facts are sufficient to make it so: most of the critical infrastructure for the most developed state is in the hands of the private sector, which thus controls the information on which any attempts to ensure security depend; and the origin of attacks on these infrastructures can be made impossible to trace, so that traditional strategies of deterrence and retaliation become irrelevant. It may or it may not be in the interests of Lloyds Bank to disclose to government authorities that a successful intrusion into its accounts had been made by a cyberattack that has cracked its security codes via the Internet, but even if a national government learned of such an attack, which ministry has jurisdiction? Should the intrusion be treated as a domestic crime? As a foreign attack? And if a foreign attack, is it by a state or a criminal conspiracy or some subnational group? Or is the entire affair the work of a disgruntled employee or simply a glitch in the software? Who has the authority to answer these questions, bearing in mind that the costs to the society of an unreported attack will almost always be greater than the costs borne by the private enterprise that suffers the initial loss, but that the private enterprise can be global while the exclusive jurisdiction of the State is, by definition, territorially limited.

The core elements of the international superinfrastructure are the telecommunications networks—which include the landline networks of long-distance telephone carriers, cellular networks, and satellite services—and the collection of information technologies that in the year 2000 was composed of 400 million computers worldwide—about 50 percent of which were in the United States, Germany having 7 percent, China 1 percent—and the Internet, a global network interconnected by means of routers that use a common set of protocols to provide communication among users then numbering about 32 million devices, and expected by 2002 to encompass about 300 million worldwide. Taken together, these three networks (telecommunications, computer, and Internet) supported over 200 million hours of connectivity every business day in 2000. The telecommunications networks are crucial for virtually all aspects of the infrastructures of most states, including their defense operations. In 2001 more than 95 percent of all internal communications by the U.S. Department of Defense went by means of the public switched network. Moreover, the pace of this increasing dependence was quickening.

So long as the nation-state dominated public affairs, it was inconceivable that states would willingly lose control of their national telecommunication industries. If it had been proposed in 1945 that the U.S. Bell System should be dismantled, objections on grounds of national security and law enforcement would almost certainly have trumped efficiency concerns. Today, the desire to bring better service at a lower cost to consumers has made the security and law arguments sound antiquated. In fact the distinctions between local and long distance and between wireline and wireless service providers are beginning to disappear. All aspects of the public switched telephone network have now been opened to competition. In the traditionally monopolistic local markets, local exchange carriers have been required to allow alternative access providers to interconnect to them. The U.S. Telecommunications Act of 1996 cleared the way for cable television operators to offer telephone and other services over their cable systems. As the structure of the industry changes, fewer services will be delivered wholly by a single provider; more often services will involve interconnection and interworking among several providers, which will inevitably mean greater reliance on what I have called the superinfrastructure. As in banking, the industry will consolidate. The Pacific Telesis–SBC and NYNEX–Bell Atlantic mergers in 2000 reflected this trend. Indeed future mergers will be international in scope, such as was presaged by British Telecom's attempted takeover of the MCI network. Thus we will see a more diverse and decentralized system that is, at the same time, far more dependent on a smaller number of electronic gateways.

Banking and finance, after having remained essentially unchanged since the Second World War, are being revolutionized through access to the superinfrastructure, interacting with a political environment that has radically changed regulatory policy. Until the 1980s, the financial services infrastructure of most countries was primarily the product of states that prohibited these institutions from entering specific lines of business, limited the ownership of various types of firms, and prevented banks from operating on an international or even national level. In some states, such as Japan and Germany, many of these constraints were still largely in force at the century's end. Once deregulation occurs, however, financial institutions need advanced telecommunications to remain competitive in the new environment. In the twenty-first century, the infrastructure of national banking and financial services will become heavily dependent on computer-controlled systems and the telecommunications systems that link them together to move instruments of value through the economy. Payment systems, perhaps the most crucial sector in banking and financial operations, rely on a small number of networked information systems to track, finalize, and account for transactions. Practically all communications in the industry use leased terrestrial circuits; and it is anticipated that the trading markets, electronic funds transfer, and other financial functions will migrate to shared networks like the Internet that are more cost-effective. The use of electronic cash is quickly increasing, with a significant impact on the volume and value of transactions flowing through electronic funds. Visa and Mastercard are international systems of banking and debit that would be impossible without this electronic linkage. In the five years from 1990 to 1995 the use of cash in all transactions decreased 5 percent, and this trend is accelerating. The number of banks is expected to continue to decline. Many financial institutions are outsourcing activities, allowing them to focus on core business functions and reduce overhead. The result of this, however, is to concentrate back-office financial functions in a handful of third-party providers connected by the super-infrastructure, so that disruption of one major outsource would affect multiple companies.

Similarly, for nearly sixty years the electric power industry reflected a well-defined pattern of mutually exclusive regulated monopolies, each serving customers in its discrete area. Utilities in the United States and Britain now must unbundle generation, transmission, and other services, enabling rivals to lease lines to send power to their customers. Companies must post data on transmission availability and rates on the Internet. Moreover, in the past, steam-driven generators were the norm, whether relying on coal or nuclear fuel. Now aero-derivative gas turbines make power more cheaply, use less fuel, and are cleaner. With the new technology, power companies can achieve comparable output with plants one-tenth the size. This means that new, smaller companies can enter the market, increasing competition and penalizing older utilities with high sunk costs in outmoded plant and equipment. Today, telecommunications networks hook up to the giant Interconnects that are the islands of the electrical power infrastructure for the developed world. Electrical power generation, transmission, and distribution are largely controlled by a multitude of automated systems that monitor, report on, and in part control the flow of energy throughout these systems. Yet as more players enter the field, the SCADA—supervisory control and data acquisition—systems that manage the flow of energy are becoming more numerous. These standardized, automated systems are linked to control centers that are linked in turn to management systems responding to the increasingly competitive business environment. Thus we have the paradox of more access to competition, meaning more competitors, and yet more centralization and dependence upon the superinfrastructure.

The pipelines that carry oil and gas, like the energy transmission lines, also are controlled by SCADA systems that rely on standardized, automated mechanisms as a way of meeting the pressures of intensified competition. These systems controlled in 2000 much of the 22,000 miles of oil pipelines and 1.2 million miles of gas pipelines, regulating the flow of oil and gas through an array of pumps, vents, valves, and storage facilities throughout the pipeline system. Here as elsewhere, the efforts toward standardization and establishment of common protocols are driven by the high cost of maintaining multiple kinds of protocols, computer hardware, and software. Many infrastructure entities look to the day when virtually all of their operations will run on networks of large computers using standard communications software throughout.

The difficulty posed by these infrastructure developments is that a cyberattack on that structure can now be launched from anywhere on the globe and can have an impact that is compounded by the interconnectivity among essential elements of the infrastructure. The rapid dependence on information that is sweeping the infrastructure is accompanied by a mutual dependency among, and a dramatic lessening of the number of, critical nodes as well as a general standardization. These developments are largely responsible for the increase in wealth that has been brought about by the new deployment of information; unavoidably they have created a situation of very high risk should that information be tampered with or interdicted. The use of information technology has grown from an option to enhance efficiency to a necessity that many parts of the infrastructure require to function.

The critical superinfrastructure provides the link between the processes of quite different organizations and thus, if compromised, has the ability to create a cascading effect, multiplying destruction exponentially. Thus, for example, a national outage of the U.S. public switched network (PSN) would not only bring almost all local service and all long-distance telephone service in North America to a halt; it would also disrupt Internet communications and cut off essential services such as air traffic control, banking and financial transactions, and even the emergency response to deal with the crisis caused by this outage.

Who would mount such an attack? Unlike conventional warfare, this type of operation would offer little strategic warning and few indications of an imminent assault. Physical attacks would be carried out by small, highly mobile units, while individuals equipped with laptop computers could launch attacks from any point on the global network. This form of warfare would be inexpensive, putting it within reach of most groups and most states. As in the world economy, the greatest asset in this conflict would be information: in this case, the information necessary to turn information technology against itself.

Where would such an attack on the critical superinfrastructure come from? It might be the result of a natural disaster, like an earthquake or flood, or of a simple accident at a critical node owing to design flaws, installation errors, or inadequate operation. Or it might be caused by an intentional act of terrorism, like the attacks on the World Trade Center that targeted both the American air traffic network and its financial services industry. The most insidious and conceivably the most damaging threat to cyber systems, however, is a cyber threat. Such threats are new, the product of the information age that gave rise to the superinfrastructure in the first place.

Cyber threats might arise from malicious insiders, from terrorists or military opponents, or organized crime, from hackers or competing industrial firms, or from the national intelligence or defense agencies of other countries.[13] National intelligence agencies may wish to siphon off data or even to insert disinformation. In a 1990s incident, organized crime electronically robbed Citibank of $10 million through its branch office in St. Petersburg, Russia; it would be idle to suppose that criminal conspiracies will not explore the possibilities of falsifying criminal records, accounts, and other data stored electronically. Hackers are often students who penetrate government and private systems for the sheer thrill of beating the system. In an era of deep suspicion of the motives of governments and large corporations, the number of such persons will surely increase as the number of persons with computer expertise and experience increases.[14] Insiders pose the most dangerous threat because they have detailed knowledge of the systems they attack and ready access to the target's own resources.

Even while economic competition is driving globalization and the centralization of risks that amounts to placing very heavy bets on a few roulette numbers, this same competition provides a strong disincentive to actions in the private sector to ensure information security. Steps that are sufficient from an economic point of view are not necessarily reasonable from the viewpoint of national security and emergency preparedness, but greater measures are more costly, and therefore competitively penalize the company that undertakes them.

Nor is it yet entirely clear what government should do. There are no unified bodies of law devoted to critical infrastructure. Rather there are elaborate fiefdoms of regulation that have evolved in separate sectors seeking to ensure service, public safety, and competition. The government needs private partners to undertake the task of protecting the information superinfrastructure, yet these are the same corporations that are often reluctant even to report break-ins or breakdowns in their operations and who are very distrustful of joint operations with the government.

At bottom, this is a national security problem, but it is also a problem for international security, because the infrastructure we must protect is increasingly international. This fact is a by-product of a much desired goal of the market-state, the creation of a world economy. If states seek to expand the opportunities for every individual, then this will necessarily lead to a globalization of the infrastructure. If a market-state attempted to interfere with this development in order to protect the national security—that is, the security of the national critical infrastructure—it would inevitably sacrifice the expansion of opportunity that is its purpose and thus the reason for which it claimed that it is important to keep the State secure in the first place.

The potency of particular threats to the State changes with each era. A modern army could be quickly suffocated if its logistical umbilical cord were severed by infrastructure attacks, while the mercenaries of the Thirty Years' War, who lived mainly by foraging, could have continued functioning. The reliance of modern armies on telecommunications and electronic computation* has created new and more valuable targets for cyberattack and weapons of mass destruction.

Yet the problem of attacks on critical infrastructure is in large part a private sector problem. If we bring to bear on this problem the strategic habits of the Long War—of the nation-state, that is—we may actually sacrifice the tort liability and corporate responsibility necessary for innovative insurance and improved security practices that would arise from the private sector responding to economic disincentives. If states (in a nation-state mentality) were to try to impose regulatory solutions, these might well be ineffective in any case: there will never be sufficient time or resources to write legal rules ahead of the imaginative cyber designer. Only experienced managers in the sectors themselves, acting daily and learning constantly, can stay ahead of this threat; regulations will always come too late.

These two aspects of the critical infrastructure problem—its private and international dimensions—are unwelcome to most states: internationalizing national security is only a little more distasteful than privatizing it. But there are really very few practical alternatives. Most of us are unlikely to be attackers in this new era, but we will probably all be defenders at one time or another. Cyber threats, in themselves, are poorly analogized to the wars of the past, which depended on violence for their essential character. Rather cyber threats are more like epidemiological threats, in which our ultimate security will lie in the good sense of private persons in many countries, cooperating through a central clearinghouse but assessing their own health and taking the appropriate measures to maintain it. To continue the metaphor, the U.S. Centers for Disease Control (CDC) and Prevention, not the Pentagon, is the model the market-state should pursue in addressing this problem.

Nevertheless, the defense planners of many developed states have an important role to play. Their first step must be to free themselves from the habits they acquired planning for nuclear strategy (just as nuclear strategy fifty years ago required that they free themselves from the habits inculcated by theories of conventional bombing). We must learn to think in terms of vulnerabilities instead of threats; of mitigation instead of fortress defense; of reconstitution instead of retaliation. These changes in our ways of thinking are as crucial to dealing with the problem of critical infrastructure protection as are the technological aspects of the problem.

Vulnerability-based strategies against chemical/biological, nuclear, or cyberattacks will depend upon *heterogeneity* (the use of multiple means of

---

*The U.S. force in Kosovo was one-tenth the size of the Desert Storm force in the Gulf War, yet it used a hundred times the bandwidth.

protection and communication), *reassessment* (the use of dynamic systems that reallocate resources automatically), *redundancy* (which depends upon excess information), *resilience* (which depends upon excess capacity), *integrity* (which depends upon strong encryption), *decentralization* (which enables the use of quarantines of both persons and networks), and *deception*. None of these concepts are new to military planners, but they have to be applied in new, defensive modalities. Our current planning—which depends entirely on detecting a computer intrusion, monitoring it, and tracking down the attacker—is hopelessly ill-suited to our situation. Such retaliatory strategies surrender initiative and permit the aggressor to soak up our resources with little more cost to him than the press of a key. Yet 90 percent of the proposed U.S. 2000 budget in this arena was earmarked for intrusion detection and prevention. The developed market-states should be spending their resources on technologies that make the critical infrastructure more slippery, more difficult to damage, more quickly reconstituted, and, above all, more deceptive.

An historical analogy may also provide some help. At the beginning of the twentieth century, many industrial societies experienced unprecedented migration from rural to urban areas. In America this was augmented by large-scale immigration from Europe. One result was the construction of vast tracts of substandard housing in densely populated city areas. At about the same time the first modern housing codes were promulgated. These set minimal standards for building construction and emergency access. But the real work of protecting cities from fires was done by private insurance companies that required compliance with these codes as a condition for insurance (which was itself a condition for mortgage financing). The increased vulnerability of critical infrastructure has been brought about by the same volcanic economic growth that the United States experienced early in the twentieth century. This vulnerability is also driven partly by consumer demand and partly by the familiar problem of single-actor transaction costs (which tend to jeopardize an entire neighborhood, for example, because the cost to any one actor of a fire does not justify the expense of organizing protection for all). Some similar sort of information security requirement for private insurance can also be useful in addressing the problem of critical infrastructure. Using the market in this way—because insurance is a globalized service—can internationalize a solution far more effectively (and more quickly) than a network of international treaties.

As with environmental threats imposed by a single irresponsible state on all others, it is highly possible that a state linked by the Internet to all other states might threaten, however inadvertently, the critical infrastructure of the entire developed world. And as with global environmental threats, rules for timely intervention are needed. In their absence, we run the risk of introducing some of the classic and familiar causes of war that, when played across the dimension of constitutional change, make the strategic innovation of a cybernated infrastructure attack the kind of tinderbox that could ignite a war in the twenty-first century.

(6)

Owing to the development of public health measures, inoculations and vaccines, and modern antibiotics the ancient practice of quarantine largely vanished from twentieth-century developed states. This coincided with the emergence in the United States of omnicompetent nation-state governments that replaced the more limited domestic authorities of the state-nation. Thus even though potential federal authority of the States expanded, with respect to quarantine, this authority lay fallow. Today we have the paradoxical situation that a threat to the entire nation by means of infectious agents in a terrorist war against the United States would confront a patchwork of state laws, only a few of which have been updated to apply to all diseases. The federal government is, statutorily, largely out of the picture and the state laws are often antiquated. Many state laws require judicial approval in order to enforce a quarantine. Other state laws restrict the authority of public health officials to share information about an individual's health status. Some states forbid the sharing of information among state agencies or even for one state to inform another state of a health emergency. In October 2001 the CDC released a model state Emergency Health Powers Act. This statute is designed to give officials the power to act decisively in the event of a biological attack or the outbreak of an infectious epidemic.

Under this statute, public health officials could compel a person to submit to a physical exam or a test without a court order. Physicians and other health workers could be forced to do this testing. While court orders would be required for quarantines officials could quarantine first and go to court afterward. Officials could compel persons to be vaccinated or treated for infectious diseases. States would have broad emergency powers to confiscate property and facilities, including subways, hospitals, and drug companies.

This statute implicates a number of significant constitutional issues: (1) Should the federal government, rather than the states, be empowered as the effective public health actor in such a crisis? Currently federal authority relies on the Stafford Act, which is far too narrow and restrictive to help in such an emergency; if, however, state and federal authorities are not clarified, we could face the prospect of paralysis or even intergovernmental violence. (2) Does the federal government have the constitutional power, in light of recent Supreme Court cases, to adopt legislation similar to that in the proposed model act? The federal government does have ample emergency powers in war and it may be that a terrorist attack could engage those authorities. But it might also be that an outbreak of an infectious epidemic will occur without the disclosure of its origin. Other federal constitutional powers, such as the commerce power, that might serve as the basis for federal action have been sharply restricted by recent caselaw as the United States moves toward market-state constitutional rules. (3) How might the civil liberties of Americans be safeguarded in such a statute, state or federal? Questions such as the limits of public health surveillance, the requirement of mandatory disease reporting, confidentiality, compulsory vaccination, testing and screening, isolation and quarantine, compulsory physical examination—all these issues implicate the Constitution's guarantee of due process and its commitment to personal and physical autonomy. Other questions might arise regarding the guarantee of equal protection. For example, in the early 1900s, San Francisco imposed a quarantine to halt a tuberculosis epidemic, but applied the quarantine only to Chinese Americans. In the 1980s HIV-infected students were often barred from public schools and several states passed laws allowing AIDS patients to be quarantined.

The potential twenty-first century conflict posed by this problem is one of civil war.

(7)

The revolution in military affairs that won the Long War is currently bringing us the market-state. The emergence of this new form of the constitutional order will be accompanied by new forms of warfare. In these final paragraphs I should like to speculate about these new forms. In other words, if the current revolution in military affairs, taken in a broader sense than simply the latest technology, is a consequence of the threefold phenomenon of nuclear and other weapons of mass destruction, international telecommunications, and the power of rapid computation, and if the market-state is the constitutional consequence of this revolution in military affairs, what is the next revolution in military affairs that is a consequence of the market-state? I venture the guess that it will be a result of advances in biogenetics and that this development will challenge the meritocracy on which the market-state depends.

Thus the knowledge and techniques that will make biological superweapons available to the market-state and its adversaries may ultimately bring about the new form that will supersede that state. First, the dispersal of these techniques to market actors—corporations that run hospitals, pharmaceutical labs, vast agribusinesses, and the like—will inevitably have the consequence of proliferating actual weapons to those who wish to destroy the market-state. Second, the open society on which the market-state depends and which it does so much to foster will find it more difficult than the nation-state to assert legal control over biogenetic knowledge and weaponizing. The public will call for measures that are highly intrusive and oppressive, and these too will undermine the ethos of the market-state. Third, the fundamental idea of the market-state—that equality means treating those equally endowed in an equal way*—will be shattered when the means of altering our natural endowment of intelligence, beauty, emotional stability, physical strength and grace, even sociability, is available at a price. The market-state will have to decide how to distribute such benefits, having thrown away the basis on which it was created to make such decisions, namely, the cultivation of natural merit. And this development creates a fertile environment for violent civil conflict.

---

*A conception quite different from the egalitarianism of the nation-state, where equality meant treating all citizens equally because citizenship was granted equally to all.

CHAPTER TWENTY-SEVEN

Peace in the Society of Market-States:
Conclusion to Book II

The means that nature employs to accomplish the development of all faculties is the antagonism of men in society, since this antagonism becomes, in the end, the cause of a lawful order of this society.

—Kant, *Idea for a Universal History
with Cosmopolitan Intent* (1784)

ALTHOUGH THERE ARE intended to be many parallels between the arguments and structure of Book I, "State of War," and Book II, "States of Peace," it is hoped that either book could stand alone. Book I addresses the State: its modern birth and its morphogenesis from chamberlains waiting on Renaissance princes to the complex and varied bureaucracies of the market-states of the twenty-first century. "States of Peace" is addressed to the collectivity of modern states. Because that collectivity is built out of individual states, the dynamic relation between strategy and constitutionalism that drove the development of the State is also reflected in the development of the society of states. There is, however, one profound difference: whereas it was violence and disorder that animated the development of the law and strategy of the State—the State's need to monopolize the control of legitimate violence within, and to be free of violent coercion outside its boundaries—it was peace and reconciliation that animated the development of the society of states—that society's need to find consensus on the legitimate basis for admission to the society and to maintain harmony and stability among its members. On November 9, 1989, twelve states met in Canberra and created the organization for Asia-Pacific Economic Cooperation (APEC). On that same day the Berlin Wall came down. The first event belongs to Book II; the second, to Book I. Who can say today for which event November 9, 1989, will be remembered in twenty-five or fifty years' time?

Book I ended with the emergence of the market-state in its various forms. These variations are the result of different historical attitudes about the degree and nature of sovereignty that is retained by the people of the State. Such differences were reflected in different provisions for human rights and the differing responsibilities that were assumed by the State for the economic security of its citizens. Some states, like the United States, hold that all government power is derived directly from a portion of the sovereignty of the People. These states tend to enforce expansive human rights for individual expression but are less supportive of the assured status and income security of citizens. Others, like the city-state of Singapore, are more authoritarian because they hold that sovereignty lies in the State and rights are granted to the People. Still others, like France, hold that while sovereignty lies in the People, it has been wholly delegated to the State for the benefit of the People, and this responsibility is reflected in the public policies of such states, which tend to be more concerned with maintaining the social contract.

Imagine a society composed of such different kinds of market-states. How does such a society achieve consensus? Does it need to achieve consensus? What might such a consensus accomplish?

One necessary step is to factor the interests of the society of states into a state's calculations of its own vital interests. One of the barriers to the consideration of the interests of the society of states has been the nonterritoriality of that society. Where is it? Over what territory does its flag fly? Who speaks for its interests? Is its jurisdiction universal? If it is everywhere, then does it supplant the jurisdiction of the individual states? If the paradigm of the legitimate constitutional form of the state is the nation-state, then must the society of states be composed of one great nation— mankind, perhaps? If the domain of the society of states is not everywhere, then is it confined to the property around the U.N. and other global organizations? Or on the high seas, beyond the littoral claims of states, in what are called "international waters"?

If we concede that the society of states is not territorial, then presumably it cannot be a sovereign. If it is not a sovereign, then it cannot generate law nor make war. It cannot set up rules for intervention, or act on those rules. If, on the other hand, we accept that sovereignty is not necessarily a matter of territoriality where would this end? Would the Red Cross be a state? Or Citicorp? Or Al Qaeda?

Nation-states could only delegate sovereignty legitimately when a larger nation was created, as for example, by the union of Egypt and Syria, which was called the United Arab Republic, or when a previous state fragmented, as for example, when Ukraine, Russia, and other republics succeeded the USSR. International bodies, like the U.N. and the ICJ, were legal bodies composed of representatives of sovereigns. They were not sovereign themselves.

Market-states can legitimately augment these representatives with agents hired by contract, that is, through markets. Such agents are nonterritorial, like other market entities. On this basis some institutions, like the IMF, would have fiduciary responsibilities to some states; this responsibility, therefore, would not axiomatically be universal. Some institutions, like NATO, could—under the terms of a contract with its constitutive partners—even wage war, though they could not make peace settlements (because, as mere agents they cannot make law). Other institutions, like the U.N., or the World Bank or the ICJ, would lapse into more circumscribed, though still valuable, roles than the ones they occupy today as representatives of the society of nation-states.

What a pluralist society of states needs are practical means of cooperation—alternatives to the nation-state institutions that span the different forms of the market-state. Agreements to set up consortia among market-states might provide one such mechanism. The very process of hammering out such agreements could be a useful way of achieving consensus. The responsibilities of these various ad hoc consortia would include the protection and advancement of the interests of the society of states—though once again, the "case-law" generated by their practices would not be universal as it would apply only to voluntary participants, and the war-fighting functions of such groups would not admit of an independent peacemaking authority. These consortia will be modeled more on multinational corporations or cartels than on states, in part because they are nonterritorial. They can either be a force for consensus and harmony—because they effectively aid the efficient functioning of the global market, human rights, and the information that links the two—or they can harden into competing alliances with limitless capacity for conflict. Corporations, after all, are designed to compete.

States recognize that it is not territoriality alone that they must defend, but rather also nonterritorial interests. Such a recognition runs against the grain of the leaders of states. Thinking of the State as essentially territorial comes naturally in light of how modern states began, and their close identification of sovereignty with the body of the prince. We even speak of the *body politic,* and also of the *territorial integrity* of the state when it is whole.

Nevertheless, threats like those posed to the critical infrastructure of states are fundamentally nonterritorial. The computer attack via the Internet that disables a power grid or a telecommunications link is not really a territorial attack. An attack on the critical superinfrastructure that binds the developed world ever more interdependently is actually an attack on the assets of the society of states, on which individual states may depend but which they do not own any more than they own a market in raw materials, or a market in currencies.

Such a change in attitude about the nonterritorial interests of states is bound to come with the advent of the market-state. Also, there will come changes in how territory itself is viewed. Each historic society of states has favored a particular means of resolving state disputes. Not surprisingly, the society of nation-states favored national partitions (quite unlike the partitions of Poland, for example, in the nineteenth century that made no pretext of accommodating national peoples). Market-states that are defined less by their territoriality and their nations will find other means appropriate to their constitutional form.

One may speculate that the umbrella, rather than the felt-tipped marker that once limned partition lines, will be one such means. The umbrella is a free-trade and/or defense zone that allows for a common legal jurisdiction as to some, but not all, issues. To put it differently, an umbrella is one outcome of a market in sovereignty. Different umbrellas may overlap. Small societies can shelter within such umbrellas—cultures too small to be viable as separate states—retaining for themselves control over essentially cultural matters.* For such umbrellas to work, however, we must weaken the promise of maximum identical human freedoms for all peoples, because the cultural control that a society wishes to retain (its religious character, for example) may infringe on maximum identical freedom. As Thomas Jefferson wrote in a letter, "the maxim of civil government should be reversed and we should say: divided we stand, united we fall."

Umbrellas of this kind might permit the reunion of states that were severed by partition: India, Bangladesh, and Pakistan; the Koreas; Rwanda, Burundi, and Tanzania; Ireland; Palestine—all the states whose insecurity threatens the stability of the society of states and, I might add, that of the United States so long as she chooses to exercise world leadership and thus inevitably attracts the hostility of otherwise remote parties. Moreover such umbrellas offer a constitutional mechanism for ameliorating one of the most significant shortcomings of the market-state, its indifference to community and to culture. Under a multicultural umbrella, many subcultures can dwell, appropriating the economic and defense advantages of a larger territorial scope while retaining the ability to develop different legal regimes within each specific domain. These subcultures will not be states, at least as we have understood the term. Let us call them "provinces." These may be provinces where feminists or fundamentalist Christians or

*Compare the Hungarian proposals for a "contractual nation," a range of government agencies and foundations that link ethnic Hungarians living in neighboring countries to Hungary. "According to this view, Hungarians abroad should be able to claim Budapest as their cultural center, Bratislava or Belgrade as their state capitals, Cluj-Napoca or Novi Sad as their regional centers, and so on." Zsuzsa Csergo and James Goldgrier, "Virtual Nationalism," *Foreign Policy* (July/August 2001): 76.

ethnic Chinese congregate, all within a larger sheltering area of trade and defense. This concept of overlapping jurisdictions offers another way in which consensus might be assisted once market-states emerge. Such markets in sovereignty can be liberating for groups that now feel confined within national sovereignties or ignored within multicultural states. But such markets can also lead to internal conflict as some groups within a state wish to trade sovereignty while others do not; and markets in sovereignty can lead to external conflict as some states feel alienated and marginalized by richer, more encompassing cartels of shared human values.*

Tentatively we may note these ten constitutional conditions for a society of market-states: (1) the maintenance of a force structure capable of defeating a challenge to peace; (2) the creation of security structures and alliances capable of dealing with the problems of population control, migration, and ecological stability; (3) a consensus among the great powers on the legitimacy of certain forms of the market-state; (4) a few clear, structural rules for any state's behavior that are enforced by arms if necessary, analogous to the society of nation-states' bar against the annexation of any territory without the consent of its inhabitants; (5) provisions for the financial assistance to great powers when these powers undertake to intervene on behalf of the peace and security of the society of states as a whole; (6) prohibitions against arms trading in nuclear materials, weapons of mass destruction (WMD), and missile technology but that permit trade in some defensive, informational technologies; (7) practices for bribing states—by enhancing their security or their wealth—in order to prevent WMD proliferation to any state but especially to major states; (8) prohibitions against wholesale attacks by the state on its own populations; (9) some general prohibition on anticompetitive trade and financial practices; (10) a consensus on the rule that no state that meets the standards of the Peace of Paris—free elections, market economy, human rights—ought to be the subject of threats of force.

These conditions are not the same as those that aimed to ensure stability in the Long War. They are not the same as those sought by the U.S. policy of containment that successfully ended that war. These conditions give greater priority to peripheral conflicts and require greater consensus. They may not cost any less, but they allocate expenditures differently. They address a new class of security problems that will not be resolved any more easily, and possibly not any more quickly, than those of the Long War. Finally, these conditions presuppose a commitment to pluralism that

---

*Some of the key cases to watch are the communities of the Walloons (Belgium), the Turks (Bulgaria), the Quebecois (Canada), Germans (Czech Republic), Magyars (Romania), the Basques and Catalans (Spain), the Irish, Welsh, and Scots (United Kingdom), and the Lombards (Italy).

is inconsistent with either relativism or exceptionalism. By pluralism is meant the view that some values are to be preferred to others, and that these preferred values are those democratic and peaceful institutions that permit individuated and diverse cultural development in the context of nonaggressive relations. The reason why the political system of the West is preferred is that it is the only system that allows *all* states, Western or not, to develop their own cultures. In a society of states committed to pluralism there are preferred values (as opposed to relativism) but no preferred states (as opposed to exceptionalism).

The above list of conditions also suggests a way in which states can decide when to use force to achieve or maintain peace, that is, it implies a calculus analogous to the Weinberger Doctrine.[1] This program assumes that states will have to reconfigure and retrain their forces to function in ambiguous environments, where the threat may not come from another state or even an identifiable aggressor, and where the line between war and crime has been smudged.

We ask the same questions that we asked before. *Which crises demand consideration for intervention?* Those with significant costs to world public order, that system of state legitimacy that relies on the ten conditions for peace outlined above. *When do these crises profit from intervention?* When intervention is likely to make a decisive difference at a cost/reward ratio that is commensurate with the significance of the risk to world public order. *Who should intervene?* Those states with the largest stakes in world public order. *What objectives should be pursued?* Restoring and maintaining the conditions for a civil society. *How is this accomplished?* By voluntary coalitions of essentially mercenary forces, compensated by contributions from all states having a stake in the outcome.[2] In Europe (and perhaps the Near East) this might mean the use of NATO forces; in Africa, Economic Community of West African States (ECOWAS) troops, augmented as necessary, and so on. The United States should take the lead in assembling such mercenary teams. As Joseph Nye has rightly said:

> the United States has to recognize a basic proposition of public-goods theory: if the largest beneficiary of a public good (such as international order) does not provide disproportionate resources toward its maintenance, the smaller beneficiaries are unlikely to do so.[3]

Such is the calculus of the society of states of peace. It is no more than a rather formulaic rendering of the commonsense judgments statesmen make every day, with the factors made a bit more perspicuous. This calculus recognizes the State's interest in a peaceful order. It contrasts with the classic calculus of a state of war, that is, that the State should not intervene when the risks of intervention in a crisis exceed the State's vital interests in the outcome.*

Expressing these rules of decision so plainly helps to determine the selection of the war aim, which we can define as that objective such that its relation to world public order yields a stake for the intervening state that exceeds the share of the risks—political and military—it is asked to bear. Such rules can also help determine the weapons to be deployed and the command structure to be used. These rules prompt leaders to offer realistic justifications for the courses of action they choose. It should not be necessary to pretend disingenuously that contemporary interventions obey the classic calculus of a state of war when the historical context for these decisions comes after the end of the Long War and in contemplation of preventing another such cataclysm. Leaders can forthrightly explain why they are intervening in situations that previously would not have been thought appropriate for intervention. To take one example: the U.S. president's speech explaining the situation in Kosovo when NATO air attacks began ought also to have explained our criteria for undertaking such attacks. The U.S. president's speech to Congress explaining our taking up arms against terrorism did so.

We have long been accustomed to think of the imperatives of the State as basically strategic, and of the issues that engage the society of states as fundamentally questions of law. We have long been accustomed to deny that a State can be compelled by other states to obey its own laws, and we usually deny that the society of states has any particular strategic objectives.

The developmental picture of the State that I have presented, however, portrays the constitutional and the strategic dimensions as intimately and inextricably interconnected. This interconnectedness between law and strategy is also a fundamental feature of the society of states. Within a single state the constitutional order determines the ways conflict is managed and rationalized domestically and abroad. For the international society of states, peace treaties perform a similar role, by attempting to solve the puzzles created by wars. In both instances, constitutions provide a society—whether it is a society of citizens or the society of states—with the means to choose among values when there is no one optimum solution. When the choices to be made are among incommensurate values, a constitution records and determines how those choices are to be made in order for them to be accorded legitimacy.

We have thought of international law as providing a largely stable background to the spread of the model of the European state around the globe.

---

*Compare Homer's description of the two cities—the City at Peace and the City at War—in his depiction of scenes on the shield of Achilles, *The Iliad*, Book XVIII, lines 491–549.

Some particular doctrines may change, but the idea of a law of nations is supposed to be more or less constant, ever expanding until it has become universal. On the basis of the portrait I have given of international law, however, this description is unjustified. International law has developed in a turbulent periodicity, changing its most basic precepts as its constituent parties, states, underwent dramatic and fundamental constitutional change. One consequence of this different understanding is that universalism no longer seems inevitable, and we can entertain the idea that the reversibility of this universalism does not mean the retrenchment or death of international law itself.

We have thought of the history of the nation-state as having begun at Westphalia. Here, too, the portrait I have drawn is somewhat different. This, too, is freeing, because it allows us to imagine that the nation-state may indeed be dying (as seems to many to be the case) without having to concede that the State itself is withering away (as seems improbable).

The Long War of the nation-state is over, having destroyed every empire that participated in it, every political aristocracy, every general staff, as well as much of the beauty of European and Asian life. Of that brief period after world markets brought relative comfort and security and before world ambition brought the destruction of societies that in retrospect appear so very unworldly, we can only say: such a period could not exist in our age.

I have called this conflict the Long War not simply because of its duration but because this length connects the world of many centuries—feudal, national, imperial, mercantile, and religious—with the world that is yet to be, the new century's world that is being born.

Two tasks lie before us: to decide, as states, when it is appropriate to use force in this new world; and to determine, as a society of states, when to collectively sanction the use of that force in this world. This is a matter of creating precedents and case law. It amounts to deploying the habits of law on behalf of strategy, and of course vice versa.

These precedents and case law, however, are not those generated by courts. We may accomplish in Bosnia a successful, long-term intervention by the society of states on world-public-order grounds; if we do, then the Yugoslav Wars will become as much a precedent in the future as the Gulf War is now. The same is true of our war on international terrorism. The rules of collective engagement will be based on how the last similar problem was approached, and on what basis we would like to see the next, future problem resolved. I believe that the combination of improvised constitutional instruments with increasingly settled case law is the appropriate method for the society of market-states. This combination is a reversal of the method of the nation-state (and to that extent may take place outside the U.N.).

This case law of the society of states must be consciously crafted. It will require political, business, and media leaders to think in terms of following and creating precedents rather than in terms of the impromptu. It will require that leaders forthrightly explain their decisions by means of doctrine, and not simply in emotive phrases. We are now in a position to write this case law through our decisions; some day, through an inability to achieve international consensus, we may no longer be in such a position, and we will regret having wasted an opportunity that would have avoided a world-rending war.

The views on international security generally prevailing today, however, are far from those that reflect a commitment to creating such case law. These views are at once very narrow and very ambitious. They are narrow because they have up to now excluded the nonterritorial threats to the State that are becoming increasingly dangerous; they are complacently ambitious because they do not recognize that the power of states to ensure their own security by conventional strategies is rapidly waning.

States are losing control of their sovereignty, especially if this is conceived in territorial terms. Once the territorial membrane collapses, then the distinction between law and strategy—the separate inner and outer modalities of the State—seems to weaken. In fact, this membrane was always a reflection of the interconnectedness of these two ideas, not of their independence. Because it was always so, implicitly, it should not alarm us now that we contemplate a world in which it is explicitly so. Like the union of time and space that once seemed so counterintuitive, the union of law and strategy is compelled by its usefulness. We simply cannot understand the development of the State and the society of states by holding either of these concepts in isolation from the other.

The threats we will soon be facing are not easily categorized as state aggressions. Indeed for the first time since the birth of the State, a state structure is no longer necessary in order to organize violence on a scale that is devastating to a society. And yet, perhaps ironically, this development makes the role of the State all the more crucial in achieving international peace and national security. This is because the shift away from retaliatory, threat-based strategies to defensive, vulnerability-based strategies will require a State—indeed will require a society of states—to successfully execute. Acting alone, the market can never coordinate the defensive tactics I have described into a general strategy. A market-state is required.

In the new era we are entering, the State will be as indispensable to peace as it was in the era of invasions that gave it birth. To stop a state's aggressions, especially against its own people, and to build international defenses against aggression that can, but need not, come from official governments will require strong states. If these missions are avoided or postponed, a new, horrifying kind of conflict may emerge in which an authoritarian market-state challenges the contentment of the rest because they are weak, and because their weakness is a threat, enabling nonstate terrorists and aggressors they cannot suppress to bring chaos everywhere. The market that encouraged this passivity will have destroyed the market-state.

So we begin a new millennium—*not* in terror but not in tranquility either; with faith and hope, but with wariness and an anxious foreboding, also. Law, strategy, and history continue, as before, to set the terms of legitimacy for the State. Although technology has changed the context for each of these fate-shaping institutions of godlike creation, the terms of legitimacy are human terms, not technological ones, written in human acts, and broken or mended by human deeds.

To act is to understand; every act reflects an understanding. My aim has been to enhance an understanding that has been called upon perhaps no more than a half dozen times in the last five hundred years to create a new world from the inherited political institutions of the old. Will we lay a long siege against ourselves or master the craft of the armorer when shields are made of secrets and not of bronze?

Advice to a Prophet

When you come, as you soon must, to the streets of our city,
Mad-eyed from stating the obvious,
Not proclaiming our fall but begging us
In God's name to have self-pity,

Spare us all word of the weapons, their force and range,
The long numbers that rocket the mind;
Our slow, unreckoning hearts will be left behind,
Unable to fear what is too strange.

Nor shall you scare us with talk of the death of the race.
How should we dream of this place without us?—
The sun mere fire, the leaves untroubled about us,
A stone look on the stone's face?

Speak of the world's own change. Though we cannot conceive
Of an undreamt thing, we know to our cost
How the dreamt cloud crumbles, the vines are blackened by frost,
How the view alters. We could believe,

If you told us so, that the white-tailed deer will slip
Into perfect shade, grown perfectly shy,
The lark avoid the reaches of our eye,
The jack-pine lose its knuckled grip

On the cold ledge, and every torrent burn
As Xanthus once, its gliding trout
Stunned in a twinkling. What should we be without
The dolphin's arc, the dove's return,

These things in which we have seen ourselves and spoken?
Ask us, prophet, how we shall call
Our natures forth when that live tongue is all
Dispelled, that glass obscured or broken

In which we have said the rose of our love and the clean
Horse of our courage, in which beheld
The singing locust of the soul unshelled,
And all we mean or wish to mean.

Ask us, ask us whether with the worldless rose
Our hearts shall fail us; come demanding
Whether there shall be lofty or long standing
When the bronze annals of the oak-tree close.

—Richard Wilbur

Epilogue

FOR FIVE CENTURIES only a state could destroy another state. And for five centuries, states have developed means of defeating other states. Entire worlds of diplomacy, international law, alliances, and naval, air, and land warfare are all predicated upon conflicts among *states*. Only states could marshal the resources to threaten the survival of other states; only states could organize societies to defend themselves against such threats. Only states could bring about peace congresses.

We are entering a period, however, when very small numbers of persons, operating with the enormous power of modern computers, biogenetics, air transport, and even small nuclear weapons, can deal lethal blows to any society. Because the origin of these attacks can be effectively disguised, the fundamental bases of the State will change.

During the second half of the hegemony of the order of nation-states—a period, that is, immediately following Hiroshima—many persons, including Albert Einstein, believed there would be either "one world or none." Fearing a nuclear holocaust, they hoped that strategy could be subordinated to world law. This fear has largely dissolved with the end of the Long War and the strategic triumph of one version of the nation-state, liberal parliamentarianism. Yet we may again soon hear this dated slogan because we will confront dangers every bit as great as we did then.

For the end of the Long War created a set of new challenges, and today a question descended from this conflict confronts the constitutional order. It is whether and how states can continue to exist with ever more ubiquitous and powerful technologies that can alter or destroy our entire environment. These technologies include weapons of mass destruction and biogenetic and cybernetic techniques. The legal institutions of the triumphant parliamentary states are committed to the protection of individual rights and civil liberties. To protect these institutions in the face of these new challenges will require a strategic ingenuity that would tax the gifts of the historic innovators described in this volume.

When a disguised attack with these new weapons occurs, and its author is not definitely identified, three deadly risks will arise: (1) a state that is unwilling or unable to suppress the elements believed to be responsible will forfeit its sovereignty and be subject to attack and even occupation; (2) a state that is the subject of an attack will sacrifice its constitutional institutions and turn on its own people—or a discrete minority within—with violence and despotic police methods; (3) a state, though disavowing responsibility, will be deemed the author of the attacks through unknown agents, and will become the target for retaliation. All three of these scenarios fall along the seam of sovereignty that separates law from strategy, and all three are laden with peril. Any one of these scenarios could lead to war, as the targets of retaliation resist.

In fact it is sometimes hard to separate the threats posed by nuclear, chemical, and biological weapons and cyberattacks, because so many of the techniques of any one of these is useful to the others. A coordinated biological attack is the dream of many terrorists; such scenarios are especially horrific when the means of coping with them, which are highly dependent on rapid information transfer, are also attacked. Furthermore, an adversary state might well want to shield itself from retaliation by operating not through its armed forces—arrayed invitingly across a desert frontier—but through shadowy agents posing as terrorists or acting through the infinitely extendable arms of the Internet.

Similarly, within a state,

> the knowledge and techniques for making biological super-weapons will become dispersed among hospital laboratories, agricultural research institutes, and peaceful factories everywhere. Only an oppressive police state could assure total government control over such novel tools for mass destruction. In a free and open democracy, those who wish to destroy the political order that they despise will inevitably find ways to acquire these tools.[1]

Such attacks will not arrive with labels that tell us whether they are the result of a terrorist's attack, or a strategic assault by another state, or just the afternoon diversions of a teenager in California. Therefore we must have governmental structures that are supple and flexible enough to react in an environment of unprecedented uncertainty. Above all we must avoid the paralysis that can seize a government when the jurisdictional lines along which we habitually act do not neatly correspond to the known facts of an incident.

Strategically the important thing to appreciate about such attacks is their essential ambiguity. Because it may not be possible to determine the source of the incursion, strategies of retaliation and deterrence, which have served us well in the past, become less useful. In such a world we must move our thinking from threat-based strategies that rely on knowing precisely who our enemy is and where he lives, to vulnerability-based strategies that try to make our infrastructure more slippery, more redundant, more versatile, more difficult to attack.

National security will cease to be defined in terms of borders alone because both the links among societies as well as the attacks on them exist in psychological and infrastructural dimensions, not on an invaded plain marked by the seizure and holding of territory. The line between the public and the private that has been the essential division between state and society has been partly effaced because most of the critical infrastructures are in the hands of the private sector. We shall have to take in new national security partners drawn from the private sector in order to protect the public good. Those states that defy this development by attempting to hold on to state-owned enterprises will steadily impoverish themselves at a rate that is slower, perhaps, but surer than those that risk vulnerability through competition and growth.

There will be no final victory in such a war. Rather victory will consist in having the resources and the ingenuity to avoid defeat.

So long, however, as states rely on a deterrence-and-retaliation model for their strategic paradigms—that is, a model that requires a threat-based analysis—they will inevitably neglect those steps, including enhanced intelligence collection, pre-emption, the development of defensive systems (including sensors), vaccinations, the prepositioning of medical supplies, and advanced methods of deception that provide the basis for operating within a different paradigm, one that relies on a vulnerability analysis. So long as states rely on a nation-state model for their international order, fruitlessly attempting to cope with new problems by trying to increase the authority of treaties, multistate conventions, or formal international institutions like the United Nations and the World Trade Organization, the society of states will fail to develop practices and precedents for regional, consensual, and market-driven arrangements that do not rely on law for enforcement. Constitutional orders that protect human rights and liberties can coexist with the consequences of the Long War only if they revolutionize their military strategies; states will only be able to pursue military strategies that enable collaboration and international consensus if they revolutionize their constitutional orders, away from the national, law-centered methods of the nation-state and toward the international, market operations of the market-state.

We are at the beginning of the sixth great revolution in strategic and constitutional affairs. The revolution in military affairs and the market-state are entering the twenty-first century together. For every state there are profound choices to be made: which military revolution to pursue (because this will affect the nature of market-state one gets, whether it is repressive or protective or aggressive); and which kind of market-state to pursue (managerial, entrepreneurial, or mercantile) because this will affect what kind of strategic capability is sought (nurturing collective goods and defensive systems, developing ever more lethal retaliatory abilities, or equipping large standing forces with global power projection). As in the past, revolutions in military affairs are symbiotically connected to transformations in the constitutional order, but neither are *mechanical*. Each depends on human decisions.

Because the nation-state puts so much reliance on law, one might conclude that in the coming era the market will replace law as the partner of strategy. That conclusion would be a mistake. Law will change, and the use of law as regulation, so favored by the nation-state, will lessen. Nevertheless the State will continue to rely on law to shape its internal order, even if the legal rules derived tend to be rules that recognize a larger role for the market. Only the State can promulgate laws. Therefore it will be crucial to develop legal processes that provide orderly and peaceful means of reflecting the popular will. Otherwise, the operations of the market-state will be reduced to the market itself. This will invite revolt.

The central point in recognizing the emergence of the market-state is not simply to slough off the decayed nation-state. It is also to emphasize the importance of developing public goods[2]—such as loyalty, civility, trust in authority, respect for family life, reverence for sacrifice, regard for privacy, admiration for political competence—that the market, unaided, is not well adapted to creating and maintaining. The market-state has to produce public goods because that is precisely what the market will not do. This need for qualities of reciprocity, solidarity, even decent manners, domestically, mirrors the need for collective goods, internationally, and thus represents not only a challenge but an opportunity for leadership.

Law and strategy will continue to be key instruments of the State. It is folly to consider steps in one of these dimensions without a sensitivity to the other. But the new context of the market-state will treat these interconnected dimensions in ways that are dissimilar to the worlds of legal regulation and strategic deterrence we are accustomed to in the nation-state. In 2001, the first year of the second Bush administration, the United States underwent a long-overdue defense review under the direction of Andrew Marshall. Its recommendations—on missile defense, force sizing, the "two and a half" war strategy, cyber and infrastructure protection—were the focus of intense scrutiny and, like the proposals in the present work, many of which they resemble, were controversial. But virtually no one in that debate observed that the profound changes urged in the Marshall Report will have equally profound consequences for the constitutional make-up of the country. Similarly, in Britain the government has pursued constitutional innovations like the devolution of power to Scotland, Wales, and Northern Ireland, a closer relationship with the European Union (including the possible adoption of a European currency), and even proportional representation in Parliament. These ideas were hotly debated in the 2001 election, and dissected in the political conversation that goes on after the election results are in, but there was little mention of how such changes will affect the willingness of citizens to volunteer for wars, to pay for expensive military technologies like missile defense, or to want to engage in expeditionary force initiatives.

When the best commentators look at the future, they seem to divide between two expectations: some, like John Keegan, expect that states will master the arts of peace and that war will wither away[3]; others, like Martin van Creveld, believe that war will degenerate into civil chaos, fought by stateless gangs.[4] One might say that the former see a future of law without war, and the latter a future of wars without law. My own view, of course, is that law and war will persist because they are mutually supportive. And this is not the worst dynamic equilibrium: a state without a strategy for war would be unable to maintain its domestic legitimacy and thus could not even guarantee its citizens' civil rights and liberties; a lawless state at war could never make peace and thus would be trapped in the cycle of violence and revenge.

The parliamentary nation-state has emerged from the Long War as triumphant. Nevertheless, we should not expect that either this form of the constitutional order or the Peace that recorded its ascendancy will be eternal. Mindful of the past, we can expect a new epochal war in which a new form of the State—the market-state—asserts its primacy as the most effective constitutional means to deal with the consequences of the strategic innovations that won the Long War. To shape, if not permanently forestall, this war to come, the society of states must organize in ways that enable it to prevent the proliferation of weapons of mass destruction, to treat expeditionary interventions as opportunities for consensus-creating coalitions, and to share information as a means of defense against disguised attacks. By these means, the next epochal war can be converted into a series of interventions and crises, instead of a world-shattering cataclysm or a stultifying and repressive world order.

It is a cliché that generals prepare to fight the last war rather than the next one. But if it is such a cliché, why haven't the generals heard it—that is, why do we persist in modeling the future on the past?

The past, it turns out, is all we know about the future. Things are usually pretty much the way they have been. About modern warfare we can say three things based on the past: that it pits one country against another; that it is waged by governments, not private parties; that the victorious party defeats its adversary.

Now it happens that we are living in one of those relatively rare periods in which the future is unlikely to be very much like the past. Indeed the three certainties I just mentioned about national security—that it is national (not international), that it is public (not private), and that it seeks victory (and not stalemate)—these three lessons of the past are all about to be turned upside down by the new age of indeterminacy into which we are plunging.

The Shield of Achilles

        She looked over his shoulder
            For vines and olive trees,
        Marble well-governed cities
            And ships upon untamed seas,
        But there on the shining metal
            His hands had put instead
        An artificial wilderness
            And a sky like lead.

A plain without a feature, bare and brown,
    No blade of grass, no sign of neighborhood,
Nothing to eat and nowhere to sit down,
    Yet, congregated on its blankness, stood
    An unintelligible multitude,
A million eyes, a million boots in line,
Without expression, waiting for a sign.

Out of the air a voice without a face
    Proved by statistics that some cause was just
In tones as dry and level as the place:
    No one was cheered and nothing was discussed;
    Column by column in a cloud of dust
They marched away enduring a belief
Whose logic brought them, somewhere else, to grief.

        She looked over his shoulder
            For ritual pieties,
        White flower-garlanded heifers,
            Libation and sacrifice,
        But there on the shining metal
            Where the altar should have been,
        She saw by his flickering forge-light
            Quite another scene.

Barbed wire enclosed an arbitrary spot
    Where bored officials lounged (one cracked a joke)
And sentries sweated for the day was hot:
    A crowd of ordinary decent folk
    Watched from without and neither moved nor spoke
As three pale figures were led forth and bound
To three posts driven upright in the ground.

The mass and majesty of this world, all
   That carries weight and always weighs the same
Lay in the hands of others; they were small
   And could not hope for help and no help came:
   What their foes liked to do was done, their shame
Was all the worst could wish; they lost their pride
And died as men before their bodies died.

   She looked over his shoulder
      For athletes at their games,
   Men and women in a dance
      Moving their sweet limbs
   Quick, quick, to music,
      But there on the shining shield
   His hands had set no dancing-floor
      But a weed-choked field.

A ragged urchin, aimless and alone,
   Loitered about that vacancy; a bird
Flew up to safety from his well-aimed stone:
   That girls are raped, that two boys knife a third,
   Were axioms to him, who'd never heard
Of any world where promises were kept,
Or one could weep because another wept.

   The thin-lipped armorer,
      Hephaestos, hobbled away,
   Thetis of the shining breasts
      Cried out in dismay
   At what the god had wrought
      To please her son, the strong
   Iron-hearted man-slaying Achilles
      Who would not live long.

—W. H. Auden

Postscript
The Indian Summer[*]

I am inclined to think that the last utterance will formulate, strange as it may appear, some hope to us now utterly inconceivable. For mankind is delightful in its pride, its assurance, and its indomitable tenacity. It will sleep on the battlefield among its own dead . . .[†]

—Joseph Conrad

WAR IS NOT a pathology that, with proper hygiene and treatment, can be wholly prevented. War is a natural condition of the State, which was organized in order to be an effective instrument of violence on behalf of society. Wars are like deaths, which, while they can be postponed, will come when they will come and cannot be finally avoided. As we have seen in the preceding pages, and as Conrad also wrote, "the life-history of the earth must in the last instance be a history of a really relentless warfare. Neither his fellows, nor his gods, nor his passions will leave a man alone."[‡] On September 11, 2001, the nascent community of market-states came to this knowledge as every society of states that preceded it has: through violence. In New York and in Washington, we slept that night among our own dead who were interred beneath rubble, as if on a battlefield.

The September attacks on the United States provide that country and its allies with an historic opportunity, even while they have dealt America an historic wound. That opportunity is the moment and the context in which to organize a grand coalition of states, with many of whose policies other

---

[*]Written after the attacks on New York and Washington, September 11, 2001.
[†]Joseph Conrad, *Notes on Life and Letters* (Pennsylvania State University, 2001), 17–18.
[‡]Ibid.

than counterterrorism the United States differs. Such coalitions, whose precise composition will shift from time to time and threat to threat, can be created and managed to fight a new epochal war composed of interventions against a variety of challenges that include terrorism—both within the State, as in the example of Serbia, and against the State, as in the case of the September attacks, and even by one state against its neighbor, as in the case of Iraq's aggression against Iran and Kuwait.

If a coalitional war against international terrorism prompts the United States, the United Kingdom, and their allies to conduct cooperative operations at the leading edge of modern technology this war could forestall the cataclysmic conflicts among great powers that modern technology makes possible. Indeed I would say that there can be no higher priority for the United States and the United Kingdom than to strengthen cooperation with Russia in a league against international terrorism, even to the extent of transforming NATO. NATO could become the meeting ground for coalitional warfare against this lethal, global menace, and could include Russia as a full member. The September attacks can be understood as the first battle in this new war. If, as some historians argue, the twentieth century began in August 1914 it may be that the twenty-first century will be said to have begun in September 2001.

The multinational mercenary terror network that Osama bin Laden and others have assembled is a malignant and mutated version of the market-state. Like other emerging market-states, it is a reaction to the strategic developments of the Long War that brought forth cultural penetration, the liberalization of trade and finance, and weapons proliferation, on an unprecedented scale. Like other states, this network has a standing army; it has a treasury and a consistent source of revenue; it has a permanent civil service; it has an intelligence collection and analysis cadre; it even runs a rudimentary welfare program for its fighters, and their relatives and associates. It has a recognizable hierarchy of officials; it makes alliances with other states; it promulgates laws, which it enforces ruthlessly; it declares wars.

This network, of which Al Qaeda is only a part, greatly resembles a multinational corporation but that is simply to say that it is a *market-state,* made possible by advances in international telecommunications and transit, rapid computation, and weapons of mass destruction. Lacking contiguous territory, Al Qaeda is a kind of virtual state, which means that our classical strategies of deterrence based on retaliation will have to be rethought. That is another way of saying that even when Afghanistan is conquered and pacified, the war against terrorism will go on.

Deterrence, assured retaliation, and overwhelming conventional force enabled victory for the coalition of parliamentary nation-states in the war that began in 1914 and only finally ended with the Peace of Paris in 1990. These strategies cannot provide a similar victory at present because what threatens the states of the world now is too easy to disguise and too hard to locate in any one place. We cannot deter an attacker whose identity or location is unknown to us, and the very massiveness of our conventional forces makes it unlikely we will be challenged openly. As a consequence, we are just beginning to appreciate the need for a shift from the sole reliance on target, threat-based strategies to defensive, vulnerability-based strategies.

Realizing that we are fighting a virtual state and not just a stateless gang helps clarify our strategy. For one thing, it suggests that controlling and diminishing the revenue stream to bin Laden's network is far more important than capturing or killing any individual. For another, it clarifies the line between mere crime—which we use law, after the fact, to prosecute— and warfare, which we use strategy, before the fact, to anticipate.

The United States is at war no less than when a conventional state launched a surprise attack in 1941, and the assault this time has come for much the same reason. Now, as then, the United States aroused fear that her global presence would threaten the ambitions of a messianic state bent on regional subjugation and domination. Then as now the alliance of which the United States is a part faces a long and bitter struggle.

The world community faces its own historic challenge in creating a constitution for the international order that will emerge from this war. Will that community—the society of states—use the discredited multilateral institutions of the nation-state as a way of frustrating action in order to control the acts of its strongest member, the United States? Or will that society simply expect every state to defend itself as best it can, spiraling into a chaos of self-help, ad hoc interventions, and sabotage? Or will that community consist of islands of authoritarianism, whose institutions focus only inward in an attempt to prevent violence by harsh police methods? Or can we learn to produce *collective goods*—like shared intelligence and shared surveillance information from shared nanosensors and shared missile and cyber defenses? Indeed the production and distribution of collective goods*—such as the coalition against international terrorism itself—may be the only way for a market-state to forestall peer competition and defeat international terrorism at the same time.

The phrase *Indian Summer*† usually evokes a pleasant sensation of warm autumn weather that gives us a second chance to do what winter will

---

*Described in Chapter 12.
†See, for example, Boris Pasternak, "Indian Summer," in *The Poems of Dr. Zhivago* (Kansas City, 1967), 26 (trans. E. M. Kayden).

make impossible. The origin of this phrase, however, is more menacing. The early American settlers were often forced to take shelter in stockades to protect themselves from attacks by tribes of Native Americans. These tribes went into winter quarters once autumn came, allowing the settlers to return to their farms. If there was a break in the approaching winter—a few days or weeks of warm, summery climate—then the tribal attacks would be resumed, and the defenseless settlers became their prey. Once again the settlers were forced to band together or to become victims, attacked one by one.

The onslaughts in the autumn of 2001 on a warm, summerlike day on the East Coast of the United States are both the herald of further savagery and the call for defenses that, if they are sustained, offer the world's best hope of avoiding a world-rending cataclysm. States that otherwise might find themselves in a violent competition can take this opportunity to cooperate in a new security structure. States that otherwise have little in common in their foreign policies have this in common: all are subject to attacks by a virtual state because a virtual state is the neighbor of all. States whose relations with the United States have been fraught in the past could now become valuable partners; states whose relations with the United States have been warm and trusted can be even more relied upon for their counsel now that our fates are more closely bound together.

The foregoing book was completed well before September 11, but the terrible events of that day were not unexpected or even unprecedented, as the text of this book discloses. Rather one had hoped that we might be spared a little longer. If those horrors inspire us now to deal realistically and creatively with the threats we face, then the sacrifice of innocents on that day may yet yield a stronger and more resilient society of the survivors. In thinking about the past, we will remember our dead, and secure the future for which they died.

We are entering a fearful time, a time that will call on all our resources, moral as well as intellectual and material. It is not unlike periods in the past when there was "a sense of anticipation, a sense of conflict, a sense of dread, a sense of the unknown."* As I write this, the world is in a mood of apprehension because many had expected that by this time other horrors would have been inflicted upon us, yet for a while little has happened. In a similar period, after the invasion of Poland but before the battles of France and Braitain, King George VI spoke to his country in a radio broadcast. He spoke of the "hard . . . waiting, [that] waiting is a trial of nerve and discipline." Finally he warned of the "dark times ahead of us."

*Peter Gomes, *Sundays at Harvard* (Cambridge, Mass: 1995), 23.

A new year is at hand. We cannot tell what it will bring. If it brings peace, how thankful we shall all be. If it brings us contingued struggle we shall remain undaunted. In the meantime, I feel that we may all find a message of encouragement in the lines which, in my closing words, I would like to say to you:

> I said to the man who stood at the Gate of the Year: "Give me a light, that I might tread safely into the unknown." And he replied, "Go out into the darkness and put your hand into the Hand of God. That shall be to you better than light and safer than a known way."

May that Almighty Hand guide and uphold us all.*

Philip Bobbitt
December 13, 2001

*Quoted in John W. Wheeler-Bennett, *King George VI: His Life and Reign* (St. Martin's Press, New York, 1958), 429–30.

Perhaps

Perhaps these thoughts of ours
will never find an audience
Perhaps the mistaken road
will end in a mistake
Perhaps the lamps we light one at a time
will be blown out, one at a time
Perhaps the candles of our lives will gutter out
without lighting a fire to warm us.

Perhaps when all the tears have been shed
the earth will be more fertile
Perhaps when we sing praises to the sun
the sun will praise us in return
Perhaps these heavy burdens
will strengthen our philosophy
Perhaps when we weep for those in misery
we must be silent about miseries of our own.

Perhaps
Because of our irresistible sense of mission
   We have no choice.

—Shu Ting
(translated by Carolyn Kizer)

APPENDIX

I should like to append three notes in order to dispel—or at least to miti-gate—the natural concerns of readers undertaking arguments and theses that are presented in the way I have chosen.

A NOTE ON EUROCENTRISM

As Steven Weinberg has thoughtfully pointed out to me in a letter, although I say that the Crimean War was the most deadly of any from 1815 to 1914, the Tai Ping Rebellion in China killed ten times as many people. Indeed throughout the historical discussion of constitutional forms, I con-centrate almost entirely—until the twentieth century—on European ex-amples. Similarly, although gunpowder was invented in Asia and conscription by force took place in tribal Africa, my discussion of strategic innovations is also confined to Europe, at least in the initial periods.

The reason for this is the State is a European political idea. The society of states first emerged in Europe at the time of the Renaissance and only in the late twentieth century encompassed the globe. The military and strate-gic innovations relevant to its development occurred in Europe and in those theatres of war with which European states were concerned. It has been suggested that it was the sheer bellicosity of Europe that accounted for its domination of the world political order. Without going so far, I will simply say that the exploitation of strategic innovation was certainly given impetus by the intense political competition among states, and vice versa. As a result, the forms of government developed in Europe were well situ-ated to compete with other forms in the Americas and in Africa and Asia.

A NOTE ON CAUSALITY

In this work I have described a recurring pattern: long periods of over a century in which the international order of states is stable, broken by an abrupt shift to epochal war that puts the constitutional basis of the warring states in play, followed by the renovation of the international order as states copy the constitutional order of the winning states, and the ratification of this new order by international congresses of peace. I have traced these patterns from the Renaissance into the twenty-first century. But I do not believe that I have discovered an historical law of general application.

Far from it. Rather I believe that at each juncture, things might have gone differently. It is the decisions of those persons who guide the State that determine whether stability or innovation will ensue. True, these decisions are confined by the "genetic material" of the State: its culture and resources. But within these constraints many real choices are possible with respect to the two dominant, mutually affecting dimensions of the State, law and strategy. The society of states we have today has been brought into being by countless acts of decision making that were not compelled by larger structures, but rather that constituted those structures. It is precisely because these choices could have been different that legitimacy is conferred—or withdrawn—by their outcome. History is the name we put to choices made.

I came across this manifesto by Rey Koslowski and Friedrich Kratochwil that seems to me very largely right on this issue. They write:

> Domestic and international actors reproduce or alter systems through their actions. Any given international system does not exist because of immutable structures, but rather the very structures are dependent for their reproduction on the practices of the actors. Fundamental change of the international system occurs when actors, through their practices, change the rules and norms constitutive of international interaction. . . . Fundamental changes in international politics occur when beliefs and identities of domestic actors are altered thereby also altering the rules and norms that are constitutive of their political practices. To the extent that patterns emerge in this process, they can be traced and explained, but they are unlikely to exhibit predetermined trajectories to be captured by general historical laws, be they cyclical or evolutionary.[1]

Causes of war will vary with particularity, owing to the local historical context, and yet will also be, very broadly, the same as ever. My claim is that the strategic innovations that prove decisive in epochal wars (most recently, the advances in international telecommunications, rapid computation, and weapons of mass destruction that won the Long War) interact with the struggle over the constitutional order (most recently, as the decaying nation-state is superseded by the emerging market-state), creating new forms of government (for example, the virtual, multinational nonterritorial regime, like the terrorist Al Qaeda) and new tactics (such as asymmetrical warfare using the latest communications technology, cartel-like coalitions, daring weapons of mass destruction that match the lucrative targets amassed by the market-state, like the World Trade Center towers, with manned cruise missiles such as fuel-fire commercial airliners).

War is inevitable not because of this interaction but because of the nature of the State, which operationalizes and magnifies a group's ability to wage conflict, and the nature of man in groups. Given that wars will occur, this historical interaction—more descriptive than causal—can manifest itself in many different events. This is a matter of human agency. Epochal wars could be great power cataclysms, or coalitional low-intensity conflicts, or high-technology nonexplosive attacks that induce economic and social collapse. This book tries to help us make choices, not forecasts.

A NOTE ON PERIODICITY

The periods I describe, and the forms of government to which they are attached, are given sharper edges than might otherwise be the case were my perspective less lengthened. But like the black border on a hemline in a Sargent painting that dissipates into streaks and then into disconnected islands of paint as one approaches the canvas more closely, my categories are composed of many disparate elements that are drawn together by my vision of their purpose.

In the states we have studied, each period is typified by great constitutional forms—princely, kingly, territorial, imperial, national—whose elements include bureaucratic establishments, the expectations of citizens as to what the State is for, the views of those citizens and of foreigners of the source of the State's legitimacy, the State's role in transnational institutions, and other matters. Like the traits shared by a family, many mixtures are possible and it may be that no single state shares with another every single element of its form. Moreover, in any period there are members of the society of states who typify earlier periods, some that are in transition, and some that are evidence of a new, challenging form.

For these reasons, it may appear that I am trying to shoehorn a complicated history into a rigid taxonomy. Sophisticated readers may find their minds flooded with counterexamples as they proceed through the historical/analytical parts of the narrative.

Indeed I am quite aware of this reaction; I tend to be a skeptical reader myself, one who suspends counterargument with difficulty. My only defense, if such it be, is this: if my general characterizations are useful, and if the reader finds himself adding examples to those periods and forms I have described, then I will feel my rather arbitrary constructions have been worthwhile. If not, I invite amendment.

NOTES

PROLOGUE

1. As Max Weber observed, the "medieval knights made feudal social organization inevitable; then its displacement by mercenary armies and later (beginning with Maurice of Orange) by disciplined troops led to the establishment of the modern State." Max Weber, *Economy and Society* (University of California Press, 1978), 904–908. It is also to Weber that we owe the idea that the State seeks a monopoly on legitimate violence. Max Weber, "Politics as Vocation," in *Essays in Sociology,* ed. H. Gerth and C. Wright Mills (Routledge, 1970), 77–78.

2. Frederick Turner, *Natural Classicism: Essays on Literature and Science* (Paragon House, 1985) and *The Culture of Hope: A New Birth of the Classical Spirit* (New York: Free Press, 1995).

INTRODUCTION: LAW, STRATEGY, AND HISTORY

1. Cf. *La Pietra Report* (2000), which affirms national histories, but of a very different kind. "Instead of assuming the nation to be the "natural" unit of historical analysis, it acknowledges a variety of relevant and interrelated geographical units of history. It urges not only the exploration of the different historical forces, including transnational ones, that made and sustained the nation and national identities but also the importance, always changing, of the nation in relation to other social units, from the town, to the transnational region, to solidarity with all peoples of color, to international corporations." Thomas Bender, "Writing National History in a Global Age," *Correspondence: An International Review of Culture and Society,* no. 7 (Winter 2000/2001): 14.

2. Hans Kelsen, *General Theory of Law and State* (Cambridge, Mass.: Harvard University Press, 1945).

3. John Austin, *Province of Jurisprudence Determined* (Cambridge, U.K.: Cambridge University Press, 1995 [1832]).

4. Niccolò Machiavelli, *The Prince,* trans. Harvey C. Mansfield, Jr. (University of Chicago Press, 1985).

5. Jean Bodin, *Six Books of the Commonwealth* (B. Blackwell, 1955 [1606]).

6. Georg Wilhelm Hegel, *The Phenomenology of the Spirit (1807),* trans. A. V. Miller and J. N. Findlay (Oxford, 1979). Also see Roger Kimball, "The Difficulty with Hegel," *New Criterion* 19 (September 2000): 4.

7. William A. Owens, "The Wrong Argument about Readiness," *New York Times* (September 1, 2000): A27.

8. See, e.g., Thomas Friedman, "It's Harder Now to Figure Out Compelling National Interests," *New York Times* (May 31, 1992): E5.
9. See A. J. P. Taylor, *The Origins of the Second World War* (Penguin, 1961) for a related argument.
10. U.S. Department of the Army, *Decisive Victory: America's Power Projection Army* (Washington, D.C.: Department of the Army, 1994). See also the *Quadrennial Defense Review* (May 1997, http://www.defenselink.mil.pubs/qdr/) and the *Bottom-Up Review* (October 1993, http://www.fas.org/man/docs/bur/).
11. Bernard Brodie, "Implications for Military Policy," in *The Absolute Weapon: Atomic Power and World Order,* ed. Bernard Brodie (Harcourt, Brace, 1946), 76.
12. Thomas C. Schelling, *Arms and Influence* (New Haven: Yale University Press, 1966).
13. Michael Howard, "Lessons of the Cold War," *Survival* 36 (1994–1995): 165.
14. Philip Bobbitt, *Democracy and Deterrence* (New York: St. Martin's Press, 1988), 286.
15. Fred Ikle, "The Next Lenin: On the Cusp of Truly Revolutionary Warfare." *The National Interest* 47 (1997): 9.
16. Bobbitt, *Democracy and Deterrence,* 19–96.
17. But see Ashton Carter and William Perry, *Preventive Defense* (Washington, D.C.: Brookings Institution, 1999).
18. Paul Bracken, "The Military after Next," *The Washington Quarterly* 16 (1993): 157.
19. Fred Iklé, "The Next Lenin."
20. See also Robert D. Kaplan, "Fort Leavenworth and the Eclipse of Nationhood," *Atlantic Monthly* (September 1996), and Martin van Creveld, *The Transformation of War* (Free Press, 1991); see also van Creveld's *The Rise and Decline of the State* (Cambridge, U.K.: Cambridge University Press, 2000).
21. Jean-Marie Guehenno, *The End of the Nation-State* (University of Minnesota Press, 1995).
22. Kenichi Ohmae, *The End of the Nation-State: The Rise of Regional Economies* (New York: Free Press, 1995).
23. Martin van Creveld, *The Rise and Decline of the State* (Cambridge, U.K., 1999). See also *Empire*.

CHAPTER ONE: THUCYDIDES AND THE EPOCHAL WAR

1. *On Justice, Power, and Human Nature: The Essence of Thucydides' History of the Peloponnesian War,* ed. and trans. Paul Woodruff (Hackett, 1993).
2. The term *Hundred Years' War* appears first to have been used in 1821 by Charles Desmichels. During this period of Anglo-French détente, Desmichels labeled the hundred years of animosity—often punctuated by long periods in which there was no actual fighting—as the Hundred Years' War. The term was picked up in Germany in 1829, and by English historians in 1870. P. J. Winter, "Sur l'origine de l'appellation de la guerre de cent ans," *Information History* 37 (1975): 20–24.
3. In contrast to the Hundred Years' War, the Thirty Years' War was named almost instantly, once the Westphalian Peace actually seemed to deliver a general settlement. The term *Thirty Years' War* was used as early as 1648 in an anonymous outline of the main events of the war, and in three other works about the war printed in 1649, 1650, and 1657. See Guenther H. S. Mueller, *Journal of Modern History* 50 (1978): iii.
4. The Punic Wars, for example, fit this pattern: although the participants thought, more than once, that hostilities had ended, and significant periods without fighting did occur, historians came to view the various Carthaginian wars as engagements in a single war because the peace settlements failed to resolve the conflicts over which the wars were fought.

5. Geoffrey Parker, *The Thirty Years' War* (Routledge and Kegan Paul, 1984); see also C. V. Wedgwood, *The Thirty Years' War* (J. Cape, 1938); P. Limm, *The Thirty Years' War* (1984); and J. H. Elliott, *Richelieu and Olivares* (Cambridge, U.K.: Cambridge University Press, 1984).

6. P. Brightwell, "Spanish Origins of the Thirty Years' War," *European Studies Review* (1979).

7. Parker, *The Thirty Years' War,* xiv.

8. Supra, n. 2.

9. Egon Friedell, *A Cultural History of the Modern Age,* trans. Charles Francis Atkinson (Knopf, 1930–1932), 15.

10. Kenneth Fowler, *The Age of Plantagenet and Valois* (Putnam, 1967), 13.

11. Anne Curry, *The Hundred Years War* (London: Macmillan, 1983).

12. Hunter R. Rawlings III, *The Structure of Thucydides' History* (Princeton University Press, 1981); Simon Hornblower, *Thucydides* (Duckworth, 1987).

CHAPTER TWO: THE STRUGGLE BEGUN: FASCISM, COMMUNISM, PARLIAMENTARIANISM, 1914–1919

1. Kurt F. Reinhardt, *Germany 2000 Years,* rev. ed., *Vol. 1, The Rise and Fall of the "Holy Empire"* (Frederick Ungar, 1961).

2. "It is usual, in analysing the constitution of 1871, to emphasize its federal character, pointing out that it betrays in every paragraph the conflicts of a thousand years of German history. But the reality is otherwise. The federal rights . . . were illusory. . . . Prussia had sufficient votes to veto constitutional changes, but more important was the fact that the Chancellor was under no necessity of consulting the council on any question of major political importance. . . . The system contrived in 1871 included a Reichstag elected by universal and equal franchise; but its powers were nugatory. . . . [I]t had no power of voting or refusing to vote taxes . . . since imperial revenue was provided partly from permanent fixed duties, partly by *pro rata* contributions from the individual federal states. . . . Finally, the Reichstag had no control over executive ministers, who were responsible only to the Prussian king who was also German emperor. . . . The German labour leader, Wilhelm Liebknecht, was therefore not wide of the mark in dubbing the Reichstag 'the fig-leaf of absolutism'; the system of government established in 1871 was, in fact, a veiled form of the monarchical absolutism vested in the king of Prussia." Geoffrey Barraclough, *Factors in German History* (B. Blackwell, 1946). It is important to note, in the debate as to whether Wilhelmine Germany was a proto-fascist state, that while many parliamentary nation-states allowed for the suspension of constitutional provisions in an emergency, the Kaiserrech and Nazi Germany permitted the chancellor to remain in office and to rule by decree even when he had lost his parliamentary majority.

3. Barraclough, *Factors in German History,* 116.

4. Fritz Fischer, *Germany's Aims in the First World War* (Norton, 1967). This is the English translation of his *Griff nach der Weltmacht* (Droste, 1961); Fritz Fischer, *World Power or Decline: The Controversy over Germany's Aims in the First World War,* trans. Lancelot Farrar, Robert Kimber, and Rita Kimber (Norton, 1974); Fritz Fischer, *War of Illusions: German Policies from 1911 to 1914,* trans. Marian Jackson (Norton, 1975); see *Krieg der Illusionem* (1969).

5. "Analysis of the origins of the First World War has therefore been profoundly influenced by the 'Fischer revolution.'" Norman Stowe, *Europe Transformed, 1878–1919* (Harvard University Press, 1984), 196, comments that "Not many historians nowadays dissent from the proposition that the German government, egged on by its generals, deliberately provoked the war of 1914." John Moses, *The Politics of Illusion* (George

Prior, 1975), 48, says that "Even Fischer's most persistent opponents such as Gerhard Ritter (1888–1967) and Golo Mann, for example, were forced to agree with him that Imperial Germany's policies unleashed the war; however, they imputed to Germany's leaders defensive rather than offensive motives." "As Fischer has forcefully stated, 'there is not a single document in the world which could weaken the central truth that in July 1914 a will to war existed solely and alone on the German side and that all arrangements on the side of the *Entente* served the defensive security of their alliance. And that will to war had been crystallising for many years previously.'" Some historians, while not disputing this, emphasize the opportunistic nature of German policy. "James Joll, *The Origins of the First World War* (Longman, 1984), 235, feels that by December 1912 German rulers had 'accepted war as inevitable' but were concerned to wage it at the most opportune time." Ruth Henig, *The Origins of the First World War* (Routledge, 1989; reprinted 1991), 43.

6. For the current status of the Fischer controversy, compare Bernd-Jurgen Wendt, "Zum Stand der 'Fischer-Kontroverse' um den Ausbruch des ersten Weltkrieges," *Annales Universitatis Scientarium Budapestinensis de Rolando Eotvos Nominatae: Section Historica* 24 (1985): 92–132 (concluding that Fischer's theses regarding the Riezler papers, the role of Bethmann Hollweg, and the continuity of German policies leading to both world wars remain unrefuted) with Wayne C. Thompson, "The September Program: Reflections on the Evidence," *Central European History* 11 (1978): 348–354 (arguing that the Riezler paper was only "a provisional catalog of possible war aims drawn up for negotiating purposes").

7. See Roger Fletcher, introduction to Fischer, *Kaiserreich to Third Reich: Elements of Continuity in German History, 1871–1945* (Allen & Unwin, 1986; reprinted Routledge, 1991).

8. Ian Kershaw, "1933: Continuity or Break in German History?" *History Today* 33 (1983): 13–18.

9. Fletcher, Introduction to Fischer, 10.

10. Edward Acton, *State and Society under Lenin and Stalin,* in *Themes in Modern European History, 1890–1945,* ed. Paul Hayes (London: Routledge, 1992).

11. Ibid., 156–157.

12. William G. Rosenberg, "Russian Labor and Bolshevik Power after October," *Slavic Review* (1985): 222–223.

13. Condoleezza Rice, "The Making of Soviet Strategy," *Makers of Modern Strategy: From Machiavelli to the Nuclear Age,* ed. Peter Paret (Princeton University Press, 1986), 648.

14. "A variety of motives lay behind this support: ideological commitment, patriotism . . . The rhetoric of class warfare in terms of which the [Five-Year] Plan was implemented struck a responsive chord. It promised a return to the heroic tradition of October and the Civil War, an attack on Bourgeois deformities, on NEP-men, kulaks and privileged members of the intelligentsia." Edward Acton, "State and Society under Lenin and Stalin," in *Themes of Modern European History, 1890–1945* (Routledge, 1992), 162–163. Note the similarity between this rhetoric and the Nazi attacks on Weimar society.

15. Rosenberg, 164–165.

16. Eugene Genovese, "The Squandered Century," *Current* (July–August 1995): 36.

17. Henig, *The Origins of the First World War,* 14.

18. Vladimir I. Lenin, *Imperialism: The Highest Stage of Capitalism* (International, 1988 [1916]).

CHAPTER THREE: THE STRUGGLE CONTINUED: 1919–1945

1. In *Mein Kampf* Hitler gave such an account. Adolf Hitler, *Mein Kampf* (F. Eher Nachf, 1941).

2. Paul Hayes, "The Triumph of Caesarism: Fascism and Nazism," in *Themes in Modern European History 1890–1945*, ed. Paul Hayes (Routledge, 1992), 176.

3. Fritz Fischer, *From Kaiserreich to Third Reich* (Allen & Unwin, 1986), 97; the interior quotes are from his work cited as n. 122 in that book.

4. Alan Bullock, *Hitler: A Study in Tyranny* (Bantam Books, 1958).

5. David E. Kaiser, *Economic Diplomacy and the Origins of the Second World War* (Princeton: Princeton University Press, 1980).

6. A.J.P. Taylor, *Origins of the Second World War* (Hamilton, 1961).

7. William L. Shirer, *The Rise and Fall of the Third Reich* (New York: Simon & Schuster, 1960).

8. See, for example, *The Origins of the Second World War Reconsidered: The A.J.P. Taylor Debate after Twenty-five Years*, ed. Gordon Martel (Allen & Unwin: 1986); and *Paths to War: New Essays on the Origins of the Second World War*, ed. Robert Boyce and Esmonde M. Robertson (New York: St. Martin's Press, 1989).

9. "The march on Rome [was in fact] a mere symbol of a triumph of political intrigue, though in order to satisfy both the squadristi and the need for a myth, it was depicted as a real and important event involving the violent seizure of power." Hayes, 177–178.

10. May 1924 (6.5%); December 1924 (3%); May 1928 (2.6%); September 1930 (18.3%); July 1932 (37.3%); November 1932 (33.1%). Richard F. Hamilton, *Who Voted for Hitler?* (Princeton University Press, 1982), 476.

11. Jacek Jedruch, *Constitutions, Elections, and Legislatures of Poland, 1493–1977: A Guide to Their History* (University Press of America, 1982); Rett R. Ludwikowski and William F. Fox, Jr., *The Beginning of the Constitutional Era* (Catholic University of America Press, 1993); Timothy Wiles, ed., *Poland between the Wars, 1918–1939* (Indiana University Polish Studies Center, 1989); Jan Karski, *The Great Powers & Poland, 1919–1945: From Versailles to Yalta* (University Press of America, 1985).

12. Kenneth B. Pyle, *The Making of Modern Japan*, 2nd ed. (D. C. Heath, 1996), 78, 87, 122–124.

13. Ibid., 116–117.

14. Ibid., 125–138.

15. Bernard Eccleston, "The State and Modernization in Japan," in *The Rise of the Modern State*, ed. James Anderson (Brighton, Sussex: Harvester Press, 1986), 204.

16. For example, with the Peace Preservation Law of 1925.

17. James B. Crowley, *Japan's Quest for Autonomy* (Princeton University Press, 1966), 116–121. For an opposing view, see Richard Storry, *A History of Modern Japan* (Penguin Books, 1960), 186–187.

18. "Teikoku Zaigo Gunjinkai Sanjunenshi," in Richard J. Smethurst, *The Social Basis for Japanese Militarism* (dissertation, University of Michigan at Ann Arbor, 1968), 22.

19. Diane Shaver Clements, *Yalta* (Oxford University Press, 1970); Richard F. Fenno, *The Yalta Conference* (Heath, 1955); Edward R. Stettinius, *Roosevelt and the Russians: The Yalta Conference* (New York: Doubleday, 1949).

CHAPTER FOUR: THE STRUGGLE ENDED: 1945–1990

1. W. S. Churchill, Speech at Fulton, Missouri, March 5, 1946.

2. H. S. Truman, Address to the U.S. Congress, March 12, 1947.

3. G. M. Malenkov, September 22, 1947, quoted in Edgar Geoffrey Rayner, *The Cold War* (Hodder & Stoughton, 1992), 17.

4. NSC 68: United States Objectives and Programs for National Security, April 14, 1950, reprinted in *American Cold War Strategy: Interpreting NSC 68*, ed. Ernest May

(Bedford Books, 1993), 32; see also Philip Bobbitt, Lawrence Freedman, and Gregory F. Treverton, eds. *U.S. Nuclear Strategy: A Reader* (New York University Press, 1989).

5. David N. Schwartz, *NATO's Nuclear Dilemmas* (Brookings Institution, 1983), chapters 1 and 2; Jane E. Stromseth, *The Origins of Flexible Response: NATO's Debate over Strategy in the 1960s* (New York: St. Martin's Press, 1988).

6. See statement by Arthur Henderson, British Secretary for Air, May 11, 1949.

7. Known as Jiang Jieshi in later transliterations of Chinese nomenclature.

8. N. S. Khrushchev, *Khrushchev Remembers,* ed. Strobe Talbott (Boston: Little, Brown, 1971).

9. This assessment was first broached by a senior Chinese diplomat in conversations with the author.

10. Although the circumstance of Nagy's judicial murder remain uncertain, the best recent scholarship can be found in György Litván, "A Nagy Imre per politikai háttere," *Világosság,* vol. 10, 1992, 743–57; and János M. Rainer, "Nagy Imre életútia," *Multunk,* vol. 4, 1992, 3–14.

11. Letter of President Eisenhower to Marshal Bulganin, November 5, 1956.

12. Kai Bird, *The Color of Truth* (Simon & Schuster, 1998), 203–206.

13. This doubled U.S. forces in Germany. In the 1950s allied forces levels in Germany were between 240,000 and 250,000. During the "flexible response" period of the mid to late sixties, force levels were just over 200,000. See Horst Menderhausen, "Troop Stationing in Germany: Value and Cost, Memorandum 588–1 PR" (Santa Monica: RAND, 1968), 8; and James D. Hessman, "U.S. Forces in Europe," *Armed Forces Journal* (July 11, 1970): 20.

14. See the Soviet Reply to Western Notes on Berlin, August 3, 1961.

15. N. S. Khrushchev, television broadcast, August 7, 1961. See also Lawrence Freedman, *Kennedy's Wars: Berlin, Cuba, Laos and Vietnam* (Oxford, 2000), 45–111.

16. *Khrushchev Remembers,* 460. This report invites skepticism in light of Khrushchev's antipathy toward Mao. See, e.g., pp. 461–479, discussing Mao Zedong and the schism.

17. Bobbitt, *Democracy and Deterrence,* 201–202.

18. In English as ". . . without firing a single shot" and ". . . without having to fire a single shot" in *Khrushchev Remembers,* 460 and 504, respectively.

19. Frederick the Great wrote in his 1747 *Instructions for His Generals*: "The greatest secret of war and the masterpiece of a skillful general is to starve his enemy. Hunger exhausts men more surely than courage, and you will succeed with less risk than by fighting. But since it is very rare that a war is ended by the capture of a depot and matters are only decided by great battles, it is necessary to use all these means to attain this object . . . War is decided only by battles and is not finished except by them. Thus they have to be fought, but it should be opportunely and with all the advantages on your side . . . The occasions that can be procured are when you cut the enemy off from his supplies and when you use favourable terrain." Reproduced in *The Roots of Strategy: A Collection of Military Classics,* ed. T. R. Phillips (Military Service, 1955), 173, 213.

20. Donald Kagan, *On the Origins of War and the Preservation of Peace* (New York: Doubleday, 1995).

21. "Son of Late Soviet Premier to Become U.S. Citizen," *Agence France-Presse,* July 11, 1999.

22. Charles Bohlen, memo to Secretary of State, April 5, 1950, *Foreign Relations of the United States I* (1950), 222.

23. See the views of McGeorge Bundy in this regard, as reported (with some skepticism) in Kai Bird, *The Color of Truth: McGeorge Bundy and William Bundy, Brothers in Arms* (Simon & Schuster, 1998), 354, citing Department of State Bulletin, February 5, 1968 (speech by Bundy).

24. Speaking at the Ninth Party Congress of the Chinese Communist Party in Beijing, April 1, 1965. Quoted in E. G. Rayner, *The Cold War* (1992), 63–64.

25. Compare Thomas Risse-Kappen, "Ideas Do Not Float Freely: Transnational Coalitions, Domestic Structures, and the End of the Cold War," *International Organization* 48 (Spring 1994): 185.

26. Vladimir Tismaneanu, *Reinventing Politics: Eastern Europe from Stalin to Havel* (New York: Free Press, 1992).

27. Michael Howard, "Hardship, Famine, and Fear," *The Financial Times,* May 6/7, 1995.

28. Eric Hobsbawm, *The Age of Extremes: A History of the World, 1914–1991* (Pantheon Books, 1991), 12.

29. Francis Fukuyama, *The End of History and the Last Man* (New York: Free Press, 1992).

30. Richard Kugler, *Commitment to Purpose: How Alliance Partnership Won the Cold War* (Santa Monica: RAND, 1993).

31. G. Craig and F. Gilbert, "Strategy in the Present and Future," in *Makers of Modern Strategy,* ed. Peter Paret (Princeton University Press, 1986), 870–871. This might also be applied with justice to the "limitations determined by political considerations"—though much criticized—applied by the U.S. in the Viet Nam War.

32. Carl von Clausewitz, *On War,* ed. and trans. Michael Howard and Peter Paret (Princeton University Press, 1976 [1832]), 87.

CHAPTER FIVE: STRATEGY AND THE CONSTITUTIONAL ORDER

1. Michael Roberts, *The Military Revolution 1556–1660* (1956), reprinted with slight changes in Michael Roberts, *Essays in Swedish History* (University of Minnesota Press, 1967), 195–225.

2. Sir George Clark, *War and Society in the Seventeenth Century* (Cambridge, U.K.: Cambridge University Press, 1958).

3. See, for example, Karen Rasler and William Thomson, "War Making and State Making and Governmental Expenditures, Tax Reviews and Global War," *American Political Science Review* 49 (1985): 491–507; Michael Mann, *States, War, and Capitalism* (Basil Blackwell, 1988); John Brewer, *The Sinews of Power* (Unwin Hyman, 1989); Niall Ferguson, *The Cash Nexus: Money and Power in the Modern World, 1700–2000* (Basic Books, 2001).

4. Parker, *The Military Revolution,* 2–3.

5. See also William McNeill, *The Pursuit of Power* (University of Chicago Press, 1982).

6. Geoffrey Parker, "The 'Military Revolution,' 1560–1660—A Myth?," *Journal of Modern History* 46 (1976).

7. Jeremy Black, *European Warfare, 1660–1815* (New Haven: Yale University Press, 1994).

CHAPTER SIX: FROM PRINCES TO PRINCELY STATES: 1494–1648

1. Compare Dante, *The Inferno,* trans. Robert Pinsky (Noonday Press, 1996), Canto III, 11.5–6, 24–25. ("No things before me not eternal.")

2. Adam Watson, *The Evolution of International Society* (Routledge, 1992), 143.

3. Eric Christiansen, *The Northern Crusades: The Baltic and the Catholic Frontier, 1100–1525* (Macmillan, 1980), 250–251.

4. See Watson, n. 106, chapters 13 and 14 generally.

5. John Keegan, *A History of Warfare* (Hutchison, 1993). His predecessor, Charles VII, had used bombards to great effect earlier in the century. Harfleur, which had successfully resisted long sieges in 1415 and 1440, fell to Charles in only seventeen days after an attack by sixteen bombards. See Christopher Allmand in *The Cambridge Illustrated History of Warfare,* ed. Geoffrey Parker (Cambridge, U.K.: Cambridge University Press, 1995).

6. Quoted in M. E. Mallet, "Diplomacy and War in Later Fifteenth Century Italy," *Proceedings of the British Academy,* 67 (1981): 267–288.

7. Keegan, *A History of Warfare,* 320–322.

8. Michael T. Clark, "Realism: Ancient and Modern," *Political Science and Politics* 26, no. 3 (September 1993): 491.

9. Samuel E. Finer, "State and Nation-Building in Europe," in *The Formation of Nation States in Western Europe,* ed. Charles Tilly (Princeton University Press, 1975), 74.

10. Wallace K. Ferguson, *Europe in Transition* (Houghton Mifflin, 1962), 153–155.

11. Such was the rise of Francesco Sforza, a *condottiere* who became Duke of Milan by exploiting the state apparatus that the Visconti had developed. Franco Catalano, *Francesco Sforza* (Dall'Oglio, 1983); Cecilia Ady, "The Invasions of Italy," *New Cambridge Modern History,* ed. G. R. Potter (Cambridge, U.K., 1960), 1, 344; Jacob Burckhardt, *The Civilization of the Renaissance in Italy,* vol. 1 (Harper & Row, 1958), 34–44.

12. See Fernand Braudel, *Civilization and Capitalism, Fifteenth–Eighteenth Century,* vol. 3, *The Perspective of the World,* trans. Sian Reynolds (Harper & Row, 1984), 120; see also Michael Knapton, "City Wealth and State Wealth in Northeast Italy, Fourteenth–Seventeenth Centuries," in *La ville, la bourgeoisie, et la genèse de l'état moderne, XIIe–XVIIIe siècles: Actes du colloque de Bielefeld, 29 novembre–1 décembre 1985,* ed. Neithard Bulst and Jean-Philippe Genet (Editions du Centre National de la Recherche Scientifique: Diffusion, Presses du CNRS, 1988).

13. Niccolò Machiavelli, last chapter in *The Prince.*

14. Michael Howard, *War in European History* (Oxford, 1976), 5.

15. Felix Gilbert, "Machiavelli: The Renaissance of the Art of War," in *Makers of Modern Strategy,* ed. Peter Paret (Princeton University Press, 1986), 12–13.

16. Machiavelli, *The Prince,* chapter 12.

17. Machiavelli, *The Discourses,* III, 31.

18. Machiavelli, *The Prince* (trans. L. Ricci, 1903: rev., 1935), 43–44.

19. John Addington Symonds, *A Short History of the Renaissance in Italy* (Scribner, 1893), 4.

20. Of which scutage, which dates from the high Middle Ages, was a harbinger.

21. Paul Kennedy, *The Rise and Fall of the Great Powers: Economic Change and Military Conflict from 1500 to 2000* (Random House, 1987), 23; see also John Ulric Nef, *War and Human Progress: An Essay on the Rise of Industrial Civilization* (Russell & Russell, 1950), 46.

22. Lynn, citing recent scholarship on state formation in early modern Europe, recognizes this link between war and emerging absolutism. See also Charles Tilly, *Coercion, Capital, and European States, A.D. 900–1990* (B. Blackwell, 1990); Brian Downing, *The Military Revolution and Political Change* (Princeton University Press, 1992); and David Kaiser, *Politics and War: European Conflict from Philip II to Hitler* (Cambridge, Mass.: Harvard University Press, 1990).

23. Adam Watson, *The Evolution of International Society* (Routledge, 1992) , 164.

24. Ibid., 146.

25. Ibid., 161.

26. Clifford Rogers, "Military Evolution," in *The Reader's Companion to Military History,* ed. Robert Cowley and Geoffrey Parker (Houghton Mifflin, 1996), 396.

27. Geoffrey Parker, *The Military Revolution*, 12.
28. Bert S. Hall and Kelly R. DeVries, "The Military Revolution Revisited," *Technology and Culture* (July 1990): 500–507, take issue with Parker but on different grounds, i.e., they assume the premise that such fortresses would affect the state's political order but deny that the effects were as large, or as attributable to fortress design, as Parker maintains; and see Simon Adams, "Tactics or Politics? The Military Revolution and Hapsburg Hegemony, 1525–1649," in *Tools of War,* ed. John A. Lynn (University of Illinois Press, 1990), 28–52, and John Lynn, "The Trace Italienne and the Growth of Armies: The French Case," *Journal of Military History* 55 (July 1991): 297–330.
29. Watson, 164.
30. Lynn, "Trace Italienne," 322, speaking of the French experience.
31. Kennedy, 70.
32. Christopher Marlowe, *The Famous Tragedy of the Rich Jew of Malta* (Da Capo Press, 1971), 7.

CHAPTER SEVEN: FROM KINGLY STATES
TO TERRITORIAL STATES: 1648–1776

1. William Shakespeare, *The Tempest,* Act I, Scene 2, lines 94–100. *The Yale Shakespeare,* ed. W. L. Cross and Tucker Brooke (Barnes & Noble, 1993), p. 1408.
2. Peter Mancias, "The Legitimation of the Modern State: A Historical and Structural Account," in *State Formation and Political Legitimacy,* ed. R. Cohen and J. D. Toland (Transaction Books, 1988), 173–176.
3. Tilly, *Coercion, Capital,* 14.
4. Michael Howard, *War in European History,* 20; "Historians indeed normally date the beginnings of 'Modern European History' from the Italian Wars which opened with the French invasion of 1494."
5. Jeremy Black, who is in a position to know, makes this claim. Jeremy Black, *European Warfare, 1660–1815* (Yale University Press, 1994), 3.
6. Parker, *The Military Revolution,* 19. In this wonderfully written and illustrated book, Parker actually provides a plate reproducing William Louis's original letter, with a diagram in the count's hand showing how the countermarch would work.
7. Richard Bonney, *The European Dynastic States, 1494–1660* (Oxford University Press, 1991), 524–525.
8. Max Weber, from *Max Weber: Essays in Sociology,* trans. and ed. H. H. Gerth and C. Wright Mills (Oxford University Press, 1946), 256–257.
9. Gunther E. Rothenberg, "Maurice of Nassau, Gustavus Adolphus, Raimondo Montecucolli, and the 'Military Revolution' of the Seventeenth Century," in *Makers of Modern Strategy: From Machiavelli to the Nuclear Age,* ed. Peter Paret (Princeton, 1986), 33.
10. Roberts, *Essays in Swedish History,* 204–205, 210; see also Paul Kennedy's observation that "each belligerent had to learn how to create a satisfactory administrative structure to meet the 'military revolution'; and of equal importance, it also had to devise new means of paying for the spiraling costs of war." Kennedy, 56.
11. McNeill, *Pursuit of Power,* 80, 95.
12. Black, *European Warfare, 1660–1815,* 4.
13. Jean Bodin, *Six Books of the Commonwealth,* ed. K. D. McRae (Harvard University Press, 1962), 200.
14. Nicholas Henshell, *The Myth of Absolutism: Change and Continuity in Early Modern European Monarchy* (Longman, 1992), 3–4.
15. Thomas Hobbes, *Behemoth,* William Olesworth, ed. (B. Franklin, 1963).

16. Konrad Repgen, "What Is a 'Religious War'?" in *Politics and Society in Reformation Europe,* ed. E. I. Kouri and Tom Scott (New York: St. Martin's Press, 1987), 319; quoted in Bonney, 550.
17. Kennedy, 52.
18. Ibid., 25.
19. A Habsburg prince was emperor from 1273 to 1291, 1298 to 1308, 1438 to 1740, and 1745 to 1806.
20. Roberts, 202.
21. Geoffrey Symcox, *War, Diplomacy, and Imperialism, 1618–1763* (Walker, 1974), 103–105.
22. Roberts, 24.
23. Quoted in Michael Roberts, *Gustavus Adolphus* (Longman, 1992), 29–30.
24. Roberts, 31.
25. Kennedy, 64–65, citing several works by Roberts ("What follows relies heavily upon the writings of Michael Roberts, . . ."), see vol 1.
26. Howard, *War in European History,* 59.
27. This account is taken from Roberts's superb *Gustavus Adolphus.*
28. E. A. Beller, "The Thirty Years War," *New Cambridge Modern History,* vol. 4 (ed. J. P. Cooper) (Cambridge, 1970), 354. Note that this is to be distinguished from "sovereignty."
29. Barbara Riebling, "Milton on Machiavelli: Representations of the State in 'Paradise Lost,'" *Renaissance Quarterly* 49 (1996): 573.
30. Kalevi J. Holsti, *Peace and War: Armed Conflicts and the International Order, 1648–1989* (Cambridge University Press, 1991), 25.
31. Ibid., 39.
32. Bonney, 525.
33. Quoted by Bonney, 531; see also Jacques B. Bossuet, *Politique tirée des propres paroles de l'Ecriture sainte,* ed. LeBrun (Droz, 1967), 114.
34. Supra, Chapter 5, n. 3.
35. See James Anderson and Stuart Hall, "Absolutism and other Ancestors," in *The Rise of the Modern State,* ed. James Anderson (Brighton, Sussex: Harvester Press, 1986).
36. Ibid.
37. Howard, *War in European History,* 37.
38. See John Theibault, "The Rhetoric of Death and Destruction in the Thirty Years' War," *Journal of Social History* 27 (Winter 1993): 272; Henry Kamen, "The Economic and Social Consequences of the Thirty Years' War," *Past and Present* 39 (1968): 44–61. Christopher Friedrichs, *The Thirty Years' War,* ed. Geoffrey Parker (Routledge, 1984), 208–215, compromises by estimating the percentage of population loss during the war at about midway between the horrific figures of Gunther Franz, *Der Dreissigjahrige Krieg und das Deutsche Volk,* 4th ed. (Fischer, 1979) and the skeptical conclusions of S. H. Steinberg, *The 'Thirty Years War' and the Conflict for European Hegemony, 1600–1660* (Norton, 1967).
39. Gordon A. Craig and Aleksander L. George, *Force and Statecraft: Diplomatic Problems of Our Time,* 2nd ed. (Oxford University Press, 1990), 6.
40. Watson, 195.
41. Wedgwood, 526.
42. See John Locke, *First Treatise on Civil Government,* undertaken to refute Filmer's *Patriarcha.*
43. Kennedy, 75.
44. *Oeuvres de Louis XIV* (1806 ed.) i, 14–18.
45. Howard, *War in European History,* 63–64.

46. William Doyle, *The Old European Order,* 2nd ed. (Oxford University Press, 1992), 265.

47. Ibid., 164.

48. Sir George Clark, "From the Nine Years War to the War of Spanish Succession," *New Cambridge Modern History,* v. VI (ed. J. S. Bromley) (Cambridge, 1971), 384.

49. Losskey, *New Cambridge Modern History,* v. VI, 191–192.

50. Quoted in Andreas Osiander, *The State System of Europe, 1640–1990* (Oxford University Press, 1994), 93–94.

51. Ibid., 94–95.

52. Watson, 193, 204.

53. Ibid., 198, 211.

54. Howard, *War in European History,* 56.

55. Voltaire, *L'Histoire du regne de Louis XIV,* Chapter 2.

56. Emmerich Vattel, *Le Droit des Gens,* Book III, Chapter 3, Sections 47–48.

57. Quoted in Geoffrey Holmes and William A. Speck, *The Divided Society: Parties and Politics in England, 1694–1716* (New York: St. Martin's Press, 1967), 96.

58. Quoted in Bernard Fay, *Louis XVI ou la fin d'un monde* (Perrin, 1955), 148.

59. *New Cambridge Modern History,* v. V, 544.

60. Ibid., 546.

61. Ibid., 552.

62. Ibid.

63. Quoted in Craig and George, 20.

64. R. R. Palmer, "Frederick the Great, Guibert, Bulow: From Dynastic to National War," in *Makers of Modern Strategy,* ed. Paret, 99.

65. See Hubert C. Johnson, *Frederick the Great and His Officials* (New Haven: Yale University Press, 1975).

66. Keegan, *History of Warfare.*

67. Ibid.

68. Ibid., 99.

69. Quoted in Palmer, 105.

70. Indeed his tactical innovations prompted innovative responses to such an extent that even the Prussian oblique order, in Jeremy Black's words, "lost its novelty." Jeremy Black, "The Seven Years' War," in *The Reader's Companion to Military History,* ed. Robert Cowley and Geoffrey Parker (Houghton Mifflin, 1996), 423.

71. By the eve of the French Revolution, Prussia included half a dozen small territories in western Germany that did not border Prussia herself.

72. Frederick II, "Military Testament of 1768," in *Die Werke Friedrichs des Grossen,* v. 6 (R. Hobbing, 1912–1914), 248; Montesquieu, *Oeuvres Complètes,* vol. 29 (Gallimard, 1951), 3; and Montesquieu, "Histoire de mon temps, preface of 1775," in *Oeuvres Complètes,* v. 2 (Gallimard, 1951), xxxviii.

73. Frederick II, "Politisches Testament von 1752," in *Die Werke Friedrichs des Grossen,* v. 7 (R. Hobbing, 1912–1914), 158. Quoted by Palmer, 105.

74. Consider Palmer, 92–93, and Craig and George, 22–23.

75. As Palmer has concluded, "The period from 1740 to 1815, opening with the accession of Frederick the Great as king of Prussia and closing with the dethronement of Napoleon as emperor of the French, saw both the perfection of the older style of warfare and the launching of a newer style which in many ways we still follow. . . . The seventeenth century, while enlarging armies beyond precedent, had advanced the principles of orderly administration and control. It had put a new emphasis on discipline . . . turned army leaders into public officials, and made armed force into the servant of government." Palmer, 91.

76. George, 22.
77. Holsti, 90.
78. Evan Luard, *War in International Society* (Tauris, 1986), 110. See also Evan Luard, *Conflict and Peace in the Modern International System: A Study of the Principles of International Order* (SUNY Press, 1988).
79. Holsti, 92.
80. Black, *European Warfare,* 85.
81. Ibid., 94.

CHAPTER EIGHT: FROM STATE-NATIONS TO NATION-STATES: 1776–1914

1. Goethe, *Faust, The Second Part of the Tragedy,* trans. Walter Kaufmann (New York: Doubleday, 1961).
2. William Doyle, *The Old European Order,* 295–296.
3. Ibid.
4. Kennedy, 143. Just as in the first part of the twentieth century, the First World War was known as "the Great War."
5. Quoted in *New Cambridge Modern History,* vol. 9, 253.
6. Ibid., 311.
7. Ibid.
8. Osiander, 196–197.
9. *New Cambridge Modern History,* vol. 9, 299.
10. Ibid., 269.
11. Philip Henry, Fifth Earl Stanhope, *Notes of Conversations with the Duke of Wellington 1831–1851* (J. Murray, 1888), 81.
12. *New Cambridge Modern History,* vol. 9, 273.
13. See Peter Paret, *Yorck and the Era of Prussian Reform, 1807–1815* (Princeton University Press, 1960), 208; and Peter Paret, *Understanding War* (Princeton University Press, 1992), 16–17.
14. Peter Paret, "Napoleon," in *Makers of Modern Strategy,* ed. Paret, 126.
15. Howard, *War in European History,* 83–84.
16. Paraphrasing ibid.
17. Charles Tristan de Montholon, *Recits de la captivité de l'empereur Napoleon* [Paris, 1847], 2:432–433; quoted by Paret, "Napoleon," 127.
18. Paret, "Napoleon," 129.
19. Ibid., 129–130.
20. Cf. David Chandler, "The Right Man in the Right Place: Napoleon Bonaparte and the Battle for Toulon, France," *History Today* 49 (June 1999): 35.
21. Black, *European Warfare,* 187.
22. James H. Billington, *Fire in the Minds of Men: Origins of Revolutionary Faith* (Transaction, 1999), 160.
23. Consider the following from Act II of Puccini's *Tosca.*
    Sciarrone: Oh such fearful news, your lordship?
    Scarpia: Why this air of anxious hurry?
    Sciarrone: All our armies are defeated. . . .
    Scarpia: All our troops are defeated? Where?
    Sciarrone: At Marengo . . .
    Scarpia (impatiently): Yes, go on, man!
    Sciarrone: No! Melas was beaten!

(Cavaradossi, who has been listening to Sciarrone with mounting agitation, now in his excitement finds the strength to stand up and confront Scarpia menacingly.)

Cavaradossi: Victorious! Victorious!

> God of vengeance appear,
> Fill the wicked with fear!
> Surge up Liberty,
> Crushing all tyranny!

Giacomo Puccini, *Tosca,* libretto by Giuseppe Giacosa and Luigi Illica after the play by Victorien Sardou, trans. Edmund Tracey (Riverman Press, 1982), 63–64.

24. Quoted by André Fugier, *La Revolution francaise et l'Empire Napoleonien* (Hachette, 1954), 265; quoted in Robert Gildea, *Barricades and Borders, Europe 1800–1914* (Oxford University Press, 1987), 49.
25. Michael Howard, *The Causes of War and Other Essays* (Temple Smith, 1983), 27.
26. With the exception of the Russian and Habsburg armies, which were drawn from multinational states. Geoffrey Best, *War and Society in Revolutionary Europe, 1770–1870* (Leicester University Press, 1982), 255.
27. "A wretch, never named but with curses and jeers!" Lord Byron, *The Poetical Works of Lord Byron,* "The Irish Avatar" (1910), 107–109.
28. See e.g., Sir Charles Webster, *The Foreign Policy of Castlereagh* (Bell, 1950).
29. See e.g., Henry Kissinger, *A World Restored* (Grosset & Dunlap, 1964).
30. New Treaty of the Allied Powers, April 3, 1815 (Vienna) (from the German Papers).
31. Craig and George, 27.
32. On September 21, 1809, Castlereagh fought a duel with Canning to defend his "honor and reputation" after he discovered that the intention to remove him from the cabinet had been long concealed. Canning, who was hit in the leg in the second round of the duel, had managed the concealment, and then denied doing so. Wendy Hinde, *Castlereagh* (Collins, 1981), 166.
33. Ibid., 99.
34. See Franklin Ford, *Europe 1780–1830,* 2nd ed. (Longman, 1989), 234.
35. Ibid., 276.
36. Quoted by Craig and George, 29.
37. Quoted by Craig and George, 31.
38. Craig and George, 31.
39. Jacques Droz, *Europe between the Revolutions, 1815–1848* (New York: Harper & Row, 1967).
40. Quoted in Droz, 217.
41. Quoted in Craig and George, 32.
42. Quoted in F. B. Artz, *Reaction and Revolution, 1814–1832* (Harper & Brothers, 1934), 161.
43. Lieven to Nesselrode, December 4, 1820: St. Petersburg Archive.
44. Quoted in Robert W. Seton-Watson, *Britain in Europe, 1789–1914* (Macmillan, 1937), 74.
45. Harold Nicolson, *The Congress of Vienna* (Constable, 1946), 268.
46. Chateaubriand to Montmorenci, August 13, 1822; see d'Antioche, Chateaubriand, 342, 348.
47. Ford, 288.
48. Paul Schroeder, *The Transformation of European Politics, 1763–1848* (Oxford: Clarendon Press, 1994).
49. Brendan Simms, "The Transformation of European Politics," *Historical Journal* 37 (December 1995): 999–1000.

50. Kissinger, *A World Restored,* 170–174.
51. John Lynn, "The Great Question Concerning the Congress of Vienna Is This: Why Was It So Successful?" *Reader's Companion to Military History,* ed. Robert Cowley and Geoffrey Parker (Houghton Mifflin, 1996), 105.
52. Lord Castlereagh, Second Marquis Londonderry, "Letter to Lord Camden," September 25, 1793; see Sir Archibald Alsion, *Lives of Lord Castlereagh and Sir C. Stewart* (Blackwood, 1861), 23.
53. Neumann to Esterhazy, September 21, 1822: Vienna State Archives Berichte, 216, ix.
54. Black, *European Warfare,* 234.
55. Charles Tilly, *Coercion, Capital and European States, A.D. 900–1990* (Blackwell, 1990), 14; see also Harold Dorn, "The Military Revolution: Military History or History of Europe?" *Technology and Culture* 32 (1991): 656, "The concept of the military revolution is primarily an attempt to account for the formation of the centralized nation-states of Europe by directing attention to the enormous costs and financial burdens associated with gunpowder weapons and the defensive systems they entailed, costs and burdens that only a politically centralized state could shoulder."
56. Brian Downing, *The Military Revolution and Political Change* (Princeton University Press, 1991), 14; see also David Kaiser, *Politics and War: European Conflict from Philip II to Hitler* (Cambridge, Mass.: Harvard University Press, 1990).
57. Christopher Davdeker, *Surveillance, Power, and Modernity* (New York: St. Martin's Press, 1990).
58. The French royal army in 1788–1789, on the eve of the revolution, had about 150,000 men; by August 1793 it had reached 645,000 and the *leveé en masse* then doubled this number.
59. Schroeder, 391.
60. Black, *European Warfare,* 237.
61. "The advanced technology of steam engines and machine made tools gave Europe decisive economic and military advantages. The improvements to the muzzle loading gun (percussion caps, rifling, etc.) were ominous enough; the coming of the breech loader vastly increasing the rate of fire was an even greater advance; and the Gatling guns, Maxims and light field artillery put the final touches to a new firepower revolution which quite eradicated the chances of successful resistance by indigenous peoples reliant upon older weapons. Furthermore, the steam driven gunboat meant that European power, already supreme in open waters, could be extended inland via major waterways like the Niger, the Indus and the Yangtze." Kennedy, 150.
62. Black, *European Warfare,* 15–16, 201, n. 62. A recent study has concluded that the Maratha artillery was more advanced than the British on several counts but that their command structure was a shambles, with fatal consequences. At Assaye, Wellington's success owed much to a bayonet charge, scarcely confirming the standard image of Western armies gunning down masses of non-European troops relying on cold steel.
63. Quoted in Michael Glover, *Napoleonic Wars* (Hippocrene Books, 1979), 129; Kennedy, 133.
64. Mira Kamdar, "Rangoon: A Remembrance of Things Past," *World Policy Journal* 16 (Fall 1999): 89.
65. Quoted by Jack R. Pole, *Political Representation in England and the Origins of the American Republic* (University of California Press, 1966), 441.
66. Black, *European Warfare,* 195.
67. Michael W. Doyle, *Empires* (Cornell University Press, 1986), 232.
68. H. G. Wells, *The Outline of History* (Newnes, 1920), 618.
69. Gildea, 178.
70. Gildea, 179.

71. Gildea, 181.
72. Michael Doyle, *Empires* (Cornell University Press, 1986), 239.
73. Kissinger, *A World Restored,* 6.
74. Quoted by Helmut Bohme, *The Foundations of the German Empire* (Oxford University Press), 113–114.
75. Hajo Holborn, "The Prusso-German School: Moltke and the Rise of the General Staff," in *Makers of Modern Strategy,* ed. Paret, 286.
76. Howard, *War in European History,* 102.
77. Hew Strachan, *European Armies and the Conduct of War* (Allen & Unwin, 1983), 114.
78. Quoted by Holborn, 288.
79. Gunther Rothenberg, "Moltke, Schlieffen, and the Doctrine of Strategic Envelopment," in *Makers of Modern Strategy,* ed. Paret, 296.
80. Howard, *War in European History,* 111.
81. Quoted by Helmut Bohme, *Deutschlands Weg zur Grossmacht* (Cologne/Berlin, 1966), 84; in Gildea, 197.
82. Lothar Gall, *Bismarck: The White Revolutionary,* vol. 1 (trans. J. A. Underwood) (Unwin Hyman, 1986), 240.
83. Ibid., 239.
84. "Flectere si nequeo superos, Acheronta movebo!" *Die politischen Recen des Fursten Bismarck: Historischkritische Gesammtausg,* vol. 2, ed. Horst Kohl (Cotta, 1892–1905), 278.
85. Gall, 300.
86. See Georges Bonnin, *Bismarck and the Hohenzollern Candidature for the Spanish Throne* (Chatto & Windus, 1957), 70–71.
87. Gall, 355.
88. Quoted in Gall, 356, and cited there.
89. Winston Churchill, *A History of the English-Speaking Peoples: The Great Democracies,* vol. 4, (Cassell, 1956–1958), 276.
90. Quoted in Gall, 359.
91. Quoted in John A. S. Grenville, *Europe Reshaped, 1848–1878* (Brighton, Sussex: Harvester Press, 1976), 358.
92. Quoted in Henry Kissinger, "Reflections of Bismarck," in *Philosophers and Kings,* ed. Dankwart A. Rustow (Braziller, 1970), 918.
93. Kessel, Moltke, 747–748; quoted by Rothenberg, 310.
94. James McPherson, *Abraham Lincoln and the Second American Revolution* (Oxford University Press, 1990), viii; see also Harold Hyman, *A More Perfect Union: The Impact of the Civil War and Reconstruction on the Constitution* (Knopf, 1973).
95. Bevin Alexander, *Robert E. Lee's Civil War* (Adams Media Corp., 1998).
96. Shelby Foote, *The Civil War: A Narrative History* (Random House, 1986).
97. *New Cambridge Modern History,* vol. 11, 273, 284–294.
98. See Paul M. Kennedy, *The Rise and Fall of the Great Powers,* which documents the repeated bankruptcies of kingly and territorial states.
99. Osiander, 312, n. 165, speech by Wilhelm before the Brandenburg regional parliament, February 24, 1892, quoted in Christian Graf von Krockow, *Die Deutschen in ihren Jahrhundert, 1890–1990* (Rowohlt, 1990), 17.

CHAPTER NINE: THE STUDY OF THE MODERN STATE

1. Guido Calabresi and Philip Bobbitt, *Tragic Choices* (New York: Norton, 1978).
2. See also Hendrick Spruyt, "Institutional Selection in International Relations: State Anarchy as Order," *International Organization* 48 (1994): 527.

3. Jeremy Black, *War and the World: Military Power and the Fate of Continents, 1450–2000* (Yale University Press, 1998), 133. "War is not always won by the big battalions and the determinist economic account that would explain success in international relations in terms of the economic strength of particular states . . . is open to question." See also Niall Ferguson, *The Pity of War* (New York: Basic Books, 1999).

CHAPTER TEN: THE MARKET-STATE

1. In his essay "The Future of the Nation-State," David Beetham makes a similar assertion: "If we consider European history, then it is only the period from the fifteenth to the nineteenth century that saw the definitive emergence of the centralized state, successfully claiming a monopoly of lawmaking and enforcement power over unified geographical territory and independence from any external authority. . . . If that process of state formation is comparatively recent in historical terms . . . it was only as late as the nineteenth century that the idea became widely accepted that the proper boundaries of the state should coincide, not with the particular territory that had been historically acquired by dynastic alliance or conquest, but with a given people, who constituted a nation." David Beetham, "The Future of the Nation-State," in *The Idea of the Modern State,* ed. Gregor McLennan, David Held, and Stuart Hall (Open University Press, 1984), 209.

2. Michael Howard, *War and the Nation-State* (Clarendon Press, 1978), 103.

3. Gregor Dallas, *At the Heart of a Tiger: Clemenceau and His World, 1841–1929* (Macmillan, 1993), 501.

4. Dwight D. Eisenhower, *Crusade in Europe* (Doubleday, 1948), 259.

5. Stalin issued orders to proceed with the development of a Soviet atomic bomb in June 1942, possibly because of information relayed by Klaus Fuchs concerning the Manhattan Project, on which he was working at Los Alamos. *Bulletin of the Atomic Scientist* (December 15, 1967); Dwight D. Eisenhower, *Mandate for Change* (New American Library, 1963), 82, n. 5; and David Holloway, "Research Note: Soviet Thermonuclear Development," *International Security* 4 (1979–1980): 192–197.

6. "Tojo Ordered Japan's Own Atomic-Bomb Project: Report," *Agence France-Presse,* July 20, 1995.

7. Aaron L. Friedberg, "The Future of American Power," *Political Science Quarterly* 7 (1994).

8. Martin van Creveld, *The Rise and Decline of the State* (Cambridge University Press, 1999), 399–401.

9. As exemplified by Timothy McVeigh's bombing of the Alfred P. Murrah Federal Building in Oklahoma City on April 19, 1995. See Tom Kenworth and Lois Romano, "Nichols Prosecutor Cites 'Avalanche of Evidence'; Closing Arguments Underway in Bombing Trial; Defense Paints Star U.S. Witness as Drug User," *Washington Post,* December 16, 1997, A8.

10. Daniel R. Headrick, *The Invisible Weapon: Telecommunications and International Politics, 1851–1945* (Oxford: Oxford University Press, 1991).

11. See e.g., Keegan, *A History of Warfare,* 305–306; and Harvey A. DeWeerd, "Churchill, Lloyd George, Clemenceau: The Emergence of the Civilian," in *Makers of Modern Strategy,* ed. Edward Mead Earle (Princeton University Press, 1944), 289.

12. Mary Fulbrook, *The Divided Nation: A History of Germany, 1918–1990* (Oxford University Press, 1991), 296.

13. Eric Helleiner, *States and the Reemergence of Global Finance: From Bretton Woods to the 1990s* (Ithaca, N.Y.: Cornell University Press, 1994).

14. Ralph Bryant, "Global Change: Increasing Economic Integration and Eroding Political Sovereignty," *Brookings Review* 12 (1994): 42.
15. Quoted in Jeffrey A. Friden, *Banking on the World: The Politics of International Finance* (Harper & Row, 1987), 114–115; see also Walter Wriston, "Technology and Sovereignty," *Foreign Affairs* 67 (1988): 63.
16. The Bush administration that took office in 2001 was, in this respect, a continuation of its predecessor, the Clinton administration. Clinton and Blair were joined in the pursuit of this new order by the Schroeder government in Germany as well. William Boston, "The Battle for Berlin: Does Gerhard Schroeder Have What It Takes to Modernize Europe's Largest Economy?" *Wall Street Journal,* September 29, 1999, R12; and William Drozdiak, "U.S. Urges 'Third Way' between European Left and Right," *Washington Post,* August 20, 1998, A23.
17. Mancias, 192: "The ideology of democracy, freedom and equality provided much of the conceptual material for the legitimation of the state. But it may be that . . . these ideas now persuade too much."
18. See, e.g., "State of the First Amendment Survey" conducted by the Center for Survey Research and Analysis, University of Connecticut, Feb. 26–Mar. 24, 1999; see also Institute for Research in Social Science, University of North Carolina, July 19, 1991, Virginia Commonwealth Poll, match #4.
19. In Poland, the media "raised expectations, then fueled frustration. It spread official propaganda; it also provided alternative information." Tomasz Goban-Klas, *The Orchestration of the Media: The Politics of Mass Communications in Communist Poland and the Aftermath* (Westview Press, 1994), 4.
20. Or in unusual cases like the BBC, partly independent, partly government controlled, the media organization is driven to seek audiences of the size of those captured by those networks that are seeking consumers.
21. Michael Howard, "Reflections on Strategic Deception," Faculty Seminar on British Studies, University of Texas at Austin, 1994.
22. See the excellent essay by A. Michael Froomkin, "The Internet as a Source of Regulatory Arbitrage," *Borders in Cyberspace: Information Policy and the Global Information Infrastructure,* ed. Brian Kahin and Charles Nesson (Cambridge, Mass.: MIT Press, 1997).
23. Robert Skidelsky, *John Maynard Keynes: A Biography* (London: Macmillan, 1983).
24. Mark V. Tushnet, "The Supreme Court 1998 Term, Foreword," 113 *Harvard Law Review* (1999), 26; see also Betty Sue Flowers, "The Economic Myth" (Center for International Business Education and Research, Graduate School Business, University of Texas at Austin, December 1995).
25. *Hopwood v. State of Texas,* 999 F. Supp. 872 (1998).
26. *U.S. v. Lopez,* 514 U.S. 549 (1995); *Roe v. Wade,* 93 S. Ct. 705 (1973); and *Griswold v. Connecticut,* 85 S. Ct. 1678 (1965).
27. Michael Walzer, "The Concept of Civil Society," in *Toward a Global Civil Society,* ed. M. Walzer (Berghahn Books, 1995), 13, 17 (emphasis supplied).
28. Ibid., 13.
29. See Peter Drucker, *The Post-Capitalist Society* (Harper Business, 1993) and Peter Drucker, "The Post-Capitalist World," *Public Interest* 109 (1992): 89; Peter Drucker, "The Age of Social Transformation," *Atlantic Monthly,* November 1994, 53.
30. It is often said that we owe to Einstein and the theory of relativity the new and characteristic point of view of this century, perhaps, it is said, even something of our "relativism" in ethics. Like the Copernican revolution that reoriented man in the solar system, this intellectual breakthrough is thought to have reoriented contemporary man. I doubt this.

In the first place (unlike the ideas of Copernicus and Kepler), there is nothing in the general or special theories of relativity that has much to do with the ordinary perceptions of everyday life. Second, there is nothing in Einstein's theories—except possibly the names of the theories themselves—that bears on relativism. Einstein's point, in fact, seems if anything rather the opposite: energy and mass can be related by virtue of their common relation to a constant, the speed of light. Third, there is another candidate that is more appropriate to this role. Einstein believed, when he presented the special theory of relativity, that the universe was composed of a single galaxy. Hubble has shown us that this is not the case, indeed that it is so far from being the case that our peripheral position in a peripheral galaxy appears to reduce us to cosmic insignificance. It is Hubble's observations that have, and will have, a profound effect on the attitude of every person to his or her life. How each person reacts to this repositioning is partly a matter of temperament, I suppose, but everyone will feel something, perhaps something like nothingness.

31. Michael Howard, *War and the Nation-State* (Clarendon Press, 1978), 14.
32. "Government Cleared in 1993 Branch Davidian Deaths," *Houston Chronicle,* September 21, 2000, A17.
33. Sanford Levinson, "The Embarrassing Second Amendment," *Yale Law Journal* 99 (1989): 637.
34. Here again, the fundamental difference between the American idea of popular sovereignty and the European idea surfaces. Whereas Europeans and Americans can agree that "a legitimate monopoly on the use of violence lies with the state, whose forces can only use violence on the authorization of responsible political leaders," the American view holds that the right to delegate this monopoly to the State lies with the people, who, as they have done in the Second Amendment, may take a residual interest, as it were, in the monopoly. The European view assumes that the State, being sovereign, has been fully delegated the sovereignty of the people and thus has the monopoly so long as it can keep it. These fundamental differences are discussed in Philip Bobbitt, *Three Dogmas of Sovereignty* (unpublished manuscript).
35. William R. Hawkins, "The Transformation of War," *National Review,* April 1991, 50.
36. And though voting mechanisms will persist, even flourish in the private sector—you will vote for the chairman of the condo association, for the trustees of the charter school, and the like—these mechanisms may be weighted just as shareholder voting is "weighted" in those institutions that reflect, rather than serve as counterweights (churches, synagogues) to, the market-state.
37. David Butler and Austin Ranney, *Referendums: A Comparative Study of Practice and Theory* (American Enterprise Institute for Public Policy Research, 1978), 34.
38. Also consider James S. Fishkin's Center for Deliberative Polling, which attempts to determine how the public would vote if it were properly educated about the issues (http://www.la.utexas.edu/research/delpol/bluebook/summary.html).
39. *Baker* v. *Carr,* 82 S. Ct. 691 (1962); and *Reynolds* v. *Sims,* 84 S. Ct. 1362 (1964).
40. Aaron L. Friedberg, "The Future of American Power," *Political Science Quarterly* 109 (Spring 1994): 5.
41. Robert E. Litan and William D. Nordhaus, *Reforming Federal Regulation* (Yale University Press, 1983), 157.

CHAPTER ELEVEN: STRATEGIC CHOICES

1. Hedley Bull, *The Anarchical Society: A Study of Order in World Politics* (New York: Columbia University Press, 1977).
2. Alan Tonelson, "Superpower without a Sword," *Foreign Affairs* 72 (Summer 1993): 166–182.

3. It is noteworthy that during the Gulf War, not one son or daughter of a member of Congress went off to war. Patrick J. Buchanan, "America's new nationalism: The new political fault line is emerging, and it will be drawn over prosperity at home vs. aid abroad," *Pittsburgh Post-Gazette,* January 3, 1994, D3.

4. Alan Tonelson, "Tremors across the America First fault line: Fearful opposition," *Washington Times,* February 18, 1992, E1.

5. U.S. Congressional Research Service.

6. Alexander Haig, interview with *Fox News,* January 14, 2001.

7. Alan Tonelson, "Beyond Left and Right: New Thinking in Foreign Policy," *Current,* May 1994, 39.

8. Christopher Layne and Benjamin Schwarz, "No New World Order: America after the Cold War," *Current,* December 1993, 26, 27.

9. "Lord Salisbury, the British prime minister at the beginning of this century, once said in exasperation about his military advisers that if they had their way they would garrison the moon to protect us from an attack from Mars." Michael Howard, *The Lessons of History* (New Haven: Yale University Press, 1991).

10. As quoted in Benjamin Schwarz and Christopher Layne, "The Case against Intervention in Kosovo," *The Nation,* April 19, 1999, 11.

11. Thomas Kuhn, *The Structure of Scientific Revolutions* (University of Chicago Press, 1970); Imre Lakatos and Paul Feyerabend, *For and Against Method: Including Lakatos's Lectures on Scientific Method and the Lakatos-Feyerabend Correspondence,* ed. Matteo Motterlini (University of Chicago Press, 1999).

12. James N. Rosenau, *Turbulence in World Politics: A Theory of Change and Continuity* (Princeton: Princeton University Press, 1990).

13. James Chace, *The Consequences of the Peace: The New Internationalism and American Foreign Policy* (Oxford: Oxford University Press, 1992).

14. Though that day of parity may still be a ways off.

15. Richard N. Rosecrance, *The Rise of the Virtual State: Wealth and Power in the Coming Century* (New York: Basic Books, 1999).

16. Zbigniew K. Brzezinski, *The Grand Chessboard: American Primacy and Its Geostrategic Imperatives* (New York: Basic Books, 1997).

17. The Western European Union is a body established in 1955 to facilitate coordination of European security and defense matters. It may soon be supplanted by the European Union's new Rapid-Reaction Force.

18. John J. Mearsheimer, *Conventional Deterrence* (Ithaca, N.Y.: Cornell University Press, 1983).

19. Kenneth Neal Waltz, *The Spread of Nuclear Weapons: More May Be Better* (International Institute for Strategic Studies, 1981).

20. A free rider is an agent who exploits a service provided by another without paying for it. New Zealand, for example, benefits from the United States's nuclear deterrent without paying for it, by, for example, allowing U.S. nuclear submarines to use New Zealand harbors.

21. James B. Steinberg, "Sources of Conflict and Tools for Stability: Planning for the Twenty-first Century" (Address at the Naval War College, Newport, Rhode Island, June 14, 1994), *Department of State Dispatch,* vol. 5, July 11, 1994, 464.

22. George Kennan, *The Cloud of Danger: Current Realities of American Foreign Policy* (Little, Brown, 1977), 41–42.

23. Tony Smith, "Making the World Safe for Democracy," *Washington Quarterly* 16 (1993): 207.

24. Alexander Hamilton, *Federalist Paper #6.* Hamilton wrote "Republics" where I have substituted "Democracies." Hamilton clearly did not mean the latter as he understood

the distinction, but contemporary readers today will better grasp this point, I think, if this substitution is made.

25. Graham E. Fuller, *The Democracy Trap: The Perils of the Post–Cold War World* (Dutton, 1991).

26. Charley Reese, "Clinton Continues U.S. Tradition of Hypocritical Meddling Abroad," *Orlando Sentinel,* May 11, 1993, A8.

27. Charles Krauthammer, "The Unipolar Moment," *Foreign Affairs* 70 (1991): 23, 24, 27.

28. William E. Odom, "NATO's Expansion: Why the Critics Are Wrong," *National Interest,* Spring 1995, 38.

29. Krauthammer, 25.

30. Jeane J. Kirkpatrick, "A Normal Country in a Normal Time," *National Interest,* Fall 1990, 40–44.

31. Krauthammer, 27.

32. Richard N. Haass, "Paradigm Lost," *Foreign Affairs* 74 (1995): 43, 44.

33. Available at www.rice.edu/projects/baker/pubs/workingpapers/efac/jan21.html.

34. Bobbitt, *Democracy and Deterrence,* 283.

35. For an elaboration of the argument for this conclusion, I refer the reader to Calabresi and Bobbitt, *Tragic Choices.*

36. "Instrucción que dio el Conde Duque a Felipe I," British Museum, Egerton MS 347, fos. 249–290.

37. It is not only intellectuals who make this error. Insofar as the movement toward a European Defense Initiative is, for many, merely a political station on the way to an integrated European defense system, coordinated by the European Union, it reflects a similar disposition, because such a defense arrangement requires a fundamental constitutional modification of the nation-states of Europe in the direction of a superstate.

CHAPTER TWELVE: STRATEGY AND THE MARKET-STATE

1. William Poundstone, *Prisoner's Dilemma: John von Neumann, Game Theory, and the Puzzle of the Bomb* (New York: Doubleday, 1992).

2. Lamar Smith, "Immigration and Welfare Reform: Finally, Taxpayers Are Being Considered," *USA Today,* March 1, 1997, 30. See also George Borjas, "Immigration and Welfare Benefits," *Congressional Testimony,* March 12, 1996. For a contrasting view, see James Bornemeier, "Study Says Newcomers Give More Than They Take," *Portland Oregonian,* December 1, 1995, A1.

3. On February 23, 1996, the Outstanding Public Debt was $5,017,056,630,040.53. This was the first time in history the U.S. national debt surpassed the $5 trillion mark.

4. R. W. Apple, Jr., "Poll Shows Disenchantment with Politicians and Politics," *International Herald Tribune,* August 14, 1995, 3, reporting on *New York Times*/CBS Poll; ironically this was reported a few pages away from a rather snide *New York Times* attack on the Clintons for refusing to reveal their private tax returns from the mid-1980s, suggesting that "the Clintons owe it to the public to . . . waive their privacy rights at the IRS" and concluding that until the Whitewater independent counsel publishes his report one cannot know whether the President and the First Lady "were truthful," "The Whitewater Tax Questions," 6.

5. Robert M. Dunn, Jr., "Has the U.S. Economy Really Been Globalized?" *Washington Quarterly,* Winter 2001, 54.

6. See the proposal by Ronald Asmus, Robert Blackwill, and F. Stephen Larrabee, "Can NATO Survive?" *Washington Quarterly,* Spring 1996, 79, for an expansion of a NATO agenda.

7. See the excellent recent books on this subject by Richard Haass, *Intervention: The Use of American Military Force in the Post–Cold War World* (Brookings Institution, 1994); and *The Reluctant Sheriff* (Council on Foreign Relations Press, 1997).

8. James Kurth, "The Decline and Fall of Almost Everything: Paul Kennedy Peers into the Future ('Preparing for the 21st Century')," *Foreign Affairs* 72 (Spring 1993): 162. "The best way—for a nation and a person—to prepare for the 21st century will be what has always been the best way to prepare for uncertainty. That is to rely not so much upon the outer supports of plans, programs and policies but upon the inner strengths of character—resiliency and resourcefulness, discipline and cooperation, endurance and courage, and, perhaps above all, faith and hope." See also James Fallows, *More like Us: Making America Great Again* (Boston: Houghton Mifflin, 1989).

9. For an excellent analysis, see Richard O. Hundley, *Past Revolutions, Future Transformations: What Can the History of Revolutions in Military Affairs Tell Us about Transforming the U.S. Military?* (Rand, 1999).

10. "One set of possibilities relates to future advances in sensor technology; these are opening up unused portions of the electromagnetic spectrum that, when matched with improved computational capabilities and deployment in space, offer the prospect for a truly transparent battlefield. . . . [E]lectronic systems may be redesigned so that they will be virtually undetectable." Dan Goure, "Is There a Military-Technical Revolution in America's Future?" *Washington Quarterly* 16 (1993): 179.

11. Ibid., 175.

12. Carter and Perry, 135. This change "began in the 1970's with the development of satellite reconnaissance, smart weapons, cruise missiles, stealth aircraft, and other breakthroughs that would not have been possible without the microchip . . ."

13. Eliot Cohen, "A Revolution in Warfare," *Foreign Affairs* 75 (1996): 37. "Admiral William Owens, former vice chairman of the Joint Chiefs of Staff, has written of a 'system of systems': through an integrated network of powerful computers and high-speed communications. This will transform the way commanders and troops see and communicate on the battlefield. In the past, information was passed around the battlefield via radio conversations or typewritten messages. Commanders got only a fraction of the information they could really use in combat. With the system of systems envisioned in Force 21, commanders will have the ability to send and receive, in digital bursts, critical information about the location of enemy and friendly forces: the rate of use of food, fuel, and ammunition; the progress of current operations; and plans for future operations.

"The effect on combat operations will be revolutionary. Every commander will have 'battlefield awareness': a constant, complete, three-dimensional picture of the battlefield. Every field unit will be better able to carry out its commander's orders because it will be able to see more clearly through the 'fog of battle.' An entire division will be able to fight as a single integrated combat system.

"In battle, when a tank commander spots enemy forces, he will have a choice. He could engage the enemy with the weapons on his tanks, or he could call in attack helicopters, artillery, strike aircraft, or naval gunfire. Because of digital technology . . . these other units will see exactly what the tank commander sees. . . . As combat is underway, the supporting logistics unit will monitor the ammunition usage, so it will be able to resupply at the time and amount needed, thereby reducing the huge logistics tail otherwise needed to support combat operations." Carter and Perry, 199.

14. Cohen, 38.

15. It had caused a complete reworking of American nuclear strategy and prompted the introduction into Europe of fast-reacting Pershing II missiles and survivable ground-launched cruise missiles.

16. Jeffrey R. Cooper, "Another View of the Revolution in Military Affairs," in *In Athena's Camp: Preparing for Conflict in the Information Age,* ed. John Arquilla and David Ronfeldt (Santa Monica: RAND, 1997), 114.

17. *Future Visions for U.S. Defense Policy, the Council on Foreign Relations Defense Policy Review,* ed. John Hillen (Council on Foreign Relations, 1998), 5–6.

18. Les Aspin, address to Jewish Institute for National Security Affairs, Washington, D.C., September 21, 1992, reprinted in Richard Haass, *Intervention,* 183–190.

19. See e.g., "A National Security Strategy of Engagement and Enlargement," The White House, February 1995; and see also "Annual Report to the President and the Congress," William S. Cohen, Secretary of Defense (1999), 3–4.

20. General Colin S. Powell, remarks to defense writers' group, September 23 1993, quoted in Harry G. Summers, *The New World Strategy: A Military Policy for America's Future* (Simon & Schuster, 1995), 139.

21. Paul Bracken defines this list a little differently, treating the "C" class candidates as states that, though they suffer problems rather than pose threats—for example, problems such as ethnic civil war (Yugoslavia), insurgency (Peru), terrorism (Egypt), civil disorder (Somalia), or infiltration such as by narcotics flows—these states nevertheless can impose demands on the U.S. military. Paul Bracken, "The Military After Next," *The Washington Quarterly* 16 (Autumn 1993): 157.

22. T. R. Fehrenbach, *This Kind of War: A Study in Unpreparedness* (Pocket Books, 1963).

23. This study was highly controversial insofar as it seemed to imply that current allies might become future competitors. See Patrick Taylor, "Pentagon Drops Goal of Blocking New Superpowers," *The New York Times,* May 24, 1992, A1; Barton Gellman, "Keeping the U.S. First; Pentagon Would Preclude a Rival Superpower," *Washington Post,* March 11, 1992, A1. See also Francis Fukuyama, "The Beginning of Foreign Policy," *The New Republic,* August 17, 1992, 24.

24. Bracken, 157.

25. Goure, 31.

26. Jeffrey Cooper, "Another View of the Revolution in Military Affairs," in *In Athena's Camp: Preparing for Conflict in the Information Age,* ed. John Arquilla and David Ronfeldt (Santa Monica: RAND, 1997), 114.

27. This figure comes from Dr. Hans Mark, former director for defense research and engineering at the United States Department of Defense.

28. Cohen, 50.

29. "An analogy might be Germany's acquisition of a modern air force in the space of less than a decade in the 1930s. At a time when civilian and military aviation technologies did not diverge too greatly, Germany could take the strongest civilian aviation industry in Europe and within a few years convert it into enormous military power, much as the United States would do a few years later with its automobile industry." Cohen, 51.

30. Howard Baker and Lloyd Cutler, "A Report Card on the Department of Energy's Nonproliferation Programs with Russia," The Secretary of Energy Advisory Board, United States Department of Energy, January 10, 2001.

31. Carter and Perry, 76–77.

32. Cohen, 51.

33. See Paul Bracken, "The Military after Next," 161. Clifford Rogers notes that although the technology has been perfected, when military organizations failed either to restructure effectively, whether through lack of funds or organizational insight, they failed to achieve the benefits of revolutionary increase in military effectiveness. Clifford J. Rogers, "The Military Revolutions of the Hundred Years War," *The Journal of Military History* (April 1993): 241–278.

34. Cohen, 53.

35. Goure, 180.

36. "To the extent that the defense sector increases its dependence on the commercial sector for the ability to support and reconstitute its forces, it will be further pushed in the direction of a revolution by necessity." Ibid.

37. "Virtually no one is considering [conflicts] where the next military will face competition from its peers or from major regional competitors that can adversely affect U.S. interests in key regions. This is *terra incognita,*" Bracken, 166.

38. Josef Joffe, "Bismarck or Britain?: Toward an American Grand Strategy after Bipolarity," *International Security* 19 (Spring 1995): 31–32.

39. Joffe describes this as "a demand for [American] services, and that translates into political profits," and he suggests that "[t]hese revenues can be nicely invested elsewhere, e.g., [in gaining] America's access to the [European] Single Market. To be in a position where all the powers need us . . . would clearly help the United States to improve the political terms of trade vis-à-vis the E.U. and to contain neo-mercantilism in general." Joffe, 113.

40. Carter and Perry, 56–57.

41. Ibid., 27.

42. Ibid., 42.

43. Ibid., 47.

44. Ibid., 120–121.

45. Martin C. Libicki, "Informational War and Peace," *Journal of International Affairs* 51 (1998): 420–421.

46. Joseph Nye and William Owens, "America's Information Edge," *Foreign Affairs* 75 (1996): 21, 28.

47. Kees van der Heijden, *Scenarios: The Art of Strategic Conversation* (Wiley, 1997), 2.

48. Ibid., 8, 7.

49. Bracken, 162.

50. See Wesley K. Clark, *Waging Modern War* (Public Affairs, 2001).

51. Barry Posen and Andrew Ross, "Competing Visions for U.S. Grand Strategy," *International Security* 21 (1997): 50–51. The Clinton administration, in its second term, plainly took these lessons of the first term to heart when it determined to prosecute a humanitarian intervention in Kosovo through the use of precision air strikes.

52. Joffe, 2.

53. Edward Luttwak, "Toward Post-Heroic Warfare," *Foreign Affairs* 74 (1995): 115.

54. See Colin L. Powell, "U.S. Forces: Challenges Ahead," *Foreign Affairs* 72 (1993): 32; and Caspar W. Weinberger, *Fighting for Peace: Seven Critical Years in the Pentagon* (Warner Books, 1990).

55. Luttwak, 109, 112.

56. Bobbitt, *Democracy and Deterrence,* 101–102.

57. Ibid., 102.

58. Roger Hilsman, "Does the CIA Still Have a Role?" *Foreign Affairs* 74 (1995): 104.

59. "The key professional argument advanced by the most senior U.S. military chiefs to reject all proposals to employ U.S. offensive air power in Bosnia rested on the implicit assumption . . . that only decisive results are worth having . . ." Luttwak, 120–121.

60. Richard Holbrooke, *To End a War* (Random House, 1998), 142–158.

61. Ivo H. Daalder and Michael E. O'Hanlon, *Winning Ugly: NATO's War to Save Kosovo* (Brookings Institution, 2000), 231.

62. Ibid., 4.

63. Ibid., 233.

64. "The rise of information technologies [has led to] the development of intelligent weapons that can guide themselves to their targets [but this] is only one and not

necessarily the most important. The variety and ever-expanding capabilities of intelligence-gathering machines and the ability of computers to bring together and distribute to users the masses of information from these sources stem [also] from the information revolution." Eliot Cohen, "A Revolution in Warfare," *Foreign Affairs* 75 (1996): 37.

65. "Spacecast 2020" (Air University, June 1994).

66. Andrew F. Krepinevich, "Cavalry to Computer: The Pattern of Military Revolution," *National Interest* (Fall 1994): 30–41.

67. Raffi Gregorian, "Global Positioning Systems: A Military Revolution for the Third World?" *SAIS Review* 13 (1993): 133.

68. For a more skeptical view of missile defense, see Joseph Cirincione and Frank von Hippel, *The Last Fifteen Minutes: Ballistic Missile Defense in Perspective* (Coalition to Reduce Nuclear Dangers, 1996).

69. Keith Payne, "Post–Cold War Deterrence and Missile Defense," *Orbis* 39 (1995): 203.

70. Hans Mark, "Pentagon Official Touts Sea-Based Missile Defense," *Aerospace Daily,* September 1, 1999, 344.

71. Eisenhower, *Crusade in Europe,* 260.

CHAPTER THIRTEEN: THE WARS OF THE MARKET-STATE

1. Machiavelli, *Discoursi* (Modern Library, 1950), 104.

2. Bodin, 200.

3. See Hume's remark that the "greatness of the state" and "the happiness of its subjects" had become interdependent. David Hume, "Of Commerce," in *Essays, Morals, Political and Literary* (Oxford University Press, 1963), 1753.

4. Pole, *Political Representation in England,* 441.

5. Burke and Napoleon, Lenin and Wilson: how surprised they might be that, in retrospect, they were struggling to give pre-eminence to the same constitutional order.

6. See Charles Tilly, *European Revolutions, 1492–1992* (Blackwell, 1993), which focuses on the role of revolution in state formation. See also Michael Richards, "How to Succeed in Revolution without Really Trying," *Journal of Social History* 28 (1995): 883.

7. Howard, "War and the Nation State," in *The State,* ed. Stephen Graubard (Norton, 1979), 101–110.

8. Geoffrey Parker, "Continuity and Change in Western Geopolitical Thought during the Twentieth Century," *International Social Science Journal* 43 (1991): 21.

9. Friedberg, "The Future of American Power," 1.

10. Anthony Giddens, *The Nation State and Violence* (Berkeley: University of California Press, 1985).

11. Peter Mancias, *The Death of the State* (New York: Putnam, 1974).

12. D. Beetham, "The Future of the Nation-State," in *The Idea of the Modern State,* ed. Gregor McLennan, David Held, and Stuart Hall (Open University Press, 1984), 208–222.

13. Hans Mark in his commencement address at St. Edwards University, Austin, Texas, Saturday, May 8, 1993.

14. See John Lynn, "Clio in Arms: The Role of the Military Variable in Shaping History," *Journal of Military History* 55 (1991): 83–95. See also Charles Tilly, *Coercion, Capital, and the European States, A.D. 90–1990* (Blackwell, 1990); David Kaiser, *Politics and War: European Conflict from Philip II to Hitler* (Harvard University Press, 1990); Brian M. Downing, *The Military Revolution and Political Change in Early Modern Europe* (Princeton University Press, 1991); Geoffrey Parker, *The Military Revolution: Military Innovation and the Rise of the West, 1500–1800* (Cambridge University Press,

1988); and David Ralston, *Importing the European Army: The Introduction of European Military Techniques and Institutions into the Extra-European World, 1600–1914* (University of Chicago Press, 1990); Jeremy Black, *War and the World: Military Power and the Fate of Continents, 1450–2000* (New Haven: Yale University Press, 1998).

15. Arthur Nussbaum, *A Concise History of the Law of Nations* (Macmillan, 1947), 238–247. It should be noted that the eighteenth century saw the same sort of optimism: Howard, *War in European History*, 73.

16. Samuel P. Huntington, "The Clash of Civilizations?" *Foreign Affairs* 72 (1993): 22.

17. "Insights and Action Items for U.S. Global Relations in the 21st Century," *Report of the Project on the Future of Global Relations*, 1997.

18. Bill Clinton, "Remarks on the Reinventing Government Initiative," *Weekly Compilation of Presidential Documents*, vol. 30, 1994, 1763.

19. Bill Clinton, "Remarks to the Joint Session of the Louisiana State Legislature in Baton Rouge, Louisiana," *Weekly Compilation of Presidential Documents*, vol. 32, 1996, 969.

20. Ibid.

21. Bill Clinton, "Address before a Joint Session of the Congress on the State of the Union," *Weekly Compilation of Presidential Documents*, vol. 33, 1997, 136.

22. Bill Clinton, "Inaugural Address," *Weekly Compilation of Presidential Documents*, vol. 33, 1997, 60. Nor is the executive the only branch of government leading the movement toward the market-state in the United States. As Mark Tushnet has observed, the U.S. Supreme Court's "federalism decisions are the most obvious examples.... *United States* v. *Lopez*, which struck down the Gun-Free Zones Act as beyond the power given Congress in the Commerce Clause; *Printz* v. *United States*, which invalidated the Brady Handgun Control Act because it forced state executive officials to implement a national program; *City of Boerne* v. *Flores*, which invalidated the Religious Freedom Restoration Act for exceeding the scope of Congress's power to remedy court-identified violations of the Free Exercise Clause; and a series of decisions restricting Congress's ability to impose retroactive monetary liability on states because such remedies violated the Eleventh Amendment." Mark V. Tushnet, "The Supreme Court 1998 Term, Foreword: The New Constitutional Order and the Chastening of Constitutional Aspiration," 113 *Harvard Law Review* 26 (1999).

INTRODUCTION: THE ORIGIN OF INTERNATIONAL LAW IN THE CONSTITUTIONAL ORDER

1. See Machiavelli's chapters in *The Prince* on "dangling the carrot" and "brandishing the stick" for a view of the state in strategic terms, i.e., those that aim for collective aggrandizement with, in principle, no limits. See Niccolò Machiavelli, *The Prince*, Chapters XV and XVII. Clifford Orwin, "Machiavelli's Unchristian Charity," *American Political Science Review* 72 (1978): 1217–1228.

2. Stanley Hoffmann, "Politics among the Nations: The Struggle for Power and Peace," *The Atlantic*, November 1985, 134.

3. Michael Howard, *The Causes of War and Other Essays*, 27.

4. Philip Bobbitt, *Three Dogmas of Sovereignty*.

5. Carl von Clausewitz, *On War*, 75.

6. Hedley Bull, "The Emergence of a Universal International Society," in *The Expansion of International Society*, ed. Hedley Bull and Adam Watson (Oxford University Press, 1984), 117.

7. Montesquieu, *Oeuvres Complètes*, vol. 2 (Gallimard, 1951), 237.

8. "Barbarus" is the Latin word for foreigner.
9. Murray Forsyth, "The Tradition of International Law," in *Traditions of International Ethics,* ed. Terry Nardin and David R. Mapel (Cambridge University Press, 1992), 24.
10. Ibid.
11. Adam Watson, *The Evolution of International Society,* 8. The most important of these limitations arises from the constitutional order of the State because this governs strategy, which is the exercise of the state's power abroad.
12. Anne-Marie Slaughter, "The Real New World Order," *Foreign Affairs* 76 (1997): 183, 195.

CHAPTER FOURTEEN: COLONEL HOUSE AND
A WORLD MADE OF LAW

1. *The Intimate Papers of Colonel House,* vol. 1, 16.
2. Ibid., 45.
3. Ibid., 46.
4. Ibid., 62.
5. Ibid., 126.
6. *Profiles in Power: Twentieth Century Texans in Washington,* ed. Kenneth E. Hendrickson, Jr., and Michael L. Collins (Harlan Davidson, 1993), 5.
7. *Intimate Papers of Colonel House,* vol. I, 114.
8. B. W. Huebsch letter, House Files, Yale University.
9. Ibid.
10. *Portland* (Maine) *Evening Telegram,* November 30, 1912.
11. *Dallas Morning News,* December 30, 1912.
12. *Hartford Courant,* December 13, 1912.
13. *Trenton Advertiser,* January 5, 1913.
14. *Philadelphia Public Ledger,* January 12, 1913.
15. "Literary Gossip," *Los Angeles Times,* February 2, 1913.
16. *Cincinnati Enquirer,* December 12, 1912.
17. *The New York Times,* January 26, 1913.
18. *Los Angeles Times,* February 2, 1913.
19. *Philadelphia Public Ledger,* January 27, 1913; see also *LaFollette's,* Madison, Wisconsin, March 29, 1913.
20. *Chicago Record Herald,* November 28, 1912.
21. *Zion's Herald,* February 19, 1913, Boston: "It would be much more interesting to know. For after all, it makes a difference who says a thing."
22. *Los Angeles Times,* March 30, 1913.
23. Milwaukee, Wisconsin, January 18, 1913: the "story is rather amateurish in places," *Chicago News,* January 18, 1913.
24. Walter Lippmann, "America's Future Pictured in a Decidedly Quaint Novel," *New York Times Book Review,* December 8, 1912, 4.
25. Franklin K. Lane, *The Letters of Franklin K. Lane,* ed. Anne Wintermute Lane and Louise Herrick Wall (Boston: Houghton Mifflin, 1922).
26. Daniel P. Moynihan, *On the Law of Nations* (Harvard University Press, 1990), 1.
27. "Why We Went to War: President Wilson's Famous Address at the Opening of the War Congress, April 2, 1917," in *President Wilson's Great Speeches and Other History Making Documents* (Stanton and Van Vliet, 1919), 17.
28. See Joyce Williams, *Colonel House and Sir Edward Grey: A Study in Anglo-American Diplomacy* (University Press of America, 1984), 22–29.
29. *The Intimate Papers of Colonel House,* vol. 1, 240 (diary date 5/9/13).

30. Almost identical to a plan set out in *Philip Dru.*
31. G. M. Trevelyan, *Grey of Fallodon* (Longmans, Green, 1946), 271.
32. *The Intimate Papers of Colonel House,* vol. 1, 262.
33. Ibid., 274–275.
34. Indeed, Spring-Rice, the British ambassador to the United States, thought that House's mission had precipitated the German action toward Austria because it signaled to the war party in Berlin that U.S. mediation might weaken their hand with the kaiser. *The Intimate Papers of Colonel House,* vol. 1, 286–287.
35. Ibid.
36. George W. Egerton, *Great Britain and the Creation of the League of Nations: Strategy, Politics and International Organization, 1914–1919* (University of North Carolina Press, 1978), citing Grey to Spring-Rice, December 22, 1914, F.O. 800/84. See also Trevelyan, 314–315. House's initial reply—that the United States could not become a party to any agreement binding members to enforce the observance of treaties, see Egerton, 25—seems to have been based on constitutional grounds having to do with the war powers of the executive. See Philip Bobbitt, "War Powers: An Essay on John Hart Ely's War and Responsibility: Constitutional Lessons of Vietnam and Its Aftermath," *Michigan Law Review* 92 (1994): 1364; (arguing that the United States can go to war on the basis of a ratified treaty without further congressional action); see also Philip Bobbitt, *Three Dogmas of Sovereignty* (noting that Congress can also supersede a treaty by statute and thus that the U.S. treaty commitment is only conditional, posing the possibility that U.S. constitutional law—the basis of congressional supersession—might come into conflict with doctrines of international law, e.g., *pacta sunt servanda*).
37. *The Nation,* March 14, 1914, quoted in A.J.P. Taylor, *The Trouble Makers: Dissent over Foreign Policy, 1792–1939* (Indiana University Press, 1958), 115.
38. Egerton, 25.
39. *The Intimate Papers of Colonel House,* vol. 1, 364.
40. Zimmerman to House, March 21, 1915.
41. *The Intimate Papers of Colonel House,* vol. 1, 433–434.
42. House Files, Yale University.
43. *The Intimate Papers of Colonel House,* vol. 2, 89.
44. *The Intimate Papers of Colonel House,* vol. 2, 90–91.
45. *The Intimate Papers of Colonel House,* vol. 2, 98.
46. Hildebrand in *Profiles in Power,* 17.
47. Patrick Devlin, *Too Proud to Fight: Woodrow Wilson's Neutrality* (Oxford University Press, 1974), 473.
48. Oliver W. Holmes, Jr., "A Soldier's Faith: An address delivered on Memorial Day, May 30, 1895, at a meeting called by the graduating class of Harvard University" (Research Publications, 1984). On this change, as on so many other subjects, Michael Howard has written with insight. See Michael Howard, *The Causes of War and Other Essays,* 27.
49. *The Intimate Papers of Colonel House,* vol. 2, 359.
50. "The Making of a President," in *Philip Dru,* 89–90.
51. *The Intimate Papers of Colonel House,* vol. 2, 359 (just as, in 1996, President Clinton ran for governor, as it were, on issues of crime, welfare reform, and the domestic economy).
52. No Democratic candidate save Madison and Buchanan had won the presidency without New York.
53. *The Intimate Papers of Colonel House,* vol. 2, 361.
54. Devlin, 686.

55. Woodrow Wilson, "An Address to a Joint Session of Congress," April 2, 1917, in *Papers of Woodrow Wilson,* vol. 41, ed. Arthur S. Link (Princeton University Press, 1966–1992), 526–527.
56. Devlin, 679.
57. *New York Times,* September 4, 1918; see also U.S. Cong. Rec., 2d sess., vol. LVI, part 10, p. 9875 (Sept. 3, 1918).
58. The quoted passage above, see TAN 559, describing the organization of the campaign is taken from Selwyn and almost perfectly tracks House's memo to Wilson. Compare the following extracts, the first from *Philip Dru,* the second a campaign memo by House from June 1916.

> "He began by eliminating all the states he knew the opposition party would certainly carry, but he told the party leaders there to claim that a revolution was brewing, and that a landslide would follow at the election. This would keep his antagonists busy and make them less effective elsewhere.
>
> "He also ignored the states where his side was sure to win. In this way he was free to give his entire thoughts to the twelve states that were debatable, and upon whose votes the election would turn. He divided each of these states into units containing five thousand voters, and, at the national headquarters, he placed one man in charge of each unit. Of the five thousand, he roughly calculated there would be two thousand voters that no kind of persuasion could turn from his party and two thousand that could not be changed from the opposition. This would leave one thousand doubtful ones to win over. So he had a careful poll made in each unit, and eliminated the strictly unpersuadable partymen, and got down to a complete analysis of the debatable one thousand. Information was obtained as to their race, religion, occupation and former political predilection. It was easy then to know how to reach each individual by literature, by persuasion or perhaps by some more subtle argument. No mistake was made by sending the wrong letter or the wrong man to any of the desired one thousand.
>
> "In the states so divided, there was, at the local headquarters, one man for each unit just as at the national headquarters. So these two had only each other to consider, and their duty was to bring to Rockland a majority of the one thousand votes within their charge. The local men gave the conditions, the national men gave the proper literature and advice, and the local men then applied it. The money that it cost to maintain such an organization was more than saved from the waste that would have occurred under the old method." E. M. House, *Philip Dru: Administrator* (Huebsch, 1912), 89–90.
>
> "House's Plan of Campaign, June 20, 1916. In preparing the organization I would suggest that the following States be classified in this way:
>
> "Class 1. Connecticut, New York, New Jersey, Maryland, West Virginia, Indiana, Missouri, Wyoming, Arizona, and New Mexico.
>
> "Class 2. Maine, Massachusetts, Ohio, Illinois, Colorado, California, Oregon, and Washington.
>
> "Class 3. Rhode Island, Wisconsin, Michigan, Minnesota, Iowa.
>
> "We should put forth our maximum effort in the States of Class 1, a strong effort in those of Class 2, and a lesser effort in those of Class 3.
>
> "There are seven states in Class 1 of prime importance, which we should and must carry. These States should be divided into units of not larger than 100,000 voters.
>
> "By having the State organizations cooperate closely with the national organization, it will not be over-difficult to have the certain Republican and certain Democratic voters of these units segregated. This can be done by writing to the

precinct chairmen in those units and obtaining from them lists of the entire electorate, putting the absolutely certain Republicans and absolutely certain Democrats
in one class and the fluctuating voters in another.

"This independent vote should be classified as to race, religion, and former affiliations. Roughly speaking, we must assume that in a unit of 100,000 voters, eighty
per cent of them will be unchangeable voters, which would leave twenty per cent
that can be influenced by argument.

"The size of these units must necessarily depend upon the size of our campaign
fund. If it is small, a larger unit will have to be considered; if sufficient money is
raised, a smaller unit can be made. The smaller the unit the more successful, of
course, will be the result.

"Literature, letters in sealed envelopes, and personal appeals should be made to
each of these doubtful voters.

"One member of the Campaign Committee should be placed in charge of the
organization of these units, with nothing else to do. He, in turn, should place one
man in charge of each unit. The duty of this man should be to keep in touch not only
with the State Executive Committee of his particular unit, but also with each one of
the doubtful voters in that unit." *The Intimate Papers of Colonel House,* vol. 2,
361–362.

59. *Philip Dru,* 44–45
60. Ronald Steel, *Walter Lippmann and the American Century* (Little, Brown, 1980), 127,
    n. 18
61. Steel, 166.
62. Steel, 130.
63. Steel, 125.
64. *The Intimate Papers of Colonel House,* vol. 3, 316, et seq.
65. Eugene V. Rostow, *Toward Managed Peace: The National Security Interests of the
    United States, 1759 to the Present* (Yale University Press, 1993), 218.
66. W. M. Knight Patterson, *Germany from Defeat to Conquest* (Allen & Unwin, 1945),
    137.
67. Woodrow Wilson, "President Wilson's Address to Congress Analyzing German and
    Austrian Peace Utterances," Joint Session, February 11, 1918," in *The Messages and
    Papers of Woodrow Wilson,* vol. 1 (Review of Reviews Corporation, 1924), 475.
68. Paul M. Kennedy, *Rise and Fall of the Great Powers,* 272.
69. Arthur Bryant, *Unfinished Victory,* 32, noted in Roy Denman, *Missed Chances* (Cas-
    sell, 1993), Chapter 2, note 3.
70. Roy Denman, *Missed Chances,* 31.
71. Denman, 32.
72. House Files, Yale University.
73. *The Intimate Papers of Colonel House,* vol. 4, 361.
74. *The Intimate Papers of Colonel House,* vol. 4, 362.
75. Edith B. Wilson, *My Memoir* (Bobbs-Merrill, 1939), 245–246.
76. See A. H. Robertson, *Human Rights in the World: An Introduction to the Study of the
    International Protection of Human Rights* (New York: St. Martin's, 1982), 118–125.
77. H. Kissinger, "The New Face of Diplomacy: Wilson and the Treaty of Versailles,"
    Diplomacy (Simon & Schuster, 1994), 218–245. My treatment is completely at odds
    with the charge of Colonel House's alleged agreement to sidetrack the league into a
    separate "annex" in order to conclude the conference, a charge that appeared conspicu-
    ously in Mrs. Wilson's *Memoirs* and in an article by her confidant, Wilson's physician,
    and that has now regrettably become an accepted part of the received history of this

period. Not only does Mrs. Wilson's view lead to many historiographical anomalies, it wholly misreads House's tactics, which endeavored to save the Wilsonian program.

78. "Seton-Watson, . . . an eloquent advocate of the Slav claims . . . [had] helped me draw up a boundary line between the two nationalities which was much nearer the truth . . . In this way [House and I] tossed about free cities and played ducks and drakes with not a few islands, and we certainly whittled down the territory which both countries claimed . . . I made a 'graph' and a map showing what we had accomplished. There was the city of Fiume and the port of Susak and a little of the adjacent territory. All the rest was assigned. 'But this area, Colonel,' I explained, 'we shall call Disputanta, and we shall place it under the administration of the League of Nations for the period of fifteen years. Then we shall end up with a free and fair election, a plebiscite . . .' The Colonel was enchanted with what he called a magical solution of all our troubles.'" Stephen Bonsal, *Suitors and Suppliants: The Little Nations at Versailles* (Prentice-Hall, 1946).

79. Quoted in Kissinger, *Diplomacy,* 235.

80. Which we know was dictated each day and was not subsequently "corrected"; see Yale Papers memorandum.

81. *The Intimate Papers of Colonel House,* vol. 4, 390.

82. *The Intimate Papers of Colonel House,* vol. 4, 488–489.

83. David H. Miller, *The Drafting of the Covenant,* vol. 1 (Putnam, 1928), 49.

84. Philip Bobbitt, "War Powers: An Essay on John Hart Ely's War and Responsibility: Constitutional Lessons of Vietnam and Its Aftermath," *Michigan Law Review* 92 (May 1994): 1364.

CHAPTER FIFTEEN: THE KITTY GENOVESE INCIDENT AND THE WAR IN BOSNIA

1. This account is largely taken from A. M. Rosenthal's excellent study of the Kitty Genovese murder, *Thirty-Eight Witnesses* (McGraw-Hill, 1964). Rosenthal's account draws upon contemporaneous interviews made in the aftermath of the murder.

2. "Calling for Help on the T," *Boston Globe,* February 3, 2000, A20.

3. Dave Lieber, "Biggest Mystery Is Why No One Called the Police," *Fort Worth Star Telegram,* October 13, 2001, 1.

4. *International Helsinki Federation for Human Rights Annual Report 1996;* see also U.S. Department of State, *Bosnia & Herzegovina Country Report on Human Rights Practices for 1996,* January 30, 1997; also Dan Smith, et al., *The State of War and Peace Atlas* (Penguin, 1997).

5. Janusz Bugajski, "Balkan Tragedy," *Orbis* 40 (1996): 638; see also Laura Silber and Alan Little, *Yugoslavia: Death of a Nation* (TV Books: Distributed by Penguin USA, 1996).

6. Ibid.

7. Warren Zimmermann, *Origins of a Catastrophe: Yugoslavia and Its Destroyers—America's Last Ambassador Tells What Happened and Why* (Times Books, 1996), 157.

8. Brigitte Hipfl, Klaus Hipfl, and Jan Jagodzinski, "Documentary Films and the Bosnia-Herzegovina Conflict: From Production to Reception," *Bosnia by Television,* ed. James Gow, Richard Paterson, and Alison Preston (British Films Institute, 1996), 34, 35, 45.

9. James Gow, *Triumph of Lack of Will: International Diplomacy and the Yugoslav War* (Hurst, 1997), 304.

10. The Bosnian minister to the U.N. later stated that members of the incoming Clinton administration had suggested that it would be more helpful to Bosnia once in office than had been the Bush administration.

11. Cf. Tyler Marshall, "Nato Issues Ultimatum to Serbs Ringing Enclave: Bosnia; Alliance Threatens Air Strikes Unless Rebels Withdraw 2 Miles from Gorazde's Center by 3 P.M. Today," *Los Angeles Times,* April 23, 1994, A1.

12. Gwen Ifill, "Clinton Defends Foreign Policy Record," *New York Times,* May 4, 1994, A12.

13. Patrick Glynn, "See No Evil: Clinton-Bush and the Truth about Bosnia," *The New Republic,* October 25, 1993, 23.

14. Ibid.

15. There was preparation on the Western side for a response to such eventualities, so especially the 2/94–9/95 ones were played up.

16. "The Sacking of Croatia," *New York Times,* September 22, 1991, E16.

17. "Erasing Bosnia's Memory," *Washington Post,* October 16, 1992, A24.

18. But see the Final Report of the Commission of Experts, published in May 1994.

19. "Crisis in Yugoslavia" (House of Representatives, June 25, 1991), *Congressional Record,* 1991, H5043.

20. "Spare Bosnia the Postmortems," *Washington Post,* October 13, 1993, C6.

21. Henry Kissinger, "Bosnia Has Never Been a Nation and Has No Specific Cultural Identity. Why Are We Intent on Preserving This Balkan No-Man's Land?" *Los Angeles Times,* May 16, 1993, M2.

22. Noel Malcolm argues that the U.S./E.C. position emboldened Milosevic to attempt to crush the Slovenia and Croatian secession movements with military force. Noel Malcolm, *Bosnia: A Short History* (New York University Press, 1994).

23. European expectations seem to have been significantly different from American ones—much more pessimistic and more willing to assume that violence is the natural state of the Balkans.

24. One report described the tarmac lot at Omarska as "a killing yard, the bodies loaded onto trucks by bulldozers. Omarska was a place where cruelty and mass murder had become a form of recreation. The guards were often drunk and singing while they tortured. A prisoner named Fikret Harambasic was castrated by one of his fellow inmates before being beaten to death. One inmate was made to bark like a dog and lap at a puddle of motor oil while a guard . . . jumped up and down on his back until he was dead. The guards would make videos of this butchery for their home entertainment." Dusan Tadic, the Bosnian Serb primarily responsible for this, was convicted of crimes against humanity by the war crimes tribunal in The Hague and sentenced to twenty years in concurrent sentences for the killing and torture of Muslim prisoners. Gillian Sharpe and Bob Edwards, "Bosnian Serb Sentenced. Gillian Sharpe reports from The Hague on the International War Crimes Tribunal's first sentencing of a Bosnian Serb war criminal. Dusan Tadic was sentenced to twenty years in concurrent sentences for the killing and torture of Muslims in prison camps," *NPR Morning Edition,* July 14, 1997.

25. Members of the American Jewish community repeatedly spoke out to call attention to the systematic violence against the Muslims in Bosnia. Notable among them for his tenacity and eloquence was Elie Wiesel.

26. Ed Vulliamy, "Middle Managers of Genocide," *The Nation,* June 10, 1996, 11.

27. See Final Report of the Commission of Experts.

28. "A Mission of Mercy for Tavnik," *New York Times,* December 6, 1992, E18.

29. Final periodic report on the situation of human rights in the territory of the former Yugoslavia submitted by Mr. Tadeusz Mazowiecki, special rapporteur of the Commission on Human Rights, pursuant to paragraph 42 of the Commission Resolution 1995/89.

30. "A Defeat for Civilization," *Wall Street Journal,* July 17, 1995, A10.

31. Dimitri Simes, "There's No Oil in Bosnia," *New York Times,* March 10, 1993, A1.
32. See U.N. Report S/26765.
33. Tigalrth-Pileser III (745 B.C.–727 B.C.) was the first Assyrian ruler to make forced resettlement a policy; under his reign half the population of a conquered land would be carried off, to be replaced by settlers from other areas.
34. Andrew Bell-Fialkoff, "A Brief History of Ethnic Cleansing," *Foreign Affairs* 72 (1993): 110.
35. Cf. William Safire, "On Language," *Houston Chronicle,* March 14, 1993 (syndicated column).
36. Christopher Hitchens reports that Jose-Maria Mendiluce, the UNHCR envoy, believes he first coined the term. Christopher Hitchens, "Appointment in Sarajevo," *The Nation,* 1992, 236.
37. Norman Cigar, *Genocide in Bosnia: The Policy of Ethnic Cleansing* (Texas A&M University Press, 1995), 18–19.
38. Cited in Rabia Ali and Lawrence Lifschultz, "Why Bosnia?," *Monthly Review* 45 (March 1994): 1; also in V. P. Gagnon, "Ethnic Nationalism and International Conflict: The Case of Serbia," *International Security* 19 (1994): 130; and in Wohlstetter, see n. 41 below.
39. See Ali and Lifschultz.
40. Classified State Department report, cited in Ali and Lifschultz; "A Last Chance," *New Yorker,* July 27, 1993, 4 (saying U.S. had one "last chance" not to become implicated in an E.C.–U.N. scheme of apartheid).
41. Albert Wohlstetter, "Creating a Greater Serbia," *The New Republic,* August 1, 1994, 22.
42. A similar account describes the first stage of operations, before systematic shelling:

> A 62-year-old Bosnian Muslim witnessed the willful killing by ethnic Serb paramilitary forces of at least 53 men, women, and children in the village of Prhovo, Bosnia. At about 3 pm on May 30, 1992, a large force of ethnic Serb paramilitary soldiers and three armored personnel carriers entered Prhovo, a village located about 7 kilometers northeast of Kjuc. The village, which contained 45 houses grouped along a main road and several small streets, had more than 150 inhabitants. The soldiers, who wore stocking masks over their faces, went from house to house searching for weapons. After finding some weapons, the soldiers proceeded to ransack the homes, break windows and doors, and pull the residents out into the streets. These men, women, and children were ordered to fold their hands behind their heads and were herded through the village to a point on the road where they were stopped and lined up. Meanwhile, the soldiers attempted to coax back into the village those residents who had run into the woods when the soldiers arrived. The soldiers announced through megaphones that the residents would not be harmed if they returned. When these people returned, the soldiers beat them severely; about 10 were beaten into unconsciousness. The assembled villagers were then told that they were free, that they need not worry anymore, and that they must place white flags on their homes to indicate the village had surrendered. During the nights of May 30–31, some people fled to the woods, while others slept in their cellars. At about 6 pm on June 1, the soldiers returned and again used megaphones to call people in from the forest. They also went from house to house, pulling people out into the streets. The male residents were beaten severely. At about 7 pm, the soldiers began murdering the residents with automatic weapons. They fired single shots, then long bursts of automatic gunfire. After the shooting stopped and the soldiers had departed, the witness, who had fled to the woods when the shooting

started, returned to the village. The murdered men, women, and children lay in the streets. Houses were burning, and their roofs were collapsing. Some women and children who had hidden in basements began coming into the street crying and looking for their loved ones.

43. David Owen, *Balkan Odyssey* (Harcourt, Brace, 1995), 355. Roger Cohen savagely commented on this passage: "In other words: to deny a people the right to defend themselves is morally defensible if it enables you to have the satisfaction of feeding them free macaroni." Roger Cohen, "Balkan Odyssey (Book Reviews)," *The New Republic*, March 11, 1996, 37.

44. Ali and Lifschultz, 28.

45. "Perisic Calls Journalist's War Crimes Questions 'Illogical,'" *World News Connection*, May 9, 2000. But see also the case of Cedomir Mihailovic, a relatively high-ranking intelligence officer, who defected to the Netherlands and presented documents and evidence to the War Crimes Tribunal that he claimed would show that the original orders for ethnic cleansing and the setting up of the camps came directly from the Milosevic regime in Belgrade. They were purported to have been written over a number of months in a variety of different offices, but forensic analysis showed that they were all produced on a single typewriter in a much shorter period of time. Mihailovic was merely trying to ingratiate himself with Western governments. Christopher Hitchens, "Minority Report," *The Nation*, June 19, 1995, 875. Dan Fesperman, "Genocide Evidence Proves Elusive: Atrocities: UN Investigators Have Failed So Far to Build a Case against Slobodan Milosevic for War Crimes in Bosnia," *Baltimore Sun*, June 10, 1999, A2.

46. "Hearing of the House National Security Committee Regarding the Proposal to Send U.S. Ground Troops to Bosnia," *Federal News Service*, November 2, 1995; see also Charles Boyd, "Making Peace with the Guilty: The Truth about Bosnia," *Foreign Affairs* 74 (September 1995): 22.

47. Gow, 301.

48. Cf. Marlise Simons, "3 Serbs Convicted in Wartime Rapes," *New York Times*, February 23, 2001, A1.

49. "I think the world should recognize that the Serbian people do have legitimate interests, especially the right to self-determination for the three million Serbs living outside the borders of Serbia and Montenegro." Heather Green, "Q&A: Diplomacy and Force in Facing the Balkan Conflict," *International Herald Tribune*, March 22, 1993, 2.

50. Owen, 342–343.

51. "Declaration on the 'Guidelines on the Recognition of New States in Eastern Europe and the Soviet Union,'" December 16, 1991, reprinted in *International Legal Materials* 31 (1992): 1487.

52. Gow, 8.

53. Stephen Hedges, Peter Cary, Bruce Auster, and Tim Zimmerman, "The Road to Ruin: Bosnia Policy and the Many Causes of Failure," *U.S. News and World Report*, December 12, 1994, 59.

54. Ibid.

55. Quoted in Leslie H. Gelb, "Euro-Bosnian Games," *New York Times*, January 31, 1993, E7.

56. See also Secretary Christopher's frequent statements that "these people have hated each other for hundreds of years." Also see General Charles Boyd's testimony, cited at n. 45, that the Serbs may at present appear more culpable than Muslims or Croats, but this is only because we are witnessing a small slice of the bigger picture involving a

"centuries old conflict." Hearing of the House National Security Committee Regarding the Proposal to Send U.S. Ground Troops to Bosnia, November 2, 1995.

57. Charles Lane, "The Death of Yugoslavia," *Washington Monthly*, April 1996, 48.

58. "Reader Feedback, What Do You Think about U.S. Intervention in Bosnia?" *Boston Globe*, May 7, 1993, 10.

59. Ibid.

60. Jeff Jacoby, "A Recipe for a Debacle," *Boston Globe*, November 30, 1995, 23.

61. Transcript, report by Tom Gjelten, "Morning Edition," *National Public Radio*, July 17, 1995. In this the president was only following his predecessor President Bush who said, on August 10, 1992, "Now the war in Bosnia . . . is a complex, convoluted conflict that grows out [of] age-old animosities. . . . Those who understand the nature of this conflict understand that an enduring solution cannot be imposed by force from outside on unwilling participants."

62. "US efforts to promote a peaceful settlement in Yugoslavia. (Statement by Principal Deputy Assistant Secretary of State Ralph Johnson) (Transcript)." *U.S. Department of State Dispatch*, vol. 2, October 21, 1991, 782.

63. Quoted by Saul Friedman, "U.S. Joins Aid Effort," *Newsday*, July 2, 1992.

64. "Clinton Mulls New Bosnia Steps," *USA Today*, May 13, 1993, A1 ("calling the crisis a 'European issue' . . .")

65. This eventually became the demand that the Vance-Owen Plan be accepted.

66. Heinz A. J. Kern, "The Clinton Doctrine: A New Foreign Policy: The White House Bosnia Retreat Shows a New Approach to the U.S. World Role—Balancing U.S. Power and Commitment. The New Doctrine Is a Mixed Blessing," *Christian Science Monitor*, June 18, 1993.

67. This remark made on CNN, *Larry King Live*, July 31, 1993.

68. At Srebrenica one desperate request by the local U.N. commander for air strikes was rebuffed on the grounds that the wrong form had been submitted.

69. "Any possible air strikes may do nothing to deter Serbian aggression. 'Will it be enough to . . . stop the shelling of Sarajevo, to bring parties to the peace table?'" Boutros-Ghali said. Johanna Neuman, "Cautious Clinton Tiptoes Nearer to Bosnia Commitment," *USA Today*, July 29, 1993, A7.

70. "A 'Terrible War' Rages On," *U.N. Chronicle* 31 (March 1994): 62.

71. Frank Murray, "Clinton Turned Down U.S. Plan for Air Strikes," *Times of London*, June 14, 1993, Overseas News.

72. Craig Whitney, "Conflict in the Balkans; the Strategy; NATO Diplomats Question Details of Plan for Air Raids," *New York Times*, July 23, 1995, A1.

73. "NATO military officers pointed out that Britain had often agreed to threaten NATO air strikes against the Serbs in principle but had balked at launching them for fear of provoking retaliation against British soldiers in the United Nations peacekeeping force in Bosnia." Ibid. See also, "The Crossing of the Mogadishu Line," *Economist*, January 13, 1996, 51.

74. Owen, 355.

75. James B. Steinberg, "International Involvement in the Yugoslavia Conflict," in *Enforcing Restraint: Collective Intervention in Internal Conflicts*, ed. Lori Fisler Damrosch (Council on Foreign Relations, 1993), 64.

76. Steinberg, 44; Leslie H. Gelb, "False Humanitarianism," *New York Times*, August 6, 1992, A23.

77. John F. Burns, "Serbs Hedging on Vows to Ease Siege in Bosnia," *New York Times*, August 7, 1993, A1.

78. "Kozyrev, U.N. Chief Oppose Armed Intervention in Ex-Yugoslavia," *Agence France-Presse*, December 26, 1992.

79. The Dayton Agreement also gives rights to Bosnian Croats and Serbs for political affiliation with Croatia and Serbia respectively.
80. "To understand the failure of international efforts and the conditions for success, it is necessary to analyse in detail what the initiatives taken actually were." (Gow, 6.)

CHAPTER SIXTEEN: THE DEATH OF THE
SOCIETY OF NATION-STATES

1. Charles Tilly, "Futures of European States," *Social Research* 59 (1992): 715.
2. G.A. Res. 2131, 20 U.N. GAOR Supp. (No. 14) 11, U.N. Doc. A/6014 (1965).
3. As one U.N. official put it, "The lesson of all this is that the U.N. does not learn lessons."
4. And also the Chinese suppression of Tibet.
5. Nevertheless, the need to keep allies on board restrained the United States at a number of points in the conflict. William Stueck, *The Korean War: An International History* (Princeton University Press, 1995), 130–142.
6. See also W. Michael Reisman, "Coercion and Self-Determination: Construing Charter Article 2(4)," *American Journal of International Law* 78 (July 1984): 642.
7. An alternative proposal was put forward by Brian Urquhart, "For a UN Volunteer Military Force," *New York Review of Books,* June 10, 1993, 3.
8. NATO having successfully made the transition from nation-state to market-state instrument.

CHAPTER SEVENTEEN: PEACE AND
THE INTERNATIONAL ORDER

1. Guicciardini wrote in his *Ricordi,* "Before the year 1494, wars were protracted, battles bloodless, the methods followed in besieging towns slow and uncertain; and although artillery was already in use, it was managed with such want of skill that it caused little hurt. Hence it came about that the ruler of a state could hardly be dispossessed. But the French, on their invasion of Italy, infused so much liveliness into our wars, that [until compensating fortifications could be introduced] whenever open country was lost, the state was lost with it." Cf. Francesco Guicciardini, *Ricordi* (Mursia, 1994).
2. A sympathetic thesis was propounded by Robert Randle in 1987 that I gratefully stumbled upon only as this book was going to press. Randle writes that "major peace settlements, such as Westphalia and Vienna, have the characteristics of constitutions; the same can be said of many lesser settlements, even those ending bi-lateral wars. Peace settlements not only bring wars to an end; they can also revise the constitution of the state system." Robert Randle, *Issues in the History of International Relations: The Role of Issues in the Evolution of the State System* (Praeger, 1987), 34. See also Christian Reus-Smit, "The Constitutional Structure of International Society and the Nature of Fundamental Institutions," *International Organization* 51 (Autumn 1997): 555. In this chapter, I shall argue that the peace settlements that conclude epochal wars are the constitutions of the society of states.
3. Randle, *Issues in the History of International Relations,* 183.
4. Randle believes that the "key patterning of interstate relations results from states' interests in issues," whereas I argue that the key pattern results from states' security needs in interaction with their domestic constitutional development—which may or may not be coextensive with the issues of the day. And Randle argues that the peace agreements are revisions of the constitutions of state systems, whereas I suggest that it is the society of states (by no means limited to its formal, juridical components) that is being reformed.

5. Cf. the opening paragraph of Hedley Bull, "The Emergence of a Universal International Society" in *The Expansion of International Society*, 117.
6. Cf. Paul Rice Doolin, *The Fronde* (Cambridge, Mass.: Harvard University Press, 1935).
7. Randle, *The Origins of Peace* (New York: Free Press, 1973) 46–47; A transformation occurs when one ordering principle replaces another. A constitution embodies ordering principles so a transformation of the society of states occurs when a new constitution of that society replaces the old.

CHAPTER EIGHTEEN: THE TREATY OF AUGSBURG

1. *New Cambridge Modern History,* vol. 1, 5.
2. Richard. Bonney, *The European Dynastic States, 1494–1660* (Oxford University Press, 1991), 81.
3. Ibid.
4. *New Cambridge Modern History,* vol. 2, 7.
5. Wilbur K. Jordan, *The Development of Religious Toleration in England,* vol. 1 (P. Smith, 1965), 37.
6. See Ben S. Trotter, "War and Government in the French Provinces: Picardy, 1470–1560," a review of David Potter's book of this title in *The Historian* 57 (Autumn 1994): 183. Potter "contends that the Hundred Years War and the Wars of Religion, seemingly motivated by issues more lofty than dynastic concerns, have eclipsed the role which the Habsburg-Valois Wars played in the development of absolute monarchy, particularly its military, administrative, and financial institutions."
7. Ronald A. Brand, "External Sovereignty and International Law," *Fordham International Law Journal* 18 (May 1995): 1688.
8. Bull and Watson, 15.
9. See Part II of Book I of the present work.
10. "The Sea of Faith / Was once, too, at the full, and round earth's shore / Lay like the folds of a bright girdle furl'd." Matthew Arnold, "Dover Beach," in *The Norton Anthology of English Literature* (Norton, 1974), 1355.
11. Adam Watson, "European International Society and Its Expansion," in *The Expansion of International Society* (ed. H. Bull and A. Watson) (Oxford, 1984), 15.
12. See S. Schumann, "Joachim Mynsinger von Frundeck: Humanist-Rechtgelehrter-Politiker (1514–1588)," Archiv fur Kulturgeschichte 1980–1981, 62–63, 159–193, arguing that "the stable period between the Peace of Augsburg and the outbreak of the Thirty Years War allowed the development of consolidated territorial states run for princes by bureaucrats drawn largely from a mostly bourgeois educated elite."
13. Judith Brown, "Courtiers and Christians: the First Japanese Emissaries to Europe," *Renaissance Quarterly* 47 (Winter 1994): 872.
14. Ibid.
15. Benedict Kingsbury and Adam Roberts, "Introduction to Hugo Grotius and International Relations," *Hugo Grotius and International Relations,* ed. Hedley Bull, Benedict Kingsbury, and Adam Roberts (Oxford University Press, 1992), 8.
16. *Political Writings, Francisco de Vitoria,* ed. Anthony Pagden and Jeremy Lawrence (Cambridge University Press, 1991): "The origin of public international law dates to Father Francisco de Vitoria and his studies of sovereign rights to claim and colonize the New World." See also "The International Community According to Francisco de Vitoria," *The Thomist* 10 (January 1947): 1–55.
17. See J. Verhoeven's essay in *Actualité de la Pensée Juridique de Francisco de Vitoria,* ed. A. Truyol y Serra, H. Mechoulan, P. Haggenmacher. A. Ortiz-Arce, P. M. Marine,

and J. Verhoeven (Bruylant, 1988), reviewed by R. Beenstra, *American Journal of International Law* 86 (1992): 181.

18. Alice J. Knight, *Las Casas: "The Apostle of the Indies"* (Neale, 1917); Francis A. McNutt, *Bartholomew de las Casas: His Life, His Apostolate, and His Writings* (Putnam, 1909); both cited by Nussbaum, n. 12, 310.

19. Vitoria, *De Indis Recenter Inventis,* II, i–vii.

20. In the heresy proceeding against Erasmus, Vitoria, as the representative of the Inquisition, judged the great humanist guilty though many of Vitoria's colleagues attempted to dissuade him. Nussbaum, 63.

21. Vitoria, *Relectio de Jure Belli,* XIII. "Having suffered a wrong is the one and only just basis for war."

22. Compare James L. Brierly, "Suarez's Vision of a World Community" and "The Realization Today of Suarez's World Community," in *The Basis of Obligation in International Law and Other Papers,* ed. Hersch Lauterpacht and C.H.M. Waldock (Oxford: Clarendon Press, 1958).

23. Francisco Suarez, *De Legibus ac Deo Legislatore,* II.xix.9.

24. See e.g., Cornelius F. Murphy, Jr., "The Grotian Vision of World Order," *American Journal of International Law* 76 (July 1982): 496–497.

25. Francisco Suarez, *Selections from Three Works,* vol. 2, ed. Carnegie, trans. Gwladys Williams, Ammi Brown, and John Waldron (Clarendon Press, 1944), 817.

26. See plates on p. 346.

27. P. Haggenmacher, "Grotius and Gentili," in Kingsbury and Roberts, 140. This is Haggenmacher's translation of a letter from Gentili to his friend John Bennett; see Holland, "Alberico Gentili," appendix no. 4, 29–30; see also Gesina H. J. van der Molen, *Alberico Gentili* (A. W. Sijthoff, 1968), 53.

28. "[A]nd thus paradoxically the Protestant refugee had come to side with the main Catholic power against the country which was steadily becoming a bastion of Calvinism." Haggenmacher, 141; see also Nussbaum, saying that Gentili's acceptance of this role was "a somewhat puzzling step for a Protestant refugee to take." Nussbaum, 76.

29. Alberico Gentili, *De Jure Belli Libri Tres,* vol. 2, ed. Carnegie, trans. John C. Rolfe (Clarendon Press, 1933), 1612, paragraph 609.

30. Compare TAN 141. This conclusion is at variance with that drawn by Francis I also on the juridical basis that the State is distinguishable from the prince. Either *conclusion* is reasonable; what is interesting is the shared *premise.*

31. See Theodor Meron, "The Authority to Make Treaties in the Late Middle Ages," *American Journal of International Law* 89 (January 1995): 14.

32. "There remains now the one question concerning an honorable cause for waging war . . . which is undertaken for no private reason of our own, but for the common interest and in behalf of others. Look you, if men clearly sin against the laws of nature and mankind, I believe that any one whatsoever may check such men by force of arms." Quoted by Meron, 114.

33. Nussbaum, 84.

34. Nussbaum, 79.

CHAPTER NINETEEN: THE PEACE OF WESTPHALIA

1. See memorandum to Louis XIII of January 1629, quoted in *New Cambridge Modern History,* vol. 4, 328.

2. Henry J. Chaytor, *European History: Great Leaders and Landmarks from Early to Modern Times,* vol. 3 (Gresham Publishing, 1915), 113.

3. As Randle observed in his monumental study of European wars and peace agreements, "The European order collapsed in the Franco-Dutch war in 1678. It did so again in 1683 with a general European war that lasted 17 years, in 1701 in the War of Spanish Succession, in 1740 in the War of Austrian Succession, and again in the Seven Years War (1756–1763) . . . In the settlements that ended all these major wars, Westphalia was approved and incorporated by reference." Randle, 70.

4. *New Cambridge Modern History,* vol. 4, 352.

5. Which was reflected in the name chosen in Philadelphia for the new American constitutional entity, the "United *States,*" just as the new name that emerged from the Bolshevik Revolution—the Union of Soviet Socialist Republics—reflected a new constitutional order.

6. Sweden had refused a Danish offer to mediate. Swedish suspicion was not without foundation: see the instructions of the Danish government to its delegates in Andreas Osiander, *The States System of Europe 1640–1990: Peacemaking and the Conditions of International Stability* (Oxford University Press, 1994), 18.

7. Ibid., 21.

8. Ibid., 19. In 1649 Christina commissioned a dramatic play entitled *La naissance de la paix,* with a book by Descartes, who had come to Stockholm and wished to honor his patroness.

9. Ibid., 26.

10. Report to Oxenstierna, quoted by Osiander, 29.

11. The French delegates reported to Mazarin that the "disposition of the princes of Germany . . . is very different from that of the princes of Italy, the latter, being very intelligent and well-advised, approving of, and wishing for, everything that may contribute to make them independent while [the German princes] are much more affected by the love of their fatherland [*beaucoup plus touchés de l'amour de leur patrie*] and cannot approve of foreigners dismembering the Empire, no matter what hope of a gain we hold out to them." D'Avaux and Servien to Mazarin, January 14, 1645, quoted by Osiander, 38.

12. Bearing in mind, as the reader must, that the emperor wore two constitutional hats, as it were: his kingship, which was derived by heredity over certain Habsburg lands, and his emperorship, which was his by the vote of the Imperial electors.

13. Randle, *The Origins of Peace,* 332.

14. Ibid., 54.

15. Osiander uncharacteristically overstates this revision, however, by saying that "the sixteenth century maxim of *cuius regio, eius religio* . . . was abandoned" and sharply reproves Holsti, McKay, and others for "serious factual errors" in maintaining otherwise. It is true that it is a common error to treat Westphalia as the agreement that introduced the "*cuius*" provision, but this principle was embraced, not abandoned, in the Westphalian settlement.

16. Karsten Ruppert, *Die Kaiserliche Politik auf dem Westfälischen Friedenskongreß (1643–1648)* (Aschendorff: 1979), 229, cited by Osiander, 48.

17. As Leo Gross wrote in the most authoritative legal commentary on the treaty, Westphalia was "a public act of disregard for . . . the papacy" that "liquidat[ed], with a degree of apparent finality the idea of the Middle Ages as an objective order of things personified by the Emperor in the Secular realm." Gross, 37.

18. Osiander, 51.

19. Ibid., 68.

20. Randle, *Issues in the History of International Relations,* 53.

21. Cicely V. Wedgwood, *The Thirty Years War* (Cape, 1938), 526.

22. *Proceedings of the American Society of International Law* 87 (March/April 1993): 325, and citations, n. 10.
23. C. G. Roelofsen, "17th Century International Politics," in Bull, Kingsbury, and Roberts, 124.
24. Ibid.
25. Quoting John Morley, who ranked it with Adam Smith's *The Wealth of Nations,* Bull, 71.
26. R. A. Falk, "On the Recent Further Decline of International Law," in *Legal Change: Essays in Honor of Julius Stone,* ed. A. R. Blackshield (Butterworths, 1983), 272; compare Bruce Ackerman's "Constitutional Moment," in Bruce A. Ackerman, *We the People: Foundations,* vol. 1, and *Transformations,* vol. 2 (Belknap Press of Harvard University Press, 1991, 1998).
27. The Latinized version of the Dutch name de Groot.
28. A notable figure described in Book I.
29. Georg Schwarzenberger, "The Grotius Factor in International Law and Relations: A Functional Approach," in Bull, Kingsbury, and Roberts.
30. Martin Wight, *Systems of States,* ed. Hedley Bull (Leicester University Press for the London School of Economics and Political Science, 1977), 127.
31. Bull, 70.
32. Bull, 75, 77.
33. William Stanley Macbean Knight, *The Life and Works of Hugo Grotius* (Oceana, 1962), 289.
34. See Bull, 79–91.
35. Cf. Quentin Skinner, *The Foundations of Modern Political Thought: The Age of Reformation,* vol. 2 (Cambridge University Press, 1978), 152–154; and see Richard Tuck, *Natural Rights Theories: Their Origin and Development* (Cambridge University Press, 1969), 67.
36. G. Mattingly, "International Diplomacy and International Law," in *New Cambridge Modern History,* vol. 3, ed. R. B. Wernham, 169–170.
37. Jean-Jacques Rousseau, *The Social Contract,* Book I, trans. Maurice Cranston (Penguin, 1968), 51.
38. Mattingly, 169.
39. Schwarzenberger, "The Grotius Factor," 306.
40. Bull, "The Importance of Grotius," 74.
41. Hugo Grotius, *De Jure Belli ac Pacis* (apud Ioannem Blaev, 1667), II.xx.40.
42. Osiander, 41.
43. Hugo Grotius, *De Jure Belli ac Pacis,* ed. and trans. W. Whewell (J. W. Parker, 1853), I.ix.
44. All of these arguments—the one at the footnote call is nowadays termed "rule utilitarian"—will be found in contemporary debates in political philosophy.
45. Murphy, 15.
46. Gottfried Wilhelm Leibniz, "Opinion on the Principles of Pufendorf," *The Political Writings of Leibniz,* ed. and trans. Patrick Riley (Cambridge University Press, 1972), 64.

CHAPTER TWENTY: THE TREATY OF UTRECHT

1. On April 11, 1713, treaties were signed between France and Britain, Portugal, Prussia, and Savoy; on November 4, between France and the United Provinces; on July 13, between Spain and Britain and Savoy and with the Dutch on June 26. The emperor

Charles concluded terms on March 6, 1714, at Rastatt, which was confirmed in a separate treaty at Baden on Nov 7, 1714; Portugal finally agreed to peace with Spain at Utrecht on February 6, 1715.

2. Bolingbroke, Henry St. John Viscount, and Gilbert Parke, *Letters and Correspondence, Public and Private, of Viscount Bolingbroke* (G.G. & J. Robinson, 1798), ii, 443, 614.

3. Bolingbroke, Henry St. John Viscount, *The Works of Lord Bolingbroke* (Frank Cass, 1967) (reprint of the 1844 edition), ii, 276 ff., 313, 302.

4. See Osiander, 111–113.

5. Bolingbroke, Henry St. John Viscount, and Gilbert Parke, *Letters and Correspondence, Public and Private, of Viscount Bolingbroke* (G.G. & J Robinson, 1798), i, 595, letter dated July 21, 1712.

6. Osiander, 119.

7. Bolingbroke, Henry St. John Viscount, *The Works of Lord Bolingbroke* (Frank Cass, 1967) (reprint of the 1844 edition), ii, 287.

8. At Utrecht, Osiander perceptively writes that "the word 'state' was used ordinarily to designate an administrative unit with the potential to be an autonomous international actor, even though it might not, and in fact often did not, possess that quality at the moment. For instance, the French instruction for the congress refers to the Spanish dominion as 'a monarchy so vast and consisting of so many states'" (Osiander, 103).

9. Bolingbroke, Henry St. John Viscount, *The Works of Lord Bolingbroke* (Frank Cass, 1967) (reprint of the 1844 edition), ii, 288.

10. Osiander, 123.

11. Quoted in Osiander, 132; see also the renunciations of the Duke of Orleans, and that of Philip V.

12. Quoted in Osiander, 127.

13. Quoted in Osiander, 128.

14. Quoted in Osiander, 131.

15. In the Austrian Netherlands, the Dutch acquired the right to garrison Namur, Tournai, Menin, Ypres, and other places. In Italy, the duke of Savoy gained Exilles, Fenestrelle, and other forts; Allesadrai, part of Montferrat, Valenza, Vigevano, and other critical places that would bar a French invasion of Italy. Various districts on the Rhine were obtained by German states, and France removed to the west bank. Brandenburg got part of Gelders, Bavaria recovered the Palatinate, and the elector at Cologne was restored: all these arrangements were thought to deter any renewed French aggression, yet not to provide a base for independent forays.

16. Randle, 261.

17. F. W. Walbank, *A Historical Commentary on Polybius* (Clarendon Press) (vol. I, 1957) (vol. II, 1967) (vol. III, 1974).

18. Murphy, 34.

19. Nussbaum, 156.

20. Robert von Mohl referred to it as "a kind of oracle with diplomats and especially with consuls," see Nussbaum, ibid.

21. Ibid., 161.

22. See e.g., *Armitz Brown* v. *United States,* 8 Cranch (12 U.S.), 110.

23. Vattel, *Le droit des gens* (Editions A. Pedone, 1998), II.i.16.

24. Reminiscent in our day of George Gilder and his descriptions of a market-state backlit by universal prosperity.

25. "Now although nature has so constituted men that they absolutely require the assistance of their fellow men if they are to live as it befits men to live, and has thus established a general society among them, yet nature cannot be said to have imposed upon

men the precise obligation of uniting together in civil society; and if all men followed [the laws of nature] subjection to civil society would be needless." Vattel, *Le droit des gens,* preface.

26. Murphy, 51; see Vattel, II.i.16.
27. Osiander, 48.

CHAPTER TWENTY-ONE: THE CONGRESS OF VIENNA

1. Carl von Clausewitz, *On War,* trans. Howard and Paret.
2. Gneisenau observed: "The Revolution has set in motion the national energy of the entire French people. . . . If the other states wish to restore the balance of power they must open and use the same resources." Also, consider the Prussian constitutional reform of 1807, discussed in *New Cambridge Modern History,* vol. 9, 367–394.
3. Thomas B. Macaulay, *Napoleon and the Restoration of the Bourbons,* ed. Joseph Hamburger (Columbia University Press, 1977), 98.
4. Kissinger, *Diplomacy,* 84.
5. Nussbaum, 178.
6. *New Cambridge Modern History,* vol. 9, 646–647: "To Vienna as guests of Francis I of Austria came King Frederick I of Württemberg, Elector William of Hesse, the Hereditary Grand Duke George of Hesse-Darmstadt, King Maximilian I, Joseph of Bavaria, King Frederick VI of Denmark and Karl August, Duke of Weimar and friend of Goethe. The King of Prussia, present himself, was accompanied by his white-haired chancellor, Prince Hardenberg, assisted by the scholarly Humboldt, and a group of experts, among them the prominent statistician, Hoffmann. Alexander I of Russia . . . was supported by the most international group of advisers at the Congress—the Russian Razumovski; Nesselrode, his foreign minister of German extraction; Stein, distinguished reformer and exile of the Prussian service; Tsartoryski of Poland; and Pozzo di Borgo, Corsican enemy of Bonaparte. . . . Talleyrand headed the French delegation. . . . Castlereagh took with him his three principal European ambassadors . . . [and] hired his own embassy staff as insurance against the Austrian spy system, at that time the most efficient in Europe. Metternich . . . was assisted by . . . a regular group of assistants and specialists, and particularly by Friedrich von Gentz, a most interesting intellectual and publicist. . . . Prominent among the lesser statesmen were Wrede, chief diplomatist for Bavaria; Cardinal Consalvi, secretary of state for the Pope; and Münster, able and experienced representative of Hanover. . . . The Congress . . . attracted to Vienna a medley of princes, aristocrats, tourists, beggars, spies and pickpockets."
7. This is discussed in Chapters 7 and 8.
8. *New Cambridge Modern History,* vol. 9, 22, citing K. Waliszewski, *Le regne d'Alexandre I,* vol. 2 (1924), 378.
9. It is interesting that Britain only signed a peace with Napoleon when the British state took a retrogressive constitutional move away from state-nationhood. It was the resignation of the Pitt cabinet over the king's refusal to assent to a law removing the disabilities of Catholics that cleared the way for a treaty with the French.
10. Treaty of Union, Concert and Subsidy between Austria, Great Britain, Prussia and Russia, March 1, 1814, art. XVI, 673 Consol. T.S. 84, 91; W. Alison Phillips, *The Confederation of Europe: A Study of the European Alliance, 1813–1823* (H. Fertig, 1966), 74–75 (discussing the importance of article XVI for Europe and also noting that the treaty was actually signed on March 10 but antedated).
11. Quoted in Osiander, 243.
12. Kissinger, *Diplomacy,* 82.

13. Quoted in Osiander, 243.
14. Quoted in Osiander, 194.
15. Osiander, 190.
16. Quoted in Osiander, 191.
17. Ibid.
18. Osiander thinks Webster owes his view to an anachronism also, but not the same one I have in mind. For Osiander, Webster is confounding twentieth century nationalism with early nineteenth century national ideas; this may be true, but it does not go to the public opinion/expediency point; whatever sort of state nationalists wanted, Webster's point is that their feelings were simply ignored rather than that they were not accommodated.
19. In contrast, for example, to the territorial state, for which such allocations were everything.
20. Osiander, 196–197.
21. Calabresi and Bobbitt, *Tragic Choices.*
22. Ibid., 41–42.
23. Talleyrand, *Memoirs,* vol. 2 (Putnam, 1891), 120.
24. Talleyrand thus spoke to the tsar: "Neither you, sire, nor the allied powers, nor I, whom you believe to possess some influence, not one of us, could give a king to France. France is conquered—and by your arms, and yet even today, you have not that power . . . In order to establish a durable state of things, and one which could be accepted without protest, one must act upon a principle. With a principle we are strong. We shall experience no resistance; opposition will, at any rate, vanish soon, and there is only one principle. Louis XVIII is a principle; he is the legitimate king of France." Talleyrand, vol. 2, 124, quoted in Osiander, 214; see also the discussion of legitimacy by Macaulay, 70–72.
25. For example, the Habsburg realms, though vast, were materially augmented by the addition of the Spanish Netherlands as compensation for the loss of the Spanish throne.
26. This was the Russian delegation; see Osiander, 229.
27. Osiander, 226.
28. Osiander, 227.
29. Osiander, 224.
30. Quoted in Osiander, 226.
31. November 4, 1814; Wellesley ix, 415.
32. October 12, 1814; Wellesley ix, 329, 331.
33. Quoted in Osiander, 187.
34. Final Report to Louis XVIII, *Talleyrand,* ii, 238, 244f. As Osiander concludes, "[I]t was the turn of the republicanism to return through the back door. Mandated parliamentary assemblies sprang up everywhere, more ambitious and more effective than their precursors in pre-revolutionary Europe," 220.
35. See Osiander, 220, n. 134.
36. Quoted in Osiander, 202.
37. Ibid.
38. Alan Palmer, *Metternich* (Harper & Row, 1972), 113.
39. Harold Nicolson, *The Congress of Vienna: A Study in Allied Unity: 1812–1822* (Viking Press, 1946), 143.
40. Palmer, 139.
41. Quoted in Osiander, 205.
42. Quoted in Osiander, 206.
43. J. G. Lockhart, *The Peacemakers 1814–1815* (Duckworth, 1932), 46.
44. This account was given by the Prussian diplomat Stein.

45. Lockhart, 49.
46. Article XIII of the Federal Act provided: "In allen deutschen Staaten wird eine land-standische Verfassung stattfinden." The term "Verfassung" was variously interpreted as either requiring a "parliamentary constitution" (by liberals) or a system of Estates (by conservatives).
47. Talleyrand, quoted in Holsti, 114.
48. It was largely taken from the code prepared by Francis Lieber for the Union Army in 1863 during the American Civil War.
49. Quoted in Nussbaum, 233.
50. Ibid.
51. Murphy, 117.
52. Quoted in Francis H. Hinsley, *Power and the Pursuit of Peace: Theory and Practice in the History of Relations between States* (Cambridge University Press, 1963), 224–225.
53. Robert B. Mowat, *The Concert of Europe* (Macmillan, 1930), vi–vii.
54. Murphy, 89.
55. Ibid.

CHAPTER TWENTY-TWO: THE VERSAILLES TREATY

1. Friedrich Nietzsche, "Thus Spake Zarathustra," in *The Portable Nietzsche,* ed. and trans. Walter Kaufmann (Viking Press, 1954), 160–161. Charles de Gaulle also spoke of states as *"monstres froids."*
2. William Langer, "A Critique of Imperialism," in *The New Imperialism: Analysis of Late Nineteenth Century Expansion,* ed. Harrison M. Wright (Heath, 1961), 98.
3. Osiander, 251.
4. For I dipt into the future; far as human eye could see.
    Saw the Vision of the world, and all the wonder that would be . . .
    Heard the heavens fill with shouting, and there rain'd a ghastly dew
    From the nations' airy navies grappling in central blue . . .
    Till the war-drum throbb'd no longer and the battle flags were furl'd
    In the Parliament of Man, the Federation of the World.
    Alfred Lord Tennyson, "Locksey Hall," in *Poems Published in 1842* (Clarendon Press, 1914), 207–220. According to his biographer, President Truman copied this stanza in his own hand and carried it with him for the next fifty years. Alonzo L. Hamby, *Man of the People: A Life of Harry S Truman* (Oxford, 1995), 13.
5. *The Messages and Papers of Woodrow Wilson,* vol. 1, 378–379.
6. Arthur Walworth, *America's Moment, 1918: American Diplomacy and the End of World War I* (Norton, 1977), 95.
7. See discussion in Chapter 14, "Colonel House and a World Made of Law."
8. 1. An open peace conference.
    2. Freedom of navigation of the seas.
    3. Reduction of trade barriers.
    4. Reduction of armament levels to "the lowest point consistent with domestic safety."
    5. "A free, open-minded, and absolutely impartial adjustment of all colonial claims."
    6. Withdrawal from Russian territory and respect for Russian political self-determination.
    7. "Belgium, the whole world will agree, must be evacuated and restored."
    8. "All French territory should be freed and the invaded portions restored."
    9. "A readjustment of the frontiers of Italy should be effected along clearly recognizable lines of nationality."

10. "The peoples of Austria-Hungary, whose place among the nations we wish to see safeguarded and assured, should be accorded the freest opportunity to autonomous development."

11. Balkan states evacuated and restored.

12. Ottoman Empire removed from Europe to allow for free passage in the Dardanelles and self-determination.

13. "An independent Polish state should be erected which should include the territories inhabited by indisputably Polish populations."

14. Establishment of the League of Nations.

9. A role played by the first Treaty of Paris with respect to the Vienna congress.

10. See Osiander, 299.

11. *The Messages and Papers of Woodrow Wilson,* vol. 1, 352.

12. Robert F. Randle, *The Origins of Peace: A Study of Peacemaking and the Structure of Peace Settlements* (Free Press, 1963), 429: "They . . . fix the structure of the then-current system in terms of the territory and resources of the belligerents. . . ." See also Osiander, 313.

13. U.S. State Department, 1942–1947, vi, 882.

14. I have consolidated several remarks of Clemenceau, including some made the next day. Quoted in Osiander, 283–284.

15. France on the northern coast of the Black Sea; Britain in Central Asia in the Transcaucasus; Japan, the United States, and Britain in Siberia; and Britain, the United States, and France in the Murmansk-Archangel region.

16. Robert Lansing, *The Peace Negotiations: A Personal Narrative* (Houghton Mifflin, 1921), 244.

17. Harold George Nicolson, *Diaries and Letters* (Atheneum, 1966–1968).

18. Larry E. Jones, *German Liberalism and the Dissolution of the Weimar Party System, 1918–1933* (University of North Carolina Press, 1988), 3.

19. Charles L. Mee, Jr., *The End of Order, Versailles, 1919* (Dutton, 1980), 267 (emphasis supplied).

20. See Herbert Spiro, *The Dialectic of Representation, 1619–1969* (University Press of Virginia, 1969).

21. Eberhard Kolb, *The Weimar Republic,* trans. P. S. Falla (London: Unwin Hyman, 1988).

22. This was characteristic of the German advances in historiography during this period; see for example, Schliemann.

23. Hegel makes this argument in the introduction to *The Philosophy of History*: Georg W.F. Hegel, *Introduction to the Philosophy of History* (Hackett, 1998), 40–56.

24. Hans Linde, "State, Sovereignty, and International Law: A Study of Three German Legal Theories," unpublished thesis (1947), 32. I would prefer to say "a misunderstanding derived from the days of feudal monarchy."

25. Ibid., 28.

26. J. J. Lador-Lederer, "Jews in Austrian Law," *East European Quarterly* 12 (1978): 129–142.

27. Leaders from Canute to Stalin have disputed this.

28. Linde, 50.

29. If Mé + E (or Mê + E), then $Z \to M$ (where M is a human act, the performance of which is Mé—or its avoidance Mê; E signifies an event, usually produced by behavior M; Z is the enforcing behavior of the official, and the arrow directed against M indicates that generally the behavior of the official is directed against the actor that is responsible for the behavior). Erich Voegelin, "Kelsen's Pure Theory of Law," *Political Science Quarterly* 42 (1927): 270.

30. "Without your calling it, the tide comes in / Without your hurling it, the earth can spin / Without your pushing them, the clouds roll by / If they can do without you duckie, so can I." "Without You," from the musical *My Fair Lady*, written by Alan Jay Lerner and Frederick Loewe.

31. Hans Kelsen, *General Theory of Law and State*, trans. Anders Wedberg (Russell & Russell, 1945), 115.

32. Cf. M. A. Bedau, "Weak Emergence," in *Philosophical Perspectives: Mind, Causation, and World*, vol. 11, ed. James Tomberlin (Blackwell, 1997), 375.

33. Compare: "the world is everything that is the case." Ludwig Wittgenstein, *Tractatus Logico-Philosophicus*, I.

34. Hans Kelsen, "Centralization and Decentralization," in *Authority and the Individual* (Harvard University Press, 1937), 239.

35. Stephen Holmes, *The Anatomy of Illiberalism* (Harvard University Press, 1993), 37. Interestingly, the left quarterly *Telos* devoted its entire Summer 1987 issue to Schmitt, introducing its subject by saying "in the present situation of political stalemate, the left can only benefit by learning from Carl Schmitt." P. Piccone and G. L. Ulmen, "Introduction to Carl Schmitt," in "Special Issue on Carl Schmitt," *Telos: A Quarterly of Critical Thought* 72 (1987).

36. M. Wiegandt, "The Alleged Unaccountability of the Academic: A Biographical Sketch of Carl Schmitt," *Cardozo Law Review* 16 (March 1995).

37. In *Political Romanticism*, he attacked the Romantics whose attitudes "preclude[d] any firm position or commitment" and for whom God as a point of reference was replaced by "the genial 'I.'" His next book, *Die Diktatur*, was also a product of the Munich period of Schmitt's life. This work included an interpretation of that provision of the Weimar Constitution—which permitted the president to assume dictatorial powers—that attracted attention owing to Schmitt's novel reading of Article 48 as both expansive in its allocation of power to suspend basic rights, but restricted in that the ultimate form of the State—the constitutional order referred to in Book I—could not be changed.

38. Carl Schmitt, *Political Theology: Four Chapters on the Concept of Sovereignty*, trans. George Schwab (Cambridge, Mass.: MIT Press, 1985).

39. Carl Schmitt, *The Crisis of Parliamentary Democracy*, trans. Ellen Kennedy (Cambridge, Mass.: MIT Press, 1985).

40. Carl Schmitt, *The Concept of the Political*, trans. George Schwab (Rutgers University Press, 1976).

41. A fifth idea is derived from this distinction: Schmitt's theory of *Grossraum*—a geographical region dominated by the general application of a particular friend/enemy distinction, affording rights to resist intervention in the area by other powers.

42. Quoted in David Dysenhaus, "Hermann Heller and the Legitimacy of Legality," 17, later published in *Oxford Journal of Legal Studies* vol. 16, 641 (1996), 22, n. 41.

43. Dysenhaus, 2.

44. As for modern-day critical legal theorists and for the Frankfurt School that was their progenitor and Schmitt's contemporary.

45. Philip Bobbitt, *Constitutional Fate: Theory of the Constitution* (Oxford: Oxford University Press, 1982).

46. Philip Bobbitt, *Constitutional Interpretation* (B. Blackwell, 1991).

47. Schmitt, *The Concept of the Political*, 26.

48. Ibid., 27.

49. Stephen Holmes, *The Anatomy of Illiberalism*, 40.

50. Quoted in Dysenhaus, 13.

51. Dysenhaus, 14.

52. In *Political Theology,* Schmitt had characterized the views of de Maistre and other counterrevolutionary philosophers as "decisionism" (*decisionem*).

53. Schmitt, *Political Theology,* 30.

54. This identification apparently ran in one direction only. Count Ciano reported that in early 1943 Mussolini said that that year would determine whether the Italians were a great people or a nation of waiters.

55. See Rolf Wiggershaus, *The Frankfurt School: Its History, Theories, and Political Significance,* trans. Michael Robertson (Polity Press, 1994); Martin Jay, *The Dialectical Imagination: A History of the Frankfurt School and the Institute of Social Research, 1923–1950* (Little, Brown, 1973); George Friedman, *The Political Philosophy of the Frankfurt School* (Ithaca, N.Y.: Cornell University Press, 1981). See also Laurent Stern, "On the Frankfurt School," *History of European Ideas* 4 (1983): 83

56. György Lukács, *History and Class Consciousness,* trans. Rodney Livingstone (MIT Press, 1971), 1.

57. Ibid., 85.

58. Judith Marcus, "The Judaic Element in the Teachings of the Frankfurt School," *1986 Yearbook of the Leo Baeck Institute* (Leo Baeck Institute, 1986), 339–353.

59. *Social Democracy and the Rule of Law: Otto Kirchheimer and Franz Neumann,* ed. Keith Tribe, trans. Leena Tanner and Keith Tribe (Allen & Unwin, 1987).

60. See lecture, *University of Kansas Law Review* 42, Summer 1994, 770.

61. *Cardozo Law Review* 17, March 1996, 826.

62. Neumann's arguments—that legal formalism can be used to combat oppression and to protect minorities—were very much an exception in the school.

63. Kirchheimer was greatly influenced by Carl Schmitt. He adopted wholesale the latter's views on direct democracy and social homogeneity, as well as Schmitt's emphasis on the "emergency exception" and the crucial role of the definitive decision, of which, both Schmitt and Kirchheimer argued, a liberal democracy was incapable.

64. Otto Kirchheimer, "The Socialist and Bolshevik Theory of the State," in *Social Democracy and the Rule of Law* (Allen & Unwin, 1987), 14.

65. William Scheuerman, *Between the Norm and the Exception* (MIT Press, 1994), 25.

66. Kirchheimer, "The Socialist and Bolshevik Theory of the State," 12–14.

67. Ibid., 10–14.

68. Otto Kirchheimer, "Weimar—And What Then?" in *Social Democracy and the Rule of Law* (Allen & Unwin, 1987), 44.

69. Scheuerman, 31–32.

70. Ibid., 26.

71. Quoted in Otto Kirchheimer, *Political Justice: The Use of Legal Procedures for Political Ends* (Princeton University Press, 1961), 287, as part of a critique of state socialist law.

72. Scheuerman, 36.

73. Kirchheimer, "The Socialist and Bolshevik Theory of the State," 18.

74. Otto Kirchheimer, "Criminal Law in National Socialist Germany," in *Studies in Philosophy and Social Science* 8 (1939): 463.

75. Otto Kirchheimer, "The Legal Order of National Socialism," in *Studies in Philosophy and Social Science* 9 (1941): 456–478.

76. Ehrhard Bahr, "The Anti-Semitism Studies of the Frankfurt School: The Failure of Critical Theory," *German Studies Review* 1 (1978): 125.

CHAPTER TWENTY-THREE: THE PEACE OF PARIS

1. Kenneth A. Oye, "Explaining the End of the Cold War: Morphological Behavioral Adaptations to the Nuclear Peace?" in *International Relations Theory and the End of*

the Cold War, ed. Richard Ned Lebow and Thomas Risse-Kappen (New York: Columbia University Press, 1995). Kenneth A. Oye has concluded that the bipolar strategic world required such enormous infusions of resources that the Soviet economy was undermined. The burdens thus imposed by the international competition structured Gorbachev's reform agenda. See also Robert Gates, *From the Shadows: The Ultimate Insiders Story of Five Presidents and How They Won the Cold War* (New York: Simon & Schuster, 1996).

2. Michael Doyle has argued that the domestic pressures for political reform persuaded the Soviet leadership to enter the international political economy in order to gain the fruits of the international market. See the final chapter, "The Future," in Michael Doyle, *Ways of War and Peace* (New York: Norton, 1997). See also Thomas Risse-Kappen, "Did 'Peace through Strength' End the Cold War? Lessons from INF," *International Security* 16 (1991): 162; and on a related note, Mancur Olson, *Power and Prosperity* (Basic Books, 2000), in which it is argued that democracy performs better economically than either communist or capitalist tyranny.

3. Compare Paulette Kurzer, "International Relations Theory and the End of the Cold War," *Political Science Quarterly* 8 (1996): 166; and Thomas Risse-Kappen, "Ideas Do Not Float Freely: Transnational Coalitions, Domestic Structures, and the End of the Cold War," *International Organizations* 48 (1994): 185.

4. See Part II, Book I.

5. Gorbachev deployed glasnost and perestroika as a response to the delegitimization of Soviet communism and as an attempt to retain control through reform: "[Counterreformation] is a self-critical show of strength with the aim of incorporating those values created against the will of [the established orthodoxy], and outside the social institutions in order to stop them [from] becoming antagonistic and subversive." Adam Michnik, "The Great Counter-Reformer," *Labor Focus and Eastern Europe* 9 (July–October 1987): 23.

6. Michnik.

7. Coit Blaker, *Hostage to Revolution: Gorbachev and Soviet Security Policy, 1985–1991* (Council on Foreign Relations, 1993), 188.

8. See Adam Michnik, "On Resistance," in Adam Michnik, *Letters from Prison and Other Essays,* trans. Maya Liatynski (University of California Press, 1985), 41, 43.

9. In this regard it is quite interesting to recall the following statements by Gorbachev at a press conference held with Mrs. Thatcher: ". . . I will tell you about an interesting conversation which I had at Stanford when I met a group of professors . . . Professor Friedman, the economist . . . had a very interesting observation to make. He recalled that, after World War II, when the U.S. set out to help the Japanese . . . to master the forms of a market economy, a group of them, specialists, arrived in Japan. His first impression . . . was that the people were wholly unprepared for working in the conditions which they wanted to propose. They were all very unhurried people. They lacked energy and initiative. They were absolutely not the right kind of human material. . . . Subsequently he quickly changed his mind. You know how the Japanese work now, he said. I met leaseholders in the Kremlin recently and they are the very people who are working under conditions which are necessary for a market economy. I was struck by their openness, judgment, experience, and initiative. They had so many proposals. That discussion ended with them sitting around preparing a proposal for the president. . . . These are already different people." Joint Press Conference, June 8, 1990, Moscow Television in FBIS-SOV, June 11, 1990. Gorbachev believed that he could make the Russian people into a disciplined and yet innovative workforce—as he thought the Americans had done with the Japanese—not, however, in order to support a parliamentary system but to advance socialism.

10. By the beginning of the twentieth century, the Russian state-nation employed about 160 full-time personnel in its secret police, and a police force of about 10,000. Its successor, the Soviet nation-state's secret police, amounted to 262,400 in 1921, excluding the NKVD. John Gray, "The Politics of Cultural Diversity," in *Postliberalism* (Routledge, 1993), 257.

11. These can be compared to Mao's Great Leap Forward, and the "Cultural Revolution."

12. Fairbanks attributes the first noticing in the West of this recurrence to Walter Laqueur. See Charles Fairbanks, "The Nature of the Beast," *The National Interest* 31 (Spring 1993): 46.

13. Vladimir Kontorovich, "The Economic Fallacy: Economic Problems and the Collapse of Communism in the Former USSR," *The National Interest* 31 (Spring 1993): 35.

14. Ibid.

15. This theory holds, roughly, that economies are so rife with distortions and compensations for them, that interventions will inevitably have unintended, indeed unpredictable consequences.

16. Kontorovich, 35.

17. Ibid.

18. Ibid.

19. Walter C. Uhler, "The Gorbachev Factor," *Bulletin of the Atomic Scientists* 53 (1997): 65.

20. Soviet forces crushed popular uprisings in East Germany (1953), Hungary (1956), Poland (1956), and Czechoslovakia (1968). There was a popular joke in Communist Hungary that while Hungarians could get a passport to travel abroad every three years, Russians were only given one every twelve years: 1944, 1956, 1968, and 1980 (Afghanistan).

21. See Zbigniew Herbert, *Barbarzynca w ogrodzie* (*Barbarian in the Garden*), trans. Michael March and Jaros Law Anders (Carcanet, 1985); Václav Havel, "The Memorandum," trans. Vera Blackwell, in *Selected Plays, 1963–83* (Faber and Faber, 1992); Milan Kundera, *Nesnesitelna lehkost byti* (*The Unbearable Lightness of Being*), trans. Michael Henry Heim (Harper & Row, 1984); and the Russian glasnost literary journal, *Glas: New Russian Writing,* available both in Russian and in English translation.

22. See Jacek Kuron's conception of "social self-organization" in *Polityka i odpowiedzialnosc* ("Aneks," 1984); György Konrád, *Antipolitics: An Essay,* trans. Richard E. Allen (Harcourt, Brace, Jovanovich, 1984); and Václav Havel, "Power of the Powerless," in *Open Letters: Selected Writings, 1965–1990,* ed. Paul Wilson (Knopf, 1991).

23. Michael R. Beschloss and Strobe Talbott, *At the Highest Levels: The Inside Story of the End of the Cold War* (Boston: Little, Brown, 1993).

24. Rey Koslowski and Friedrich Kratochwil, "Understanding Change in International Politics: The Soviet Empire's Demise and the International System," *International Organization* 48 (Spring 1994): 215.

25. Ibid. Compare Raymond Garthoff, *The Great Transition: American-Soviet Relations and the End of the Cold War* (Brookings Institution, 1994), for a contrary view.

26. Kontorovich, 43.

27. Pierre Lelloche, "Kohls Apart: Schemes of Reunification," *The New Republic,* March 19, 1990, 12.

28. Brian Beedham, "Baker and the Old One-Three-Two," *The Economist* 316 (September 1, 1990): S10.

29. Philip Zelikow and Condoleezza Rice, *Germany Unified and Europe Transformed: A Study in Statecraft* (Cambridge, Mass.: Harvard University Press, 1995).

30. Ibid.

31. James A. Baker, "The Common European Interest: America and the New Politics Among Nations," *U.S. Department of State Dispatch*, vol. 1, September 3, 1990, 36.

32. Michael F. Miley, "The CSCE Process and The Question of Sovereignty," *Southern University Law Review* 19 (1992): 123.

33. S. Roth, "The CSCE 'Charter of Paris for a New Europe,'" *Human Rights Law Journal* 11, no. 3–4 (1990): 374.

34. Note Miley, 116.

35. "Conference on Security and Cooperation in Europe: Charter of Paris for a New Europe and Supplementary Document to Give Effect to Certain Provisions of the Charter," *International Legal Materials* 30 (January 1991): 1993.

36. R. W. Apple, Jr., "Summit in Europe: 34 Leaders Adopt Pact Proclaiming a United Europe," *New York Times,* November 22, 1990, A1.

37. Roth, 374. In a later article R. W. Apple observed that when "wars turn things upside down, the politicians, craving stability, always start trying to institutionalize the new world order. After Napoleon came the Holy Alliance, after World War I, the League of Nations, after World War II the United Nations. So last week [a congress of states] had a go, around a hexagonal table in Paris, at inventing something to replace the cold war."

38. At Paris, President Bush proclaimed that the "Cold War is over. In signing the Charter of Paris we have closed a chapter of history." The *New York Times* commented that the Charter of Paris marked "the final denouement of the global conflict that began a half century ago." See Apple, "Summit in Europe."

39. *Le Monde,* November 21, 1990. The summit at Paris spoke on behalf of the society of nation-states, it should be noted, in contrast to the Congress of Vienna, which spoke for the society of state-nations.

40. Roth, 375.

41. Thomas Buergenthal, "CSCE Rights," *George Washington Journal of International Law and Economics* 25, no. 2 (1991): 361.

42. "Conference on Security and Cooperation in Europe: Document of the Moscow Meeting on the Human Dimension, Emphasizing Respect for Human Rights, Pluralistic Democracy, the Rule of Law and Procedures for Fact Finding," *International Legal Materials,* 30 (October 3, 1991): 1672.

43. Buergenthal, 380–381 (emphasis supplied).

44. Quoted in Daniel Patrick Moynihan, "The Time and Place for International Law," *Washington Post,* April 1, 1990, C7.

45. Harold Hongju Koh, "A World Transformed," *Yale Journal of International Law* 20 (Summer 1995): ix.

46. See David Kennedy, "The Move to Institutions," *Cardozo Law Review* 8 (1987): 844; and Nathaniel Berman, "But the Alternative Is Despair: European Nationalism and the Modernist Renewal of International Law," *Harvard Law Review* 106 (1993): 1792.

47. Koh, 1045.

48. Daniel Westberg, "The Relations between Positive and Natural Law in Aquinas," *Journal of Law & Religion* 11 (1994–95): 1.

49. Martin van Gelderen, "The Challenge of Colonialism: Grotius and Vitoria on Natural Law and International Relations," *Grotiana* 14/5 (1993–94): 3–37.

50. See Dennis Patterson, *Law and Truth* (Oxford: Oxford University Press, 1996).

51. Karl N. Llewellyn, *The Bramble Bush: On Our Law and Its Study* (Oceana Publications, 1951; first published 1930). This shocking remark was an extension of Holmes's celebrated observation that "Law is nothing more pretentious than the prediction of what courts will in fact do," perhaps via Cook, who had suggested, regarding this passage, that "[t]he word 'courts' should include some other more or less similar

officials." W. W. Cook, "The Logical and Legal Bases of the Conflict of Laws," *Yale Law Journal* 33 (1924): 457.

52. Abram Chayes, et al., *International Legal Process* 1 (1968): xi (emphasis supplied); see also William N. Eskridge, Jr., and Philip P. Frickey, "An Historical and Critical Introduction to Henry M. Hart, Jr. and Albert M. Sacks, The Legal Process," *The Legal Process: Basic Problems in the Making and Application of Law* (Foundation Press, 1994); ciii, note 232, dxiv, note 286, cxxxii, note 346, describing the origin of Chayes and Ehrlich's work in the legal process materials, cited in Koh, n. 94.

53. See Roger Fisher, "Bringing Law to Bear on National Governments," *Harvard Law Review* 74 (1961): 1130.

54. Akehurst, Michael, *A Modern Introduction to International Law,* 7th ed. (rev. ed., Peter Malanczuk) (Routledge, 1997), 6.

55. Ibid.

56. Akehurst, 2; see also Akehurst, "Custom as a Source of International Law," *British Year Book of International Law* 47 (1974–75): 1.

57. Tom J. Farer, "Human Rights in Law's Empire: The Jurisprudence War," *American Journal of International Law* 85 (1991): 117.

58. Ibid., 118.

59. François, Duc de La Rochefoucauld, *Maxims,* trans. Leonard Tancock (Penguin Books, 1959), 65.

60. Despite the fact that Europe, and especially Germany, were early contributors to legal realism, note the German *Interessenjurisprudenz* and *Freie Rechtslehre,* acknowledged by Llewellyn, as well as Geny's *Libre recherche scientifique.*

61. "An examination of the Collected Courses of the Hague Academy of International Law . . . reveals that European scholarship in international law . . . [has] continued largely in the traditional, non-theoretical, doctrinal vein. International legal scholarship in other countries followed this doctrinal, Eurocentric pattern." Cf. Yasuaki Onuma, "Japanese International Law in the Postwar Period—Perspectives on the Teaching and Research of International Law in Postwar Japan," *Japanese Annual of International Law* 33 (1990): 25, 44.

62. Farer, 117.

63. Some say the earliest known writing is a treaty.

64. Oscar Schachter, *International Law in Theory and Practice: General Course in Public International Law* (Academic Publishers, 1982), 24.

65. Ibid., 25.

66. Cf. Thomas Franck, "The Case of the Vanishing Treaties," *American Journal of International Law* 81 (1987): 763.

67. Schachter, *International Law in Theory and Practice,* 44.

68. Oscar Schachter, "The Legality of Pro-Democratic Invasion," *American Journal of International Law* 78 (1984): 645, 649.

69. See Leland M. Goodrich, Edvard Hambro, and Anne P. Simons, *Charter of the United Nations* (Columbia University Press, 1969), 629–632.

70. Oscar Schachter, "United Nations Law in the Gulf Conflict," *American Journal of International Law* 85 (July 1991): 464.

71. Compare the strikingly similar hypothetical exercise used by Justice Hugo Black in his Charpentier Lectures to ridicule the position of Justice Frankfurter; see Hugo L. Black, "The Bill of Rights," *New York University Law Review* 35 (1960): 877–878. It suggests that even the plainest of the textual provisions of the Bill of Rights of the U.S. Constitution could be overridden by an appeal to extratextual values, like necessity.

72. Most of McDougal's most important early work is collected in Myres S. McDougal and Associates, *Studies in World Public Order* (Yale University Press, 1960), although

in many ways McDougal's Hague lectures provide more insight into the development of his unique framework. Other important articles, although only a limited selection from a vast corpus, include: Myres S. McDougal, "Law as a Process of Decision: A Policy-Oriented Approach to Legal Study," *Natural Law Forum* 1 (1956): 53; Myres S. McDougal, "Some Basic Theoretical Concepts about International Law: A Policy-Oriented Framework of Inquiry," *Journal of Conflict Resolution* 4 (1960): 337; Myres S. McDougal and W. Michael Reisman, "The World Constitutive Process of Authoritative Decision," *Journal of Legal Education* 19 (1967): 253; Myres S. McDougal, Harold D. Lasswell, and W. Michael Reisman, "Theories about International Law: Prologue to a Configurative Jurisprudence," *Virginia Journal of International Law* 8 (1968): 188; Myres S. McDougal, "International Law and Social Science: A Mild Plea in Avoidance," *American Journal of International Law* 66 (1972): 77; Myres S. McDougal and W. Michael Reisman, "International Law in Policy-Oriented Perspective," in *The Structure and Process of International Law,* ed. Ronald St. J. Macdonald and Douglas M. Johnston (Martinus Nijhoff, 1983), 103 [hereinafter Policy-Oriented Perspective]. On the contributions of his many students, see the Festschrift published on the occasion of his retirement: *Toward World Order and Human Dignity,* ed. W. Michael Reisman and Burns H. Weston (Free Press, 1976) [hereinafter *Toward World Order*], also containing a complete bibliography of works by and relating to McDougal; see also "International Law and International Relations Theory: A Dual Agenda," *American Journal of International Law* 87 (1993): 205.

73. Anthony Kronman, "Jurisprudential Responses to Legal Realism," *Cornell Law Review* 73 (1988): 335; Jan Vetter, "Postwar Legal Scholarship on Judicial Decision-making," *Journal of Legal Education* 33 (1983): 412.

74. As Anne-Marie Burley (herself one of the most insightful and distinguished of McDougal's heirs) concluded, "Although many of his students profited from his insights when turned to their own purposes, McDougal's most prominent disciple and heir to his jurisprudential approach is W. Michael Reisman." See, e.g., W. Michael Reisman, "A Theory about Law from the Policy Perspective," in *Law and Policy,* ed. D. N. Weisstub (Osgoode Hall Law School, 1976), reprinted as abridged in Myres S. McDougal and W. Michael Reisman, *International Law Essays: A Supplement to International Law in Contemporary Perspective* (Foundation Press, 1981), 1; and [other] co-authored works also written with McDougal.

75. Reisman, 273.

76. Richard Falk, "Casting the Spell: The New Haven School of International Law," *Yale Law Journal* 104 (1995): 1991–92.

77. Reisman, 277.

78. See generally Myres S. McDougal, "Legal Bases for Securing the Integrity of the Earth-Space Environment," *Annals of the New York Academy of Sciences* 184 (1971): 380; Myres S. McDougal and Harold D. Lasswell, "The Identification and Appraisal of Diverse Systems of Public Order," *American Journal of International Law* 53 (1959): 1; Winston Nagan, "Civil Process and Power: Thoughts from a Policy-Oriented Perspective," *University of Florida Law Review* 39 (1987): 453; W. Michael Reisman, "A Theory about Law from the Policy Perspective," in *Law and Policy,* ed. Weisstub, 75.

79. See for example, Samuel P. Huntington's well-known argument in *The Clash of Civilizations.*

80. Emphasis supplied. Paula Wolff, "McDougal's Jurisprudence: Utility, Influence, Controversy," *Proceedings of the American Society of International Law* 79 (April 25–27, 1985): 270–271. One might add that even if there is a universal consensus on what people want for themselves, it does not follow, alas, that there is an identical consensus on what we are prepared to accord to others.

81. Ibid., 284.
82. Franck, 765.
83. Louis Henkin, *How Nations Behave* (Columbia University Press, 1979), 40; see also Louis Henkin, "Force, Intervention and Neutrality in Contemporary International Law," *Proceedings of the American Society on International Law* 57 (1963): 168.
84. Ervin H. Pollack, *Jurisprudence, Principles and Applications* (Ohio State University Press, 1979), 788.
85. Dean Acheson, "The Arrogance of International Lawyers," *International Law* 2 (1968): 592; and also Dean Acheson, *Fragments of My Fleece* (Norton, 1971), 156.
86. "The law is what the judges say it is," Charles E. Hughes, *The Supreme Court of the United States* (Columbia University Press, 1928), 120; "the Constitution is what the Supreme Court says it is," Charles E. Hughes, *Addresses and Papers of Charles Evans Hughes* (Putnam, 1908), 139–141.
87. *Proceedings of the American Society of International Law* 13 (1963): 14.
88. See John Lewis Gaddis, "The Tragedy of Cold War History," *Diplomatic History* 17 (1993): 1.
89. Vladislav Zubok and Constantine Pleshakov, "Great Britain," in *The Origins of the Cold War in Europe: International Perspectives,* ed. David Reynolds (New Haven: Yale University Press, 1994).
90. "The Soviet occupation of the Western Ukraine and Byelorussia from 1939–41 provide an example of how the Soviet system foreshadowed the policies Stalin would pursue after World War II. The entire program of phony elections, purges and mass shootings was carried out during the invasion of Poland in 1939." The security police murdered 400,000 persons and expelled another 1.5 million to the interior. Jacob Heilbrun, "Who Writes the History: Neo-Revisionism and the Cold War," *Current,* December 1994, 12.
91. Quoted by Heilbrun, ibid.
92. Douglas Brinkley, *Dean Acheson: The Cold War Years 1953–71* (Yale University Press, 1992); see also Dean Acheson, *Present at the Creation: My Years at the State Department* (Norton, 1969); and Gaddis Smith, *Dean Acheson* (Cooper Square Publishers, 1972).
93. Brinkley, p. 66.
94. Perhaps women will not fall prey to this conceit; in Acheson's day there were virtually no females at the Harvard Law School.
95. See David McCullough, *Truman* (Simon & Schuster, 1992), 760–761.
96. Acheson, "The Arrogance of International Lawyers," 592.
97. Brinkley, *Dean Acheson;* also quoted in Hodgson.
98. Acheson, "The Arrogance of International Lawyers," 598.
99. Bobbitt, *Tragic Choices,* 18.
100. Karl N. Llewellyn, *The Bramble Bush;* this is also a popular assertion in critical legal studies.
101. Wolff, "McDougal's Jurisprudence," 272.
102. Judith Gail Gardam, "Gender and Non-Combatant Immunity" (Symposium: Feminist Inquiries into International Law), *Transnational Law and Contemporary Problems* 3 (1993): 345.
103. Hilary Charlesworth, Christine Chinkin, and Shelly Wright, "Feminist Approaches to International Law," *American Journal of International Law* 85 (1991).
104. The constitution of the society of state-nations was very different: the Ottoman Empire was not admitted to this society until 1856.
105. David A. Westbrook, "Islamic International Law and Public International Law: Separate Expressions of World Order," *Virginia Journal of International Law* 33 (Summer 1993): 829.

106. See also David N. Kennedy, "A New Stream of International Law Scholarship," *Wisconsin International Law Journal* 7 (1998): 1, and his book *International Legal Structures* (Nomos, 1987); James Boyle, "Ideas and Things: International Legal Scholarship and the Prison-House of Language," *Harvard International Law Journal* 26 (1985): 327; and Phillip Trimble, "International Law, World Order and Critical Legal Studies," *Stanford Law Review* 42 (1990): 811; and Nigel Purvis, "Critical Legal Studies in Public International Law," *Harvard Journal of International Law* 32 (1991): 81.

107. Bobbitt, *Constitutional Interpretation*.

108. "Law is something we do, not something we have as a consequence of something we do. Sometimes our activities in law—deciding, proposing, persuading—may link up with specific ideas we have at those moments; but often they do not, and it is never the case that this link must be made for the activities that are law to be law. Therefore the causal accounts of how those inner states come into being, accounts that often lose their persuasiveness in contact with the abundance of the world, are really beside the point. If we want to understand the ideological and political commitments in law, we have to study the grammar of the law, that system of logical constraints that the practices of legal activities have developed in our particular culture." Ibid., 24.

109. See for example, Gunnar Schuster, "Extraterritoriality of Securities Laws: An Economic Analysis of Jurisdictional Conflicts," *Law and Policy in International Business* 26 (1994): 165; Joel Trachtman, "The Theory of the Firm and the Theory of International Economic Organization: Toward Comparative Institutional Analysis," in *Symposium: Institutions for International Economic Integration, Northwestern Journal of International Law and Business* 17 (Winter–Spring 1996–97): 470.

110. Michael J. Sandel, *Liberalism and the Limits of Justice* (Cambridge, U.K.: Cambridge University Press, 1998).

111. Ronald Dworkin, *Law's Empire* (Cambridge, Mass.: Harvard University Press, 1986).

112. See Thomas Franck's *Fairness in International Law and Institutions* (Oxford University Press, 1995) for a sophisticated and even charming exposition of how Rawls's work might be applied to the issue of legitimacy in international law.

113. Jürgen Habermas, *Between Facts and Norms: Contributions to a Discourse Theory of Law and Democracy* (Studies in Contemporary German Social Thought), trans. William Rehg (Cambridge, Mass.: MIT Press, 1996).

114. James Brierly, *The Law of Nations,* 6th ed. (Oxford University Press, 1963), 51.

115. *Proceedings of the American Society of International Law,* vol. 86, 120.

116. See Jack Balkin for argument that deconstruction can be put to conservative uses; and Bruce Ackerman, in *We the People: Foundations* (Belknap Press, Harvard, 1991), 320–322, and Frederick Schauer in "Constitutional Positivism," *Connecticut Law Review* 29 (Spring 1993), for arguments that formalism can be put in service of liberal ideals.

117. These are discussed in some detail in *Constitutional Fate* (1982) and *Constitutional Interpretation* (1991).

118. James A. Baker III, with Thomas DeFrank, *The Politics of Diplomacy: Revolution, War and Peace* (New York: Putnam, 1995).

CHAPTER TWENTY-FOUR: CHALLENGES TO THE NEW INTERNATIONAL ORDER

1. Having looked at this question when I was writing *Democracy and Deterrence,* I have less sympathy with those scholars who argue that the United States need not have dropped atomic bombs on Hiroshima and Nagasaki because the Japanese were

obviously losing the war and thus could have been induced to surrender without an American invasion.

2. For an excellent discussion, see "Japanese Nuclear Weapons," in *Asia-Pacific: Issues and Developments* (National Security Planning Associates, 1997), 23.

3. Lawrence Freedman, "The 'Proliferation Problem' and the New World Order," 2 (manuscript in possession of the author); see also Lawrence Freedman, "Great Powers, Vital Interests and Nuclear Weapons," *Survival* 4 (Winter 1994/95).

4. Kenneth N. Waltz, *The Spread of Nuclear Weapons: More May Be Better* (1981).

5. See Lawrence Freedman, "Great Powers, Vital Interests and Nuclear Weapons, supra n. 3, 36.

6. This speech is reproduced in *Churchill's "Iron Curtain" Speech Fifty Years Later,* ed. James W. Muller (with assistance from the Churchill Center) (University of Missouri Press, 1999).

7. Martin Van Creveld, *Nuclear Proliferation and the Future of Conflict* (Macmillan, 1993), 122.

8. Supplying other states with ballistic missile defense can strengthen the credibility of American commitment. This is because it avoids the theorem described in *Democracy and Deterrence,* which holds that any American effort to cure "decoupling"—the abandonment of the European or any extended theatre—risks "uncoupling"—the confinement of nuclear war to an extended theatre while the U.S. remains a sanctuary. See Bobbitt, *Democracy and Deterrence,* 99–109.

9. See Richard Betts, "The New Threat of Mass Destruction," *Foreign Affairs* 77 (1998): 31.

10. Cf. Colin G. Calloway, *New Worlds for All: Indians, Europeans, and the Remaking of Early America* (Baltimore: Johns Hopkins University Press, 1997), 33–38.

11. George W. Christopher and Julie Pavlin, "Biological Warfare: A Historical Perspective," *Journal of the American Medical Association* 278 (1997): 412.

12. Robert Koch (1843–1910) discovered mycobacterium tuberculosis as the agent of human tuberculosis in 1871. His postulates are these: an infectious disease is caused by a pathogen organism; that organism must be obtained in pure culture; the organism obtained in culture must reproduce in experimental animals; the pathogen organism must be recovered from the animals used for the experiment so vaccines can be produced.

13. This was Ken Alibek, the former deputy director of Biopreparat, a network of institutes responsible for weapons research and the production of pathogen agents.

14. See Ronald Atlas, "Combating the Threat of Biowarfare and Bioterrorism: Defending against Biological Weapons Is Critical to Global Security," *BioScience* 9 (1999): 465, from which much of the background provided in this account is taken. The CIA reported in 1995 that seventeen countries—Bulgaria, China, Cuba, Egypt, India, Iran, Iraq, Israel, Laos, Libya, North Korea, Russia, South Africa, South Korea, Syria, Taiwan, and Viet Nam—were researching or stockpiling weapons for germ warfare.

15. Ibid. See M. Leitenberg, "The Conversion of Biological Warfare Research and Development Facilities to Peaceful Uses," in *Control of Dual Threat Agents: The Vaccines for Peace Program,* ed. Erhard Geissler and John P. Woodall (Oxford University Press, 1994), 77.

16. Brad Roberts, in *Washington Quarterly,* Winter 1995, 5; see also *Biological Weapons: Weapons of the Future?,* vol. 15, ed. Brad Roberts (Center for Strategic and International Studies, 1993).

17. A United States Office of Technology Assessment Report concluded that a small private plane with 220 pounds of anthrax spores flying over Washington, D.C., on a north to south route trailing an invisible mist would kill a million people on a day with mod-

erate wind. Even a single warhead of anthrax spores, OTA estimates, would kill 30,000 to 40,000 persons, more in fact than an Hiroshima-size nuclear weapon.

18. A Japanese attack using cholera agents on Changteh in 1941 led to an estimated 10,000 casualties and 1,700 deaths among Japanese troops.

19. The anthrax released from the Soviet lab near Sverdlovsk in 1979 may have been specially bred to be resistant to antibiotics and specifically engineered to attack adult males. Antibiotics failed to prevent the deaths of over 1,000 civilians, but three times as many men as women died and not a single child.

20. Though it was ultimately unable to seal its borders against communication. Arthur C. Clarke, who early on speculated about the geosynchronous satellite, observed that "[r]adio waves have never respected frontiers, and from an altitude of 36,000 kilometers, national boundaries are singularly inconspicuous." Satellites enable persons with such decentralized devices as a simple transistor radio or television to receive information beyond the control of national authorities.

21. It is worth noting that a team of researchers at Malvern, Worcestershire, given a task of improving the reliability of RAF radar equipment, hit upon the idea of putting an entire circuit on a block of silicon a half-inch square. This concept was not operationalized until 1958 by Roger Kilby at Texas Instruments.

22. Quoted in Walter B. Wriston, "Clintonomics," *Vital Speeches,* vol. 59, April 1, 1993, 376.

23. Peter Drucker, "The Changed World Economy," *Foreign Affairs* 64 (1986): 777–778.

24. Wriston, 379.

25. Ibid., 380.

26. Ibid.

27. Ask not what your country can do for you (nation-state) or what you can do for your country (state-nation), but what, with your country's help, you can do for yourself (market-state).

28. C. Fred Bergsten, "The World Economy after the Cold War," *Foreign Affairs* 69 (1990): 98.

29. Ibid.

30. According to the *CIA World Factbook 2000,* current U.S. external debt stands at $862 billion. The Bureau of the Public Debt does not provide percentage breakdowns by nation. According to Peter Hadfield, "Japan holds a large chunk of U.S. national debt—$500 billion worth, according to some estimates," "Japan backs away from bond threat," *USA Today,* June 25, 1997, 10B. But see Claire Mencke, "Prices Flat Despite Bullish Data: Japan Rumors, Iraq Events Cited," *Investor's Business Daily,* November 17, 1997, B14. " 'There's no real evidence of this yet, but people in the market are very fearful of it because of Japan's super-large Treasury holdings,' *MCM Money Watch* economist Astrid Adolfson said, 'noting that Japan holds about $321 billion of the $1.3 trillion of Treasury debt outstanding.' "

31. Drucker, 786.

32. See Robert Gilpin, *War and Change in World Politics* (Cambridge University Press, 1981), 235.

33. Robert P. Kadlec, "Biological Weapons for Waging Economic Warfare," in *Battlefield of the Future,* ed. Barry R. Schneider and Lawrence E. Grinter (Air University Press, 1995), 251.

34. Drucker, 771.

35. David Sapsford, *Real Primary Commodity Prices: An Analysis of Long-Run Movements,* International Monetary Fund Internal Memorandum, May 17, 1985 (unpublished).

36. Drucker, 773.

37. Ibid., 781; see also Walt Rostow, "The Terms of Trade in Theory" and "The Terms of Trade in Practice," in *The Process of Economic Growth* (Norton, 1953), 168.

38. Robert W. Kates, "Expecting the Unexpected?" *Environment* 38 (1996): 6.

39. William McNeill, *Plagues and Peoples* (Anchor Press, 1976), 254.

40. Some knowledgeable commentators expect that advances in biotechnology will obviate this problem by allowing us to grow organs cheaply.

41. Methyl chloride, for example, killed more than a hundred people in a Cleveland hospital in 1929 when it leaked into a ventilation system following an explosion in an X-ray lab.

42. Kates, n. 38.

43. SALADIN: And I a Mussulman. Between us is the Christian. Now, but one of all these three religions can be true. A man like you stands not where accident of birth has cast him. If he so remain, it is from judgment, reason, choice of best. Impart to me your judgment; let me hear the reasons I've no time to seek myself.

Saladin then gives Nathan a few hurried moments to contemplate on this question alone. After a soliloquy by Nathan, Saladin returns to be told this story.

NATHAN: In gray antiquity there lived a man in Eastern lands who had received a ring of priceless worth from a beloved hand. Its stone, an opal, flashed a hundred colors, and had the secret power of giving favor, in sight of God and man, to him who wore it with a believing heart. What wonder then this Eastern man would never put the ring from off his finger, and should so provide that to his house it be preserved forever? Such was the case. Unto the best beloved among his sons he left the ring, enjoining that he in turn bequeath it to the son who should be dearest; and the dearest ever, in virtue of the ring, without regard to birth, be of the house the prince and head. You understand me, Sultan?

SALADIN: Yes; go on!

NATHAN: From son to son the ring descending, came to one, the sire of three; of whom all three were equally obedient; whom all three he therefore must with equal love regard. And yet from time to time now this, now that, and now the third,—as each alone was by, the others not dividing his fond heart, appeared to him the worthiest of the ring; which then, with loving weakness, he would promise to each in turn. Thus it continued long. Be he must die; and then the loving father was sore perplexed. It grieved him thus to wound two faithful sons who trusted in his word; but what to do? In secrecy he calls an artist to him, and commands of him two other rings, the pattern of his own; and bids him neither cost nor pains to spare to make them like, precisely like to that. The artist's skill succeeds. He brings the ring, and e'en the father cannot tell his own. Relieved and joyful, summons he his sons, each by himself; to each one by himself he gives his blessing, and his ring—and dies. You listen, Sultan?

SALADIN: (who, somewhat perplexed, has turned away)—Yes; I hear, I hear. But bring your story to an end . . .

NATHAN: Return we to our rings. As I have said, the sons appealed to law, and each took oath before the judge that from his father's hand he had the ring,—as was indeed the truth; and had received his promise long before, one day the ring, with all its privileges, should be his own,—as was not less the truth. The father could not have been false to him each one maintained; and rather than allow upon the memory of so dear a father such stain to rest, he must against his brothers, though gladly he would nothing but the best believe of them, bring charge of treachery; means would he find the traitors to expose, and be revenged on them.

SALADIN: And now the judge? I long to hear what words you give the judge. Go on!

NATHAN: Thus spoke the judge: Produce your father at once before me, else from my tribunal do I dismiss you. Think you I am here to guess your riddles? Either would you wait until the genuine ring shall speak?—But hold! A magic power in the true ring resides, as I am told, to make its wearer loved—pleasing to God and man. Let that decide. For in the false can no such virtue lie. Which one among you, then, do two love best? Speak! Are you silent? Work the rings but backward, not outward? Loves each one himself the best? Then cheated cheats are all of you! The rings all three are false. The genuine ring was lost; and to conceal, supply the lost, the father made three in place of one.

SALADIN: Oh, excellent!

NATHAN: Go, therefore, said the judge, unless my counsel you'd have in place of sentence. It were this: accept the case exactly as it stands. Had each his ring directly from his father, let each believe his own genuine. 'Tis possible your father would no longer his house to one ring's tyranny subject; and certain that all three of you he loved, loved equally, since two he would not humble, that one might be exalted. Let each one to his unbought, impartial love aspire; each with the others vie to bring to light the virtue of the stone within his ring; Let gentleness, a hearty love of peace, beneficence, and perfect trust in God, come to its help. Then if the jewel's power among your children's children be revealed, I bid you in a thousand, thousand years again before this bar. A wiser man than I shall occupy this seat, and speak. Go!—Thus the modest judge dismissed them.

CHAPTER TWENTY-FIVE: POSSIBLE WORLDS

1. Joseph Nye, Jr., "Peering into the Future," *Foreign Affairs* 73 (1994): 82.
2. Ibid.
3. See *Scenario Planning: Forging a Link with Strategic Decision Making* (Corporate Executive Board, 1999), 51; and Arie de Geus, *The Living Company* (Harvard Business School Press, 1997); David Mason, "Scenario-Based Planning Decision Model for the Learning Organization," in *Planning Review*, vol. 22, March/April 1994; Ian Wilson, "The Effective Implementation of Scenario Planning: Changing the Corporate Culture," in *Learning from the Future: Competitive Foresight Scenarios*, ed. Liam Fahey (Wiley, 1998).
4. *Scenario Planning,* supra n. 3.
5. Ibid., 19–21.
6. For an excellent treatment of the scenario process see Peter Schwartz, *The Art of the Long View* (New York: Doubleday, 1991).
7. *Public Global Scenarios* 1992–2020, 2 (Shell International Petroleum Company, 1992). "[T]he purpose of scenario planning is not to pinpoint future events but to highlight large-scale forces that push the future in different directions. It's about making these forces visible, so that if they do happen, the planner will at least recognize them. It's about helping make better decisions today. Scenario planning begins by identifying the focal issue or decision. There are an infinite number of stories that we could tell about the future; our purpose is to tell those that matter, that lead to better decisions."
8. *Global Trends 2015: A Dialogue about the Future with Nongovernment Experts* (National Intelligence Council 2000–02, Dec. 2000), 12. The following "assumed facts" for the scenario period are taken from this document.
9. See *National Intelligence Estimate on Ballistic Missile Threat,* declassified (U.S. GPO, 1999).

10. Walt W. Rostow, "2050: An Essay on the 21st Century," 29 (ms.).
11. Ibid.
12. Paul Domjan, "Future Scenarios" (2001) (unpublished manuscript).
13. Ibid., 9.
14. William Greider, *One World, Ready or Not: The Manic Logic of Global Capitalism* (Simon & Schuster, 1997), 167–168; this is basically a description of Germany's policy in the late 1990s.
15. Roger Rainbow, in *Scenarios for the Future.*
16. Fukuyama, xiv.
17. Ibid., 77.
18. Ibid., 48.
19. This is a paraphrase of Bernard Lewis, "The Roots of Muslim Rage: Why So Many Muslims Deeply Resent the West, and Why Their Bitterness Will Not Be Easily Mollified," *The Atlantic Monthly,* September 1990, 48.
20. See Benjamin Barber, *Jihad v. McWorld* (Ballantine Books, 1995); and Patrick Glynn, "The Age of Balkanization," *Commentary* 96 (July 1993): 21–24.
21. *Seven Tomorrows: Seven Scenarios for the Eighties and Nineties* (MCB University Press, 1982), 150 et seq.
22. Joseph Jaworski, *Synchronicity* (Berrett-Koehler, 1996): 164; see also *Tragic Choices.*
23. Quoting a speech by R. Kako, who was chairman of Canon, Inc., at the time.

CHAPTER TWENTY-SIX:
THE COMING AGE OF WAR AND PEACE

1. *Global Trends 2015: A Dialogue about the Future with Nongovernment Experts,* 12.
2. President Clinton's January 18, 1998, State of the Union Address.
3. E.g. Don DeLillo, *Underworld* (Scribner, 1997), 76. "Now that power is in shatters or tatters and now that those Soviet borders don't even exist in the same way, I think we understand, we look back, we see ourselves clearly, and them as well. Power meant something thirty, forty years ago. It was stable, it was focused, it was a tangible thing. It was greatness, danger, terror, all those things. And it held us together, the Soviets and us. Maybe it held the world together. You could measure things. You could measure hope and you could measure destruction. Not that I want to bring it back. It's gone, good riddance. But the fact is . . . Many things that were anchored to the balance of power and the balance of terror seem to be undone, unstuck. Things have no limits now. Money has no limits. I don't understand money anymore. Money is undone. Violence is undone, violence is easier now, it's uprooted, out of control, it has no measure anymore, it has no level of values . . ."
4. Richard Danzig, *The Big Three: Our Greatest Security Risks and How to Address Them* (Institute for National Strategic Studies, 1999).
5. Michael Doyle, "Kant, Liberal Legacies and Foreign Affairs," *Philosophy and Public Affairs* 12 (1983): 205, 323.
6. Thomas Schwartz and Kiron Skinner, "The Myth of Democratic Pacifism," *Wall Street Journal,* January 7, 1999, A10.
7. At the same time that the pope was condemning war among Christians the Church was murdering Cathars, Albigensians, Waldensians, and others. See Wolfgang Wackernagel, "Two Thousand Years of Heresy: An Essay," *Diogenes* 47 (Fall 1999): 134; or, for a more entertaining account, see David Roberts, "In France, an Ordeal by Fire and a Monster Weapon Called 'Bad Neighbor': Cathars, Nonviolent Christian Heretics, Victims of the Inquisition in the Thirteenth Century," *Smithsonian* 22 (May 1991): 40.

8. R. James Woolsey, "On National Security Challenges in the 21st Century," *National Security Law Report* 23 (January/February 2001): 5.

9. Rules, and also techniques.

10. See testimony of Michael Beschloss, Ed Turner, and Ted Koppel before the House Foreign Affairs Committee in *Impact of Television on U.S. Foreign Policy* (U.S. GPO, 1994).

11. "The defining moment was when Walter Cronkite announced on nationwide television after the Tet Offensive that he didn't believe we had any further reason to be in Vietnam." Interview with Senator John McCain, March/April 2000, Association of Graduates, West Point.

12. David Anderson, "Is Libel Law Worth Reforming?" *University of Pennsylvania Law Review* 140, no. 2 (December 1991): 487.

13. In the twelve months prior to July 1994, the Defense Department detected 3,600 computer intrusions on military networks. Admiral McConnell, former head of the National Security Agency (NSA), has stated that computer intruders, in his view, have already included foreign intelligence agencies, criminals, terrorists, and members of the computer underground. A 1996 GAO report estimates, on rather slender evidence it must be said, that as many as 250,000 attempts to penetrate Defense Department computer systems occurred in 1995, and that twice that many would occur in 1997. When the Defense Department has attempted to penetrate its own systems, it succeeded in over 7,800 attempts—an 87 percent success rate, fewer than 5 percent of which attempts were even detected and fewer than 1 percent of which were reported up the chain of command.

14. An October 1996 Ernst & Young survey of corporate executives disclosed that 78 percent of respondents reported financial losses from the preceding two years that were attributable to information security problems and computer viruses. And there are escalating grounds for concern. In 1998 identified computer viruses increased from 8,000 to 12,000 within the past year, and they continued to grow at an estimated 300 per month. Intruders have compromised nearly all elements of the PSN: switching systems, operations, administration, maintenance and provisioning systems, and packet data networks. They have regularly attacked the networks linked to the PSN. And they have demonstrated great skill at manipulating data networks including the ATM (asynchronous transfer mode) networks and the synchronous optical networks (SONET).

CHAPTER TWENTY-SEVEN:
PEACE IN THE SOCIETY OF MARKET-STATES

1. For an excellent discussion of the debate surrounding this doctrine, see Richard Haass, *Intervention: The Use of American Military Force in the Post–Cold War World* (Brookings Institution, 1994).

2. For a different proposal, see Richard Haass, *The Reluctant Sheriff* (Council on Foreign Relations).

3. Joseph Nye, "Redefining the National Interest," *Foreign Affairs* 78 (July/August 1999): 28.

EPILOGUE

1. Fred Ikle, *The National Interest,* March 1, 1997.

2. Michael Walzer, "The Concept of Civil Society," in *Toward a Global Civil Society,* ed. Michael Walzer (Berghahn Books, 1995), n. 342.

3. John Keegan, *History of Warfare:* see Chapter 6, n. 5.

4. Martin van Creveld, *The Rise and Decline of the State* (Cambridge, U.K.: Cambridge University Press, 2000).

APPENDIX

1. Rey Koslowski and Friedrich V. Kratochwil, "Understanding Change in International Politics: The Soviet Empire's Demise and the International System" (Symposium: The End of the Cold War and Theories of International Relations), *International Organization* 48 (Spring 1994): 15.

BIBLIOGRAPHY

Acheson, Dean, *Fragments of My Fleece* (New York: Norton, 1971).

———, *Present at the Creation: My Years in the State Department* (New York: Norton, 1969).

Ackerman, Bruce A., *We the People: Foundations,* vol. 1 and *Transformations,* vol. 2 (Cambridge, Mass.: Belknap Press of Harvard University Press, 1991, 1998).

Acton, Edward, "State and Society under Lenin and Stalin," in *Themes in Modern European History, 1890–1945,* ed. Paul Hayes (London: Routledge, 1992).

Akehurst, Michael, *A Modern Introduction to International Law,* 7th ed., rev. ed., Peter Malanczuk (London: Routledge, 1997).

Alexander, Bevin, *Robert E. Lee's Civil War* (Holbrook, Mass.: Adams Media Corp., 1998).

Alighieri, Dante, *The Inferno,* trans. Robert Pinsky (New York: Noonday Press, 1996).

Alison, Sir Archibald, *Lives of Lord Castlereagh and Sir C. Stewart* (London: W. Blackwood and Sons, 1861).

Anderson, James, ed., *The Rise of the Modern State* (Brighton, Sussex: Harvester Press, 1986.

Arend, Anthony, *Pursuing a Just and Durable Peace: John Foster Dulles and International Organization* (New York: Greenwood Press, 1988).

Artz, F. B., *Reaction and Revolution, 1814–1832* (New York: Harper & Brothers, 1934).

Austin, John, *Province of Jurisprudence Determined* (Cambridge, U.K.: Cambridge University Press, 1995 [1832]).

Barber, Benjamin, *Jihad v. McWorld* (New York: Ballantine Books, 1995).

Barraclough, Geoffrey, *Factors in German History* (Oxford: B. Blackwell, 1946).

Bedau, M. A., "Weak Emergence," in *Philosophical Perspectives: Mind, Causation, and World,* ed. James Tomberlin (Oxford: Blackwell Publishers, 1997).

Beschloss, Michael R., and Strobe Talbott, *At the Highest Levels: The Inside Story of the End of the Cold War* (Boston: Little, Brown, 1993).

Best, Geoffrey, *War and Society in Revolutionary Europe, 1770–1870* (Leicester: Leicester University Press, 1982).

Billington, James H., *Fire in the Minds of Men: Origins of Revolutionary Faith* (New Brunswick, N.J.: Transaction, 1999).

Bird, Kai, *The Color of Truth: McGeorge Bundy and William Bundy, Brothers in Arms* (New York: Simon & Schuster, 1998).

Black, Jeremy, *European Warfare, 1660–1815* (New Haven: Yale University Press, 1994).

———, *War and the World: Military Power and the Fate of Continents, 1450–2000* (New Haven: Yale University Press, 1998).

Blacker, Coit, *Hostage to Revolution: Gorbachev and Soviet Security Policy, 1985–1991* (New York: Council on Foreign Relations Press, 1993).

Bobbitt, Philip, *Democracy and Deterrence* (New York: St. Martin's Press, 1988).

Bobbitt, Philip, and Guido Calabresi, *Tragic Choices* (New York: Norton, 1978).

Bobbitt, Philip, Lawrence Freedman, and Gregory F. Treverton, eds., *U.S. Nuclear Strategy: A Reader* (New York: New York University Press, 1989).

Bodin, Jean, *Six Books of the Commonwealth* (Oxford: B. Blackwell, 1955 [1606]).

———, *Six Books of the Commonwealth,* ed. K. D. McRae (Cambridge, Mass.: Harvard University Press, 1962).

Bohme, Helmut, *Deutschlands Weg zur Grossmacht* (Cologne/Berlin: Kiepenheuer & Witsch, 1966).

———, *The Foundations of the German Empire* (Oxford: Oxford University Press, 1971).

Bonney, Richard, *The European Dynastic States, 1494–1660* (Oxford: Oxford University Press, 1991).

Bonnin, Georges, *Bismarck and the Hohenzollern Candidature for the Spanish Throne* (London: Chatto & Windus, 1957).

Bonsal, Stephen, *Suitors and Suppliants: The Little Nations at Versailles* (New York: Prentice-Hall, 1946).

Bossuet, Jacques B., *Politique tirée des propres paroles de l'Ecriture sainte,* ed. LeBrun (Geneva: Droz, 1967).

Boyce, Robert, and Esmonde M. Robertson, eds., *Paths to War: New Essays on the Origins of the Second World War* (New York: St. Martin's Press, 1989).

Braudel, Fernand, *Civilization and Capitalism, 15th–18th Century* (New York: Harper & Row, 1982–84).

Breuer, William B., *Race to the Moon: America's Duel with the Soviets* (Westport, Conn.: Praeger, 1993).

Brewer, John, *The Sinews of Power* (London: Unwin Hyman, 1989).

Brierly, James, *The Law of Nations,* 6th ed. (Oxford: Oxford University Press, 1963).

Brinkley, Douglas, *Dean Acheson: The Cold War Years, 1953–71* (New Haven: Yale University Press, 1992).

Brodie, Bernard, "Implications for Military Policy," in *The Absolute Weapon: Atomic Power and World Order,* ed. Bernard Brodie (New York: Harcourt, Brace, 1946).

Brodie, Bernard and Fawn, *From Crossbow to H-Bomb* (Bloomington: Indiana University Press, 1973).

Brzezinski, Zbigniew K., *The Grand Chessboard: American Primacy and Its Geostrategic Imperatives* (New York: Basic Books, 1997).

Bull, Hedley, *The Anarchical Society: A Study of Order in World Politics* (New York: Columbia University Press, 1977).

Bull, Hedley, and Adam Watson, eds., *The Expansion of International Society* (Oxford: Oxford University Press, 1984).

Bull, Hedley, Benedict Kingsbury, and Adam Roberts, eds., *Hugo Grotius and International Relations* (Oxford: Oxford University Press, 1992).

Bullock, Alan, *Hitler: A Study in Tyranny* (New York: Bantam Books, 1958).

Butler, David, and Austin Ranney, *Referendums: A Comparative Study of Practice and Theory* (Washington, D.C.: American Enterprise Institute for Public Policy Research, 1978).

Calloway, Colin G., *New Worlds for All: Indians, Europeans, and the Remaking of Early America* (Baltimore: Johns Hopkins University Press, 1997).

Carter, Ashton, and William Perry, *Preventive Defense* (Washington, D.C.: Brookings Institution, 1999).

Catalano, Franco, *Francesco Sforza* (Milan: Dall'Oglio, 1983).

Chace, James, *The Consequences of the Peace: The New Internationalism and American Foreign Policy* (Oxford: Oxford University Press, 1992).

Chaytor, Henry J., *European History: Great Leaders and Landmarks from Early to Modern Times* (London: Gresham Publishing Company, 1915).

Christiansen, Eric, *The Northern Crusades: The Baltic and the Catholic Frontier, 1100–1525* (London: Macmillan, 1980).

Churchill, Winston, *A History of the English-Speaking Peoples: The Great Democracies* (London: Cassell, 1956–58).

Cirincione, Joseph, and Frank von Hippel, *The Last 15 Minutes: Ballistic Missile Defense in Perspective* (Washington, D.C.: Coalition to Reduce Nuclear Dangers, 1996).

Clark, Sir George, *War and Society in the Seventeenth Century* (Cambridge, U.K.: Cambridge University Press, 1958).

Clausewitz, Carl von, *On War,* trans. J. J. Graham (London: K. Paul, Trench, Trubner, 1908).

———, *On War* ed. and trans. Michael Howard and Peter Paret (Princeton: Princeton University Press, 1976 [1832]).

Clements, Diane Shaver, *Yalta* (Oxford: Oxford University Press, 1970).

Cohen, Ronald, and Judith D. Toland, eds., *State Formation and Political Legitimacy* (New Brunswick, N.J.: Transaction Books, 1988).

Cooper, Jeffrey, "Preparing for Conflict in the Information Age," in J. Arquilla and D. Rosenfeldt, eds., *In Athena's Camp* (Santa Monica: RAND, 1997).

Cowley, Robert, and Geoffrey Parker, eds., *The Reader's Companion to Military History* (Boston: Houghton Mifflin, 1996).

Craig, Gordon A., and Aleksander L. George, *Force and Statecraft: Diplomatic Problems of Our Time* (Oxford: Oxford University Press, 1983).

Craig, Gordon A., and F. Gilbert, "Strategy in the Present and Future," in *Makers of Modern Strategy,* ed. Peter Paret (Princeton: Princeton University Press, 1944).

Creveld, Martin van, *Nuclear Proliferation and the Future of Conflict* (London: Macmillan, 1993).

———, *The Rise and Decline of the State* (Cambridge, U.K.: Cambridge University Press, 1999).

———, *The Transformation of War* (New York: Free Press, 1991).

Crowley, James B., *Japan's Quest for Autonomy* (Princeton: Princeton University Press, 1966).

Curry, Anne, *The Hundred Years War* (London: Macmillan, 1983).

Daalder, Ivo H., and Michael E. O'Hanlon, *Winning Ugly: NATO's War to Save Kosovo* (Washington, D.C.: Brookings Institution, 2000).

Dallas, Gregor, *At the Heart of a Tiger: Clemenceau and His World, 1841–1929* (London: Macmillan, 1993).

Damrosch, Lori Fisler, ed., *Enforcing Restraint: Collective Intervention in Internal Conflicts* (New York: Council on Foreign Relations Press, 1993).

Danzig, Richard, *The Big Three: Our Greatest Security Risks and How to Address Them* (Washington, D.C.: National Defense University Press, 1999).

Davdeker, Christopher, *Surveillance, Power, and Modernity* (New York: St. Martin's Press, 1990).

DeLillo, Don, *Underworld* (New York: Scribner, 1997).

Denman, Roy, *Missed Chances* (London: Cassell, 1996).

Devlin, Patrick, *Too Proud to Fight: Woodrow Wilson's Neutrality* (Oxford: Oxford University Press, 1974).

Doolin, Paul Rice, *The Fronde* (Cambridge, Mass.: Harvard University Press, 1935).

Doyle, Michael W., *Empires* (Ithaca, N.Y.: Cornell University Press, 1986).

————, *Ways of War and Peace* (New York: Norton, 1997).

Doyle, William, *The Old European Order,* 2nd ed. (Oxford: Oxford University Press, 1992).

Downing, Brian M., *The Military Revolution and Political Change in Early Modern Europe: Origins of Democracy and Autocracy in Early Modern Europe* (Princeton: Princeton University Press, 1991).

Droz, Jacques, *Europe between the Revolutions, 1815–1848* (New York: Harper & Row, 1967).

Drucker, Peter, *The Post-Capitalist Society* (New York: HarperBusiness, 1993).

Dworkin, Ronald, *Law's Empire* (Cambridge, Mass.: Harvard University Press, 1986).

Dziak, John W., *Chekisty: A History of the KGB* (Lexington, Mass.: Lexington Books, 1988).

Eccleston, Bernard, "The State and Modernization in Japan," in *The Rise of the Modern State,* ed. James Anderson (Brighton, Sussex: Harvester Press, 1986).

Eisenhower, Dwight D., *Crusade in Europe* (New York: Doubleday, 1948).

————, *Mandate for Change* (New York: New American Library, 1963).

Elliott, J. H., *Richelieu and Olivares* (Cambridge, U.K.: Cambridge University Press, 1984).

Fahey, Liam, ed., *Learning from the Future: Competitive Foresight Scenarios* (New York: John Wiley, 1998).

Fallows, James, *More like Us: Making America Great Again* (Boston: Houghton Mifflin, 1989).

Fay, Bernard, *Louis XVI ou la fin d'un monde* (Paris: Perrin, 1955).

Fehrenbach, T. R., *This Kind of War: A Study in Unpreparedness* (New York: Pocket Books, 1963).

Fenno, Richard F., *The Yalta Conference* (Boston: Heath, 1955).

Ferguson, Niall, *The Pity of War* (New York: Basic Books, 1999).

Ferguson, Wallace K., *Europe in Transition, 1300–1520* (Boston: Houghton Mifflin, 1962).

Fischer, Fritz, *The Civilization of the Renaissance in Italy* (New York: Harper, 1958).

————, *Germany's Aims in the First World War* (New York: Norton, 1967). (English translation of his *Griff nach der Weltmacht* [Dusseldorf: Droste, 1961].)

————, *From Kaiserreich to the Third Reich: Elements of Continuity in German History, 1871–1945,* trans. Roger Fletcher (London: Allen & Unwin, 1986).

————, *War of Illusions: German Policies from 1911 to 1914* (New York: Norton, 1975).

————, *World Power or Decline: The Controversy over Germany's Aims in the First World War,* trans. Lancelot Farrar, Robert Kimber, and Rita Kimber (New York: Norton, 1974).

Fitzgerald, F. Scott, *The Great Gatsby* (New York: Scribner's, 1953).

Foote, Shelby, *The Civil War: A Narrative History* (New York: Random House, 1986).

Ford, Franklin, *Europe, 1780–1830,* 2nd ed. (London: Longman, 1989).

Fowler, Kenneth, *The Age of Plantagenet and Valois* (New York: Putnam, 1967).

Franck, Thomas, *Fairness in International Law and Institutions* (Oxford: Oxford University Press, 1995).

Friden, Jeffrey A., *Banking on the World: The Politics of International Finance* (New York: Harper & Row, 1987).

Friedell, Egon, *A Cultural History of the Modern Age,* trans. Charles Francis Atkinson (New York: Knopf, 1930–1932).

Friedman, George, *The Political Philosophy of the Frankfurt School* (Ithaca, N.Y.: Cornell University Press, 1981).

Friedrich II, Kung au Prussen, *Die Werke Friedrichs des Grossen,* 10 vol. (Berlin: Hobbing, 1912–1914).

Fugier, André, *La Revolution française et l'Empire Napoleonien* (Paris: Hachette, 1954).

Fukuyama, Francis, *The End of History and the Last Man* (New York: Free Press, 1992).

Fulbrook, Mary, *The Divided Nation: A History of Germany, 1918–1990* (Oxford: Oxford University Press, 1991).

Fuller, Graham E., *The Democracy Trap: The Perils of the Post–Cold War World* (New York: Dutton, 1991).

Garthoff, Raymond, *The Great Transition: American-Soviet Relations and the End of the Cold War* (Washington, D.C.: Brookings Institution, 1994).

Gates, Robert, *From the Shadows: The Ultimate Insiders Story of Five Presidents and How They Won the Cold War* (New York: Simon & Schuster, 1996).

Gentili, Alberico, *De Jure Belli Libri Tres,* Carnegie Endowment for International Peace, trans. John C. Rolfe (Oxford: Clarendon Press, 1933).

Geus, Arie de, *The Living Company* (Cambridge, Mass.: Harvard Business School Press, 1997).

Giddens, Anthony, *The Nation State and Violence* (Berkeley: University of California Press, 1985).

Gilbert, Felix, "Machiavelli: The Renaissance of the Art of War," in *Makers of Modern Strategy,* ed. Peter Paret (Princeton: Princeton University Press, 1986).

Gildea, Robert, *Barricades and Borders, Europe 1800–1914* (Oxford: Oxford University Press, 1987).

Gilpin, Robert, *War and Change in World Politics* (Cambridge, U.K.: Cambridge University Press, 1981).

Glover, Michael, *Napoleonic Wars* (New York: Hippocrene Books, 1979).

Goodrich, Leland M., Edvard Hambro, and Anne P. Simons, *Charter of the United Nations: Commentary and Documents* (New York: Columbia University Press, 1969).

Gow, James, *Triumph of the Lack of Will: International Diplomacy and the Yugoslav War* (London: Hurst, 1997).

Gow, James, Richard Paterson, and Alison Preston, eds., *Bosnia by Television* (London: British Film Institute, 1996).

Graubard, Stephen, ed., *The State* (New York: Norton, 1979).

Greider, William, *One World, Ready or Not: The Manic Logic of Global Capitalism* (New York: Simon & Schuster, 1997).

Grenville, John A. S., *Europe Reshaped 1848–1878* (Brighton, Sussex: Harvester Press, 1976).

Grotius, Hugo, *De Jure Belli ac Pacis,* ed. and trans. W. Whewell (London: J. W. Parker, 1853).

Guehenno, Jean-Marie, *The End of the Nation-State* (Minneapolis: University of Minnesota Press, 1995).

Haass, Richard, *Intervention: The Use of American Military Force in the Post–Cold War World* (Washington, D.C.: Brookings Institution, 1994).

———, *The Reluctant Sheriff* (New York: Council on Foreign Relations, 1997).

Habermas, Jürgen, *Between Facts and Norms: Contributions to a Discourse Theory of Law and Democracy,* Studies in Contemporary German Social Thought, trans. William Rehg (Cambridge, Mass.: MIT Press, 1996).

Hamilton, Richard F., *Who Voted for Hitler?* (Princeton: Princeton University Press, 1982).

Hart, Henry M., Jr., and Albert M. Sacks, *The Legal Process: Basic Problems in the Making and Application of Law* (Westbury, N.Y.: Foundation Press, 1994).

Havel, Václav, "The Memorandum," trans. Vera Blackwell, in *Selected Plays, 1963–83* (London: Faber and Faber, 1992).

———, *Open Letters: Selected Writings, 1965–1990,* ed. Paul Wilson (New York: Knopf, 1991).

Hayes, Paul, "The Triumph of Caesarism: Fascism and Nazism," in *Themes in Modern European History, 1890–1945*, ed. Hayes (London: Routledge, 1992).

Headerick, Daniel, *The Invisible Weapon, Telecommunications and International Politics, 1851–1945* (Oxford: Oxford University Press, 1991).

Hegel, W. F., *Introduction to the Philosophy of History* (Indianapolis: Hackett, 1998).

Heijden, Kees van der, *Scenarios: The Art of Strategic Conversation* (New York: John Wiley, 1997).

Helleiner, Eric, *States and the Reemergence of Global Finance: From Bretton Woods to the 1990s* (Ithaca, N.Y.: Cornell University Press, 1994).

Henig, Ruth, *The Origins of the First World War* (London: Routledge, 1989).

Hendrickson, Kenneth E., Jr., and Michael L. Collins, eds., *Profiles in Power: Twentieth Century Texans in Washington* (Arlington Heights, Ill.: Harlan Davidson, 1993).

Henkin, Louis, *How Nations Behave* (New York: Columbia University Press, 1979).

Henry, Philip, Fifth Earl Stanhope, *Notes of Conversations with the Duke of Wellington, 1831–1851* (London: Murray, 1888).

Henshell, Nicholas, *The Myth of Absolutism: Change and Continuity in Early Modern European Monarchy* (London: Longman, 1992).

Hillen, John, ed., *Future Visions for U.S. Defense Policy, The Council on Foreign Relations Defense Policy Review* (New York: Council on Foreign Relations Press, 1998).

Hinde, Wendy, *Castlereagh* (London: Collins, 1981).

Hinsley, Francis H., *Power and the Pursuit of Peace: Theory and Practice in the History of Relations between States* (Cambridge, U.K.: Cambridge University Press, 1963).

Hobsbawm, Eric, *The Age of Extremes: A History of the World, 1914–1991* (New York: Pantheon Books, 1994).

Holmes, Geoffrey, and William A. Speck, *The Divided Society: Parties and Politics in England, 1694–1716* (New York: St. Martin's Press, 1967).

Holmes, Stephen, *The Anatomy of Antiliberalism* (Cambridge, Mass.: Harvard University Press, 1993).

Holsti, Kalevi J., *Peace and War: Armed Conflicts and the International Order, 1648–1989* (Cambridge, U.K.: Cambridge University Press, 1991).

Hornblower, Simon, *Thucydides* (London: Duckworth, 1987).

Howard, Michael, *The Lessons of History* (New Haven: Yale University Press, 1991).

———, *War and the Nation-State* (Oxford: Clarendon Press, 1978).

Hume, David, *Essays, Morals, Political and Literary* (Oxford: Oxford University Press, 1963).

Hundley, Richard O., *Past Revolutions, Future Transformations: What Can the History of Revolutions in Military Affairs Tell Us about Transforming the U.S. Military?* (Santa Monica: RAND, 1999).

Hyman, Harold, *A More Perfect Union: The Impact of the Civil War and Reconstruction on the Constitution* (New York: Knopf, 1973).

Jay, Martin, *The Dialectical Imagination: A History of the Frankfurt School and the Institute of Social Research, 1923–1950* (Boston: Little, Brown, 1973).

Jedruch, Jacek, *Constitutions, Elections, and Legislatures of Poland, 1493–1977: A Guide to Their History* (Washington, D.C.: University Press of America, 1982).

Johnson, Hubert C., *Frederick the Great and His Officials* (New Haven: Yale University Press, 1975).

Johnson, Paul, *The Birth of the Modern World Society* (New York: HarperCollins, 1991).

Joll, James, *The Origins of the First World War* (London: Longman, 1984).

Jones, Larry E., *German Liberalism and the Dissolution of the Weimar Party System, 1918–1933* (Chapel Hill: University of North Carolina Press, 1988).

Jordan, Wilbur K., *The Development of Religious Toleration in England* (Gloucester, Mass.: P. Smith, 1965).

Kaiser, David E., *Economic Diplomacy and the Origins of the Second World War* (Princeton: Princeton University Press, 1980).

———, *Politics and War: European Conflict from Philip II to Hitler* (Cambridge, Mass.: Harvard University Press, 1990).

Kagan, Donald, *On the Origins of War and the Preservation of Peace* (New York: Doubleday, 1995).

Kahin, Brian, and Charles Nesson, eds., *Borders in Cyberspace: Information Policy and the Global Information Infrastructure* (Cambridge, Mass.: MIT Press, 1997).

Karski, Jan, *The Great Powers and Poland, 1919–1945: From Versailles to Yalta* (Washington, D.C.: University Press of America, 1985).

Keegan, John, *A History of Warfare* (New York: Knopf, 1993).

Kelsen, Hans, "Centralization and Decentralization," in *Authority and the Individual* (Cambridge, Mass.: Harvard University Press, 1937).

———, *General Theory of Law and State* (Cambridge, Mass.: Harvard University Press, 1945).

———, *General Theory of Law and State,* trans. Anders Wedberg (New York: Russell & Russell, 1945).

Kennan, George, *The Cloud of Danger: Current Realities of American Foreign Policy* (Boston: Little, Brown, 1977).

Kennedy, David, *International Legal Structures* (Baden-Baden: Nomos, 1987).

Kirchheimer, Otto, *Political Justice: The Use of Legal Procedures for Political Ends* (Princeton: Princeton University Press, 1961).

———, *Studies in Philosophy and Social Science* (London: Allen and Unwin, 1987).

Kissinger, Henry, "The New Face of Diplomacy: Wilson and the Treaty of Versailles," in *Diplomacy* (New York: Simon & Schuster, 1994).

———, *A World Restored* (New York: Grosset and Dunlap, 1964).

Kohl, Horst, ed., *Die Politischen Reden des Fursten Bismarck: Historischkritische Gesammtausg* (Stuttgart: Cotta, 1892–1905).

Kolb, Eberhard, *The Weimar Republic,* trans. P. S. Falla (London: Unwin Hyman, 1988).

Konrád, György, *Antipolitics: An Essay,* trans. Richard E. Allen (New York: Harcourt, Brace, Jovanovich, 1984).

Kouri, E. I., and Tom Scott, eds., *Politics and Society in Reformation Europe* (New York: St. Martin's Press, 1987).

Knight, Alice J., *Las Casas, "The Apostle of the Indies"* (New York: Neale Publishing Company, 1917).

Knight, William Stanley Macbean, *The Life and Works of Hugo Grotius* (New York: Oceana, 1962).

Khrushchev, N. S., *Khrushchev Remembers,* ed. Strobe Talbott (Boston: Little, Brown, 1970).

Kuhn, Thomas, *The Structure of Scientific Revolutions* (Chicago: University of Chicago Press, 1970).

Kundera, Milan, *Nesnesitelna lehkost byti* (The Unbearable Lightness of Being), trans. Michael Henry Heim (New York: Harper & Row, 1984).

Kugler, Richard, *Commitment to Purpose: How Alliance Partnership Won the Cold War* (Santa Monica: RAND, 1993).

Lakatos, Imre, and Paul Feyerabend, *For and Against Method: Including Lakatos' Lectures on Scientific Method and the Lakatos-Feyerabend Correspondence* (Chicago: University of Chicago Press, 1999).

Langer, William, *The "New Imperialism": Analysis of Late Nineteenth-Century Expansion,* ed. Harrison M. Wright (Boston: Heath, 1961).

———, ed., *Rise of Modern Europe,* 20 vol. (New York: Harper & Row, 1936–1985).

Lansing, Robert, *The Peace Negotiations: A Personal Narrative* (Boston: Houghton Mifflin, 1921).

Lauterpacht, Hersch, and C.H.M. Waldock, eds., *The Basis of Obligation in International Law, and Other Papers* (Oxford: Clarendon Press, 1958).

Leibniz, Gottfried Wilhelm, *The Political Writings of Leibniz,* ed. and trans. Patrick Riley (Cambridge, U.K.: Cambridge University Press, 1972).

Leitenberg, M., *Control of Dual Threat Agents: The Vaccines for Peace Program,* ed. Erhard Geissler and John P. Woodall (Oxford: Oxford University Press, 1994).

Lenin, Vladimir I., *Imperialism: The Highest Stage of Capitalism* (New York: International, 1988 [1916]).

Limm, Peter, *The Thirty Years War* (London: Longman, 1984).

Litan, Robert E., and William D. Nordhaus, *Reforming Federal Regulation* (New Haven: Yale University Press, 1983).

Llewellyn, Karl N., *The Bramble Bush: On Our Law and Its Study* (New York: Oceana Publications, 1951 [1930]).

Lockhart, J. G., *The Peacemakers, 1814–1815* (London: Duckworth, 1932).

Ludwikowski, Rett R., and William F. Fox, Jr., *The Beginning of the Constitutional Era* (Washington, D.C.: Catholic University of America Press, 1993).

Macaulay, Thomas B., *Napoleon and the Restoration of the Bourbons,* ed. Joseph Hamburger (New York: Columbia University Press, 1977).

Machiavelli, Niccolò, *The Discourses,* III (London: Penguin Books, 1970).

———, *Il Discorsi* (New York: Modern Library, 1950).

———, *The Prince,* trans. Harvey C. Mansfield, Jr. (Chicago: University of Chicago Press, 1985).

MacNutt, Francis A., *Bartholomew de las Casas: His Life, His Apostolate, and His Writings* (New York: Putnam, 1909).

Malcolm, Noel, *Bosnia: A Short History* (New York: New York University Press, 1994).

Mancias, Peter, *The Death of the State* (New York: Putnam, 1974).

Mann, Michael, *States, War and Capitalism* (Oxford: Basil Blackwell, 1988).

Marcus, Judith, *1986 Yearbook of the Leo Baeck Institute* (New York: Leo Baeck Institute, 1986).

Marlowe, Christopher, *The Famous Tragedy of the Rich Jew of Malta* (New York: Da Capo Press, 1971).

Martel, Gordon, ed., *The Origins of the Second World War Reconsidered: The A.J.P. Taylor Debate after Twenty-five Years* (London: Allen & Unwin, 1986).

May, Ernest, ed., *American Cold War Strategy: Interpreting NSC 68* (Boston: Bedford Books, 1993).

McDougal, Myres S., and W. Michael Reisman, *International Law Essays: A Supplement to International Law in Contemporary Perspective* (Westbury, N.Y.: Foundation Press, 1981).

McDougal, Myres S., and Associates, *Studies in World Public Order* (New Haven: Yale University Press, 1960).

McLennan, Gregor, David Held, and Stuart Hall, eds., *The Idea of the Modern State* (Philadelphia: Open University Press, 1984).

McNeill, William, *Plagues and Peoples* (Garden City, N.J.: Anchor Press, 1976).

———, *The Pursuit of Power* (Chicago: University of Chicago Press, 1982).

McPherson, James, *Abraham Lincoln and the Second American Revolution* (Oxford: Oxford University Press, 1990).

Mearsheimer, John J., *Conventional Deterrence* (Ithaca, N.Y.: Cornell University Press, 1983).

Mee, Charles L., Jr., *The End of Order, Versailles, 1919* (New York: Dutton, 1980).

Michnik, Adam, *Letters from Prison and Other Essays,* trans. Maya Liatynski (Berkeley: University of California Press, 1985).

Miller, David H., *The Drafting of the Covenant* (New York: Putnam, 1928).

Miscamble, Wilson, *George Kennan and the Making of American Foreign Policy, 1947–1950* (Princeton: Princeton University Press, 1992).

Molen, Gesina H. J. van der, *Alberico Gentili* (Leiden: A. W. Sijthoff, 1968).

Montesquieu, *Oeuvres Complètes* (Paris: Gallimard, 1951).

Moses, John, *The Politics of Illusion* (London: George Prior, 1975).

Mowat, Robert B., *The Concert of Europe* (London: Macmillan, 1930).

Moynihan, Daniel P., *On the Law of Nations* (Cambridge, Mass.: Harvard University Press, 1990).

Muller, James W., ed., *Churchill's "Iron Curtain" Speech Fifty Years Later* (Columbia, Mo.: University of Missouri Press, 1999).

Nardin, Terry, and David R. Mapel, eds., *Traditions of International Ethics* (Cambridge, U.K.: Cambridge University Press, 1992).

Neal, Larry, ed., *War Finance,* 3 vols. (Brookfield, Vt.: Edward Elgar, 1994).

New Cambridge Modern History, 14 vol. (Cambridge, U.K.: Cambridge University Press, 1957–1979).

Nicolson, Harold, *The Congress of Vienna: A Study in Allied Unity: 1812–1822* (New York: Viking Press, 1946).

———, *The Congress of Vienna* (London: Constable, 1946).

Nietzsche, Friedrich, *The Portable Nietzsche,* ed. and trans. Walter Kaufmann (New York: Viking Press, 1954).

Nussbaum, Arthur, *A Concise History of the Law of Nations* (New York: Macmillan, 1947).

Ohmae, Kenichi, *The End of the Nation-State: The Rise of Regional Economies* (New York: Free Press, 1995).

Olson, Mancur, *Power and Prosperity* (New York: Basic Books, 2000).

O'Neill, Robert, and D. M. Horner, eds., *New Directions in Strategic Thinking* (London: Allen & Unwin, 1981).

Osiander, Andreas, *The States System of Europe, 1640–1990: Peacemaking and the Conditions of International Stability* (Oxford: Oxford University Press, 1994).

Owen, David, *Balkan Odyssey* (New York: Harcourt Brace, 1995).

Oye, Kenneth A., *International Relations Theory and the End of the Cold War,* ed. Richard Ned Lebow and Thomas Risse-Kappen (New York: Columbia University Press, 1995).

Palmer, Alan, *Metternich* (New York: Harper & Row, 1972).

Parker, Geoffrey, *The Military Revolution: Military Innovation and the Rise of the West, 1500–1800* (Cambridge, U.K.: Cambridge University Press, 1988).

———, *The Thirty Years War* (London: Routledge and Kegan Paul, 1984).

Paret, Peter, *Understanding War* (Princeton: Princeton University Press, 1992).

———, *Yorck and the Era of Prussian Reform, 1807–1815* (Princeton: Princeton University Press, 1966).

Patterson, Dennis, *Law and Truth* (Oxford: Oxford University Press, 1996).

Patterson, W. M. Knight, *Germany from Defeat to Conquest* (London: Allen & Unwin, 1945).

Pipes, Richard, *Russia under the Old Regime* (London: Weidenfeld & Nicolson, 1974).

Pole, Jack R., *Political Representation in England and the Origins of the American Republic* (Berkeley: University of California Press, 1966).

Pollack, Ervin Harold, *Jurisprudence: Principles and Applications* (Columbus: Ohio State University Press, 1987).

Prall, Stuart E., ed. *The Puritan Revolution: A Documentary History* (Garden City, N.Y.: Anchor Books, 1968).

Pyle, Kenneth B., *The Making of Modern Japan,* 2nd ed. (Boston: Heath, 1996).

Ralston, David, *Importing the European Army: The Introduction of European Military Techniques and Institutions into the Extra-European World, 1600–1914* (Chicago: University of Chicago Press, 1990).

Randle, Robert F., *Issues in the History of International Relations: The Role of Issues in the Evolution of the State System* (Westport, Conn.: Praeger, 1987).

———, *The Origins of Peace: A Study of Peacemaking and the Structure of Peace Settlements* (New York: Free Press, 1973).

Rawlings, Hunter R., III, *The Structure of Thucydides' History* (Princeton: Princeton University Press, 1981).

Rayner, Edgar G., *The Cold War* (London: Hodder & Stoughton, 1992).

Reinhardt, Kurt F., *Germany 2000 Years,* rev. ed., *Vol. 1, The Rise and Fall of the "Holy Empire"* (New York: Frederick Ungar, 1961).

Reisman, W. Michael, *Law and Policy,* ed. David N. Weisstub (Toronto: Osgoode Hall Law School, 1976).

Reisman, W. Michael, and Burns H. Weston, eds., *Toward World Order and Human Dignity* (New York: Free Press, 1976).

Rice, Condoleezza, "The Making of Soviet Strategy," in *Makers of Modern Strategy: From Machiavelli to the Nuclear Age,* ed. Peter Paret (Princeton: Princeton University Press, 1986).

Roberts, Michael, *Essays in Swedish History* (Minneapolis: University of Minnesota Press, 1967).

———, *Gustavus Adolphus* (New York: Longman, 1992).

———, *The Military Revolution, 1560–1660* (Belfast: M. Boyd, 1956).

Rosecrance, Richard N., *The Rise of the Virtual State: Wealth and Power in the Coming Century* (New York: Basic Books, 1999).

Rosenau, James N., *Turbulence in World Politics: A Theory of Change and Continuity* (Princeton: Princeton University Press, 1990).

Rosenthal, Abraham M., *Thirty-Eight Witnesses* (New York: McGraw-Hill, 1964).

Rostow, Eugene V., *Toward Managed Peace: The National Security Interests of the United States, 1759 to the Present* (New Haven: Yale University Press, 1993).

Rostow, Walt, *The Process of Economic Growth* (New York: Norton, 1953).

Rousseau, Jean-Jacques, *The Social Contract, Book I,* trans. Maurice Cranston (London: Penguin, 1968).

Rustow, Dankwart A., ed., *Philosophers and Kings* (New York: Braziller, 1970).

Sandel, Michael J., *Liberalism and the Limits of Justice* (Cambridge, U.K.: Cambridge University Press, 1998).

Scenerio Planning: Forging a Link with Strategic Decision Making (Washington, D.C.: Corporate Executive Board, 1999).

Schachter, Oscar, *International Law in Theory and Practice: General Course in Public International Law* (Boston: Kluwer Academic Publishers, 1982).

Schelling, Thomas C., *Arms and Influence* (New Haven: Yale University Press, 1966).

Schmitt, Carl, *The Concept of the Political,* trans. George Schwab (New Brunswick, N.J.: Rutgers University Press, 1976).

———, *The Crisis of Parliamentary Democracy,* trans. Ellen Kennedy (Cambridge, Mass.: MIT Press, 1985).

————, *Political Theology: Four Chapters on the Concept of Sovereignty,* trans. George Schwab (Cambridge, Mass.: MIT Press, 1985).

Schneider, Barry R., and Lawrence E. Grinter, eds., *Battlefield of the Future: 21st Century Warfare Issues* (Maxwell Air Force Base, Ala.: Air University Press, 1995).

Schroeder, Paul, *The Transformation of European Politics, 1763–1848* (Oxford: Clarendon Press, 1994).

Schwartz, David N., *NATO's Nuclear Dilemmas* (Washington, D.C.: Brookings Institution, 1983).

Schwartz, Peter, *The Art of the Long View* (New York: Doubleday, 1991).

Seton-Watson, Robert W., *Britain in Europe, 1789–1914* (London: Macmillan, 1937).

Shaw, Albert, Ed. *The Messages and Papers of Woodrow Wilson* (New York: Review of Reviews Corporation, 1924).

Shirer, William L., *The Rise and Fall of the Third Reich* (New York: Simon & Schuster, 1960).

Silber, Laura, and Alan Little, *Yugoslavia: Death of a Nation* (New York: TV Books: Penguin USA, 1996).

Skidelsky, Robert, *John Maynard Keynes: A Biography* (London: Macmillan, 1983).

Skinner, Quentin, *The Foundations of Modern Political Thought: The Age of Reformation* (Cambridge, U.K.: Cambridge University Press, 1978).

Smethurst, Richard J., "Teikoku Zaigo Gunjinkai Sanjunenshi," in *The Social Basis for Japanese Militarism* (Dissertation, Ann Arbor: University of Michigan, 1968).

Smith, Gaddis, *Dean Acheson* (New York: Cooper Square Publishers, 1972).

Steel, Ronald, *Walter Lippmann and the American Century* (Boston: Little, Brown, 1980).

Stettinius, Edward R., *Roosevelt and the Russians: The Yalta Conference* (New York: Doubleday, 1949).

Storry, Richard, *A History of Modern Japan* (London: Penguin Books, 1960).

Stowe, Norman, *Europe Transformed, 1878–1919* (Cambridge, Mass.: Harvard University Press, 1984).

Stromseth, Jane E., *The Origins of Flexible Response: NATO's Debate over Strategy in the 1960s* (New York: St. Martin's Press, 1988).

Stueck, William, *The Korean War: An International History* (Princeton: Princeton University Press, 1995).

Suarez, Francisco, *De Legibus ac Deo Legislatore.* (Madrid: Consejo Superiore de Investigations Cietificas, 1967).

————, *Selections from Three Works,* Carnegie Endowment for International Peace, trans. Gwladys Williams, Ammi Brown, and John Waldron (Oxford: Clarendon Press, 1944).

Summers, Harry G., *The New World Strategy: A Military Policy for America's Future* (New York: Simon & Schuster, 1995).

Symcox, Geoffrey, *War, Diplomacy, and Imperialism, 1618–1763* (New York: Harper Torchbooks, 1974).

Symonds, John Addington, *A Short History of the Renaissance in Italy* (New York: Scribner, 1893).

Taylor, Alan J. P., *Origins of the Second World War* (London: Hamish Hamilton, 1961).

————, *The Trouble Makers: Dissent over Foreign Policy, 1792–1939* (Bloomington: Indiana University Press, 1958).

Tilly, Charles, *Coercion, Capital, and European States* (Oxford: Blackwell, 1992).

————, *European Revolutions, 1492–1992* (Oxford: Blackwell, 1993).

Tilly, Charles, ed., *The Formation of Nation States in Western Europe* (Princeton: Princeton University Press, 1975).

Tismaneanu, Vladimir, *Reinventing Politics: Eastern Europe from Stalin to Havel* (New York: Free Press, 1992).

Trevelyan, G. M., *Grey of Fallodon* (London: Longmans, 1946).

Tribe, Keith, ed., *Social Democracy and the Rule of Law: Otto Kirchheimer and Franz Neumann,* trans. Leena Tanner and Keith Tribe (London: Allen & Unwin, 1987).

Tuck, Richard, *Natural Rights Theories: Their Origin and Development* (Cambridge, U.K.: Cambridge University Press, 1979).

Turner, Frederick, *The Culture of Hope: A New Birth of the Classical Spirit* (New York: Free Press, 1995).

———, *Natural Classicism: Essays on Literature and Science* (Paragon House, 1985).

Tushnet, Mark, and Vicki C. Jackson, *Comparative Constitutional Law* (Westbury, Conn.: Foundation Press, 1999).

Vattel, Emmerich de, *Le Droit des Gens* (Editions A. Pedone, 1998).

Vitoria, Francisco de, *Actualité de la Pensée Juridique de Francisco de Vitoria,* ed. A. Truyol y Serra, H. Mechoulan, P. Haggenmacher. A. Ortiz-Arce, P. M. Marine, and J. Verhoeven (Geneva: Bruylant, 1988).

———, *Political Writings, Francisco de Vitoria,* ed. Anthony Pagden and Jeremy Lawrence (Cambridge, U.K.: Cambridge University Press, 1991).

Waliszewski, K., *Le regne d'Alexandre I* (1924).

Waltz, Kenneth Neal, *The Spread of Nuclear Weapons: More May Be Better* (London: International Institute for Strategic Studies, 1981).

Walzer, Michael, ed., *Toward a Global Civil Society* (Oxford, New York: Berghahn Books, 1995).

Walworth, Arthur, *America's Moment, 1918: American Diplomacy and the End of World War I* (New York: Norton, 1977).

Watson, Adam, *The Evolution of International Societies: A Comparative Historical Analysis* (London: Routledge, 1992).

Weber, Max, *From Max Weber: Essays in Sociology,* trans. and ed. Hans H. Gerth and Charles W. Mills (Oxford: Oxford University Press, 1946).

Webster, Sir Charles, *The Foreign Policy of Castlereagh* (Bell, 1950).

Wedgwood, Cicely V., *The Thirty Years War* (London: Cape, 1938).

Weinberger, Caspar W., *Fighting for Peace: Seven Critical Years in the Pentagon* (New York: Warner Books, 1990).

Wells, H. G., *The Outline of History* (London: George Newnes, 1920).

Wiggershaus, Rolf, *The Frankfurt School: Its History, Theories and Political Significance,* trans. Michael Robertson (Polity Press, 1994).

Wight, Martin, *Systems of States,* ed. Hedley Bull (Leicester: Leicester University Press for the London School of Economics and Political Science, 1977).

Wiles, Timothy, ed., *Poland between the Wars, 1918–1939* (Bloomington: Indiana University Polish Studies Center, 1989).

Williams, Joyce, *Colonel House and Sir Edward Grey: A Study in Anglo-American Diplomacy* (Washington, D.C.: University Press of America, 1984).

Wilson, Edith B., *My Memoir* (Bobbs-Merrill, 1939).

Wilson, Woodrow, *Papers of Woodrow Wilson,* ed. Arthur S. Link (Princeton: Princeton University Press, 1966–1992).

———, *President Wilson's Great Speeches and Other History Making Documents* (Chicago: Stanton and Van Vliet, 1919).

Zelikow, Philip, and Condoleezza Rice, *Germany Unified and Europe Transformed: A Study in Statecraft* (Cambridge, Mass.: Harvard University Press, 1995).

Zimmermann, Warren, *Origins of a Catastrophe: Yugoslavia and Its Destroyers—America's Last Ambassador Tells What Happened and Why* (New York: Times Books, 1996).

ACKNOWLEDGMENTS

The Shield of Achilles was begun in 1990 as a series of honorary lectures to be delivered in 1992 at St. Mary's Law School before I left government service in 1993. Dean Barbara Aldave was responsible for that original invitation for which I am most grateful. The expanded written version of these lectures was largely complete when I re-entered government in 1997. These valuable opportunities for government service came my way owing to the invitations of Robert Kimmitt, undersecretary of state for political affairs in the Bush administration, and James B. Steinberg, deputy national security advisor to President Clinton.

I would not have been able to serve, however, without the leaves of absence from my professorship at the University of Texas that were arranged by Deans Mark Yudof and Michael Sharlot, and the indulgence of Kings College, London, during the interim that Lawrence Freedman, Gibson Gayle, and Brian and Aleksandra Marsh made possible.

When the war in Kosovo ended in the summer of 1999, I again left government and returned to London in order to prepare the manuscript for publication. In September I resumed teaching at the University of Texas and at year's end I sent the manuscript to publishers in what I knew was, and would probably always remain, an uncompleted form. Along the way many persons have read the manuscript and given me detailed comments. I especially wish to acknowledge five persons—Hans Mark, Mark Sagoff, Steven Weinberg, Paul Woodruff, and Lawrence Wright—for their dedication to trying to improve this work by giving me extensive, line-by-line comments on what is, after all, a long book. Eric Weinmann's immense erudition saved me from many errors; if some still lurk in this thicket of words, it is my sole responsibility.*

In addition to his many helpful suggestions, I am further indebted to Sir Michael Howard for his characteristically thoughtful foreword.

Betty Sue Flowers introduced me to the Shell Scenario project; that acquaintance with this important method—as explicated for me by Napier Collyns and Roger Rainbow—and her pathbreaking monograph, "The Economic Myth," have informed all of the discussion about future decisions that this book marries to its historical analysis. I would have written a book on these themes, but *this* book is Betty Sue's.

My wise and profound editor, Ashbel Green, has been both incisive and gentlemanly. His is a classic taste and to the extent this book, though large, is properly proportioned, it is his doing. If there is an informal collegium of literary editors he is its dean. My agents Glen Hartley and Lynn Chu brought him the manuscript (and Harriet Rubin brought them to me), for which I am deeply grateful. Stuart Proffitt, another editor of surpassing distinction, has provided me with his incomparable assistance for which many writers—but none more than I—are thankful.

*I should also like to thank the copyeditor, Susanna Sturgis, for whose labors I am grateful and of whom I thought when I came across this passage in a letter from the English critic James Agate: "Dear Cardus:—Re your *Ten Composers*. Have corrected your spelling. Also your Italian, German, French and occasionally your English. Have put your French accents right. Have emended your quotations . . . Titivated your titles. In places made the clumsy felicitious. Verified your keys. Rationalized your punctuation . . . In short, I have put this entrancing book right in all matters of fact and left only its errors of taste and judgment." Jacques Barzun, "James Agate and His Nine Egos," in *A Jacques Barzun Reader*, 94 (New York, 2002).

There are no words in these thousand pages, nor in any book, sufficient to thank Yvonne Tocquigny for her daily encouragement.

Jennifer Lamar, my resourceful and talented secretary, has brought this manuscript through many drafts. Her skill and patience have been tried, but not found wanting. My two research assistants, Paul Domjan and his successor John Tannous (both I am pleased to say Marshall Scholars now at Oxford), were indispensable. Thierry Joffrain, of the many law students I drafted from time to time for this project, stands out even in such an able field. Jory Lange helped prepare the index with meticulous care.

I would also like to thank a number of friends who encouraged me in this long task: James Adams, Michael Beschloss, James Billington, Sidney Blumenthal, Arnaud de Borchgrave, Michael Boudin, Richard Danzig, Bob Inman, Simon Jenkins, Nicholas Lemann, Sanford Levinson, Hans Linde, Roger Louis, Richard Markovits, Dennis Patterson, Henry Reath, Michael Reisman, Elspeth Rostow, Walt Rostow, Steven Simon, Strobe Talbott, Stuart Taylor, Ruth Wedgwood, and Philip Ziegler. Morris Abram, Charles Black, and Barbara Jordan did not live to see the publication of the manuscript we so often discussed, but I cannot forget them here any more than I shall ever be able to forget them.

Despite all this heroic assistance and inspiring aid, I am sorely conscious of the shortcomings that persist in this work, and of my own ignorance. There are many scholars on whose labors I have depended. Yet I have no desire to be a synthesizer or compiler; what I offer is an original, though I hope not idiosyncratic, set of theses with practical and theoretical implications. I do not believe that the study of the past resolves present controversies but I am sure that thinking about the past can illuminate our present problems; that thinking about the past in the context of the future, and vice versa, will be fruitful for new approaches to our current dilemmas. Perhaps this conviction is owed to my unusual personal history; I sometimes think that not only was I supposed to write this book but that I am perhaps one of the few who would. That is because for the last twenty-five years I have led a double life.

As a teacher, I have divided my life between Texas and England. In the United States, I have taught constitutional law at the University of Texas; in the United Kingdom, I have taught the history of nuclear strategy, first at Oxford and later at Kings College, London. Abroad I have taught only strategy; at home I have taught only law.

Overlain on this life of teaching and writing has been another life as a public official. I have served in all three branches of the U.S. government and in both Democratic and Republican administrations. At various times I have been associate counsel to the president for intelligence and international security at the White House; the counselor on international law at the State Department; the legal counsel to the Senate Select Committee on the Iran-Contra Affair and author of the Senate Report *Covert Action in a Democratic Society.* Until returning to academic life in the fall of 1999 I served in a series of senior positions at the National Security Council: director for intelligence; senior director for critical infrastructure; and finally as the senior director for strategic planning.

No doubt this fragmented and multiple existence accounts for the different voices one encounters on reading this book, but more important, this life has given me an unusual array of vantage points that is rarely found in a single professional career and for which I am grateful to the persons named and to many others unnamed. It is precisely these perspectives—national and international, public and private, strategic and constitutional—that at the beginning of the twenty-first century are coming together in the life of the State, an institution that has hitherto been defined by keeping these perspectives logically and politically distinct.

This book is the confluence of all these strands—law, history, and strategy—as these have been interwoven with a life in and out of government. It could not really be otherwise. As Valery wrote, "In fact there is no theory that is not a fragment, carefully prepared, of some autobiography."

ANNOTATED INDEX

ABC Problem: should the U.S. structure its forces to deal with peer nations, mid-level developing nations with modern forces and primitive weapons of mass destruction (WMD) or militarily ineffectual but dangerous states and non-state actors? 299

Acton, Edward, 27, 832, 889

Adolphus, Gustavus (1594–1632): Swedish king 1611–1632 during the Thirty Years' War, 69, 70, 73, 96, 99, 100–14, 130, 504, 508, 512, 516–17, 837–8, 898

Akashi, Yasushi (1931–): U.N. administrator in Bosnia; supervised Cambodian peace talks and elections 1993, 445, 459

Alba, Duke of (also Alva, Fernando Alvarez de Toledo) (1508–1583): Spanish commander in Low Countries, 494, 495

Alexander I (1777–1825): Russian tsar (1801–1825) represented Russia at Congress of Vienna (1814–1815), 150, 162, 869

Aquinas, Thomas (1225–1274): Jesuit philosopher, 77, 87, 491, 877

Article 2(4): U.N. Charter provision outlawing aggression by one state against another, 473, 863; compare Article 51, a provision recognizing each state's right to defend itself

Articles 42 and 43 of the U.N. Charter: U.N. Charter provisions authorizing the Security Council to use armed forces to maintain international peace and security, 169, 256, 433, 463, 473–4

Aspin, Les (1938–1995): U.S. secretary of defense (1993–1994), 298, 850

Athens: Greek city-state that flourished in the fifth century B.C., 8, 21, 332

Augustine, St. (354–430): Christian philosopher, author of *Confessions* and *The City of God,* 77

Austin, John (1790–1859): English jurist, 6, 565–7, 585–6, 589–90, 641, 829, 845–6, 852, 889–90

Ayala, Balthazar (1548–1584): Spanish military figure and jurist, 489, 494–6, 499

Badinter Commission: E.U. tribunal that establishes criteria for international recognition of states emerging from former Eastern and Central European communist countries, 449, 463

Baker, James (1930–): U.S. political figure; White House chief of staff (1981–1985, 1992–1993); secretary of the treasury (1985–1988); secretary of state (1989–1992), 280, 431–3, 612, 626–33, 635, 662, 846, 876, 881

balance of power, 90, 121, 124, 126, 129–33, 153, 155, 162, 169, 171–2, 233, 258–60, 263–65, 271, 278–9, 309, 344, 360, 383, 521, 523–7, 532, 534, 537, 539–40, 543, 550–3, 555, 559–60, 869, 886

Barraclough, Geoffrey, 26, 831, 889

Bartholomew, Reginald, 457

Beetham, David, 336, 844, 852

politician; led Free French in World War II; French provisional president (1945–1946); prime minister (1958–1959); president (1959–1969), 251, 630, 730, 871

Desert Storm: U.S. war plan in Gulf War (1991), 249, 295, 793

deterrence: a strategy, often pertaining to nuclear weapons, intended to dissuade an opponent from certain actions through threats, 11–5, 48–9, 52, 235, 244, 310, 328–9, 400, 620, 680–3, 686, 689–91, 713, 726, 759, 788, 812–4, 820–1

Diplomatic Revolution of 1748, 143

Douhet, Guilio (1869–1930): Italian military strategist; early advocate of military significance of air power, 325

Doyle, Michael, 178, 184, 202, 266, 839–40, 842–3, 875, 886, 891

Drucker, Peter 699, 707, 845, 883, 892

Dukakis, Michael, 10

Eagleburger, Lawrence Sidney: U.S. diplomat; deputy secretary of state (1989–1992); secretary of state (1992–1993), 428, 445–6, 451

economic sanctions, 265, 313, 318–20, 460, 462–3, 466, 656

Edict of Nantes (1598): recognized minority Protestant rights within Catholic France, 108, 125

Emmanuel II, Victor (1820–1878): king of Sardinia-Piedmont (1849–1861); king of Italy (1861–1878, first modern king of unified Italy), 183

England, 22, 25, 35, 78, 81, 83, 94, 96, 117–18, 122, 126, 128–31, 135, 149, 155, 159, 161, 201, 334–5, 368, 380, 382, 385, 390, 486, 487, 497, 511, 521, 546, 554, 902

entrepreneurial state: seeks leadership through the production and marketing of collective goods that the world's states want, 283–4, 286, 288–9, 292–3, 336–7

epochal war: a war that challenges and ultimately changes the basic constitutional structure of the State, by linking strategic to constitutional innovations, 8, 10, 22–3, 30, 64, 67, 88, 109–11, 127, 146,

146, 151, 203, 333, 334–6, 342, 346, 383, 487, 504, 520–1, 539, 556, 571, 575, 638, 661, 720–1, 778–9, 815, 820, 826, 830

ethnic cleansing: to expel ethnic groups from a State, through terror or extermination, 226, 276, 286, 289, 310, 316, 326, 338, 423–4, 426, 429–30, 434, 437–44, 446–7, 450–1, 458–9, 466, 481, 726, 731, 861

euro: common currency proposed for E.U., 234, 312, 701, 703, 728, 742–3, 753

European Defense Community, 253, 746

European Union (E.U.), 9, 234, 256, 261, 268, 270, 282, 286–7, 290, 326, 421, 446, 449, 452, 455, 463, 468–9, 475, 633, 674, 676, 687, 702–3, 727, 743, 746–50, 755, 770, 776–7, 782, 815, 847–8, 851, 908

extended deterrence: the nuclear threat by which nonhomeland theatres and other interests are protected, 14, 328–9, 620–1, 634, 689, 713, 731, 744

fascism, 24–6, 29, 31, 34, 36–9, 41, 43, 215, 332, 384, 571, 578, 603–5, 607–8, 610, 626, 673, 675, 677–8, 698, 781

Federalist Papers (1787–1788): series of newspaper articles, by Alexander Hamilton, James Madison, and John Jay; the most important document interpreting the U.S. Constitution on the basis of historical argument, 84, 177, 515, 536, 655, 661, 683

Fehrenbach, T. R., 300, 850, 892

Filmer, Sir Robert (d.1653): English political philosopher associated with absolutism, 121

First Partition of Poland (1772), 138

Fischer, Fritz (1908–1999): demonstrated that the German Imperial Government had planned and deliberately started the First World War and had pursued expansionist aims scarcely differing from the policies of the Third Reich, 26, 35, 831–3, 892

Ford, Gerald, (1913–): U.S. president (1974–1977), 10, 297, 322, 627

Fouquet, Nicolas (1615–1680): French financial administrator, 123

A NOTE ABOUT THE AUTHOR

Philip Bobbitt was born in Austin, Texas, and educated at Princeton, Oxford, and Yale. He currently holds the Walker Centennial Chair in Constitutional Law at the University of Texas. Formerly he was a fellow at Nuffield College, Oxford, where he was a member of the Oxford Modern History faculty and later a fellow at King's College, London, in the War Studies Department. He has served as associate counsel to the president for intelligence and national security, legal counsel to the Senate Select Committee on the Iran-Contra Affair, the counselor on international law at the Department of State, as well as director of intelligence, senior director for critical infrastructure, and senior director for strategic planning at the National Security Council. He has written previous books on constitutional law, social choice, and nuclear strategy. He lives in Austin, Washington, and London.

A NOTE ON THE TYPE

The text of this book was set in a typeface called Times New Roman, designed by Stanley Morison for *The Times* (London), and introduced by that newspaper in 1932.

Among typographers and designers of the twentieth century, Stanley Morison was a strong forming influence, as typographical adviser to the Monotype Corporation of London, as a director of two distinguished English publishing houses, and as a writer of sensibility, erudition, and keen practical sense.

In 1930 Morison wrote: "Type design moves at the pace of the most conservative reader. The good type-designer therefore realizes that, for a new font to be successful, it has to be so good that only very few recognize its novelty. If readers do not notice the consummate reticence and rare discipline of a new type, it is probably a good letter." It is now generally recognized that in the creation of Times Roman, Morison successfully met the qualifications of his theoretical doctrine.

Composed by Stratford Publishing Services, Brattleboro, Vermont
Printed and bound by R. R. Donnelley & Sons, Harrisonburg, Virginia
Designed by Robert C. Olsson